Western Film Series
of the Sound Era

For Midnight, Butterscotch,
Charlie, Oreo, Fred and Macy

Western Film Series of the Sound Era

Michael R. Pitts

McFarland & Company, Inc., Publishers
Jefferson, North Carolina

ALSO BY MICHAEL R. PITTS
AND FROM MCFARLAND

RKO Radio Pictures Horror, Science Fiction and Fantasy Films, 1929–1956 (2015)

Western Movies: A Guide to 5,105 Feature Films, 2d ed. (2013)

Allied Artists Horror, Science Fiction and Fantasy Films (2011)

Columbia Pictures Horror, Science Fiction and Fantasy Films, 1928–1982 (2010)

Poverty Row Studios, 1929–1940: An Illustrated History of 55 Independent Film Companies, with a Filmography for Each (1997; paperback 2005)

Charles Bronson: The 95 Films and the 156 Television Appearances (1999; paperback 2003)

Horror Film Stars, 3d ed. (2002)

Hollywood and American History: A Filmography of Over 250 Motion Pictures Depicting U.S. History (1984)

The present work is a reprint of the illustrated case bound edition of Western Film Series of the Sound Era, *first published in 2009 by McFarland.*

LIBRARY OF CONGRESS CATALOGUING-IN-PUBLICATION DATA

Pitts, Michael R.
Western film series of the sound era / Michael R. Pitts.
p. cm.
Includes bibliographical references and index.

ISBN 978-1-4766-7237-3 ∞
softcover : acid free paper

1. Western films — United States — History and criticism.   I. Title.
PN1995.9.W4P57   2018   791.436'278 — dc22   2008042863

BRITISH LIBRARY CATALOGUING DATA ARE AVAILABLE

© 2009 Michael R. Pitts. All rights reserved

No part of this book may be reproduced or transmitted in any form or by any means, electronic or mechanical, including photocopying or recording, or by any information storage and retrieval system, without permission in writing from the publisher.

On the cover: Poster art from the 1937 film *Hills of Old Wyoming*, with William Boyd and George "Gabby" Hayes (Paramount Pictures/Photofest)

Printed in the United States of America

McFarland & Company, Inc., Publishers
Box 611, Jefferson, North Carolina 28640
www.mcfarlandpub.com

Table of Contents

Preface 1

Billy Carson 3
Billy the Kid 21
Cheyenne Harry 34
The Cisco Kid 43
Dr. Monroe 64
The Durango Kid 68
Frontier Marshals 113
Hopalong Cassidy 118
The Irish Cowboys 175
John Paul Revere 180
Lightning Bill Carson 183
The Lone Ranger 190
The Lone Rider 208
Nevada Jack McKenzie 219
The Range Busters 232
Ranger Bob Allen 254
Red Ryder 259
Renfrew of the Royal Mounted 284
The Rough Riders 290
Rough Ridin' Kids 300

Table of Contents

Royal Canadian Mounted Police 303

The Singing Cowgirl 320

The Texas Rangers 322

The Three Mesquiteers 340

The Trail Blazers 384

Wild Bill Elliott 391

Wild Bill Hickok 399

Wild Bill Saunders 412

Winnetou 415

Zorro 429

Bibliography 457
Index 459

Preface

Westerns have always been one of the most popular of movie genres, dating back to the cinema's infancy with *The Great Train Robbery* in 1903. Series westerns took off not long after that when G.M. Anderson starred as "Broncho Billy" for Essanay, eventually headlining and directing nearly 400 one-; and two-reel installments between 1907 and 1916. By 1910, the western was firmly established with the moviegoing public and would reach its zenith in the mid–1930s when more than two dozen cowboy stars were making series cowboy movies. Although it was first thought that outdoor productions would not adapt well to sound, the talkie *In Old Arizona* (1929) proved this to be false and the western continued in popularity with numerous oater series being produced well into the early 1950s.

This volume examines thirty western film series made during the sound era. To be included, the series must have a continuing character or characters or be based on a particular theme, such as the "Royal Canadian Mounted Police" films taken from the works of James Oliver Curwood. Most of the western film series that are examined here focus on a character or multiple characters, such as the triad hero concept in the series "The Range Busters," "The Three Mesquiteers," "The Rough Riders" and "The Trail Blazers." More often, though, a series was about a single hero portrayed by a particular western star, such as William Boyd's Hopalong Cassidy, Johnny Mack Brown's Nevada Jack McKenzie, Tim McCoy's Lightning Bill Carson and the trio of series starring Bill Elliott. In a number of cases, a series would have a comedy sidekick who would often be on a par with the hero, such as Al St. John's character Fuzzy Q. Jones in the "Billy the Kid" and "Billy Carson" outings, Guy Wilkerson in the "Texas Rangers" productions and Smiley Burnette in most of the "Durango Kid" affairs.

In making series westerns, the studios hoped to keep moviegoers coming back for each installment, much like with weekly serial chapters. Western series entries were usually spread out over a period of weeks or months and box office returns determined series longevity. The "Hopalong Cassidy" and "Durango Kid" series each contained more than 60 features, with "The Three Mesquiteers" not far behind. Cassidy ran theatrically for 13 years, Durango for eight years and the Mesquiteers for seven years. "Billy Carson," "Nevada Jack McKenzie" and "The Range Busters" had better than average runs while a few such as "Rough Ridin' Kids" and "The Singing Cowgirl" lasted only three or four installments.

Purists may argue that other series deserve to be included in the book but these lack the criterion of featuring a continuing lead character. The films of Gene Autry and Roy Rogers are omitted because they were all individual features without any continuous plots other than having the stars use their own names for the characters they portrayed. Just the opposite is true for such series as Allan Lane's "Action Westerns" (1944–45) and "Famous Westerns" (1947–53) for Republic, and the "Range Rider" series Tex Ritter did for Grand National (1936–

38). These oaters had a continuing star playing a different character in each feature. Also omitted are silent films and short subjects unless they are part of a bigger overall character in the sound era, for example "The Cisco Kid" and "Zorro." Perhaps one exception is "Cheyenne Harry," a character Harry Carey played more than a dozen times in the silent days and reprised for two sound features.

The series included in this book mainly were produced from the 1930s into the early 1950s excepting "Winnetou," which was made in Europe in the 1960s. Television basically shut down the series western but the "Winnetou" features revived the concept and proved to be hugely popular, especially overseas. Their popularity spawned a batch of new series, including "Django," "Sabata," "Sartana" and "Trinity," but few of these outings ever made it to the U.S., unlike the "Winnetou" features, which were all released stateside. (Also, many of the Winnetou-inspired series were not originally made around a continuing character but were retitled and redubbed to make them appear to be a "Django" or "Sartana" feature when factually they were not. For those interested in delving into the complicated world of these European series offshoots, the best source is Thomas Weisser's *Spaghetti Westerns—The Good, the Bad and the Violent: 558 Eurowesterns and Their Personnel, 1961–1977*, published by McFarland in 1992.)

For each serial covered in this volume, a brief introduction to the history of the character or characters is first provided, including discussion of appearances in mediums such as books, stage, radio or television. This is followed by chronologically arranged synopses and analyses of the movies in the serial. A filmography providing the production, cast and crew information, also chronologically arranged, follows the discussion of the movies.

I would like to thank Larry Shuman for suggesting the concept for this book and Ray White and Francis M. Nevins for the help they provided in its writing. Viewing these wonderful old films again and writing about them has been a most enjoyable experience for me and I hope learning about the western film series of the sound era will provide the same enjoyment for the reader.

BILLY CARSON

PRC's evolution of the Billy the Kid (q.v.) series into a Billy Carson series was a simple one: The company only changed the name of star Buster Crabbe's character. There have been a number of reasons given for this metamorphosis: parental groups objected to children having a positive association with a known outlaw, exhibitors felt the same way or thought that Billy the Kid had run his course as a box office draw, or that Crabbe appeared too mature to be playing a character with the moniker of "kid." Whatever the reason, the transition was a smooth one, and outside the character name, there appears to be little difference between Crabbe's last Billy the Kid entry, *Blazing Frontier*, and the initial Billy Carson offering, *Devil Riders*, both 1943 releases. Advertising for the series gave Carson's horse, Falcon, star billing along with Crabbe, and Wally West continued to be the star's stunt double.

Crabbe would make 23 Billy Carson features, with Al St. John continuing in the role of Fuzzy Q. Jones. By this time the Neufeld brothers had ended their "Lone Rider" (q.v.) series, thus freeing St. John to work solely with Crabbe. Sigmund Neufeld continued to produce while his sibling, Sam Newfield, directed. The co-stars made a likable duo and gave the otherwise rather threadbare productions more than passable entertainment value. In *Hollywood Corral* (1976), Don Miller noted that director Newfield "seemed to bring added vigor to his work" as the Carson character took over. He added, "Minor performers might blow their lines without retakes and some of the interior sets looked ready for the scrap pile, but the new-found exuberance was a blessing." Regarding the two stars, Miller said, "Crabbe was coasting in his hero role, but his easygoing manner combined with genuine skill made it look good. St. John had honed his Fuzzy character to a sharp comic point." David Rothel opined in *Those Great Cowboy Sidekicks* (1984), "The Buster/Fuzzy series for PRC was never well-produced; the budgets only allowed for the cheesiest of sets, static camera setups, and scripts that often seemed to be made up as they prepared to roll the film in the camera. The main thing the series had going for it (if not the only thing) was the pleasant chemistry exuded by the two stars. It was as if they knew they were entangled in a hopeless mishmash of Western celluloid, but would, nevertheless, attempt to entertain all us kids who had plunked down our dimes at the box office. In short, Buster and Fuzzy didn't take the series too seriously and, therefore, just had fun with it. We in the audience could do the same."

The Billy Carson features, like the Billy the Kid ones which preceded them, were PRC's bread and butter. Exhibited at smaller venues than "A" productions, they were potent enough at the box office to help keep the company afloat for most of the 1940s with the two stars each earning about one thousand dollars per feature. That, along with the Neufelds' salaries, probably accounted for about one-half of the budget for each production. The series had a better than average run, with Buster Crabbe playing Billy the Kid or Billy Carson in a total of three dozen features from 1941 to 1946.

For a long time, film book authors maintained that each of the Billy the Kid–Billy Carson films were a carbon copy of the other, all cheaply made and cheap-looking with only the barest of entertainment values. With the coming of the video age, however, and the renewed popularity of "B" westerns, the series has been re-evaluated and while it still maintains its reputation for

Buster Crabbe and Falcon in the "Billy Carson" series.

cheapness, a look at the individual features show the Kid-Carson films to be more individualistic than previously thought. Certainly this can be said for the Carsons, since the uniformity of the Billy the Kid outlaw-now-good-guy character was dropped in favor of the more commonly accepted cowboy hero called Billy Carson.

The initial Billy Carson series entry, *Devil Riders* (1943), told of gang leader Del Stone (Charles King) and his cohort, crooked lawyer Jim Higgins (John Merton), trying to cause trouble between stage line owner Tom Farrell (Frank LaRue) and Pony Express partners Billy Carson (Crabbe) and Fuzzy Jones (St. John). Farrell has a government contract to construct a road through an area called the Badlands, where Stone has his hideout. When the outlaws attack the stagecoach carrying Farrell's daughter Sally (Patti McCarty), Billy comes to her rescue. Stone then has his men bushwhack Farrell and Billy is blamed. Tom, however, clears Carson and the two rivals come to realize someone is out to destroy their friendship. As a result, Billy and Fuzzy volunteer to continue building the road project until Tom is able to resume his duties as the director of the construction. When Farrell's men refuse to work because they have not been paid, Billy quells the uprising and lends Sally the money she needs, and she asks him to become a partner in the stage line. Higgins and Stone hire gunman Steve Lacey (Bud Osborne) to destroy the stagecoach operation but after causing a great deal of havoc he is captured by Billy. A ruse is then devised by Billy and the local sheriff (Steve Clark) in which Lacey accidentally causes Higgins to reveal illegal activities with Stone, and the lawyer is arrested. Stone escapes but is caught by Billy and the outlaw gang is arrested. After Billy and

Fuzzy use Farrell's stagecoach to take needed serum to a nearby town, the two relinquish their Pony Express business and become partners with the Farrells. *Devil Riders* contained plenty of fights and riding action plus an amusing square dance sequence in which St. John displayed comedy choreography. A hillbilly band, which included Tex Williams, performed the songs "It Don't Mean Anything Now" and "She's Mine." While Ed Cassidy received billing as the town doctor, an unbilled actor actually performed the role.

Devil Riders was released in November, 1943, and it was followed by *Frontier Outlaws* in March, 1944. In the area of Wolf Valley, prospectors Billy (Crabbe) and Fuzzy (St. John) are being forced off their gold claim by gunman Rusty Bradford (Frank Ellis), who has been hired by dishonest lawyer Barlow (Charles King) and his partner Taylor (Jack Ingram). The two crooks want to control the area but Billy beats Bradford to the draw in a gunfight, killing the outlaw. When Barlow accuses Billy of murdering Bradford, Billy turns himself in, while Fuzzy informs Billy's girlfriend Pat Clark (Frances Gladwin) and her rancher mother, Ma Clark (Marin Sais), about the shooting. The trial judge (Emmett Lynn) drops the charges against Billy but puts him in jail for thirty days to protect him from the crooks. During that time, Barlow and Taylor have their gang terrorize the vicinity. The judge lets Billy out of jail and he joins the sheriff (Edward Cassidy) in fighting the lawlessness. Ma Clark is about to lose her ranch due to a mortgage she owes Barlow and the latter has his men rustle her cattle so she cannot pay her debt. When Billy and Fuzzy find out Barlow has stolen their gold, they take it back and give it to Ma, who then pays off the crook. Billy takes the gold back from Barlow and then adopts the disguise of Mexican bandit Jose Gonzalez and offers to buy stolen cattle from Barlow. When the crook sends his men to rustle the cattle, they are arrested by Fuzzy and the sheriff. Billy then outguns both Barlow and Taylor, arresting the two badmen. During the proceedings, Tex Williams sings "Don't Waste No Worry Over Me."

Shortly after the release of *Frontier Outlaws* came *Thundering Gun Slingers*, also issued in March, 1944. Here Billy (Crabbe) investigates the hanging of his uncle (George Chesebro), a rancher accused of rustling the cattle of his neighbor, Jeff Halliday (Karl Hackett). The lynching, which appalled both Halliday and his daughter Beth (Frances Gladwin), was really instigated by saloon proprietor Steve Kirby (Charles King), who uses violence in order to get ranchers to sell out cheap so he can take control of the area. When Kirby finds out about Carson's investigation, he sends his henchmen Slade (Jack Ingram) and Dawson (Kermit Maynard) to bushwhack him, but Billy is warned by Fuzzy (St. John), the local doctor. Kirby rides to the Halliday ranch and tells him that

Advertisement for *Thundering Gun Slingers* (PRC, 1944).

Billy has come to avenge his uncle's hanging. Billy accuses Halliday of the crime and challenges him to a gunfight, but this is stopped by Fuzzy and Beth. In town, Kirby tells Billy he must pay off a debt owed to him by his uncle before he can take control of the Carson ranch. This causes a fistfight between Billy and Kirby. The crook then orders the killing of Halliday, which is carried out by Slade. Billy witnesses the killing and chases Slade just as Beth arrives on the scene, making her believe Billy murdered her father. Billy is arrested for the crime but the injured Slade goes to Fuzzy for treatment and the doctor sets Billy free. Slade and Dawson have been given orders by Kirby to evict Beth from her ranch but she is saved by Billy and Fuzzy, with Billy shooting Slade and capturing Dawson. When the sheriff (Budd Buster) and his posse come to the Halliday ranch looking for Billy, Beth sends them in the wrong direction and Billy forces a confession out of Dawson, implicating Kirby in the crimes. Back in town, Billy beats Kirby in a fight and the crook is arrested.

Unlike the previous two series entries, *Valley of Vengeance*, issued in the spring of 1944, did not contain musical interludes. Much of the storyline is told in flashback as we learn how Billy (Crabbe) and Fuzzy (St. John) first met as children, when they were the only survivors of a wagon train attack. Adopted by different families, they are reunited two decades later in King City and vow to find those responsible for the murder of their families. The story begins with Billy and Fuzzy coming to King City to accuse Dave Carr (Lynton Brent) of really being Andrew Carberry, the lawyer who led the wagon train into the deadly ambush and who stole their parents' land claims. Carr attempts to shoot Billy, who kills him in self-defense. Billy and Fuzzy then find deeds made out to King Brett (Jack Ingram); Billy tells him to return the land he has stolen. The

Lobby card for *Valley of Vengeance* (PRC, 1944) picturing Buster Crabbe and Evelyn Finley.

local sheriff, Barker (Glenn Strange), who is owned by Brett, tries to arrest Billy and Fuzzy but a federal marshal (Ed Cassidy) takes over the case. The marshal is looking into charges by Billy's rancher boss (John Elliott) of Brett's corruption. Billy and Fuzzy tell the marshal about the childhood events which led them back to King City where Brett, realizing they might uncover his crooked deals, orders gunman Burke (Charles King) to kill them. Helen Miller (Evelyn Finley), Brett's secretary, overhears him and she warns Billy and Fuzzy. When Brett tries to blow up Billy's employer's water supply, Billy and Fuzzy, who is a munitions expert, stop them with dynamite and force the gang into a nearby shack where the outlaws surrender. With the evidence of the stolen deeds, the marshal arrests Burke and Carr, and Helen tells Billy and Fuzzy her older sister was one of those killed in the wagon train attack.

In the fifth Billy Carson film, *Fuzzy Settles Down*, issued in summer 1944, Billy (Crabbe) and Fuzzy (St. John) receive the reward for capturing bank robbers. They ride to the town of Red Rock where outspoken newspaper editor John Martin (John Elliott) has been murdered and his business is about to be foreclosed. Martin's daughter Edith (Patti McCarty) does not have the money to buy the newspaper so Billy and Fuzzy purchase it and ask her to stay on and run it. Barlow (Charles King), the rancher who is behind the lawlessness, orders his gang to continue to harass local ranchers as well as sabotage the building of a telegraph line which will connect Red Rock with the rangers. When Fuzzy takes money raised by the ranchers to build the line, he is attacked by Barlow's men and accused of stealing the funds. In order to free Fuzzy, Billy goes to Barlow's ranch looking for evidence and is followed by Pete (John Merton), one of the gang. Billy beats Pete in a fight and then finds the stolen money at the ranch. As a result, Pete agrees to testify against his boss. In town, Billy and Pete confront Barlow, who shoots Pete. Billy, however, tosses a gun to the wounded man, who kills Barlow. Billy leaves town and Fuzzy gives his interest in the newspaper to Edith and follows him.

Rustlers' Hideout, which came out in September, 1944, had Billy (Crabbe) and Fuzzy (St. John) leading a cattle drive near Teton City. The cattle are to be sold to Dave Crockett (Hal Price), the owner of the local meat packing plant. Banker Stanton (John Merton) and saloon proprietor Shaw (Charles King) want to bankrupt Crockett and take over his business. They hire gambler Hammond (Lane Chandler) to cheat Crockett's son Jack (Terry Frost) at cards but Billy proves the gambler is crooked. Hammond then tries to blackmail Shaw but the latter warns him to leave town. The gambler decides to sell his information to Billy but is knocked out during a fight. Billy leaves and Hammond recovers, only to be accosted by Jack who wants his money back. They too fight but the gambler is shot from ambush just as Jack fires his gun. Jack thinks he has killed the gambler but the sheriff (Ed Cassidy), after finding Hammond's body, blames Billy. Meanwhile Billy goes to see Dave Crockett and along the way he meets the man's daughter Barbara (Patti McCarty). Crockett has been forced to mortgage his ranch and business in order to pay off a note to Stanton, who plans to ruin Crockett by stealing Carson's herd. At the ranch, Billy is accused of murdering Hammond and is later arrested by the sheriff but Fuzzy sets him free. In Teton City, Jack tells Billy and Fuzzy he murdered Hammond but Carson informs him that the gambler was killed by a bullet that was not from his gun. Billy then asks Jack to assemble men to protect the cattle herd and they are able to thwart Stanton and Shaw's rustlers. The crooks then plan to poison a water hole but Crockett and his daughter see them doing this. Shaw shoots Dave and takes Barbara prisoner. Although wounded, Dave manages to warn Billy and he follows the crooks into town. There Shaw shoots Stanton after catching him looting his safe. Billy arrives and subdues Shaw, proving it was the saloon owner's gun which killed Hammond. With Shaw under arrest, Billy frees Barbara and then he and Fuzzy complete their cattle drive.

During his tenure at PRC, director Sam Newfield directed a number of horror films: *The Mad Monster* (1942), *Dead Men Walk* (1943, with Al St. John as a villager, *The Black Raven* (1943), *The Monster Maker* (1944), and *The Flying Serpent* (1946). Several films in the "Billy Carson" series also incorporated the horror motif, beginning with *Wild Horse Phantom*, issued in the fall of 1944. One of PRC's first really successful features was the 1940 Bela Lugosi starrer *The Devil Bat*,

Lobby card for *Rustlers' Hideout* (PRC, 1944) showing Charles King and Buster Crabbe.

and the main prop from that film, a giant bat, was again used in *Wild Horse Phantom*. Most of the film's action took place in a spooky mine which was supposedly haunted, not only by the giant bat but also by a specter emitting a piercing cry, much like the villain played by Sheldon Lewis in the Ken Maynard starrer *Tombstone Canyon* (Sono-Art World Wide, 1933). Michael H. Price and John Wooley noted in *Forgotten Horrors 3* (2003), "Measured by H.P. Lovecraft's scares-are-where-you-find-'em policy, the film's overall tone is not of horrific intent, given the greater concern with reclaiming a fortune and saving a bunch of honest ranchers from economic ruin. But for a rousing moment, there, the classic elements of an *el cheapo* horror movie fell decisively into place, in a testament to the wisdom of the resourceful frugality that defines independent filmmaking."

Wild Horse Phantom, released in October, 1944 (just in time for Halloween), told of Billy (Crabbe) and a prison warden (John Elliott) working out a plan to let convict Link Daggett (Kermit Maynard) escape with cohorts Lucas (Bob Cason), Kallen (Frank Ellis) and Moffett (Frank McCarroll). Billy would then follow the quartet and find out where they hid money they stole from the Piedmont Bank. Daggett forces another prisoner, Tom Hammond (Robert Meredith), to make the jail break with him, but when he refuses to join the gang on the outside, Daggett shoots him. Hammond manages to make it to the cabin of his friend Fuzzy (St. John), and before dying tells him about Daggett and the prison break. Fuzzy then joins forces with Billy and they trail the outlaws to the Wild Horse Mine where Daggett has stashed the stolen money. Daggett cannot remember in which tunnel he hid the loot and while he and his gang are searching, they are spooked by the sound of maniacal laughter. Billy and Fuzzy are captured by the outlaws but manage to escape and take Lucas prisoner. Fuzzy stays to guard Lucas and Billy goes after the other three outlaws but spots the man making the cries and follows him to a nearby ranch. There he meets Marian Garnet (Elaine Morey), who asks him why he is trailing her father, Ed Garnet (Budd Buster), the owner of the mine. The local banker (Hal Price) arrives and tells Garnet he will repossess his ranch and mine if he does make his mortgage payment. Billy then learns the money stolen by the Daggett gang belonged to area ranchers, including Garnet. At the mine, Fuzzy is chased by a huge bat and Lucas manages to escape and find Daggett, who he taunts for not finding the money. Daggett shoots Lucas. When Fuzzy stumbles across the dead man's body, he accidentally opens a wall where the loot is hidden. Garnet shows up and takes the money as Fuzzy runs in search of Billy. Daggett and Kallen then have a falling out and Daggett wounds Kallen. Billy chases Daggett, who is killed by Kallen. Billy convinces Garnet to give up the stolen money and he takes it to the banker and pays off the ranchers' debts.

December of 1944 saw the release of two more "Billy Carson" features, *Oath of Vengeance* and *The Drifter*. In the former, Billy (Crabbe) and Fuzzy (St. John) decide to purchase a general store but they find that the area is torn by a feud between ranchers and farmers. Secretly behind the feud is banker Steve Kinney (Jack Ingram), who wants to control the entire countryside. He makes the ranchers think the farmers are stealing their cattle and at the same time he urges the ranchers to stop the farmers from selling their crops. As a result, both will go broke and he will foreclose on all. Billy tries to convince rancher Dale Kirby (Mady Laurence) to stop the hostilities but she refuses to listen. When Billy sees one of the Kirby cowhands bushwhacked, he wounds the assailant, who turns out to be one of Kinney's hired guns, Bart (John L. Cason). The shooting gets Fuzzy on the trail of Mort (Charles King), another of Kinney's men, but he is fired upon by Steve and loses him. Mort then accuses farmer Dan Harper (Karl Hackett) of the killing of the Kirby employee and before he can go on trial the outlaws break him out of jail and take him prisoner. Billy tracks the outlaws, overpowers Mort and forces him to confess that Kinney is behind the lawlessness. Once Billy beats Kinney in a fight and the latter is arrested, there is peace between the ranchers and farmers. Dale offers Billy the job of ranch foreman but he refuses and rides away. When the postmistress (Marin Sais) announces she plans to wed Fuzzy, he too leaves town.

The eighth and final 1944 "Billy Carson" release was *The Drifter*. Its rather complicated plot offered Crabbe dual roles, that of Billy Carson and his lookalike, sharpshooter Drifter Davis. The film has Davis working for a traveling medicine show, using his gun act as a front for his outlaw activities with Dirk Trent's (Jack Ingram) gang. Following a bank robbery, Davis is arrested by the local sheriff (Jimmy Aubrey) who believes he is cowboy Billy Carson (also Crabbe). When Billy comes into town the next day, the sheriff thinks he has escaped and takes him back to jail where he meets his doppelganger. Billy then decides to impersonate Davis and bring his gang to justice. In Centerville, Billy joins the medicine show and gets orders from Trent to rob a stagecoach. Meanwhile, Billy's old friend Fuzzy (St. John) arrives in town to see him but Billy rebuffs him and, in turn, is scolded by show owner Sally Dawson (Carol Parker). Fuzzy trails Billy and thwarts the stage robbery and takes the money to bank examiner Simms (Ray Bennett), a secret cohort of Trent. Believing Billy is still in jail, Fuzzy sets Drifter free but, realizing he made an error, he recaptures him and leaves him tied up in an abandoned cabin. Drifter manages to escape and when Billy arrives with Fuzzy, Davis attacks him. Confused, Fuzzy knocks out Billy and he and Drifter tie him up. Drifter then rides into town to see Trent as Sally arrives at the cabin and convinces Fuzzy he has the wrong man. Davis carries off the stagecoach robbery but is murdered by Trent after he delivers the gold to him. Billy and Fuzzy show up and arrest Trent and Simms and take them to jail. Sally offers Billy the job of sharpshooter with her show.

Seven more "Billy Carson" features were released in 1945, beginning with *His Brother's Ghost*, which came out in February. Like the earlier *Wild Horse Phantom*, it treaded into supernatural territory and provided St. John with dual roles. It has King County rancher Billy (Crabbe) being brought in by old pal Andy Jones (Al St. John) since Billy had success in rounding up an outlaw gang, one similar to the marauders raiding sharecroppers in the Wolf Valley region. Billy follows a man (Roy Brent) he saw snooping around Andy's ranch to the spread of another rancher, Thorne (Charles King), whom he accuses of being behind the raids. One of Thorne's men knocks out Billy from behind and they tie him up and take him with them on a series of raids which result in the deaths of several sharecroppers. Billy manages to escape but when he returns to Andy's ranch he finds his pal has been mortally wounded in a shootout with Thorne's men. Andy asks Billy to send for his brother Jonathan (St. John), a sheep farmer who calls himself Fuzzy. When Fuzzy arrives, Andy asks that he carry out an impersonation of him until the marauders can be stopped, and Fuzzy agrees. The local physician, Doc Packard (Karl Hackett), who is in cahoots with Thorne, declares Andy dead and that night he is buried by Billy, Fuzzy and his ranch hands. Thorne sends two of his men to make sure Andy is dead; when Fuzzy shows up, the two are frightened away from the ranch. Fuzzy then follows them to their hideout and again scares the gang members. To show his men Andy is really dead, Thorne has them open Andy's grave but Fuzzy again returns to frighten the outlaws. When one of the gang wants to quit, Thorne kills him. Billy and Fuzzy organize the sharecroppers and ranchers for a showdown with the outlaws and after a fight between Billy and henchman Jarrett (John L. Cason), the latter is frightened into a confession when he sees Fuzzy, thinking he is Andy's ghost. Jarrett tells them that Thorne and Packard are behind the crimes and they are partners with the local deputy sheriff, Bentley (Archie Hall). Billy and Fuzzy go to Bentley's office and he too is spooked by the sight of Fuzzy and is about to confess when Thorne shoots him. Thorne tries to escape but is stopped by Billy after a fight. Fuzzy then declares himself the area judge and sheriff and he sentences Thorne and his gang to prison.

In *Shadows of Death*, issued in April, 1945, Billy (Crabbe) is hired by railroad agent Dave Haneley (Karl Hackett) to help him find out the route the company plans to take. Since the line is supposed to run to Red Rock, Billy rides there in the guise of a cattle buyer. Hostel owner Steve Landreau (Charles King) has overheard Billy and Dave's conversation and later he and his cohorts Butch (Bob [John L.] Cason) and Frisco (Frank Ellis) murder the agent and steal his railroad map. Before heading to Red Rock, Billy finds the murdered Haneley; when he realizes that the map is missing, he believes the agent was killed for it. Landreau and his pals also come to Red Rock where he opens a gambling house, fleecing local rancher Clay Kincaid (Edward Hall), much to the chagrin of his girlfriend, Babs Darcy (Dona Dax). The local sheriff, barber and justice of the peace, Fuzzy Jones (St. John) confronts Landreau about cheating his friend Clay but is thrown out of the gambling house. Billy arrives and fights with Butch and Frisco. Fuzzy then introduces him to Babs, making Clay jealous; this causes the girl to break their engagement. Billy tells Fuzzy he is looking for Haneley's killer and he suspects Steve and he searches the latter's office for the map but cannot find it. Clay continues to lose money to Landreau, who wants his ranch since he knows that land will be used by the railroad to extend its new line. Billy tries unsuccessfully to stop Clay from putting up his ranch as security for his gambling debts and Clay threatens to kill him. Wanting both Billy and Clay out of the way, Landreau tries to set up a gunfight between the two men. Fuzzy tries to stop Clay from riding into town but is thwarted by Landreau. At the gambling house, Clay is wounded by gunfire from Landreau's men but Billy shoots Butch, and Fuzzy does the same to Frisco. Landreau tries to escape with the map but Billy stops him, now having the evidence to jail the murderer. When Clay recovers from his wounds, he and Babs are married by Fuzzy.

Although a rather lumbering effort in the "Billy Carson" series, *Shadows of Death* does have some amusing moments. Both Emmett Lynn and Jimmy Aubrey have funny cameos as bathtub users at Fuzzy's tonsorial parlor. St. John also milks quite a bit of comedy out of a couple of scenes. While shaving bad guy Frisco (Frank Ellis), he accidentally drops a straight razor down his back, splitting open the man's coat and shirt. Toward the end of the film, Fuzzy tries trimming a customer's (Budd Buster) beard but he cannot satisfy the man. First he is made to look like Ulysses S. Grant and then he is turned into an Abraham Lincoln lookalike.

One of the highlights of the series was *Gangster's Den* (1945), which featured Charles King (usually a dastardly villain) in a comedy role. King, who began his screen career as a comedian in the *Mike and Ike* series of two-reelers for Universal in 1927, is cast as a lovable drunk. His scenes with St. John highlight an otherwise typical plot; in the course of the action, Fuzzy meets barfly King. Needing a bodyguard, Fuzzy tells King he is "big and ugly enough" for the part with Charlie replying, "I was a pretty baby." Asked how much the job pays, Fuzzy tells him, "All your drinks and grub. Do you want the job?" Charlie replies, "Forget the grub and I do."

Coming out in the early summer of 1945, *Gangster's Den* had Billy (Crabbe) and Fuzzy (St. John) as gold miners who refuse to sell their claim to corrupt lawyer Horace Black (I. Stanford Jolley), who also wants the ranch belonging to siblings Ruth (Sydney Logan) and Jimmy Lane (Michael Owen). He also wants to buy Taylor's (Karl Hackett) saloon since he thinks it is built over the entrance to a valuable gold claim. When Jimmy loses at gambling, he asks Black for a loan and the lawyer has him sign an IOU which is really the deed to the family ranch. Taylor, afraid of Black, sells the saloon to Fuzzy, who uses the gold he prospected with Billy to pay for the property. Gambler Curt (Kermit Maynard), a cohort of Black, tells his boss about the sale and they plan to ambush Fuzzy. Ruth learns what is happening and wounds Curt and then rides to Billy and Jimmy for help. Jimmy is wounded in a battle with Black's gang and later Billy finds that Taylor has been murdered and the gold Fuzzy paid him is missing. When a deputy (Wally West) attempts to serve foreclosure papers on the ranch, Jimmy realizes he has been duped by Black. Jimmy wounds the deputy, who is later killed by Black, who then blames Jimmy for his murder. When Billy sees Black burning the deputy's shirt, he realizes his friend is innocent and he has Fuzzy tell the lawyer he wants to sell him the saloon. They also spread the rumor that Taylor is still alive and is at the Lane ranch. There Billy forces Black's henchman Dent (George Chesebro) to admit he killed Taylor at his boss' behest. Black purchases the saloon from Fuzzy with the stolen gold but when henchman Curt finds out Dent has been arrested, he figures Black has double-crossed them. Curt and Black have a shootout and they end up killing each other. When Fuzzy realizes the cellar under the saloon houses only weaver's looms, he gives the property to its cook (Emmett Lynn) and he and Billy return to gold mining.

Stagecoach Outlaws, released in the summer of 1945, begins with Billy (Crabbe) saving Linda Bowen (Frances Gladwin) from masked outlaws during a stagecoach robbery. Jed Bowen (Ed Cassidy), Linda's father and the stage line owner, offers Billy the job of protecting his operation. Billy declines the offer. The man behind the robbery, saloon keeper Steve Kirby (I. Stanford Jolley), wants the line to carry bullion from the area's growing mining business. Kirby tells his cohorts Slade (Bob [John L.] Cason) and Dawson (Kermit Maynard) to go to a nearby town and break gunslinger Matt Brawley (Robert Kortman) out of jail so he can join their gang. Brawley, however, sets himself free by fooling deputy Fuzzy (St. John) and locking him in a cell. When Slade and Dawson arrive at the jail, they think Fuzzy is Brawley; they free him and he goes with them to the town of Red River. There Billy sees his old pal Fuzzy and then trails him when he rides with Slade and Dawson to a ghost town hotel. Dawson gets the drop on Billy but he manages to escape after hearing the two outlaws try and find out where Fuzzy, who they think is Brawley, has hidden money from his various robberies. Billy agrees to aid Bowen after questioning Kirby's efforts to buy the franchise. Using a disguise, Billy takes a payroll intended for the stagecoach in a buckboard while the strong box on the coach contains washers. Kirby forces Fuzzy to rob the stagecoach as Brawley comes to Red Rock trying to find out who is impersonating him. Billy rides to the ghost town to warn Fuzzy and finds that Slade and Dawson are holding Linda prisoner. While Fuzzy leads Brawley and Slade away from the ghost town, Billy beats Dawson in a fight. Returning to the deserted hotel, Fuzzy helps Billy subdue the two outlaws. They return the outlaws to Red Rock and there Dawson is shot by Kirby before he can implicate him. Billy shoots Kirby, bringing an end to the outlaws' terror reign. Fuzzy returns Brawley to jail.

Border Badmen and *Fighting Bill Carson* were both issued in October, 1945. The first to come out was *Border Badmen* and in it Fuzzy (St. John) convinces Billy (Crabbe) to accompany him to Cedar Creek to collect an inheritance left to him by a distant cousin, Stockton. They find a toll gate keeper murdered and Deputy Sheriff Spencer (Ray Bennett) arrests them for the killing, the body being that of the town sheriff, Bentley. The two are ordered released, however, by Merritt (Charles King), the former superintendent of the ranch Fuzzy expects to inherit. Merritt is in cahoots with Spencer, town banker Gillian (Archie Hall), hotel owner Evans (Budd Buster) and Jim Bates (Steve Clark), the mayor of the town, in a scheme to use the Stockton estate to purchase the area around Cedar Creek. The group plan to substitute saloon girl Roxie (Marilyn Gladstone) for another heir, Helen Stockton (Lorraine Miller). When they try to kidnap the young woman, they are opposed by Billy and Fuzzy. Taken to a remote cabin, the trio manages to escape and they go to the home of the deceased sheriff's widow (Marin Sais), who tells them her husband was murdered because he was the only one in town who could identify Helen. Billy and Fuzzy go back to town and Billy identifies himself as a Stockton heir and finds letters from Helen in Bates' room. Bates is stabbed and Billy and Fuzzy play a game of cat and mouse with the crooks through a secret passage between the hotel rooms. Learning that Helen has been kidnapped, Billy and Fuzzy force some of the gang members to reveal that Merritt kidnapped the girl and, locating Roxie, they make her admit she was posing as Helen. Going to the hotel, the duo subdue Merritt and Spencer and free Helen as Evans tries to kill Billy but fails. Evans then turns on Merritt, saying he was behind the murders. At a probate hearing, Helen receives her inheritance and Fuzzy gets one dollar and all his cousin's debts.

The second October, 1945, series release, *Fighting Bill Carson* had the title character (Crabbe) save Clay Allison (I. Stanford Jolley) and his niece, Jeanne Darcy (Kay Hughes), from outlaws during a payroll wagon robbery. During the holdup, Billy shoots and kills outlaw Steve (Budd Buster); the latter's brother Cass (Kermit Maynard), another robber, vows revenge. Although Allison set up the banking system in the town of Eureka, he does not want the job of bank president since he plans to rob the bank once all of its deposits are in place. Instead he urges the townspeople to make Fuzzy (St. John) the bank president. Fuzzy hires Jeanne to work as a teller and she informs her uncle of the combination to the bank's safe. She tells her uncle that Billy and Fuzzy suspect him of being behind the holdup and he arranges for her to lure Billy away from town so he can be ambushed by Allison's cohort Cass and Joe (John L. Cason). Billy manages to escape from the outlaw as Allison robs the bank's safe. After Billy tells Allison that Jeanne has confessed to her part in his scheme, Joe tries to kill Billy but is instead shoot dead. Billy and Allison then have a fistfight with the crook being beaten and forced to return the money he stole. When Jeanne asks Billy to forgive her, she is accidentally killed by Cass, who was trying to shoot Billy. Billy then kills Cass.

Prairie Rustlers, issued in November, 1945, again offered Crabbe dual roles and it also gave St. John an opportunity to display his acrobatic abilities in a scene in which he does bicycle riding tricks, the character of Fuzzy Jones having won a bicycle in a raffle. Crabbe played Billy Carson and his lookalike cousin Jim Slade, who blames Billy for putting him behind bars. Slade is the leader of a rustling gang which kills the town's sheriff (Wally West), forcing café owner-deputy sheriff Fuzzy (St. John) to take over the lawman's job. When Slade and his gang come to town, Fuzzy mistakes Slade for Billy and is knocked down by the outlaw. When Billy does arrive, Fuzzy confronts him but Billy manages to convince him of his true identity. Helen Foster (Evelyn Finley), the daughter of rancher Dan Foster (Karl Hackett), asks Fuzzy to recommend a trail boss for their upcoming cattle drive and Fuzzy suggests Billy, who turns down the job. Slade's men, Matt (I. Stanford Jolley) and Vic (Kermit Maynard), offer to help Helen and a fight breaks out between them and Billy. Matt goes to the Foster ranch and convinces Dan and Helen to hire him as their trail boss. When Billy tries to stop them, they order him off their property. Billy then trails Matt to the gang's hideout where he finds Slade, and the two fight. Outlaws kidnap Billy the next night and take him to their hideout. The next day the outlaws try to rustle the Fosters' cattle and Slade wounds Dan. He then goes back to the hideout and changes clothes with prisoner Billy, with the latter being blamed for the rustling.

Kermit Maynard and Buster Crabbe in *Prairie Rustlers* (PRC, 1945).

Matt and Helen take Billy into town but Fuzzy refuses to arrest him and helps him to escape. Billy returns to the hideout and forces Slade to again change clothes with him. Slade knocks Billy down and runs from the shack but Matt mistakes him for Billy and shoots him, with Billy gunning down Matt. Billy becomes the town marshal and Fuzzy returns to his café.

The final seven "Billy Carson" features were issued in 1946, beginning in January of that year with *Lightning Raiders*. *Variety* called it "a run-of-the-mill western ... with enough action, gun fights and juvenile comedy to satisfy the customers who go for this type of thing. Two stars have built up quite a following for themselves and their names on the marquee should make the film do okay in its usual spot on a weekend dualer." The plot has Billy (Crabbe) and Fuzzy (St. John) investigating a series of mail robberies. Billy finds it odd that while the bandits take the mailbags, they do not bother gold shipments. Following a holdup, the duo trails the robbers to an abandoned mining camp and rout them. They ride to Murray's (Karl Hackett) ranch and he tells them he plans to sell his mine to Frank Hayden (Steve Darrell), the town banker. An assay report shows his mine contains only low-grade ore but Billy tells him the report has been altered. Billy comes to believe Murray is behind the robberies and is faking the assayer's reports so he can buy up all the mines. Because Hayden has given many of them loans, the locals refuse to believe Billy's theory. Hayden decides to get Billy and Fuzzy out of the way by framing them for the robberies. When Fuzzy is found with a letter retrieved from trailing the holdup gang, he is jailed, but escapes. Fuzzy then leads Hayden and his gang out of town and Billy opens the crook's safe and finds other altered reports which lead to Hayden's arrest.

Romance enters Fuzzy's life in *Gentlemen with Guns*, released in March of 1946. Here Billy (Crabbe) comes to see his pal Fuzzy (St. John) and finds him at odds with rancher Jim McAllister (Steve Darrell), who does not want Fuzzy to sell some of his land but instead wants to buy his water rights. Billy also learns that Fuzzy plans to marry Matilda Boggs (Patricia Knox), who he met via a lonely hearts club. To get Fuzzy out of the way, McAllister tells the sheriff (Budd Buster) that Fuzzy has been rustling his cattle and he then sends henchman Ed Slade (George Chesebro) to Fuzzy's ranch. While there, Slade is shot and Fuzzy is blamed for the crime. Slade, however, was only faking; after Fuzzy is arrested, he rides to McAllister's hideout. Matilda arrives in town and after Fuzzy sees the beautiful woman he breaks out of jail to be with her. The young woman, however, only wants Fuzzy's money and she tells McAllister she will sell him Fuzzy's ranch once he is hanged for Slade's killing. Slade also falls for Matilda and proposes to her but she sends word to Fuzzy to leave his hiding place so they can be married. When Fuzzy sees Slade leave his ranch, he tells Billy, who gives chase to the supposedly dead man but loses him. Billy, however, does get back to the ranch in time to stop the wedding while McAllister tries to instigate a lynch mob to get Fuzzy out of the way. Billy then locates Slade and gets him back to town, exonerating Fuzzy. Billy defeats McAllister in a fight and the unwed Matilda leaves town.

Ghost of Hidden Valley, which came out in June, 1946, was another series entry to include the horror motif in his plot. An abandoned ranch near Hidden Valley is used by gang leader Blackie Dawson (Charles King) to hide stolen cattle. It is an ideal hideout since the place is supposed to be haunted. When the owner of the property, Henry Trent (John Meredith), arrives with his butler Tweedle (Jimmy Aubrey), Billy (Crabbe) and Fuzzy (St. John), who were friends of Henry's father, escort them to the ranch. Although Fuzzy fears ghosts, he and Billy stay the night at the ranch and the next day they find a footprint near the ranch house and then narrowly miss being shot. Neighbor Kaye Dawson (Jean Carlin), Blackie's niece, pays Henry a visit and the two are attracted to each other. Dawson's boss, Arnold (Zon Murray), orders him to kill Henry but Dawson refuses and wants to end the cattle rustling. After finding cattle tracks on the ranch, Billy comes to believe the rustlers are using it as a hideout and he also recognizes Arnold as a wanted outlaw. Kaye tells her uncle she loves Henry and fears for his safety. The gang kidnaps Henry, and Arnold tries to force him to sign over his ranch, but Dawson comes to his defense. As a result, Arnold kills Dawson and plans to frame Billy for the murder. Billy, however, proves

Arnold is actually wanted killer Jim Slade and he brings the outlaw to justice. As a result, Trent and Kaye wed.

Released in July, 1946, *Prairie Badmen* had Fuzzy (St. John) working for a touring medicine show run by Doc Lattimer (Ed Cassidy) and his children, Linda (Patricia Knox) and Don (John L. Buster). When outlaws spook the medicine wagon horses, Billy (Crabbe) stops them and is invited to ride with the group. In the next town, Doc is accosted by outlaws Cal (Charles King), Lon (Kermit Maynard) and Steve (John L. Cason). Cal later asks Don if his father knew outlaw Bill Thompson (Frank Ellis). Cal then demands that Doc give him the map he got from Thompson which reveals the hiding place of gold bars the outlaw had stolen. Doc denies any knowledge of Thompson and the map, but after the outlaws are run off by Billy and Fuzzy he tells them the wounded Thompson had indeed given him such a map. Wanting to get away from traveling, Don steals the map and goes to a shack, the hiding place of the gold. He is trailed there by the gang and by Billy and Fuzzy. A fight ensues after Fuzzy stampedes the gang's horses and Billy and Fuzzy capture the outlaws. Doc gives the gold bars to the local sheriff (Steve Clark) and receives a reward.

Terrors on Horseback and *Overland Riders* were released in August, 1946. The former has Fuzzy (St. John) invite his friend Billy (Crabbe) to come to Canyon City to meet his niece who will arrive by stagecoach. Outlaws, however, attack the stage and rob it, murdering all the passengers. Fuzzy vows revenge for his niece's killing and he and Billy trace the gang to the outlaw town of Pecos City. Having met saloon singer Roxie (Patti McCarty) while on their way to town, they get a lead from her which takes them to the livery stable owned by Ed Sperling (Karl Hackett) since the girl was riding a horse used by one of the stage attackers. They find Sperling at the local bar and after a fight breaks out, Billy questions a gambler (Kermit Maynard) who admits he was hired by Ben Taggart (Bud Osborne) to take part in the robbery. The gambler is shot before he can name the person behind the crime. Heading to the town of Red Post to see Taggart, Billy and Fuzzy meet deputy sheriff Jim Austin (Steve Darrell) and they tell him of their suspicions. One of Taggart's men (Frank Ellis) tells him about Billy and Fuzzy, and Taggart has his gang capture the pair. Taggart tells Billy and Fuzzy that the murders were committed by gang members, including Luke Gordon (George Chesebro) and a man named Buck. Billy and Fuzzy manage to escape and locate Gordon, who says Buck committed the murders. As they return to Canyon City, Gordon is murdered but Billy plots a ruse, saying that Gordon is still living in order to capture Buck. When Billy finally captures Buck, he is shown to be the deputy sheriff.

Overland Riders had Billy (Crabbe) rescuing Fuzzy (St. John) and Jean Barkley (Patti McCarty) from a stagecoach holdup, with Fuzzy being surprisingly ungrateful. Fuzzy goes to the land office and tries to buy some land from agent Vic Landreau (Jack Ingram), who refuses to sell. Landreau is behind the holdup because the wants the Barkley ranch and surrounding land for himself. Billy escorts Jean to the ranch of her father, Jeff Barkley (Slim Whitaker), and Landreau arrives and offers to buy the spread since he has a mortgage on the place. Jeff refuses since he has the money to pay off the mortgage. Fuzzy then tries to buy land from Barkley, who also refuses him, and Fuzzy blames Billy. Billy trails Fuzzy, who is bushwhacked by Landreau's gang, and rescues him. When Barkley goes to town to pay off his mortgage, he is murdered by Landreau, who takes the money. After Fuzzy finds the murdered man he is arrested for the crime but Billy believes he is innocent. Billy remembers that the money was blood-stained from the holdup and after Fuzzy tells him the railroad plans to build through the Barkley property, Billy realizes that Landreau is behind the crimes. Although Jean plans to sell the ranch to Landreau, Billy stops her and then breaks into Vic's safe and finds the blood-stained currency. Landreau and his men are arrested by the sheriff (Bud Osborne) and Billy and Fuzzy hire on as trail drivers for Jean.

The final "Billy Carson" feature, *Outlaws of the Plains*, came out in September 1946 and it too had horror overtones. The ghost of a long-dead Indian chief speaks to Fuzzy (St. John) and tells him there is gold near Cortez Rock. Fuzzy goes there and finds gold nuggets but is accused of trespassing. The land owner, Nord Finner (Charles King), offers to sell him the property. The spirit's voice tells Fuzzy to find investors for the purchase and he decides to include his pal Billy (Crabbe), although the spirit warns him against Billy. Billy is ambushed on his way to see Fuzzy but escapes as Fuzzy gets area ranchers to invest in the purchase, since they think he can see into the future. Billy does not believe in Fuzzy's story and becomes worried because some of the ranchers have mortgaged their land to invest in his scheme. Rancher Henry Reed (Karl Hackett) observes the spirit talking to Fuzzy, recognizing him as a member of Finner's gang. Before Reed can reveal the truth, he is killed, but Billy locates the killer and forces him to confess. When Billy decides to take the spirit's place, he is captured by the gang and left unconscious. He revives in time to tell the sheriff (Bud Osborne) what has happened and they round up Finner and his gang. Although Finner planted the gold nuggets in order to get a big sale, the locals do become rich because a railroad agent (Slim Whitaker) offers them a huge sum for their land.

While filming *Outlaws of the Plains* in 1946, Crabbe finally got fed up with the Neufelds' cost-cutting and quit the series. Quickly the brothers cast Lash LaRue as Cheyenne Davis and continued on, keeping St. John as Fuzzy Q. Jones. Crabbe worked for the Neufelds again in the television series *Captain Gallant of the Foreign Legion*, also known as *Captain Gallant* and *Foreign Legionnaire*. It ran on both NBC-TV and ABC-TV between 1955 and 1963 before being syndicated. Crabbe co-starred in the series with his son, Cullen "Cuffey" Crabbe, and another Fuzzy, Fuzzy Knight, for 65 half-hour episodes, filmed in North Africa.

Crabbe continued his film career after the Billy Carson series, appearing in the Westerns *Last of the Redmen* (1947), *Gun Brothers* (1956), *The Lawless Eighties* (1957), *Badman's Country* (1958), *Gunfighters of Abilene* (1960), *The Bounty Killer* and *Arizona Raiders* (both 1965) as well as the serials *Pirates of the High Seas* (1950) and *King of the Kongo* (1952). He worked in television and authored two books, *Buster Crabbe's Energistics* (1977) and *Buster Crabbe's Arthritis Exercise Book* (1980). He often won championships in the seniors' swimming division. In the 1970s and early 1980s he was a guest at Western film conventions and he closed out his film career in *The Comeback Trail* (filmed in 1970 but not given much exposure until 1982), *Swim Team* (1979) and *The Alien Dead* (1980). He died in 1983; at the time he was a member of the planning committee for the 1984 Los Angeles Olympic Games.

As noted, St. John continued with the Fuzzy Q. Jones role in a new PRC series starring Lash LaRue in the role of Marshal Cheyenne Davis. After eight 1947 releases, the studio became Eagle Lion and LaRue and St. John signed with producer Ron Ormond for a Western Adventure Production series. They did a dozen features for the company between 1948 and 1952, ending with *Frontier Phantom*, which marked the finale of St. John's nearly 40-year film career. While working with both Crabbe and LaRue at PRC, St. John had made personal appearances, both solo and in tandem with the two stars. Following the demise of his film career, he toured for the next decade, dying on January 31, 1963, just before a scheduled theater appearance in Georgia.

Filmography

Devil Riders (PRC, 1943, 56 minutes) Producer: Sigmund Neufeld. Director: Sam Newfield. Screenplay: Joe (Joseph) O'Donnell. Photography: Robert Cline. Editor: Bob Crandall. Sound: Lyle Willey. Production Manager: Bert Sternbach. Assistant Director: Melville De Lay.

Cast: Buster Crabbe (Billy Carson), Al St. John (Fuzzy Q. Jones), Patti McCarty (Sally Farrell), Charles King (Del Stone), John Merton (Jim Higgins), Kermit Maynard (Red), Frank La Rue (Tom Farrell), Jack La Rue (Turner), George Chesebro (Curley), Hank Bell (Jed Clark), Steve Clark (Sheriff), Bud Osborne (Steve Lacey), Al Ferguson (Al), Rose Plummer (Woman at Dance), Jimmy Aubrey, Ralph Bucko, Roy Bucko, Artie Ortego (Citizens), Art Dillard, Bert Dillard, Frank Ellis, Herman Hack, Kansas Moehring (Henchmen), Curley Dresden (Posse Rider), Big Slicker Quartet [Tex Williams, Deuce Spriggins, Smokey Rogers, Don Weston] (Musicians).

Frontier Outlaws (PRC, 1944, 58 minutes) Producer: Sigmund Neufeld. Director: Sam Newfield. Screenplay: Joe (Joseph) O'Donnell. Photography: Robert Cline. Editor: Holbrook N. Todd. Sound: Art Smith. Production Manager: Bert Sternbach. Assistant Director: Melville De Lay.

Cast: Buster Crabbe (Billy Carson), Al St. John (Fuzzy Q. Jones), Frances Gladwin (Pat Clark), Marin Sais (Ma Clark), Charles King (Barlow), Jack Ingram (Taylor), Kermit Maynard (Wallace), Edward (Ed) Cassidy (Sheriff), Emmett Lynn (Judge James Ryan), Budd

Buster (Bartender), Bert Dillard (Bert), Frank Ellis (Rusty Bradford), Ray Henderson (Dave), Wally West (Cowboy), Dan White (Stage Guard), Silver Harr, John L. Cason, Tex Cooper (Ranchers), Jimmy Aubrey, George Morrell, Horace B. Carpenter, Jack Tornek (Bar Customers), Silver Tip Baker (Stage Driver), Herman Hack, Carl Mathews, Artie Ortego (Henchmen), Tex Williams (Singer).

Thundering Gun Slingers (PRC, 1944, 60 minutes) Producer: Sigmund Neufeld. Director: Sam Newfield. Screenplay: Fred Myton. Photography: Robert Cline. Editor: Holbrook N. Todd. Art Director: Paul Palmentola. Sound: Glen Glenn. Production Manager: Bert Sternbach. Assistant Director: Melville De Lay.

Cast: Buster Crabbe (Billy Carson), Al St. John (Fuzzy Q. Jones), Frances Gladwin (Beth Halliday), Charles King (Steve Kirby), Jack Ingram (Vic Dawson), Karl Hackett (Jeff Halliday), Kermit Maynard (Ed Slade), Budd Buster (Sheriff), George Chesebro (Dave Carson), Hank Bell (Bartender Hank), Cactus Mack, Ray Henderson, Augie Gomez (Henchmen), Roy Bucko, Herman Hack (Bar Customers), George Morrell (Townsman).

Valley of Vengeance (PRC, 1944, 56 minutes) Producer: Sigmund Neufeld. Director: Sam Newfield. Screenplay: Joseph O'Donnell. Photography: Jack Greenhalgh. Editor: Holbrook N. Todd. Sound: Glen Glenn. Production Manager: Bert Sternbach. Special Effects: Ray Mercer. Assistant Director: Melville De Lay.

Cast: Buster Crabbe (Billy Carson), Al St. John (Fuzzy Q. Jones), Evelyn Finley (Helen Finley), Glenn Strange (Marshal Barker), Charles King (Burke), John Merton (Burt), Lynton Brent (David Carr/Andrew Carberry), Jack Ingram (Rance "King" Brett), Bud Osborne (Dad Carson), Nora Bush (Ma Carson), Steve Clark (Happy), Donald Mayo (Youthful Billy Carson), David Polonsky (Youthful Fuzzy Q. Jones), John Elliott (Dan Stewart), Hank Bell (Mr. Jones), Ed Cassidy (Marshal Riley), Budd Buster (Parsons), Jimmy Aubrey, Jess Cavin, Morgan Flowers, George Morrell, Dan White (Settlers), John L. Cason, Curley Dresden, Carl Matthews, Wally West, Ben Corbett (Henchmen), Pascale Perry (Charlie), Artie Ortego (Deputy), Herman Hack (Cook), Merrill McCormick, Ray Henderson (Men in Saloon), Tex Cooper (Onlooker).

Fuzzy Settles Down (PRC, 1944, 60 minutes) Producer: Sigmund Neufeld. Director: Sam Newfield. Screenplay: Louise Rousseau. Photography: Jack Greenhalgh. Editor: Holbrook N. Todd. Sound: Glen Glenn. Production Manager: Bert Sternbach. Special Effects: Ray Mercer. Assistant Director: Melville De Lay.

Cast: Buster Crabbe (Billy Carson), Al St. John (Fuzzy Q. Jones), Patti McCarty (Edith Martin), Charles King (Lafe Barlow), John Merton (Pete), Frank McCarroll (Rusty), Hal Price (Sheriff), John Elliott (John Martin), Edward [Ed] Cassidy (Rancher Weaver), Robert Hill (Bidder), Edward Peil, Sr. (Carson City Marshal), Ted Mapes, Tex Palmer (Bank Robbers), Horace B. Carpenter (Man in Office), Ray Jones (Henchman), Artie Ortego, Wally West, Steve Clark, Ben Corbett, John L. Cason (Red Rock Citizens), Holly Bane, Herman Hack, Dan White, Jack Tornek, Morgan Flowers, George Morrell (Townsmen), Ray Henderson, Chick Hannon, Jimmy Aubrey, Hank Bell, Silver Tip Baker (Men in Saloon).

Rusters' Hideout (PRC, 1944, 60 minutes) Producer: Sigmund Neufeld. Director: Sam Newfield. Screenplay: Joseph O'Donnell. Photography: Jack Greenhalgh. Editor: Holbrook N. Todd. Sound: Glen Glenn. Production Manager: Bert Sternbach. Assistant Director: Melville De Lay.

Cast: Buster Crabbe (Billy Carson), Al St. John (Fuzzy Q. Jones), Patti McCarty (Barbara), Charles King (Buck Shaw), John Merton (Harry Stanton), Terry Frost (Jack Crockett), Hal Price (Dave Crockett), Lane Chandler (Hammond), Al Ferguson (Steve), Frank McCarroll (Squint), Ed Cassidy (Sheriff), Steve Clark (Ed Lowery), John L. Cason (Charlie Green), Wally West (Deputy), Bud Osborne (Henchman), Ed Peil, Sr. (Gambler).

Wild Horse Phantom (PRC, 1944, 56 minutes) Producer: Sigmund Neufeld. Director: Sam Newfield. Screenplay: George Milton [Milton Raison & George Wallace Sayre]. Photography: Jack Greenhalgh. Editor: Holbrook N. Todd. Sound: Arthur Smith. Production Manager: Bert Sternbach. Special Effects: Ray Mercer. Assistant Director: Harold E. Knox.

Cast: Buster Crabbe (Billy Carson), Al St. John (Fuzzy Q. Jones), Elaine Morey (Marian Garnet), Kermit Maynard (Link Daggett), Budd Buster (Ed Garnet), Hal Price (Cliff Walters), Robert Meredith (Tom Hammond), Frank Ellis (Kallen), Frank McCarroll (Moffett), Bob [John L.] Cason (Lucas), John Elliott (Prison Warden), Slim Whitaker (Prison Guard), Reed Howes (Jim Brooks), Bud Osborne (Bill), Steve Clark, George Morrell, Herman Hack, Curley Dresden, Hank Bell, Ed Peil, Sr., Jack Tornek (Ranchers), Jimmy Aubrey (Henchman).

Oath of Vengeance (PRC, 1944, 57 minutes) Producer: Sigmund Neufeld. Director: Sam Newfield. Screenplay: Fred Myton. Photography: Robert Cline. Editor: Holbrook N. Todd. Sound: Arthur Smith. Production Manager: Bert Sternbach. Special Effects: Ray Mercer. Assistant Director: Harold E. Knox.

Cast: Buster Crabbe (Billy Carson), Al St. John (Fuzzy Q. Jones), Mady Laurence (Dale Kirby), Jack Ingram (Steve Kinney), Charles King (Mort), Marin Sais (Ma), Karl Hackett (Dan Harper), Kermit Maynard (Red), Hal Price (Sheriff), Frank Ellis (Vic), John L. Cason (Bart), Frank McCarroll, Augie Gomez, Herman Hack (Henchmen), Jimmy Aubrey (Deputy Sheriff), Jack Kinney, Rose Plummer, Hank Bell, Jack Evans, Morgan Flowers (Settlers), Wally West, Ray

Henderson, Ralph Bucko, Tex Palmer (Cowboys).

The Drifter (PRC, 1944, 61 minutes) Producer: Sigmund Neufeld. Director: Sam Newfield. Screenplay: Patricia Harper. Photography: Robert Cline. Editor: Holbrook N. Todd. Production Manager: Bert Sternbach. Sound: Lyle Willey. Assistant Director: Melville De Lay.

Cast: Buster Crabbe (Billy Carson/Drifter Davis), Al St. John (Fuzzy Q. Jones), Carol Parker (Sally Dawson), Jack Ingram (Dirk Trent), Kermit Maynard (Jack), Roy Brent (Sam), George Chesebro (Blackie), Ray Bennett (Simms), Jimmy Aubrey (Sheriff Perkins), Slim Whitaker (Marshal Hodges), Robert Hill (Thomas Barton), Wally West (Henchman), Herman Hack, Foxy Callahan (Citizens).

His Brother's Ghost (PRC, 1945, 58 minutes) Producer: Sigmund Neufeld. Director: Sam Newfield. Screenplay: George Milton [Milton Raison & George Wallace Sayre]. Photography: Jack Greenhalgh. Editor: Holbrook N. Todd. Sound: Arthur Smith. Production Manager: Bert Sternbach. Assistant Director: Harold E. Knox.

Cast: Buster Crabbe (Billy Carson), Al St. John (Fuzzy Q. Jones/Andy Jones), Charles King (Thorne), Karl Hackett (Doc Packard), Archie Hall (Bentley), Roy Brent (Yeager), Bud Osborne (Magill), Bob [John L.] Cason (Jarrett), Frank McCarroll (Madison), George Morrell (Foster), Richard Alexander, Carl Mathews, Charles Soldani, Art Dillard (Henchmen), Frank Ellis, Herman Hack, Jimmy Aubrey, Ray Henderson (Ranchers), Rube Dalroy (Citizen).

Shadows of Death (PRC, 1945, 59 minutes) Producer: Sigmund Neufeld. Director: Sam Newfield. Screenplay: Fred Myton. Photography: Jack Greenhalgh. Editor: Holbrook N. Todd. Art Director: Paul Palmentola. Sound: Glen Glenn. Special Effects: Ray Mercer. Assistant Director: Melville De Lay.

Cast: Buster Crabbe (Billy Carson), Al St. John (Fuzzy Q. Jones), Dona Dax (Babs Darcy), Charles King (Steve Landreau), Karl Hackett (Dave Haneley), Edward Hall (Clay Kincaid), Frank Ellis (Frisco), Bob [John L.] Cason (Butch), Emmett Lynn (Man in Bathtub), Bud Osborne, Budd Buster (Barber Shop Customers), Jack Baxley (Sheriff), Wally West (Deputy), Jimmy Aubrey (Drunk), Frank McCarroll (Henchman), George Morrell, Ray Henderson, Rube Dalroy (Citizen), Jack Tornek, Jack Evans (Men Playing Checkers), Art Dillard, Lew Morphy (Poker Players).

Poster for *Wild Horse Phantom* (PRC, 1944).

Gangster's Den (PRC, 1945, 55 minutes) Producer: Sigmund Neufeld. Director: Sam Newfield. Screenplay: George Plympton. Photography: Jack Greenhalgh. Editor: Holbrook N. Todd. Sound: Charles Althouse. Production Manager: Bert Sternbach. Special Effects: Ray Mercer. Assistant Director: Jack Vance.

Cast: Buster Crabbe (Billy Carson), Al St. John (Fuzzy Q. Jones), Sydney Logan (Ruth Lane), Charles

King (Butch), Emmett Lynn (Webfoot), Kermit Maynard (Curt), Edward [Ed] Cassidy (Sheriff), Stan [I. Stanford] Jolley (Horace Black), George Chesebro (Dent), Karl Hackett (Taylor), Michael Owen (Jimmy Lane), John L. Cason (Burke), Wally West (Deputy), Herman Hack (Mine Guard), Steve Clark (Bartender), Jimmy Aubrey (Henchman), Artie Ortego (Townsman), Frank McCarroll, Art Fowler, Jack Montgomery, Morgan Flowers (Card Players), Art Mix, Matty Roubert, Jack Evans, Horace B. Carpenter, Fox Callahan, Victor Cox, Rube Dalroy (Bar Customers).

Stagecoach Outlaws (PRC, 1945, 58 minutes) Producer: Sigmund Neufeld. Director: Sam Newfield. Screenplay: Fred Myton. Photography: Jack Greenhalgh. Editor: Holbrook N. Todd. Sound: Glen Glenn. Production Manager: Bert Sternbach. Special Effects: Ray Mercer. Assistant Director: William O'Connor.

Cast: Buster Crabbe (Billy Carson), Al St. John (Fuzzy Q. Jones), Frances Gladwin (Linda Bowen), Ed Cassidy (Jed Bowen), I. Stanford Jolley (Steve Kirby), Kermit Maynard (Vic), Bob [John L.] Cason (Joe), Robert Kortman (Matt Brawley), Steve Clark (Sheriff), Wally West (Virge), Hank Bell (Hank), Victor Cox (Tim), Roy Bucko (Gus), Herman Hack (Sal), Jimmy Aubrey, Frank McCarroll, Tex Cooper (Saloon Customers), George Morrell, Jack Evans, Rube Dalroy (Townsmen), Rose Plummer (Townswoman).

Border Badmen (PRC, 1945, 55 minutes) Producer: Sigmund Neufeld. Director: Sam Newfield. Screenplay: George Milton [Milton Raison & George Wallace Sayre]. Photography: Jack Greenhalgh. Editor: Holbrook N. Todd. Sound: Lyle Willey. Production Manager: Bert Sternbach. Music: Frank Sanucci. Assistant Director: William O'Connor.

Cast: Buster Crabbe (Billy Carson), Al St. John (Fuzzy Q. Jones), Lorraine Miller (Helen Stockton), Charles King (Merritt), Raphael [Ray] Bennett (Deputy Spencer), Archie Hall (Gillian), Budd Buster (Peter Evans), Marilyn Gladstone (Roxie), Marin Sais (Mrs. Bentley), Slim Whitaker (Dolan), Wally West (Max), Steve Clark (Mayor Jim Bates), Bud Osborne (Deputy), Roy Bucko (Davis), Henry Hall (Judge), Frank Ellis (Bennett), Ray Henderson (Pete), Bob [John L.] Cason, Ray Jones, Victor Cox (Henchmen).

Fighting Bill Carson (PRC, 1945, 53 minutes) Producer: Sigmund Neufeld. Director: Sam Newfield. Screenplay: Louise Rousseau. Photography: Jack Greenhalgh. Editor: Holbrook N. Todd. Sound: Lyle Willey. Music: Frank Sanucci. Production Manager: Bert Sternbach. Assistant Director: William O'Connor.

Cast: Buster Crabbe (Billy Carson), Al St. John (Fuzzy Q. Jones), Kay Hughes (Jeanne Darcy), Stan [I. Stanford] Jolley (Clay Allison), Kermit Maynard (Cass), Bob [John L.] Cason (Joe), Budd Buster (Steve), Bud Osborne (Sheriff), Wally West (Hal), Lynton Brent, Augie Gomez (Henchmen), Jimmy Aubrey (Bank Customer), Roy Bucko, Jack Tornek, Rube Dalroy, Fox Callahan, George Morrell, Ray Jones (Townsmen), Rose Plummer (Townswoman).

Prairie Rustlers (PRC, 1945, 56 minutes) Producer: Sigmund Neufeld. Director: Sam Newfield. Screenplay: Fred Myton. Photography: Jack Greenhalgh. Editor: Holbrook N. Todd. Sound: Lyle Willey. Production Manager: Bert Sternbach. Music: Lee Zahler. Assistant Director: William O'Connor.

Cast: Buster Crabbe (Billy Carson/Jim Slade), Al St. John (Fuzzy Q. Jones), Evelyn Finley (Helen Foster), Karl Hackett (Dan Foster), I. Stanford Jolley (Matt), Bud Osborne (Bart), Kermit Maynard (Vic), Tex Williams (Vocalist), Wally West (Lawman), Jimmy Aubrey (Cook), Dorothy Vernon (Minnie), John L. Cason (Gus), Al Ferguson (Posse Rider), Dean Eaker, George Bamby (Band Members), George Morrell, Carl Mathews, Herman Hack, Tex Cooper, Ray Jones, Al Haskell, Jack Evans (Townsmen).

Lightning Raiders (PRC, 1945, 61 minutes) Producer: Sigmund Neufeld. Director: Sam Newfield. Screenplay: Elmer Clifton. Photography: Jack Greenhalgh. Editor: Holbrook N. Todd. Sound: Lyle Willey. Production Manager: Bert Sternbach. Special Effects: Ray Mercer. Music Director: Lee Zahler. Assistant Directors: Lou Perlof & Stanley Neufeld.

Cast: Buster Crabbe (Billy Carson), Al St. John (Fuzzy Q. Jones), Mady [Lawrence] Laurence (Jane Wright), Henry Hall (George Wright), Steve Darrell (Frank Hayden), I. Stanford Jolley (Kane), Karl Hackett (Jim Murray), Roy Brent (Al Phillips), Marin Sais (Mrs. Loren), Al Ferguson (Paul Loren), Budd Buster (Sheriff Nord), John L. Cason (Gordon), Frank Ellis (Gibbs), Bert Dillard (Deputy Sheriff Bert), Victor Cox (Stagecoach Driver), Carl Mathews (Posse Rider), Jack Evans, Bob Burns, Rube Dalroy, Herman Hack (Saloon Customers), Tex Cooper, Rose Plummer (Citizens).

Gentlemen with Guns (PRC, 1946, 53 minutes) Producer: Sigmund Neufeld. Director: Sam Newfield. Screenplay: Fred Myton. Photography: Jack Greenhalgh. Editor: Holbrook N. Todd. Sound: Lyle Willey. Production Manager: Bert Sternbach. Effects: Ray Mercer. Music Director: Lee Zahler. Assistant Director: Stanley Neufeld.

Cast: Buster Crabbe (Billy Carson), Al St. John (Fuzzy Q. Jones), Patricia Knox (Matilda Boggs), Steve Darrell (Jim McCallister), George Chesebro (Ed Slade), Karl Hackett (Judge), Budd Buster (Sheriff), Frank Ellis (Red Cassidy), George Morrell (Townsman), Herman Hack, Jack Evans, Bert Dillard, Art Dillard (Saloon Customers).

Ghost of Hidden Valley (PRC, 1946, 56 minutes) Producer: Sigmund Neufeld. Director: Sam Newfield. Screenplay: Ellen Coyle. Photography: Art Reed. Editor: Holbrook N. Todd. Sound: Glen Glenn. Production Manager: Bert Sternbach. Special Effects: Ray Mercer. Music Director: Lee Zahler. Assistant Director: Stanley Neufeld.

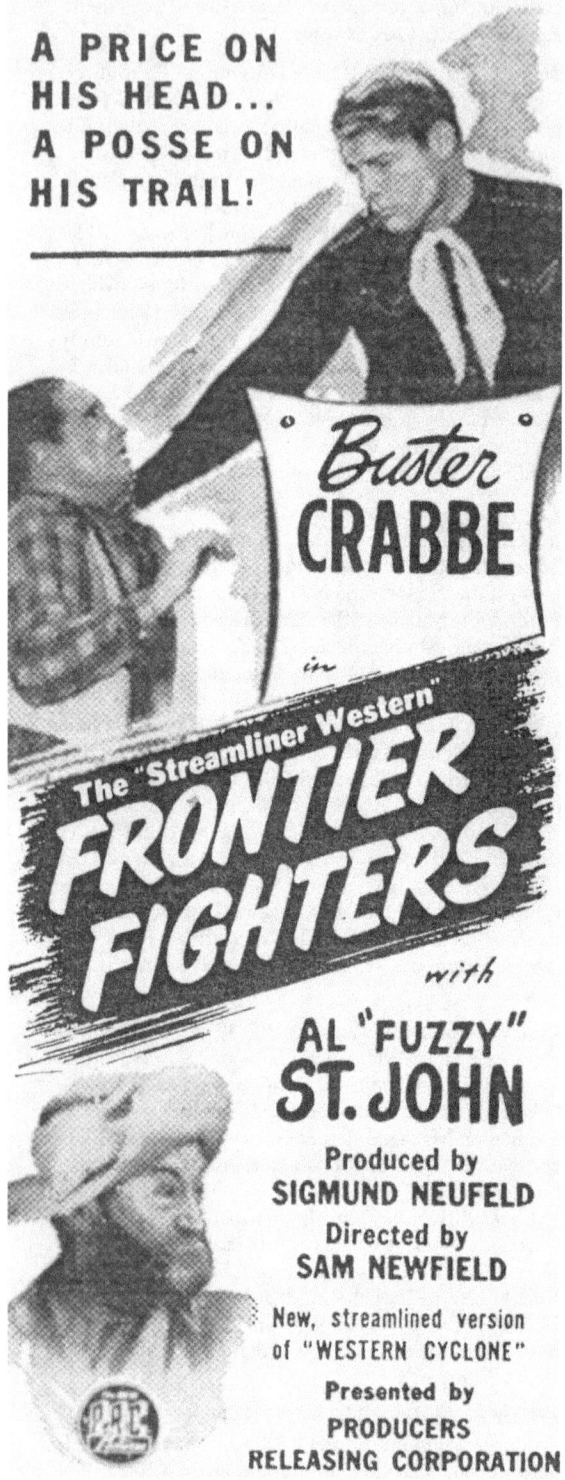

Cast: Buster Crabbe (Billy Carson), Al St. John (Fuzzy Q. Jones), Jean Carlin (Kaye Dawson), John Meredith (Henry Trenton), Charles King (Ed "Blackie" Dawson), Jimmy Aubrey (Tweedle), Karl Hackett (Jed), John L. Cason (Buck Sweeney), Silver Harr (Stagecoach Guard), Burt [Bert] Dillard (Stagecoach Driver), Zon Murray (Arnold/Jim Slade), George Morrell, Bob Burns, Milburn Morante (Homesteaders), Wally West, Ray Henderson (Henchmen), Herman Hack (Citizen), Victor Adamson [Denver Dixon] (Saloon Customer), Jack Evans (Card Player).

Prairie Badmen (PRC, 1946, 55 minutes) Producer: Sigmund Neufeld. Director: Sam Newfield. Screenplay: Fred Myton. Photography: Robert Cline. Editor: Holbrook N. Todd. Sound: Glen Glenn. Production Manager: Bert Sternbach. Special Effects: Ray Mercer. Music Director: Lee Zahler. Assistant Director: Stanley Neufeld.

Cast: Buster Crabbe (Billy Carson), Al St. John (Fuzzy Q. Jones), Patricia Knox (Linda Lattimer), Charles King (Cal), Ed Cassidy (Doc Lattimer), Kermit Maynard (Lon), John L. Cason (Steve), Steve Clark (Sheriff), Frank Ellis (Bill Thompson), John L. Buster (Don Lattimer).

Terrors on Horseback (PRC, 1946, 55 minutes) Producer: Sigmund Neufeld. Director: Sam Newfield. Screenplay: George Milton [Milton Raison & George Wallace Sayre]. Photography: Jack Greenhalgh. Editor: Holbrook N. Todd. Sound: Lyle Willey. Produc-

Above, right and opposite: Advertisements for re-edited versions of PRC films.

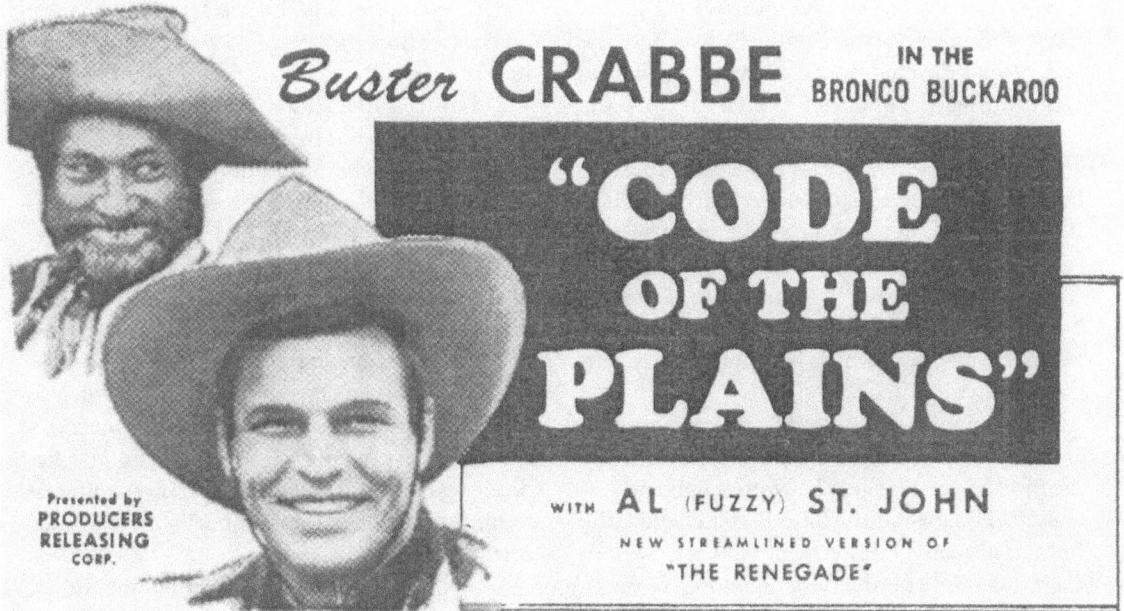

tion Manager: Bert Sternbach. Special Effects: Ray Mercer. Music Director: Lee Zahler. Assistant Director: Stanley Neufeld.

Cast: Buster Crabbe (Billy Carson), Al St. John (Fuzzy Q. Jones), Patti McCarty (Roxie), I. Stanford Jolley (Grant Barlow), Kermit Maynard (Wagner), Henry Hall (Doc Jones), Karl Hackett (Ed Sperling), Marin Sais (Mrs. Bartlett), Budd Buster (Sheriff Jed Bartlett), Steve Darrell (Deputy Jim Austin/Buck), Steve Clark (Cliff Adams), Bud Osborne (Ben Taggart), Al Ferguson, Lane Bradford (Bushwhackers), Frank Ellis (Conners), George Morrell (Bartender), George Chesebro (Luke Gordon), Jack Kirk (Jack Ryan), Herman Hack, Jack Evans (Saloon Customers).

Overland Riders (PRC, 1946, 53 minutes) Producer: Sigmund Neufeld. Director: Sam Newfield. Screenplay: Ellen Coyle. Photography: Jack Greenhalgh. Editor: Holbrook N. Todd. Sound: Earl Sitar. Production Manager: Bert Sternbach. Special Effects: Ray Mercer. Assistant Director: Stanley Neufeld.

Cast: Buster Crabbe (Billy Carson), Al St. John (Fuzzy Q. Jones), Patti [McCarty] McCarthy (Jean Barkley), Slim Whitaker (Jeff Barkley), Bud Osborne (Sheriff Oliver), Jack O'Shea (Vic Landreau), Frank Ellis (Cherokee), Al Ferguson (Tug Wilson), Bob [John L.] Cason (Hank Fowler), George Chesebro (Jim Rance), Lane Bradford (Deputy Sheriff), Jimmy Aubrey (Deputy Sheriff Joe), Wally West (Henchman).

Outlaws of the Plains (PRC, 1946, 56 minutes) Producer: Sigmund Neufeld. Director: Sam Newfield. Screenplay: A. Frederic Evans. Story: Elmer Clifton. Photography: Jack Greenhalgh. Editor: Holbrook N. Todd. Sound: Elden Ruberg. Production Manager: Bert Sternbach. Special Effects: Ray Mercer. Music Director: Lee Zahler. Assistant Director: Stanley Neufeld.

Cast: Buster Crabbe (Billy Carson), Al St. John (Fuzzy Q. Jones), Patti McCarty (Kitty Reed), Charles King, Jr. (Nord Finner), Karl Hackett (Henry Reed), Jack O'Shea (Ralph Emory), Bud Osborne (Sheriff), Budd Buster (Tom Wilson), Slim Whitaker (Agent Graham), John L. Cason (Joe Dayton), Jimmy Aubrey (Rancher), Lane Bradford, Roy Brent, Al Ferguson, Frank Ellis, George Morrell, Ray Henderson (Citizens).

BILLY THE KID

The famed outlaw Billy the Kid (1859–91) was immortalized in print and later on film, with MGM doing two big-budget productions, both called *Billy the Kid*, in 1930 and in 1941. Johnny Mack Brown had the title role in the early talkie with Robert Taylor essaying the part in the 1941 remake. Sandwiched between them was PRC's series of the adventures of a whitewashed Billy the Kid. When the studio was known as Producers Distributing Corporation (PDC), it was announced that George Houston would star in eight "Billy the Kid" adventures for the 1939–40 season, but the series never materialized. Early in 1940, PDC was bankrupt and the studio was reorganized as Producers Releasing Corporation (PRC) with its main output coming from Sigmund Neufeld Productions with financial backing from Pathe Labs, both of which had sunk money into the floundering PDC.

Sigmund Neufeld Productions was located at 1440 North Gower Street in Hollywood, while the PRC offices were at 1422 North Highland Avenue in Hollywood; George R. Batcheller, the former head of Chesterfield Pictures, was in charge of PRC's production. Sigmund Neufeld's wife, Ruth, was vice-president of Sigmund Neufeld Productions and his brother, Sam Newfield (real name: Samuel Neufeld), was the company's secretary. Bert Sternbach was its production manager and casting director, while Jack Greenhalgh was the head of the camera department, Holbrook N. Todd was the editor, Hans Weeren was the chief sound engineer, Fred Preble was stage manager, and Johnny Lange and Lew Porter headed the music department.

The Neufeld brothers were natives of New York City. Sigmund Neufeld (1896–1979) produced more than 130 features films between 1932 and 1956, while his sibling, Sam Newfield (1899–1964), directed twice that many movies, beginning with short subjects in 1926 and graduating to features, with *Wolf Dog* being his final film in 1958. Jack Greenhalgh (1904–71), also a Gotham native, began in films in the 1920s as an assistant cameraman and from 1935 to 1953 he photographed approximately 200 features. Holbrook N. Todd (1906–72) edited some 200 movies between 1931 and 1957 and he returned to edit *Las Vegas Hillbillys* in 1966 and *Hillbillys in a Haunted House* the next year. He also served as associate producer of *Urubu* in 1948. Melville De Lay (1899–1947) worked as assistant director for the Neufelds and, between 1930 and 1946, he was either second unit director or assistant director on over 100 features. He directed *The Mystic Hour* (1934) and *Law of the Saddle* (1943), a "Lone Rider" (q.v.) entry. He also was associate producer on four features in 1946–47 before dying of a heart attack.

For its initial season, 1940–41, PRC advertised 15 features but by the next year it had nearly tripled that number. Most of the movies were directed by Sam Newfield, who was so busy he also used the pseudonyms Sherman Scott and Peter Stewart. He used both monikers for the first half-dozen entries in the studios "Billy the Kid" series starring Bob Steele in the title role. Co-starring with Steele was silent film comic Al St. John, who continued the character of Fuzzy Jones, which he had created in a series with Fred Scott for Spectrum Pictures from 1936 to 1938. The first five Steele features also co-starred Carleton Young as a third saddle pal, although not in a continuing role.

Bob Steele (1907–88) (real name: Robert Bradbury) was one of the most popular Western film stars when he took over the lead in the "Billy the Kid" series in 1940. He had been a star for more than a dozen years, having begun at Film Booking Offices (FBO) in the late 1920s. After a series with Syndicate in 1929, he made his sound debut for Tiffany in *Near the Rainbow's End* (1930) and during the 1930s he headlined series for Tiffany, World Wide, Monogram, Supreme, Republic and Metropolitan. In 1939 he received critical acclaim for his work as Curley in the film version of John Steinbeck's *Of Mice and Men*. Al St. John (1893–1963) grew up in show business and got into films as a result of being the nephew of Roscoe "Fatty" Arbuckle. Beginning in 1913 he worked for Mack Sennett and during the 1920s he starred in short comedies for Paramount, Fox and Educational. A master of physical comedy, St. John made an easy transition to sound and by the mid–1930s he was specializing in Westerns, usually as a comedy sidekick. Carleton Young (1907–71) was an active character actor in films beginning in 1936 and on occasion he played leading roles. Possessing a distinctive voice, he also worked in radio where he starred in "The Adventures of Ellery Queen" (NBC, 1942–43) and "The Count of Monte Cristo" (Mutual, 1946–52). He was also very active in television.

While MGM announced its plans for a big-budget remake of *Billy the Kid* starring Robert Taylor in 1940, PRC beat its much bigger counterpart to the punch and by the time the Taylor film was released in the spring of 1941, PRC already had five of its Bob Steele "Billy the Kid" features in theatrical release. The first of these was *Billy the Kid Outlawed*, which came out in the summer of 1940. In its brisk 52 minutes, the feature tells how Billy (Steele), along with pals Fuzzy Jones (Al St. John) and Jeff Travis (Carleton Young), becomes a hunted outlaw. Billy, Fuzzy and Jeff return to Lincoln City, New Mexico, after a cattle drive to find two of their friends have been murdered. The victims, brothers, opposed the activities of outlaws led by Lige Ellis (John Merton) and were murdered by his gang. Lige, however, secretly works for general store owners Pete Morgan (Joe McGuinn) and Sam Daly (Ted Adams), who want to control the area. Billy befriends John Fitzgerald (Walter McGrail) and his daughter Molly (Louise Currie) after rescuing them from a runaway stagecoach. Fitzgerald confides to Billy that he is a judge sent to investigate the lawlessness around Lincoln City. Morgan and Daly have the judge murdered and, after Daly is elected sheriff, he declares Billy and his friends wanted outlaws. Billy vows revenge for the murder of his friends and he robs Morgan and Daly's store and carries out other acts of sabotage against the two. This causes the reward on his head to increase drastically. Seeking to get Billy out of the way, Morgan and Daly convince Molly and Dave Hendricks (Kenne Duncan), the judge's former law partner, to tell Billy he is being offered a pardon. When he comes to discuss the pardon, the outlaw gang fire on him but in a shootout he and his pals kill Morgan and Daly and rout the gang. Despite Molly and Hendricks' assurance the pardon is real, Billy does not believe them and rides away.

The second outing, *Billy the Kid in Texas*, came out in the fall of 1940 and this time Billy (Steele) is in Texas where he observes an express wagon robbery and then takes the stolen money away from the thieves. Later he meets pal Fuzzy (St. John) in town but the outlaws spot Billy and ambush him. The owner of the express office, Mary Barton (Terry Walker), takes care of him, and when the stolen money is returned to Mary, leading citizen Jim Morgan (Frank LaRue) appoints Billy the town sheriff and Fuzzy his deputy. Outlaw leaders Dave (Charles King) and Flash (John Merton) hire gunman Gil Cooper (Carleton Young) to dispose of Billy. When the Kid and Gil meet for a showdown, they realize they are long-lost brothers and Billy makes Gil promise to go straight. When Dave and Flash find out that Gil is Billy's brother, they take him prisoner, and at the same time, Mary finds a Billy the Kid wanted poster and tells Morgan that the sheriff is an outlaw. The crooks also capture Billy and Fuzzy and announce their plans to rob Mary's express wagon. Billy, Fuzzy and Gil escape and rob the wagon themselves but are arrested by Morgan and a posse. The outlaw gang later steals the money from a safe in the sheriff's office. Billy, Fuzzy and Gil escape and follow the thieves, capturing them and recovering the money. Billy and Fuzzy then ride away as Gil takes over the job as the town lawman. *Variety* complained the film was "much duller than the previous ones [sic]," adding, "More implausible passages and situations than usual creep into the story." Regarding the star, the trade paper noted, "Steele is not as good as usual as Billy in this yarn. He suffers from inane lines and worse episodes." The feature was also released as *Battling Outlaw*.

The last 1940 "Billy the Kid" series release was *Billy the Kid's Gun Justice*, issued in December. With bounty hunters on their trail, Billy (Steele), Fuzzy (St. John) and Jeff Blanchard (Young) head for the latter's uncle ranch. Along the way they rescue pretty Ann Roberts (Louise Currie), who is being run off her land by Buck Mason (Rex Lease) and his partner Ed Baker (Charlie King), cattlemen who want her ranch. The trio rides home with Ann only to discover her place was the one Jeff thought belonged to his uncle, who has disappeared according to Ann's father (Forrest Taylor). Billy finds out Cobb Allen (Al Ferguson) sold the Roberts the ranch and that he has also been forcing homesteaders to pay for water he diverted from their spreads. Billy tries to get Allen to return the money he took from the ranchers but barely escapes from Cobb's gang. Fuzzy then convinces Allen that a fortune is buried on a nearby ranch and from the map he is shown, Cobb recognizes the Roberts place and decides to buy it legally. Mason and Baker also want the property and try to outbid Allen but when they reach an impasse, they join forces to buy the place, outbidding Billy. The Kid then takes the money and gives it to the homesteaders. Jeff has overheard Baker tell Mason that Allen killed his uncle and he goes to the sheriff (Ted Adams), who arrests Allen and lets the wanted Billy escape.

Billy the Kid's Range War was issued in January 1941. Its involved story has outlaw Buck (Rex Lease) posing as Billy the Kid (Steele) in carrying out a rash of robberies. Fuzzy (St. John) rescues the real Billy from arrest at the hands of their friend, Marshal Jeff Carson (Carleton Young), and Sheriff Black (Ted Adams), who want him for the murder a freight company owner who was building a nearby road in order to get a government mail contract. Sheriff Black is really in cahoots with steamboat line owner Williams (Karl Hackett), who is after the mail contract for his business. Ellen Gorhman (Joan Barclay), the murdered man's daughter, is the ward of her father's friend Leonard (Milton Kibbee). He is also working with Black and Williams but becomes upset when he finds out it was Williams who ordered Gorhman's murder and also had the victim's ranch foreman killed and replaced with one of his own men, Jenkins (Howard Masters). Romero (Julian Rivero) overhears the meeting between the crooks and tells Billy and Fuzzy. Billy kidnaps Jenkins and pretends to be him. Billy continues the work on the road but Jeff arrests him and Fuzzy breaks him out of jail. When Ellen refuses to sell Williams her business, he plans to kill her but Leonard objects and Williams has him murdered by Buck, who is now working for the crook. Ellen sees Buck escape and since he is riding Billy's pinto horse, she thinks it was the Kid who killed her guardian. Ellen then decides to sell to Williams, but Billy stops the action. When Buck arrives on Billy's pinto, she realizes she was wrong about the Kid. Before Buck can confess to killing Leonard, Williams shoots him. Williams then says he has plans to dynamite the new road and as Fuzzy takes him prisoner, Billy rides to stop the explosion. Billy and Fuzzy then supervise the work completing the road and Ellen gets the mail contract. She offers the duo the job of running the freight line but they are forced to refuse when a posse shows up after the still wanted Billy the Kid. *Variety* called it "[o]ne of the less vigorous westerns. Meller is based on story material that impresses as too flimsy, though fist fights, a bit of gunplay and conventional horse-chase occasionally relieve tedious sequences ... Steele handles assignment capably." The film was later released in 16mm as *Texas Trouble*.

Sam Newfield directed the first four "Billy the Kid" films as Peter Stewart but for the last two starring Bob Steele he helmed as Sherman Scott. The first of these, and the fifth series entry, was *Billy the Kid's Fighting Pals*, which came out in the spring of 1941. Later shown on television as *Trigger Men*, the feature has wanted outlaws Billy (Steele), Fuzzy (St. John) and Jeff (Carleton Young) arrive in the border town of Paradise which is being terrorized by outlaws. When thugs Badger (Charles King) and Burke (Curley Dresden) force newspaperman Mason (Budd Buster) to leave town, Billy takes over the operation after beating Badger in a fight. Bartender Lopez (Julian Rivero) writes the purchase contract and bank owner Hardy (Ed Peil, Sr.) and his niece Ann (Phyllis Adair) make Billy welcome. It is then learned that Mason has been murdered. Unknown to Billy, Hardy is in league with Badger in a plan to take over the town and use it to construct a smuggling tunnel under the Mexican border. Badger orders his men to kill Fuzzy and Billy but they fail and Billy captures Badger and leaves him in Ann's custody. Ann tells Billy that Badger has escaped, but after a shootout with Fuzzy, Badger is again placed in jail. There he confesses to Billy about Hardy's plan to take over the town and that he and Ann are lovers. When the sheriff (George Chesebro) arrives, Lopez, who is really a Mexican operative, gives him proof of Hardy and Badger's activities, with Billy, Fuzzy and Jeff leaving town.

Steele's final "Billy the Kid" feature was *Billy the Kid in Santa Fe*, released in the summer of 1941. Found guilty of a killing he did not commit, Billy is rescued from hanging by pals Fuzzy (St. John) and Jeff (Rex Lease). After the trio stops rustlers from raiding Pat Walker's (Marin Sais) ranch, they head to Santa Fe in search of Texas Joe (Dave O'Brien), a gambler who was paid by cattleman Hank Baxter (Frank Ellis) to give false testimony at Billy's trial. The Kid believes Santa Fe bar owner Steve Barton (Charles King) had him framed and in Santa Fe he runs across an old friend, Silent Don Vincent (Dennis Moore). Barton frames Texas Joe for murder as Billy is put in charge of local law enforcement. He goes to arrest

Texas Joe and finds him at Vincent's shack but Barton's men let him out of jail. Barton's cohort Bert Davis (Karl Hackett), the real killer, leads a posse which finds Texas Joe and hangs him. Vincent, who was Texas Joe's brother, seeks revenge by killing all the posse members but is wounded and saved by Pat. Realizing his motive for the killings, Jeff and his deputies form a court and declare Vincent not guilty. Billy arrives at Pat's ranch to arrest Vincent but Fuzzy and Jeff tell him of the jury's verdict and he sets Vincent free.

In *Billy the Kid in Santa Fe*, the part of Jeff was portrayed by Rex Lease (1901–66), who previously had villain roles in *Billy the Kid's Gun Justice* and *Billy the Kid's Range War*. Lease had starred in Westerns for Tiffany, World Wide, Syndicate and Superior before appearing in supporting roles in scores of oaters into the mid–1950s.

After making the sixth "Billy the Kid" feature, Steele signed with Republic Pictures and proceeded to appear in its "Three Mesquiteers" (q.v.) series. PRC hired Buster Crabbe to take over as William Bonney with St. John remaining as Fuzzy Jones. Born Clarence Linden Crabbe, Buster Crabbe (1907–83) was sometimes billed as Larry "Buster" Crabbe. A native of California, he won a gold medal in swimming at the 1932 Los Angeles Olympic Games and the next year starred in two adventure movies, *King of the Jungle* for Paramount and the serial *Tarzan the Fearless* for Principal. At Paramount he worked in a variety of roles, including appearing in ten features based on the works of Zane Grey between 1933 and 1937. His greatest fame, however, came at Universal where he headlined three "Flash Gordon" serials between 1936 and 1940 as well as the cliffhangers *Red Barry* (1938) and *Buck Rogers* (1939).

Crabbe's first "Billy the Kid" series release was *Billy the Kid Wanted*, issued in the fall of 1941.

Bob Steele and Rex Lease in *Billy the Kid in Santa Fe* (PRC, 1941).

Sam Newfield continued to direct the series using the *nom de screen* Sherman Scott. For this entry, Dave O'Brien made his first appearance in the role of Jeff. Tired of being a wanted man, Fuzzy (St. John) departs from his friends Billy (Crabbe) and Jeff (O'Brien) and decides to become a farmer. In Paradise Valley he is told the settlers are being cheated by land company owner Matt Brawley (Glenn Strange), who uses his water rights and company store to keep them in his debt. Outlaw gang leader Jack Saunders (Charles King) wants part of Brawley's action but the latter refuses, saying he controls the area's new sheriff (Slim Whitaker). After Fuzzy gets into a fight with Brawley, he is arrested but he gets a note smuggled to Billy and Jeff and they break him out of jail. Billy decides to help the homesteaders by robbing Brawley's store and giving them the supplies. Brawley hires Saunders to kill Billy but he also plots to have the sheriff arrest Billy, since he knows Brawley will be no match for the Kid. Before the gunfight, however, Billy and Jeff cook up a plot to denounce each other, with Jeff pretending to join Saunders and Billy aligning himself with Brawley. Billy also gets the homesteaders to unite. When the Brawley and Saunders gangs meet for a showdown, Billy shoots Saunders and Fuzzy arrives with the homesteaders and the two gangs are captured. Homesteader Stan Harper (Howard Masters), who sheltered Billy, Fuzzy and Jeff when they came to Paradise Valley, is made the new sheriff. *Variety* thought it "routine fare" adding, "Crabbe fits nicely into the title role, although not looking particularly like a cowpuncher." The reviewer noted that Sam Newfield's son, Joey, "has a wonderful bit." He portrayed the son of homesteader Harper at the beginning of the film, looking after his sick mother (Choti Sherwood), whose condition alerts Fuzzy to the plight of the homesteaders.

Billy the Kid's Round-Up was released late in 1941. Running 58 minutes, it was later cut by ten minutes for television showings. In it Glenn Strange plays the role of Vic Landreau, a bad guy character name which would again be used in *Tumbleweed Trail* (1942), a "Frontier Marshals" (q.v.) entry, as well as in another "Billy the Kid" feature, *The Kid Rides Again* (1943); both times Charles King played the part. *Billy the Kid's Round-Up* also had Carleton Young return in the role of Jeff, the last time he would play the character.

Taking place in Gila Valley, *Billy the Kid's Round-Up* had Billy (Crabbe), Fuzzy (St. John) and Jeff (Young) called in by the local sheriff, Jim Hanley (Slim Whitaker), to look into the criminal activities of saloon owner Landreau (Strange). Landreau plans to run Deputy Sheriff Ed Slade (Charles King) against Hanley but the latter is murdered before he can reveal the name of the local outlaw gang leader to newspaper owner Dan Webster (John [Elliott] Webster) and his daughter Betty (Joan Barclay). When Butch Holcomb (Dennis Moore) tries to shoot Billy, he is captured and admits he was sent by Landreau, who wants the Kid out of the way. Billy goes to town and confronts Landreau, who denies hiring Butch. When Landreau's men try to wreck Webster's printing press, Billy stops them and Betty nominates Fuzzy to be the town's new lawman. The outlaws kidnap Betty but Billy rescues her. They capture Slade and force him to confess in writing about Landreau's activities; the confession is printed by Webster. Billy and Landreau have a

Advertisement for *Billy the Kid's Round-Up* (PRC, 1941).

fight and Vic is arrested. Since he has been elected sheriff, Fuzzy stays in Gila Valley as Billy and Jeff depart.

Billy the Kid Trapped, the first of five series films in 1942, was released in February of that year. In this one, Bud McTaggart (1910–49) took over the role of Jeff Walker, pal of Billy (Crabbe) and Fuzzy (St. John). The plot has the trio being saved from the gallows by an outlaw gang that has been using their identities and committing a series of crimes, including the murder for which they were about to be hanged. When Billy, Fuzzy and Jeff save Sheriff Masters (Ted Adams) during a shootout with the gang, they convince him of their innocence. In Mesa City, the trio finds out that crook Stanton (Glenn Strange) is behind the outlaws and he has gang leader Red Burton (Jack Ingram) appointed sheriff. Using the guise of the Kid and his pals, Stanton's gang robs a stagecoach. The driver, Dave Evans (Eddie Phillips), the brother of the previous sheriff who was murdered by the outlaws, comes to believe that it was Billy who killed his sibling. Fuzzy and Jeff chase the outlaws and get back the stolen money and Dave's sister Sally (Anne Jeffreys) provides Billy with an alibi. Sheriff Masters arrives in town and enlists Dave's help in bringing the outlaw gang to justice. When a judge (Walter McGrail), who is coming to town to try Stanton and his men, is attacked by the gang, Billy, Fuzzy and Jeff surprise the outlaws by being his fellow stagecoach passengers. One of the outlaws (Budd Buster) admits it was Stanton who killed Dave's brother. Stanton shoots the confessor but is captured by Billy and the gang is arrested. Masters becomes Mesa City's new sheriff and hires Dave as his deputy.

Dave O'Brien returned to the role of Jeff, now called Jeff Travis, in *Billy the Kid's Smoking Guns*, which arrived in theaters in the spring of 1942. When outlaws abduct a rancher (Curley Dresden), Billy (Crabbe), Fuzzy (St. John) and Jeff (O'Brien) save the man's son (Joe Newfield) from the gang and take him home to his mother (Joan Barclay), who is also being harassed. The local sheriff (Ted Adams), actually the gang leader, takes the rancher to Doc Hagen (Milton Kibbee), who murders him. Billy finds out the local ranchers' protective organization, which owns the only store, is taking over local ranches in lieu of the credit it gave to the settlers. The head of the association, Morgan (John Merton), who is aware the government plans to buy up the area, is behind the foreclosures. He is in league with Hagen, who orders Billy's murder, because the Kid has decided to help the settlers fight the association. Billy, Fuzzy and Jeff start their own general store, but Hagen tries to sabotage their supply wagons. While searching Hagen's office, Billy finds proof that the doctor is behind the lawlessness. The sheriff tries to arrest the Kid, but it is he who is taken prisoner. Billy then unites the ranchers into a posse as Hagen and Morgan begin to foreclose on the ranches. Fuzzy does not realize that Hagen is behind the crimes and when Jeff is shot by the gang, he takes him to the doctor. Billy rides to Jeff's rescue and then threatens Hagen with his own poison. As a result, the doctor confesses to the crimes as the posse rounds up Morgan and his gang.

Law and Order, released in the summer of 1942, was the first series entry which did not carry the name Billy the Kid in the title, although alternately it was called *Billy the Kid in Law and Order* and *Billy the Kid's Law and Order*, and in England it was retitled *Double Alibi*. For the role of Jeff Travis, Dave O'Brien was now billed as Tex O'Brien. This time out Billy (Crabbe) finds he is the lookalike of Lieutenant Ted Morrison (also Crabbe), the commander of the fort where Billy, Fuzzy (St. John) and Jeff (O'Brien) have been taken prisoner. Billy, wearing Morrison's uniform, escapes with his pals only to be fired upon. Finding an invitation to the wedding of Morrison's aunt, Mary Todd (Sarah Padden), Billy and his friends decide to investigate. The blind Mary does not realize that her fiancé, George Fremont, is really an imposter, Simms (Hal Price). Simms has been planted by Mil Crawford (Charles King), the justice of the peace, who wants to control Mary's estate. Crawford has his henchman Turtle (John Merton) murder the real Fremont as well as Morrison. When Billy impersonates Morrison, Mil tries to get him lynched but he is saved by Fuzzy who identifies him as Mary Todd's nephew. When the real Fremont's niece, Linda (Wanda McKay), arrives for the wedding, she agrees to aid Billy in exposing Simms and she stops the proceedings to announce he is an imposter. Billy captures Crawford and his gang is jailed. Linda decides to stay on and take care of Mary.

The triad heroes concept, which had been with the "Billy the Kid" films since the series' inception in 1940, ended with *Sheriff of Sage Valley*, shown in the fall of 1942. In it, Dave O'Brien portrayed the character of Jeff for the final time. The feature offered Crabbe another dual role, this time as Bill Bonney and his long-lost brother, outlaw Kansas Ed Bonney. When the sheriff of Sage Valley is killed during a holdup which Billy, Fuzzy (St. John) and Jeff (O'Brien) are unable to stop, the trio does not realize that fellow passengers Janet (Maxine Leslie) and Sloane (Charles King) are also involved. The two work for Kansas Ed (Crabbe), an outlaw who wants to control the town. When Mayor Harrison (Hal Price) refuses to extend Ed's lease on his gambling house, Ed has him shot but Billy saves the mayor and the latter offers him the job of Sage Valley sheriff. Billy refuses. After a killing at the casino, Harrison warns Ed to clear out and again Harrison is attacked. This time Billy agrees to become the town's lawman as Ed names Sloane the town's new mayor. Billy beats Sloane in a fight and arrests him but comes to realize that Ed may he the brother he thought was dead. He also believes he has been made to pay for Ed's crimes. Janet is able to lure Billy to Ed's hideout where he is captured and forced to exchange clothes with his brother. As a result, the ranchers think Billy is now one of the crooks but Fuzzy and Jeff help him to escape. The three are then captured and jailed by the ranchers but Harrison, who has recuperated from being shot, sets them free. Ed captures the trio but Jeff, after taking a beating from Ed, revives and snares the gang and shoots Ed, who is engaged in a fight to the death with Billy. Before dying, Ed admits he is Billy's brother. The ranchers demand that Billy, Fuzzy and Jeff be arrested but the mayor lets them escape. *Variety* dubbed it "an indie-made western that ranks with the best in the field although palpably having cost less than most."

The last 1942 series release, *The Mysterious Rider*, issued in November, is set in the ghost town of Laramie, whose citizens have abandoned it after being terrorized by outlaws. Billy (Crabbe) and Fuzzy (St. John) arrive there and find former sheriff Dalton Sykes (John Merton) searching for a vein of gold discovered by a rancher he had murdered. Sykes also plans to kill Billy, whom he blames for local lawlessness, and Fuzzy, but the two end up rescuing Martha (Caroline Burke) and Johnny Kincaid (Edwin Brian), the children of the murdered rancher, who have arrived to take over their father's ranch. At the ranch, Fuzzy plays the dead man's violin and the outlaws think his ghost has come back to haunt them. When the violin is broken in a fight, the map to the gold

Advertisement for *Sheriff of Sage Valley* (PRC, 1942).

vein is revealed. Sykes learns about the map but Billy gives him a bogus copy while Johnny is sent to a nearby town for the marshal (Ted Adams). When he realizes he has been duped, Sykes returns to get the real map and tries to kill Billy and Fuzzy, but Johnny and the lawman arrive and he is arrested. The feature was later reissued in a 40-minute version called *Panhandle Trail*.

Six more "Billy the Kid" releases came out in 1943, beginning with January's *The Kid Rides Again*, also called *Billy the Kid Rides Again*. The plot has Fuzzy (St. John) running a saddle shop in the town of Sundown. Wanted for a robbery he did not commit, Billy (Crabbe) seeks sanctuary there, feeling that Tom (Glenn Strange) and Mort Slade (I. Stanford Jolley) have framed him. He also believes the brothers are head of an outlaw gang terrorizing local ranchers. When the ranchers cannot pay their mortgages, Mort buys them. Billy and Fuzzy go to the Slade hideout where Mort is overheard planning to ruin banker Ainsley (Ed Peil, Sr.) who will not sell him any more ranch foreclosures. Billy tries to warn the banker and his daughter Joan (Iris Meredith) but they think he is an outlaw and refuse to believe him. When Vic Landreau (Charles King), Mort's gunman, forces Billy into a fight, he is killed and the Kid is arrested. Mort then robs Ainsley's bank and although Fuzzy frees Billy from jail, he is then blamed for the robbery. Mort tells the townspeople that Ainsley's bank is broke and Billy promises Joan he will try and recover the stolen money. At the Slade hideout, Billy finds the bank money and he and Fuzzy capture the gang. Billy gives the money back to Ainsley and turns Tom Slade over to the law. Billy is then forced to shoot Mort in self-defense.

With the next series entry, *Fugitive of the Plains*, director Sam Newfield used his own name for the rest of the series. Released in March, 1943, it was also called *Billy the Kid in Fugitive of the Plains* and later was reissued as *Raiders of Red Rock*, running 38 minutes. This entry, like several others in the series, featured a female villain. Unlike most Western film series, several entries in the "Billy the Kid" and later "Billy Carson" (q.v.) films offered women on the wrong side of the law. This effort tells of Billy (Crabbe) trying to prove his innocence involving crimes along the Mexican border. Billy and Fuzzy (St. John) ride to the town of Red Rock where the Kid is blamed for the murder of a deputy. Following the trail of the culprits, they come upon the hideout of Kate Shelby (Maxine Leslie) and her outlaw gang. Billy and Fuzzy join the gang despite the protests of henchman Dillon (Jack Ingram). Billy and Fuzzy capture two of the gang and as Kate plans a bank robbery, two more of her men disappear. Realizing that Billy is behind the abductions, Kate captures him but the sheriff (Karl Hackett) chases Kate and her gang. Kate is shot but before dying she shoots Dillion, preventing him from killing Billy. The sheriff then realizes Billy and Fuzzy are innocent of any crimes.

In *Western Cyclone*, released in the spring of 1943, Billy (Crabbe) stages a fake stagecoach holdup to impress passenger Senator Peabody (Milton Kibbee) how much trouble fellow passenger Governor Jim Arnold (Karl Hackett), who is riding with his niece Mary (Marjorie Manners) and banker Dirk Randall (Glenn Strange), is having with lawlessness in the region of Dry Springs. Later the governor confides to Billy that he believes someone is trying to unseat him. It turns out Randall is after the office and he hires Ace Harmon (Charles King), a saloon proprietor, to frame Billy for the murder of his henchman Rufe Meeker (Jack Ingram). Billy is arrested for killing Rufe after a shootout but Fuzzy finds evidence that another gun was used to commit the crime. Billy is tried and sentenced to be hanged and Fuzzy is arrested for weapons theft but the two manage to escape from jail. Finding out Billy is still at large, Randall has Mary kidnapped and says he will let her go if Billy gives himself up. Billy agrees but the sheriff (Hal Price) sets him free and they concoct a ruse that Mary has escaped. Randall sends henchman Jake (Artie Ortego) to find Mary. Billy and Fuzzy follow him to the gang's hideout, capture Jake and set Mary free. Harmon robs the bank and shoots Billy. Randall then murders Harmon and returns to town saying that Billy did the deed. Billy, however, was only wounded and he tells the sheriff it was Randall who committed the crimes. The film was re-released in a 39-minute version re-titled *Frontier Fighters*.

Cattle Stampede, also known as *Billy the Kid in Cattle Stampede*, came out in August, 1943. After outlaw Ed Dawson (Hansel Werner) saves

Billy (Crabbe) and Fuzzy (St. John) from being captured by his gang, he asks the duo to aid his rancher father Sam Dawson (Ed Cassidy) and sister Mary (Frances Gladwin), whose cattle herds are being rustled. The culprit is Dawson's foreman, Brandon (Charles King), who is in cahoots with corrupt land baron Coulter (Glenn Strange). When Brandon's scheme is revealed, Dawson asks Billy to take over as foreman, not knowing he is a wanted man. Billy and Fuzzy organize area ranchers into a patrol and Billy then robs Coulter's stolen money from a stagecoach and places it in the local bank. Mary, a passenger on the stagecoach, thinks Billy is really an outlaw until she is kidnapped by Coulter, who plans to hold her hostage so her father will sign over his ranch to him. Coulter's henchman, Elkins (Frank Ellis), reveals that his boss has taken Mary. Billy and Fuzzy lead the ranchers to the outlaw's hideout and after a shootout the girl is set free.

In July's *The Renegade*, Billy (Crabbe) comes to the aid of banker John Martin (Karl Hackett) and his daughter Julie (Lois Ranson), friends of his pal Fuzzy (St. John). Robberies have emptied Martin's Pine Bluff bank and when he returns from a nearby town with borrowed money he is attacked by outlaws and the money is stolen. Behind the scheme is Hill (Ray Bennett), the town's mayor, who wants the nearby land because of oil deposits. Hill's henchman Pete (Tom London) claims that Martin has been embezzling money from his own bank and Billy arrives in time to save the banker from being lynched. Since area ranchers have been threatened with foreclosures, Billy and Fuzzy check the county records but are ambushed by another henchman, Goodwin (George Chesebro), who the Kid is forced to shoot. The sheriff (Jack Rockwell) sets Billy free but arrests Martin on a warrant sworn out by Pete. He is released when stolen bank money is found on Goodwin. Pete and his gang try to bushwhack Billy and Fuzzy, and during the fight Billy discovers a pool of oil, thus making him aware of the motive for the crimes. They capture the gang and then find evidence in Hill's office, along with the rest of the stolen bank money. Hill is arrested and the locals realize they are going to be rich. In 1947 the feature was revamped into a 38-minute version called *Code of the Plains*.

The final "Billy the Kid" series film, *Blazing Frontier*, also called *Billy the Kid in Blazing Frontier*, was released in the fall of 1943. Like the earlier *Fugitive of the Plains*, it is set in Red Rock County where railroad agent Luther Sharp (I. Stanford Jolley) and railroad detective chief Ward Tragg (Frank Hagney) have cheated the ranchers out of their land through crooked contracts. Lem Barstow (Milton Kibbee), the ranchers' lawyer, asks Billy (Crabbe) to look into the matter. In Red Rock, Billy catches Tragg cheating at cards but when the railroad detective learns the Kid's identity he tries to hire him to help get rid of the now unruly settlers. Billy refuses and instead claims that Fuzzy (St. John) is a notorious gunman who will aid Tragg. Sharp and Tragg tell Fuzzy to rob the stagecoach carrying the money Sharp has swindled out of the settlers. Fuzzy commits the robbery but gives the money to the settlers, whom Billy convinces to use it to buy a ranch. When Tragg finds out that Barstow has asked for an investigation by a railroad official (John Elliott), he orders his gang to destroy the lawyer's house. Fuzzy, who is still a member of the gang, sends a warning to Billy and Barstow and the two escape. When Tragg gets a lynch mob after Barstow, he is arrested for his own safety but Billy sets him free and the two prevent the railroad official from being captured by the gang. During a shootout, several gang members are killed and the two crooks are arrested. The settlers then buy back their land from the railroad.

The character name of Billy the Kid was changed to Billy Carson and Crabbe and St. John would star in 23 "Billy Carson" (q.v.) series entry from 1943 to 1946.

Filmography

Billy the Kid Outlawed (PRC, 1940, 52 minutes) Producer: Sigmund Neufeld. Director: Peter Stewart [Sam Newfield]. Screenplay: Oliver Drake. Photography: Jack Greenhalgh. Editor: Holbrook N. Todd. Production Manager: Bert Sternbach. Music Directors: Johnny Lange & Lew Porter. Assistant Director: Melville De Lay.

Cast: Bob Steele (Billy the Kid), Al St. John (Fuzzy Jones), Louise [Currie] Curry (Molly Fitzgerald), Carleton Young (Jeff Travis), John Merton (Lige Ellis), Joe McGuinn (Pete Morgan), Ted Adams (Sam Daly), Walter McGrail (Judge John Fitzgerald), Hal Price (Sheriff Long), Kenne Duncan (Dave Hendricks), Reed Howes (Whitey), George Chesebro (Tex), Steve Clark (Shorty), Budd Buster (Clem), Jack Perrin, Sherry Tansey [James Sheridan], Carl Mathews (Henchmen).

Billy the Kid in Texas (PRC, 1940, 63 minutes) Producer: Sigmund Neufeld. Director: Peter Stewart [Sam Newfield]. Screenplay: Joseph O'Donnell. Photography: Jack Greenhalgh. Editor: Holbrook N. Todd. Sound: Hans Weeren. Music Directors: Johnny Lange & Lew Porter. Production Manager: Bert Sternbach. Sets: Ernest Graber. Assistant Director: Melville De Lay.

Cast: Bob Steele (Billy the Kid), Al St. John (Fuzzy Jones), Terry Walker (Mary Barton), Carleton Young (Gil Cooper/Gil Bonney), Charles King (Dave), John Merton (Flash), Frank La Rue (Jim Morgan), Charles [Slim] Whitaker (Windy), Lew Meehan (Saloon Owner), Wally West (Posse Rider), Oscar Gahan, Ray Henderson (Saloon Customers), Augie Gomez (Pete), Curley Dresden, Pascale Perry, Art Dillard, Chick Hannon (Henchmen), Merrill McCormick, Sherry Tansey [James Sheridan], George Morrell, Tex Palmer, Jack Evans, Ben Corbett, Herman Hack, Denver Dixon [Victor Adamson], Al Haskell (Citizens).

Also called *Battling Outlaw*.

Billy the Kid's Gun Justice (PRC, 1940, 57 minutes) Producer: Sigmund Neufeld. Director: Peter Stewart [Sam Newfield]. Screenplay: Joseph O'Donnell. Photography: Jack Greenhalgh. Editor: Holbrook N. Todd. Production Manager: Bert Sternbach. Music: Johnny Lange & Lew Porter. Music Director: David Chudnow. Assistant Director: Melville De Lay.

Cast: Bob Steele (Billy the Kid), Al St. John (Fuzzy Jones), Louise Currie (Ann Roberts), Carleton Young (Jeff Blanchard), Charlie [Charles] King (Ed Baker), Rex Lease (Buck Mason), Ken [Kenne] Duncan (Bragg), Forrest Taylor (Tom Roberts), Ted Adams (Sheriff), Al Ferguson (Cobb Allen), Karl Hackett (Martin), Ed Peil, Sr. (Dave Barlow), Julian Rivero (Carlos), Blanca Vischer (Juanita), Oscar Gahan, George Morrell (Settlers), Richard Cramer (Bartender), Curley Dresden (Posse Leader), Wally West, Joe McGuinn, Carl Mathews, Augie Gomez (Henchmen).

Billy the Kid's Range War (PRC, 1941, 60 minutes) Producer: Sigmund Neufeld. Director: Peter Stewart [Sam Newfield]. Screenplay: William Lively. Photography: Jack Greenhalgh. Editor: Holbrook N. Todd. Production Manager: Bert Sternbach. Sound: Hans Weeren. Sets: Ernest Graber. Music Directors: Johnny Lange & Lew Porter. Assistant Director: Melville De Lay.

Cast: Bob Steele (Billy the Kid), Al St. John (Fuzzy Jones), Joan Barclay (Ellen Gorhman), Carleton Young (Marshal Jeff Carson), Rex Lease (Buck), Milton Kibbee (Leonard), Karl Hackett (Williams), Ted Adams (Sheriff Black), Julian Rivero (Miguel Romero), Stephen Chase (Dave Hendrix), Howard Masters (Ab Jenkins), Buddy Roosevelt (Spike), Ralph Peters (Jailer), Blanca Vischer (Girl in Cantina), George Chesebro, Wally West, Tex Palmer, Sherry Tansey [James Sheridan], Tex Palmer, Carl Mathews (Henchmen), John Ince (Hawkins), Curley Dresden, Milburn Morante, Jack Tornek (Road Workers).

16mm title: *Texas Trouble*.

Billy the Kid's Fighting Pals (PRC, 1941, 59 minutes) Producer: Sigmund Neufeld. Director: Sherman Scott [Sam Newfield]. Screenplay: George Plympton. Photography: Jack Greenhalgh. Editor: Holbrook N. Todd. Production Manager: Bert Sternbach. Sound: Hans Weeren. Sets: Ernest Graber. Music Director: David Chudnow. Assistant Director: Melville De Lay.

Cast: Bob Steele (Billy the Kid), Al St. John (Fuzzy Jones), Phyllis Adair (Ann Hardy), Carleton Young (Jeff), Charles King (Badger), Curley Dresden (Burke), Edward Peil, Sr. (Hardy), Hal Price (Burrows), George Chesebro (Sheriff), Forrest Taylor (Hanson), Budd Buster (Mason), Julian Rivero (Lopez), Stanley Price (Marshal Mason), Wally West (Red), Sherry Tansey [James Sheridan], Art Dillard, Ray Henderson (Henchmen), Frank Ellis, Al Taylor (Lynch Mob Members), Milburn Morante, George Morrell, Jack Evans, Jack Tornek (Saloon Customers).

TV title: *Trigger Men*.

Billy the Kid in Santa Fe (PRC, 1941, 61 minutes) Producer: Sigmund Neufeld. Director: Sherman Scott [Sam Newfield]. Screenplay: Joseph O'Donnell. Photography: Jack Greenhalgh. Editor: Holbrook N. Todd. Production Manager: Bert Sternbach. Sound: Hans Weeren. Sets: Fred Preble. Music: Johnny Lange & Lew Porter. Assistant Director: Melville De Lay.

Cast: Bob Steele (Billy the Kid), Al St. John (Fuzzy Jones), Rex Lease (Jeff), Marin Sais (Pat Walker), Dennis Moore (Silent Don Vincent), Karl Hackett (Bert Davis), Steve Clark (Allan), Hal Price (Sheriff), Charles King (Steve Barton), Frank Ellis (Hank Baxter), Dave O'Brien (Texas Joe Benson), Kenne Duncan (Scotty), John Elliott (Judge), Art Dillard (Regan), Ray Henderson (Mike), Wally West (Deputy), George Morrell (Bartender), Curley Dresden (Luke), Chick Hannon, Foxy Callahan (Bushwhackers), Artie Ortego, Roy Bucko (Lynch Mob Members), Oscar Gahan, Jack Evans (Gamblers), Reed Howes, Denver Dixon [Victor Adamson] (Henchmen), Herman Hack (Rustler), Milburn Morante, Barney Beasley (Men in Courtroom), George Hazel (Bar Customer), Henry Wills (Cowboy), Jack Tornek, Herman Howlin (Citizens).

Billy the Kid Wanted (PRC, 1941, 62 minutes) Producer: Sigmund Neufeld. Director: Sherman Scott [Sam Newfield]. Screenplay: Fred Myton. Photography: Jack Greenhalgh. Editor: Holbrook N. Todd. Production Manager: Bert Sternbach. Music Director: David Chudnow. Assistant Director: Melville De Lay.

Cast: Buster Crabbe (Billy the Kid), Al St. John (Fuzzy Jones), Dave O'Brien (Jeff), Glenn Strange (Matt Brawley), Charles King (Jack Saunders), Howard

Masters (Stan Harper), Choti Sherwood (Jane Harper), Joe Newfield (Joey Harper), Budd Buster (Store Owner), Frank Ellis (Bart), Slim Whitaker, Steve Clark (Lawmen), Reed Howes, Ray Henderson, Art Dillard, Al Taylor, Pascale Perry (Deputies), Kenne Duncan, Wally West, Archie Hall, Curley Dresden, Augie Gomez (Henchmen), George Morrell, Chick Hannon (Homesteaders).

Billy the Kid's Round-Up (PRC, 1941, 58 minutes) Producer: Sigmund Neufeld. Director: Sherman Scott [Sam Newfield]. Screenplay: Fred Myton. Photography: Jack Greenhalgh. Editor: Holbrook N. Todd. Production Manager: Bert Sternbach. Sets: Vin Taylor. Sound: Hans Weeren. Assistant Director: Melville De Lay.

Cast: Buster Crabbe (Billy the Kid), Al St. John (Fuzzy Jones), Carleton Young (Jeff), Joan Barclay (Betty Webster), Glenn Strange (Vic Landreau), Charles King (Ed Slade), Slim Whitaker (Sheriff Jim Hanley), John [Elliott] Webster (Dan Webster), Dennis Moore (Butch Holcomb), Richard Cramer (Harry the Bartender), Curley Dresden (Curley), Kenne Duncan (Joe), Oscar Gahan, Herman Hack, Horace B. Carpenter, Denver Dixon [Victor Adamson], George Morrell, Tex Phelps, Barney Beasley, Tex Cooper, Lew Morphy (Citizens), Art Dillard, Augie Gomez, Wally West (Henchmen), Jim Mason, Jack Evans, Morgan Flowers (Bar Customers), Tom Smith (Voter).

Billy the Kid Trapped (PRC, 1942, 59 minutes) Producer: Sigmund Neufeld. Director: Sherman Scott [Sam Newfield]. Screenplay: Joseph O'Donnell. Photography: Jack Greenhalgh. Editor: Holbrook N. Todd. Production Manager: Bert Sternbach. Sound: Hans Weeren. Music: Johnny Lange & Lew Porter. Assistant Director: Melville De Lay.

Cast: Buster Crabbe (Billy the Kid), Al St. John (Fuzzy Jones), Bud McTaggart (Jeff Walker), Anne [Jeffreys] Jeffries (Sally Crane), Glenn Strange (Stanton), Walter McGrail (Judge Jack McConnell), Ted Adams (Sheriff John Masters), Jack Ingram (Red Burton), Milton Kibbee (Judge Clarke), Eddie Phillips (Dave Evans), Budd Buster (Montana), George Chesebro (Deputy Sheriff Curley), Richard Cramer (Gus the Bartender), Ralph Bucko (Sheriff Steve Evans), Ray Henderson (Charley), Wally West (Pete), Jimmy Aubrey, Art Dillard, Bert Dillard, Curley Dresden, Augie Gomez, Cactus Mack, Carl Mathews (Henchmen), Oscar Gahan, Jack Evans, Jim Mason, Horace B. Carpenter, Hank Bell, Roy Bucko, Jack Tornek, Herman Hack, Jack Kinney, Pascale Perry (Bar Customers).

Billy the Kid's Smoking Guns (PRC, 1942, 58 minutes) Producer: Sigmund Neufeld. Director: Sherman Scott [Sam Newfield]. Screenplay: George Milton [George W. Sayre & Milton Raison]. Photography: Jack Greenhalgh. Editor: Holbrook N. Todd. Production Manager: Bert Sternbach. Sound: Hans Weeren. Music Directors: Johnny Lange & Lew Porter. Special Effects: Ray Mercer. Assistant Director: Melville De Lay.

Cast: Buster Crabbe (Billy the Kid), Al St. John (Fuzzy Jones), Dave O'Brien (Jeff Travis), John Merton (Morgan), Joan Barclay (Mrs. Howard), Milton Kibbee (Dr. Hagen), Ted Adams (Sheriff Carson), Karl Hackett (Hart), Frank Ellis (Carter), Slim Whitaker (Roberts), Joe Newfield (Dickie Howard), Curley Dresden (Tom Howard), George Morrell, Steve Clark, Chick Hannon, Budd Buster, Foxy Callahan (Ranchers), Art Dillard, Bert Dillard (Henchmen), Lou Fulton (Victim).

British title: *Smoking Guns*.

Law and Order (PRC, 1942, 57 minutes) Producer: Sigmund Neufeld. Director: Sherman Scott [Sam Newfield]. Screenplay: Sam Robins. Photography: Jack Greenhalgh. Editor: Holbrook N. Todd. Production Manager: Bert Sternbach. Music Director: Leo Erdody. Assistant Director: Melville De Lay.

Advertisement for *Billy the Kid Trapped* (PRC, 1942).

Cast: Buster Crabbe (Billy the Kid/Lieutenant Ted Morrison), Al St. John (Fuzzy Jones), Tex [Dave] O'Brien (Jeff Travis), Sarah Padden (Mary Todd), Wanda McKay (Linda Fremont), Charles King (Mil Crawford), Hal Price (Simms), John Merton (Turtle), Ken [Kenne] Duncan (Durgan), Ted Adams (Sheriff Jeff), George Morrell (George Fremont), Kermit Maynard (Corporal), Steve Clark, Herman Hack (Wedding Guests), Bert Dillard (Joe), Carl Mathews (Henchman), Jack Kirk (Stagecoach Driver), Art Dillard (Orderly), Jimmy Aubrey, Wally West, Hank Bell, Tex Cooper, Augie Gomez (Citizens).

British title: *Double Alibi*.

Sheriff of Sage Valley (PRC, 1942, 57 minutes) Producer: Sigmund Neufeld. Director: Sherman Scott [Sam Newfield]. Screenplay: George W. Sayre & Milton Raison. Photography: Jack Greenhalgh. Editor: Holbrook N. Todd. Production Manager: Bert Sternbach. Sound: Hans Weeren. Assistant Director: Melville De Lay.

Cast: Buster Crabbe (Billy the Kid/Kansas Ed), Al St. John (Fuzzy Jones), Tex [Dave] O'Brien (Jeff), Maxine Leslie (Janet), Charles King (Sloane), John Merton (Nick), Kermit Maynard (Slim Jenkins), Hal Price (Mayor Jed Harrison), Budd Buster (Tim Pine), Jimmy Aubrey (Bartender), Jack Kirk (Stagecoach Guard), Al Taylor (Croupier), Merrill McCormick, Frank Ellis, Art Dillard, Carl Mathews, Dan White (Ranchers), Lynton Brent, Curley Dresden, Ray Henderson (Henchmen), Jack Evans (Bar Customer), Bert Dillard (Guard).

The Mysterious Rider (PRC, 1942, 57 minutes) Producer: Sigmund Neufeld. Director: Sherman Scott [Sam Newfield]. Screenplay: Steve Braxton [Sam Robins]. Photography: Jack Greenhalgh. Editor: Holbrook N. Todd. Production Manager: Bert Sternbach. Sound: Hans Weeren. Assistant Director: Melville De Lay.

Cast: Buster Crabbe (Billy the Kid), Al St. John (Fuzzy Jones), Caroline Burke (Martha Kincaid), John Merton (Dalton Sykes), Edwin Brian (Johnny Kincaid), Jack Ingram (Trigger Larsen), Slim Whitaker (Rufe), Kermit Maynard (Joe), Ted Adams (U.S. Marshal), Jimmy Aubrey (Deputy), Bert Dillard (Luke), Frank Ellis, Joe Phillips, Augie Gomez (Henchmen).

Reissued as *Panhandle Trail*, running 40 minutes.

The Kid Rides Again (PRC, 1943, 60 minutes) Producer: Sigmund Neufeld. Director: Sherman Scott [Sam Newfield]. Screenplay: Fred Myton. Photography: Jack Greenhalgh. Editor: Holbrook N. Todd. Production Manager: Bert Sternbach. Sound: Hans Weeren. Music: Leo Erdody. Assistant Director: Melville De Lay.

Cast: Buster Crabbe (Billy the Kid), Al St. John (Fuzzy Jones), Iris Meredith (Joan Ainsley), Glenn Strange (Tom Slade), Charles King (Vic Landreau), I. Stanford Jolley (Mort Slade), Ed Peil, Sr. (John Ainsley), Ted Adams (Sheriff), Karl Hackett (Sheriff Henry), Slim Whitaker (Texas Lawman), Jim Mason (Gus the Bartender), Snub Pollard (Saloon Employee), Steve Clark (Bank Customer), Kenne Duncan, Frank McCarroll, Roy Bucko (Saloon Customers), Tex Phelps (Deputy), Tex Cooper (Doctor), Curley Dresden (Henchman), Milburn Morante, Al Haskell, Rose Plummer (Citizens).

Also called *Billy the Kid Rides Again*.

Fugitive of the Plains (PRC, 1943, 56 minutes) Producer: Sigmund Neufeld. Director: Sam Newfield. Screenplay: George W. Sayre. Photography: Jack Greenhalgh. Editor: Holbrook N. Todd. Production Manager: Bert Sternbach. Sound: Hans Weeren. Assistant Director: Melville De Lay.

Cast: Buster Crabbe (Billy the Kid), Al St. John (Fuzzy Jones), Maxine Leslie (Kate Shelly), Jack Ingram (Dillon), Kermit Maynard (Spence), Karl Hackett (Sheriff Sam Packard), Hal Price (Sheriff Dave Connelly), George Chesebro (Baxter), Frank Ellis (Dirk), John Merton (Deputy), Curley Dresden (Curley), Art Dillard (Pete), Carl Sepulveda (Tex), Jimmy Aubrey, Budd Buster, Tex Harper (Deputies), Hank Bell (Stagecoach Driver), Artie Ortego, Kansas Moehring (Henchmen).

Also called *Billy the Kid in Fugitive of the Plains*; reissued as *Raiders of Red Rock*, running 38 minutes.

Western Cyclone (PRC, 1943, 62 minutes) Producer: Sigmund Neufeld. Director: Sam Newfield. Screenplay: Patricia Harper. Photography: Robert Cline. Editor: Holbrook N. Todd. Production Manager: Bert Sternbach. Sound: Hans Weeren. Assistant Director: Melville De Lay.

Cast: Buster Crabbe (Billy the Kid), Al St. John (Fuzzy Jones), Marjorie Manners (Mary Arnold), Karl Hackett (Governor Jim Arnold), Milton Kibbee (Senator Peabody), Glenn Strange (Dirk Randall), Charles King (Ace Harmon), Hal Price (Sheriff Hastings), Kermit Maynard (Hank), Jack Ingram (Rufe Meeker), Steve Clark (Roberts), Lane Bradford (Joe), Lou Fulton (Deputy Sheriff Pete), Frank McCarroll (Red), Artie Ortego (Jake), Charles Murray, Jr., Frank Ellis, Bert Dillard, Al Haskell, Wally West (Henchmen), Herman Hack (Butch), Hank Bell (Bartender), Jack Evans, George Hazel, Barney Beasley, Jack Tornek (Saloon Customers), Robert Hill (Judge), Jimmy Aubrey, Art Dillard, Rube Dalroy, Victor Cox, Morgan Flowers, George Morrell, Lew Morphy (Citizens).

Reissued as *Frontier Fighters*, running 39 minutes.

Cattle Stampede (PRC, 1943, 58 minutes) Producer: Sigmund Neufeld. Director: Sam Newfield. Screenplay: Joseph O'Donnell. Photography: Robert Cline. Editor: Holbrook N. Todd. Production Manager: Bert Sternbach. Sound: Corson Jowett. Assistant Director: Melville De Lay.

Cast: Buster Crabbe (Billy the Kid), Al St. John (Fuzzy Jones), Frances Gladwin (Mary Dawson), Glenn Strange (Coulter), Charles King (Brandon), Ed Cassidy (Sam Dawson), Hansel Werner (Ed Dawson), Ray

Bennett (Stone), Frank Ellis (Elkins), Steve Clark (Turner), Roy Brent (Slater), John Elliott (Dr. George Arnold), Budd Buster (Jensen), Reed Howes (Dan Kelly), Carl Mathews, Art Dillard, Curley Dresden, Roy Bucko (Henchmen), Ted Adams, Tex Cooper, Hal Price, Ray Jones, Rose Plummer (Citizens), Hank Bell (Stagecoach Driver), George Morrell (Rancher), Wally West (Rider), Frank McCarroll (Fighter), Ray Jones (Spectator), Ed Peil, Sr. (Banker).

Also called *Billy the Kid in Cattle Stampede*.

The Renegade (PRC, 1943, 58 minutes) Producer: Sigmund Neufeld. Director: Sam Newfield. Screenplay: George Milton [George W. Sayre & Milton Raison]. Photography: Robert Cline. Editor: Holbrook N. Todd. Production Manager: Bert Sternbach. Sound: Hans Weeren. Assistant Director: Melville De Lay.

Cast: Buster Crabbe (Billy the Kid), Al St. John (Fuzzy Jones), Lois Ranson (Julie Martin), Karl Hackett (John Martin), Ray Bennett (Mayor Hill), Frank Hagney (Saunders), Jack Rockwell (Sheriff), Tom London (Pete), George Chesebro (Bart Goodwin), Jimmy Aubrey, Jack Montgomery (Bushwhackers), Wally West, Dan White (Henchmen), Milburn Morante, Art Dillard, Silver Harr (Citizens), Jack Evans, Jack Tornek (Saloon Customers).

Reissued in 1947 as *Code of the Plains*, running 38 minutes.

Blazing Frontier (PRC, 1943, 58 minutes) Producer: Sigmund Neufeld. Director: Sam Newfield. Screenplay: Patricia Harper. Photography: Robert Cline. Editor: Holbrook N. Todd. Production Manager: Bert Sternbach. Sound: Hans Weeren. Assistant Director: Melville De Lay.

Cast: Buster Crabbe (Billy the Kid), Al St. John (Fuzzy Jones), Marjorie Manners (Helen Barstow), Mil [Milton] Kibbee (Lem Barstow), I. Stanford Jolley (Luther Sharp), Frank Hagney (Ward Tragg), Kermit Maynard (Deputy Sheriff Pete), George Chesebro (Deputy Sheriff Slade), Frank Ellis (Deputy Sheriff Biff), Kenne Duncan (Clark), Robert Hill (John Trainer), Slim Whitaker (Sheriff), Pascale Perry, Morgan Flowers (Deputy Sheriffs), Budd Buster (Newton), Charles King (Auction Bidder), Cactus Mack (Tom), Chick Hannon, Jack Evans, Augie Gomez, Rube Dalroy (Homesteaders), Hank Bell (Bartender), Bert Dillard (Stagecoach Guard), Curley Dresden, Frank McCarroll (Henchmen), Tex Palmer, Ray Jones, Bill Wolfe, Herman Hack, Jimmy Aubrey, Barney Beasley (Saloon Customers), John Elliott (Railroad Official).

Also called *Billy the Kid in Blazing Frontier*.

CHEYENNE HARRY

Harry Carey created the role of Cheyenne Harry in the 1916 feature film *A Knight of the Range* and he continued to play the character in 18 more silent films for Universal from 1917 to 1919. Two decades after first performing the part, Carey revived Cheyenne Harry in two features, *Aces Wild* and *Ghost Town*, for Commodore Pictures. Regarding his portrayal of Cheyenne Harry, Jon Tuska wrote in *Views & Reviews* (Spring, 1973), "Harry Carey as a screen cowboy was quite dissimilar to William S. Hart. His personality was engaging with a comfortable self-sufficiency. He was incapable of Hart's moral intensity and lacked utterly Hart's penchant for sustained melodrama. Carey's natural humor and charm resulted in a characterization that, in some ways, anticipated Will Rogers."

Harry Carey (1878–1947) was born Henry DeWitt Carey II in the Bronx, New York, the son of a judge. Following in his father's footsteps, he studied law at Hamilton Institute and New York University before poor health sidelined his career intentions and he wrote a play, *Montana*, in which he starred for the next five years. After *Heart of Alaska*, his second stage effort, bombed, he began working in films in 1909 at Biograph, eventually becoming a leading man in D.W. Griffith productions. Carey moved west as a member of the Griffith company, signed with Universal in 1915 and was soon headlining a series of westerns as well as screenwriting, producing and directing.

The first "Cheyenne Harry" production was a five-reel outing called *A Knight of the Range*, which Jacques Jaccard directed and Carey wrote, thus the actor created as well as played Cheyenne Harry. The leading lady was Olive Golden and she and Carey were married in 1920. Released in February 1916, *A Knight of the Range* also marked the acting debut of Hoot Gibson, although he had been associated with films since 1910 as a stuntman. The plot had cowboy Cheyenne Harry (Carey) coming to the aid of a friend, Bob Graham (Gibson), who has been induced to take part in a robbery. Both men love Bess Dawson (Golden) and she has chosen Graham, so Cheyenne convinces a posse that he (Harry) was the one involved in the holdup. After Graham lets Cheyenne take the blame, Bess finds out the truth. Bob loses his life in a shootout and Bess marries the exonerated Cheyenne. Released by Universal, as were all the silent Harry Carey–Cheyenne Harry films, the feature was produced by Red Feather Photoplays.

Next Carey portrayed Cheyenne Harry in two short western features directed by John Ford, under the name Jack Ford. (During the silent era, the two men would collaborate on over two dozen motion pictures.) *The Soul Herder* and *Cheyenne's Pal* were produced by Bison Motion Pictures and released in 1917; both are now lost to the ages.

Ford made his feature directorial debut with *Straight Shooting*, a Butterfly Picture production released in the summer of 1917. Shot in Newhall, California, this seven-reeler is one of the few full-length silent "Cheyenne Harry" productions that survives today. Rancher Thunder Flint (Duke Lee) wants to rid the range of farmers and he tells Sam Turner (Hoot Gibson) to order homesteader Sweetwater Sims (George Berrell) to leave although Sam loves Sim's daughter Joan (Molly Malone). After the ranchers take control of the farmers' waterhole, Flint hires outlaws Cheyenne Harry (Carey) and Placer Fremont (Vester Pegg) to carry out his orders and run off the Sims family. Sims' son Tom (Ted Brooks) is murdered by the ranchers and a repentant Cheyenne offers to help the farmers. When Flint and Fremont learn of his actions, the rancher tells Placer to kill Cheyenne. Cheyenne and Fremont meet in a front street showdown with Placer getting killed. When Sam finds out that the ranchers plan to unite and exterminate the homesteaders, he tells Cheyenne, who has Joan gather the farmers at the Sims ranch. He then rides to Devil's Valley to enlist the help of outlaw Black Eyed Pete (Milt Brown) and his gang. Sam joins the farmers in fighting the ranchers but they are outnumbered until Cheyenne arrives with Pete and his men and the attackers are defeated. Cheyenne, who loves Joan, decides to leave. When Sam finds out that Joan also wants Cheyenne, he tells her where to find him. *The Moving Picture World* noted, "[T]he riding and fighting episodes are enacted with dash and enthusiasm."

Carey and director Ford worked together on two more "Cheyenne Harry" Butterfly Picture productions, *The Secret Man* and *A Marked Man*, both issued in October 1917. The former, co-written by Ford, had Cheyenne Harry (Carey) breaking out of prison and getting on a train. Passenger Henry Beaufort (Morris Foster) is going to the ranch of his rich uncle where he once secretly wed Molly (Edith Sterling), who is loved by Deputy Sheriff Chuck Fadden (Hoot Gibson). When Beaufort's servant Pedro (Steve Clements) gets drunk and wrecks his employer's wagon, Beaufort's little girl Elizabeth (Elizabeth Janes) is found by Cheyenne, who is on the run from the local sheriff (Vester Pegg), Molly's brother. Unable to locate water for the injured child, Cheyenne turns himself over to the lawman, who tries to kill Beaufort because he thinks he seduced his sister. At Molly's goading, Fadden lets Cheyenne out of jail and he stops the confrontation. Learning that his uncle, who did not like Molly, has died, Beaufort reunites with his wife as both Chuck and Cheyenne depart.

A Marked Man had outlaw Cheyenne Harry (Carey) falling in love with Molly Young (Molly Malone) and promising her and her father (Harry Rattenberry) that he will go straight. When one of his former comrades, Ben Kent (Vester Pegg), arrives in the area, Cheyenne lets himself be talked into taking part in a stagecoach holdup. During the robbery, the driver is killed; Cheyenne is arrested, tried and sentenced to hang for the crime. When the sheriff (Bill Gettinger) finds out that Cheyenne's mother (Mrs. Anna Townsend) is about to arrive to visit with her son, he agrees to let her think Cheyenne is an honest man. When she leaves, Cheyenne goes back to jail but is soon set free when one of the passengers identifies Ben Kent as the killer. Cheyenne and Molly are then free to marry.

John Ford, who would direct the rest of the *Cheyenne Harry* films starring Carey, next helmed **Bucking Broadway**, which came out at the end of 1917. Carey wrote the script for this five-reel Harry Carey Production. In the previous outings, Cheyenne Harry (Carey) had been an outlaw but in this one he is a ranch foreman who is in love with his employer's (L.M. Wells) daughter, Molly

(Molly Malone). Strockbroker Thornton (Vester Pegg) is also attracted to the girl and he convinces her to come with him to New York City. When he tries to seduce her she sends for Cheyenne. In the big city, Cheyenne gets involved with gangsters but they aid him in finding Molly, who is with Thornton at a nightclub. The two men fight over the young woman, with Cheyenne winning and taking Molly back home. *Bucking Broadway* is one of the few surviving "Cheyenne Harry" productions.

The Phantom Riders, the first of five 1918 "Cheyenne Harry" outings, was issued in January. Future serial director Henry MacRae wrote this effort which had rancher Cheyenne Harry (Carey) standing up to cattleman Dave Bland (Bill Gettinger), who wants all of Paradise Creek for himself. Bland is married to Molly (Molly Malone), who was forced into the nuptials but loves Cheyenne. To rid the range of other ranchers, Bland hires an outlaw called the Unknown (Vester Pegg) and his Phantom Riders. The raiders rustle Cheyenne's herd and beat him badly and when he recovers he finds the Unknown in a saloon and kills him. The Phantom Riders then corner Cheyenne as Molly rides for the Forest Rangers; during a shootout, Dave Bland is killed. With peace restored, Cheyenne and Molly are free to wed.

Ford and Carey co-authored the story for *Wild Women*, which came out in February 1918. Unlike the previous series entries that had rather austere storylines, this outing was more of a fantasy comedy. The plot had Cheyenne Harry (Carey) and the cowboys at the Circle-L Ranch taking part in a San Francisco rodeo to raise money for a cowpuncher's wife who needs an expensive operation. Winning most of the prize money, the boys go to a Hawaiian cabaret where they imbibe Honolulu cocktails and Cheyenne passes out and dreams that he and his pals are shanghaied. Tired of being forced to scrub the ship's deck, the cowboys mutiny and wind up in the Hawaiian Islands where the ugly queen (Martha Mattox) wants to wed Cheyenne. He gets away from her and falls in love with a beautiful princess (Molly Malone), but before he can kiss her he wakes up. Promising never again to partake of cocktails, Cheyenne and his pals head back to the Circle-L.

George Hively, who worked on the scripts for the first six Universal "Cheyenne Harry" features, adapted Frederick R. Bechdolt's *Popular Magazine* story "Back to the Right Trail" for *Thieves' Gold*, issued in March 1918. In this one, Cheyenne Harry (Carey) is a bored cowpoke working at Savage's (L.M. Wells) ranch. He agrees to help highwayman Curt Simmons (Vester Pegg), who uses the money he steals to finance rebels in Mexico. While playing cards with Simmons and his cohort Betoski (Harry Tenbrook), Cheyenne shoots Betoski after being insulted by him and then gets drunk and helps Curt rob a stagecoach. While being chased by a posse, Cheyenne spots a runaway buggy driven by his friend Uncle Larkin (John Cook). He brings it to a halt, meeting passenger Alice Norris (Molly Malone), who has come to visit Savage and his wife (Helen Ware). Savage comes to Cheyenne's defense after he is arrested and soon gets him out of jail. Returning to the ranch, Cheyenne falls in love with Alice but when she finds out he killed a man she rejects him and plans to return to her fiancé. After a shootout with Simmons, Cheyenne is left unconscious as Alice finds him and decides to stay.

The next series entry, *Hell Bent*, released in July 1918, was thought to be lost until a print was located in the Czechoslovak Film Archive. A story collaboration between Carey and Ford, it was about Cheyenne Harry (Carey) coming to Rawhide where he befriends Cimmaron Bill (Duke Lee) and is infatuated with dance hall girl Bess Thurston (Neva Gerber). Outlaw Beau Ross (Joseph Harris) also wants Bess and he gets her brother Jack (Vester Pegg) to join his gang. Beau then kidnaps Bess and waylays Cheyenne, who manages to escape by beating Jack in a fight and stealing his clothes. Dressed as Jack, Cheyenne captures Beau and the two are forced to trek across the desert to the nearest water hole. When they get there, the two men find the hole is dry. Beau dies but Cimmaron saves Cheyenne.

Eugene B. Lewis, who would work on the scenarios for the next five "Cheyenne Harry" features, wrote *Three Mounted Men*, issued in October 1918. The somewhat convoluted plot had Cheyenne Harry (Carey) and fellow prison inmate Buck Masters (Joe Harris) hating each other. The warden's (Charles Hill Mailes) crooked son (Harry Carter) enlists Buck's aid in covering up his thefts in the prison's record books and he gets Buck a pardon. Once released, Buck tries to blackmail his benefactor and the man gets Cheyenne a pardon so he can put Masters back behind bars. Cheyenne tracks Buck to a small town where he meets and falls in love with saloon girl Lola Masters (Neva Gerber), unaware that she and Buck are siblings. When he finds out that Masters is planning a bank heist, Cheyenne tells the warden's son who sends his deputies to arrest him. Realizing he has hurt Lola by causing the arrest of her brother, Cheyenne brings him back to his sister, who makes him promise he will go straight.

Seven Universal "Cheyenne Harry" films were released in 1919, beginning with *Roped* in January. In this lost feature, which was issued as a Universal Special Attraction, Cheyenne Harry (Carey) is a rich rancher who advertises for a housekeeper and ends up marrying one of the applicants, Aileen Judson-Brown (Neva Gerber). A year later the happy couple has a baby but Aileen's social-climbing mother (Molly McConnell) wants her to divorce Cheyenne and marry wealthy Ferdie Van Duzen (Arthur Shirley). Cheyenne's mother-in-law takes the baby and tells Cheyenne it has died and that Aileen no longer wants him. Cheyenne sadly returns to his ranch but the Judson-Browns' butler (J. Farrell MacDonald) informs him the child is still alive. When Cheyenne locates Alice and the baby, he learns that she is still in love with him. Leaving her mother, Aileen takes the baby back to the ranch with Cheyenne.

Eugene B. Lewis adapted his short story "Hell's Neck" for *A Fight for Love*, which came to theaters in March 1919. It had cattle thief Cheyenne Harry (Carey) escaping across the Canadian Border, making friends with an Indian tribe and fighting whiskey-running half-breed Black Michael (Joe Harris) over a pretty maiden (Princess Neola May). The vengeful Black Michael informs the Mounties about Cheyenne and he rides away and meets Kate McDougal (Neva Gerber), the daughter of a trading post operator (Mark Fenton). When Black Michael and three of his cohorts try to abduct Kate, she is saved by Cheyenne and the local priest (J. Farrell MacDonald). Cheyenne is then accused of killing the tribe's chief as Black Michael kidnaps Kate and takes her to an island where Cheyenne has taken sanctuary. The two men again fight, with Cheyenne forcing the half-breed to admit he killed the chief. Black Michael falls to his death from a precipice. Returning to the trading post, Cheyenne and Kate announce they will wed.

Next came *Bare Fists*, released in May 1919. When the marshal (Joseph Girard) of a Kansas border town is murdered, his son Cheyenne Harry (Carey) vows revenge. He kills two of the murderers but his mother (Mrs. Anna Townsend) makes him swear to never again wear a gun. Cheyenne loves beautiful Conchita (Betty Schade), as does Boone Travis (Joe Harris), who kills a man and places the blame on Cheyenne. Sentenced to hang, Cheyenne is allowed to see his mother and when she tells him that his young brother Bud (Howard Enstedt) was branded by rustlers, he makes a getaway. Cheyenne captures Travis and his gang and gets the evidence he needs to prove his innocence and return to Conchita.

The following two series entries, *Riders of Vengeance* and *The Ace of the Saddle*, both issued in the summer of 1919, were billed as Universal Special Attractions. Ford and Carey wrote the story for *Riders of Vengeance*, a very austere melodrama that begins with Cheyenne Harry's (Carey) fiancée (Clita Gale) and parents (Alfred Allen, Jennie Lee) being gunned down on his wedding day. Returning to the town of Mesquite a year later, Cheyenne methodically hunts down and kills the murderers except for Gale Thurman (Joe Harris). When Thurman's fiancée (Seena Owen) is hurt in a stagecoach robbery, Cheyenne takes her to the cave where he lives and nurses her back to health. Thurman tracks Harry and the girl to the cave and they are attacked by Apaches. During the fight, Gale informs Cheyenne that he took no part in killing his loved ones but dies during the shootout. After defeating the Indians, Cheyenne and the young woman find they have fallen in love.

George Hively returned to do the scenario for *Ace of the Saddle*, which had Cheyenne Harry (Carey) fighting rustlers but getting no help from the local sheriff (Joe Harris) who is working with the outlaws. Cheyenne asks neighboring county Sheriff Faulkner (Duke R. Lee) to help but he cannot enforce the law across county lines. Cheyenne falls for Faulkner's daughter Madeline (Peggy Pearce). Hating guns, Madeline implores

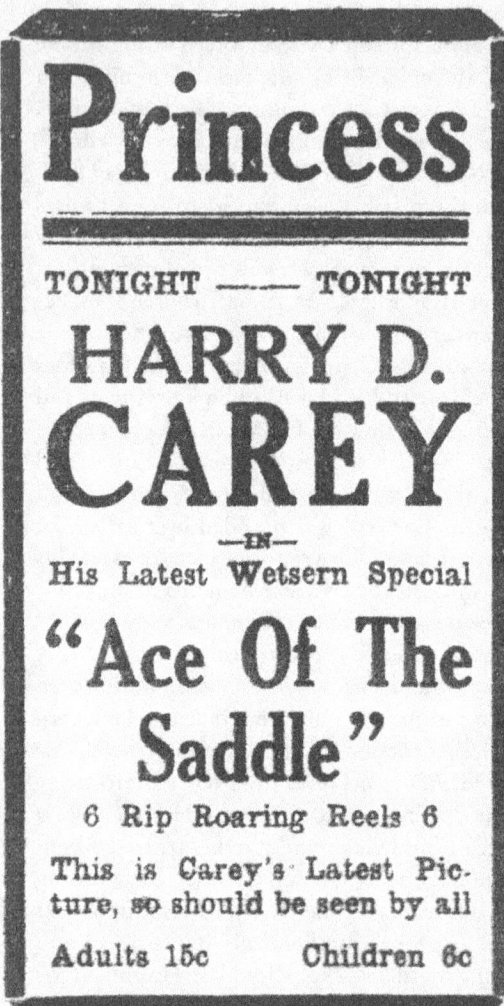

Advertisement for *Ace of the Saddle* (Universal, 1919).

November 1919. Three of the film's six reels have survived. In this light comedy, rancher Cheyenne Harry (Carey) refuses to sell his spread to rich cattleman John Merritt (J. Barney Sherry), owner of the Merritt Packing Company. After attempts are made on his life, Cheyenne is forced off his ranch because of a discrepancy in his land title and Merritt buys the property. Cheyenne then travels to Merritt's Chicago estate and is mocked by the man's daughter Helen (Kathleen O'Connor) and her society friends. Returning to the West, Cheyenne robs the packing company's payroll shipments and writes Merritt to credit the money taken to his account. Helen comes to the ranch and Cheyenne kidnaps her but the two fall in love. When her father shows up with lawmen, Helen tells her dad she loves Cheyenne and the two men come to an agreement.

The final silent "Cheyenne Harry" feature, *Marked Men*, is the best known because it was based on Peter B. Kyne's 1913 novel *The Three*

Cheyenne to give up his six-shooters and he agrees. Since the outlaws heed the code of not shooting an unarmed man, they poison his water hole. When Cheyenne lures some of the gang into Faulkner's county, they are arrested but the dishonest sheriff sets them free and they kidnap Madeline. Strapping on his guns, Cheyenne saves Madeline and gets the gang into a cabin where they unknowingly drink some of the poisoned water. The crooked sheriff and the other outlaws are arrested and Cheyenne and Madeline plan to wed.

Carey and Ford again wrote a story for the series with *A Gun Fightin' Gentleman*, released in

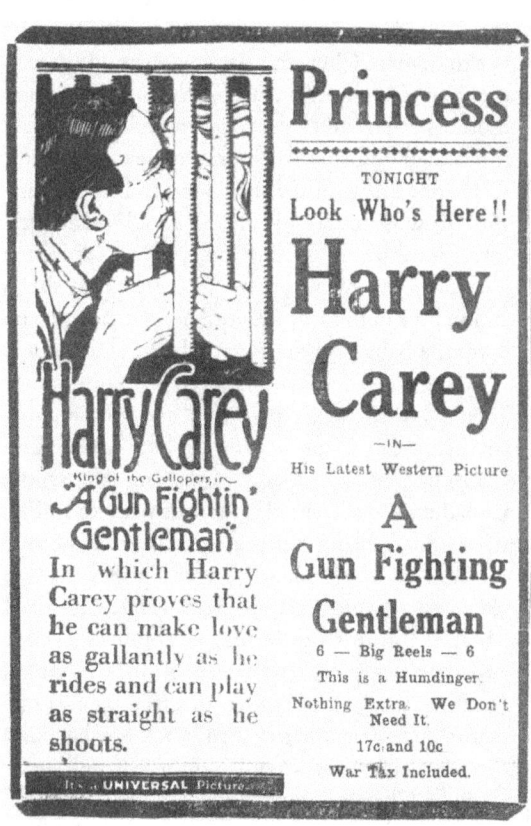

Advertisement for *A Gun Fightin' Gentleman* (Universal, 1919).

Godfathers. Released at the end of 1919, it had escaped convicts Cheyenne Harry (Carey), Tom Gibbons (Joe Harris) and Tony Garcia (Ted Brooks) coming to Trade Rat where Cheyenne falls for Ruby Merrill (Winifred Westover). They rob the bank and escape into the desert where they find a dying woman and her baby. She begs them to take the infant to its godparents and the three agree to do so. During the trek across the desert, Tom and Tony die but Cheyenne manages to get the little one to Trade Rat where he hands it over to Ruby and the sheriff (Charles Le Moyne), who arrests him. The lawman finds out the child is his nephew and he petitions the governor for a pardon for Cheyenne. When the pardon is issued, Cheyenne and Ruby marry and raise the baby.

Marked Men was the second time Carey had played the lead in the Peter B. Kyne yarn for Universal, having starred in the studio's 1916 version, *The Three Godfathers*, which was directed by Edward J. LeSaint. The studio shot the story for a third time in 1930 as *Hell's Heroes* and MGM filmed it in 1936 as *The Three Godfathers*. A dozen years later, John Ford directed yet another version of *The Three Godfathers* for MGM and it was dedicated to the memory of Harry Carey, who had died the year before.

In August 1919, W.W. Hodkinson Corporation, through Pathe Exchange, released the seven-reel feature *The Westerners* in which Roy Stewart starred as Cheyenne Harry. Although top-billed, Stewart basically had a supporting role in a tale of vengeance involving Black Mike Lafond (Robert McKim), a half-breed Indian who is thrown out of a wagon train by Jim Buckley (Wilfred Lucas) for insulting a woman. The vengeful Lafond murders a passenger, Prue Welch (Mildred Manning), the wife of a professor (Graham Pettie), and steals their small child. Black Mike raises the girl as his daughter, Molly (Mildred Manning), and fifteen years later he forces her to work as a dance hall girl in his saloon. Buckley is now a businessman in the community and Black Mike turns the locals against him, forcing Jim to flee. Cheyenne Harry (Roy Stewart), who loves Molly, helps Buckley fight Lafond. When Black Mike tries to ambush Jim, the two men fight and Buckley throws Lafond off a cliff. Jim Buckley is exonerated and Cheyenne and Molly plan to marry.

Carey left Universal in 1922 and signed with Films Booking Office (FBO) where he made a series of westerns released via the states' rights market. He remained with FBO until 1926 when he went to work for two seasons at Pathe and in 1928–29 he and his wife toured in vaudeville. In 1930 he starred in MGM's *Trader Horn*, one of the greatest adventure films ever made. In the 1930s he was very active in movies, often appearing in westerns and serials. He portrayed Tucson Smith in RKO Radio's 1935 "Three Mesquiteers" (q.v.) feature *Powdersmoke Range*, the same year he headlined a quartet of "B" westerns for Artclass Pictures, and in 1936 he again played Cheyenne Harry in two features for Commodore Pictures, *Aces Wild* and *Ghost Town*.

William Berke produced and Harry Fraser directed both sound "Cheyenne Harry" features. In his Artclass films, Carey rode a steed called Sonny, the Marvel Horse, and the animal was also featured in the Commodore productions. *Aces High*, issued in January 1936, was the first of the two films, and in it former marshal Cheyenne Harry Morgan (Carey) is headed for Durango when he meets up with Slim (Roger Williams) and Heck (Chuck Morrison) who accompany him to town and promptly lock him in jail. They locate their boss, Kelton (Theodore Lorch), who recognizes Cheyenne as his nemesis from a decade before. He attempts to shoot Cheyenne but is stopped by Slim, who tells him it would be bad business. Kelton orders the men to set Cheyenne free and when Kelton tries to run newspaperman Anson (Phil Dunham) out of town, Cheyenne stops him, becoming a partner in the newspaper. He hires Snowflake (Fred "Snowflake" Toones) to work for him and then rides to see teenager Martha Woods (Gertrude Messinger), whose late father, a friend of the ex-lawman, was murdered. She tells him that her father and Kelton argued over papers about her dad's mine. When Kelton, Slim and Heck show up, Cheyenne throws them off the Woods property. Kelton decides to double-cross Slim and Heck and cleans out his safe and hides the booty in the Woods mine, but he is seen by Cheyenne, who is taking Martha to town to stay with Anson and help work on the newspaper. Since Cheyenne has challenged him to a gunfight that evening, Kelton orders Slim and Heck to blow up the newspaper office and his safe. They bungle the first job, only breaking a window, but set the fuse on the safe and leave as Cheyenne comes to Kelton's office for the Woods mine papers. The two men fight and Kelton knocks out Cheyenne, who barely manages to escape injury when the safe explodes. Kelton rides out of town, followed by Heck and Slim, who shoots Snowflake when he stops him from taking Cheyenne's horse Sonny. The dying Snowflake asks Cheyenne to care for his mule Aloysius. Cheyenne and the sheriff (William McCall) chase the crooks as Kelton stops at the mine to get the stolen money. When Slim and Heck take it away from him, he shoots them. Riding away, Kelton is thrown from his horse and he and Cheyenne have a showdown on a suspension bridge with both men falling into the river. The sheriff shoots Kelton as Cheyenne swims to shore. Leaving Martha with Anson, Cheyenne, Sonny and Aloysius head south to the mining country near Ghost Town.

Filmed in Kernville, California, *Aces Wild* got its title from the poker game that villain Kelton played with the sheriff. Carey, dressed in black, was well into his fifties when he made the feature but he was a stalwart hero whose laconic personality added greatly to the film's entertainment value. In one scene, Martha asks Cheyenne if he is worried about the showdown he may have with Kelton. He tells her, "Sundown's got to come to all of us sometime. Why worry?" Francis Walker doubled for the star during the fight and riding sequences.

The second sound "Cheyenne Harry" outing, *Ghost Town*, released in February 1936, was a sequel to *Aces Wild*. Taking up from the first film, it had Cheyenne Harry Morgan (Carey), his horse Sonny and Aloysius the mule going to Ghost Town, once a prosperous community called Seward. Partners Abe Rankin (Phil Dunham) and Jim "Mac" MacCall (Earl Dwire) hope to revive the area by finding gold in their mine, the Royal Flush. MacCall plans to invest $10,000 in the project as assayer Bud Ellis (David Sharpe) informs Abe that the ore they have mined is of high quality. Overhearing this is Gannon (Roger Williams), who works for Rankin and MacCall, and promoter Murrell (Lee Shumway), who wants to buy the mine. The two men are working with Blackie (Chuck Morrison) and Rose (Jane Novak), who has opened a Ghost Town boarding house in anticipation of the mine's revival. As MacCall drives in his old flivver from Soledad with the cash, he meets up with Cheyenne Harry, who he knew from years before. After they part, Cheyenne hears shots and sees three men firing at Mac; he stops them and finds the old man badly injured. Cheyenne locates the money and when the three attackers approach the ambush site, he hides. When Gannon is unable to find the cash, he says the old man has died and leaves with his cohorts, Murrell and Blackie. Gannon and Blackie go to Rose and tell her they plan to get the money, which they believe is hidden in the mine, and with Murrell they all will leave town. After Gannon informs the sheriff (Ed Cassidy) that he saw MacCall attacked, he goes with the lawman to

Advertisement for *Ghost Town* (Commodore, 1936).

Cheyenne's camp; when they find the cash there, Cheyenne is arrested and taken to jail. The sheriff hides the money in his house and orders Bud to guard it while his daughter Billie (Ruth Findlay) takes Cheyenne his dinner. While the lawman is gone, Cheyenne fashions a noose and drags over the keys to his cell and after talking to Billie about the mine he escapes and locks her in the cell. The crooks attack Bud and steal the money and Cheyenne, seeing them escape, frees the young man and tells him to get Billie and take a doctor to MacCall, who is hidden in the mine's left tunnel. Cheyenne then trails the crooks heading for the mine and when they corner Bud and Mac in a tunnel, Cheyenne sets off an explosion and the sheriff and his deputy (Francis Walker) arrest the thieves. As Cheyenne is about to leave town, he asks for a hundred dollar loan from now prosperous bankers Rankin and MacCall. Telling them he plans to head south to the Rio Grande River, he leaves Aloysius with them in payment.

Aces Wild and *Ghost Town* belied their Poverty Row origins to become a satisfying finale to the character of Cheyenne Harry, as well as Harry Carey's "B" western starring career. He continued, however, to make films like *Border Café* (1937), *The Law West of Tombstone* (1938), *The Spoilers* (1942), *The Angel and the Badman* and *Duel in the Sun* (both 1947), and *Red River* (1948). One of filmdom's best character actors, he also appeared in the features *The Prisoner of Shark Island* (1936), *Mr. Smith Goes to Washington* (1939), *They Knew What They Wanted* and *Beyond Tomorrow* (both 1940), *The Shepherd of the Hills* and *Among the Living* (both 1941), *The Great Moment* (1944), *Sea of Grass* (1947) and *So Dear to My Heart* (1948), which was released the year after his death due to complications from a spider bite.

Filmography

A Knight of the Range (Universal, 1916, 7 reels) Director: Jacques Jaccard. Scenario: Harry Carey.
Cast: Harry Carey (Cheyenne Harry), Olive Golden (Bess Dawson), Hoot Gibson (Bob Graham), William Canfield (Gentleman Dick), Bud Osborne (Sheriff), A.D. Blake (Nick), Bill Gettinger [William Steele] (Buck), Peggy Coudray (Dolores).

The Soul Herder (Universal, 1917, 3 reels) Director: Jack [John] Ford. Scenario: George Hively. Photography: Ben F. Reynolds.
Cast: Harry Carey (Cheyenne Harry), Jean Hersholt (Priest), Molly Malone, Fritzi Ridgeway, Vester Pegg, Hoot Gibson, Duke R. Lee, Bill Gettinger [William Steele], Elizabeth James.
Also called *The Sky Pilot*.

Cheyenne's Pal (Universal, 1917, 2 reels) Director: Jack [John] Ford. Scenario: Jack [John] Ford & Charles J. Wilson. Photography: Friend Baker.
Cast: Harry Carey (Cheyenne Harry), Gertrude Astor (Dance Hall Girl), Pete Carey (Cactus), Jim Corey (Nosy Jim), Hoot Gibson, Vester Pegg, Bill Gettinger [William Steele], Steve Pimento, Ed Jones (Cowboys).
Also called *Cactus My Pal* and *A Dumb Friend*.

Straight Shooting (Universal, 1917, 71 minutes) Director: Jack [John] Ford. Scenario: George Hively. Photography: Ben F. Reynolds & George Scott.
Cast: Harry Carey (Cheyenne Harry), Molly Malone (Joan Sims), Duke R. Lee (Thunder Flint), Vester Pegg (Placer Fremont), Hoot Gibson (Sam Turner), Milt Brown (Black Eyed Pete), George Berrell (Sweetwater Sims), Ted Brooks (Tom Sims).
Also called *Joan of Cattle Country*.

The Secret Man (Universal, 1917, 5 reels) Director-Story: Jack [John] Ford. Scenario: George Hively. Photography: Ben F. Reynolds.
Cast: Harry Carey (Cheyenne Harry), Edith Sterling (Molly Beaufort), Vester Pegg (Sheriff Bill), Hoot Gibson (Chuck Fadden), Steve Clements (Pedro), Bill Gettinger [William Steele] (Foreman), Elizabeth Janes (Elizabeth Beaufort).
Also called *The Round-Up* and *Up Against It*.

A Marked Man (Universal, 1917, 5 reels) Director: Jack [John] Ford. Scenario: George Hively. Photography: John W. Brown.
Cast: Harry Carey (Cheyenne Harry), Molly Malone (Molly Young), Harry Rattenberry (Mr. Young), Vester Pegg (Ben Kent), Mrs. Anna Townsend (Harry's Mother), Bill Gettinger [William Steele] (Sheriff), Hoot Gibson.

Bucking Broadway (Universal, 1917, 5 reels) Producer: Harry Carey. Director: Jack [John] Ford. Scenario: George Hively. Photography: Ben F. Reynolds & John W. Brown.
Cast: Hoot Gibson (Cheyenne Harry), Molly Malone (Molly Malone), Gertrude Astor (Gladys), L.M. Wells (Mr. Malone), Vester Pegg (Thornton), Bill Gettinger [William Steele] (Foreman), Martha Mattox (Store Customer).
British title: *Slumbering Fires*.

The Phantom Riders (Universal, 1918, 5 reels) Producer: Harry Carey. Director: Jack [John] Ford. Scenario: George Hively. Story: Henry MacRae. Photography: Ben F. Reynolds & John W. Brown.

Cast: Harry Carey (Cheyenne Harry), Molly Malone (Molly Grant), Bill Gettinger [William Steele] (Dave Bland), Buck Connors (Pebble Grant), Vester Pegg (The Unknown), Jim Corey (Foreman).

Working title: *Range War*.

Wild Women (Universal, 1918, 5 reels) Producer: Harry Carey. Director: Jack [John] Ford. Scenario: George Hively. Story: Harry Carey & Jack [John] Ford. Photography: Ben F. Reynolds & John W. Brown.

Cast: Harry Carey (Cheyenne Harry), Molly Malone (Princess), Martha Mattox (Queen), Edward Jones (Pelon), Vester Pegg (Pegg), E. Van Beaver (Boss), Wilfred Taylor (Slugger).

Thieves' Gold (Universal, 1918, 5 reels) Director: Jack [John] Ford. Scenario: George Hively, from the story "Back on the Right Trail" by Frederick R. Bechdolt. Photography: Ben F. Reynolds & John W. Brown.

Cast: Harry Carey (Cheyenne Harry), Molly Malone (Alice Norris), Vester Pegg (Curt Simmons), L.M. Wells (Mr. Savage), John Cook (Uncle Larkin), Helen Ware (Mrs. Savage), Harry Tenbrook (Colonel Betoski), Martha Mattox (Mrs. Larkin), Millard K. Wilson.

Hell Bent (Universal, 1918, 6 reels) Director: Jack [John] Ford. Scenario-Story: Harry Carey & Jack [John] Ford. Photography: Ben F. Reynolds.

Cast: Harry Carey (Cheyenne Harry), Neva Gerber (Bess Thurston), Duke R. Lee (Cimmaron Bill), Vester Pegg (Jack Thurston), Joseph Harris (Beau Ross), Steve Clements, Millard K. Watson.

Three Mounted Men (Universal, 1918, 6 reels) Director: Jack [John] Ford. Scenario-Story: Eugene B. Lewis. Photography: Ben F. Reynolds & John W. Brown.

Cast: Harry Carey (Cheyenne Harry), Neva Gerber (Lola Masters), Joe Harris (Buck Masters), Harry Carter (Warden's Son), Ruby Lafayette (Mrs. Masters), Charles Hill Mailes (Warden), Mrs. Anna Townsend (Harry's Mother), Ella Hall.

Also called *Three Wounded Men*.

Roped (Universal, 1919, 6 reels) Director: Jack [John] Ford. Scenario-Story: Eugene B. Lewis. Photography: John W. Brown. Production Supervisor: James C. Bradford.

Cast: Harry Carey (Cheyenne Harry), Neva Gerber (Aileen Judson-Brown), Molly McConnell (Mrs. Judson-Brown), Arthur Shirley (Ferdie Van Duzen), J. Farrell MacDonald (Butler).

A Fight for Love (Universal, 1919, 6 reels) Producer: P.A. (Pat) Powers. Director: Jack [John] Ford. Scenario: Eugene B. Lewis, from his story "Hell's Neck." Photography: Ben F. Reynolds & John W. Brown.

Cast: Harry Carey (Cheyenne Harry), Neva Gerber (Kate McDougal), Joe Harris (Black Michael), Mark Fenton (Angus McDougal), J. Farrell MacDonald (Priest), Princess Neola May (Indian Maiden), Edith Johnson, Betty Schade, Chief Big Tree, Dark Cloud.

Bare Fists (Universal, 1919, 6 reels) Producer: P.A. (Pat) Powers. Director: Jack [John] Ford. Scenario: Eugene B. Lewis. Story: Bernard McConville. Photography: John W. Brown.

Cast: Harry Carey (Cheyenne Harry), Betty Schade (Conchita), Joe Harris (Boone Travis), Vester Pegg (Lopez), Molly McConell (Conchita's Mother), Anna May Walthall (Ruby), Howard Enstedt (Bud), Joseph Girard (Harry's Father).

Riders of Vengeance (Universal, 1919, 6 reels) Producer: P.A. (Pat) Powers. Director: Jack [John] Ford. Scenario: Eugene B. Lewis. Story: Harry Carey & Jack [John] Ford. Photography: John W. Brown.

Cast: Harry Carey (Cheyenne Harry), Seena Owen (The Girl), Joseph [Joe] Harris (Gale Thurman), J. Farrell MacDonald (Buell), Alfred Allen (Harry's Father), Jennie Lee (Harry's Mother), Clita Gale (Virginia), Vester Pegg, Betty Schade, M.K. [Millard] Wilson.

The Ace of the Saddle (Universal, 1919, 6 reels) Producer: P.A. (Pat) Powers. Director: Jack [John] Ford. Scenario: George Hively. Story: Frederick J. Jackson. Photography: John W. Brown.

Cast: Harry Carey (Cheyenne Harry), Joe Harris (Crooked Sheriff), Duke R. Lee (Sheriff Faulkner), Peggy Pearce (Madeline Faulkner), Jack Waters (Inky O'Day), Vester Pegg (Gambler), William Courwright (Storekeeper), Zoe Rae, Howard Enstedt (Children), Ed [King Fisher] Jones.

Working title: *A Man of Peace*.

The Westerners (W.W. Hodkinson, 1919, 70 minutes) Producer: Benjamin B. Hampton. Director: Edward Sloman. Scenario: E. Richard Shayer, from the novel by Stewart Edward White. Titles: Stewart Edward White. Photography: John F. Seitz. Technical Advisor: Clark Comstock.

Cast: Roy Stewart (Cheyenne Harry), Robert McKim (Black Mike Lafond), Wilfred Lucas (Jim Buckley), Mildred Manning (Prue Welch/Molly Lafond), Mary Jane Irving (Little Molly Welch), Graham Pettie (Professor Welch), Frankie Lee (Dennis), Clark Comstock (Lone Wolf), Dorothy Hagar (Bismarck Annie).

A Gun Fightin' Gentleman (Universal, 1919, 5 reels) Producer: P.A. (Pat) Powers. Director: Jack [John] Ford. Scenario: Hal Hoadley. Story: Harry Carey & Jack [John] Ford. Photography: John W. Brown.

Cast: Harry Carey (Cheyenne Harry), J. Barney Sherry (John Merritt), Kathleen O'Connor (Helen Merritt), Harry Meter (Earl of Jollywell), Lydia Titus (Helen's Aunt), Duke R. Lee (Buck Regan), Joe Harris (Seymour), Johnnie Cooke (Sheriff), Ted Brooks (Youngster).

Marked Men (Universal, 1919, 6 reels) Producer: P.A. (Pat) Powers. Director: Jack [John] Ford. Scenario: H. Tipton Steck, from the novel *The Three Godfathers* by Peter B. Kyne. Photography: John W. Brown. Editors: Frank Lawrence & Frank Atkinson.

Cast: Harry Carey (Cheyenne Harry), J. Farrell MacDonald (Placer), Joe Harris (Tom Gibbons), Ted Brooks (Tony Garcia), Winifred Westover (Ruby Merrill), Charles Le Moyne (Sheriff Cushing).

Also called *Trail of Shadows*.

Aces Wild (Commodore, 1936, 58 minutes) Producer: William Berke. Director: Harry Fraser. Screenplay: Weston Edwards. Story: Monroe Talbot. Photography: Robert Cline. Editor: Arthur A. Brooks. Sound: Corson Jowett. Assistant Director: William L. Nolte.

Cast: Harry Carey (Cheyenne Harry Morgan), Gertrude Messinger (Martha Woods), Ted [Theodore] Lorch (Kelton), Roger Williams (Slim Bartlett), Chuck Morrison (Heck), Phil Dunham (Anson), Snowflake [Fred Toones] (Snowflake), Ed Cassidy (Blacksmith), William McCall (Sheriff), Bill Patton, Francis Walker (Citizens), Jack Evans (Saloon Customers), Ray Henderson (Rider), Sonny, the Marvel Horse, Aloysius the Mule (Themselves).

Ghost Town (Commodore, 1936, 56 minutes) Producer: William Berke. Director: Harry Fraser. Screenplay: Weston Edwards. Story: Monroe Talbot. Photography: Robert Cline. Editor: Arthur A. Brooks. Music Director: Lee Zahler. Art Director: Jim Morahan. Sound: C. [Clifford] Ruberg. Assistant Director: Louis Germonprez.

Cast: Harry Carey (Cheyenne Harry Morgan), Ruth Findlay (Billie Blair), Jane Novak (Rose), David Sharpe (Bud Ellis), Lee Shumway (Mr. Murrell), Edward [Ed] Cassidy (Sheriff Blair), Roger Williams (Ed Gannon), Phil Dunham (Abe Rankin), Earl Dwire (Jim "Mac" MacCall), Chuck Morrison (Blackie Hawkes), Francis Walker (Deputy Sheriff Frank), Horace Murphy (Henry), Bart Carre (Slim), Sonny, the Marvel Horse, Aloysius the Mule (Themselves).

THE CISCO KID

Using the pen name O. Henry, William Sydney Porter (1862–1910) wrote over 400 short stories, and one of the most enduring has been "The Caballero's Way," published in 1907, which introduced the Cisco Kid. From this lone literary source sprung a western character who has encompassed not only films, but also radio, television, comic books and various merchandising. Ironically, the literary Cisco has almost nothing to do with the popular cultural figure. In the short story, the Cisco Kid is a murderous bandit who exacts a terrible revenge on the girl who betrayed him. For the most part, his incarnation in films and other pop culture outlets have him as the Robin Hood of the Old West.

The Cisco Kid came to films just seven years after the publication of the O. Henry story when Éclair American produced *The Caballero's Way* in 1914. Filmed in Tucson, Arizona, it starred William R. Dunn as Cisco and Edna Payne as his unfaithful lover, Tonia. The feature was distributed by Universal, the same studio that brought the story to the screen again in 1919 as *The Border Terror*, with Vester Pegg as the Cisco Kid and Yvette Mitchell as Tonia.

The first major Cisco Kid production, and perhaps the most important feature made about the character, was Fox's all-talking *In Old Arizona* (1929), starring Warner Baxter as the Cisco Kid. Baxter was so impressive in the part that he won an Academy Award as Best Actor. The role was originally scheduled to be played by the film's co-director, Raoul Walsh. Walsh, however, lost an eye in a freak accident and Baxter took over the characterization and Irving Cummings became the feature's co-director. Some 70 years after its release, *In Old Arizona* still has its charm, although it appears to be a bit creaky and somewhat stagebound in its emoting by a cast trying to adapt to talkies. Still it makes surprisingly good use of the sound and for the audience of its time it was full of novelties like the noise of horses' hoofs, ham and eggs cooking on a stove and most importantly, the use of music in a western. Lew Brown, Ray Henderson and Buddy G. DeSylva wrote its haunting theme song, "My Tonia," which sold thousands of copies in sheet music with Warner Baxter's picture emblazoned on its cover. In addition, Nick Lucas' recording of the song for Brunswick Records was a major seller. Despite its somewhat tarnished reputation today, *In Old Arizona* was the first important sound western.

Advertisement for *In Old Arizona* (Fox, 1929).

Warner Baxter (1891–1951) had been a stage actor before coming to films in 1914 and was the leading man in such silent efforts as *All Women* (1918), *Those Who Dance* (1924), *Mannequin*, *Aloma of the South Seas* and *The Great Gatsby* (all 1926), and *Ramona* and *West of Zanzibar* (both 1928), before making his sound debut as the Cisco Kid. Co-starring in *In Old Arizona* was Edmund Lowe (1890–1971), who also began his career on stage before eventually moving to Broadway and then into films. Equally at home on stage or on the screen, he made his movie debut in 1915 and appeared in numerous features; his most famous part came as Sergeant Quirt in Raoul Walsh's 1926 success *What Price Glory?*

Taking place in 1898, *In Old Arizona* had the Cisco Kid (Warner Baxter), a dashing bandito with a $5,000 reward on his head, holding up a stagecoach and taking its Wells Fargo strongbox. When word of the robbery gets back to the local Army commandant (Roy Stewart), he orders Sergeant Mickey Dunn (Edmund Lowe) to bring in the Kid, dead or alive. In town for a shave and a bath, Cisco meets Dunn in Giuseppe's (Henry Armetta) barbershop and the two become friends; Dunn later learns Cisco's identity from the area blacksmith (James Marcus). Meanwhile, Cisco goes to see his girlfriend, Tonia Maria (Dorothy Burgess), a seductive two-timer, who is warned about her promiscuous ways by her servant Bonita (Soledad Jiminez). The Kid gives Tonia presents and makes love to her before sending the girl into town to tell Dunn he has left the area. Mickey is attracted to the Mexican girl and arrives at her house, just as Cisco rides away. The sergeant romances the amorous Tonia and promises to take her with him to New York City upon his transfer to Governor's Island. Cisco rustles a herd of cattle and when a trio of outlaws (Tom Santschi, Frank Campeau, Pat Hartigan) try to murder him, he kills two of them and scares off the third. Dunn takes Tonia to his camp where she finds out he is trailing Cisco but after he offers her the reward for the bandit she agrees to help him capture her lover. Cisco, who has purchased a white mantilla for Tonia, returns and overhears Dunn and the girl plot his downfall, with Tonia telling Mickey she wants the Kid dead. After Dunn departs, Cisco appears and gives her the mantilla. While he is putting away his horse, she writes a note to the sergeant telling him Cisco is back and sends it to him via Bonita; the Kid intercepts the missive. In its place he sends word to Dunn that he will be wearing Tonia's clothes and the mantilla as she rides away as a decoy. Mickey returns to the girl's casa and, when Cisco departs, Tonia, wearing the mantilla, wave goodbye to him. Dunn shoots her as the Kid rides away.

So popular was Baxter's portrayal of the Cisco Kid that he played a similar character in the 1930 Fox release *The Arizona Kid* and the next year he was Cisco again in the two-reel Masquers Club of Hollywood production *The Slippery Pearls*, a comedy featuring nearly every big name in the film industry, which was distributed by Paramount.

In 1931 Fox re-teamed Baxter and Lowe as Cisco and Sergeant Dunn for a sequel to *In Old Arizona*, called *The Cisco Kid*. Irving Cummings also returned to direct and the feature reused the song "My Tonia" and added a new one composed by Baxter called "Song of the Cisco Kid." James Bradbury, Jr., and John Webb Dillon also reprised their roles from the 1929 film as Lowe's military buddies. Again taking place just prior to 1900, *The Cisco Kid* had Army Sergeant Michael Patrick "Mickey" Dunn (Lowe) still out to collect the $5,000 reward on his nemesis, the Cisco Kid (Baxter). Rustling cattle with fellow outlaws Lopez (Charles Stevens) and Gordito (Chris-Pin Martin), the Kid spies Dunn and his army cohorts Dixon (Bradbury, Jr.) and Bouse (Dillon) and he tells Gordito to shoot at him to make the soldiers think he is rustling his and Lopez's herd. Cisco escapes to Carrizo where he has a run-in with Sheriff Tex Ransom (Frederick Burt) over the affections of beautiful Carmencita (Conchita Montenegro). Wounded by the lawman, the Kid escapes and is nursed back to health by Sally Benton (Nora Lane), a widow who is about to lose her ranch to the sheriff and his crooked cohort, banker Enos Hankins (Willard Robertson). To save Sally's ranch, Cisco robs Hankins' bank and is nearly shot by the newly arrived Dunn, but Carmencita pretends to be injured and the bandit makes a getaway. Dunn rides to the ranch and apprehends Cisco but lets him go after finding out he robbed the bank to help the widow and her children. Writing in *The Western* (1983), Phil Hardy noted, "Baxter's charming and surprisingly complex interpretation overcomes the naiveties of the plot."

Baxter portrayed the bandit for the third and final time in 1939's 20th Century–Fox production *Return of the Cisco Kid*, directed by Herbert I. Leeds, who would helm three more Cisco Kid features in the next two years. Shot mostly on location in Arizona, the film also saw Chris-Pin Martin return in the role of Gordito, a part he would play in the next six series outings. Martin (1893–1953) entered films in 1925 and until his death appeared in over 130 feature films. His portrayal of Gordito as a fat, greasy character was popular with American audiences but proved offensive to Latin Americans.

Taking place in 1900, *Return of the Cisco Kid* opened with the bandit (Baxter) being shot by a firing squad whose members do not know that the guns they used were loaded with blanks. That night, Cisco's friends Gordito (Martin) and Lopez (Cesar Romero) exhume his coffin and they go north into Arizona where they meet Colonel Bixby (Henry Hull) and his niece Ann Carver (Lynn Bari), who are going to a ranch they have purchased. When Bixby and Ann's stagecoach is held up, the Kid stops the robbery but in town the two find out that their partner's son, Alan Davis (Kane Richmond), has been jailed by crooked land owner Sheriff McNally (Robert Barrat), who holds the deed to their property. The sheriff arrests Bixby and Ann but Cisco breaks them and Alan out of jail; Davis is wounded in the escape. Having fallen in love with Ann, Cisco leaves the trio with Mama Soledad (Soledad Jiminez) and pretends to be a cattle buyer who wants to purchase the Bixby place. At first the sheriff refuses to sell but after Cisco offers him $100,000 he agrees and the Kid robs the lawman's bank to pay for the ranch. McNally tries to trap the bandit but instead has to give up the deed to the Bixby spread. When Cisco finds out Ann loves Alan, he sends the young man into the trap McNally set for him but after learning that Ann never cared for him, he sets out to rescue Alan. As McNally and a group of Mexican rurales wait for him, Cisco manages to circle around and capture them. Forcing McNally to agree to leave Bixby, Ann and Alan alone, the Kid rides away and he, Lopez and Gordito head back to Mexico. *Variety* called the film "a fast-paced western ... [a] compact interweave of comedy and rather lusty excitement."

Nearly 40 when he portrayed the Cisco Kid for the third and final time, Baxter relinquished the role to Cesar Romero, who would star in six more series episodes. In the early 1940s, Baxter suffered a nervous breakdown but returned to the screen to star in Columbia's popular "Crime Doctor" series from 1943 to 1946 as well as headlining a number of "B" pictures for the studio. Suffering from arthritis, he died in 1951 of pneumonia. Romero (1907–94), who played Lopez in *The Cisco Kid Returns* before assuming the mantle of O. Henry's character, was of Cuban ancestry. Starting out as a ballroom dancer, he came to Broadway in 1927 and made his film debut in *The Shadow Laughs* in 1933. Thereafter he appeared in scores of films, both as a star and featured performer, and he also was in numerous TV programs, starring in the 1954 series *Passport to Danger*. He was most famous, however, for playing the Joker in nineteen episodes of ABC-TV's *Batman* from 1966 to 1968.

Herbert I. Leeds directed Romero's first starring series entry, *The Cisco Kid and the Lady*, which was released late in 1939. Lensed at Lone Pine, California, it had the Kid (Romero) and his pal Gordito (Martin) stopping robbers from attacking a man and his infant son. Gang leader Jim Harbison (Robert Barrat) pretends to also aid them as the man dies leaving the trio the baby and a map to his gold mine. When the outlaws try to get rid of Cisco and Gordito, they learn that the two have destroyed their parts of the map after memorizing them. When schoolmarm Julie Lawson (Marjorie Weaver) comes by on another stagecoach, Cisco leaves the infant, whom he has dubbed Junior (Gloria Ann White), with her. In town the Kid romances dancer Billie Graham (Virginia Field), Harbison's girlfriend, as the gang leader plans to ambush Cisco and Gordito. When Julie's fiancé, Tommy Bates (George Montgomery), arrives in town, he mistakenly thinks the baby belongs to her and they have a falling out. Tommy also is jealous of Cisco although the bandit is attracted to Billie, who knows his identity. Thinking Cisco has stolen Harbison's portion of the map, which she covets, the dancer has the Kid, Gordito and Bates put in jail. Cisco then tells Harbison to dress like him and rob a stagecoach so the Kid will be set free. Breaking out of jail, the Kid and Gordito force justice of the peace Pop Saunders (James Burke) to marry Julie and Tommy while soldiers hunt for Harbison, believing he is the Cisco Kid. Giving the gold mine to Julie, Tommy and the baby, Cisco and Gordito leave the area with Billie after Harbison is killed by the soldiers.

The first of four 1940 series entries, *Viva Cisco Kid* was directed by former actor Norman Foster. It had the Kid (Romero) abandoning his unfaithful girlfriend Helena (Jacqueline Dalya) and forcing his friend Gordito (Martin) to desert his fiancée (Inez Palange), with both promising to give up women. However, when they stop a stagecoach robbery, Cisco falls in love with passenger Joan Allen (Jean Rogers) and escorts her and the coach into the town of Towash. Saloon keeper Hank Gunther (Harold Goodwin), the boss of the outlaws, learns that the robbery attempt was unsuccessful and the money he was after is now in the express office. He tells his cohort, Jesse Allen (Minor Watson), Joan's father, to get the money and that night Jesse warns Joan to leave town. Cisco also tells the girl that he is no good for her and will also ride away as a sky pilot, Moses (Nigel De Brulier), sees Jesse rob the express office. Hank kills Moses, and Jesse confesses his crime to Joan and rides into Mexico. Joan goes after him and meets Cisco and Gordito, who are captured by posse members who blame them for Moses' killing. Escaping, the Kid and Gordito leave Joan with Gunther, who takes her to the Sugar Loaf Mine where the real gang leader, "The Boss" (Stanley Fields), makes her a prisoner. Jesse saves Cisco and Gordito from being arrested and they head to the mine where the Kid and his pal try to join the gang. Gunther and his men capture Jesse and the Boss places Cisco, Gordito, Joan and her father in a mine tunnel. A gang member (Ray Teal) sets off an explosion and the mine collapses, killing all the gang members and trapping Cisco, Gordito, Joan and Jesse. The four escape after Gordito follows a rabbit which finds an opening. Jesse agrees to return the stolen money as Cisco, after being kissed by Joan, and Gordito ride away.

Lucky Cisco Kid, directed by H. Bruce Humberstone, came out in the summer of 1940 and had Cisco (Romero) and Gordito (Martin) hijack a stagecoach before being chased by Sergeant Dunn (Dana Andrews) and his soldiers. They leave the coach and split up before going to a small Arizona town where Cisco flirts with Lola (Mary Beth Hughes), a saloon singer and Dunn's girlfriend. Gordito joins a church group and later he and the Kid hear Judge McQuade (Willard Robertson) denounce them for their various crimes. The two caballeros come to realize they are being impersonated and blamed for offenses they did not commit. When stagecoach driver Tex (Dick Rich) recognizes Cisco and Gordito, he calls for their arrest but the two ride out of town to aid rancher Emily Lawrence (Evelyn Venable) after her son Tommy (Johnny Sheffield) claims their spread is being raided by the Kid and his men. As a result, Cisco and Gordito hire on at the Lawrence ranch and find out Emily is in debt to McQuade, who wants the ranch. Cisco is shot while witnessing a stagecoach holdup and he is blamed for the crime but is shielded by Emily. Lola announces that Bill Stevens (Joseph Sawyer), one of her suitors, robbed the stagecoach and both he and Cisco are brought to McQuade. Gordito robs the judge's safe and gets proof that McQuade and Stevens are partners and that Stevens had robbed the ranchers in the guise of the Cisco Kid. Lola gets the reward money for the capture of the outlaw gang and she persuades Dunn to let Cisco and Gordito go free. *Variety* considered it "a standard western" but "better entertainment than past two releases of the group."

Otto Brower directed *The Gay Caballero*, which came out in the fall of 1940. Production at Lone Pine had to be suspended for two months after Romero broke his leg during filming. Set in 1889, it found the Cisco Kid (Romero) and Gordito (Martin) learning from a young woman (Jacqueline Dalya) that her fiancé had been accused of being Cisco and was murdered by Joe Turner (Edmund MacDonald), the foreman of her employer, ranch owner Kate Brewster (Janet Beecher). The two caballeros then stop a stagecoach robbery and meet passengers George Wetherby (C. Montague Shaw) and his daughter Susan (Sheila Ryan), who are buying land from Kate Brewster. Cisco and Gordito go with George and Susan, who are from England, to the Brewster ranch and there they learn that Kate's nephew Billy (Robert Sterling) has just become a deputy sheriff. That evening, Turner describes how the Cisco Kid raided the Brewster ranch but Wetherby is determined to stay in the West. Kate and Turner are in cahoots trying to drive the Wetherbys out of the area since the Englishman's purchase will split the Brewster ranch. Planning to rob the stagecoach carrying Wetherby's money, Kate informs Cisco that she knows his true identity and she orders the local sheriff (Hooper Atchley) to arrest him. George and Billy distrust Cisco but Susan remains loyal to him as Cisco is blamed for a stagecoach robbery carried out by Turner, who impersonated him. The Kid eludes capture but Gordito is taken into custody. When Cisco tries to free his friend the next day, he too is arrested but both men manage to break jail. Cisco shoots Turner in a showdown and he and Gordito stop Kate from taking Wetherby's funds; during a chase, Kate is killed when her wagon overturns. After explaining things to George and his daughter, and urging them not to tell Billy, Cisco rides away with Gordito, with both of them being chased by the sheriff and his men.

Herbert I. Leeds returned to direct the final two 20th Century–Fox Cisco Kid outings, *Romance of the Rio Grande* and *Ride on Vaquero*, both 1941 releases. The former, issued at the beginning of the year, was the only Cisco Kid feature to be based on a novel, Katherine Fullerton Gerould's 1932 book *Conquistador*. Allegedly a remake of the 1931 film *The Cisco Kid*, it had almost nothing to do with that feature but instead told of Rancho Santa Margarita owner Don Fernando de Vega (Pedro de Cordoba) sending for his Spanish-born grandson, Don Carlos Hernandez (Romero). Don Fernando does not care for his nephew, Ricardo de Vega (Ricardo Cortez), and wants to leave his vast Arizona ranch to his grandson. Masked men Carver (Raphael [Ray] Bennett) and Manuel (Trevor Bardette) attack the stagecoach carrying Carlos and try to murder him but he is saved by the Cisco Kid (Romero) and his pal Gordito (Martin). Realizing that the badly wounded Carlos is his lookalike, Cisco takes the wounded man to innkeeper Mama Lopez (Inez Palange), and then he and Gordito ride to the Vega hacienda where Cisco impersonates Carlos. There they meet not only Don Fernando and Ricardo, but also Rosita (Patricia Morison), Carlos' intended bride, and Maria (Lynne Roberts), the Don's ward. Both Ricardo and Rosita are surprised to see Carlos since they were behind the effort to have him killed so they could marry and control the ranch after Don Fernando's death. Although Cisco and Gordito had planned to rob the Vega rancho, Cisco becomes very fond of the Don as well as Maria and comes to realize that Ricardo and Rosita were the ones who ordered Carlos' killing. After a mysterious assailant murders Don Fernando, Cisco believes Ricardo will also try to murder him. The next day, while accompanying Ricardo and his men on a tour of the rancho, he and Gordito are attacked and during a shootout Manuel is killed. Ricardo and Carver escape to Mama Lopez' place where they realize the real Carlos is alive and that Cisco is an imposter. Mama Lopez warns the two caballeros and they are able to get away from the Vega rancho and save Carlos, who Carver planned to murder. Cisco, Gordito and Carlos then formulate a plan by which Cisco goes back to the rancho as Carlos and Maria tells him she loves Cisco and that it was Ricardo who tried to kill him, thinking she is talking to Carlos. After overhearing Ricardo and Rosita argue, Cisco proposes marriage to Rosita and she accepts, thinking she is going to marry Carlos. Ricardo, however, learns she betrayed him; Rosita shoots him but before dying he kills her. As Cisco and Gordito ride away the next day, Carlos begins to romance Maria.

One of the best entries in the post–Warner Baxter Cisco Kid films, *Romance of the Rio Grande* had Lynne Roberts singing "Ride on Vaquero" and "You'll Find Your Answer in My Eyes." This is somewhat ironic since the film's other leading lady, Patricia Morison, was also a concert vocalist who later headlined the 1949 Broadway musical *Kiss Me Kate*.

Ride on Vaquero was also the title of the final Cesar Romero Cisco Kid film, which came to theaters in the spring of 1941. Its storyline told of the Kid's (Romero) lady love, Dolores (Joan Woodbury), turning him and Gordito (Martin) over to the cavalry for reward money. The two are accused of a series of kidnappings and Colonel Warren (Paul Harvey) offers Cisco and Gordito a chance to clear their names by finding the real culprits. Cisco is not interested in the offer until he finds out the outlaws have killed a family friend and kidnapped the murdered man's son, Carlos Martinez (Robert Lowery). Riding to the Martinez rancho, the two learn that Carlos' wife, Marguerita (Lynne Roberts), has placed a mortgage on the place in order to get ransom money from banker Dan Clark (Edwin Maxwell). In town, Cisco meets a former lover, Sally Slocum (Mary Beth Hughes), a dancer at a saloon owned by Sleepy (Paul Sutton) and Redge (Don Costello). When he tells her he is helping Marguerita, Sally agrees not to reveal his identity. Going to the site where the ransom is to be paid, he sees Redge and town sheriff Johnny Burns (Arthur Hohl) collect the money. He follows the duo to Clark's office and deduces that the trio is behind the Martinez killing. After Cisco and Gordito find Carlos in a remote cabin, they are arrested by the sheriff and put in jail. Marguerita does not believe Cisco's story about the three men killing her father-in-law and kidnapping her husband in order to get control of the Martinez rancho. Cisco also believes it was Sally who revealed his identity to the sheriff, although she is innocent. After Cisco learns that Colonel Warren has been killed in an Indian raid, Sally helps him and Gordito break jail. Cisco tricks the banker, Sheriff Burns and Redge into signing confessions. Sally keeps the trio at gunpoint until the army can arrive to arrest them as Cisco and Gordito ride away.

20th Century–Fox planned to continue the series with *The Cisco Kid Rides Again* but Romero joined the Armed Forces at the beginning of World War II and the production was cancelled.

After a four-year hiatus, the Cisco Kid returned to the screen when Monogram producer Philip N. Krasne obtained the screen rights to the O. Henry character. Krasne, who co-produced the first three Monogram "Charlie Chan" productions, hired Duncan Renaldo to portray Cisco and Martin Garralaga to play his partner, Pancho. Renaldo had already played a Latin American cowboy hero, Rico, in Republic's "The Three Mesquiteers" (q.v.) series. Garralaga did a less stereotyped portrayal of Pancho, in comparison to Chris-Pin Martin's work as Gordito. Ironically, Garralaga, who was also an opera singer, was afraid of horses. When the trio of films Krasne did with Renaldo and Garralaga for Monogram in 1945 were later released to television, the characters of Cisco and Pancho were redubbed Chico and Pablo.

The first of the Monogram productions, *The Cisco Kid Returns*, directed by John P. McCarthy,

Duncan Renaldo as the "Cisco Kid."

was issued in February 1945. Cisco (Duncan Renaldo) and Pancho (Martin Garralaga) halt the wedding of the Kid's former girlfriend, Rosita Gonzales (Cecilia Callejo), to cantina proprietor John Harris (Roger Pryor), a cohort of Paul Conway (Anthony Warde), who is out to steal the estate of businessman Stephen Page (Walter Clinton). Later Cisco finds Page, who has been ambushed, and agrees to the dying man's request that he look after his daughter Nancy (Sharon Smith). Page was killed by Jennings (Cy Kendall), who works for Harris. Cisco is accused of the murder and of kidnapping the young girl. After the local priest (Fritz Leiber) tells Cisco and Pancho to grant Page's dying wish, the duo accompanies a woman, Elizabeth Page (Vicky Lane), who claims to be Nancy's mother, and her maid (Jan Wiley), to the Page estate. When Rosita sees Cisco with Elizabeth, she becomes jealous and tells Harris that the Kid is harboring the Page girl. Harris then plans to turn Nancy over to Conway but before doing so he demands that Conway make him a partner. When Cisco tries to romance the maid, he is nearly captured by the sheriff (Bud Osborne) and his men but he is rescued by Pancho. Cisco finds a new refuge for Nancy and then has Pancho bring take Conway, Elizabeth and her maid, and the lawman to the mission, where he claims Nancy is hidden. Cisco proves Elizabeth is a fake hired by Conway to impersonate Mrs. Page and that Conway was fired by Page before he was murdered. The maid then confesses and Conway and Elizabeth are arrested as Cisco and the sheriff ride to apprehend Harris and Jennings. After the outlaws are behind bars, Rosita returns to Cisco.

Phil Rosen helmed the second Monogram entry, *In Old New Mexico*, released in the spring of 1945. Basically a murder mystery in a western setting, the feature had Cisco (Renaldo) and Pancho (Garralaga) robbing a stagecoach and taking nurse Ellen Roth (Gwen Kenyon) with them. Ellen has been falsely accused of murdering a patient for her money. Going to the town of Gilda, Cisco tries to find out who owns the post office box where the dead woman sent a series of letters. He finds out it belongs to saloon proprietor Will Hastings (Norman Willis), a man unknown to Ellen, who is hiding at a local mission. Ellen tells Cisco that her employer was murdered by Dr. Wills (Richard Gordon); back in town, the Kid learns from saloon singer Dolores (Aurora Roche) that Hastings told her he was going to be rich. After a fracas with Hastings, Cisco leaves town when the sheriff (Lee "Lasses" White) shows up. He later returns and forces the saloon owner to admit he was the murdered woman's nephew and heir. Cisco then sets a trap to capture the killer by offering to turn Ellen over to him for a hefty reward. After Ellen is arrested, Cisco and Pancho make the local newspaper printer (Edward Earle) release a story saying that Ellen is innocent and that Dr. Wills has been arrested for the killing. Cisco then offers to silence Ellen for Hastings and when Wills comes to Gilda, the Kid captures him and takes him to the mission. Wills confesses to Ellen that he and Hastings carried out the killing, and the doctor and his boss are arrested.

South of the Rio Grande, the third and final 1945 Monogram series entry, was directed by genre veteran Lambert Hillyer, and was issued in the fall of that year. Its story was written by Johnston McCulley, the creator of "Zorro" (q.v.), and it had the Cisco Kid (Renaldo) and Pancho (Garralaga) come to the aid of old friend Esteban Robena only to find out that he and his family were murdered by Miguel Sanchez (George J. Lewis), a district official, and his men. The two

Lobby card for *In Old New Mexico* (Monogram, 1945).

save another rancher, Manuel Gonzales (Tito Renaldo), from being shot by Sanchez's men as Marvel's sister, Dolores (Lillian Molieri), is abducted and taken to Mia Grande, where she is forced to sing in Sanchez's cantina. Manuel asks Cisco and Pancho to lead the local ranchers in fighting the corrupt Sanchez and they agree to do so. After a government inspector is killed by Sanchez's men, Cisco impersonates the man and he arrives at the cantina as Sanchez's girlfriend Pepita (Armida) becomes jealous of her lover's attentions to Dolores. When Pepita learns that Dolores is Manuel's sister, she tries to tell Sanchez but is prevented by Luis (Pedro Regas) and Mama Maria (Soledad Jiminez), Dolores' protectors. When Pepita does manage to escape and inform Sanchez of Dolores' true identity, Cisco orders Pancho to shoot the girl. Cisco then romances Pepita, who informs him of Sanchez's crooked activities, which include rustling cattle and murdering those who oppose him. Realizing the game is up, Sanchez and his henchman Torres (Francis McDonald) plan to take the money they have stolen, murder Cisco and flee across the border. Cisco traps Sanchez and orders him to write a confession; when the crook pulls a gun on him, the Kid kills him. The ranchers then capture the Sanchez gang and Dolores is freed.

Although *South of the Rio Grande* was a fairly interesting feature, it was heavily padded with music. A dubbed Renaldo sang two songs while Armida performed "El Tecolote" and "Esa Moreno" and Lillian Molieri sang "Te Perdi" and "Adios Amor," with both women being accompanied by The Guadalajara Trio. The feature also proved to be Renaldo's last Cisco Kid film for a while since he then left the series to do war work for the U.S. government.

Scott R. Dunlap, who had produced Monogram's "The Range Busters" and "Nevada Jack

McKenzie' (q.v.) series, took over the reins of "Cisco Kid" features in 1946 with Gilbert Roland playing the title role. The half dozen films Roland made as Cisco were slanted more toward the adult market than the usual "B" westerns. Roland's Cisco smoked, drank tequila and romanced every beautiful woman he met in sharp contrast to most cowboy film heroes who did not smoke, drink or chase girls. The Roland series was given a bigger budget than had been allotted to the Renaldo features and as a result the studio produced six well-made and entertaining Cisco Kid outings. Regarding his work as the O. Henry character, Roland once said, "My Cisco Kid might have been a bandit, but he fought for the poor and was a civilized man in the true sense of the word." Martin Garralaga, who had played Pancho in the Renaldo outings, appeared in the first four Roland Ciscos but not as a sidekick. The initial quartet of films also featured a series theme song, "Ride, Amigos, Ride," composed by Charles Rosoff and Eddie Cherkose. It was sung by members of Cisco's gang since the first four series features had him as the leader of an outlaw band which robbed the rich and gave to the poor.

A native of Mexico, Gilbert Roland (1905–94) began working in Hollywood films in 1918 as an extra and within a few years he was starring in features like *The Plastic Age* (1925), *Camille* (1927) and *The Woman Disputed* (1928). He had no trouble making the transition to sound and in 1930 he starred in the English and Spanish versions of MGM's *Men of the North*. He was quite active in both English- and Spanish-language films in the 1930s and early 1940s and, following the Cisco Kid features, he continued to star in numerous motion pictures. In his sixties he headlined several westerns produced in Europe, including *Sam Cooper's Gold*, *Any Gun Can Play* and *Between God, the Devil and a Winchester* (all 1968) and *Johnny Hamlet* (1972). He was especially impressive as the vengeful patron in his final western, *Barbarosa*, in 1982. As an inside joke, Roland would use parts of his real name, Luis Antonio Damaso de Alonso, as the Cisco Kid's actual moniker. (In fact, Roland used the name Luis Alonso when starring in Mexican films in the 1930s and 1940s.)

Roland's initial Cisco Kid feature was *The Gay Cavalier*, released in March 1946. It, and the next three Ciscos, was directed by William Nigh. The film introduced a new sidekick for Cisco, Nacho Galindo in the role of Baby. It also featured two songs, "The Gay Caballero" and "One Kiss," both sung by leading lady Ramsay Ames, their composer. Taking place in 1850, it had bandit leader Cisco (Roland) making a stop at his father's grave before finding out that someone has taken his identity and stolen money given by the local peons to construct a new church. The culprit is Lawton (Tristram Coffin), a businessman who intends to wed Angela Geralda (Helen Gerard), the daughter of rancher Don Felipe Geralda (Martin Garralaga), who hopes the marriage will save his fortunes. Angela's sister Pepita (Ramsay Ames) does not care for Lawton and urges her sister not to marry him. At the Geralda hacienda, Lawton claims that the Cisco Kid committed the robbery but the bandit, who has also come to the ranch, convinces Pepita of his innocence and tries to make Lawton confess to the crime, but he is pursued by Lewis (John Merton), Lawton's cohort. Angela plans to marry Lawton to help her father but she is really in love with Juan (Drew Allen), who overhears Lawton and Lewis reveal the whereabouts of the stolen money. He tells Cisco about the money and along with Cisco's partner Baby (Nacho Galindo) they go to the gang's hideout at the Mountain of Shadows and capture all the outlaws except for Graham (Frank LaRue). While Cisco takes the money to the local padre (Joseph Burlando), Lawton talks Don Felipe into signing over his property to him in return for marrying Angela. When Cisco learns of this, he rushes to the ranch with Juan, halts the wedding and confronts Lawton. The two engage in a sword duel; when Lawton tries to shoot Cisco, he is stopped by Baby. Lawton is arrested and Angela and Juan plan to marry as the Cisco Kid and his gang ride away, Cisco having reluctantly bid farewell to Pepita.

Three months later came the release of *South of Monterey*, which had the Cisco Kid (Roland) and his band helping the poor in Southern California who are being harassed by crooked officials. Bennett (Harry Woods), the tax collector, is behind the lawlessness and he tries to make the police chief, Commandante Auturo Morales (Martin Garralaga), force his sister Maria (Marjorie Riordan) to marry him. Because Maria loves rancher Carlos Mandreno (George J. Lewis), Bennett tells Auturo to frame Carlos on a cattle rustling charge and put him in jail. The Cisco Kid arrives in town with his partner Baby (Frank Yaconelli), who pretends to be a blind troubadour, and learns that the money Carlos was to have received for selling his herd has been stolen by a mystery man called the Silver Bandit because he rides a horse with a silver saddle. Since Cisco also uses a silver saddle, he is chased by a posse and wounded but seeks sanctuary with Maria, who takes care of him. Cisco then goes back to town where he flirts with saloon singer Carmelita (Iris Flores), Auturo's girlfriend. Maria announces she will marry Bennett if Carlos is set free. When Auturo slaps Carmelita, Cisco defends her; she accidentally reveals his identity and he is arrested. Feeling remorse, Carmelita helps Cisco and Carlos escape from jail and the two men ride to Bennett's mountain hideout. Bennett tells Auturo he plans to take the money he has stolen from the locals and make a getaway. The commandante, disguised as Cisco, robs a stagecoach and shoots the driver. Cisco and Juan realize that Auturo is the Silver Bandit but before they can capture him he is shot by Bennett. Cisco then fights it out with Bennett, killing him, and he later tells Maria her brother died defending himself against the crooked tax collector. Maria and Carlos are reunited as Cisco, Baby and their gang leave.

South of Monterey featured Frank Yaconelli in the part of Cisco's sidekick Baby, a role he would also play in the next two series entries. A native of Italy, Yaconelli (1898–1965) worked in silent pictures before doing character roles in the sound era, later working at Monogram in westerns starring Tom Keene and Jack Randall. He continued to portray ethnic characters in films through the mid–1950s. During that time he was also featured in the Edward D. Wood Jr.-produced stage show "The Tom Keene Revue."

Probably the best of the Gilbert Roland Cisco Kid adventures was *Beauty and the Bandit* for which the star, with no screen credit, provided additional dialogue. Although it was a fast-moving production with a solid plot, its main asset was beautiful Ramsay Ames as Jeanne Du Bois, who implausibly masquerades as a young man in the feature's early sequences. The feature also had usual villain Glenn Strange as a sailor friend of the Cisco Kid, singing the sea shanty "Blow the Man Down." The plot had the Cisco Kid (Roland) meeting an old sailor friend (Strange) and learning that a wealthy Frenchman, Du Bois, has just arrived by boat and is planning to take a chest full of silver to the town of San Marino. Cisco pretends to be a police official and rides with Du Bois while Cisco's gang, led by his sidekick Baby (Frank Yaconelli), robs the stagecoach and hides the silver, replacing it with rocks. The silver was to be used to buy land obtained cheaply by land speculator Doc Walsh (William Gould) after his partner, Dr. Valegra (Martin Garralaga), had poisoned the local grain supplies. Cisco tries to spend the night in Du Bois' room, upon their arrival in San Marino; he is surprised to find out that his traveling companion is actually a beautiful woman, Jeanne Du Bois (Ramsay Ames), who is aware he stole her silver. Walsh finds out the silver is missing and Jeanne informs him it is safely hidden. Police Captain Jorge (George J. Lewis) arrests several members of his gang, but Cisco and Baby rescue them. At the gang's hideout, Jeanne professes her love for Cisco who scolds the young woman when he finds out she will sell the land she plans to purchase to high bidders in Europe. Back in town, Cisco and Jeanne see the local peons dying from eating the poisoned grain and Cisco makes Valegra give him an antidote. Regretting her involvement in the scheme, Jeanne pays Walsh for the land and then burns the deeds. Hoping to kill Cisco, Walsh confines Jeanne to one of the rooms in his hotel and throws his voice in an effort to confuse the bandit. During a shootout in the dark, however, it is Walsh who is shot by the Cisco Kid. After Cisco says goodbye to Jeanne, Jorge tries to arrest him but the Kid makes a getaway and rides off with his gang. During the scene at Cisco's camp, Ramsay Ames serenaded the bandit with the song "Vieni, Cher Cher Ton Baiser."

In *Riding the California Trail*, issued early in 1947, the Cisco Kid (Roland) rides into the town of San Lorenzo with his cohort Baby (Frank Yaconelli) and their gang and flirts with dancer Raquel (Teala Loring), whose boyfriend, Raoul (Ted Hecht), is about to wed wealthy Dolores Ramirez (Inez Cooper). Raquel tells Cisco that Raoul is only marrying Dolores for her money (she is known as "The Angel of San Lorenzo" because of her work with the poor). When Raoul finds Cisco with Dolores, he starts a fight and takes a beating; Cisco and his men soon leave town. Incognito, Cisco and Baby go to the Ramirez hacienda with the bandit claiming to be Don Luis Tomas Pasquale Alonso Salazar, the son of an old family friend. He is welcomed by Dolores' uncle Don Jose (Martin Garralaga) and finds out that the young woman plans to give her wealth to the needy. Dolores tells Cisco she will marry Raoul because it was her late father's wish but when Raoul arrives he accuses the Kid of being an imposter and they engage in a sword fight with Cisco winning. The hacienda housekeeper (Marcelle Gradville) asks Cisco to stop the marriage. Back in town, Cisco learns from Raquel that Dolores' late father's will leaves all his money to his brother Don Jose upon Dolores' marriage to Raoul. Cisco then robs Raoul of a 500,000 peso note given him by Don Jose and goes back to the Ramirez hacienda where he forces footman Pablo (Gerald Echaverria) to reveal where Don Jose keeps his papers. There Cisco finds the fake will giving him the estate when Dolores marries and he shows this to the young woman in front of her uncle. Raoul, who has been set free by Raquel, shows up and tries to shoot Cisco but is stopped by Baby. Cisco and Raoul fight with swords with Raoul being defeated as the police arrive. Dolores helps Cisco to escape and he tells her he may return. During the proceedings, Inez sang "Mi Amor Yo Volvio" and Ramsay Hill can be seen doubling for Gilbert Roland in several action sequences.

After four Cisco Kid productions, producer Scott R. Dunlap was promoted to executive assistant at Monogram and Jeffrey Bernerd took over as the series producer. This brought about several changes, including William Nigh being replaced as director by Christy Cabanne and Chris-Pin Martin returning as Cisco's sidekick in the revived role of Pancho. The sidekick character was decidedly cleaned up in comparison to Martin's previous characterization of Gordito. Also for the last two series entries, Gilbert Roland received on-screen credit for additional dialogue and the bandit's gang was eliminated.

The first Jeffrey Bernerd series production, *Robin Hood of Monterey*, came out in the fall of 1947, nine months after the previous Cisco Kid production. Here Cisco (Roland) and Pancho (Martin) save wounded Eduardo Belomonte (Travis Kent), the son of an old friend, from a trio of ambushers. Eduardo tells them he caught his stepmother, Maria Belmonte (Evelyn Brent), kissing her supposed cousin Don Ricardo Gonzales (Jack LaRue) with Maria convincing his father, Don Carlos Belmonte (Pedro de Cordoba), that he, Eduardo, had made a pass at her. A short time later, Don Carlos is murdered and Eduardo is blamed and runs away, leaving behind his fiancée Lolita (Donna [Martell] De Mario). Telling Eduardo to stay hidden, Cisco and Pancho ride to the Belmonte hacienda where Don Ricardo has taken a fancy to Lolita, who is now forced to work as a servant. Cisco recognizes Maria as a former entertainer wanted for murdering her employer and the two agree not to reveal each other's identities as Cisco steals a bullet from Maria's small pistol. In Pueblo de San Blas, Cisco gets confirmation from the local doctor (Julian Rivero) that the bullet from Maria's gun was like the one that killed her husband. On Maria's orders, Don Ricardo tells the village alcalde (Nestor Paiva) about Cisco being in town. The bandit and his pal are captured when they stop to help Lolita, who has fled the Ramirez hacienda. The next day Cisco is shot by a firing squad but, Cisco having bribed one of the jailers, blanks were used in the shooting. He breaks Pancho out of jail and learns that Eduardo has gone to the hacienda, where he is captured. After the young man's arrest, Cisco is able to show the alcalde the evidence that Eduardo is innocent because of the matching bullets from Maria's gun; the two set a trap for the widow. She later tries to bribe Cisco into silence. When he refuses, she attempts to kill him but she and Don Ricardo are arrested by the alcalde and Eduardo is set free. Although Cisco offers to give himself up for arrest, the alcalde permits him and Pancho to escape.

The final Gilbert Roland Cisco Kid feature, *King of the Bandits*, came out in November 1947. It opens with Pancho (Martin) dreaming that he and Cisco (Roland) are shot by a firing squad and upon awaking he warns his friend to stay out of Arizona. Finding out there is a $500 reward there for Cisco, the two men save saddle maker Pedro Gomez (Pat Goldin) from being lynched because he was suspected of helping the bandit. The three men then aid Alice Mason (Angela Greene) and her mother (Laura Treadwell) after their stagecoach is attacked by bandits who stole their jewels. They accompany the women to a nearby mission where Alice asks Cisco to find her brother Frank (William Bakewell), a cavalry captain. At the Ace High Saloon, the Kid finds out that Smoke Kirby (Anthony Warde) and his gang have been masquerading as Cisco and Pancho and committing a series of robberies. When Cisco learns Smoke has given Alice's locket to saloon girl Connie (Cathy Carter), he returns it to her and goes with Alice, with whom he has fallen in love, and her mother to Fort Roberts where they are to meet Frank, who has been ordered by his commander (Boyd Irwin) to arrest the bandit. Before they arrive, Smoke tries to kill Cisco in a duel but fails. When Frank and his men come on the scene, Smoke tells them that Cisco stole the jewels and he and Pancho are put behind bars. Pedro aids the two in escaping but Frank is blamed and is sentenced to a court martial. Cisco and Pancho trail Smoke to his hideout where the outlaw's men desert him. Desperate, Smoke heads back to El Rio on foot but is stalked by Pancho, who corners him in a saloon and makes him confess to the stagecoach robbery. Frank is set free as Cisco gives Pedro money to go into business and reluctantly bids farewell to Alice.

The final batch of Cisco Kid series westerns were released by United Artists between 1948 and 1950. Philip N. Krasne returned as producer and Duncan Renaldo resumed playing the starring part, also becoming associate producer. These Inter–American Productions had Cisco without a mustache for the first time on the talking screen. Cast in the role of Pancho was Leo Carrillo, who at first turned down the offer but was persuaded to accept it by Renaldo who told him that Pancho was the Sancho Panza counterpart to Cisco's Don Quixote. A native of California, Carrillo (1881–1961) was the son of a mayor of Los Angeles and spoke five languages. After college he worked as a newspaper cartoonist before going into vaudeville and the theater. He made his Broadway debut in 1915 and came to films toward the end of the silent era. He made his biggest impact in sound films, often cast as gangsters. He also played likable Spanish villains, especially in westerns. Among his many pre–Pancho features

Advertisements for *The Valiant Hombre* (Monogram, 1949).

were *Lasca of the Rio Grande* (1931), *Parachute Jumper* (1933), *Viva Villa* (1934), *Moonlight Murder* and *The Gay Desperado* (both 1936), *20 Mule Team* (1940), *Horror Island* (1941) and *Frontier Badmen* (1943). Carrillo's interpretation of Pancho, with his mangled English and malapropos such as "Let's went," made him an audience favorite, especially after the series was transferred to television in 1950.

Issued late in 1948, *The Valiant Hombre* was the first of a trio of series features directed by Wallace Fox. It introduced the rousing Cisco Kid theme song composed by Albert Glasser, which was also used in the later television series. Cisco (Renaldo) and Pancho (Carrillo) learn of the disappearance of prospector Paul Mason (John James) from Joe Haskins (Guy Beach), who is trying to feed Mason's heartbroken dog Daisy. Joe tells them that Mason struck a rich claim he planned to record but disappeared before he could make the filing. When Joe is murdered, Cisco and Pancho are blamed by the sheriff (Stanley Andrews) and put in jail. The two manage to escape and prove their innocence and the lawman then arrests the real killer (Gene Roth), who is also murdered. Cisco finds out that a stagecoach driven by his friend Whiskers (Lee "Lasses" White) is carrying Linda Mason (Barbara Billingsley), the missing man's sister. Saloon owner Lon Lansdell (John Litel) has kidnapped Mason and is holding him hostage, threatening to harm Linda if Mason won't reveal the location of his gold strike. Cisco suspects Lansdell after Mason's dog sniffs at him and he abducts Linda to protect her from the saloonkeeper. After taking her to a remote shack, they are captured by Lansdell and his gang; Cisco and Pancho are tied up as the young woman is taken to the outlaws' hideout. Cisco and Pancho overpower their guards, who they tie up loosely; when they get loose, our heroes trail them to the hideout where a shootout takes place. The gang members give up and Lansdell falls from a cliff trying to escape.

In *The Gay Amigo*, released in the spring of 1949, Cisco (Renaldo) and Pancho (Carrillo) are mistaken for outlaw gang leaders by Cavalry Captain Lewis (Kenneth MacDonald) when they are observed near a holdup. Finding a dead bandit with a decorous belt, the two ride into town where Lewis arrests them in a cantina. Released due to lack of evidence, Cisco and Pancho are trailed by Sergeant McNulty (Joe Sawyer) on Lewis' orders. When the two comrades find out that newspaper editor Stoneman (Walter Baldwin) wants them back in jail, they go back to the cantina where they see waitress Rosita (Armida) wearing the dead bandit's belt. She tells them it was a gift from Bill Brack (Fred Kohler, Jr.), who operates the local smithy. When Stoneman's friend Ed Paulsen (Sam Flint) is murdered, Cisco and Pancho are arrested for the crime but manage to escape and hold up a stagecoach. The two then force newspaper typesetter Thompson (Billy Wayne) to set up a story about the holdup. Stoneman, who is the real robber, arrives and Cisco takes his loot and locks him and Thompson in a closet. The newspaper editor gets free. Brack, who is his partner, wants his share of the stolen loot but Thompson tells him he was robbed by Cisco and Pancho. When the two men try to skip town with gold they had previously stolen, they are apprehended by Cisco and Pancho, who hold them for Lewis. *Variety* noted, "Pic has some neat turns, providing surprises and laughs."

Issued in the early summer of 1949, *The Daring Caballero* found the Cisco Kid (Renaldo) and Pancho (Carrillo) coming across a young runaway, Bobby Del Rio (Mickey Little), who had been living at the local mission after his father, banker Patrick Del Rio (David Leonard), was arrested for murder. Returning the boy to the padre (Pedro de Cordoba) at the mission and promising Bobby to help his father, Cisco masquerades as a waiter at the Grubstake Café, takes food to the jail and sets Patrick free. Hiding him in the mission's cellar, Cisco and Pancho learn from Del Rio that he found that money was missing from his bank and was accused of killing his clerk. At the trial, another bank worker, Hodges (Charles Halton), testified against Del Rio and he was sentenced to be hung. In town, Cisco meets the prosecuting attorney-mayor, Brady (Stephen Chase), who he once knew in Sonora under the name Barton. Becoming leery of Hodges, Cisco has the banker give him two $500 bills in exchange for gold coins of the same value. When the town marshal (Edmund Cobb) arrests Pancho, Cisco forces Brady to telephone the lawman and have his pal set free. Showing Del Rio the two bills he got from Hodges, the banker tells Cisco that the serial numbers for the missing money are on a list given to Kippee Valez (Kippee Valez), the daughter of an old friend and also a clerk in the bank. When Hodges tells Brady that Bobby is living at the mission, they go there and try to find out if the boy knows the whereabouts of his father. As the two men look around the mission, Cisco and Pancho successfully hide Del Rio. Pancho then goes to Kippee to get the serial number list and she tells him it is at the bank. When Cisco goes to the bank and finds the key to the safe deposit box containing the list, he is attacked by Brady, who is knocked out by Cisco. Accompanied by Cisco and Pancho, Kippee goes to the bank and shows them the list but it does not match the bills provided by Hodges. Cisco finds the stolen money in another safety deposit box as they hear Brady and Hodges approaching. The two crooks go into the vault and Cisco locks them in and orders Pancho to find Judge Perkins (Frank Jaquet), who presided over Del Rio's trial. When Hodges goes to sleep, Brady switches the stolen money to his own safety deposit box. The next day, Cisco and Pancho has the jury from the trial meet in the bank with the judge and he has Kippee open the vault, freeing Hodges and Brady. When Cisco opens Brady's safety deposit box containing the stolen money, Hodges kills the mayor and is later sentenced to hang. Patrick is set free and is reunited with his son.

The penultimate United Artists Cisco Kid feature, *Satan's Cradle*, released in October, 1949, was directed by genre veteran Ford Beebe. Here the Cisco Kid (Renaldo) and Pancho (Carrillo) come across a sky pilot, Henry Lane (Byron Foulger), who has been run out of the New Mexico town of Silver City by lawyer Steve Gentry (Douglas Fowley) and his men. Since Cisco and Pancho were on the way to town to meet saloon owner Lil Mason (Ann Savage), because of her reputed beauty, they take Henry with them. At Lil's Silver Lode Saloon, Cisco announces that Henry will hold Sunday services and the trio then go to work turning a vacant building into a church. Gentry orders his henchman Idaho (George DeNormand) to murder Cisco but Pancho saves him by falling from the church roof, enabling Cisco to shoot the man in self-defense. Cisco, Pancho and Henry leave town and the preacher is hidden at a mountain hideaway called Satan's Cradle. Henry informs Cisco and Pancho that Lil claims to be the widow of the town's murdered founder but that a courthouse fire in Oklahoma destroyed the marriage certificate. Returning to town, Cisco uses a ruse to make Lil misstate her supposed marriage date as Gentry tries to get the drop on the Kid but he and Pancho manage to escape and Gentry draws up a quick claim deed giving him all Lil's property. Gentry and his men then trail Cisco and Pancho to Satan's Cradle but the two get away after shooting four gang members. At the mine where the town's founder was killed, Cisco and Pancho look for clues as Gentry and his henchman Rocky (Buck Bailey) dynamite the place; the comrades manage to survive. Lil and her friend, dance hall girl Belle (Claire Carleton), plan to leave town after Gentry tells them he killed Cisco and Pancho. Cisco goes to Lil's room and asks her to tell the sheriff what she knows about Gentry. The lawyer overhears the conversation and fires at Lil as Pancho ropes and ties up Rocky. Gentry tries to escape but he is tracked down and shot in self-defense by Cisco. When Lil agrees to turn state's evidence, Cisco and Pancho leave town in search of another beautiful woman in San Lorenzo, California.

Derwin Abrahams, who directed several "Hopalong Cassidy" and "Durango Kid" (q.v.) features, helmed the final United Artists Cisco Kid adventure, *The Girl from San Lorenzo*, issued in February 1950. It was scripted by Ford Beebe, who directed *Satan's Cradle*. When the Cisco Kid (Renaldo) and Pancho (Carrillo) are falsely accused of holding up stagecoaches, they elude a sheriff and his posse and go to San Lorenzo where Pancho gets a letter from his grandmother asking him to go to Cactus Wells. Since his grandmother has been deceased for several years, the two decide to investigate. Rancher McCarger (Leonard Penn) tries to shoot Cisco but Nora Malloy (Jane Adams) grabs his arm, with Cisco wounding the rancher. When Cisco and Pancho visit McCarger, he shows them a letter from Sheriff Ed Marlowe (Lee Phelps) claiming that Cisco murdered McCarger's brother in Cactus Wells. Cisco denies the charge and promises to investigate. He and Pancho head to the town, also Nora's destination, where she is to marry Jerry Todd (Bill Lester). When Cisco and Pancho witness Kansas (Don C. Harvey) and Rusty (Wes Hudman) pretending to be them and holding up a stagecoach, they prevent the robbery and aid the wounded driver, Jerry Todd. They take him to Cactus Wells and then go to Nora's house where they hide when the sheriff and his men arrive. When the wounded Jerry is brought to the house, he is questioned by Cisco and Pancho but the sheriff and his men return and they are arrested. Kansas and Rusty break them out of jail and take them to the gang's cave hideout. Cisco and Pancho overpower Kansas and escape with Cisco holding up a stagecoach and taking its express box. When Kansas and Rusty rob the same conveyance, they find out they have been beaten to the bullion shipment by Cisco and Pancho. The two comrades then go back to town and inform the sheriff of Kansas and Rocky's impersonation. The two outlaws work for station agent Ross (Byron Foulger) who gives himself away by checking on stolen money in his safe as Cisco and the sheriff observe him. When the rest of the gang arrives at the station, they are arrested and the sheriff sends McCrager a letter telling him Ross, not Cisco, murdered his brother.

Although the Cisco Kid series came to an end with *The Girl from San Lorenzo*, the character had its greatest wave of popularity when the *Cisco Kid* television series began broadcasting in 1950 (156 episodes, running through 1955 and syndicated by Ziv). *The Cisco Kid* was the first western TV series filmed in color and as a result it remains a popular program to this day. Renaldo and Carrillo continued their roles as Cisco and Pancho and in the series they rode horses named Diablo and Loco, respectively. In addition to the series, the two stars had lucrative careers making personal appearances, in tandem and separately.

Carrillo's final film was the title role in the Mexican made *Pancho Villa Returns* in 1950; fol-

Duncan Renaldo and Diablo make a personal appearance, circa 1970.

lowing the *Cisco Kid* television series he retired to his Southern California ranch. Although he was nearly 75 when the TV series ended, he did his own riding and many of the stunts while portraying Pancho. He died in 1961, the same year his best-selling book, *The California I Love*, was published. Renaldo appeared in two 1951 features, *The Capture* and *The Lady and the Bandit*, before giving his full attention to the *Cisco Kid* TV programs. Following the end of the series, he continued to make personal appearances until 1970 and then retired. He and Carrillo did very little with merchandising for the series since neither wanted to exploit their characters in that fashion. Their images, however, were used to advertise several breads such as Tip-Top and Butternut, the latter sponsoring the TV show in Chicago for thirteen years. In the mid–1970s, Renaldo began appearing at film conventions and festivals and in 1980 he did the illustrations for the poetry book *Drifter's Dream*; his planned autobiography was never published. Renaldo died in 1980. The last time he and Leo Carrillo appeared together was in 1959 in a tribute to Carrillo on NBC-TV's *This is Your Life*.

O. Henry's famous Robin Hood of the Old West came to radio in 1942 via the *Cisco Kid* series on the Mutual network. Jackson Beck played Cisco and Louis Sorin was Pancho on the series that ran until the end of 1945. Two years later the series was revived over the Don Lee Pacific Coast Network and syndicated nationwide by Ziv for 630 broadcasts through 1956. Jack Mather, who sounded a lot like Duncan Renaldo, starred as Cisco, and Harry Lang was Pancho, a role also played for a short time by Mel Blanc.

The Cisco Kid's comic book career began in 1944 with a one-shot outing called "Cisco Kid Comics," published by Bernard Bailey. In 1950 Dell Comics began their "Cisco Kid" series, running for 41 issues through 1958. These comics showed Cisco and Pancho in the likeness of Duncan Renaldo and Leo Carrillo. There was also a syndicated newspaper Cisco Kid comic strip that ran at the same time as the Dell Comics.

Continuing its policy of never leaving well enough alone, Hollywood brought the O. Henry character back to the screen in 1994 with the telefeature *The Cisco Kid*, starring Jimmy Smits in the title role and Cheech Marin as Pancho. The production was directed by Luis Valdez, who had previously helmed the box office success, *La Bamba* (1987), a biopic of singer Ritchie Valens. This new version had Cisco becoming a revolutionary aiding the Juarista cause in Mexico in the post–Civil War period. As to be expected of left-wing Hollywood, the feature portrayed Gringos in a decidedly unfavorable manner.

The Cisco Kid takes place in Mexico in 1867 during the war between the occupying forces of Austrian Emperor Maximilian, whom French King Napoleon II had placed in Mexico during the American Civil War, and Benito Juarez and his followers. The Cisco Kid (Smits) and Pancho (Marin) meet in jail where they are about to be executed, Cisco for trying to help a prostitute, Libertad (Lorena Victoria) escape from a government brothel, and Pancho for revolutionary activities. When gunmen stop the executions, Cisco and Pancho escape and ride to a small village where they take money collected by the French from poor peons and meet Dominique (Sadie Frost), the niece of French army commander Dupre (Bruce Payne) and fiancée of his right hand man, Lieutenant Colonel Delacroix (Ron Perlman). Although Cisco wants to keep the money, Pancho convinces him to return it to the people. While Cisco makes a deal with the revolutionaries to sell them weapons obtained from two ex–Confederates, Washam (Tony Amendola) and Lundquist (Tim Thomerson), the two Americans join forces with Dupre to liberate the town of San Miguel, which is on the way to the Gulf of Mexico, from the Juaristas. On Christmas Day, Washam, Lundquist and their men steal a statue of the child Jesus from the church, killing many people. Cisco and Pancho are in attendance during the attack and vow to recover the statue. Going to the pueblo of Cueros, the two learn of a caballero competition, with Cisco winning and getting an invitation to the governor's palace, where he will get a prize. Since both Cisco and Pancho think the statue is hidden in the palace, they attend the ball, where Pancho finds the statue and Cisco romances Dominique. The two are recognized, however, and are arrested and held prisoner in a brothel where Libertad helps them to escape. While Dominique is abducted by the rebels, who make it look like the crime was committed by Cisco, the Kid and Pancho return to the Juristas with the statue and guns. Cisco, however, offends one of the leaders, Dona Josefa (Teresa Lagunes), and Pancho when he asks for a receipt for the guns so he can prove he had not been running guns in Texas. Just as Cisco and Pancho have a falling out over his request, news comes that the French army is on its way and the Juristas prepare for battle as Cisco sets out to rescue Dominique, with whom he has fallen in love. Pancho carries the statue across the countryside, enticing the peasants to join the fight as Cisco locates Dominiaue in Cueros and brings her back to the Jurista camp. The decisive battle takes place the next day with Cisco killing Commander Dupre and disarming Delacroix. With the battle won, Benito Juarez (Luis Valdez) arrives on the scene and thanks Cisco for his aid in defeating the French. After Dona Josefa gives Cisco the money for the guns and the letter he requested he bids farewell to Dominique, who is going back to France, and Pancho, who has promised his wife (Yareli Arizmendi) he will give up revolutionary life. Riding away, Cisco is rejoined by Pancho and they head out for new adventures.

Telecast on U.S. TV early in 1994 by the Turner Broadcasting System, *The Cisco Kid* was filmed on location in Mexico and a highlight was its use of authentic locations depicting the rural Mexico of 1867. For the climactic battle scenes, over 400 period uniforms were rented for realistic detail. Regarding the relationship between Cisco and Pancho, the *New York Daily News* mistakenly mentioned previous "casting of non–Latinos in these roles" which probably accounts for the additional opinion, "Both roles have been reworked so that Cisco — *a la* Batman — is a gentleman of means, crusading for justice, riding the western plains in search of selfhood and the meaning of life. Whereas, Pancho is no longer the drunken idiot, but is instead a brave individual — cheerful and intelligent." More on the mark was Jeff Jarvis, who wrote in *TV Guide*, "The stars bring charm to their dusty fight, dance, and rodeo scenes, but the movie tells its story flatly, without surprise or excitement."

Filmography

The Caballero's Way (American Éclair–Universal, 1914, 2 reels) Director: Webster Cullison. Story: O. Henry.

Cast: William R. Dunn (The Cisco Kid), Edna Payne (Tonia), Jack W. Johnston (Lieutenant Sandridge), Hal Wilson (Tonia's Father).

The Border Terror (Universal, 1919, 2 reels) Director: Harry Harvey. Screenplay: H. Tipton Steck, from the story "The Caballero's Way" by O. Henry.

Cast: Vester Pegg (The Cisco Kid), Yvette Mitchell (Tonia).

In Old Arizona (Fox, 1929, 95 minutes) Directors: Raoul Walsh & Irving Cummings. Screenplay: Tom Barry, from the story "The Caballero's Way" by O. Henry. Photography: Arthur Edeson. Editor: Louis R. Loeffler. Song: Lew Brown, Buddy G. DeSylva & Ray Henderson. Sound: Edmund Hansen. Assistant Directors: Archibald Buchanan, Frank Powolny & Charles Woolstenhulme.

Cast: Warner Baxter (The Cisco Kid), Edmund Lowe (Sergeant Mickey Dunn), Dorothy Burgess (Tonia Maria), J. Farrell MacDonald (Tad), Soledad Jiminez (Bonita), Fred Warren (Pianist-Singer), Henry Armetta (Giuseppe), Tom Santschi, Frank Campeau, Pat Hartigan (Rustlers), Roy Stewart (Colonel), James Bradbury, Jr. (Joe), John Webb Dillon (Joe's Friend), Frank Nelson, Duke Martin (Cowboys), James Marcus (Blacksmith), Joe Brown (Bartender), Alphonse Ethier (Sheriff), Helen Lynch (Saloon Girl), Ed Peil, Sr., Jim Farley (Citizens), Ivan Linow (Russian), Lola Salvi (Italian Girl), Chris-Pin Martin (Caballero).

The Cisco Kid (Fox, 1931, 61 minutes) Producer: William Goetz. Director: Irving Cummings. Screenplay: Alfred A. Cohn. Photography: Barney McGill. Editor: Alex Troffey. Music: George Lipschultz. Songs: Warner Baxter, Lew Brown, Buddy G. DeSylva & Ray Henderson. Art Director: Joseph Wright. Sound: George B. Costello. Assistant Directors: Earl Rettig & Charles Woolstenhulme.

Cast: Warner Baxter (The Cisco Kid), Edmund Lowe (Sergeant Mickey Dunn), Conchita Montenegro (Carmencita), Nora Lane (Sally Benton), Frederick Burt (Sheriff Tex Ransom), Willard Robertson (Enos Hankins), James Bradbury, Jr. (Dixon), Jack [John Webb] Dillon (Bouse), Charles Stevens (Lopez), Chris-Pin Martin (Gordito), Rita Flynn (Dance Hall Girl), Douglas Haig (Billy Benton), Marilyn Knowlden (Annie Benton), Consuelo Castillo de Bonzo (Maria).

Return of the Cisco Kid (20th Century–Fox, 1939, 70 minutes) Producer: Kenneth Macgowan. Director: Herbert I. Leeds. Screenplay: Milton Sperling. Photography: Charles G. Clarke. Editor: James B. Clark. Music Director: Cyril J. Mockridge. Art Directors: Richard Day & Wiard B. Ihnen. Sound: Roger Heman & Arthur von Kirbach. Costumes: Gwen Wakeling. Sets: Thomas Little. Technical Advisor: Ernesto A. Romero. Assistant Director: Sidney Bowen.

Cast: Warner Baxter (The Cisco Kid), Lynn Bari (Ann Carver), Cesar Romero (Lopez), Henry Hull

(Colonel Jonathan Bixby), Kane Richmond (Alan Davis), C. Henry Gordon (Mexican Captain), Robert Barrat (Sheriff McNally), Chris-Pin Martin (Gordito), Adrian Morris (Deputy Sheriff Johnson), Soledad Jiminez (Mama Soledad), Harry Strang (Deputy Sheriff), Arthur Aylesworth (Stagecoach Driver), Paul E. Burns (Hotel Clerk), Victor Kilian (Bartender), Eddy Waller (Stagecoach Guard), Ruth Gillette (Flora), Ward Bond (Tough Guy), Gino Corrado (Waiter), Ralph Dunn (Guard), Herbert Heywood (Proprietor), Ethan Laidlaw (Luke), Charles Tannen (Bank Teller), Lee Shumway (Gang Member).

The Cisco Kid and the Lady (20th Century–Fox, 1939, 74 minutes) Executive Producer: Sol M. Wurtzel. Associate Producer: John Stone. Director: Herbert I. Leeds. Screenplay: Frances Hyland. Story: Stanley Rauh. Photography: Barney McGill. Editor: Nick De Maggio. Music Director: Samuel Kaylin. Art Directors: Richard Day & Chester Gore. Sound: George Leverett & William H. Anderson. Sets: Thomas Little. Costumes: Herschel. Assistant Director: Jasper Blystone.

Cast: Cesar Romero (The Cisco Kid), Marjorie Weaver (Julie Lawson), Chris-Pin Martin (Gordito), George Montgomery (Tommy Bates), Robert Barrat (Jim Harbison), Virginia Field (Billie Graham), Harry Green (Teasdale), Gloria Ann White (Junior), John Beach (Stevens), Ward Bond (Walton), J. Anthony Hughes (Drake), James Burke (Pop Saunders), Harry Hayden (Sheriff), James Flavin (Sergeant O'Riley), Ruth Warren (Effie Saunders), Eddy Waller (Stagecoach Driver), Adrian Morris (Drunk), Ivan Miller (Post Commander), Virginia Brissac (Seamstress), Eddie Dunn (Jailer), Arthur Rankin, Harry Strang, Lester Dorr (Telegraph Operators), Paul Sutton (Saloon Customer), Paul E. Burns (Jake).

Viva Cisco Kid (20th Century–Fox, 1940, 70 minutes) Executive Producer: Sol M. Wurtzel. Director: Norman Foster. Screenplay: Samuel G. Engel & Hal Long. Photography: Charles Clarke. Editor: Norman Colbert. Music Director: Samuel Kaylin. Art Directors: Richard Day & Chester Gore. Sound: William H. Anderson & Bernard Freericks. Sets: Thomas Little. Costumes: Herschel. Assistant Director: Sam Schneider.

Cast: Cesar Romero (The Cisco Kid), Jean Rogers (Joan Allen), Chris-Pin Martin (Gordito), Minor Watson (Jesse Allen), Stanley Fields (Boss), Nigel De Brulier (Moses), Harold Goodwin (Hank Gunther), Francis Ford (Proprietor), Charles Judels (Pancho), Harrison Greene (Frank Snodgrass Benson), LeRoy Mason (Gang Leader), Tom London (Marshal), Jim Mason (Lem), Hank Worden (Deputy Sheriff), Eddy Waller (Stagecoach Driver), Ray Teal (Gang Member), Bud Osborne (Kennedy), Paul Sutton (Joshua), Mantan Moreland (Memphis), Paul Kruger (Jack), Willie Fung (Wang), Frank Darien (Express Office Agent), Jacqueline Dalya (Helena), Margaret Martin (Helena's Mother), Inez Palange (Pancho's Fiancée).

Lucky Cisco Kid (20th Century–Fox, 1940, 67 minutes) Producer: Sol M. Wurtzel. Associate Producer: John Stone. Director: H. Bruce Humberstone. Screenplay: Robert Ellis & Helen Logan. Story: Julian Johnson. Photography: Lucien N. Andriot. Editor: Fred Allen. Music Director: Cyril J. Mockridge. Art Directors: Richard Day & Chester Gore. Sound: Bernard Freericks & William H. Anderson. Sets: Thomas Little. Costumes: Helen A. Myron. Assistant Director: Aaron Rosenberg.

Cast: Cesar Romero (The Cisco Kid), Mary Beth Hughes (Lola), Dana Andrews (Sergeant Dunn), Evelyn Venable (Emily Lawrence), Chris-Pin Martin (Gordito), Willard Robertson (Judge McQuade), Joe Sawyer (Bill Stevens), Johnny Sheffield (Tommy Lawrence), William Royle (Sheriff), Francis Ford (Court Clerk), Otto Hoffman (Ed Stoke), Dick Rich (Stagecoach Driver Tex), Bob Hoffman, Boyd "Red" Morgan (Soldiers), Harry Strang (Corporal), Gloria Roy (Dance Hall Girl), Lillian Yarbo (Queenie), Adrian Morris, Jimmie Dundee, William Pagan (Stagecoach Passengers), Lew Kelly (Stagecoach Dispatcher), Milton Kibbee (Wells Fargo Agent), Sarah Edwards (Spinster), Frank Lackteen (Murdered Gang Member), James Flavin, Thornton Edwards (Ranch Foremen), Henry Roquemore (Diamond), Syd Saylor (Hotel Clerk), Blackie Whiteford (Spike), Ethan Laidlaw, Frank Ellis (Gang Members), Spencer Charters (Hotel Guest).

The Gay Caballero (20th Century–Fox, 1940, 58 minutes) Producers: Walter Morosco & Ralph Dietrich. Director: Otto Brower. Screenplay: John Larkin. Story: Walter Bullock & Alfred Duffy. Photography: Edward Cronjager. Editor: Harry Reynolds. Music Director: Emil Newman. Art Directors: Richard Day & Chester Gore. Sound: Arthur von Kirbach & Harry M. Leonard. Sets: Thomas Little. Costumes: Herschel. Assistant Director: William Eckhardt.

Cast: Cesar Romero (The Cisco Kid), Sheila Ryan (Susan Wetherby), Robert Sterling (Billy Brewster), Chris-Pin Martin (Gordito), Janet Beecher (Kate Brewster), Edmund MacDonald (Joe Turner), Jacqueline Dalya (Carmelita), C. Montague Shaw (George Wetherby), Hooper Atchley (Sheriff McBride), George Magrill, LeRoy Mason (Deputy Sheriffs), Jim Pierce, Ethan Laidlaw, John Byron (Gang Members), Tom London (Rancher), Dave Morris (Stagecoach Passenger), Jack Stoney (Stagecoach Guard), Lee Shumway (Stagecoach Driver), Frank Lackteen (Peon).

Romance of the Rio Grande (20th Century–Fox, 1940, 72 minutes) Executive Producer: Sol M. Wurtzel. Director: Herbert I. Leeds. Screenplay: Harold Buchman & Samuel G. Engel, from the novel *Conquistador* by Katherine Fullerton Gerould. Photography: Charles Clarke. Editor: Fred Allen. Music Director: Emil Newman. Songs: Abel Baer & I. Wolfe Gilbert. Art Directors: Richard Day & Chester Gore. Production Manager: William Koenig. Sound: George Leverett & Harry M. Leonard. Sets: Thomas Little. Costumes: Herschel. Assistant Director: Charles Hall.

Cast: Cesar Romero (The Cisco Kid/Don Carlos Hernandez), Patricia Morison (Rosita), Lynne Roberts (Maria), Ricardo Cortez (Ricardo de Vega), Chris-Pin Martin (Gordito), Aldrich Bowker (Padre Martinez), Joseph MacDonald (Carlos), Pedro de Cordoba (Don Fernando de Vega), Inez Palange (Mama Lopez), Raphael [Ray] Bennett (Carver), Trevor Bardette (Manuel), Tom London (Marshal), Eva Puig (Marta), Francis Ford (Stagecoach Driver).

Ride on Vaquero (20th Century–Fox, 1941, 64 minutes) Executive Producer: Sol M. Wurtzel. Director: Herbert I. Leeds. Screenplay: Samuel G. Engel. Photography: Lucien Andriot. Editor: Louis Loeffler. Music Director: Emil Newman. Art Directors: Richard Day & Chester Gore. Sound: Harry M. Leonard & George Leverett. Sets: Thomas Little. Costumes: Herschel. Dance Supervisor: Eduardo Cansino.

Cast: Cesar Romero (The Cisco Kid), Mary Beth Hughes (Sally Slocum), Lynne Roberts (Marguerita Martinez), Chris-Pin Martin (Gordito), Robert Lowery (Carlos Martinez), Ben Carter (Watchman Buffinch), William Demarest (Bartender Barney), Robert Shaw (Cavalry Officer), Edwin Maxwell (Dan Clark), Paul Sutton (Sleepy), Don Costello (Redge), Arthur Hohl (Sheriff Johnny Burns), Irving Bacon (Jailer), Dick Rich (Curly), Paul Harvey (Colonel Warren), Joan Woodbury (Dolores), Hector V. Sarno (Miguel), Frank Orth (Auctioneer Murphy), Paco Moreno (Gypsy), Joe Whitehead (Joe), Paul Kruger (Hank), Alec Craig (Walter Limey), Victor Potel (Ole), Max Wagner (Partner), Edgar Edwards (Sergeant), James Flavin (Officer), Eva Puig (Maria), Philip Van Zandt (Blacksmith).

The Cisco Kid Returns (Monogram, 1945, 64 minutes) Producer: Philip N. Krasne. Associate Producer: Dick L'Estrange. Director: John P. McCarthy. Screenplay: Betty Burbridge. Photography: Harry Neumann. Editor: Marty Cohen [Martin G. Cohn]. Music: Albert Glasser. Music Director: David Chudnow. Sound: Glen Glenn. Sets: Ted Driscoll. Assistant Director: Eddie Davis.

Cast: Duncan Renaldo (The Cisco Kid), Martin Garralaga (Pancho), Roger Pryor (John Harris), Cecilia Callejo (Rosita Gonzales), Fritz Leiber (Padre), Jan Wiley (Jeanette), Sharon Smith (Nancy Page), Vicky Lane (Julia/Elizabeth Page), Anthony Warde (Paul Conway), Bud Osborne (Sheriff), Eva Puig (Senora Tia), Cy Kendall (Jennings), Emmett Lynn (Sheriff), Bob Duncan, Elmer Napier (Deputy Sheriffs), Carl Mathews (Deputy Sheriff Bill), Jerry Shields (Pedro), Walter Clinton (Stephen Page), Neyle Morrow (Attendant).

TV title: *The Daring Adventurer*.

In Old New Mexico (Monogram, 1945, 62 minutes) Producer: Philip N. Krasne. Associate Producer: Dick L'Estrange. Director: Phil Rosen. Screenplay: Betty Burbridge. Photography: Arthur Martinelli. Editor: Martin Cohn [Martin G. Cohn]. Music: David Chudnow. Song: Hershey Martin & Mayris Chaney. Sound: Glen Glenn. Sets: Ted Driscoll. Assistant Director: Seymour Roth.

Cast: Duncan Renaldo (The Cisco Kid), Martin Garralaga (Pancho), Gwen Kenyon (Ellen Roth), Pedro de Cordoba (Father Angelo), Norman Willis (Will Hastings), [Lee] "Lasses" White (Sheriff Clem Petty), Frank Jaquet (Stagecoach Passenger), Aurora Roche (Dolores), Edward Earle (Printer), Donna Dax (Belle), John [Laurenz] Lawrence (Al), Richard Gordon (Tom "Doc" Wills), James [Jim] Farley (Telegrapher Hank), Carr-Bert Dancers (Entertainers), Ken Terrell (Deputy Sheriff Cliff), Harry Depp (Printer), Bud Osborne (Stagecoach Driver), The Jesters (Musicians).

Also called *The Cisco Kid in Old New Mexico*; working title: *The Case of the Missing Medico*.

South of the Rio Grande (Monogram, 1945, 62 minutes) Producer: Philip N. Krasne. Director: Lambert Hillyer. Screenplay: Victor Hammond & Ralph Bettinson. Story: Johnston McCulley. Photography: William Sickner. Editor: William Austin. Music Director: Edward J. Kay. Song: J. Castelleone & Louis Herscher. Art Director: Dave Milton. Sound: Glen Glenn. Sets: Vin Taylor. Assistant Director: Eddie Stein.

Cast: Duncan Renaldo (The Cisco Kid), Martin Garralaga (Pancho), Armida (Pepita), The Guadalajara Trio (Musicians), George J. Lewis (Miguel Sanchez), Lillian Molieri (Dolores Gonzales), Francis McDonald (Torres), Charles Stevens (Sebastian), Pedro Regas (Luis), Soledad Jiminez (Mama Maria), Tito Renaldo (Manuel Gonzalez), Joe Dominguez (Gang Member).

Also called *The Cisco Kid in South of the Rio Grande*; working title: *Song of the Border*.

The Gay Cavalier (Monogram, 1946, 65 minutes) Producer: Scott R. Dunlap. Director: William Nigh. Screenplay: Charles Belden. Photography: Harry Neumann. Editor: Fred Maguire. Songs: Ramsay Ames, Eddie Cherkose & Charles Rosoff. Art Director: Ernest R. [E.R.] Hickson. Sound: Frank McWhorter. Production Manager: Charles J. Bigelow. Costumes: Harry Bourne. Special Effects: Larry Glickman & Mario Costegnaro. Assistant Director: Edward [Eddie] Davis.

Cast: Gilbert Roland (The Cisco Kid), Martin Garralaga (Don Felipe Geralda), Nacho Galindo (Baby), Ramsay Ames (Pepita Geralda), Helen Gerald (Angela Geralda), Tristram Coffin (Lawton), Drew Allen [Gil Frye] (Juan), Iris Flores (Lonely Senora), John Merton (Lewis), Frank LaRue (Graham), Joseph Burlando (Padre), Pierre Andre, Iris Bocignon (Dancers), Terry Frost, Pierce Lyden, Artie Ortego, Dusty Rhodes, Delmar Costello, Ralph Johns, Alex Montoya, Jack La Tour, Gabriel Peralta, Bob Butt, Mike J. Rodriguez (Gang Members), Clem Fuller (Buggy Driver), Lynton Brent (Coach Guard), Elvira Aldana (Humming Girl), George J. Lewis, Wally West, Dorothy Michaels, Don Driggers (Wedding Guests), Ernie Adams, Jack Cheatham, Larry Steers (Creditors), Raphael [Ray]

Bennett (Miguel), Dee Cooper, Eddie Majors (Bandits), Ted Mapes (Coach Driver).

South of Monterey (Monogram, 1946, 63 minutes) Producer: Scott R. Dunlap. Director: William Nigh. Screenplay: Charles Belden. Photography: Harry Neumann. Editor: Fred Maguire. Music Director: Edward J. Kay. Songs: Eddie Cherkose, Gladys Flores, Edward J. Kay & Charles Rosoff. Art Director: Ernest [E.R.] Hickson. Sound: Frank McWhorter. Sets: Vin Taylor. Costumes: Harry Bourne. Production Manager: Charles J. Bigelow. Assistant Director: Eddie Davis.

Cast: Gilbert Roland (The Cisco Kid), Martin Garralaga (Commandante Auturo Morales), Frank Yaconelli (Baby), Marjorie Riordan (Maria Morales), Iris Flores (Carmelita), George J. Lewis (Carlos Mandreno), Harry Woods (Bennett), Terry Frost (Morgan), Rosa Turich (Lola), Wheaton Chambers (Padre), Nick Thompson (Jailer Pedro), Felipe Turich (Old Man), Drew Allen [Gil Frye] (Man at Bar), Joe Dominguez (Messenger), Lane Bradford, Wally West, Blackie Whiteford (Outlaws), Ray Jones, Roy Bucko (Posse Members), George DeNormand (Stagecoach Driver).

Beauty and the Bandit (Monogram, 1946, 69 minutes) Producer: Philip N. Krasne. Director: William Nigh. Screenplay: Charles Belden. Photography: Harry Neumann. Editor: Fred Maguire. Music Director: Edward J. Kay. Songs: Eddie Cherkose, Gordon Clark & Charles Rosoff. Art Director: Ernest [E.R.] Hickson. Sound: Franklin Hansen. Sets: Vin Taylor. Costumes: Harry Bourne. Production Manager: Charles J. Bigelow. Makeup: Harry Ross. Assistant Director: Eddie Davis.

Cast: Gilbert Roland (The Cisco Kid), Martin Garralaga (Dr. Juan Federico Valegra), Frank Yaconelli (Baby), Ramsay Ames (Jeanne Du Bois), Vida Aldana (Lolita), George J. Lewis (Captain Jorge), William Gould (Doc Wells), Dimas Sotello (Farmer), Felipe Turich (Poisoned Farmer), Antonio Damas (Luis), Glenn Strange (Bill), Joe Dominguez (Peon), Artie Ortego, Alex Montoya, Robert O'Byrne (Gang Members).

Working title: *Cisco and the Angel.*

Riding the California Trail (Monogram, 1947, 59 minutes) Producer: Scott R. Dunlap. Director: William Nigh. Screenplay: Clarence Upson Young. Photography: Harry Neumann. Editor: Fred Maguire. Song: Edward J. Kay & Gladys Flores. Sound: Tom Lambert & John Kean. Production Manager: Charles J. Bigelow. Sets: Vin Taylor. Makeup: Harry Ross. Costumes: Harry Bourne. Assistant Director: Eddie Davis.

Cast: Gilbert Roland (The Cisco Kid), Martin Garralaga (Don Jose Ramirez), Frank Yaconelli (Baby), Teala Loring (Raquel), Inez Cooper (Dolores Ramirez), Ted Hecht (Raoul), Marcelle Grandville (Rosita), Gerald Echaverria (Pablo), Julia Kent (Flower Seller), Eve Whitney (Maria), Frank Marlo (Captain), Rosa Turich (Cook), Alex Montoya (Lieutenant), Tony Roux (Manager).

Robin Hood of Monterey (Monogram, 1947, 57 minutes) Producer: Jeffrey Bernerd. Director: Christy Cabanne. Screenplay: Bennett Cohen. Additional Dialogue: Gilbert Roland. Photography: William Sickner. Editor: Roy Livingston. Music: Edward J. Kay. Art Director: Ernest [E.R.] Hickson. Production Supervisor: Glenn Cook. Sound: Earl Sitar & John Kean. Sets: Vin Taylor. Makeup: Harry Ross. Assistant Director: Eddie Davis.

Cast: Gilbert Roland (The Cisco Kid), Chris-Pin Martin (Pancho), Evelyn Brent (Maria Belmonte/Maria Sanchez), Jack La Rue (Don Ricardo Gonzales), Pedro de Cordoba (Don Carlos Belmonte), Donna [Martell] De Mario (Lolita), Travis Kent (Eduardo Belmonte), Thornton Edwards (El Capitan), Nestor Paiva (Alcalde), Ernie Adams (Pablo), Julian Rivero (Dr. Martinez), Felipe Turich (Guard), Alex Montoya (Juan), Fred Cordova (Manuel), George Navarro (Gambler).

King of the Bandits (Monogram, 1947, 64 minutes) Producer: Jeffrey Bernerd. Director-Story: Christy Cabanne. Screenplay: Bennet Cohen. Additional Dialogue: Gilbert Roland. Photography: William Sickner. Editor: Roy Livingston. Music Director: Edward J. Kay. Art Director: Ernest [E.R.] Hickson. Sound: Tom Lambert & Dean Spencer. Production Supervisor: Glenn Cook. Sets: Vin Taylor. Makeup: Harry Ross. Assistant Director: Eddie Davis.

Cast: Gilbert Roland (The Cisco Kid), Angela Greene (Alice Mason), Chris-Pin Martin (Pancho), Anthony Warde (Smoke Kirby), Laura Treadwell (Mrs. Mason), William Bakewell (Captain Frank Mason), Rory Mallinson (Burl), Pat Goldin (Pedro Gomez), Cathy Carter (Connie), Boyd Irwin (Colonel Wayne), Antonio Filauri (Padre), Jasper Palmer (U.S. Marshal), Bill Cabanne (Orderly), Frank Marlo (Polo), Guy Teague (Jack), James Harrison (Leader), George Douglas (Guard), Douglas Aylesworth (Trooper), Gene Roth (Marshal), Jack O'Shea (Bartender), Bill Neff (Captain).

The Valiant Hombre (United Artists, 1948, 61 minutes) Producer: Philip N. Krasne. Associate Producer: Duncan Renaldo. Director: Wallace Fox. Screenplay: Adele Buffington. Photography: Ernest Miller. Editor: Martin G. Cohn. Music: Albert Glasser. Sound: Ferrol Redd. Production Manager: Dick L'Estrange. Unit Manager: Ben Chapman. Sets: Tom Thompson. Makeup: Ted Larsen. Costumes: Bert Offord. Property Master: Charles Henley. Assistant Director: Buddy Messinger.

Cast: Duncan Renaldo (The Cisco Kid), Leo Carrillo (Pancho), John Litel (Lon Lansdell), Barbara Billingsley (Linda Mason), John James (Paul Mason), Stanley Andrews (Sheriff Dodge), Lee "Lasses" White (Whiskers), Guy Beach (Old Joe Haskins), Gene Roth (Bartender Pete), Ralph Peters (Deputy Sheriff Clay), Terry Frost (Brett), Frank Ellis (Dudley), George DeNormand (Lefty), Herman Hack (Hank), Ed Peil, Sr. (Hotel Clerk Miller), Hank Bell (Sheriff), Bert Dillard (Deputy Sheriff), George Morrell, Rube Dalroy (Citizens).

The Gay Amigo (United Artists, 1949, 62 minutes) Producer: Philip N. Krasne. Associate Producer: Duncan Renaldo. Director: Wallace Fox. Screenplay: Doris Schroeder. Photography: Ernest Miller. Editor: Martin G. Cohn. Music: Albert Glasser. Art Director: Frank Dexter. Sound: Ferrol Redd. Production Manager: Dick L'Estrange. Makeup: Ted Larsen. Sets: Vin Taylor. Assistant Directors: Bud Messinger & Larry Chapman.

Cast: Duncan Renaldo (The Cisco Kid), Leo Carrillo (Pancho), Armida (Rosita), Joe Sawyer (Sergeant McNulty), Walter Baldwin (Stoneham), Fred Kohler, Jr. (Bill Brack), Kenneth MacDonald (Captain Lewis), George DeNormand (Corporal), Clayton Moore (Lieutenant), Fred Crane (Duke), Helen Servis (Old Maid), Beverly Jons (Blonde), Bud Osborne (Stagecoach Driver), Sam Flint (Ed Paulsen), Lee Tung Foo (Lee), Dick Elliott (Passenger), Al Ferguson (Customer), Billy Wayne (Thompson).

TV title: *The Daring Rogue.*

The Daring Caballero (United Artists, 1949, 60 minutes) Producer: Philip N. Krasne. Associate Producer: Duncan Renaldo. Director: Wallace Fox. Screenplay: Betty Burbridge. Story: Frances Kavanaugh. Photography: Lester White. Editor: Marty [Martin G.] Cohn. Music: Albert Glasser. Art Director: Edward Jewell. Sound: Garry Harris. Sets: Helen Hansard. Makeup: Arthur Dupuis. Costumes: Robert Richards. Production Assistant: Mel Mark. Property Master: Gene Stone. Assistant Director: Louis Germonprez.

Cast: Duncan Renaldo (The Cisco Kid), Leo Carrillo (Pancho), Kippee Valez (Kippee Valez), Charles Halton (Ed J. Hodges), Pedro de Cordoba (Father Leonardo), Stephen Chase (Mayor Brady/Barton), David Leonard (Patrick Del Rio), Edmund Cobb (Sheriff J.B. Scott), Frank Jaquet (Judge Perkins), Mickey Little (Bobby Del Rio).

TV title: *Guns of Fury.*

Satan's Cradle (United Artists, 1949, 60 minutes) Producer: Philip N. Krasne. Associate Producer: Duncan Renaldo. Director: Ford Beebe. Screenplay: Jack Benton [J. Benton Cheney]. Photography: Jack Greenhalgh. Editor: Martyn [Martin G.] Cohn. Music: Albert Glasser. Art Director: Frank Sylos. Sound: Ben Winkler. Sets: Helen Hansard. Makeup: Arthur Dupuis. Costumes: Sidney Dunham. Production Assistant: Mel Mark. Assistant Director: Louis Germonprez.

Cast: Duncan Renaldo (The Cisco Kid), Leo Carrillo (Pancho), Ann Savage (Lil Mason), Douglas Fowley (Steve Gentry), Byron Foulger (Henry Lane), Claire Carleton (Belle), Buck Bailey (Rocky), George DeNormand (Idaho), Wes Hudman (Peters).

The Girl from San Lorenzo (United Artists, 1950, 58 minutes) Producer: Philip N. Krasne. Director: Derwin Abrahams. Screenplay: Ford Beebe. Photography: Kenneth Peach. Editor: Marty [Martin G.] Cohn. Music: Albert Glasser. Art Director: Fred Preble. Sound: Hugh McDowell. Sets: Harry Reif. Makeup: Arthur Dupuis. Costumes: Robert B. Harris. Production Assistant: Mel Mark. Property Master: Eugene C. Stone. Assistant Director: Louis Germonprez.

Cast: Duncan Renaldo (The Cisco Kid), Leo Carrillo (Pancho), Jane Adams (Nora Malloy), Bill Lester (Jerry Todd), Byron Foulger (Ross), Don C. Harvey (Kansas), Lee Phelps (Sheriff Ed Marlowe), Edmund Cobb (Wooly), Leonard Penn (Tom McCarger), David Sharpe (Blackie), Wes Hudman (Rusty), Henry Wills (Stagecoach Guard).

A.k.a. *Don Amigo.*

The Cisco Kid (Turner Pictures, 1994, 91 minutes Color) Producers: Robert Katz, Gary M. Goodman & Barry Rosen. Executive Producer: Moctesuma Esparaza. Associate Producer: Ramiro Jaloma. Director: Luis Valdez. Screenplay: Luis Valdez & Michael Kane. Photography: Guillermo Navarro. Editor: Zach Staenberg. Music: Joseph Juan Gonzalez. Art Director: Theresa Wachter. Sets: Hermelindo "Melo" Hinojosa. Costume Design: Graciela Mazon. Production Design: Joe Aubel. Casting: Iris Grossman. Makeup Supervisor: Mark Sanchez. Production Supervisor: Carolyn Caldera. Set Dressers: Eduardo Serrano & Juan Carlos Serrano.

Cast: Jimmy Smits (The Cisco Kid), Cheech Marin (Pancho), Sadie Frost (Dominique), Bruce Payne (General Martin Dupre), Ron Perlman (Lieutenant Colonel Delacroix), Tony Amendola (Washam), Tim Thompson (Lundquist), Pedro Armendariz [Jr.] (General Montano), Phil Esparza (Kessler), Clayton Landey (Van Boose), Charles McCaughan (Haynie), Tony Pandolfo (Alain Vitton), Roger Cudney (Alcott), Joaquin Garrido (Lopez), Guillermo Rios (Hernandez), Miguel Sandoval (Hidalgo), Tomas Goros (Trevino), Rufino Echegoyen (Aparicio), Teresa Lagunes (Dona Josefa), Honorato Magaloni (General Gutierrez), Luis Valdez (Benito Juarez), Yareli Arizmendi (Rosa Rivera), Marisol Valdez (Linda Rivera), Julius Jansland (Antonio Rivera), Mario Ecati Zapata (Juanito Rivera), Mario Alberto (Hector Rivera), Boris Peguero (Eduardo Rivera), Maya Zapaa (Alicia Rivera), Gerardo Zepeda (Guerrero), Lorena Victoria (Libertad), Valentina Ponzanneli (Old Woman), Pedro Altamirano (Prison Guard), Gerardo Martinez (Soldier in Dungeon), Rojo Grau (Firing Squad Leader), Guido Bolanos (Guard), Roberto Olivo, Roberto Antunez (Farmers), Pablo Zuack (French Officer), Lakin Valdez (Small Boy), Mario Valdez (San Miguel Citizen), Luisa Coronel, Amelia Zapata, Alexandra Vicencio (Women), Moctesuma Esparza (Bishop), Susan Benedict, Corrina Duran, Patricia Brown, Claire Lewin, Carolyn Caldera, Herendia Silva (Spies).

Dr. Monroe

Charles Starrett made over forty westerns for Columbia Pictures from 1935 to 1941 before the studio starred him in the "Dr. Monroe" series. Based on the character created by James L. Rubel in a series of books, the films told of a medical man in the West and his attempts to champion justice. Although only a trio of features were made, they are among the best of Starrett's cowboy movies and the star considered them the apex of his long sagebrush career. The films are sometimes referred to as the "Medico" series.

Director Lambert Hillyer (1893–1969), who helmed all three, had previously directed Starrett in *The Durango Kid* (1940) and *The Pinto Kid* (1941), and he would imbue the series with the qualities that had made him a favorite of such genre stars as William S. Hart, Tom Mix and Buck Jones. A native of Indiana, Hillyer started out in the newspaper business before turning to writing, which eventually led him to Hollywood, where he began directing in 1917. Also a writer and producer, he worked for most of the major studios in the silent era, before joining Columbia in the early 1930s, where he made some of Buck Jones' finest talkies, including *One Man Law* (1931), *The Forbidden Trail* and *The Sundown Rider* (both 1932) and *The Man Trailer* (1934). At Universal he did two of that studio's successful horror thrillers, *The Invisible Ray* and *Dracula's Daughter* (both 1936) and he also worked at Republic, RKO Radio and Monogram. Beginning in 1943 he worked for the latter studio exclusively in westerns through 1949, except for a couple of Tom Neal mystery featurettes, *The Hat Box Mystery* and *The Case of the Baby Sitter*, both 1947 Screen Guild releases. Before retiring in the early 1950s, Hillyer also worked in television, including the *Cisco Kid* series.

The three "Dr. Monroe" features were based on novels written in the 1930s by James L. Rubel. Later he wrote the westerns *The Bounty Hunter* (1946) and *Thunder Valley* (1957) as Mason MacRae; he also used the pseudonym Timothy Hayes. Under his own name he penned the novels *Eli Donovan* (1950), about a female detective, *No Business for a Lady* (1950) and *The Wanton One* (1960).

The initial "Dr. Monroe" outing, *The Medico of Painted Springs*, released in June, 1941, was based on Rubel's 1934 novel of the same title and was produced by Jack Fier. Also called *The Doctor's Alibi*, its plot had Dr. Steven Monroe (Charles Starrett) arriving in the town of Painted Springs to conduct medical exams of men wanting to join the Rough Riders and fight in the Spanish-American war. The community is torn by a feud between cattlemen and sheep raisers. Dr. Monroe is called to treat Nancy Richards (Terry Walker), a rancher's daughter, and sheepman Ed Gordon (Ray Bennett), both of whom have been shot during a gunfight between the rival factions. Fred Burns (Wheeler Oakman), another cattle raiser, is behind all the trouble since he wants to steals his neighbors' herds and blame it on the sheepmen. Steven and Nancy are attracted to each other, much to the chagrin of her father's (Ben Taggart) foreman Kentucky Lane (Richard Fiske); Burns tries to cause further trouble between the men, which results in a fistfight between the doctor and the foreman. When Steven knocks out Lane and departs, Burns' henchman Pete (Chuck Hamilton) shoots Lane and leaves him for dead. Burns has the sheriff (Edmund Cobb) arrest Monroe for killing Lane, but the foreman is revived by the doctor long enough to name his assailant. As a result, the sheriff's wife (Edythe Elliott) releases the doctor and stops a gun battle between the rival factions. When Nancy accuses Burns of being behind all the trouble, he has Pete kidnap her, but Steven and Nancy's father and his men show up and the girl is rescued. Monroe forces a confession out of Pete, causing the arrest of Burns and an end to the feuding.

As was common with program westerns of the period, *The Medico of Painted Springs* included music, here performed by a group called The Simp-Phonies which contributed a song, "Corny Troubles." Three other tunes were also featured: "Lonely Rangeland," "Rocking and Rolling in the Saddle" and "We'd Just as Soon Fiddle or Fight."

With the second series entry, *Thunder Over the Prairie*, released late in July of 1941, William Berke took over as producer (he would continue with the final entry, *Prairie Stranger*, issued two months later). *Thunder Over the Prairie* was based on Rubel's 1935 novel *The Medico Rides*. Monroe (Starrett), doing post graduate work in New York City, accepts a position at Bellevue Hospital while

Eileen O'Hearn and Charles Starrett in *Thunder Over the Prairie* (Columbia, 1941).

his roommate, Roy Mandan (Stanley Brown), a Native American, gives up his studies to return home to Rock City. There he joins his brother Clay (David Sharpe) in helping to build an irrigation project to bring water to the area, which has been plagued by lack of rain and dust storms. The head of the project, Henry Clayton (Jack Rockwell), is not only charging the workers for their labor but is also using second-rate material to construct a dam. Monroe, unhappy with his hospital work, soon joins Roy and works to help the poor people of the area and befriends a young boy, Timmy Wheeler (Danny Mummert). Steven is befriended by Bones (Cliff Edwards), who is also studying medicine. After a falling out with Clayton's cohorts Taylor (Donald Curtis) and Hartley (Joe McGuinn), the Mandan brothers are fired and they decide to round up wild horses to sell to the construction company. Although they bring in strays, Roy and Clay are accused of rustling and, in trying to escape from a posse, Roy is shot. His sister, Nona (Eileen O'Hearn), brings Monroe to save Roy and the doctor tries to convince the brothers to turn themselves in to the law. Before they can do so, Clayton orders the dam, which has been weakened by a storm, dynamited and then blames the Mandans, based upon the false testimony of Timmy's father, Dave Wheeler (Ted Adams), a night watchman. When Timmy is hurt, Dave confesses to Monroe that he lied about the brothers dynamiting the dam while Clay and his tribesmen stampede a wild horse herd into town, breaking up Roy's trial. During the stampede, Roy shoots Hartley and Timmy is fatally hurt. Before dying, Hartley implicates Clayton and his cohorts and they are arrested. Roy and Clay are then proven innocent.

Cliff "Ukulele Ike" Edwards and Cal Shrum

Charles Starrett and Cliff Edwards in *Thunder Over the Prairie* (Columbia, 1941).

and His Rhythm Rangers provided a trio of songs composed by Shrum and Billy Hughes: "Diggin' in the Cold, Cold Ground," "Headin' for Home" and "Saddle Tramps." Edwards (1895–1971) was a Missouri native who sang and strummed the ukulele to international fame. In the 1920s he sold over 70 million records, the most popular being "June Night" and "Ja Da." He starred on Broadway, where he introduced the George Gershwin tune "Lady Be Good," and later on radio. With the coming of the talkies he introduced "Singin' in the Rain" in MGM's *Hollywood Revue of 1929* (1929) and then developed into a character actor in scores of motion pictures. He often was a sidekick in "B" westerns. He was the voice of Jiminy Crickett singing "When You Wish Upon a Star" in *Pinocchio* (1940) and in the 1950s he worked in various Disney television productions. He died destitute in 1971.

The final "Dr. Monroe" series feature, *Prairie Stranger*, came out in September, 1941. It was based on Rubel's book *The Medico Rides the Trail* (1926). This time out Monroe (Starrett) and his pal Bones (Cliff Edwards) take over the practice of a recently deceased physician in the town of Red Fork. When the older Dr. Westridge (Edmund Cobb) arrives in town, the locals desert Monroe for the more seasoned doctor and he is forced to take a job as a cowboy on a ranch owned by Jud Evans (Forbes Murray) and his daughter Sue (Patti McCarty). When rival rancher Jim Dawson (Frank La Rue) learns that Westridge has been in prison, he forces the medical man to concoct a poison which he uses on Evans' cattle, hoping to run him out of business. When Bones comes across a mysterious bottle in the bunkhouse, he has Monroe test its contents, and it proves to be poison. When Dawson finds Monroe with the bottle, he has him arrested. Steven manages to escape, becoming a wanted man. When Westridge objects about Monroe's persecution, Dawson orders his cohort Barton (Archie Twitchell) to kill the doctor. At the undertaker's (Jim Corey) office, Monroe and Bones locate the bullet which killed Westridge and during a square dance Bones takes all the unholstered guns. The murder bullet is linked to Barton, who tries to escape in a buggy belonging to Sue. Monroe overtakes the buggy, rescues Sue and captures Barton, who implicates Dawson in the crimes.

For this entry, the musical interludes were provided by Edwards and Lew Preston and His Ranch Hands. Preston composed the songs "Doin' It Right," "Lit'l Darlin'" and "I'm Just a Small Town Scally-wag"; the feature also included the Lopez Wallingham tune "I'll Be a Cowboy 'Till I Die."

After *Prairie Stranger*, Charles Starrett would continue making cowboy pictures for Columbia and in 1945 he would commence his best known work for the studio, the "Durango Kid" (q.v.) series.

Filmography

The Medico of Painted Springs (Columbia, 1941, 58 minutes) Producer: Jack Fier. Executive Producer: Irving Briskin. Director: Lambert Hillyer. Screenplay: Winston Miller & Wyndham Gittens, from the novel by James L. Rubel. Photography: Benjamin H. Kline. Editor: Mel Thorsen. Songs: The Simp-Phonies, Eddy Cunningham, Enright Busse & Frank Wilder. Sound: John Goodrich. Assistant Director: Milton Carter.

Cast: Charles Starrett (Dr. Steven Monroe), Terry Walker (Nancy Richards), Ben Taggart (Ben Richards), Ray Bennett (Ed Gordon), Wheeler Oakman (Fred Burns), Richard Fiske (Kentucky Lane), Edmund Cobb (Sheriff Blaine), Edythe Elliott (Mrs. Blaine), Bud Osborne (Karns), Steve Clark (Ellis), Chuck Hamilton (Pete), The Simp-Phonies (Musicians), Art Mix, Lloyd Bridges (Cowboys), Jim Corey (Slim), Buck Connors (Old Man), Hank Bell (Driver), Eddie Laughton (Deputy Sheriff), John Tyrrell (Bartender), George Huggins (Bearded Soldier), Carl Sepulveda (Man with Tattoo).

A.k.a. *The Doctor's Alibi*.

Thunder Over the Prairie (Columbia, 1941, 60 minutes) Producer: William Berke. Executive Producer: Irving Briskin. Director: Lambert Hillyer. Screenplay: Betty Burbridge, from the novel *The Medico Rides* by James L. Rubel. Photography: Benjamin H. Kline. Editor: Burton Cramer. Songs: Cal Shrum & Billy Hughes. Assistant Director: Milton Carter.

Cast: Charles Starrett (Dr. Steven Monroe), Cliff Edwards (Bones Malloy), Eileen O'Hearn (Nona Mandan), Stanley Brown (Roy Mandan), Danny Mummert (Timmy Wheeler), David Sharpe (Clay Mandan), Jack Rockwell (Henry Clayton), Joe McGuinn (Hartley), Donald Curtis (Taylor), Ted Adams (Dave Wheeler), Budd Buster (Judge Merriwether), Cal Shrum & His Rhythm Rangers (Musicians), Steve Clark (Sheriff), Murdock MacQuarrie (Mandan), Eddie Laughton (Prosecutor), John Tyrrell (Messenger Boy), Francis Sayles (Corbin), Horace B. Carpenter (Citizen).

Prairie Stranger (Columbia, 1941, 58 minutes) Producer: William Berke. Executive Producer: Irving Briskin. Director: Lambert Hillyer. Screenplay: Winston Miller, from the novel *The Medico Rides the Trail* by James L. Rubel. Photography: Benjamin H. Kline. Editor: James Sweeney. Songs: Lew Preston & Lopez Wallingham. Art Director: Perry Smith. Sound: Jack Haines. Assistant Director: Thomas [Tommy] Flood.

Cast: Charles Starrett (Dr. Steven Monroe), Cliff Edwards (Bones Malloy), Patti McCarty (Sue Evans), Forbes Murray (Jud Evans), Frank La Rue (Jim Dawson), Archie Twitchell (Barton), Francis Walker (Craig), Edmund Cobb (Dr. Westridge), James [Jim] Corey (Undertaker), Russ Powell (Whittling Jones), Lew Preston & His Ranch Hands (Musicians), Chester Conklin (Cook), Monty Collins (Salesman), Hank Bell (Driver), George Sherwood (Sheriff), Edward Hearn (Vet), Lynn Lewis (Wallflower), John Tyrrell (Bartender), George Morrell (Injured Man), Ray Jones, Jack Tornek (Citizens), Rube Dalroy (Saloon Customer).

THE DURANGO KID

For a decade, Charles Starrett had been headlining westerns for Columbia Pictures, beginning with *The Gallant Defender* in 1935. During that time he had ranked in the *Motion Picture Herald*'s poll of top ten money-making western stars except in 1943 when no poll was taken. By the mid–1940s, however, it was becoming evident that something was needed to keep the Starrett series going. Incoming producer Colbert Clark decided to bring back the masked avenger character of the Durango Kid, a part Starrett portrayed in a feature of that title in 1940. Clark's move proved to be a good one and from 1945 to 1952 the actor portrayed the masked man in 64 features, retaining his berth as one of the top moneymakers in the cowboy film field.

As one might expect from a series that ran for so many features over a seven-year period, the Durango Kids tended to vary in quality, although they never seemed to lose their appeal. In *Heroes of the Range* (1987), Buck Rainey wrote, "The Durango stories were the Western stereotype stripped down to the mare's back.... The theory that the grinding out of the same plot, with only minor variations, will still result in a successful film, particularly if it happens to be a Western, is nowhere more strongly (and somewhat mistakenly) illustrated [than] in the Durango Kid series.... The same old stagecoach holdup, the same old suave villain masquerading as a benefactor, the same old cattle stampede and a few other standard props were constantly assembled by producer Clark, and while the result probably produced no audible complaints from oater fans, the whole series seemed rather tired." Regarding the star he noted, "Starrett, however, competently performs his chores in all 63 [sic] entries...."

Without doubt, it was the acting ability and screen charisma of Charles Starrett which kept him working as a western star for Columbia Pictures for seventeen years and it was his immense popularity, especially with youngsters, which made the Durango Kid films the second longest running "B" western series, in both years and numbers, after "Hopalong Cassidy" (q.v.). Starrett (1904–86) was a Massachusetts native whose father founded the Starrett Precision Tool Company, which operates to this day. Brought up in a wealthy home, he attended prep school, where he became involved in acting, and then Dartmouth College, where he excelled in football. As a result of the latter activity, he made his film debut in *The Quarterback* (1926), which was filmed at Dartmouth. After graduation he worked in stock before making his Broadway debut in 1929 in *Claire Adams*. As a result he was signed by Paramount, where he remained until going to Columbia in 1935. During his early '30s, he was on loan to other studios more often than he worked at his home base. Among his best remembered roles were the lead in the independent production *The Viking* (1931), a football player in Paramount's *Touchdown* (1932), and the tortured leading man in MGM's *The Mask of Fu Manchu* (1932). He also top-lined several programmers from Chesterfield, including *Murder on the Campus* (1933), *Stolen Sweets, Green Eyes, Sons of Steel* (all 1934) and *A Shot in the Dark* (1935), a murder mystery which took place at Dartmouth.

When Tim McCoy left Columbia in 1935, the studio hired Starrett to take over as its western film hero and in the next ten years he headlined nearly 70 oaters. In 1940 the studio placed Starrett in its "Dr. Monroe" (q.v.) westerns but after only a trio of efforts, copyright problems caused the highly regarded series to be halted. Music, mainly provided by the Sons of the Pioneers, was a part of Starrett's westerns from almost the beginning and would continue in his Durango Kid features, although more often than not the musical interludes tended to slow the plot or bring it to a complete halt. Country and western greats Jimmie Davis (two-term governor of Louisiana), Ernest Tubb, Jimmy Wakely and Ozie Waters were among the singers in Starrett's Columbia oaters. Sidekicks too were a staple in the star's features and they included crooner Donald Grayson, singer-comic Cliff "Ukulele Ike" Edwards, Russell Hayden, Arthur Hunnicutt and Dub Taylor.

Starrett headlined 35 westerns for Columbia before starring in *The Durango Kid* in 1940. Directed by veteran Lambert Hillyer, it told of rancher Bill Lowry (Starrett) trying to find his father's killer, the crime being blamed on nesters by rival Mace Ballard (Kenneth MacDonald), the real culprit. When the neighboring Winslow ranch is destroyed by Ballard's raiders, Bill moves the owner (Forrest Taylor) and his pretty daughter Nancy (Luana Walters) to nearby Hidden Valley and then takes on the guise of the avenging Durango Kid. The masked man steals Ballard's money and gives it to local homesteaders as Marshal Trayboe (Melvin Lang) appoints Bill his deputy with orders to bring in the Durango Kid. When the locals become tired of the lawlessness and decide to leave Hidden Valley, Nancy takes their funds, planning on leaving the money with Bill, but she is captured by Ballard and his gang. Using the girl as bait, Ballard manages to also capture the Durango Kid, who has come to her rescue. The marshal, however, has followed Bill; he and his men surround Ballard's ranch and the crook is killed. Bill then reveals he is the Durango Kid and he and Nancy plan to wed. The Sons of the Pioneers figured in the plot as homesteaders as well as contributing the quartet of songs "Lullabye," "The Prairie Sings," "There's a Rainbow Over the Range" and "Yippi-Ti Your Troubles Away," all composed by group members Bob Nolan and Tim Spencer. In *Hollywood Corral* (1976), Don Miller said, "It hit about average, moving well and with some okay action."

Jack Fier produced *The Durango Kid* and he would do the same with *Sagebrush Heroes* five years later. This feature was an anomaly in the Durango Kid series in that Starrett portrayed a radio actor who plays the character over the air and also in real life, in order to stop injustice. Luci Ward's script had radio entertainer Steve Randall (Starrett), famous for his program about the Durango Kid, and his band touring with a rodeo. When Steve's wallet is stolen by orphan Marty Jones (Elvin Field), local newspaper reporter Connie Pearson (Constance Worth) convinces Steve to give Marty a break by having him sent to the Sunshine Ranch, a boys' home run by Tom Goodwin (Forrest Taylor). When Marty finds out that supposedly good Samaritan Goodwin is using the ranch as a front for cattle theft and child labor, he runs away with another boy (Bobby Larson) whose brother was murdered because he learned of Goodwin's activities. They meet Steve and his troupe and he sends the boys back to the ranch, and then goes to town and informs Connie and her employer (Vernon Dent) of the boys' claims. When they refuse to believe him, Steve decides to actually become the Durango Kid and expose Goodwin. Steve and his bandsman Jimmy (Jimmy Wakely) wire the Sunshine Ranch for sound and use the local doctor, Webb (Joel Friedkin), to help them get Goodwin to admit to his activities, with the confession being broadcast. As a result, the local sheriff (Edmund Cobb) arrests Goodwin and his gang and Webb is made the new head of the boys' home. Jimmy Wakely and Ozie Waters and His Saddle Pals performed four songs in the feature: "Hold That Critter Down," "I've Sold My Saddle for an Old Guitar," "Ride 'em Cowboy" and "Yippi-Ti Your Troubles Away."

The Durango Kid series kicked off in earnest with the April, 1945, release of *The Return of the Durango Kid*, under the auspices of producer Colbert Clark, who would remain in that capacity for the entire seven-year run. Jack Fier would stay with the Durango unit as its production manager. Derwin Abrahams, who had helmed several of the

Charles Starrett as "The Durango Kid," riding Raider.

Charles Starrett as "The Durango Kid."

"Hopalong Cassidy" (q.v.) features, directed, and he would also do the next two Durango Kid outings. Tex Harding served as Starrett's sidekick for the first eight series features and he also sang, although it has been claimed he was dubbed by James T. "Bud" Nelson, who was also cast in bit parts. Various musical groups like The Jesters, Bob Wills and His Texas Playboys, Spade Cooley and Al Trace and His Silly Symphonists provided the musical interludes during the series' first season. In the Durango Kid series, Starrett rode a beautiful white horse named Raider and his stunt double was Ted Mapes, who also played supporting roles in many of the films. In the episodes, the character of the Durango Kid was dressed all in black, including a black mask and hat.

The Return of the Durango Kid offered a rather complicated plot taking place in 1875 Texas, with Bill Blaydon (Charles Starrett) on the way to Silver City to clear the name of his late father who was framed. His stagecoach is held up by outlaws with passenger Paradise Flo (Jean Stevens) steering the gang to the location of a payroll shipment. In town, the owner of the stage line, Buckskin Liz (Betty Roadman), tells Bill that saloon owner Kirby (John Calvert) is behind the holdups and he goes to his place of business in order to get back his father's watch, stolen by the badmen. After retrieving the watch, Steve is offered a job by Liz driving her coaches along with Jim (Tex Harding) and Curly (Britt Wood). A masked man, the Durango Kid, relieves Kirby and his men of the money they stole and leaves it at the stage depot. Realtor Wagner (Hal Price) tries to buy out Liz, which makes Steve suspicious as the Durango Kid continues to harass Kirby's gang. He also uses various tactics to brew discontent between Kirby and his cohort Wagner as well as gang members Ringo (Paul Conrad) and Cherokee (Ray Bennett). Bill eventually tricks Wagner into confessing that his father was framed but the realtor is murdered by Kirby, with Bill being arrested for the crime. Paradise, who wants to get away from her employer Kirby, sneaks a gun into Bill's cell but he gives it to the sheriff (Dick Botiller) who then allows him a day to prove his innocence. As the Durango Kid, Bill splits up Kirby's gang and then tells Ringo that Kirby plans to turn on him. When Ringo confronts Kirby, he is shot but before dying he accuses Kirby of killing Wagner. The Durango Kid then tries to capture Kirby but is forced to kill him. Tex Harding "crooned" "Old Pinto" while The Jesters performed "He Holds the Lantern (While His Mother Cuts the Wood)" and "Why They Fiddle Out the Polka." Although the series was an immediate hit with cowboy film fans, *The Return of the Durango Kid* was somewhat listless, even lacking most of the fisticuffs associated with Starrett westerns.

The action perked up a bit with the next entry, *Both Barrels Blazing*, issued in May, 1945. Dub Taylor, who had been Starrett's comedy sidekick in five previous Columbia outings, returned in that capacity for this feature and would do so for the next half-dozen Durango Kid flicks. Also back was the comedy singing group The Jesters, who performed "Cowboys and Indians" and "Sidekick Joe" as well as joining Tex Harding on "Look Before You Leap." Harding soloed on "A Lonely Cowboy" which he crooned to leading lady Pat Parrish. The film took place in 1880 with Texas Ranger Kip Allen (Starrett) taking a leave of absence from his job and traveling to New Mexico Territory where as the Durango Kid he tries to capture train robber Dan Cass (Robert Barron).

Poster for *The Return of the Durango Kid* (Columbia, 1945).

grandfather's mine are actually smelted coins. When Grubstake is bushwhacked by the Durango Kid, Kip follows the thief; it turns out to be Tex, who wants to protect Gail by sending the stolen money back to the U.S. Treasury. Realizing he has been duped by Lucky, Grubstake tries to aid Kip and Tex in capturing the outlaw but Kirby shoots the old man. Lucky also turns on his henchman, Nevada (Charles King), and leaves him for dead. Before dying, Nevada tells Kip that the stolen money is in Thorpe's safe. Kip confronts Thorpe and outshoots the badman, bringing him to justice. With Tex planning to marry Gail, Kip heads off to look into trouble in Antelope Valley.

Released in August, 1945, the next series entry, *Rustlers of the Badlands*, does indeed take place in Antelope Valley, New Mexico, with cavalry scouts Steve Lindsay (Charles Starrett), Tex Harding (Tex Harding) and Cannonball (Dub Taylor) looking into cattle rustling. Steve obtains a legal document stolen from Sally Boylston (Sally Bliss), whose uncle, rancher Andrew Boylston (Steve Clark), has been kidnapped. In town, Boylston's foreman Jim Norton (George Eldredge) accuses Steve of stealing the document and he is convicted and sentenced to die. Tex and Cannonball come to his rescue and

When Cass is shot by saloon owner Lucky Thorpe (Alan Bridge), the Kid is blamed since Lucky wants the stolen loot and later hides it in an abandoned mine. Kip enlists the aid of old friend Tex (Tex Harding), now a miner, and the two come to believe that Lucky is behind the killing. Thorpe's good luck charm is old prospector Grubstake (Emmett Lynn), who asks the gambler's help when he finds out his granddaughter Gail (Pat Parrish) is coming to Long Bend for a visit. Lucky then decides to use Grubstake as a shill, making it look like the old man struck it rich and having this as a means to get rid of the stolen gold. Gail arrives and is feted with a party as Tex falls for her and later finds out the nuggets from her

Steve then assumes the guise of the Durango Kid and visits Sally, who tells him that Norton plans to take a cattle herd to an army post. The three scouts stop the cattle drive and chase the bandits to their hideout where they find, and free, Boylston. Tex and Sally take her uncle to town while the sheriff (Karl Hackett) accuses Steve and Cannonball of being cattle thieves and puts them in jail. Steve is able to escape and as the Durango Kid he goes to Boylston's ranch and finds Norton's bank book. Steve then demands that Norton cut him in for one-half of his money and the two head to the gang's hideout where Steve shoots it out with the crooks as Cannonball and the sheriff arrive and the outlaws are arrested. This time

Jack Rockwell and Charles Starrett in *Both Barrels Blazing* (Columbia, 1945).

out the music was provided by Al Trace and His Silly Symphonists doing "Hey! Louella" and "Yodelin' Kate" as Tex Harding sang "Dusty Saddle on the Ole Barn Wall."

Carolina Cotton and Spade Cooley's Band, including Tex Williams and Deuce Spriggins, furnished the songs in *Outlaws of the Rockies*, issued in August of 1945. This one told of Steve Williams (Starrett) being hired as sheriff of Corvalis in order to bring in a gang supposedly led by Dan Lanning (I. Stanford Jolley); the outlaws have been raiding local miners. After one of the robberies, Steve captures one of the gang, his old friend Tex (Tex Harding), who claims to be innocent and later escapes from jail. Feeling Steve intentionally let his friend escape, the locals try to arrest the sheriff but he manages to get away and he goes to the Rimrock Mine where he finds owner Jane Stuart (Carole Mathews) and her foreman Cannonball (Dub Taylor) hiding Tex. They lock up Steve, and Tex escapes only be captured by the gang but he is rescued by the Durango Kid. The wounded Tex returns to the Rimrock while Durango lures the gang away. He is later ambushed by the outlaws but is saved by Tex. The two men then decide to work together but end up being captured by the law. After Jane brings a gold shipment to the bank, the real gang leader, peddler Honest Dan Chantry (Philip Van Zandt), has his men steal it and while the sheriff is after the gang, Cannonball helps Steve and Tex break jail. The two come upon Chantry and his wagon and they become suspicious when they notice the wagon wheels sinking into the ground. They follow Chantry to the gang's hideout and find the stolen gold in his wagon. When the outlaws try to kill Steve and Tex with a wagon filled with gunpowder, Steve shoots at the wagon and causes an explosion which weakens the gang and they are arrested. With Steve and Tex cleared, Tex remains in Corvalis with Jane while Steve goes off to new adventures. The songs performed in the film were "Do Ya or Don't Cha?," "Hilda Was a Darn Good Cook," "I'll Come Ridin' Home to You" and

"You'll Know What It Means to Be Blue," all composed by Spade Cooley and Smokey Rogers. *Variety* termed it "a weak western" whose "lack of originality and poor attempts at humor groove it for the grade-school kids."

Outlaws of the Rockies marked the feature directorial debut of Ray Nazarro, who would go on to direct over three dozen entries in the Durango Kid series. A native of Massachusetts, Nazarro (1902–86) worked as an assistant director in two-reelers for Educational Pictures before joining Columbia in 1934 as an assistant and second unit director. In regards to Nazarro's work on the Durango series, Don Miller stated in *Hollywood Corral* (1976), "Nazarro's style was enigmatic.... [His] directing had a slapdash, nervous energy, the narratives pushed along pumpily. Nazarro didn't spend the time choreographing fistic encounters, which are difficult to film, but instead would settle for a fast and not too realistic haymaker from Starrett."

Next came *Blazing the Western Trail*, issued in October, 1945, which took place in 1870 and told of Jeff Waring (Starrett) and Tex Harding (Tex Harding) riding to the town of Quanto Basin to visit Jeff's uncle Dan Waring (Steve Clark), the manager of Forrest Brent's (Alan Bridge) stage line. Brent has hired gunman Jim McMasters (Mauritz Hugo) to drive competitor Bob Halliday (Nolan Leary) out of business. Dan learns what is happening and threatens to expose Brent but is murdered by McMasters, with the crime being blamed on Halliday. Jeff and Tex arrive just after the killing and Jeff accepts the position with Brent left open by his uncle's death while Halliday's daughter Mary (Carole Mathews) and helper Cannonball (Dub Taylor) are left to run their stagecoach line. Jeff tells Tex he suspects Brent of being behind his uncle's murder and he investigates as the Durango Kid. While Durango foils Brent's gang in their attempts to put the Hallidays out of business, Jeff and Tex fake a fight with Tex taking a job with Mary. He later dresses as the Durango Kid in order to dispel Brent's suspicion that Jeff is the masked avenger. Since both the Brent and Halliday lines are vying for a mail contract, the government inspector (Frank La Rue) sanctions a race between the two competitors with the winner getting the contract. The race begins with Jeff riding with Brent while Tex goes with Carole, but Jeff drops off the stagecoach during the event and becomes the Durango Kid and takes over driving Mary's vehicle when Tex is wounded by one of Brent's men. Mary wins the race and Jeff gets McMasters to confess to killing his uncle on Brent's orders. Jeff then overpowers Brent and takes him to the sheriff (Edmund Cobb). While Tex remains with Mary, whose father has been exonerated, Jeff rides off to Nevada.

Blazing the Western Trail was a fairly entertaining Durango Kid entry highlighted by musical numbers performed by Bob Wills and His Texas Playboys, featuring vocals by Tommy Duncan on "Time Changes Everything," "Ida Red" and "Liza Jane." Tex Harding soloed on "I Wonder If You Feel the Way I Do." Another plus for the entry was Cannonball's rustic romance with lunchroom proprietor Nellie, humorously portrayed by Virginia Sale. The feature was the first of four Durangos directed by Vernon Keays, who also did the next one, *Lawless Empire*.

Bob Wills and His Texas Playboys were back in *Lawless Empire*, which came out in mid–November of 1945. This time the Durango Kid (Starrett) comes to the aid of minister Tex Harding (Tex Harding) and his sister Vicky (Mildred Law), as they try to stop Duke Flinders (Ethan Laidlaw) and his gang from driving a family of homesteaders out of Dry Gulch. Duke and his men trail the masked man to a camp where he finds only cowboys Steve Ransom (Starrett) and Bob (Bob Wills) and their hired hands (The Texas Playboys). In town, Duke tells his employer, town boss Blaze Howard (John Calvert), about the masked man and saloon worker Cannonball (Dub Taylor) hears Howard order Durango's murder. Jeff is offered the job of town marshal by Tex and refuses, but later agrees to take the position when offered it by Howard. Steve tells Cannonball he believes the town's former sheriff, his brother, was murdered and he wants to avenge his death. When the Durango Kid stops the outlaws from breaking up a homesteaders' rally, the people unite, capture Duke and take him to Steve, who upsets them by letting the badman out on bail. Jeff believes someone else is working with Howard and Duke as the Durango Kid takes money from Blaze so the settlers can build a church. When Duke is captured by Durango, he announces he wants to quit the gang but is murdered by the local physician, Doc Weston (Forrest Taylor), the mastermind behind the lawlessness. When the newspaper editor (Tom Chatterton) tells Jeff that Doc Weston treated his brother for a minor wound which caused his death, Jeff realizes the doctor is in cahoots with Howard. Blaze and Weston try to set a trap for the Durango Kid by letting Cannonball overhear them planning Tex's murder. The two crooks then get the drop on the masked man at Harding's home but are forced to flee when Tex and Cannonball arrive with a group of nesters. Weston and Howard try to start a cattle stampede in order to make their escape but they are arrested by Steve. This time out, Bob Wills and His Texas Playboys performed "Dev'lish Mary" and "Stay a Little Longer" while Tex Harding, leading lady Mildred Law and the Bob Wills group sang the Rev. W.D. Stevens' classic hymn "Farther Along."

The final 1945 series feature, *Texas Panhandle*, came out late in December and featured music by the Spade Cooley Band and singer Carolina Cotton. Taking place in 1890, it has Secret Service operative Steve Buckner (Starrett) resigning his post and heading to Texas where he becomes a scout on a wagon train led by Tex Harding (Tex Harding) and Cannonball (Dub Taylor), who is attacked by bandits and saved by the Durango Kid. The leader of the gang, Slash (George Chesebro), gets the drop on Cannonall, rearms his gang and forces the homesteaders to go to Crow Springs, which is run by crooked realtor Ace Galatin (Forrest Taylor). The land in the area belonged to Ann Williams's (Nanette Parks) late father but Galatin tells her he died without a will and that the territory is available for settlement. Once the settlers arrive in Crow Springs, Galatin has them sign over their land deeds to him and he hires Steve, who is a lawyer, to handle the legal transactions. The Durango Kid discovers that Galatin holds Ann's father deed which wills the land to her and he takes it from the realtor; later he blows open the realtor's safe and finds it contains stolen government gold. Galatin learns that Steve is a government agent but the lawman manages to escape with the help of Tex and Cannonball. At Ann's ranch, the Durango Kid tells her the truth about her father's will. Galatin and his gang arrive and try to unmask him but are driven off by Tex, Cannonball and the homesteaders. The Durango Kid rides to town where he arrests Ace and recovers the gold. As a result, Steve rejoins the Secret Service and Ann gives the homesteaders the land they have registered. The musical interludes had Spade Cooley's Band performing "Shame on You," "Heavenly Range" (both written by Cooley, the latter with Smokey Rogers and Bob Wills), and Tommy Duncan's "Take Me Back to Tulsa." Tex Harding crooned "At Sunset" and Carolina Cotton sang and yodeled her composition, "I Love to Yodel."

Frontier Gun Law was the first Durango film for 1946 and it was the final series appearances by Tex Harding and Dub Taylor, the latter having little do to as the driver of a stagecoach attacked by a gang called The Phantoms which terrorize ranchers around Mesa City. Jim Stewart (Starrett) arrives in town on the stage to purchase a ranch from paraplegic newspaperman Matt Edwards (Weldon Heyburn). He finds out that another rancher, Tex Harding (Tex Harding), is suspected of being the head of the gang because his spread has never been attacked. After Stewart moves into his new home, it is raided and a cowhand killed, so he becomes the Durango Kid in order to find the culprit. Stewart discovers that the outlaws use newspaper advertising to inform gang members about raids and after another attack the sheriff (Frank LaRue) arrests Tex, although Stewart believes him to be innocent. The Durango Kid aids Tex in getting out of jail. Back at the Harding ranch, they are attacked by the raiders as Tex's sister Kitty (Jean Stevens) goes into town to get the sheriff. The lawman and his posse capture the gang but their leader escapes and the Durango Kid goes back to town and meets with Edwards. Using the ruse of setting the editor's leg blanket on fire, Durango proves the newspaperman is the gang leader and arrests him. The music in the feature was provided by Al Trace and His Silly Symphonists, along with Jack Guthrie, whose Capitol recording of "Oklahoma Hills" was one of the top country records of 1945.

Smiley Burnette joined the Durango Kid series in *Roaring Rangers* (released in February, 1946), and he would remain for the rest of the series. Having already been the sidekick to Gene Autry, Roy Rogers, Eddie Dew and Sunset Carson at Republic, Burnette brought with him a fan following which certainly enhanced the popular-

Poster for *Frontier Gunlaw* (Columbia, 1946).

shows "All Star Western Theater" and "Melody Roundup." From 1950 to 1953 he starred on radio in the syndicated "Smiley Burnette Show" (nearly 300 episodes); the series used the star's composition "It's My Lazy Day" as its theme song.

Roaring Rangers started the Durango series tradition of having Starrett's character named Steve. That name had been used in many of the star's earlier features but other given names had also been assigned to Starrett's characters. From now until the series ended, however, Starrett always played someone named Steve, although the surnames varied in each entry. The feature also marked director Ray Nazarro's return for six outings and it included not only vocalizing by Smiley Burnette but also Merle Travis and His Bronco Busters. Barry Shipman's script had Steve Cameron (Starrett), alias the Durango Kid, and his pal Smiley (Burnette), coming to outlaw-ridden Powder River at the behest of young Larry Connor (Mickey Kuhn), the son of beleaguered lawman Jeff Conner (Jack Rockwell). Bar owner Taggert (Edmund Cobb) is behind the lawlessness and is working with Jeff's dishonest brother Bill Conner (Ed Cassidy). After meeting Jeff and his daughter Doris (Adelle Roberts), Steve accepts the post of deputy sheriff while Taggert assigns his henchman Slade (Ted Mapes) to murder the Durango Kid, whom Larry has claimed is coming to town. Slade takes on the guise of Durango to discredit him and Larry is later shot while spying on him and his henchmen. While Larry is taken to the state capital for medical help, the sheriff forms a posse to hunt down the Durango Kid, whom he thinks shot his son. While he is gone, Taggert has him removed from office and takes over as sheriff. The Durango Kid uses a ruse to capture Slade wearing his costume and turns him over to

ity of the Durango features. He also composed and performed dozens of songs in the films although his bumbling comedy character and silly ditties sometimes proved irritating to cowboy fans wanting more hard riding, fights and shootouts. During the six years he worked on the Durango Kid series, Burnette continued to make personal appearances, recorded for the record labels ARA and Bullet, and guest starred on the radio

Poster for *Roaring Rangers* (Columbia, 1946).

gert. During the proceedings, Burnette performed his self-penned "Lazy Daily Dozes" and "A New Ten Gallon Hat"; the feature also included the traditional "The Old Chisholm Trail."

The third of ten 1946 Durango Kid releases, *Gunning for Vengeance*, was issued in March. Taking place in 1888, it has Steve Landry (Charles Starrett) protecting trail drives from outlaws. While en route to the town of Split Rock to become its new lawman, he rescues Jenkins (Nolan Leary) and his teenage daughter Elaine (Marjean Neville) from renegades. In town he deputizes his old pal, blacksmith Smiley (Burnette), and then tries to arrest Curley (Robert Kortman), the man who shot Jenkins. Curley, however, manages to escape from Belle Madden's (Phyllis Adair) saloon, and Steve and Smiley form a posse and pursue the outlaw, who crosses the state line. Disguised as the Durango Kid, Steve follows Curley and returns him to Split Rock. Belle is in cahoots with Jim Clayburn (Lane Chandler), head of the saloonkeepers' league, who gets the citizens riled up as a diversion in order to break Curley out of jail. When the plans fails because the outlaws cannot break an automatic lock invented by Smiley, Jim plans to kidnap Elaine. Belle, who likes the girl, convinces him to let the teenager stay with her. As Durango hunts for Elaine, Smiley learns of her whereabouts and rides to find the masked man and together they shoot it out with the gang as Clayburn goes back to town for Elaine. As the young girl tries to escape, Belle comes to her aid and is shot by Clayburn. Elaine manages to get to Steve and Smiley and warn them they will be attacked by the outlaws. The Durango Kid and Smiley get the drop on Clayburn and his men and

the sheriff. The gang, however, attacks the stage carrying the lawman, Doris and Slade and causes it to crash but Durango is able to save the trio. Although Steve plans to make Slade confess, Taggert murders his henchman and Cameron finds out that Bill thinks his brother is still alive and plans to murder him. Steve trails Bill and shoots him before he can kill Jeff, who then arrests Tag-

bring them to justice. For this affair, Burnette wrote and sang a trio of songs, "Hominy Grits," "Smithy's a Liar" and "Twenty Long Years," while Curt Barrett and the Trailsmen contributed "The Belle of Sonora Is Mine."

For the April, 1946, Durango Kid series release *Galloping Thunder*, Burnette contributed the songs "The Fife," "Gettin' Some Sleep" and "The Wind Sings a Cowboy Song," while Merle Travis and His Bronco Busters did "Texas Home, Here I Come," composed by Travis and Tex Atkinson. This one took place in 1880 with cattlemen's agent Steve Reynolds (Starrett) assigned to look into horse rustling in Split Rock, Arizona, where banker Grat Hanlon (Richard Bailey) is the secret head of the outlaws. Cowpoke Smiley (Burnette) is after the reward for capturing the gang and is saved by Steve from Hanlon's men, who suspect him of being the Durango Kid. In town, Smiley decides to become an undertaker while Steve meets Jud Temple (Adelle Roberts), Hanlon's fiancée. The crook tries to turn the locals against Durango by having one of his underlings dress like the masked avenger and rob the bank. Steve goes undercover as outlaw Buck McCloud and learns that Hanlon plans to rustle ranchers' horses which he promised to drive to a military outpost. The Durango Kid stops the gang from stampeding the herd as the ranchers, joined by Steve, shoot it out with the outlaws and Reynolds brings in Hanlon. Footage from this feature would be reused in the later Durango Kid adventures *Challenge of the Range* (1949) and *Cyclone Fury* (1951).

The next month brought *Two-Fisted Stranger*, another 1880 adventure, which featured Grand Ole Opry star Zeke Clements performing his self-penned "You're Free Again" and "Will You Meet Me Little Darlin,'" while Smiley Burnette did two of his compositions, "Trombone Song" and "Someone Swell," the latter written with Hank Penny. In this one, lawman Steve Gordon (Starrett) becomes the sheriff of a Nevada town after its lawman (Jack Rockwell) is murdered by an outlaw gang. With the help of deputy Smiley (Burnette), Steve hunts for the outlaws whose boss is Brady (Lane Chandler), who works for bank president Martin (Davison Clark). When the bank is robbed, the Durango Kid recovers the money and returns it to Martin. Steve and Smiley later find raw diamonds on the banker's land. Martin sells shares of the area only to find out the diamonds are fake ones planted by Brady. When the two men face off, Brady knocks out Martin, kidnaps his daughter Jennifer (Doris Houck) and tries to escape with the bank's money. The Durango Kid rescues Jennifer and, after proving that Brady seeded Martin's land with fake diamonds, he captures the crook and his gang.

Issued in July, 1946, *The Desert Horseman* had Steve Godfrey (Starrett) out to clear his name after being framed for the robbery of a cavalry paymaster. He comes to see his friend, rancher Tom Jarvis (Bud Osborne), who was also framed for the crime, but finds he has been murdered. At the Jarvis ranch he meets the new owner, the murdered man's niece, Mary Ann (Adelle Roberts), and the cook, Smiley (Burnette), an old friend. Jarvis' lawyer, Sam Treadway (Richard Bailey), is working with outlaw Rex Young (John Merton) in a scheme to force Mary Ann to sell them her ranch but when their gang attempts to harass the young woman, they are run off by the Durango Kid. Durango also foils Young's attempt to force Mary Ann to sign over a quick claim deed to her property and later Steve becomes suspicious of Treadway. One of the lawyer's cohorts (Riley Hill) finds a wanted poster in Steve's belongings and Gordon is arrested by the sheriff (Jack Kirk). When Smiley finds out the lawyer has plans to meet Mary Ann in the hills, he helps Steve break jail. Smiley and the ranch hands then capture Young and his outfit as the Durango Kid fights it out with Treadway and saves Mary Ann's life. This outing featured music by Walt Shrum and the Colorado Hillbillies, a group which included Tex Williams. They performed "I Wish I Could Be a Singing Cowboy," with an unbilled female vocalist, and "There's a Tear in Your Eye," written by Shrum and Robert Hoag, while Burnette contributed his self-penned "He Was an Amateur Once" and "Ring the Bell."

The next month saw the release of *Heading West*, with music by Hank Penny and His Plantation Boys who did the traditional "Sally Goodin'" and "Bless Your Heart," composed by band members Penny and Harold Hensley. Burnette also did two of his own songs, "The Old Ice Cream Freezer" and "Scaredy Cat Blues." Here Indian agent Steve Randall (Starrett) and his pal Smiley (Burnette) ride to Bonanza City where Steve's friend, mining business co-owner Jim Mallory (Hal Taliaferro), sells out to his partner Rance Hudson (Norman Willis). Rance hires Curley Curlew (Bud Geary) and his brother Red (Frank McCarroll) to rob and kill Mallory and after doing so the two refuse to give Hudson the money. When the Curlew brothers try to rob a mine gold shipment, they are stopped by the Durango Kid. Later, Steve and Smiley volunteer to ride shotgun for mine owner Sam Parker's (Nolan Leary) next shipment. Steve and Smiley find the Curlews' hideout and the Durango Kid takes some of their money to Hudson, who then vows revenge on the brothers. During a gun battle between the two rival gangs, the Durango Kid takes their gold and gives it to Parker as Hudson's men wipe the Curlew bunch. Hudson then has his gang rob Parker's stagecoach. When he tries to escape with the gold, he is killed by the Durango Kid in a shootout.

The fall of 1946 brought *Landrush*, a tepid tale about land surveyor Steve Harmon (Starrett) assigned to work on government land (known as Free Territory) which is also the hideout of Claw Hawkins (Bud Geary) and his gang. The outlaws want to keep a settlers' wagon train out of the area and they attack and rob the group but are routed by the Durango Kid. In the nearby town of Border Plain, newspaper editor Jake Parker (Emmett Lynn) wants the badge of Sheriff Collins (Bud Osborne), whom he believes is in cahoots with Hawkins; he is supported by dentist-carpenter Smiley (Burnette). When Hawkins uses marked bills from a robbery to try and bribe Jake, the newspaperman rejects the offer. He is beaten and his office ransacked by the gang, who are run off by Steve and Smiley. The Durango Kid then breaks up the gang and saves Jake's daughter Mary (Doris Houck) from their clutches. Later the gang tries to top homesteaders from staking claims in the Free Territory by starting a brush fire but Steve puts it out and as the Durango Kid he chases Hawkins and his men to their hideout. Garvey (Stephen Barclay), a gang member, turns on Claw and kills him and then is arrested by the Durango Kid. This time around the music was provided by Ozie Waters and His Colorado Rangers with public domain material like Benjamin Russell Hanby's "Darling Nellie Grey" and Stephen Foster's "De Camptown Races" and "Oh! Susanna," while Burnette did his "Dentist Song." Footage from the feature was later reused in *Streets of Ghost Town* (1950).

Ozie Waters and his group were back performing "Louisville Lady" and "The Trail That Has No End" in the November, 1946, release, *Terror Trail*. In this one Burnette sang his own numbers, "Peg Leg Bandit" and "Way Down Low." It had Red Butte saloon owner Duke Catlett (Lane Chandler) fomenting tensions between cattlemen and sheepherders as he plans to swindle Karen Kemp (Barbara Pepper) and her brother Rocky (Elvin Field) by having them robbed by his cohort Waco (Ted Mapes). The Durango Kid thwarts the robbery and later his alter ego, rancher Steve Haverley (Starrett), stops at Smiley's (Burnette) trading wagon to visit with his old friend. While Catlett decides to go ahead with his sheep deal with Karen, rancher Matson (Zon Murray) tells Steve that sheep men are infiltrating their lands and he wants a range war. Steve, who preaches moderation, suspects that someone besides the sheep herders is behind the trouble and he becomes suspicious of Rocky who has made an alliance with Waco and his men. Posing as a guard, Durango finds out that Catlett plans to rustle Karen's sheep herd. When the saloon owner tries to get Karen to help him rob Steve, she refuses and is made a prisoner. Smiley rescues Karen and they ride to warn Steve and stop the gang as Rocky is nearly killed during a stampede but is saved by the Durango Kid. Durango, Smiley and the combined cattle and sheep ranchers round up the Catlett gang as Rocky vows to give up lawlessness.

The Durango Kid series closed out 1946 with a poor effort called *The Fighting Frontiersman* in which Ranger Steve Reynolds (Starrett) and Smiley (Burnette) come to the town of Twin Forks at the behest of saloon girl Dixie (Helen Mowery) following the abduction of prospector Cimarron Dobbs (Emmett Lynn), who had found gold left in the area by the army of Santa Ana. Dobbs has been kidnapped by saloon owner John Munro (Robert Filmer), who orders his gang to kill any strangers coming into the town. As Steve and Smiley post a reward for information on the whereabouts of Cimarron, Munro offers Dixie half of the treasure if she will find out its location from the prospector. After convincing the old

Poster for *The Fighting Frontiersman* (Columbia, 1946).

cheaply made and mediocre western series, it captured the fancy of the public and in 1946 Starrett was ranked number six in the *Motion Picture Herald*'s annual poll of top money-making cowboy stars, up one notch from the previous year. The 1946 *Boxoffice* poll returned him to the top ten (he had not made the list for 1945). Except for a no-show in 1949, Starrett would remain in eighth, ninth or tenth position in the *Boxoffice* poll through 1952 while he would remain in sixth position in the *Motion Picture Herald* poll through 1949, going to seventh in 1950, up to fourth in 1951 and ninth in 1952. Smiley Burnette also made the two trade paper polls for his work in the Durango series. The *Motion Picture Herald* listed him in fifth place in 1946, seventh in 1947, ninth from 1948 through 1950, and seventh again in 1951 and 1952. *Boxoffice* had him sixth from 1946 through 1948, eighth in 1949 and 1950, seventh in 1951 and eighth again in 1952.

There were nine low-budget Durango Kid releases in 1947. As Don Miller noted in *Hollywood Corral* (1976), "[T]he Durango Kid series became cheap. Not the kind of raw cheapness of the earlier, war-restricted Starretts, when the action made up for it; rather, a kind of unpleasant tackiness that skimped on sets, action and production niceties. [Director Ray] Nazarro kept the films moving, but toward no particular goal. The Durango films soon became merely 55 minutes of milling around." Regarding the two series stars, Miller noted, "Starrett had become so firmly rooted in his Western milieu that he could hardly make a false step, and indeed he became a saving grace. Burnette tried hard, but his comedy became more puerile with each film."

The initial 1947 series release, *South of the Chisholm Trail*, was a reworking of Columbia's big-budget *Texas* (1941), which starred William Holden, Claire Trevor, Glenn Ford and George Bancroft and was directed by George Marshall. Derwin Abrahams helmed this one-hour version which told of the coming of the railroad to Abilene, Kansas, in the 1870s. During a celebration put on by promoter Big Jim Grady (Frank Sully), horseshoe peddler Smiley (Burnette) is nearly injured in a wrestling match before being rescued by his pal Steve Haley (Starrett). When Smiley is falsely accused of robbery, the Durango Kid finds the stolen loot, frees him and later returns the

man she is in league with the Durango Kid, Dixie tells Cimarron to draw a map to the treasure, but she is followed by Durango who sets Dobbs free. Smiley and several townsmen defeat the gang in a shootout while Munro dies in an explosion he set to kill Durango. Steve then tells the citizens of the town the treasure will be used to improve the area. Hank Newman and the Georgia Crackers performed Bob Newman's "Following the Trail" in the film along with two more public domain songs, Stephen Foster's "Old Folks at Home" and "Little Brown Jug" by Joseph E. Winner. Burnette also did a trio of his own ditties, "Coyote Chorus," "Don't Be Mad at Me" and "Swamp Woman Blues."

Although the Durango Kid was basically a

Steve and the ranchers, the gang is killed and Walker is arrested.

Jock Mahoney, who first doubled for Charles Starrett in *Frontier Gunlaw*, and had since mostly replaced Ted Mapes as the star's stuntman, had a featured role as one of George Chesebro's henchmen; he had made his series acting debut in *The Fighting Frontiersman* playing an outlaw. Also in the supporting cast was Fred F. Sears, who would also work as a dialogue coach and then in 1949 become a director. Hank Newman and the Georgia Crackers provided the songs "Down in Abilene" and "I'd Learn to Yodel" while Burnette sang the traditional "Frog Went a Courtin'" and a trio of his own songs, "I Got the Sillies," "I'd Make a Hit with You" and "King of Pain."

March of 1947 saw the release of *The Lone Hand Texan* which had the Durango Kid coming to the aid of oilman Sam Jason (Fred F. Sears), whose drilling projects are being sabotaged by outlaws. Durango is really cowboy Steve Driscoll (Starrett), a friend of Sam's. Steve asks financial aid from rich rancher Clarabelle Adams (Mary Newton), a widow who has caught the eye of store clerk Smiley (Burnette), much to the chagrin of his employer, Hattie Hatfield (Maudie Prickett). Clarabelle refuses Steve's request and after he finds out she has been contacted by a big oil company, he begins to suspect she is working with her foreman Scanlon (George Chesebro) in putting Jason out of business so she can take over his operations. While Smiley refuses to believe Steve about Clarabelle, she tells Scanlon to kill Boomer Kildea (Robert Stevens), a wildcatter who has gone to work for Jason. Durango saves Boomer and then helps Sam in calling a town meeting to raise funds to save his business. When Steve and Sam try to take the money invested by the locals, they are robbed by Scanlon in the guise of the Durango Kid. Steve then becomes Durango and chases the impersonator to Clarabelle's ranch

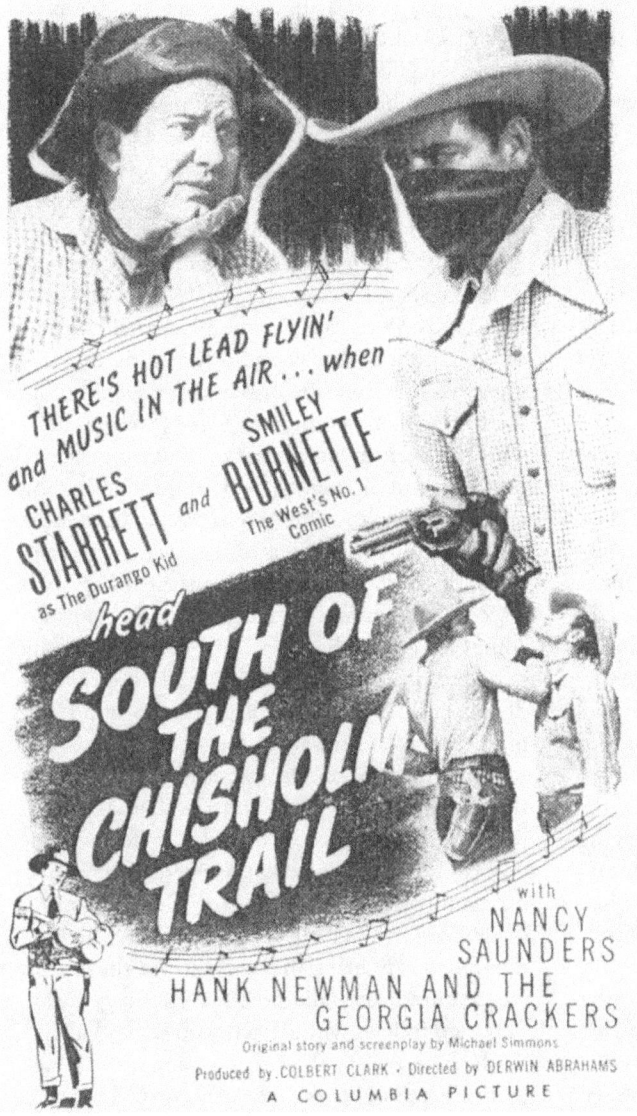

Poster for *South of the Chisholm Trail* (Columbia, 1947).

money. While Steve accepts rancher Pop Grant's (Frank LaRue) offer to help local ranchers fight an outlaw gang, Smiley goes to work for veterinarian Doc Walker (George Chesebro), one of the leaders of the crooks. When Pop is murdered at a cattlemen's meeting, both Smiley and Steve, who has been offered a rustling job by Walker, realize the vet is involved in the lawless activities. When he finds out that Grady is the brains behind the outlaws, Steve accepts Walker's offer and is forced to shoot Big Jim. Walker and his gang then try to rob the cattle exchange but in a shootout with

where a gunfight ensues. Smiley arrives with reinforcements and Clarabelle, Scanlon and their men are arrested as Jason's oil well brings in a gusher. Mustard and Gravy appeared as the entertainer pals of Smiley who aid him in helping Durango capture the crooks and they performed "Birthday Song" and "We Had a Big Time" in the feature while Burnette sang his own compositions "Never Say 'Love You' on a Postcard" and "Smart Aleck Crow." During the shooting of this feature, Starrett became a real-life hero when he was able to maneuver a stagecoach he was driving from slamming into a group of extras after the horses were spooked.

West of Dodge City, one of the low points of the Durango Kid series, came out in March of 1947, just a few weeks after *The Lone Hand Texan*. Mustard and Gravy were back singing "The Circus Parade" and "Satchel Up and Go" and Burnette contributed two songs he wrote, "Can't Cry for Laughin'" and "Cricket Song." This arid production told of the murder of rancher John Avery (Nolan Leary) by Henry Hardison (Fred F. Sears), a corrupt merchant who wanted Avery's land for a power project reservoir. Surveyor Steve Ramsey (Starrett), who had been hired by Avery, saw the attack by outlaws on the stagecoach carrying Avery and Hardison and in Silver Bend, newspaperman Smiley (Burnette) accuses the businessman of being behind Avery's killing. After Hardison claims Avery was in favor of the reservoir, Steve tells Smiley that the murdered man never agreed to the project. When Smiley prints an article disputing Hardison's claim, the merchant's henchman Borger (I. Stanford Jolley) and his men try to take over the newspaper office but are run off by the Durango Kid. While Steve tells the locals that the Avery ranch will not serve as a reservoir, the murdered man's son Danny (Glenn Stuart) wants to sell Hardison the property but is opposed by his sister Anne (Nancy Saunders). Hardison then frames Danny for a robbery and has him arrested; his men terrorize Anne into selling the property. The Durango Kid orders Hardison out of town and the crook decides to flood the Avery ranch. He manages to carry out his plan but is nearly drowned himself before being saved by Durango. The merchant is arrested, Danny is set free, and the Avery ranch is saved.

In *Law of the Canyon* (April, 1947), government agent Steve Langtry (Starrett) pretends to be a meek merchant planning to open a business in Jackson City. He is robbed and wounded by the Hood gang but is rescued by prospector Smiley (Burnette) and taken into town where he is treated by Dr. Middleton (Fred F. Sears). Since the local sheriff, Coleman (George Chesebro), cannot perform his duties due to ill health, the doctor advises Steve to pay the ransom on his stolen supply wagons. The sheriff's daughter, Mary (Nancy Saunders), tells Steve to resist the blackmail attempt as the Durango Kid saves his incoming replacement wagons from the outlaws, as well as rescuing the lawman's young son Spike (Buzz Henry), who has been pursuing the outlaw gang. Steve, however, ends up being jailed for not fighting the crooks but Smiley helps him to escape. Both Steve and Smiley are suspicious of the doctor and Smiley replaces the serum in his medical bag with water. Gang member Fletcher (Zon Murray) comes to believe that Steve and Durango are the same person. When Steve goes back to Dr. Middleton to be treated for his gunshot wound, the physician gives him an injection and Steve pretends to lose consciousness. Middleton, who is the leader of the outlaws, and Fletcher take Steve to their hideout but are spotted by Smiley, who reports to the sheriff, who has recovered from being drugged by the doctor. Smiley, Coleman and a posse head to the gang's hideout where the Durango Kid is fighting the outlaws and the crooks are captured; the fake doctor makes a getaway. Durango follows Middleton, who falls off a cliff. With the outlaw gang behind bars, Steve heads to another assignment. For this entry, Texas Jim Lewis and His Lone Star Cowboys entertained with "I'm Riding the Trail Back Home" and "Way Back in Grandpa's Day," both composed by Lewis, while Burnette did two more of his ditties, "Huntin' Trouble" and "With My Luck."

The late spring of 1947 saw the release of *Prairie Raiders* on which Derwin Abrahams took over as director. Ozie Waters and His Colorado Rangers returned to perform "My Country and You Dear" and "Roll on Little Dogie," and Burnette did "Nasty Rabbits" and "The Thieving Burro," which he composed. Here Starrett is another government agent, Steve Bolton, who leases Bronc Masters' (Robert Scott) government land in Whispering Range in order to round up wild mustangs for the Army. Bronc, however, thinks Steve has lied to him when realtor Spud Henley (Hugh Prosser) comes up with a lease from the Secretary of the Interior on the land, as he plans to sell the animals to fertilizer and glue factories. When Spud's men try to stop Steve from contacting Washington about the matter, they are run off by the Durango Kid, who takes Henley's lease. The gang is thwarted by Durango when they plan to attack Steve; Spud orders them to stampede a horse herd into town and load them into boxcars. Masters, however, sets the mustangs free as Durango meets with Meeker (Sam Flint), the interior secretary, who is visiting the town. Meeker tells him that Henley's lease is a fake. Durango rides to the Masters ranch where Bronc is about to be arrested for horse theft by the sheriff (Steve Clark), upon a complaint by Henley. Durango shows the lawman the forged document and then beats Henley in a fight. Smiley Burnette basically had a secondary role as Masters' ranch hand while leading lady Nancy Saunders had even less to do as Bronc's fiancée.

Derwin Abrahams also directed the next two Durango Kid releases, *The Stranger from Ponca City* and *Riders of the Lone Star*, both released in the summer of 1947. The former, although a Columbia production, was partially filmed at the Providencia Ranch at Universal City and brought back Texas Jim Lewis and His Lone Star Cowboys performing Lewis' "Hootenanny Annie" and Cindy Walker's "Hill Billy Lil," while Burnette did a trio of his silly ditties, "Catfish Take a Look at That Worm," "Law and Order" and "Top It." The plot had Ponca City being divided between law-abiding citizens and outlaws with Steve Larkin (Starrett) arriving in the area to buy a ranch, although café owner Smiley (Burnette) warns him against the transaction. When Steve captures two outlaws about to attack Sheriff Tug Carter (Paul Campbell), he is offered the lawman's job by merchant Carmody (Forrest Taylor), but he refuses. Steve goes to the ranch to purchase it from realtor Terry Saunders (Virginia Hunter) and later the Durango Kid comes to Terry's rescue when outlaws try to rob her. The realtor then goes to Carmody's store in order to register the ranch sale and Flip Dugan (Jim Diehl), a gunman, tries to stop her but is thwarted by Durango, who then escapes attack by the outlaws. After Steve is ambushed by the gang, he, Smiley and Texas Jim (Texas Jim Lewis) look for clues and find a broken spur which belongs to Dugan. Again escaping from the gang, the masked man returns to his alter ego Steve, who tells Carmody he plans to have a party at his ranch for all the citizens. During the festivities, Carmody overhears Steve tell the sheriff he thinks the outlaws will try to rustle cattle during the party. Since he is the leader of the gang, Carmody goes to tell his men and is followed by Steve, Smiley, the sheriff and some ranchers. The lawman and his men arrest the gang and Durango captures Carmody.

The second summer 1947 release, *Riders of the Lone Star*, came out in August. It featured Curly Williams and His Georgia Peach Pickers performing "Let Me By" and "Oh Monah," with Burnette doing "Grandpa Frog" and "Prairie Dog Lament," which he wrote. Here Starrett is Ranger Steve Mason, who arrives at the Gold Rock Mine with his friend Smiley (Burnette), a singer-magician. After being attacked by outlaws, they meet the mine's owner, Doris McCormick (Virginia Hunter), and teenager Mike Morton (Mark Dennis), the ward of alcoholic Faro (George Chesebro). The boy has been told that his father was an outlaw but he does not believe the story and wants to be reunited with him. Mike is kidnapped by crooks, then saved by the Durango Kid. As Smiley and some musicians (Curly Williams and His Georgia Peach Pickers) put on a show for the miners, Steve comes to suspect that Murdock (Steve Darrell) might be Mike's father since he is using the man's rifle. In reality, Murdock is after money stolen years before by Morton and he believes the outlaw is the Durango Kid. At Mike's birthday party, Faro gives him a map showing the location of the hidden loot and the boy is abducted by Murdock's gang. Durango is told by Faro where the money is stashed and he follows the crooks. During a shootout, Faro, who is really Morton, takes a bullet aimed at Mike as Durango and the sheriff (Eddie Parker) round up the gang. *The Hollywood Reporter* stated that *Riders of the Lone Star* would be the last Durango feature but apparently Columbia had a change of heart since the series ran for another five years.

Ray Nazarro resumed directing the Durango Kid series with *Buckaroo from Powder River*, released in October, 1947. This one had cowpoke

Steve Lacey (Starrett) pretending to be hired gunman McCall (Frank McCarroll), after taking from the badman a letter in which he is offered a job by gang leader Pop Ryland (Forrest Taylor). Pop has been persuaded by his sons Clint (Douglas D. Coppin) and Dave (Casey MacGregor) to hire McCall to murder his rebellious stepson Tommy (Paul Campbell), who refuses to go along with their scheme to steal counterfeit territorial bonds. Joining the Ryland gang, Steve uses his Durango Kid disguise to stop a holdup and then he fakes killing Tommy, whom he takes to a hideout where the young man's sweetheart, Mollie (Eve Miller), waits for him. Clint suspects Steve of being the Durango Kid and he and the gang capture barber Smiley (Burnette), a friend of Lacey's, and try to force a confession out of him only to be thwarted by the masked man. While searching the Ryland house for proof of a counterfeiting operation, Steve is forced to kill Clint. Pop pretends to surrender, tries to kill Steve and is himself shot. With the rest of the gang under arrest, Tommy plans to marry Mollie. Again Burnette sang two of his songs, "Cecil Could See What He Wanted to See" and "Sure Sounds Good to Me," while the Cass County Boys, who usually worked with Gene Autry, did "When I Saw Sweet Nellie Home" and the traditional "Carry Me Back To Old Virginny" by James A. Bland. The feature also had Ted Mapes back as Starrett's stunt double.

By this time, stock footage from previous Durango Kid features was beginning to show up in new series entries, never more blatantly than in the final 1947 release, *Last Days of Boot Hill*, which used many scenes from *Both Barrels Blazing* to flesh out its slim plotline. In Sunset Pass, Texas, Treasury agent Steve Duncan (Starrett) shows up looking for government gold stolen by Lucky Thorpe (Alan Bridge), who was tried and hung after being captured by the Durango Kid. Lucky's widow, Clara Brent (Mary Newton), who is also searching for the gold, blames the masked man for her husband's death. Clara enlists the aid of ranch foreman McCoy (J. Courtland Lytton), who feels the money rightfully belongs to Lucky's daughter Paula (Virginia Hunter), who arrives with her fiancé Frank Rayburn (Paul Campbell). In town, Steve starts a saloon brawl with badman Bronc Peters (Robert J. Wilke) in order to get thrown in jail so he can have a secret talk with Deputy Sheriff Smiley (Burnette). He relates to Smiley how Thorpe stole the government gold and used prospector Grubstake (Emmett Lynn) as a front in exchanging it for cash. When Grubstake finds out what Thorpe is doing, he agrees to aid the Durango Kid in trapping him, but the prospector is murdered. Since Steve believes Thorpe hid the gold on his ranch, he goes to McCoy and gets a job. After Paula and Frank take over the ranch, Clara and her brother, Reed Brokaw (Bill Free), hire a gunman (John L. Cason) to kill the young woman but she is saved by Durango. Steve tells Paula and Frank he is a government agent after the money, which is eventually found by Clara and Reed. Durango stops Clara from murdering Paula, the siblings are arrested and the gold is sent to Washington. The Cass County Boys were back singing "Inside Looking Out" and "Texas Belle" while Burnette contributed "Giddy Up Jericho" and "On My Way Back Home."

Eight Durango Kid features were released in 1948, beginning with *Six-Gun Law* in January. Barry Shipman's screenplay had rancher Steve Norris (Starrett) thinking he shot the local sheriff, Brackett (Ethan Laidlaw), after being falsely accused of cattle theft. Actually the shooting was a ruse set up by Boss Decker (Hugh Prosser), the leader of an outlaw gang, to control Steve (the gun Steve used contained blanks). Boss then makes Steve the new sheriff and forces him to carry out his will as his gang murders Brackett. Steve, who loses faith with the locals by working with Decker, decides to keep the job until he can turn himself over to the soon to be arriving U.S. marshal, Reed (Pierce Lyden). When Decker orders his men to rob the bank, the money is taken first by the Durango Kid and left with Jeff's close friend, Bret Wallace (George Chesebro), who is shot by the outlaws. Before dying, Wallace rides to photographer Smiley's (Burnette) house and tells him that he was shot by Decker's men. Decker blames Wallace's son, Jim (Paul Campbell), for the bank robbery and orders Steve to arrest him. The sheriff carries out the orders but lets Jim's sister June (Nancy Saunders) get away so she can inform Smiley about the arrest. Durango hands Jim over to Smiley for safekeeping and Decker then tries to have Steve murdered when he finds out he plans to work with Marshal Reed.

He also orders Reed killed but Steve gets him safely to town where the U.S. marshal hears Decker and the gang own up to killing Brackett, and Durango brings in Decker. For this affair, Curly Clements and His Rodeo Rangers performed "Cowboy Shindig" and Burnette contributed "Around the Clock" and "If I Were the Boss."

J. Benton Cheney, who wrote a number of the "Hopalong Cassidy" (q.v.) features, contributed a fairly interesting whodunit script for the series' next outing, *Phantom Valley*, released in February, 1948. Ozie Waters and His Colorado Rangers made a return singing the traditional ballads "The Big Corral" and "Streets of Laredo" as Burnette did his own "I'll Be Glad to See You." Phantom Valley marshal Steve Collins (Starrett) comes to the rescue of stableman Smiley (Burnette) who is being pursued by marauders after he tried to stop them from attacking homesteader Jim Durant (Sam Flint) and Jancy Littlejohn (Virginia Hunter), the daughter of attorney Sam Littlejohn (Joel Friedkin). Jim and Jancy had just removed the homesteaders' funds from the local bank and the outlaws kidnapped Jim. Steve and Smiley find Jancy and return her to town. Rancher Bob Reynolds (Robert Filmer) is blamed for the robbery and later the Durango Kid finds Durant's wagon at the man's home. Steve arranges for a bank loan for the homesteaders so they can pay their taxes. When he and Smiley get the money, they are attacked by outlaws but elude them. When rancher Ben Theibold (Fred F. Sears) finds out there is oil on his land in Pennsylvania, he is shot and badly wounded and the outlaws attack other ranchers, blaming the crimes on the homesteaders. The capture of gang member Frazer (Zon Murray) by Steve proves the homesteaders are innocent but the outlaw is shot before he can reveal the name of his boss. Suspects Reynolds and Littlejohn are arrested but quickly set free by gang member Crag Parker (Mikel Conrad) who plans to kill them but is stopped by Durango. Telling the two men to keep undercover at Deep Springs, Steve and Smiley inform Jancy that her father has been killed but the next day Steve goes to the outlaws' hideout and finds she is their leader. Jancy tells Steve that Sam is not her real father and she plans to take control of Phantom Valley. Before she can kill the lawman, Smiley, Reynolds and Littlejohn arrive. When Jancy tries to escape, Crag accidentally kills her. The outlaws are arrested and Smiley is made the valley's deputy marshal.

West of Sonora, issued in March, 1948, featured The Sunshine Boys, a group which would appear in a half-dozen Durangos as well as tour with Starrett in his Durango Kid stage act. In this film they performed "Dese Bones Gonna Rise Again" and "The Glory Trail" while Burnette did "I Ain't Gonna Do Tomorrow" and "Lil Indian." The feud between the Clinton and Murphy families makes up the plot of this outing, with Steve Rollins (Starrett) being made a deputy sheriff by his friend, Sico City sheriff Jeff Clinton (George Chesebro). Clinton is trying to rescue his granddaughter Penny (Anita Castle), who has been kidnapped by her other grandfather, hook-handed outlaw Black Murphy (Steve Darrell). Steve saves badly injured prospector Jack Bascom (Emmett Lynn), who has just made a gold strike, from marauders and takes him to Murphy's camp, where his life is saved by an operation. Jeff tries to make peace between Jeff and Murphy, not knowing that Jeff's brother Sandy (Hal Taliaferro) is behind the lawlessness blamed on Murphy. When Sandy tries to ambush Murphy, the Durango Kid thwarts the effort and takes Penny back to Jeff. Wanting the gold claim for himself, Sandy murders Bascom; Murphy, blamed for the crime, is arrested by Steve after he demands Penny's return. Sandy and his two cohorts (Robert J. Wilke, Lynn Farr) try to get Murphy lynched but are stopped by the Durango Kid. When Steve finds out that Bascom has left his gold claim to Anita, he asks his pal Smiley (Burnette) to protect her as Sandy burns down the local land registration office hoping to destroy proof of the child's gold claim. Steve, however, has removed the records. Sandy plans to murder both Jeff and Penny in order to get control of the mine. The Durango Kid stops Sandy from shooting Jeff and Murphy and then chases him into town where Sandy plans to murder the little girl. Durango captures one of Sandy's henchmen, who tells him his boss murdered Jack Bascom. As Sandy is about to shoot Penny, the Durango Kid stops him and the child is reunited with her grandfathers, who end their feud. One amusing scene had Burnette filling in for a no-show female singer and dressed to the hilt as "Fifi Latour."

Whirlwind Riders, issued in the spring of 1948, dealt with the brief period in the early 1870s when the Texas Rangers were disbanded and replaced by the corrupt state police. Western music great Doye O'Dell and the Radio Rangers performed "Give Me Texas" and the folk song "Jimmy Crack Corn" while Burnette contributed the ditties "Fiddlin' Fool" and "Lookin' Poor, Feelin' Rich." The story had former Texas Ranger Steve Lanning (Starrett), supposedly a wanted man, saving his pal, traveling repairman Smiley (Burnette), a former Ranger, from state police thugs. He does so in the guise of the masked Durango Kid. Later, in the town of Indian Springs, Steve stops bully Red Jordan (Eddie Parker), a state policeman, from roughing up youngster Tommy Ross (Little Brown Jug) and wins the friendship of the boy's father, cattleman Homer Ross (Philip Morris). When Steve and Smiley talk with newspaper editor Bill Webster (Patrick Hurst), Steve says he is working undercover to get evidence against the crooked lawmen controlled by entrepreneur Tracy Beaumont (Fred F. Sears). Beaumont cheats Homer at cards and tries to get him to front for him as the commissioner of the West Texas state police. At the same time he finds out that Steve is a wanted man and tries to enlist him in the force. The Durango Kid tells Homer to take the job so he can get evidence against Beaumont. Tommy realizes that Durango and Steve are the same person. After Durango stops the police from taking the ranchers' cattle to pay back taxes, Beaumont has his henchman Buff (Jack Ingram) dress like the masked man and rob the local bank. Tommy, however, recognizes Buff and the outlaw takes him to Beaumont; the boy admits Durango and Steve are one. The boy is taken to the outlaws' hideout where Steve rescues him as Beaumont and Buff plan to frame Durango for the holdup. Steve gets back into town in Smiley's wagon as Homer receives a letter from the state saying that the Texas Rangers have been reinstated. When Homer brings the news to Beaumont and Buff, Durango arrests the outlaws and recovers the money they have stolen. When Beaumont tries to kill the masked man, he is shot by Ross. Scripter Norman S. Hall later reworked this tale for the 1952 Gene Autry Columbia vehicle *Night Stage to Galveston*.

Released in the summer of 1948, *Blazing Across the Pecos* was a tawdry effort about outlaws using Indians to raid rancher Matt Carter's (Thomas Jackson) trading posts in order to put him out of business. Pecos Flats mayor Ace Brockway (Charles Wilson) is behind the scheme and one of his men, Buckshot (Jack Ingram), mistakenly thinks he has killed the Durango Kid. Cowboy Steve Blake (Starrett) arrives in town and stops a drunk Buckshot from shooting at a saloon run by Mike Doyle (Pat O'Malley). As a result, Brockway hires him to work as deputy sheriff under incompetent lawman Smiley (Burnette), who also runs the local beanery. Newspaper editor Jim Traynor (Paul Campbell) informs Steve that he believes the mayor is giving rifles to Chief Bear Claw (Chief Thundercloud) and his braves so they will attack Carter and force him out of the area. After a raid on Carter's wagon by the Indians, the Durango Kid takes the rifles promised to Bear Claw. Buckshot, who thinks Steve and Traynor are working together, hires gunman Ballard (Frank McCarroll) to kill the newspaperman. When Ballard tries to murder Jim, he is shot by Steve. Carter plans to sell his cattle in order to get more supplies for his trading posts. Jim prints a story about the cattle drive and Ace and Buckshot try to steal Carter's money but are stopped by Durango. Ace then has Bear Claw and his braves rustle the herd but, using smoke signals, Durango convinces the chief to return the cattle to Carter. When Brockway finds out that Bear Claw has told the military about his part in the raids, he decides to rob Carter and make his escape, but he is captured by Steve and Smiley, who also arrest Buckshot. Leading lady Patricia White, better known as Patricia Barry, had little to do as Carter's daughter. Red Arnall and the Western Aces performed "Goin' Back to Texas" and the traditional "Crawdad Song" as Burnette contributed his tunes "That's All Brother" and "It Ain't Much Help." The comedy highlight of this anemic entry had bumbling Smiley trying to paint a sign and being scared by Steve, thus getting his foot caught in a bucket. Trying to get his foot out, he kicks the bucket off and it lands on the head of tough gunman Ballard. "Is anybody in there?" Smiley asks, as he taps on the bucket covering the outlaw's head.

Trail to Laredo, issued in the late summer of 1948, had Jim Bannon in a co-starring role; the next year, the actor would have the lead in a quartet of "Red Ryder" (q.v.) features. In this one, the Cass County Boys were back with "Flo from St. Joe Mo" and "Go West Young Lady," which they did with leading lady Virginia Maxey, while Smiley Burnette sang his "It's My Turn" and "The Yodeler." This one had the Durango Kid telling Dan Parks (Jim Bannon), co-owner of a freight operation with Walt Morgan (George Chesebro), to watch out for boxes of ringbolts. Finding one of these boxes, Dan opens it and sees that it contains gold. When Morgan finds out, he tells the sheriff (John Merton); Dan is accused of being part of a smuggling operation and is forced to go into hiding. Cowboy Steve Ellison (Starrett) comes to town looking for Dan, who is an old friend, and is followed by his partner, Smiley (Burnette), a treasury agent working undercover as a painter. Steve meets saloon girl Classy (Virginia Maxey) who is looking after Dan's son Ronnie (Tommy Ivo), Dan comes out of hiding and tells them he is being framed by Morgan, who is in league with saloon proprietor Fenton (Hugh Prosser), the head of the smugglers. The sheriff arrives and arrests Dan as Durango visits Morgan, who is later murdered by outlaw Blaze (John L. Cason) on Fenton's orders. A masked Blaze breaks Dan out of jail, and Dan is blamed for the killing of Morgan. Smiley alerts the sheriff about Blaze and the lawman leads a posse to the gang's hideout where a shootout takes place as Durango takes back the gold hidden there. In order to trap Fenton, Steve sets up a meeting with Dan but the saloon owner kidnaps Ronnie. Durango offers Fenton a deal to exchange the gold he has for cash. As the saloon owner admits his involvement in the lawlessness and the murder of Morgan, the sheriff overhears and Fenton is arrested. Ronnie is reunited with his father, who has been exonerated.

Released in the fall of 1948, *El Dorado Pass* told of cowboy Steve Clayton (Starrett) being accused of stealing $20,000 from Mexican rancher Don Martinez (Harry Vejar) during a stagecoach holdup. He is arrested and jailed, but his buddy, barber Smiley (Burnette), aids him in getting free. As the Durango Kid, Steve learns that the stolen gold is being held by another rancher, Page (Steve Darrell), who was going to sell Martinez some thoroughbred horses. Durango meets with Page and tells him he can exchange the gold for dollars. The plan goes awry, however, when Page's gang stops Steve from turning their boss and the gold over to the law. Page is killed by his own men (who think he has double-crossed them) and Steve is taken hostage as they plan to murder him and then claim the reward. Smiley follows the gang to the hideout and helps Steve to escape. The Durango Kid goes to the sheriff (Rory Mallinson) and leads him and a posse to the hideout, where the gang is captured. When Steve, who has been cleared of the robbery charges, returns the gold to Don Martinez, his daughter Dolores (Elena Verdugo) tells him to thank Durango. Shorty Thompson sang the traditional "The Yellow Rose of Texas" and Eddie Dean and Glenn Strange's classic "On the Banks of the Sunny San Juan," while Burnette performed his own "Black, Black Jack of All Trades."

The final 1948 series release, December's *Quick on the Trigger*, was a cheapjack affair with music by The Sunshine Boys who did "Better Get Down and Pray" and "Midnight Flyer" as Burnette contributed his tunes "Bugle Boy" and "Ring Eye Rhythm." The plot, such as it was, had Sheriff Steve Warren (Starrett) being tried for the murder of outlaw Fred Reed (Russell Arms). During the trial, Steve tells how he was on the trail of an outlaw gang robbing a stagecoach line owned by Nora Reed (Helen Parrish), Fred's sister. Following a holdup, Steve captured Fred but before he could name the gang leader he was shot and Nora accused him of murdering her brother. Prosecuting attorney Garvey Yager (Lyle Talbot) gets a conviction and Steve is sentenced to hang. Steve's friend Smiley (Burnette) breaks him out of jail and as the Durango Kid Steve sets out to get the evidence needed to clear his name. He learns that Yager is really a former convict who forged his law diploma and that he rigged Steve's conviction in order to get revenge because it was Steve's father, a judge, who sent him to prison. Steve then sets a trap for Yager and his henchman, surveyor Alfred Murdock (George Eldredge), and gets them to confess to Reed's killing. The two crooks are arrested and Steve resumes his lawman duties.

Eight more Durango Kid adventures appeared in theaters in 1949, beginning in February with *Challenge of the Range*. This outing used footage from a previous entry, *Galloping Thunder*, to tell its tale of cowboy Steve Roper (Starrett) becoming involved in a range war with a gang of outlaws trying to take the property of Jim Barton (Henry Hall). Barton believes rancher Cal Matson (Steve Darrell) is out to run off all the homesteaders in order to enlarge his property. In town, Steve becomes acquainted with author Smiley (Burnette), who is researching a book on range wars, and later accepts a job with the Farmer's Association after beating Reb (William [Billy] Halop), Matson's son, in a shooting contest. Following another raid, Barton and Matson have a showdown with Barton being shot and Matson arrested for his murder. The Durango Kid notices that the fatal shot was fired from another location and he later finds papers signed by farmers giving the association any vacated properties. Association members Largo (Robert Filmer) and Collins (George Chesebro) come under suspicion after Largo sends a warning to Reb that his dad will be lynched and another to the local sheriff (Pat O'Malley) saying that Reb will break his father out of jail. As a result, Steve believes the two are after the valley's water rights. When Largo tries to shoot Manson, Durango attempts to stop him but it is Collins who kills Largo. The Barton and Matson families reconcile with Reb and Judy (Paula Raymond), Barton's daughter, planning to wed. Here The Sunshine Boys vocalized "The More We Get Together" and the traditional "The Old Scrubbin' Bucket," while Burnette performed two more of his compositions, "I Kin Dance" and "My Home Town."

Desert Vigilante, issued in the spring of 1949, featured The Georgia Crackers singing "The Sky Over California" and Jimmy Wakely's "I'll Never Let You Go, Little Darlin'" as Burnette sang his "He Don't Like Work" and "I Can Be as Bad as That." Here undercover agent Steve Brooks (Starrett) investigates silver smuggling near the Mexican border town of San Feliz where he plans to see bedridden Angel (Mary Newton), the mother of Bob Gill (Paul Campbell), who was murdered during an ambush. He goes to the Lazy Z Ranch, owned by Betty Long (Peggy Stewart), to see Angel, who is a guest there, and finds the place has been searched by outlaws. In town, Steve meets with Bob's employer, lawyer Thomas Hadley (Tristram Coffin), and informs him of his mission. Outlaw Bill Martin (George Chesebro) demands that Steve give him silver which Bob was supposed to have from illegally exchanging stolen certificates for it in Mexico. A fight ensues and Steve escapes back to the Lazy Z where ranch cook Smiley (Burnette) thinks ghosts are in the cellar, although it is really the outlaws looking for missing silver certificates. They are found by Hadley and Angel, who is not really Gill's mother, the two being the leaders of the smuggling operation. Martin and his gang try to get the certificates from Hadley but they are later taken by the Durango Kid, who also saves Bob's brother Jim (Tex Harding) after Hadley tries to have him ambushed. Angel and Hadley get more silver and hide it in the ranch's cellar as Durango informs Jim of his brother's killing and says that he thinks Hadley is to blame. In an attempt to get the silver, Martin and his gang stampede the ranch's cattle but are captured by Steve and Jim. Martin escapes and shoots Hadley and Angel. Martin then tries to get away through a secret tunnel which goes into

Poster for *Desert Vigilante* (Columbia, 1949).

Mexico, but Steve follows him and on the other side of the border the outlaw is arrested by the Mexican police. As Steve rides away, Jim remains with Betty. The film marked the return of former series co-star Tex Harding; the mine sequences were shot at Bronson Caves in Hollywood's Griffith Park.

Laramie, released in May, 1949, featured the noted Victor recording artist Elton Britt, famous for his yodeling and for singing the million seller "There's a Star Spangled Banner Waving Somewhere," in the role of a singing sergeant. Taking place in 1868, it had Steve Holden (Starrett), a peace commissioner, trying to stop an Indian uprising. He visits a fort run by Colonel Dennison (Fred F. Sears), an old friend. There he meets regiment scout Cronin (Robert J. Wilke), who is behind a scheme to start an uprising in order to sell rifles to the Indian tribes. When Chief Eagle (Shooting Star) and his son Running Wolf (Jay Silverheels) come to the fort to meet with Dennison and Steve, the chief is shot and killed. Steve tries to capture the shooter but fails as Running Wolf is incarcerated. When Dennison refuses to set the young brave free, the Durango Kid lets him out of the guardhouse. Steve then enlists the aid of shoemaker Smiley (Burnette) in finding someone with a boot whose distinctive print was found near the site where the fatal shot was fired. As Cronin encourages Running Wolf and his tribe to attack the settlers, Smiley realizes that the boot he is trying to find belongs to the regiment scout. He tells Steve this news and the two, along with Dennison's son (Tommy Ivo), set up a plan to capture Cronin, who murdered the chief. When Cronin's guilt is proved to Running Wolf, and the killer arrested, the range war is averted. The feature used stock footage from *Stagecoach* (1939) with Starrett wearing an outfit to match the one worn by John Wayne in the John Ford film. (Tim Holt, Yakima Canutt and Cliff Lyons can be spotted in this stock footage.) Britt sang his popular composition "Chime Bells" along with the traditional "Mollie Darling," while Burnette performed his "The Happy Cobbler" and "Who Don't."

Released in the summer of 1949, *The Blazing Trail* featured Slim Duncan and Hank Penny performing their songs "Cheer Up" and "Want a Gal from Texas" as Burnette did his "Extra, Extra!" and "You Put Me on My Feet (When You Took Her Off My Hands)" with Duncan and Penny. Barry Shipman's script was basically a mystery set in Bradytown with Sheriff Steve Allen (Starrett) investigating the murder of Old Mike Brady (Robert Malcolm). Among the suspects are the dead man's brothers Sam (Steve Darrell) and Kirk (Steve Pendleton) and also Full House Patterson (Jock O'Mahoney), who had a falling out with Mike over a card game. The victim's will, witnessed by attorney Luke Masters (Fred F. Sears) and his niece Janet (Marjorie Stapp), along with illiterate cowpoke Jess Williams (Trevor Bardette), divided his property between the surviving brothers with Williams getting a worthless mine known as Mike's Folly. The Durango Kid suspects Sam and Williams but the bullet that killed Mike does not fit either of their guns. After asking newspaper editor Smiley (Burnette) for a sample of Mike's handwriting, Steve finds out the bullet came from Sam's weapon. Sam too is murdered as evidence that Mike's will was illegal disappears. To smoke out the culprit, Steve has Smiley print a story about gold being discovered in Sam's mine and Janet helps him to find a new will hidden in a secret panel at Brady's home. Steve tells Smiley to print the new will in his newspaper and then goes to the mine where he finds Sam and Jess. Deducing that Jess is not illiterate, Steve accuses him of murdering Brady with Luke's gun as well as writing the second will, giving him the mine. Sam is arrested and Steve then exposes the fact that the gold he thought he was loading was actually printer's type. A good deal of the plot was narrated by Starrett's character.

The next month brought *South of Death Valley*, a torpid tale of cowboy Steve Downey (Starrett) trying to find out who murdered his brother-in-law, a miner with a claim near Nugget City. Rancher Molly Tavish (Gail Davis) warns Steve not to work the dead man's mine because the cattlemen think their herds are being poisoned by pollution caused by the miners, who have unleashed tainted underground streams. When a fight starts between the ranchers and miners, it is stopped by the Durango Kid, who is told by the Tavishes to talk with the local sheriff, Smiley (Burnette). While Tommy Tavish (Richard Emory) is the main murder suspect, Steve questions miner Sam Ashton (Fred F. Sears), who gave his brother-in-law the money he needed to work his claim. Upon orders from Ashton, his men try unsuccessfully to murder Steve. Henchman Bead (Clayton Moore) does succeed in killing Tommy and places the blame on Steve. Another brother, Scotty Tavish (Lee Roberts), attempts to shoot Steve and Smiley is forced to arrest Downey, who escapes from jail and finds poison in the office of the local assayer, drunkard Mullen (Jason Robards). Bead thinks he has killed Steve, who goes into hiding as Ashton blames Scotty for his murder. The Durango Kid comes to the young man's aid and helps him and his sister make a getaway. By pretending to be a ghost, Steve gets a confession from Mullen that he is in cahoots with Ashton in putting strychnine in the local water supply. The Durango Kid and trails the outlaws to his mine where he sees them putting sacks of gold in wagons. He manages to get the drop on the gang as Smiley, Molly and Scotty arrive to help Durango capture them. Tommy Duncan and the Western All-Stars performed "Rock-A-Bye, Baby (Rock-A-Bye Jailbird)" and "Saturday Night in San Antone" while Burnette added a duo of tunes from his repertoire, "The Ever-Lovin' Marshal," done with Tommy Duncan, and "(You Won't Be Takin' It with You) When You Go."

Footage from *Galloping Thunder* appeared in another series entry, *Bandits of El Dorado*, issued in the fall of 1949. (As a consequence, Kermit Maynard ended up with two parts in the latter feature: He was a stage guard in the *Galloping Thunder* stock shots and a holdup man in new footage for *Bandits of El Dorado*.) The Barry Shipman script seemed to include some plot elements previously used in "Hopalong Cassidy" (q.v.) features as well as from Edgar Wallace's 1926 novel *The Dark Eyes of London*. The plot had Texas Ranger Captain Richard Henley (Fred F. Sears), Mexican Rurales Colonel Jose Vargas (George J. Lewis) and geologist Charles Bruton (John Dehner) headed by stagecoach to Copper City to investigate the disappearance of wanted outlaws into Mexico. A masked man murders Henley but before dying he claims the killer was Steve Carson (Starrett); this is actually all a ruse to give Carson a crime record so he can work undercover. He then goes to merchant Morgan (Clayton Moore), who at first refuses to help him and then demands money in exchange for a hideout. When entertainer Smiley (Burnette) recognizes Steve, Morgan tells his cohort Bruton that Steve may be a lawman. Steve finds out the location of the outlaws' hideout from Morgan's partner, Tucker (John Doucette), while Henley, who is dressed as a peon, warns Steve that Bruton has set a trap for him. Bruton murders Tucker for his betrayal and then captures Henley, who is rescued by Durango. The masked man fights it out with Bruton, who confesses he murdered all the escaping outlaws in his charge after taking their money. Mustard and Gravy, who appeared in blackface as Smiley's protégés, were back doing "The Last Great Day" while Burnette provided his songs "The Rich Get Richer" and "Tricky Senor."

Screenwriter Barry Shipman next penned another sagebrush whodunit for the series in *Horsemen of the Sierras*, which came to theaters in the autumn of 1949. In it, country singer T. Texas Tyler sang "Fair Weather Baby," which he wrote with Harold Hensley, and Scotty Wiseman's "Remember Me, I'm the One Who Loves You." Burnette performed his own "Tonight's My Night to Howl." The story concerned Steve Saunders (Starrett), a United States marshal, investigating the murder of a surveyor working on the Grant ranch, whose owner was supposedly murdered by foreman Ellory Webster (George Chesebro), who died during a fire. The ranch was left to juvenile Robbie Grant (Tommy Ivo), who runs away from a children's home by stealing Steve's horse and gets sanctuary in Sheriff Smiley's (Burnette) jail. The murdered man's will is being contested by several relatives, including Don Grant (Jock O'Mahoney), while the locals claim the ranch is haunted by his ghost. The Durango Kid meets with Patty McGregor (Lois Hall), the sister of the murdered surveyor, who works for hotel owner Phineas Grant (Jason Robards), another claimant to the estate. When Duke Webster (John Dehner), who also is contesting the will, tries to murder Steve, he is arrested, but is set free by Phineas, who has kidnapped Robbie. Both feuding families, the Grants and the Websters, try to find out who is pretending to be the ranch ghost but end up in a fight which is stopped by Durango, who arrests Duke and Phineas. When the masked man announces he knows there is oil on the ranch and that Duke and Phineas are in cahoots, the two men turn on each other with Duke announcing that Phineas murdered Robbie's dad and Phineas saying that Duke did away with the surveyor. Ellory, who pretended to be the ghost, reappears and Robbie gets his inheritance.

The final 1949 Durango outing, a tepid effort called *Renegades of the Sage*, took place in the post–Civil War era and had Steve Duncan (Starrett), an agent for the Secret Service, on the trail of a gang tearing down territorial telegraph lines. The main suspect is Lynn Braden (Trevor Bardette), a medical student who carried out the same kind of work for the Confederacy during the war. Steve, ambushed and left for dead by outlaws, is rescued by cowboy Smiley (Burnette) and taken to a trading post run by Braden and his daughter Ellen (Leslie Banning). Now known as Miller, the medical man tends to Steve's wounds; he later saves the life of a boy (Jerry Hunter) by performing a difficult operation. As a result, Braden tells Steve the truth about his identity and the Durango Kid gets evidence that the gang who attacked him is run by Sloper (Douglas Fowley), the brains behind the telegraph lines sabotage. Miller aids Steve in stopping the gang from attacking a supply train and during the melee Sloper dies. With Miller exonerated, Steve sets out on another case. This outing had Burnette singing his songs "Let Me Sleep" and "Pussy Foot"; "America" and "I'm Grateful for Small Favors" were also performed. *Variety*, which reviewed the film nearly a year after its initial release, said it was "heavy in the action department"; sported "a better-than-average story for a low-budget western"; and that it "provides a large dose of gunplay and a minimum of dialog."

The year 1949 saw the initial publication of the Durango Kid comic books by Magazine Enterprises. Starrett was shown on the covers either in full color photos, as in the first five issues, or insert photographs. The comics presented Durango's alter ego as Secret Service agent Steve Brand, who had a rotund sidekick named Muley Pike. (The Smiley Burnette character could not be used in the comics since the comedian has his own comic book with Fawcett.) The Durango Kid comic books were published from 1949 to 1955; in 1990, AC Comics began reprinting some of the strips. The Durango Kid was also in "Best of the West," also published by Magazine Enterprises, and "Great Western," both coming out in the early 1950s. With the demise of the Magazine Enterprises series in 1955, a Spanish-language version of the strip, "El Durango Kid," was begun by the company and these continued until 1959.

Trail of the Rustlers was the first of eight Durango Kid movies issued to theaters in 1950. Eddie Cletro and His Roundup Boys joined Burnette in providing the film's musical interludes "I Should Say," "I Wish I'd Said That" and "Shoot Me Dead for That One," all of which Smiley composed. This one had the Durango Kid earning the hatred of the Mahoney family, which is secretly trying to run off ranchers so they can control the range land around the town of Rio Perdito, by killing one of the clan as he tries to escape from jail. The dead man's brother, Chick Mahoney (Don C. Harvey), dresses like Durango and attacks the ranchers. Cowboy Steve Armitage (Starrett) finds out that Durango has been blamed for the murder of the father of Mary Ellen (Gail Davis) and Tod Hartley (Tommy Ivo). Pretending sympathy, Mrs. Mahoney (Mira McKinney), the mother of the clan, comforts the siblings. Meanwhile, Steve meets old pal Smiley (Burnette), who has received an authorization letter permitting him to buy ranch land around the town. The Mahoneys try to kill Steve but are stopped by the Durango Kid, who is seen by Tod; the masked man is able to convince him that he did not murder his father. Durango robs a stagecoach carrying money for Smiley to purchase land but it is later found by Mrs. Mahoney in Steve's possessions. The money is given to Smiley while Tod finds a secret river on his family's ranch and he tells the Mahoneys. The old lady orders cohorts Bob (Chuck Roberson) and Jake (Boyd "Red" Morgan) to abduct the boy and hide him until the family can get control of the Hartley spread. The Durango Kid rescues Tod and then stops Chick, who is dressed to look like him, from forcing Smiley to carry out the sale. The Mahoney family is put behind bars and the local water problem is solved as Tod plans to be like Durango by dressing like him and riding a horse called Raider Jr. (Raider was the masked man's horse, his alter ego Steve rode a steed named Bullet and Smiley's horse was called Ringeye.)

Next came April's *Outcasts of Black Mesa*, which used stock footage in telling its story of mine owner Steve Norman (Starrett) being

Martha Hyer and Charles Starrett in *Outcast of Black Mesa* (Columbia, 1950).

framed for the murder of his partner Walt Dorn (William Gould) after the man's daughter, Ruth (Martha Hyer), says she saw him try to kill a third partner, Ted Thorp (Lane Chandler). Steve manages to get away from the sheriff (Stanley Andrews) and as the Durango Kid he asks photographer Smiley (Burnette) to get information on Dayton (William Haade), a gunfighter he suspects did the killing. Although Dayton proves to be a wanted killer, Steve is arrested, tried and sentenced to hang; Smiley gets him out of jail. As the Durango Kid he learns that Dayton was hired by phony local doctor Andrew Vanig (Richard Bailey), who wanted the three mine partners out of the way so he could marry Ruth and obtain the property. Durango captures Dayton after a showdown but Vanig escapes only to be killed in a stagecoach wreck. Ozie Waters was back to sing "Just Sittin' Around in Jail" while Burnette did his songs "Donkey Engine" and "Nobody Fires the Boss." *Variety* noted that the feature "lines up the proper amount of chases and fights for the Saturday matinee juv trade" but added, "Production shaves the budget mighty close, tossing in quite a bit of footage from other Starrett pix as well as reprising a number of new scenes shot for this one...."

In June 1950 came *Texas Dynamo*, a mild affair with Slim Duncan returning with the song "Let's Rally One and All" as Burnette contributed his compositions "Fickle Finger of Fate" and "Kitty Loved the Calliope." Steve Drake (Charles Starrett) arrives in Beckton, Colorado, at the behest of its founder, only to find him murdered. The crime was committed by vigilante leader Stanton (John Dehner), who convinces the dead man's daughter Julie Beck (Lois Hall) to become the town's mayor. Once elected, she institutes Stanton's plan that prohibits all but members of a citizens' league, who are all vigilantes, from carrying weapons. When the Durango Kid is seen, he is blamed for the killing as Stanton hires the Texas Dynamo (Ethan Laidlaw), a gunman, to murder him. The Dynamo, however, dies after being bitten by a snake and Steve pretends to be the gunfighter as Stanton and his men frame Bill Beck (Jock O'Mahoney), Julie's brother, on a bank robbery charge. Durango then enlists the help of his friend Smiley (Burnette) in proving that Stanton and the vigilantes are behind the lawlessness and Durango makes Stanton confess to the killing.

Streets of Ghost Town, issued in August, 1950, was akin to a picture puzzle in that it was made up of whole parts and bits and pieces of previous Durango films strung together with new footage to create a surprisingly entertaining programmer. Most of the old footage came from *Gunning for Vengeance* and *Landrush*; the main musical number, Ozie Waters and His Colorado Rangers singing "Oh Susanna," was also lifted from the latter title. The only other song in the film was Burnette's rendition of the traditional "Streets of Laredo" replete with new lyrics by the comic. Containing tinges of mystery and horror, the story told of undercover agent Steve Woods (Starrett) coming to the ghost town of Shadeville with his friend Smiley (Burnette) and Sheriff Dodge (Stanley Andrews) in search of over one million dollars in stolen funds. They suspect that Bart Selby (Frank Fenton) and his gang are also looking for the money taken from them in a double cross by outlaw Bill Donner (George Chesebro). Steve relates to the sheriff how Selby and his gang stole the money with Donner and another gang member, Wicks (John L. Cason), hiding it in Devil's Cave in a Spanish mine vault. Donner, who left Wicks to die in the vault, is later captured by the Durango Kid and sent to prison but escapes. He is caught by Selby and is blinded for refusing to reveal the location of the treasure. He makes his way to Dusty Creek and is sent back to prison where he supposedly died in a fire. That night, however, Smiley thinks he sees Donner's ghost and the three men spy Tommy Donner (Brown Jug), the supposedly dead man's nephew, who is also looking for the gold. The boy takes their supplies so they head back to Dusty Creek where they meet Tommy's sister Doris (Mary Ellen Kay), who insists on going back with them to Shadeville. Steve, Smiley, Dodge, Doris and Dodge's deputy Kirby (Jack Ingram) go to the ghost town where Tommy tells his uncle, who is still alive, he has found the mine entrance. Selby and his gang show up and shoot Donner, and Selby makes Tommy take him to the mine. The Durango Kid rescues the boy but the gang captures Smiley and Dodge. After Tommy is reunited with Doris, Kirby takes them both to Selby. Returning with them to the vault door, Selby finds the now mad Donner in the vault and murders the blind man as Doris and Tommy get away and Durango kills Selby. Durango promises Tommy a reward for finding the gold, which will be returned to the U.S. mint. In several scenes, Jock Mahoney can be easily spotted doubling for Starrett as the Durango Kid.

Having previously directed *Desert Vigilante* and *Horsemen of the Sierras* in 1949, Fred F. Sears returned to helm the next series entry, *Across the Badlands*, released in the fall of 1950. He would direct ten of the remaining seventeen Durango features, the other seven being done by Ray Nazarro. A native of Massachusetts, Sears (1913–57), as previously noted, was an actor and dialogue coach in the Durango series before taking over as director. During his career he acted in some forty features and directed over fifty, sometimes performing in his own features. Among his later directorial efforts were *Ambush at Tomahawk Gap* (1953), *The Miami Story* (1954), *Cell 2455—Death Row*, *Chicago Syndicate*, *Apache Ambush* and *Inside Detroit* (all 1955), the well-done chillers *The Werewolf* and *Earth vs. the Flying Saucers* (both 1956), the musicals *Rock Around the Clock* (1956) and *Don't Knock the Rock* (1957), *The Night the World Exploded* and *The Giant Claw* (both 1957) and *Badman's Country* (1958).

Sears also directed the next three Durango outings, beginning with *Across the Badlands*, issued in September, 1950. Barry Shipman's screenplay told of former Texas Ranger Steve Ransom (Starrett) coming to San Feliz at the behest of railroad chief Banion (Charles Evans), who wants him to find out who is behind a gang of thugs who are attacking surveyors looking for the lost Ranahan Trail, which supposedly runs through the desert to the town. Sheriff Crocker (Stanley Andrews) suspects stagecoach line owner Jeff Carson (Hugh Prosser), since the railroad would put him out of business. Steve is shot at on his way to town and he manages to get the gun fired at him and takes it to gunsmith Smiley (Burnette) for identification. There he meets hotel owner Rufus Downey (Dick Elliott), a relative of the man who found the lost trail, and Eileen Carson (Helen Mowery), Jeff's daughter. Smiley says the gun belongs to Carson, who later claims it was lost. One of the gang members, Bart (Robert S. Cavendish), incites the locals to hang Carson but he is saved by the Durango Kid. Claiming the Ranahan Trail is a fake, Carson informs Durango that its founder actually murdered those who supposedly used the trail and took their goods and money. Both Steve and Carson believe Downey is behind the recent lawlessness and set out to find the massacre site. Another gang member, Duke Jackson (Robert J. Wilke), finds out his twin brother Keno (also Wilke) has escaped from jail and a plan is hatched where Duke will supposedly find the trail and Keno will pretend to be him in San Feliz. When Smiley and Carson locate the massacre site and report to Steve, he goes to the sheriff and the two set out to arrest Downey. Along the way, Crocker gets the drop on Steve and admits to being the gang leader. Steve is able to defeat Crocker in a fight and as Durango he brings in the sheriff's gang, clearing Carson. In this one, Harmonica Bill is back dueting with Burnette on the tune "Harmonica Bill," which Smiley wrote. Burnette also did his "I'm Telling Myself I Ain't Afraid."

Raiders of Tomahawk Creek, released in the fall of 1950, was a tale about five silver rings made by an Indian tribe's medicine man for an old prospector, with the possessors of the rings being murdered. Since the killings are done with a tomahawk, the Indians are blamed by the locals but newly appointed agent Steve Blake (Starrett) does not agree. When rancher Jeff Calhoun is murdered and his ring stolen, the former Indian agent, Randolph Dike (Edgar Dearing), takes the man's younger brother Billy (Billy Kimbley) to amateur detective Smiley (Burnette), Steve's friend. Learning that another rancher was murdered earlier, Steve goes to see the man's daughter, Janet Clayton (Kay Buckley), who informs him that her father also had a silver ring. When Smiley and Billy are caught spying on the Indians they are chased by several braves but are saved by the Durango Kid. Durango talks to Chief Flying Arrow (Paul Marion) about the rings; he denies knowledge of the murders but does say that the tribe's medicine man made the rings. When another rancher is killed, Dike tells the sheriff (Paul McGuire) that Steve is the murderer because he too is wearing a silver ring; Steve is arrested. During his arraignment the following day, Dike's henchman Saunders (Lee Morgan) tries to steal his ring but it has been hidden by Smiley. Smiley and Billy then track Dike and his men but are caught; Billy breaks away and rides for help. The Durango Kid arrives and rescues Smiley and the gang is captured. Durango returns the rings to Flying Arrow, who shows him that the rings, when combined, reveal the location of a silver mine. In this outing, Burnette performed two more of his songs, "The Grasshopper Polka" and "I'm Too Smart for That."

Released in December, 1950, *Lightning Guns* was a compact yarn in which Burnette did a trio of his ditties, "Bathtub King," "Our Whole Family's Smart" and "Ramblin' Blood in My Veins." Cowboy Steve Brandon (Charles Starrett) comes to Piute Valley to see his friend, Sheriff Rob Saunders (Jock O'Mahoney), and fights masked raiders who attack a dam project. He finds out that Luke Atkins (William Norton Bailey) is constructing a dam in order to provide water for himself and other ranchers and the project is opposed by another cattleman, Captain Dan Saunders (Edgar Dearing), Rob's father. The lawman is in love with Luke's daughter Susan (Gloria Henry) and the feud between their fathers is causing friction in their romance. Since the other ranchers believe Dan is the leader of the raiders, his son is forced to form a posse and arrest him for the murder of a banker. Dan is about to be hung when he is saved by the Durango Kid, who takes him to jail. Merchant Jud Norton (Raymond Bond) agrees to pay for the dam's completion but demands a mortgage on Atkins' ranch. He then orders his men to free Dan and raid the dam site, placing the blame on the elder Saunders. The Durango Kid trails the gang to their hideout, finding out Norton is their boss. Steve has his traveling salesman pal Smiley (Burnette) watch Norton as the Durango Kid captures the outlaws and puts them behind bars. Durango then proves to the ranchers that Jud Norton is responsible for the raids and Dan is vindicated.

Ray Nazarro was back to helm the final Durango release for 1950, *Frontier Outpost*; Fred F. Sears appears in the film as an army investigator. Released at the end of December, it also features musicians Hank Penny and Slim Duncan; Burnette sings his songs "Live to Eat" and "Twista." Undercover agents Steve Lawton (Starrett) and Smiley (Burnette) are on the trail of outlaws stealing government gold shipments sent to Fort Navajo. The Durango Kid, however, steals the gold first and Steve and Smiley take it by stagecoach to the fort, accompanied by Alice Tanner (Lois Hall), the wife of commanding officer Captain Tanner (Paul Campbell). Upon arrival, they find the fort is deserted except for Army investigator Copeland (Fred F. Sears) who tells the two agents to report to military headquarters in Santa Fe. Once they leave, civilian government agent Forsythe (Steve Darrell), the leader of the outlaws, murders Copeland and the stagecoach driver (Bud Osborne) and abducts Mrs. Tanner. Forsythe then telegraphs his gang to murder Steve and Smiley and steal the gold but the two manage to escape. Upon arrival in Santa Fe, Steve is arrested for robbery and murder. He breaks out of jail and as the Durango Kid he locates and rescues Captain Tanner. There is a shootout with the gang; Forsythe is killed and the rest of the gang is arrested. Steve rescues Alice and reunites her with her husband.

Although the Saturday matinee western was quickly becoming passé due to the inroads of television, Columbia still continued to profit from the Durango Kid series and another eight adventures of the masked man came to theaters in 1951. The beginning of the year also saw Starrett appearing in his first non-western role in thirteen years when he guest starred on an episode of the ABC-TV series *Faith Baldwin Broadcast Theater* (January 27, 1951). The episode was entitled "A Shot in the Dark," the same title as the actor's 1935 feature for Chesterfield Pictures. It was to be the last time he played a part other than the Durango Kid.

The initial 1951 Durango outing, *Prairie Roundup*, issued in January, returned director Sears to the series with a fast-paced adventure containing a complicated plot in which the Durango Kid was literally chasing himself. It opens with ex–Texas Ranger Steve Carson (Starrett) being arrested for killing the Durango Kid, an impersonator trying to halt a robbery. Although his pal Smiley (Burnette) knows his true identity, Steve swears him to silence. The real culprit is the dead man's partner, Hank Edwards (Don C. Harvey), and after Steve is tried and convicted, Smiley breaks him out of jail and the two head to Santa Fe, trailing Edwards. There the outlaw and his other partner, Poker Joe (Paul Campbell), work for Buck Prescott (Frank Fenton), the head of the local cattle company. The crooked Prescott was once run out of Texas by Steve and he now works with the sheriff (Frank Sully) in a scheme to cheat local ranchers. When a herd is on its way to market, Prescott's gang stampedes it, causing the ranchers to sell their surviving cattle below market prices. Following the murder of a rancher by Edwards so his cattle can be mixed with Prescott's, Steve and Smiley come upon the man's body and are accused of killing him by Toni Eaton (Mary Castle), the daughter of cattleman Jim Eaton (George Baxter). After Steve explains what happened, Toni asks him to be trail boss on the cattle herd her dad has going to New Mexico. On the trail, Smiley finds out that another rancher, Kelly (Forrest Taylor), had his herd stampeded and in Santa Fe Steve saves the man when he is attacked by Edwards and Poker Joe. Prescott's men then stampede the Eaton cattle, forcing Steve to sell the remainder at a loss to Prescott, whom he accuses of starting the charge. Toni blames Steve for the raid although her father accepts his story, but after Steve thwarts another stampede by Prescott's gang, Buck offers a reward for him and the Durango Kid accepts the offer to kill Steve. Durango, however, robs the local stagecoach of the money Prescott needs to buy a cattle herd. After a fight, Steve captures Poker Joe, but Edwards gives him a gun so he can escape. Durango wounds Joe and then shows him the gun he received contains blanks and the outlaw admits Prescott and Edwards have stolen cattle corralled in Lost Valley. Back in Santa Fe, Toni agrees to sell Prescott her remaining herd but Durango arrives and stops the deal, wounding the sheriff and shooting Prescott. Now under arrest, Edwards and Poker Joe admit that Steve is innocent and Toni returns home to form a cattle company. The Sunshine Boys were back in this edition singing "Ride on the Golden Range in the Sky" while

Burnette contributed his "Deep Froggie Blues" and "Snack Happy."

Sears also helmed *Ridin' the Outlaw Trail*, which came out in February, 1951. Its music was provided by Pee Wee King and His Golden West Cowboys and Burnette performed his composition "I'm a Sucker for a Bargain." With a plot similar to *Both Barrels Blazing*, the adventure finds Texas Ranger Steve Forsythe (Starrett) on the trail of Sam Barton (Lee Morgan) for gold theft. Arriving in Spring Rock, Texas, Barton is murdered by crook Ace Conley (Jim Bannon) and his partner Reno (Chuck Roberson) and they make local blacksmith Smiley (Burnette) melt the gold into bullion which they hide in an old mine. Ace blackmails old prospector Pop Willard (Edgar Dearing), forcing him pass off the bullion as having been discovered by Pop. Willard, an ex-convict, does not want his daughter Betsy (Sunny Vickers) to know he spent time in prison, although her fiancé, Sheriff Tom Chapman (Peter Thompson), is aware of his past. Steve comes to Spring Rock and recognizes Pop; the sheriff tells him about his background and his attempts to make a new life for himself and his daughter. Smiley then informs Steve about the gold and the Durango Kid finds the mine where he halts the smelting and then informs the sheriff of Ace's activities. Durango and Chapman have a shootout with Ace and Reno and the two crooks are arrested. Steve returns the gold to the government while Betsy remains unaware of her father's criminal past.

Director Ray Nazarro returned to the Durangos to direct what may well be his best series entry, *Fort Savage Raiders*, released in March, 1951. For once a Durango adventure did not have a leading lady and it had only one song, Burnette's "Full Speed Ahead." A rather grim affair, the feature told of cavalry Captain Michael Craydon (John Dehner) becoming mentally unhinged when he is not allowed to see his sick child. He deserts but is captured and incarcerated; he escapes along with several other men imprisoned for murder. The escapees form an outlaw gang, led by Craydon, which raids military posts and ranches. Steve Drake (Starrett), a civilian, is enlisted by Colonel Sutter (Fred F. Sears) to form a group of men to hunt down and capture the gang which has been dubbed the Fort Savage Raiders. Steve agrees and gets his friends Smiley (Burnette), Old Cuss (Trevor Bardette) and Rog Beck (Frank Griffin) to join him. Since the mission is a military one, the men are forced to answer to a recent West Point graduate, Lieutenant James Sutter (Peter Thompson), the colonel's son. Disguised as prospectors, the men seek out the raiders but are continually hampered by young Sutter's inexperience and desire to stick to protocol. When the company is endangered due to Sutter's conceit, they are rescued by the Durango Kid. The lieutenant continues to mishandle the mission; after again being saved by Durango, he tries to arrest the masked man. Eventually Steve becomes fed up with Sutter and beats him in a fight, forcing the military man to let him led the mission. As a result they are able to corral Craydon in a cave, where Steve shoots him, as the rest of the gang is captured.

The next two series films, *Snake River Desperadoes* and *Bonanza Town,* were directed by Sears, with the former being issued in May, 1951. The plot had Department of Indian Affairs officer Steve Reynolds (Starrett) looking into the murder of Jason Fox (Sam Flint), a government man investigating the illegal sale of firearms to Indian tribes. Finding a letter on Fox addressed to trading post operator Jim Haverly (Monte Blue), Steve visits the merchant and meets his nephew Billy (Tommy Ivo), who is a friend of Little Hawk (Brown Jug), the son of Indian chief Black Eagle (Charles Horvath). A vigilante group is formed to stop the attacks, which are really caused by outlaws dressed in Indian costumes. When Billy and Little Hawk find a shipment of rifles outside the town of Stardale, they report it to the Durango Kid, who then stops the vigilantes from attacking Black Eagle's village. Entertainer Smiley (Burnette), who came to town with his coronet band on the stagecoach on which Fox was killed, tries to help Billy get the rifles, but is captured by the Indians. As a result, Steve and Jim go to see Black Eagle but they are attacked and Steve is left for dead. The Durango Kid comes to the Indian village and hears Jim tell the chief he needs to buy rifles from him to fight the vigilantes. After Jim departs, Steve tells Black Eagle that the whites will not attack his tribe and he returns to town with Smiley and a peace treaty. When Smiley shows the citizens the treaty, Jim claims it is a fraud and that Steve has been killed; Steve shows up to prove him wrong. Haverly, who is behind the lawlessness, berates his henchman Brandt (Boyd "Red" Morgan) for not killing Steve and then orders his men to dress as Indians and raid the town in an effort to negate the treaty. At a party celebrating the signing of the treaty, word comes of an imminent Indian attack and the vigilantes unite to fight back despite Steve's protestations. Billy sends a smoke signal to the Indians warning them of the vigilantes' plan but is taken prisoner by his uncle, who also captures Little Hawk. Billy manages to escape and reports to Steve. In a showdown with Durango, Haverly is killed, thus bringing peace to the area. Accompanied by his polka band, Burnette performed "Brass Band Polka," which he wrote.

Bonanza Town, released in the summer of 1951, was a sequel to *West of Dodge City* and contained quite a bit of footage from that production. Burnette wrote the songs "It All Goes to Show Ya" and "Rootie Toot" for the film and in it he performed them with Slim Duncan. Starting off with footage from *Whirlwind Raiders* in which the Durango Kid saves Smiley (Burnette) during a runaway, the feature had Treasury Department agent Steve Ramsey (Starrett) looking for outlaw Henry Hardison (Fred F. Sears), who stole $30,000 in marked bills. Steve informs his friend, tinker Smiley, that he believes Hardison is hiding in Bonanza Town, which is run by crook Krag Boseman (Myron Healey) with opposition by Judge Anthony Dillon (Luther Crockett). Judge Dillon is confronted by a U.S. marshal (Paul McGuire), who plans to arrest him for his involvement in a bribery and murder case, but the lawman is shot in the back by Hardison, the judge's brother. Passerby Bill Trotter (Al Wyatt) is accused of the killing by Krag and his henchman Smoker (Charles Horvath) and placed under arrest, despite the protests of the judge's son, Bob Dillon (Ted Jordan). Bob asks the Durango Kid to head the local vigilantes in freeing Trotter as Steve meets with Krag and becomes his bodyguard. Boseman pays Ramsey with some of the marked money he is seeking and he tells Smiley, now the town barber, that he believes Krag and Hardison are working together to control the town. He relates how Hardison murdered a rancher (Nolan Leary) near Heela Pass in order to get his property and how his various machinations resulted in his setting an explosion to divert a river and allegedly being drowned as a result. Steve confronts the judge about Hardison being alive and Dillon signals Ramsey that his brother is in the next room. Hardison kills Dillon for his disloyalty but his chased by the Durango Kid, who shoots him from the top of a building as he tries to get out of town with the stolen money. This Durango entry also did not have a leading lady unless one counts the appearance of Nancy Saunders in footage from *West of Dodge City*.

Females were also sparse in *Cyclone Fury*, issued in September, 1951, which brought back director Ray Nazarro. It included footage from *Galloping Thunder*, *Landrush* and *Prairie Raiders*; its musical numbers, "Gettin' Some Sleep" and "The Wind Sings a Cowboy Song," performed by Burnette and Merle Travis and His Bronco Busters, were lifted from *Galloping Thunder*. The story told of government agent Steve Reynolds (Charles Starrett) leasing Arizona grazing land to Bronc Masters (Robert E. Scott) so he can round up and tame wild mustangs for military use. Bronc is murdered and Steve suspects foul play, especially after he is attacked by a quartet of men. At a meeting to award the horse delivery contract, Grat Hanlon (Clayton Moore) is the high bidder until Steve produces the new owner of Masters' Flying M Ranch, Indian boy Johnny (Louis Lettieri), Bronc's adopted son. Steve agrees to deliver the cattle in Johnny's name. Grat orders his henchman (Richard Alexander) to kill the boy but he fails, although Johnny falls out of a window and sustains a broken leg. Placing the boy in the care of his pal Smiley (Burnette), who has opened a funeral parlor, Steve then sends Smiley to give a message to Johnny's tribe to start rounding up wild mustangs. Grat's men attack Smiley, who is saved by the Durango Kid. The Indians get the message but the outlaws rob the bank of the money the army planned to use to buy the horses; it is retrieved by Durango. Grat then tries to get a higher military authority to give him the contract and he orders his henchman Bunco (Robert J. Wilke) to murder Steve, but the government man escapes and sends Smiley to aid in rounding up the horse herd, which must be in town that evening. Durango also enlists the aid of local Indian tribes in bringing in the mustangs. Grat returns with a new contract which will take effect if Johnny's horses are not delivered on time but Bunco tells him the herd is on its way so Grat orders his men to stampede the mustangs. Durango and the ranchers have a shootout with the gang, which is routed, and the masked man chases Grat into town and beats him in a fight. Smiley leads the horses into the town's corrals, with Johnny winning the government contract. Grat is jailed for Masters' murder.

The dearth of femininity in the Durango series continued with another Ray Nazarro effort, *The Kid from Amarillo*, which came out in the fall of 1951. Taking place in Texas in 1890, it had Treasury Agent Steve Ransom (Starrett), along with fellow agents Smiley (Burnette) and Tom Mallory (Harry Lauter), trying to stop a silver smuggling operation along the Mexican border. Mallory, pretending to be a boxer, joins the gang run by rancher Jonathan Cole (Fred F. Sears). Cole is also in charge of a prison farm on the U.S. side of the border and the prisoners there build roads. Although he is unable to connect Cole to the smuggling, Steve notices that the prisoners wear chains to work but not when they come back. Smiley gets himself caught by the gang and this also leads to Mallory's identity being revealed and both agents are held prisoner in the penal camp. Smiley and Tom find out that the silver is being melted into links for the chains worn by the prisoners and this is the way the metal is being smuggled across the border. The Durango Kid attacks a wagon carrying the silver ingots and takes it back to the camp where he sets Smiley and Tom free. Enlisting the aid of the Mexican rurales, the three agents capture the gang and then head to Cole's ranch where, after a shootout, the outlaws are arrested. The film was remade as an episode of the *Tales of the Texas Rangers* (ABC-TV, 1958–59), which had series star Harry Lauter in the same part he played in the Durango feature.

Sears directed the next three Durango efforts, beginning with the final 1951 release, *Pecos River*, which came out in December. The title is misleading as the feature contains no river, let alone the Pecos River. The musical interludes are worse than ever, with Burnette and Harmonica Bill doing "The Eye Song" from "Three Blind Mice," and Stephen Foster's "Old Folks at Home" with new lyrics by Smiley, plus the "Harmonica Bill Medley" comprised of "O Where, O Where, Has My Little Dog Gone" and "Beethoven's Symphony No. 6 (Pastoria)." The film, however, does give Jock Mahoney, who continued to be Starrett's stunt double, his best series role to date as dude Jack Mahoney, a recent college graduate who has come home to Arizona to surprise his father, Coulter stagecoach driver Old Henry Mahoney (Edgar Dearing). Old Henry and the Durango Kid have just saved oculist Smiley (Burnette) from outlaws with Old Henry killing one of the bandits. The gang's leader, Pop Rockland (Steve Darrell), along with his sons Mose (Zon Murray) and Sniffy (Paul Campbell), swear revenge on Mahoney. Working incognito, Post Office investigator Steve Baldwin (Starrett) comes to town to take a job at the Coulter Stage Lines, run by Betty Coulter (Delores Sidener), and he is impressed with the way Jack beats up bullies Mose and Sniffy. He and Betty take the young man to see Old Henry, who has been murdered by Pop. Jack vows revenge and after his dad's funeral the Durango Kid teaches the young man to shoot a gun as Steve ingratiates himself with the Rocklands after taking over as Old Henry's replacement. Jack follows Steve to the outlaws' hideout but is taken prisoner and nearly pushed off a cliff before being rescued by the Durango Kid. Jack drives the Coulter stage the Rockland gang plans to rob. The local sheriff (Frank Jenks) rides in the stagecoach and is wounded during a gun battle with the gang as Durango comes to the rescue. Betty leads a posse in arresting the Rocklands as Durango saves the sheriff before the stagecoach goes over a bridge mined by the outlaws. As Steve and Smiley head off to new adventures, Jack stays with Betty to run the stage line.

The final half dozen Durango Kid adventures came out in 1952, beginning with *Smoky Canyon*, released in January. Taking place in the 1880s in Montana, it told of two ranchers, Roberta "Rob" Woodstock (Dani Sue Nolan) and Carl Buckley (Tristram Coffin), agreeing to a range war to mitigate recent court rulings in favor of sheepmen who have been encroaching on their ranges. Unknown to Rob, Buckley is secretly working with a syndicate to keep up the price of beef by preventing Montana cattle from reaching Eastern packers. Rob's former fiancé, Jack Mahoney (Jack [Jock] Mahoney), who has been falsely accused of murdering her father (Frank O'Connor), finds sheepman Johnny Big Foot (Charles Stevens), who has been attacked by Buckley's men, and takes him to sheep rancher Wyler (Forrest Taylor) after the Durango Kid leads Sheriff Bogart (Larry Hudson) and his posse away from Jack. In the town of Timber Rock, Steve Brent (Starrett) meets local tour guide Smiley (Burnette) but refuses to work for Rob because she is a woman as Durango hears Jack's side of the story and vows to help him clear his name. Trying to instigate more trouble, Buckley has his men burn Rob's land and steal her cattle, blaming the sheepherders and Durango. Rob then hires Steve to capture Durango but Jack blames Steve when Johnny Big Foot is found murdered. Sheepman Spade (Sandy Sanders) is a spy for Buckley and he tells his boss that Jack is out to get Steve as Rob joins Buckley and the sheriff in a plan to capture Jack. Feeling remorse, Rob goes to warn Jack, who ambushes Steve. Rob comes along while the two men fight and she knocks out Steve so Jack can escape. Later, the Durango Kid obtains Buckley's records, proving he works for the syndicate, and takes them to Sheriff Bogart. Risking being caught, Jack goes to Rob and tells her Buckley set the fire which burned her range and that her dad was murdered because he knew about Carl's lawless activities. The two head to Smoky Canyon for a showdown with Buckley but are captured by his gang. Buckley sets off an explosion to start a cattle stampede and his henchman Lars (Chris Alcaide) is trampled to death. Durango arrives to set Jack and Rob free as the fleeing Buckley and Bogart are killed by falling boulders caused by the stampede. Spade, who has been subdued in a fight with Smiley, clears Jack's name, and the young man is made sheriff and reunited with Rob. Burnette wrote and performed two songs, "Daydream Lariat" and "It's Got to Get Better Before It Gets Worse." The feature used stock footage from *Storm Over Wyoming*, a 1950 RKO Radio production starring Tim Holt.

The Hawk of Powder River, which came out in February, 1952, had a half-breed known as The Hawk (Clayton Moore) heading a gang which robs stagecoaches in the region of Wild River. U.S. Marshal Steve Martin (Starrett) comes to the area and enlists the aid of photographer Smiley (Burnette) in finding the outlaw who has murdered all the previous sheriffs. When the latest lawman, Clark Mahoney (Sam Flint), is killed by The Hawk, his son Jack (Jack [Jock] Mahoney) takes over the job and an attempt is made on his life but he is saved by the Durango Kid. Durango manages to capture The Hawk and takes him to Jack, who puts him in jail. In order to infiltrate the outlaw gang, Steve gets himself arrested and he helps The Hawk break jail. As a result, he joins the gang but well-meaning Smiley nearly causes Steve to be found out. After locating the money taken by the outlaws, Steve tells Smiley to inform Jack about The Hawk's next robbery and the Durango Kid stops the holdup and kills The Hawk in a shootout. Jack and Smiley round up the remainder of the outlaws, bringing peace to Wild River. During the proceedings, Burnette sang two more of his compositions, "Chief Pocatello from the Cherokee" and "Pedro Enchilada."

Ray Nazarro was back to direct the next three Durangos, beginning with the April, 1952, release *Laramie Mountains*, which was filmed at Corriganville. This one had Burnette presenting two more of his silly songs, "Come, Come to the Mess" and "Sloop, Sloop, Sloop." The involved, somewhat tiresome plot told of Indian attacks on supply trains in the Laramie Mountains after many years of peace. Swift Eagle (Jack [Jock] Mahoney), a white man reared by Indians, is believed to be behind the raids. Fort Tourney commanding officer Major Markham (Fred F. Sears) enlists the aid of Paul Drake (Rory Mallinson), a deserter, and Carson (Zon Murray) in an effort to murder Chief Lone Tree (John War Eagle). Since the military has arranged a meeting with the two Indians, Drake tells Markham to incite Swift Eagle to violence so the soldiers can legally attack the tribe. When previously wounded Lieutenant Pierce (Marshall Reed) wants Swift Eagle arrested for attacking the supply trains, a fight starts and Drake and Carson almost attack the Indians when they are halted by the Durango Kid. At the fort, Markham is condemned by Steve Holden (Starrett), an Indian Affair agent, for upsetting Swift Eagle. Later, the major goes into the mountains to confer with Henry Mandel (Robert J. Wilke), the man behind the raids. Mandel wants the area removed from Indian territory so he can stake a claim on the gold-rich area. After a failed meeting with Lone Tree, Steve finds his escort murdered and Durango demands an explanation from Swift Eagle, who claims his people had nothing to do with the massacre. Discovering half of a horseshoe at the site, Swift Eagle proves to Steve that the Indians are innocent. Back at the fort the company cook, Sergeant Smiley (Burnette), tries to tell Markham that Drake is a deserter but is stopped by Carson. After a failed meeting between Markham and Lone Tree, in which Swift Eagle prevents Drake from shooting the chief, the Indians agree not to fight until Steve finds the other half of the horseshoe. Steve trails Drake and Carson and overhears Mandel tell them to murder Markham with an Indian knife. Returning to the fort, Steve asks Smiley to bring Markham to the outlaws' cave but Smiley's dog steals the map Steve gives him and Pierce tries to arrest Holden, who makes a getaway. Steve and Swift Eagle are captured by Drake at the cave as Smiley gets back the map and takes Markham and his men to the location. Steve and Swift Eagle manage to get free and hold off Mandel and his gang with Indian weapons until Markham and his men arrive to arrest the outlaws.

The Rough, Tough West, which was issued in June, 1952, gave Jock Mahoney, again billed as Jack, a meaty role as a "good badman" and it also spotlighted Carolina Cotton as his singer girlfriend. The plot had cowpoke Steve Holden (Starrett) arriving in Hard Rock to visit an old friend, Big Jack Mahoney (Mahoney), with whom he once served in the Texas Rangers. Big Jack and his cohort Fulton (Marshall Reed) control the town and miner Jordan MacCrea (Bert Arnold) plans to kill Big Jack. Steve and Big Jack meet at the latter's saloon where Carolina (Carolina Cotton), Jack's lady friend, is the singer. Although Steve turns down Big Jack's offer to work for him, he decides to stay on as the town marshal after Jordan makes an attempt on his friend's life. Although Big Jack is friendly with a crippled boy, Buzz Barett (Tommy Ivo), Fulton tries to shut down the local newspaper run by Buzz's grandmother Matty (Valerie Fisher); Jordan tries to stop him. The two men fight but are stopped by the Durango Kid. The incident causes friction between Steve and Big Jack as local miners find out they will have to pay a huge toll to bring their gold ore from the mountains on a road controlled by Fulton and his men. The miners want to resort to violence but are stopped by Durango, who tells them to use pack mules and bypass the road. Fulton and his men kidnap Buzz and try to force him to tell them the mule train's route but he is rescued by Durango. Fulton then tries to get the same information from old Pete Walker (Fred F. Sears), a friend of Big Jack's, as Buzz overhears and rides to warn the miners. He is too late, however, and the Durango Kid fails to stop the robbery; the boy is injured in the attack. When Big Jack tries to help the boy, he is dismissed by Matty. After Fulton murders Pete, Mahoney decides to give back the gold taken from the miners. Big Jack and Fulton fight with Jack being wounded. Fulton and his men set fire to the newspaper office, trapping Buzz inside. Big Jack tries to rescue the boy but is overcome by smoke as the fire gets out of hand and burns down Hard Rock. Steve manages to rescue Big Jack and Buzz after Fulton and his gang are arrested. Big Jack, who plans to marry Carolina, announces he will rebuild the town. Burnette, who had little to do in the film as Hard Rock's fire chief, sang his "Fire of '41" while Carolina Cotton performed her composition "You Gotta Get a Guy with a Gun" and "Cause I'm in Love," with Pee Wee King and His Band, who also did "You Don't Need Love Anymore," with the vocal by Redd Stewart, and "The More We Get Together." Although he did not direct this one, Fred F. Sears had two roles in the production: He was bearded miner Peter Walker and also the town physician. The film was redone as an episode of *Tales of the Texas Rangers* (ABC-TV, 1958–59).

The final Durango Kid feature directed by Ray Nazarro, *Junction City*, came out in July, 1952. The Sunshine Boys were back singing the gospel "Glory Train" while Burnette did his own "Li'l Injun." Barry Shipman's script told of stagecoach driver Jack Mahoney (Jack [Jock] Mahoney) being arrested by Sheriff Jeff Clinton (George Chesebro) for kidnapping mining heiress Penny Sanderson (Kathleen Case). When the young woman is not found, Jack is accused of murdering her and is tried and sentenced to hang. Cowboy Steve Rollins (Starrett) and his pal Smiley (Burnette) set out to solve the mystery of Penny's disappearance. Steve is aware that years before, the Durango Kid helped Penny, then a child, get her inheritance by ending a long-standing feud between her grandfathers. Durango finds out that

Lobby card for *The Rough, Tough West* (Columbia, 1952).

Penny's guardians, Emmett (John Dehner) and Ella Sanderson (Mary Newton), pretend to be worried about the girl although they were unkind to her when she lived with them. Penny is found in hiding by Durango and she informs him that she lives in fear of her life because of her guardians who want her dead so they can inherit the gold mine. Steve and Smiley expose the machinations of the Sandersons and Jack is vindicated.

Fred F. Sears returned to direct the last Durango Kid release, *The Kid from Broken Gun*, issued in the late summer of 1952. Again The Sunshine Boys sang in the feature as did Burnette, who performed another song he wrote, "It's the Law." Set in New Mexico in 1875, it had former boxer Jack Mahoney (Jack [Jock] Mahoney), who was once billed as "The Kid from Broken Gun," on trial for the murder of Matt Fallon (Chris Alcaide) over the affections of Jack's lady friend, attorney Gail Kingston (Angela Stevens), who is defending Jack at his trial. Prosecuting attorney Kiefer (Myron Healey) proves that Jack had a bad temper and that he was forced to give up boxing because of his vicious ring tactics. Steve Reynolds (Starrett), Jack's pal, testifies in his behalf, and with another friend, Smiley (Burnette), he finds out that Doc Handy (Pat O'Malley) may be able to supply Jack with an alibi. Handy, who was watching over a strongbox filled with gold being stored in the town's express office, is murdered before he can testify. Jack is convicted and given the death sentence but Steve continues to investigate and he finds out it was Gail who murdered Fallon in order to frame Jack so she could get the gold. Gail then orders Jack's murder and her gang waylays the sheriff (Mauritz Hugo) and are about to kill Jack when he is rescued by the Durango Kid. Durango and Smiley make the court reconvene and the masked avenger supplies the necessary evidence to prove Gail killed Fallon, in league with Martin Donohugh (Tristram Coffin), her express company boss lover, and Jack is freed. *Variety* called it "a complicated program western" and complained, "The plot is too involved and too much of the action is talked out.... Footage is padded out with generous use of clips from older Starrett oaters, spotted via flashbacks that are tied in with the story being told."

After more than sixty releases, the Durango Kid packed it in with *The Kid from Broken Gun*, although star Starrett was in good company since most of the other cowboy matinee heroes had given up the silver screen: Roy Rogers quit the year before, Tim Holt's last starrer was also in 1952, and Gene Autry would leave the screen in 1953. Although he had offers to bring the Durango Kid to television, as Rogers and Autry did with their screen characters, Starrett opted to retire after being a western film hero for seventeen years and starring in over 130 cowboy pictures. He was just behind William Boyd in starring in the greatest number of films portraying the same character and he had the longest tenure of any western star with one studio. Following retirement, Starrett traveled extensively with his wife Mary and also did promotional work for his family's business, the Starrett Precision Tool Company. In the 1980s he made several appearances at western film conventions. A founding member of the Screen Actors Guild, Starrett died March 22, 1986, in Borrego Springs, California.

Following the demise of the Durango Kid series, Smiley Burnette remained at Columbia where he did six features in 1953 with Gene Autry, ending his film career with the man he started it with in 1935. For the next decade he continued to tour with his road show, appearing all across the United States, and in the late 1950s he recorded albums for the Cricket and Starday labels. He also toured with Autry and appeared on numerous radio and television programs and in 1959 he was a regular on ABC-TV's *Ozark Jubilee* starring Red Foley. From 1963 to 1967 he portrayed train engineer Charlie Pratt on *Petticoat Junction* on CBS-TV and he also played the role in several episodes of the same network's *Green Acres*. One of the most popular and best-loved of western comedians, Burnette died February 16, 1967. In 1998 he was given the Western Music Association Award.

Unlike most Columbia films, the Durango Kid series was not released to television and the movies went unseen, except for private collectors, long after the end of their theatrical run. In recent years a few of the Durangos have been telecast as well as being issued on tape and DVD, but the majority of the series is still unavailable. Although the Durango Kid films were never popular with the critics, the series had a contingent of loyal followers. Unlike many continuing series, the features did not decline toward the end but actually seemed to somewhat improve. While the overall series was never of a particular high quality, the movies provided the kind of fare demanded by the Saturday matinee crowd. Produced on low budgets, the Durangos always made money for Columbia and thanks to the charisma of Starrett and the juvenile following of Burnette, they remain one of the most enduring of western film series.

Filmography

The Durango Kid (Columbia, 1940, 61 minutes) Producer: Jack Fier. Director: Lambert Hillyer. Screenplay: Paul Franklin. Photography: John Stumar. Editor: Richard Fantl. Songs: Bob Nolan & Tim Spencer.

Cast: Charles Starrett (Jim Lowery/The Durango Kid), Luana Walters (Nancy Winslow), Kenneth MacDonald (Mace Ballard), Francis Walker (Steve), Forrest Taylor (Ben Winslow), Melvin Lang (Marshal Trayboe), Bob Nolan & The Sons of the Pioneers [Bob Nolan, Tim Spencer, Lloyd Perryman, Pat Brady, Hugh Farr, Karl Farr] (Musicians), Frank LaRue (Sam Lowry), Ralph Peters (Taylor), Jack Rockwell (Mr. Evans), Marin Sais (Mrs. Evans), Roger Gray (Jergens), Jack Kirk, Steve Clark, George Russell (Gang Members), John Tyrrell, Silver Tip Baker (Citizens).

Sagebrush Heroes (Columbia, 1945, 55 minutes) Producer: Jack Fier. Director: Benjamin Kline. Screenplay: Luci Ward. Photography: George Meehan. Editor: Aaron Stell. Songs: Fleming Allen, Bob Nolan, Roy Rogers & Tim Spencer. Art Directors: Lionel Banks & Perry Smith. Sound: Lambert Day. Sets: Fay Babcock. Assistant Director: Wilbur McGaugh.

Cast: Charles Starrett (Steve Randall/The Durango Kid), Dub Taylor (Cannonball), Constance Worth (Connie Pearson), Jimmy Wakely (Jimmy), Ozie Waters & His Saddle Pals (Musicians), Elvin Field (Marty Jones), Bobby Larson (Tim), Forrest Taylor (Tom Goodwin), Joel Friedkin (Dr. Webb), Lane Chandler

(Colton), Paul [Conrad] Zaremba (Brady), Eddie Laughton (Layton), John Tyrrell (Finley), Vernon Dent (Editor Haynes), Davison Clark (Judge), Edmund Cobb (Sheriff Barnes), Budd Buster (Moore), Jessie Arnold (Mrs. Barnes), Ted French (Thompson).

Working title: *Heroes of the Sagebrush.*

The Return of the Durango Kid (Columbia, 1945, 58 minutes) Producer: Colbert Clark. Director: Derwin Abrahams. Screenplay: J. Benton Cheney. Photography: Glen Gano. Editor: Aaron Stell. Songs: Lanny Grey, Roy Jacobs, Sol Marcus, Al J. Neiburg, Eddie Seiler & Arthur Terker. Art Directors: Lionel Banks & Charles Clague. Sets: John W. Pascoe.

Cast: Charles Starrett (Bill Blaydon/The Durango Kid), Tex Harding (Jim), Jean Stevens (Paradise Flo), John Calvert (Leland "Lee" Kirby), The Jesters (Musicians), Britt Wood (Stagecoach Driver Curly), Ray Bennett (Cherokee), Betty Roadman (Buckskin Liz Bancroft), Elmo Lincoln (Luke Blaine), Francis Walker (Deputy Sheriff), Dick Botiller (Sheriff), Steve Clark (Murdered Gambler), Paul [Conrad] Zaremba (Ringo), Hal Price (Thomas J. Wagner), Carl Sepulveda (Tom Richards), Tex Palmer (Saloon Helper), William Desmond, Carl Mathews, Wally West, Lew Morphy, Herman Hack, Dan White, Ted Mapes (Gang Members), Jack Evans, Philip Kieffer (Citizens), James T. "Bud" Nelson (Pedestrian), Robert Walker (Saloon Customer).

Working title: *Stolen Time.*

Both Barrels Blazing (Columbia, 1945, 57 minutes) Producer: Colbert Clark. Director: Derwin Abrahams. Screenplay: William Lively. Photography: George Meehan. Editor: Henry Batista. Songs: Mario Silva. Art Director: Charles Clague. Sets: John W. Pascoe.

Cast: Charles Starrett (Kip Allen/The Durango Kid), Tex Harding (Tex Harding), Dub Taylor (Cannonball), Pat Parrish (Gail Radford), The Jesters (Musicians), Alan Bridge (Lucky Thorpe), Charles King (Nevada), Emmett Lynn (J. Horace "Grubstake" Higginbotham), Robert Barron (Dan Cass), Jack Rockwell (Captain Rogers), Edward Howard (Spike), John L. Cason (Chad), Bert Dillard (Lefty Dean), Tex Palmer (Stagecoach Driver), Hansel Warner (Barney), James T. "Bud" Nelson, Dan White (Gang Members), Wally West, Rube Dalroy (Citizens).

British title: *The Yellow Streak.*

Rustlers of the Badlands (Columbia, 1945, 55 minutes) Producer: Colbert Clark. Director: Derwin Abrahams. Screenplay: J. Benton Cheney. Story: Richard Hill Wilkinson. Photography: George Meehan. Editor: Aaron Stell. Music Director: Mischa Bakaleinikoff. Songs: Sam Braverman, William Brookhouse, Charles Cody, Frank Davis, Jerry Levy, Burt Rice, Mickey Stoner, Al Trace & Ben Trace. Art Director: Charles Clague. Sound: Lodge Cunningham. Sets: John W. Pascoe. Production Manager: Jack Fier. Assistant Director: Wilbur McGaugh.

Cast: Charles Starrett (Steve Lindsay/The Durango Kid), Tex Harding (Tex Harding), Dub Taylor (Cannonball), Sally Bliss [Carla Balenda] (Sally Boylston), George Eldredge (Jim Norton), Edward Howard (Regan), Ray Bennett (Blake), Karl Hackett (Sheriff Mallory), James T. "Bud" Nelson, Frank McCarroll, Carl Sepulveda (Gang Members), Al Trace & His Silly Symphonists (Musicians), Nolan Leary (Dr. Burton), Steve Clark (Andrew Boylston), Edmund Cobb (Tom), Ted Mapes (Packard), Jack Ingram (Major Ostrand), Frank LaRue (Emerson), Frank Ellis (Cowboy), Bud Osborne (Stagecoach Driver), Ted French (Cook).

British title: *By Whose Hand?*

Outlaws of the Rockies (Columbia, 1945, 55 minutes) Producer: Colbert Clark. Director: Ray Nazarro. Screenplay: J. Benton Cheney. Photography: George Kelley. Editor: Aaron Stell. Music: Marlin Skiles. Songs: Spade Cooley & Smokey Rogers. Art Director: Charles Clague. Sound: Philip Faulkner. Assistant Director; Carter De Haven, Jr.

Cast: Charles Starrett (Steve Williams/The Durango Kid), Tex Harding (Tex Harding), Dub Taylor (Cannonball), Carole Mathews (Jane Stuart), Carolina Cotton (Singer), Spade Cooley (Spade), Philip Van Zandt (Honest Dan Chantry), George Chesebro (Bill Jason), I. Stanford Jolley (Ace Lanning), Jack Rockwell (Sheriff Hall), Tex Williams, Deuce Spriggins (Musicians), Frank LaRue (Tom Drake), Frank Lanning (Banker), Steve Clark (Sheriff Potter), Kermit Maynard, Ted Mapes, Nolan Leary, John Tyrrell (Deputy Sheriffs), James T. "Bud' Nelson (Pete), Victor Travers, Horace B. Carpenter, Herman Hack (Citizens), Frank O'Connor (Miner Pete), Roy Bucko (Gang Member).

British title: *A Roving Rogue.*

Blazing the Western Trail (Columbia, 1945, 60 minutes) Producer: Colbert Clark. Director: Vernon Keays. Screenplay: J. Benton Cheney. Photography: George Meehan. Editor: Henry Batista. Songs: Tommy Duncan & Bob Wills. Art Director: Charles Clague. Sets: John W. Pascoe.

Cast: Charles Starrett (Jeff Waring/The Durango Kid), Tex Harding (Tex Harding), Dub Taylor (Cannonball/Ethelbert), Carole Mathews (Mary Halliday), Bob Wills & His Texas Playboys [Bob Wills, Tommy Duncan, Noel Boggs, Cameron Hill, Joe Holley, Alex Brashear, Monte Mountjoy, Jimmy Wyble] (Musicians), Alan Bridge (Forrest Brent), Nolan Leary (Bob Halliday), Edmund Cobb (Sheriff Turner), Steve Clark (Dan Waring), Virginia Sale (Nellie), Mauritz Hugo (Jim McMasters), Ethan Laidlaw (Santry), John Tyrrell (Perkins), Frank LaRue (U.S. Postal Inspector Spencer), James T. "Bud" Nelson (Deputy Sheriff), Budd Buster (Passenger), Ted Mapes, Robert Williams, Chick Hannon, Edward Howard (Gang Members).

British title: *Who Killed Waring?*

Lawless Empire (Columbia, 1945, 60 minutes) Producer: Colbert Clark. Director: Vernon Keays. Screenplay: Bennett Cohen. Story: Elizabeth Beecher. Photography: George Meehan. Editor: Paul Borofsky. Songs: Tommy Duncan, the Rev. W.D. Stevens & Bob Wills. Art Director: Charles Clague. Sound: Lambert Day. Sets: John W. Pascoe. Assistant Director: Wilbur McGaugh.

Cast: Charles Starrett (Steve Ranson/The Durango Kid), Tex Harding (the Rev. Tex Harding), Dub Taylor (Cannonball), Mildred Law (Vicky Harding), Bob Wills & His Texas Playboys [Bob Wills, Tommy Duncan, Leon McAuliffe, Noel Boggs, Joe Holley, Al Stricklin, Millard Kelso, Jimmy Wyble] (Musicians), John Calvert (Blaze Howard), Ethan Laidlaw (Duke Flinders), Forrest Taylor (Doc Weston), Johnny Walsh (Marty Foster), Lloyd Ingraham (Mr. Murphy), Jack Rockwell (Jed Stevens), Jessie Arnold (Mrs. Arnold), George Chesebro (Lenny), Tom Chatterton (Sam Enders), Jack Kirk (Cattle Buyer), Boyd Stockman (Skids), John Tyrrell (Bartender Johnny), Frank LaRue, Edward Howard, Chick Hannon, Joe Galbreath, James T. "Bud" Nelson (Homesteaders).

British title: *Power of Possession*.

Texas Panhandle (Columbia, 1945, 58 minutes) Producer: Colbert Clark. Director: Ray Nazarro. Screenplay: Ed Earl Repp. Photography: George Kelley. Editor: Paul Borofsky. Music Director: Mischa Bakaleinikoff. Music Supervisor: Paul Mertz. Songs: Spade Cooley, Carolina Cotton, Tommy Duncan, Helen Hagstrom, Smokey Rogers, Mario Silva, Serge Walter & Bob Wills. Art Director: Charles Clague. Sound: Jack Goodrich. Production Manager: Jack Fier. Assistant Director: Carter De Haven, Jr.

Cast: Charles Starrett (Steve Buckner/The Durango Kid), Tex Harding (Tex Harding), Dub Taylor (Cannonball), Nanette Parks (Ann Williams), Carolina Cotton (Carolina), Spade Cooley Band [Spade Cooley, Smokey Rogers, Deuce Spriggins, Joaquin Murphy, Johnny Weis, Muddy Berry, Frank Buckley, Dean Eaker, Spike Featherstone, Gibby Gibson] (Musicians), Tex Williams (Singer), Jody Gilbert (Millicent), William Gould (Chief James Harrington), George Chesebro (Slash), Forrest Taylor (Ace Galatin), Budd Buster (Martin), Hugh Hooker (Shorty), Robert Walker (Bartender), Ted Mapes (Trig), Jack Kirk (Bistro), Edward Howard (Dinero), Ray Jones (Homesteader), Tex Palmer (Gang Member).

Frontier Gun Law (Columbia, 1946, 60 minutes) Producer: Colbert Clark. Director: Derwin Abrahams. Screenplay: Bennett Cohen. Story: Victor McLeod. Photography: Glen Gano. Editor: Aaron Stell. Music Director: Mischa Bakaleinikoff. Songs: Al Hoffman, Jerry Livingston, Al Trace & Nate Wexler. Art Director: Charles Clague. Sound: Edward Bernds. Sets: John W. Pascoe. Production Manager: Jack Fier. Assistant Director: Wilbur McGaugh.

Cast: Charles Starrett (Jim Stewart/The Durango Kid), Tex Harding (Tex Harding), Dub Taylor (Cannonball), Jean Stevens (Kitty), Weldon Heyburn (Matt Edwards), Jack Rockwell (Hank Watson), Frank LaRue (Sheriff Kincaid), John Elliott (Pop Evans), Robert Kortman (Mace), Stanley Price (Sam), Al Trace & His Silly Symphonists (Musicians), Jack Guthrie (Musician), Hank Worden (Pete), John Tyrrell (Stableman), Bill Nestell (Saloon Customer).

British title: *Menacing Shadows*; working titles: *Phantom Outlaws* and *Prairie Raiders*;

Roaring Rangers (Columbia, 1946, 58 minutes) Producer: Colbert Clark. Director: Ray Nazarro. Screenplay: Barry Shipman. Photography: George Kelley. Editor: Jerome Thoms. Music Director: Mischa Bakaleinikoff. Songs: Smiley Burnette, Alice Hawthorne, Lee Penny & Bob Wills. Art Director: Charles Clague. Sound: Howard Fogetti. Production Manager: Jack Fier. Assistant Director: James Nicholson.

Cast: Charles Starrett (Steve Randall/The Durango Kid), Smiley Burnette (Smiley Butterbean), Adelle Roberts (Doris Connor), Merle Travis & His Bronco Busters [Merle Travis, Slim Duncan, Alan Reinhart, Red Murrell] (Musicians), Jack Rockwell (Sheriff Jeff Connor), Ed Cassidy (Bill Connor), Edmund Cobb (Taggert), Mickey Kuhn (Larry Connor), Ted Mapes (Slade), Teddy Infuhr (Urchin), Kermit Maynard, Jack Kirk (Ranchers), Gerald Mackey (Scrud), Robert J. Wilke (Outlaw Boss), Herman Hack, Carol Henry, Chick Hannon, Tommy Coats (Gang Members), Nolan Leary, Chuck Baldra, George Morrell, John Tyrrell, Frank O'Connor, Blackie Whiteford, Robert Williams, Tex Harper, Frank Fanning (Citizens), Tex Terry, Jack Tornek, Lew Morphy, Roy Bucko (Saloon Customers), Ethan Laidlaw (Messenger).

Also called *False Hero*; working title: *Powder River*.

Gunning for Vengeance (Columbia, 1946, 54 minutes) Producer: Colbert Clark. Director: Ray Nazarro. Screenplay: Louise Rosseau & Ed Earl Repp. Photography: George Kelley. Editor: Paul Borofsky. Music Director: Mischa Bakaleinikoff. Songs: Curt Barrett, Smiley Burnette & Charley Wilkin. Art Director: Charles Clague. Sound: Philip Faulkner. Assistant Director: Carter De Haven, Jr.

Cast: Charles Starrett (Steve Landry/The Durango Kid), Smiley Burnette (Smiley), Marjean Neville (Elaine Jenkins), Curt Barrett & The Trailsmen [Curt Barrett, Slim Duncan, Rudy Sooter, Bud Dooley, Stanley Ellison] (Musicians), Phyllis Adair (Belle Madden), Lane Chandler (Jim Clayburn), George Chesebro (Mike), Frank LaRue (Mayor Garry), Robert Kortman (Curley), Nolan Leary (Jenkins), Frank Fanning (Dr. Hawkins), Dick Rush (Banker), John Tyrrell (Deputy Sheriff), Jack Kirk (Raider), Herman Hack, Tommy Coats, Matty Roubert, Chick Hannon, Blackie Whiteford, Herman Howlin (Gang Members), Robert Williams (Shorty), Bob Reeves (Saloon Customer).

Also known as *Jail Break*; working title: *Burning the Trail*.

Galloping Thunder (Columbia, 1946, 54 minutes) Producer: Colbert Clark. Director: Ray Nazarro. Screenplay: Ed Earl Repp. Photography: George Kelley. Editor: Richard Fantl. Music Director: Mischa

Bakaleinikoff. Songs: Tex Atkinson, Smiley Burnette & Merle Travis. Art Director: Charles Clague. Sound: Jack Haynes. Production Manager: Jack Fier. Assistant Director: Carter De Haven, Jr.

Cast: Charles Starrett (Steve Reynolds/The Durango Kid), Smiley Burnette (Smiley), Adelle Roberts (Jud Temple), Merle Travis & His Bronco Busters (Musicians), Richard Bailey (Grat Hanlon), Edmund Cobb (Barstow), Kermit Maynard (Krag), John Merton (Regan), Forrest Taylor (Colonel Collins), Curt Barrett (Nate), Ray Bennett (Wyatt), Nolan Leary (Curt Lawson), Budd Buster (Barber), Merrill McCormick, Roy Butler (Ranchers), Bob Reeves (Cowboy), Gordon Harrison (Indian).

Working title: *Bronco Busters*

Two-Fisted Stranger (Columbia, 1946, 51 minutes) Producer: Colbert Clark. Director: Ray Nazarro. Screenplay: Robert Lee Johnson. Story: Robert Lee Johnson & Peter Whitehead. Photography: Vincent Farrar. Editor: Paul Borofsky. Songs: Smiley Burnette, Zeke Clements & Hank Penny. Art Director: Charles Clague. Sound: Jack Haynes. Production Manager: Jack Fier. Sets: Richard Mansfield. Assistant Director: Carter De Haven, Jr.

Cast: Charles Starrett (Steve Gordon/The Durango Kid), Smiley Burnette (Smiley), Doris Houck (Jennifer Martin), Zeke Clements (Entertainer), Lane Chandler (Brady), Davison Clark (J.P. Martin), George Chesebro (Doyle), Maudie Prickett (Widow Simpson), Jack Rockwell (Sheriff Condon), Ted Mapes (Duke Benson), Frank O'Connor (Mr. O'Connor), Charles Murray, Jr. (Ted Randolph), I. Stanford Jolley, Edmund Cobb, Matty Roubert, Herman Hack, Tommy Coats, Frank Ellis (Gang Members).

British title: *High Stakes*.

The Desert Horseman (Columbia, 1946, 54 minutes) Producer: Colbert Clark. Director: Ray Nazarro. Screenplay: Sherman Lowe. Photography: L.W. O'Connell. Editor: Paul Borofsky. Music Director: Mischa Bakaleinikoff. Songs: Smiley Burnette, Sammy Cahn, Saul Chaplin & Robert Hoag. Art Director: Charles Clague. Sets: Richard Mansfield. Assistant Director: Carter De Haven, Jr.

Cast: Charles Starrett (Steve Godfrey/The Durango Kid), Smiley Burnette (Smiley), Adelle Roberts (Mary Ann Jarvis), Walt Shrum & His Colorado Hillbillies (Musicians), Richard Bailey (H.H. "Sam" Treadway), John Merton (Rex Young), Tommy Coats (Baldy), Riley Hill (Eddie), Jack Kirk (Sheriff), George Morgan (Pete), Bud Osborne (Tom Jarvis), Tex Williams (Entertainer), Herman Hack, Bert Dillard (Gang Members), Tex Cooper (Citizen).

Working title: *Phantom of the Desert*; British title: *Checkmate*.

Heading West (Columbia, 1946, 54 minutes) Producer: Colbert Clark. Director: Ray Nazarro. Screenplay: Ed Earl Repp. Photography: George B. Meehan. Editor: Henry Batista. Music Director: Mischa Bakaleinikoff. Songs: Smiley Burnette, Mel Foree, Harold Hensley, Hank Penny & Fred Rose. Art Director: Charles Clague. Sound: Jack Haynes. Production Manager: Jack Fier. Sets: Richard Mansfield. Assistant Director: William O'Connor.

Cast: Charles Starrett (Steve Randall/The Durango Kid), Smiley Burnette (Smiley), Doris Houck (Anne Parker), Hank Penny & His Plantation Boys [Hank Penny, Harold Hensley, Noel Boggs, Sanford Williams, Fenton Reynolds] (Musicians), Norman Willis (Rance Hudson), Hal Taliaferro [Wally Wales] (Jim Mallory), Bud Geary (Blaze "Curley" Curlew), Frank McCarroll (Red Curlew), John Merton (Kelso), Nolan Leary (Sam Parker), Tom Chatterton (Dr. Wyatt), Tommy Coats (Carter), Charles Soldani (Indian), Matty Roubert, Stanley Price, Dick Botiller, Herman Hack (Gang Members).

Working title: *Massacre Mesa*; British title: *The Cheat's Last Throw*.

Landrush (Columbia, 1946, 53 minutes) Producer: Colbert Clark. Director: Vernon Keays. Screenplay: Michael Simmons. Photography: George B. Meehan. Editor: James Sweeney. Songs: Smiley Burnette & Stephen Foster. Art Director: Charles Clague. Sound: Philip Faulkner. Sets: George Montgomery. Assistant Director: William O'Connor.

Cast: Charles Starrett (Steve Harmon/The Durango Kid), Smiley Burnette (Smiley), Doris Houck (Mary Parker), Ozie Waters & His Colorado Rangers (Musicians), Steve Barclay (Caleb Garvey), Emmett Lynn (Jake Parker), Robert Kortman (Sackett), Bud Geary (Claw Hawkins), Curt Barrett (Minister), Nolan Leary (Jenkins), Bud Osborne (Sheriff Jim Collins), George Chesebro (Bill), Herman Hack (Fred), George Hoey (Sweeper), Scotty Harrell (Entertainer Scotty), Roy Butler (Prospector), John Hawks (Stagecoach Driver), Ted French, George Russell, Ethan Laidlaw (Gang Members), Russell Meeker (Citizen), John Tyrrell, Sam Garrett (Cavalrymen).

British title: *The Claw Strikes*.

Terror Trail (Columbia, 1946, 56 minutes) Producer: Colbert Clark. Director: Ray Nazarro. Screenplay: Ed Earl Repp. Photography: George B. Meehan. Editor: Aaron Stell. Songs: Smiley Burnette. Art Director: Charles Clague. Sets: Richard Mansfield.

Cast: Charles Starrett (Steve Haverley/The Durango Kid), Smiley Burnette (Smiley), Barbara Pepper (Karen Kemp), Ozie Waters & His Colorado Rangers (Musicians), Lane Chandler (Duke Catlett), George Chesebro (Drag), Zon Murray (Bart Matson), Elvin Field (Rocky Kemp), Robert Barron (Jed), Wesley Tuttle (Entertainer), Ted Mapes (Waco), Jack Evans (Wrangler), Budd Buster (Stagecoach Driver), Matty Roubert, Tommy Coats, Billy Dix (Gang Members), Edward Howard, Bill Clark (Cowboys), George Morrell (Citizen).

Working title: *Renegade Range*.

The Fighting Frontiersman (Columbia, 1946, 62 minutes) Producer: Colbert Clark. Director: Derwin Abrahams. Screenplay: Ed Earl Repp. Photography: Philip Tannura. Editor: Jerome Thoms. Music Director: Mischa Bakaleinikoff. Songs: Smiley Burnette, Stephen Foster, Bob Newman & Joseph E. Winner. Art Director: Charles Clague. Sound: Lambert Day. Sets: Robert Bradfield. Production Manager: Jack Fier. Assistant Director: Carter De Haven, Jr.

Cast: Charles Starrett (Steve Reynolds/The Durango Kid), Smiley Burnette (Smiley), Helen Mowery (Dixie King), Hank Newman & The Georgia Crackers (Musicians), Robert Filmer (John Munro), George Chesebro (Rankin), Emmett Lynn (Cimmaron Dobbs), Zon Murray (Slade), Jim Diehl (Blaze), Maudie Prickett (Barber Kate), Jacques O'Mahoney [Jock Mahoney] (Waco), Frank Ellis (Frank), Frank LaRue (Roberts), Herman Hack (Chuck), Russell Meeker (Bartender), Jack Evans, Jack Tornek, Foxy Callahan, Victor Cox, Kit Guard (Citizens), George Plues, Ray Jones, Blackie Whiteford, Ben Corbett (Saloon Customers).

Working title: *Big Bend Badman*; British title: *Golden Lady*.

South of the Chisholm Trail (Columbia, 1947, 58 minutes) Producer: Colbert Clark. Director: Derwin Abrahams. Story-Screenplay: Michael Simmons. Photography: George Kelley. Editor: Paul Borofsky. Music Director: Mischa Bakaleinikoff. Songs: Smiley Burnette & Hank Newman. Art Director: Charles Clague. Sound: Lambert Day. Assistant Director: Carter De Haven, Jr.

Cast: Charles Starrett (Steve Haley/The Durango Kid), Smiley Burnette (Smiley), Nancy Saunders (Nora Grant), Hank Newman & His Georgia Crackers (Musicians), Frank Sully (Big Jim Grady), Jim Diehl (Herk), Jack Ingram (Chet Tobin), George Chesebro (Doc Walker), Frank LaRue (Pop Grant), Jacques O'Mahoney [Jock Mahoney] (Thorpe), Eddie Parker (Sheriff Palmer), Peter Perkins, Victor Holbrook, Pierce Lyden, Lane Bradford, Ray Elder (Gang Members), Fred F. Sears (Johnson), Chuck Hamilton (Bellows), Joseph Palma, Victor Travers, Cy Malis, Ethan Laidlaw, Merrill McCormick (Ranchers), Kermit Maynard (Deputy Sheriff), Sam Lufkin, Kernan Cripps (Cattle Buyers), John Tyrrell, Thomas Kingston (Cashiers), John L. Cason (Fight Patron), Robert Barron (Deputy Marshal), Milton Kibbee (Referee), Steve Clark, Herman Hack, Kit Guard, Rube Dalroy, Jack Evans (Citizens), Blackie Whiteford (Messenger).

Working title: *The Outlaw Tamer*.

The Lone Hand Texan (Columbia, 1947, 54 minutes) Producer: Colbert Clark. Director: Ray Nazarro. Screenplay: Ed Earl Repp. Photography: George Kelley. Editor: Paul Borofsky. Songs: Smiley Burnette, Doris Fisher & Allan Roberts. Art Director: Charles Clague. Sound: Lambert Day. Sets: Frank Kramer. Location Manager: Ralph Black. Casting: Victor Sutker. Assistant Director: William O'Connor.

Cast: Charles Starrett (Steve Driscoll/The Durango Kid), Smiley Burnette (Smiley), Mustard & Gravy [Frank Rice & Ernest L. Stokes] (Musicians), Mary Newton (Clarabelle Adams), Fred F. Sears (Sam Jason), Maudie Prickett (Hattie Hatfield), George Chesebro (Scanlon), John L. Cason, George Russell (Outlaws), Robert [Kellard] Stevens (Boomer Kildea), Jim Diehl (Straw Boss), Jasper Weldon (Coachman Williams), Post Park (Stagecoach Driver), Art Dillard (J.E. Clark), Matty Roubert (Gang Member), Herman Hack, Blackie Whiteford (Well Workers).

Working title: *Blue Prairie*; British title: *The Cheat*.

West of Dodge City (Columbia, 1947, 56 minutes) Producer: Colbert Clark. Director: Ray Nazarro. Screenplay: Bert Horswell. Photography: George Kelley. Editor: Paul Borofsky. Music Director: Mischa Bakaleinikoff. Songs: Smiley Burnette, Frank Rice & Ernest L. Stokes. Art Director: Charles Clague. Sound: Philip Faulkner. Sets: Robert Bradford. Assistant Director: William O'Connor.

Cast: Charles Starrett (Steve Ramsey/The Durango Kid), Smiley Burnette (Smiley), Nancy Saunders (Anne Avery), Mustard & Gravy [Frank Rice & Ernest L. Stokes] (Musicians), Glenn Stuart (Danny Avery), Stan [I. Stanford] Jolley (Borger), George Chesebro (Hod Barker), Bob [Robert J.] Wilke (Adams), Nolan Leary (John Avery), Steve Clark (Sheriff Howard), Zon Murray (Dirk), Marshall Reed (Flint), Tom Chatterton (Office Manager), Bud Osborne (Stagecoach Driver), Almira Sessions (Mrs. Throckbottom), Jim Diehl (Banker).

Working title: *Trigger Law*.

Law of the Canyon (Columbia, 1947, 57 minutes) Producer: Colbert Clark. Director: Ray Nazarro. Screenplay: Eileen Gray. Photography: George Kelley. Editor: Burton Kramer. Songs: Smiley Burnette, Ike Cargill & Tex Jim Lewis. Art Director: Harold MacArthur. Sets: David Montrose.

Cast: Charles Starrett (Steve Langtry/The Durango Kid), Smiley Burnette (Smiley), Nancy Saunders (Mary Coleman), Buzz Henry (Spike Coleman), Texas Jim Lewis & His Lone Star Cowboys [Billy Liebert, Harold Hensley, Buddy Hayes, Spud Goodall] (Musicians), George Chesebro (Sheriff Coleman), Edmund Cobb (T.D. Wilson), Fred F. Sears (Dr. Middleton), Zon Murray (Fletcher), Jack Kirk (Wagon Driver Ben), Robert J. Wilke (Knife Thrower), Frank Marlo (Blackie), Douglas D. Coppin (Hotel Clerk), Stanley Price (Man in Road), Art Dillard (Wagon Driver), Tommy Coats (Trail Herder).

British title: *The Price of Crime*.

Prairie Raiders (Columbia, 1947, 55 minutes) Producer: Colbert Clark. Director: Derwin Abrahams. Screenplay: Ed Earl Repp. Photography: George Kelley. Editor: Paul Borofsky. Songs: Smiley Burnette. Art Director: Charles Clague. Sound: Lambert Day. Sets: David Montrose. Assistant Director: William O'Connor.

Cast: Charles Starrett (Steve Bolton/The Durango

Kid), Smiley Burnette (Smiley), Nancy Saunders (Ann Bradford), Robert Scott (Bronc Masters), Ozie Waters & His Colorado Rangers (Musicians), Hugh Prosser (Bart "Spud" Henley), Lane Bradford (Stark), Ray Bennett (Flagg), Douglas D. Coppin (Hotel Clerk Briggs), Steve Clark (Sheriff), Tommy Coats (Shorty), Frank LaRue (Bradford), John L. Cason (Cinco), Sam Flint (Secretary of Interior Meeker), Scotty Harrell, Eddie Kirk (Entertainers).

Working title: *Whispering Range*.

The Stranger from Ponca City (Columbia, 1947, 56 minutes) Producer: Colbert Clark. Director: Derwin Abrahams. Screenplay: Ed Earl Repp. Photography: George Kelley. Editor: Burton Kramer. Songs: Smiley Burnette, Texas Jim Lewis & Cindy Walker. Art Director: Charles Clague. Sound: Jack Goodrich. Sets: David Montrose. Assistant Director: William O'Connor.

Cast: Charles Starrett (Steve Larkin/The Durango Kid), Smiley Burnette (Smiley), Virginia Hunter (Terry Saunders), Texas Jim Lewis & His Lone Star Cowboys [Texas Jim Lewis, Billy Liebert, Buddy Haynes, Charlie Linville] (Entertainers), Paul Campbell (Deputy Marshal Tug Carter), Forrest Taylor (Grat Carmondy), Jim Diehl (Flip Dugan), Jacques O'Mahoney [Jock Mahoney] (Tensleep), John Carpenter (Duke), Harmonica Bill [William Russell] (Cook), Bud Osborne (Ranger Jed), Ted Mapes (Fargo), Tom McDonough (Bill), Kermit Maynard, Charles Hamilton (Gang Members), Roy Butler (Rancher).

Riders of the Lone Star (Columbia, 1947, 55 minutes) Producer: Colbert Clark. Director: Derwin Abrahams. Screenplay: Barry Shipman. Photography: George Kelley. Editor: Paul Borofsky. Songs: Smiley Burnette, Eddie Kirk & Joe Pope. Art Director: Harvey Gillett. Sound: Lambert Day. Sets: David Montrose. Assistant Director: William O'Connor.

Cast: Charles Starrett (Steve Mason/The Durango Kid), Smiley Burnette (Smiley), Virginia Hunter (Doris McCormick), Curly Williams & His Georgia Peach Pickers (Entertainers), Steve Darrell (Murdock), Edmund Cobb (Blake), George Chesebro (Faro), Mark Dennis (Mike Morton), Lane Brandford (Rank), Ted Mapes (Slade), Peter Perkins (Brock), Eddie Parker (Sheriff Banning), Nolan Leary (Dr. Jones).

Buckaroo from Powder River (Columbia, 1947, 55 minutes) Producer: Colbert Clark. Director: Ray Nazarro. Screenplay: Norman S. Hall. Photography: George Kelley. Editor: Paul Borofsky. Songs: James A. Bland, Smiley Burnette, J. Fletcher & Frances Kyle. Art Directors: Charles Clague & Harvey Gillett. Sound: Howard Fogetti. Sets: David Montrose. Assistant Director: William O'Connor.

Cast: Charles Starrett (Steve Lacey/The Durango Kid), Smiley Burnette (Smiley), Eve Miller (Molly Parnell), Forrest Taylor (Pop Ryland), Paul Campbell (Tommy Ryland), The Cass County Boys [Jerry Scoggins, Bert Dodson, Fred S. Martin] (Entertainers), Douglas D. Coppin (Clint Ryland), Philip Morris (Sheriff Parnell), Casey MacGregor (Dave Ryland), Ted Adams (Lon Driscoll), Edmund Cobb (Taggart), Ethan Laidlaw (Ben Trask), Phil Arnold (Barbershop Customer), Buster Brodie (Bald Man), Roy Butler (Tom), Kermit Maynard (Stagecoach Guard), Frank McCarroll (McCall), Tex Palmer (Stagecoach Driver).

Working title: *Blazing Through Cimarron*.

Last Days of Boot Hill (Columbia, 1947, 55 minutes) Producer: Colbert Clark. Director: Ray Nazarro. Screenplay: Norman S. Hall. Photography: George Kelley. Editor: Paul Borofsky. Songs: Smiley Burnette, Milton Drake, Harry Meerson, Belmont Parker & Harry Zimmer. Art Director: Charles Clague. Sound: Lambert Day. Sets: David Montrose. Assistant Director: William O'Connor.

Cast: Charles Starrett (Steve Waring/The Durango Kid), Smiley Burnette (Smiley), Virginia Hunter (Paula Thorpe), Paul Campbell (Frank Rayburn), Mary Newton (Clara Brent), The Cass County Boys [Jerry Scoggins, Bert Dodson, Fred S. Martin] (Entertainers), Bill Free (Reed Brokaw), J. Courtland Lytton (Dan McCoy), Robert J. Wilke (Bronc Peters), Syd Saylor (Hank), Alan Bridge (Forrest "Lucky" Thorpe/Forrest Brent), John L. Cason (Chad), Blackie Whiteford (Gang Member), Victor Cox (Sheriff), Carole Mathews (Mary Halliday), Emmett Lynn (J. Horace "Grubstake" Higginbotham), Charles King (Nevada), Nolan Leary (Bob Halliday), Tex Harding (Tex), Steve Clark (Dan Waring), Robert Barron (Dan Cass), Mauritz Hugo (Jim McMasters), John Tyrrell (Perkins).

British title: *On Boot Hill*.

Six-Gun Law (Columbia, 1948, 54 minutes) Producer: Colbert Clark. Director: Ray Nazarro. Screenplay: Barry Shipman. Photography: George Kelley. Editor: Henry DeMond. Songs: Smiley Burnette & Curly Clements. Art Director: Charles Clague. Sound: Lambert Day. Sets: David Montrose. Assistant Director: Gilbert Kay.

Cast: Charles Starrett (Steve Norris/The Durango Kid), Smiley Burnette (Smiley), Nancy Saunders (June Wallace), Paul Campbell (Jim Wallace), Hugh Prosser (Boss Decker), Curly Clements & the Rodeo Rangers (Musicians), George Chesebro (Bret Wallace), Billy Dix (Crowl), Robert J. Wilke (Larson), John L. Cason (Ben), Ethan Laidlaw (Sheriff Brackett), Pierce Lyden (Marshal Jack Reed), Bud Osborne (Stagecoach Driver Barton), Budd Buster (Duffy), Louis "Slim" Gaunt (Drunk Cowboy).

Phantom Valley (Columbia, 1948, 56 minutes) Producer: Colbert Clark. Director: Ray Nazarro. Screenplay: J. Benton Cheney. Photography: George Kelley. Editor: Paul Borofsky. Songs: Smiley Burnette. Art Director: Charles Clague. Sets: David Montrose.

Cast: Charles Starrett (Steve Collins/The Durango Kid), Smiley Burnette (Smiley), Virginia Hunter (Janice "Jancy" Littlejohn), Ozie Waters & the Colorado Rangers (Musicians), Joel Friedkin (Samuel Littlejohn),

Robert Filmer (Bob Reynolds), Mikel Conrad (Crag Parker), Zon Murray (Frazer), Sam Flint (Jim Durant), Fred F. Sears (Ben Theibold), Teddy Infuhr (Chips), Jerry Jerome (Bart), Denver Dixon (Citizen).

Working title: *Call of the Prairie.*

West of Sonora (Columbia, 1948, 55 minutes) Producer: Colbert Clark. Director: Ray Nazarro. Screenplay: Barry Shipman. Photography: Ira H. Morgan. Editor: Jerome Thoms. Songs: Smiley Burnette. Art Director: Charles Clague. Sound: Josh Westmoreland. Sets: George Montgomery.

Cast: Charles Starrett (Steve Rollins/The Durango Kid), Smiley Burnette (Smiley), George Chesebro (Sheriff Jeff Clinton), Anita Castle (Penelope Clinton), The Sunshine Boys [Eddie Wallace, Freddie Daniel, M.H. Richman, J.D. Sumner] (Musicians), Hal Taliaferro [Wally Wales] (Sandy Clinton), Robert J. Wilke (Brock), Emmett Lynn (Jack Bascom), Lynn Farr (Dickson), Blackie Whiteford (Three Strike O'Toole), Lloyd Ingraham (Old Man).

Whirlwind Raiders (Columbia, 1948, 54 minutes) Producer: Colbert Clark. Director: Vernon Keays. Screenplay: Norman S. Hall. Photography: M.A. Anderson. Editor: Paul Borofsky. Songs: Smiley Burnette, Daniel Decatur, Emmett & Leon Rice. Art Director: Charles Clague. Sets: David Montrose.

Cast: Charles Starrett (Steve Lanning/The Durango Kid), Smiley Burnette (Smiley), Fred F. Sears (Tracy Beaumont), Nancy Saunders (Claire Ross), Little Brown Jug [Don Kay Reynolds] (Tommy Ross), Doye O'Dell & the Radio Rangers (Musicians), Jack Ingram (Captain Buff Tyson), Philip Morris (Homer Ross), Patrick Hurst (Bill Webster), Eddie Parker (Red Jordan), Lynn Farr (Slim), Maudie Prickett (Mrs. Wallace), Frank LaRue (Wilson), Russell Meeker (Charlie the Bartender).

British title: *State Police.*

Blazing Across the Pecos (Columbia, 1948, 54 minutes) Producer: Colbert Clark. Director: Ray Nazarro. Screenplay: Norman S. Hall. Photography: Ira H. Morgan. Editor: Richard Fantl. Songs: Joseph Brockman, Smiley Burnette & John Cornell. Art Director: Charles Clague. Sound: Jack Goodrich. Sets: Sidney Clifford. Assistant Director: Gilbert Kay.

Cast: Charles Starrett (Steve Blake/The Durango Kid), Smiley Burnette (Marshal Smiley Burnette), Patricia White [Patricia Barry] (Lola Carter), Paul Campbell (Jim Traynor), Charles Wilson (Mayor Ace Brockway), Thomas Jackson (Matt Carter), Red Arnall & the Western Aces (Musicians), Jack Ingram (Buckshot Thomas), Chief Thundercloud (Chief Bear Claw), Pat O'Malley (Mike Doyle), Jock O'Mahoney [Jock Mahoney] (Bill Wheeler), Paul Conrad (Sleepy Larsen), Pierce Lyden (Mr. Jason), Post Park (Stagecoach Driver), Jack Evans, Blackie Whiteford, Jack Tornek (Citizens), Ralph Bucko (Messenger).

British title: *Under Arrest.*

Trail to Laredo (Columbia, 1948, 54 minutes) Producer: Colbert Clark. Director: Ray Nazarro. Screenplay: Barry Shipman. Photography: Henry Freulich. Editor: Paul Borofsky. Music: Smiley Burnette, Sammy Cahn, Saul Chapin, Ed McDermott & Don Roseland. Art Director: Charles Clague. Sound: Lambert Day. Sets: David Montrose. Assistant Director: Gilbert Kay.

Cast: Charles Starrett (Steve Ellison/The Durango Kid), Smiley Burnette (Smiley), Jim Bannon (Dan Parks), Virginia Maxey (Classy), Tommy Ivo (Ronnie Parks), Hugh Prosser (Fenton), The Cass County Boys [Jerry Scoggins, Bert Dodson, Fred S. Martin] (Musicians), George Chesebro (Walt Morgan), Robert J. Wilke (Duke), John L. Cason (Blaze), John Merton (Sheriff Kennedy), Ted Mapes (Chuck), Bob Reeves (Ranger Captain).

El Dorado Pass (Columbia, 1948, 56 minutes) Producer: Colbert Clark. Director: Ray Nazarro. Screenplay: Earle Snell. Photography: Rex Wimpy. Editor: Burton Kramer. Music Director: Mischa Bakaleinikoff. Songs: Smiley Burnette, Eddie Dean & Glenn Strange. Art Director: Carl Anderson. Sound: Frank Goodwin. Sets: Frank Kramer. Production Manager: Jack Fier. Makeup: Leonard Ingleman. Assistant Director: Earl Bellamy.

Cast: Charles Starrett (Steve Clayton/The Durango Kid), Smiley Burnette (Smiley), Elena Verdugo (Dolores), Steve Darrell (Page), Rory Mallinson (Sheriff Tom Wright), Ted Mapes (Dodd), Stanley Blystone (Barlow), Gertrude Chorre (Sunflower), Harry Vejar (Don Martinez), Blackie Whiteford (Gang Member).

Working title: *Crossroads of the West*; British title: *Desperate Men.*

Quick on the Trigger (Columbia, 1948, 54 minutes) Producer: Colbert Clark. Director: Ray Nazarro. Screenplay: Elmer Clifton. Photography: Rex Wimpy. Editor: Paul Borofsky. Music Director: Mischa Bakaleinikoff. Songs: Smiley Burnette, Hy Heath, Fred Rose & The Sunshine Boys. Art Director: Charles Clague. Sound: Russell Malmgren. Sets: Frank Kramer. Production Manager: Jack Fier. Assistant Director: Paul Donnelly.

Cast: Charles Starrett (Steve Warren/The Durango Kid), Smiley Burnette (Smiley), Lyle Talbot (Garvey Yager), Helen Parrish (Nora Reed), George Eldredge (Alfred Murdock), The Sunshine Boys [Eddie Wallace, J.D. Sumner, Freddie Daniel, M.H. Richman] (Musicians), Ted Adams (Sheriff Martin Oaks), Alan Bridge (Judge Kormac), Russell Arms (Fred Reed), Budd Buster (Telegrapher), Bud Osborne (Stagecoach Driver), Russell Meeker (Jury Foreman), Tex Cooper (Juror), George Morrell (Citizen), Sandy Sanders, Blackie Whiteford (Gang Members).

Working title: *Gun Brand*; British title: *Condemned in Error.*

Challenge of the Range (Columbia, 1949, 56 minutes) Producer: Colbert Clark. Director: Ray Nazarro. Screenplay: Ed Earl Repp. Photography: Rex Wimpy. Editor: Paul Borofsky. Songs: Smiley Burnette, Doris

Fisher & Allan Roberts. Art Director: Charles Clague. Sound: Russell Malmgren. Sets: David Montrose. Production Manager: Jack Fier. Assistant Director: Paul Donnelly.

Cast: Charles Starrett (Steve Roper/The Durango Kid), Smiley Burnette (Smiley), Paula Raymond (Judy Barton), William [Billy] Halop (Reb Matson), Steve Darrell (Cal Matson), Henry Hall (Jim Barton), Robert Filmer (Grat Largo), The Sunshine Boys [Eddie Wallace, Freddie Daniel, M.H. Richman, J.D. Sumner] (Musicians), George Chesebro (Lon Collins), Leroy Johnson, Emile Avery (Cowboys), Frank McCarroll (Dugan), John L. Cason (Spud Henley), Edmund Cobb, Kermit Maynard, Matty Roubert, Ray Bennett, Cactus Mack (Gang Members), Pat O'Malley (Sheriff), Milton Kibbee (Ezra), Marshall Reed (Rider), Frank O'Connor (Saunders), Rose Plummer (Citizen).

British title: *Moonlight Raid*.

Desert Vigilante (Columbia, 1949, 56 minutes) Producer: Colbert Clark. Director: Fred F. Sears. Screenplay: Earle Snell. Photography: Rex Wimpy. Editor: Paul Borofsky. Songs: Smiley Burnette & Jimmy Wakely. Art Director: Charles Clague. Sets: David Montrose.

Cast: Charles Starrett (Steve Brooks/The Durango Kid), Smiley Burnette (Smiley), Peggy Stewart (Betty Long), Mary Newton (Angel), George Chesebro (Bill Martin), The Georgia Crackers (Musicians), Paul Campbell (Bob Gill), Tex Harding (Jim Gill), Jack Ingram (Border Patrol Sergeant), I. Stanford Jolley (Ace), Ted Mapes, George Morrell, Blackie Whiteford, Sandy Sanders, Lew Morphy, Roy Bucko (Gang Members), Jerry Hunter (Indian Boy).

Laramie (Columbia, 1949, 55 minutes) Producer: Colbert Clark. Director: Ray Nazarro. Screenplay: Barry Shipman. Photography: Rex Wimpy. Editor: Paul Borofsky. Songs: Elton Britt, Smiley Burnette & Bob Miller. Art Director: Charles Clague. Sets: James Crowe.

Cast: Charles Starrett (Steve Holden/The Durango Kid), Smiley Burnette (Smiley), Fred F. Sears (Colonel Ron Dennison), Tommy Ivo (Denny Dennison), Elton Britt (Singing Sergeant), Bob [Robert J.] Wilke (Cronin), George Lloyd (Sergeant Duff), Myron Healey (Lieutenant Reed), Shooting Star (Chief Eagle), Jay Silverheels (Running Wolf), Jim Diehl (Brecker), Rodd Redwing (Indian Lookout), Nolan Leary (Senator Briggs), John L. Cason, Ethan Laidlaw (Gang Members), Kermit Maynard (Stagecoach Driver).

The Blazing Trail (Columbia, 1949, 58 minutes) Producer: Colbert Clark. Director: Ray Nazarro. Screenplay: Barry Shipman. Photography: Ira H. Morgan. Editor: Paul Borofsky. Songs: Floyd Bartlett, Smiley Burnette, Slim Duncan, George La Verne & Hank Penny. Art Director: Charles Clague. Sets: Frank Tuttle.

Cast: Charles Starrett (Steve Allen/The Durango Kid), Smiley Burnette (Smiley), Fred F. Sears (Luke Masters), Steve Darrell (Sam Brady), Jock [Mahoney] O'Mahoney (Full House Patterson), Trevor Bardette (Jess Williams), Hank Penny, Slim Duncan (Musicians), Steve Pendleton (Kirk Brady), Robert Malcolm (Old Mike Brady), John L. Cason (Cotton), Frank McCarroll, Herman Hack (Deputy Sheriffs), John Merton (Guard), Frank O'Connor (County Recorder), George Morrell, Rube Dalroy (Citizens), Jack Evans, Blackie Whiteford (Newspaper Purchasers), Merrill McCormick (Witness).

British title: *The Forged Will*.

South of Death Valley (Columbia, 1949, 55 minutes) Producer: Colbert Clark. Director: Ray Nazarro. Screenplay: Earle Snell. Photography: Fayte Browne. Editor: Paul Borofsky. Songs: Smiley Burnette, Effie I. Canning, Milton Drake & Mrs. Tommy Duncan. Art Director: Charles Clague. Sets: George Montgomery. Makeup: Bob Schiffer.

Cast: Charles Starrett (Steve Downing/The Durango Kid), Smiley Burnette (Smiley), Fred F. Sears (Sam Ashton), Lee Roberts (Scotty Tavish), Richard Emory (Tommy Tavish), Clayton Moore (Bead), Tommy Duncan & His Western All Stars (Musicians), Jason Robards (Porter Mullen), Chuck Hamilton, Kermit Maynard (Gang Members), Jack Evans, Blackie Whiteford, George Morrell, George Sowards (Citizens).

British title: *River of Poison*.

Bandits of El Dorado (Columbia, 1949, 54 minutes) Producer: Colbert Clark. Director: Ray Nazarro. Screenplay: Barry Shipman. Photography: Fayte Browne. Editor: Paul Borofsky. Songs: Smiley Burnette, Frank Rice & Ernest L. Stokes. Art Director: Charles Clague. Sets: George Montgomery.

Cast: Charles Starrett (Steve Carson/The Durango Kid), Smiley Burnette (Smiley), George J. Lewis (Colonel Jose Vargas), Fred F. Sears (Captain Richard Henley), John Dehner (Charles Bruton), Clayton Moore (B.F. Morgan), Mustard & Gravy [Frank Rice & Ernest L. Stokes] (Musicians), Jock [Mahoney] O'Mahoney (Ranger Tim Starling), John Doucette (Tucker), Max Wagner (Paul), Henry Kulky (Bartender Spade), Edmund Cobb, John Merton, Ray Bennett (Bank Robbers), Kermit Maynard (Bank Robber/Stagecoach Guard), Jack Evans (Stage Line Employee), Carl Mathews (Texas Ranger), Monte Montague, Blackie Whiteford (Saloon Customers), Merrill McCormick, Jack Tornek, Victor Cox, Herman Hack, Al Haskell, Ray Jones (Citizens), Ted Mapes (Rider).

British title: *Tricked*.

Horsemen of the Sierras (Columbia, 1949, 56 minutes) Producer: Colbert Clark. Director: Fred F. Sears. Screenplay: Barry Shipman. Photography: Fayte Browne. Editor: Paul Borofsky. Songs: Smiley Burnette, Harold Hensley, T. Texas Tyler & Scotty Wiseman. Art Director: Charles Clague. Sound: Jack Haynes. Sets: George Montgomery. Production Manager: Jack Fier. Assistant Director: Gilbert Kay.

Cast: Charles Starrett (Steve Saunders/The Durango

Kid), Smiley Burnette (Sheriff Smiley), T. Texas Tyler (Entertainer), Lois Hall (Patty McGregor), Tommy Ivo (Robin "Robbie" Grant), John Dehner (Duke Webster), Jason Robards (Phineas Grant), Daniel M. Sheridan (Morgan Webster), Jock [Mahoney] O'Mahoney (Don Grant), George Chesebro (Ellory Webster), Emile Avery, Ethan Laidlaw, Charles Soldani (Gang Members).

British title: *Remember Me*.

Renegades of the Sage (Columbia, 1949, 56 minutes) Producer: Colbert Clark. Director: Ray Nazarro. Screenplay: Earle Snell. Photography: Fayte Browne. Editor: Paul Borofsky. Songs: Smiley Burnette, Henry Carey, Gene De Paul, Don Raye & Samuel Francis Smith. Art Director: Charles Clague. Production Manager: Jack Fier. Assistant Director: Gilbert Kay.

Cast: Charles Starrett (Steve Duncan/The Durango Kid), Smiley Burnette (Smiley), Leslie Banning (Ellen Miller/Ellen Braden), Trevor Bardette (Miller/Lynn Braden), Douglas Fowley (Sloper), Jock [Mahoney] O'Mahoney (Lieutenant Hunter), Fred F. Sears (Lieutenant Jones), Jerry Hunter (Johnny), George Chesebro (Laborer), Frank McCarroll (Drew), Selmer Jackson (Brown).

British title: *The Fort*.

Trail of the Rustlers (Columbia, 1950, 55 minutes) Producer: Colbert Clark. Director: Ray Nazarro. Screenplay: Victor Arthur. Photography: Fayte Browne. Editor: Paul Borofsky. Songs: Smiley Burnette. Art Director: Charles Clague. Sets: George Montgomery.

Cast: Charles Starrett (Steve Armitage/The Durango Kid), Smiley Burnette (Smiley), Gail Davis (Mary Ellen Harley), Tommy Ivo (Tod Harley), Mira McKinney (Mrs. Mahoney), Don C. Harvey (Chick Mahoney), Eddie Cletro & His Roundup Boys (Musicians), Myron Healey (Ben Mahoney), Chuck Roberson (Bob), Gene Roth (Sheriff Dave Wilcox), Boyd "Red" Morgan (Jake), Herman Hack (Rancher), Blackie Whiteford (Citizen), Post Park (Stagecoach Driver).

Outcasts of Black Mesa (Columbia, 1950, 54 minutes) Producer: Colbert Clark. Director: Ray Nazarro. Screenplay: Barry Shipman. Story: Elmer Clifton. Photography: Fayte Browne. Editor: Paul Borofsky. Songs: Smiley Burnette & Frances Clark. Art Director: Charles Clague. Sets: Sidney Clifford. Makeup: Leonard Engelman.

Cast: Charles Starrett (Steve Norman/The Durango Kid), Smiley Burnette (Smiley), Martha Hyer (Ruth Dorn), Richard Bailey (Andrew Vaning), Stanley Andrews (Sheriff Grasset), William Haade (Dayton), Lane Chandler (Ted Thorp), William Gould (Walt Dorn), Bob [Robert J.] Wilke (Curt), Charles "Chuck" Roberson (Kramer), Ozie Waters (Singer).

British title: *The Clue*.

Texas Dynamo (Columbia, 1950, 54 minutes) Producer: Colbert Clark. Director: Ray Nazarro. Screenplay: Barry Shipman. Photography: Fayte Browne. Editor: Paul Borofsky. Songs: Smiley Burnette & Frances Clark. Art Director: Charles Clague. Sound: Frank Goodwin. Sets: George Montgomery. Production Manager: Jack Fier. Makeup: Leonard Engelman.

Cast: Charles Starrett (Steve Drake/The Durango Kid), Smiley Burnette (Smiley), Lois Hall (Julia Beck), Jock [Mahoney] O'Mahoney (Bill Beck), John Dehner (Stanton), George Chesebro (Kroger), Emil Sitka (Turkey), Fred F. Sears (Hawkins), Gregg Barton (Luke), Slim Duncan (Musician).

British title: *Suspected*.

Streets of Ghost Town (Columbia, 1950, 54 minutes) Producer: Colbert Clark. Director: Ray Nazarro. Screenplay: Barry Shipman. Photography: Fayte Browne. Editor: Paul Borofsky. Songs: Smiley Burnette & Stephen Foster. Art Director: Charles Clague. Sets: George Montgomery. Assistant Director: R.M. Andrews.

Cast: Charles Starrett (Steve Woods/The Durango Kid), Smiley Burnette (Smiley), George Chesebro (Bill Donner), Mary Ellen Kay (Doris Donner), Stanley Andrews (Sheriff Dodge), Frank Fenton (Bart Selby), Don Reynolds "Brown Jug" [Don Kay Reynolds] (Tommy Donner), Ozie Waters & His Colorado Rangers (Musicians), John L. Cason (John Wicks), Jack Ingram (Deputy Sheriff Kirby), Nolan Leary (Jenkins), Robert Kortman (Sackett), Emmett Lynn, Doris Houck (Homesteaders), Dick Rush (Banker), John Tyrrell (Deputy Sheriff).

Across the Badlands (Columbia, 1950, 55 minutes) Producer: Colbert Clark. Director: Fred F. Sears. Screenplay: Barry Shipman. Photography: Fayte Browne. Editor: Paul Borofsky. Songs: Smiley Burnette. Art Director: Charles Clague. Sound: Jack Haynes. Production Manager: Jack Fier. Sets: Fay Babcock. Makeup: Leonard Engelman. Assistant Director: Lee Lukather.

Cast: Charles Starrett (Steve Ransom/The Durango Kid), Smiley Burnette (Smiley), Helen Mowery (Eileen Carson), Stanley Andrews (Sheriff Crocker), Bob [Robert J.] Wilke (Duke Jackson/Keno Jackson), Dick Elliott (Rufus Downey), Hugh Prosser (Jeff Carson), Robert S. Cavendish (Bart), Charles Evans (Gregory Banion), Paul Campbell (Pete), Harmonica Bill [William Russell] (Musician), Richard Alexander (Thug), Bob Woodward (Gang Member).

British title: *The Challenge*.

Raiders of Tomahawk Creek (Columbia, 1950, 55 minutes) Producer: Colbert Clark. Director: Fred F. Sears. Screenplay: Barry Shipman. Story: Eric Freiwald & Robert Schaefer. Photography: Fayte Browne. Editor: Paul Borofsky. Songs: Smiley Burnette. Art Director: Charles Clague. Sound: Russ Malmgren. Sets: Louis Diage. Production Manager: Jack Fier. Makeup: Gordon Hubbard. Assistant Director: Gilbert Kay.

Cast: Charles Starrett (Steve Blake/The Durango Kid), Smiley Burnette (Smiley), Edgar Dearing (Randolph Dike), Kay Dearing (Janet Clayton), Billy Kimbley (Billy Calhoun), Paul Marion (Chief Flying Arrow), Paul McGuire (Sheriff), Bill Hale (Jeff Calhoun), Lee Morgan (Saunders), Ted Mapes (Gang Member).

Lightning Guns (Columbia, 1950, 55 minutes) Producer: Colbert Clark. Director: Fred F. Sears. Screenplay: Victor Arthur. Story: Bill Milligan. Photography: Fayte Browne. Editor: Paul Borofsky. Music Director: Mischa Bakaleinikoff. Songs: Smiley Burnette. Art Director: Charles Clague. Sound: George Cooper. Sets: George Montgomery. Assistant Director: Willard Reineck.

Cast: Charles Starrett (Steve Brandon/The Durango Kid), Smiley Burnette (Smiley), Gloria Henry (Susan Atkins), William Norton Bailey (Luke Atkins), Edgar Dearing (Captain Dan Saunders), Raymond Bond (Jud Norton), Jock [Mahoney] O'Mahoney (Sheriff Rob Saunders), Chuck Roberson (Hank Burch), Frank Griffin (Jim Otis), Joel Friedkin (Crawley), George Chesebro (Blake), Ken Houchins (Musician), Billy Williams (Guard), Merrill McCormick (Gang Member).

Working title: *Taking Sides*.

Frontier Outpost (Columbia, 1950, 55 minutes) Producer: Colbert Clark. Director: Ray Nazarro. Screenplay: Barry Shipman. Photography: Fayte Browne. Editor: Paul Borofsky. Music Director: Mischa Bakaleinikoff. Songs: Smiley Burnette. Art Director: Charles Clague.

Cast: Charles Starrett (Steve Lawton/The Durango Kid), Smiley Burnette (Smiley), Lois Hall (Alice Tanner), Steve Darrell (Forsythe), Fred F. Sears (Copeland), Bob [Robert J.] Wilke (Krag Benson), Paul Campbell (Captain Tanner), Jock [Mahoney] O'Mahoney (Lieutenant Peck), Bud Osborne (Stagecoach Driver), Charles "Chuck" Roberson (Gopher), Pierre Watkin (Colonel Warrick), Dick Wessel (Sergeant Murphy), Hank Penny, Slim Duncan (Musicians), Everett Glass (Chalmers).

Prairie Roundup (Columbia, 1951, 53 minutes) Producer: Colbert Clark. Director: Fred F. Sears. Screenplay: Joseph O'Donnell. Photography: Fayte Browne. Editor: Paul Borofsky. Music Director: Mischa Bakaleinikoff. Songs: Smiley Burnette. Art Director: Charles Clague. Sound: Lambert Day. Production Manager: Jack Fier. Sets: David Montrose. Assistant Director: Wilbur McGaugh.

Cast: Charles Starrett (Steve Carson/The Durango Kid), Smiley Burnette (Smiley), Mary Castle (Toni Eaton), Frank Fenton (Buck Prescott), The Sunshine Boys [Eddie Wallace, Freddie Daniel, M.H. Richman, J.D. Sumner] (Musicians), Frank Sully (Sheriff), Paul Campbell (Poker Joe), Forrest Taylor (Dan Kelly), George Baxter (Jim Eaton), Lane Chandler (Red Dawson), John L. Cason (Barton), Al Wyatt (Masked Man), Glenn Thompson (Pete), Ace Richmond (Curtis), Don C. Harvey (Hawk Edwards), Blackie Whiteford (Citizen).

Ridin' the Outlaw Trail (Columbia, 1951, 56 minutes) Producer: Colbert Clark. Director: Fred F. Sears. Screenplay: Victor Arthur. Photography: Fayte Browne. Editor: Paul Borofsky. Music Director: Mischa Bakaleinikoff. Songs: Smiley Burnette. Art Director: Charles Clague. Sound: Howard Fogetti. Production Manager: Jack Fier. Assistant Director: Gilbert Kay.

Cast: Charles Starrett (Steve Forsythe/The Durango Kid), Smiley Burnette (Smiley), Sunny Vickers (Betsy Willard), Edgar Dearing (Pop Willard), Peter Thompson (Sheriff Tom Chapman), Jim Bannon (Ace Conley), Lee Morgan (Sam Barton), Chuck Roberson (Reno), Pee Wee King & the Golden West Cowboys (Musicians), Frank McCarroll (Guard), Ethan Laidlaw, Guy Teague (Gang Members).

Fort Savage Raiders (Columbia, 1951, 54 minutes) Producer: Colbert Clark. Director: Ray Nazarro. Screenplay: Barry Shipman. Photography: Henry Freulich. Editor: Paul Borofsky. Music Director: Ross DiMaggio. Songs: Smiley Burnette. Art Director: Charles Clague. Sound: George Cooper. Sets: George Montgomery. Assistant Director: Paul Donnelly.

Cast: Charles Starrett (Steve Drake/The Durango Kid), Smiley Burnette (Smiley), John Dehner (Captain Michael Craydon), Trevor Bardette (Old Cuss), Peter Thompson (Lieutenant James Sutter), Fred F. Sears (Colonel Sutter), Dusty Walker (Blonde), John L. Cason (Gus), Frank Griffin (Rog Beck), Sam Flint (Colonel Markham).

Snake River Desperadoes (Columbia, 1951, 55 minutes) Producer: Colbert Clark. Director: Fred F. Sears. Screenplay: Barry Shipman. Photography: Fayte Browne. Editor: Paul Borofsky. Music Director: Ross DiMaggio. Music Supervisor: Paul Mertz. Songs: Smiley Burnette. Art Director: Charles Clague. Sound: Jack Goodrich. Production Manager: Jack Fier. Sets: George Montgomery.

Cast: Charles Starrett (Steve Reynolds/The Durango Kid), Smiley Burnette (Smiley), Monte Blue (Jim Haverly), Don Reynolds "Brown Jug" [Don Kay Reynolds] (Little Hawk), Tommy Ivo (Billy Haverly), Boyd "Red" Morgan (Brandt), George Chesebro (Josh "Dad" Haverly), John Pickard (Dodds), Charles Horvath (Chief Black Eagle), Sam Flint (Jason Fox), Duke York (Pete), Herman Hack (Citizen), Al Wyatt (Gang Member).

Bonanza Town (Columbia, 1951, 56 minutes) Producer: Colbert Clark. Director: Fred F. Sears. Screenplay: Barry Shipman & Bert Horswell. Photography: Henry Freulich. Editor: Paul Borofsky. Music Director: Mischa Bakaleinikoff. Songs: Smiley Burnette & Slim Duncan. Art Director: Charles Clague. Sound: Russell Malmgren. Sets: George Montgomery. Assistant Director: Gilbert Kay.

Cast: Charles Starrett (Steve Ramsey/The Durango Kid), Smiley Burnette (Smiley), Fred F. Sears (Henry Hardison), Luther Crockett (Judge Anthony Dillon),

Myron Healey (Krag Boseman), Charles Horvath (Smoker), Slim Duncan (Slim), Al Wyatt (Bill Trotter), Paul McGuire (Marshal John Reed), Vernon Dent (Barber Shop Customer), Nancy Saunders (Anne Avery), Glenn Stuart (Danny Avery), I. Stanford Jolley (Borger), George Chesebro (Hod Barker), Robert J. Wilke (Adams), Nolan Leary (John Avery), Steve Clark (Sheriff Howard), Zon Murray (Dirk), Marshall Reed (Flint), Bud Osborne (Stagecoach Driver), Guy Teague, George Magrill (Gang Members), Ted Jordan (Bob Dillon).

British title: *Two-Fisted Agent*.

Cyclone Fury (Columbia, 1951, 53 minutes) Producer: Colbert Clark. Director: Ray Nazarro. Screenplay: Barry Shipman & Ed Earl Repp. Photography: Henry Freulich. Editor: Paul Borofsky. Music Director: Mischa Bakaleinikoff. Music Supervisor: Paul Mertz. Songs: Smiley Burnette. Art Director: Charles Clague. Sets: George Montgomery.

Cast: Charles Starrett (Steve Reynolds/The Durango Kid), Smiley Burnette (Smiley), Clayton Moore (Grat Hanlon), Bob [Robert J.] Wilke (Bunco), Fred F. Sears (Captain Barham), Merle Travis & His Bronco Busters (Musicians), Louis Lettieri (Johnny Masters), George Chesebro (Bret Fuller), Frank O'Connor (Doctor), Jay Silverheels (Chief Running Wolf), Edmund Cobb (Barstow), Kermit Maynard, Ray Bennett, Matty Roubert (Gunmen), Slim Duncan (Fiddler), John Merton, Lane Bradford (Gang Members), Frank Moran (Cook), Robert E. Scott (Brock Masters), Richard Alexander (Big Henchman), Lew Morphy (Wrangler).

Working title: *Cyclone Canyon*.

The Kid from Amarillo (Columbia, 1951, 56 minutes) Producer: Colbert Clark. Director: Ray Nazarro. Screenplay: Barry Shipman. Photography: Fayte Browne. Editor: Paul Borofsky. Music Director: Mischa Bakaleinikoff. Songs: Smiley Burnette. Art Director: Charles Clague. Sound: Lambert Day. Sets: James Crowe. Assistant Director: James Nicholson.

Cast: Charles Starrett (Steve Ransom/The Durango Kid), Smiley Burnette (Smiley), Harry Lauter (Tom Mallory), Fred F. Sears (Jonathan Cole), Don Megowan (Rakim), Scott Lee (Snead), Guy Teague (Dirk), Charles Evans (Jason Summerville), George J. Lewis (Don Jose Figaroa), Henry Kulky (Zeno), George Chesebro (El Loco), The Cass County Boys [Jerry Scoggins, Bert Dodson, Fred S. Martin] (Musicians).

British title: *Silver Chains*.

Pecos River (Columbia, 1951, 55 minutes) Producer: Colbert Clark. Director: Fred F. Sears. Screenplay: Barry Shipman. Photography: Fayte Browne. Editor: Paul Borofsky. Music Director: Mischa Bakaleinikoff. Songs: Smiley Burnette. Art Director: Charles Clague. Sound: Lambert Day. Sets: James Crowe.

Cast: Charles Starrett (Steve Baldwin/The Durango Kid), Smiley Burnette (Smiley), Jack [Jock] Mahoney (Jack Mahoney), Delores Sidener (Betty Coulter), Steve Darrell (Pop Rockland), Frank Jenks (Sheriff Denning), Harmonica Bill [William Russell] (Entertainer), Paul Campbell (Sniff Rockland), Zon Murray (Mose Rockland), Maudie Prickett (Mrs. Peck), Eddie Fetherston (Mr. Grey), Edgar Dearing (Old Henry Mahoney), Frank McCarroll, Al Haskell, Blackie Whiteford (Citizens).

British title: *Without Risk*.

Smoky Canyon (Columbia, 1952, 55 minutes) Producer: Colbert Clark. Director: Fred F. Sears. Screenplay: Barry Shipman. Photography: Fayte Browne. Editor: Paul Borofsky. Music Director: Mischa Bakaleinikoff. Songs: Smiley Burnette. Art Director: Charles Clague. Sets: Louis Diage. Assistant Director: James Nicholson.

Cast: Charles Starrett (Steve Brent/The Durango Kid), Smiley Burnette (Smiley), Jack [Jock] Mahoney (Jack Mahoney), Dani Sue Nolan (Roberta "Rob" Woodstock), Tristram Coffin (Carl Buckley), Larry Hudson (Sheriff Bogart), Chris Alcaide (Lars), Sandy Sanders (Spade), Charles Stevens (Johnny Big Foot), Boyd "Red" Morgan (Joe), Leroy Johnson (Ace), Frank O'Connor (Jim Woodstock), Blackie Whiteford, Chick Hannon (Citizens), Dick Botiller (Rancher), Gerald Mohr (Narrator).

The Hawk of Powder River (Columbia, 1952, 54 minutes) Producer: Colbert Clark. Director: Fred F. Sears. Screenplay: Howard J. Green. Photography: Fayte Browne. Editor: Paul Borofsky. Music Director: Mischa Bakaleinikoff. Songs: Smiley Burnette. Art Director: Charles Clague. Sound: Frank Goodwin. Assistant Director: Paul Donnelly.

Cast: Charles Starrett (Steve Martin/The Durango Kid), Smiley Burnette (Smiley), Jack [Jock] Mahoney (Jack Mahoney), Clayton Moore (The Hawk), Eddie Parker (Skeeter), Jim Diehl (Al Travis), Lane Chandler (George), Syd Saylor (Yank-Em-Out Kennedy), John L. Cason (Duke), Leroy Johnson (Smoky), Jack Carry (Pete), Sam Flint (Clark Mahoney), Donna Hall (Young Woman).

Laramie Mountains (Columbia, 1952, 54 minutes) Producer: Colbert Clark. Director: Ray Nazarro. Screenplay: Barry Shipman. Photography: Fayte Browne. Editor: Paul Borofsky. Music Director: Mischa Bakaleinikoff. Songs: Smiley Burnette. Art Director: Charles Clague. Sound: Russell Malmgren. Sets: James Crowe. Assistant Director: Jack Corrick.

Cast: Charles Starrett (Steve Holden/The Durango Kid), Smiley Burnette (Smiley), Jack [Jock] Mahoney (Swift Eagle), Fred F. Sears (Major Markham), Marshall Reed (Lieutenant Pierce), Rory Mallinson (Paul Drake/Bill Turner), Zon Murray (Carson), John War Eagle (Chief Lone Tree), Robert J. Wilke (Henry Mandel), Boyd "Red" Morgan (Jeff Kruller), Frank McCarroll (Soldier), Jay Silverheels (Running Wolf), Chris Alcaide (Gang Member).

The Rough, Tough West (Columbia, 1952, 54 minutes) Producer: Colbert Clark. Director: Ray Nazarro. Screenplay: Barry Shipman. Photography: Fayte

Browne. Editor: Paul Borofsky. Music Director: Mischa Bakaleinikoff. Songs: Smiley Burnette, Carolina Cotton, Stan Jones, Pee Wee King & Redd Stewart. Art Director: Charles Clague. Sound: Lambert Day. Sets: Frank Tuttle. Assistant Director: Jack Corrick.

Cast: Charles Starrett (Steve Holden/The Durango Kid), Smiley Burnette (Smiley), Jack [Jock] Mahoney (Big Jack Mahoney), Carolina Cotton (Carolina), Pee Wee King & the Golden West Cowboys (Musicians), Marshall Reed (Fulton), Fred F. Sears (Pete Walker/Doctor), Bert Arnold (Jordan MacCrea), Tommy Ivo (Buzz Barrett), Valerie Fisher (Matty Barrett), Boyd "Red" Morgan (Bill), Tommy Kingston (Blackjack Dealer), Redd Stewart (Singer), Hank Garland (Guitarist), Ethan Laidlaw, Bob Woodward (Gang Members), Ben Corbett (Miner), Frank Ellis (Saloon Customer).

Junction City (Columbia, 1952, 54 minutes) Producer: Colbert Clark. Director: Ray Nazarro. Screenplay: Barry Shipman. Photography: Henry Freulich. Editor: Paul Borofsky. Music Director: Mischa Bakaleinikoff. Songs: Smiley Burnette, Ace Richman, Audrey Lee Smith, J.O. Smith & Eddie Wallace. Art Director: Charles Clague. Sound: Russell Malmgren. Sets: Frank Tuttle. Assistant Director: Paul Donnelly.

Cast: Charles Starrett (Steve Rollins/The Durango Kid), Smiley Burnette (Smiley), Jack [Jock] Mahoney (Jack Mahoney), Kathleen Case (Penny Sanderson), John Dehner (Emmett Sanderson), Steve Darrell (Black Murphy), George Chesebro (Sheriff Jeff Clinton), Mary Newton (Ella Sanderson), Robert Bice (Bleaker), Hal Price (Sheriff), Hal Taliaferro [Wally Wales] (Sandy Clinton), Chris Alcaide (Jarvis), Bob Woodward (Keely), Joel Friedkin (Boggs), Harry Tyler (Giles), The Sunshine Boys [Eddie Wallace, J.D. Sumner, M.H. Richman, Freddie Daniel] (Musicians).

The Kid from Broken Gun (Columbia, 1951, 55 minutes) Producer: Colbert Clark. Director: Fred F. Sears. Screenplay: Barry Shipman & Ed Earl Repp. Photography: Fayte Browne. Editor: Paul Borofsky. Musical Director: Mischa Bakaleinikoff. Songs: Smiley Burnette. Art Director: Charles Clague. Sound: George Cooper. Assistant Director: Willard Reineck.

Cast: Charles Starrett (Steve Reynolds/The Durango Kid), Smiley Burnette (Smiley), Jack [Jock] Mahoney (Jack Mahoney), Angela Stevens (Gail Kingston), Tristram Coffin (Martin Donohugh), Myron Healey (Kiefer), Helen Mowery (Dixie King), Mauritz Hugo (Sheriff), Edgar Dearing (Judge Halloway), Chris Alcaide (Matt Fallon), Pat O'Malley (Doc Handy), John L. Cason (Chuck), Eddie Parker (Al), Edward Hearn (Jury Foreman), Charles Horvath (Joe), The Sunshine Boys [Eddie Wallace, J.D. Sumner, M.H. Richman, Freddie Daniel] (Musicians).

FRONTIER MARSHALS

After the "Billy the Kid" and "The Lone Rider" (qq.v.) series, producer Sigmund Neufeld and his brother, director Sam Newfield, launched a third "B" western set for PRC called "Frontier Marshals." Production-wise the new series was almost a carbon copy of the others, with Jack Greenhalgh handling the camera, Holbrook N. Todd editing, Bert Sternbach as production manager, Hans Weeren handling sound, and Melville De Lay working as assistant director. There was also contrived plotting, mostly outdoor locales, cheap production values and canned background music. Like "The Lone Rider," the "Frontier Marshals" films contained songs, putting them in the musical westerns category.

Since the singing cowboy came into vogue in the mid-1930s, PRC decided to have its new series top heavy with music. Thus two of the series' three lead heroes were singing cowboys, played by Bill (Cowboy Rambler) Boyd and Art Davis. Since neither was noted for their thespian abilities, third billing went to the more established Lee Powell. When Boyd and Davis were not making music in the films, the plots had the three "Frontier Marshals" on the trail of various outlaws for a half-dozen features, all released in 1942.

Although he had never been in films before, Bill (Cowboy Rambler) Boyd (1910–1977) got top billing, probably on the strength of having the same name as William Boyd, the star of the very popular "Hopalong Cassidy" (q.v.) series, which in 1942 began being released by United Artists, after seven years under the Paramount banner. In fact, for a time in the 1930s before he became Hoppy, William Boyd had used the screen moniker of Bill Boyd in order to avoid confusion with another actor, William (Stage) Boyd (1890–1935). The Cowboy Rambler Boyd was a native of Texas who, with his younger brother Jim, became interested in music at an early age, and in 1932

Art Davis in the "Frontier Marshals."

they formed the group The Cowboy Ramblers, which also included fiddler Art Davis. The group began recording for Victor Records in 1934 and the next year had a best seller with "Under the Double Eagle." The band's sound was basically country-western swing; Bill Boyd and His Cowboy Ramblers recorded over 200 songs for Victor Records through the early 1950s. Art Davis (1913–1987) left the group in the mid–1930s and came to Hollywood, first working for Gene Autry. From 1935 to 1939 he appeared in sixteen sagebrush yarns, usually as a fiddler and/or singer. In 1939 he was billed as Larry Mason in *The Adventures of the Masked Phantom*.

Lee Powell (1908–1944) was cinematically the most established of the three stars, having played the lead in the popular Republic serial *The Lone Ranger* in 1937. The next year he headlined another Republic cliffhanger, *The Fighting Devil Dogs*, but he was unable to maintain the momentum and the six films he did for PRC proved to be his only starring series. He did, however, team with crooner Art Jarrett and comic Al St. John for the Grand National oater *Trigger Pals*, a 1939 release which was to be the first of a series (which failed to materialize). He also had a good supporting role as Captain Roka in the 1940 Universal serial *Flash Gordon Conquers the Universe* starring Buster Crabbe in the title role.

The "Frontier Marshals" series kicked off with *Texas Manhunt* (1942) which Don Miller in *Hollywood Corral* (1976) termed a "dud." He added, "Nor did the series improve. Boyd, Davis and Powell failed to click together, and received no help from the production side." As noted, Sam Newfield directed all six series efforts and for each he used the pseudonym, Peter Stewart. Bill Boyd and Art Davis used their own names throughout the series but the opener had Lee Powell playing Marshall Lee Clark, although the last five entries his character used his name. With Bill (Cowboy Rambler) Boyd and Art Davis appearing a bit portly in the saddle, the main heroic action was left up to Powell, who handled the chores admirably when the budgets permitted.

By now the motif of having Nazis invade the range was in vogue and *Texas Manhunt* told of spy Otto Reuther (Arno Frey) enlisting the aid of businessman Clay (Karl Hackett) and cattle buyer Jensen (Frank Hagney) in his plans to stop the

Lee Powell in the "Frontier Marshals."

supply of beef cattle to the government by various methods of sabotage. When café owner Carol Price (Julie Duncan) becomes suspicious of Reuther, she informs radio announcers Bill Boyd and Art Davis (themselves) and they broadcast that Reuther boards with Clay and that recently broke Jensen has mysteriously come into money. Clay and Jensen try to ambush Bill and Art but the two are saved by government agent Lee Clark (Powell), who has been sent to the area to look into the sabotage activities. Jensen tries to mislead Clark by joining forces with him, since Clark believes Clay is behind the illegal activities. Lee captures Clay and then tells the ranchers they can combine their herds and send them to market via train. Jensen's gang plan to blow up the railroad tracks and henchman Hank Smith (Frank Ellis) takes Carol prisoner. The young woman escapes and warns Lee as Reuther is killed by a bomb planted in Carol's wagon. The cattle make it safely to market and Clark arrests Jensen and his gang. Bill Boyd and Johnny Martin wrote the song "When I Had My Pony on the Range" for the film.

Johnny Lange and Lew Porter were the head of the music department at Sigmund Neufeld Productions, which financed the "Frontier Marshals" features for PRC, and for the series second entry, *Raiders of the West*, they composed "Remember Me" and "Whispering Winds." Boyd provided the songs "Sunset Trail To Texas," written with Audrey Fisher, and "Tell Me Why My Daddy Don't Come Home," which he composed with Hal Burns and Earl Nunn. This outing had the three heroes as government agents masquerading as horse auctioneers as they investigate a counterfeiting operation. Joseph Rand (John Elliott), an engraver for the U.S. Mint, is held hostage in an old house by Duke Mallory (Charles King) and his gang and forced to make bogus currency. Mallory uses his dude ranch as a front and when they catch him passing counterfeit money, agent Lee Powell (himself) suspects Duke is part of the gang. When Lee tries to interest Mallory in more fake bills, the latter refuses but rides immediately to the hideout and is followed by Bill Boyd and Art Davis (themselves), who are partners with Powell. Bill and Art, however, are arrested by Mallory for the murder of a homesteader actually killed by Duke's gang. The local sheriff (Slim Whitaker) and judge (Milton Kibbee) know Bill and Art are innocent and allow them to escape jail. Mallory agrees to buy Lee's fake money as the lawmen are then able to prove Mallory has been passing counterfeit currency at his dude ranch. Mallory, however, captures Lee but he is freed by dude ranch hostess Lola Andre (Virginia Carroll), who is really Rand's daughter. Bill and Art find Rand but are attacked by Mallory's gang. Lee rides to their rescue, being followed by Lola and a posse which captures the outlaws.

Next came *Rolling Down the Great Divide* which sported the title tune composed by Boyd and Leon Payne, plus a trio of songs by Lange and Porter: "I'll Be Wishing," "It's All Over Now" and "Roaming in Wyoming." Its plot had another patriotic theme, that of ranchers selling their horse herds for government use. Café owner Joe Duncan (Glenn Strange) and his gang want the herds for the same purpose and blame their rustling activities on once wealthy cattleman Lem Bartlett (John Elliott). Government marshal Lee Powell (himself) investigates and learns that short-wave radio transmissions are used to aid the rustlers. Gang member Dale (Jack Ingram) runs the short-wave radio wagon under the guise of it being a traveling recording studio. Lee's co-workers Bill Boyd and Art Davis (themselves) are hired by Duncan to entertain in his café, where the radio operations are headquartered. Lee catches the gang trying to rustle horses but they escape. Dale, however, warns Duncan and they stage another raid. When Lee sees Duncan using a short-wave radio, he realizes he is behind the thefts and then later finds the entrance to the gang's hideout. Waitress Rita (Wanda McKay) tries to warn Lee that Duncan knows his identity and the café owner captures both of them. When Bill and Art approach Dale about making a recording, they too are captured but sing a song over the mobile radio giving their whereabouts. Lee and Rita hear the song and are able to escape. They go to the sheriff (Jack Holmes) who rounds up a posse and they ride to the hideout and capture the gang.

Since the series took place during the first full year of World War II, the draft was taking its toll on available young actors as noted again by Don Miller in *Hollywood Corral*: "In the fourth entry, *Tumbleweed Trail*, Powell was forced to go through the motions of a knock-down, drag-out

Advertisement for *Raiders of the West* (PRC, 1942).

brawl with aging Jack Rockwell, bald and in precarious physical condition. No budgetary consideration for a double, so poor Rockwell had to puff through the charade, with Powell seemingly embarrassed by the exertion." For *Tumbleweed Trail* Boyd and Dick Reynolds wrote the title song while Davis collaborated with Lange and Porter on "What Can I Do" and Lange and Porter provided "Down the Moonlit Trail" and "The Tide Has Turned."

Tumbleweed Trail is a confused effort about a gang of outlaws operating in south Oklahoma just over the Texas border. Marshals Bill Boyd and Art Davis (themselves) arrest Vic Landreau (Charles King), charging him with leading the gang, but they cannot make the charges stick and the sheriff (Frank Hagney) lets him go. When Bill fights with Vic, the sheriff arrests him while Art meets with their partner Lee Powell (himself), who then demands the sheriff release Bill. The head badman is actually saloon owner Mort Slade (Jack Rockwell), who has his gang run the marshals out of town. Lee then meets with local ranchers and asks them to aid him in finding out who is really behind the gang. Bill tries to romance Slade's daughter Linda (Marjorie Manners), who causes him to be captured by her father's men. A vigilante group led by the marshals capture the sheriff and then let him go, hoping he will lead them to his boss. Linda overhears Lee say Bill has escaped and he and Art follow her to the hideout and rescue Bill. Back in town, Lee has a confrontation with Slade, whom he arrests after beating him in a fight.

The fifth series entry, *Prairie Pals*, was basically a reworking of *Raiders of the West*. This time Wainwright (Jack Holmes), a famous scientist who has developed a formula for extracting gold from a specific type of rock, is held hostage and forced to work for Ace Shannon (I. Stanford Jolley), whose gang has been terrorizing the Elkhorn area. Marshals Bill Boyd and Art Davis (themselves) infiltrate the gang, which is fronted by Mitchell (Charles King). The local sheriff (Karl Hackett) tells another marshal, Lee Powell (himself), that he suspects Shannon is responsible for the lawlessness, since Lee is trying to find the missing scientist. Wainwright, meanwhile, informs Shannon of the whereabouts of a large gold deposit. When his gang plans to raid the ranch, Bill and Art notify Lee and the attempt is thwarted. Seeking information, Lee goes to Shannon's office and finds Betty Wainwright (Esther Estrella) looking for information which might lead her to her missing father. She has been working as an entertainer in Shannon's saloon. Lee and Betty follow Shannon to his hideout where they rescue Wainwright, and Lee arrests Shannon. Mitchell captures Bill and Art as Shannon escapes but Lee brings a posse and rounds up the crooks.

Lange and Porter provided four songs for the proceedings: the title tune, "Just So Long, Not Goodbye, Dear," "Think of Me Darling, While I'm Away" and "Prairie Moon." The duo originally composed the latter tune for the Fred Scott starrer *Songs and Bullets* (Spectrum, 1938). Also included in the feature was the Gene Autry-Fred Rose composition "You'll Be Sorry."

The final series entry was *Along the Sundown Trail* for which Lange and Porter wrote "Nobody's Fault But My Own," "Ridin' Free" and the title song. The plot had mine foreman Bert Fleming (Jack Ingram) secretly working for rival mine owner Salter (Charles King), who has been switching the ore from his worthless mine with that of Fleming's boss, Pop Lawrence (Karl Hackett). When a lawman disappears, Marshal Lee Powell (himself) asks fellow lawmen Bill Boyd and Art Davis (themselves) to investigate. They pretend to be entertainers and are hired by Salter, who also owns a saloon. Lee is able to prove that Pop's tungsten mine is rich in ore and with the aid of a deputy (Ted Adams) he prevents Lawrence's ore wagons from being hijacked. Determined to get Pop's mine so he can sell it to a syndicate for a half million dollars, Salter gets Lawrence's hot-headed son Joe (Howard Masters) drunk and then murders Pop, making Joe think he killed the old man. Salter then tells Pop's daughter Susan (Julie Duncan) that Lee shot her father. After forcing Joe to sign the Lawrence mine over to him, Salter kills Joe and captures Susan. Lee, Bill and Art arrive at Salter's hideout and capture the outlaw, charging him with the murders of Pop and Joe.

Seeing the handwriting on the wall, the ever-frugal Neufeld brothers dropped the "Frontier Marshals" and replaced it with another hero triad series, "The Texas Rangers" (q.v.). Powell and Davis went into the military while Boyd continued fronting the Cowboy Ramblers; he would continue to do so into the mid–1950s after which he became a Dallas disc jockey. Boyd lived to see the "B" western revival in the 1970s and attended a few fan conventions before his death in 1977. After the war, Davis resumed his musical career and in 1949 he and his Rhythm Riders were in the Astor short *A Cowboy's Holiday*. In 1975 he recorded an album for White Hat Records and he also appeared at western film conventions and remained an active performer until his death in 1987. Lee Powell did not live to continue his movie career. Joining the Marines in 1942, he died July 30, 1944, after seeing action in Tarawa, Saipan and Tinian in the Marianas Islands. He was awarded the Purple Heart.

Filmography

Texas Manhunt (PRC, 1942, 60 minutes) Producer: Sigmund Neufeld. Director: Peter Stewart [Sam Newfield]. Screenplay: William Lively. Photography: Jack Greenhalgh. Editor: Holbrook N. Todd. Production Manager: Bert Sternbach. Sound: Paul Schumtz. Songs: Johnny Lange, Lew Porter, Bill Boyd & Art Davis. Assistant Director: Melville De Lay.

Cast: Bill (Cowboy Rambler) Boyd (Himself), Art Davis (Himself), Lee Powell (Marshal Lee Clark), Julie Duncan (Carol Price), Frank Hagney (Walter Jensen), Karl Hackett (Paul Clay), Dennis Moore (Jim Rogers), Frank Ellis (Hank Smith), Arno Frey (Otto Reuther), Eddie Phillips (Nate Winters), Kenne Duncan (Lake), Forrest Taylor (Horace Atkinson), Frank La Rue (Dr. McKenzie).

Raiders of the West (PRC, 1942, 60 minutes) Producer: Sigmund Neufeld. Director: Peter Stewart [Sam Newfield]. Screenplay: Oliver Drake. Photography: Jack Greenhalgh. Editor: Holbrook N. Todd. Production Manager: Bert Sternbach. Sound: Hans Weeren. Songs: Bill Boyd. Assistant Director: Melville De Lay.

Cast: Bill (Cowboy Rambler) Boyd (Himself), Art Davis (Himself), Lee Powell (Himself), Virginia Carroll (Lola Rand/Lola Andre), Charles King (Duke Mallory), Glenn Strange (Hank Reynolds), Rex Lease (Joe), Slim Whitaker (Sheriff), Milton Kibbee (Judge), Lynton Brent (Morton), Eddie Dean (Pete), William Desmond, Reed Howes, Hal Price, Carl Mathews, George Morrell (Townsmen), Gale Sherwood (Gwen), Arch Hall (Tex), Snowflake [Fred Toones] (Snowflake Jones), Bill Cody, Jr. (Juvenile), Frank Ellis (Deputy), John Elliott (Joseph Rand), Kenne Duncan (Harris), Lane Bradford, Tex Palmer (Henchmen), Hank Bell (Kansas McFarland), John L. Cason (Gene), Curley Dresden (Sam), Fred MacKaye (Gambler), Wally West (Court Spectator), Carl Sepulveda (Slim).

Rolling Down the Great Divide (PRC, 1942, 59 minutes) Producer: Sigmund Neufeld. Director: Peter Stewart [Sam Newfield]. Screenplay: George Milton [Milton Raison & George Wallace Sayre]. Photography: Jack Greenhalgh. Editor: Holbrook N. Todd. Production Manager: Bert Sternbach. Songs: Johnny Lange & Lew Porter. Assistant Director: Melville De Lay.

Cast: Bill (Cowboy Rambler) Boyd (Himself), Art Davis (Himself), Lee Powell (Himself), Wanda McKay (Rita), Glenn Strange (Joe Duncan), Karl Hackett

(Pete), Jack Holmes (Sheriff Snowden), Ted Adams (Martin), Jack Ingram (Dale), John Elliott (Lem Bartlett), Dennis Moore, George Chesebro (Henchmen), Hank Bell (Foreman Jim), Frank Ellis (Rancher), Blackie Whiteford, Curley Dresden (Drunks), Horace B. Carpenter, Jack Roper, Tex Palmer (Citizens).

Tumbleweed Trail (PRC, 1942, 57 minutes) Producer: Sigmund Neufeld. Director: Peter Stewart [Sam Newfield]. Screenplay: Fred Myton. Photography: Jack Greenhalgh. Editor: Holbrook N. Todd. Production Manager: Bert Sternbach. Sound: Hans Weeren. Songs: Bill Boyd & Art Davis. Assistant Director: Melville De Lay.

Cast: Bill (Cowboy Rambler) Boyd (Himself), Art Davis (Himself), Lee Powell (Himself), Marjorie Manners (Linda Slade), Jack Rockwell (Mort Slade), Charles King (Vic Landreau), Karl Hackett (Sheriff Barlow), George Chesebro (Curt Bachman), Frank Hagney (Sheriff), Reed Howes (Croupier), Steve Clark (Dealer), Maxine Leslie (Marge Davis), Dan White, Tex Palmer, Bert Dillard, Augie Gomez, Curley Dresden (Henchmen), Art Dillard (Jack), Jack Evans (Rancher), George Morrell (Hank Slocum), Jack Montgomery (Saloon Customer).

Prairie Pals (PRC, 1942, 58 minutes) Producer: Sigmund Neufeld. Director: Peter Stewart [Sam Newfield]. Screenplay: Patricia Harper. Photography: Jack Greenhalgh. Editor: Holbrook N. Todd. Production Manager: Bert Sternbach. Songs: Johnny Lange & Lew Porter. Assistant Director: Melville De Lay.

Cast: Bill (Cowboy Rambler) Boyd (Himself), Art Davis (Himself), Lee Powell (Himself), Esther Estrella (Betty Wainwright), Charles King (Mitchell), John Merton (Ed Blair), Jack Holmes (Mr. Wainwright), Kermit Maynard (Crandall), I. Stanford Jolley (Ace Shannon), Al St. John (Hank Stoner), Karl Hackett (Sheriff), Bob Burns (Deputy), Bert Dillard (Mine Guard), Al Taylor (Rancher), Frank Ellis, Frank McCarroll, Carl Mathews, Curley Dresden (Henchmen), Jack Kinney, Art Dillard, Morgan Flowers (Bar Customers), Bill Patton, George Morrell (Citizens).

Along the Sundown Trail (PRC, 1942, 57 minutes) Producer: Sigmund Neufeld. Director: Peter Stewart [Sam Newfield]. Screenplay: Arthur St. Claire. Photography: Jack Greenhalgh. Editor: Holbrook N. Todd. Production Manager: Bert Sternbach. Sound: Hans Weeren. Songs: Johnny Lange & Lew Porter. Assistant Director: Melville De Lay.

Cast: Bill (Cowboy Rambler) Boyd (Himself), Art Davis (Himself), Lee Powell (Himself), Julie Duncan (Susan Lawrence), Charles King (Ben Slater), Jack Ingram (Bert Fleming), Karl Hackett (Pop Lawrence), John Merton (Jake), Howard Masters (Joe Lawrence), Kermit Maynard (Curley Morgan), Al St. John (Crandall), Jack Holmes (Marlowe), Hal Price (Sheriff Kincaide), Ted Adams (Deputy Casey), Frank Ellis (Miner), Reed Howes, Jimmy Aubrey, Art Dillard (Bar Customers), Curley Dresden (Bartender), Steve Clark (Croupier), Tex Palmer, Roy Bucko (Teamsters), Herman Hack, Ralph Bucko, Augie Gomez (Citizens).

HOPALONG CASSIDY

From 1907 to 1941, Clarence E. Mulford (1883–1956) wrote 28 novels and several short stories about the character of Hopalong Cassidy. As the books progressed, the character changed from rough-hewn young cowpoke to a middle-aged gunfighter and occasional law officer, withered and bow-legged in appearance. When producer Harry "Pop" Sherman acquired the film rights to the character, he wanted to cast James Gleason in the role but ended up hiring William Boyd, who transformed Hopalong Cassidy into a handsome, good-natured and stalwart hero. Boyd even eschewed the character's traditional Western garb, instead mainly wearing an all-dark outfit and a light bandana with a cowhead clip. The transformation resulted in a series of very entertaining productions from 1935 to 1948 and continuing on television and radio and via merchandising.

While both Mulford, who never liked the cinematic Cassidy, and Sherman deserve credit for bringing Hopalong Cassidy to the public, it was Boyd who made the character a popular hero for countless fans from the mid–1930s to the present day. Born in Oklahoma in 1895, Boyd drifted to Hollywood in 1919, landing extra work in films. By the mid–1920s he had become a leading man and starred in several Cecil B. DeMille films, including *The Road to Yesterday* (1925), *The Volga Boatman* (1926) and *King of Kings* (1927), and D.W. Griffith's *Lady of the Pavements* (1929). Boyd easily made the transition to sound, mainly working for Pathe in features like *High Voltage* (1929). In the silent days he had headlined the western

William Boyd as "Hopalong Cassidy."

The Last Frontier (1926) and in 1931 he did the same in *The Painted Desert*, which brought Clark Gable his first good notices. By now the actor was billing himself as Bill Boyd in order to avoid confusion with William "Stage" Boyd, who was also making talking pictures. At RKO, Bill Boyd starred in a number of solid programmers like *Carnival Boat* and *Men of America* (both 1932) and *Lucky Devils* and *Emergency Call* (both 1933) but after the other Boyd made headlines for being involved in a wild party, Bill Boyd found himself working on Poverty Row in quickies such as *Port of Lost Dreams* (1934) and *Racing Luck* (1935). Being signed to play Hopalong Cassidy literally revived Boyd's career and provided him with the role of a lifetime.

The first series feature, *Hop-Along Cassidy*, released in the late summer of 1935, was based on Mulford's 1912 novel *Hopalong Cassidy Enters*, which became the film's reissue title. This solid one hour's entertainment was lensed at Lone Pine and Red Rock Canyon, California, and takes place in the days before barbed wire fences. The feature begins with Bill Cassidy (William Boyd) returning to the syndicate-owned Bar 20 ranch and being hired as line foreman by boss Buck Peters (Charles Middleton), an old friend. While ranch hands Uncle Ben (George Hayes) and Red Connors (Frank McGlynn, Jr.) are glad to see Cassidy, their many tales of his valor cause friction between Cassidy and hotheaded cowpoke Johnny Nelson (Jimmy Ellison). Cassidy learns that Peters is having trouble with neighbor Jim Meeker (Robert Warwick), whose herds are straying onto Bar 20 land in search of water. Unknown to both men, Meeker's foreman, Pecos Jack Anthony (Kenneth Thomson), is instigating the trouble by working with rustler Frisco (Frank Campeau) and his gang, who have been stealing both ranchers' cattle and murdering their cowhands. When Johnny finds some of Meeker's cattle on Bar 20 land he runs them off, meeting Mary Meeker (Paula Stone), the rancher's daughter, and being shot at by Pecos Jack, whose actions are thwarted by Cassidy. Smitten with Mary, Johnny goes to a party at the Meeker ranch where he has an altercation with Pecos Jack but is rescued from a lynch mob by Cassidy, Uncle Ben and Red. Cassidy, however, is shot in the leg, which causes him to walk with a limp. Convinced there is a concerted effort to cause friction between Peters and Meeker, Cassidy discovers how both men's cattle brands have been changed to a third brand; with this information, Peters convinces Meeker to aid him in finding the culprit. When Uncle Ben discovers that the rustlers are hiding in Thunder Mesa, he is shot in the back by Pecos Jack but he lives long enough to write a message in the dust, giving the location. Cassidy discovers his mur-

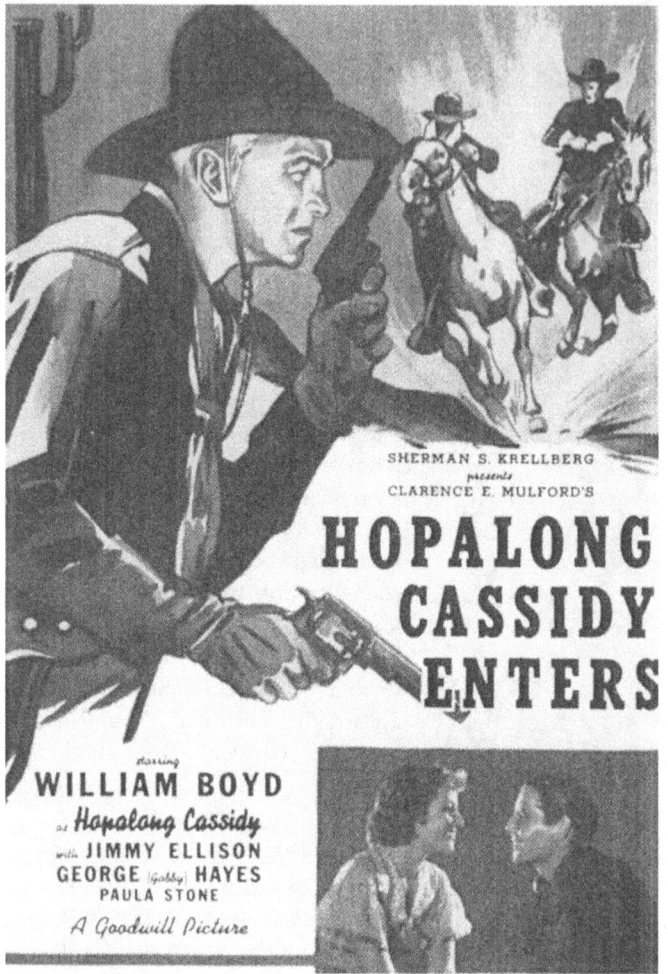

Advertisement for *Hopalong Cassidy Returns*, a re-issue of *Hop-Along Cassidy* (Paramount, 1935).

"You didn't stand a chance, did you, old-timer?" The film also explains how Cassidy got his nickname: After being shot in the leg while rescuing Johnny Nelson from the lynch mob, he recovers but has a noticeable limp. In response to the situation, Cassidy says, "I guess I'll just hop along."

Adding to the success of the series entry was the casting of James Ellison, billed as Jimmy, as Johnny Nelson, and George Hayes in the part of Uncle Ben. The twenty-five-year-old Ellison began acting in stock companies before coming to films in 1932 and the Cassidy series hurled him into the public eye. Between 1935 and 1937 he would portray the role in eight series entries. Hayes (1885–1969) came to films in the early 1920s from vaudeville but only began making an impression with the coming of sound, often working for producers Trem Carr and Paul Malvern. It was in Malvern's Monogram Lone Star westerns with John Wayne, that Hayes began to develop the crusty, lovable range character which would become Windy Halliday in the Cassidy series and "Gabby" in films with Roy Rogers, Randolph Scott and others.

The second series entry, *The Eagle's Brood*, was released in the fall of 1935, based on Mulford's 1931 novel *Hopalong Cassidy and the Eagle's Brood*. Unlike the initial film, which stayed fairly close to its literary source, this outing (and most subsequent ones) had little to do with the book. It was, however, a very strong production which helped to build the foundation for the Hopalong Cassidy series' success. The film opens with Big Henry (Addison Richards) and his cutthroats ambushing and murdering a young couple for the gold they are carrying, with their son Pablo (George Mari) witnessing the crime. The gold was intended for the boy's grandfather, the once notorious outlaw El Torro (William Farnum), now living south of the border as Pedro Sanchez. Dancer Dolores (Nana Martinez [Joan Woodbury]) comes upon the crime scene and rescues Pablo, intending to take him to her boyfriend boss, Big Henry, the operator of the local saloon.

dered friend and the message, unites the Bar 20 and Meeker cowhands and they attack the outlaws in their lair. After a fierce fight, the rustlers are defeated and the cowardly Pecos Jack falls to his death from a cliff in an effort to escape. Although he loves Mary, Johnny leaves her behind to join Cassidy, Buck and Red, who plan to purchase their own spread in Wyoming.

Astride his beautiful white horse Topper, Boyd made a dashing cinema hero and *Hop-Along Cassidy* proved to be a well-made beginning to the series. With its scenic locales and theme song "Followin' the Stars," the feature was fast-paced and highly entertaining. When first shown, there were probably few dry eyes in theaters when Cassidy finds the murdered Uncle Ben and intones,

When she finds out it was Big Henry who committed the crime, she hides the boy in a remote cabin as Sanchez arrives to find his grandson. Sanchez borrows a horse from deputy sheriff Johnny Nelson (Jimmy Ellison), who later joins his boss, Sheriff Bill Cassidy (William Boyd), in search of El Torro, who has been sighted. Cassidy, however, rides into a quicksand pit and is rescued by Sanchez, whom Cassidy arrests. Sanchez pleads with the lawman to find his grandson and Cassidy lets El Torro return to Mexico. Cassidy and Johnny turn in their badges. In Big Henry's saloon, Dolores plans to tell Cassidy where Pablo is hidden, but she is murdered by Big Henry. When Henry's cohort Ed (John Merton) threatens to kill grizzled bartender Spike (George Hayes), Cassidy accidentally shoots Ed, and Henry enlists him for his gang. Another gang member, Mike (Frank Shannon), tries to kill Cassidy but ends up being dragged to death by his own horse. When Johnny finds red clay on Dolores' boots, Spike tells him it came from Red Mountain, the place where Pablo is hidden. Johnny finds the boy but is shot by another gang member, Steve (Paul Fix), who trailed him. While trying to get Cassidy, Big Henry shoots Steve and then leaves for Red Mountain in order to kill Johnny and the boy. Spike tries to warn Cassidy and is shot but before dying he tells him of Henry's plans. Cassidy follows Henry to Red Mountain and the two fight, with Big Henry falling from a cliff. Cassidy and Johnny then take the boy home to his grandfather.

Since the character that George Hayes played in *Hop-Along Cassidy* was killed, here the actor was given the role of bartender Spike, a good-badman part and the kind he sometimes played in the John Wayne Monogram Lone Star series. In the next series film, *Bar 20 Rides Again*, the third and last series entry for 1935, he would initiate the role of Windy, which would become Windy Halliday. *The Eagle's Brood* greatly benefited from a strong supporting cast, which included silent film star William Farnum as El Torro, Addison Richards as the cold-blooded Big Henry, Joan Woodbury as the hapless Dolores and Dorothy Revier as saloon girl Dolly, who has a brief flirtation with Cassidy. Like the initial outing, the film was directed by Howard Bretherton, who would helm the first six features in the series.

In *Bar 20 Rides Again*, Frank McGlynn, Jr., returned as Red Connors. It was also the first entry to give billing to a musical group, Chill Wills and His Avalon Boys. Bar 20 foreman Hopalong Cassidy (William Boyd) comes to the aid of an old friend, Jim Arnold (Howard Lang), whose Wyoming ranch is being raided by an outlaw called Nevada and his gang. Jim does not want the help of Johnny Nelson (Jimmy Ellison), because Johnny is in love with Jim's daughter Margaret (Jean Rouverol), who has come home from finishing school and is engaged to marry neighboring rancher George Perdue (Harry Worth). Johnny rides on before Hoppy to Wyoming while Nevada and his men rustle Jim's herd with gang member Cinco (Al St. John) getting killed. After they arrive in Wyoming, Hoppy pretends to be gambler Tex Riley while Red Connors joins Jim's workers. Windy (George Hayes), an old desert rat, is befriended by Tex and takes him to the Perdue ranch where he announces he plans to kill Johnny. Perdue, who is really Nevada, wants Johnny out of the way because of Margaret and he asks Tex to join his gang. Nevada then takes Tex to Johnny and the latter two engage in a fake gunfight, with Johnny supposedly getting killed. When Tex learns that Nevada plans another raid, he and Windy try to send a smoke signal to the Arnold ranch but end up starting a brush fire. Nevada and his gang try to kill Tex and Windy but Johnny arrives and they escape back to the Arnold ranch where the two sides engage in a gun battle. Perdue is killed and Jim gets back his stolen cattle as Windy finds out that Tex Riley is really Hopalong Cassidy and he agrees to join the Bar 20 outfit. Johnny returns home with Hoppy, Red and Windy but announces he plans to come back and marry Margaret.

Based on Mulford's 1926 novel *Bar-20 Rides Again*, the film contained several of the book's characters and a bit of its plot, but overall it was not a faithful adaptation. It was, however, a top-notch production, as noted by Don Miller in *Hollywood Corral* (1976): "*Bar 20 Rides Again* amply showed how good the Hoppys were capable of being, and as it evolved how good they were going to be." Miller praised the feature's gunfight climax as well as the work of director Howard Bretherton, cameraman Archie Stout and editor Edward Schroeder, as well as the use of Gluck's

George Hayes and William Boyd in *Bar 20 Rides Again* (Paramount, 1935).

"Dance of the Furies" as musical background. Also of note is that the villain portrayed by Harry Worth idolized Napoleon Bonaparte and tried to emulate his military tactics in taking over the Arnold ranch.

Released in March, 1936, *Call of the Prairie* was the first of four Hopalong Cassidy adventures that year and, like its predecessors, it was supposedly based on a Mulford work, this time *Hopalong Cassidy's Protégé* (1926), but had little to do with the novel. George Hayes is an outlaw, for the last time, while Chill Wills and His Avalon Boys sing the feature's title song. Returning from selling Bar 20 cattle in Omaha, Hopalong Cassidy (William Boyd) finds that Johnny Nelson (Jimmy Ellison) has taken to drinking and gambling with no good Sam Porter (Alan Bridge) and his gang. One of the gang members, crusty Shanghai Charles McHenry (George Hayes), learns from an inebriated Johnny that Hoppy has returned with a large amount of cash from the cattle sale. That night Sam, Tom Slade (Al Hill) and the rest of the gang rob Bar 20 foreman Buck Peters (Howard Lang) and frame Johnny for the crime. Peters, who gave the robbers letters instead of money, orders Hoppy to prove Johnny's innocence in twelve hours or he will press charges against the young man. Porter orders Shanghai to kill Johnny but the cowpoke manages to escape. Hoppy captures Slade, and while on the lam Johnny saves Linda McHenry (Muriel Evans), Shanghai's daughter, when her horse bolts. Shanghai breaks Slade out of jail as the gang captures Johnny and plans to kill him, but he is saved by Cassidy. The two round up the gang as the dying Porter shoots Shanghai, who survives and returns the stolen Bar 20 money.

Call of the Prairie continued the fine pace of the Hopalong Cassidy series as Fred Romary stated in his notes for its Image Entertainment DVD release: "The Cassidy features were drawing family audiences into the theaters. Hopalong Cassidy was beginning to overshadow Bill Boyd, and Boyd's portrayal showed more intelligence, charm, and humor with each successive feature. Like a sculptor with raw clay, he was molding the character with qualities that hold up in viewing these features today."

Issued in the spring of 1936, *Three on the Trail* was supposedly based on the 1921 Mulford novel *Bar-20*, but outside of a few characters and situations it had little to do with the book. In the town of Mesquite, Hopalong Cassidy (William Boyd) and Johnny Nelson (Jimmy Ellison) save schoolmarm Mary Stevens (Muriel Evans) from the evil machinations of saloon owner Pecos Kane (Onslow Stevens). The duo take Mary with them to the Bar 20 ranch and along the way they see a stagecoach being held up by Kane's gang, who had been informed by corrupt Sheriff Sam Corwin (John St. Polis) about a gold shipment. Johnny is hurt trying to stop the robbery. At the same time, another Bar 20 wrangler, Windy (George Hayes), observes a murder in Kane's saloon. The Bar 20 men agree to put an end to Kane and his lawless element and try to get rancher Ridley (Claude King) to help them but he refuses.

Advertisement for *Three on the Trail* (Paramount, 1936).

When the sheriff tries to arrest Johnny on the trumped-up charge of robbing the stagecoach, Hoppy demands the lawman have a warrant. At Kane's saloon, Johnny sees one of the robbers but the sheriff refuses to arrest him. Hoppy and Johnny are kidnapped by Kane's gang while Kane and Corwin convince Ridley that the two Bar 20 men raided his cattle. Hoppy and Johnny manage to escape on foot and later, while crossing a desert, they get the upper hand on Corwin and his deputies and take their horses. Hoppy convinces Ridley of his innocence and they lead a posse in attacking Kane's saloon, not knowing Mary is being held hostage. Johnny rescues his sweetheart as Hoppy uses dynamite to blow up the saloon. Injured during the shootout, Hoppy makes sure the reward money for bringing in the gang goes to Johnny so he can wed Mary.

Heart of the West, released in the summer of 1936, bore only a slight resemblance to the 1932 Mulford novel *Mesquite Jenkins, Tumbleweed*, on which it was supposedly based. The title tune, written by Victor Young and Sam Coslow, was sung during the credits by British crooner Al Bowlly, then vocalist with Ray Noble and His Orchestra. Hopalong Cassidy (William Boyd) and Johnny Nelson (Jimmy Ellison) are hired by rancher John Trumbull (Sidney Blackmer) to drive his cattle to market. On their way to Trumbull's Tumbling-L Ranch, they come upon cowpoke Windy (George Hayes), who has been ambushed and shot by two men while delivering a breed bull to Jim Jordan's (Charles Martin) Three-J Ranch. Saxon (Ted Adams), one of the attackers, is injured by the bull and is taken prisoner by Hoppy. While in town, Hoppy learns that Jordan has won a court case against Trumbull and has vowed to keep John's cattle off his range by constructing a fence in Black Valley. Trumbull continues his fight with Jordan although he loves the latter's sister Sally (Lynn Gabriel). When Trumbull's foreman Tom Patterson (John Rutherford) tries to start a fight with the unarmed Jordan, Hoppy stops him. He and Johnny quit their jobs at the Tumbling-L. Trumbull has his men rescue Saxon from the Three-J and continues with plans to destroy Jordan's fences and keep stolen cattle in Black Valley. Hoppy decides to work for Jordan and is made foreman of the ranch; he orders Windy to get posts for the fence project but Trumbull's men steal his wagon and try to burn the posts. Johnny, who was supposed to stay at the Three-J to protect Sally, goes into town for supplies, sees the burning wagon and puts out the fire. Trumbull finds Sally alone at the ranch and makes a pass at her and she scratches his face. Later, Trumbull tells Jordan that he and Mary plan to wed but Johnny sees the scratches on his face. Jim, Hoppy and Johnny take him back to the ranch where they find Sally. Trumbull then declares a range war and plans to have his partner Barton (Fred Kohler) drive a herd of rustled cattle over Jordan's land and into Black Valley. After Patterson and his men are captured by the Bar 20 cowboys, Jordan and his cowhands successfully fight off Trumbull and his gang. Trumbull orders Barton to turn back his herd but he refuses and Hoppy is forced to stop them with dynamite. The herd turns back and Trumbull is killed in the stampede. Hoppy and Nelson return to the Bar 20 but Johnny promises to come back to see Sally at the fall roundup.

The next series outing, *Hopalong Cassidy Returns* was based on Mulford's 1924 novel of the same title although it had almost nothing to do with the literary work. Released in October, 1936, its plot found Hoppy (Boyd) and his younger brother Buddy (William Janney) coming to Mesa Grande at the behest of the town's newspaperman, Bob Saunders (John Beck), a paraplegic. After a miner (Irving Bacon) is murdered for his gold claim, Saunders writes an editorial about the crime and the town's crooked sheriff, Blackie Felton (Stephen Morris [Morris Ankrum]), resigns and leads the citizens in making Bob the new marshal. Hoppy saves saloon owner Lilli Marsh (Evelyn Brent) when her horse runs away with her, not knowing she is behind the lawlessness. Lilli's right hand man, Clairborne (Grant Richards), sadistically murders Saunders, with Hoppy taking over the lawman's job with assistance from his old friend Windy Halliday (George Hayes). When Lilli acquires the murdered miner's gold claim, Hoppy realizes she is behind the outlaw menace and urges her to depart. Hoppy arrests Clairborne who admits that Felton killed the miner and he also reveals the location of the gang's hideout. Hoppy, Buddy, Windy and local ranchers attack the hideout with Buddy being captured but saved by his brother; the gang is defeated.

Back in town, Lilli stops Blackie from ambushing Hoppy, with whom she has fallen in love, and is mortally wounded, dying in Hoppy's arms. Hoppy kills Blackie as Buddy decides to stay in the area with Mary Saunders (Gail Sheridan), the sister of the murdered newsman.

Hopalong Cassidy Returns was the first series feature without James Ellison as Johnny Nelson and it was the initial entry to use the full character name Windy Halliday for the grizzled cowpoke portrayed by Hayes. It was also the first of six series entries to be directed by Nate Watt* and provided the initial series appearance for Stephen Morris, whose work would highlight a number of the Cassidy efforts, later under the name Morris Ankrum.

The final 1936 entry, December's *Trail Dust*, was taken from the Mulford book of the same title, published two years earlier. It was said to be Mulford's favorite of the Hoppy features, one he wanted remade with William Boyd on a much bigger budget. The feature brought James Ellison back as Johnny Nelson and in it he crooned the Harry Tobias-Jack Stern compositions "Beneath a Western Sky" and "Wide Open Spaces."

Hoppy (Boyd) unites ranchers in taking their cattle to market when the local cattle association buyer (Kenneth Harlan) will not give them a fair price. Rancher Lewis (Harold Daniels) has his cohorts Tex Anderson (Stephen Morris [Morris Ankrum]) and Joe Wilson (Ted Adams) hire on as drovers with Hoppy in order to use delaying tactics so his (Lewis') herd will be the first to reach market. While on the drive, Hoppy and Johnny (Ellison) rescue Beth Clark (Gwynne Shipman) after she has been thrown by her horse. She tells them that her father, trail cutter Sheriff John Clark (John Elliott), has disappeared. Lewis pretends to be a trail cutter and tries to further delay the Hoppy herd; he also has his gang attack Hoppy's chuck wagon, driven by Windy (Hayes), and burn its provisions. Windy goes to trader Waggoner (Dick Dickinson) for supplies but is attacked with Hoppy not only saving him but running off longtime enemy Waggoner and his gang and getting the supplies needed for the trail drive. After Johnny learns that John Clark is being held prisoner by Lewis, two of Hoppy's men, Red (Earl Askam) and Skinny (Tom Halligan), are murdered with Tex suspected of being the culprit. While Beth rides for help, Hoppy starts a brush fire to scare off Lewis' herd and Wilson knocks out Windy and steals dynamite from his wagon, planning to blow up Hoppy's herd when they come through a pass outside of town. Hoppy kills Wilson and Tex and helps the wounded Windy. Beth arrives with Saunders and his men, the gang is captured and the girl is reunited with her father, who escaped from captivity. Once the cattle herd is sold, Hoppy heads to Mexico and is joined by Johnny and Windy.

Leisurely paced, *Trail Dust* reused long shots of the cattle herd first shown in *Heart of the West*. One amusing sequence had Windy giving Johnny lessons in romancing Beth. Fred Romary, in the notes for the feature's Image Entertainment DVD release, said the film "concerns itself with the stark reality of hunger, despair and economic turmoil reflective of life during the Depression of the 1930s.... Once again Nate Watt shows splendid handling of a slow but strongly plotted screenplay and characters making the lengthy film seem fast-paced. Archie Stout's superbly dramatic cinematography of the stark outdoor scenery almost reaches impressionistic proportions."

By this time the Hopalong Cassidy features were so popular with the moviegoing public that Boyd was ranked fourth in the annual *Motion Picture Herald* poll of top money-making western film stars. From 1937 to 1941 he was second in the poll each year, behind only Gene Autry. In 1937, *Boxoffice* magazine began a similar poll and Boyd was ranked third. He finished second in that poll in both 1938 and 1939, was third in 1940 and back to second in 1941. The series features cost around $60,000 each, higher than most program westerns, and had financial returns in excess of three times their production costs. As the star of the series, Boyd made around $100,000 a year.

---

*Regarding Watt's taking over as director, Don Miller wrote in Hollywood Corral (1976), "[T]he film was supplied with action, but of a remarkably violent sort, verging on the sadistic." He noted the "graphic scene" where the newspaper editor is roped in his wheelchair and dragged to death and the finale in which villain Blackie "is gunned down by Cassidy at point blank range — with a second pistol shot following, just to make sure."

Borderland, released in February, 1937, was the first of a half-dozen series releases that year; it was based on Mulford's 1922 book *Bring Me His Ears* but it had almost no relationship to the literary work other than locale. Filmed near Joshua Tree, California, in the Mojave Desert, the feature had Ellison, in his final series appearance, warbling the title song; at 81 minutes it was the longest running Hopalong Cassidy feature. The production was dominated by the performance of Stephen Morris (later Morris Ankrum) as a supposedly stupid townsman who is really the notorious bandit "The Fox." *Borderland* also gave Boyd a broader part than usual, for the plot called for him to pretend to be a outlaw on the run, one with a cold, calculating disposition who even showed unkindness to a little girl (Charlene Wyatt). The finale was particularly exciting with a wounded Hoppy holding the Fox at bay, waiting rescue by a posse as he slowly bleeds to death from a gunshot inflicted by the bandit.

Texas Ranger Hoppy (Boyd) is assigned to ferret out a notorious outlaw called The Fox, whose gang has been attacking ranches along the U.S.–Mexican border. Going undercover, Hoppy takes the guise of an escaped convict and turns on his pals, Ranger Johnny (Ellison) and oldtimer Windy (Hayes). In the Mexican village of El Rio, Hoppy boards at a house run by Grace Rand (Nora Lane), along with Johnny and Windy, who have followed him, and a half-wit called Loco (Stephen Morris [Morris Ankrum]), who does odd jobs. Loco, however, is really the Fox, who kills one of his men (George Chesebro) for disobeying orders and replaces him with Dandy Morgan (Alan Bridge). Hoppy finds the murdered man and notices a paper with strange cuts, similar to one he found at a remote cabin, the Fox's hideout. The Fox orders a henchman (Leo J. Mahan) to kill Johnny, but Hoppy shoots the outlaw and takes the unconscious Johnny back to Grace's boardinghouse. When Hoppy sees Loco making the paper cutouts, he thinks he works for the Fox and sets up a ruse to trap the outlaw. He joins Dandy in a plan to rustle cattle but at the same time alerts Mexican Secret Service Colonel Gonzales (Trevor Bardette), who has been masquerading as a street singer, to have his men ready to capture the Fox's gang. Becoming leery of Hoppy, the Fox gets him to come to his cabin at the head of Cloudburst Canyon by kidnapping Windy and little Molly Rand (Charlene Wyatt), Grace's daughter. When Hoppy gives up his guns, the Fox sets Windy and Molly free. In a fight, Hoppy disarms the outlaw but receives a bad leg wound. Gonzales and his men, along with Johnny, arrive on the scene and shoot it out with the gang as Hoppy, losing a great deal of blood, tries to hold the Fox at bay. When the gang is defeated, Johnny comes to Hoppy's rescue as Gonzales arrests the Fox. Hoppy and Johnny's friendship is renewed when Hoppy tells Johnny that he rescued him after he was shot by the Fox's henchman.

Ellison departed the Hopalong Cassidy series after *Borderland*, having become disgruntled with producer Harry Sherman. Ellison co-starred in Cecil B. DeMille's big-budget *The Plainsman* (1937) for Paramount. He wanted a series of his own and Sherman promised to star him in a group of features based on the works of Rex Beach. When this failed to happen, Ellison asked to be released from his contract and he signed with RKO Radio where he starred in many features before returning to a western series with the "Irish Cowboys" (q.v.) in 1950. Picked to replace Ellison in the Hoppy series was Russell Hayden (1910–81), whom producer Sherman thought would be ideal for the role of Lucky Jenkins, although his only film experience had been on the other side of the camera as a technician. Sherman's choice, however, would prove to be a good one and Hayden would co-star in 27 Hopalong Cassidy features between 1937 and 1941, continuing the triad hero concept of the series.

Released in the spring of 1937, *Hills of Old Wyoming* introduced the title song written by Leo Robin and Ralph Rainger; it would become a perennially popular western ballad. The feature was based on Mulford's 1933 novel *The Round-Up* and like nearly all the Cassidy photoplays it had little to do with its alleged source. The story had Wyoming ranch owner Hoppy (Boyd) trying to find out who is behind cattle rustling in the area, the culprits thought to be Indians from a local reservation. Indian agent Andrews (Stephen Morris [Morris Ankrum]) is behind the trouble and Hoppy, along with pals Windy (Hayes) and Lucky Jenkins (Hayden), become suspicious of him after his cohort, Lone Eagle

(Steve Clemente), tries to frame Hoppy on a rustling charge. Andrews has Lone Eagle murdered, hoping the Indians will put the blame on Hoppy, who brings the murdered man's body to the tribe's leader (Chief Big Tree) and promises to find the culprit. With Windy and Lucky kept as hostages, the chief allows Hoppy to go; he returns and proves to the chief that bullets from Andrews' gun killed Lone Eagle. When Andrews finds out that Hoppy and his pals, along with the Indians, are out to get him, he tries to escape but is captured, bringing peace back to the area.

An amusing subplot in *Hills of Old Wyoming* had both Lucky and Windy involved in romances; Windy with general store owner Ma Hutchins, played by silent film star Clara Kimball Young, and Lucky with her pretty daughter, Alice (Gail Sheridan). The highlight of the feature, though, was its scenic locales and their exploitation by cameraman Archie Stout. At 78 minutes, however, the feature tended to drag until its exciting finale.

Next came *North of the Rio Grande*, issued early in the summer of 1937, supposedly taken from the 1925 Mulford book *Cottonwood Gulch*. With his entry, cinematographer Russell Harlan replaced Stout, but the high visual standards of the series continued. Here Hoppy (Boyd) takes the guise of big-talking gunman Wild Bill "Dynamite" Magroo in an effort to get revenge on an outlaw called the Lone Wolf, who murdered his younger brother Buddy Cassidy. In the town of Cottonwood Gulch, Hoppy makes friends with saloon girl Faro Annie (Bernadene Hayes), much to the chagrin of her boss, Ace Crowder (John Rutherford), the Lone Wolf's partner. As Magroo, Hoppy robs a stagecoach and hides the loot but is warned by Crowder not to interfere in local affairs. Cassidy then visits Buddy's widow Mary (Lorraine Randall) at her Bar Q ranch. Deputy Sheriff Plunkett (Al Ferguson), who has trailed Hoppy on Crowder's orders, tries to murder him but is himself killed. The head (Lee Colt [Lee J. Cobb]) of the local railroad tells Crowder to hire Hoppy to bring in the Lone Wolf as the masked outlaw, who wears a large ring, hires Hoppy to steal a shipment of gold. Hoppy then tells the railroad man the true nature of his business in Cottonwood Gulch and returns the money he had stolen. He is then sent to Henry Stoneman (Stephen Morris [Morris Ankrum], the town banker, whom Hoppy recognizes as the Lone Wolf from the ring he wears. Stoneman ties up Hoppy and plans to skip town with the money he and Crowder have amassed. When Crowder finds out he has been double-crossed, he sets out after Stoneman, who forces Windy (Hayes) to engineer the local train out of town. When Annie sees Hoppy's horse outside Stoneman's office, she unties him as Hoppy's pal Lucky (Hayden) leads a gang of railroad men after Crowder and Stoneman. The outlaws are captured. Lucky is wounded and nearly killed when he gets his foot caught in a train track, but is saved by Hopalong. Although Hoppy and Lucky are afraid that Windy was killed when the train jumped the tracks and went over a cliff, they find the grizzled oldtimer in a bunch of cactus. He managed to jump off the train while Stoneman was killed in the crash.

The mid-summer of 1937 saw the release of *Rustlers' Valley*, a top-notch entry taken from the 1924 Mulford novel of the same name; the film was closer to the original source than most of the Hoppy screen efforts. The story opens with Lucky (Hayden) framed for the robbery of a $20,000 mine payroll by ranch foreman Taggart (Ted Adams). Taggart works for Glen Randall (Stephen Morris [Morris Ankrum]), who is in cahoots with businessman Cal Howard (Lee Colt [Lee J. Cobb]). Howard is working with bank president Clem Crawford (Oscar Apfel) in buying up local ranches at a cheap price in order to sell the land to an Eastern syndicate planning to construct an irrigation dam. In trying to get away from the sheriff (John Beach) and his posse, Lucky is thought to be drowned in a river flowing through Black Canyon and a saddened Hoppy (Boyd) and Windy (Hayes) decide to investigate. The two attend an engagement party for Howard and Agnes Randall (Muriel Evans), whose father is Glen Randall. Howard plans to take over the Randall ranch by marrying Agnes and then have Crawford foreclose on a loan to Randall since his spread is coveted by the syndicate. At the party, Lucky reveals himself to Hoppy and Windy. Howard becomes jealous of Hoppy's attentions to Agnes, who breaks off her engagement to him. Windy hides Lucky in nearby Lost Canyon while Hoppy is hired as Randall's foreman when Taggart quits.

When Hoppy finds out from Windy that Howard helped Taggart get clear of a murder charge some years before, Hoppy confronts the businessman, who orders Taggart to kill him. He also tells Taggart to rustle the Randall cattle and hide them in Lost Canyon so Randall will not have the collateral needed to pay his bank loan to Crawford. When Windy and Lucky find the stolen cattle in Lost Canyon, they tell Hoppy, who then comes to Agnes' rescue after she is shot at by Taggart because she is riding Hoppy's horse. Trailing Taggart to the gang's hideout, Hoppy captures him and Howard as a posse surrounds the place. As Howard manages to get the drop on Hoppy, Windy and Lucky push large rocks onto the gang's shack and Hoppy escapes. Howard, Taggart and the remaining gang members are arrested.

Filmed at the ghost town in Columbia, California, *Rustlers' Valley* contained a well-staged climactic shootout between the outlaws and the posse, with the huge boulders being pushed down a hill and onto the gang's hideout a highlight. The sequence was reused in the film's 1942 remake *Lost Canyon*. Villain Lee J. Cobb, billed as Lee Colt, would later star in the popular NBC-TV television series *The Virginian* from 1962 to 1966. Interestingly, the feature cast usual villain Morris Ankrum as the heroine's kindly father.

The late summer of 1937 saw the issuance of *Hopalong Rides Again*, allegedly based on Mulford's 1923 book *Black Buttes*. Shot at Lone Pine, California, it was another sturdy entry in the series, made more so by the appearance of silent western star William Duncan (1879–1961) in the role of Bar 20 boss Buck Peters. A native of Scotland, Duncan worked in the physical culture field before coming to films in 1911. By the mid-teens he was a major star of serials and in 1922 he signed with Universal. He left films in 1925 but returned in the 1930s, also appearing as Buck Peters in two 1938 releases, *Bar 20 Justice* and *The Frontiersman*, and 1939's *Law of the Pampas*. The film was also the first of 28 series entries directed by Lesley Selander (1900–79), a native of California who came to films in 1919 as a laboratory assistant before turning to cinematography. After working as an assistant director in the mid–1930s, he made his directorial debut in 1936, helming Buck Jones in *Ride 'Em Cowboy*. Before retiring in 1968 he directed over 130 films, mostly Westerns.

Hopalong Rides Again has Bar 20 ranch foreman Hoppy (Boyd) ordered by his boss Buck Peters (William Duncan) to drive a large herd over the Black Buttes trail, where a stampede had killed two cowhands the year before. Ranch hand Lucky (Hayden), who is romancing Buck's niece, Laura (Lois Wilde), helps Hoppy and his sidekick Windy (Hayes) round up the cattle for the drive.

Poster for *Hopalong Rides Again* (Paramount, 1937).

Horace Hepburn (Harry Worth), a paleontology professor doing dinosaur research for a museum, stops at the Bar 20 to get a horseshoe replacement and he tells Hoppy that his sister Nora Blake (Nora Lane) owns a spread in nearby Grass Valley. Hoppy, who is in love with Nora, welcomes Horace but Windy, who does the horseshoeing, becomes wary of the man after finding dynamite in his wagon. Bar 20 rider Keno (Ernie Adams) is fired by Hoppy after he tries to shoot Lucky; Keno then tells Hepburn, who is the head of a rustling gang, about the upcoming trail drive. Hepburn and his gang use dynamite to stampede the herd with Buck's young nephew Artie (William King) being injured. Since Artie cannot be moved, Windy stays with the boy while Hoppy orders Lucky to take the herd to market and return in eight days with the proceeds from the sale. Suspecting that Horace is involved in the stampede, Hoppy visits Nora and tells her about Lucky's trip, knowing he will be overheard by her brother. Windy sees Horace and his men changing the Bar 20 brand to appear to be Nora's, and Hoppy shows her the evidence without telling her that Horace is involved. Although still weak, Artie distracts Windy and rides back to the Bar 20 to get Buck and the ranch hands. When gang member Blackie (John Rutherford) refuses to bushwhack Hoppy, Horace shoots him as Buck and his men arrive and rout the rustlers. Horace tries to escape by dynamiting a nearby hill but the dying Blackie shoots him, setting off an explosion which kills Hepburn. Hoppy does not tell Nora about her brother's criminal activities.

The final 1937 series outing, *Texas Trail*, came out in November and had no connection with the literary work on which it was supposed to be based, Mulford's 1923 novel *Tex*. At the beginning of the Spanish-American War, Hoppy (Boyd), who is training volunteers for Teddy Roosevelt's Rough Riders, is ordered by an Army major (Karl Hackett) to bring in 500 wild horses in a week, for military use. Heading to Ghost Creek Canyon with several men, including his pals Windy (Hayes) and Lucky (Hayden), Hoppy splits his drovers into two units and in less than a week they round up the needed mustangs. Black Jack Carson (Alexander Cross), with whom Lucky is a rival for the affections of schoolmarm Barbara Allen (Judith Allen), plans to take over the herd and sell it on the open market. He has his men put ten of his horses into the herd and then he and his gang attack the cowboys' camp, taking them prisoner. Carson then tries Hoppy and his men as horse thieves and leaves them tied up as they (Carson's gang) take the herd to market. Boots (Billy King), the young son of the major, becomes concerned when Hoppy does not arrive with the cattle and he rides to the campsite and, finding the men tied up, sets them free. Carson's cohort Hawks (Robert Kortman) tries to alert his boss that the cowboys have been turned loose but he is killed when he falls on his own knife. In order to stampede the herd, Hoppy has Lucky set a fire; the cowboys then fight a pitched battle with the outlaws as the horses run from the blaze. Barbara rides to the fort to get help from the cavalry. Hoppy drives the horse herd across a river and then single-handedly holds off Carson and his gang until Barbara arrives with the soldiers and the outlaws are subdued. The horses are then driven to the fort. As Hoppy and his pals prepare to join the Rough Riders, Lucky kisses Barbara goodbye.

Texas Trail was the only Hoppy feature directed by David Selman, a veteran director of Columbia westerns with Tim McCoy and Charles Starrett. Containing a fast-moving plot and the usual fine photography and scenic backgrounds, the feature did contain a scene which surprisingly did not draw the ire of the censors. When Barbara overhears a henchman telling Carson that Hoppy and his men have escaped, she is in her bedroom which is right next to Carson's bedroom. Evidently the schoolteacher and the cattleman lived together in the same house.

Lesley Selander returned to direct *Partners of the Plains*, the first of seven 1938 Hoppy screen adventures; released in January of that year, it was allegedly based on the 1918 Mulford novel *The Man from Bar 20: A Story of Cow-Country*. The fairly light-hearted romp is dominated by Gwen Gaze as self-centered Londoner Lora Drake, who comes to the LD Ranch, which she co-owns, with her Aunt Martha (Hilda Plowright) and her fiancé, Ronald Harwood (John Warburton). When she tries to use her position to control ranch foreman Hoppy (Boyd), he quits. She has him arrested for taking a ranch horse. Deciding to play her game, Hoppy has himself released from

Poster for *Partners of the Plains* (Paramount, 1938).

jail in Lorna's custody and the two become attracted to each other. Also arriving in the area is outlaw Scar Lewis (Alan Bridge), who has gotten out of prison a year early for good behavior and swears revenge on Hoppy for putting him behind bars. Scar comes to realize that Ronald is jealous of Hoppy and convinces him to kill his rival but he fails. When Lorna decides to raise sheep instead of cattle on the ranch, Hoppy warns her it will start a range war. She discharges him but he will not leave because he is still in her custody.

Lorna then argues with Ronald and breaks off their engagement. Scar and his henchman Doc Galer (Al Hill) plan to murder Hoppy by having him take Lorna to a remote cabin which they plan to dynamite. Ronald convinces ranch hand Baldy Morton (Harvey Clark) that Lorna wants to see Hoppy at the cabin but Hoppy is suspicious. He and Lucky (Hayden) have a shootout with Galer, who is killed. Ronald reveals Scar's plan to them. Ronald prevents the dynamite from exploding but a brush fire ensues and Hoppy saves Lorna when it surrounds the cabin. Hoppy and Ronald are joined by Lucky and the ranch hands in a gunfight with Scar and his gang; the ex-convict is shot by Lucky and the outlaws are captured. Lorna then obeys Hoppy's order to return to the ranch. Later she and her aunt leave for a visit to California while Ronald decides to stay on at the LD ranch.

Like *Hopalong Rides Again*, *Partners of the Plains* allowed Hoppy to fall in love. One amusing scene had Lucky telling Baldy that he needs to dress for dinner in evening clothes, which Baldy takes to mean a night shirt. For this feature and the next, *Cassidy of Bar 20*, Hayes took a hiatus from the series and was replaced in *Partners of the Plains* by Harvey Clark as comedy relief Baldy. Regarding the overall production, *Variety* noted, "[Harry] Sherman spends more on his sagebrush mellers than the ordinary producer and he gets more than average results. Among other things he employs good writers and good directors. Additionally, Sherman seems to take care in selecting his cast and tries to get away a little from conventional types, particularly as to heroines." The trade paper called leading lady Gwen Gaze "a welcome change" although the reviewer suspected her singing "Moonlight on the Sunset Trail" was dubbed.

Frank Darien played Pappy, the comedy relief, in the next Hoppy entry, *Cassidy of Bar 20*, released in February, 1938; it supposedly came from Mulford's 1929 book *Me an' Shorty*. Nora Lane returned as Hoppy's sweetheart, Nora Blake, a part she did previously in *Hopalong Rides Again*. Telling the Bar 20 boys to wait for him for two weeks, Hoppy (Boyd) and his friends Lucky (Hayden) and Pappy (Darien) ride to the aid of Nora (Nora Lane), who co-owns the T.D. Rancho with Tom Dillon (John Elliott). On the way they are shot at by Dillon's daughter Mary (Margaret Marquis), who mistakes them for the outlaws who have been rustling the ranch's cattle. Later they meet crook Jeff Caffrey (Carleton Young), who is in league with Clay Allison (Robert Fiske), a businessman who is really the leader of the gang which is tearing down barbed wire fences and running stolen cattle over T.D. range. Jeff gets the local sheriff (Edward Cassidy) to arrest Hoppy, Lucky and Pappy for the crimes and at a trial Hoppy pleads guilty in order to get into the gang. Given probation, Hoppy and Lucky go to work for Allison while Pappy is placed in the custody of hotel owner Ma Caffrey (Gertrude W. Hoffman), Jeff's mother. Hoppy leaves to investigate the rustling and Lucky, who is covering his trail, is shot by Jeff. Mary stops Jeff from killing Lucky and tries to convince Jeff to quit working for Allison. When Dillon refuses to sell him his half of the T.D. Rancho, Clay kills him but finds out that Jeff saw him commit the crime. Pappy finds an underground passage out of the jail and escapes. Planning to rustle all the area's unbranded cattle for himself, Allison is confronted by Cassidy who has sent Lucky for the Bar 20 wranglers. Holding off Clay and his men, Hoppy has Jeff arrested for Dillon's murder but the young man later finds the underground passage and, after escaping, he is murdered by Allison. Before dying, Jeff gives his mother one of Clay's special-made bullets, proving that Allison was his murderer. When Clay's gang arrive at the T.D. Rancho to shoot Hoppy, they are met by the Bar 20 boys and driven back to town. Hoppy and Pappy get to the hotel in time to stop Allison from killing Ma McCaffrey, who has confronted him about her son's murder. Hoppy shoots Clay, the outlaws are arrested and peace is restored.

Romance for Hoppy continued in the next series release, *Heart of Arizona*, which came out in the spring of 1938, supposedly based on Mulford's 1930 novel *The Deputy Sheriff*. Young Artie (Billy King) arrives at the Bar 20 ranch to spend the summer with his uncle Buck Peters (John Elliott). Meanwhile, Belle Starr (Natalie Moorhead) is released from prison after five years but the local sheriff, Hawley (John Beach), wants her out of the area. Bar 20 foreman Hoppy (Boyd) comes to Belle's defense by giving her his horse so she can go to Gunsmoke Canyon where she is reunited with her daughter Jackie (Dorothy Short). Wrangler Lucky (Hayden) is smitten with Belle and, to take his mind off her, Hoppy has him lead a herd of cattle to a new pasture. While Lucky and cowpoke Twister (Leo J. McMahon) are out with the herd, Jackie is thrown from her horse and Lucky takes her home. Twister is in cahoots with Belle's crooked foreman Ringo (Alden Chase) and the two rustle the herd. The next day

Poster for *Heart of Arizona* (Paramount, 1938).

the sheriff arrests Lucky for stealing cattle but he escapes at the urging of pal Windy (Hayes), and Buck Peters refuses to prosecute him. Hiding out at Belle's ranch, Lucky falls in love with Jackie while Belle harbors her own romantic feelings for Hoppy. After Ringo kills Twister to keep him quiet, Hoppy finds his body and this leads him to an abandoned mine which is being used as a slaughter pit. The mine is on land belonging to Trimmer Winkler (Lane Chandler); Hoppy accuses him of cattle rustling. Trimmer rides to meet Ringo, who is his partner, while the sheriff tries to arrest Lucky, who is shot. Realizing that Lucky has an alibi on the night of the latest cattle rustling, the sheriff leaves him with Belle and Jackie. Belle now realizes that Ringo is behind the lawlessness and is putting the blame on her. When Ringo steals all of her cattle, Hoppy becomes Belle's foreman and he marks a few steers and then traces them to Winkler after he purchases them from Ringo. The sheriff tries to arrest the two men after finding them with the marked cattle, but he is shot by Winkler. Ringo then leads his rustling gang to Belle's ranch where she, Hoppy and Jackie try to hold them off as Windy uses a mirror signal to get help from the Bar 20. When Ringo attempts to murder Hoppy, Belle takes the bullet intended for him, as the Bar 20 wranglers arrive to fight the gang. Hoppy kills Ringo, and Windy shoots Trimmer as he tries to ambush Lucky. Dying in Hoppy's arms, Belle is laid to rest among the rocks she loved.

Regarding the feature, Fred Romary wrote in his Image Entertainment DVD liner notes that it had "a strong screenplay by Norman Houston" and was "a departure from the formatted Hopalong Cassidy series.... [H]ere is a film rich in strong character studies, some almost spiritual at times. Especially defined are the spirited female players. A love story as well as a frontier adventure. Again, Russell Harlan's cinematography is picture-perfect, framing the many moods sensitively. In today's vernacular, this might be considered a woman's film."

Bar 20 Justice, released in June, 1938, was credited to the 1912 novel *Buck Peters, Ranchman* by Mulford and John Wood. Hoppy (Boyd) comes to the aid of mine owner Ann Dennis (Gwen Gaze) after her husband Denny (John Beach) is mysteriously murdered, the culmination of several supposed accidents at their Freeze-On mine. With the aid of Lucky (Hayden), Hoppy convinces the miners to stay on the job and appoints Les Martin (Dick Dickinson) night watchman after he is recommended by mine foreman Slade (Paul Sutton), whom Hoppy does not trust. Lucky abducts Martin and takes him to the Bar 20 ranch and Hoppy has Windy (Hayes) take over as guard. Pretending to be deaf and addled, Windy spies miners from the rival Devil-May-Care claim, owned by Frazier (Pat J. O'Brien), working the Dennis operation. Finding a secret door between the two claims, Hoppy is able to verify that the gold from the Devil-May-Care mine actually came from the Freeze-On. When Hoppy and Slade take Duke (Walter Long), Denny's killer, to a remote shack, the two men turn on Hoppy and he is tied up and left to die when they set the building on fire. Windy rescues Hoppy while Ann goes to Bar 20 owner Buck Peters (William Duncan) for help. Lucky arrives with Buck and his men and they attack Frazier and his miners. Hoppy subdues Frazier in a fight and the gang is arrested.

Issued theatrically in the summer of 1938, *Pride of the West* had a convoluted plotline which very little to do with its supposed source, Mulford's 1920 book *Johnny Nelson*. Rancher Hoppy (Boyd) is asked by Mary (Charlotte Field) and Dick Martin (Billy King) to help their father, Sheriff Tom Martin (Earle Hodgins), investigate a gold robbery in which Lucky (Hayden) was wounded. The sheriff feels that banker Caldwell (Kenneth Harlan) wants him out of office so that he (Caldwell) and his former business partner, real estate agent Nixon (James Craig), can buy up all the nearby ranch land and thus control the area water rights. Finding the robbers' hideout, Hoppy marks bags of gold and then has Martin take a posse out on a wild goose chase so the bandits can bring the loot into town. Windy (Hayes) and Lucky inform Hoppy that the gold was brought to Caldwell and Nixon; the trio hold up the crooks and take the gold to Windy's shack. Hoppy returns to town and pretends he never left Sing Loo's (Willie Fung) restaurant but the two are tied up by the crooks who then ride to the shack. Seeing Caldwell and Nixon leave town, Dick rings a church bell which is a signal for the sheriff and his posse to return. As Windy and Lucky try to fight off the crooks, Dick unties Hoppy, who follows the posse to Windy's shack. Ordering a ceasefire, Hoppy turns Windy and Lucky over to the law. Back at the jail he uses the marked money bags to prove that Caldwell and Nixon and their gang stole the gold and the crooks are arrested.

In Old Mexico, released in September, 1938, was a follow-up to *Borderland* although it was supposedly based on Mulford's 1927 book *Corson of the JC*. The beautifully photographed and well-paced western, the only series film to be directed by Edward D. Venturini, featured the Aaron Gonzales song "Muchachita" which was sung by Jane (later Jan) Clayton, the future wife of co-star Hayden. Trevor Bardette repeated the role of Colonel Gonzales from the previous outing, but Paul Sutton was cast as the notorious outlaw "The Fox" (the part previously played by Stephen Morris [Morris Ankrum]).

Bar 20 buckaroos Hoppy (Boyd), Windy (Hayes) and Lucky (Hayden) ride south of the border after receiving a note from Colonel Gonzales (Bardette); the colonel had previously aided Hoppy in sending the Fox (Sutton) to jail. Along the way, the trio gets directions to the Gonzales rancho from a woodcutter, who is really the Fox in disguise. The three men are welcomed at the rancho by Gonzales' father, Don Carlos (Al Garcia), although he knows nothing about the missive sent by his son to Hoppy. Also at the hacienda are Don Carlos' spritely daughter Anita (Clayton), who is enamored of Cassidy, and her American companion Janet Leeds (Betty Amann). Housekeeper Elena (Anna Demetrio) takes an immediate shine to Windy, hoping to make him her fifth husband. During dinner, a message is thrown through a window concerning Don Carlos' son; the men head out in search of him and find that he has been murdered. Before dying, Gonzales wrote the letters "zor" in the sand, the only clue to the crime. The murder was committed by the Fox in revenge for Gonzales sending him to prison; Hoppy and Don Carlos deduce this was the man who murdered the colonel. Becoming suspicious of Janet, Hoppy plays a waiting game in investigating the crime, much to the chagrin of Lucky and Anita. Hoppy keeps company with Anita and the two decide to go riding in the desert where she holds him at gunpoint and tells him she is the Fox's sister, something he had already presumed, and that she had helped her brother escape from prison. After Hoppy takes her gun away, the Fox gets the drop on Hoppy but he shoots the outlaw and lets Janet escape. Along with Windy, Hoppy starts leading the Fox back to the hacienda. The killer's gang attacks Lucky and Anita, who have been looking for clues in defiance of Hoppy's orders. Windy is shot and Hoppy tells him to ride to the rancho for help as he, Lucky and Anita hold off the gang. Despite a second wound, Windy rides to Don Carlos who leads his men in forcing the gang to surrender, just as Hoppy is running out of ammunition. The Fox tries to use a knife to murder Hoppy, whose last bullet kills the outlaw. Hoppy and Lucky ride to the hacienda to see Windy, who is being nursed back to health by Elena.

The final 1938 Hopalong Cassidy feature, *The Frontiersmen*, issued at the end of the year, was yet another outing supposedly based on Mulford's novel *Bar 20* without any similarities in plot. Here Bar 20 foreman Hoppy (Boyd) is forced to order Artie Peters (Dickie Jones), the nephew of ranch owner Buck Peters (William Duncan) and his wife Amanda (Clara Kimball Young), to attend school although he and the other students detest their teacher Miss Snooks (Emily Fitzroy). After the schoolboys tie up Miss Snooks, town mayor Jud Thorpe (Charles "Tony" Hughes) has Hoppy restore order while he and his men rustle Bar 20 cattle. Thorpe is really the notorious outlaw Dan Rawley. When Hoppy finds one of the Bar 20 men has been killed during the raid, he suspects Thorpe, who is defeated in his plan to bring in a strict teacher by Hoppy, who asks the school board for a more gentle instructor. This turns out to be Easterner June Lake (Evelyn Venable), who boards at the Bar 20 and quickly wins over Artie as well as the Bar 20 hands, who quit work on a new corral to polish up the schoolhouse. When only Artie attends the first day of classes, the cowboys round up the other students and take them to class. Both Lucky and Windy are attracted to June, as is Thorpe. Hoppy follows Buck's orders and moves a large cattle herd to mountain pasture for grazing. Both Windy and Lucky propose marriage to June but she accepts Thorpe's proposal, despite Hoppy's protest. While the mayor gives out diplomas at the school's graduation ceremonies, his men wait to rustle the Bar

20 herd. One of Thorpe's men, Buster Sutton (Roy Barcroft), turns on the mayor and tries to kill him, calling out his real name before Thorpe shoots him. Although Thorpe makes a getaway, he is followed by Hoppy and the Bar 20 boys; the outlaw and his gang are captured. With June promising to return for classes the next fall, Hoppy realizes he also has feelings for her.

Regarding the feature, *Variety* commented, "Well-constructed oats opera ... differs chiefly from the others in that there is stronger romantic interest developed and a group of singing schoolboys figures in the prairie school episodes. Emphasis on schoolday sequences hold back robust western action until the last 15 minutes when it is doubly concentrated.... St. Brendan Boy's Choir, cast as a group of school youngsters, lend a distinct musical touch to the outdoor opus with their vocalizing."

The first of five 1939 series releases, *Sunset Trail*, came out in February. Rancher John Marsh (Kenneth Harlan) sells his cattle herd for $30,000 to gambling house owner Monte Keller (Robert Fiske). As Marsh heads east with his wife Ann (Charlotte Myers) and their daughter Dorrie (Jane [Jan] Clayton) on a stagecoach, Keller leads his men in an ambush, kills Keller and takes back the money. Ann goes to a banker (Alphonse Ethier) for help and he tells her to go back to Silver City and open a dude ranch. Since Ann remembers some of the serial numbers on the paper money stolen from her husband, the banker promises to send Hoppy (Boyd) to investigate the crimes. When Hoppy gets a letter from the banker explaining the situation, he tells Windy (Hayes) and Lucky (Hayden) to ride to Silver City but once they are there they must promise to pretend to not know him. Turning down financial help from Keller, who is romantically interested in her, Ann sets up the Flying T Guest Ranch although she does agree to let his henchman Steve Dorman (Anthony Nace) work at the ranch. After having a run-in with Keller in Silver City, Windy and Lucky go to the Flying T and are hired despite Steve's objections. Paying guests of the dude ranch include aged Furbush (Maurice Cass), spinster Abigail Snodgrass (Kathryn Sheldon) and dandified dude William Harold Cassidy, really Hoppy in disguise. Steve becomes jealous of Lucky's attentions to Dorrie and they fight. The

Poster for *Sunset Trail* (Paramount, 1938).

disguised Hoppy gambles at Keller's place and wins some bills with the same serial numbers as those stolen from Ann's husband. While supposedly taking a lesson in stud poker from Steve, Hoppy confronts him about the bills and the two fight. After a chase, Hoppy is forced to kill Steve in self-defense, thus revealing his real identity. During a poker game, Hoppy not only wins back the money Keller stole but he also exposes him as a crook. As Hoppy and Ann leave town on the stagecoach, Keller's cohort Walker (Glenn Strange) arrives with the news that Steve has been killed by Hoppy. Keller leads his gang in pursuit of the stagecoach, but they are stopped by the arrival of Lucky and the trail patrol. Although he suffers a shoulder wound, Hoppy kills Keller. Windy, trying to elude Abigail's attentions, rides out of Silver City ahead of Hoppy and Lucky. During the course of the feature, Jane (Jan) Clayton serenaded Russell Hayden with the song ""A Cowgirl Dreams On."

Although allegedly based on the 1928 Mulford novel *Mesquite Jenkins, Sunset Trail* had very little to do with the book; the next series entry, *Silver on the Sage*, was supposedly taken from Mulford's *On the Trail of the Tumbling T*, published in 1935. A cattle herd led by Windy (Hayes) and Lucky (Hayden) is rustled, prompting Dave Talbot (Stanley Ridges), foreman of the Lazy J Ranch where the cattle herd was headed, to attack Lucky. Lucky accuses him of being involved in the rustling. Lazy J owner Tom Hamilton (Frederick Burton) wants to settle the argument with the local marshal (Jack Rockwell) but when Lucky takes out after a sniper he returns to find Hamilton murdered and Talbot missing. In town, the lawman says Talbot was playing cards at the time of the killing at Earl Brennan's (also Stanley Ridges) gambling house and this is confirmed by gambler Bill Thompson, really Hoppy (Boyd) incognito. Lucky breaks out of jail and is followed to a supposedly poisoned water hole at the desert's edge by Hoppy and Windy. There Cassidy finds the water hole is not poisoned and he also informs Lucky and Windy that Talbot was not playing cards with him at the time of the murder. Telling Windy and Lucky to stay hidden, Hoppy continues to investigate the killing but his cover is soon blown by Brennan who plans to kill him and raid the Hamilton ranch, now run by the dead man's daughter Barbara (Ruth Rogers). When Lucky finds out about Brennan's plans, he warns Barbara, but she has her men tie him up, thinking he killed her father. Talbot tries to ambush Hoppy, but Hoppy gets the advantage of him and takes him to the marshal with proof that Brennan and Talbot are twins and that Brennan shot Hamilton. After a shootout with the law, the gang manages to get out of town as Hoppy takes a posse to the Hamilton ranch and sets Lucky free. He then follows the Brennan gang to a desert hideout where he sets a fire which brings the marshal and his posse, brining an end to the lawlessness.

With *The Renegade Trail*, issued in the summer of 1939, the series gave up any pretense of being taken from Mulford's works other than crediting him for his characters. Bar 20 men Hoppy (Boyd) and Lucky (Hayden) ride to the town of Cactus Springs to see Windy (Hayes), who has been named marshal. Also arriving is escaped convict Smoky Bob Joslin (Russell Hopton), who teams with another ex-con, Traynor (John Merton), in a scheme to rustle the cattle on the ranch of his wife, Mary Joyce (Charlotte Wynters), with the aid of notorious cattle rustler Stiff Hat Bailey (Roy Barcroft). Mary has not told her little boy, Joey (Sonny Bupp), the truth about his father; the youngster thinks his dad died a hero fighting for his country. The boy is also enthralled by Windy's tales of the heroics of Hoppy, who goes to work at Mary's Circle J Ranch when her foreman (Jack Rockwell) finds out that Bailey is in the area. While prodding cattle into their pens, Joey falls off a rail and Hoppy risks his life to save the boy, who sustains a broken leg. Joslin confronts Mary and threatens to tell the truth about himself to their son unless she pretends he is her brother Bennett. When Hoppy meets Joslin, he realizes he is lying; Mary tells him the truth and begs Hoppy to let her husband go free for the youngster's sake. Hoppy reluctantly agrees. After leaving the Circle J, Joslin and Traynor lock Mary in the tool shed and then join with Bailey to rustle the ranch's herd. While trailing the rustlers, Lucky is ambushed but he is saved by Hoppy, who sends his wounded friend back to the ranch in a chuck wagon. There Jenkins shoots Traynor and frees Mary. Taking Joey, the three head to town but are overtaken by the Bailey gang. As Joslin holds the three prisoners, Bailey and his men raid the stockade; the foreman and his men surrender to the outlaws as Hoppy circles around and gets the drop on the gang. When Joslin is about to tell Joey the truth about himself, Mary stops him as Lucky jumps Joslin and the horses bolt. Windy arrives and shoots Joslin while Hoppy saves Mary and Joey.

By now, the Hopalong Cassidy series was incorporating more music into its productions. Here The King's Men serenade Hoppy with "Hi Thar, Stranger," slowing up the film's plot flow and action. On the other hand, their rendering of "Lazy Rolls the Rio Grande" was nicely incorporated into the plot with the singers portraying cowboys ending their day's work. The latter song was recorded by Rudy Vallee on Varsity Records (no. 8211). *The Renegade Trail*, an otherwise satisfying series outing, included a continuity error: In one scene Hoppy refers to ranch foreman Slim as Red, a cowhand portrayed in the feature by future genre star Eddie Dean. The film also marked the final appearance of Hayes as Windy Halliday in the series.

Range War, released in the fall of 1939, has Hoppy (Boyd) hired by banker Higgins (Kenneth Harlan) to look into the theft of $25,000 that he loaned rancher Jim Marlow (Matt Moore). Marlow had planned to use the money to build a railroad around the property of cattleman Buck Collins (Willard Robertson), thus preventing him from charging ranchers high tolls for running herds across his land. Riding with Lucky (Hayden), Hoppy meets cowpoke Speedy McGinnis (Britt Wood) and the trio travel to a mission where Hoppy visits an old friend, Padre Jose (Pedro de Cordoba), and also meets Marlow's daughter Ellen (Betty Moran). Trying to ferret out the crooks, Hoppy has Higgins loan Marlow more money and then Hoppy and Speedy rob the stagecoach carrying the cash and are chased by two outlaws. The sheriff (Glenn Strange), having been informed of the plan by Hoppy, arrests all of them and takes them to jail. Hoppy outsmarts a deputy (Earle Hodgins) and all four men escape from jail and head to the outlaws' hideout. There Speedy observes Collins' cohort Dave Morgan (Francis McDonald) dividing up the stolen loot and is nearly shot by the man but is saved by Hoppy. Hoppy and Speedy then tie up the outlaws and ride with them to the mission, leaving Morgan to inform Collins of his plans. Sending Ellen to get help from her father, Hoppy and Speedy hold off the outlaws who are subdued upon the arrival of Marlow and his men.

Britt Wood (1895–1965), a veteran vaudeville comedian and harmonica player, appeared in seven Hopalong Cassidy features, four of them in the role of Speedy McGinnis. Producer Harry Sherman hoped the character would catch on with the public as did George Hayes as Windy Halliday, but it was not to be, as noted by David Rothel in *Those Great Cowboy Sidekicks* (1984): "The Speedy character was rather intriguing for a film or two, but familiarity soon bred discontent, if not contempt. He was an interesting codger to ride to town with once or twice, but you wouldn't want him as a constant trail mate. In short, Speedy didn't wear well."

The final 1939 series outing, November's *Law of the Pampas*, was a leisurely paced murder mystery set in Argentina. Nate Watt returned to direct this series entry. To compensate for the absence of Windy Halliday from the proceedings, the script had Sidney Toler, most famous for his many screen portrayals of Charlie Chan, as a methodical ranch foreman whose nickname was El Melancolio (The Worrier) because of his pessimistic outlook on life. The feature also marked William Duncan's final appearance as Bar 20 owner Buck Peters. At the Arizona Territorial Rodeo Fair, Bar 20 foreman and deputy marshal Hoppy (Boyd) is introduced by his boss Buck Peters (William Duncan) to his guests, Argentine rancher Jose Valdez (Pedro de Cordoba), his grandson Ernesto (Jojo la Sadio), his son-in-law Ralph Merritt (Sidney Blackmer) and his melancholy foreman Don Fernando Ramirez (Sidney Toler). After Hoppy saves Ernesto from being gored by a rampaging wild bull, Buck agrees to sell Valdez half of his cattle herd and he orders Hoppy and Lucky (Hayden) to accompany the herd, which after an overland drive will be shipped to Argentina by rail and boat. During the roundup, Fernando tells Cassidy that Valdez's son Carlos, Ernesto's father, and his daughter Rosita, Merritt's wife, both had met tragic deaths, Carlos while cleaning a gun and Rosita from falling from a cliff while riding. Once they are in Argentina at the Valdez rancho, Hoppy becomes convinced that Carlos and Rosita were both murdered and he is concerned because Merritt was away on business when both crimes were committed. After finding Merritt with dancing girl Chiquita (Steffi Duna), he investigates further and Merritt becomes suspicious, ordering his henchmen Slim (Glenn Strange) and Curly (Eddie Dean) to kill Hoppy if he continues snooping. Hoppy and Lucky have a brawl in a local cantina with Slim and Curly. Merritt then orders Chiquita to send a message to Hoppy for a rendezvous as he plans to shoot him upon arrival. Hoppy gets the drop on Merritt, who he now knows is wanted outlaw Slim Woolsey, but Chiquita forces him to drop his gun and he is taken prisoner. When Hoppy induces

Merritt to admit he has no plans to marry Chiquita, the girl rides to the rancho for help as Hoppy makes a successful breakaway and heads to the nearest gaucho camp for reinforcements. When Chiquita arrives at the rancho, Fernando has Lucky put Valdez and Ernesto in a wagon and they seek sanctuary in a nearby cave. Merritt and his men follow them, but they are trailed by Hoppy and the gauchos. Merritt and his gang overtake the wagon as it breaks down but in a gunfight with the gauchos they are defeated. As Merritt tries to escape, he is stopped by Hoppy using a bolo. With Merritt's plan to murder Valdez and Ernesto and take over the rancho thwarted, Hoppy and Lucky return home to the Bar 20.

Law of the Pampas contains quite a bit of comedy and, like most series entries, saves the real action for the finale. There is considerable humorous byplay between the characters of Hoppy, Lucky and Fernando, whom Lucky jokingly refers to as Ferdy. While the character of Fernando is basically a forlorn one, he becomes animated in the presence of his wife, hacienda housekeeper Dolores (Anna Demetrio). One amusing scene has Dolores arrive at the cattle camp to see her husband, who tells her she is needed at the rancho. He asks Hoppy and Lucky to help him get his overweight wife back on her mule, who instead tries to run away. Rather than try and lift Dolores, Hoppy volunteers to ride to the rancho and let them know of her whereabouts.

Lesley Selander returned to direct four of the five 1940 releases, beginning with *Santa Fe Marshal*, issued in January. Here Hoppy (Boyd), working undercover for the government, is trying to find out who is behind the lawlessness in the silver mining region of Del Oro. Along the way he aids medicine man Doc Bates (Earle Hodgins) and his pretty daughter Paula (Bernadene Hayes), whose show wagon has broken down. Becoming a partner with Bates, Hoppy takes the guise of a mind reader and in town he rescues Ma Burton (Marjorie Rambeau), whose horse has bolted. She invites him to stay at her boarding house; he tells her he is an escaped convict and he has his buddy Lucky (Hayden) pretend to be a lawman on his trail. When Bates obtains from the room of known outlaw Blake (Kenneth Harlan) a watch which has the initials of a payroll carrier murdered at the Gardner Silver Mine, owned by John Gardner (Jack Rockwell), he shows it to Hoppy who begins to think Ma may be involved in the robberies. He then tries to get Ma and her boys to take part in a bogus robbery in order to trap them, but Ma finds out that Hoppy is really a lawman and captures him and Gardner; after robbing the mine, she leaves them to die in a fire. Paula, who overheard Ma's plans and tried to warn Hoppy, is taken prisoner by gang member Tex Barners (George Anderson). Lucky rides to the mine and liberates Hoppy and Gardner and the trio capture the outlaws and set Paula free.

Variety commented on this feature, "It introduces considerably more romantic interest and adds a shakerful of comedy. Latter is welcome and can't miss and the former is not so abundant as to get in the way. Difficulty, however, is that they consume footage that might have gone to brawling, shooting and hard riding, which is at a minimum." The reviewer also commended Earle Hodgins for his role of Doc Bates, calling him "excellent" and adding, "His humorous mixing of curing fluids from water and tea, and the spiels, with their interlined wisecracks going over the head of the natives, are truly part of the early American scene." The trade paper also referred to Bernadene Hayes' role as "Boyd's ticker interest."

Howard Bretherton returned to direct *The Showdown*, issued in March, 1940. It also brought back Britt Wood (as comedy relief Speedy McGinnis) and Morris Ankrum (resuming the villainous chores he had previously done billed as Stephen Morris). The story had Speedy (Wood) drafted to introduce Baron Rendor (Ankrum) to the people upon his arrival at the railroad station in Sundance, Nevada. Sue Willard (Jane [Jan] Clayton), a stowaway on the train masquerading as a boy, also gets off at Sundance. Hoppy (Boyd) saves Sue when she nearly falls under the train; when he finds out she is not a boy, she explains that she is the niece of local horse breeder Colonel Rufe White (Wright Kramer). The Baron, who is traveling with his valet Harry Cole (Donald Kirke), has come to Sundance to look at White's horses (he is representing a European syndicate interested in racehorses, especially the colonel's best racer, Warlock). Sue rides with Lucky (Hayden), Speedy, the Baron and his valet to the White ranch where for the first time the colonel meets the daughter of his late sister. White and the Baron negotiate the sale of the horses and the colonel asks Hoppy to ship his horses to auction in San Francisco if the Baron, who must wire his employers, does not buy them. When Hoppy finds out there have been no telegrams sent from Sundance to Europe, he becomes suspicious; after the Baron tries to cheat him in a card game he is wary of the visitor. Hoppy marks the money he won from the Baron and then Bowman (Roy Barcroft) and his men, who are in league with the Baron, take it from him. Lucky becomes jealous of Hoppy over Sue. Colonel White intercepts a letter to Sue from her attorneys informing her that she is the rightful owner of the White ranch and that the colonel usurped it from her mother. The colonel denounces Sue and has the town marshal (Eddie Dean) arrest her. Hoppy and Lucky come to her defense but the Baron arrives with the money for the horse herd and Hoppy brands him an imposter because it is the marked money that was stolen from him by Bowman and his gang. During a scuffle, the colonel dies from a heart attack and Hoppy finds the letter which exonerates Sue. The young woman then asks Hoppy to drive her horse herd to market but this makes Lucky jealous and he joins up with the Baron, a fake who really wants the horses for bets at county fairs. The crooks tie up Hoppy and leave him in a barn which they set on fire, but he manages to escape, along with Speedy, who was sleeping in the barn. With Bowman and his cohort Johnson (Kermit Maynard) and their gang, the Baron rustles the horses and hides in a wagon covered with hay. Lucky is forced to drive the wagon at gunpoint but Hoppy enters the wagon and fights with the Baron and then orders Lucky, who has been shot, to jump as the wagon careens off a cliff, killing the imposter. The marshal and his posse arrest the gang members after a shootout. Sue decides to stay at the ranch and hires Lucky to be her foreman. During the proceedings, the King's Men sang "Mi Solo Amor."

Hidden Gold was released in June, 1940, with Lesley Selander returning to direct. This likable affair has Hoppy (Boyd) and Lucky (Hayden) coming to visit Speedy (Wood), who now operates a mining claim, and is in debt to store owner Matilda Purdy (Ethel Wales). Their real mission is to investigate a series of express gold robberies involving the mine of Ed Colby (Minor Watson), once a notorious outlaw. Colby is in partnership with mining company owner Ward Ackerman (George Anderson), who is really the mastermind behind the holdups (he has been stealing gold from Colby's mine and claiming it is from his own operations). While investigating the most recent holdup, Hoppy and Lucky meet Jane Colby (Ruth Rogers), Ed's daughter, who asks Cassidy to become foreman of her father's mine; Hoppy is suspicious of Colby because of his past and refuses. After Colby is shot, Ackerman plans to make fellow mine owner Hendricks (Roy Barcroft) the foreman, so Hoppy agrees to take the job. Hoppy soon notices that the quality of ore coming out of the mine has deteriorated and one of the miners, Sanford (Walter Long), nearly causes his death by weakening mine timbers, resulting in a ceiling collapse. When Lucky finds outside ore being smuggled into the mine, he is forced to kill Sanford and then reports his findings to Hoppy as Hendricks and his men raid Speedy's claim. Hoppy follows the gang's tracks to an old mine shaft owned by Ackerman and realizes that the mining company owner is one of the outlaws. After Speedy finds gold on his claim, Hoppy uses the nuggets to capture the outlaws by sending out a new shipment. After the stagecoach is robbed, Hoppy joins forces with Logan (Eddie Dean), leader of the miners' peace enforcers, and his men, along with the miners, in converging on the outlaw hideout at Ackerman's supposedly deserted mine shaft. The gang is trapped in the mine with Hoppy shooting Hendricks and capturing Ackerman, thus proving Colby was not guilty of the robberies.

Next came *Stagecoach War*, released in the summer of 1940. This time out, the King's Men contributed a trio of songs as singing outlaws: "Hold Your Horses," "Lope-Along Road" and "Westward Ho." The plot had Bar 20 cowpokes Hoppy (Boyd), Lucky (Hayden) and Speedy (Wood) leading a cattle herd to Blue Sky when they stop a runaway stagecoach which has just been robbed by a gang of singing bandits, lead by Smiley (Rad Robinson). The stagecoach is owned by Jeff Chapman (J. Farrell MacDonald), to whom the trio are supposed to deliver the cattle. The Bar 20 men take the injured Chapman to his ranch where they meet his daughter Shirley (Julie

Carter), who is in love with rival stagecoach operator Neal Holt (Harvey Stephens), who wants Chapman's mail contract. Twister Maxwell (Frank Lackteen), Holt's stable foreman, in is league with Smiley and his gang and supplies them with information on mineral shipments. When Speedy finds a horseshoe, which fits Twister's horse, at the scene of the holdup, Hoppy feels that Holt may be involved in the robberies and gets him to agree to a stagecoach race, with the mail contract going to the winner. Lucky successfully drives Chapman's stagecoach but is forced to pull aside on a mountain curve when he sees Shirley, with whom he is in love, in Holt's vehicle. The locals who bet on Chapman want to lynch Lucky for throwing the race, but Hoppy comes to his rescue, explaining that his pal pulled up to save Shirley's life since it appeared the two coaches were about to crash. Holt agrees with Hoppy and the race is declared a draw. As a result, Chapman agrees to let Shirley marry Neal. When the singing outlaws try another robbery, they are rounded up by the Bar 20 trio.

Stagecoach War was probably the flattest of the Hopalong Cassidy series to date. Even though it ran only one hour, it was a draggy affair not helped by singing villains and their trio of ditties. The feature lacked strong villains, since the outlaws were portrayed by the King's Men, with member Rad Robinson as gang leader Smiley. *Variety* correctly called it "a weak one in comparison with previous quality," adding, "Not that William Boyd is any the less virile as the savior of all that's good and pure in the sagebrush, but the scripter appears to have done him and the cast dirt this time. The dialog sounds more Vassar than Cripplecreek."

If *Stagecoach War* was one of the weaker moments in the Hopalong Cassidy series, its follow-up *Three Men from Texas* is considered by many to be one of the best, if not *the* best. Directed by Lesley Selander and written by Norton S. Parker, it introduced Andy Clyde in the role of California Carlson, a part he would play for the remainder of the series and later on radio. Clyde (1892–1967) was a native of Scotland who came to Hollywood in 1919 and through the influence of his friend Jimmy Finlayson began working for Mack Sennett. He rose from bits to supporting roles during the 1920s, even headlining two-reelers, often in the guise of an old man. With the coming of sound he became Sennett's top comic and in 1932 he joined Educational Pictures. Two years later he began a series of comedy two-reelers for Columbia (77 entries before culminating in 1956). He was also in demand for supporting roles in feature films, but made his greatest cinema impact in the role of California Carlson.

Three Men from Texas told of raiders attacking haciendas and towns in California with Santa Carmen banker Ed Thompson (Davison Clark) writing to Texas Ranger Captain Andrews (Morgan Wallace) asking for help. Andrews offers the assignment to Hoppy (Boyd), who declines because he wants to return to the Bar 20 ranch when his term of service expires. Lucky (Hayden) jumps at the chance, hoping to go west to meet beautiful senoritas, and gets the job. After Hoppy and Lucky part company, Hoppy finds a dying cowboy (Wen Wright) whose horse herd has been rustled. The trail leads him to a shack where he meets long-winded California Carlson (Clyde) who at first claims to be a badman who thinks Hoppy is really a wanted outlaw, Ben Stokes (Glenn Strange). When Hoppy realizes that California works for Gardner (Dick Curtis), the leader of the rustlers, he arrests him. As they ride to town, Hoppy and California are attacked by Gardner, Stokes and their men who want to kill the ranger and silence the talkative California. The frightened California ends up aiding Hoppy arrest three of the gang members, although Gardner and Stokes escape. When Hoppy learns that the two outlaws are heading for California, he asks Andrews to send him there with California Carlson as his guide; the Ranger captain makes Hoppy a U.S. marshal. On the way to Santa Carmen, Hoppy and California see Pico Serrano (Thornton Edwards) and his men rob a stagecoach. California once saved Serrano's life and the bandit tells the two men that gringos stole his hacienda, forcing him and many others into a life of crime in order to survive. In Santa Carmen, Hoppy is reunited with Lucky, the town's marshal, but is disheartened to learn that he is planning a showdown with bar owner Bruce Morgan (Morris Ankrum), who is allied with Gardner and Stokes. When Hoppy tries to stop him, Lucky locks him in jail with California and Ed Thompson. Thompson's clerk (John "Skins" Miller) releases the trio in

time for Hoppy to prevent a wounded Lucky from being gunned down by Morgan's men. During a shootout with the outlaws, Hoppy, Lucky and California escape and take refuge in Serrano's mountain hideout, where a smitten Lucky is nursed back to health by Pico's pretty daughter Paquita (Esther Estrella). Hoppy organizes a posse of local rancheros and miners and when elderly Don Ricardo Velez (Carlos De Valdez) is evicted from his hacienda by Morgan's henchman Dave (George Lollier) and his outlaws, Serrano and his men join Hoppy and the posse and take back the hacienda. Serrano then gets the drop on Hoppy, takes his gun and orders Dave and his cohorts

Left: Poster for *Three Men from Texas* (Paramount, 1940). *Below:* Andy Clyde, William Boyd and Russell Hayden in *Three Men from Texas* (Paramount, 1940).

hanged. In revenge, Morgan and his gang attack Serrano's stronghold and while many of the defenders manage to escape, Paquita is mortally wounded. As a result, Hoppy enlists the aid of the locals and with Pico's men they ride into Santa Carmen and pin Morgan and his gang in his Diamond Horseshoe Bar. In the shootout, Hoppy beats Gardner in a fistfight, California kills Stokes and a badly wounded Pico strangles Morgan to death before dying. With peace restored to the town, Hoppy and Lucky ride back to Texas with newly appointed marshal California deciding to join them.

The year 1941 was the high watermark for the series in regards to the number of releases: Ten new Hopalong Cassidy features appeared in theaters that year, kicking off with another high-grade effort, *Doomed Caravan*, issued in January. It was again directed by Lesley Selander; this time the script was co-written by Norton S. Parker and Johnston McCulley, the creator of Zorro (q.v.). Unfortunately the film's production was delayed for four months when Boyd suffered a leg injury during shooting in the High Sierras. Again set in frontier California, the feature began with Hoppy (Boyd) and Lucky (Hayden) taking a convoy of gold to Crescent City Freight Company owner Jane Travers (Minna Gombell). Upon arriving, they find Jane and her men in a shootout with a gang which has set fire to her storehouses and robbed her wagon trains in an effort to put her out of business. Working for Jane is California Carlson (Clyde), who left the Bar 20 to return to his home state. After running off the marauders, Jane tells Hoppy that she has asked for an escort of army troopers for her next shipment and Hoppy agrees to go along as a guard. The man behind the robberies, merchant Stephen Westcott (Morris Ankrum), wants to control all the area shipping. He orders his henchman Ferber (Pat J. O'Brien) and his gang to attack the troopers, steal their clothes and take their place guarding the wagon trains. After seeing the motley "troopers" arrive in town, Hoppy becomes suspicious and later finds evidence the real troopers were murdered. Hoppy and his men attack the convoy, run off the outlaws and escort Jane and her wagons safely to the town of Eldorado, where Jane's friend Diana Westcott (Georgia Hawkins) is greeted by Stephen Westcott, her uncle. Hoppy takes a dislike to Westcott and consults the governor, Don Pedro (Jose Luis Tortosa), who tells him he has called for state troopers to settle the unrest between the local Americans and Mexicans. The village priest (Martin Garralaga) believes the trouble is being caused by rancher Ed Martin (Trevor Bardette), who openly advocates the rights of the poor but is secretly in league with Westcott. When Lucky, who is smitten with Diana, unwittingly tells her uncle about the coming of the troopers, Westcott wants to immediately take over the town but Martin dissuades him. Westcott then suggests to Don Pedro that he hold a fiesta to unite the area factions but during the event Martin and his men take everyone prisoner; Martin declares himself provisional governor and confiscates Jane's property. Hoppy manages to escape and he and Diana, who has overheard her uncle talking with Martin, take refuge with California. In the guise of a priest, Hoppy smuggles guns to Lucky and Jane and her men, who are imprisoned in a stockade. As Martin plans to murder the prisoners with a firing squad, they turn on their captors and Martin is shot by Lucky when he tries to knife Hoppy. The Bar 20 boys, along with Jane and her men, then defeat the outlaws and a fleeing Westcott is roped off his horse by Hoppy and arrested. Don Pedro resumes his duties as governor and Jane returns with her wagons to Crescent City.

Howard Bretherton was back to direct *In Old Colorado*, issued late in March, 1941. Another stout Hopalong Cassidy feature, it took place in Colorado in 1890 with Arrow H cattle rancher George Davidson (Stanley Andrews) stringing barbed wire across his land to keep out cattle belonging to newcomers Ma Woods (Sarah Padden), Jim Stark (Eddy Waller) and other nesters. When Davidson's foreman, Joe Weiler (Morris Ankrum), threatens to shoot Ma when she cuts the barbed wire, Davidson stops him, saying the nesters will not be able to sell cattle in time to pay off their mortgages. Ma's daughter Myra (Margaret Hayes) suggests she contact Bar 20 owner Buck Peters about buying her herd and he agrees, sending foreman Hoppy (Boyd) with $20,000 in cash to cement the deal. Word of the sale gets around Cooperstown and Hoppy, who is traveling with Lucky (Hayden) and California (Clyde), is robbed of the money by Blackie Reed (Weldon Heyburn) and his men. Blackie is in cahoots with Weiler and Ma's foreman, Hank Merritt (James Seay), who has been fomenting the trouble between Davidson and the nesters in hopes of driving all of them off the range so they can take over the land. Hoppy tells the local sheriff (Morgan Wallace) about the robbery and Davidson offers to sell the Bar 20 his cattle at half the price offered to Ma and the other nesters. Hoppy tells Davidson he will considers his offer and he, Lucky and California head to Ma's ranch where he plans to work incognito. When the rustlers attack Ma's herd, Myra is nearly killed but is saved by Hoppy. As a result, the Bar 20 boys are hired to work for Ma but when Davidson blows his cover by demanding an answer to his offer, Hoppy tells him and Ma that he thinks a third party is behind the trouble and asks for them to call a truce. The Bar 20 men follow Merritt to the rustlers' hideout but Weiler gets the drop on them. The trio manage to escape, returning in time to stop the rustlers from stealing the nesters' cattle. When Davidson announces he will back their notes, Weiler shoots him. Lucky manages to lasso Merritt, and the ranchers join the sheriff in rounding up Reed and his gang. Hoppy trails Weiler, capturing him and finding the stolen $20,000 in the money belt stolen during the robbery. Davidson recovers from his wounds and both he and Ma offer the Bar 20 boys jobs, but the trio opts to return home.

In Old Colorado had more than its share of comedy, with California becoming entangled with a slick hombre (Philip Van Zandt) who fleeces him in the old shell game. Also supposedly supplying mirth was Cliff Nazarro as Nosey Haskins, Ma's jack-of-all-trades. Unfortunately, Nazarro's double-talk did nothing more than slow up the scenes in which he appeared.

Derwin Abrahams, who had served as assistant director on the previous 27 Hopalong Cassidy features, was promoted to director with April's *Border Vigilantes*. This fast-paced, compact effort had Hoppy (Boyd) coming to the aid of his friend, rancher Dan Forbes (Morris Ankrum). Accompanied by his pals Lucky (Hayden) and California (Clyde), Hoppy finds out that Forbes suspects that the local vigilante group (of which he is a member) has been infiltrated because the group has been unable to stop recent stagecoach robberies. The leader of the vigilantes is businessman Henry Logan (Victor Jory), who is actually head of the outlaws; when he learns of Hoppy's arrival, he orders Hoppy and Forbes murdered. At Gunsight Pass, Logan's henchman Big Ed Stone (Hal Taliaferro) wings Forbes but is shot and left for dead by Hoppy. Arriving in Silver City, Hoppy tells Forbes and his daughter Helen (Frances Gifford) not to reveal his identity but after the Bar 20 men thwart a heist, the outlaws terrorize the area. Hoping to catch the gang, Hoppy and Forbes switch silver and when the real ore disappears, Hoppy is blamed until it is revealed that California accidentally mixed up the shipments, with the silver being safe at Forbes' ranch. Hoppy, Lucky and California trail Logan and his men to their hideout and Hoppy is injured during a shootout. He outwits the gang by using exploding bullets which make it appear they are surrounded. Logan and his cohorts are placed under arrest and the Bar 20 boys go back to Texas.

The series' streak of top-notch productions continued with *Pirates on Horseback*, released in May, 1941. Britt Wood had returned to the series in a small role in *Border Vigilantes* and he did the same in this entry, playing an ill-fated miner and making the most of a character who is killed off during the first ten minutes. The production also greatly benefited from the presence of Eleanor Stewart, who had previously been the leading lady to sagebrush stalwarts Tex Ritter, Bob Steele, the Three Mesquiteers (q.v.), Bob Allen, Tom Keene, Jack Randall and Ken Maynard; she would appear in two more Hopalong Cassidy outings, *Riders of the Timberline* the same year and *Mystery Man* in 1944.

Pirates on Horseback opens with prospector Ben Pendleton (Wood) coming into the town of Rimrock with his mule and announcing that he has made a big gold strike by locating the lost El Dorado mine. The sheriff (Henry Hall) warns him to keep quiet but saloon keeper-gambler Ace Gibson (Morris Ankrum) sends his cohorts Watson (William Haade) and Carter (Dennis Moore) to make Pendleton reveal the location of his mine. During a shootout, Pendleton is killed. When this news reaches the Bar 20, California (Clyde) realizes he is a relative of the murdered man and the heir to his claim. Hoppy (Boyd) and Lucky (Hayden) accompany California to Pendleton's Red Butte's home. There they meet Trudy (Eleanor

Stewart), Pendleton's niece and also an heir to the property. The four work together to locate the mine and Hoppy finds a cryptic note left by Pendleton stating that it was in the sunset shadow of an eagle. Gibson overhears them discussing the message and he has his men ambush Hoppy, who becomes suspicious of the gambler. When California comes to town with news he has found nuggets at the old mine on Pendleton's place, it starts a stampede to the place until the nuggets turn out to be mushrooms. Ace then tries to alienate Trudy from the Bar 20 men by claiming that they are confidence men who swindle single women out of their money. She orders Hoppy, Lucky and California off the Pendleton homestead but that evening Hoppy figures out the code and uncovers the mine under Pendleton's woodshed. Ace and his men capture them; Watson and Carter are left to guard them as Gibson takes Trudy to town to file charges against the trio. Once in town, the gambler tries to force Trudy to sell him her property for $5,000 and she refuses. The Bar 20 boys manage to overpower their captors and Hoppy rides to Rimrock where he rescues Trudy and turns Ace over to the sheriff. Trudy and California sell their mine for $500,000 and the young woman goes back to the Bar 20 with Hoppy and Lucky, as California excitedly rides ahead to claim a prize he won at the county fair.

The feature kept up the series' high standard for plot and performances and Russell Harlan's photography of some particularly spectacular landscapes is an added plus. The murder of Ben Pendleton is a brutal one for the series. In the film's climactic fight scene between Hoppy and Ace Gibson, one-time cowboy star Ted Wells can be easily spotted doubling for Boyd.

Released in the fall of 1941, *Wide Open Town* was a reworking of the earlier *Hopalong Cassidy Returns* replete with Evelyn Brent repeating her role of a female gang leader who finds herself romantically drawn to Hoppy. Hoppy (Boyd), Lucky (Hayden) and California (Clyde) come to the town of Gunsight in search of rustled Bar 20 cattle. Along the way Hoppy attempts to rescue saloon owner Belle Langtry (Brent) when her horse stampedes, but he soon learns that the attractive woman has control of the situation. She is the leader of a gang opposed by newspaperman Jim Stuart (Morris Ankrum) and his daughter Joan (Bernice Kay [Cara Williams]). Belle's cohort Steve Fraser (Victor Jory) murders a miner (George Cleveland) and finds out the location of his mine, and Belle files on the claim. When the Bar 20 men arrive in town, they stop Fraser and his gang from wrecking the newspaper office (Stuart wrote an editorial condemning Belle and her activities). Hoppy then accepts the job of town marshal and goes to Belle's saloon saying he intends to clean up the town. Hoppy plans to capture the outlaws by announcing the shipment of money via stagecoach. During a shootout, California is slightly wounded, two of the bandits are killed and another, Ed Stark (Glenn Strange), is arrested. While Belle tries to romance Hoppy, California lets Stark escape from jail and the Bar 20 men trail him to the gang's hideout where most of the outlaws are arrested and the stolen cattle recovered. One of the gang (Roy Barcroft) eludes capture and he tells Fraser what happened. Taking Belle and Joan prisoners, Fraser orders his men to cover the town and ambush Hoppy and the local ranchers when they arrive to arrest them. Joan manages to fire a warning shot but when Fraser threatens to kill her the gun battle halts. Belle tries to help Joan escape and Steve shoots her but Hoppy, who has received a shoulder wound, breaks in and fights with Fraser who dies falling from a window. Both Hoppy and Belle recover from their injuries and remain friendly although Belle will have to serve a prison sentence for her crimes.

Wide Open Town proved to be Hayden's final appearance in the Hopalong Cassidy series after a total of 27 features. During that time he also appeared in the Paramount westerns *The Mysterious Rider* (1938), *Heritage of the Desert* (1939) and *Knights of the Range* and *The Light of Western Stars* (both 1940). After leaving the studio he signed with Columbia where from 1941 to 1944 he appeared in 16 westerns as well as two Universal oaters, *Frontier Law* (1943) and *Marshal of Gunsmoke* (1944). Hired to replace Hayden as Johnny Nelson in the Cassidy series was Brad King (1918–91) who would play the role in the next five 1941 Hoppy releases.

Riders of the Timberland, issued in the fall of 1941, took Hoppy to lumberjack country with The Guardsmen Quartet as lumbermen singing the robust balled "The Fighting Forty." While King appeared rather stilted as the new Johnny Nelson, the feature was enhanced by a top-notch supporting cast, with usual villain Victor Jory playing a good guy French-Canadian lumber camp foreman, silent stars Anna Q. Nilsson and J. Farrell MacDonald in a mid-life romance and former sagebrush heroes Wally Wales (billed here as Hal Taliaferro) and Tom Tyler excelling as slimy villains. For the second time Eleanor Stewart made a fetching and resourceful heroine in a Cassidy adventure. The plotline had timber wolf Preston Yates (Edward Keane) hiring Ajax Lumber Company representative Ed Petrie (Hal Taliaferro) to make sure that lumberman Jim Kerrigan (J. Farrell MacDonald) does not complete his contract with the company. Yates wants to drive Kerrigan out of business so he can take control of pristine mountain forests belonging to the lumberman. Petrie has Bill Slade (Tom Tyler) infiltrate Kerrigan's work gang, using explosives, fires and ambushes to slow the tree cutting. After refusing a loan from affectionate friend and businesswoman Donna Ryan (Anna Q. Nilsson), Kerrigan writes to his old buddy Buck Peters at the Bar 20 ranch who sends his foreman, Hoppy (Boyd), with a $15,000 loan. Hoppy and Johnny (King) arrive at the lumber camp where they meet California (Clyde), who is working there as a cook. Following an accident which badly injures a worker, Slade goads the crew into quitting. Kerrigan and his foreman, Baptiste (Victor Jory), are desperate to get a new crew but all of their requests meet with refusals until Kerrigan's daughter Elaine (Eleanor Stewart) arrives by train with a gang of lumberjacks called the Fighting Forty. Petrie and his men try to run off the new workers but they are badly beaten in a street fight, and work resumes at the Kerrigan camp. After Slade and some men fail to sabotage the camp, Hoppy trails them into town and learns that Petrie is giving the orders. Hoppy and Kerrigan work out a scheme to capture the saboteurs by having Hoppy alienate himself by pretending to cheat at cards. This causes Petrie to introduce him to Yates, and Hoppy supposedly sets out a plan to start a forest fire and put Kerrigan out of business. The plan is actually a ruse to capture the gang but in the fracas Kerrigan is badly wounded and Baptiste blames Hoppy, and he and Johnny are locked in a tool shed. As Hoppy and Johnny dig their way out, Kerrigan tells Elaine the truth and she rides into town, being preceded by Baptiste and the Fighting Forty. Slade, who has escaped capture, rides to town to warn Petrie who plans to blow up a nearby dam and deluge the lumber camp. Baptiste and his men are about to waylay Hoppy when Elaine arrives with the news of Hoppy's innocence and they join forces to try and stop Petrie. Riding a log hoisted by cable, Hoppy and Johnny get to the dam where a shootout occurs between the lumbermen and the saboteurs. Hopalong manages to find the dynamite and throws it at the saboteurs, killing Petrie, Slade and their men. With Kerrigan able to fulfill his contract, California decides to go back to the Bar 20 with Hoppy and Johnny.

Nearly as good as *Riders of the Timberlane* was *Stick to Your Guns*, released in September, 1941. In it, Boyd also took on the role of gambler Tex Riley, a part he played earlier in *Bar 20 Rides Again*. Music also played a bigger factor in this effort with the Jimmy Wakely Trio singing "My Kind of Country" and "On the Strings of My Lonesome Guitar" and joining Brad King on "Blue Moon on the Silver Sage." This time out Bar 20 owner Buck Peters (Joe Whitehead) sends Hoppy (Boyd), Johnny (King) and California (Clyde) to Nevada to aid local cattlemen in fighting a rustling gang lead by Nevada Teale (Dick Curtis), whose gang is headquartered in the Snake Buttes area. Stopping in the town of Verde, Hoppy talks with old foe Long Ben (Charles Middleton), who has a grudge to settle with Teale and his gang; he tells Cassidy how to find them. Posing as gambler Tex Riley, Hoppy, along with California, rides into Nevada's camp and is soon accepted as a gang member, while Johnny meets with local ranchers and unites them in forming a posse to arrest the outlaws. Johnny learns the whereabouts of Snake Buttes from old prospector Jud Winters (Henry Hall), who lives with his pretty granddaughter June (Jacqueline [Jennifer] Holt). As Riley, Hoppy tries to start a rivalry between the gang members with outlaw Concho (Robert Kortman) shooting Elbows (Ian MacDonald) in the back and in turn being gunned down by henchman Carp (Jack Rockwell). As Hoppy sets a smoldering signal fire for the posse, the group is joined by Jud and June. After Hoppy is forced to kill gunman Layton (Kermit Maynard) in self-defense, camp cook Charlie (Tom Ung) is blamed for the fire, which serves as a signal to the posse as to the outlaws' hideout. Two henchmen, Duby (Frank Ellis) and Ed (Mickey Eissa), wing Jud but Ed is killed by the posse as Duby makes it back to the hideout. Now suspicious of Riley, Nevada sends his cohort Gila (Weldon Heyburn) to see Long Ben, who tells him the truth about Hoppy's identity only to be gunned down by Gila. When Gila returns with the news, Hoppy shoots him. He and California escape and join the posse, which has been trapped in a box canyon by the gang. During a shootout, most of the outlaws are killed and the rest surrender, with Hoppy outdrawing Nevada. With the rustled cattle returned to their owners, the Bar 20 trio head back home.

Also released in September, 1941, was *Twilight on the Trail*, which was co-scripted by actress Ellen Corby. Director Howard Bretherton returned to the series for this one and the next outing, *Outlaws of the Desert*. Again the Jimmy Wakely Trio provided the music, including the title song by Ralph Rainger and Leo Robin which was first introduced in Paramount's *The Trail of the Lonesome Pine* five years before. They also performed "The Funny Old Hills" and trio member Johnny Bond's classic "Cimmaron." Here Rangers Hoppy (Boyd), California (Clyde) and Johnny (King) pretend to be Eastern dudes investigating area cattle rustling. They use the guise as a favor to friend Jim Brent (Jack Rockwell), owner of the Circle Y Ranch, a victim of the rustlers. Johnny attempts to romance Jim's daughter Lucy (Wanda McKay) but she wants nothing to do with him and doubts the usefulness of the citified detectives. Hoppy learns from Jim that cattle tracks always lead to the cabin of prospector Steve Farley (Frank Austin) and then disappear but Farley claims to know nothing about the stolen cattle. When Johnny is winged while defending the cattle herd, Brent's foreman, Nat Kervy (Norman Willis), the head of the rustling operation, becomes suspicious after his cohort Tim Gregg (Tom London) tells him the detectives are good riders and shooters. Going through their belongings, Kervy finds out that Hoppy, Johnny and California are rangers and he tries to lead them into an ambush but fails. After observing riders entering Farley's barn and covering their tracks, Hopalong and California find a hidden door in the barn which leads to an old mine where the stolen cattle are secreted. They are taken prisoners, but Johnny sees their horses being led into the barn and he goes to Brent who accompanies him back to Farley's place along with some of his men and Kervy. Hoppy and California manage to escape and join the ranchers in a shootout with the gang. As Hoppy pursues Kervy through the mine shaft, the gang is arrested. Kervy is also subdued and turned over to the law.

The last two 1941 Hopalong Cassidy outings, *Outlaws of the Desert* and *Secret of the Wastelands*, were both issued in November. Previous adventures had the Bar 20 bunch in Mexico and Argentina and *Outlaws of the Desert* had them in Arabia. This time out Hoppy (Boyd), California (Clyde) and Johnny (King) accompany neighbor Charles Grant (Forrest Stanley), who travels to Arabia with his wife Jane (Nina Guilbert) and daughter Susan (Jean Phillips) to purchase desert stallions as cavalry horses for the government. In the Sahara Desert, they come to the defense of a caravan which is being raided and their guide, Yussuf (George J. Lewis), leads them to the camp of Sheik Suleiman (Duncan Renaldo), the caravan's destination. Although he refuses to sell Grant any horses, Suleiman gives Hoppy two white horses as a reward for saving his property from the raiders. In a nearby oasis, Susan has made friends with siblings Nicki (Alberto Morin) and Marie Karitza (Luli Deste). Nicki and Grant are kidnapped while scouting for horses. When $50,000 is demanded for the abducted men, Hoppy goes back to Suleiman's camp and learns from him that the likely kidnapper is Faran El Kader (Jean Del Val). The Bar 20 men leave for Kader's camp and Susan, who has cabled home for the ransom money, is also kidnapped by Marie and Nicki, who are really married crooks. Aided by Yussuf, Hoppy manages to capture Kader and the Karitzas and frees Grant and his daughter. They return to Suleiman's camp which is attacked by Kader's tribesmen. Hoppy uses an old Apache ruse to defeat the marauders as Suleiman bests Kader in a sword duel. Hoppy and his pals return home with the Grants, who have secured the horses they needed.

Derwin Abrahams returned to direct *Secret*

of the Wastelands, based on Bliss Lomax's 1940 novel, and incorporating Clarence E. Mulford's characters. The plotline had a mystery motif, something that would dominate later series episodes. Hoppy (Boyd), along with pals California (Clyde) and Johnny (King), is hired to lead an archaeological expedition to the ancient ruins of Pueblo Grande. The party consists of Dr. Birdsall (Gordon Hart), an archaeologist, his niece Jennifer Kendall (Barbara Britton), Professor Stubbs (Hal Price), United States Mint representative Clay Elliott (Keith Richards) and Chinese cook Doy Kee (Lee Tung Foo). Chinese trader Moy Soong (Soo Yong) and her lawyer Slade Salters (Douglas Fowley) and three henchmen follow the group into the desert and an attempt is made on Hoppy's life. Elliott finds gold nuggets which suggest to Hoppy the Chinese may be involved in other acts of sabotage plaguing the expedition. At Pueblo Grande, Dr. Birdsall finds a statue of Buddha, and Jennifer disappears. When the group's water supply is sabotaged and Doy Kee is found murdered, Hoppy forces the members to go to the nearby town of Piute. Unbeknownst to them, Salters takes over the diggings. Johnny becomes upset when Hoppy refuses to go to the law over Jennifer's disappearance; Hoppy instead meets with Moy Soong and gets a promise that Jennifer will be returned if he will keep silent. Johnny, however, tells the sheriff (Jack Rockwell), who follows Hoppy and Moy Soong with a posse. Hoppy helps the Chinese make it back to Pueblo Grande; to escape a shootout with the lawmen, they take him to a secret valley, which the Chinese have cultivated for years using gold from the ruins to support their efforts. The elders ask Hoppy how to obtain the area legally and he tells them to stake a claim on the land. When gold-hungry Elliott tries to run away, Hoppy knocks him out. As the posse makes its way into the valley, Hoppy rides to Piute to file a land claim for the Chinese. He arrives at the same time as Salters, whom he defeats in a fistfight before filing the claim. The grateful Chinese thank Cassidy and permit Birdsall to resume his exploration.

Secret of the Wastelands proved to be the series' final Paramount release. The studio sold some of its productions to United Artists and included in the deal were the Hoppy features. Thus producer Harry Sherman relocated to United Artists where he would finance another baker's dozen Cassidy releases. The feature also marked Brad King's last outing as Johnny Nelson. Joining the series with the first United Artists release, *Undercover Man*, was Jay Kirby as Breezy Travers, soon to be called Johnny Travers. Kirby (1920–64), whose real name was William George, would play the part in six features, but he made no more of an impression than did Brad King.

Harry Sherman (1884–1952), who had been in the film business since the mid-teens, also produced a number of other westerns during his tenure with Hopalong Cassidy. Among them were *The Mysterious Rider* (1938), *The Llano Kid* and *Heritage of the Desert* (both 1939), *Boss of Bullion City*, *The Light of Western Stars* and *Cherokee Strip* (all 1940), *Parson of Panamint* (1941), *American Empire* (1942) and *Buffalo Bill* (1944).

In contrast to the ten Hoppy releases in 1941, only two series entries came out in 1942 under the United Artists banner, both directed by Lesley Selander. The first was *Undercover Man*, released in October. Its involved story took place in 1887 with raiders working on both sides of the United States and Mexican borders, attacking ranches and mines. Commandante Don Thomas Gomez (Antonio Moreno) rides into Texas with his men to visit his old friend, Texas Rangers Captain John Hawkins (Jack Rockwell), asking for help in ending the lawlessness. Hawkins suggests that Hoppy (Boyd) handle the investigation. When Hoppy, California (Clyde) and Breezy Travers (Jay Kirby) ride to Gomez's hacienda, they are ambushed but scare off their attackers. At the hacienda, the trio meets Senor Gomez and his daughter Dolores (Esther Estrella) and his companions, widowed Dona Louise Saunders (Nora Lane) and her son Bob (Alan Baldwin). Breezy is smitten with Dolores while California likes Gomez's cook, rotund Rosita (Eva Puig), the fiancée of the commandante's assistant, Miguel (Chris-Pin Martin). Two attacks are made on mule trains; after the second, rancher Chavez (Tony Roux) tells Gomez he saw Hoppy leading the raiders. Gomez assigns Miguel to keep watch on Hoppy and his friends. When another attack takes place in Texas, witnesses claim it was Gomez who was leading the outlaws. While meeting with Sheriff Hawkins, Hoppy is warned by his deputy, Ed Carson (John Vosper), that Gomez may be behind the attacks. Hoppy and Gomez realize that someone has been impersonating both of them in order to cause friction between Americans and Mexicans. After California accidentally stumbles into a deserted wine cellar which leads to a cave, the men find clothes and horses matching those worn by Hoppy and Gomez. When Bob is seen leaving the hacienda, Hoppy, California and Breezy trail him and see him meet with the outlaws who refuse to let him quit the gang. Going to the office of a nearby lawman (Earle Hodgins), Hoppy finds a wanted poster which reveals the identity of the gang leader. When the raiders attack another freight wagon, Hoppy, local ranchers and the Texas Rangers unite to round up the gang. Carson shoots a rider dressed like Hoppy and riding a white horse and it turns out to be Dona Louise, who says she was forced to aid the outlaws in order to protect her son from a false murder charge for which he was being blackmailed. As she is about to name the gang leader, Carson pulls a gun on the group and tries to escape but is arrested by Hoppy, who proclaims that the wanted poster revealed Carson to be wanted outlaw Idaho Pete Jackson. As Hoppy and Breezy plan to return to the Bar 20, California is shocked to learn his planned marriage to Rosita is off since her supposedly dead husband has returned home to her and their brood of children.

The second 1942 release, December's *Lost Canyon*, was a competent remake of the 1937 series feature *Rustlers' Valley*. The finale (huge boulders being pushed onto the outlaws' shack) was lifted from the earlier film with the villains, played by Lee J. Cobb, Ted Adams and Al Ferguson, being easily spotted in the new entry. The feature also had the Sportsmen Quartette sing "Jingle, Jangle, Jingle" which was popularized that year on Capitol Records by Tex Ritter. A bit more compact that the first version, this outing had Johnny (Kirby) happen upon a bank robbery in which a guard is killed, and being blamed for the crime by Wade Haskell (Karl Hackett), foreman of rancher-lawyer Jeff Burton (Douglas Fowley). In attempting to escape from a posse, Johnny jumps to his apparent death into a river, saddening his friends Hoppy (Boyd) and California (Clyde) who believe in his innocence. When Johnny shows up alive, Hoppy hides him in an old cabin and he and California set out to find the real killer. The Bar 20 men are friendly with rancher Tom Clark (Herbert Rawlinson) and his daughter Laura (Lola Lane), who breaks off her engagement to Burton because of his overbearing ways. Hoppy finds out that Burton has been trying to buy spreads, and from banker Zack Rogers (Guy Usher) he learns that the lawyer was part-owner of the mine whose payroll was stolen in the bank holdup. California then uncovers the fact that Haskell is in debt to Burton for having gotten him cleared of a rustling charge. Hoppy faces Burton with the evidence at the same time Rogers is forced to call in the note on Clark's ranch. While denying knowledge of the crimes, Burton tells Haskell to murder Hoppy and have their gang rustle Clark's cattle so he will not be able to pay off his note. When Johnny sees Clark's cattle being rustled, he tries to warn Hoppy but is arrested by the local sheriff (Hugh Prosser) who also wants to take in Hoppy and California for aiding him. Laura, who has been riding Hoppy's white horse, is shot at by Haskell, who mistook her for Hoppy. She is found with only a slight wound by the Bar 20 men, who have escaped from the sheriff. The trio then follow Burton, Haskell and their gang to their remote hideout where Burton makes plans to blame the rustling on Clark. While Hoppy gets the drop on Burton and Haskell in their shack, the gang has a shootout with the sheriff and his posse. Johnny and California demolish the shack by rolling boulders onto its roof. Hoppy is not hurt and the crooks are arrested.

Since there were only two Hopalong Cassidy releases in 1942, Boyd fell behind Gene Autry and Roy Rogers in that year's *Motion Picture Herald* poll of top moneymaking western stars but he was back up to second place for the years 1943 to 1945, after only Roy Rogers. He was also third in the 1942 *Boxoffice* poll, a position he also held in 1944 and 1945 with no poll being conducted in 1943.

The year 1943 resulted in seven series releases, the initial one being *Hoppy Serves a Writ*, issued in March. It was the first of sixteen series features to be directed by George Archainbaud (1890–1959), whose career dated back to 1917. In the 1930s he helmed some top-notch features for RKO including *The Silver Horde* (1930), *Lost*

Squadron (1932), *Thirteen Women* and *The Penguin Pool Murder* (both 1932) and *Murder on the Blackboard* (1934). He moved to Paramount in the mid–1930s and began making westerns with the Hoppy series, eventually directing Gene Autry's last features for Columbia in the early 1950s. Also appearing in *Hoppy Serves a Writ* was Robert Mitchum, who was making his film debut after working in little theater. He was introduced to producer Harry Sherman by an artists' manager, Paul Wilkins, and would appear in seven Hoppy productions in a row, the series proving to be his launching pad to stardom.

Hoppy Serves a Writ returned the series to its literary origins, being based on Mulford's 1941 novel of the same title (Mulford's final Hoppy tale). Wells Fargo stagecoach driver California (Clyde) is robbed by the Jordan brothers: scar-faced Tom (Victor Jory), Steve (George Reeves) and Greg (Hal Taliaferro). Later California and Deputy Sheriff Johnny Travers (Kirby) find the outlaws' horses, which have been stolen, but are prevented by law from crossing the Texas border into Oklahoma Territory in search of the robbers. Hoppy (Boyd), the sheriff of Twin Rocks, decides to go into Oklahoma in search of the outlaws after a complaint by TC Ranch owner Todd Colby (Roy Barcroft), who has been the victim of several raids. Taking the guise of cattle buyer Jones, Hoppy stops at the ranch of Ben Hollister (Forbes Murray), where he also meets Ben's daughter Jean (Jan Christy) and her boyfriend, Steve Jordan. Not given a friendly welcome, he rides to Mesa City where he stops Tom Jordan from manhandling Jim Belman (Earle Hodgins), the desk clerk and bartender at the local hotel and saloon. Although told to stay in Texas, California and Johnny follow Hoppy and meet Jean, who Johnny thinks is the victim of a runaway horse, only find out she was in a race with Steve. In Mesa City, the two Bar 20 men see Hoppy beat up Tom for trying to cheat him in a poker game, but Hoppy refuses to acknowledge them. In talking to store owner Danvers (Byron Foulger), Hoppy learns Hollister paid off a bill with Wells Fargo money that had been stolen in the stagecoach robbery. When the Jordans learn of this, they decide to murder Hollister since it was Tom who gave him the $500 bill. Realizing Hollister is in danger, the Bar 20 boys ride to his ranch and warn him and Jean in time and they manage to run off the Jordan brothers. Hollister then hires California and Johnny as ranch hands but California is abducted by the outlaws, who beat him in an effort to find out who his employer is. Leaving California unconscious, the Jordans decide to steal Hollister's cattle and change the brands as Hoppy and Johnny rescue California. He has overheard the brothers' rustling plans and the trio find Steve changing brands; they take him back to the cabin he shares with his brothers and there they find the stolen Wells Fargo money. Hoppy lets Steve escape as the Bar 20 men herd the stolen cattle to the river which separates Texas and Oklahoma Territory. The Jordans and their men follow but are met by a posse on the Texas side of the line. Attempting to escape, they are lassoed by Hoppy and arrested. With the cattle returned to Hollister, Hoppy, California and Johnny start home with Johnny promising to return to see Jean.

The feature proved to be an entertaining and exciting one, with an especially well-staged saloon brawl between Boyd and Victor Jory. The title, *Hoppy Serves a Writ*, proved to be a bit of a misnomer, since at the finale it was actually California who shows the outlaws the arrest warrant (it is quite soggy by the time he gets it to them).

Lesley Selander returned to direct *Border Patrol*, issued in the spring of 1943. Again dealing with troubles along the U.S.–Mexican border, the feature was dominated by Russell Simpson as tyrant Orestes Krebs, who rules a mountainous area north of the border with an iron fist, using Mexican workers and prisoners as slaves in his silver mine. When the vaquero riding with missing Don Enrique Perez (George Reeves) is murdered after crossing the border into the United States, the border patrol sends Texas Rangers Hoppy (Boyd), California (Clyde) and Johnny (Kirby) to meet with Mexican Commandant La Barca (Duncan Renaldo), who says that 25 of his countrymen answered an advertisement to work at the Silver Bullet Mine but none of them returned. He also tells them Perez was sent to investigate and he asks the Rangers' aid in finding the missing men. La Barca's daughter Inez (Claudia Drake) dines with the men and expresses her distrust in the American trio. She trails Hoppy and his pals when they leave for the silver mine. Once there, they are shot at by lookouts Quinn (Robert Mitchum) and Barton (Cliff Parkinson). Quinn escapes to warn his boss, Orestes Krebs (Russell Simpson), while Barton is taken prisoner and admits to killing the vaquero. He leads them to a rundown town where they meet Krebs, who says he is the mayor, sheriff and judge of the Commonwealth of Silver Bullet. He also announces that he is arresting them for murder and horse theft and he holds a trial in the town saloon. When Inez rides into Silver Bullet, Krebs tells her that the trio killed Perez and she testifies against them. Hoppy, California and Johnny are sentenced to be hanged. Hoppy tells Inez to ask to see the mine and Krebs takes her on a tour after having his forced labor locked away from sight. Perez, who is among the prisoners, leaves his hat which Inez sees; he also calls to her through a mine shaft. Back in town, Inez offers to make dinner for Krebs and the condemned men and when the town cook (Earle Hodgins) is not looking, she puts a revolver and bullets in the food. Finding the gun and bullets, Hoppy and his pals overpower their jailer (Pierce Lyden) and make a getaway, taking Inez with them. Going to the mine, they set the prisoners free and Inez is reunited with Perez. Krebs follows with his gang but Hoppy organizes the prisoners in using mine wagons to encircle the outlaws. After a shootout, the henchmen surrender as Krebs tries to make a getaway; Hoppy captures Krebs. Back in town, California is made the new judge and he orders Krebs to pay his former slaves before Hoppy arrests him for enforcing involuntary servitude. Johnny, who is smitten with Inez, is upset when he finds out she is engaged to Perez.

One of the best of the United Artists Hoppy releases, *Leather Burners* (issued in May, 1943) was based on the 1940 novel of the same title by Bliss Lomax, with Mulford's characters incorporated into the plotline. It was the final feature film of director Joseph E. Henaberry (1888–1976) who began his career in 1913 as an actor before turning to direction under the supervision of D.W. Griffith. During the silent era he directed some of the screen's most popular film stars and with the coming of sound he worked on the East Coast directing short subjects. From the late 1930s until 1957 he directed films for the U.S. Army Signal Corps. *Leather Burners* started out as a traditional western but moved into the genres of mystery and horror with a deformed madman hiding in an old mine and directing lawlessness intended to make him a dictator.

Rancher Johnny (Kirby) sends for his friends Hoppy (Boyd) and California (Clyde) when a fellow rancher is murdered by the raiders who have been terrorizing the area. When Hoppy and California arrive in the town of Buckskin, they see mine company president Dan Slack (Victor Jory) being shot; Slack survives because the bullet hit his pocket watch. Hopalong notices that the bullet is cold. Slack offers the two men jobs guarding the shipment trains from his mines but they refuse; he also tells them that local ranchers are sabotaging his water lines. Hoppy and California ride to Johnny's ranch where they meet his girlfriend Sharon Longstreet (Shelley Spencer) and her little brother Bobby (Bobby Larson), children of the murdered rancher. At a meeting of the local cattlemen, Hoppy refuses to help them unless he is paid and he later tells California he took this tack because he feared for Johnny's life since he believes one of the ranchers is a traitor. Hoppy and California agree to work for Slack, whom they suspect is behind the trouble. Harrison Brooke (George Reeves), Sharon's lawyer, tells them he believes Slack is to blame for the lawlessness. At the rundown Palace Hotel, desk clerk Sooky Withers (Christian Rub) tells the Bar 20 men about Sam Bucktoe (George Givot), who brought prosperity to the area by making a huge gold strike and building the hotel, which has not been occupied for five years. He also informs them that Bucktoe was killed in a mine shaft collapse but that his ghostly voice can still he heard in the mine. Hoppy writes to the marshal of Salt Lake City asking for information on Slack but telegrapher Lafe (Hal Taliaferro), gives Hoppy a fake response. Realizing he has been fooled, Hoppy and California tie up Lafe and then let him escape and follow him; Lafe dies when his saddle cinch breaks and he falls into a gorge. The Bar 20 men see a gang rustling Johnny's cattle and they run them off and start to take the herd back to Travers' spread. Rancher Bart Healey (Forbes Murray), who was leading the rustlers and is in cahoots with Slack, tells Johnny that his friends are rustling his cattle. Despite protests from Bart, who wants to hang Hoppy and California, Johnny lets them go but the local sheriff (Cal Shrum) tries to arrest them; they take his guns. Meeting with Sharon, Hoppy asks her to keep an eye on the ranchers; later she tells him that Bart and the sheriff have formed a posse and are looking for him and California. Hoppy and Sharon follow a gang member to Coffin Canyon where they find a deserted corral but are forced to flee when the outlaws arrive on the scene. Later Bobby trails Hoppy and California back to the corral and when the Bar 20 men find a hidden mine opening they send the boy back with a message for Sharon to give to the sheriff. In the mine, the two men see Slack who has come to see Bucktoe, who is still alive and the leader of the rustling gang. Upset at Slack's failures, Bucktoe tries to kill him by loosening mine timbers but Slack escapes deeper into the mine. There Hoppy and California find the stolen cattle kept in pens where they are butchered and sent out in cars under ore from the mine. Johnny, Brooke, the sheriff and his posse arrive at the mine and attack the gang members who are pinned at the mine entrance with Hoppy and California on the other side. The insane Bucktoe, who wants to run out all the area ranchers so he can control the entire valley, murders Slack and then sets the cattle free, causing a stampede through the mine tunnel. Bobby, who has followed the posse, is nearly trampled by the cattle but saved by Hoppy; the stampede causes a cave-in which kills Bucktoe. During the gun battle, Bart shoots Brooke, who is only injured, and is killed by Johnny. The gang is arrested. When Hoppy and California head back to the Bar 20, Johnny goes with them since he found out Sharon is in love with Brooke.

Lesley Selander returned to direct the next two Hoppy efforts, *Colt Comrades* and *Bar 20*, with the former (coming out in June, 1943) based on the 1939 novel of the same title by Bliss Lomax; the leading lady was Lois Sherman, daughter of producer Harry Sherman. For this outing, Hoppy was back in an all-dark outfit after having worn lighter pants, shirts and hats in previous efforts. The story had government agents Hoppy (Boyd), California (Clyde) and Johnny (Kirby) out to capture Dirk Mason (Robert Mitchum), who robbed the mail and murdered a freight agent; Mason works for banker Jeb Hardin (Victor Jory). When Mason goes to him for help, Hardin and his henchman Joe Brass (Douglas Fowley) refuse to aid him. Trailed into town by the three agents, Mason takes refuge in the saloon but is soon captured by Hoppy and is killed by Brass, head of the town's vigilante committee, before he can talk. Both Hardin and Hoppy want the $5,000 reward money and the banker sets aside his claim when Hoppy agrees to invest the money locally. Hardin holds the mortgage on the Whitlock ranch, which he wants to control for its water rights. Hoppy, California and Johnny go to the Whitlock ranch and meet the owners, Lin Whitlock (George Reeves) and his sister Lucy (Lois Sherman). After much discussion, the five agree to form a partnership and Hoppy sends California to pay Hardin the $500 water bill owed for the month. In the saloon, he is hoodwinked out of the money by Wildcat Willy (Earle Hodgins), who shows him "proof" there is oil under the Whitlock ranch. The other partners are unhappy with California for throwing away their money and after two weeks Hardin, who had promised to extend the bill for 30 days, has the water shut off. Hoppy, Johnny and rancher Varney (Herbert Rawlinson) try to get the water turned on again but without success. The drill that Willy has set up on the Whitlock ranch brings up water, enough for the entire valley. When Hardin refuses to buy Whitlock cattle, Hoppy calls a meeting of ranchers and forms an alternate cattlemen's association, since the banker runs the local one for his own profit. Hardin and Brass, however, put fake brands on Varney's cattle and accuse Hoppy and his pals of being rustlers; they are forced to flee. Returning to the Whitlock ranch, Hoppy learns from Willy that Hardin was Mason's boss and had him killed. Hoppy deduces that the mail robbery was the banker's way of getting the local ranchers' cattle sale contracts. California lures the vigilantes out of town by telling them that Hoppy and Johnny want to turn themselves in. The two men then return to town and take Hardin prisoner and search is office, finding the cattle contracts. Giving Lucy and Willy the contracts, Hoppy sends them out to form a posse. When the vigilantes return, they are caught between the government agents and the ranchers and are forced to surrender as Hoppy whips Hardin in a fistfight. With the trouble settled, Hoppy, California and Johnny return to the Bar 20 to help Buck Peters fight rustlers.

Colt Comrades was Jay Kirby's final series outing; George Reeves, who had played support-

Dustine Farnum, Betty Blythe, William Boyd, Andy Clyde and Robert Mitchum in *Bar 20* (United Artists, 1943).

ing parts in several of the Hoppy features, took over the third position in the triad hero concept for one time in *Bar 20*, released in the fall of 1943. It was allegedly based on Mulford's first Cassidy novel of the same title, published in 1907. The leading lady, Dustine Farnum, was the daughter of silent film star Dustin Farnum. Here Bar 20 cowboys Hoppy (Boyd), California (Clyde) and Lin Bradley (Reeves) are on their way to the Stevens ranch to purchase cattle when they meet a stagecoach carrying Mrs. Stevens (Betty Blythe), her daughter Marie (Dustine Farnum) and a friend, Mark Jackson (Victor Jory). The Bar 20 men thwart stagecoach robber Quirt Rankin (Francis McDonald) and his gang although the outlaws do escape with jewelry which belongs to Richard Adams (Robert Mitchum), Marie's fiancé. At the Stevens ranch, Richard stops the cattle sale because he will not allow the Stevenses to use the money to replace the stolen jewelry. Hoppy is robbed of the cash he planned to use to pay for the cattle. Jackson, who wants the Stevens ranch and is the mastermind behind the robbery, offers to loan Richard money in return for a note for the deed to his ranch. Lin sees some of the bills Richard got from Jackson and recognizes it as part of the currency stolen from Hoppy, and he comes to believe Richard was involved in the holdup. Trailing Richard to the gang's hideout, where he hopes to retrieve his jewelry, Lin takes back the money while Hoppy and California capture Quirt and his gang. After identifying Jackson as his boss, Quirt is killed by the outlaws. Hoppy, California and Lin are arrested for the stagecoach robbery and murder of Quirt. Cassidy convinces Richard to let him try and prove Jackson's guilt by having him escape from jail, impersonating Quirt. Jackson and his men try to kill Hoppy, but they are prevented by Richard as Hoppy brings in Jackson and the gang. Marie and Richard plan to get married and sell Hoppy their cattle.

George Reeves was a plus factor for the Cassidy series but after this one appearance as one of the leads he was called into the military and the tertiary role was taken over by Jimmy Rogers (1915–2000), playing a character of the same name. The son of humorist-actor Will Rogers, Jimmy had none of his father's charisma and his screen persona was even more of a deficit to the series than either Brad King or Jay Kirby. Unfortunately he would play the part in the last six Cassidy offerings produced by Harry Sherman. The first of these was *False Colors*, issued in November, 1943. It was directed by George Archainbaud and, except for Rogers, it was a fairly strong entry. Bar 20 boys Hoppy (Boyd), California (Clyde), Jimmy Rogers (Rogers) and Bud Lawton (Tom Seidel) are delivering cattle to the railroad when Bud is ambushed by two men, Sonora (Glenn Strange) and Lefty (Pierce Lyden). In Denton, Bud finds out that his father has died and that he has inherited his ranch, the Diamond Hitch. He goes to a lawyer (Earle Hodgins) and signs papers making the other three Bar 20 men his partners in the spread, and is then murdered by Sonora and Lefty. The two murderers work for lawyer Mark Foster (Douglass Dumbrille), the executor of the Lawton property, who hires Kit Moyer (also Seidel), a lookalike for Bud, to impersonate him so Foster can get the ranch which controls the water rights to the entire valley near Poncho. In town the imposer meets Bud's sister Faith (Claudia Drake) and alienates her by wanting to sell the ranch. Also in town are Hoppy, California and Jimmy, who have come to look over the Lawton spread. They try to get jobs at the ranch but Moyer refuses to hire them. Hoppy tells Faith he was a friend of her father and urges her to keep Jimmy on to look after the livestock. Back in town, Hoppy meets with Judge Stevens (Sam Flint) and tells him he believes Bud is a fake and that he and his partners legally own part of the ranch. At the saloon, California gets into a fight with one of Foster's men, Rip Austin (Robert Mitchum), who is beaten by Hoppy. At the Diamond Hitch, Hoppy accuses Moyer of being an imposter and produces the partnership agreement signed by the real Bud Lawton. Foster then claims the Bar 20 men are imposters and they are forced to flee but end up being captured when California receives a slight injury. Faith is given the partnership agreement by Hoppy as he and his pals are ushered out of their cell by Sheriff Martin (Roy Barcroft), who claims he does not want to be part of a lynching. When Hoppy sees Sonora and Lefty waiting outside to ambush them, he turns on the sheriff, who is in cahoots with Foster, and locks him and the two outlaws in a jail cell. Hoppy then gets the drop on Moyer, who overhears Foster plan to have him killed and make it look like a suicide. Foster shoots Moyer and tries to get the locals to lynch Hoppy. The outlaw survives and implicates the lawyer who is beaten in a brawl by Hoppy. With the gang arrested, Jimmy plans to stay on at the Diamond Hitch as the foreman but changes his mind and returns to the Bar 20 with Hoppy and California.

The final 1943 Cassidy feature, *Riders of the Deadline*, came out in December. Its script had been used earlier for the 1941 Don "Red" Barry Republic western *Desert Bandit*. Richard Crane, who played the part of Tim Mason, replaced John James who had been drafted into the military. Lesley Selander directed this tale of Texas Rangers Hoppy (Boyd), California (Clyde) and Jimmy (Rogers) being joined on the force by rancher Tim Mason (Crane), who has lost all his money playing cards with Gunner Madigan (Anthony Warde). Although he no longer has the funds to pay the loan on his ranch, banker Simon Crandall (William Harrigan) agrees to extend the note in exchange for letting him run wagons across Tim's ranch. Crandall is the head of a smuggling gang. When Tim refuses his request, he is beaten by Nick Drago (Robert Mitchum), one of Crandall's henchmen. Hoppy, California and Jimmy capture the wagon but the driver is killed and Tim is arrested for the crime by the head of the Rangers, Captain Jennings (Herbert Rawlinson). After Hoppy assures Tim's sister Sue (Frances Woodward) that Tim will not go to trial, another of Crandall's men, lawman Martin (Hugh Prosser), murders Tim and accuses Hoppy of trying to aid Tim in escaping from jail. In order to get to the bottom of the case, Hoppy purposely alienates himself from Jennings and the Rangers and pretends to join Gunner and steals back the captured supply wagon. Letting himself be arrested, Hoppy reports to Jennings, who lets him escape. Crandall begins running the Mason ranch, supposedly to help pay off the family debt. Sue and her employee Sourdough (Earle Hodgins) find boxes filled with guns and are taken prisoner by Madigan and his men. While Hoppy frees Sue and Sourdough, Madigan goes to Crandall wanting his share of the smuggling operation. The banker shoots him. As Drago attempts to murder Hoppy, he is shot by California and Jimmy, and Crandall and his gang is put behind bars. Hoppy then becomes a captain with his own unit, which includes California and Jimmy.

Texas Masquerade, first shown in February, 1944, was the first of a quartet of Cassidy features that year. Directed by George Archainbaud, it opened with Hoppy (Boyd), California (Clyde) and Jimmy (Rogers) stopping a robbery and arresting wanted outlaw Sam Nolan (Francis McDonald). The victim, lawyer James Corwin (Nelson Leigh), is badly hurt; Hoppy takes him to the Bar 20 to recover and has Nolan put in jail. Since Corwin has given Hoppy permission to use his identity, Hoppy sends California and Jimmy ahead to the southern Texas town of Glenby, which has been plagued by raiders known as the Night Riders. Once in Glenby, California and Jimmy are hired to work at the Lazy W Ranch co-owned by Virginia Curtis (Mady Correll) and Corwin, who is her cousin. Hoppy comes to town as Corwin, acting like an Eastern dude, and he is harassed by saloon owner Ace Maxson (Don Costello), a cohort of attorney J.K. Trimble (Russell Simpson), the real leader of the Night Riders. When Hoppy refuses to sell his part of the ranch to Trimble, the lawyer orders his men to evict rancher John Martindale (J. Farrell MacDonald) and his wife Emma (June Terry Pickrell). Hoppy and California are shot at in a cactus-ridden area called Satan's Garden, the marauder's hideout. Hoppy succeeds in getting the drop on Al (Pierce Lyden) and Jeff (John Merton), two of Virginia's ranch hands who actually are in cahoots with Trimble. Back at the ranch, a suspicious Virginia forces Hoppy's hand and he reveals his true identity to her. She tells him she thinks Trimble is the leader of the Night Riders. Deputy Sheriff Lou Sykes (Bill Hunter), a thug in Trimble's employ and Maxson's brother-in-law, and honest but cowardly Sheriff Rowbottom (Robert McKenzie) serve eviction papers on Martindale, who shoots and kills Sykes when he manhandles Emma. Hoppy and his pals hear the shots and ride to the Martindale ranch where John shows them a pool of black liquid, with Hoppy realizing that Trimble wants the area ranches because there is oil in the ground. Maxson and a posse arrive at the Martindale ranch and try to hang John but Hoppy stops them; the rancher is taken to jail. Sam Nolan, who has escaped from prison, arrives in town and Trimble and Maxson hire him to take Sykes' place. Recognizing Hoppy, he organizes a raid by the Night Riders on the Lazy W. At the ranch, Nolan gets the drop on Hoppy who manages to pull a gun out of a drawer and kill him. Hoppy holds off the outlaws until California, Jimmy and Corwin arrive with a posse and surround the gang. The sheriff tells Hoppy that Trimble has gone to Satan's Garden and Hoppy follows him there. The lawyer dies when he falls into a pool of quicksand. The Bar 20 boys head home as Virginia and James look forward to the appraisal of their oil holdings.

Texas Masquerade's opening montage of the Night Riders at work came from previous features. The next outing, *Lumberjack*, not only returned Hoppy to the logging country of *Riders of the Timberlane*, it incorporated a fight sequence from that feature and was a reworking of the 1941 release, which was also directed by Lesley Selander. At the Bar 20 ranch, Buck Peters' (Herbert Rawlinson) daughter Julie (Ellen Hall) secretly marries Ben Jordan (John Whitney), a lumberman who is shot and killed. Only Buck, who has been injured, can identify the killer but he cannot travel so he sends his foreman, Hoppy (Boyd), and ranch hand Jimmy (Rogers) with Julie to logging country near Pine Rock to forestall the sale of Jordan's property due to back taxes. Hoppy stops the tax sale and Julie pays the amount owed, saving the logging operation which is coveted by land developer Clyde Fenwick (Francis McDonald). Also in Pine Rock is California (Clyde), a former Bar 20 ranch hand, and homesteader Big Joe Williams (Charles Morton), who has been working for Jordan. Against Hoppy's advice, Julie signs a contract with Fenwick to supply wooden ties to the railroad, despite the fact he and his partner Daniel Keefer (Douglass Dumbrille) have been foreclosing on area settlers. Although Julie tells Hoppy to return to the Bar 20, he decides to stay after Jimmy realizes that Taggart (Hal Taliaferro), Keeper's foreman, is the man who shot Jordan. Hoppy has Jimmy ride to the Bar 20 to get Buck Peters as Taggart is put in charge of Julie's logging crew and told to hold up work so she will be unable to fulfill the contract and lose the property. When Julie confronts Taggart, he hits her. Hoppy comes to her rescue and is forced to fight the entire logging crew until California takes Hoppy and Julie to safety. Big Joe Williams offers to put together for Julie a new crew made up of squatters who were owed money by Jordan. With Hoppy in charge, the new crew works ahead of schedule. When it becomes apparent that Julie will be able to complete the contract, Fenwick tells Taggart to sabotage the operation. California finds out about Taggart's plan and tells the loggers, who are aided by the returning Jimmy and Buck Peters and a crew from the Bar 20. Defeating the crooks, Buck identifies Taggart as Jordan's murderer and the gang is arrested. Fenwick and Keeper escape; Jimmy captures Keeper but Fenwick manages to place dynamite at a nearby dam. Hoppy finds the explosive and throws it near a tree. After the explosion, the tree crashes into a shack, killing the hiding Fenwick. Julie turns the logging property over to Big Joe and the men who helped her and she goes back to the Bar 20 with her father, Hoppy, California and Jimmy.

Lumberjack included the Ozie Waters song "The Place Your Heart Calls Home"; the next Hoppy release, *Mystery Man*, issued in May, 1944, had Waters as a singing cowboy performing another of his tunes, "Tie a Saddle String Around Your Troubles." Directed by George Archainbaud, it had Hoppy (Boyd), California (Clyde) and Jimmy (Rogers) leading a cattle drive from the Bar 20 to the Circle J Ranch in Texas. They stop a bank robbery committed by outlaws led by Bud Trilling (Don Costello); some of the gang members are captured. Jimmy is nearly killed but is saved by stagecoach passenger Diane Newall (Eleanor Stewart), whose father, Sam Newhall (Forrest Taylor), is the local sheriff. Marshal Blane (Jack Rockwell) questions the outlaws but they refuse to identify their leader. Bud poses as an Easterner and is able to break his men out of jail and then plans to rustle the Bar 20 cattle. That night the outlaws spook the Bar 20 men's horses and steal the herd but Hoppy and his men find their mounts and get back the rustled livestock. Pretending to be a sheriff, Bud rides into the Bar 20 camp, gets the drop on Hoppy and his crew, ties them up and steals their papers. Hoppy manages to break free but Red (Pierce Lyden), one of the gang, sees the escape and rides to warn Trilling. The outlaws plan to take the herd to the Circle J and sell them, pretending to be Bar 20 men. Hoppy and Rogers follow the outlaws but California has to stay behind because his horse goes lame. Trilling, posing as Hoppy, tells Sheriff Newhall that he and his men are being followed by rustlers and the lawman urges him to continue on to the Circle J. The sheriff arrests Hoppy and Jimmy when they arrive in town; Diane gets Jimmy set free although Hoppy remains behind bars. When California arrives he too is put in jail. Diane sets the Bar 20 men free and, taking a shortcut to the Circle J, they drive the cattle and the rustlers into Fox Canyon where they engage in a gun battle. Trilling is shot and the rest of the gang is captured, with the sheriff apologizing to Hoppy. With the cattle sale completed, the Bar 20 boys return home with Jimmy promising to come back to Diane.

Lesley Selander directed the last 1944 Hoppy release, *Forty Thieves*, which also proved to be his final series entry. The title refers to a band of outlaws, made up of three different gangs, who band together to stop Hoppy from bringing law and order to the Arizona Territory. The feature begins with a montage of scenes from previous features showing Hoppy (Boyd) rounding up various outlaw gangs, including the lassoing scene from the finale of *Hoppy Serves a Writ*. Having run all the outlaws out of the territory, Hoppy is up for re-election as county sheriff with California (Clyde) as his campaign manager. California and Jimmy (Rogers) are also his deputies, with Hoppy becoming the parole officer of Tad Hammond (Douglass Dumbrille), whom he put behind bars five years before. When saloon proprietor Jerry Doyle (Kirk Alyn) tells his old friend Hammond that Hoppy is responsible for his poor business, the parolee suggests he run against Hoppy in the election. A reluctant Doyle agrees and Hammond succeeds in uniting three gangs run out of the area by Hoppy, the Ike Simmons (Glenn Strange) and Jess Clanton (Hal Taliaferro) bands and another headed by the Garms brothers, Sam (Jack Rockwell) and Joe (Robert Kortman). While Judge Reynolds (Robert Frazer) and his daughter Katherine (Louise Currie) conduct the election, Hammond has the outlaws move to the outskirts of town and tell incoming ranchers the voting has been postponed. When Buck Peters (Herbert Rawlinson) and his men refuse to believe the crooks, a shootout takes place and Buck rides to town to get help from Hoppy, who succeeds in arresting the outlaws. While Hoppy is out of town, Clanton starts a fight and Simmons stuffs the ballot box. When Hoppy returns with his prisoners, he finds out he has lost the election. That evening, Hammond offers a reward for anyone who kills Hoppy. Hoppy shows up and has a shootout in Doyle's saloon, and tells the baddies to be out of town in twelve hours. Examining the ballots, Hoppy and Judge Reynolds realize the votes against Hoppy are counterfeit. A shootout takes place as the outlaws try to ambush Hoppy, who is slightly wounded. California kills Clanton as the judge and other citizens take up arms and force the gang out of town. Jimmy and Katherine take the stagecoach to the state capitol to see the governor and request he order a new election, but they are waylaid by Hammond and his gang. Tad sends a message to Hoppy to meet him at Big Horn Butte and he rides there with Doyle, with whom he has exchanged clothes and horses. Hammond and Simmons murder Doyle, thinking he is Hoppy, who circles around the outlaws. Jimmy is able to set himself free and Buck and the Bar 20 men arrive, resulting in a gun battle with the gang. Surrounded, the outlaws surrender but Hammond attempts to escape. He and Hoppy fight it out on a suspension bridge with Hammond falling to his death. Hoppy decides to return to the Bar 20 as California declares his candidacy for sheriff until he hears his duties will also encompass patrolling the lawless Indian Territory.

A sturdy entry in the series, *Forty Thieves* proved to be the last United Artists release from Harry Sherman Productions. Sherman would produce only two more westerns, *Ramrod* (1947) and *Four Faces West* (1948), before retiring after more than thirty years in the film business. Like Sidney Toler had done earlier with the Charlie Chan character, Boyd bought the rights to Hopalong Cassidy and launched Hopalong Cassidy Productions, which would make an additional dozen Hoppy features with continued distribution through United Artists. These features are generally considered inferior to the Harry Sherman productions but they had the asset of having Rand Brooks in the role of Lucky Jenkins. Probably best remembered as Scarlett O'Hara's first husband in *Gone with the Wind* (1939), Brooks (1918–2003) brought exuberance to the revived Jenkins part and proved to be a far better sidekick to Hoppy than Brad King, Jay Kirby or Jimmy Rogers.

George Archainbaud would direct all twelve of the remaining Hopalong Cassidy features, beginning with *The Devil's Playground*, released late in 1946; it was the first new Hoppy film in nearly eighteen months. Lewis J. Rachmil (1908–84), who was art director for the series from 1936 to 1941 and had served as associate producer since then, would get producer credit on all of the twelve new features while Boyd, sometimes uncredited, would serve as executive producer. Comparing well with previous series outings, *The Devil's Playground* told of Bar 20 men Hoppy (Boyd), California (Clyde) and Lucky (Brooks) riding through hostile desert country known as the Devil's Playground and hearing a mysterious rider; Hoppy tells the superstitious California it's a ghost, an Indian maiden who haunts the area. Returning to their line shack, the three men find a woman, Lucy Evans (Elaine Riley), who has been wounded and trusts no one. Going back to the Devil's Playground, Hoppy meets Judge Morton (Robert Elliott) and his confederates, Roberts (Francis McDonald), Wolfe (Everett Shields) and Shorty (John George). The judge tells Hoppy they are looking for his daughter who is mentally deranged and who tried to commit suicide. The next morning Hoppy returns to the line shack with the judge and his men only to find the mystery woman has fled. The Bar 20 cowboys then ride into town where the deputy sheriff (Earle Hodgins) tells them Morton does not have a daughter and that the judge is looking for gold stolen by Curly Evans (Ned Young), who was sentenced to prison by Morton. Going back to the Devil's Playground, the three men find Shorty murdered; Hoppy remembers that the man tried to tell him something earlier but was silenced by his comrades. When they bring the body back to town, the sheriff (Joseph J. Greene) and his posse arrest Morton and his men but one of them, Roberts, claims he killed Shorty in self-defense. The sheriff puts Morton and his men in jail along with Hoppy and his pals. Hoppy spots Lucy across the street dressed in clothes she took from California. Using the ruse of suffering from food poisoning, Hoppy and his friends escape from jail and, using a copy of a crude map left by Shorty, they locate Lucy, who informs them Morton is not her father and that he wants her map which shows the location of the gold. She agrees to return to town with the Bar 20 men but once there Morton and his men, who have left the jail with the sheriff, steal the map. Hoppy, California, Lucky and Lucy outrace Morton and his pals to the place where the gold is hidden and find Evans, who has escaped from prison with plans to return the gold to the bank in Soledad. The group manages to get the gold back to the Bar 20 line shack but there they are surrounded by Morton and his men and soon run out of ammunition. Hoppy surrenders but sets fire to blankets in the cabin, causing a diversion which lets him get the drop on the outlaws. The sheriff arrives with a posse and the gang is taken into custody. Evans and Lucy, who is his wife, go back with the gold.

Fool's Gold came out early in 1947 and, like its predecessor it contained scenic locales and excellent photography by Mack Stengler, who lensed all twelve Hopalong Cassidy Productions. While well-made, this one suffered from lethargy, something that would plague several of the later entries. An added plus was Jane Randolph as the fetching, but tough, heroine. Here Hoppy (Boyd) agrees to help his friend Colonel Landy (Forbes Murray) find his son Bruce (Stephen Barclay), who has become involved with an outlaw gang after running away from the military following an altercation with a superior officer. Unknown to his pals California (Clyde) and Lucky (Brooks), Hoppy leaves for Twin Buttes posing as a cattleman. Near the town he meets a hostile prospector (Earle Hodgins) and later he is denied lodgings at the Twin Buttes Stagecoach Inn by Jessie Dixon (Jane Randolph), who thinks Hoppy is really Captain William Thompson, a man sent to arrest her lover, Bruce. Leaving town, Hoppy stops a runaway wagon driven by Jessie's father, Professor Dixon (Robert Emmett Keane), who studies spiders. The professor forces his daughter to give Cassidy a room at their hotel and he also plans to have Bruce lead his gang in stealing $200,000 in gold from the cavalry. He wants the money to compensate him for the ten years he was forced to spend in a military prison. Having followed their friend, California and Lucky arrive in Twin Buttes as peddlers while Dixon forces a reluctant Bruce to promise to carry out the robbery. When a tarantula is planted in Hoppy's hotel room, he suspects Dixon. Later he is knocked out by gang member Blackie (Wee Willie Davis), who plans to drown him; Blackie is killed by California. The Bar 20 men go to Dixon's cabin in a place called the Craggs and find it filled with jars containing deadly spiders along with a gold-thinning outfit and lots of copper bars. Hoppy concludes that Dixon plans to cover the bars with a layer of gold and put them in the place of the government gold shipment, which they plan to steal. Jessie takes Hoppy to Bruce's cabin but he is captured by Dixon and his men. Along with California and Lucky, he is tied up in Dixon's cabin with the professor having taken the tops off three jars containing poisonous spiders. Hoppy manages to free himself and his friends by using a pocketknife. When Dixon returns they tie him up and go after the gang. Jessie arrives at the shack and finds her father has been killed by one of the tarantulas meant for the Bar 20 men. The gang, dressed as soldiers, sign for the government gold from a military detail led by Lieutenant Anderson (Glen Gallagher). Hoppy, California and Lucky get the drop on the gang as they are in the act of carrying off the gold. Jessie goes back with Bruce, who will face a military tribunal, while the Bar 20 cowboys return home.

The third Hopalong Cassidy Production, *Unexpected Guest* (March, 1947), would set the tone for several of the features that would follow, having mystery and horror overtones. Ande Lamb's screenplay had Hoppy (Boyd) and Lucky (Brooks) accompanying California (Clyde) to the ranch of his late cousin Hiram Baxter for the reading of his will. On the trail they are fired upon by a mysterious masked phantom. Once at the Baxter ranch, California learns from family lawyer Potter (John Parrish) that he is one of six people who will benefit from the estate; each time one of them dies, the survivors will split that person's inheritance. Claiming that the estate is nearly worthless, Potter suggests the heirs sell the property, which makes Hoppy suspicious. California and two other relatives, Ruth Baxter, Hiram's niece (Patricia Tate), and Phineas Phipps (Joel Friedkin), decide not to sell; Phipps is later shot. Hoppy hears another heir, the dead man's stepson, Ralph Baxter (Ned Young), claim that Matt Ogden (Robert B. Williams), to whom he is in debt, tried to kill him and that he has a deal with Potter. During the night, Cassidy and Lucky follow Ruth to a meeting with still another heir, housekeeper Matilda Hackett (Una O'Connor), who believes in spirits. The housekeeper tells Ruth that voices have informed her that the young woman should ride the next day to a hidden canyon in order to find important information. Hoppy too hears the voice and the Bar 20 men follow Ruth, who they see fall into a hole in the ground. They rescue Ruth and Lucky takes her home. Hoppy and California discover an oil well hidden on the Baxter ranch. At the ranch house, Hoppy locates a secret panel in the library containing account books which belonged to Ruth's father. He insists that Potter is trying to steal money from the estate; the lawyer manages to get away through a secret passage but is fatally shot by a hooded figure. Hoppy hears the shot and unmasks the killer, Hiram Baxter. The rancher had only pretended to be dead in order to kill off his heirs and he has used a bullhorn to make Matilda think she was hearing spirit voices.

With its mystery angle, hidden panels, masked phantom and ghost voices, *Unexpected Guest* was not without entertainment value, although it eschewed fighting, riding and gunplay for mystery, low-key lighting and too much talk. A pleasant departure from the usual western series plot, it greatly benefited from the presence of Una O'Connor as the superstitious Matilda; this fine character actress had previously added so much to the horror classics *The Invisible Man* (1933) and *The Bride of Frankenstein* (1935). *Unexpected Guest* continued the series penchant for weird characters since *The Devil's Playground* had a maniac out for revenge and *Fool's Gold* featured a villain who used spiders to kill off his enemies. The tradition would continue with *Dangerous Venture* (May, 1947), which dealt with the legend of ghost Indians, a lost Aztec tribe and hidden treasure.

Hoppy was back wearing a black outfit in *Dangerous Venture*, a one-hour excursion which was one of the better later features. It begins with Hoppy (Boyd), California (Clyde) and Lucky (Brooks) stopping ranchers Dan Morgan (Harry Cording) and Bill Kane (Francis McDonald) from shooting Jose (Neyle Morrow), a young warrior of the Talnec tribe, whom they accuse of cattle rustling. The Lazy L herd has actually been rustled by Morgan's men dressed as Indians; the Talnecs, a ghost tribe which lives on a nearby mesa, are being blamed. The Bar 20 men ride to town where the marshal (Jack Quinn) tells Hoppy that the Talnecs are a peaceful tribe and that only Morgan and Kane have been making complaints about them. Hoppy also meets pretty Dr. Sue Harmon (Betty Alexander), the daughter of an archaeologist whose work the young woman is continuing with the assistance of Dr. Atwood (Douglas Evans). The two archaeologists believe that the Talnec tribe is the last remnants of the Aztecs and they are planning an expedition to the mesa where the tribe lives. Sue asks Hoppy and his pals to join them as added protection. Meeting with Jose's grandfather, Xeoli (Fritz Leiber), Hoppy promises him the expedition will not tamper with the tribe's burial grounds, which contain gold and other priceless artifacts. During the trek into the area, Hoppy is shot at by Kane, who is dressed as an Indian. After Atwood learns that Hoppy thinks Morgan is behind the lawlessness, he makes a deal with the rancher for a fifty-fifty split on all treasures they find in the Talnec burial grounds. In order to rustle a herd of cattle, Morgan has some of his men dress as Indians and they raid the expedition's camp. One of the gang members, Red (Ken Tobey), is killed. Hoppy becomes suspicious of Atwood, who fled the camp before the raid, and he and his friends pretend to return to the Bar 20 but keep watch on the expedition and see Atwood join Morgan and Kane and their men in going to the burial grounds. There the crooks find Jose and shoot him. He is found by Xeoli, who blames Hoppy and tries to capture him for a fire sacrifice. Hoppy easily disarms Xeoli who, humiliated, returns to his tribe and tells Jose's sister Talu (Patricia Tate) that he will sacrifice himself to the fire god. The young woman, however, is intent on bringing in Hoppy but mistakes California for him; she takes him to the stronghold where he is tied to a sacrificial altar. Hoppy trails Morgan,

Kane and Atwood after they loot the Talnec burial grounds and he sees Lucky and Sue, who were instructed to stay behind, arrive on the scene. After a shootout with the outlaws, the trio follow tracks which lead them to the Talnec camp where Hoppy rescues California; they are attacked by Morgan, Kane and Atwood. The greedy Atwood falls into the sacrificial fire trying to steal an artifact and Kane is killed by Hoppy as Morgan is forced to surrender.

The next series outing, *The Marauders*, came out in the summer of 1947 and again had a plot with a mystery motif. It opens with the Bar 20 trio (Boyd, Clyde, Brooks) holing up in a deserted church in Coltsville, a ghost town, in order to escape a storm. During the night they hear organ music and meet Mrs. Crowell (Mary Newton) and her daughter Susan (Dorinda Clifton). The two women tell them that Mrs. Crowell's husband was the minister at the church but that he was killed and that various mysterious events, including shootings and kidnappings, have left the town deserted except for the two women and their friend, Deacon Black (Ian Wolfe). When a beam falls on the church organ, Cassidy fears someone is out to murder Susan. The next day the Bar 20 men stop Riker (Harry Cording) and his wrecking crew from demolishing the church, and that night they keep the gang from setting fire to the building. Meeting with old friend Tom Connell (Earle Hodgins), the county clerk, Hoppy learns that Black's sister has been trying to buy up land. After returning to the church, where he, California, Lucky and the Crowells have been holed up, Hoppy begins to suspect Mrs. Crowell of being involved with the gang and he also notices a romance between Lucky and Susan. A wounded oil driller (Dick Bailey) staggers into the church and collapses and one of the gang tries to break in through the bell tower but falls to his death. The dead man turns out to be Black. The driller comes to and tells Hoppy that Black is the head of the gang that wants the land because it is rich in oil. Tom Connell and a posse arrive and arrest Riker and his men. The Bar 20 cowboys plan to return home, although California has taken a liking to Mrs. Crowell and Lucky promises to return to Susan.

Next came one of the weaker entries in the series, *Hoppy's Holiday*, released almost simultaneously with *Dangerous Venture*. Although trade shown at 70 minutes, it was cut by ten minutes for theaters and still moved at a lethargic pace. Vacationers Hoppy (Boyd), California (Clyde) and Lucky (Brooks) arrive at the Mesa City festival where California buys a new suit and valise as he plans to enter a square dance contest. During the festivities, the town's bank is robbed of money intended for a local irrigation project. One of the robbers, Ace (Holly Bane), runs into California and accidentally picks up his suitcase. When California finds the stolen money in the grip left behind by the robber, he decides to conceal it in the hotel's dumbwaiter but is seen by Jed (Jeff Corey), the hotel clerk, and is arrested by the sheriff (Donald Kirke). As Hoppy and Lucky look into the matter, Jed tries to run off with the money but is stopped by Hoppy, who receives a flesh wound from Dunning (Leonard Penn), who kills Jed. Dunning, chief of the irrigation project, is also the leader of the gang which held up the bank. Taking flight in one of the newfangled

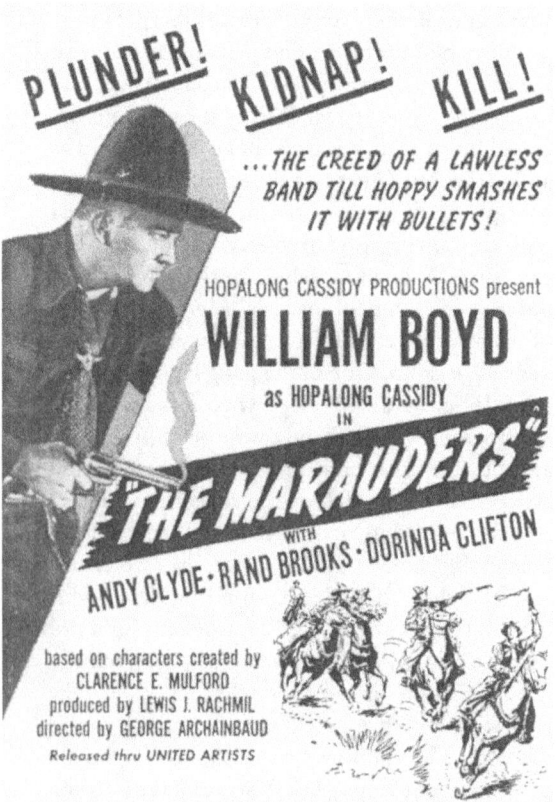

Poster for *The Marauders* (United Artists, 1947).

gasoline-driven motor cars, Dunning and his men are chased by a posse and take shelter in a remote shack but surrender after a gunfight with the lawmen. Back in town, Hoppy tells the sheriff he found the money after it was stolen and mailed it to hotel owner Patton (Andrew Tombes). With the crime solved, the Bar 20 men continue their holiday.

Hoppy's Holiday was the last series entry for 1947. For the year, Boyd was ranked third in the *Motion Picture Herald* poll of top moneymaking western stars after having been second for the years 1943 through 1945 and not appearing in the 1946 poll since one Cassidy feature was released that year. On the other hand, the similar *Boxoffice* poll listed him third in 1944 and 1945, fifth in 1946 and fourth in 1947.

The first 1948 series feature, March's *Silent Conflict*, was even duller than *Hoppy's Holiday*. Its only interest came in the odd plot contrivance of having the villain use hypnotism to control his victims. Hoppy (Boyd), California (Clyde) and Lucky (Brooks) are in charge of a drive for the cattlemen's association. Hoppy becomes worried about Lucky who has become lax in his duties and has been keeping company with gambler Speed Blaney (James Harrison). After the cattle sale, the Bar 20 men stop for the night at the Boulder Inn where Blaney shows up along with medicine show barker Doc Richards (Earle Hodgins) and his niece Rene (Virginia Belmont). California tells Hoppy that Lucky is in debt to Blaney but has saved the money to pay the gambler. Richards gives Lucky an herbal tea drink which makes him sleep and then hypnotizes him. Hoppy finds the cattle money missing the next day, and since Lucky has disappeared, he suspects him of the theft. Hoppy and California try to find Lucky, who has joined Richards and Rene. Blaney and his men deny knowing about the theft; when the cattlemen's association members show up, Hoppy promises to retrieve the money. While staying at a shack with Rene and Lucky, Richards sees Hoppy and California riding toward them, hypnotizes Lucky and orders him to kill his friends. Hoppy is able to get behind Lucky and knock him out. When he recovers, Lucky joins his pals in confronting Richards. The cattlemen, led by rancher Randall (Forbes Murray), show up and Hoppy gives them the money for their herd; Richards is arrested. With *Silent Conflict*, Boyd received on-screen billing as executive producer and he would continue to do so for the final five features in the series.

Hoppy was back wearing a light-colored outfit in the April, 1948, release *The Dead Don't Dream* which had him as a cowboy Philo Vance trying to solve a series of murders at a remote hotel in what turned out to be a leisurely, and fairly entertaining, mystery movie. Hoppy (Boyd), California (Clyde) and Lucky (Brooks), all wearing their Sunday finest, are on the way to the Last Chance Inn for Lucky's wedding to Mary Benton (Mary Tucker). Upon arrival, the trio is told by wheelchair-bound innkeeper Jeff Potter (John Parrish) that the wedding has been postponed due to the disappearance of Mary's uncle, prospector Jim Benton. After meeting miner Earl Wesson (Leonard Penn), whose gold claim is next to Benton's, Hoppy goes with him to the Benton mine and there they find the prospector murdered. Wesson sends his partner, Bart Lansing (Francis McDonald), to get the sheriff. Mary tells California she is not sure if she really wants to marry Lucky, and Hoppy witnesses an argument between Potter and his brother Larry (Bob Gabriel). Prospector Jesse Williams (Stanley Andrews), an old friend of Hoppy's, takes a room at the inn and he tells Hoppy that another prospector disappeared earlier while staying at the Last Chance. The next day Williams is gone; the Bar 20 men find some of his belongings being burned by Duke (Richard Alexander), the inn's handyman. Sheriff Thompson (Forbes Murray) comes to the inn to investigate Benton's murder and Lucky has to tell Mary about the homicide. He also sees her uncle's will which made her the sole heir to the gold he deposited in a nearby bank. After Hoppy and Thompson find that Benton's body is missing from the mine, the lawman decides to spend the night in the murdered man's room at the inn since he suspects that Larry Potter, who is wanted for murder in Texas, is the killer. That night Hoppy sees Mary leave with Wesson, her former boyfriend, and then finds that the lawman is missing. Finding Larry in the marshal's room, Hoppy and Jenkins chase him but he is shot by an unknown assailant; they return his body to the inn. Wesson tells Hoppy that he and Lansing are pulling up stakes but first plan to form a posse to look for the killer. He also offers their gold claim to Jeff Potter. That night Hoppy stays in Benton's room and learns that the bed's canopy lowers, thus suffocating the occupant. When Lansing comes into the room, Hoppy gets the drop on him and he admits to the murders. Wesson takes Hoppy prisoner and the three men go into the cellar of the inn where a fight ensues. Lucky and Duke, who is fed up working for the killers, come to his rescue and they capture Wesson and Lansing, who are taken to jail by the new marshal (Don Haggerty). Mary breaks off her engagement to Lucky and plans to go back East as the Bar 20 men head home after getting an invitation from Jeff Potter to come back to his hostel.

Sinister Journey, released in June, 1948, had Hoppy garbed in a light-colored outfit with a black scarf. Hoppy (Boyd), California (Clyde) and Lucky (Brooks) are on their way to Wheeler to meet with railroad vice president Tom Smith (Stanley Andrews). Hoppy rides ahead of his pals and stops at a ranch house where Lee Garvin (John Kellogg) asks his help because his wife Jessie (Elaine Riley) is ill. Hoppy soon realizes she is suffering from locoweed poisoning and is able to help the young woman. The Bar 20 men stay for supper and learn that Jessie is Tom's daughter and Lee is a brakeman for the railroad; Tom was opposed to their marriage and dislikes his son-in-law. Tom also suspects that Lee is responsible for a series of accidents plaguing the railroad line. The three men agree to work for Tom in trying to find out who is responsible for the sabotage but Lee becomes resentful, thinking they are spying on him, and he picks a fight with Lucky. Lee finds hobo Ben Watts (Will Orlean) sleeping in one of the railroad cars and Watts recalls they were cellmates in prison. Not wanting his wife and father-in-law to know he has a record, Lee gives Watts money, which is witnessed by Hoppy. Jessie and Lee have an argument and she returns to her father, who is shot at by his secretary, Harmon Roberts (Don Haggerty), Lee's one-time romantic rival for Jessie. The blame for the shooting is placed on Watts, who is killed by Roberts before he can reveal the truth to Hoppy. Since he feels Roberts is behind the sabotage, Hoppy convinces Lee to talk with Tom but he is slugged by Roberts who murders Tom and puts the blame on Lee. With Roberts having papers which give him Tom's interest in the railroad, Jessie decides to go with him on a train to the east, unaware that Roberts and his henchman, railroad yard boss Banks (Harry Strang), have had a falling-out over money. The Bar 20 men locate Lee before he is arrested for Tom's murder. With a made-up claim that Banks is turning state's evidence against Roberts, Hoppy causes the man to confess; he is arrested for murder and forgery by the marshal (Herbert Rawlinson). Lee and Jessie are reconciled and Jessie tells Hoppy that Lee will be the new vice-president of her railroad.

Sinister Journey was a rather listless affair but the next month it was followed by *Borrowed Trouble*, a compact, somewhat tongue-in-cheek entry which contained quite a bit of comedy. It greatly benefited from Anne O'Neal's performance as a prim, but gritty, schoolteacher. Back in a black outfit, Hoppy (Boyd), along with California (Clyde) and Lucky (Brooks), delivers a herd to cattle dealer Groves (Herbert Rawlinson) and then they all head into town where Steve Mawson's (John Parrish) newly opened saloon is a bane to school marm Miss Abbott (Anne O'Neal). The new saloon is located next to her school and she is upset because Mawson broke his word and opened up the place instead of building a general store as he promised. In retaliation, she throws apples at the saloon and breaks its windows with Mawson blaming Big Dome Saloon owner-rival Dink Davis (Cliff Clark). Mawson orders his men to do the same to Davis' saloon as Hoppy talks with Miss Abbott, who admits breaking Mawson's windows. That night the schoolteacher is kidnapped and taken to Mawson's remote cabin. Hoppy blames the saloon owner for the abduction. One of Miss Abbott's pupils gives Hoppy directions to the cabin and he and Lucky rescue the woman after a shootout with her guards. As Davis accuses Mawson of kidnapping the schoolteacher and orders him out of town, Hoppy, Lucky and Miss Abbott arrive at Mawson's saloon and Hoppy accuses Davis of the abduction. He pulls a gun on Cassidy and tries to escape but Miss Abbott uses an apple to knock the gun out of his hand and Hoppy shoots him. The local sheriff (Earle Hodgins), who is always late on the scene, arrives and announces he is also the town's undertaker. Thanking Hoppy for clearing him of the kidnapping charge, Mawson agrees to buy

Davis' saloon and give it to Miss Abbott for a new schoolhouse.

Hoppy was back wearing a light-colored outfit in the penultimate series entry, *False Paradise*, released in September, 1948. Anne Larson (Elaine Riley) and her father, retired entomology professor Alonzo Larson (Joel Friedkin), purchase the Paradise Ranch, which is next to the one owned by Hoppy (Boyd), California (Clyde) and Lucky (Brooks). After seeing the dilapidated condition of the ranch, the professor and his daughter realize they were cheated by land agent Bentley (Kenneth MacDonald). Hoppy believes there is silver under the Larson property and gets a loan from banker Waite (Cliff Clark) to start mining operations. Waite, however, is working with Bentley and tells him about the loan and he rushes out to the ranch to buy it back; Hoppy arrives and throws him off the place. Bentley and Waite plant miners Buck (Richard Alexander) and Sam (Zon Murray) as spies and the two try to sabotage the mining operations. Smelting company representative Radley (George Eldredge) signs a contract with Larson to take all the mine's silver. Waite orders his men to cause a cave-in, not knowing the miners have hit a wall of solid rock. Buck and Sam plant dynamite in the mine but are caught by the professor, whom they overpower and pin under a boulder. Hoppy arrives on the scene, shoots both men and rescues Larson but is unable to prevent the dynamite from exploding. The blast opens up a rich silver vein. Waite hires Deal (Don Haggerty) to work for Larson. After Cassidy sees Deal report to Waite prior to a silver shipment, he takes precautions. When the outlaws attack the silver wagons, one of them is filled with armed miners. Bentley tries to use boulders to halt the wagons but Hoppy and Lucky stop him. Back in Waite's office, Hoppy gets the drop on Bentley and Waite and takes them to the smelter where Larson pays off the bank loan. Hoppy then orders Bentley, Waite and their gang out of the territory as Lucky romances Anne.

False Paradise was a fairly fast-paced affair, in contrast to the finale Hopalong Cassidy feature, *Strange Gamble*, which came out in October, 1948. A somewhat confused effort, it had Hoppy (Boyd), California (Clyde) and Lucky (Brooks) as federal men working undercover as outlaws in search of counterfeiters. Near Silver City they rescue Nora Murphy (Elaine Riley) who is trying to drive a stagecoach containing her intoxicated brother Sid (William F. Leicester) and his seriously ill wife Mary (Joan Barton). Upon arrival in Silver City, the town boss, Mordigan (James Craven), refuses them lodgings but Doc White (Joel Friedkin) gives Mary his room at the hotel. After Sid tells Mordigan he has purchased the Silver Belle mine, he is found dead in the boss' saloon, and soon Mary also dies. Wanting Hoppy out of the way, Mordigan has his henchman Longhorn (Francis McDonald) start a stampede which nearly kills the Bar 20 men while they sleep. Getting money from Mordigan for damages to his property, Hoppy buys Wong's (Lee Tung Foo) restaurant and Nora pretends to be his fiancée. She tells Hoppy that her father found the Silver Belle mine but has not been seen. Hoppy finds John Murphy (Herbert Rawlinson), Nora's father, who works for Mordigan. Doc White is shot by Mordigan's henchman Pete (Robert B. Williams) but before dying he tells Hoppy to look out for De Lara (Alberto Morin), a Mexican government agent. Mordigan's men capture De Lara and take him to the mine to kill him but Hoppy arrives and arrests the gang, reuniting Nora with her father, who was being forced to work as a counterfeiter. Murphy and Nora then plan to reopen the mine while De Lara goes back to Mexico and the Bar 20 trio return home.

While it seemed the Hopalong Cassidy series went out with a whimper with *Strange Gamble*, just the opposite occurred because Boyd, in purchasing the rights to the character, also obtained the television rights which would eventually make him a fortune. The Cassidy features were sold to NBC and became one of the most popular items in those early days of television, starting a Hopalong Cassidy craze which would make the character far more popular than it had ever been in theaters. As a result, Boyd continued to be one of the top moneymaking film cowboys, ranking fifth in the *Motion Picture Herald* poll in 1948, seventh in 1949 and fifth again in 1950. Even as late as 1952, six years after the release of the final Cassidy feature, he was listed in tenth position. In the similar *Boxoffice* poll, Boyd was fifth in 1948 and 1949 and fourth in 1950.

Due to the popularity of the network TV showings of the Hoppy movies, the star formed

William Boyd Productions and headlined the *Hopalong Cassidy* TV show which ran initially from 1949 to 1951 on NBC although it remained on the network well into 1954. Boyd served as executive producer for the filming of forty half-hour TV shows which co-starred Edgar Buchanan as Red Connors. In addition, the final twelve theatrical features, to which Boyd owned the rights, were re-edited into 25-minute installments of the TV series, for a total of 52 segments. During the 1950–51 television season, *Hopalong Cassidy* was the ninth most popular program with a rating of 39.9.

Another offshoot of the Cassidy craze was a radio series which ran from early 1952 to March, 1954, starring Boyd as Hoppy with Andy Clyde and Joe Duval as California Carlson. A total of 104 programs were broadcast; from January until September, 1950, the series was on the Mutual network and was sponsored by General Foods, which continued with the program for the rest of its run on CBS. From April through December, 1952, repeats were broadcast on CBS and sponsored by Cella Vineyards.

Boyd also starred as Hopalong Cassidy in a series of Capitol Records which were released between 1950 and 1955. Issued both as albums and singles in 33, 45 and 78 rpm formats, the titles were "Hopalong Cassidy and the Singing Bandit" (CBX-3058), "Hopalong Cassidy and the Square Dance Hold-Up" (CBX-3075), "Hopalong Cassidy and the Two Legged Wolf" (CAS-3109), "Hopalong Cassidy and the Story of Topper" (CAS-3110), which was reissued on SM-1001 as "My Horse Topper;" "Hopalong Cassidy and the Mail Train Robbery" (CAS-3164), "Hopalong Cassidy and the Sheep Rustlers" (CAS-3197) and "Hopalong Cassidy and a Boy's Best Friend" (CAS-3231). There was also a ten-inch album called "Hoppy's Good Luck Coin/The Legend of Phantom Scout Pass" (30128).

Although Hopalong Cassidy had been in comic books since 1942, the TV revival of the character brought about an abundance of Hoppy comics. From 1942 to 1944 Hopalong had been a part of Fawcett's "Master Comics" series and the company issued a solo "Hopalong Cassidy" comic book in 1943. Fawcett revived Cassidy for a series of comic books which ran from 1946 to 1953 and the next year DC Comics began its "Hopalong Cassidy" comic books which ran until 1959. Hopalong was also a part of "Real Western Hero," published by Fawcett from 1948 to 1950 and thereafter William Boyd appeared in nine issues of the series. From 1950 to 1953 Cassidy was also a part of Fawcett's "Six Gun Heroes" comics and for a time the character was in the series when it was taken over by Charlton Publications. Finally the star himself was featured in twenty-three issues of "Bill Boyd Western," published by Fawcett from 1950–1952.

Thanks to the popularity of the Hopalong Cassidy films, the Mulford books about the character were widely read. In 1950, four new Hopalong Cassidy novels appeared, written by Louis L'Amour under the pseudonym Tex Burns. They were *The Riders of High Rock*, *The Rustlers of West Fork*, *Troubleshooter* and *The Trails to Seven Pines*. In addition a number of child-oriented Hoppy books appeared in the early 1950s from various publishers. Among them were a trio of 1950 volumes published by Bonnie Book, *Hopalong Cassidy and His Young Friend Danny*, *Hopalong Cassidy Lends a Hand* and *Hopalong Cassidy Makes New Friends*. There were also three books from the Samuel Lowe Company, *Hopalong Cassidy and the Stolen Treasure*, *Hopalong Cassidy and the Stampede* and *Hopalong Cassidy Comes to Rimrock*. In 1951 Whitman published the hardcover book *Hopalong Cassidy and the Two Young Cowboys* and the same year Little Golden Books released *Hopalong Cassidy and the Bar 20 Cowboys*. The year 1951 also saw the publication of *Hopalong Cassidy Musical Roundup*, a song folio from Nacio Publications. There were also a number of *Hopalong Cassidy Annual* and *Hopalong Cassidy Stories* volumes published in Great Britain in the 1950s.

By the time the Hoppy craze hit in 1950, Boyd and the character he played were synonymous in the minds of the public. As Hoppy, Boyd's picture emblazoned the covers of such national publications as *Life*, *Look* and *Time* and the marketplace was flooded with Hopalong Cassidy merchandising which included movie-related items like toys, pop-up books, sheriff's badges, binoculars and coloring books. There was a plethora of other Hoppy merchandise such as postcards, paper napkins, good luck coins, wrist watches, table covers, mugs, knives, play money, thermos jugs, Christmas ornaments, puzzles, kerchiefs, key rings, pewter coins, hair barrettes, shot glasses, coasters and wallets, just to name a few. There were also food endorsements for bread, milk and potato chips plus Hoppy's picture on milk carton lids and tabs. In addition there was the Hoppy's Troopers club, which exemplified the Hopalong Code of Conduct, and the star donated large sums of money to children's hospitals and homes. In 1951 Boyd opened an amusement park called Hoppy Land and that year he was shown in the Columbia Screen Snapshots short *Hopalong in Hoppy Land*. Having previously appeared in five Screen Snapshots shorts dating back to 1930, Boyd's final film appearance came in 1955 in another entry in the series, *Hollywood Bronc Busters*.

Like most cowboy film stars, Boyd had made personal appearances since the inception of the Cassidy series but beginning in 1950 he and his wife Grace Bradley were constantly traveling, promoting the Hopalong Cassidy image and its products. In 1952 Boyd appeared as Cassidy in a guest role in Cecil B. DeMille's *The Greatest Show on Earth* and the next year he narrated the thirteen-minute short *Little Smokey: The True Story of America's Forest Fire Preventin' Bear*, also known as *Little Smokey*. Although he continued to make public appearances through 1960, Boyd's last television airing as Hoppy came in a 1956 episode of the CBS-TV series *The Jackie Gleason Show*.

In 1952 a "new" Hopalong Cassidy feature film appeared in Europe. It was called *Les Nouvelles Aventures d'Hopalong Cassidy* in France and *De Nieuwe Avonturen von Hopalong Cassidy* in Belgium, both titles translating as *The New Adventures of Hopalong Cassidy*. The feature was made up of three episodes of the *Hopalong Cassidy* TV series which co-starred Edgar Buchanan as Red Connors. One of the episodes, "The Jinx Wagon," guest starred Myron Healey, while another, "Outlaw's Reward" featured Elaine Riley, who brightened several of the latter Hoppy features as leading lady.

Boyd, a multi-millionaire by the end of the 1950s, retired to Palm Springs where he lived for the rest of his life with his fourth wife Bradley, whom he married in 1937. In 1968 he underwent cancer surgery and he died on September 12, 1972. Over the years, the Hopalong Cassidy films have retained their popularity, being constantly available to the public in theaters, on television and through VHS recordings and DVDs. Hopalong Cassidy, as portrayed by William Boyd, was a hero to millions and remains one of America's true cinema legends.

Filmography

Hop-Along Cassidy (Paramount, 1935, 60 minutes) Producer: Harry Sherman. Executive Producer: Henry Herzbrun. Associate Producer: George Green. Director: Howard Bretherton. Screenplay: Doris Schroeder, from the novel *Hopalong Cassidy Enters* by Clarence E. Mulford. Additional Dialogue: Harrison Jacobs. Photography: Archie Stout. Editor: Edward Schroeder. Song: Sam H. Stept & Dave Franklin.

Cast: William Boyd (Bill "Hopalong" Cassidy), Jimmy Ellison (Johnny Nelson), Paula Stone (Mary Meeker), George Hayes (Uncle Ben), Kenneth Thomson (Pecos Jack Anthony), Frank McGlynn, Jr. (Red Connors), Charles Middleton (Buck Peters), Robert Warwick (Jim Meeker), Willie Fung (Salem), Frank Campeau (Frisco), Jim Mason (Tom Shaw), Ted Adams (Hall), Franklyn Farnum (Doc Riley), John Merton, Wally West, Monte Rawlins (Party Guests), Pascale Perry (Outlaw Guard), Sid Jordan (Cowboy).

Reissue title: *Hopalong Cassidy Enters*.

The Eagle's Brood (Paramount, 1935, 61 minutes) Producer: Harry Sherman. Associate Producer: George Green. Director: Howard Bretherton. Screenplay: Doris Schroeder & Harrison Jacobs, from the novel by Clarence E. Mulford. Photography: Archie Stout. Editor: Edward Schroeder. Music: Sam H. Stept. Sound: Earl Sitar. Assistant Director: Ray Flynn.

Cast: William Boyd (Bill "Hopalong" Cassidy), Jimmy Ellison (Johnny Nelson), William Farnum (El Toro/Senor Pedro Chavez), George Hayes (Spike), Addison Richards (Big Henry), Nana Martinez [Joan Woodbury] (Dolores), Frank Shannon (Mike), Dorothy Revier (Dolly), Paul Fix (Steve), Al Lydell (Pop), John Merton (Ed), George Mari (Pablo Chavez), Juan Torena (Esteban), Henry Sylvester (Sheriff), Cliff Lyons (Cowboy), Jim Corey, Rube Dalroy (Saloon Customers).

Bar 20 Rides Again (Paramount, 1935, 61 minutes) Producer: Harry Sherman. Associate Producer: George Green. Director: Howard Bretherton. Screenplay: Doris Schroeder & Gerald Geraghty, from the novel by Clarence E. Mulford. Adaptation: Doris Schroeder. Photography: Archie Stout. Editor: Edward Schroeder. Song: Sam H. Stept & Dave Franklin. Sound: Earl Sitar. Assistant Director: Ray Flynn.

Cast: William Boyd (Bill "Hopalong" Cassidy), Jimmy Ellison (Johnny Nelson), Jean Rouverol (Margaret Arnold), George Hayes (Windy), Harry Worth (George "Nevada" Perdue), Frank McGlynn, Jr. (Red Connors), Howard Lang (Jim Arnold), Ethel Wales (Clarissa "Clary" Peters), Paul Fix (Gila), J.P. McGowan

(Buck Peters), Joe Rickson (Herb Layton), Al St. John (Cinco), John Merton (Carp), Frank Layton (Elbows), Chill Wills & His Avalon Boys (Musicians), Jim Mason, Jack Kirk, Chuck Baldra (Gang Members), Tracy Layne (Wagon Driver), Sid Jordan (Stagecoach Driver).

Call of the Prairie (Paramount, 1936, 63 minutes) Producer: Harry Sherman. Associate Producer: George Green. Director: Howard Bretherton. Screenplay: Doris Schroeder & Vernon Smith, from the novel *Hopalong Cassidy's Protégé* by Clarence E. Mulford. Photography: Archie Stout. Editor: Edward Schroeder. Art Director: Lewis J. Rachmil. Music Director: Boris Morros. Song: Tot Seymour & Vee Lawnhurst. Sound: Earl Sitar. Assistant Director: Ray Flynn.

Cast: William Boyd (Hopalong Cassidy), Jimmy Ellison (Johnny Nelson), Muriel Evans (Linda McHenry), George Hayes (Charlie "Shanghai" McHenry), Chester Conklin (Sheriff Sandy McQueen), Alan Bridge (Sam Porter), Willie Fung (Wong), Howard Lang (Buck Peters), Hank Mann (Tom the Bartender), Al Hill (Tom Slade), James [Jim] Mason (Hoskins), John Merton (Arizona), The Avalon Boys [Chill Wills, Walter Trask, Art Green, Don Brookins] (Musicians), John St. Polis (Jim), Robert McKenzie (Café Owner), Tom London (Dealer), Pascale Perry (Bank Customer), Denver Dixon (Townsman).

Three on the Trail (Paramount, 1936, 67 minutes) Producer: Harry Sherman. Associate Producer: George Green. Director: Howard Bretherton. Screenplay: Doris Schroeder & Vernon Smith, from the novel *Bar 20* by Clarence E. Mulford. Photography: Archie Stout. Editor: Edward Schroeder. Music Director: Boris Morros. Sound: Earl Sitar. Costumes: Albert Kennedy. Special Effects: Mel Wolf. Assistant Director: Ray Flynn.

Cast: William Boyd (Hopalong Cassidy), Jimmy Ellison (Johnny Nelson), Onslow Stevens (Pecos Kane), Muriel Evans (Mary Stevens), George Hayes (Windy), Claude King (J.P. Ridley), William Duncan (Buck Peters), Clara Kimball Young (Rose Peters), John St. Polis (Sheriff Sam Corwin), Ernie Adams (Idaho), Al Hill (Kit Thorpe), Ted Adams (Jim Trask), John Rutherford (Lewis), Lita Cortez (Conchita), Franklyn Farnum (Deputy Sheriff), Joe Rickson (Gabby), Lew Meehan (Bartender), Artie Ortego (Gang Members), Hank Bell (Party Dancer), Jack Montgomery (Murdered Cowboy).

Working title: *Bar 20 Three*.

Heart of the West (Paramount, 1936, 60 minutes) Producer: Harry Sherman. Associate Producer: George Green. Director: Howard Bretherton. Screenplay: Doris Schroeder, from the novel *Mesquite Jenkins, Tumbleweed* by Clarence E. Mulford. Photography: Archie Stout. Editor: Edward Schroeder. Song: Sam Coslow & Victor Young, sung by Al Bowlly. Special Effects: Mel Wolf. Assistant Directors: Ray Flynn & Theodore Joos.

Cast: William Boyd (Hopalong Cassidy), Jimmy Ellison (Johnny Nelson), George Hayes (Windy Jenkins), Sidney Blackmer (John Trumbull), Lyn Gabriel (Sally Jordan), Fred Kohler (Barton), Warner Richmond (Johnson), John Rutherford (Tom Patterson), Walter Miller (Whitey), Charles Martin (Jim Jordan), Ted Adams (Saxon), Robert McKenzie (Tim Grady), Leo J. McMahon (Jessup), John Elliott (Judge), Roy Bucko (Jenkins).

Hopalong Cassidy Returns (Paramount, 1936, 74 minutes) Producer: Harry Sherman. Associate Producer: Eugene Strong. Director: Nate Watt. Screenplay: Harrison Jacobs, from the novel by Clarence E. Mulford. Photography: Archie Stout. Editor: Robert Warwick. Art Director: Lewis J. Rachmil. Sound: Earl Sitar. Special Effects: Mel Wolf. Costumes: Al Kennedy. Assistant Directors: D.M. [Derwin] Abrahams & U.O. Smith.

Cast: William Boyd (Hopalong Cassidy), George Hayes (Windy Halliday), Gail Sheridan (Mary Saunders), Evelyn Brent (Lilli Marsh), Stephen Morris [Morris Ankrum] (Blackie Felton), William Janney (Buddy Cassidy), Irving Bacon (Peg Leg Holden), Grant Richards (Bob Claiborne), John Beck (Bob Saunders), Al St. John (Luke), Ernie Adams (Tim Benson), Joe Rickson (Buck), Ray Whitley (Davis), Claude Smith (Dugan), Gwynne Shipman (Saloon Girl), William J. O'Brien (Bartender Sandy), Bill Nestell (Pete the Blacksmith), Leo J. McMahon (Cowboy), Frank Ellis, Bob Burns, Bud McClure, Jack Montgomery (Gamblers), George Plues, Jim Corey, Hank Bell (Saloon Customers).

Trail Dust (Paramount, 1936, 76 minutes) Producers: Harry Sherman. Associate Producer: Eugene Strong. Director: Nate Watt. Screenplay: Al Martin, from the novel by Clarence E. Mulford. Photography: Archie Stout. Editor: Robert Warwick. Music Arranger: Charles Bradshaw. Music Chorus Director: Billy Hamer. Songs: Harry Tobias, Jack Stern & Claudia Humphrey. Sound: Earl Sitar. Special Effects: Mel Wolf. Costumes: Al Kennedy. Assistant Directors: D.M. [Derwin] Abrahams & Harry Knight.

Cast: William Boyd (Hopalong Cassidy), Jimmy Ellison (Johnny Nelson), George Hayes (Windy Halliday), Stephen Morris [Morris Ankrum] (Tex Anderson), Gwynne Shipman (Beth Clark), Britt Wood (Lanky Smith), Dick Dickinson (Waggoner), Earl Askam (Red), Alan Bridge (Tom Babson), John Beach (Hank), Ted Adams (Joe Wilson), Tom Halligan (Skinny), Dan Wolheim (Borden), Harold Daniels (Sheriff Lewis), Emmet Daly (George), Al St. John (Al), Kenneth Harlan (Bowman), George Chesebro (Saunders), Robert Drew [Bob Woodward] (Bob), John Elliott (Sheriff John Clark), Leo J. McMahon (Cowboy).

Borderland (Paramount, 1937, 81 minutes) Producer: Harry Sherman. Associate Producer: Eugene Strong. Director: Nate Watt. Screenplay: Harrison Jacobs, from the novel *Bring Me His Ears* by Clarence E. Mulford. Photography: Archie Stout. Editor: Robert Warwick.

Art Director: Lewis J. Rachmil. Sound: Earl Sitar. Special Effects: Mel Wolf. Wardrobe: Al Kennedy. Assistant Directors: D.M. [Derwin] Abrahams & Harry Knight.

Cast: William Boyd (Hopalong Cassidy), Jimmy Ellison (Johnny Nelson), George Hayes (Windy Halliday), Stephen Morris [Morris Ankrum] (Loco/The Fox), John Beach (Texas Ranger Bailey), Charlene Wyatt (Molly Rand), Nora Lane (Grace Rand), Trevor Bardette (Colonel Gonzales), Earle Hodgins (Major Stafford), Alan Bridge (Dandy Morgan), George Chesebro (Tom Parker), John St. Polis (Doctor), Charles [Slim] Whitaker (Rancher), J.P. McGowan (El Rio Sheriff), Harry Bernard (El Rio Bartender), Frank Ellis (Frank), Karl Hackett, Robert Walker (Tourists), Francis Walker, Ralph Bucko, Ralph Bucko (Rangers), Leo J. McMahon, Ed Cassidy (Gang Members), Buffalo Bill, Jr. (Card Player), Herman Hack, Jim Corey (Saloon Customers), Frosty Royce (Cowboy), Jack Evans, Cliff Parkinson (El Rio Citizens), Joe Dominguez (Mexican).

Hills of Old Wyoming (Paramount, 1937, 78 minutes) Producer: Harry Sherman. Director: Nate Watt. Screenplay: Maurice Geraghty, from the novel *The Round-Up* by Clarence E. Mulford. Photography: Archie Stout. Editor: Robert Warwick. Music: Ralph Rainger. Song: Leo Robin & Ralph Rainger. Art Director: Lewis J. Rachmil. Sound: Earl Sitar. Special Effects: Mel Wolf. Production Manager: Harry Knight. Costumes: Al Kennedy. Assistant Director: D.W. [Derwin] Abrahams.

Cast: William Boyd (Hopalong Cassidy), George Hayes (Windy Halliday), Russell Hayden (Lucky Jenkins), Stephen Morris [Morris Ankrum] (Agent Andrews), Gail Sheridan (Alice Hutchins), John Beach (Saunders), Clara Kimball Young (Ma Hutchins), Earle Hodgins (Thompson), Steve Clemente (Lone Eagle), Chief Big Tree (Indian Chief), George Chesebro (Peterson), Paul Gustine (Daniels), Leo J. McMahon (Steve), John Powers (Smiley), Jim Mason (Deputy Sheriff).

North of the Rio Grande (Paramount, 1937, 70 minutes) Producer: Harry Sherman. Director: Nate Watt. Screenplay: Jack [Joseph] O'Donnell, from the novel *Cottonwood Gulch* by Clarence E. Mulford. Photography: Russell Harlan. Editor: Robert Warwick. Art Director: Lewis J. Rachmil. Production Manager: Harry Knight. Props: Hugh Donovan. Assistant Directors: D.W. [Derwin] Abrahams & U.O. Smith.

Cast: William Boyd (Hopalong Cassidy), George Hayes (Windy Halliday), Russell Hayden (Lucky Jenkins), Stephen Morris [Morris Ankrum] (Henry Stoneham/The Lone Wolf), Bernadene Hayes (Faro Annie), John Rutherford (Ace Crowder), Walter Long (Patrick "Bull" O'Hara), Lee Colt [Lee J. Cobb] (Wooden), Al Ferguson (Deputy Sheriff Jim Plunkett), John Beach (Clark), Lorraine Randall (Mary Cassidy), Richard Cramer, George Plues (Card Players), Harry Bernard (Bartender), Lee Brooks (Jess), Lafe McKee, Bill Nestell, Horace B. Carpenter, Fred Burns, Silver Tip Baker (Jurors), Hank Bell, William H. O'Brien, Ted Billings (Waiters), Al Haskell (Fiddle Player), Herman Hack, Carl Mathews, Cliff Lyons, Buck Morgan (Saloon Customers), Charles Murphy (Dancer), Cliff Parkinson (Jerry), George Morrell (Roulette Player).

Rustlers' Valley (Paramount, 1937, 61 minutes) Producer: Harry Sherman. Director: Nate Watt. Screenplay: Harry O. Hoyt, from the novel by Clarence E. Mulford. Photography: Russell Harlan. Editor: Sherman Rose. Supervising Editor: Robert Warwick. Art Director: Lewis J. Rachmil. Production Manager: Harry Knight. Wardrobe: Al Kennedy. Props: Henry Donovan. Assistant Directors: D.M. [Derwin] Abrahams & U.O. Smith.

Cast: William Boyd (Hopalong Cassidy), George Hayes (Windy Halliday), Russell Hayden (Lucky Jenkins), Stephen Morris [Morris Ankrum] (Glen Randall), Muriel Evans (Agnes Randall), Lee Colt [Lee J. Cobb] (Cal E. Howard), Ted Adams (Taggart), Al Ferguson (Joe), John Beach (Sheriff Boulton), John St. Polis (Crawford), Leo J. McMahon (Art), Dot Farley (Mrs. Anson), Bernadene Hayes (Alice), John Powers (Stuttering Party Guest), Horace B. Carpenter, Ben Corbett (Party Guests).

Hopalong Rides Again (Paramount, 1937, 65 minutes) Producer: Harry Sherman. Director: Lesley Selander. Screenplay: Norman Houston, from the novel *Black Buttes* by Clarence E. Mulford. Photography: Russell Harlan. Editor: Robert Warwick. Art Director: Lewis J. Rachmil. Production Manager: Ralph Ravenscroft. Sound: Earl Sitar. Props: Henry Donovan. Special Effects: Harry Redmond. Assistant Directors: D.M. [Derwin] Abrahams & Theodore Joos.

Cast: William Boyd (Hopalong Cassidy), George Hayes (Windy Halliday), Russell Hayden (Lucky Jenkins), William Duncan (Buck Peters), Lois Wilde (Laura Peters), William [Billy] King (Artie Peters), Nora Lane (Nora Blake), Harry Worth (Professor Horace Hepburn), John Rutherford (Blackie), Ernie Adams (Keno), Frank Ellis (Dirk), William J. O'Brien (Shorty), Blackjack Ward (Slim), Ben Corbett, Artie Ortego (Gang Members).

Working title: *Cassidy Bar 20*.

Texas Trail (Paramount, 1937, 59 minutes) Producer: Harry Sherman. Director: David Selman. Screenplay: Jack [Joseph] O'Donnell, from the novel *Tex* by Clarence E. Mulford. Additional Dialogue: Harrison Jacobs. Photography: Russell Harlan. Editor: Sherman Rose. Art Director: Lewis J. Rachmil. Production Manager: Roger Ravenscroft. Sound: Karl Zint. Props: Henry Donovan. Wardrobe: Al Kennedy. Assistant Directors: D.M. [Derwin] Abrahams & Theodore Joos.

Cast: William Boyd (Hopalong Cassidy), George Hayes (Windy Halliday), Russell Hayden (Lucky Jenkins), Judith Allen (Barbara Allen), Billy King (Boots McCready), Rafael [Ray] Bennett (Brad), Alexander Cross (Black Jack Carson), Robert Kortman (Hawks),

Karl Hackett (Major McCready), Jack Rockwell (Shorty), John Beach (Smokey), Philo McCullough (Jordan), John Judd (Lieutenant), Ben Corbett (Guard), Clyde Kinney (Courier), Leo J. McMahon (Corporal), Earle Hodgins (Major Jordan), John Powers (Cook), Cliff Parkinson (Gang Member).

Partners of the Plains (Paramount, 1938, 70 minutes) Producer: Harry Sherman. Director: Lesley Selander. Screenplay: Harrison Jacobs, from the novel *Man from Bar 20: A Story of Cow-Country* by Clarence E. Mulford. Photography: Russell Harlan. Editor: Robert Warwick. Song: Ralph Freed & Burton Lane. Art Director: Lewis J. Rachmil. Production Manager: Eugene Strong. Sound: Earl Sitar. Wardrobe: Al Kennedy. Props: Henry Donovan. Special Effects: Harry Redmond. Assistant Directors: D.M. [Derwin] Abrahams & Theodore Joos.

Cast: William Boyd (Hopalong Cassidy), Russell Hayden (Lucky Jenkins), Harvey Clark (Baldy Morton), Gwen Gaze (Lorna Drake), Hilda Plowright (Aunt Martha), John Warburton (Ronald Howard), Al Bridge (Scar Lewis), Al Hill (Doc Galer), Earle Hodgins (Sheriff), John Beach (Benson), Bud McClure (Joe), Herman Hack, Jim Corey (Gang Members), Hank Bell (Citizen).

Cassidy of Bar 20 (Paramount, 1938, 59 minutes) Producer: Harry Sherman. Director: Lesley Selander. Screenplay: Norman Houston, from the novel *Me an' Shorty* by Clarence E. Mulford. Photography: Russell Harlan. Editor: Sherman A. Rose. Art Director: Lewis J. Rachmil. Production Manager: Eugene Strong. Wardrobe: Earl Moser. Props: Henry Donovan. Assistant Directors: D.M. [Derwin] Abrahams & Theodore Joos.

Cast: William Boyd (Hopalong Cassidy), Russell Hayden (Lucky Jenkins), Frank Darien (Pappy), Nora Lane (Nora Blake), Robert Fiske (Clay Allison), John Elliott (Tom Dillon), Margaret Marquis (Mary Dillon), Gertrude W. Hoffman (Ma Caffrey), Carleton Young (Jeff Caffrey), Gordon Hart (Judge Jed Belcher), Edward [Ed] Cassidy (Sheriff Hawley), John Beach, Wen Wright, Jim Toney (Cowboys), Charles Murphy (Tex).

Heart of Arizona (Paramount, 1938, 68 minutes) Producer: Harry Sherman. Associate Producer: J.D. Trop. Director: Lesley Selander. Screenplay: Harrison Jacobs & Norman Houston, from the novel *The Deputy Sheriff* by Clarence E. Mulford. Photography: Russell Harlan. Editor: Sherman A. Rose. Sound: Earl Sitar. Wardrobe: Earl Moser. Props: Henry Donovan. Assistant Directors: D.M. [Derwin] Abrahams & Theodore Joos.

Cast: William Boyd (Hopalong Cassidy), George Hayes (Windy Halliday), Russell Hayden (Lucky Jenkins), John Elliott (Buck Peters), Billy King (Artie Peters), Natalie Moorhead (Belle Starr), Dorothy Short (Jackie Starr), Alden Chase (Don Ringo), John Beach (Sheriff Hawley), Lane Chandler (Trimmer Winkler), Leo J. McMahon (Twister), Lee Phelps (Ranger Captain), Robert McKenzie (Stagecoach Driver), Ben Corbett (Cowboy).

Bar 20 Justice (Paramount, 1938, 70 minutes) Producer: Harry Sherman. Associate Producer: J.D. Trop. Director: Lesley Selander. Screenplay: Harrison Jacobs & Arnold Belgard, from the novel *Buck Peters, Ranchman* by Clarence E. Mulford. Photography: Russell Harlan. Editor: Robert Warwick. Art Director: Lewis J. Rachmil. Sound: Karl Zint. Wardrobe: Earl Moser. Props: Henry Donovan. Special Effects: Harry Redmond. Assistant Directors: D.M. [Derwin] Abrahams & Theodore Joos.

Cast: William Boyd (Hopalong Cassidy), George Hayes (Windy Halliday), Russell Hayden (Lucky Jenkins), Gwen Gaze (Ann Dennis), William Duncan (Buck Peters), Pat J. O'Brien (Frazier), Paul Sutton (Slade), John Beach (Denny Dennis), Joe De Stefani (Perkins), Walter Long (Duke Pierce), Bruce Mitchell (Ross), Dick Dickinson (Les Martin), Wen Wright (Jim).

Pride of the West (Paramount, 1938, 56 minutes) Producer: Harry Sherman. Associate Producer: J.D. Trop. Director: Lesley Selander. Screenplay: Nate Watt, from the novel *Johnny Nelson* by Clarence E. Mulford. Photography: Russell Harlan. Editor: Sherman A. Rose. Music Director: Boris Morros. Song: Harry Tobias & Jack Stern. Art Director: Lewis J. Rachmil. Sound: Glenn Rominger. Wardrobe: Earl Moser. Props: Henry Donovan. Assistant Directors: D.M. [Derwin] Abrahams & Theodore Joos.

Cast: William Boyd (Hopalong Cassidy), George Hayes (Windy Halliday), Russell Hayden (Lucky Jenkins), Earle Hodgins (Sheriff Tom Martin), Charlotte Field (Mary Martin), Billy King (Dick Martin), Kenneth Harlan (Mr. Caldwell), Glenn Strange, Art Mix (Gang Members), James Craig (Nixon), Bruce Mitchell (Detective), Earl Askam (Dutch), Henry Otho (Slim), Leo J. McMahon (Johnson), Wen Wright, George Morrell, Horace B. Carpenter, Jess Cavin, Jim Toney (Citizens), Willie Fung (Sing Loo), Johnny Luther (Vocalist), Charles Murphy (Ed).

In Old Mexico (Paramount, 1938, 67 minutes) Producer: Harry Sherman. Director: Edward D. Venturini. Screenplay: Harrison Jacobs, from the novel *Corson of the JC* by Clarence E. Mulford. Photography: Russell Harlan. Editor: Robert Warwick. Music: Gregory Stone. Music Director: Boris Morros. Song: Aaron Gonzales. Art Director: Lewis J. Rachmil. Sound: Earl Sitar. Wardrobe: Earl Moser. Props: Henry Donovan. Assistant Directors: D.M. [Derwin] Abrahams & Theodore Joos.

Cast: William Boyd (Hopalong Cassidy), George Hayes (Windy Halliday), Russell Hayden (Lucky Jenkins), Paul Sutton (The Fox), Al Garcia (Don Carlos Gonzales), Jane [Jan] Clayton (Anita Gonzales), Trevor Bardette (Colonel Gonzales), Betty Amann (Janet Leeds), Anna Demetrio (Elena), Glenn Strange (Burke), Tony Roux (Pancho), Fred Burns, Cliff Parkinson (Gang Members).

The Frontiersman (Paramount, 1938, 74 minutes) Producer: Harry Sherman. Director: Lesley Selander. Screenplay: Norman Houston, from the novel *Bar-20* by Clarence E. Mulford. Additional Dialogue: Harrison Jacobs. Photography: Russell Harlan. Editor: Sherman A. Rose. Art Director: Lewis J. Rachmil. Music Director: Boris Morros. Sound: Earl Sitar. Wardrobe: Earl Moser. Props: Henry Donovan. Assistant Directors: D.M. [Derwin] Abrahams & Theodore Joos.

Cast: William Boyd (Hopalong Cassidy), George Hayes (Windy Halliday), Russell Hayden (Lucky Jenkins), Evelyn Venable (June Lake), William Duncan (Buck Peters), Clara Kimball Young (Amanda Peters), Charles "Tony" Hughes (Dan Rawley), Dickie Jones (Artie Peters), Roy Barcroft (Buster Simon), Emily Fitzroy (Miss "Snooksie" Snooks), John Beach (Quirt), Robert Mitchell & His St. Brendan's Boys Choir (Choir), Dorothy Vernon, Jack Evans, George Morrell, Rube Dalroy, Charles Brinley, Jess Cavin (Citizens), Blackjack Ward (Rustler), Jim Corey (Cowboy).

Sunset Trail (Paramount, 1939, 69 minutes) Producer: Harry Sherman. Director: Lesley Selander. Screenplay: Norman Houston, from the novel *Mesquite Jenkins* by Clarence E. Mulford. Photography: Russell Harlan. Editor: Robert Warwick. Music Director: Ed Paul. Song: Stanley Cowan & Bobby Worth. Art Director: Lewis J. Rachmil. Sound: Earl Sitar. Wardrobe: Earl Moser. Props: Henry Donovan. Assistant Directors: D.M. [Derwin] Abrahams & Theodore Joos.

Cast: William Boyd (Hopalong Cassidy), George Hayes (Windy Halliday), Russell Hayden (Lucky Jenkins), Charlotte Wynters (Ann Marsh), Jane [Jan] Clayton (Dorrie Marsh), Robert Fiske (Monte Keller), Kenneth Harlan (John Marsh), Anthony Nace (Steve Dorman), Kathryn Sheldon (Abigail Snodgrass), Maurice Cass (E. Prescott Furbush), Alphonse Ethier (Banker), Glenn Strange (Walker), Claudia Smith (Mary Rogers), Jack Rockwell (Stagecoach Driver Bill), Tom London (Trail Patrol Captain Jake), Jerry Jerome (Dude), Al Ferguson (Gang Member), Wen Wright, Frank Ellis, Jim Corey, Jim Toney (Cowboys), Fred Burns (Trail Patrol Rider), Horace B. Carpenter (Citizen), Charles Murphy (Stagecoach Guard), Bob Woodward, Ralph Bucko, Roy Bucko (Saloon Customers).

Working title: *Silver Trail Patrol*.

Silver on the Sage (Paramount, 1939, 68 minutes) Producer: Harry Sherman. Associate Producer: J.D. Trop. Director: Lesley Selander. Screenplay: Maurice Geraghty, from the novel *On the Trail of the Tumbling T* by Clarence E. Mulford. Photography: Russell Harlan. Editor: Robert Warwick. Music Director: Boris Morros. Song: Leo Robin & Ralph Rainger. Art Director: Lewis J. Rachmil. Sound: William Wilmarth. Wardrobe: Earl Moser. Props: Henry Donovan. Assistant Directors: D.M. [Derwin] Abrahams & Theodore Joos.

Cast: William Boyd (Hopalong Cassidy), George Hayes (Windy Halliday), Russell Hayden (Lucky Jenkins), Ruth Rogers (Barbara Hamilton), Stanley Ridges (Earl Brennan/Dave Talbot), Frederick Burton (Tom Hamilton), Jack Rockwell (Marshal), Roy Barcroft (Ewing), Ed Cassidy (Pierce), Wen Wright (Lane), Sherry Tansey [James Sheridan] (Martin Brennan), Jim Corey (Baker), Bruce Mitchell (Bartender), Bud McClure, Hank Bell (Deputy Sheriffs), Herman Hack, George Morrell, Dick Dickinson (Gamblers), Frank O'Connor (Juror).

Working title: *Riders of the Range*.

The Renegade Trail (Paramount, 1939, 59 minutes) Producer: Harry Sherman. Director: Lesley Selander. Screenplay: Harrison Jacobs & John Rathmell. Photography: Russell Harlan. Editor: Sherman A. Rose. Music: Phil Ohman. Music Director: Boris Morros. Song: Foster G. Carling & Phil Ohman. Art Director: Lewis J. Rachmil. Sound: William Wilmarth. Wardrobe: Earl Moser. Props: Henry Donovan. Assistant Directors: D.M. [Derwin] Abrahams & Theodore Joos.

Cast: William Boyd (Hopalong Cassidy), George Hayes (Windy Halliday), Russell Hayden (Lucky Jenkins), Charlotte Wynters (Mary Joyce), Russell Hopton (Bob "Smoky" Joslin), Roy Barcroft (Stiff Hat Bailey), John Merton (Tex Traynor), Sonny Bupp (Joey Joyce), Eddie Dean (Red), The King's Men [Ken Darby, Rad Robinson, Bud Linn, Jon Dodson] (Singers), Jack Rockwell (Slim Baker), Robert Kortman (Haskins), John Wallace (Cookie), Leo J. McMahon (Cattle Prodder), Blackjack Ward, Cliff Lyons (Gang Members).

Working title: *Arizona Bracelets*.

Range War (Paramount, 1939, 65 minutes) Producer: Harry Sherman. Director: Lesley Selander. Screenplay: Sam Robins. Additional Dialogue: Walter Roberts. Story: Josef Montiague. Photography: Russell Harlan. Editor: Sherman A. Rose. Music: Victor Young. Art Director: Lewis J. Rachmil. Sound: Earl Sitar. Wardrobe: Earl Moser. Props: Henry Donovan. Assistant Director: D.M. [Derwin] Abrahams.

Cast: William Boyd (Hopalong Cassidy), Russell Hayden (Lucky Jenkins), Britt Wood (Speedy McGinnis), Pedro De Cordoba (Padre Jose), Willard Robertson (Buck Collins), Matt Moore (Jim Marlow), Betty Moran (Ellen Marlow), Kenneth Harlan (Charles Higgins), Francis McDonald (Dave Morgan), Don Latorre (Felipe), Glenn Strange (Sheriff), Earle Hodgins (Deputy Sheriff Fenton), Stanley Price (Agitator), Jason Robards, Wen Wright (Ranchers), Eddie Dean (Pete), Raphael [Ray] Bennett (Stokey), George Chesebro (Gang Member), Rad Robinson (Cowboy), Tom Smith (Railroad Worker), Herman Hack, George Morrell, Pascale Perry (Citizen).

Working title: *Lawful Outlaws*.

Law of the Pampas (Paramount, 1939, 72 minutes) Producer: Harry Sherman. Associate Producer: Joseph W. Engel. Director: Nate Watt. Screenplay: Harrison Jacobs. Photography: Russell Harlan. Editor: Carrol Lewis. Supervising Editor: Sherman A. Rose. Music:

Victor Young. Art Director: Lewis J. Rachmil. Sound: Earl Sitar. Wardrobe: Earl Moser. Assistant Director: D.M. [Derwin] Abrahams.

Cast: William Boyd (Hopalong Cassidy), Russell Hayden (Lucky Jenkins), Sidney Toler (Don Fernando Ramirez), Steffi Duna (Chiquita), Sidney Blackmer (Ralph Merritt), Pedro De Cordoba (Jose Valdez), William Duncan (Buck Peters), Anna Demetrio (Dolores Ramirez), Eddie Dean (Curly Naples), Glenn Strange (Slim Schultz), Jojo La Sadio (Ernesto "Tito" Valdez), The King's Men [Ken Darby, Rad Robinson, Bud Linn, Jon Dodson] (Singers), Johnny Luther, Roy Brent, George Sowards (Gang Members), Tony Roux (Gaucho), Martin Garralaga (Gaucho with Bolo), Herman Hack, George Plues, Tex Phelps (Rodeo Onlookers), Jack Montgomery (Man Starting Fight).

Working title: *Argentina.*

Santa Fe Marshal (Paramount, 1940, 68 minutes) Producer: Harry Sherman. Associate Producer: Joseph W. Engel. Director: Lesley Selander. Screenplay: Harrison Jacobs. Photography: Russell Harlan. Editor: Sherman A. Rose. Music: Victor Young. Art Director: Lewis J. Rachmil. Sound: Charles Althouse. Wardrobe: Earl Moser. Props: Henry Donovan. Assistant Director: D.M. [Derwin] Abrahams.

Cast: William Boyd (Hopalong Cassidy), Russell Hayden (Lucky Jenkins), Marjorie Rambeau (Ma Burton), Bernadene Hayes (Paula Bates), Earle Hodgins (Doc Bates), Britt Wood (Axel), Kenneth Harlan (Blake), William Pagan (Flint), George Anderson (Tex Barnes), Jack Rockwell (John Gardner), Eddie Dean (Marshal), Fred Graham (Bartender Dan), Horace B. Carpenter (Sam), Frank Ellis (Onlooker), Robert McKenzie (Citizen), George Morrell (Man with Glasses), Cliff Parkinson, Duke Green, Billy Jones (Gang Member).

Working title: *Medicine Show.*

The Showdown (Paramount, 1940, 65 minutes) Producer: Harry Sherman. Director: Howard Bretherton. Screenplay: Harold Kusel & Donald Kusel. Story: Jack Jungmeyer. Photography: Russell Harlan. Editor: Carrol Lewis. Music: Foster G. Carling & John Leipold. Song: Foster G. Carling & Phil Ohman. Art Director: Lewis J. Rachmil. Sound: Charles Althouse. Wardrobe: Earl Moser. Props: Henry Donovan. Assistant Director: D.M. [Derwin] Abrahams.

Cast: William Boyd (Hopalong Cassidy), Russell Hayden (Lucky Jenkins), Britt Wood (Speedy McGinnis), Morris Anrkum (Baron Rendor), Jane [Jan] Clayton (Sue Willard), Wright Kramer (Colonel Rufe White), Donald Kirke (Harry Cole), Roy Barcroft (Bowman), Eddie Dean (Marshal), Kermit Maynard (Johnson), Walter Shumway (Snell), The King's Men [Ken Darby, Rad Robinson, Bud Linn, Jon Dodson] (Singers), Snub Pollard (Pianist), Eddy Chandler (Clerk), Murdock MacQuarrie (Zeke), George Morrell (Citizen), Jim Corey, Ray Jones (Saloon Customers).

Working title: *Gun Chores.*

Hidden Gold (Paramount, 1940, 60 minutes) Producer: Harry Sherman. Associate Producer: Joseph W. Engel. Screenplay: Gerald Geraghty & Jack Merserveau. Photography: Russell Harlan. Editor: Carrol Lewis. Music Director: Irvin Talbot. Art Director: Lewis J. Rachmil. Sound: Charles Althouse. Wardrobe: Earl Moser. Props: Harry Donovan. Assistant Director: D.M. [Derwin] Abrahams.

Cast: William Boyd (Hopalong Cassidy), Russell Hayden (Lucky Jenkins), Minor Watson (Ed Colby), Ruth Rogers (Jane Colby), Britt Wood (Speedy McGinnis), Ethel Wales (Matilda Purdy), Lee Phelps (Sheriff Cameron), Roy Barcroft (Hendricks), George Anderson (Ward Ackerman), Eddie Dean (Logan), Raphael [Ray] Bennett (Fleming), Jack Rockwell (Pete), Walter Long (Sanford), Robert Kortman, Cliff Parkinson, Art Dillard (Gang Members), Bruce Mitchell (Jim), Merrill McCormick (Citizen).

Working title: *Man from Bar-20.*

Stagecoach War (Paramount, 1940, 63 minutes) Producer: Harry Sherman. Associate Producer: Joseph W. Engel. Screenplay: Lesley Selander. Screenplay: Norman Houston & Harry F. Olmsted. Photography: Russell Harlan. Editor: Sherman A. Rose. Music: John Leipold. Songs: Foster G. Carling & Phil Ohman. Music Director: Irvin Talbot. Art Director: Lewis J. Rachmil. Sound: Charles Althouse. Wardrobe: Earl Moser. Props: Henry Donovan. Assistant Director: D.M. [Derwin] Abrahams.

Cast: William Boyd (Hopalong Cassidy), Russell Hayden (Lucky Jenkins), Julie Carter (Shirley Chapman), Harvey Stephens (Neal Holt), J. Farrell MacDonald (Jeff Chapman), Britt Wood (Speedy McGinnis), Rad Robinson (Smiley), Eddy Waller (Quince), Frank Lackteen (Maxwell), Jack Rockwell (Matt Gunther), Eddie Dean (Tom), The King's Men [Ken Darby, Bud Linn, Jon Dodson] (Singers), Robert Kortman (Campfire Outlaw), Rod Cameron, Johnny Luther, Frank Ellis, Merrill McCormick (Cowboys), Hank Bell, Denver Dixon, George Morrell, Victor Cox (Citizens), Tex Palmer, George Sowards (Gang Members).

Three Men from Texas (Paramount, 1940, 73 minutes) Producer: Harry Sherman. Associate Producer: Joseph W. Engel. Screenplay: Norton S. Parker. Photography: Russell Harlan. Editor: Carrol Lewis. Supervising Editor: Sherman A. Rose. Music: Victor Young. Art Director: Lewis J. Rachmil. Sound: Charles Althouse. Wardrobe: Earl Moser. Props: Henry Donovan. Assistant Director: D.M. [Derwin] Abrahams.

Cast: William Boyd (Hopalong Cassidy), Russell Hayden (Lucky Jenkins), Andy Clyde (California Carlson), Morris Ankrum (Bruce Morgan), Morgan Wallace (Captain Andrews), Thornton Edwards (Pico Serrano), Esther Estrella (Paquita Serrano), Davison Clark (Ed Thompson), Dick Curtis (Gardner), George Lollier (Dave), Glenn Strange (Ben Stokes), Neyl Marx [Neyle Morrow] (Juanito), Wen Wright (Button), Carlos De

Valdez (Don Ricardo Velez), Lucio Villegas (Ramon), Roy Butler (Sam), Frank Ellis (Randy), Cliff Parkinson (Stagecoach Driver), Michael Vallon (Mayor), Charles Murphy (Stagecoach Guard), John "Skins" Miller (Herman), George Morrell (Gambler), Jim Corey, Tex Phelps, Chuck Morrison, Herman Hack, Bill Nestell, Jack King, Ralph Bucko, Roy Bucko (Gang Members), Fred Burns, Bob Burns (Rancher), Frank McCarroll, Milburn Morante (Citizens).

British title: *Ranger Guns West*.

Doomed Caravan (Paramount, 1941, 62 minutes) Producer: Harry Sherman. Associate Producer: Joseph W. Engel. Director: Lesley Selander. Screenplay: J. Benton Cheney & Johnston McCulley. Photography: Russell Harlan. Editor: Carrol Lewis. Supervising Editor: Sherman A. Lowe. Music Directors: Irving Talbot & John Leipold. Art Director: Lewis J. Rachmil. Sound: Charles Althouse. Sets: Emile Kuri. Wardrobe: Earl Moser. Props: Henry Donovan. Assistant Director: D.M. [Derwin] Abrahams.

Cast: William Boyd (Hopalong Cassidy), Russell Hayden (Lucky Jenkins), Andy Clyde (California Carlson), Minna Gombell (Jane Travers), Morris Ankrum (Stephen Westcott), Georgia Hawkins (Diana Westcott), Trevor Bardette (Ed Martin), Pat J. O'Brien (Jim Ferber/Sergeant Spencer), Raphael [Ray] Bennett (Pete Gregg), Jose Luis Tortosa (Governor Don Pedro), Martin Garralaga (Frey Sebastian), Wen Wright (Cowboy), Fred Burns (Luke), Charles Murphy (Fiesta Guest), Art Dillard (Gang Member).

In Old Colorado (Paramount, 1941, 66 minutes) Producer: Harry Sherman. Associate Producer: Joseph W. Engel. Director: Howard Bretherton. Screenplay: Norton S. Parker & J. Benton Cheney. Photography: Russell Harlan. Editor: Carrol Lewis. Music Director: Irvin Talbot. Art Director: Lewis J. Rachmil. Sound: Charles Althouse. Sets: Emile Kuri. Wardrobe: Earl Moser. Props: Henry Donovan. Assistant Director: D.M. [Derwin] Abrahams.

Cast: William Boyd (Hopalong Cassidy), Russell Hayden (Lucky Jenkins), Andy Clyde (California Carlson), Margaret Hayes (Myra Woods), Morris Ankrum (Joe Weiler), Sarah Padden (Harriet "Ma" Woods), Cliff Nazarro (Nosey Haskins), Stanley Andrews (George Davidson), James Seay (Hank Merritt), Morgan Wallace (Sheriff Jack Collins), Weldon Heyburn (Blackie Reed), Eddy Waller (Jim Stark), John Beach, Wen Wright (Cowboys), Ted Wells (Bill), Philip Van Zandt (Shell Game Crook), Bill Nestell (Blacksmith), Henry Wills (Jim), Curley Dresden, Denver Dixon (Gang Members).

Working titles: *Bullets and Bandits* and *Cattle Train*.

Border Vigilantes (Paramount, 1941, 63 minutes) Producer: Harry Sherman. Associate Producer: Joseph W. Engel. Director: Derwin Abrahams. Screenplay: J. Benton Cheney. Photography: Russell Harlan. Editor: Robert Warwick. Supervising Editor: Sherman A. Lowe. Music Directors: Irvin Talbot & John Leipold. Song: Sam Coslow & Pauline Bouchard. Art Director: Lewis J. Rachmil. Sound: Charles Althouse. Assistant Director: Frederick Spencer.

Cast: William Boyd (Hopalong Cassidy), Russell Hayden (Lucky Jenkins), Andy Clyde (California Carlson), Frances Gifford (Helen Forbes), Victor Jory (Henry Logan), Ethel Wales (Aunt Jennifer Forbes), Morris Ankrum (Dan Forbes), Tom Tyler (Yager), Hal Taliaferro [Wally Wales] (Big Ed Stone), Jack Rockwell (Hank Weaver), Britt Wood (Lafe Willis), Edward Earle (Stevens), Wen Wright (Frank), John Beach, Johnny Luther, Ted Wells, Lem Sowards, Herman Howlin, Joe Garcia, Chuck Morrison (Gang Members), Curley Dresden, Fox Callahan (Bank Guards), Hank Bell (Stable Owner), Al Haskell, Tex Cooper (Card Players), Hank Worden (Wagon Driver), Henry Wills (Cowboy), Arthur Thalasso (Bartender), Jess Cavin (Saloon Customer), Charles Murphy, George Sowards (Vigilantes).

Pirates on Horseback (Paramount, 1941, 66 minutes) Producer: Harry Sherman. Associate Producer: Joseph W. Engel. Director: Lesley Selander. Screenplay: Ethel La Blanche & J. Benton Cheney. Photography: Russell Harlan. Editor: Carrol Lewis. Supervising Editor: Sherman A. Lowe. Music: John Leipold & Maurice Lawrence. Art Director: Lewis J. Rachmil. Sound: Charles Althouse. Wardrobe: Earl Moser. Sets: Emile Kuri. Props: Henry Donovan. Assistant Director: Frederick Spencer.

Cast: William Boyd (Hopalong Cassidy), Russell Hayden (Lucky Jenkins), Andy Clyde (California Carlson), Eleanor Stewart (Trudy Pendleton), Morris Ankrum (Ace Gibson), William Haade (Bill Watson), Dennis Moore (Jud Carter), Henry Hall (Sheriff John Blake), Britt Wood (Ben Pendleton), Jack Rockwell (Stable Owner), Chief Thundercloud (Flying Cloud), Bruce Mitchell (Bartender), Wen Wright, Henry Wills, George Sowards (Gang Members), Chuck Morrison (Tall Cowboy), Tom Smith (Card Player), Ray Henderson, Tex Harper, Silver Tip Baker (Saloon Customers).

Wide Open Town (Paramount, 1941, 79 minutes) Producer: Harry Sherman. Associate Producer: Lewis J. Rachmil. Director: Lesley Selander. Screenplay: J. Benton Cheney & Harrison Jacobs, from the novel *Hopalong Cassidy Returns* by Clarence E. Mulford. Photography: Russell Harlan. Editor: Carrol Lewis. Supervising Editor: Sherman A. Rose. Music Director: Irvin Talbot & John Leipold. Art Director: Ralph Berger. Sound: Charles Althouse. Sets: Emile Kuri. Wardrobe: Earl Moser. Props: Henry Donovan. Assistant Director: Frederick Spencer.

Cast: William Boyd (Hopalong Cassidy), Russell Hayden (Lucky Jenkins), Andy Clyde (California Carlson), Evelyn Brent (Belle Langtry), Victor Jory (Steve Fraser), Morris Ankrum (Jim Stuart), Bernice Kay [Cara Williams] (Joan Stuart), Kenneth Harlan (Tom Wilson), Roy Barcroft (Red), Glenn Strange (Ed Stark), Ed Cassidy (Reed Jackson), Jack Rockwell (Rancher),

George Cleveland (Pete Carter), Frank Darien (Pop), Robert Kortman (Blackie), Wen Wright (Spike), Lee Shumway (Bartender Sandy), Chuck Morrison (Joe), Ethan Laidlaw (Waiter), Edward Brady, Hank Bell (Citizens).

Working titles: *Men of action* and *Law Comes to Gunsight*.

Riders of the Timberlane (Paramount, 1941, 59 minutes) Producer: Harry Sherman. Associate Producer: Lewis J. Rachmil. Director: Lesley Selander. Screenplay: J. Benton Cheney. Photography: Russell Harlan. Editor: Fred Feitshans, Jr. Supervising Editor: Sherman A. Lowe. Music: John Leipold. Music Director: Irvin Talbot. Song: Grace Hamilton & Jack Stern. Art Director: Ralph Berger. Sound: Charles Althouse. Sets: Emile Kuri. Wardrobe: Earl Moser. Assistant Director: Glenn Cook.

Cast: William Boyd (Hopalong Cassidy), Andy Clyde (California Carlson), Brad King (Johnny Nelson), Victor Jory (Baptiste Deschamp), Eleanor Stewart (Elaine Kerrigan), J. Farrell MacDonald (Jim Kerrigan), Anna Q. Nilsson (Donna Ryan), Tom Tyler (Bill Slade), Edward Keane (Preston Yates), Hal Taliaferro [Wally Wales] (Ed Petrie), Mickey Eissa (Foreman Larry), The Guardsmen Quartet (Singing Loggers), Frank Miller, Herman Hack, Hank Bell, Tex Phelps (Loggers), Tex Cooper (Saloon Customer).

Working title: *Timber Wolves*.

Stick to Your Guns (Paramount, 1941, 63 minutes) Producer: Harry Sherman. Associate Producer: Lewis J. Rachmil. Director: Lesley Selander. Screenplay: J. Benton Cheney. Photography: Russell Harlan. Editor: Carrol Lewis. Supervising Editor: Sherman A. Rose. Music: John Leipold. Songs: Smiley Burnette, Ralph Freed, Frank Loesser, Jimmy McHugh, Sam H. Stept & Jimmy Wakely. Music Director: Irvin Talbot. Art Director: Ralph Berger. Sound: Charles Althouse. Sets: Emile Kuri. Wardrobe: Earl Moser. Assistant Director: Glenn Cook.

Cast: William Boyd (Hopalong Cassidy), Andy Clyde (California Carlson/California Jack), Brad King (Johnny Nelson), Jacqueline [Jennifer] Holt (June Winters), Dick Curtis (Nevada Teale), Weldon Heyburn (Gila), Henry Hall (Jud Winters), Jack Rockwell (Carp), Ian MacDonald (Elbows), Kermit Maynard (Layton), Charles Middleton (Long Ben), Joe Whitehead (Buck Peters), Jack C. Smith (Tex), Jack Trent (Red), Homer Holcomb (Lanky Smith), Tom London (Waffles), Tom Ung (Chinese Charlie), Mickey Eissa (Ed), The Jimmy Wakely Trio [Jimmy Wakely, Johnny Bond, Dick Reinhart] (Singing Cowboys), Bob Card (Frenchy), Robert Kortman (Concho), Frank Ellis (Duby), Frank Mills (Bartender), Robert Barron (Saloon Customer), Herman Hack, Charles Murphy, Lew Morphy, Roy Bucko (Gang Members), Silver Tip Baker (Citizen).

Twilight on the Trail (Paramount, 1941, 57 minutes) Producer: Harry Sherman. Associate Producer: Lewis J. Rachmil. Director: Howard Bretherton. Screenplay: J. Benton Cheney, Ellen Corby & Cecile Kramer. Editor: Fred Feitshans, Jr. Supervising Editor: Sherman A. Rose. Music: John Leipold. Songs: Louis Alter, Johnny Bond, Sidney D. Mitchell, Ralph Rainger & Leo Robin. Music Director: Irvin Talbot. Art Director: Ralph Berger. Sound: Charles Althouse. Sets: Emile Kuri. Wardrobe: Earl Moser. Assistant Director: Glenn Cook.

Cast: William Boyd (Hopalong Cassidy), Andy Clyde (California Carlson), Brad King (Johnny Nelson), Wanda McKay (Lucy Brent), Jack Rockwell (Jim Brent), Norman Willis (Nat Kervy), Robert Kent (Ash Drake), Tom London (Tim Gregg), Frank Austin (Steve Farley), The Jimmy Wakely Trio [Jimmy Wakely, Johnny Bond, Dick Reinhart] (Singing Cowboys), Robert Kortman (Guard), Hal Taliaferro [Wally Wales], Kermit Maynard, Jim Corey (Cowboys), Frank Ellis (Charlie), Bud Osborne, Herman Hack (Gang Members), Clem Fuller (Stagecoach Driver), John Powers (Passenger).

Outlaws of the Desert (Paramount, 1941, 66 minutes) Producer: Harry Sherman. Associate Producer: Lewis J. Rachmil. Director: Howard Bretherton. Screenplay: J. Benton Cheney & Bernard McConville. Photography: Russell Harlan. Editor: Carrol Lewis. Supervising Editor: Sherman A. Lowe. Music: John Leipold. Music Director: Irvin Talbot. Art Director: Ralph Berger. Sound: Charles Althouse. Sets: Emile Kuri. Wardrobe: Earl Moser. Assistant Director: Glenn Cook.

Cast: William Boyd (Hopalong Cassidy), Andy Clyde (California Carlson), Brad King (Johnny Nelson), Duncan Renaldo (Sheik Suleiman), Jean Phillips (Susan Grant), Forrest Stanley (Charles Grant), Nina Guilbert (Jane Grant), Luli Deste (Marie Karitza), Alberto Morin (Nicki Karitza), George J. Lewis (Yussuf), Jean Del Val (Faran El Kaer), Jamiel Hasson (Ali), Mickey Eissa (Salim), George Woolsey (Major Crawford), Ted Wells, Charles Murphy (Cowboys), Bill Nestell (Waukegan Man).

Working titles: *The Sheik of Buffalo Butte*.

Secret of the Wastelands (Paramount, 1941, 66 minutes) Producer: Harry Sherman. Associate Producer: Lewis J. Rachmil. Director: Derwin Abrahams. Screenplay: Gerald Geraghty, from the novel by Bliss Lomax. Photography: Russell Harlan. Editor: Fred Feitshans, Jr. Supervising Editor: Sherman A. Lowe. Music: John Leipold. Song: Jack Scholl & Phil Boutelje. Music Director: Irvin Talbot. Art Director: Ralph Berger. Sound: Charles Althouse. Sets; Emile Kuri. Wardrobe: Earl Moser. Assistant Director: John Sherwood.

Cast: William Boyd (Hopalong Cassidy), Andy Clyde (California Carlson), Brad King (Johnny Nelson), Soo Young (May Soong), Barbara Britton (Jennifer Kendall), Douglas Fowley (Slade Salters), Keith Richards (Clay Elliott), Richard Loo (Quan), Lee Tung Foo (Doy Kee), Gordon Hart (Dr. Malcolm Birdsall), Earl Gunn (Clanton), Ian MacDonald (Hollister), John

Rawlins (Williams), Roland Got (Yeng), Hal Price (Professor Balto Stubbs), Jack Rockwell (Sheriff Mulhall), Bill Nestell (Dealer), Charles Murphy (Gang Member).

Working title: *Ghosts of Rimrock*.

Undercover Man (United Artists, 1942, 64 minutes) Producer: Harry Sherman. Associate Producer: Lewis J. Rachmil. Director: Lesley Selander. Screenplay: J. Benton Cheney. Photography: Russell Harlan. Editor: Carrol Lewis. Supervising Editor: Sherman A. Lowe. Music Director: Irvin Talbot. Art Director: Ralph Berger. Sound: L.J. Meyer. Sets: Emile Kuri. Wardrobe: Earl Moser. Assistant Director: Glenn Cook.

Cast: William Boyd (Hopalong Cassidy), Andy Clyde (California Carlson), Jay Kirby (Breezy Travers), Antonio Moreno (Commandante Don Tomas Gonzales), Nora Lane (Dona Louise Saunders), Chris-Pin Martin (Miguel), Esther Estrella (Dolores Gonzales), John Vosper (Deputy Sheriff Ed Carson/Idaho Pete Jackson), Eva Puig (Rosita Lopez), Alan Baldwin (Bob Saunders), Jack Rockwell (Captain John Hawkins), Pierce Lyden (Bart), Tony Roux (Chavez), Earle Hodgins (Sheriff Blackford), Ted Wells (Jim Wilson), Cliff Parkinson (Rancher Cook), Martin Garralaga (Cortez), Frank Ellis (Gang Member), Ben Corbett (Ambusher), George Sowards, Lem Sowards (Cowboys), Joe Dominguez (Caballero).

Lost Canyon (United Artists, 1942, 62 minutes) Producer: Harry Sherman. Associate Producer: Lewis J. Rachmil. Director: Lesley Selander. Screenplay: Harry O. Hoyt, from the novel *Rustlers' Valley* by Clarence E. Mulford. Photography: Russell Harlan. Editor: Carrol Lewis. Song: Frank Loesser & Joseph J. Lilley. Music Director: Irvin Talbot. Art Director: Ralph Berger. Sound: William Wilmarth. Sets: Emile Kuri. Wardrobe: Earl Moser. Assistant Director: Glenn Cook.

Cast: William Boyd (Hopalong Cassidy), Andy Clyde (California Carlson), Jay Kirby (Johnny Travers), Lola Lane (Laura Clark), Doug [Douglas] Fowley (Jeff Burton), Herbert Rawlinson (Tom Clark), Guy Usher (Zack Rogers), Karl Hackett (Wade Haskell), Hugh Prosser (Sheriff Jim Stanton), Robert Kortman (Joe), The Sportsmen [Bill Days, John Rang, Thurl Ravenscroft, Max Smith] (Singing Cowboys), Gertrude Astor (Mrs. Anson), Henry Wills (Henry), Bill Nestell (Deputy Sheriff), Si Jenks (Square Dance Caller), Alieth Hansen (Banjo Player), Spade Cooley (Fiddle Player), Cliff Parkinson (Sniper), John L. Cason, Merrill McCormick (Gang Members), Milburn Morante, Herman Hack, Jack Evans, Dorothy Vernon, George Morrell, Charles Murphy (Citizens), Frank Mills (Customer), Lee J. Cobb, Ted Adams, Al Ferguson (Outlaws in Cabin).

Hoppy Serves a Writ (United Artists, 1943, 67 minutes) Producer: Harry Sherman. Associate Producer: Lewis J. Rachmil. Director: George Archainbaud. Screenplay: Gerald Geraghty, from the novel by Clarence E. Mulford. Photography: Russell Harlan. Editor: Sherman A. Rose. Music Director: Irvin Talbot. Art Director: Ralph Berger. Sound: William Wilmarth. Sets: Emile Kuri. Wardrobe: Earl Moser. Assistant Director: Glenn Cook.

Cast: William Boyd (Hopalong Cassidy), Andy Clyde (California Carlson), Jay Kirby (Johnny Travers), Victor Jory (Tom Jordan), George Reeves (Steve Jordan), Jan Christy (Jean Hollister), Hal Taliaferro [Wally Wales] (Greg Jordan), Forbes Murray (Ben Hollister), Bob [Robert] Mitchum (Rigney), Byron Foulger (Mr. Danvers), Earle Hodgins (Jim Belman), Roy Barcroft (Tod Colby), Herman Hack (Gang Member), Steve Clark, Ben Corbett, Bob Burns (Card Players), Cliff Parkinson (Guard), Roy Bucko (Rider).

Working title: *Texas Law*.

Border Patrol (United Artists, 1943, 65 minutes) Producer: Harry Sherman. Associate Producer: Lewis J. Rachmil. Director: Lesley Selander. Screenplay: Michael Wilson. Photography: Russell Harlan. Editor: Sherman A. Rose. Music Director: Irvin Talbot. Art Director: Ralph Berger. Sound: William Wilmarth. Sets: Emile Kuri. Wardrobe: Earl Moser. Assistant Director: Glenn Cook.

Cast: William Boyd (Hopalong Cassidy), Andy Clyde (California Carlson), Jay Kirby (Johnny Travers), Russell Simpson (Orestes Krebs), Claudia Drake (Inez LaBarca), George Reeves (Don Enrique Perez), Duncan Renaldo (Commandant LaBarca), Pierce Lyden (Loren), Bob [Robert] Mitchum (Quinn), Cliff Parkinson (Barton), Herman Hack (Turner), Dan White (Martin), Robert Kortman, Bill Nestell (Guards), Earle Hodgins (Cook), Hugh Prosser (Mine Boss), Henry Wills, Leo J. McMahon, Charles Murphy (Cowboys), Merrill McCormick, Denver Dixon (Miners), Roy Bucko (Wagon Driver).

Working title: *Missing Men*.

Leather Burners (United Artists, 1943, 66 minutes) Producer: Harry Sherman. Associate Producer: Lewis J. Rachmil. Director: Joseph E. Henaberry. Screenplay: Jo Pagano, from the novel by Bliss Lomax. Photography: Russell Harlan. Editor: Carrol Lewis. Music: Samuel Kaylin. Music Director: Irvin Talbot. Art Director: Ralph Berger. Sound: William Wilmarth. Sets: Emile Kuri. Wardrobe: Earl Moser. Assistant Director: Glenn Cook.

Cast: William Boyd (Hopalong Cassidy), Andy Clyde (California Carlson), Jay Kirby (Johnny Travers), Victor Jory (Dan Slack), George Givot (Sam Bucktoe), Shelley Spencer (Sharon Longstreet), Bobby Larson (Bobby Longstreet), George Reeves (Harrison Brooke), Hal Taliaferro [Wally Wales] (Lafe), Forbes Murray (Bart Healy), Bob [Robert] Mitchum (Randall), Christian Rub (Snooky Withers), Robert Kortman (Blackie), Cal Shrum (Sheriff Martin), Herman Hack (Jim), Bill Nestell (Bartender), Bob Burns, Merrill McCormick, Jack Casey (Ranchers), George Morrell, Kit Guard (Citizens), Art Mix (Posse Member).

Colt Comrades (United Artists, 1943, 65 minutes) Producer: Harry Sherman. Associate Producer: Lewis J. Rachmil. Director: Lesley Selander. Screenplay: Michael Wilson, from the novel by Bliss Lomax. Photography: Russell Harlan. Editor: Fred W. Berger. Music Director: Irvin Talbot. Art Director: Ralph Berger. Production Manager: Dick Johnston. Sound: Jack Noyes. Sets: Emile Kuri. Wardrobe: Earl Moser. Assistant Director: Glenn Cook.

Cast: William Boyd (Hopalong Cassidy), Andy Clyde (California Carlson), Jay Kirby (Johnny Travers), Lois Sherman (Lucy Whitlock), Victor Jory (Jeb Hardin), George Reeves (Lin Whitlock), Douglas Fowley (Joe Brass), Herbert Rawlinson (Varney), Earle Hodgins (Wildcat Willie), Bob [Robert] Mitchum (Dirk Mason), Jack Mulhall (Postmaster), Russell Simpson (Sheriff), Dewey Robinson (Bartender Sam), Art Dillard (Red), William Gould, Jack Shannon, Cliff Lyons, Bill Wolfe (Ranchers), Fred Kohler, Jr., Henry Wills, Blackjack Ward, Jim Corey, Ralph Bucko, Roy Bucko (Vigilantes), Tex Phelps (Checker), George Sowards (Rider), Tex Cooper (Saloon Customer), George Plues (Gang Member).

Bar 20 (United Artists, 1943, 55 minutes) Producer: Harry Sherman. Associate Producer: Lewis J. Rachmil. Director: Lesley Selander. Screenplay: Norman Houston, Morton Grant & Michael Wilson, from the novel by Clarence E. Mulford. Photography: Russell Harlan. Editor: Carrol Lewis. Music Director: Irvin Talbot. Art Director: Ralph Berger. Sound: Jack Noyes. Sets: Emile Kuri. Wardrobe: Earl Moser. Assistant Director: Glenn Cook.

Cast: William Boyd (Hopalong Cassidy), Andy Clyde (California Carlson), George Reeves (Lin Bradley), Dustine Farnum (Marie Stevens), Victor Jory (Mark Jackson), Douglas Fowley (Slash), Betty Blythe (Mrs. Stevens), Bob [Robert] Mitchum (Richard Adams), Francis McDonald (Quirt Rankin), Earle Hodgins (Tom), Henry Wills, Roy Bucko (Gang Members).

Working title: *Bar 20 Three*.

False Colors (United Artists, 1943, 65 minutes) Producer: Harry Sherman. Associate Producer: Lewis J. Rachmil. Director: George Archainbaud. Screenplay: Bennett Cohen. Photography: Russell Harlan. Editor: Fred W. Berger & Carrol Lewis. Music Director: Irvin Talbot. Art Director: Ralph Berger. Sets: Emile Kuri. Wardrobe: Earl Moser. Assistant Director: Glenn Cook.

Cast: William Boyd (Hopalong Cassidy), Andy Clyde (California Carlson), Jimmy Rogers (Jimmy Rogers), Douglass Dumbrille (Mark Foster), Tom Seidel (Bud Lawton/Kit Moyer), Claudia Drake (Faith Lawton), Bob [Robert] Mitchum (Rip Austin), Glenn Strange (Sonora), Pierce Lyden (Lefty), Roy Barcroft (Sheriff Clem Martin), Sam Flint (Judge Stevens), Earle Hodgins (Jay Griffin), Elmer Jerome (Jed Stevers), Glen Walters (Tall Dancer), Tom London, Bob Burns, George Morrell, Franklyn Farnum, Denver Dixon (Citizens), Jack Montgomery (Gambler), Frank O'Connor (Party Guest), Dan White (Saloon Customer).

Riders of the Deadline (United Artists, 1943, 70 minutes) Producer: Harry Sherman. Associate Producer: Lewis J. Rachmil. Director: Lesley Selander. Screenplay: Bennett Cohen. Photography: Russell Harlan. Editors: Fred W. Berger & Walter Hannemann. Supervising Editor: Carrol Lewis. Music Director: Irvin Talbot. Art Director: Ralph Berger. Production Manager: Dick Johnston. Sound: Jack Noyes. Sets: Emile Kuri. Wardrobe: Earl Moser. Assistant Director: Glenn Cook.

Cast: William Boyd (Hopalong Cassidy), Andy Clyde (California Carlson), Jimmy Rogers (Jimmy Rogers), Frances Woodward (Sue Mason), William Harrigan (Simon Crandall), Bob [Robert] Mitchum (Nick Drago), Richard Crane (Tim Mason), Anthony Warde (Gunner Madigan), Hugh Prosser (Sheriff), Herbert Rawlinson (Captain Jennings), Jack Rockwell (Tex), Earle Hodgins (Sourdough), Monte Montana (Private Calhoun), Jim Bannon (Tex), Bill Beckford (Kilroy), Pierce Lyden (Sanders), Herman Hack, Art Felix (Gang Members), Robert Walker, Cliff Parkinson, Roy Bucko (Rangers).

Texas Masquerade (United Artists, 1944, 58 minutes) Producer: Harry Sherman. Associate Producer: Lewis J. Rachmil. Director: George Archainbaud. Screenplay: Norman Houston & Jack Lait, Jr. Photography: Russell Harlan. Editor: Walter Hannemann. Supervising Editor: Carrol Lewis. Music Director: Irvin Talbot. Art Director: Ralph Berger. Sound: Jack Noyes. Sets: Emile Kuri. Wardrobe: Earl Moser. Assistant Director: Glenn Cook.

Cast: William Boyd (Hopalong Cassidy), Andy Clyde (California Carlson), Jimmy Rogers (Jimmy Rogers), Don Costello (Ace Maxson), Mady Correll (Virginia Curtis), Francis McDonald (Sam Nolan), Russell Simpson (J.K. Trimble), J. Farrell MacDonald (John Martindale), Nelson Leigh (James Corwin), Robert McKenzie (Marshall Rowbottom), June Terry Pickrell (Emma Martindale), Pierce Lyden (Al), Bill Hunter (Deputy Lou Sykes), John Merton (Jeff), Snub Pollard (Waiter), George Morrell (Piano Player), Bob Burns (Saloon Customer), Ralph Bucko, Roy Bucko (Gang Members).

Lumberjack (United Artists, 1944, 65 minutes) Producer: Harry Sherman. Associate Producer: Lewis J. Rachmil. Director: Lesley Selander. Screenplay: Barry Shipman & Norman Houston. Photography: Russell Harlan. Editor: Fred W. Berger. Supervising Editor: Carrol Lewis. Song: Ozie Waters & Forrest Johnson. Music Director: Irvin Talbot. Art Director: Ralph Berger. Sound: Jack Noyes. Sets: Emile Kuri. Wardrobe: Earl Moser. Assistant Director: Glenn Cook.

Cast: William Boyd (Hopalong Cassidy), Andy Clyde (California Carlson), Jimmy Rogers (Jimmy Rogers), Douglass Dumbrille (Daniel J. Keefer), Ellen

Hall (Julie Jordan), Francis McDonald (Clyde Fenwick), Ethel Wales (Aunt Abby Peters), Hal Taliaferro [Wally Wales] (Taggart), Charles Morton (Big Joe Williams), Herbert Rawlinson (Buck Peters), Frances Morris (Mrs. Williams), John Whitney (Ben Jordan), Jack Rockwell (Sheriff Miles), Henry Wills (Slade), Bob Burns (Justice of the Peace), Earle Hodgins (Parson), Pierce Lyden (Gang Member), Bill Nestell (Thug), Hank Worden (Logger).

Working title: *Timber*.

Mystery Man (United Artists, 1944, 58 minutes) Producer: Harry Sherman. Associate Producer: Lewis J. Rachmil. Director: George Archainbaud. Screenplay: J. Benton Cheney. Photography: Russell Harlan. Editors: Fred W. Berger & Carrol Lewis. Song: Ozie Waters & Forrest Johnson. Music Director: Irvin Talbot. Art Director: Ralph Berger. Sound: Jack Noyes. Sets: Emile Kuri. Wardrobe: Earl Moser. Assistant Director: Glenn Cook.

Cast: William Boyd (Hopalong Cassidy), Andy Clyde (California Carlson), Jimmy Rogers (Jimmy Rogers), Don Costello (Bud Trilling), Eleanor Stewart (Diane Newhall), Francis McDonald (Bert Rogan), Forrest Taylor (Sheriff Sam Newhall), Jack Rockwell (Marshal Ted Blane), John Merton (Bill), Pierce Lyden (Ted), Bob Burns (Tom Hanlon), Ozie Waters (Tex), Bob Baker (Cowboy), Bill Nestell (Larry), Lew Meehan (Deputy Sheriff), Hank Bell (Deputy Sheriff Ed), Art Mix (Robber), George Morrell (Citizen), Herman Hack, Henry Wills, Lew Morphy (Gang Members), Bill Hunter (Joe).

Working title: *Thundering Hoofs*.

Forty Thieves (United Artists, 1944, 61 minutes) Producer: Harry Sherman. Associate Producer: Lewis J. Rachmil. Director: Lesley Selander. Screenplay: Michael Wilson & Bernie Kamins. Photography: Russell Harlan. Editor: Carrol Lewis. Music: Mort Glickman. Music Director: David Chudnow. Art Director: Ralph Berger. Sound: Jack Noyes & William H. Lynch. Sets: Emile Kuri. Wardrobe: Earl Moser. Props: Henry Donovan. Special Effects: Mario Castegnaro. Assistant Director: George Tobin.

Cast: William Boyd (Hopalong Cassidy), Andy Clyde (California Carlson), Jimmy Rogers (Jimmy Rogers), Douglass Dumbrille (Tad Hammond), Louise Currie (Katherine Reynolds), Kirk Alyn (Jerry Doyle), Herbert Rawlinson (Buck Peters), Robert Frazer (Judge Reynolds), Glenn Strange (Ike Simmons), Hal Taliaferro [Wally Wales] (Jess Clanton), Jack Rockwell (Sam Garms), Robert Kortman (Joe Garms), Earle Hodgins (Tipsy Voter), Bill Nestell (Bartender), Herman Hack, Richard Botiller, Tex Harper (Gang Members), Lew Morphy, George Sowards (Gamblers), Hank Worden (Buckboard Driver), Denver Dixon (Citizen).

The Devil's Playground (United Artists, 1946, 65 minutes) Producer: Lewis J. Rachmil. Director: George Archainbaud. Screenplay: Ted Wilson. Photography: Mack Stengler. Editor: Fred W. Berger. Music: David Chudnow. Art Director: Harvey T. Gillett. Sound: Frank Hansen. Sets: George Mitchell. Wardrobe: Earl Moser. Assistant Director: George Tobin.

Cast: William Boyd (Hopalong Cassidy), Andy Clyde (California Carlson), Rand Brooks (Lucky Jenkins), Elaine Riley (Lucy Evans), Robert Elliott (Judge Jack Morton), Joseph J. Greene (Sheriff Porky), Francis McDonald (Roberts), Ned [Nedrick] Young (Curly Evans), Earle Hodgins (Deputy Dan'l), George Eldredge (U.S. Marshal), Everett Shields (Wolfe), John George (Shorty), Dewey Robinson (Deputy Sheriff Ed Garrity), Herman Hack (Gang Member), Jack Evans, Blackie Whiteford (Saloon Customers), Henry Wills (Wagon Driver), Merrill McCormick (Rider), Hank Bell (Gambler), Tex Cooper (Citizen).

Fool's Gold (United Artists, 1947, 63 minutes) Producer: Lewis J. Rachmil. Director: George Archainbaud. Screenplay: Doris Schroeder. Photography: Mack Stengler. Editor: Fred W. Berger. Music: David Chudnow. Production Design: Harvey T. Gillett. Sound: Harry Lindgren. Sets: George Mitchell. Wardrobe: Earl Moser. Assistant Director: George Tobin.

Cast: William Boyd (Hopalong Cassidy), Andy Clyde (California Carlson), Rand Brooks (Lucky Jenkins), Jane Randolph (Jessie Dixon), Robert Emmett Keane (Professor Dixon), Stephen Barclay (Bruce Landy), Harry Cording (Duke), Earle Hodgins (Sandler), Bob Bentley (Barton), Wee Willie Davis (Blackie), Forbes Murray (Colonel Jed Landy), Glen Gallagher (Lieutenant Anderson), Ben Corbett (Sergeant), Fred "Snowflake" Toones (Speed), Johnny Luther, George Sowards (Cowboys).

Working title: *Twin Buttes*.

Unexpected Guest (United Artists, 1947, 61 minutes) Producer: Lewis J. Rachmil. Director: George Archainbaud. Screenplay: Ande Lamb. Photography: Mack Stengler. Editor: Fred W. Berger. Music: David Chudnow. Art Director: Harvey T. Gillett. Sound: Frank Hansen. Sets: George Mitchell. Wardrobe: Earl Moser. Assistant Director: George Tobin.

Cast: William Boyd (Hopalong Cassidy), Andy Clyde (California Carlson), Rand Brooks (Lucky Jenkins), Una O'Connor (Mathilda Hackett), John Parrish (David J. Potter), Patricia Tate (Ruth Baxter), Ned [Nedrick] Young (Ralph Baxter), Earle Hodgins (Joshua Colter), Joel Friedkin (Phineas Phipps), Robert B. Williams (Matt Ogden), William Ruhl (Sheriff).

Working title: *Whispering Walls*.

Dangerous Venture (United Artists, 1947, 59 minutes) Producer: Lewis J. Rachmil. Director: George Archainbaud. Screenplay: Doris Schroeder. Photography: Mack Stengler. Editor: Fred W. Berger. Music: David Chudnow. Art Director: Harvey T. Gillett. Sound: Frank Hansen. Sets: George Mitchell. Wardrobe: Earl Moser. Assistant Director: George Tobin.

Cast: William Boyd (Hopalong Cassidy), Andy Clyde (California Carlson), Rand Brooks (Lucky Jenkins), Fritz Leiber (Chief Xeoli), Douglas Evans (Dr. Grimes Atwood), Harry Cording (Dan Morgan), Betty Alexander (Dr. Sue Harmon), Francis McDonald (Bill Kane), Neyle Morrow (Jose), Patricia Tate (Talu), Bob Faust (Stark), Ken [Kenneth] Tobey (Red), Jack Quinn (Marshal), Bill Nestell (Pete).

The Marauders (United Artists, 1947, 63 minutes) Producer: Lewis J. Rachmil. Executive Producer: William Boyd. Director: George Archainbaud. Screenplay: Charles Belden. Photography: Mack Stengler. Editor: Fred W. Berger. Music: David Chudnow & Paul Sawtell. Art Director: McClure Capps. Sound: Max Hutchinson. Sets: George Mitchell. Assistant Director: George Templeton.

Cast: William Boyd (Hopalong Cassidy), Andy Clyde (California Carlson), Rand Brooks (Lucky Jenkins), Ian Wolfe (Edwin "Deacon" Black), Dorinda Clifton (Susan Crowell), Mary Newton (Mrs. Crowell), Harry Cording (Riker), Earle Hodgins (Tom Connell), Dick Bailey (Driller), Richard Alexander (Smitty), Herman Hack (Gang Member).

TV title: *King of the Range*.

Silent Conflict (United Artists, 1948, 61 minutes) Producer: Lewis J. Rachmil. Executive Producer: William Boyd. Director: George Archainbaud. Screenplay: Charles Belden. Photography: Mack Stengler. Editor: Fred W. Berger. Music: Darrell Calker. Art Director: Jerome Pycha, Jr. Sound: Frank McWhorter. Sets: George Mitchell. Wardrobe: Earl Moser. Assistant Director: William D. Faralla.

Cast: William Boyd (Hopalong Cassidy), Andy Clyde (California Carlson), Rand Brooks (Lucky Jenkins), Virginia Belmont (Rene Richards), Earle Hodgins (Doc Richards), James Harrison (Speed Blaney), Forbes Murray (Randall), John Butler (Clerk), Herbert Rawlinson (Yardman), Richard Alexander, Don Haggerty, Leo J. McMahon (Ranchers), George Magrill (Bartender).

Working title: *Without Honor*.

Hoppy's Holiday (United Artists, 1948, 60 minutes) Producer: Lewis J. Rachmil. Executive Producer: William Boyd. Director: George Archainbaud. Screenplay: J. Benton Cheney, Bennett Cohen & Ande Lamb. Story: Ellen Corby & Cecile Kramer. Photography: Mack Stengler. Editor: Fred W. Berger. Music: David Chudnow. Art Director: Harvey T. Gillett. Sound: Frank Hansen. Sets: George Mitchell. Wardrobe: Earl Moser. Assistant Director: George Tobin.

Cast: William Boyd (Hopalong Cassidy), Andy Clyde (California Carlson), Rand Brooks (Lucky Jenkins), Andrew Tombes (Mayor Frank Patton), Leonard Penn (Dunning), Jeff Corey (Jed), Mary Ware (Gloria Patton), Donald Kirke (Sheriff), Hollis [Holly] Bane (Ace), Gil Patric (Hill), Frank Henry (Bart), Johnny Luther (Fiddler), Ben Corbett, Jack Evans, Jack Montgomery, Bob Burns, Rube Dalroy, Kansas Moehring, Tex Cooper, Denver Dixon, Roy Bucko (Citizens), Glen Walters (Tall Woman).

The Dead Don't Dream (United Artists, 1948, 62 minutes) Producer: Lewis J. Rachmil. Executive Producer: William Boyd. Director: George Archainbaud. Screenplay: Francis Rosenwald. Photography: Mack Stengler. Editor: Fred W. Berger. Music: Darrell Calker. Art Director: Jerome Pycha, Jr. Sound: Frank McWhorter. Sets: George Mitchell. Wardrobe: Earl Moser. Assistant Director: William D. Faralla.

Cast: William Boyd (Hopalong Cassidy), Andy Clyde (California Carlson), Rand Brooks (Lucky Jenkins), John Parrish (Jeff Potter), Leonard Penn (Earl Wesson), Mary Tucker (Mary Benton), Francis McDonald (Bart Lansing), Richard Alexander (Duke), Bob Gabriel (Larry Potter), Stanley Andrews (Jesse Williams), Forbes Murray (Sheriff Thompson), Don Haggerty (Second Sheriff).

Working title: *Coward's Castle*.

Sinister Journey (United Artists, 1948, 59 minutes) Producer: Lewis J. Rachmil. Executive Producer: William Boyd. Director: George Archainbaud. Screenplay: Doris Schroeder. Photography: Mack Stengler. Editor: Fred W. Berger. Music: Darrell Calker. Art Director: Jerome Pycha, Jr. Sound: Tom Lambert. Sets: George Sawley. Wardrobe: Earl Moser. Assistant Director: William D. Faralla.

Cast: William Boyd (Hopalong Cassidy), Andy Clyde (California Carlson), Rand Brooks (Lucky Jenkins), Elaine Riley (Jessie Garvin), John Kellogg (Lee Garvin), Don Haggerty (Harmon Roberts), Stanley Andrews (Tom Smith), Harry Strang (Banks), John Butler (Storekeeper), Herbert Rawlinson (Marshal Reardon), Will Orlean (Ben Watts), Wayne C. Treadway, Snub Pollard (Engineers).

Alternate title: *Two Gun Territory*; Working title: *The Railroad Story*.

Borrowed Trouble (United Artists, 1948, 59 minutes) Producer: Lewis J. Rachmil. Executive Producer: William Boyd. Director: George Archainbaud. Screenplay: Charles Belden. Photography: Mack Stengler. Editor: Fred W. Berger. Music: Darrell Calker. Art Director: Jerome Pycha, Jr. Sound: Tom Lambert. Sets: George Sawley. Wardrobe: Earl Moser. Assistant Director: William D. Faralla.

Cast: William Boyd (Hopalong Cassidy), Andy Clyde (California Carlson), Rand Brooks (Lucky Jenkins), Anne O'Neal (Miss Abbott), John Parrish (Steve Mawson), Cliff Clark (Dink Davis), Helen Chapman (Lola Blair), Earle Hodgins (Sheriff), Herbert Rawlinson (Mr. Groves), Don Haggerty (Lippy), James Harrison (Rocks), Clarke Stevens, George Sowards (Gang Members), Eilene Janssen, Nancy Stowe, Jimmy Crane, Bill O'Leary, Norman Ollestad, Jr. (School Children), Byron Foulger (Bartender Mike), Herman Hack, Al Thompson (Saloon Customers).

False Paradise (United Artists, 1948, 59 minutes) Producer: Lewis J. Rachmil. Executive Producer: William Boyd. Director: George Archainbaud. Screenplay: Harrison Jacobs. Photography: Mack Stengler.

Editor: Fred W. Berger. Music: Ralph Stanley [Raoul Kraushaar]. Art Director: Jerome Pycha, Jr. Sound: Earl Sitar. Sets: George Sawley. Wardrobe: Earl Moser. Assistant Director: William D. Faralla.

Cast: William Boyd (Hopalong Cassidy), Andy Clyde (California Carlson), Rand Brooks (Lucky Jenkins), Elaine Riley (Anne Larson), Cliff Clark (Gerald Waite), Joel Friedkin (Professor Alonzo Larson), Kenneth MacDonald (Bentley), Don Haggerty (Deal), George Eldredge (Mr. Radley), Richard Alexander (Buck), Zon Murray (Sam), William Norton Bailey (Miner).

Strange Gamble (United Artists, 1948, 61 minutes) Producer: Lewis J. Rachmil. Executive Producer: William Boyd. Director: George Archainbaud. Screenplay: Doris Schroeder, Bennett Cohen & Ande Lamb. Photography: Mack Stengler. Editor: Fred W. Berger. Music: Ralph Stanley [Raoul Kraushaar]. Art Director: Jerome Pycha, Jr. Sound: Earl Sitar. Sets: George Sawley. Wardrobe: Earl Moser. Makeup: Philip Scheer. Assistant Director: William D. Faralla.

Cast: William Boyd (Hopalong Cassidy), Andy Clyde (California Carlson), Rand Brooks (Lucky Jenkins), Elaine Riley (Nora Murray), James Craven (Mordigan), Robert B. Williams (Pete Walters), Alberto Morin (Ramon De Lara), Joel Friedkin (Doc White), Herbert Rawlinson (John Murray), Francis McDonald (Longhorn), William F. Leicester (Sid Murray), Joan Barton (Mary Murray), Lee Tung Foo (Wong), Dewey Robinson (Bartender Joe), George Sowards (Gang Member).

Les Nouvelles Aventures d'Hopalong Cassidy (The New Adventures of Hopalong Cassidy) (Ibis Films, 1952, 75 minutes) Producer: Toby August. Executive Producer: William Boyd. Director: George Archainbaud. Screenplay: Cecile Kramer & Eric Freiwald. Music: Dave Kahn.

Episodes:

"OUTLAW'S REWARD"

Cast: William Boyd (Hopalong Cassidy), Edgar Buchanan (Red Connors), Elaine Riley (Nancy Mathews), William Haade (Al), Denver Pyle (Vic James), John Alvin (Frank Scott), Harlan Warde (Dr. Glenn Scott).

"THE JINX WAGON"

Cast: William Boyd (Hopalong Cassidy), Edgar Buchanan (Red Connors), Myron Healey (Rick Bayless), Thurston Hall (Dan Clemens), Kathleen Case (Ginny Clemens), Steve Conte (Lait), Paul E. Burns (Sandy Morgan), Michael Thomas (Jeff Clemens).

UNKNOWN TITLE

Cast: William Boyd (Hopalong Cassidy), Edgar Buchanan (Red Connors).

Belgian title: *De Nieuwe Avonturen von Hopalong Cassidy* (The New Adventures of Hopalong Cassidy).

THE IRISH COWBOYS

Producer Ron Ormond signed a deal with Lippert Pictures in 1949 to produce two dozen program westerns through 1954, a half dozen a year. To star in these features, Ormond teamed former "Hopalong Cassidy" (q.v.) alumnus James Ellison and Russell Hayden with genre veterans Raymond Hatton and Fuzzy Knight as their sidekicks. Like Anne Jeffreys in Republic's "Wild Bill Elliott" (q.v.) series, Betty [Julie] Adams played the leading lady and each feature had a supporting cast of familiar faces such as Tom Tyler, George J. Lewis, Dennis Moore, John Cason, Stanley Price, George Chesebro, Bud Osborne and Jimmie Martin. The series was so cheap that it could not compete in the dying "B" western theatrical market and lasted for only six 1950 releases.

Today "The Irish Cowboys" series is not held in high regard. One of the main reasons is that the films were shot simultaneously over a brief period with all the various sequences, such as ranch, saloon, outdoor riding, fights, etc., being filmed at the same time using the same costumes, with the six features then pieced together, often using chunks of footage from older productions. Each feature began and ended with the four leads riding side by side although the scripts varied from film to film as to how they interacted with each other. The two main stars were billed as Jimmie "Shamrock" Ellison and Russ "Lucky" Hayden and while the latter wore traditional cowboy garb, Ellison was outfitted in a buckskin suit similar to the one he wore in Cecil B. DeMille's *The Plainsman* (1936). Needless to say, the same crews were used on each picture, all of them directed by Thomas Carr, with Ron Ormond collaborating with Maurice Tombragel on the scripts (the majority of "The Irish Cowboys" were remakes). In all the films, the leading lady was named Ann.

Hostile Country, released late in March 1950, opened the series; it was a remake of the 1935 Bob Steele starrer *No Man's Range*. Its somewhat complicated story had Shamrock Ellison (Ellison) and his pal Lucky Hayden (Hayden) trying to find Shamrock's stepfather Henry Oliver (George Chesebro) in order to get his half of the family ranch left to him by his late mother. Meeting rancher Ann Green (Adams) and her foreman, Deacon Hall (Knight), they get work at Colonel Pat Higgins' (Hatton) ranch. Oliver's men have shut off a pass which the other ranchers need to drive their cattle to market; the Brady brothers, Tom (Tom Tyler) and Ed (John L. Cason), try to enlist more gunman to keep the pass closed. After being ordered off the Oliver ranch, Shamrock and Lucky go to town where they get into a poker game. When another player (George J. Lewis) is caught cheating, he pulls a gun on Shamrock and is shot by Lucky. The man is identified as Henry Oliver. The two cowboys get out of town and are hidden from the sheriff (Stanley Price) by the Brady brothers, who force them to join their gang. When government envoy Lane (J. Farrell MacDonald) offers to purchase Ann's horses, Higgins and Deacon attempt to open up the pass but are stopped by the Bradys and their thugs. Shamrock and Lucky halt the gunfight. At the Oliver ranch, Shamrock finds his stepfather who says he was held prisoner by the Brady brothers who want his spread. As Shamrock and Oliver are being forced to dig their graves, Lucky comes to their rescue. Lucky and Shamrock dynamite the blockage at the pass, letting Ann's herd get through. They then enlist the aid of the sheriff and capture the Brady boys. After Ann is paid for the horses, Shamrock and Lucky disagree as to which one of the two she should wed. *Variety* thought it "an okay addition to the Saturday matinee market, featuring a lot of riding, shooting and horseplay."

The second series outing, *Marshal of Heldorado*, came out in April 1950; it too was a remake of an earlier Bob Steele western, *The Rider of the Law* (1935). Despite its title, the film took place in Apache, Arizona, where bank owner the Colonel (Hatton) gives the job of sheriff to buffalo hunter Lucky (Hayden) because the mayor (Knight) cannot keep the office filled due to the lawless element. Easterner Shamrock Ellis (Ellison), a dude riding a mule, also arrives in town and rents Lucky's cabin where he sees brothers Doc (Dennis Moore) and Jake Tulliver (John L. Cason) shoot each other over hidden loot. Shamrock tells Lucky to take the credit for killing the brothers as the stolen money is returned to the Colonel whose daughter Ann (Adams) makes Shamrock a deputy sheriff. While being shaved by barber Razor Tulliver (Stephen Carr), a brother of the dead men, Shamrock's identity as a federal marshal is revealed. While Ann has her father give Shamrock a job in his bank, the Colonel, who has embezzled money to aid local settlers, is warned of his identity by Razor. Another Tulliver sibling, Nate (George J. Lewis), tries to murder Shamrock, who gets the drop on him and kills the assailant. Razor then tells the Colonel to leave the bank's safe unlocked so he and another brother, Mike Tulliver (Tom Tyler), can rob it and get rid of Shamrock. Not wanting to be a part of the killing, the Colonel reveals the plan to Shamrock and the two join Lucky and Ann in fighting it out with the Tullivers and their men. Deputizing the town's barflies, Shamrock and Lucky capture the outlaws. With the money taken from them, the Colonel is able to pay off the settlers' mortgages.

The third series entry, *Crooked Creek*, came to theaters shortly after *Marshal of Heldorado* and while it was not a remake of a previous film it did contain quite a bit of stock footage from Bob Steele's mid–1930s westerns for Supreme Pictures. It reused the old plot devise of the hero out to avenge the murder of his family by an outlaw gang. It begins in 1860 with Shamrock Ellison (Ellison) witnessing the murder of his parents (George Chesebro, Helen Gibson) by the Gentry gang, who steal his father's initialed ring. The outlaws are after a gold shipment sent out by Deacon (Knight), who is promised by the local sheriff, the Colonel (Hatton), that it will get through safely. Also after the gold is outlaw Lucky (Hayden), who wants to raise enough money to send his sister Ann (Adams), who wants him to reform, to school in the east. After shooting Butch (Stephen Carr), one of the gang members, Shamrock is made a deputy by the sheriff (Stanley Price) and goes to Lucky's home where he meets Ann and Gentry (George J. Lewis). While Shamrock offers to aid the wounded Butch, Ann has to fend off the advances of another gang member, Kent (John L. Cason). Kent then tries to get Lucky's other men to go with Gentry and his gang and Ann rides to tell her brother. When Lucky sees Kent trying to molest Ann, he has lye thrown in his eyes; as Kent tries to shoot him, Shamrock intervenes. Seeing his father's ring on a shelf in the kitchen, Shamrock is told by Ann that it was a present from Kent. When Kent returns to Lucky's house after Ann, he is shot by Shamrock. The gang is captured by the sheriff and his posse, with Shamrock killing Gentry.

Colorado Ranger, the next "Irish Cowboys" affair, came out in May 1950; it was a remake of the 1934 Mascot serial *The Marines Are Coming*. After meeting at a saloon, gunman Shamrock (Ellison), Lucky (Hayden) and the Colonel (Hatton) flee approaching rangers and ride to Cactus Junction where the crooked sheriff (Stanley Price) makes them deputies and pays them to run off the last remaining settlers. Rancher Jim Morgan (Stephen Carr) wants all the land for himself and he controls the lawman. He also has been able to keep the homesteaders from claiming their land due to a dishonest survey he has commissioned. One of the remaining ranchers, Ann (Adams), meets with her friend Deacon (Knight) who tells her she cannot file on her land. In town, Shamrock, Lucky and the Colonel get into a fight with Loco Joe (John L. Cason) and his men and put them under arrest. Shamrock then rides to Ann's ranch where finds her tending a baby that she leaves with him when she rides to a rancher's meeting. As Lucky and the Colonel show up to help tend the infant, Ann finds out that the three men are in Morgan's pay and she returns home, disarms them and locks them in her cellar. Morgan gets Loco Joe and his boys out of jail and pays them to get rid of the settlers, only to be locked in a jail cell with the sheriff by the outlaws. When Joe and his gang ride to Ann's ranch, she manages to lock them in a bedroom and free Shamrock, Lucky and the Colonel. Shamrock goes to get Deacon but the settlers do not believe his story and chase him back to the ranch. Breaking out of the bedroom, Loco Joe wounds Lucky and tries to set fire to the ranch house but he is stopped by Shamrock, who then shows the settlers his Colorado Ranger credentials. Lucky and the Colonel also have papers showing they are rangers as the gang is subdued. Ann tells Shamrock that the baby belongs to her brother and the ranger promises to return to her.

In *West of the Brazos*, released early in June 1950, the character played by Hayden has lost his hearing due to cannon fire during the Civil War. The plot had Shamrock Ellison (Ellison) and Lucky X. Hayden (Hayden) riding to see the former's mother at her ranch near Brazos and being attacked by the Cyclone Kid (John L. Cason) and his gang. (They have mistaken Shamrock for Marshal Charlie Blythe [Stanley Price], who is on their trail.) The marshal, wounded in the shootout, makes Shamrock a deputy and says the gang is headed for Brazos. In order for the lawman to receive the reward for the capture of the gang, Shamrock assumes his identity, not knowing he is the heir to the ranch of his (Shamrock) mother, who died a few weeks before. Gang members Sam (Tom Tyler) and Ricco (Dennis Moore) rob a stagecoach and bring Cyclone a letter naming Ellison the heir to the spread that is wanted for lease by an oil company. Cyclone has already filed claim to the property using Ellison's name and orders

James Ellison as "Shamrock" in the "Irish Cowboys."

Sam and Ricco to shoot Shamrock but it is Ricco who is wounded. Having placed Marshal Blythe at Manuel's (George J. Lewis) sheep ranch to recover, Shamrock takes Ricco to Cyclone's spread and then goes to see Ann Green (Adams), an old friend who informs him of his mother's passing. She also tells him that someone identified as his brother has made a claim to the ranch. Cyclone announces to the Brazos sheriff, the Colonel (Hatton), that he shot outlaw Ricco. At a court hearing, Judge Deacon (Knight) is stopped from ruling on Cyclone's land claim by Shamrock, whose identity is verified by Ann and Lucky. When Cyclone accuses Shamrock of being the Cyclone Kid, the judge has him arrested but he and Lucky make an escape. The gang leader and Sam plan to murder Blythe. The two outlaws become members of the posse trailing Shamrock and Lucky but at Manuel's ranch, Blythe identifies the Cyclone Kid, who is beaten in a fight with Shamrock and is arrested along with Sam. By reading the couple's lips, Lucky informs the Colonel and Judge Deacon that Shamrock and Ann plan to get married.

The final "Irish Cowboys" movie, *Fast on the Draw*, came out at the end of June 1950, although like the rest of the films in the series it was not shown in some locales until much later. Like *Crooked River*, it opened with a young Shamrock witnessing the murder of his family, including his lawman father (George Chesebro), by outlaws; as a result, he grows up with a fear of guns. Years later, rodeo performer Shamrock (Ellison) and his pal Lucky (Hayden) stop a stagecoach holdup and take the vehicle into Mesa City, Arizona, where one of the passengers, Ann (Adams), urges her sheriff father, the Colonel (Hatton), to make them deputies. When the Colonel offers Shamrock the post of marshal of the town of Lawless, he refuses but later asks for time to think about it as Deacon (Knight), a friend of the lawman, holds the badge for him. The Colonel then informs Ann that Shamrock's father killed his brother. When a rock with a note attached and signed by "The Cat" orders Shamrock out of town, he agrees to take the marshal job on the condition that Lucky be made his deputy. The Cat orders his henchman Tex (John L. Cason) to murder Shamrock and Lucky as Ann informs Shamrock that her father no longer trusts him. When the Colonel finds out that Shamrock is seeing Ann he tries to shoot him, but the previously gun-shy Shamrock shoots the gun from his hand. When someone else tries to ambush Shamrock, he and Lucky learn that the express office is being robbed; they follow but lose the robbers. The two then form a posse and trail the gang to their hideout where Tex wants his share of the loot from the Cat. Shamrock arrives, shoots Tex and arrests the Cat, who turns out to be Deacon. With the gang under arrest and the express office gold recovered, the Colonel makes amends with Shamrock, who is no longer gun-shy. A remake of the 1935 Johnny Mack Brown starrer *Branded a Coward*, this film's plot had the novelty of one of the heroes turning out to be the villain.

At the time of the production of the "Irish Cowboy" series, stars Jimmy "Shamrock" Ellison and Russ "Lucky" Hayden, were billed under those names when they made a guest appearance as themselves in the 1950 Lippert release *Everybody's Dancin,'* a western musical starring Spade Cooley, who co-produced.

Following the demise of the Irish Cowboys, Ellison headlined two 1950 westerns, *I Killed Geronimo* and *The Texan Meets Calamity Jane*, before ending his screen career by co-starring with Johnny Mack Brown in a half-dozen series oaters released by Monogram in 1951–52. A guest at several western film conventions in the 1970s and 1980s, he died in 1993. Hayden briefly starred in ABC-TV's live western series *The Marshal of Gunsight Pass* in 1950 and then supported Gene Autry in two 1951 Columbia releases, *Texans Never Cry* and *Valley of Fire*, before producing a trio of syndicated television series, *Cowboy G-Men* (1952–53), in which he co-starred with Jackie Coogan; *Judge Roy Bean* (1955–57), where he played a Texas Ranger; and *26 Men* (1957–59). The series were filmed at his Pioneer Town Ranch, a 32,000 acre spread where many other films and TV series were lensed. His final screen credit was as one of the assistant directors on the Las Vegas–filmed *The Mummy and the Curse of the Jackal*, which was made in 1969 but not issued on video until 1985, four years after Hayden's death.

Series leading lady Adams (1926–) changed her name to Julie Adams and starred in features like *Bend of the River*, *Horizons West* and *The Lawless Breed* (all 1952), *The Man from the Alamo* (1953), *Creature from the Black Lagoon* (1954), *The*

Private War of Major Benson (1955), *Away All Boats* (1956), *The Gunfight at Dodge City* (1959), *Raymie* (1960), *The Underwater City* (1962), *The Valley of Mystery* (1967), *McQ* (1974), *The Killer Inside Me* (1976) and *The Fifth Floor* (1980). She also appeared in scores of TV series and co-starred on *The Jimmy Stewart Show* (NBC-TV, 1971–72).

Knight went on to appear in two more "B" western series before the genre succumbed to television in the early 1950s. Born J. Forrest Knight in West Virginia, Fuzzy Knight (1901–76) entered show business after graduating from the University of West Virginia. He worked in vaudeville and nightclubs before appearing on Broadway in 1927 and coming to Hollywood in the early 1930s. Of his many screen roles, he is probably best remembered for *The Trail of the Lonesome Pine* (1936) in which he sang "When It's Twilight on the Trail." His first western series sidekick part came in four 1937–38 Bob Baker features at Universal; at the same studio he co-starred with Johnny Mack Brown in 21 films between 1939 and 1942 and in seven more when Tex Ritter joined Brown in 1942–43. At Universal he also co-starred in series westerns with Tex Ritter, Russell Hayden, Rod Cameron, Eddie Dew and Kirby Grant and with the latter he did seven features in 1945–46. Following the "Irish Cowboys" outings he made eight films with Whip Wilson at Monogram in 1951–52 and four with Bill Elliott at the same studio in 1952–53. Knight was also well-known for the role of Fuzzy in the television series *Captain Gallant of the Foreign Legion* (NBC-TV, 1955–57).

Filmography

Hostile Country (Lippert, 1950, 59 minutes) Producer: Ron Ormond. Associate Producer: Ira Webb. Director: Thomas Carr. Screenplay: Ron Ormond & Maurice Tombragel. Photography: Ernest Miller. Editor: Hugh Winn. Music: Walter Greene. Art Director: Fred Preble. Sound: Glen Glenn & Harry Eckles. Special Effects: Ray Mercer. Sets: Theodore Offenbecker. Costumes: Bert Henrikson. Dialogue Director: Gloria Welsch. Assistant Director: F.O. Collings.

Cast: Jimmie "Shamrock" Ellison (Shamrock Ellison), Russ "Lucky" Hayden (Lucky Hayden), Raymond Hatton (Colonel Pat Higgins), Fuzzy Knight (Deacon Hall), Betty [Julie] Adams (Ann Green), Tom Tyler (Tom Brady), George J. Lewis (Jim Knowlton), John L. Cason (Ed Brady), Stanley Price (Sheriff), Dennis Moore (Pete), George Chesebro (Henry Oliver), Bud Osborne (Agate), Jimmie Martin (Fred), J. Farrell MacDonald (Lane), I. Stanford Jolley (Bartender), Cliff Taylor (Grandfather), Judith Webster (Marie), George Sowards (George), James Van Horn (Ranch Hand), Wally West (Deputy Sheriff), Carl Mathews, Ray Jones (Gamblers).

TV title: *Outlaw Fury*.

Marshal of Heldorado (Lippert, 1950, 63 minutes) Producer: Ron Ormond. Associate Producer: Ira Webb. Director: Thomas Carr. Screenplay: Ron Ormond & Maurice Tombragel. Photography: Ernest Miller. Editor: Hugh Winn. Music: Walter Greene. Art Director: Fred Preble. Sound: Glen Glenn & Harry Eckles. Special Effects: Ray Mercer. Sets: Theodore Offenbecker. Costumes: Bert Henrikson. Dialogue Director: Gloria Welsch. Assistant Director: F.O. Collings.

Cast: Jimmie "Shamrock" Ellison (Shamrock Ellison), Russ "Lucky" Hayden (Lucky Hayden), Raymond Hatton (The Colonel), Fuzzy Knight (Deacon), Betty [Julie] Adams (Ann), Tom Tyler (Mike Tulliver), George J. Lewis (Nate Tulliver), John L. Cason (Jake Tulliver), Stanley Price (Marshal), Stephen Carr (Razor Tulliver), Dennis Moore (Doc Tulliver), George Chesebro (Zeke Stanton), Bud Osborne (Brad), Jimmie Martin (Ben), Cliff Taylor (Doctor), Ned Roberts (Bartender Ned), Jack Hendricks (Zero), Wally West (Bagen), James Van Horn (Citizen), Carl Mathews, Jack Geddes (Saloon Customers).

Also called *Blazing Guns*.

Crooked River (Lippert, 1950, 58 minutes) Producer: Ron Ormond. Associate Producer: Ira Webb. Director: Thomas Carr. Screenplay: Ron Ormond & Maurice Tombragel. Photography: Ernest Miller. Editor: Hugh Winn. Music: Walter Greene. Art Director: Fred Preble. Sound: Glen Glenn & Harry Eckles. Special Effects: Ray Mercer. Sets: Theodore Offenbecker. Costumes: Bert Henrikson. Dialogue Director: Gloria Welsch. Assistant Director: F.O. Collings.

Cast: Jimmie "Shamrock" Ellison (Shamrock Ellison), Russ "Lucky" Hayden (Lucky), Raymond Hatton (The Colonel), Fuzzy Knight (Deacon), Betty [Julie] Adams (Ann), Tom Tyler (Weston), George J. Lewis (Gentry), John L. Cason (Kent), Stephen Carr (Butch), Stanley Price (Sheriff), Dennis Moore (Bob), George Chesebro (Dad Ellison), Bud Osborne (Stagecoach Driver Bud), Jimmie Martin (Dick), Cliff Taylor (Dr. E.J. Jones), Helen Gibson (Ma Ellison), Carl Mathews (Cherokee), George Sowards, Scoop Martin, Joe Phillips (Ranchers).

TV title: *The Last Bullet*.

Colorado Ranger (Lippert, 1950, 58 minutes) Producer: Ron Ormond. Associate Producer: Ira Webb. Director: Thomas Carr. Screenplay: Ron Ormond & Maurice Tombragel. Photography: Ernest Miller. Editor: Hugh Winn. Music: Walter Greene. Art Director: Fred Preble. Sound: Glen Glenn & Harry Eckles.

Special Effects: Ray Mercer. Sets: Theodore Offenbecker. Costumes: Bert Henrikson. Dialogue Director: Gloria Welsch. Assistant Director: F.O. Collings.

Cast: Jimmie "Shamrock" Ellison (Shamrock Ellison), Russ "Lucky" Hayden (Lucky Hayden), Raymond Hatton (The Colonel), Fuzzy Knight (Deacon), Betty [Julie] Adams (Ann), Tom Tyler (Pete), George J. Lewis (Tony), John L. Cason (Loco Joe), Stanley Price (Sheriff Bradley), Stephen Carr (Jim Morgan), Dennis Moore (Juan), George Chesebro (Jenkins), Bud Osborne (Regan), Jimmie Martin (Sandy), Gene Roth (Barber), I. Stanford Jolley (Bartender Charlie), Joseph Richards (Infant).

Also called *Guns of Justice*.

West of the Brazos (Lippert, 1950, 59 minutes) Producer: Ron Ormond. Associate Producer: Ira Webb. Director: Thomas Carr. Screenplay: Ron Ormond & Maurice Tombragel. Photography: Ernest Miller. Editor: Hugh Winn. Music: Walter Greene. Art Director: Fred Preble. Sound: Glen Glenn & Harry Eckles. Special Effects: Ray Mercer. Sets: Theodore Offenbecker. Costumes: Bert Henrikson. Dialogue Director: Gloria Welsch. Assistant Director: F.O. Collings.

Cast: Jimmie "Shamrock" Ellison (Shamrock Ellison), Russ "Lucky" Hayden (Lucky X. Hayden), Raymond Hatton (The Colonel), Fuzzy Knight (Judge Deacon), Betty [Julie] Adams (Ann Green), Tom Tyler (Sam), George J. Lewis (Manuel), John L. Cason (The Cyclone Kid), Stanley Price (Marshal Charlie Blythe), Stephen Carr (Rusty), Dennis Moore (Ricco), George Chesebro (Deputy Sheriff), Bud Osborne (Stagecoach Driver), Jimmie Martin (Joe), Gene Roth (Attorney Wagner), Judith Webster (Judy Gibson), Cliff Taylor (Doctor).

Also called *Rangeland Empire*.

Fast on the Draw (Lippert, 1950, 55 minutes) Producer: Ron Ormond. Associate Producer: Ira Webb. Director: Thomas Carr. Screenplay: Ron Ormond & Maurice Tombragel. Photography: Ernest Miller. Editor: Hugh Winn. Music: Walter Greene. Art Director: Fred Preble. Sound: Glen Glenn & Harry Eckles. Special Effects: Ray Mercer. Sets: Theodore Offenbecker. Costumes: Bert Henrikson. Dialogue Director: Gloria Welsch. Assistant Director: F.O. Collings.

Cast: Jimmie "Shamrock" Ellison (Shamrock Ellison), Russ "Lucky" Hayden (Lucky Hayden), Raymond Hatton (The Colonel), Fuzzy Knight (Deacon/The Cat), Betty [Julie] Adams (Ann), Tom Tyler (Gang Leader), George J. Lewis (Pedro), John L. Cason (Tex), Stanley Price (Carter), Dennis Moore (Dick), George Chesebro (Sam Ellison), Bud Osborne (Stagecoach Driver), Jimmie Martin, Carl Mathews, Scoop Martin, Bud Hooker, Joe Phillips (Gang Members), Helen Gibson (Ma Ellison), I. Stanford Jolley, Roy Butler (Bartenders), Ray Jones (Saloon Customer), George Plues (Stagecoach Driver), Cliff Taylor (Doctor), Judy Webster (Girl).

Also called *Sudden Death*.

JOHN PAUL REVERE

Republic Pictures was continually on the lookout for new Western stars and series and with some fanfare the studio initiated a search for the star of its planned new series on Texas Ranger John Paul Revere, also called Johnny Revere. Eventually Eddie Dew was signed to play the part and solid box office draw Smiley Burnette was added as his comedy sidekick. Despite all the hoopla, the series went nowhere with Dew withdrawing after only two outings to be briefly replaced by studio stalwart Bob Livingston. "John Paul Revere" is one of the least remembered of the Western film series of the 1940s.

A native of Washington state, Eddie Dew (1909–72) had been working in films since 1937, having appeared in some 70 feature films, mostly in bits although he had a supporting role in Republic's serial *King of the Texas Rangers* (1941) and the "B" Westerns *Sunset in Wyoming* (1941), *Shadows on the Range* (1942) and *King of the Cowboys* (1943). He had the physical build for the role of John Paul Revere and he was more than passable in both the acting and action departments. Unfortunately, the first series entry, *Beyond the Last Frontier* (1943), had a stodgy script and an attention-catching performance by villain Robert Mitchum, both of which tripped up Dew's chance at stardom.

Howard Bretherton (1896–1969) directed dozens of films in the sound era, specializing in Westerns. He helmed *Beyond the Last Frontier*, but it was hardly one of his best outings. It told of Texas Ranger John Paul Revere (Dew) becoming a member of the outlaw gang of Big Bill Hadley's (Harry Woods), whose headquarters is beyond Ranger jurisdiction in the Texas Panhandle.

Johnny lets Rangers Frog Millhouse (Burnette), Sarge Kincaid (Ernie Adams) and Major Cook (Charles Miller) know the gang plans to rob a stagecoach carrying medicine. In a nearby town, Sarge meets his son Steve (Richard Clarke) and the latter's pal, Trigger Dolan (Robert Mitchum), who does not approve of Sarge's desire for his son to join the Rangers. Trying to stop the stage robbery, Sarge is killed by Hadley, who persuades Dolan to join the Rangers to find out the identity of the informant in his gang. Kidnapping Steve, Hadley gives Dolan the new Ranger's identity papers and he is welcomed at the Ranger post as a new recruit. He soon tells Hadley that Johnny Revere is the informant but Frog and another ranger (Jack Kirk) stop Hadley from murdering Revere. When Johnny thwarts an attempt by Hadley's gang to smuggle guns, he covers up for Dolan's participation in the raid and ends up confined to quarters. Realizing that Revere tried to help him, Dolan tries to quit the gang but Hadley tells him he will kill Steve unless Dolan retrieves the wagons with the stolen guns. Dolan agrees to carry out the mission but when Frog arrives on the scene, Hadley knocks him out and leaves him in the burning barn where the gun wagons were housed. Dolan rescues Frog before rejoining the gang. Frog begs Revere and the Rangers to trail Hadley's gang and when Hadley spots them he accuses Dolan of a double cross. During the fight between the gang and outlaws, Dolan sides with the rangers and receives a flesh wound before the crooks are captured and Hadley is killed when a wagon falls on him. As a result of his good deeds, Dolan is backed by Revere and Frog when he enlists in the Rangers, and he is accepted.

Although *Beyond the Last Frontier* was intended to launch Eddie Dew's starring career, it instead started Robert Mitchum on his path to stardom. Mitchum had supporting roles in seven "Hopalong Cassidy" (q.v.) movies and had appeared in a few other films, but it was his flashy performance as the good-badman in *Beyond the Last Frontier* which impressed audiences and critics alike. Typical was the reviewer for *The Motion Picture Herald* which lauded his performance, saying it overshadowed that of Dew. When Mitchum signed an exclusive contract with RKO in 1944, his first assignment was to star in two Zane Grey westerns, *Nevada* (1944) and *West of the Pecos* (1945), before being launched as the star of "A" productions.

Hoping to breathe some life into its "John Paul Revere" series, Republic used the topical plot ploy of having cowgirls fighting outlaws on the range as part of the war effort in *Raiders of Sunset Pass* (1943), but even direction by serial expert John English could not help the situation. This time John Paul Revere (Dew) and Frog Millhouse, (Burnette) investigators for the Texas Cattle Commission, come to the aid of Dad Mathews (Charles Miller), whose herds are being rustled due to the lack of cowboys, since most of the latter have joined the military. Gang leader Henry Judson (LeRoy Mason) wants to put Mathews out of business and take over his contract selling cattle to the government. Since Mathews' daughter Betty (Jennifer Holt) is an expert rider, Revere suggests that she and her female friends band together and work as cowgirls, protecting the cattle herds and communicating with walkie-talkies; the young women's parents give permission with the stipulation they will not be hurt. Hudson hires gunman Tex Coburn (Kenne Duncan) to break up their operation. When one of the women (Maxine Doyle) is injured defending the cattle herd, Dad orders the other females back to their homes. At the same time, Johnny captures gang member Lefty Lewis (Roy Barcroft) who claims that Mathews is a former outlaw convicted of murder two decades before. Dad lets Lefty escape but later Frog overhears Lefty tell Judson he did the killing for which Mathews was convicted. The gang, however, captures Frog and stages another raid on the Mathews' cattle herd. Using a walkie-talkie, Frog contacts Betty and her cohorts who are riding with Revere in search of the outlaws. Finding the gang's hideout, Johnny sets Frog free and in a shootout Lefty is mortally wounded. Before dying he confesses to his crime, exonerating Dad Mathews. Judson and the gang are captured and Johnny and Frog get silver spurs from the cowgirls.

Following the making of *Raiders of Sunset Pass*, Dew's Republic contract was terminated and he went to Universal where he co-starred with Rod Cameron in a series of six solid Westerns for the 1944–45 season. He was replaced as Revere by Bob Livingston, who signed with Republic after having worked at PRC in its "Lone Rider" (q.v.) series. Burnette continued as Frog Millhouse.

The next series entry, *Pride of the Plains* (1944) was a definite improvement over the first two outings. Johnny Revere (Livingston), an inspector for the state game commission, and fellow inspector and veterinarian Frog Millhouse (Burnette) travel to Cherokee County to look into a series of wild horse stampedes. The stampedes have been caused by rancher Dan Hurley (Kenneth MacDonald) who wants to see the revocation of laws protecting wild horses so he can kill them and sell their meat. When another rancher, Bradford (Charles Miller), is advised by his foreman, Jasper Darwin (Budd Buster), to protect the wild horse herd, Hurley uses Darwin's trained horse Black Cloud to trample him, thus making it look like he was killed by a wild horse. Later Hurley paints Black Cloud white and uses him to kill Bradford, with the local sheriff, Kenny Revere (Steve Barclay), vowing to kill the animal. It was Kenny, the sweetheart of Joan (Nancy Gay), Bradford's daughter, who alerted Johnny (his brother) and Frog about the stampedes. Johnny gets proof that a captured stallion is innocent but Kenny demands a trial. Johnny and Frog take the horse into the hills for protection and Hurley hides the animal in his cabin. There Johnny realizes that Black Cloud has been painted and that he is the killer horse. When the sheriff arrives at the cabin, a fight ensues and Black Cloud tramples Hurley, proving the wild stallion's innocence. As Kenny and Joan announce they will be married, Johnny and Frog set the stallion free.

Pride of the Plains breathed new life into the Revere series; even better was *Beneath Western Skies* (1944). Johnny Revere (Bob Livingston) is now a for-hire lawman who comes to the town of Stokesville at the request of his former teacher, Carrie Stokes (Effie Laird). The town is plagued by a gang led by Bull Rinker (LeRoy Mason), who is secretly in league with banker Sam Webster (Frank Jaquet) in a scheme to run off all the citizens and take over the area. Also working with them is deputy Rod Barrow (Kenne Duncan), who works for sheriff Frog Millhouse (Burnette), whose nephew Tadpole (Joe Strauch, Jr.) is injured during one of the gang's raids. When Johnny arrives in town he is arrested for shooting gang member Hank (Bud Geary) who ambushed another outlaw wanting to quit the gang. Frog lets Johnny escape so he can join Rinker's gang but unknowingly gives away his identity to Barrow, who informs Bull. During a fight, Johnny is knocked out and gets amnesia and is then convinced by the gang that he really is an outlaw. When Frog tries to arrest Johnny, another fight ensues and Johnny regains his memory. Johnny and Frog then ride for town in order to stop Webster and Bull from taking over. After a brawl, the gang is arrested. Burnette wrote and performed the song "Travelin' Man" in the feature.

With *Beneath Western Skies*, the "John Paul Revere" series ended on a high note. Livingston and Burnette would partner for another 1944 Republic Western, *The Laramie Trail*, in which Livingston was Johnny Rapidas and Burnette continued his Frog Millhouse character. Continuing at Republic, Burnette then starred in four Sunset Carson oaters before heading to Columbia where he co-starred with Charles Starrett in the long-running "Durango Kid" (q.v.) series. Livingston would remain with Republic for another four years, appearing in both starring and supporting roles.

Eddie Dew did well in the oaters he made with Rod Cameron at Universal and after that he toured in *The Red Mill*. From 1950 into the late 1960s he played supporting roles in both movies and television but by the early 1950s he worked mainly as a director. As Edward Dew he directed feature films like *Naked Gun* (1956) and *Wings of Chance* (1961) but is best remembered for directing 32 episodes of the TV series *Sergeant Preston of the Yukon* between 1955 and 1957, as well as two religious series, *The Living Bible* in 1952 and *The Old Testament Scriptures* in 1958, the latter produced by the Lutheran Church.

Filmography

Beyond the Last Frontier (Republic, 1943, 60 minutes) Associate Producer: Louis Gray. Director: Howard Bretherton. Screenplay: Morton Grant & John K. Butler. Photography: Bud Thackery. Editor: Charles Craft. Music: Mort Glickman. Art Director: Russell Kimball. Set Decorator: Charles Thompson. Sound: Ed Borschell. Assistant Director: Derwin Abrahams.

Cast: Eddie Dew (John Paul Revere), Smiley Burnette (Frog Millhouse), Lorraine Miller (Susan

Cook), Bob [Robert] Mitchum (Trigger Dolan), Harry Woods (Big Bill Hadley), Ernie Adams (Sarge Kincaid), Richard Clarke (Steve Kincaid), Charles Miller (Major Cook), Kermit Maynard (Clyde Barton), Jack Kirk (Ranger Slade), Wheaton Chambers (Doctor), Ted Wells, Curley Dresden (Rangers), Art Dillard, Henry Wills, Cactus Mack, Al Taylor (Henchmen), Frank O'Connor (Bartender), Jack Rockwell (Rangers Recruiter), Post Park (Stagecoach Driver).

Raiders of Sunset Pass (Republic, 1943, 57 minutes) Associate Producer: Louis Gray. Director: John English. Screenplay: John K. Butler. Photography: John MacBurnie. Editor: Harry Keller. Music: Mort Glickman. Art Director: Russell Kimball. Sound: Edwin Borschell. Assistant Director: Joseph Dill.

Cast: Eddie Dew (John Paul Revere), Smiley Burnette (Frog Millhouse), Jennifer Holt (Betty Mathews), LeRoy Mason (Henry Judson), Roy Barcroft (Lefty Lewis/Dan Dowling), Charles Miller (Dad Mathews), Maxine Doyle (Sally Meehan), Mozelle Cravens (Carol), Nancy Worth (Janice Clark), Kenne Duncan (Tex Coburn), Jack Kirk (George Meehan), Budd Buster (Nevada Jones), Jack Rockwell (Sheriff Dale), Jack Ingram, Frank McCarroll, Al Taylor (Rustlers), Isabel La Mal, Dorothy Andre (Cowgirls), Fred Burns, Hank Bell, Kansas Moehring (Old Cowboys), George Byron, Larry Stewart.

Pride of the Plains (Republic, 1944, 55 minutes) Associate Producer: Louis Gray. Director: Wallace Fox. Screenplay: John K. Butler & Bob Williams. Story: Oliver Drake. Photography: John MacBurnie. Editor: Charles Craft. Music: Mort Glickman. Art Director: Fred Ritter. Set Decorator: Charles Thompson. Sound: Fred Stahl. Assistant Director: Art Siteman.

Cast: Bob Livingston (Johnny Revere), Smiley Burnette (Frog Millhouse), Nancy Gay (Joan Bradford), Stephen Barcley [Steve Barclay] (Kenny Revere), Kenneth MacDonald (Dan Hurley), Charles Miller (Grant Bradford), Kenne Duncan (Snyder), Jack Kirk (Steve Craig), Bud Geary (Gerard), Yakima Canutt (Bowman), Budd Buster (Jasper Darwin), Bud Osborne (Benson), Horace B. Carpenter (Citizen), Kansas Moehring (Henchman).

Beneath Western Skies (Republic, 1944, 56 minutes) Associate Producer: Louis Gray. Director: Spencer Gordon Bennet. Screenplay: Albert de Mond & Bob Williams. Story: Albert de Mond. Photography: Ernest Miller. Editor: Charles Craft. Song: Smiley Burnette. Sound: Richard Tyler. Assistant Director: Harry Knight.

Cast: Bob Livingston (Johnny Revere), Smiley Burnette (Frog Millhouse), Effie Laird (Carrie Stokes), Frank Jaquet (Samuel Webster), Tom London (Earl Phillips), Charles Miller (Lem Toller), Joe Strauch, Jr. (Tadpole Millhouse), LeRoy Mason (Bull Rinker), Kenne Duncan (Deputy Rod Barrow), Charles Dorety (Drunk), Jack Kirk (Wainwright), Bud Geary (Hank), Forrest Taylor (Doctor), Robert Kortman (Walker), Budd Buster (Boone), Jack Ingram, Marshall Reed, Bob Wilke, Tom Steele, Cliff Parkinson, Roy Bucko (Henchmen), Kansas Moehring (Deputy Sheriff), Jess Cavin, Horace B. Carpenter (Citizens).

LIGHTNING BILL CARSON

Tim McCoy signed with Sam Katzman's Victory Pictures in 1938 to star in the "Lightning Bill Carson" series of eight westerns. The star was paid $4,000 per film and the pictures themselves were budgeted at between $8,000 and $10,000 with domestic grosses of between $50,000 and $60,000 each. Usually filmed in three to five days, the features had indoor filming at the Monogram studios but were mostly outdoor affairs which gave McCoy an opportunity to use various disguises as his federal marshal character worked undercover. Ben Corbett, who had previously co-starred in the 1933–34 "Bud 'n Ben" series of shorts for Reliable, portrayed Carson's sidekick Magpie in seven of the eight releases after playing a gang member in the initial outing.

McCoy (1891–1978) was a Michigan native who moved to Wyoming and worked as a cowboy before service in World War I. After the war he became adjutant general of Wyoming and in 1922 he helped hire 500 Indians to appear in *The Covered Wagon* (1923), becoming their supervisor and translator. He also did trick riding in the film and this led to a supporting role in *The Thundering Herd* (1925) followed by a job as technical director of *The Vanishing American* (1926). In 1927 he was signed by MGM to star in a series of westerns supervised by David O. Selznick. He headlined 15 oaters for the studio between 1927 and 1929 with Joan Crawford as his leading lady in *Winners of the Wilderness* (1927) and *The Law of the Range* (1928). With the coming of sound, McCoy did a short for Fox, *A Night on the Range* (1929), and two Universal serials, *The Indians Are Coming* (1930) and *Heroes of the Flames* (1931), before signing with Columbia. Between 1931 and 1935, McCoy starred in 32 features for Columbia, all but eight of them westerns. During the 1935–36 theatrical season, McCoy headlined ten westerns for Puritan Pictures, the seventh being *Lightnin' Bill Carson* (1936).

Sam Newfield directed *Lightnin' Bill Carson*, which was released theatrically in the spring of 1936; it was co-produced by his brother, Sigmund Neufeld. Marshal Bill Carson (McCoy) is on the trail of outlaw Breed Hawkins (John Merton), who tried to kill him, and his partner, the Pecos Kid (Rex Lease). In San Jacinto, Hawkins plans a stagecoach holdup with Stack Stone (Karl Hackett), a hotel proprietor, and they get the Pecos Kid to join them. Pecos, whose brother is Silent Tom Rand (Harry Worth), warns his sibling that Carson is in the area and goes to Hawkins' hideout where Breed knocks him out for not joining in the robbery, which was thwarted by the sheriff (Jack Rockwell) and his posse. When he comes to, Pecos witnesses the murder of a deputy sheriff (Edmund Cobb) by Breed and escapes to his brother's place. Carson sees Pecos ride away from the hideout and after finding the lawman murdered, he rides to Rand's house and arrests Pecos, informing the two men that he knows they are brothers. Telling Stack he has arrested Hawkins, Carson is able to obtain a confession from the hotel man which exonerates Pecos. But before Carson can get to him, the sheriff and his men hang Pecos. Silent Tom Rand takes revenge by murdering the sheriff and his posse, but in a showdown with Carson he deliberately uses a gun without bullets and is killed by the lawman.

When McCoy signed with Victory Pictures to do the "Lightning Bill Carson" series, he helped formulate the character which producer Sam Katzman felt would appeal to the Saturday matinee crowd. Billed on-screen as Colonel Tim McCoy, he headlined the first series entry, *Lightning Carson Rides Again*, which was released in the fall of 1938. Sam Newfield returned to direct; he would helm all the series' eight outings. The film opens with Gannon (Ted Adams) and his gang ambushing Paul Smith (Bob Terry), a bank messenger, and his driver (Herman Hack), who is killed. As most of the gang trail Paul, who escapes on foot, henchman Shorty (Ben Corbett) retrieves the money. Paul's mother, Katherine Smith (Jane Keckley), wires her brother, Captain William

Advertisement for *Lightning Carson Rides Again* (Victory, 1938).

Carson (McCoy) of the Justice Department, asking him to help Paul. Giving up a planned fishing trip, Carson disguises himself as Jose Fernandez and attends a hearing on the robbery during which Gannon testifies that Paul murdered his driver and stole the bank's money; the sheriff (Frank LaRue) offers a $5,000 reward for Paul. Carson reveals his true identity to his sister and Smith's fiancée, Sally (Joan Barclay), and promises to get to the bottom of the matter. At a café run by Hogan (Slim Whitaker), Jose gambles with Gannon and his men and ends up beating Shorty in a fight and winging fellow gang member Jim (Reed Howes) in a shootout. Gannon then enlists Jose as a gang member and asks him to take the stolen bank money south of the border where it can be exchanged for different currency. Paul sends his mother a note saying he is going to California to try and clear his name and Carson writes to his assistant (James Flavin) asking him to keep his nephew undercover. When Sally smiles at Jose, Jim becomes suspicious and goes to the Smith ranch, where he finds Carson's horse and clothes. Jose joins Gannon and his gang in pulling off another robbery. When the gang members wait for their real boss, Jim shows up and accuses Jose of being Carson. The boss arrives and tries to kill the marshal but instead shoots Gannon. The sheriff and his men arrest the gang as Carson follows and captures the fleeing boss, who turns out to be bank clerk Ross (Frank Wayne). Although Carson is about to get a new assignment, he and Paul ride away for a fishing trip. McCoy first used his Mexican disguise in Puritan's *Border Caballero* (1936).

Six Gun Trail, issued in November 1938, introduced Ben Corbett in the role of Lightning Bill Carson's associate, Magpie. It also permitted McCoy to engage in another ethnic impersonation, this time as a Chinese. A band of outlaws pull off a big diamond heist, leaving one of their members, Joe Willis (Karl Hackett), after he is wounded. Captured by the law, Willis is forced into a confession by Captain William Carson (McCoy), who then heads to the border community of Edge Town with Magpie (Corbett). The outlaws are there trying to find someone to fence the gems and Carson meets with saloon singer Midge (Nora Lane), who is on parole thanks to the marshal. Midge is in love with the gang leader, Jim Wilson (Alden Chase), and when the outlaws see the two lawmen, there is a shootout with Tim and Magpie making a getaway. The gang captures Magpie who pretends to be a vagabond named Foolish; he tells them Carson was murdered by a Chinese. Disguised as Sam Sung, Carson arrives in town, engages Foolish as his servant, and opens an antique show, buying diamonds from Midge. In a poker game with the outlaws, Sam Sung wins all their money and they decide to use him as the fence for the stolen diamonds. When Wilson and his men arrive with the gems, Carson engages them in a shootout; he and Magpie capture the gang. Midge is injured during the fracas but Carson lets her go free.

Early in *Six Gun Trail*, Carson extracts a confession from outlaw Joe Willis by graphically describing the punishments the crook might suffer, details of hanging and the gas chamber, if he does not reveal the truth. This plot ploy was used earlier by McCoy's character in *Bulldog Courage* and again in the "Rough Riders" (q.v.) outing *The Gunman from Bodie* (1941). The feature also included two songs by Johnny Lange and Lew Porter, "Moon on the Prairie" and "When a Cowboy Sings a Lullaby." The former was sung by leading lady Nora Lane, while the second song was crooned by Hal Carey.

Another Lange-Porter dittie, "Across the Boundary Line," was sung by Art Davis in the series' next outing, *Code of the Cactus*, which came to theaters in February 1939. Davis would later co-star with McCoy in PRC's *Texas Marshal* (1941), also directed by Sam Newfield using the name Peter Stewart. In *Code of the Cactus* Davis had only a minor role as a singing outlaw in a modern-day tale of gangsters using semi-trucks and machine guns to rustle cattle. Carson (McCoy), who has lost a government packing contract to crook Blackston (Forrest Taylor), is enlisted by his pal Magpie (Corbett) and Joan (Dorothy Short) after their ranch has been raided. Carson masquerades as a Mexican named Miguel and finds out that Blackston's henchman Thurston (Ted Adams) and his gang are doing the rustling in order to supply cattle to meet their boss' contract. Carson steals several of the outlaws' trucks, forcing Thurston to make him a partner. Revealing his true identity to Magpie, Carson goes to his ranch where he meets Joan and range detective Bob Swane (Dave O'Brien), who he assigns to watch the gang's hideout. Ranch foreman James (Alden Chase) abducts Swane and, after Miguel stops the outlaws from raiding Magpie and Joan's place, James finds out the Mexican is really Carson. He goes to Thurston and, when Miguel shows up at the hideout, he is told that James informed the ranchers of the raid and that he should decide James' fate. Realizing his true identity is known by the gang, Carson shoots his way out of the hideout and takes Swane with him. Blackton then decides to run the gang himself and orders a blockade be built to stop the trucks that ranchers are using to take their cattle to market. With Carson's help, the ranchers break through the obstacle and the sheriff (Slim Whitaker) and his posse round up the rustlers. Bob and Joan decide to marry as Carson returns home to await another adventure.

In the fourth series entry, *Texas Wildcats*, released in the spring of 1939, Carson takes on the guise of a masked man called the Phantom, who robs shipments belonging to wealthy Jim Burrows (Forrest Taylor), the man who murdered his partner. Burrows posts a $5,000 reward for the capture of the masked man who is seen by Molly Arden (Joan Barclay). When Molly's brother Ed (Dave O'Brien) tries to shoot the Phantom, she stops him and the masked man rides away. In town, Carson pretends to be a gambler; when he exposes dealer Ace (Reed Howes) as a crook, he is hired by saloon owner Reno (Ted Adams) to run his games. Carson's lawman partner Magpie (Corbett), pretending to be a prospector, arrives in town as Barrows' son Mort (Bob Terry) tells his dad he believes Ed has found gold on his ranch and that they should foreclose on its mortgage. Mort goes to the Arden ranch and proposes to Molly, who rejects him. When the money the Ardens need to pay their mortgage arrives, Mort gets Ed drunk and tries to cheat him at cards but Carson refuses to deal. Ed is shot and robbed of his money. After he is taken home, the outlaws try to break into the Arden ranch house but are stopped by Carson. Burrows hires a detective, Durkin (Slim Whitaker), to rid the area of the Phantom and Carson overhears them plot to blame Reno for Ed's shooting and the robbery. They plant the money in Reno's office but Carson finds it, orders Durkin out of town, and hands the money over to Magpie to give to Burrows to pay off the Ardens' debts, saying it was given to him by the Phantom. Molly thinks the Phantom shot her brother and she accuses Carson of being the masked man; just as Burrows is about to have him arrested by his henchman Al (Frank Ellis), Magpie shows up and says the Phantom has kidnapped Ed. While Burrows and his men join Molly in trying to capture the Phantom, Carson tells Magpie that he believes Mort kidnapped Ed because of the gold on his land and that it was Mort who carried out the shooting and robbery. The two then ride to the gang's hideout where Carson corners Mort as Magpie holds off his cohorts. Burrows, who arrives with his men, accidentally shoots his son and then confesses to killing Carson's partner, with Ed overhearing. Overpowering Magpie, the outlaws are about to break into the hideout when Molly and the posse show up and they are arrested. Molly then apologizes to Carson for thinking he shot and robbed her brother. There were no songs in this outing; as with *Lightning Carson Rides Again*, the only score was canned music used during the chase sequences.

Outlaws' Paradise had McCoy in dual roles, Lightning Bill Carson and gunman Trigger Mallory. Mallory is about to be released from prison but is kept inside so his lookalike, Justice Department investigator Carson, can infiltrate his gang which has stolen negotiable bonds from the postal service. Taking on the guise of Mallory, Carson joins the outlaw gang and is welcomed by everyone except the wary Slim Marsh (Ted Adams). Carson also meets Mallory's girlfriend, Jessie (Joan Barclay), and she too falls for the ruse. Fellow agent Magpie (Corbett) comes to the area to warn Carson that Mallory has escaped from prison but is unable to find him since he is riding with the gang. When Bill slips away to contact his superiors, he is followed by Marsh; the two shoot it out with Carson forced to kill Slim. Mallory arrives in town and tells Jessie about Carson impersonating him; when he finds Magpie spying on them, Trigger imprisons him. Mallory then goes to the outlaws' headquarters to fight it out with Carson as Magpie escapes. Carson manages to get away from the gang after fighting with Trigger and he and Magpie meet and work out a plan to capture the outlaws. They successfully round up the crooks and Carson puts Trigger Mallory back behind bars.

Straight Shooter, released in August 1939, began with gang leader Ben Martin (George Morrell) being murdered by his cohorts who are after the $500,000 in stolen bonds they took during a train robbery. The killers, Brainard (Ted Adams), Slade (Reed Howes) and Luke Green (Forrest Taylor), search the dead man's ranch house and begin digging for the bonds when they are seen by Jack "Magpie" Benson (Corbett), who claims he is looking for a job. The trio throw Magpie off the ranch as FBI undercover agent Lightning Bill Carson (McCoy) comes upon Margaret Martin (Julie Sheldon) when her car's engine overheats. Carson uses the name Sudden Sam Brown and later comes to Margaret's aid when Green tries to scare her off the Martin ranch by telling her it is haunted. Since the ranch is going to be auctioned off to take care of overdue taxes, Tim, Margaret and Brainard all try to convince the sheriff (Budd Buster) to sell it to them but he refuses. The morning of the auction, Sam ties up Brainard and outbids Margaret and Luke for the property and then meets with Magpie, who tells him about the gang digging on the Martin spread. That night at the ranch house, Margaret informs Brown that she is Ben's niece and that he had written to her mother about the value of a portrait of himself. Slade spies on the two and reports back to Brainard, who offers to buy the ranch from Sam, who refuses to sell. Brainard orders Luke to steal the portrait but they find it not longer contains the information they need. Green accuses Brainard of double crossing him and he is murdered by Slade, with Sam being blamed for the killing. The sheriff arrests Brown but he escapes. The lawman goes to the Martin ranch and informs Margaret and Magpie that Sam Brown is wanted for murdering Luke Green. The sheriff leaves a deputy (Wally West) to watch the ranch; Brainard and his men show up, dry gulch the deputy and tie him up, and then try to force Magpie and Margaret to hand over the paper giving the location of the bonds. To protect Margaret, Magpie gives Brainard the paper and he admits that he and his men stole the bonds. Carson, who has freed the deputy, gets the drop on the crooks and reveals his true identity. He says he found the bonds under the ranch house floor and sent them to Washington D.C. After Brainard and his men are arrested, Carson romantically offers Margaret half interest in the ranch. *Variety* complained, "Action fans won't find much to cheer about in this one. Little effort and limited finances are very evident. It plods through a story that's vague and uninteresting, building little suspense, and the emoting of the entire cast leaves plenty to be desired." The reviewer also noted the "flock of footage devoted to chases.... [A]t one point the camera swings back and forth between three lone riders converging on one point so many times it seems to go on forever."

A little more than two weeks after the release of *Straight Shooter*, *Fighting Renegade*, the series' penultimate effort, was in theaters. It featured a title song, "Men of the Prairie," but the rest of the music in the feature was canned and reserved for action sequences. This time Carson (McCoy) is disguised as Mexican cowboy El Puma, who has been hired to help convoy an archaeological expedition in search of Indian treasure. The group is being led by Professor Lucius Lloyd (Forrest Taylor) and Marian Willis (Joyce Bryant), whose father was allegedly killed by Carson on an expedition six years before. The duo are using Marian's father's diary which gives the location of the treasure with a map. Also on the expedition are Old Dobie (Budd Buster), who claims El Puma cannot be trusted, and government man Magpie (Corbett), who stands up for the Mexican, and Marian's fiancé, Dr. Jerry Leonard (Dave O'Brien), who is jealous of El Puma. Upon his arrival, El Puma argues with Professor Lloyd and leaves but is recognized by Magpie as Carson. He tells Magpie he believes Marian's father was murdered by expedition foreman Link Benson (Ted Adams) but he needs proof. Professor Lloyd is killed by Old Dobie, who steals the diary and places the blame on El Puma. He offers the diary to Benson, who plans to abduct Margaret, the only one on the expedition who can decipher the Indian script in which the diary is written. Getting greedier, Old Dobie then offers the map to El Puma, telling him about the kidnap plot against Margaret. El Puma gets to Margaret first and steals her away but sets her free after she informs him that the map gives the treasure's location in Broken Mesa. Old Dobie then rides to tell Benson as Marian and Magpie go for the sheriff (Reed Howes). Carson and Benson fight it out at Black Mesa with Carson putting the expedition foreman under arrest as Old Dobie admits he killed Professor Lloyd.

The final series entry, *Trigger Fingers*, issued in November, 1939, gave McCoy the opportunity to use still another disguise, that of a gypsy. The story told of a series of raids and cattle rustling by the Lawson County Gang, with a $5,000 reward being offered for the band. When the outlaws rob rancher Jim Bolton (John Elliott), one of the gang members, Johnson (Kenne Duncan), is forced to leave behind his horse. The animal is found by Deputy Sheriff Jerry Walsh (Malcolm "Bud" McTaggart), the boyfriend of Bolton's daughter Jessie (Jill Martin), who sends the fingerprints found on the horse's saddle to the Federal Bureau of Investigation. Since the horse had been stolen from the U.S. Army, FBI agents Carson (McCoy), Magpie (Corbett) and Margaret (Joyce Bryant), are assigned to investigate. Masquerading as gypsies, they stop at the Bolton ranch where they read Jessie's fortune and get fingerprints, including ranch foreman Crane (Forrest Taylor), who is working for gang leader Bert Lee (Carleton Young), a rancher. Lee orders his cohorts Johnson and Mort (Ralph Peters) to lure the gypsies to the gang's hideout where he plans to murder them in case they are federal agents. At the hideout, Carson plays cards with the gang and gets their fingerprints on the deck but Bert spies the activity and a fight ensues in which gang member Thurston (Ted Adams) is injured and Mort is killed. Carson, Magpie and Margaret escape and later determine that the fingerprints are identical to those found on the stolen horse's saddle. Lee sets up a plan to frame Bill for Mort's murder. He gets Bolton and Crane to help him organize a posse of ranchers to hunt down the gypsies as Jessie informs Deputy Walsh. Bill rides to the Bolton ranch and is held captive by Jessie until he proves his identity to her; he and Walsh then go to save Magpie and Margaret from Lee and his gang. The two men manage to waylay the ranchers as Lee rides back to the hideout, pursued by Carson. As Lee, Thurston and Johnson wait to ambush him, Carson sneaks in by the back door and gets the drop on the outlaws. Magpie arrives with Deputy Walsh and the gang members are placed under arrest. Jessie then suggests that Carson, Magpie and Margaret vacation at the Bolton ranch for a few days but the FBI agents are ordered to Twin Peaks to investigate the murder of a comrade.

The *Variety* reviewer noted a major incongruity in the film's plot regarding the character of Magpie: "[H]e's sent to bring McCoy into the case on the sly, then comes into the territory with him garbed in gypsy getup, but with a pan as familiar as the shape of a baseball and gets away with it." The writer also noted that the feature had two leading ladies and was particularly taken with Joyce Bryant as FBI agent Margaret, who the scribe wrote "is a looker [and] appeared capable enough to do better by a larger assignment." The beautiful and talented Joyce Bryant was McCoy's leading lady in the seventh series entry, *Fighting Renegade*.

Although the Victory Pictures series had come to an end, McCoy continued to work with director Sam Newfield in seven westerns during the 1940–41 theatrical season. These oaters were made by Newfield's brother, Sigmund Neufeld, whose production company was doing films for the newly formed Producers Distributing Corporation (PDC). After the 1940 release of the first effort, *Texas Renegades*, the studio changed its name to Producers Releasing Corporation (PRC) and under that banner issued the remaining half-dozen McCoy features. After that, McCoy signed to co-star with Buck Jones and Raymond Hatton in Monogram's "Rough Riders" (q.v.) series.

Filmography

Lightnin' Bill Carson (Puritan, 1936, 73 minutes) Producers: Sigmund Neufeld & Leslie Simmonds. Director: Sam Newfield. Screenplay: [George] Arthur Durlam & Joseph O'Donnell. Photography: Jack Greenhalgh. Editor: Jack [John] English. Music Director: Lee Zahler. Assistant Director: William O'Connor.

Cast: Tim McCoy (Lightnin' Bill Carson), Lois January (Dolores Costello), Rex Lease (Fred Rand/The Pecos Kid), Harry Worth (Silent Tom Rand), Karl Hackett (Stack Stone), John Merton (Breed Hawkins), Joseph Girard (Mount), Lafe McKee (Don Costello), Edmund Cobb (Deputy Sheriff Sam Bates), Roger Williams (Deputy Sheriff Jed), Dick Botiller (Dick Morgan), Jimmy Aubrey (Pete), Jack Rockwell (Sheriff), Arthur Thalasso (Blacksmith), Wally West, Francis Walker, Ray Henderson (Deputy Sheriffs), Slim Whitaker, Frank Ellis (Gunmen), Harrison Greene (Bartender), George Morrell, Clyde McClary (Gamblers), Artie Ortego (Gang Member), Franklyn Farnum, Jack Evans (Citizens), Herman Hack, Oscar Gahan, Barney Beasley, Tom Smith (Saloon Customers).

Lightning Bill Carson Rides Again (Victory, 1938, 57 minutes) Producer: Sam Katzman. Director: Sam Newfield. Screenplay: E.R. O'Darsi. Photography: Marcel Le Picard. Editor: Holbrook N. Todd. Song: Johnny Lange & Lew Porter. Production Manager: Ed W. Rote. Assistant Director: Bert Sternbach.

Cast: Colonel Tim McCoy (Lightning Bill Carson/Jose), Joan Barclay (Sally), Frank Wayne (Ross), Ted Adams (Chuck "Broken Hand" Gannon), Bob Terry (Paul Smith), Jane Keckley (Katherine Smith), Ben Corbett (Shorty), Karl Hackett (Gray), Frank LaRue (Sheriff Armstrong), James Flavin (Agent Tom), Slim Whitaker (Hogan), Forrest Taylor, James Sheridan [Sherry Tansey], Dick Moorehead (Gang Member), Wally West (Gilroy).

Six Gun Trail (Victory, 1938, 59 minutes) Producer: Sam Katzman. Director: Sam Newfield. Screenplay: E.R. O'Darsi. Photography: Marcel Le Picard. Editor: Holbrook N. Todd. Songs: Johnny Lange & Lew Porter. Production Manager: Ed W. Rote. Assistant Director: Charles Henry.

Cast: Tim McCoy (Lightning Bill Carson/Sam Sung), Nora Lane (Midge), Ben Corbett (Magpie/Foolish), Alden Chase (Jim Wilson), Ted Adams (Spokesman), Donald Gallaher (Tracy), Bob Terry (Mac), Karl Hackett (Joe Willis), Frank Wayne (Messenger), Hal Carey (Singer), Jack "Tiny" Lipson (Gus), Lew Porter (Piano Player), Ray Henderson (Gang Member), Herman Hack, George Morrell (Deputy Sheriffs), James Sheridan [Sherry Tansey], Buck Morgan (Gang Members), Wally West, Oscar Gahan, Jimmy Aubrey, Artie Ortego, Clyde McClary, Barney Beasley, Rube Dalroy (Saloon Customers).

Code of the Cactus (Victory, 1939, 56 minutes) Producer: Sam Katzman. Director: Sam Newfield. Screenplay: Edward Halperin. Photography: Marcel Le Picard. Editor: Holbrook N. Todd. Songs: Johnny Lange & Lew Porter. Sound: Hans Weeren. Sets: Fred Preble. Production Manager: Ed W. Rote. Assistant Director: Bert Sternbach.

Cast: Tim McCoy (Lightning Bill Carson/Miguel), Ben Corbett (Magpie), Dorothy Short (Joan), Ted Adams (Thurston), Alden Chase (James), Dave O'Brien (Bob Swane), Forrest Taylor (Blackton), Bob Terry (Lefty), Slim Whitaker (Sheriff Burton), Frank Wayne (Jake), Art Davis (Hank), Robert Walker (Agent), Lew Porter (Piano Player), George Morrell (Deputy Sheriff), Milburn Morante (Old Timer), Clyde McClary, Jack King (Ranchers), Tex Palmer (Rider), Kermit Maynard, Carl Sepulveda, James Sheridan [Sherry Tansey], Jimmy Aubrey, Jim Corey, Carl Mathews, Bob Card, Lee Burns (Gang Members), Reed Howes (Pictured Man).

Texas Wildcats (Victory, 1939, 56 minutes) Producer: Sam Katzman. Director: Sam Newfield. Screenplay: George H. Plympton. Photography: Marcel Le Picard. Editor: Holbrook N. Todd. Sound: Glen Glenn. Sets: Fred Preble. Production Manager: Ed W. Rote. Assistant Director: Bert Sternbach.

Cast: Tim McCoy (Lightning Bill Carson/The Phantom), Joan Barclay (Molly Arden), Ben Corbett (Magpie McGillicuddy), Forrest Taylor (Jim Burrows), Ted Adams (Reno), Avando Reynaldo (Rita), Bob Terry (Mort Burrows), Dave O'Brien (Ed Arden), Frank Ellis (Al), Reed Howes (Ace), Slim Whitaker (Detective Durkin), Wally West, James Sheridan [Sherry Tansey], Herman Hack, Carl Mathews (Gang Members), Frank Wayne, Milburn Morante, Clyde McClary (Gamblers), George Morrell (Bartender), Denver Dixon (Saloon Customer).

Outlaws' Paradise (Victory, 1939, 62 minutes) Producer: Sam Katzman. Director: Sam Newfield. Story & Screenplay: Basil Dickey. Photography: Marcel Le Picard. Editor: Holbrook N. Todd. Songs: Johnny Lange & Lew Porter. Sound: Glen Glenn. Sets: Fred Preble. Assistant Director: Bert Sternbach.

Cast: Tim McCoy (Lightning Bill Carson/Trigger Mallory), Joan Barclay (Jessie Treadwell), Ben Corbett (Magpie McGillicuddy), Ted Adams (Slim Marsh), Forrest Taylor (Eddie), Bob Terry (Steve), Don Gallaher (Mort), Dave O'Brien (Meggs), Jack Mulhall (Warden), Lloyd Whitlock (Newsman), Ed Cassidy (Banker), Wally West (Bank Teller), Jack "Tiny" Lipson (Toby), Frank Wayne (Dickson), Jack C. Smith (Guard), Carl Mathews (Gang Member), George Morrell (Citizen).

Straight Shooter (Victory, 1939, 54 minutes) Producer: Sam Katzman. Director: Sam Newfield. Screenplay: Basil Dickey & Joseph O'Donnell. Story: Basil Dickey. Photography: Arthur Reed. Editor: Fred Bain. Sound: Hans Weeren. Sets: Fred Preble. Production Manager: Ed W. Rote. Assistant Director: Bert Sternbach.

Cast: Tim McCoy (Lightning Bill Carson/Sudden Sam Brown), Julie Sheldon (Margaret Martin), Ben Corbett (Magpie/Jack Benson), Ted Adams (Brainard), Reed Howes (Slade), Forrest Taylor (Luke Green), Budd Buster (Sheriff E.D. "Ed" Long), Carl Mathews (Lane), Wally West (Deputy Sheriff Ned), Dan White (Deputy Sheriff), George Morrell (Ben Martin).

Fighting Renegade (Victory, 1939, 53 minutes) Producer: Sam Katzman. Director: Sam Newfield. Story & Screenplay: William Lively. Photography: Art [Arthur] Reed. Editor: Holbrook N. Todd. Sound: Hans Weeren. Production Manager: Ed W. Rote. Assistant Director: Bert Sternbach.

Cast: Tim McCoy (Lightning Bill Carson/El Puma), Joyce Bryant (Marian Willis), Ben Corbett (Magpie), Ted Adams (Link Benson), Budd Buster (Old Dobie),

Dave O'Brien (Dr. Jerry Leonard), Forrest Taylor (Professor Lucius Lloyd), Reed Howes (Sheriff), John Elliott (Prospector), Artie Ortego (Pedro), Frank Wayne (Stagecoach Driver), Tom Smith (El Puma Henchman), Wally West, Herman Hack, Dan White, Carl Mathews, Chick Hannon, Tex Palmer (Gang Members).

Trigger Fingers (Victory, 1939, 53 minutes) Producer: Sam Katzman. Director: Sam Newfield. Story & Screenplay: Basil Dickey. Photography: Bill [William] Hyer. Editor: Holbrook N. Todd. Sound: Hans Weeren. Sets: Fred Preble. Production Manager: Ed W. Rote. Assistant Director: Bert Sternbach.

Cast: Tim McCoy (Lightning Bill Carson/Gypsy), Ben Corbett (Magpie), Jill Martin [Harley Wood] (Jessie Bolton), Joyce Bryant (Margaret/Rosita), Carleton Young (Bert Lee), Ted Adams (Jeff Thurston), John Elliott (Jim Bolton), Malcolm "Bud" McTaggart (Deputy Sheriff Jerry Walsh), Ralph Peters (Mort Hodges), Forrest Taylor (Crane), Kenne Duncan (Johnson), Budd Buster (Gila Cattlemen's Association Spokesman), Wally West (Express Office Agent), Herman Hack (Murdered Driver), Bob Terry, Carl Mathews (Gang Members), Chick Hannon, Tex Palmer (Posse Members).

THE LONE RANGER

One of the most enduring of all western film heroes, "The Lone Ranger" had its beginning in radio in the early 1930s at radio station WXYZ in Detroit, Michigan. Inspired by Johnston McCulley's character "Zorro" (q.v.), and more particularly Douglas Fairbanks' interpretation of that character, the Lone Ranger was created by writer Fran Striker with the aid of station manager Brace Beemer and supervised by George W. Trendle. From its regional start, the series went national, eventually spreading out to film, literature, pulps, comic strips, comic books, television and merchandising. After more than 70 years, the Lone Ranger remains one of the most popular American fictional heroes.

George Stenius first portrayed the title character when "The Lone Ranger" debuted on radio January 31, 1933, on WXYZ; he was followed five months later by Jack Deeds, then James Jewell, who both did the role briefly, before Earl Graser took over the part until 1941. Toward the end of 1933 the program began its national broadcast on the Quality Group (later the Mutual network), airing three times a week. Beginning early in 1938, the show was transcribed and by the end of that year Brace Beemer became the program's announcer. When Graser was killed in an automobile accident, Beemer took over the role in 1941. The next year the show switched to ABC. The series ran until the fall of 1954 for a total of nearly 3,400 broadcasts. Throughout its 23-year run, John Todd portrayed the masked man's loyal Indian companion Tonto, except for a brief period when the role was done by Louis Morango. The series was rebroadcast on ABC from 1954 to 1956 and on NBC during the 1955–56 season.

Regarding the radio program, Jim Harmon and Donald F. Glut wrote in *The Great Movie Serials: Their Sound and Fury* (1972), "With immortal background themes such as *William Tell Overture* and *Les Preludes* and the magnificent booming voice of Brace Beemer, the most memorable of the radio actors, the scripts by Fran Striker were virtual textbooks on how to construct radio drama or pulp fiction in general. The combination was unbeatable. The Lone Ranger rode beyond the limits of popular entertainment, and became an imperishable part of Americana."

The initial book about the character, *The Lone Ranger,* written by Gaylord Dubois, was published in 1936 by Grosset and Dunlap and in later years it was re-edited and then re-written by Fran Striker. Striker also wrote 17 more Lone Ranger books for Grosset and Dunlap between 1938 and 1956 (Pinnacle Books reprinted all 18 volumes in 1978). Some of the books were condensed by Whitman Publishers into Big Little Books and Better Little Books with the publisher putting out around 15 of these ten cent volumes as well the 1940 hardback *The Lone Ranger*, based on the radio program, and a 1950 Tall Better Little Book entitled *Secret of Somber Cavern*. Other volumes were originals by Whitman, such as *The Lone Ranger Outwits Crazy Cougar* (1968) by George S. Elrick. In 1951 Sandpiper Books published *The Lone Ranger's New Deputy*. Little Golden Books published a trio of Lone Ranger volumes beginning in 1954 with *The Lone Ranger* by Steffi Fletcher, followed by *The Lone Ranger and Tonto* (1957) by Charles Spain Verral and *The Lone Ranger and the Talking Pony* (1958) by Emily Brown.

In 1937, a pulp periodical entitled *The Lone Ranger Magazine* began publication and the next year King Features Syndicated started distributing the newspaper comic strip *The Lone Ranger*; it ran until 1971. For the first year it was drawn by Ed Kressy and thereafter by Charles Flanders. The syndicated strip ran in some 250 daily newspapers and in over 50 foreign publications. From 1938 until 1947, Dell Publishing Company reprinted the strips as comic books and in 1948 the company started the *Lone Ranger* comic book series, running for 145 issues until 1962. Over the years there were also a number of Lone Ranger and Tonto quarterly and annual comics as well as several giveaways.

The character's first film appearance came in the 15-chapter Republic serial *The Lone Ranger* (1938). Five script writers (Barry Shipman, George W. Yates, Franklyn Adreon, Ronald Davidson, Lois Eby) adapted Fran Striker's radio serial to the screen in an action-packed and highly entertaining cliffhanger. Five actors (Hal Taliaferro [Wally Wales], Herman Brix [Bruce Bennett], Lee Powell, Lane Chandler and George [Montgomery] Letz) were cast as Texas Rangers, with one of them also being the Lone Ranger. To further muddy the waters, the actor who portrayed the Lone Ranger, while in that guise, had his voice dubbed by Billy Bletcher. As the serial progressed, one after another of the characters was killed off, leaving only one, the Lone Ranger, at the finale. Throughout the proceedings, the taciturn Chief Thunder Cloud portrayed Tonto. The serial assembled one of the largest casts ever appearing in a cliffhanger, including many noted character performers associated with western movies at the time.

The initial chapter, "Heigh-Yo Silver," took place in post–Civil War Texas in 1865 with crook Captain Smith (Stanley Andrews) and his band of thugs trying to take over the Pecos area. Government tax collector Colonel Marcus Jeffries (Forbes Murray) arrives and he is captured and ordered killed by Smith, who takes his identity. When Texas Ranger Captain Rance (Edmund Cobb) and his men come to put an end to Smith's harsh collection ways, they are massacred by the outlaws with only one man surviving. He is nursed back to health by Tonto (Chief Thunder Cloud) and he joins up with four other Rangers in vowing revenge for the killings. The five Rangers, Bob Stuart (Hal Taliaferro), Bert Rogers (Herman Brix), Allen King (Lee Powell), Dick Forrest (Lane Chandler), and Jim Clark (George Letz), move into a deserted stockade next to a cave, where the Lone Ranger conceals his mask and guns. When called upon to fight Smith and his minions, one of the Rangers puts on the mask and rides a white horse called Silver (Silver King) to the rescue. President Abraham Lincoln (Frank McGlynn, Sr.) sends George Blanchard (George Cleveland) to the Pecos area to investigate charges of fraud and when he arrives with his daughter Joan (Lynne Roberts), Smith vows to get them out of the way. He orders his henchman, Joe Sneed (Maston Williams), who previously set up the massacre of the Ranger band, to place dynamite at the nearby fort, the Blanchards' destination. After the Lone Ranger averts disaster at the beginning of the second installment, he takes badman Kester (John Merton) prisoner and sends him back to Blanchard with word that the fake Jeffries' men had imprisoned Texas Rangers. The federal inspector confronts Jeffries who ignores him since Lincoln has been assassinated and his authority is ended. In order to get rid of the Rangers for good, Jeffries allows them to leave the fort in a wagon train and then has his men dynamite a pass to kill them. The Lone Ranger and Tonto save the wagons so Jeffries sends his men to ambush the masked man. Joan tries to warn him and they are almost killed after falling into a pit. Using another ploy, Jeffries has a fake falling-out with his henchman Taggart (Raphael [Ray] Bennett), who attempts to form an alliance with the masked man, but the Lone Ranger sees through the ruse only to be hit in the head with a rock. He is saved by Tonto as Taggart sends the Rangers to rescue a priest (William Farnum), held prisoner at a mill filled with blasting powder.

Lee Powell in *The Lone Ranger* (Republic, 1938).

When it explodes, Jim Clark is killed and the Lone Ranger nearly dies when he falls into a geyser hole during a fistfight with Taggart in a cave. Jeffries then frames the Lone Ranger and Tonto for the murder of several Indians by placing silver bullets by their bodies. A captured Tonto is nearly roasted alive until he is rescued by the masked man, who convinces the tribesmen of their innocence. When Jeffries attempts to get gunpowder to his minions, he sends Joan along as a hostage but when the wagon she is riding turns over, the Lone Ranger saves her. After Jeffries replaces the silver he collected as taxes with Confederate currency, the Rangers obtain the silver only to have the gang take it back. The outlaws hide the silver in a well and the Rangers, in the guise of poor Mexicans, find it but two of them are trapped in the well which the outlaws intend to blast. They find a tunnel that lets them escape but are captured by a cavalry unit although the Lone Ranger manages to get away and deliver the silver to a military outpost. He loses a silver spur, however, and Kester attempts to trap him only to find all of the four remaining Rangers are each missing a spur. When Jeffries decides to marry Joan, the Lone Ranger and Tonto try to rescue her but are trapped in a burning house by the outlaws. They manage to escape through a trap door. The gang leader then recovers the silver and hides it in a saloon. When the masked man goes there to recover it, he fights with the gang and is nearly overpowered until aided by Tonto. Ranger Dick Forrest falls off a cliff in a fight with gang member Felton (Tom London). He is taken to a nearby cave by Joan and the Rangers and they are pinned there by the gang, with the cave's roof collapsing. Forrest dies in the collapse as Rangers King and Rogers try to go for assistance. The gang surrounds Tonto, Blanchard, Joan and Sammy Cannon (Sammy McKim), a young boy who aided them, but the Lone Ranger arrives with a cavalry unit. The masked man and Jeffries then engage in a fight and both fall off a cliff. The Lone Ranger survives and vows to continue to battle lawlessness.

The surviving Ranger, the Lone Ranger, was Allen King, who was played by Lee Powell. Following the release of the serial, Powell made personal appearances as the Lone Ranger with a circus, which caught the attention of the character's copyright holders. He also starred in the 1939 Republic cliffhanger *Daredevils of the Red Circle*, which reunited him with Herman Brix [Bruce Bennett] and directors William Witney and John English. After that, Powell headlined PRC's "Frontier Marshals" (q.v.) series. In conjunction with *The Lone Ranger*, Grosset and Dunlap published a small book called *The Texas Renegades* in 1938, its plot based on the cliffhanger. The year 1938 also saw another tie-in, the song "Hi-Yo Silver," which was popularized on Bluebird Records by Dick Todd with Larry Clinton and His Orchestra.

The serial *The Lone Ranger* proved to be a huge success with audiences and Republic followed it with *The Lone Ranger Rides Again*, which came to theaters a year after the original chapter play. Again Witney and English directed with Shipman, Adreon, Ronald Davidson and newcomer Sol Shor doing the screenplay, which was based on uncredited Gerald Geraghty's story. Also in 15 chapters, the serial starred Robert Livingston as the Lone Ranger with Chief Thunder Cloud

Poster for *The Lone Ranger Rides Again* (Republic, 1939).

returning as Tonto. Livingston was one of Republic's brightest stars, having headlined a number of features, including playing Zorro in *The Bold Caballero* (1936) as well as one of the leads in its "The Three Mesquiteers" (q.v.) series. The Lone Ranger sequel also used the triad hero concept from the Mesquiteers, with the masked man not only being aided by Tonto, but also by a Mexican caballero (Duncan Renaldo). The plot had the Lone Ranger (Livingston), now called Bill Andrews, coming to the aid of San Ramon Valley settlers who are being harassed by raiders. Their wagon train leader, Jed Scott (William Gould), asks for Andrews' help in thwarting cattle baron Craig Dolan (J. Farrell MacDonald), who does not want the newcomers on his range. The Lone Ranger, however, learns that Dolan's nephew, Bart (Ralph Dunn), is the real culprit and he enlists Tonto (Chief Thunder Cloud) and caballero Juan Vasquez (Renaldo) in fighting Bart and his gang. At the finale, Dolan plans to wipe out the settlers who have taken refuge in a fort by blowing it up. The Lone Ranger arrives in time to save the day and then orders the settlers to move back before they are harmed. Bart tries to find out why the wagon loaded with dynamite did not explode and while he is doing so, it is detonated and he is killed, thus ending his reign of terror. Although having the same expansive production values of its predecessor, the follow-up lacked the mystery appeal of the first serial and its plotline was rather mundane.

In 1940 Republic issued a feature version of *The Lone Ranger* called *Hi-Yo Silver*, with this 69-minutes version greatly compacting the cliffhanger's story. In addition, new footage was added with Raymond Hatton playing an old-timer who relates the masked man's adventures to a young boy (Dickie Jones). Since the two Republic serials were out of circulation for many years, this was the only version of the 1938 chapter play available until the serial's recent DVD debut.

Around the time of the release of the Republic serials, a major merchandising campaign got underway promoting the Lone Ranger. The character was licensed to appear on a myriad of products, ranging from toys to clothing and food products. The campaign continues to this day, with its greatest popularity from the 1940s into the 1960s, when the Lone Ranger was especially popular due to the character's radio and television programs.

The Lone Ranger came to television in September 1949 with Clayton Moore as the title character and Jay Silverheels playing Tonto. The series ran for eight seasons on ABC-TV and was the first show the network had in the Nielsen ratings' top ten programs. It was so popular that its reruns were shown on Saturday mornings from 1953 to 1960 on CBS-TV and on Sunday afternoons on ABC-TV from 1957 to 1960 and on Wednesday afternoons from 1960 to 1961. It also was shown on NBC-TV on Saturdays during the 1961–62 season. Since that time the series had remained a popular syndicated item with Moore and Silverheels permanently affixed in the public mind as the Lone Ranger and Tonto. Moore left the series in 1952 in a salary dispute and was replaced by John Hart until 1954 when his money demands were met. Hart portrayed the Lone Ranger in 52 episodes with Moore headlining the remaining 169 segments of the series.

Moore (1914–99) was a Chicago native who first worked as a circus aerialist and model before military service. He started in films in 1938 as a stuntman and bit player. In the early 1940s he developed into a leading man, mainly in "B" pictures and serials, but he also played villainous characters. He considered the Lone Ranger a role of a lifetime and following the TV series' demise he continued to make personal appearances as the masked man. Silverheels (1912–80) was born Harold J. Smith in Canada on the Six Nations Indiana Reservation in Ontario. He was a Mohawk Indian of the Iroquois Nation. Coming to Hollywood in 1933 as a member of a lacrosse team, he became a professional boxer before he began working in films; he made scores of appearances as Native Americans.

In 1952, Apex Film Corporation released *The Legend of the Lone Ranger*, made up of the first three episodes of the TV series. It told the story of the origin of the Lone Ranger character, his mask, his horse Silver, silver bullets and his never-ending fight for justice. The film begins with six Texas Rangers, under the command of Captain Dan Reid (Tristram Coffin), being led into an ambush by half-breed Collins (George J. Lewis) at the behest of outlaw gang leader Butch Cavendish (Glenn Strange). All of the men are

Clayton Moore as the Lone Ranger.

massacred with only the captain's brother, John Reid (Moore), surviving. Badly injured, he is found by Indian Tonto (Silverheels), who nurses him back to health. Years before, when Tonto was a boy, his tribe had been attacked and he was saved by John Reid, who he calls Kimosabe, or Trusty Scout. Upon his recovery, Reid decides to wear a mask, made from his brother's vest, to hide his identity in his quest for justice, and call himself The Lone Ranger. Tonto agrees to team up with him in capturing the Cavendish gang. Collins, who was ambushed and left for dead by Cavendish, tries to kill the masked man but falls to his death from a cliff. The Lone Ranger and Tonto then head to Wild Horse Valley where they come upon a white stallion about to be gored by a buffalo. The Ranger kills the buffalo and nurses the horse back to health; it becomes his steed Silver. The two men go to the town of Colby and at the ranch of ex–Ranger Jim Blaine (Ralph Littlefield) they witness the murder of a judge by Cavendish, who is winged by Blaine. Taking Jim into his confidence, the Lone Ranger and Tonto bring him to a abandoned silver mine which the masked man plans to use to make silver bullets, a symbol of justice by law. He then sends Tonto into town for Sheriff Taylor (Walter Sande), who comes to the mine and learns about the killing of the judge. The lawman agrees to work with the Ranger and Tonto in capturing Cavendish, whose wounds are being treated by Doc Drummond (George Chesebro). The outlaw tells the physician he plans to take over the town of Colby and that he has killed several prominent citizens and replaced them with his own men. The doctor refuses to go along with his scheme as the Lone Ranger and Taylor arrive and capture Cavendish. The gang shows up and the Lone Ranger manages to get away as Tonto is refused help in town by crooked Deputy Sheriff Corey (Guy Wilkerson). The Lone Range and Tonto meet and return to recapture Cavendish and set the sheriff and the doctor free. Leaving the supposedly unconscious Cavendish behind, the four men return to town where the Lone Ranger, with the aid of Doc Drummond, jails Cavendish's cohorts. The Lone Ranger, Tonto, Sheriff Taylor and Doc Drummond then form a posse and fight it out with Cavendish and the remainder of the gang. Cavendish tries to make a getaway but is captured by the Lone Ranger and all the gang members are jailed. The Lone Ranger and Tonto then ride away to continue their fight for justice.

The TV episodes that make up *The Legend of the Lone Ranger* were remade in color in 1955 as "The Lone Ranger Rides Again." In 1954 Jack Wrather bought the rights to the Lone Ranger from the Campbell-Trendle Agency of Detroit for three million dollars and retold the history of the character in this one-hour TV special starring Moore and Silverheels, with Glenn Strange repeating the Butch Cavendish role. The program aired February 12 and 13, 1955 on both ABC-TV and CBS-TV and it was rerun on CBS-TV on February 1, 1958. Also filmed in color were the final 39 episodes of the television series *The Lone Ranger*, shown on ABC-TV during the 1956–57 season.

In 1956 the Wrather Corporation produced the feature-length motion picture *The Lone Ranger* with Moore and Silverheels continuing their TV roles. This Warner Bros. release, filmed in WarnerColor, was lensed near Kanab, Utah, and co-starred Bonita Granville, the wife of Wrather. Also in the cast was Lane Chandler, who two decades before had been one of the five Texas Rangers in Republic's *Lone Ranger* serial. With a budget of almost $500,000, the feature proved to be a very enjoyable affair that boasted beautiful photography and locales combined with an interesting storyline.

The Lone Ranger began with the masked man (Moore) and Tonto (Silverheels) stopping renegade Indians from attacking rancher Pete Ramirez (Perry Lopez) near the town of Brasada. The ranger has come to the area to meet with the territorial governor (Charles Meredith) who wants his aid in stopping the local conflict between the ranchers and Indians, so the territory can apply for statehood. The official is the guest of wealthy rancher Reece Kilgore (Lyle Bettger), who is alienated from his wife Welcome (Bonita Granville) over the way he is raising their daughter Lila (Beverly Washburn) as a tomboy who will eventually take over his ranch empire. At a mission, the Ranger masquerades as an old prospector and meets with the governor, but later identifies himself and agrees to investigate the lawlessness. Going to the local Indian reservation, the Lone Ranger and Tonto confer with Indian Chief Red

Poster for *The Lone Ranger* (Warner Bros., 1956).

before murdering the old man and blaming the crime on the Indians. In Abilene, Cassidy and his men pick up a shipment of dynamite for Kilgore from storeowner Tripp (Malcolm Atterbury). After Ramirez, who has hired on the trial drive as a wrangler, sees the explosives, he is also killed by Cassidy. When the cowboys return, the Ranger sends Tonto into Brasada to inquire about Ramirez. There he is attacked by Cassidy and nearly lynched by the locals; the Lone Ranger comes to his rescue. The Ranger later gets the storekeeper to admit that the explosives were taken by Kilgore's men. Back at the Indian reservation, the Ranger and Tonto find young brave Angry Horse (Michael Ansara) trying to usurp control of the tribe from the ailing Chief Red Hawk by preparing the warriors for battle. Later they observe four Indians set fire to a field. After capturing the quartet, they take them to the sheriff and prove to him they are white men disguised as braves. The masked man then asks the lawman to ride to the governor for help and he and Tonto attempt to stop a confrontation between the ranchers and the Indians. With trouble brewing, Kilgore sends Lila away but soon after an arrow with the little girl's scarf is found shot into the door of his ranch house. When the Lone Ranger and Tonto go back to the Indian reservation, they see the little girl being tormented by the children there and the masked man offers to fight Angry Horse for her custody. After a grueling confrontation, the Ranger defeats the brave and takes Lila home where Welcome tells him that her husband, who she now detests, is forming a group of men to attack the Indians at Pilgrim's Crossing, the site of an earlier Indian massacre. The Lone Ranger goes to Spirit Mountain to stop Kilgore from obtaining dynamite to use against the Indians. He is wounded and left for dead by the rancher and Cassidy, but is found by Tonto. The Ranger's horse, Silver, brings in a mule carrying the dynamite and the masked man and Tonto use the explosives to keep the two factions from fighting when they meet at Pilgrim's Crossing. Sheriff

Hawk (Frank De Kova), an ailing old man who promises to keep the peace although he says white men have desecrated Spirit Mountain, a sacred spot to the tribe. In town, Kilgore's foreman, Cassidy (Robert J. Wilke), rounds up men for a cattle drive and is warned by Sheriff Kimberley (John Pickard) and Indian Agent Muller (Lee Roberts) to steer clear of the Indian reservation. During the cattle drive, Cassidy rustles a small herd belonging to the sheriff's father (Hank Patterson),

Clayton Moore as the Lone Ranger and Jay Silverheels as Tonto.

Kimberley returns with the cavalry and announces he has a warrant for Kilgore's arrest for government treaty violations and killing Ramirez. The rancher denounces Cassidy as Ramirez's murderer and his foreman shoots him and tries to escape but is captured by the Lone Ranger. Welcome and Lila take sanctuary at the local mission and later, after Cassidy is sentenced to hang, she tells the padre (Edward Colmans) that she and Lila plan to stay on and run the Kilgore ranch and clear the family name. The Lone Ranger and Tonto ride away.

After eight seasons, the *Lone Ranger* television series ceased production but the Wrather Corporation produced a second Lone Ranger feature film, *The Lone Ranger and the Lost City of Gold*, issued theatrically in 1958. Like its predecessor, the production was well-made and well-written, boasted scenic locales and excellent photography. Moore and Silverheels repeated the leading roles. Genre veteran Lesley Selander, who had directed some of the "Hopalong Cassidy" and "Red Ryder' (qq.v.) series entries, helmed the fast-paced project. The feature also included a song, "Hi-Ho Silver," composed by Lenny Adelson and Les Baxter, which was performed by a male chorus during a brief prologue sequence which retold the origins of the Lone Ranger legend.

In *Lost City of Gold*, the masked man (Moore) and Tonto (Silverheels) see hooded raiders murdering an Indian. Our heroes take the man's child to the local padre (Ralph Moody), where he is cared for by Indian maiden Paviva (Lisa Montell). The padre tells the Ranger and his companion that the area around Arizona's San Dorea has been plagued by lawlessness. When Tonto rides to town to get Dr. Rolfe (Norman Frederic [Dean Fredericks]) to examine the baby, he is badly beaten by thugs Brady (Douglas Kennedy) and Wilson (Lane Bradford) on the orders of the town's prejudiced sheriff-saloon owner Matthison (Charles Watts). The Lone Ranger and Tonto meet Indian brave Red Bird (Maurice Jara) who tells them the legend of the Lake of Fire, which was formed centuries before by a huge ball of fire from the sky that wiped out Spanish conquistadors who were threatening his tribe. At the ranch of beautiful widow Fran Henderson (Noreen Nash), her foreman-lover Brady gives her part of a medallion, one he stole from the Indian whom he and his men murdered. She believes that the medallion, when complete, will show a map to one of the lost Seven Cities of Gold sought by Coronado. Since she and Brady are behind the local raids, she has him and his gang rob one of her own mine pay wagons to avert suspicion. The Lone Ranger, however, comes to feel she knows something about the lawlessness and visits her in the guise of Bret Reagan, a bounty hunter. Fran is attracted to Reagan, much to the chagrin of Brady, who orders him off the ranch. Paviva, who loves Dr. Rolfe, begs him to admit he

Poster for *The Lone Ranger and the Lost City of Gold* (United Artists, 1958).

is really an Indian but he refuses, fearing he will lose his practice. Following the death of another Indian who has a medallion piece stolen, the Lone Ranger and Tonto go to the local reservation and meet Chief Tomache (John Miljan), a sick old man who tells them that long ago he found the medallion and broke it into pieces and gave them as gifts. One went to his daughter who married a white trader and was now in the possession of the grandson he had never seen. When another Indian with a medallion piece is attacked, he is saved by the Lone Ranger and Tonto as Red Bird and his braves capture one of the raiders, Travers (Bill Henry), and take him to their village. While they are trying to get the truth out of him, Brady and Wilson sneak up and Brady kills Travers. Before dying, Travers tells Red Bird about Brady. When the Lone Ranger finds out, he goes back to visit Fran, disguised as Reagan. He informs her he has the last needed part of the medallion and the woman tells him of the city of gold and agrees to get rid of Brady and join forces with him. When Paviva is insulted in town by the sheriff, Tonto comes to her defense and is badly beaten, causing Dr. Rolfe to admit he is the grandson of Chief Tomache. He also shows the townspeople the part of the medallion he possesses. After treating Tonto's wounds, the doctor, Paviva and the baby head to the Indian village but find it deserted as the tribe is at the Lake of Fire for an annual ceremony. Brady informs Fran that Reagan is a fraud and that Dr. Rolfe has the part of the medallion they need; he and his men go the village for it, but two of the outlaws are killed by the physician and Tonto. The Lone Ranger arrives and shoots Wilson. Brady gets the drop on the doctor and takes the medallion piece, as well as the baby as a hostage. The Lone Ranger's horse, Silver, forces him to put down the baby and the foreman is wounded by the masked man but makes it back to Fran's ranch. There she completes the medallion and then kills Brady with an antique hatchet when he tries to take it from her. When the Lone Ranger shows up, Fran tries to put the blame on Brady but he tells her federal marshals are on the way and she will soon be placed in their custody. At the Indian village, Dr. Rolfe is united with his grandfather. The Lone Ranger, Tonto and others find the golden city hidden in a cave; the wealth from the cave, which is on Indian land, will be used to build a hospital.

In 1961, Sundown Productions made a pilot for a projected CBS-TV series called *Return of the Lone Ranger* with the title role played by Tex Hill, who was known as "The Singing Cowboy." The project failed to sell.

The next year the Wrather Corporation took the 39 episodes from the final (1956–57) TV season of *The Lone Ranger* and edited them into 13 feature films, each containing three episodes. Action prologue introductions were added to each of the telefeatures, which were released to local television stations by Gray-Schwartz Enterprises. The titles were *Champions of Justice, Count the Clues, Justice of the West, The Lawless, Masquerade, More Than Magic, Not Above Suspicion, One Mask Too Many, The Search, Tale of Gold, Trackers, The Truth* and *Vengeance Vow*.

In 1964, Gold Key Comics began reprinting Dell's "The Lone Ranger" comic books and in 1975 started publishing new stories until the magazine ceased production two years later. In 1977, a three-part Lone Ranger comic book was done in Sweden.

An animated television series called *The Lone Ranger*, produced by Halas & Batchelor Cartoon Films, was aired on Saturday mornings on CBS-TV from 1966–69 with Michael Rye and Shepard Menken supplying the voices of the Lone Ranger and Tonto. In 1980 the two characters were part of CBS-TV's animated series *The Tarzan/Lone Ranger Adventure Hour*, a program which combined reruns of *Tarzan* with new Lone Ranger and Zorro (q.v.) episodes. William Conrad did the voice of the masked man and Ivan Naranjo was Tonto. The series was produced by Filmation Associates.

In 1970 John Hart and Jay Silverheels made guest appearances as the Lone Ranger and Tonto in the little seen Warner Bros. feature film *The Phynx*. A decade later, the Wrather Corporation announced it planned to make a new Lone Ranger feature film but quickly drew public ire and unwanted bad publicity when it obtained a court order forbidding Clayton Moore from wearing the Lone Ranger mask.* The resulting feature film, *The Legend of the Lone Ranger*, issued theatrically in 1981, was a dud. In *The New York Times*, Janet Maslin wrote one of its kinder reviews, saying, "There's a certain magic to the Lone Ranger story that not even this listless version has been able to erase. But the film is more depressing than exhilarating, since it owes so much more to commercials than to other movies, and since it so

---

**Moore, who had retired from acting in 1959, had continued to make personal appearances and television commercials, sometimes with Jay Silverheels, and the court action resulted in such a public outcry that he was more than ever in demand. Since he could no longer wear the mask, Moore donned dark glasses for public appearances and TV work. By the mid-1980s the Wrather Corporation relented and asked that the injunction be lifted, and Moore again wore the Lone Ranger mask.*

Advertisement for *The Legend of the Lone Ranger* (Universal, 1981).

patently values blandness over spice." Like most reviewers and watchers, she commented on the miscasting of Klinton Spilsbury in the title role, describing him as "pleasant but nondescript." Overall she called the feature "standard, halfhearted adventure fare." More to the point was Phil Hardy in *The Western* (1983), who called the film a "dismal resurrection" which made the Lone Ranger "too contemporary and camp a hero." Spilsbury did not speak in the film as his voice had to be dubbed by James Keach. Producer Jack Wrather's wife, Bonita Granville, who was the leading lady in the 1956 *The Lone Ranger*, had a bit role in the production and former TV Lone Ranger John Hart was featured as a newspaper editor. Costing in excess of $18 million, the production had a domestic gross of $12.6, making it one of the bigger box office fiascos of 1981.

The Legend of the Lone Ranger retold the story of how Texas Ranger John Reid (Spilsbury) was saved by Indian Tonto (Michael Horse) from ambushers Butch Cavendish (Christopher Lloyd) and his outlaws. Donning a mask, riding a silver steed and using silver bullets, he and Tonto then set out to avenge the killings of his comrades, including his brother Captain Dan Reid (John Bennett Perry), and bring law and justice to the west. Mixed in the convoluted plot were such historical characters as Wild Bill Hickok (Richard Farnsworth), General George A. Custer (Lincoln Tate) and Buffalo Bill Cody (Ted Flicker). A major part of the story, and the film's climax, had the Lone Ranger and Tonto out to save President Ulysses S. Grant (Jason Robards) from a planned abduction by Cavendish, who seeks to rule Texas.

It is ironic that this multimillion dollar production would die a quick box office death, while Clayton Moore's popularity should continue to grow. By the 1980s he was regarded as a true American hero and this image has remained permanently fixed in the public's mind. Moore continued to make personal appearances well into the 1990s and his best-selling autobiography *I Was That Masked Man* was published in 1996. Moore died December 28, 1999. In 1985 he told an interviewer, "The Lone Ranger is a great character, a great American. Playing him made me a better person."

Silverheels did not live to see Moore's renewed popularity (or to see an increase in his own). He died March 5, 1980, following a long illness. After the *Lone Ranger* series ended, he started the Indian Actors Workshop in Hollywood and during the 1970s he worked the harness racing circuit across the United States. The year before his death, he became the first American Indian to have a star in Hollywood's Walk of Fame.

Although *The Legend of the Lone Ranger* flopped, renewed interest in the character caused the New York Times Syndicate to start a new "Lone Ranger" comic strip in 1981. Published for three years; it was written by Cary Bates and drawn by Russ Heath. In 1993, Pure Imagination Publishing did a comic book compiling some of the strips. In 1994, a quartet of comic books, "The Lone Ranger and Tonto," was published by Topps Comics.

In 2003 the masked man and Tonto returned in the television feature film *The Lone Ranger*, produced by Turner Network Television. This sad affair eschewed most of the characteristics of the Lone Ranger legend. For example, "The William Tell Overture" was replaced by a rock music soundtrack and Tonto's English rivaled that of the Lone Ranger, who was presented as a Boston law student and not a Texas Ranger. No longer called John Reid, but now carrying the moniker of Luke Hartman (Chad Michael Murray), the character comes to the west and sees his Texas Ranger brother Harmon (Sebastian Spence) murdered in an ambush. Injured himself, he is saved by Tonto (Nathaniel Arcand), who is involved in the magic arts. Luke falls in love with Tonto's sister Alope (Anita Brown) and vows to avenge his brother's murder by becoming the Lone Ranger. Although set in the 19th century, much of the film's dialogue was contemporary hip, and for the first time, a Lone Ranger film contained nudity when Alope went skinny dipping. Needless to say, the telefeature passed quietly into oblivion although it apparently was the pilot for a proposed new TV series.

A year prior to the TV movie, Columbia Pictures announced it had optioned a new Lone Ranger movie project to be done by Red Wagon Productions. By the end of 2004, it was announced that the feature was nearing production but within six months it had been postponed and at the end of 2007 Red Wagon Productions was no longer involved in the apparently moribund project. In 2006, however, a new "Lone Ranger" comic book was published by Dynamite Entertainment. Originally planned as a six-issue series, its immediate success caused it to become a continuing publication and it was nominated in the Eisner Awards for best new comic book series in 2007.

Filmography

The Lone Ranger (Republic, 1938, 15 Chapters) Supervisor: Robert M. Beche. Associate Producer: Sol C. Siegel. Directors: William Witney & John English. Screenplay: Barry Shipman, George W. Yates, Franklyn Adreon, Ronald Davidson & Lois Eby, from the radio serial by Fran Striker. Photography: William Nobles. Editors: Edward Todd & Helene Turner. Music Director: Alberto Columbo. Production Manager: Al Wilson. Unit Manager: Mack D'Agostino.

Cast: Silver King (Silver the Horse), Chief Thunder Cloud (Tonto), Lynn[e] Roberts (Joan Blanchard), Stanley Andrews (Captain Smith), George Cleveland (George Blanchard), William Farnum (Father McKim), Hal Taliaferro [Wally Wales] (Bob Stuart), Herman Brix [Bruce Bennett] (Bert Rogers), Lee Powell (Allen King), Lane Chandler (Dick Forrest), George [Montgomery] Letz (Jim Clark), John Merton (Kester), Sammy McKim (Sammy), Tom London (Felton), Raphael [Ray] Bennett (Taggart), Maston Williams (Joe Snead/Thompson), Frank McGlynn, Sr. (Abraham Lincoln), Edmund Cobb (Captain Rance), Forbes Murray (Colonel Marcus Jeffries), Jack Perrin (Morgan), Reed Howes (Lieutenant Brown), Ted Adams (Drake), Jack Rockwell (Regan), Charles Thomas (Blake), Slim Whitaker (Perkins), Walter James (Joe Cannon), Carl Stockdale (Haskins), Murdock MacQuarrie (Matt Clark), Jane Keckley (Mrs. Clark), Charles King (Morley), Lafe McKee (Bushwhacked Rancher), George Mari (Pepito), Allan Cavan (Major Brennan), Frankie Marvin, Bob Card (Fort Soldiers), Philip Armenta (Dark Cloud), Griff Barnett, Ben Wright, Wendle Gill, Ed Diaz, Frank Chrysler, Leon Bellas, John Bacon, John Baaca, Oscar Hancock, Henry Olivas, Roy Kennedy, Buck Hires, Wally Wilson, Perry Pratt (Ranchers), Edna Lawrence (Marina), J.W. Cody (Running Elk), Hank Bell (Wagon Train Settler), Bob Kortman, Art Dillard, Al Taylor, Curley Dresden, Ray Henderson, Forrest Burns, Post Park, Art Felix, George Plues, Vinegar Roan, Bert Dillard, Duke Taylor, Bill Yrigoyen, Joe Yrigoyen, Loren Riebe, Al Rimpau, John Slater, Burt Tatum, Bobby Thompson, Shorty Woods, John Goodwin, Jerry Frank, Ray Elliott, Al Delmar, Jack Casey, Jerry Brown, John Bristol, John Brahme, Wesley Hopper, Henry Isabell, Chuck Jennings, Glen Johnson, Elmer Napier, Harry Mack, Al Lorenzen, Ike Lewin, Gunner Johnson, Ken Cooper, Frank LeFever, Eddie Juaregui (Troopers), Frank Levya (Pedro), Yakima Canutt (Soldier), Jimmy Hollywood, Duke Green (Guards), Fred Burns (Holt), Tex Cooper (Texan), Inez Cody (Squaw), Frank Ellis, Jack Ingram, Jack Kirk, Bud Osborne, Blackie Whiteford (Gang Members), George Magrill, Carl Saxe (Sentries), Millard McGowan (Gunslinger), Francis Sayles (Carpetbagger), Charles Williams (Reporter), Billy Bletcher (Voice of the Lone Ranger), Earl Graser (Hi-Yo Silver Voice).

Chapter titles: 1) Heigh-Yo Silver; 2) Thundering Earth; 3) The Pitfall; 4) Agents of Treachery; 5) The

Steaming Cauldron; 6) Red Man's Courage; 7) Wheels of Despair; 8) Fatal Treasure; 9) The Missing Spur; 10) Flaming Fury; 11) The Silver Bullet; 12) Escape; 13) The Fatal Plunge; 14) Messengers of Doom; 15) The Last of the Rangers.

Feature version: *Hi-Yo Silver* (1940).

The Lone Ranger Rides Again (Republic, 1939, 15 Chapters) Associate Producer: Robert Beche. Directors: William Witney & John English. Screenplay: Barry Shipman, Franklyn Adreon, Ronald Davidson & Sol Shor, from the radio serial by Fran Striker. Photography: William Nobles & Edgar Lyons. Editors: Edward Todd & Helene Turner. Music Director: Alberto Columbo. Production Manager: Al Wilson. Unit Manager: Mack D'Agostino.

Cast: Robert Livingston (The Lone Ranger/Bill Andrews), Chief Thunder Cloud (Tonto), Duncan Renaldo (Juan Vasquez), Jinx Falken[berg] (Sue Dolan), Ralph Dunn (Bart Dolan), J. Farrell MacDonald (Craig Dolan), William Gould (Jed Scott), Rex Lease (Evans), Henry Otho (Paul Daniels), John Beach (Hardin), Glenn Strange (Thorne), Stanley Blystone (Murdock), Edwin [Eddie] Parker (Hank), Al Taylor (Colt), Carleton Young (Logan), Silver King (Silver the Horse), Wheeler Oakman (Manny), Buddy Roosevelt (Slade), Ernie Adams (Doc Grover), Roger Williams (Sheriff), Lew Meehan (Lynch), Griff Barnett (E.B. Tully), Ted Wells (Cass), Frank Ellis (Joe Parker), Buddy Messinger (Rance), Robert McClung (Danny Daniels), Ralph LeFever (Stagecoach Driver Bill), George Burton (Ed Powers), Howard Chase (Martin Gibson), Eddie Dean (Cooper), Jack Kirk (Deputy Sheriff Sam Lawson), Cecil Kellogg (Mack), Bert Dillard (Rex), Monte Montague (Tucker), Joe Perez (Diego Vasquez), Betty Roadman (Ma Daniels), Walter Wills (Doctor), Forrest Taylor (Judge Miller), Tom Smith (Simkins), Bob Robinson (Blackie), Buddy Mason (Luke), Tommy Coats (Striker), Slim Whitaker, Jim Corey (Wagon Raiders), Horace B. Carpenter, Cactus Mack (Lynch Mob Members), Post Park (Stagecoach Driver), Art Dillard (Stagecoach Guard), Jack Montgomery (Smith), David Sharpe, Art Felix, Chick Hannon, Fred Schaefer, Charles Regan (Cave Outlaws), Howard Hickey (Holmes), Barry Hays (George), Duke R. Lee (Deputy Sheriff), Charles B. Murphy (Voter), Lafe McKee, Charles Hutchison, Augie Gomez, Nelson McDowell (Citizens), Herman Hack, Duke Taylor, Forrest Burns, Wesley Hopper, Bill Yrigoyen, Joe Yrigoyen, Bud Wolfe (Posse Members), Ted Mapes (Cowboy), Francis Walker, Carl Sepulveda (Gang Members), Blackjack Ward (Safe Robber), Billy Bletcher (Voice of the Lone Ranger).

Chapter titles: 1) The Lone Ranger Returns; 2) Masked Victory; 3) The Black Raiders; 4) The Cavern of Doom; 5) Agents of Deceit; 6) The Trap; 7) The Lone Ranger at Bay; 8) Ambush; 9) Wheels of Doom; 10) The Dangerous Captive; 11) Death Below; 12) Blazing Peril; 13) Exposed; 14) Besieged; 15) Frontier Justice.

Hi-Yo Silver (Republic, 1940, 69 minutes) Feature version of *The Lone Ranger* (1938) with additional Cast: Raymond Hatton (Old Timer Smokey), Dickie Jones (Boy).

The Legend of the Lone Ranger (Apex Film Corporation, 1952, 75 minutes) Producer: Jack Chertok. Director: George B. Seitz, Jr. Screenplay: George B. Seitz, Jr., from the radio serial by Fran Striker. Photography: Mack Stengler. Editor: Axel Hubert. Art Director: Harry H. Poppe. Editorial Supervisor: Jack Ruggiero. Assistant Director: Lester Guthrie.

Cast: Clayton Moore (The Lone Ranger/John Reid), Jay Silverheels (Tonto), Glenn Strange (Butch Cavendish), George J. Lewis (Collins), Tristram Coffin (Captain Dan Reid), Walter Sande (Sheriff Two Gun Taylor), George Chesebro (Doc Drummond), Ralph Littlefield (Blaine), Jack Clifford (Jerry), Guy Wilkerson (Deputy Sheriff Corey), Frank Fenton (Ranger Captain), Horace Murphy (Jessup).

The Lone Ranger (Warner Bros., 1956, 86 minutes) Producer: Willis Goldbeck. Director: Stuart Heisler. Screenplay: Herb Meadow. Photography: Edwin DuPar. Editor: Clarence Kolster. Music: David Butolph. Art Director: Stanley Fleischer. Sound: M.A. Merrick. Sets: G.W. Berntsen. Makeup: Gordon Bau. Assistant Director: Robert Farfan.

Cast: Clayton Moore (The Lone Ranger), Jay Silverheels (Tonto), Lyle Bettger (Reece Kilgore), Bonita Granville (Welcome Kilgore), Perry Lopez (Pete Ramirez), Robert J. Wilke (Cassidy), John Pickard (Sheriff Sam Kimberley), Beverly Washburn (Lila Kilgore), Michael Ansara (Angry Horse), Frank De Kova (Chief Red Hawk), Charles Meredith (Governor), Mickey Simpson (Powder), Zon Murray (Goss), Lane Chandler (Chip Walker), Lee Roberts (Indian Agent John Muller), Malcolm Atterbury (Phineas Tripp), Edward Colmans (Padre), William Schallert (Secretary Clive), Robert Williams (Marshal), Hank Patterson (Rancher Kimberley), Elmore Vincent (Mr. Abernathy), Hal Taggart (Joe Branch), Rush Williams (Knuckles), Kermit Maynard (the Rev. Purdy), Robert Filmer, Paul Power (Businessmen), Fred Kelsey (Citizen), Robert Malcolm (Rancher).

The Lone Ranger and the Lost City of Gold (United Artists, 1958, 81 minutes) Producers: Sherman A. Harris & Jack Wrather. Director: Lesley Selander. Screenplay: Robert Schaefer & Eric Freiwald. Photography: Kenneth Peach. Editor: Robert S. Golden. Music: Les Baxter. Song: Lenny Adelson & Les Baxter. Art Director: James D. Vance. Sound: Philip Mitchell. Sets: Charles Thompson. Makeup: Layne Britton. Production Supervisor: Hugh McCollum. Assistant Director: Willard M. Reineck.

Cast: Clayton Moore (The Lone Ranger), Jay Silverheels (Tonto), Douglas Kennedy (Ross Brady), Charles Watts (Sheriff Oscar Mattison), Noreen Nash (Frances "Fran" Henderson), Ralph Moody (Padre Vincente Esteban), Lisa Montell (Paviva), John Miljan (Chief Tomache), Norman Fredric [Dean Fredericks]

(Dr. James Rolfe), Maurice Jara (Red Bird), Bill [William] Henry (Travers), Lane Bradford (Wilson), Belle Mitchell (Caulama), Bob Woodward (Gang Member), Herman Hack (Saloon Customer).

Champion of Justice (Wrather Corporation, 1962, 75 minutes) Producer: Sherman A. Harris. Executive Producer: Jack Wrather. Photography: William Whitley. Editor: Everett Dodd. Sound: Philip Mitchell. Sets: Harry Reif. Makeup: Ben Lane. Production Manager: Hugh McCollum. Story Editor: Bertram Millhauser.

Cast: Clayton Moore (The Lone Ranger), Jay Silverheels (Tonto).

Episodes:

"CHAMPION OF JUSTICE"

Director: Oscar Rudolph. Screenplay: Robert Schaefer & Eric Freiwald. Wardrobe: Dick Bachler. Assistant Directors: Gene Anderson, Jr., & George Loper.

Guest Cast: Dennis Moore (Dallas), Florence Lake (Mama Angel), Brad Jackson (The Calico Kid), Linda Wrather (Easter), Carlos Vera (Manuelo Sanchez).

"BLIND WITNESS"

Director: Earl Bellamy. Screenplay: Robert Leslie Bellem. Assistant Director: Gene Anderson, Jr.

Guest Cast: Myron Healey (Steve Grody), Kate Riehl (Kay Ellsworth), Zon Murray (Luke Grody), Byron Foulger (Joe Benson), William Fawcett (Tom Ellsworth).

"CLOVER IN THE DUST"

Director: Earl Bellamy. Screenplay: Doane Hoag. Assistant Director: George Loper.

Guest Cast: Don C. Harvey (Ben Ranson), Syd [Sydney] Mason (Matt Thorne), Harry Strang (Jeff Yeomans), Dan Barton (Tom Yeomans).

Count the Clues (Wrather Corporation, 1962, 75 minutes) Producer: Sherman A. Harris. Executive Producer: Jack Wrather. Photography: William Whitley. Editor: Everett Dodd. Makeup: Ben Lane. Production Supervisor: Hugh McCollum. Story Editor: Bertram Millhauser.

Cast: Clayton Moore (The Lone Ranger), Jay Silverheels (Tonto)

Episodes:

"THE WOODEN RIfle"

Director: Earl Bellamy. Screenplay: Doane Hoag. Sound: William Brady. Wardrobe: John Zacha. Assistant Director: Mark Sandrich, Jr.

Guest Cast: Rand Brooks (Al Sommers), Barbara Ann Knudson (Nancy Sommers), Bill [William] Challee (Deputy Sheriff Jed Crawley), Paul Engle (Danny Sommers), Sydney Mason (Ed Dekker).

"THE SHERIFF OF SMOKE TREE"

Director: Oscar Rudolph. Screenplay: Wells Root. Sound: William Brady. Wardrobe: John Zacha.

Guest Cast: Slim Pickens (Joe Boley), Mickey Simpson (Slim Peake), Tudor Owen (Mason), John Beradino (Lem Crater), Ron Hagerthy (Buck Webb).

"GHOST TOWN FURY"

Director: Earl Bellamy. Screenplay: Robert Schaefer & Eric Freiwald. Sound: Philip Mitchell. Sets: Harry Reif. Wardrobe: Dick Bachler. Assistant Director: George Loper.

Guest Cast: Richard Crane (Jimmy Clanton), Steven Ritch (Blackhawk), House Peters [Jr.] (Vic Clanton), Baynes Barron (Wade Clanton), Carlos Vera (Keo).

Justice of the West (Wrather Corporation, 1962, 75 minutes) Producer: Sherman A. Harris. Executive Producer: Jack Wrather. Photography: William Whitley. Editor: Everett Dodd. Makeup: Ben Lane. Production Manager: Hugh McCollum. Story Editor: Bertram Millhauser.

Cast: Clayton Moore (The Lone Ranger), Jay Silverheels (Tonto).

Episodes:

"NO HANDICAP"

Director: Oscar Rudolph. Screenplay: Tom Seller. Sound: William Brady. Wardrobe: John Zacha.

Guest Cast: Will Wright (Marshal Griff Allison), Ron Hagerthy (Deputy Sheriff Jim Hannan), Jim Parnell (Billy Douglas), Gary Marshall (Johnny Allison), John Beradino (Cole Douglas).

"QUICKSAND"

Director: Earl Bellamy. Screenplay: Robert Leslie Bellem & Walter A. Tompkins. Music Supervisor: Elias Al Friede. Sound: William Brady. Wardrobe: John Zacha. Assistant Director: Mark Sandrich, Jr.

Guest Cast: Henry Rowland (Steve Grote), Robert Burton (Ben Sutherland), Denver Pyle (Vance Kiley), Ric Roman (Black Hawk).

"OUTLAW MASQUERADE"

Director: Earl Bellamy. Screenplay: Robert Schaefer & Eric Freiwald. Sound: Philip Mitchell. Sets: Harry Reif. Wardrobe: Dick Bachler. Assistant Director: George Loper.

Guest Cast: Richard Crane (Billy), House Peters [Jr.] (Frank Cameron), Steven Ritch (Rado), Joseph Crehan (Governor).

The Lawless (Wrather Corporation, 1962, 75 minutes) Producer: Sherman A. Harris. Executive Producer: Jack Wrather. Photography: William Whitley. Makeup: Ben Lane. Production Manager: Hugh McCollum. Story Editor: Bertram Millhauser.

Cast: Clayton Moore (The Lone Ranger), Jay Silverheels (Tonto).

Episodes:

"THE RETURN OF DON PEDRO O'SULLIVAN"

Director: Oscar Rudolph. Screenplay: Tom Seller. Editor: Everett Dodd. Sound: William Brady. Wardrobe: John Zacha. Assistant Director: Gene Anderson, Jr.

Guest Cast: Tudor Owen (Don Pedro O'Sullivan), George J. Lewis (Jose), Maria Monay (Conchita Colleen), John Beradino (Dutch Regan), Mickey Simpson (Matt Hinshaw), Joe [Joseph] Vitale (Colonel Carlos Ortega).

"THE TARNISHED STAR"
Director: Earl Bellamy. Screenplay: Doane Hoag. Editor: Everett Dodd. Sound: Philip Mitchell. Sets: Harry Reif. Wardrobe: Dick Bachler. Assistant Director: Gene Anderson, Jr.
Guest Cast: Myron Healey (Marshal Vince Barrett), Mercedes Shirley (Martha Barrett), William Fawcett (Elias Rush), Zon Murray (Bart Rennick), Paul Engle (Jackie Barrett).

"SLIM'S BOY"
Director: Earl Bellamy. Screenplay: Doane Hoag. Editor: Frank Capacchione. Supervising Editor: Everett Dodd. Sound: Philip Mitchell. Wardrobe: Dick Bachler. Assistant Director: George Loper.
Guest Cast: Louise Lewis (Amy Masters), Trevor Bardette (Marshal Sam Masters), Pierce Lyden (Gil Ryan), Bob Roark (Tom Bartlett), John L. [Bob] Cason (Luke).

Masquerade (Wrather Corporation, 1962, 75 minutes) Producer: Sherman A. Harris. Executive Producer: Jack Wrather. Director: Earl Bellamy. Photography: William Whitley. Makeup: Ben Lane. Production Manager: Hugh McCollum. Story Editor: Bertram Millhauser.
Cast: Clayton Moore (The Lone Ranger), Jay Silverheels (Tonto).
Episodes:

"THE TURNING POINT"
Screenplay: Charles Larson. Editor: Frank Capacchione. Supervising Editor: Everett Dodd. Sound: Philip Mitchell. Wardrobe: Dick Bachler. Assistant Director: George Loper.
Guest Cast: Pierce Lyden (Earl Bennett), Margaret Stewart (Amy Stack), Paul Campbell (John Stack), George Barrows (Ray Torgeson), John L. [Bob] Cason (Sam Donald).

"CODE OF HONOR"
Screenplay: Robert Schaefer & Eric Freiwald. Editor: Everett Dodd. Sound: William Brady. Wardrobe: John Zacha. Assistant Director: Mark Sandrich, Jr.
Guest Cast: Rand Brooks (Trooper Phillips), Helene Marshall (Ellen Davis), Paul Engle (Tim Davis), John Maxwell (Colonel Strickland), John Cliff (Captain), Sandy Sanders (Yancy Johnson).

"DEAD-EYE"
Screenplay: Robert Leslie Bellem & Wells Root. Editor: Frank Capacchione. Supervising Editor: Everett Dodd. Wardrobe: Dick Bachler. Assistant Director: Gene Anderson, Jr.
Guest Cast: Myron Healey (Tanner), Zon Murray (Jake Beaudry), William Fawcett (Dallas "Dead-Eye" Jones).

More Than Magic (Wrather Corporation, 1962, 75 minutes) Producer: Sherman A. Harris. Executive Producer: Jack Wrather. Photography: William Whitley. Editor: Everett Dodd. Makeup: Ben Lane. Production Manager: Hugh McCollum. Story Editor: Bertram Millhauser.
Cast: Clayton Moore (The Lone Ranger), Jay Silverheels (Tonto).
Episodes:

"OUTLAWS IN GREASEPAINT"
Director: Oscar Rudolph. Screenplay: Tom Seller. Music Supervisor: Elias Al Friede. Sound: William Brady. Wardrobe: John Zacha. Assistant Director: Gene Anderson, Jr.
Guest Cast: Tom Brown (DeWitt Faversham), Mary Ellen Kay[e] (Lavinia Faversham), John Pickard (Lem Hollister), Ben Welden (Jim Waddell).

"HOT SPELL IN PANAMINT"
Director: Earl Bellamy. Screenplay: Hilary Creston Rhodes. Sound: William Brady. Wardrobe: John Zacha. Assistant Director: Mark Sandrich, Jr.
Guest Cast: Rand Brooks (Marshal Roy Bell), Barbara Knudson (Sarah Edwards), William Challee (Cal Ames), Sydney Mason (Big Hoe Hunsacker), John Cliff (Bradley).

"WHITE HAWK'S DECISION"
Director: Earl Bellamy. Screenplay: Robert Schaefer & Eric Freiwald. Music Supervisor: Ralph Cushman. Sound: Philip Mitchell. Wardrobe: Dick Bachler. Assistant Director: Gene Anderson, Jr.
Guest Cast: Harry Lauter (Frank Carter), Louis Lettieri (Arrowfoot), Robert Swan (Fleet Horse), Charles Stevens (White Hawk), Edmund Hashim (Little Hawk), Holly Bane (Dave),

Not Above Suspicion (Wrather Corporation, 1962, 75 minutes) Producer: Sherman A. Harris. Executive Producer: Jack Wrather. Photography: William Whitley. Editor: Everett Dodd. Makeup: Ben Lane. Production Manager: Hugh McCollum. Story Editor: Bertram Millhauser.
Cast: Clayton Moore (The Lone Ranger), Jay Silverheels (Tonto),
Episodes:

"MISSION FOR TONTO"
Director: Earl Bellamy. Screenplay: Tom Seller. Music Supervisor: Elias Al Friede. Sound: William Brady. Wardrobe: John Zacha. Assistant Director: Mark Sandrich, Jr.
Guest Cast: Gregg Barton (Cash Wade), Lane Bradford (Duke Wade), Robert Burton (Chad Bannion), Florence Lake (Emmy Corkle), Tyler MacDuff (Kip Holloway).

"JOURNEY TO SAN CARLOS"
Director: Earl Bellamy. Screenplay: Charles Larson. Sound: Philip Mitchell. Wardrobe: Dick Bachler. Assistant Director: Gene Anderson, Jr.
Guest Cast: Myron Healey (Ben Murray), Melinda Byron (Sally Walker), Rick Vallin (Chief Blue Feather), Joe [Joseph] Sargent (Jed Walker), Harry [Strang] Strange (Colonel Ray Wickstrom).

"THE AVENGER"
Director: Oscar Rudolph. Screenplay: Robert Leslie Bellem & Herbert Purdom. Story: Herbert Purdom.

Music Supervisor: Elias Al Friede. Sound: Philip Mitchell. Wardrobe: John Zacha. Assistant Director: Gene Anderson, Jr.

Guest Cast: Tris [Tristram] Coffin (Ben Jordan), Roy Barcroft (Baxter Crowe), Dennis Moore (Brad Stacy), Francis McDonald (Judge Talbot), Alan Wells (Sheriff Mark Rote).

One Mask Too Many (Wrather Corporation, 1962, 75 minutes) Producer: Sherman A. Harris. Executive Producer: Jack Wrather. Photography: William Whitley. Editor: Everett Dodd. Makeup: Ben Lane. Production Manager: Hugh McCollum. Story Editor: Bertram Millhauser.

Cast: Clayton Moore (The Lone Ranger), Jay Silverheels (Tonto).

Episodes:

"Canuck"

Director: Oscar Rudolph. Screenplay: Orville Hampton. Story: Edmund Kelso. Music Supervisor: Elias Al Friede. Sound: William Brady. Wardrobe: John Zacha. Assistant Director: Gene Anderson, Jr.

Guest Cast: Tris [Tristram] Coffin (Dan Slauson), Roy Barcroft (Marshal Roy Dillon), Virginia Christine (Cecile Charron), Peter Miles (Etienne Charron), Jason Johnson (Tom Burrows).

"The Prince of Buffalo Gap"

Director: Earl Bellamy. Screenplay: Tom Seller. Sound: Philip Mitchell. Wardrobe: Dick Bachler. Assistant Director: George Loper.

Guest Cast: Jim Bannon (Matt Cagle), Gabor Curtiz (Baron von Koenig), Michael Winkleman (Chip Truett), Robert Crosson (Prince Maxmillian).

"The Counterfeit Mask"

Director: Earl Bellamy. Screenplay: Doane Hoag. Sound: William Brady. Wardrobe: John Zacha. Assistant Director: Mark Sandrich, Jr.

Guest Cast: Bill [William] Challee (Blade), Sydney Mason (Sheriff Brad Calloway), Paul Engle (Joe Wilkins), John Cliff (Keller), Stacy Keach [Sr.] (Jay).

The Search (Wrather Corporation, 1962, 75 minutes) Producer: Sherman A. Harris. Executive Producer: Jack Wrather. Director: Earl Bellamy. Photography: William Whitley. Editor: Everett Dodd. Makeup: Ben Lane. Production Manager: Hugh McCollum. Story Editor: Bertram Millhauser.

Cast: Clayton Moore (The Lone Ranger), Jay Silverheels (Tonto).

Episodes:

"The Cross of Santo Domingo"

Screenplay: Tom Seller. Music Supervisor: Elias Al Friede. Sound: William Brady. Wardrobe: John Zacha. Assistant Director: Mark Sandrich Jr.

Guest Cast: Denver Pyle (Arley McQueen), Jeanne Bates (Amy McQueen), John [Johnny] Crawford (Tommy McQueen), Gregg Barton (Brick Norton), Ric Roman (Father Juan), Larry Johns (Sheriff Hobart), Lane Bradford (Jed).

"Christmas Story"

Screenplay: Robert Schaefer & Eric Freiwald. Music Supervisor: Elias Al Friede. Sound: William Brady. Wardrobe: John Zacha. Assistant Director: Mark Sandrich, Jr.

Guest Cast: Aline Towne (Mary Talbot), Mary Newton (Martha Hammond), Robert Burton (Josh Hammond), Jimmy Baird (Robby Talbot), Bill [William] Henry (Ben Talbot), Lane Bradford (George Stark), Terry Frost (Miner), Gregg Barton (Thug).

"Breaking Point"

Screenplay: Robert Leslie Bellem & Hilary Creston Rhodes. Sound: Philip Mitchell. Wardrobe: Dick Bachler. Assistant Director: George Loper.

Guest Cast: Keith Richards (Dan Peters), Richard Crane (Sheriff), Brad Morrow (Lenny Peters), House Peters [Jr.] (Mark Slade), Charles Wagenheim (Griff Peters).

Tale of Gold (Wrather Corporation, 1962, 75 minutes) Producer: Sherman A. Harris. Executive Producer: Jack Wrather. Photography: William Whitley. Sound: Philip Mitchell. Makeup: Ben Lane. Wardrobe: Dick Bachler. Production Manager: Hugh McCollum. Story Editor: Bertram Millhauser.

Cast: Clayton Moore (The Lone Ranger), Jay Silverheels (Tonto).

Episodes:

"Quarter Horse War"

Director: Earl Bellamy. Screenplay: Jack Natteford. Editor: Everett Dodd. Assistant Director: Gene Anderson, Jr.

Guest Cast: Harry Lauter (Sheriff Ed McGuire), Mae Morgan (Hazel Halliday), Bill [William] Tannen (Major Halliday), Charles Stevens (Chief Iron Hand), George Mather (Mark Allen), Holly Bane (Barney).

"Decision for Chris McKeever"

Director: Oscar Rudolph. Screenplay: Tom Seller. Editor: Hal Gordon. Assistant Director: Gene Anderson, Jr.

Guest Cast: George Mather (Chris McKeever), Bill [William] Tannen (Seth McKeever), Robert Swan (Ward McKeever).

"A Harp for Hannah"

Director: Earl Bellamy. Screenplay: Herb Purdom. Editor: Everett Dodd. Assistant Director: George Loper.

Guest Cast: Louise Lewis (Hannah Dubbs), Trevor Bardette (Walter Dubbs), Pierce Lyden (Reese Talman), Ralph Sanford (Sheriff Wirt), Bob Roark (Wes Talman).

Trackers (Wrather Corporation, 1962, 75 minutes) Producer: Sherman A. Harris. Executive Producer: Jack Wrather. Photography: William Whitley. Makeup: Ben Lane. Production Manager: Hugh McCollum. Story Editor: Bertram Millhauser. Assistant Director: Gene Anderson, Jr.

Cast: Clayton Moore (The Lone Ranger), Jay Silverheels (Tonto).

Episodes:

"GHOST CANYON"

Director: Earl Bellamy. Screenplay: Melvin Levy. Story: Fran Striker. Editor: Hal Gordon. Sound: Philip Mitchell. Wardrobe: Dick Bachler.

Guest Cast: Harry Lauter (Drake), Mike Ragan [Holly Bane] (Sloat), Ed [Edmund] Hashim (Bright Eagle), Charles Stevens (Imbray), Robert Swan (Willy Moon).

"THE TROUBLE AT TYLERVILLE"

Director: Oscar Rudolph. Screenplay: Charles Larson. Editor: Everett Dodd. Sound: William Brady. Wardrobe: John Zacha.

Guest Cast: Tom Brown (Roy Hillman), Mary Ellen Kay[e] (Ann Tyler), Ben Welden (Ed Lacey), Francis McDonald (Sheriff), John Pickard (Jess Tyler), Charles Aldridge (Jonas).

"TWISTED TRACK"

Director: Earl Bellamy. Screenplay: Robert Schaefer & Eric Freiwald. Editor: Everett Dodd. Sound: Philip Mitchell. Wardrobe: Dick Bachler.

Guest Cast: Gregg Barton (Frank Miller), Robert Burton (Ed Powell), Tyler MacDuff (Clint Harkey), Bill [William] Henry (Wynn Harkey), Terry Frost (Bully).

The Truth (Wrather Corporation, 1962, 75 minutes) Producer: Sherman A. Harris. Executive Producer: Jack Wrather. Photography: William Whitley. Makeup: Ben Lane. Production Manager: Hugh McCollum. Story Editor: Bertram Millhauser. Assistant Director: Gene Anderson, Jr.

Cast: Clayton Moore (The Lone Ranger), Jay Silverheels (Tonto).

Episodes:

"THE LAW AND MISS AGGIE"

Director: Oscar Rudolph. Screenplay: Tom Seller. Editor: Frank Capacchione. Sound: Philip Mitchell. Wardrobe: Dick Bachler.

Guest Cast: Florence Lake (Aggie Turner), Dennis Moore (Kag), Max Baer (Sampson), Brad Jackson (Chip Turner/White Eagle), Joe [Joseph] Vitale (Flying Cloud).

"THE BANKER'S SON"

Director: Earl Bellamy. Screenplay: Robert Leslie Bellem & Charles Larson. Editor: Everett Dodd. Sound: Philip Mitchell. Sets: Harry Reif. Wardrobe: Dick Bachler.

Guest Cast: Jim Bannon (Marshal Hendricks), Ron Hagerthy (Fred Bryan), Pat Lawless (Bill Nichols), Hank Worden (Bruckner), Ewing Mitchell (Tom Bryan).

"THE LETTER BRIDE"

Director: Earl Bellamy. Screenplay: Wells Root. Editor: Everett Dodd. Sound: William Brady. Wardrobe: John Zacha.

Guest Cast: Dennis Moore (Slick Friley), Slim Pickens (Ed Jones), Claire Carleton (Jennie), Victor Sen Yung (Lee Po), John Beradino (Ray Boone), Tudor Owen (Sheriff Ike Kane), Judy Dan (Mah Lin Soong), Joe [Joseph] Vitale (J.S. Forgan).

Vengeance Vow (Wrather Corporation, 1962, 75 minutes) Producer: Sherman A. Harris. Executive Producer: Jack Wrather. Director: Earl Bellamy. Photography: William Whitley. Editor: Everett Dodd. Makeup: Ben Lane. Production Manager: Hugh McCollum. Sound: Philip Mitchell. Wardrobe: Dick Bachler. Story Editor: Bertram Millhauser.

Cast: Clayton Moore (The Lone Ranger), Jay Silverheels (Tonto).

Episodes:

"THE COURAGE OF TONTO"

Guest Cast: Jim Bannon (Greg), Francis McDonald (Lew Pearson), Ewing Mitchell (Major Jonathan), Maurice Jara (Chief Gray Horse), Joel Ashley.

"MESSAGE FROM ABE"

Guest Cast: James Griffith (Phil Beach), Maggie O'Bryne (Ann Beach), Mauritz Hugo (Lefty Malone), Harry Strang (Old Man Hawkins).

"TWO AGAINST TWO"

Guest Cast: Eugenia Paul (Maria Mendoza), Baynes Barron (Vic Foley), Garry Murray (Danny Mendoza).

The Legend of the Lone Ranger (Universal, 1981, 98 minutes) Producers: Jack Wrather, Lew Grade & Walter Coblenz. Executive Producer: Martin Strarger. Director: William A. Fraker. Screenplay: Ivan Goff, Michael Kane, Ben Roberts & William Roberts. Adaptation: Gerald B. Derloshon. Photography: Laszlo Kovacs. Editor: Thomas Stanford. Music: John Barry. Art Director: David M. Haber. Sets: Phil Abramson. Production Design: Albert Brenner. Costumes: Noel Taylor. Assistant Director: Charles Okun.

Cast: Klinton Spilsbury (The Lone Ranger/John Reid), Michael Horse (Tonto), Christopher Lloyd (Butch Cavendish), Matt Clark (Sheriff Wiatt), Juanin Clay (Amy Striker), Jason Robards (Ulysses S. Grant), John Bennett Parry (Captain Dan Reid), David Hayward (Collins), John Hart (Lucas Striker), Richard Farnsworth (Wild Bill Hickok), Lincoln Tate (General George A. Custer), Ted Flicker (Buffalo Bill Cody), Marc Gilpin (Young John Reid), Patrick Montoya (Young Tonto), David Bennett (General Aurelio Rodriguez), Rick Traeger (German Stagecoach Passenger), James Bowan (Gambler), Kit Wong (Chinese Stagecoach Passenger), Daniel Nunez (Way Station Agent), R.L. Tolbert (Stagecoach Driver), Clay Boss (Stagecoach Guard), Jose Rey Toledo, Max Cisneros (Chiefs), Ted White (Mr. Reid), Chere Bryson (Mrs. White), Jim Burke (Stephenson), James Lee Crite (Walter), Jeff Ramsey (Alcott), Bennie E. Dobbins (Lopez), Henry Wills (Little), Greg Walker (Rankin), Michael Adams (Palmer), Ben Bates (Post), Bill Hart (Carner), Larry Randles (Stacy), Robert F. Hoy (Perlmutter), Ted Gehring (Dale Wesley Stillwell), Buck Taylor (Robert Edward Gatlin), Tom R. Diaz (Eastman), Chuck Hayward (Wald), Tom Laughlin (Neeley), Terry Leonard

(Valentine), Steve Meador (Russell), Joe Finnegan (Westlake), Roy Bonner (Richardson), John M. Smith (Whitloff), Rock Taylor (Robert Edward Gatlin), Kenneth Lingad (Pablo/Manuel), Bonita Granville (Woman), James Keach (Voice of the Lone Ranger).

The Lone Ranger (WB Television Network, 2003, 95 minutes) Producers: Susanne Daniels, Mel Efros, Eric Ellenbogen, Joseph Penner, Stacy Tile & Cathy M. Frank. Director: Jack Bender. Screenplay: Jonathan Penner & Stacy Tile. Photography: Steven Fierberg. Editors: Mark Melnick & Luis Colina. Music: Roger Neill. Production Design: Sandy Veneziano. Costumes: Karyn Wagner. Production Manager: Burt Burnam. Production Executive: Ed Milkovich. Casting: Dan Shaner.

Cast: Chad Michael Murray (The Lone Ranger/Luke Hartman), Nathaniel Arnold (Tonto), Anita Brown (Alope), Fay Masterson (Grace Hartman), Sebastian Spence (Harmon Hartman), Dylan Walsh (Kansas City Haas), Wes Studi (Kulakinah), Bradford Tatum (Tyron), Jeffrey Nording (James Landry), Lauren German (Emily Landry), Tod Thawley (Tera), Gil Birmingham (One Horn), Paul Schulze (Sheriff Landry), David Franco (Chandler), Martha Hackett (Margaret), Mike Weinberg (Junior Harmon), Antoinette Broderick (Julia), Cassie Pappas (Amy), Laura Beth Cohen (Stella), Joel Marshall (Hotel Guest), Brian J. White (Joseph Freedman), James Kyson Lee (Dr. Li).

THE LONE RIDER

Following its success with the "Billy the Kid" (q.v.) series, Sigmund Neufeld Productions launched a second group of westerns, "The Lone Rider," in 1941. In the new series, Al St. John continued his characterization of Fuzzy Jones, the comedy sidekick of Tom Cameron, alias the Lone Rider. The character was basically a singing cowboy variation of the Lone Ranger; opera baritone George Houston was cast in the role. In 1939, when PRC was still called Producers Distributing Corporation (PDC), the studio announced that Houston would play Billy the Kid in eight features but when the films finally materialized, Bob Steele was William Bonney.

Houston (1896–1944) was a New Jersey native who served in World War I. Having majored in voice and music teaching at the Institute of Musical Arts (later Juilliard School of Music) in New York City, he then launched a career in opera. By the late 1920s he was appearing in Broadway musicals and he began making films in the mid–1930s, eventually starring as singing sailors for Grand National in *Captain Calamity* (1936) and *Wallaby Jim of the Islands* (1937). For the studio he also portrayed Wild Bill Hickok in *Frontier Scout* (1938), which marked his first teaming with St. John. Houston would star in eleven "Lone Rider" outings for PRC, all released in 1941 and 1942. During that time he operated the American Music Theater in Pasadena, California, which performed opera in English. It is believed that he did the PRC series in order to help finance this singing group. In *Hollywood Corral* (1976), Don Miller said, "That [Houston] was possessed of a fine baritone was unquestioned—Houston was undoubtedly the best singer among the cowboys, on the basis of pure vocalistics…. But he was afflicted with the curse of most opera-type belters, stolidity. Generally unsmiling and in short supply of humor, Houston often seemed preoccupied, probably musing on better days at the opera with Verdi and Puccini, rather than high noons on the PRC prairies with Charlie King and I. Stanford Jolley." Miller did note, however, "He had some acting ability and could present a believable version of rough-and-tumble when called upon to do so."

Lew Porter and Johnny Lange, heads of the music department at Sigmund Neufeld Productions, composed the songs sung by Houston, including his theme song "I'm the Lone Rider," which was performed during the opening credits of each feature. Houston usually belted out two or three songs during each production, the action coming to a halt for the recitals. In this star's case, however, this procedure tended not to get unnerving since Houston had such an excellent and ingratiating singing voice. Houston's singing and

St. John's comedy antics elevated what otherwise would have been a rather mundane, typical western film series.

The Lone Rider Rides On, the series' initial entry, was issued early in 1941, and told the background of the title character. As a boy (Bobby Winkler), Tom Cameron witnesses the murder of his family by marauders. Twenty years later, Tom (Houston) is now the avenging Lone Rider, who is out to get those who killed his parents and little brother. Near the town of Flat Rock he finds a murdered man with a deed to a nearby ranch. The deed was signed by Frank Mitchell (Tom London) who is in cahoots with local crooks, including Curly Robinson (Lee Powell), who want to force the murdered man's sister, Sue Brown (Hillary Brooke), off the ranch and take over. In town, Tom stops Mitchell's gang from harassing store owner Fuzzy (St. John). Mitchell frames Tom for the murder of Sue's brother; he is found guilty and sentenced to hang by Judge Graham (Karl Hackett), who Tom remembers as the leader of the marauders who murdered his family. Fuzzy helps Tom escape and the Lone Rider then plans to stop the gang, only to learn that Curly is really his younger brother.

Also called *The Lone Rider Galloping to Glory*, the film not only introduced the series' theme "I'm the Lone Rider" but it also had Houston singing "Roll Along Prairie Wagon" and doing a comedy duet with St. John on "Nobody's Fault But My Own." The film, a good introduction to "The Lone Rider," was helped by the appearance of Hillary Brooke as the leading lady; she would have the same chore in *The Lone Rider in Frontier Fury* later in the year. Of special interest was the casting of Lee Powell as Jim Cameron, the Lone Rider's younger brother, raised by outlaws to be one of them. During a scuffle between the siblings near the finale, a birthmark identifies Jim, who willingly ends up taking a bullet to save his older brother, thus permitting warbling Tom Cameron to continue his exploits. Powell would soon star in Sigmund Neufeld Productions' "Frontier Marshals" (q.v.) for PRC.

Released in March, 1941, the series' second entry, *The Lone Rider Crosses the Rio*, now had the character of Fuzzy Jones (St. John) as Tom Cameron's (Houston) full-time sidekick. Here the duo head to Mexico in order to avoid an outlaw gang and there they learn that the area is being plagued by El Puma (Charles King) and his band of robbers. At Alta Mesa, Tom becomes involved in trying to stop a romance between the son (Howard Masters) of his friend, the town's mayor (Thornton Edwards), and a cantina singer (Roquell Verria) whose father (Julian Rivero) hides Tom's true identity. After Tom and Fuzzy plan a fake kidnapping of his son, the mayor comes to believe that Tom is El Puma, when the latter's gang actually does abduct the young man and hold him for ransom. It is then up to Tom and Fuzzy to rescue the kidnap victim and bring in El Puma and his gang. While *Variety* liked the film's star, music and comedy, it also pinpointed the main drawback of the entire series: "Major trouble with 'Lone Rider' is that the characterization has not etched clearly enough. It's a picture of a hero looking for something to become heroic about. Action, too, is ratherly (sic) thinly spread out and more of the familiar rough-and-tumble would be helpful."

The fall of 1941 brought *The Lone Rider in Ghost Town* with Tom (Houston) and Fuzzy (St. John) coming to the aid of a rancher friend (Steve Clark) and getting involved in a plot by crooked saloon owner Sinclair (Alden Chase) to steal a gold mine. Tom is alerted to trouble when an old prospector pal, Mooshide (Budd Buster), is forbidden by Sinclair to enter a supposed deserted ghost town. In reality, Sinclair has imprisoned in the mine a mining engineer (Edward Peil, Sr.) who has an option on the property. At the site, Tom runs across the engineer's daughter Helen (Alaine Brandes [Rebel Randall]), who is searching for her father. When one of Sinclair's gang members, Gordon (Reed Howes), is kidnapped and forced to confess by Tom, he is shot on Sinclair's orders. Tom is arrested for killing Gordon, who is really still alive. Tom locates Gordon and tries to take him to town but the outlaw is murdered and Tom finds the engineer and tries to prevent Sinclair from stealing the ghost mine from him. Despite its rather spooky atmosphere, the film sported a quartet of songs: "Sweet Suzannah," "Under Prairie Skies," "In Old Spring Valley" and "Old Cactus Joe," plus the title theme. *Variety* thought it "fair enough western fare."

Hillary Brooke returned as the leading lady in *The Lone Rider in Frontier Fury*, released around

Lobby card for *The Lone Rider Crosses the Rio* (PRC, 1941).

the same time as the series' previous entry. She portrayed Georgia Deering, a young Chicago woman who comes West to inherit the ranch left to her by her uncle (John Elliott), whose murder is being blamed on Tom Cameron (Houston). The real culprits are ranch foreman Clyde Barton (Archie Hall) and crooked lawyer Case Murdock (Ted Adams), who want the spread for themselves. After ranch hand Loco (Budd Buster) tries to turn in Tom, Georgia starts to believe in his innocence. Tom tells Fuzzy (St. John) to protect Georgia as he tries to find out who murdered her uncle. In Wagonwheel Gap, Tom comes to the aid of barmaid Midge (Virginia Card), whose father, Malone (Karl Hackett), is an outlaw. Malone tries to kidnap Georgia but Tom leaves a clue for Fuzzy as he also learns the identity of the murderer of Georgia's uncle.

Released in the United Kingdom as *Frontier Fury*, this fairly action-filled series outing is somewhat interesting for a couple of members of its cast. Archie Hall (1908–78) is better known as Arch Hall, Sr., a sometimes producer-director whose army career was the basis for the 1961 feature *The Last Time I Saw Archie*, starring Robert Mitchum. Hall would appear in a number of PRC westerns for the Neufeld brothers. Virginia Card, who portrayed the fill-fated Midge Malone, was an actress-singer who was married to George Houston.

The Lone Rider Ambushed was another series entry released in the fall of 1941. This time out Tom (Houston) takes the guise of his lookalike, outlaw Keno Harris (also Houston), who is about to be released from prison after serving five years for bank robbery. Tom convinces the sheriff to let him pose as Keno and infiltrate the gang now run by Blackie Dawson (Frank Hagney) in order to find the buried loot. Joining the gang, Tom is able to convey to the law the gang's plans and its mem-

Advertisement for *The Lone Rider in Frontier Fury* (PRC, 1941).

bership begins to dwindle. Keno's sweetheart, saloon singer Linda (Maxine Leslie), suspects Tom is an imposter but he convinces her to try to get Keno to go straight and return the money. Upon Tom's orders, Fuzzy (St. John) trails Keno after his release. Refusing to listen to Linda about returning the money, Keno ambushes Tom and changes clothes with him as Blackie orders Tom's murder. It is Keno, however, who is shot by the gang as Tom and Fuzzy race to defeat the outlaw gang.

The Lone Rider Ambushed afforded Houston the opportunity to portray dual roles and it also gave him a trio of passable songs: "Ridin,' Roamin' on the Prairie," "If It Hadn't Been for You" and "Without You, Darling, Life Won't Be the Same."

The last 1941 "Lone Rider" release was *The Lone Rider Fights Back* and in it Tom (Houston) and Fuzzy (St. John) come to the aid of Jean Dennison (Dorothy Short), whose rancher uncle has been murdered. Realtor George Clarke (Frank Hagney) has found out there is gold in the area and he is trying to use fake foreclosures to take over the ranch she has inherited from her uncle. Tom infiltrates Clarke's gang but the realtor distrusts him and orders three of his men, Mitter (Charles King), Gandon (Frank Ellis) and Williams (Dennis Moore), to ambush Tom. Overhearing this, Fuzzy warns Tom, who picks a fight with Williams, who gets away on Tom's horse only to be mistaken for the Lone Rider by the other gang members and murdered. Clarke accuses Tom of the killing and he is arrested; Jean gives the realtor a quick-claim deed to her ranch in order to get bond money for Cameron. Tom and Fuzzy then work out a scheme to cause the outlaws to fight among themselves, bringing about their demise and restoring Jean's ranch to her.

An interesting plot ploy in *The Lone Rider Fights Back* has Tom and Fuzzy using a microphone and amplifier to convince the sheriff (Hal Price) he is surrounded in order to get themselves released from jail. In the cast is Dennis Moore as outlaw Al Williams; he was soon to join the series, making for a triad hero group. Two songs also highlighted the feature, "Where the West Begins" and "It's All Over Now."

Houston would star in five more "Lone Rider" episodes in 1942, beginning with *The Lone Rider and the Bandit*, which was also called *Murrieta and the Lone Rider* because of its use of the character of outlaw Joaquin Murrieta in the plot. Crooked saloon proprietor Luke Miller (Glenn Strange) wants all the mining claims around Big Horn and he hires Jed Corbett (Carl Sepulveda) to pretend to be Murrieta and terrorize the area so the miners will sell him their stakes. Believing Murrieta is operating in the area, Sheriff Smoky Moore (Dennis Moore) asks Tom (Houston) and Fuzzy (St. John) to come and find the outlaw. They arrive in Big Horn masquerading as musicians. Impersonating Murrieta, Tom stops Miller's men from burning Laura Hicks' (Vicki Lester) house, as she has refused to sell her claim to the saloon owner. Miller believes Tom is Murrieta and tells this to vigilantes who arrest Tom, Fuzzy and the sheriff, but the three escape jail. When Corbett again tries to burn Laura's home, Tom stops him and forces him to confess that Miller is behind all the trouble.

The Lone Rider and the Bandit is a fairly actionful programmer which also sported a quartet of Houston songs: "I'm the Best Man in the West," "Down the Moonlit Trail," "Rainbow Valley" and "Prairie Cabin I Love." The most interesting aspect of the film, however, is the casting of Dennis Moore (1908–64) as Sheriff Smoky. For the rest of the series he would portray a character called Smoky and, starting with the next series entry, *The Lone Rider in Cheyenne*, he would be billed as Dennis "Smoky" Moore. Sometimes billed as Denny Meadows, Moore appeared in scores of films, beginning in the mid–1930s, with the bulk of them being westerns. Although he usually played supporting roles he occasionally had star parts, the "Lone Rider" films offering him his first taste of series stardom, although he did headline the Bud 'n Ben short *West on Parade* (1934) and the features *Fangs of the Wild* (1939) and *Law of the Wolf* (1941).

Next came *The Lone Rider in Cheyenne* which contained the songs "When Cowboys Start Ridin'" and "Prairie Trail." Here Tom (Houston), Fuzzy (St. John) and Smoky (Moore) are government agents; when Smoky is framed for a bank robbery in Pecos City, Tom and Fuzzy come to his rescue. The trio later go back to Pecos City to help Smoky's adoptive father, Sheriff Bill Hastings (Jack M. Holmes), fight lawlessness. Smoky recognizes the mayor, Mort Saunders (Roy Barcroft), as the leader of the gang who tried to frame him. Working undercover, Tom agrees to help Saunders get rid of Hastings so he can become the new sheriff. Convincing Smoky he is trying to capture the gang, Tom and Fuzzy hatch a plot to bring in Saunders but when a bank robbery goes awry, Smoky is blamed for the crime and nearly hanged. Tom convinces Saunders' arrested henchman Pete (George Chesebro) that the lynch mob is really coming for him and he writes a confession implicating his boss.

The third 1942 series release was *The Lone Rider in Texas Justice*, which had British showings simply as *The Lone Rider*. Here Houston sang "Ride, Cowboy, Ride," "There's Only One Rose in Texas" and "We Will Meet in the Valley," in the involved story of a female bandit leader, Nora Mason (Claire Rochelle), using the ranch of her friend Kate Stewart (Wanda McKay), the daughter of ex-outlaw Jack Stewart (Karl Hackett), to hide stolen cattle. When crooked rancher Huxley (Slim Whitaker) demands that Sheriff Smoky Moore (Moore) arrest Jack, who claims he was falsely convicted of cattle theft, a lynch mob tries to hang Smoky and Jack. Tom (Houston) and Fuzzy (St. John) come to their rescue. When Jack is murdered during a cattle raid, Fuzzy wants Smoky to arrest Tom fearing he would be lynched since he was trying to use the rustling to reveal the real gang leader. Smoky releases Tom from jail and the latter goes to a local mission disguised as a priest and finds Nora is keeping the padre (Julian Rivero) a prisoner; one of her men, Tremmer (Archie Hall), has taken the padre's place. Locating stolen cattle in a box canyon on Kate's ranch, Tom leads the locals there. Nora and her gang are arrested and Tom, Fuzzy and Smoky then decide to become gold prospectors in the Klondike.

The far north country is nowhere to be seen in the next outing, *Border Roundup*, also known as *The Lone Rider in Border Roundup*. Crook Blackie (Charles King) is after the location of rancher Jeff Sloane's (John Elliott) gold strike and he has henchman Indian Pete (Nick Thompson) murder Jeff's friend Sourdough (Jimmy Aubrey) and then blames the crime on Marshal Smoky Moore (Moore), who was attempting to aid Sloane, who has been kidnapped by Blackie. Fellow lawmen Tom (Houston) and Fuzzy (St. John) rescue Smoky. Banker Masters (I. Stanford Jolley), Blackie's boss, tells Sloane's daughter Amy (Patricia Knox) that it was Tom who abducted her father and murdered Sourdough. Amy comes to believe in Tom's innocence and agrees to help the lawmen capture the real culprits. When Amy goes with Masters to see her father, she uses a homing pigeon to alert Tom. Fuzzy is able to find the location of the gang's hideout and the lawmen lead a posse there, rounding up the gang and freeing Sloane.

This entry had Houston singing "There's a Cabin in the Clearing," "When a Cowboy Rides" and "The Rollin' Hills." The cast also included another singer, Gale Sherwood, who would later gain fame as Nelson Eddy's singing partner. Here billed as Dale Sherwood, she has the small role of a waitress.

Houston's final film was *Outlaws of Boulder Pass* in which he sang "Let's Keep Roamin' the Prairie" and "The Grass Is Always Green in Sunshine Valley." When Smoky Hammer (Moore) is waylaid by marauders, he is rescued by Tom (Houston) and Fuzzy (St. John). Recovering from his injuries, Smoky decides to keep hidden in order to find out who is responsible for the attack on him. His sister Tess (Marjorie Manners), who thinks Sid Clayton (Karl Hackett) is her father, objects to his charging high tolls to other ranchers driving cattle across their range. Gil Harkness (I. Stanford Jolley) is behind the lawlessness, believing he has killed Smoky. He plans to get rid of Tess so his underling Clayton will get full control of the ranch. Tom and Fuzzy save Tess when Harkness' gang attacks her and she hires them as ranch hands. Smoky robs the toll-takers and the locals believe he is a ghost. When Harkness proposes to Tess, Smoky proves he is not a ghost and tells Tess the truth about them being siblings. Tom causes Harkness and Clayton to have a falling-out and Smoky pretends to be his father's ghost, scaring Clayton into a confession that Harkness murdered Smoky and Tess' father. Harkness kills Clayton but is captured by Tom.

Released in November, 1942, *Outlaws of Boulder Pass* is a solid series entry thanks to its "detour into backwater superstition" (Michael H. Price & George E. Turner, *Forgotten Horrors 2* [2001]). The authors added, "The finale, where [Dennis] Moore pretends to be his long-dead father in order to spook a confession out of the bad guys, is a keeper."

Houston left the series in 1942, being replaced by Robert Livingston. Houston then concentrated on his operatic company, which was planning a national tour sponsored by the Theater Guild when he died of a heart attack on November 12, 1944.

The character name of Tom Cameron for the Lone Rider was retained in Robert Livingston's first series entry, *Overland Stagecoach*, issued late in 1942. Livingston's contract with Republic Pictures ended upon his leaving "The Three Mesquiteers" (q.v.) the previous year. Using his real name of Robert Randall, he appeared as the romantic interest in PRC's *The Black Raven* (1943), also made for Sigmund Neufeld Productions. Upon taking the lead in the "Lone Rider" series, however, he reverted to the Livingston moniker, billed as either Robert or Bob. With the departure of Houston, songs were dropped from the series and the characters of Tom Cameron, Fuzzy Jones and Smoky Moore were not used a triad heroes as in previous entries, although they do unite to fight lawlessness.

In *Overland Stagecoach*, St. John's Fuzzy Jones is a stagecoach driver whose line is in jeopardy due to the building of a railroad. Fuzzy's boss (John Elliott) is killed trying to sabotage the rail company and his partner Harlan Kent (Glenn Strange) continues the fight. He also wants to murder the dead man's daughter Susan (Julie Duncan) so he can have the stage line for himself. Fuzzy sends for his friend Tom Cameron, the Lone Rider (Livingston), who becomes convinced there is trouble when his friend Smoky Moore (Moore) is ambushed by Kent's gang on his way to take the job of railroad construction foreman. Tom saves Smoky as Kent uses gang member Pete (Budd Buster), who hides in a secret seat-box in the stagecoach, to sabotage the railroad construction with dynamite. Fuzzy, who has made disparaging remarks about the railroad, is blamed and Tom hides him in friend Pedro's (Julian Rivero) café. Eventually Kent takes Susan hostage but Tom, Fuzzy and Smoky stop the stagecoach in which Kent has the young woman hidden. When she is found, Kent is arrested and Susan takes over the stage operation.

Dennis Moore departed from the "Lone Rider" series after *Overland Stagecoach* and in 1943 co-starred in four entries in Monogram's "The Range Busters" (q.v.) series. He later co-starred in some Jimmy Wakely Monogram oaters and in 1950 he appeared in all six "Irish Cowboys" (q.v.) entries for Lippert Pictures. He mostly did supporting parts in westerns and starred in the serials *Raiders of Ghost City* (1944), *Perils of the Wilderness* and *Blazing the Overland Trail* (both 1956).

The character of Smoky Moore, now played by one-time cowboy star Lane Chandler, was retained for *Wild Horse Rustlers*, which was released in the summer of 1943. While all the other series films took place in the old West, this entry was a modern-day drama using the then-popular topic of Nazis spies invading the range, this time to sabotage horse herds for the Fatherland. For the first time, St. John's character was called Fuzzy Q. Jones, the complete name given him in the "Billy the

Kid–Billy Carson" series. With this outing, Tom Cameron is now called Tom "Rocky" Cameron.

The plot has Tom (Livingston) and Fuzzy (St. John) purchasing horses from a Texas ranch for use by the United States Cavalry. Just as they arrive at the ranch owned by Ellen Walden (Linda Leighton), they manage to save foreman Smoky Moore (Lane Chandler) from being shot by cowpoke Collins (Stanley Price), who manages to escape. Collins is working for Nazi spy Hans Beckmann (also Chandler), who is Smoky's twin brother. Beckmann is under orders to destroy all the horses intended for government use and he wants Smoky dead so he can takes his place. When Collins tries to quit the gang, Beckmann kills him and later blames the crime on Tom and Fuzzy. The Nazis kidnap Smoky, and Hans goes to the ranch with his gang, pretending to be his twin. Tom and Fuzzy break jail and Tom later tries to make Beckmann think Collins is talking to him through a bunkhouse window. Realizing that Beckmann is impersonating Smoky and that the spies are after the horses, Tom and Fuzzy stop a load of poisoned hay intended for the ranch. Burning the hay, Tom tells Ellen and Beckmann, who still poses as Smoky, that he is a government purchasing agent but later he tells Beckmann he is a rustler and gains his confidence. Tom is able to rescue Smoky, and Fuzzy brings the sheriff (Karl Hackett) and his posse; they unmask Beckmann and his gang as spies.

With *Death Rides the Plains*, the Lone Rider became just Rocky Cameron. Its plot dealt with a deadly swindle by crooks Gowdey (Ray Bennett) and Rogan (I. Stanford Jolley), who sold the Circle C ranch to unsuspecting buyers and then murdered them for the purchase money. Fuzzy (St. John) arrives at the Circle C to help run it for the new owner, one of the crooks' victims. He is run off the spread as the gang shoots and robs another buyer, James Marshall (John Elliott), but he is saved by Rocky Cameron (Livingston). He later rescues Marshall's daughter Virginia (Nica Doret) from the outlaws and then, working undercover, he tells Gowdey he wants part of his operation. The gang kills Marshall and puts the blame on Rocky and Fuzzy, but Rocky manages to convince Virginia they are innocent. With the aid of another buyer, Edward Simms (Karl Hackett), Rocky and Fuzzy are able to catch the gang and Rogan implicates Gowdey. The latter escapes after killing Rogan but is captured by Rocky, and Fuzzy turns the Circle C over to Virginia.

Law of the Saddle, also called *The Lone Rider in Law of the Saddle*, was released in the summer of 1943. Here Rocky (Livingston) and Fuzzy (St. John) try to stop crook Steve Kinney (Lane Chandler), who pillages small towns with his gang after being elected sheriff. The gang plans to take over Kingston and tries to kidnap Gayle Kirby (Betty Miles), the fiancée of Sheriff Dave Barstowe (Reed Howes), but fail when Rocky and Fuzzy come to her rescue. Dave becomes jealous of Rocky, who is later falsely accused of killing Gayle's father (John Elliott). Rocky is put in jail but Fuzzy helps him to escape. Rocky forces Kinney henchman Vic Dawson (Frank Ellis) to implicate his boss in the crimes. Dave captures the gang while Rocky pursues Kinney, killing him in a gunfight.

This feature was the only "Lone Rider" film not directed by Sigmund Neufeld's brother, Sam Newfield. Instead it was done by Newfield's assistant director, Melville De Lay. While he usually worked as a production manager or assistant director, De Lay did direct *Mystic Hour* for Progressive Pictures in 1934. The difference between his style and Sam Newfield's was noted by Don Miller in *Hollywood Corral* (1976): "Newfield was straight on with his cameras and meant business, which is why he lasted so long and made so many pictures. De Lay was his assistant, and assumed full helming of *Law of the Saddle* when Newfield took a breather. De Lay used panning shots, a variety of angles, instilled a lot of pace in the action and a lot of vigor in the actors, turned out one of the better PRC Westerns, and never directed another feature. You figure it out." Since De Lay died a couple of years after the film was made, perhaps his health did not permit him to direct full-time.

Sam Newfield returned with *Wolves of the Range*, released in the early summer of 1943. Taking place in Arizona, it had Cattlemen's Association chief Harry Dorn (I. Stanford Jolley) plotting with his pal Adams (Kenne Duncan) to get control of the area and sell it to a corporation wanting to set up an irrigation project. To do so, the two use their gang to terrorize the locals into selling. Rancher Bob Corrigan (Karl Hackett) is attacked by the gang but is saved by Rocky

Al St. John, Julie Duncan, Dennis Moore, Art Mix, Chick Hannon, Art Dillard and Budd Buster in *Overland Stagecoach* (PRC, 1942).

(Livingston) and Fuzzy (St. John). Banker Dan Brady (Ed Cassidy), who planned to loan ranchers money until a drought ends, is murdered by Dorn's henchmen Hammond (Jack Ingram) and Davis (Frank Ellis). The Lone Rider captures the killers but a crooked judge (Bob Hill) sets them free, despite the fact that Brady's daughter Ann (Frances Gladwin) testified that Dorn had threatened her father's life. With the bank about to fail, Rocky rides to a nearby town to retrieve $50,000 belonging to Ann but on the way back he is bushwhacked and develops amnesia due to a head wound. Dorn causes Rocky to be arrested for robbery and Fuzzy consults a fakir (Slim Whitaker) who sells him medallions for protection. Fuzzy sets Rocky free with the bullets fired at him by deputies lodging in the medallions. Rocky and Fuzzy head out of town trailed by the Dorn gang which, in turn, is followed by Corrigan and the other ranchers. After a gunfight, the gang is captured, and Rocky and Fuzzy head back to town to get Dorn. During a

Advertisement for *Death Rides the Plains* (PRC, 1943).

Poster for *Law of the Saddle* (PRC, 1943).

fight with Dorn, Rocky is hit in the head and his memory returns. Dorn is arrested and Rocky remembers where he hid the money.

Wolves of the Range contains an amusing performance by Slim Whitaker, usually a baddie but cast here as the fortune teller, Pasha. The amnesia plot ploy would be revived the next year at Republic when Livingston headlined the "John Paul Revere" (q.v.) series entry *Beneath Western Skies*.

The final "Lone Rider" feature, *Raiders of Red Gap*, came out in the summer of 1943. This time Rocky (Livingston) aids his partner Fuzzy (St. John), who has been mistaken for killer Butch Crane (Roy Brent), who has been hired by cattle company owner Jack Bennett (Charles King). Bennett wants the local range land in order to build packing plants so he will not have to pay for cattle shipments. When Fuzzy is mistaken for Crane by Bennett's men, Rocky convinces Bennett that Fuzzy is really the outlaw. Bennett offers Fuzzy money to kill local rancher Jim Roberts (Ed Cassidy), who is leading the ranchers in fighting the cattle company owner. When the real Crane arrives, Rocky tells Bennett he is the real hired gunman, as Fuzzy tries to ingratiate himself with Roberts and his daughter Jane (Myrna Dell). They do not believe him, however, and Fuzzy is arrested and put in jail. Rocky frees Fuzzy from jail as Crane convinces Bennett of his identity and the two plan to attack the Roberts ranch. Crane is captured by Rocky and Fuzzy. Learning of Bennett's plans, Rocky heads to the Roberts ranch while Fuzzy gets Jim to round up all the ranchers for a showdown. The gang is subdued during a gun battle and Rocky captures Bennett after a fistfight.

Following the "Lone Rider" series, Livingston re-signed with Republic Pictures and immediately took over its "John Paul Revere" character for two entries before working in both starring and supporting roles for the company. Leaving Republic in 1948, Livingston freelanced in both films and television until the mid–1950s. He left films in 1958 after a guest appearance as himself in *Once Upon a Horse* ... but in the mid–1970s he starred in three features for Independent-International Pictures, including the comedy-western *Blazing Stewardesses* (1975).

With the end of the "Lone Rider" films, St. John continued his Fuzzy Q. Jones characterization in PRC's "Billy Carson" (q.v.) series, also made by Sigmund Neufeld Productions.

Filmography

The Lone Rider Rides On (PRC, 1941, 61 minutes) Producer: Sigmund Neufeld. Director: Sam Newfield. Screenplay: Joseph O'Donnell. Photography: Jack Greenhalgh. Editor: Holbrook N. Todd. Production Manager: Bert Sternbach. Sound: Hans Weeren. Art Director: Fred Preble. Songs: Johnny Lange & Lew Porter. Assistant Director: Melville De Lay.

Cast: George Houston (Tom Cameron/The Lone Rider), Hillary Brooke (Sue Brown), Al St. John (Fuzzy Jones), Karl Hackett (Judge Graham), Lee Powell (Jim Cameron/Curly Robinson), Forrest Taylor (Sheriff), Tom London (Frank Mitchell), Frank Hagney (Bill), Frank Ellis (Pete Daly), Curley Dresden (Jerry), Buddy Roosevelt (Joe), Al Bridge (Pat Cameron), Isabel La Mal (Ma Cameron), Harry Harvey, Jr. (Young Jim Cameron), Bobby Winkler (Young Tom Cameron), Don Forrest (Eddie), Robert Kortman (Dave), Richard Cramer (Bartender), Steve Clark (Settler), Wally West,

Jay Wilsey [Buffalo Bill Jr.], Lew Meehan, Augie Gomez (Henchmen), George Morrell, Herman Hack, Ray Henderson (Citizens).

Reissued in 16mm as *Rider of the Plains*.

The Lone Rider Crosses the Rio (PRC, 1941, 63 minutes) Producer: Sigmund Neufeld. Director: Sam Newfield. Screenplay: William Lively. Photography: Jack Greenhalgh. Editor: Holbrook N. Todd. Production Manager: Bert Sternbach. Sound: Hans Weeren. Art Director: Ernest Graber. Assistant Director: Melville De Lay.

Cast: George Houston (Tom Cameron/The Lone Rider), Al St. John (Fuzzy Jones), Roquell Verria (Rosalie), Charles King (Ward Jarvis/El Puma), Julian Rivero (Pedro), Alden Chase (Deputy Hatfield), Thornton Edwards (Manuel Tores), Howard Masters (Francisco Tores), Jay Wilsey [Buffalo Bill Jr.] (Bart), Frank Ellis (Fred), Frank Hagney (Marty), Phillip [Felipe] Turich (Lieutenant Mendoza), Steve Clark (Steve), Curley Dresden (Jeff), Joe Dominguez (Rurale), Lane Bradford (Posse Rider), Carl Mathews (Bar Customer), George Morrell (Cantina Customer), Wally West, James Sheridan, Art Dillard, Ray Henderson (Henchmen).

Also known as *Across the Border*.

The Lone Rider in Ghost Town (PRC, 1941, 64 minutes) Producer: Sigmund Neufeld. Director: Sam Newfield. Screenplay: Joseph O'Donnell. Photography: Jack Greenhalgh. Editor: Holbrook N. Todd. Production Manager: Bert Sternbach. Sound: Hans Weeren. Songs: Johnny Lange & Lew Porter. Assistant Director: Melville De Lay.

Cast: George Houston (Tom Cameron/The Lone Rider), Al St. John (Fuzzy Jones), Alaine Brandes [Rebel Randall] (Helen Clark), Budd Buster (Moosehide Larsen), Frank Hagney (O'Shea), Alden Chase (Bob Sinclair), Reed Howes (Jim Gordon), Charles King (Roberts), George Chesebro (Jed), Edward Peil, Sr. (Clark), Archie Hall (Partner), Jack Ingram (Trail Boss), Lane Bradford (Boardwalk Cowboy), Byron Vance (Cowboy), Frank Ellis (Red), Steve Clark (Jim Madison), Jay Wilsey [Buffalo Bill Jr.], Curley Dresden (Henchmen), Don Forrest (Brent), Wally West, Herman Hack, Chick Hannon, Augie Gomez (Saloon Customers), Dan White (Citizen).

Reissued in 16mm as *Ghost Town*.

The Lone Rider in Frontier Fury (PRC, 1941, 53 minutes) Producer: Sigmund Neufeld. Director: Sam Newfield. Screenplay: Fred Myton. Photography: Jack Greenhalgh. Editor: Holbrook N. Todd. Production Manager: Bert Sternbach. Sound: Hans Weeren. Sets: Vin Taylor. Songs: Johnny Lange & Lew Porter. Assistant Director: Melville De Lay.

Cast: George Houston (Tom Cameron/The Lone Rider), Al St. John (Fuzzy Jones), Hillary Brooke (Georgia Deering), Karl Hackett (Matt Malone), Ted Adams (Case Murdock), Archie Hall (Clyde Barton), Budd Buster (Loco), Virginia Card (Midge Malone), Edward Peil, Sr. (Rancher), John Elliott (Jim Bowen), Tom London (Curley), Frank Ellis (Joe), Dan White (Card Player), Reed Howes, Tex Palmer, Augie Gomez (Henchmen), Horace B. Carpenter, Milburn Morante (Saloon Customers), Wally West, Ben Corbett, Curley Dresden (Ranch Hands).

British title: *Frontier Fury*.

The Lone Rider Ambushed (PRC, 1941, 63 minutes) Producer: Sigmund Neufeld. Director: Sam Newfield. Screenplay: Oliver Drake. Photography: Jack Greenhalgh. Editor: Holbrook N. Todd. Production Manager: Bert Sternbach. Sound: Hans Weeren. Sets: Vin Taylor. Songs: Johnny Lange & Lew Porter. Assistant Director: Melville De Lay.

Cast: George Houston (Tom Cameron/The Lone Rider/Keno Harris), Al St. John (Fuzzy Jones), Maxine Leslie (Linda), Frank Hagney (Blackie Dawson), Jack Ingram (Charlie Davis), Hal Price (Sheriff), Ted Adams (Deputy Slim Pettit), George Chesebro (Pete), Ralph Peters (Gus the Bartender), Charles King (Ranch Hand), Steve Clark (Ranch Foreman), Tex Palmer (Cowboy), Lew Porter (Lew the Piano Player), Ray Henderson (Posse Rider), Wally West (Citizen), Lyndon Brent, Curley Dresden, Carl Mathews, Bill Nestell, Dan White, Roy Brent, Art Dillard, Curley Dresden, Ray Jones, Augie Gomez, Barney Beasley (Henchmen).

The Lone Rider Fights Back (PRC, 1941, 64 minutes) Producer: Sigmund Neufeld. Director: Sam Newfield. Screenplay: Joseph O'Donnell. Photography: Jack Greenhalgh. Editor: Holbrook N. Todd. Production Manager: Bert Sternbach. Sound: Hans Weeren. Sets: Vin Taylor. Songs: Johnny Lange & Lew Porter. Music Director: David Chudnow. Assistant Director: Melville De Lay.

Cast: George Houston (Tom Cameron/The Lone Rider), Al St. John (Fuzzy Jones), Dorothy Short (Jean Dennison), Dennis Moore (Al Williams), Frank Hagney (George Clarke), Charles King (Mitter), Frank Ellis (New Gandon), Hal Price (Sheriff), Curley Dresden (Bailey), Pascale Perry (Adams), Walter James (Bartender), Horace B. Carpenter, Milburn Morante, George Morrell (Saloon Customers), Jack O'Shea, Wally West, Merrill McCormick (Henchmen), Art Mix (Cowboy).

The Lone Rider and the Bandit (PRC, 1942, 54 minutes) Producer: Sigmund Neufeld. Director: Sam Newfield. Screenplay: Steve Braxton [Sam Robins]. Photography: Jack Greenhalgh. Editor: Holbrook N. Todd. Production Manager: Bert Sternbach. Sound: Paul Schmutz. Songs: Johnny Lange & Lew Porter. Assistant Director: Melville De Lay.

Cast: George Houston (Tom Cameron/The Lone Rider), Al St. John (Fuzzy Jones), Dennis Moore (Sheriff Smokey Moore), Vicki Lester (Laura Hicks), Glenn Strange (Luke Miller), Jack Ingram (Joe), Milton Kibbee (Sam Turner), Carl Sepulveda (Jed Corbett), Eddie Dean (Younger Miner), Slim Whitaker (Older Miner), Slim Andrews (Piano Player), Kenne Duncan

(Saloon Henchman), Curley Dresden (Harris), Frank Ellis (Zeke the Bartender), Jack Kirk (Stage Driver), Merrill McCormick (Raider), Oscar Gahan (Miner), Wally West, Milburn Morante, Tex Phelps, George Morrell, Pascale Perry (Citizens), Steve Clark, Rube Dalroy, Augie Gomez, Jack Kinney (Citizens).

The Lone Rider in Cheyenne (PRC, 1942, 59 minutes) Producer: Sigmund Neufeld. Director: Sam Newfield. Screenplay: Elizabeth Beecher. Story: Oliver Drake. Photography: Jack Greenhalgh. Editor: Holbrook N. Todd. Production Manager: Bert Sternbach. Songs: Johnny Lange & Lew Porter. Musical Director: David Chudnow. Assistant Director: Melville De Lay.

Cast: George Houston (Tom Cameron/The Lone Rider), Al St. John (Fuzzy Jones), Dennis "Smoky" Moore (Smoky Moore), Ella Neal (Betty Tolliver), Roy Barcroft (Mort Saunders), Ken [Kenne] Duncan (Deputy Walt), Lynton Brent (Dirk Larkin), Milt [Milton] Kibbee (Joe Carson), Jack M. Holmes (Sheriff Bill Hastings), Karl Hackett (Mayor Dan Blodgett), Jack Ingram (Jed Saunders), George Chesebro (Pete Haynes), Curley Dresden (Lefty Higgins), Lew Porter (Piano Player), Jack Kirk (Driver), Ray Henderson (Payroll Guard), Richard Cramer (Bartender), Wally West, Al Taylor (Henchmen), Edward Peil, Sr. (Citizen), Milburn Morante (Checkers Player), Tex Palmer, Hank Bell, Pascale Perry, Jack Evans, Augie Gomez (Saloon Customers).

The Lone Rider in Texas Justice (PRC, 1942, 58 minutes) Producer: Sigmund Neufeld. Director: Sam Newfield. Screenplay: Steve Braxton [Sam Robins]. Photography: Jack Greenhalgh. Editor: Holbrook N. Todd. Production Manager: Bert Sternbach. Songs: Johnny Lange & Lew Porter. Assistant Director: Melville De Lay.

Cast: George Houston (Tom Cameron/The Lone Rider), Al St. John (Fuzzy Jones), Dennis "Smoky" Moore (Sheriff Smoky Moore), Wanda McKay (Kate Stewart), Claire Rochelle (Nora Gilpin), Archie Hall (Padre Tremmer), Slim Whitaker (Huxley), Edward Peil, Sr. (Ed Hannigan), Karl Hackett (Jack Stewart), Julian Rivero (Padre Jose), Dirk Thane, Art Dillard (False Padres), Curley Dresden (Curley), Jack Montgomery (Davis), Steve Clark, Merrill McCormick (Ranchers), Frank Ellis (Henchman), Horace B. Carpenter (Lynch Mob Member).

British title: *The Lone Rider*; reissued as *Texas Justice*.

Border Roundup (PRC, 1942, 57 minutes) Producer: Sigmund Neufeld. Director: Sam Newfield. Screenplay: Stephen Worth [Joseph O'Donnell]. Photography: Jack Greenhalgh. Editor: Holbrook N. Todd. Production Manager: Bert Sternbach. Songs: Johnny Lange & Lew Porter. Musical Director: David Chudnow. Assistant Director: Melville De Lay.

Cast: George Houston (Tom Cameron/The Lone Rider), Al St. John (Fuzzy Jones), Dennis "Smoky" Moore (Smoky Moore), Patricia Knox (Amy Sloane), Charles King (Blackie), I. Stanford Jolley (Masters), Edward Peil, Sr. (Sheriff), Jimmy Aubrey (Sourdough), John Elliott (Jeff Sloane), Dale [Gale] Sherwood (Waitress), Nick Thompson (Indian Pete), Frank Ellis (Joe Gardner), Jack Kirk (Mattox the Blacksmith), Lynton Brent (Sam), Curley Dresden (Bert), Herman Hack, Ray Henderson (Deputies), Dan White (Counterman).

Also called *The Lone Rider in Border Roundup*.

Outlaws of Boulder Pass (PRC, 1942, 58 minutes) Producer: Sigmund Neufeld. Director: Sam Newfield. Screenplay: Steve Braxton [Sam Robins]. Photography: Jack Greenhalgh. Editor: Holbrook N. Todd. Production Manager: Bert Sternbach. Sound: Hans Weeren. Songs: Johnny Lange & Lew Porter. Assistant Director: Melville De Lay.

Cast: George Houston (Tom Cameron/The Lone Rider), Al St. John (Fuzzy Jones), Smoky [Dennis] Moore (Smoky Hammer), Marjorie Manners (Tess Hammer/ Tess Clayton), I. Stanford Jolley (Gil Harkness), Karl Hackett (Sidney "Sid" Clayton), Charles King (Jake), Ted Adams (Sheriff), Ken [Kenne] Duncan (Mulie), Frank Ellis (Ringo), Jimmy Aubrey (Deputy), Milburn Morante (Andrews), George Morrell (Johnson), Tex Palmer (Stage Driver), Budd Buster (Rancher), Ray Henderson (Rider), Steve Clark, Charlie Murray, Jr., Bert Dillard, Art Fowler (Henchmen), Art Dillard (Posse Member).

Overland Stagecoach (PRC, 1942, 58 minutes) Producer: Sigmund Neufeld. Director: Sam Newfield. Screenplay: Fred Myton & Steve Braxton [Sam Robins]. Story: Fred Myton. Photography: Jack Greenhalgh. Editor: Holbrook N. Todd. Production Manager: Bert Sternbach. Music: Leo Erdody. Assistant Director: Melville De Lay.

Cast: Robert [Bob] Livingston (Tom Cameron/The Lone Rider), Al St. John (Fuzzy Jones), Smoky [Dennis] Moore (Smoky Moore), Julie Duncan (Susan Clark), Glenn Strange (Harlen Kent), Ted Adams (Sheriff), Julian Rivero (Pedro), Budd Buster (Pete), Art Mix (Jitters), John Elliott (Jeff Clark), Charles King (Jake), George Morrell (Doctor), Kenne Duncan, Jimmy Aubrey, Chick Hannon, Art Dillard, Bert Dillard (Posse Members), Tex Cooper, Jack Casey, Lew Morphy (Citizens), Rose Plummer (Stage Passenger), Roy Brent, Herman Hack, Dan White, Jack Evans, Augie Gomez, Barney Beasley, Frank McCarroll, Jack Tornek (Railroad Employees), Milburn Morante (Agent).

Wild Horse Rustlers (PRC, 1943, 58 minutes) Producer: Sigmund Neufeld. Director: Sam Newfield. Screenplay: Joe [Joseph] O'Donnell & Steve Braxton [Sam Robins]. Photography: Jack Greenhalgh. Editor: Holbrook N. Todd. Production Manager: Bert Sternbach. Sound: Hans Weeren. Music Director: Leo Erdody. Assistant Director: Melville De Lay.

Cast: Robert [Bob] Livingston (Tom "Rocky" Cameron/The Lone Rider), Al St. John (Fuzzy Jones), Lane Chandler (Smoky Moore/Hans Beckmann),

Linda Leighton (Ellen Walden), Frank Ellis (Jake Greene), Stanley Price (Bruce Collins), Karl Hackett (Sheriff), Jimmy Aubrey (Guard), Ben Corbett, Curley Dresden, Artie Ortego (Deputies), Kansas Moehring, Silver Harr (Henchmen).

Death Rides The Plains (PRC, 1943, 53 minutes) Producer: Sigmund Neufeld. Director: Sam Newfield. Screenplay: Joe [Joseph] O'Donnell. Story: Patricia Harper. Photography: Robert Cline. Editor: Holbrook N. Todd. Production Manager: Bert Sternbach. Sound: Hans Weeren. Music Director: David Chudnow. Assistant Director: Melville De Lay.

Cast: Bob Livingston (Rocky Cameron/The Lone Rider), Al St. John (Fuzzy Jones), Nica Doret (Virginia Marshall), Ray Bennett (Ben Gowdey), I. Stanford Jolley (Rogan), George Chesebro (Trent), John Elliott (James Marshall), Kermit Maynard (Jed), Slim Whitaker (Sheriff), Karl Hackett (Edward Simms), Frank Ellis (Sam), Curley Dresden, Wally West, Kansas Moehring (Deputies), Jimmy Aubrey, Dan White (Citizens), Hank Bell (Bartender), Lane Bradford, Milburn Morante, Oscar Gahan, Tex Cooper, Art Dillard, George Morrell, Tex Palmer, Jack Evans, Art Fowler, Rube Dalroy, Ralph Bucko, Roy Bucko, Jack Tornek, Lew Morphy (Saloon Customers).

Law of the Saddle (PRC, 1943, 59 minutes) Producer: Sigmund Neufeld. Director: Melville De Lay. Screenplay: Fred Myton. Photography: Robert Cline. Editor: Holbrook N. Todd. Production Manager: Bert Sternbach. Assistant Director: Al Schnee.

Cast: Robert Livingston (Rocky Cameron/The Lone Rider), Al St. John (Fuzzy Jones), Betty Miles (Gayle Kirby), Lane Chandler (Steve Kinney), John Elliott (Dan Kirby), Reed Howes (Sheriff Dave Barstowe), Curley Dresden (Joe), Al Ferguson (Bart), Frank Ellis (Vic Dawson), Jimmy Aubrey (Jailer), Bob [Robert F.] Hill (Tom), Bert Dillard (Hank), Jack Evans, Jack Tornek (Ranchers), Wally West, Al Taylor (Cowboys), Herman Hack, Foxy Callahan, Lew Morphy, Bill Wolfe (Citizens), Victor Adamson [Denver Dixon], George Morrell, Pascale Perry (Saloon Customers).

Also known as *The Lone Rider in Law of the Saddle.*

Wolves of the Range (PRC, 1943, 60 minutes) Producer: Sigmund Neufeld. Director: Sam Newfield. Story-Screenplay: Joseph O'Donnell. Photography: Robert Cline. Editor: Holbrook N. Todd. Production Manager: Bert Sternbach. Sound: Hans Weeren. Assistant Director: Melville De Lay.

Cast: Robert Livingston (Rocky Cameron/The Lone Rider), Al St. John (Fuzzy Jones), Frances Gladwin (Ann Brady), I. Stanford Jolley (Harry Dorn), Karl Hackett (Bob Corrigan), Ed Cassidy (Dan Brady), Jack Ingram (Hammond), Kenne Duncan (Adams), Budd Buster (Ben Foster), Bob [Robert F.] Hill (Judge Brandon), John Elliott (Doctor), Slim Whitaker (Fortune Teller Pasha), Milton Kibbee (Rancher), Lester Dorr (Bank Clerk), Roy Brent (Bill Davis), Reed Howes, Wally West, Art Dillard, Bert Dillard (Henchmen), Jimmy Aubrey (Man on Street), Augie Gomez (Man on Porch), Morgan Flowers, Al Haskell, Ray Jones, Cactus Mack, Jack Tornek, Tom Smith, Rose Plummer (Bank Customers), Art Fowler, Chick Hannon, George Morrell, Roy Bucko, Fox Callahan, Murdock MacQuarrie (Citizens), Lew Morphy (Man at Bank Door).

Raiders of Red Gap (PRC, 1943, 57 minutes) Producer: Sigmund Neufeld. Director: Sam Newfield. Screenplay: Joseph O'Donnell. Photography: Robert Cline. Editor: Holbrook N. Todd. Production Manager: Bert Sternbach. Assistant Director: Melville De Lay.

Cast: Bob Livingston (Rocky Cameron/The Lone Rider), Al St. John (Fuzzy Jones), Myrna Dell (Jane Roberts), Ed Cassidy (Jim Roberts), Charles King (Jack Bennett), Slim Whitaker (Green), Kermit Maynard (Foreman Bradley), Roy Brent (Butch Crane), Frank Ellis (Jed), George Chesebro (Sheriff Evans), Reed Howes, Curley Dresden, Merrill McCormick (Henchmen), George Morrell, Wally West (Roberts' Employees), Pascale Perry (Rancher).

NEVADA JACK MCKENZIE

Following the death of Buck Jones in the Cocoanut Grove fire in Boston late in 1942, Monogram was forced to halt its "Rough Riders" (q.v.). series. Scott R. Dunlap, the producer of "The Rough Riders," was seriously hurt in the conflagration but recovered and in 1943 he and the studio launched a new series, "Nevada Jack McKenzie," which not only utilized scripts that Jess Bowers (Adele Buffington) had prepared for "The Rough Riders" but also co-starred Raymond Hatton, continuing the Sandy Hopkins character. The leading role, written for Buck Jones, was given a name change, becoming Nevada Jack McKenzie; Great Western Productions, which made the films for Monogram release, signed Johnny Mack Brown to star.

Brown (1904–74) first gained fame as an All-American football halfback at the University of Alabama in the mid–1920s. Eschewing offers to go professional, he instead came to Hollywood, where Metro-Goldwyn-Mayer signed him in 1927. He appeared in the silents *The Divine Woman*, *Our Dancing Daughters* and *Annapolis* (all 1928), before successfully making the transition to sound in *Coquette* (1929) and *Montana Moon* (1930). Thereafter he appeared in a variety of features but seemed more at home in westerns like *Billy the Kid* (1930), *The Great Meadow* and *Lasca of the Rio Grande* (both 1931), *The Vanishing Frontier* (1932) and the 1933 Mascot serial *Fighting with Kit Carson*. He began starring in series "B" westerns for Supreme in 1935 and '36 and Republic in 1936 and '37. In 1937 he signed a contract at Universal, where he headlined 29 features and three serials before coming to Monogram in 1943. Beginning in 1940, he was ranked in the top ten money-making western stars in polls conducted by both *Motion Picture Herald* and *Boxoffice*.

The initial "Nevada Jack McKenzie" feature, *The Ghost Rider*, was released in the spring of 1943. Directed by Wallace W. Fox, it told of crooked bar owner Lash Edwards (Harry Woods) trying to get control of all the property in the area of Dead Creek. He has his men Zack Saddler (Edmund Cobb) and Steve Cook (Charles King) force slaughterhouse operator Patrick McNally (Jack Daley) to sign over his property to him; Cook then shoots McNally. Before dying, McNally is found by Nevada Jack McKenzie (Brown) and predates a deed to the property and gives it to him. McKenzie, who is known as the Ghost Rider, is out to revenge the murder of his family years before. McKenzie comes to the aid of the dead man's son, Joe (Tom Seidel); when Lash's men try to force the young man off his father's land, McKenzie stops them with the property agreement. U.S. Marshal Sandy Hopkins (Raymond Hatton), pretending to be the local sheriff, investigates the killing and is tied up by McKenzie as is Joe. McKenzie then makes himself a partner with Lash in the slaughterhouse enterprise, a deal overheard by Joe. After Sandy and Joe get free, the lawman learns the location of the gang's hideout and he and Joe go there only to find McKenzie has killed Cook, one of the murderers of his folks, in self-defense. McKenzie is arrested for shooting Cook but Sandy lets him go since he has arrested Lash and his men for the killing of a trio of federal marshals. While Sandy urges McKenzie to join the U.S. Marshals, he decides to continue on his revenge mission.

The Nevada Jack McKenzie and Sandy Hopkins characters were first united as a team in the series' second entry, *The Stranger from Pecos*, issued in the summer of 1943. It was directed by genre veteran Lambert Hillyer, who would helm 13 of the series' 20 productions. The story had McKenzie (Brown) taking the advice of Sandy Hopkins (Hatton) and joining the U.S. Marshals and being assigned to stop land thefts around the community of Blakewell. After witnessing the robbery and murder of rancher Bud Salem (Kermit Maynard) by Harmon (Charles King),

Lobby card for *The Ghost Rider* (Monogram, 1943) picturing Raymond Hatton and Johnny Mack Brown.

McKenzie takes the money the outlaw stole. He later sees Harmon and his men shoot ex-lawman Bill Barstow (Robert Frazer). Before dying, Barstow asks McKenzie and Sandy to help his son Tom (Kirby Grant) start a new ranch, but Harmon frames the young man for Salem's killing. In town, McKenzie meets restaurant owner Clem Martin (Steve Clark) and his daughter Ruth (Christine McIntyre), who believe in Tom's innocence. While Harmon plans to incite a lynch mob against Tom by letting him escape from jail, McKenzie aids the young man first and hides him with the Martins. Sandy helps Bud Salem's brother, Bert (Edmund Cobb), in saving his ranch by fixing the cards in a poker game so the stolen money won by Salem can be used to pay off banker Ward (Sam Flint). McKenzie infiltrates the Harmon gang but Clem mistakenly informs the banker that the local sheriff (Roy Barcroft) is crooked and that a federal lawman is working on the case, not knowing the banker and the sheriff are in cahoots. Ward tells Clem to hide Tom in a remote shack and then sends Harmon and his men after them. McKenzie aids the two men in evading the gang and then uses the ruse of telling Harmon about Sandy and turning him over to the gang. When Ward shows up, McKenzie and Sandy capture the outlaws and Clem Martin is made the town judge. As Tom and Ruth announce their wedding plans, McKenzie and Sandy promise to return for the nuptials.

The fall of 1943 saw the release of *Six Gun Gospel*, which had U.S. Marshals McKenzie (Brown) and Sandy (Hatton) coming to the town of Goldville to stop a series of robberies. Saloon proprietor Ace Benton (Kenneth MacDonald) wants to run off all the area ranchers so he can buy their land cheaply and resell it to a railroad that plans to run through the town. Sandy is mistaken for a parson and befriended by Jane Simms (Inna Gest) and Mary Daily (Mary MacLaren) after Jack stops Benton's men from harassing him. Finding out that Jane's father, Bill Simms (Kernan Cripps), will have to give up his claim unless he can make a bullion shipment, Sandy agrees to be the guard on the next transport, which will be driven by Dan Baxter (Eddie Dew), Jane's boyfriend. After Ben Dailey (Jack Daley), Mary's husband, refuses to sell Benton his land at a cheap price, the saloon owner's henchmen murder him; McKenzie and Sandy trail them to their hideout. Although McKenzie is snared by the outlaws, he pretends to be wanted, while Sandy joins Dan on the express run. Getting away from the hideout, McKenzie aids Sandy and Dan in fighting the robbers, who are taken prisoner. Benton forces Bill Simms to sign over his property to him but when he finds out about his men being arrested, he plans to ambush McKenzie when he comes to town with the stagecoach. The lawmen, however, put gang member Durkin (Roy Barcroft) in McKenzie's place and when they arrive in town he begs Benton not to kill him. Jack and Sandy steal into the saloon and get the drop on Ace and the remainder of his gang, and Simms is set free.

Outlaws of Stampede Pass came out the next month; Johnston McCulley, the creator of "Zorro" (q.v.), provided the story. Federal lawman McKenzie (Brown) arrives in the area of Yucca City working undercover as a cattle buyer in order to ferret out a gang of rustlers. When cattleman Tom Evans (Jon Dawson) is ambushed by outlaws who have rustled his cattle, McKenzie rescues him and takes him to the home of blacksmith Jeff Lewis (Sam Flint) and his daughter Mary (Ellen Hall). The blacksmith suggests that McKenzie call in Tom's uncle, Marshal Sandy Hopkins (Hatton), who comes to town in the guise of a dentist. McKenzie, Sandy and Jeff come up with a plan to arrest cattle buyer Ben Crowley (Harry Woods), the leader of the rustlers. When McKenzie sets up a meeting with Crowley, he is taken prisoner and removed to the outlaws' hideout. Crowley then orders his henchman Gus (Art Mix) to finish off Tom but instead he is shot by Sandy. The recovered Evans helps Sandy in looking for McKenzie, who manages to get the better of his captor, Steve Carse (Charles King), and he starts a shootout with the gang. Hearing the gunshots, Sandy and Steve locate the hideout and aid McKenzie in capturing the gang. Back in town, Crowley plans to kill the blacksmith but Sandy and McKenzie stop him and put the crook behind bars. Tom is able to get back his stolen cattle and he and Mary decide to wed.

The final series entry for 1943, *The Texas Kid*, came out in late November and had Marshal Reed dominating the proceedings in the title role. Here U.S. Marshal McKenzie (Brown) is on the trail of a gang of outlaws led by Scully (Edmund Cobb).

A member of the gang is MacLaine, known as The Kid (Marshall Reed), who leaves the outfit after killing a member who murdered his folks. While McKenzie and fellow lawman Sandy (Hatton) trail The Kid, he becomes friendly with Nancy Drew (Shirley Patterson), who had to sell her trading post to Naylor (Robert Fiske) after the murder of her father by robbers. Naylor is working with Scully in trying to run off the local ranchers in order to get their land because another stagecoach line is being planned by his Eastern employers. Sandy poses as a peddler and McKenzie hides in his wagon to avoid being killed by Scully and his men. Later McKenzie backs the Kid's plan to carry a payroll shipment to its destination and he then puts on a mask and pretends to attack the stagecoach being driven by MacLaine. The Kid, who has set up a plan to double cross Scully, throws off the strongbox and it is retrieved by McKenzie, who now believes MacLaine is in cahoots with the gang. When Scully finds out that The Kid did not bring the payroll, he orders him to be shot as McKenzie and Sandy find out he actually hid the money on the stage. They ride to The Kid's rescue but he dies from his wounds as they arrest the gang. They then grant MacLaine's last wish: The money he helped the gang steal is given to Nancy so she can open another trading post.

Johnston McCulley provided a second series story for *Raiders of the Border*, issued early in 1944. This one found federal marshals McKenzie (Brown) and Sandy (Hatton) assigned to the Mesa City area where rustlers are trading stolen cattle herds for stolen jewels. Claiming to be deaf, Sandy finds out that trading post wagon driver Whiskey Watkins (Ernie Adams) has nearly enough money to buy out his boss, Bonita Bayne (Ellen Hall), the fiancée of rancher Joe (Craig Woods). Watkins works clandestinely for saloonkeeper Blackie (Stanley Price), who orders his murder because he has become too verbose. McKenzie witnesses the killing and tells Sandy to get a job at the trading post, replacing Watkins. Bonita agrees to sell the post and marry Joe as McKenzie pretends to be a buyer and spends the night there, causing trouble with Joe's foreman, Steve Rowan (Richard Alexander). Steve works with Blackie who is controlled by hermit Harsh (Raphael [Ray] Bennett), who dwells in an earth-covered Navajo hut and makes pottery. Harsh orders Steve to steal a herd of cattle for trade with jewel fence McGee (Edmund Cobb). Steve also incites trouble between McKenzie and Joe over Bonita, and Jack meets with Harsh about possibly purchasing some of his pottery if he buys the trading post (he later sees the hermit confer with Steve). During the night, McKenzie and Sandy see Steve trying to steal Joe's cattle with the rancher being wounded by his foreman. McKenzie shoots Steve while Sandy takes the injured Joe to the trading post. After capturing two of the rustlers, McKenzie goes into town for a showdown with McGee, who manages to escape. The next day Sandy comes to Harsh's hut for a pottery shipment and McGee arrives to warn his boss about McKenzie. One of the pots break, revealing jewels secreted there. McKenzie rides up and shoots McGee, and Harsh tries to get the drop on Sandy, who shoots him with a derringer. The lawmen then arrest Blackie and the remainder of the gang.

Next came *Partners of the Trail*, an April 1944 release. The town of Rawbone has been plagued by a series of killings and federal lawmen McKenzie (Brown) and Sandy (Hatton) have been assigned to investigate. On the way to town, the stagecoach in which McKenzie is riding is held up by outlaws, and the driver is killed. Jack drives the coach into town where Sandy is working incognito as a cook. There McKenzie meets the sheriff, Dobbey (Hal Price), and Trigger (Jack Ingram), his deputy. Both have been appointed by the head of the local land and water company, J.D. Edwards (Robert Frazer). McKenzie also meets Doc Applegate (Lloyd Ingraham), who has been out of town investigating the murder of a friend, and who leaves a sealed envelope, which supplies the motive for the killing, in the safe at the Wells Fargo office, which is run by Joel Dixon (Craig Woods). Joel is engaged to Kate Hilton (Christine McIntyre), whose father was a recent murder victim. After meeting with McKenzie and Sandy, Doc, who sent for the lawmen, is murdered by Clint Baker (Marshall Reed), who works for Edwards. The gunman is arrested by McKenzie and put in jail but Edwards has Trigger silence Baker. Although they thought the motive for the area lawlessness was water rights, the two lawmen come to realize it was the discovery of gold that has instigated the trouble. McKenzie tells Joel to fetch

Doc's letter from his safe, but Edwards' henchmen steal it first. Trigger arrests McKenzie for the theft. The robbers take the letter to Edwards, who finds out it reveals the location of a rich gold claim; he has his men stake out the area. Edwards also learns that McKenzie is a U.S. marshal and he tells Trigger to kill him but Sandy stops the outlaw. The two lawmen trail outlaw Swanky (Ted Mapes) to the gold claim as Edwards calls a meeting of the ranchers to buy their spreads. Nevada breaks up the get-together, tells the ranchers they own gold-rich land and arrests the crooks.

Law Men followed three weeks later. Again the federal men (Brown and Hatton) are on the trail of outlaws, this time bank robbers in the vicinity of Verdeen. When Sandy shoots a holdup man during a robbery, he claims to be a shoemaker and is offered a vacant boot shop by businessman Pop Haynes (Hal Price). McKenzie, who also witnessed the robbery, trails the three escaping outlaws to their Bear Paw Draw hideout and then goes back to town to confer with Sandy, both believing the gang has an informer. At the hideout, McKenzie pretends to be an outlaw who wants to join the gang but he is not trusted by Gus (Art Fowler) and the other henchmen. Bank owner Bradford (Robert Frazer) is told of his losses by teller Clyde Miller (Kirby Grant). He later meets with saloon proprietor Slade (Edmund Cobb), the leader of the outlaw gang. Bradford is in cahoots with Slade because he wants to get all the ranch land in the area. At his boot shop, Sandy meets Phyllis (Jan Wiley), Clyde's girlfriend, who tells him he should room at her Auntie Mac's (Isabel Withers) boarding house. Slade outlines the next gold shipment robbery to his gang. That night at the boarding house, Clyde expresses surprise about the outlaws knowing about the gold being in the bank. McKenzie tells Sandy of the upcoming robbery and says not to let the gold be placed on the stagecoach. The next day he and Clyde replace it with sand. Bradford finds out about the plan and decides to frame Clyde, who has told him that a federal marshal is on the case. Suspecting McKenzie, when Bradford tells Slade to get rid of him, henchman Killifer (Marshal Reed) accepts the assignment but mistakenly kills another gang member, Nickel Plate (Ted French). Clyde leaves on the stagecoach with Curley (Ted Mapes), another gang member, driving as Bradford tells Phyllis that he gave Clyde some securities the day before and that he is worried about him. McKenzie meets with Sandy and the two follow the stagecoach that is held up by Slade and his men. Finding only sand in the strong box, Slade believes that Bradford has double crossed him. Clyde is taken hostage and as gang member Simmons (Ben Corbett) drives him and the stage to town, Slade and the rest of his men go to face Bradford. McKenzie and Sandy overtake the stagecoach and rescue Clyde and the three ride to town where Bradford has promised Slade he will give him the stolen gold, which is still in the bank. Curley shows up with the stagecoach and accuses Clyde of being one of the robbers. Bradford tries to incite the locals against his clerk when McKenzie and Clyde burst into Slade's saloon and arrest the banker for his crimes. Slade attempts to ambush McKenzie but is shot by Sandy as Jack wounds Killifer, and Clyde shoots Curley. Clyde is exonerated and he and Phyllis plan to marry as the townspeople throw their badly fitting shoes and boots at Sandy. This entry provided Raymond Hatton a chance to sing a brief rendition of "Jesse James."

Range Law came out in July 1944 with the two lawmen (Brown and Hatton) trying to stop the hanging of rancher Pop McGee (Steve Clark) for cattle theft, at the behest of the man's friend, Boots Annie (Sarah Padden). McKenzie helps Pop break out of jail and has him hide in a remote shack and then learns that a horseshoe he found in McGee's corral belongs to saloon owner Phil Randall's (Jack Ingram) horse. Randall wants Pop's land because it is the site of a rich silver deposit; he plans to buy the spread for back taxes. When Randall's henchman Dawson (Stanley Price) tells him that McKenzie is a lawman, the saloon owner orders his death. Dawson shoots at McKenzie and the marshal is declared dead by Sandy, as the local sheriff (Hugh Prosser), who is in cahoots with Randall, goes after the assassin. The bullets, however, hit rolled-up blankets and the unharmed McKenzie goes with Sandy to find Dawson, who has been shot by Randall. The lawmen find the wounded gunman and McKenzie takes him back to town. Sandy is arrested by the sheriff but is given an alibi by Randall, who realizes that McKenzie is still alive. Leaving Dawson at Annie's, McKenzie goes for a doctor and Sandy finds the dying outlaw who tells him that Randall framed Pop. When rancher Jim Bowen (Marshall Reed) takes food to McGee, he is followed by the outlaws who capture the two men. McKenzie and Sandy rescue Pop and Bowen and then return to town and stop Randall from buying the McGee ranch. Randall is arrested and the sheriff is killed in self-defense by McKenzie. *Variety* thought it a "fairly diverting dual western," adding, "Picture shows good overall supervision by Charles J. Bigelow."

Five weeks later, *West of the Rio Grande* came to theaters. The plot had federal marshal Sandy (Hatton) called in by Sheriff Tom Boyd (Jack Rockwell) to act as an election judge, although he poses as a schoolteacher, as voters decide on a new county seat. The contest is between Centerville and Keenesburgh, which is run by crooked Martin Keene (Kenneth MacDonald). Boyd is murdered by Nate Todd (Art Fowler) and Lucky Cramer (Hugh Prosser) on Keene's orders; gunfighter Wade Gunnerson (John Merton) is appointed in his place. Gunnerson is on his way to Keenesburgh on a stagecoach with McKenzie (Brown) and another U.S. marshal, veteran Trooper Meade (Lloyd Ingraham), an enemy of Keene. During the trip, Gunnerson kills a sheriff who tries to arrest him on a murder charge and McKenzie shoots the gunman and takes his identity. In town, McKenzie pretends to be Gunnerson and is hated by Boyd's son, Denny (Dennis Moore). McKenzie then helps Keene keep the local ranchers in line by taking their cattle for back taxes and stopping an uprising lead by Denny. Judge Darcy (Frank LaRue) sets up a plan to make sure the voting is fair and the ballots are properly delivered. Denny and Lucky are given the task of bringing in ballots from the town of Northfolk and as they do so, the outlaws attack Denny and try to steal the ballots; they are stopped by McKenzie. The ballots arrive safely as the federal marshals appoint Trooper Meade as the new sheriff. When McKenzie tells Keene to hand over his records, the crook tries to murder him but is himself shot and killed. As Sandy rounds up the rest of the outlaws, Centerville is named the new county seat.

Released in September 1944, *Land of the Outlaws* had the U.S. marshals (Brown and Hatton) summoned by Dan Broderick (John Merton), whose Blue Boy mine ore shipments are being hijacked on the way to the smelter. Broderick stops using the services of freight line owner Frank Carson (Stephen Keyes) and decides to use his own wagons in making the shipments. Ed Hammond (Hugh Prosser), a saloon proprietor who is behind the robberies, orders his henchman Slim Carter (Art Fowler), Broderick's mine foreman, to replace his boss' ore with a low-grade quality which will force the mine owner to sell his property at a cheap price. McKenzie comes to town and takes a job as head gambler at Hammond's saloon while Sandy starts working for Carson. Sandy later reveals that his new boss had served time in prison for stagecoach holdups, and McKenzie reveals his identity to Broderick. Jack urges the mine owner to rehire Carson and when an ore shipment is made, he and Sandy observe a hijack attempt and capture Vic (Tom Quinn), one of the robbers. Bart Green (Charles King), one of Hammond's men, is the leader of the hijackers. Carter changes the smelter's report on the ore that was shipped, and then slips Vic a gun filled with blanks. When the prisoner tries to shoot McKenzie and the sheriff (Steve Clark), he is shot by them but before dying implicates Carter. Since the smelter's report did not properly identify the ore shipped, McKenzie requests an inspection of the mine but Frank's fiancée, Ellen (Nan Holiday), informs Hammond that Jack is a federal marshal. Carter leads the mine inspection and has one of the outlaws, Sam (Bob Woodward), plant explosives so the lawman will be killed. McKenzie, however, refuses to let Carter leave the mine until he admits Hammond was the mastermind behind the hijackings. The two men escape from the mine before it explodes and McKenzie returns to town and arrests Hammond and his gang.

The final two 1944 series releases, *Law of the Valley* and *Ghost Guns*, both came out in November. The former had Sandy (Hatton) receiving a letter from an old friend, Luke Stone (Horace B. Carpenter), asking for help, and he and his partner McKenzie (Brown) go to Green Valley where the man's niece, Ann Jennings (Lynne Carver), tells them her uncle is in hiding and fears for his life. She takes them to her uncle but they find he has been murdered. McKenzie deduces that a masked man, whom he wounded earlier, is the culprit. When he finds out that local businessmen Dan Stanton (Edmund Cobb), Condon (Tom Quinn) and Miller (Charles King) have taken over the Stone ranch, McKenzie confronts Condon and informs him that he and Sandy were Stone's partners. Sandy and Ann take her uncle's body to the sheriff (Hal Price) and on the way to the ranch, Hopkins stops two men from ambushing McKenzie. The two lawmen see Condon and Miller meet with Al Green (Marshall Reed), the masked man wounded by McKenzie. They try to capture Green but he gets away only to be mistakenly shot by Condon's men. In town, McKenzie meets lawyer Tom Findley (Kirk Barron) who informs him that Miller and Condon dammed the stream on the Stone ranch in order to deprive the local ranchers of water so they would have to sell their spreads. The two crooks planned to sell the land to the railroad but they had to get Stone out of the way because he threatened to sue them. Calling a meeting of the ranchers, McKenzie suggests bringing back the water by dynamiting the dam. Once this is accomplished, McKenzie tells Stanton to give him the ranchers' deed and he discovers Stanton has murdered Miller. Stanton tells the sheriff that McKenzie committed the crime, but once Jack's true identity is revealed, Stanton and Condon are arrested.

Ghost Guns had Indian Springs rancher Ann Jordan (Evelyn Finley) asking for help after outlaws kill her father and raid area ranches. U.S. marshals McKenzie (Brown) and Sandy (Hatton) are assigned to look into the matter. Sandy, working undercover as a cowboy, and McKenzie come to Ann's ranch where they find her and Aunt Sally (Sarah Padden) tending to Ted Connors' (Riley Hill) wounds. He and his two brothers were ambushed by rustlers and he was the only one to survive. Ann had gone into town for drunken Doc Edwards (Ernie Adams) and there she confronted crook Matson (John Merton) and his stooge, newly appointed judge Kelbro (Frank LaRue). Matson plans to terrorize the local ranchers so they will leave and he can get their spreads to sell to an incoming railroad. While they are at the ranch, McKenzie and Sandy witness another attempt on Ted's life, and McKenzie tells Doc to say Connors has died. In town, Sandy is able to obtain proof that Kelbro is a fake and then he trails the gang as they try to rustle Ann's cattle. The rustlers capture Sandy and accuse him of killing the Connors brothers but McKenzie comes to his rescue and demands he be given a trial. Back in town, McKenzie and Sandy get Kelbro's forged papers and Sandy heads to the state capitol as McKenzie and Ted aid Ann in stopping the rustling. When the outlaws try to waylay Sandy's stage, McKenzie stops them, and later captures gang member Waco (Jack Ingram). At Ann's ranch, McKenzie confronts Waco who sees Ted and thinks he is a ghost. As a result, the rustler implicates Matson but henchman Bart (John L. Cason) reports Waco's capture to his boss. Matson leads his gang in an assault on Ann's ranch but Doc, who overhears their plans, goes to tell McKenzie, and the two men ride to the ranch to help Ted and Aunt Sally. Ann joins up with Sandy and they return to the ranch, catching the outlaws in a crossfire, with Matson and his men being defeated. McKenzie and Sandy then learn that Ann and Ted plan to wed.

Five "Nevada Jack McKenzie" features came out in 1945, beginning in January with *The Navajo Trail*. Here Sandy (Hatton) witnesses the killing of Texas Rangers Sergeant Trevor (Jasper L. Palmer) by outlaw Slim Ramsey (Raphael [Ray] Bennett). When McKenzie (Brown) arrives and learns of the murder, he trails Ramsey to a remote cabin and the outlaw believes him to be another wanted man, Rocky Saunders. In order to capture all the area outlaws, McKenzie continues the charade. Slim introduces him to gang leader Jack Farr (Edmund Cobb). Gang member Tabor (Tom Quinn) is shot by Farr for failing to carry out orders, and McKenzie moves him to the cabin of Mary Trevor (Jennifer Holt), the daughter of the murdered ranger. Sandy shows up with horses he claims to have taken from Indians and tries to sell them to Farr, but his true identity is soon revealed to the crook. When some of the gang members locate Tabor at Mary's cabin and overhear him tell Paul Mason (Riley Hill), another Texas Ranger, about the gang, they go to their boss who rides with his men to kill Tabor, Mary and Paul. The Ranger, however, locates Nevada and Sandy and the three rescue the victims and arrest Farr and his gang.

The next month, *Gun Smoke*, with a plot ripe with mystery elements, was released. It had McKenzie (Brown) and Sandy (Hatton) on a bear hunting trip and finding several bodies in an overturned stagecoach. One of the dead passengers, archaeologist Hinkley, was after Indian treasure. Going to Pawnee, the dead man's home, McKenzie meets Jane Condon (Jennifer Holt), a restaurant operator whose late father was Hinkley's partner. When outlaws Cyclone (Marshall Reed) and Whity (Kansas Moehring) harass Shag (Dimas Sotello), an Indian who had worked with Hinkley, McKenzie tries to save him but he is too late as the man dies of gunshot wounds. The two hoodlums carried out the killing on orders from saloon man Lucky Baker (Raphael [Ray] Bennett), who wants the treasure. McKenzie accuses Baker of ordering Shag's killing and fights it out with his henchman Knuckles (Wen Wright), whom he defeats. Sandy shows up in town as a medicine peddler and he and McKenzie reveal their identities to Jane. Also arriving in town is Joel Hinkley (Riley Hill), the murdered man's son. He has a map to the treasure site and is attacked by Lucky's men but is saved by Nevada and Sandy. As a result, the lawmen go with Joel to the treasure site, a cave containing Indian graves, and they find Cyclone and Whity there. After shooting the two outlaws, the trio take the treasure and Sandy keeps it while Joel informs Baker that McKenzie tried to steal it from him. The saloon men orders Knuckles and his gang to rob the stagecoach on which Sandy is riding; after Knuckles gets the gold, he decides to keep it for himself. Knuckles tells his boss he failed to get the treasure as the lawmen take them and the rest of the gang into custody. McKenzie and Sandy then have to further postpone their vacation so they can attend Jane and Joel's wedding.

Stranger from Santa Fe came out in June 1945. Outlaw Manning (John Merton) forces a stranger to take part in a holdup, in which Dale Grimes (Joann Curtis) is a participant. Manning makes the stranger take rings from Dale and then leaves the man without a horse. The man finds his own mount and rides to Marsha Earley's (Beatrice Gray) Bar X ranch and identifies himself as Roy Ferris, the new foreman, hired by her late father. Ferris is actually U.S. Marshal McKenzie (Brown), who is working with Sandy (Hatton) in tracking an outlaw gang. McKenzie gives jobs to Sandy as well as to Dan Murray (Jimmie Martin), who was previously fired. When Manning arrives at the ranch, McKenzie confronts him and kills him in a gunfight. A mysterious rider observes the shooting and reports it to Ned Grimes (Jack Ingram), Dale's brother, who has been courting Marsha but really wants her ranch. After McKenzie and Sandy reveal to Dan they are federal lawmen, they are arrested by the sheriff (Steve Clark) since Dale identified McKenzie as the man who robbed her and Marsha believes Dan was involved in Manning's shooting. The trio, however, manage to break out of jail so Dan can stop Marsha from marrying Grimes. Murray locks up Grimes and abducts Marsha but the sheriff lets Ned go and leaves to form a posse. At Grimes' Circle G ranch, McKenzie, Sandy and Dan fight with the crook and his gang. When the sheriff arrives, McKenzie shows him the money taken in the stagecoach holdup, which was hidden in Ned's barn. Grimes, Dale and their men are arrested and McKenzie and Sandy stay on to see Marsha and Dan get married.

The Lost Trail, issued in the fall of 1945, was a remake of "The Range Busters'" (q.v.) initial outing, *Arizona Bound* (1941). McKenzie (Brown) stops a stagecoach robbery and takes the driver, wounded Ned Turner (Riley Hill), to his girlfriend, stage line owner Jane Burns (Jennifer Holt), whose father was murdered in a similar holdup. At the Burnsville saloon, McKenzie pretends to be a cattle buyer and meets the owner, John Corbett (Kenneth MacDonald), who wants to run Jane out of business so he can control all the area freight operations. Sandy (Hatton) arrives in town with a calf to sell to McKenzie, but ends up becoming the new sheriff after showing his ability with a gun. When mine owners Jones (Frank LaRue) and Mason (Steve Clark) express unwillingness to ship their ore on Jane's line, Corbett promises them a better deal. McKenzie then offers to drive Jane's wagon with the recovering Ned as the guard. As McKenzie suggests a different route for the run, Sandy informs Corbett of the change of plans and the next day the outlaws rob the stagecoach and openly implicate McKenzie in the holdup. Back in town, McKenzie is arrested and put in jail while Sandy is held captive by Corbett. An elderly man (Milburn Morante) frees Sandy, who comes to McKenzie's rescue. After dispersing a lynch mob, Sandy tells Jane that the gold was never shipped and is still in her office safe. McKenzie goes to the saloon and gets the drop on Corbett and his men but a shootout takes place and McKenzie beats the saloon owner in a fistfight. The gang is put in jail and Ned becomes the town's new lawman. Unlike other entries in the series, this one had musical interludes (supplied by the Shrum brothers, Cal and Walt).

The final 1945 series release, *Frontier Feud*, came out in November. Here Jack McKenzie (Brown) and Sandy (Hatton) become involved in a range feud between Joe Davis (Dennis Moore) and partners Bill Corey (Steve Clark) and Don Graham (Jack Ingram). When Jack finds a murdered cowboy, he tells the locals he is the man's brother and the two ranchers, Davis and Corey, blame each other for the killing. McKenzie shoots Burnett (Ted Mapes) after he wounds Corey, and Graham declares that Davis ordered Burnett, his employee, to kill Corey although Joe is engaged to Blanche Corey (Christine McIntyre), Bill's daughter. The local sheriff (Jack Rockwell) makes McKenzie a deputy as Sandy goes to work for Davis. Joe's loan is denied an extension by banker Chalmers (Frank LaRue), who is in cahoots with Graham in taking over the Davis ranch. Although McKenzie's ruse about being the murdered cowboy's brother is revealed, he arrests Joe and tells the sheriff he is a federal marshal. Joe's foreman, Sam Murphy (Edwin Parker), announces he will get his boss out of jail but in reality he is working with Graham. The crooks agree to set Joe free and then murder him as Murphy and his men will rustle Joe's cattle so they cannot be sold to pay off his loan. McKenzie tries to stop the breakout and is abducted by the outlaws but Sandy captures Graham and sets McKenzie free. The two lawmen stop the gang from taking Joe out of jail and after a shootout the outlaws are arrested and McKenzie captures Chalmers. McKenzie and Sandy then leave town after finding out Joe and Blanche will be married.

The penultimate "Nevada Jack McKenzie" adventure, *Border Bandits*, came out early in 1946. It had Sandy (Hatton) bringing in his pal McKenzie (Brown) after rancho owner Gonzales (Lucio Villegas) receives a message telling him to hand over the family's jewels. While the two lawmen find the local sheriff murdered, Deputy Sheriff Spike (John Merton), Pepper (Tom Quinn) and Dutch (Bud Osborne), all wearing masks, hold up Gonzales and demand the jewels; before he can retrieve them, he is shot by Dutch. Steve Halliday (Riley Hill), who wants to marry Celia (Rosa del Rosario), Gonzales' granddaughter, pursues the robbers but is wounded. Steve is taken to town by Celia and her employee Jose (Charles Stevens) so he can be cared for by drunken Doc Bowles (Steve Clark), who has been tossed out of the local saloon but befriended by McKenzie. When Steve is able to talk, Dutch accuses McKenzie of the killing and arrests him, while Sandy finds the murdered Gonzales. Doc repays McKenzie's kindness by getting him out of jail and the lawman goes to the rancho and stops Pepper as he attempts to kill Sandy and Jose. McKenzie then takes Pepper and Sandy to jail and tells Dutch to put them behind bars. There Sandy tries to find out from Pepper who is behind the lawlessness, but the outlaw is shot before he can talk. Steve tells his uncle, John Halliday (Frank LaRue), the owner of the local land and water operation, that McKenzie is a federal marshal, not knowing that his uncle is the gang's leader. When Jose brings the Gonzales jewels to John Halliday so they will be safe, he is shot by the businessman, but McKenzie arrests him before he can dispose of the servant's body. The jewels are returned to Celia and she and Steve get married. *Variety* noted, "Pace of this film is too leisurely for the average action fan. Formula story of sheriff vs. badmen unwinds without any finesse to make up for fatal deficiencies in the fisticuff and gunplay departments."

The last series entry, *The Haunted Mine*, followed in February 1946. The story had McKenzie (Brown) and Sandy (Hatton) being assigned by their superior officer (Frank LaRue) to investigate several mysterious deaths connected with a supposedly haunted mine inherited by Mrs. Durant (Claire Whitney) and her daughter Jenny (Linda Johnson). Located near Buckeye, a ghost town, the mine also took the life of owner Frank Durant, who drowned there. McKenzie finds the body of a man whose bandana contains gold dust and he is later accused of killing him by men who also work for the deceased's boss, gang leader Steve Twining (John Merton). Twining wants the Durant mine because he has found a rich gold vein and he has another henchman, Blackie (Marshall Reed), steal the Durants' cattle. McKenzie is brought to town and Twining convenes a jury, which includes Sandy, who is pretending to be a barber. After a guilty verdict, McKenzie is given a last wish for a shave and Sandy helps him escape through a hidden tunnel. Jenny and her admirer Dan McLeod (Riley Hill) try to stop Mrs. Durant from signing over the mine to Twining but fail, although McKenzie manages to get back the deed. As he is reading it, a mystery man knocks him out and nearly slits his throat but is scared off by Sandy. When Dan is beaten by the outlaws because they think he stole the deed, he is rescued by the lawmen. After giving Mrs. Durant the deed, McKenzie and Dan ride to the mine as Twining and his men try to make her to give them the document. At the mine, Blackie shoots at Jack and Dan but they later find him with his throat slit. The mystery man attacks Dan but is stopped by McKenzie as Sandy forces the outlaws off the Durant ranch. Arriving at the mine, Sandy is accosted by the mystery man and knocks him out. Twining, who has captured Jenny, arrives with his men and a shootout takes place with McKenzie rescuing Jenny and capturing a fleeing Twining, who confesses to flooding the mine shaft, to conceal the vein of ore, resulting in Durant's drowning. The mystery man (Raphael [Ray] Bennett) was a crazed barber who killed anyone associated with the mine after his son died there. After reporting back to his superior officer, McKenzie goes on vacation.

After 20 features, the "Nevada Jack McKenzie" series was becoming mundane. Each film seemed pretty much like its predecessor with the two lawmen being summoned to a western town plagued by outlaws controlled by a boss who was after the area's land, either for a railroad sale or for valuable minerals. McKenzie and Sandy usually worked undercover and separately until the finale when they teamed to rout the bad guys. Many of the stories ended with a young couple involved in the proceedings getting married. The two heroes would then go their separate ways until their next similar adventure. David Rothel noted in *Those Great Cowboy Sidekicks* (1984), "The films were moderately well produced considering the limited budgets that Monogram allocated, but they never compared favorably with the flashy production quality in any Republic Pictures product. Many of the Brown-Hatton scripts plodded along with an overabundance of stale dialogue and a paucity of action."

Ironically, Brown and Hatton would team for another 23 features at Monogram following the halt of the "Nevada Jack McKenzie" series. Their final trio of films at Monogram in 1948 co-starred Max Terhune.

After Hatton departed Monogram, Brown starred in 22 more "B" westerns for the studio from 1948 to 1952, six with James Ellison. Under the Allied Artists banner he also co-starred in the bigger budget features *Stampede* (1949) and *Short Grass* (1950). Following the end of his cowboy films starring career, Brown made a guest appearance in the 1953 production *The Marshal's Daughter* and then operated a restaurant for many years. In the mid–1960s he returned to films for featured roles in *The Bounty Killer* and *Requiem for a Gunfighter* (both 1965) and *Apache Uprising* (1966); he died in 1974. Like several other "B" western stars, Brown had a comic book series named for him, beginning with Dell Publishing's *Four Color* that ran from 1950–59. His comics were also a part of Dell's *Giant Series Western Roundup* from 1952 to 1957.

After leaving Monogram, Hatton continued to freelance in films as a character actor and he appeared in all six entries in Lippert's "Irish Cowboys" (q.v.) series in 1950. After 1950 he was very active in television and he continued in that medium and films well into the 1960s. His final western was *Requiem for a Gunfighter* (also with Brown) in 1965 and two years later he did his last movie, *In Cold Blood*. Between 1909 and 1967, Hatton appeared in over 400 films.

Filmography

The Ghost Rider (Monogram, 1943, 54 minutes) Producer: Scott R. Dunlap. Director: Wallace W. Fox. Screenplay: Jess Bowers [Adele Buffington]. Photography: Harry Neumann. Editor: Carl L. Pierson. Music: Edward Kay. Art Director: Ernest [E.R.] Hickson. Sound: Glen Glenn. Production Supervisor: Charles J. Bigelow. Assistant Director: William Strohbach.

Cast: Johnny Mack Brown (Nevada Jack McKenzie/The Ghost Rider), Raymond Hatton (Sandy Hopkins), Harry Woods (Lash Edwards), Beverly Boyd (Julie Wilson), Tom Seidel (Joe McNally), Edmund Cobb (Zack Saddler), Bud Osborne (Lucky Howard), George DeNormand (Red), Bill Hunter, Wally West

(Gang Members), Artie Ortego (Roy Kern), Charles King (Steve Cook), Milburn Morante (John Wilson), Bill Nestell (Bartender Bill), Jack Daley (Patrick McNally), Horace B. Carpenter (Old Man), Ray Miller (Scudder), Art Fowler (Jess), George Morrell (Pete the Bartender), Jess Cavin (Citizen), Herman Hack, Foxy Callahan, Kansas Moehring, Ralph Bucko, Roy Bucko (Saloon Customers).

The Stranger from Pecos (Monogram, 1943, 57 minutes) Producer: Scott R. Dunlap. Director: Lambert Hillyer. Screenplay: Jess Bowers [Adele Buffington]. Photography: Harry Neumann. Editor: Carl L. Pierson. Music: Edward Kay. Art Director: Ernest [E.R.] Hickson. Sound: Glen Glenn. Production Supervisor: Charles J. Bigelow. Assistant Director: William Strohbach.

Cast: Johnny Mack Brown (Nevada Jack McKenzie), Raymond Hatton (Sandy Hopkins), Kirby Grant (Tom Barstow), Christine McIntyre (Ruth Martin), Steve Clark (Clem Martin), Edmund Cobb (Bert Salem), Sam Flint (Jonathan Ward), Charles King (Harmon), Roy Barcroft (Sheriff Ben), Bud Osborne (Gus), Artie Ortego (Ed), L.W. [Lynton] Brent (Deputy Sheriff Joe), Milburn Morante (Telegrapher Pete), Robert Frazer (Bill Barstow), Frosty Royce (Gang Member), Kermit Maynard (Bud Salem), Tom London (Deputy Sheriff Steve), George Morrell, Carol Henry (Citizens), Herman Hack, Chick Hannon, Lew Morphy, Ralph Bucko, Roy Bucko (Saloon Customers).

Six Gun Gospel (Monogram, 1943, 55 minutes) Producer: Scott R. Dunlap. Director: Lambert Hillyer. Screenplay: Jess Bowers [Adele Buffington] & Ed Earl Repp. Photography: Harry Neumann. Editor: Carl L. Pierson. Music: Edward Kay. Sound: Glen Glenn. Production Supervisor: Charles J. Bigelow. Assistant Director: William Strohbach.

Cast: Johnny Mack Brown (Nevada Jack McKenzie), Raymond Hatton (Sandy Hopkins), Inna Gest (Jane Simms), Eddie Dew (Dan Baxter), Kenneth MacDonald (Ace Benton), Edmund Cobb (Waco), Roy Barcroft (Durkin), Bud Osborne (Joe), Isabel Withers (Almira), Mary MacLaren (Mary Dailey), Jack Daley (Ben Dailey), Artie Ortego (Ed), L.W. [Lynton] Brent (Steve), Milburn Morante (Zeke), Kernan Cripps (Bill Simms), Tom London (Murdered Gambler), Lew Porter (Piano Player), Jack Evans, Chick Hannon, Lew Morphy, Rube Dalroy, Jack Tornek (Saloon Customers).

Outlaws of Stampede Pass (Monogram, 1943, 58 minutes) Producer: Scott R. Dunlap. Director: Wallace W. Fox. Screenplay: Jess Bowers [Adele Buffington]. Story: Johnston McCulley. Photography: Marcel Le Picard. Editor: Carl L. Pierson. Music: Edward Kay. Sound: Glen Glenn. Production Supervisor: Charles J. Bigelow. Assistant Director: Theodore Joos.

Cast: Johnny Mack Brown (Nevada Jack McKenzie), Raymond Hatton (Sandy Hopkins), Ellen Hall (Mary Lewis), Jon Dawson (Tom Evans), Harry Woods (Ben Crowley), Charles King (Steve Carse), Edmund Cobb (Hank), Sam Flint (Sam Lewis), Mauritz Hugo (Slick), Art Mix (Gus), Herman Hack (Ed), Artie Ortego (Joe), Milburn Morante (Zeke), Eddie Burns (Red), Dan White (Curt), Hal Price (Bartender Pete), Cactus Mack (Ed), Kansas Moehring (Taylor), Denver Dixon, Curley Dresden, Tex Cooper, Rube Dalroy, Bud Wolfe (Saloon Customers).

The Texas Kid (Monogram, 1943, 56 minutes) Producer: Scott R. Dunlap. Director: Lambert Hillyer. Screenplay: Jess Bowers [Adele Buffington]. Story: Lynton Wright Brent. Photography: Harry Neumann. Editor: Carl L. Pierson. Music: Edward Kay. Sound: Glen Glenn. Production Supervisor: Charles J. Bigelow. Assistant Director: Theodore Joos.

Cast: Johnny Mack Brown (Nevada Jack McKenzie), Raymond Hatton (Sandy Hopkins), Marshall Reed (The Kid/MacLaine), Shirley Patterson (Nancy Drew), Robert Fiske (Naylor), Edmund Cobb (Scully), George J. Lewis (Rocky), Cyril Ring (Tim Atwood), Lynton Brent (Jess), Stanley Price (Ed), Bud Osborne (Steve), Kermit Maynard (Alex), John Judd (Roy), Charles King (Red Grogan), Horace B. Carpenter, Fred Hoose (Ranchers), Harry Tenbrook, Joe Phillips (Gang Members).

Also called *The Adventures of the Texas Kid*.

Raiders of the Border (Monogram, 1944, 58 minutes) Producer: Scott R. Dunlap. Executive Producer: Trem Carr. Director: John P. McCarthy. Screenplay: Jess Bowers [Adele Buffington]. Story: Johnston McCulley. Photography: Harry Neumann. Editors: Carl L. Pierson & John C. Fuller. Art Director; Ernest [E.R.] Hickson. Sound: Glen Glenn. Production Supervisor: Charles J. Bigelow. Assistant Director: Theodore Joos.

Cast: Johnny Mack Brown (Nevada Jack McKenzie), Raymond Hatton (Sandy Hopkins), Craig Woods (Joe), Ellen Hall (Bonita Bayne), Raphael [Ray] Bennett (Harsh), Edmund Cobb (McGee), Ernie Adams (Whiskey Watkins), Dick Alexander (Steve Rowan), Lynton Brent (Davis), Stanley Price (Blackie), Ben Corbett, Kermit Maynard, Herman Hack, Kansas Moehring (Gang Members).

Partners of the Trail (Monogram, 1944, 55 minutes) Producer: Scott R. Dunlap. Executive Producer: Trem Carr. Director: Lambert Hillyer. Story-Screenplay: Frank H. Young. Photography: Harry Neumann. Editor: Carl Heim. Music: Edward Kay. Sound: Glen Glenn. Assistant Director: Ed Stein.

Cast: Johnny Mack Brown (Nevada Jack McKenzie), Raymond Hatton (Sandy Hopkins), Craig Woods (Joel Dixon), Christine McIntyre (Kate Hilton), Marshall Reed (Clint Baker), Joe Eggerton (Hilton), Jack Ingram (Trigger), Harry F. [Hal] Price (Dobbey), Lynton Brent (Lem), Lloyd Ingraham (Doc Applegate), Ben Corbett (Duke), Ted Mapes (Swanky), Steve Clark (Colby), Robert Frazer (J.D. Edwards), Slim Whitaker (Stagecoach Driver Pete), Wally West (Saloon Customer), Al Taylor, Kansas Moehring (Ranchers), Chick Hannon (Bartender), Bill Wolfe (Citizen).

Law Men (Monogram, 1944, 54 minutes) Producer: Scott R. Dunlap. Director: Lambert Hillyer. Story-Screenplay: Glenn Tryon. Photography: Harry Neumann. Editor: John C. Fuller. Music: Edward Kay. Sound: Glen Glenn. Production Supervisor: Charles J. Bigelow. Assistant Director: Ed Stein.

Cast: Johnny Mack Brown (Nevada Jack McKenzie), Raymond Hatton (Sandy Hopkins), Jan Wiley (Phyllis), Kirby Grant (Clyde Miller), Robert Frazer (Bradford), Edmund Cobb (Slade), Art Fowler (Gus), Harry F. [Hal] Price (Pop Haynes), Marshall Reed (Killifer), Isabel Withers (Auntie Mac), Ben Corbett (Simmons), Ted Mapes (Curley Balou), Steve Clark (Wilson), Bud Osborne (Hardy), Ted French (Nickel Plate), Jack Rockwell (Murdered Sheriff), Bob Woodward (Gambler), Denver Dixon, Artie Ortego (Saloon Customers), George Morrell, Jack Evans, Ray Jones, Rube Dalroy (Citizens).

Range Law (Monogram, 1944, 57 minutes) Producer: Scott R. Dunlap. Executive Producer: Trem Carr. Director: Lambert Hillyer. Story-Screenplay: Frank H. Young. Photography: Harry Neumann. Editor: John C. Fuller. Music: Edward Kay. Sound: Glen Glenn. Production Supervisor: Charles J. Bigelow. Assistant Director: Theodore Joos.

Cast: Johnny Mack Brown (Nevada Jack McKenzie), Raymond Hatton (Sandy Hopkins), Ellen Hall (Lucille Gray), Sarah Padden (Boots Annie), Lloyd Ingraham (Judge Cal Bowen), Marshall Reed (Jim Bowen), Jack Ingram (Phil Randall), Art Fowler (Swede Larson), Hugh Prosser (Sheriff Jed Hawkins), Stanley Price (Dawson), Steve Clark (Pop McGee), Harry F. [Hal] Price (Zeke), Ben Corbett (Joe), Bud Osborne (Davis), Lynton Brent (Baxter), George Morrell (Cassidy), Kansas Moehring (Evans), Milburn Morante (Bartender), Horace B. Carpenter (Turnkey), Foxy Callahan (Cowboy), Denver Dixon, Chick Hannon, Artie Ortego, Tex Palmer (Saloon Customers).

Working title: *Hangman's Law*.

West of the Rio Grande (Monogram, 1944, 57 minutes) Producer: Scott R. Dunlap. Director: Lambert Hillyer. Story-Screenplay: Betty Burbridge. Photography: Arthur Martinelli. Editor: John C. Fuller. Music: Edward Kay. Art Director: Dave Milton. Sound: Glen Glenn. Production Supervisor: Charles J. Bigelow. Assistant Director: Theodore Joos.

Cast: Johnny Mack Brown (Nevada Jack McKenzie), Raymond Hatton (Sandy Hopkins), Dennis Moore (Denny Boyd), Christine McIntyre (Alice Darcy), Lloyd Ingraham (Trooper Meade), Kenneth MacDonald (Martin Keene), Frank LaRue (Judge Darcy), Art Fowler (Nate Todd), Hugh Prosser (Lucky Cramer), Edmund Cobb (Curly), Steve Clark (Doc Ely), Jack Rockwell (Sheriff Tom Boyd), Hal Price (Pop Grimsby), John Merton (Wade Gunnerson), Lynton Brent (Harris), Al Ferguson (Stagecoach Guard Joe), Pierce Lyden (Nick Towne), George Morrell (Hank Judd), Bud Osborne (Rich), Chick Hannon (Wilson), Tommy Coats (Rancher), Post Park (Stagecoach Driver Sam), Foxy Callahan (Citizen).

Working title: *One Man Law*.

Land of the Outlaws (Monogram, 1944, 59 minutes) Producer: Scott R. Dunlap. Director: Lambert Hillyer. Story-Screenplay: Joseph O'Donnell. Photography: Harry Neumann. Editors: John C. Fuller & Pierre Janet. Music: Edward Kay. Sound: Glen Glenn. Sets: Vin Taylor. Production Supervisor: Charles J. Bigelow. Assistant Director: Bobby Ray.

Cast: Johnny Mack Brown (Nevada Jack McKenzie), Raymond Hatton (Sandy Hopkins), Nan Holliday (Ellen), Stephen Keyes (Frank Carson/Frank Carr), Hugh Prosser (Ed Hammond), Charles King (Bart Green), Tom Quinn (Vic), Steve Clark (Sheriff), John Merton (Dan Broderick), Art Fowler (Slim Carter), Bud Wolfe (Drake), John Judd (Jim), Ray Elder (Clint), Chick Hannon (Joe), Bob [John L.] Cason (Curly), Kansas Moehring (Jed), Bob Woodward (Sam), Dick Rush (Bartender Charlie), George Morrell, Rube Dalroy (Citizens), Jack Evans (Saloon Customer).

Working title: *Fool's Gold*.

Law of the Valley (Monogram, 1944, 58 minutes) Producer: Scott R. Dunlap. Director: Howard Bretherton. Screenplay: Joseph O'Donnell. Photography: Marcel Le Picard. Editors: Jack Foley & Pierre Janet. Music: Edward Kay. Sound: Glen Glenn. Sets: Vin Taylor. Production Supervisor: Charles J. Bigelow. Assistant Director: Theodore Joos.

Cast: Johnny Mack Brown (Nevada Jack McKenzie), Raymond Hatton (Sandy Hopkins), Lynne Carver (Ann Jennings), Kirk Barron (Tom Findley), Edmund Cobb (Dan Stanton), Charles King (Miller), Tom Quinn (Condon), Steve Clark (Slim Roberts), Hal Price (Sheriff), Marshall Reed (Al Green), George DeNormand (Red Adams), George Morrell (Jenkins), Charles McMurphy (Bartender), Horace B. Carpenter (Luke Stone), Snub Pollard, Rose Plummer (Citizens), George Sowards, Dee Cooper (Gang Members), Bud Pope (Saloon Customer).

Ghost Guns (Monogram, 1944, 60 minutes) Producer: Scott R. Dunlap. Director: Lambert Hillyer. Screenplay: Frank H. Young. Story: Bennett Cohen. Photography: Marcel Le Picard. Editors: J.M. [Jack] Foley & Pierre Janet. Music: Edward Kay. Sets: Vin Taylor. Production Supervisor: Charles J. Bigelow. Assistant Director: Theodore Joos.

Cast: Johnny Mack Brown (Nevada Jack McKenzie), Raymond Hatton (Sandy Hopkins), Evelyn Finley (Ann Jordan), Riley Hill (Ted Connors), Ernie Adams (Doc Edwards), Sarah Padden (Aunt Sally), Jack Ingram (Waco), Tom Quinn (Stringer), Frank LaRue (Kelbro), John Merton (Matson), Steve Clark (Steve), Marshall Reed (Black Jack), George Morrell (Station Agent), Bob [John L.] Cason (Bart), Ray Jones (Tex), Dick Rush (Bartender), Jack Evans, Chick Hannon

(Citizens), Dee Cooper (Gang Member), Dick Dickinson (Saloon Victim).

Working title: *Ghost of Indian Springs*.

The Navajo Trail (Monogram, 1945, 56 minutes) Producer: Scott R. Dunlap. Director: Howard Bretherton. Screenplay: Frank H. Young. Story: Jess Bowers [Adele Buffington]. Photography: Marcel Le Picard. Editors: William Austin & Arthur H. Bell. Music: Edward Kay. Sound: Glen Glenn. Sets: Vin Taylor. Production Supervisor: Charles J. Bigelow. Assistant Director: Bobby Ray.

Cast: Johnny Mack Brown (Nevada Jack McKenzie), Raymond Hatton (Sandy Hopkins), Jennifer Holt (Mary Trevor), Riley Hill (Paul Mason), Edmund Cobb (Jack Farr), Raphael [Ray] Bennett (Slim Ramsey), Charles King (Red), Tom Quinn (Tober), Mary MacLaren (Stella Ramsey), Bud Osborne (Brad), Earl Crawford (Joe), Josh [John] Carpenter (Steve), Jim Hood (Rusty), Jasper L. Palmer (Sergeant Trevor).

Working titles: *Navajo Trails* and *the Texas Terror*.

Gun Smoke (Monogram, 1945, 57 minutes) Producer: Scott R. Dunlap. Director: Howard Bretherton. Screenplay: Frank H. Young. Photography: Marcel Le Picard. Editors: J.M. [Jack] Foley & Arthur H. Bell. Music: Edward Kay. Sound: Glen Glenn. Sets: Vin Taylor. Production Supervisor: Charles J. Bigelow. Production Manager: Bobby Ray. Assistant Director: Eddie Davis.

Cast: Johnny Mack Brown (Nevada Jack McKenzie), Raymond Hatton (Sandy Hopkins), Jennifer Holt (Jane Condon), Riley Hill (Joel Hinkley), Wen Wright (Knuckles), Raphael [Ray] Bennett (Lucky Baker), Steve Clark (Soda), Marshall Reed (Cyclone), Bob [John L.] Cason (Red), Louis Hart (Pete), Frank Ellis (Duce), Roy E. Butler (Sheriff), Kansas Moehring (Whity), Dimas Sotello (Shag), Elmer Napier (Cactus), Jack Baxley (Bartender), Horace B. Carpenter (Man in Pawnee), Chick Hannon (Gang Member), George Morrell (Citizen).

Working title: *Saddle Smoke*.

Stranger from Santa Fe (Monogram, 1945, 56 minutes) Producer: Scott R. Dunlap. Director: Lambert Hillyer. Screenplay: Jess Bowers [Adele Buffington], from the story "Pilgrim Ramrod for Hell's Range" by Charles N. Heckelmann. Photography: Harry Neumann. Editor: Jack Milner. Music: Frank Sanucci. Sound: Glen Glenn. Sets: Vin Taylor. Production Supervisor: Robert [Bobby] Ray. Assistant Director: Eddie Davis.

Cast: Johnny Mack Brown (Nevada Jack McKenzie), Raymond Hatton (Sandy Hopkins), Beatrice Gray (Marsha Earley), Joann Curtis (Dale Grimes), Jimmie Martin (Dan Murray), Jack Ingram (Ned Grimes), John Merton (Cy Manning), Tom Quinn (Bill), Steve Clark (Sheriff), Jack Rockwell (Stagecoach Driver), Bud Osborne (Clint), Hal Price (Telegrapher Hymer), Dick Dickinson (Justice of the Peace), Ray Elder, Louis Hart (Gang Members), Eddie Parker (Jessie Balbo), Henry Wills (Deputy Sheriff Ed), Horace B. Carpenter (Citizen).

The Lost Trail (Monogram, 1945, 57 minutes) Producer: Scott R. Dunlap. Director: Lambert Hillyer. Screenplay: Jess Bowers [Adele Buffington]. Photography: Marcel Le Picard. Editor: Jack Milner. Music: Frank Sanucci. Art Director: Dave Milton. Sound: Glen Glenn. Sets: Vin Taylor. Production Supervisor: Charles J. Bigelow. Assistant Director: Eddie Davis.

Cast: Johnny Mack Brown (Nevada Jack McKenzie), Raymond Hatton (Sandy Hopkins), Jennifer Holt (Jane Burns), Riley Hill (Ned Turner), Kenneth MacDonald (John Corbett), Edwin Parker (Bill), John Ince (Bailey), Frank LaRue (Jones), Steve Clark (Mason), Milburn Morante (Zeke), Lynton Brent (Hall), Frank McCarroll (Joe), Dick Dickinson (Ed), Henry Vroom (Tom), John Bridges (Dr. Brown), Walt Shrum & His Colorado Hillbillies, Cal Shrum & His Rhythm Rangers (Musicians), Denver Dixon, Tex Cooper, Cactus Mack, George Morrell (Citizens), Chick Hannon, Victor Cox, Ray Henderson (Gang Members), Carl Mathews, Jack Tornek, Ralph Bucko (Saloon Customers).

Frontier Feud (Monogram, 1945, 54 minutes) Producer: Scott R. Dunlap. Director: Lambert Hillyer. Screenplay: Jess Bowers [Adele Buffington], from the story "The Last Outpost in Hell" by Charles N. Heckelmann. Photography: Harry Neumann. Editor: Dan Milner. Music: Frank Sanucci. Art Director: Vin Taylor. Sound: Glen Glenn. Production Supervisor: Charles J. Bigelow. Assistant Director: Eddie Davis.

Cast: Johnny Mack Brown (Nevada Jack McKenzie), Raymond Hatton (Sandy Hopkins), Dennis Moore (Joe Davis), Christine McIntyre (Blanche Corey), Jack Ingram (Don Graham), Edwin Parker (Sam Murphy), Frank LaRue (Chalmers), Steve Clark (Bill Corey), Jack Rockwell (Sheriff Clancy), Mary MacLaren (Sarah Morgan), Edmund Cobb (Nat Moran), Lloyd Ingraham (Si Peters), Ted Mapes (Slade Burnett), Lynton Brent (Red), Terry Frost, Wally West, Pierce Lyden, Frank McCarroll (Gang Members), Horace B. Carpenter (Saloon Customer), Dan White, Ray Jones (Citizens), Ray Henderson (Cowboy), Rube Dalroy (Gambler).

Border Bandits (Monogram, 1946, 57 minutes) Producer: Scott R. Dunlap. Director: Lambert Hillyer. Screenplay: Frank H. Young. Photography: William A. Sickner. Editor: Carrol Lewis. Music: Frank Sanucci. Art Director: Vin Taylor. Sound: Glen Glenn. Production Supervisor: Charles J. Bigelow. Assistant Director: Eddie Davis.

Cast: Johnny Mack Brown (Nevada Jack McKenzie), Raymond Hatton (Sandy Hopkins), Riley Hill (Steve Halliday), Rosa del Rosario (Celia Nogales), John Merton (Deputy Sheriff Spike), Tom Quinn (Pepper), Frank LaRue (John Halliday), Steve Clark (Doc Bowles), Charles Stevens (Jose), Lucio Villegas (Senor Gonzales), Bud Osborne (Dutch), Pat R. McGee

(Cupid), Terry Frost (Windy), Ray Jones, Rube Dalroy (Citizens), Julia Villirea (Senora).

The Haunted Mine (Monogram, 1946, 52 minutes) Producer: Scott R. Dunlap. Director: Derwin Abrahams. Screenplay: Frank H. Young. Story: Elizabeth [Betty] Burbridge. Photography: Harry Neumann. Editor: Fred Maguire. Music: Edward Kay. Art Director: Vin Taylor. Sound: Glen Glenn. Production Supervisor: Charles J. Bigelow. Assistant Director: Theodore Joos.

Cast: Johnny Mack Brown (Nevada Jack McKenzie), Raymond Hatton (Sandy Hopkins), Linda Johnson (Jenny Durant), Riley Hill (Dan McLeod), John Merton (Steve Twining), Raphael [Ray] Bennett (Mystery Man), Claire Whitney (Mrs. Durant), Marshall Reed (Blackie), Bob Butt (Kirk Tracy), Terry Frost (Bill Mead), Lynton Brent (Skyball), Leonard St. Leo (Stirrup), Frank LaRue (U.S. Marshal Matterson), Ray Jones (Citizen).

THE RANGE BUSTERS

Range Busters, Inc., was formed in 1939 with George Weeks as its president-producer. The company signed Ray Corrigan and Max "Alibi" Terhune, who were starring in Republic's "The Three Mesquiteers" (q.v.) series, to headline a similar triad cowboy grouping called "The Range Busters." Singer-actor John King was inked to play the third member of the triumvirate. A deal was signed with Monogram Pictures to release the features which were produced by Range Busters, Inc., a subdivision of Phoenix Productions and George W. Weeks Productions. The first nine outings were distributed in the United Kingdom by New Realm/Renown. The films were to be shot at Ray Corrigan's ranch in Simi Valley, California, with the star getting a percentage of the profits.

Corrigan and Terhune's contracts with Republic were expiring and they both chose to leave the studio to do "The Range Busters." The new series was not only in direct competition with their Mesquiteers outings but it was also considered a rip-off of the Republic features, albeit on a lower production scale. In *Hollywood Corral* (1976), Don Miller's reaction to the series' opener, *The Range Busters*, pretty much summed up the differences between the Monogram and Republic offerings: "[T]he production was far below the classy Republic brand, [but] the tatty appearance wasn't too big a drawback." The traditional song "Home on the Range" was used as the series theme and in most of the films the stars rode the same horses: Flash, a white horse, was Crash's steed, while Dusty rode either Tex or Marko, and Alibi's horse was dubbed Banjo.

"The Range Busters" was the brainchild of George W. Weeks (1885–1953), who produced over three dozen features between 1929 and 1943. In 1929 he produced the Eddie Dowling starrer *Rainbow Man* for Sono-Art before moving to Paramount. He left films in 1933 and returned with the "Range Busters" series. During the interim he headed up the sales departments at Monogram and Grand National. In 1942 he produced another Monogram release, *War Dogs*, which was directed by S. Roy Luby, who helmed most of the Range Busters. Anna Bell Ward was associate producer for sixteen Range Busters outings and she also served as costume designer for the entry *Rock River Renegades*.

Whatever artistic merit "The Range Busters" may have had was probably engendered by Luby, who directed the majority of the films and edited all twenty-four series outings using the name Roy Claire. Luby (1904–76) began working in films with Max Fleischer's silent "Out of the Inkwell" cartoon series in 1918; the next year he edited the "Mutt and Jeff" series. Between 1931 and 1952 he edited over one hundred features and from 1934 to 1943 he directed thirty-two films, beginning with the Wills Kent production *Range Warfare* in 1934. As Roy Clair he scripted Kent's 1935 Montie Montana starrer *Circle of Death* and after working on the Range Busters he directed the exploitation features *Black Market Babies* and *Confessions of a Vice Baron* (both 1943). In the 1950s he edited such TV series as *Rocky Jones, Space Ranger* and *The Adventures of Wild Bill Hickok* and he ended his film career as associate producer of the features *I'll Give My Life* (1960) and *A Letter to Nancy* (1965).

Since a number of popular cowboy stars like Gene Autry and Roy Rogers were using their own names in their films, the "Range Busters" series billed its stars as Ray "Crash" Corrigan, John "Dusty" King and Max "Alibi" Terhune, the same monikers they used in each of the features. The nickname "Crash" for Corrigan came from his playing the character of Crash Corrigan in Republic's serial *Undersea Kingdom* (1936). "Alibi" for Terhune was close to the Lullaby character he did in "The Three Mesquiteers." The "Dusty" for King was probably used because it had the ring of a Western character; some sources claim it was suggested by Corrigan. The Dusty character was pretty much the equivalent of Stony Brooke in the Mesquiteers outings except that in the Range Busters, King sang a song or two, keeping in form with the popularity of cowboy crooners in "B" Westerns.

King (1909–87) was born Miller McLeod Everson and began working as a singer in radio before joining Ben Bernie's band as a vocalist. With Bernie he made his first film, *Stolen Harmony*, in 1935 and thereafter played small roles in features until obtaining the title role in the 1937 Universal serial *Ace Drummond*. After that he was a leading man in "B" pictures. Not only did he croon in the Range Busters outings but he also composed some of the songs.

The Range Busters, the series' initial entry (August, 1940), proved to be a good launch for the Corrigan-King-Terhune triad teaming. The Range Busters, Crash (Corrigan), Dusty (King) and Alibi (Terhune), join forces and ride to the Circle T Ranch near the town of Paso Lobo to help their friend, ranch owner Homer Thorp (Horace Murphy), who has written asking for their aid in solving a series of mysterious murders on his spread. In town they rescue Homer's daughter Carol (Luana Walters) from the attentions of businessman Torrence (LeRoy Mason), who wants to buy the Circle T. Carol tells them her father has been murdered and she offers the boys jobs. Local chemist Doc Stengle (Frank LaRue), a close friend of the Thorp family, tells them the ranch is haunted by a ghostly presence known as the Phantom. The Range Busters go to the Thorp ranch and the next morning they are shot at while in the bunkhouse. Leaving Alibi to watch the ranch, Crash and Dusty try to find out who shot at them and come across the abandoned Circle T Mine which Torrence and his gang use to smuggle guns across the border. Dusty chases Torrence and his men as Crash returns to the ranch where Alibi has begun to suspect that Carol's supposedly blind Uncle Rolf (Earle Hodgins) may be faking his affliction. Capturing Dusty, Torrence sends his horse back to the Circle T. Crash and Alibi set out in search of their friend but become suspicious of what appear to be planted clues along the trail. The two are able to outsmart the gang members guarding Dusty and they set him free. Crash informs the local sheriff (Karl Hackett) about the smuggling operation and that night the Range Busters and the law round up the gang. Torrence escapes to the Circle T where he ties up Carol; Crash arrives and they fight. Just as he is about to reveal who is behind the killings, a shot is fired from Uncle Rolf's room, killing Torrence. Meanwhile, Dusty and Alibi take the tunnel from the mine and it leads them to the ranch house and they help Crash corner the killer, who turns out to be Doc Stengle. The chemist had learned that the mine was rich in gold and he used the guise of the Phantom to kill off Homer Thorp so he could purchase the ranch. Although both Crash and Dusty are smitten with Carol and want to stay at the Circle T, the Range Busters ride off to new adventures.

The trio of stars meshed well together in *The Range Busters* and the film proved actionful with plenty of fistfights and chases. It also had a horror motif with a mysterious phantom killer, a spooky mine tunnel and a series of murders. The plot had two villains: the crooked, lecherous Torrence and the masked Phantom. In addition, the feature offered the light-hearted camaraderie between its stars, comedy interludes involving Alibi's dummy Elmer, and King crooning a couple of Johnny Lange-Lew Porter songs, "Beneath the Mellow Moon" and "Get Along Little Cowboy." At the beginning, the film even offered an explanation as to why the Max Terhune character was called Alibi; the name change, from Lullaby to Alibi, came about because Elmer got him into so much trouble, Max always had to "alibi" for him. There were a couple of drawbacks, however, because the feature apparently took place in the Old West, yet tire tracks were visible in some scenes and the ranch house was wired for electricity.

Next came *Trailing Double Trouble*, in October, 1940. In addition to an action-filled plot, the feature offered Texas champion rope twirler Rex Felker and a musical interlude by the Jimmy Wakely Trio. Crash (Corrigan), Dusty (King) and Alibi (Terhune) witness the ambush of a man (Kenne Duncan) who entrusts them with his baby before dying. The trio decide to investigate the killing while the dead man's sister Marion Horner (Lita Conway) enlists the aid of a family friend, lawyer Jim Moreland (Roy Barcroft), in finding her missing nephew. Moreland is the baby's guardian and it was he who ordered the killing to get possession of the Horner ranch which contains a rich gravel deposit. The lawyer plans to get a hefty state contract for the gravel. To get the Range Busters out of the way, Moreland tells his cohort Kirk (Tom London) to frame them for the killing. When Kirk tries to abduct the infant, Alibi substitutes Elmer in its place. Looking for Amos Hardy (Jack Rutherford), a suspect in the case, the Range Busters fight it out with Kirk and the gang and then ride to the Horner ranch where Marion tells them that Hardy has offered to buy the property and that Moreland is the baby's executor. Wanting Marion out of the way, Moreland orders his men to take her to a remote cabin but Crash and Dusty find evidence in the lawyer's office tying him to the state gravel contract. The trio lead Moreland and his men along with the sheriff (Forrest Taylor) and a posse to the canyon where Marion is hidden and there they show the lawman the contract. Hardy, who was in league with Moreland, confesses that he and the lawyer ordered the ranch owner's murder. After Hardy and Moreland are arrested, Marion is set free. The feature began a running gag of having the trio order milk while at the local saloon, this causing much consternation for Richard Cramer, who played the bartender in many of the series entries.

The final series feature for 1940, *West of Pinto Basin*, was issued in November. Crash (Corrigan), Dusty (King) and Alibi (Terhune) arrive in Pinto Basin to look into a series of stagecoach robberies. The stolen money was to be used to pay for the construction of the Medicine Hat Dam which is needed by ranchers to save their arid land. While gambling at the local saloon, Alibi loses the trio's horses in a card game and the three end up getting into a fight with the owner, Harvey (Tristram Coffin), and his gang. Harvey is behind the robberies in an attempt to bring the dam project to a standstill and get the ranches for a cheap price. The Range Busters get jobs working for bank president Joan Brown (Gwen Gaze) who does not know that her teller Summers (Phil Dunham) is working with Harvey, informing him about the times of the money shipments. The saloon owner has one of his cohorts accuse the Range Busters of robbing the stages and the sheriff (Bud Osborne) puts them in jail. Harvey then breaks them out from behind bars and tries to frame them for the next holdup but they turn the tables on him by committing the robbery themselves. The trio then rounds up Harvey and his gang and turns the money over to Joan. Des Moines, Iowa, singing-yodeling cowboy Jerry Smith contributed a trio of his self-penned songs in the feature: "Rhythm of the Saddle" and "Ridin' the Trail Tonight," which he also performed, and "That Little Prairie Gal of Mine," crooned by John King. *Variety* felt the film "is no rave among westerns, but grooved nearly enough to the average to satisfy."

Trail of the Silver Spurs, issued in January, 1941, was the first of eight series features for that year. Like *The Range Busters*, it had a horror-mystery plot involving a phantom, a supposedly haunted mine and ghost writing. Following the killing of two men (Frank Ellis, Carl Mathews) suspected of looting the Denver Mint, a miner known as the Jingler (I. Stanford Jolley), because he always wears spurs, strikes gold in the desert and turns it in to the government. Undercover agents Crash (Corrigan), Dusty (King) and Alibi (Terhune) are sent to investigate since the color of the gold does not match that of ore found in Arizona, where he claims to have made the strike. The trio stay in the ghost town of Bottle Neck and during the night Alibi sees a phantom wind the clock in the deserted hotel where they are sleeping. Later they hear gunshots and witness a shootout between three men, one of whom turns out to be Dan Nordick (Milburn Morante), the owner of the town. Nordick's daughter Nancy

John King and Ray Corrigan in *The Range Busters* (Monogram, 1940).

(Dorothy Short) tells Dusty the town was once prosperous but after the gold ran out it became deserted. Crash follows Dan to the mine and is shot at by a mysterious stranger (George Chesebro) who runs away when Dusty and Alibi approach.

To lift Dan's spirits, Alibi salts the mine with gold and as a result the area is swamped with prospectors. All along the Jingler has been using the cellar at the town hotel as his headquarters and it is there he has hidden gold he stole from the Den-

Max Terhune and Elmer.

ver Mint. The Jingler threatens to expose the Range Busters for starting a phony gold rush and when they refuse to leave the area he tells the miners they have been cheated by Nordick, who has sold them mine shares at a low price. Crash tells Alibi to get Nancy and her father out of town as the mob, led by miner Stoner (Eddie Dean), takes after Crash and Dusty. Back in town, the stranger who shot at Crash finds the entrance to the Jingler's hideout through the hotel's clock. While rummaging through the cellar he is caught by the Jingler and in an effort to buy his life, he offers him a map leading to a rich vein of gold in Nordick's mine. The Jingler shoots the man but Crash, who has returned to town with Dusty, hears the shot and captures him. Trying to bribe the two Range Busters, he takes them to the cellar where they arrest him after seeing the gold bars from the government mint. When it is learned that gold still exists in the Nordick mine, the prospectors return and Bottle Neck again prospers.

The feature is a fairly eerie affair lightened by the amusing byplay between Crash and Dusty, and Alibi's interludes with Elmer. John King sang the Lew Porter-Johnny Lange tune "A Rainbow's Riding the Range" along with the traditional "Goodbye Old Paint," on which he is accompanied by Eddie Dean. The film's main drawback is the use of stock footage in the boomtown sequences. The obviously big-budget footage does not match well with the overall Poverty Row look of the feature.

Another good entry in the series, *The Kid's Last Ride*, came out in February, 1941. Crash (Corrigan), Dusty (King) and Alibi (Terhune) ride to the town of Canyon City where they have been commissioned by the Citizens Committee to rid the area of lawlessness. They are attacked by gunmen and their horses are stolen, forcing them to walk to town. Once there, they are sworn in as marshals and, after breaking up a saloon fight, they meet the local schoolmarm, Sally Rowell (Luana Walters), who seeks their aid in ridding the schoolhouse of an unwanted skunk. They learn she is the daughter of the deceased judge who sentenced the brother of Robert Harmon (Al Bridge) and Bart Gill (Glenn Strange) to death. The two are really outlaws, the Breeden Brothers, and they have sworn revenge

Poster for *Trail of the Silver Spurs* (Monogram, 1941) with the title misspelled.

on Sally and her younger brother Jimmy (Edwin Brian); they saddle Jimmy with gambling debts and then force him to take part in a robbery. The Range Busters stop the robbery; Jimmy is injured in the shootout and goes to Sally, who hides him in a cabin. Crash locates the cabin but Sally holds him off at gunpoint while Jimmy runs away. Seeing the Breedens approach, Jimmy rides away on Crash's horse in order to protect Sally but is shot by the outlaws. The crooks then attack the cabin but are arrested by Crash, Dusty and Alibi. After Jimmy dies from his wounds, the Range Busters leave the now peaceful Canyon City.

The Kid's Last Ride was highlighted by a well-staged saloon brawl between Corrigan and Glenn Strange and by the comedy song "It's All a Part of the Game," performed by Crash, Dusty and Alibi. John King crooned "The Call of the Wild" in a sequence where he romances Luana Walters, who had also been the leading lady in *The Range Busters*. *Variety* complained, "Poor, eye-straining photography and weak songs, packed up in an overly dramatic story...."

Time travel was the plot crux of *Tumble Down Ranch in Arizona*, released in the spring of 1941. Corrigan and King not only play the Crash and Dusty characters, but also their descendants. Modern-day university student Johnny King (John King) comes to believe that people can travel back in time. At the Tucson Rodeo he meets Ray Corrigan (himself) and the two soon discover that their fathers, Crash Corrigan and Dusty King, were part of the famous Old West Range Busters. Thrown by a horse during competition, Johnny finds himself in the year 1900 with Corrigan at his side. They are joined by Alibi (Max Terhune) who has been helping Judge Jones (John Elliott) and his daughter Dorothy (Sheila Darcy), whose wagon has been attacked by outlaws. The judge has been sent by the government to preside in lawless Cactus City. Dusty takes him and Dorothy to their destination while Crash and Alibi go to Corrigan's mother's (Marian Kerby) ranch. He finds the place run-down since the ranch hands have gone to work for the railroad, a venture sponsored by hotel owner Gallop (Quen Ramsey). The Joneses arrive in town with Dusty and go to the sheriff, Nye (Jack Holmes), not knowing he is in league with Gallop. When the lawman comes to the aid of two gunmen who attacked the judge and his daughter, the Range Busters move the Joneses to Mother Corrigan's ranch for protection. Gallop wants Mrs. Corrigan's property which the railroad needs for a right-of-way and he gets his partner, politician Slocum (James Craven), to trick the old lady into signing over her deed, under the guise of a cattle contract. When surveyors show up on the Corrigan spread, the Range Busters wreck their equipment but Sheriff Nye arrests Mrs. Corrigan. When he receives evidence against Gallop and Slocum, Judge Jones deputizes Crash, Dusty and Alibi, whom the sheriff then arrests for Gallop's murder. Alibi catches Slocum with incriminating evidence, proving he is the killer. Crash and Dusty escape from the sheriff and aid Alibi in bringing in Slocum; they also arrest Nye. As the Range Busters are being thanked for returning law and order to the town, Dusty awakes in the hospital with Dorothy's daughter as his nurse.

The University of Arizona Glee Club was featured in *Tumble Down Ranch in Arizona*; the group not only accompanied John King on the title song but also on "Wake Up with the Dawn" and "All Hail Arizona." The song "Tumble Down Ranch in Arizona" was composed by Bill Watters and Howard Steiner and was recorded by bandleader Frankie Masters. The Watters-Steiner team also wrote "Wake Up with the Dawn."

Wrangler's Roost, which came out in the early summer of 1941, had Crash (Corrigan), Dusty (King) and Alibi (Terhune) as U.S. marshals on the trail of a bandit with the same trademarks as the long-missing Black Bart. Going to Apache Butte, Crash pretends to be a gambler and romances pretty Molly Collins (Gwen Gaze), much to the chagrin of Dusty. Molly's father, Joe Collins (Jack Holmes), is an alcoholic who is being helped by the local sky pilot, Deacon Stewart (Forrest Taylor). Gambling den operators Miller (George Chesebro) and Brady (Frank Ellis) are out to get the Collins ranch and sell it to the railroad for a needed right-of-way. Miller, who has been posing as Black Bart, robs a stagecoach and then tries to buy the Collins Ranch only to find it has been donated to Stewart for a church. When Brady and his men try to break up a church social, Stewart stops them with a gun. The next night he plays Collins' hand in a poker game, winning back a loan Joe got from Miller. As a result, Crash becomes suspicious that Stewart may be Black Bart. During a stagecoach robbery, Crash shoots at a man he thinks is Black Bart but the bandit escapes and along the road shoots Stewart. The preacher tells Crash he was once Black Bart but that he had no part in the recent robberies. Crash then trails the robber to a cabin where Dusty and Alibi are being held prisoner by Brady. During a fight, Miller accidentally shoots Brady and is in turn shot by Dusty. The recovering Deacon Stewart tells Joe and Molly the truth about his past but the Range Busters refuse to arrest him since they have solved the recent crime wave. During the proceedings, John King sang the title tune and "Joggin.'"

Next was *Fugitive Valley*, coming out in late July, 1941. It featured a heroine called The Whip, a cross between Zorro and Lash LaRue. The plot had Sheriff Warren (Tom London) and his jailer (Edward Peil, Sr.) in cahoots with lawman Crash (Corrigan) in infiltrating an outlaw gang run by a bandit, the Whip. They arrest Crash for stagecoach robbery and place him in a cell with Red Langdon (Robert Kortman), a member of the Whip's gang. Dusty (King) helps the two escape and Red takes them to Fugitive Valley, a town without law. There they meet Gray (Glenn Strange), who beats Crash in a fight when his authority is challenged. Crash and Dusty then join the gang and rob a stagecoach in which Alibi (Terhune) is traveling incognito as trickster Hammo the Great. He and Elmer are taken to the gang's hideout to entertain the outlaws but Alibi uses pigeons to take messages to Sheriff Warren. In town, Crash and Dusty meet and romance Ann Savage (Julie Duncan), the assistant of the local doctor (Edward Brady). Unbeknownst to them and the bandits, Ann is really the Whip, the leader of a gang out to prove that businessman Brandon (Reed Howes) is backing Gray, and that Brandon has stolen Ann's father's ranch. When Ann finds out that Brandon is heading to town with the money from the gang's recent robberies, she and her gang attack him and take the loot. After talking with the sheriff, Brandon becomes suspicious and alerts Gray, who plans a robbery and waits to find out who tells Warren. The Range Busters are forced to reveal their identities and Alibi is knocked out as Crash and Dusty ride to warn the sheriff and his posse about an ambush from Gray's gang. Ann and her boys ride into town, find Alibi and locate money in Gray's safe which matches the currency they took from Brandon. The sheriff and his posse are pinned down by the outlaws but Crash and Dusty come to their rescue and rout the gang, chasing them back to Fugitive Valley. There they are caught in a crossfire between the Whip's gang and the law and are forced to surrender. Crash and Dusty find out that Ann is the Whip, and that she is working on the side of the law. The two want to stay with Ann but Alibi concocts a fake message which carries the trio out of Fugitive Valley.

Fugitive Valley, one of the better outings in the series, never takes itself too seriously. Terhune has quite a bit of screen time in the guise of magician Hammo the Great as he performs magic tricks and comedy with Elmer. One amusing sequence has Crash and Dusty vying for Ann's affections and being diagnosed with a contagious disease, since their tongues have turned blue from eating blueberry pie. King does a nice job crooning the songs "My Little Prairie Annie" and "Riding Along." In keeping with the series policy of featuring western singers in the cast, Texas native Doye O'Dell sings "The Old Chisholm Trail" and also enacts the role of the Whip's chief henchman. While Glenn Strange and Robert Kortman are effective as the bad guys, they never appear to be very dangerous, and the chief villain, played by Reed Howes, only shows up in a couple of scenes. Corrigan and Strange engage in a short but rousing fight, one of the best of the series. *Variety* noted that the film "is on a par footing with any of their previous entries, which, plus their growing fame, adds up to powerful boxoffice prospects."

It was back to the horror-mystery angle in the next Range Busters release, *Saddle Mountain Roundup*, a remake of the Beacon's Guinn "Big Boy" Williams starrer, *Big Boy Rides Again* (1935). William L. Nolte, who was production manager on the series, got story credit since he wrote the original screenplay for the Beacon release. Issued late in the summer of 1941, *Saddle Mountain Roundup* began during a terrible thunderstorm with rancher Magpie Harper (John Elliott) fearing for his life. The rancher has hired Crash (Corrigan), Dusty (King) and Alibi (Terhune) to guard his horse herd while it is on the way to market and he sends for the trio. Magpie has also decided to forego signing an agreement with fellow rancher Jack Henderson (Steve Clark) until his lawyer, Dan Freeman (Jack Mulhall), can finalize the contract. Magpie is very fond of Freeman's daughter Nancy (Lita Conway) and considers her his only family. Henderson believes that Magpie's foreman, Blackie Stone (George Chesebro), has been stealing his boss' horses and the two argue. When his servant Fang Way (Willie Fung) serves Magpie his dinner, he gives part of it to his pet raven and the bird dies. Realizing he was about to be poisoned, Magpie writes a note to the Range Busters but is shot before he can reveal the location of money he has hidden on his ranch. Fang Way puts the note in his pocket when he finds his employer dead, not realizing its importance. On the way to Magpie's ranch, Crash and Dusty are shot at but fail in their attempt to capture their attacker. At the ranch they learn about their friend's murder from Blackie. The local sheriff (Jack Holmes) is more interested in fishing than in solving the case. Freeman informs Crash and Dusty that Magpie left no money in his bank account and they tell him that Alibi is bringing the proceeds from the sale of the horses. Alibi is abducted and left tied up in a remote cabin, the money being hidden inside Elmer. Crash follows Fang Way and finds the note Magpie had written while Dusty, exploring Magpie's house, is knocked out and falls into a mine tunnel below the structure. Freeman reads Magpie's will which leaves almost all of his estate to Nancy. Dusty awakens and follows the mine tunnel, locating and rescuing Alibi. Crash finds Blackie murdered and returns to the ranch where Fang Way has been attacked. When they spy a mysterious figure in the mine tunnel, Dusty and Alibi give chase. The phantom escapes through a trap door, runs through the house and rides away. Crash follows and captures the murderer: Freeman. Henderson then tells the trio that Freeman wanted Magpie's money for himself and that he had also killed Blackie who had been blackmailing him. With the case solved, Crash and Dusty want to stay and romance Nancy but Alibi convinces them to go with him to Denver to get Elmer a new hair piece. During the proceedings, King sang two songs for which he wrote the lyrics, "The Doggone Dogie Got Away" and "That Little Green Valley of Mine." Hick comic Cousin Harold Goodwin, cast as a ranch hand, contributed "Little Brown Jug."

Tonto Basin Outlaws, issued in October, 1941, had Crash (Corrigan), Dusty (King) and Lullaby (Terhune) wanting to join Teddy Roosevelt's Rough Riders and fight in the Spanish-American War only to be assigned as undercover agents looking into the rustling of cattle intended for Army use. While Denver reporter Jane Blan-

Advertisement for *Tonto Basin Outlaws* (Monogram, 1941).

Lobby card for *Tonto Basin Outlaws* (Monogram, 1941).

chard (Jan Wiley) begs her editor (Rex Lease) for a chance to cover the rustling story, Crash goes to his boyhood home of North Butte pretending to be a cowhand looking for work. There he meets his childhood chum Jeff "Weasel" Miller (Tristram Coffin), who he once saved from drowning. Miller, who owns the West Wyoming Cattle Company and most of the town, is the ringleader of the cattle theft gang. Stark (Edmond Cobb), one of Miller's henchmen, tells him that Crash is one of the Range Busters and is responsible for him going to prison. Wanting to keep tabs on Crash, Miller hires him to run his hotel. Meanwhile, Jane has gone to work in Miller's café and both Crash and Dusty flirt with her although she thinks Crash is an outlaw and Dusty a range detective. Alibi learns from a stagecoach driver (Budd Buster) that money taken in a recent robbery was going to the government. Crash takes Jane riding but sends her back to town in order to observe a cattle herd which is soon rustled with one of the cowboys, Bill Brown (Art Fowler), being injured. Crash takes him back to town where Miller pretends to be outraged by the raid, although he was the one who ordered the rustling. Alibi finds out that the stolen stagecoach money had been in a strongbox consigned to Miller; going to the man's office looking for evidence, he is accidentally locked in the closet. The next day Dusty spies Ricks (Ted Mapes), a man he once sent to prison, coming out of Miller's office and he follows him only to be trailed by Jane. To get her safely out of the way, Dusty locks her in a cabin but she is rescued by Stark, who then captures Dusty, who has seen the gang rustling cattle. Jane follows Stark and Dusty and is able to help Dusty escape. Finding the telegram connecting Miller to the robberies on Elmer, Crash goes to Miller's office, and Alibi breaks out of the closet; the two escape from Miller and Ricks. When Ricks tries to shoot Crash, Miller stops him and tells his former pal they are now even. As Crash and Alibi hole up in the hotel, Miller arouses the locals against them and a gunfight ensues. Brown, however, will not join Miller and his gang and rides out of town, meeting the returning Dusty and Jane. The trio cause a cattle stampede through the town which crushes the walls of Miller's office, bringing about the downfall of the crook and his gang.

Tonto Basin Outlaws, a fairly entertaining entry, is marred by ill-matched stock footage of cattle herds, rustling and the finale stampede. Its strong point is beautiful leading lady Jan Wiley who is quite ingratiating as the very feminine but tough-minded newspaper reporter out to get a big scoop. During the course of the picture she is romanced by Dusty who sings "Cabin of My Dreams" which King co-wrote with Jean George. Genre veteran Hank Bell has three roles in the movie: He is seen as citizens Luke and Slim and briefly appears as a man leaving the military recruiting office.

The final 1941 series release, *Underground Rustlers*, came out in November. Its plot evolved from the great gold conspiracy of 1869 when Eastern financiers tried to corner the gold market. As a result, Colorado and California are ordered by

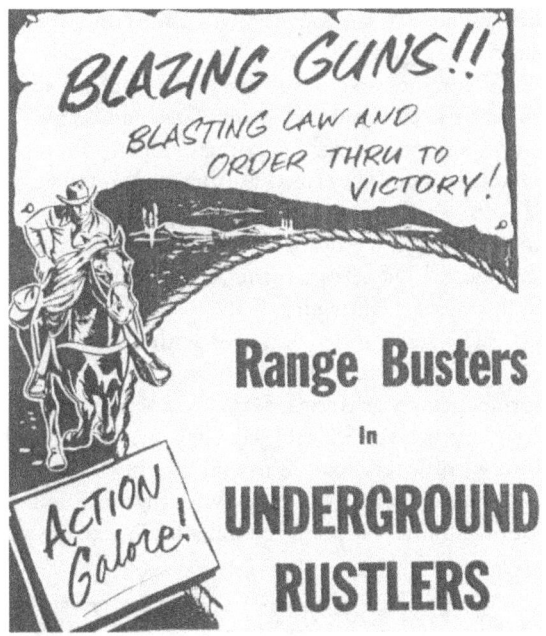

Advertisement for *Underground Rustlers* (Monogram, 1941).

the government to increase mining operations and Range Busters Crash (Corrigan), Dusty (King) and Alibi (Terhune) are sent to Gold Butte to look into a series of bullion robberies. Alibi and Elmer go into the area as peddlers and at a relay station meet up with Crash and Dusty, who are attracted to a pretty stagecoach passenger, Irene Bently (Gwen Gaze), whose father, Jim Bently (Forrest Taylor), is head of the local smelting operations. During the ride, Crash announces he suspects Bently of being behind the robberies, not realizing he is Irene's father. When they see a buckboard driver being attacked by three bandits, the Range Busters come to the rescue and are able to catch one of the holdup men, Joe (Carl Mathews), who they take to jail. The buckboard was carrying gold hidden in potato sacks; the trio returns it to mining engineer Martin Ford (Robert Blair). Alibi begins to think that Coyote Gold Mine owner Tom Harris (Tom London) may have been one of the robbers, not knowing Harris is in cahoots with Ford in a scheme to dig a tunnel from his mine to Bently's smelter and steal the gold shipments. After Ford agrees to set up a fake stagecoach shipment in order to lure the robbers, the Range Busters become suspicious of him although Ford claims Bently is behind the rob-

beries. In order to get his freedom, Joe accuses Bently of being his boss and the sheriff (Bud Osborne) arrests Bently but is forced to let him go after Joe is murdered in his cell by Ford. To clear his name, Bently gives Ford the combination to the smelter safe and Ford orders Harris and another henchman, Jake (Steve Clark), to loot it but Alibi gets the drop on them. During a shootout, Alibi pretends to be mortally wounded and Harris and Jake accuse him of the robbery. The Range Busters, along with the sheriff and government man Ward (Edward Peil, Sr.), arrange for an inquest. At the time it is to take place, Harris and Jake plan to complete the tunnel and carry off the robbery. When they break into the safe, the two henchmen are captured by Crash and Dusty. At the inquest, Alibi's "ghost" arises and accuses Ford of the robberies and of "making Elmer an orphan." Ford tries to escape but is subdued by Crash. As they leave town, Irene brings the Range Busters a telegram from President Ulysses S. Grant thanking them for stopping the gold robberies.

Underground Rustlers gave the lion's share of its action to Max Terhune, who not only carried off solo undercover work but also pretended to be his own ghost at the inquest finale. In addition, he and Elmer had several amusing scenes as he peddled a variety of wares, calling himself a purveyor and not a peddler. "The price is cheap, folks," Alibi would tell a crowd with Elmer replying, "Yeah, like the materials." Among the offered items were unbreakable suspenders and a comb which promoted hair growth. The feature also included the usual amusing rivalry between Crash and Dusty over the leading lady, giving Dusty the opportunity to croon "Followin' the Trail" and "Sweetheart of the Range."

The first of seven 1942 series releases, *Thunder River Feud*, came out in January of that year. By this time the entries were beginning to stall somewhat as noted by this one's emphasis on comedy over plot and action. It opens at the Tucson Rodeo with Crash (Corrigan) beating out Dusty (King) for the championship belt although Dusty pulls a prank and has his picture taken as Crash, thus getting all the publicity. The two then learn that pretty Maybelle Pembroke (Jan Wiley) is returning to the family ranch from an Eastern school. When they find out that Alibi (Terhune) used to work there, they convince him to join his cowboys to the location with Buck and Tex starting a gunfight between the two rival ranchers. When the two crooks disappear, Dusty is able to halt the confrontation while Crash and Alibi stop Taggart and his henchmen from robbing Harrison's safe. The thieves are captured and there is peace between the Harrison and Pembroke families. During the proceedings, King sang "What a Wonderful Day." Again the appearance of Jan Wiley was a definite plus.

The series slide continued with *Rock River Renegades* (February, 1942), although it did give former genre star Kermit Maynard a sizable role. In it he portrayed Sheriff Luke Graham, who is in love with Grace Ross (Christine McIntyre), the daughter of local newspaper owner Richard Ross (John Elliott). Not only is Graham criticized by

Advertisement for *Thunder River Feud* (Monogram, 1942).

them in taking a vacation at the ranch. To impress the young lady, Crash claims to be Gerald Griswold, a noted writer, and Dusty gets a job at the ranch, claiming to be Crash. Maybelle loves Grover Harrison (Carleton Young), whose rancher father, Colonel Harrison (Rick Anderson), is feuding with her father, Jim Pembroke (Jack Holmes), over a fence line. Instigating trouble between the two families is Dick Taggart (George Chesebro), Pembroke's ex-foreman, who has been stealing cattle from both ranches. When Taggart tries to murder Grover and put the blame on Pembroke, Alibi saves the young man much to the delight of Maybelle. Alibi tells Jim Pembroke that someone is causing the trouble between him and Harrison as Taggart orders his henchmen Tex (Carl Mathews) and Buck (Ted Mapes) to loot Harrison's safe. During Maybelle's birthday party, Pembroke is told that Harrison's cowhands are destroying his fence and he takes

Poster for *Rock River Renegades* (Monogram, 1942).

Ross for not stopping road agents plaguing the Rock River area, he also has a romantic rival in saloon keeper-realtor Jim Dawson (Weldon Heyburn), who is actually the leader of the outlaws. Needing help, the sheriff sends for the Range Busters. Crash (Corrigan) and Dusty (King) stop a stagecoach robbery on their way to town. Alibi (Terhune), who takes a job as a typesetter at Ross' newspaper, finds out that Dawson has started rumors that Crash and Dusty are outlaws working with the sheriff. Since the robbers' tracks always vanish into thin air, Graham and Dusty try to follow them while Crash escapes an attack from the gang. When Grace decides to marry Dawson, the Range Busters try to delay the ceremony, but after another robbery with the stage driver being killed, Ross forms a vigilante group and appoints Dawson its leader. In order to stop Grace from marrying Dawson, the trio detain the judge (Budd Buster) who is to perform the ceremony. This causes Dawson to panic, and he order his men to get all the money they have hidden at the hideout. Due to his investigations, Graham is able to report to Grace and her father that Dawson is wanted in Dodge City for murder. Following Dawson and his men to the hideout, the Range Busters round up the gang and prove that the disappearing horse tracks were caused by reversed horseshoes. After Grace marries Graham, the Range Busters leave Rock River. This feature had King performing "Prairie Serenade" and "Oh, My Darling Clementine."

A bit better was *Boot Hill Bandits* which came out in the spring of 1942. Here Crash (Corrigan) rides into the town of Sundance where he meets his nemesis, the Mesquite Kid (I. Stanford Jolley), in the Traveler's Roost saloon and hotel. Crash has been invited to the town by the local lawman, Tolliver (Steve Clark), who wants him to take the job of county marshal. After Crash disarms the gunman, the Mesquite Kid challenges him to a gunfight. Both men have made dates to meet with the hostel's owner, Brand Bolton (John Merton), who wants the Kid to eliminate Crash because he (Bolton) is afraid the lawman will investigate a series of stagecoach robbers (Bolton is the gang leader). Crash takes a shine to singer May Meadows (Jean Brooks), who arrives in town just before the Mesquite Kid returns. Dusty (King) and Alibi (Terhune) also come to town, just after the Kid returns with a henchman (Merrill McCormick). The badmen try to ambush Crash in the saloon, and Dusty and Alibi think their friend has been killed, until the Kid walks out and falls dead. Following the gunfight, the town's mayor, Noah Smyth (Budd Buster), swears Crash in as county marshal. The Range Busters join the sheriff in trying to protect a wagon carrying a mine payroll and Crash spots it as a runaway. He leaps onto the wagon, which explodes. Maverick (Glenn Strange), a dimwit working for Bolton, finds Crash's badge and takes it to his boss. Bolton pays Maverick a reward and orders him out of the county but instead Maverick tries to steal the payroll and kills Joe (Carl Mathews), one of Bolton's men, who is guarding the strongbox. Just as Maverick is about to get the money, a ragged Crash appears. Maverick, thinking Crash is a ghost, backs away from him and falls off a cliff. Dusty and Alibi find Crash and take him to the sheriff, along with the mine payroll. They decide that Crash should pretend to be dead in order for them to investigate the case more freely. Bolton, trying to impress May, gives the singer Crash's badge as a souvenir and she immediately takes it to the sheriff, who then links Bolton to the robberies. The real boss of the robberies warns Bolton to keep the badge hidden, unaware his underling has given it to the singer. When Alibi and May go riding, Bolton has his henchman Stack Stoner (George Chesebro) kidnap them. Unable to retrieve the badge from May, he takes them to a remote cabin. There Alibi uses Elmer to outsmart the drunken Stoner, and he and May escape. Dusty trails Bolton, who tries to shoot him. After a fight, Dusty takes Bolton to jail where he is confronted by Crash, May and the sheriff. As a result he agrees to help them capture the mastermind and he sets up a meeting at the gang's hideout where Mayor Smyth, Bolton's boss, is captured. When he tries to escape, Smyth is killed by a townsman (Milburn Morante). Crash then gives up his marshal's job and rides away with Dusty and Alibi.

Boot Hill Bandits had the interesting subplot of the sheriff being a Union veteran and the man who shot the mayor a former Confederate, but both men united in fighting the lawlessness plaguing Sundance. Also well-done is the shootout between Crash and the Mesquite Kid. The actual event is not shown, with reaction shots of the faces of the witnesses outside the saloon being used in its place. The film also includes a well-staged fight between Dusty and Bolton; Glenn Strange is quite good as the scar-faced Maverick, the same type of role he would play in PRC's *The Mad Monster* (1942) and *The Black Raven* (1943). Jean Brooks made a beautiful and dignified leading lady; she does little vocalizing although her character is billed as the "Songbird of the West." Also on the minus side is the scene where Glenn Strange's double falls off the cliff onto obviously padded brush.

Texas Trouble Shooters, released in July, 1942, found Range Busters Crash (Corrigan), Dusty (King) and Alibi (Terhune) on vacation near Buckhorn, Texas. When Alibi hears a cry for help, he is unable to wake his lazy partners and he goes it alone, rescuing Bret Travis (Roy Harris), who has been shot and left for dead on a runaway buckboard. The injured Bret tells Alibi he has come from Amarillo to claim his half of an inheritance left to him by his late uncle. When Crash and Dusty learn that the other half of the estate goes to the uncle's pretty daughter Judy Wilson (Julie Duncan), they concur with Alibi's plea to help Travis. Leaving Bret to recover, the trio travels to the Lazy W ranch, which has been left to Travis and Judy. There Alibi finds out that family lawyer Roger Denby (Glenn Strange) has brought in Wade Evans (Eddie Phillips), pretending he is Bret. Dusty pretends to be a old friend of Judy's late father while Crash gets himself hired by Denby as the Lazy W's new foreman. While Crash and Dusty try to romance Judy, Crash learns that her late father had discovered oil on a section of his ranch. When another rancher, Bill Ames (Steve Clark), is brought to the Lazy W by Denby and proposes leasing that section for grazing his cattle, the Range Busters suspect Denby of trying to get the spread for himself. Ames reveals the identity of Crash, Dusty and Alibi to Denby, who orders his gang to capture Dusty and Bret. Fighting it out with Denby, Crash forces the lawyer to confess to the kidnapping as well as the murder of Judy's father and the attempt on Bret's life. The gang is arrested and Bret comes to the Lazy W to collect his inheritance. King sang "Light of Western Skies" and "Deep in the Heart of Texas" in the feature.

The autumn of 1942 saw the issuance of *Arizona Stage Coach*. The feature gets off to a silly start with Dusty (King) being hung upside down and forced to sing the Rudy Sooter song "Where the Green Grass Grows High in the Mountains" in order to carry out a bet with Crash (Corrigan) and Alibi (Terhune). Arriving on the scene are Wells Fargo attorney Larry Meadows (Forrest Taylor) and his niece Dorrie Willard (Nell O'Day). Meadows asks the trio to hunt down highwaymen who have been carrying out stagecoach robberies in the vicinity of Stoney Creek and he invites them to visit Dorrie and her brother Ernie (Roy Harris) at their Diamond W ranch. Riding to the area, the Range Busters come upon a stage holdup and they chase the robber, who eludes them. When the stagecoach arrives at the junction, the driver, Jake (Steve Clark), reports the robbery to Wells Fargo agent Tim Douglas (Charles King), who offers to take Dorrie, who was a passenger, to meet her brother. At the Diamond W, Ernie discovers that his partner, Tex Laughlin (Stanley Price), is the robber and he is forced to kill him in self-defense. Ernie then takes the stolen money into town as the Range Busters find Tex's body and he is identified by Douglas and Dorrie. Douglas intercepts a posse led by Sheriff Denver (Jack Ingram), who tries to arrest Ernie for the robbery. Eluding the law, Ernie goes back to the ranch and tells Dorrie and the Range Busters what happened. They urge him to take refuge at a remote line shack while Crash, Dusty and Alibi investigate. Ernie, however, is soon captured by Strike (Kermit Maynard) and Ace (Carl Mathews), who are henchmen of Douglas, the brains behind the outlaw gang. The crooks force Ernie to pretend he is their leader during the next robbery and Jake identifies him to the law. The Range Busters hatch a plot to catch the gang by sending $10,000 via the Wells Fargo to the Dry Gulch Ranch in Arizona. The trio, in disguise, then robs the stagecoach before the gang make their attempt, much to the surprise of Jake and shotgun guard Dan (Frank Ellis), who are in cahoots with Douglas. Dorrie goes to Douglas for help and tells him the identity of the Range Busters and he has Strike drive her to the gang hideout to see her brother. The Range Busters force a confession out of Jake who identifies Douglas as the gang leader, but he is overheard by Dan who rides to inform his boss. Strike then turns on Douglas and tries to escape but he is shot by gang member Red (Slim Whitaker), who was told to ambush Ernie. Red is shot by the sheriff as the Range Busters attack the hideout. Douglas rides away and is captured by Crash, and Ernie subdues Red. Crash and Dusty want to stay at the Diamond W with Dorrie but Alibi cooks up a scheme with the sheriff, who has fallen in love with the girl, to get them to leave.

Arizona Stage Coach is a fairly entertaining feature which moves along at a good clip but it has several deficiencies. It contains too many scenes in which Elmer works alone without the obvious needed benefit of Alibi and it cannibalizes from other series entries: The chase sequences are lifted from *West of Pinto Basin* and many of the outdoor shots are from *Wrangler's Roost*. One highlight is King's vocalizing on "Red River Valley." The plot ploy of hiding money inside Elmer was used previously in *Saddle Mountain Roundup*.

The feature proved to be Corrigan's last appearance in the series for a time. Replacing him was David Sharpe, in the second-billed role of Davy. As a result, John King moved up to top billing and he also took over Crash's white horse. David Sharpe (1910–80) was a native of St. Louis, Missouri, who grew up in Hollywood where he worked in pictures as a child performer. In the early 1930s he co-starred in Hal Roach's series of two-reelers, "The Boy Friends," and later did a trio of "Young Friends" features for producer William Berke. For Berke he also co-starred with Flash the Dog in some two-reel action dramas and he did supporting roles in numerous features, including many "B" westerns, before turning to stunt work in the late 1930s. He continued to act, however, and had a starring role in the 1941 Monogram feature *Silver Stallion* before joining the Range Busters. Along with Richard Talmadge and Yakima Canutt, he is regarded as one of Hollywood's greatest stuntmen.

With the departure of Corrigan, Robert Tansey took over the direction of the Range Busters; S. Roy Luby continued to edit the features under the Roy Claire moniker. The first feature starring the trio of King, Sharpe and Terhune was *Texas to Bataan*, released in October, 1942. Taking place on the eve of the Second World War, it told of Range Busters Dusty (King), Davy (Sharpe) and Alibi (Terhune), being employed by Tom Conroy (Steve Clark) to take his horses to Bataan, in the Philippines, for use by the United States Army soldiers based there. Another rancher, Richards (Frank Ellis), has been having his horse herds poisoned and stampeded and the Range Busters agree to investigate the matter. Following tire tracks from Richards' ranch, the trio is fired upon by the occupants of a large truck which, when stopped at a roadblock, is found to be carrying rifles manufactured in Japan. The assailants are rescued by Cookie (Escolastico Baucin), an employee of Conroy's who turned out to be a Japanese spy. Since Cavalry Captain Anders (Kenne Duncan) has approved the sale of Conroy's horses, the Range Busters drive the herd to Galveston, Texas, leaving behind Conroy's daughter Dallas (Marjorie Manners), who is being courted by both Dusty and Davy. From Galveston, Dusty and Davy take the horses via a freighter to the Philippines and deliver them to Captain Anders. While in a café, they see Cookie and overhear him tell German spy Miller (Guy Kingsford) that Richards is an Axis agent. They get Cookie and themselves arrested, and Anders frees Dusty and Davy and tells them an American harbor may be attacked. Back home, Dusty and Davy rejoin Alibi and the three confront Richards, who is shot by Davy when he tries to escape. The trio finds a cache of dynamite on the agent's ranch. Following the bombing of Pearl Harbor, the Range Busters join the military. During the proceedings, King warbled his self-penned "My Pony and Me" as well as "Goodbye Old Paint."

Next came *Trail Riders*, issued in December, 1942. Following the murder of his lawman son (Kenne Duncan), border marshals chief Jim Hammond (Steve Clark) calls in Range Busters Dusty (King), Davy (Sharpe) and Alibi (Terhune) to help thwart lawlessness in Gila Springs, Arizona. Upset by their friend's murder, the trio gives up a vacation and are sworn in as marshals. When they get to Gila Springs, Ed Cole (Charles King), the head of the local vigilantes, orders them out of town. The Range Busters go to the ranch of Mike Rand (Forrest Taylor), a friend of Hammond's; Mike's son Jeff (Lynton Brent) is in cahoots with Cole, who is really the chief of the local outlaws. Going to the ranch, Dusty, Davy and Alibi rescue

Rand's daughter Mary (Evelyn Finley) when her buckboard horses run away; she believes they are bandits. As Jeff shoots at the trio, Davy goes after him while Hammond ranch hand Tiny (Jack Curtis) pulls a gun on Dusty and Alibi. Back at the ranch, the Range Busters tell Hammond they are lawmen, and when Jeff shows up, Davy acts like he does not know him. Alibi trails Jeff into town and sees him talking with Cole, who then becomes friendly to the Range Busters. Ace Alton (Kermit Maynard), a Cole cohort who was once put in jail by the lawmen, starts a saloon brawl with them. Jeff is injured but rescued by the Range Busters. They take him back to the Hammond ranch where he owns up to being part of the outlaw gang and vows to help his father and the marshals bring them to justice. As a ruse they spread a rumor that the local bank contains a great deal of money and when the gang tries to rob it they are confronted by Dusty, Davy, Alibi and Jeff. When Cole tries to kill the lawmen, Jeff stops him but is knocked down as Cole escapes. The rest of the gang is captured and Davy beats Cole in a fistfight. With law and order now in Gila Springs, the Range Busters go back to their vacation. King sang Stephen Foster's public domain song "Oh Susanna" in the film, thus saving production costs.

Two Fisted Justice, released in January, 1943, was the first of a half-dozen Range Busters that year. This time Dusty (King), Davy (Sharpe) and Alibi (Terhune) are hired by Wells Fargo manager Bert Newsome (Lynton Brent) to stop highwaymen who murdered the sheriff of Dry Gulch and are terrorizing the area. Near the town, Davy sees a stagecoach holdup but is unable to catch the outlaws. In Dry Gulch, he goes to see contact Joan Hodgins (Gwen Gaze) whose father, Will Hodgins (John Elliott), owns the general store. Davy beats up Trigger Farley (Charles King), who tried to harass Joan for not selling him ammunition. When Davy rides out of town, Trigger follows and shoots him in the back. Dusty arrives in Dry Gulch looking for Davy and stops gang leader Decker (George Chesebro) from shooting Hodgins, who then takes Dusty to his ranch where Davy is recovering. The citizens' committee hires the Range Busters as the new marshals and the trio sets a trap to catch the outlaws. They break into Decker's safe only to find it empty since Trigger has taken the gang's stolen loot to their hideout. Decker wants to fight Dusty and has his men attack him but Davy, Alibi and the town's citizens shoot it out with the gang and bring them to

Poster for *Trail Riders* (Monogram, 1942).

Advertisement for *Two Fisted Justice* (Monogram, 1943).

justice. King crooned another of his own compositions, "Go to Sleep Little Cowboy."

The horror-mystery angle returned in *Haunted Ranch*, the 20th series outing, issued in February, 1943. It proved to be the final Range Busters film for both John King and David Sharpe as well as director Robert Tansey. Taking still another vacation, the Range Busters (King, Sharpe, Terhune) receive orders from U.S. Marshals chief Hammond (Steve Clark) to look into the murder of Reno Red, who years before robbed the Denver Mint and probably hid the bullion on his ranch near Stony Bend. The other members of Red's gang, Rance Austin (Glenn Strange), Chuck (Charles King), Ed (Bud Osborne) and Danny (Tex Palmer), are trying to scare everyone off the ranch, the Triangle W, so they can search for the stolen gold. Learning that Red left the property to his nephew, outlaw Hank Travers (Augie Gomez), and a niece, Helen Weston (Julie Duncan), from back East, Rance orders Danny to murder Travers. The Range Busters witness the shooting and as Davy tracks down Danny, the dying Travers gives Dusty and Alibi the letter confirming his inheritance. Capturing Danny, Davy takes him to jail while Dusty decides to impersonate Travers and goes to the ranch, where he hears strange noises. When the cook, Sam (Fred "Snowflake" Toones), arrives with Helen, he tells Dusty he is the only worker on the ranch since the house is filled with strange sounds like cries in the night, organ playing, and rattling chains. After Davy turns Danny over to Marshal Hammond, he enlists in Teddy Roosevelt's Rough Riders and his pal, Deputy Rex (Rex Lease), is sent to aid Dusty and Alibi. Both Dusty and Rex vie for Helen's affections as they try to learn the name of the tune, Reno Red's favorite, which they must play on the organ in order to claim the inheritance. Realizing that Dusty is an imposter, Rance goes to the ranch and then has the sheriff (Budd Buster) arrest him as Alibi and Rex tell Julie and Sam their real identities. Planning to kill Dusty, Rance breaks him out of jail as Ed wounds the sheriff; Alibi and Rex arrive and drive the outlaws away. As the Range Busters take the sheriff into their confidence, Rance and his men ride to the ranch and take Helen prisoner while Chuck and Ed realize the organ is made of steel and is probably the hiding place of the bullion. The Range Busters arrive with Sam, who ran away when Helen was captured, and they engage the outlaws in a fight. Sam picks up a music box which plays "Little Brown Jug," the tune needed to open the side of the organ, revealing the gold. Rance and his men are put under arrest with the gold to be returned to the government mint. Dusty plans to follow Davy into the Rough Riders.

While fairly atmospheric and nicely paced,

Haunted Ranch obviously suffered from some script re-write during production. About halfway through filming, David Sharpe entered the military and he was hastily replaced by genre veteran Rex Lease. The scene where a badly dubbed Davy tells Hammond he is going to join the Rough Riders uses an obvious double for Sharpe, shot from the back. This is followed by a recruiting office scene lifted from *Tonto Basin Outlaws*. On the plus side is Steve Clark repeating the role of Hammond, which he did originally in *Trail Riders*, and there is some nice comedy interplay between bad guys Charles King and Bud Osborne as they try to decipher the combination of the organ. Charlie tells Bud he learned to play the organ after he had "mastered the mandolin." King sang "Where the Prairie Hills Meet the Sky" and also briefly did "Clementine."

In March, 1943, came *Land of Hunted Men* which gave last-billed Fred "Snowflake" Toones a fairly large part in the proceedings, making sort of a fourth Range Buster, much like Rex Lease in the previous *Haunted Ranch*. The feature also brought back Ray Corrigan and introduced Dennis Moore in the role of Denny. In addition, S. Roy Luby resumed duties as director. The plot told of Denny (Moore) being injured while chasing highwaymen and hiding out in a line shack with fellow Range Busters Crash (Corrigan) and Alibi (Terhune). Since crook Faro Wilson (Charles King) claims Denny was a robber, Crash tells their cook Snowflake (Fred "Snowflake" Toones) to investigate Wilson. When Crash and Alibi go to see Sheriff Wallace (Steve Clark), they find out that Pelham (John Merton), manager of a local mine, is upset at the lawman because of the payroll robberies. Since the sheriff thinks Faro is involved in the lawlessness, Crash and Alibi masquerade as cattle buyers and go to Faro's saloon, where Snowflake is employed. Crash wins a lot of money gambling and Snowflake warns him that Faro plans to accuse him of cheating in order to recover the winnings. After a fight, Crash and Alibi escape and spend the night at Dad Oliver's (Forrest Taylor) farm, where both men are attracted to Oliver's daughter Dorrie (Phyllis Adair). When Faro's gang tries to find Crash and Alibi, they end up in a shootout with Denny at the line shack; Crash and Alibi arrive and chase the baddies away. Snowflake brings Crash the money he won at Faro's saloon, and Crash asks him to have the sheriff check the serial numbers. Another mine payroll shipment is planned by Pelham, but Snowflake finds out the mine manager is in cahoots with Faro and he warns the sheriff. When the serial numbers on Crash's money match those from the stolen payroll, the Range Busters and the sheriff realize Faro is behind the robberies. When Faro and his gang attack the payroll wagon, they are surrounded by the Range Busters and turned over to the sheriff.

The series returned to patriotic themes, as exemplified earlier in *Texas to Bataan,* with its next two entries, *Cowboy Commandos* and *Black Market Rustlers*. Released in June, 1943, *Cowboy Commandos* had the Range Busters (Corrigan, Moore, and Terhune) about to go to New York City for a war bond drive with trick rider Joan Cameron's (Evelyn Finley) rodeo show. The tour is postponed, however, when Joan finds out her lawman brother has been murdered. She and the Range Busters come to the aid of her uncle, Dan Bartlett (Steve Clark), whose efforts to mine magnacite, which contains magnesium, for the war effort are being sabotaged. When Dan says foreign agents are behind the lawlessness, Crash agrees to take over the local sheriff's job while Denny and Alibi hire on at the mine. As planned, Alibi gets himself fired by Bartlett and goes to the local saloon where he announces he will get even with him. The saloon is run by weakling Werner (Budd Buster) and his strong-willed wife Kate (Edna Bennett). Two mine workers, Fraser (John Merton) and Mario (Frank Ellis), overhear Alibi's rantings. During the robbery of a wagon carrying magnacite, Deputy Slim (Johnny Bond) is injured; Crash catches robber Fred (George Chesebro) and takes him back to jail where Mario shoots him before he can talk. The masked Mario thinks he also killed Crash, who was actually unhurt. Alibi discovers a hidden room attached to the saloon where the local Nazis have their headquarters. When he hears the saboteurs plan to blow up the mine, he rides to tell Joan, who has taken over the handling of the office affairs, and she gets the news to Crash and Denny. As the agents plant the dynamite, Slim lets the air out of Kate's tires so she cannot get away as ordered by Werner, the head of the spy operation. At the mine, a shootout takes place between the Range Busters and the saboteurs. Werner and Mario try to escape but are captured by Crash and Dusty. The film's main drawback was its constant loud music and a highlight was Johnny Bond singing the Johnny Lange song "I'll Get the Fuehrer as Sure as Shootin.'"

Issued in August, 1943, *Black Market Rustlers* was even more of a propaganda piece with a foreword denouncing the sale of beef on the black market; at the finale, Ray Corrigan speaks directly to the audience about aiding the war effort by not dealing with black marketeers. Here Crash (Corrigan), Denny (Moore) and Alibi (Terhune) come to the town of Winston to investigate the rustling of cattle herds with the beef being sold on the black market. When Crash finds the body of the investigator who asked their help, he is accused of the crime by Slade (George Chesebro), the real killer. Crash is put in jail by the sheriff (Carl Sepulveda) but Alibi, an old friend of the sheriff, shows him the letter asking the Range Busters to investigate the local rustling. While Crash pretends to remain a prisoner, Denny gets a job at Fred Prescott's (Steve Clark) ranch where he flirts with the owner's pretty daughter Linda (Evelyn Finley). That night, Crash comes to the Prescott ranch; Slade and his cohort Kyper (Frank Ellis) drive by and Slade tries to kill Prescott but fails. Crash and Denny then tell the Prescotts they are working undercover and enlist their support in fighting the rustlers. Crash and Alibi search Slade's property and find a large truck which they believe is being used to transport the stolen cattle. When Denny spies a gang near the cattle herd at Prescott's ranch, he captures one of the guards, Perry (John Merton), and takes him to Prescott. Bartender Jake (Hal Price) becomes suspicious of Alibi, so saloon owner Corbin (Glenn Strange), the gang leader, tells Jake to give him knockout drops; Alibi only pretends to take them and collapses. After hearing Corbin's plans for a final rustling effort at the Prescott ranch, Alibi reports the news to Crash who confronts Corbin. After a brawl, the gang leader is arrested. With the sheriff and a posse standing by, Denny captures truck driver Bill (Carl Mathews) and replaces him with Prescott cowhand Slim (Hank Worden). When the rustlers try to round up the cattle, Crash, Denny and Alibi ride out from the back of the truck and capture the outlaws. With the gang in jail, Alibi puts all their guns in a barrel designed to collect scrap metal for the war effort. Music was provided by the Austin Family and ukulele player Art Fowler, who also played a cowboy. Little Jean Austin sang and yodeled "You Wink at Me and I'll Wink at You" and Jim Austin sang "Wait for the Wagon" followed by an instrumental of "I'm a Ridin' Old Paint."

The final series film, *Bullets and Saddles*, was released in the fall of 1943. When outlaws terrorize rancher Charlie Craig (Budd Buster) and his family, he asks Marshal Claiburn (Forrest Taylor) for more help. The lawman seems reluctant so Craig vows to form a vigilante committee. Jack Hammond (Glenn Strange) orders his thugs Blair (Steve Clark) and Webber (Ed Cassidy) to murder cattle buyer Tex Landers (Silver Harr) and then blame the crime on Craig. As a result, his mother (Rose Plummer) sends for the Range Busters (Corrigan, Moore, Terhune), since she helped raise Crash. Alibi is sent to investigate Hammond's saloon, the Wayside Inn. There he sees the bartender, Webber (Ed Cassidy), try to get the locals riled up against Craig, who has found the outlaws' hideout and tries to capture Blair. When the gang runs him off, Craig tries to escape in his buckboard but is shot; after a wreck the outlaws leave him for dead. The next day the Range Busters find him alive and take him back to his ranch as henchman Mike (John Merton) tells Hammond that Craig is still alive. When Crash tries to spy on Hammond, Webber gets the drop on him and takes him to his boss but Crash manages to turn the tables on the crooks and escape. Dusty hears Hammond tell his men they will burn down the Craig house and rustle all his cattle. Alibi moves Mother Craig and her granddaughter, Laura (Julie Duncan), to a barn as Webber and henchman Butch (Joe Garcia) set fire to the Craig house. As the crooks rustle Craig's cattle, he joins the sheriff and the Range Busters in fighting them. After a gun battle, the gang is subdued and Crash and Denny capture the fleeing Hammond and Blair. Alibi presents a confession from Mike which clears Craig of killing Landers. The Craigs invite the Range Busters to visit them after their new home is constructed.

Although a fairly fast-paced affair, *Bullets and Saddles* had its gunfight finale literally lifted from the earlier *Fugitive Valley*. In fact, Robert Kortman as an outlaw is easily spotted although he had no other part in the proceedings. To complicate matters further, Tom London is audibly called the sheriff while Forrest Taylor had the part in the rest of the feature. Both of these scenes are from *Fugitive Valley*.

The Range Busters proved to be Ray Corrigan's final association with "B" Western series films. He would continue to take acting roles, most often using his ape suit in a variety of jungle and horror features. He also enacted the title role in the classic sci-fi programmer *It! The Terror From Beyond Space* in 1958. He spent most of his time developing Corriganville in Simi Valley, California. Not only the Range Busters movies, but scores of other Western and outdoor features were filmed on the property which also became an amusement park. In 1965 Corrigan sold the business to Bob Hope for $2.8 million, and it was renamed Hopetown. After that, Corrigan moved to Oregon, where he worked in real estate development and film production. During the 1970s he was a guest at several Western film conventions. He died August 10, 1976.

Following the demise of the Range Busters, Max Terhune returned to the stage, touring solo and with entertainers such as Tex Ritter and Wally Fowler. He resumed film work in 1944, co-starring with Ken Maynard and Eddie Dean in *The Harmony Trail*; it was reissued as *White Stallion* three years later. During the 1948–49 season he co-starred in eight oaters with Johnny Mack Brown at Monogram and he later had roles in *Rawhide* (1951) and *Giant* (1956), along with working in such TV series as *I Love Lucy*, *Annie Oakley* and *The Lone Ranger*. In the early 1950s he had his own TV program, *Alibi's Tent Show*, on KNX-TV in Hollywood. During the late 1950s and into the 1960s he and Elmer were featured at Corriganville and later Hopetown, and he continued to make personal appearances until his death on June 5, 1973.

After military service in World War II, John King returned to Hollywood and attempted to resume his career as a cowboy star but the production company for which he was working went out of business and he moved to Arizona where he operated a garage and worked in automobile sales. Some years later he moved to La Jolla, California, where he owned and operated a restaurant. Like Corrigan and Terhune, he hit the Western

Max Terhune in the late 1960s.

film convention trail in the 1970s before his death on November 11, 1987.

David Sharpe returned to Hollywood after the war and resumed his career, both as an actor and stuntman. Over the years he doubled for many big stars like Glenn Ford, Alan Ladd and Audie Murphy and he continued to do stunt work well into the 1970s before dying March 30, 1980. He had suffered with Parkinson's Disease for several years. Dennis Moore also continued his acting career following the demise of the Range Busters, mainly doing supporting roles in scores of films and TV shows, including the "Irish Cowboys" series for Screen Guild in 1950. He died March 1, 1964.

A footnote to the Range Busters came in the early 1950s when Corrigan and Terhune teamed with Monte Hale's brother, Bill Hale, to star in a 30-minute television pilot, *Buckskin Rangers*. Filmed at Corriganville, it was written by William

L. Nolte, the production manager for the Range Busters features, and directed by Frank McDonald. The supporting cast included Tom Keene, Virginia Herrick, Kermit Maynard, Lane Bradford and Ted Mapes.

Filmography

The Range Busters (Monogram, 1940, 56 minutes) Producer: George W. Weeks. Associate Producer: Anna Bell Ward. Director: S. Roy Luby. Screenplay: John Rathmell. Photography: Ed [Edward] Linden. Editor: Roy Claire (S. Roy Luby). Art Director: Fred Preble. Music Director: Frank Sanucci. Songs: Johnny Lange & Lew Porter. Sound: Glen Glenn. Production Manager: Melville Shyer. Property Master: Bill Billings.

Cast: Ray Corrigan (Crash), John King (Dusty), Max Terhune (Alibi), Luana Walters (Carol Thorp), LeRoy Mason (Torrence), Earle Hodgins (Uncle Rolf Thorp), Frank LaRue (Doc Stengle), Kermit Maynard (Wyoming), Bruce King (Wall), Duke [Carl] Mathews (Rocky), Horace Murphy (Homer Thorp), Karl Hackett (Sheriff Dod Clayburne), Herman Hack (Joe), Ed Brady (Frightened Cowhand), Hank Worden, Jimmie Widener (Cowboys).

Trailing Double Trouble (Monogram, 1940, 56 minutes) Producer: George W. Weeks. Associate Producer: Anna Bell Ward. Director: S. Roy Luby. Screenplay: Oliver Drake. Story: George H. Plympton. Photography: Edward Linden. Editor: Roy Claire (S. Roy Luby). Music Director: Frank Sanucci. Songs: Johnny Lange & Lew Porter. Sound: Glen Glenn. Production Manager: William L. Nolte.

Cast: Ray Corrigan (Crash), John King (Dusty), Max Terhune (Alibi), Lita Conway (Marion Horner), Nancy Louise King (Horner Baby), Roy Barcroft (Jim Moreland), Forrest Taylor (Sheriff), Jack Rutherford (Amos Hardy), Tom London (Kirk), Carl Mathews (Drag), Ken [Kenne] Duncan (Bob Horner), Rex Felker (Texas Champion Roper), Jimmy Wakely's Rough Riders [Jimmy Wakely, Johnny Bond, Dick Reinhart] (Musicians), Richard Cramer (Jake the Bartender), Frank Ellis (Gang Member).

West of Pinto Basin (Monogram, 1940, 60 minutes) Producer: George W. Weeks. Associate Producer: Anna Bell Ward. Director: S. Roy Luby. Screenplay: Earle Snell. Story: Elmer Clifton. Photography: Edward Linden. Editor: Roy Claire (S. Roy Luby). Music Director: Frank Sanucci. Songs: Jerry Smith. Sound: Glen Glenn. Production Manager: William L. Nolte.

Cast: Ray Corrigan (Crash), John King (Dusty), Max Terhune (Alibi), Gwen Gaze (Joan Brown), Tristram Coffin (Harvey), Dirk Thane (Hank), George Chesebro (Lane), Carl Mathews (Joe), Bud Osborne (Sheriff), Jack Perrin (Ware), Phil Dunham (Summers), Budd Buster (Jeff Jones), Jerry Smith (Musician/Stagecoach Guard), Johnny Luther (Stagecoach Guard), Richard Cramer (Bartender), Bud McClure (Stagecoach Driver).

Working title: *Triple Threat*.

Trail of the Silver Spurs (Monogram, 1941, 58 minutes) Producer: George W. Weeks. Associate Producer: Anna Bell Ward. Director: S. Roy Luby. Screenplay: Earle Snell. Story: Elmer Clifton. Photography: Robert Cline. Editor: Roy Claire (S. Roy Luby). Music Director: Frank Sanucci. Songs: Johnny Lange & Lew Porter. Sound: Glen Glenn. Production Manager: William L. Nolte.

Cast: Ray Corrigan (Crash), John King (Dusty), Max Terhune (Alibi), I. Stanford Jolley (The Jingler), Dorothy Short (Nancy Nordick), Milt [Milburn] Morante (Dan Nordick), George Chesebro (Wilson), Eddie Dean (Stoner), Frank Ellis, Carl Mathews (Murdered Men), Chuck Baldra (Rider).

The Kid's Last Ride (Monogram, 1941, 55 minutes) Producer: George W. Weeks. Associate Producer: Anna Bell Ward. Director: S. Roy Luby. Screenplay: Earle Snell. Photography: Robert Cline. Editor: Roy Claire (S. Roy Luby). Music Director: Frank Sanucci. Sound: Glen Glenn. Production Manager: William L. Nolte.

Cast: Ray Corrigan (Crash), John King (Dusty), Max Terhune (Alibi), Luana Walters (Sally Rowell), Edwin Brian (Jimmy Rowell), Al Bridge (Robert Harmon/Jim Breeden), Glenn Strange (Bart Gill/Ike Breeden), Frank Ellis (Walsh), John Elliott (Disher), George Havens (Student), George Morrell (Fleming), Tex Palmer (Tex), Al Haskell (Blackie), Jack Evans, Ray Jones, Roy Bucko (Gamblers), Jack Baxley (Jack), Walter James (Bartender), Carl Mathews (Gang Member), Herman Hack, Jack Montgomery (Saloon Customers).

Tumble Down Ranch in Arizona (Monogram, 1941, 60 minutes) Producer: George W. Weeks. Associate Producer: Anna Bell Ward. Director: S. Roy Luby. Screenplay: Milton Raison. Photography: Robert Cline. Editor: Roy Claire (S. Roy Luby). Songs: E.C. Monroe, Dorothy H. Monroe, Howard Steiner & Bill Watters. Sound: Glen Glenn. Production Manager: William L. Nolte.

Cast: Ray Corrigan (Crash/Crash Jr.), John King (Dusty/Johnny King), Max Terhune (Alibi), Sheila Darcy (Dorothy Jones/Dorothy's Daughter), Marian Kerby (Mother Rogers), Quen Ramsey (Gallop), James Craven (Dan Slocum), John Elliott (Judge Uriah Jones), Jack Holmes (Sheriff Nye), Steve Clark (Shorty Gill), Sam Bernard (Café Owner), Rex Felker (Rope Twirler), The University of Arizona Glee Club (Singers), Doye O'Dell (Surveyor/Musician), Rudy Sooter (Musician), Carl Mathews (Cliff Mason), Tex Palmer (Tombstone Regan), Oscar Gahan, Tex Cooper, Tom Smith (Jurors), Frank Ellis (Gambler), Frank McCarroll (Cowboy), Chick Hannon (Gang Member), Lew Meehan, Herman Hack, Denver Dixon, Bud McClure, Jack Evans (Saloon Customers).

Wrangler's Roost (Monogram, 1941, 57 minutes) Producer: George W. Weeks. Associate Producer: Anna Bell Ward. Director: S. Roy Luby. Screenplay: John Vlahos & Robert Finkle. Story: Earle Snell. Photography: Robert Cline. Editor: Roy Claire (S. Roy Luby). Music Director: Frank Sanucci. Sound: Glen Glenn. Production Manager: William L. Nolte.

Cast: Ray Corrigan (Crash), John King (Dusty), Max Terhune (Alibi), Forrest Taylor (Deacon Stewart/Black Bart), Gwen Gaze (Molly Collins), George Chesebro (Miller), Frank Ellis (Bully Brady), Jack Holmes (Joe Collins), Walter Shumway (Grover), Tex Palmer, Carl Mathews, Frank McCarroll (Gang Members), Jim Corey, Buck Moulton, Roy Bucko (Gamblers), Hank Bell, Bob Card (Stagecoach Drivers), Horace B. Carpenter, Emma Tansey, Herman Hack, George Morrell, Tex Cooper, Silver Tip Baker (Church Members), Al Haskell, Ray Jones, Tex Phelps, Jack Evans (Saloon Customers), Chick Hannon (Citizen).

Fugitive Valley (Monogram, 1941, 56 minutes) Producer: George W. Weeks. Associate Producer: Anna Bell Ward. Director: S. Roy Luby. Screenplay: John Vlahos & Robert Finkle. Story: Oliver Drake. Photography: Robert Cline. Editor: Roy Claire (S. Roy Luby). Music Director: Frank Sanucci. Songs: Jean George & Harry Tobias. Sound: Glen Glenn. Production Manager: William L. Nolte.

Cast: Ray Corrigan (Crash), John King (Dusty), Max Terhune (Alibi/Hammo the Great), Julie Duncan (Ann Savage), Glenn Strange (Gray), Robert Kortman (Red Langdon), Edward Brady (Dr. Steve), Tom London (Sheriff Warren), Reed Howes (Jim Brandon), Carl Mathews (Slick), Edward Peil, Sr. (Eddie), Doye O'Dell (Jim), Ray Jones (Teamster).

Saddle Mountain Roundup (Monogram, 1941, 59 minutes) Producer: George W. Weeks. Associate Producer: Anna Bell Ward. Director: S. Roy Luby. Screenplay: Earle Snell & John Vhalos. Story-Production Manager: William L. Nolte. Photography: Robert Cline. Editor: Roy Claire (S. Roy Luby). Music Director: Frank Sanucci. Songs: Jean George, John King & Joseph Winner. Sound: Glen Glenn.

Cast: Ray Corrigan (Crash), John King (Dusty), Max Terhune (Alibi), Lita Conway (Nancy Henderson), Jack Mulhall (Dan Freeman), Willie Fung (Fang Way), John Elliott (Magpie Harper), George Chesebro (Blackie Stone), Jack Holmes (Sheriff), Steve Clark (Jack Henderson), Carl Mathews (Bill), Cousin Harold Goodwin (Himself), Al Ferguson (Gang Leader), Tex Palmer (Gang Member).

Tonto Basin Outlaws (Monogram, 1941, 60 minutes) Producer: George W. Weeks. Associate Producer: Anna Bell Ward. Director: S. Roy Luby. Screenplay: John Vlahos. Story: Earle Snell. Photography: Robert Cline. Editor: Roy Claire (S. Roy Luby). Music Director: Frank Sanucci. Song: Jean George & John King. Sound: Glen Glenn. Production Manager: William L. Nolte.

Cast: Ray Corrigan (Crash), John King (Dusty), Max Terhune (Alibi), Jan Wiley (Jane Blanchard), Tristram Coffin (Jeff "Weasel" Miller), Edmund Cobb (Jim Stark), Ted Mapes (Ricks), Art "Dustbowl" Fowler (Bill Brown), Carl Mathews (Ed), Reed Howes (Captain T.L. Jameson), Rex Lease (Managing Editor Stanley), Edward Peil, Sr. (Photographer), Budd Buster (Fake Stagecoach Driver), Frank Ellis, Jim Corey, Tex Palmer, Art Dillard (Gang Members), Bud McClure (Stagecoach Driver), Denver Dixon, Bert Dillard, Rube Dalroy, George Morrell, Jack Evans, Jack Tornek (Citizens), Hank Bell (Slim/Luke/Man Leaving Recruiting Station), Chick Hannon, Foxy Callahan (Enlistees).

Underground Rustlers (Monogram, 1941, 56 minutes) Producer: George W. Weeks. Associate Producer: Anna Bell Ward. Director: S. Roy Luby. Screenplay: Bud Tuttle & Elizabeth Beecher. Story: John Rathmell. Adaptation & Dialogue: John Vlahos. Photography: Robert Cline. Editor: Roy Claire (S. Roy Luby). Music Director: Frank Sanucci. Songs: Mickey Ford, Jean George, Roy Ingraham & Harry Tobias. Production Manager: William L. Nolte.

Cast: Ray Corrigan (Crash), John King (Dusty), Max Terhune (Alibi), Gwen Gaze (Irene Bently), Robert Blair (Martin Ford), Forrest Taylor (Jim Bently), Tom London (Tom Harris), Steve Clark (Jake Smith), Bud Osborne (Sheriff), Edward Peil, Sr. (Ward), Richard Cramer (Charlie the Bartender), Carl Mathews (Joe), John Elliott (Gold Orator), Rudy Sooter (Guitarist Toby), Tex Palmer (Ed), Buck Connors (Old Man), Post Park (Stagecoach Driver), Roy Bucko (Stagecoach Guard), Milburn Morante, Denver Dixon, Frank McCarroll, Tex Cooper, George Morrell (Citizens), Tex Phelps (Saloon Customer).

Thunder River Feud (Monogram, 1942, 58 minutes) Producer: George W. Weeks. Associate Producer: Anna Bell Ward. Director: S. Roy Luby. Screenplay: John Vlahos. Story: Earle Snell. Photography: Robert Cline. Editor: Roy Claire (S. Roy Luby). Music Director: Frank Sanucci. Song: Jean George. Sound: Glen Glenn. Production Manager: William L. Nolte.

Cast: Ray Corrigan (Crash), John King (Dusty), Max Terhune (Alibi), Jan Wiley (Maybelle Pembroke), Jack Holmes (Jim Pembroke), Rick Anderson (Colonel Harrison), Carleton Young (Grover Harrison), George Chesebro (Dick Taggart), Carl Mathews (Tex), Budd Buster (Sheriff), Ted Mapes (Buck), Steve Clark (Shorty Branscomb), Rudy Sooter (Guitarist), Hal Price (Merchant), Jimmy Aubrey (Photographer), Tex Palmer (Gang Member).

Rock River Renegade (Monogram, 1942, 56 minutes) Producer: George W. Weeks. Director: S. Roy Luby. Screenplay: John Vlahos & Earle Snell. Story: Faith Thomas. Photography: Robert Cline. Editor: Roy Claire (S. Roy Luby). Music Director: Frank Sanucci. Songs: Jean George & Pete Montrose. Sound: Corson Jowett. Costume Design: Anna Bell Ward. Production Manager: William L. Nolte.

Cast: Ray Corrigan (Crash), John King (Dusty), Max Terhune (Alibi), Christine McIntyre (Grace Ross), John Elliott (Richard E. "Dick" Ross), Weldon Heyburn (Jim Dawson/Phil Sanford), Kermit Maynard (Marshal Luke Graham), Frank Ellis (Chuck), Carl Mathews (Joe), Richard Cramer (Ed the Bartender), Tex Palmer (Tex), Budd Buster (Judge), Steve Clark (Gang Member), Hank Bell (Bill Davis).

Boot Hill Bandits (Monogram, 1942, 58 minutes) Producer: George W. Weeks. Associate Producer: Anna Bell Ward. Director: S. Roy Luby. Screenplay: [George] Arthur Durlam. Photography: Robert Cline. Editor: Roy Claire (S. Roy Luby). Music Director: Frank Sanucci. Sound: Corson Jowett. Production Manager: William L. Nolte.

Cast: Ray Corrigan (Crash), John King (Dusty), Max Terhune (Alibi), Jean Brooks (May Meadows), John Merton (Brand Bolton), Glenn Strange (Maverick), I. Stanford Jolley (The Mesquite Kid), Steve Clark (Sheriff Jed Tolliver), George Chesebro (Stack Stone), Richard Cramer (Corn Hawkins), Budd Buster (Mayor Noah Smyth), Milburn Morante (Cameron), James [Jimmy] Aubrey (Drunk), Carl Mathews (Joe), Hank Bell (Hank), Denver Dixon (Citizen/Posse Member), Merrill McCormick (The Mesquite Kid's Henchman), Snub Pollard (Bartender), Archie Ricks (Gambler), Harry Willingham (Deputy Sheriff Harry), Ray Henderson (Deputy Sheriff), James Sheridan [Sherry Tansey], Wally West, Jack Tornek, Tom Smith, Jack Evans (Citizens), Tex Palmer (Gang Member), Herman Hack, Bert Dillard (Saloon Customers).

Texas Trouble Shooters (Monogram, 1942, 55 minutes) Producer: George W. Weeks. Associate Producer: Anna Bell Ward. Director: S. Roy Luby. Screenplay: Arthur Hoerl. Story: Elizabeth Beecher. Photography: Robert Cline. Editor: Roy Claire (S. Roy Luby). Music Director: Frank Sanucci. Sound: Glen Glenn. Production Manager-Assistant Director: William L. Nolte.

Cast: Ray Corrigan (Crash), John King (Dusty), Max Terhune (Alibi), Julie Duncan (Judy Wilson), Glenn Strange (Roger Denby), Roy Harris [Riley Hill] (Bret Travis), Eddie Phillips (Wade Evans), Frank Ellis (Duke), Ted Mapes (Slim), Kermit Maynard (Pete), Gertrude W. Hoffman (Grannie Wilson), Steve Clark (Bill Ames), Jack Holmes (Perry), Richard Cramer (Mike the Bartender), Carl Mathews (Gang Member).

Arizona Stage Coach (Monogram, 1942, 52 minutes) Producer: George W. Weeks. Associate Producer: Richard Ross. Director: S. Roy Luby. Screenplay: Arthur Hoerl. Story: Oliver Drake. Photography: Robert Cline. Editor: Roy Claire (S. Roy Luby). Music Director: Frank Sanucci. Song: Rudy Sooter. Sound: Lyle Willey. Production Manager: William L. Nolte.

Cast: Ray Corrigan (Crash), John King (Dusty), Max Terhune (Alibi), Nell O'Day (Dorrie Willard), Charles King (Tim Douglas), Roy Harris [Riley Hill] (Ernie Willard), Kermit Maynard (Strike Cardigan), Carl Mathews (Ace), Slim Whitaker (Red), Slim Harkey (Panhandle), Steve Clark (Jake), Frank Ellis (Dan), Jack Ingram (Sheriff Denver), Stanley Price (Tex Laughlin), Forrest Taylor (Uncle Larry Meadows), Richard Cramer (Joe the Bartender), Eddie Dean (Gang Member), Jimmy Aubrey, Milburn Morante, Denver Dixon, Herman Hack (Saloon Customers).

Texas to Bataan (Monogram, 1942, 56 minutes) Producer: George W. Weeks. Associate Producer: Richard Ross. Director: Robert Tansey. Screenplay: Arthur Hoerl. Photography: Robert Cline. Editor: Roy Claire (S. Roy Luby). Music Director: Frank Sanucci. Song: John King. Production Manager: William L. Nolte.

Cast: John King (Dusty), David Sharpe (Davy), Max Terhune (Alibi), Marjorie Manners (Dallas Conroy), Steve Clark (Tom Conroy), Budd Buster (Tad Kelton), Escolastico Baucin (Cooke), Frank Ellis (Ken Richards), Kenne Duncan (Captain Anders), Guy Kingsford (Miller), Al Ferguson, Carl Mathews, Tex Palmer, Tom Steele (Gang Members).

Also known as *The Long, Long Trail*.

Trail Riders (Monogram, 1942, 55 minutes) Producer: George W. Weeks. Associate Producer: Anna Bell Ward. Director-Story: Robert Tansey. Screenplay: Frances Kavanaugh. Photography: Robert Cline. Editor: Roy Claire (S. Roy Luby). Music Director: Frank Sanucci. Song: Stephen Foster. Production Manager: William L. Nolte. Assistant Directors: Bobby Ray & Don Verk.

Cast: John King (Dusty), David Sharpe (Davy), Max Terhune (Alibi), Evelyn Finley (Mary Rand), Forrest Taylor (Mike Rand), Charles King (Ed Cole), Kermit Maynard (Ace Alton), Lynton Brent (Jeff Rand), Jack Curtis (Tiny), Steve Clark (Marshal Jim Hammond), Kenne Duncan (Marshal Frank Hammond), Richard Cramer (Jake the Bartender), Frank LaRue (Jamison), Bud Osborne (Red), Frank Ellis, Tex Palmer, Augie Gomez (Gang Members).

Also known as *Overland Trail*.

Two Fisted Justice (Monogram, 1943, 54 minutes) Producer: George W. Weeks. Associate Producer: Anna Bell Ward. Director: Robert Tansey. Screenplay-Story-Production Manager: William L. Nolte. Photography: Robert Cline. Editor: Roy Claire (S. Roy Luby). Music Director: Frank Sanucci. Song: John King. Sound: Lyle Willey.

Cast: John King (Dusty), David Sharpe (Davy), Max Terhune (Alibi), Gwen Gaze (Joan Hodgins), Joel Davis (Sonny Hodgins), John Elliott (Will Hodgins), Charles King (Trigger Farley), George Chesebro (Decker), Frank Ellis (Harve), Cecil Weston (Miss Adams), Hal Price (Sam), Lynton Brent (Bert Newsome), Kermit Maynard (Joe), Richard Cramer (Ed the Bartender), Carl Mathews (Slim), Augie Gomez (Hank), Tex Palmer (Gang Member), Denver Dixon, Rose Plummer, Jack Curtis (Stagecoach Passengers), Milburn Morante, Jack Evans (Saloon Customers).

Haunted Ranch (Monogram, 1943, 54 minutes) Producer: George W. Weeks. Director: Robert Tansey. Screenplay: Harriett [Elizabeth] Beecher. Story: Arthur Hoerl. Photography: Robert Cline. Editor: Roy Claire (S. Roy Luby). Music Director: Frank Sanucci. Song: John King. Sound: Lyle Willey. Production Manager: William L. Nolte. Assistant Production Manager: Jim Hawthorne.

Cast: John King (Dusty), David Sharpe (Davy), Max Terhune (Alibi), Julie Duncan (Helen Weston), Glenn Strange (Rance Austin), Charles King (Chuck), Bud Osborne (Ed), Rex Lease (Deputy Sheriff Rex), Snowflake [Fred Toones] (Sam), Budd Buster (Sheriff), Tex Palmer (Danny), Steve Clark (Marshal Hammond), Augie Gomez (Hank Travers), Carl Mathews (Deacon), Jimmy Aubrey (Jim the Bartender), Hank Bell (Enlistee).

Land of Hunted Men (Monogram, 1943, 58 minutes) Producer: George W. Weeks. Associate Producer: Clark Paylow. Director: S. Roy Luby. Screenplay: Elizabeth Beecher. Story-Production Manager: William L. Nolte. Photography: James Brown. Editor: Roy Claire (S. Roy Luby). Music Director: Frank Sanucci. Sound: Lyle Willey.

Cast: Ray Corrigan (Crash), Dennis Moore (Denny), Max Terhune (Alibi), Phyllis Adair (Dorrie Oliver), Charles King (Faro Wilson), John Merton (Pelham), Ted Mapes (Piebald), Frank McCarroll (Tabasco), Forrest Taylor (Dad Oliver), Steve Clark (Sheriff Andy Wallace), Snowflake [Fred Toones] (Snowflake), Augie Gomez (Augie), Hank Bell (Stagecoach Driver), Carl Sepulveda, Tex Palmer (Gang Members), Jack Evans, Ray Jones, Al Haskell (Saloon Customers).

Cowboy Commandos (Monogram, 1943, 52 minutes) Producer: George W. Weeks. Director: S. Roy Luby. Screenplay: Elizabeth Beecher. Story-Assistant Director: Clark Paylow. Photography: Edward Kull. Editor: Roy Claire (S. Roy Luby). Music Director: Frank Sanucci. Song: Johnny Lange. Sound: Lyle Willey. Production Manager: William L. Nolte.

Cast: Ray Corrigan (Crash), Dennis Moore (Denny), Max Terhune (Alibi), Evelyn Finley (Joan Cameron), Johnny Bond (Deputy Slim), Budd Buster (Werner), John Merton (Larry Fraser), Frank Ellis (Mario), Steve Clark (Uncle Dan Bartlett), Edna Bennett (Katie Werner), Bud Osborne (Hans), George Chesebro (Fred), Ray Jones, Pascale Perry (Deputy Sheriffs), Hank Bell (Pete), Augie Gomez, Artie Ortego (Mine Guards), Jack Evans, Herman Hack, Kansas Moehring, Carl Sepulveda (Gang Members), Archie Ricks, Jack Tornek, Denver Dixon, Foxy Callahan (Saloon Customers).

Black Market Rustlers (Monogram, 1943, 58 minutes) Producer: George W. Weeks. Director: S. Roy Luby. Screenplay: Patricia Harper. Photography: Edward Kull. Editor: Roy Claire (S. Roy Luby). Music Director: Frank Sanucci. Songs: James Austin. Sound: Lyle Willey. Production Manager: William L. Nolte. Assistant Director: Clark Paylow.

Cast: Ray Corrigan (Crash), Dennis Moore (Denny), Max Terhune (Alibi), Evelyn Finley (Linda Prescott), Steve Clark (Fred Prescott), Glenn Strange (Corbin), Carl Sepulveda (Sheriff Harley), George Chesebro (Slade), Hank Worden (Slim), Frank Ellis (Kyper), John Merton (Parry), Frosty Royce (Ed), James Austin, Little Jean Austin, Ingrid Austin, Art Fowler (Entertainers), Claire McDowell (Mrs. Prescott), Hal Price (Jake), Carl Mathews (Bill), Foxy Callahan (Deputy Sheriff), Stanley Price, Tex Palmer (Gang Members), Bert Dillard (Citizen), George Morrell, Dick Rush, Tom Smith (Ranchers), Wally West (Cowboy), Tex Cooper, Rube Dalroy, Barney Beasley (Saloon Customers).

Bullets and Saddles (Monogram, 1943, 54 minutes) Producer: George W. Weeks. Associate Producer: Anna Bell Ward. Director: Anthony Marshall. Screenplay: Elizabeth Beecher. Story: Arthur Hoerl. Photography: Edward Kull. Editor: Roy Claire (S. Roy Luby). Music Director: Frank Sanucci. Sound: Lyle Willey. Production Manager: William L. Nolte. Assistant Director: Clark Paylow.

Cast: Ray Corrigan (Crash), Dennis Moore (Denny), Max Terhune (Alibi), Julie Duncan (Laura Craig), Budd Buster (Charlie Craig), Rose Plummer (Mother Craig), Forrest Taylor (Marshal Claiburn), Glenn Strange (Jack Hammond), Steve Clark (Blair), John Merton (Mike Selts), Ed Cassidy (Webber), Joe Garcia (Butch), Silver Harr (Tex Landers), Wally West, Victor Cox (Posse Riders), Frank McCarroll, Carl Mathews (Gang Members), Denver Dixon, Jack Evans, George Morrell (Saloon Customers), Robert Kortman (Outlaw), Tom London (Sheriff), Hal Price (Citizen Firing Gun).

Also called *Vengeance in the Saddle.*

RANGER BOB ALLEN

After doing eight westerns for Columbia Pictures with Ken Maynard, producer Larry Darmour signed Bob Allen to star in the "Ranger Bob Allen" series that ran for a half-dozen entries. Spencer Gordon Bennet directed all the films while Nate Gatzert supplied the screenplays. Most of the features contained music and the first three featured Buzzy Henry playing juvenile supporting parts. Also spotlighted was the hero's steed, Pal the Wonder Horse; Wally Wales, using the name Hal Taliaferro, supported Allen in four of the six outings. Despite an appealing hero, a bevy of beautiful leading ladies (Iris Meredith, Elaine Shepard, Louise Small, Eleanor Stewart, Martha Tibbetts), good supporting casts and passable stories with plenty of action, the "Ranger Bob Allen" series failed to catch on with the public.

Just as Gene Autry was using his real name for his screen characters, Columbia sought to identify Bob Allen with the Ranger role he portrayed. Allen (1906–98) was born Theodore Baehr in Mount Vernon, New York, and attended Dartmouth University where he took part in sports and dramatics. For a time he worked in banking and then became an aviator before stage work. He was an extra in *The Quarterback* (1926) and became active in films in 1930 before working on Broadway and then signing with Columbia Pictures in 1934. There he was in such productions as *The Black Room*, *Crime and Punishment* and *Love Me Forever* (all 1935) and *Craig's Wife* (1936), as well as supporting Tim McCoy in a trio of 1935 releases, *Law Beyond the Range*, *Fighting Shadows* and *The Revenge Rider*. His work in these "B" westerns resulted in Allen starring in this Columbia series.

The Unknown Ranger, released in the fall of 1936, told of newcomer Bob Allen (Allen) working at Jim Wright's (Edward Hearn) ranch and falling in love with Jim's daughter Ann (Martha Tibbetts). A rival rancher, Van (Harry Woods), also wants Ann and he warns Bob to stay away from her. Older hand Chuckler (Hal Taliaferro [Wally Wales]) informs Bob that he believes Van is using a stallion to raid the area ranchers' horse herds. Van, his henchman Quirt (Robert Kortman) and their men come upon his horse fighting with a wild stallion just as Wright, Bob and Chuckler arrive on the scene. Both ranchers attempt to capture the wild stallion and a contest is held to see who can break the horse. Quirt is thrown as is Van who attempts to shoot the animal but is stopped by Bob. After Chuckler is also thrown, Bob manages to tame the stallion and names him Pal. Van tries to start a fight with Bob but Wright orders him and his men off his ranch and Ann rebuffs his attentions. With the opening of the railroad, Wright wants to be the first rancher to send his cattle to market by rail and he plans a drive to the pickup place as Van decides to steal the cattle and take them across the border. While Wright and the rest of his men go on the cattle drive, Bob stays behind with Chuckler, who was hurt when he was thrown by Pal. Bob tells Chuckler he is really a Texas Ranger out to arrest Van and his men for rustling. Van, Quirt and their men drive off all of Wright's horses but are scared away by Allen and Chuckler. Bob then saddles Pal and rides after the gang as the runaway horses mix with the cattle drive and stampede into Westville, wrecking the town during the celebration ceremonies for the railroad's opening. Bob captures Van, who is jailed for cattle rustling and horse stealing, and promises to return to Ann.

Genre veteran Wally Wales used the name Hal Taliaferro for the first time in *The Unknown Ranger* and he would continue with the moniker for the remainder of his screen career. Buzzy Henry, who played the heroine's pesky little brother, did both rope and riding tricks in the feature. A trio of songs, "Cowboy, Cowboy Where Have You Been," "I Lost My Heart on the Prairie" and "Frankie's Flaming Fandango," by Lee Zahler and Dave Ormont were used in the feature. The latter was framed in a very amusing sequence and sung by Hal Taliaferro as the ranch hands, including Art Mix, Francis Walker and Cactus Mack, danced in the bunkhouse.

The second series outing, *Rio Grande Ranger*, came out late in 1936 and was a remake of the 1931 Buck Jones feature *Border Law* which the star remade for Columbia three years later as *The Fighting Ranger*. The plot had Texas Rangers Bob Allen (Allen) and Hal (Hal Taliaferro [Wally Wales]), on the trail of Jim Sayres (Paul Sutton) and his gang, who are headquartered in Shonto, south of the U.S.–Mexican border. In an attempt to get the outlaws into Ranger territory, Bob takes the guise of outlaw Smoke and Hal ingratiates himself with Sayres and informs him there is a reward for Smoke's capture. On his way to Shonto, Bob comes to the aid of Sandra Cullen (Iris Meredith) and her little brother Buzzy (Robert "Buzzy" Henry) who are attacked by a wild steer. Sandra and Buzzy's father, cattle drive boss John

Bob Allen as "Ranger Bob Allen."

Cullen (John Elliott), ask Bob to remain at their camp but he heads to Shonto where he overpowers Sayre's henchman Sneed (Tom London). Casino proprietor Sayre asks Bob to work for him and gives him the job of leading the raid on the Cullen cattle. Sneed, who has been fired by Sayre, tells Cullen of the impending raid, and Bob is forced to escape from his cowpunchers. While Sandra comes to Bob's defense, he and Hal are taken prisoner by the Sayre gang but when they find out the gang intends to kidnap Sandra and Buzzy they escape and are followed by the outlaws. Once the two Rangers get Sayre and his men across the border, they are arrested. Bob informs Sandra that he is a lawman and they resume their romance.

Next came the January 1937 release *Ranger Courage* that briefly featured the song "The Old Arapaho Trail." This one began with the old ploy of white villains dressed as Indians robbing a wagon train. Bull (Walter Miller) and his gang attack a convoy led by Daniel Harper (William Gould), who is traveling with his daughter Alice (Martha Tibbetts) and young son Buzzy (Buzzy Henry). The little boy manages to get through the attack line and ride to the nearest Texas Ranger station where Lieutenant Caps (Buffalo Bill, Jr.) dispatches his men, including Ranger Bob Allen (Allen), to aid the settlers. The raiders ride off when the Rangers appear. Bob investigates the attack and finds cowboy boot tracks left by the marauders. He gets permission to work undercover as a prospector and teams up with gambler Doc (Horace Murphy) and old-timer Judge (George Morrell). They head to the town of Hopi where Bob notices that tassels worn by Bull match those found at the scene of the raid. When the wagon train arrives in town, Bull tries to flirt with Alice. Bob stops him, beats Bull in a fight and orders him out of town. When Indian Tall Feather (J.W. Cody) tells Bob he was abducted by the outlaws and that their hideout is in Devil's Basin, the Ranger goes in pursuit of the gang but Bull and his men capture him. Bull gives henchman Snakey Joe (Harry Strang) Bob's badge and tells him to take it to the Cullen wagon train which is being escorted by Lieutenant Caps and his men. Snakey Joe tells Caps he has been ordered to another area and when the Rangers leave, Bull and his boys attack the convoy, planning to drive the wagons through a pass where dynamite has been planted. With the help of his horse Pal, Bob escapes and manages to turn the wagons around but the one carrying the settlers' money, driven by Alice, is pursued by Bull and his men. Bob comes to Alice's rescue as the gang is caught in their own explosion. Ken Maynard and his horse Tarzan can be glimpsed in stock footage taken from a previous Larry Darmour production.

Law of the Ranger, which came to theaters in the spring of 1937, takes place in Gateway Valley where crook Nash (John Merton) wants to control the water rights by building a dam and reservoir. He kills rancher Baldwin (Jimmy Aubrey) as newspaperman Polk (Lafe McKee) and his daughter Evelyn (Elaine Shepard) openly oppose his actions. Two State Rangers, Bob (Allen) and Wally Hood (Hal Taliaferro [Wally Wales]), arrive to investigate, working undercover as homesteaders with Bob out to file a property claim. After Nash's man Pete (Tom London) starts a fight with Bob and loses, Bob and Wally are welcomed to town by Polk and Evelyn. When Nash suggests that Bob file on the Baldwin property, Polk and his daughter believe he is in cahoots with the crook and they take the suggestion of their employee Zeke (Ernie Adams) and plan to send for the State Rangers. Zeke, however, tells crook Snippy (George Morrell) who informs Nash and Pete. The next morning Evelyn is trailed by Pete and Wes (Bud Osborne), who are captured by Bob and Wally. Telling Evelyn they are Rangers, the two set out to bring in Nash and his gang. Bob reports to his superior officer, Lieutenant Wells (Buffalo Bill, Jr.), and then frees Pete and Wes. Bob rides to Oreville, leaving Wally at the Baldwin property, but arrives after Nash, who has been given land registration forms by Zeke, who has also come to file on the ranch. Pete and the gang run Wally off the Baldwin property and when Bob returns, Nash claims the land belongs to him. Evelyn, who saw Wally being run off and went to the ranch, claims she was holding the property for Bob since she is one of the filers. Nash and his men start shooting as Bob and Evelyn take refuge in the ranch house. Wally, who has gone to the Ranger encampment on foot, shows up with Lieutenant Wells and his men and the crooks are surrounded. Bob and Evelyn then decide to share the ranch.

Reckless Ranger, released just a couple of weeks after *Law of the Ranger*, was a remake of the 1928 Tom Tyler starrer *When the Law Rides*. It offered Allen dual roles of a Texas Ranger and his murdered brother. Jim Allen (Allen) organizes sheep ranchers and has them apply for government grazing rights for their herds and as a result he is abducted and hung on the orders of cattleman Barlow (Harry Woods), who has purchased 20,000 head of cattle and wants the grazing rights for himself. Jim's wife Mary (Mary MacLaren) sends their little son Jimmie (Buddy Cox) to neighboring rancher Chet Newton (Jack Perrin) for help and he calls the Texas Rangers. Ranger Captain Andrews (Lane Chandler) assigns Bob Allen (also Allen) to search for Jim, who is his brother; he takes Ranger Jay (Dirk Thane) with him. They find Jim and then go to the Newton ranch where Bob meets Chet's sister Mildred (Louise Small). After telling Mary and Jimmie about what happened to Jim, Bob, Jay and Chet get on the trail of the lynchers and arrest three of them. The men are identified by Mary. In order to catch the gang leader, Bob pretends to be Jim. In town, Barlowe sees him and thinks he has been double-crossed. After Barlowe's henchman Steve (Bud Osborne) and his men unsuccessfully try to ambush Jay, who is taking the prisoners to jail, one of the lynchers, Mort (Jack Rockwell), escapes. Captain Andrews informs Mildred by telephone that Mort knows Allen is a Ranger. Leaving a message for her brother, Mildred takes Jimmie to the Allen ranch that is raided by Barlowe and his men but they are run off by Bob. Bob then tells Chet, who has found his sister's note, to round up all the sheep ranchers. Bob rides to Barlowe's ranch, where Mildred and Jimmie are held hostage. Mildred helps the boy to escape but gang member Snager (Roger Williams), who pretends to be a sheep man, follows him but is thwarted by Bob, who tells Jimmie to ride and bring Chet and the sheep men to Barlowe's ranch. There Bob gets the drop on Barlowe but is forced to fight Mort while Barlowe tries to make a getaway. After having beaten Mort, the Ranger pursues Barlowe who falls to his death from a cliff. Chet arrives with the sheep ranchers and they round up the rest of the gang, and Bob captures Snager. Bob is then free to romance Mildred.

The last "Ranger Bob Allen" feature, *The Rangers Step In*, came out in August 1937. It told of Ranger Bob's (Allen) family having a lengthy feud with the Warren clan, led by Jed Warren (Lafe McKee). Bob is in love with Jed's daughter Terry (Eleanor Stewart), and the two want to marry and end the quarrel. Breck Warren (Hal Taliaferro [Wally Wales]), Jed's son, claims that Bob rustled his dad's cattle; the *real* culprit is Martin (John Merton) who wants both the Allen and Warren spreads in order to sell them to the railroad for a right-of-way. When Bob's superior officer, Captain Thomas (Jay Wilsey [Buffalo Bill, Jr.]), tries to make peace between the two families, both Bob and Jed agree but Breck starts a fight with Bob. Martin then orders Breck murdered and Bob is blamed for the crime as another Warren brother, Fred (Jack Ingram), incites the townspeople into a lynch mob. Bob, who has been dismissed from the Rangers, manages to escape from jail and says farewell to Terry but as he is being chased by a posse led by Martin he meets two men (Richard Cramer, Arthur Millett) from the railroad who have come to purchase the right-of-way from Martin. He then rides to the Warren ranch and exposes Martin's plot to buy the ranches. When the marshal (Jack Rockwell) arrives, Jed tells him that Bob did not shoot his son. Bob then captures Martin and returns to the Rangers but is granted a month's leave so he and Terry can be married.

Following the six "Ranger Bob Allen" series, producer Larry Darmour starred Jack Luden in four Columbia "B" westerns that highlighted the heroics of a dog named Tuffy. After appearing in *The Awful Truth* (1937), Allen departed from Columbia Pictures and signed with 20th Century–Fox where he was in films like *Meet the Girls* and *Up the River* (both 1938) and *Winner Take All* (1939) before going to Republic to co-star in *Fighting Thoroughbreds* (1939). After working for producer Walter Wanger in *Winter Carnival* in 1940, Allen returned to the stage where he appeared in many productions including "Kiss Them for Me," "Showboat," "Junior Miss" and "Auntie Mame" and during the early 1950s he was active in television. Over the years, Allen (who was also billed as Robert Allen and Bob "Tex" Allen) did scores of commercial films and television commercials. His last movies were *Exorcism at Midnight* (1979) and *Raiders of the Living Dead* (1986), in which he wore the Ranger outfit he used in the "Ranger Bob Allen" series. A frequent guest at film conventions in the 1980s and 1990s, he continued to make TV commercials until his death in 1998.

Filmography

The Unknown Ranger (Columbia, 1936, 58 minutes) Producer: Larry Darmour. Director: Spencer Gordon Bennet. Screenplay: Nate Gatzert. Photography: James S. Brown, Jr. Editor: Dwight Caldwell. Songs: Lee Zahler & Dave Omont. Sound: Tom Lambert. Assistant Director: Jesse Duffy.

Cast: Bob Allen (Ranger Bob Allen), Martha Tibbetts (Ann Wright), Harry Woods (Van), Hal Taliaferro [Wally Wales] (Chuckler), Buzzy Henry (Buzzy Wright), Robert Kortman (Quirt), Edward Hearn (Jim Wright), Oscar Gahan, Rudy Sooter, Robert Hoag (Musicians), Art Mix, Francis Walker, Ray Henderson (Cowboys), Al Taylor (Frank), Buck Moulton (Buck), Merrill McCormick (Bearded Cowboy), Tex Palmer (Wagon Driver), Allan Cavan (Ranger Captain), Cactus Mack (Jake), Lew Meehan, Bud McClure, Bob Card, Art Dillard, Jack King (Gang Members), Robert McKenzie (Mayor), Horace B. Carpenter (Old Rancher), Henry Hall, Eva McKenzie (Citizens), Bud Jamison (Bartender), Rube Dalroy (Saloon Customer).

Rio Grande Ranger (Columbia, 1936, 54 minutes) Producer: Larry Darmour. Director: Spencer Gordon Bennet. Screenplay: Nate Gatzert. Story: Jacques Jaccard & Celia Jaccard. Photography: James S. Brown, Jr. Editor: Dwight Caldwell. Music Director: Lee Zahler. Song: Jack C. Smith. Sound: Tom Lambert. Assistant Director: J.A. [Jesse] Duffy.

Cast: Bob Allen (Ranger Bob Allen/Smoke), Iris Meredith (Sandra Cullen), Paul Sutton (Jim Sayres), Hal Taliaferro [Wally Wales] (Ranger Hal Garrick), Robert [Buzzy] Henry (Buzzy Cullen), John Elliott (John Cullen), Tom London (Sneed), Slim Whitaker (Jack), Jack Rockwell (Captain Winkler), Henry Hall (General Green), Ed Cassidy (Marshal), Frank Ellis (Frank), Art Mix, Jack Ingram, Dick Botiller, Jim Corey, Bud McClure, Jack King, Ray Jones, Al Taylor, George Plues (Gang Members), Art Dillard (Cowboy), Jack C. Smith (Bartender).

Ranger Courage (Columbia, 1937, 59 minutes) Producer: Larry Darmour. Director: Spencer Gordon Bennet. Screenplay: Nate Gatzert. Photography: James S. Brown, Jr. Editor: Dwight Caldwell. Music Director: Lee Zahler. Sound: Tom Lambert. Assistant Director: J.A. [Jesse] Duffy.

Cast: Bob Allen (Ranger Bob Allen), Martha Tibbetts (Alice Harper), Walter Miller (Bull), Buzzy Henry (Buzzy Harper), Bud Osborne (Steve), Robert Kortman (Toady), Harry Strang (Snakey Joe), William Gould (Daniel Harper), Horace Murphy (Doc), Franklyn Farnum (Cousin Joe Harper), Buffalo Bill, Jr. [Jay Wilsey] (Lieutenant Caps), George Morrell (Judge), Oscar Gahan, Rudy Sooter, Lloyd Perryman, Robert Hoag, Cactus Mack (Musicians), J.W. Cody (Tall Feather), Lafe McKee (Stable Owner), Buck Moulton (Pete), Bob Reeves (Sergeant), Frank Ball (Sam), Nate Gatzert (Brown), Jack King (Blackie), Gene Alsace (Guard), Horace B. Carpenter (Marshal), Bob Burns, Jack Evans, Silver Tip Baker, Jack Tornek (Settlers), Tex Palmer, Al Taylor, George Hazel (Gang Members), Jim Corey (Horseshoe Player), Eva McKenzie (Mrs. Brown).

Law of the Ranger (Columbia, 1937, 58 minutes) Producer: Larry Darmour. Director: Spencer Gordon Bennet. Screenplay: Nate Gatzert. Story: Jesse Duffy & Joseph Levering. Photography: James S. Brown, Jr. Editor: Dwight Caldwell. Sound: Tom Lambert. Assistant Director: Jesse Duffy.

Cast: Bob Allen (Ranger Bob Allen), Elaine Shepard (Evelyn Polk), John Merton (Bill Nash), Hal Taliaferro [Wally Wales] (Ranger Wally Hood), Lafe McKee (Editor Polk), Tom London (Pete West), Charles [Slim] Whitaker (Steve), Ernest [Ernie] Adams (Zeke), Lane Chandler (Cal Williams), Buffalo Bill, Jr. [Jay Wilsey] (Lieutenant Wells), Jimmy Aubrey (Baldwin), George Morrell (Snippy), Frank Ball (Land Registrar John), Bud Osborne (Wes), Herman Hack (Ranger Dan),

Wally West, Ray Henderson (Rangers), Arthur Millett (Stable Owner), Francis Walker, Bill Patton, Al Taylor, Tex Palmer, Jim Corey, Ralph Bucko (Gang Members).

Reckless Ranger (Columbia, 1937, 59 minutes) Producer: Larry Darmour. Director: Spencer Gordon Bennet. Screenplay: Nate Gatzert. Story: Jesse Duffy & Joseph Levering. Photography: Bert Longnecker. Editor: Dwight Caldwell. Assistant Director: J.R. [Jesse] Duffy.

Cast: Bob Allen (Ranger Bob Allen/Jim Allen), Louise Small (Mildred Newton), Jack Perrin (Chet Newton), Mary MacLaren (Mary Allen), Harry Woods (Bill Barlowe), Buddy Cox (Jimmie Allen), Jack Rockwell (Mort), Slim Whitaker (Steve), Roger Williams (Snager), Lane Chandler (Captain Dan Andrews), Dirk Thane (Ranger Jay), Frank Ball (Bascomb), Oscar Gahan, Rudy Sooter, Lloyd Perryman (Musicians), Lafe McKee, Robert McKenzie, Herman Hack, Chick Hannon, Jack Tornek (Sheep Ranchers), Arthur Millett (Marshal), Tommy Coats (Les), Jim Corey, Tex Palmer, Al Taylor, Bud Pope, George Plues (Gang Members), Archie Ricks, Jack King (Rangers), Jack Evans (Prisoner), Eva McKenzie (Social Organizer), Jim Corey, Buck Morgan, Tex Cooper, Victor Cox (Citizens).

The Rangers Step In (Columbia, 1937, 58 minutes) Producer: Larry Darmour. Director: Spencer Gordon Bennet. Screenplay: Nate Gatzert. Story: Jesse Duffy & Joseph Levering. Photography: James S. Brown, Jr. Editor: Dwight Caldwell. Music Director: Lee Zahler. Assistant Director: J.A. [Jesse] Duffy.

Cast: Bob Allen (Ranger Bob Allen), Eleanor Stewart (Terry Warren), John Merton (Martin), Hal Taliaferro [Wally Wales] (Breck Warren), Jack Ingram (Fred Warren), Jack Rockwell (Marshal), Jay Wilsey [Buffalo Bill, Jr.] (Captain Thomas), Lafe McKee (Jed Warren), Robert Kortman (Wes), Harry Harvey (Dude), Joseph Girard (Mark Allen), Herman Hack (Ranger Dugan), Harry Tenbrook (Deputy Sheriff), Richard Cramer, Arthur Millett (Land Buyers), Lew Meehan, Ray Jones, Jack King, George Plues (Gang Members), Francis Walker, Eddie Juarequi (Rangers), Billy Townsend (Boy), Tex Palmer (Cowboy), Artie Ortego, Bert Dillard, Eva McKenzie, Jack Evans (Citizens), Art Dillard, Ray Henderson, Al Taylor (Riders).

RED RYDER

Comic strip cowboy hero Red Ryder was created by Stephen Slesinger (1901–53) and drawn by Fred Harman (1902–82), who first drew the character as Bronc Peeler in 1933; by 1938 he had become Red Ryder. Syndicated by Newspaper Enterprises Association, the comic strip reached its peak in the 1940s when it appeared in some 750 newspapers and had a readership of 14 million. Its popularity resulted in Red Ryder appearing in a number of other entertainment media, including comic books, books, merchandising, movies and radio. The comic strip ran until 1964.

Red Ryder's first comic book appearance came in 1939 in Dell Publications' "Crackerjack Funnies" and the Harman character would continue in this series until the spring of 1941. In 1940, Slesinger's Hawley Publications issued the first "Red Ryder" comic book in a series which mainly featured newspaper reprints of the adventures of Ryder, his horse Thunder and Little Beaver, his young Navaho Indian pal. In 1941, Dell Comics took over the publication of the series, running for 151 issues into 1957. In later years the title was changed from "Red Ryder" to "Red Ryder Ranch Magazine" and finally "Red Ryder Ranch Comics." Red Ryder appeared in giveaway comics for such businesses as Buster Brown Shoes and Langendorf Bread. Little Beaver was also featured in four issues of "Four Color Series" comics from Dell between 1949 and 1951 and that year the company began a "Little Beaver" series that ran for eighteen issues into 1958.

The first Red Ryder novel, published by Whitman's Better Little Books in 1939, was entitled *Red Ryder and Little Beaver on Hoofs of Thunder*. Nine more Ryder Better Little Books followed: *Red Ryder and the Fighting Westerner* (1940), *Red Ryder and the Code of the West* (1941), *Red Ryder and Western Border Guns* (1942), *Red Ryder and the Outlaw of Painted Valley* (1943), *Red Ryder in Range War* (1945), *Red Ryder and the Squaw-Tooth Rustlers* (1946), *Red Ryder and the Rimrock Killer* and *Red Ryder and the Secret Canyon* (both 1948) and *Red Ryder and Circus Luck* (1949). In 1941, Whitman published *Red Ryder Paint Book* and the same year released two novels, *Red Ryder and the Secret of Wolf Canyon* by S.S. Stevens and *Red Ryder and the Mystery of the Whispering Walls* by R.R. Winterbotham. The company followed these with *Red Ryder and the Adventure of Chimney Rock* (1946) by H.C. Thomas, *Red Ryder and the Secret of the Lucky Mine* (1947) by Carl W. Smith, *Red Ryder and the Riddle of Roaring Range* (1951) and *Red Ryder and the Thunder Trail* (1956), both by Jerry McGill. In addition to books and comic books, Red Ryder was also merchandised via cowboy hats, toy guns and BB guns, etc.

The character came to films in the 12-chapter Republic serial *Adventures of Red Ryder* (1940) that was advertised as being based on "the famous NEA newspaper cartoon." Starring in the title role was Donald Barry, who was billed as Don "Red" Barry, a screen moniker he would use on and off for the rest of his career. Born Don Barry d'Acosta, Barry (1911–80) was a Texas native who began working in films in 1932. After making a favorable impression in supporting roles in Republic westerns, especially the "Three Mesquiteers" (q.v.) series feature *Wyoming Outlaw* (1939), he was assigned to play the Ryder role. As a result of the cliffhanger's success, Republic signed him to star in "B" westerns and between 1940 and 1943 he headlined 29 oaters for the studio. In addition, Republic starred him in a number of non-westerns, including *The Traitor Within* and *Remember Pearl Harbor!* (both 1942), *The West Side Kid* (1943), *My Buddy* (1944), *The Chicago Kid* (1945), the *film noir* classic *The Last Crooked Mile* (1946), *Madonna of the Desert*, *Lightnin' in the Forest* and *Train to Alcatraz* (all 1948). After leaving Republic, Barry remained very active in films, both in starring and character roles. He headlined a "B" western series for Lippert in 1949–50 and continued to appear in numerous cowboy movies until his death by suicide in 1980.

In 1940, Republic announced it would produce a serial called *The Lone Star Texas Ranger* but the owners of the Lone Ranger copyright objected to the title and it was replaced on the studio's schedule by *Adventures of Red Ryder*. Directed by the team of William Witney and John English, the cliffhanger was an action-packed, quickly paced thriller that was very popular with movie audiences. The involved story had the Santa Fe Railroad Company planning to expand through the area around Mesquite with local banker Calvin Drake (Harry Worth) wanting to buy up all the range land in order to sell it for a huge profit. In league with Ace Hanlon (Noah Beery), Drake and his gang begin a series of raids in order to force out the ranchers. When rancher Ira Withers (Ed Cassidy) is murdered by the outlaws, Colonel Tom Ryder (William Farnum) and his son Red Ryder (Barry) start a vigilante group to rid the area of the gunmen. Colonel Ryder is murdered, by gang member One-Eye Chapin (Robert Kortman), as is Sheriff Andrews (Lloyd Ingraham), who leaves behind a daughter, Beth (Vivian [Austin] Coe). Red Ryder captures one of the gang, Shark (Ray Teal), and with his young Indian friend Little Beaver (Tommy Cook) takes him to the new lawman, Dade (Carleton Young), who is really working with Drake and Hanlon. One of the ranchers about to lose her ranch is Red's aunt, the Duchess (Maude Pierce Allen). Hanlon assigns gang member Pecos Bates (Bud Geary) to kill Shark before he can talk and he carries out his assignment but dies while fighting with Red. Red helps the ranchers to get a loan to repair their properties. While Drake and Hanlon

Don "Red" Barry and Tommy Cook in *Adventures of Red Ryder* (Republic, 1940).

order their men to steal the funds, Red and Cherokee Sims (Hal Taliaferro) stop some of the bandits but others manage to take the money. Trying to get funding for the ranchers, Red enters a Wells Fargo stagecoach race but is kidnapped by the outlaws. Little Beaver aids in his escape and he enters the race, winning the $5,000 prize. When one of the gang members (Ernest Sarracino) tries to steal the money, a gun battle takes place with a citizen being killed as a result. Red is blamed and put in jail by Sheriff Dade but he manages to escape and he and Little Beaver trail the thief to the gang's hideout. Before the outlaw is accidentally shot by one of his cohorts, he writes a confession in charcoal on a tabletop; after being captured by the posse, Red reveals this to Dade. When the crooked lawman tries to destroy the confession, he is trapped by Red and Little Beaver. Red then sets out for a showdown with Drake, who dies in a fall from a suspension bridge.

David Sharpe doubled for Barry for the many hazardous and exciting stunts in *Adventures of Red Ryder*. While the serial made Barry a star, he disliked the part because he thought it miscast him. It was during the production of the cliffhanger that Barry married Peggy Stewart, who would later portray the heroine in many Republic "B" westerns (including a dozen Red Ryder features) and serials.

The character came to radio on February 3, 1942 when the "Red Ryder" series debuted on NBC's Blue Network. Reed Hadley starred as Red with Little Beaver being played by Tommy Cook, who performed the role in the 1940 serial. Cook alternated the part with Frank Breese and in the fall of 1942 the series switched to the Mutual network. For a time the actors did the show on Mondays, Wednesdays and Fridays for Don Lee/Mutual and then repeated the same scripts on Tuesdays, Thursdays and Saturdays on the Blue Network. After that, Langendorf Bread took over the sponsorship of the program and it continued to be broadcast mainly on the West Coast by the Don Lee Network and Mutual. Carlton Kadell took over the role of Red Ryder in 1945 and the next year Brooke Temple became Red until the series ended in 1951. Henry Blair played Little Beaver from 1944 to 1947, followed by Johnny McGovern (1947–50) and Sammy Ogg (1950–51). The supporting cast included Martha Wentworth as the Duchess (she would also play the part in seven Republic features), Arthur Q. Bryan as Rawhide Rolinson and Horace Murphy as Buckskin Blodgett. Among the show's announcers were Ben Alexander and Art Gilmore. The series' theme song was "The Dying Cowboy."

Republic had purchased the screen rights to the Ryder character in order to produce the 1940 serial but the studio did not make any further Ryder movies until 1944 when it cast Bill Elliott as the red-headed avenger, whom the radio series dubbed "America's Most Famous Fighting Cowboy." Elliott signed with Republic where he was first billed as Wild Bill Elliott in a series (q.v.) of eight films of the same name in 1943–44 before playing Red Ryder. For the first eight Ryder features he was paid $3,750 per film and this was raised by one thousand dollars per movie when he signed for a second batch in 1945.

After having co-starred with Elliott in the "Wild Bill Elliott" series, George "Gabby" Hayes continued the part of Gabby in the first two "Red Ryder" features, *Tucson Raiders* and *Marshal of Reno*, both released in 1944. Alice Fleming was cast as the Duchess and Bobby Blake played Little Beaver. Alice Fleming (1882–1952) first appeared in films in the silent era, doing five features between 1919 and 1922. She returned to movies in 1937 and during the next decade appeared in over 40 films. Born Michael Gubitosi in 1933, New Jersey native Robert Blake was billed as Mickey Gubitosi when he played the role of a sniveling character called Mickey in some forty MGM "Our Gang" shorts from 1939 until the series' demise in 1944. By 1942 he was being billed as Bobby "Mickey" Blake and when he signed for the Red Ryder films he became Bobby Blake. The actor later referred to the Republic series as "the commode of my life."

Each of the Republic Red Ryder features began with the hero and Little Beaver stepping out of the pages of a large Ryder book with Bill Elliott firing off three shots from both of his two guns and Little Beaver shooting two arrows, leading into the movie. *Tucson Raiders*, the first Red Ryder feature film, released in the spring of 1944, was directed by veteran serial specialist Spencer Gordon Bennet. The story had Red Ryder (Elliott) and Little Beaver (Blake) coming to Painted Valley at the behest of the Duchess (Fleming).

Wild Bill Elliott as "Red Ryder."

Red, who saved Little Beaver when a bursting dam had killed his tribe, stops some ruffians from disrupting a meeting held by Gabby (Hayes) on a statehood petition. At the Duchess' ranch the two meet rancher Beth Rogers (Peggy Stewart) and her Aunt Hannah (Ruth Lee), territorial bank president Jeff Stark (LeRoy Mason), and ranch foreman Tom Hamilton (John Whitney), Beth's beau. Stark is secretly working with territorial governor York (Stanley Andrews) in using bank funds to purchase all the area's transportation lines, and with Hannah, who wants her niece's ranch. When Stark tells York that the Duchess has sent for Judge James Wayne (Tom Chatterton), the two crooks plot to kill him. They order Sheriff Kirk (Ed Cassidy) and Deputy Logan (Edward Howard) to carry out the job but they end up shooting a minister (Karl Hackett), whom Red tries to save. After the man dies, Kirk accuses Red of the murder and has Hannah slip him a gun filled with blanks so the sheriff can shoot him when he tries to escape jail. Little Beaver switches the gun intended for Red with that of the sheriff and Ryder makes a getaway as Stark has his gang rob a stagecoach and place the blame on Red. Stark is seen by Gabby and Little Beaver giving a coded note to Hannah to deliver to the sheriff; Gabby steals it and breaks the code. As a result, Red intercepts a stagecoach carrying Judge Wayne and the two develop a plan to capture the outlaws. When the gang robs the stage, they also kidnap Little Beaver, who has followed Ryder, and take him to their hideout. The Duchess forces Hannah to reveal her association with the crooks and the location of their hideout. Ryder, Gabby and Hamilton rescue Little Beaver and during a gunfight Stark and the sheriff are killed. Before Red and Little Beaver depart, Judge Wayne marries Beth and Tom.

Another serial ace, Wallace Grissell, directed the next adventure, *Marshal of Reno*, released in the summer of 1944. Taking place in the mid–1890s, it told of the rivalry between the towns of Blue Springs and Rockland in being made the county seat. Newspaperman John Palmer (Herbert Rawlinson) wants to become rich by promoting Rockland and he hires outlaws to carry out a series of lawless acts which give Blue Springs a bad name. The gang robs a stagecoach and wounds Judge Holmes (Tom Chatterton), but are captured by Red (Elliott), former marshal of Reno, Gabby (Hayes) and Little Beaver (Blake). A posse also brings in two area newcomers, Danny Boyd (Jay Kirby) and Lee Holden (Blake Edwards). Kellogg (Jack Kirk), who secretly works for Palmer, helps Holden to escape and then kills him so he cannot identify the other gang members who took his and Boyd's horses. Red saves Danny from a lynch mob but the young man says he will avenge his friend's murder. Palmer gives Danny a job while Judge Holmes recuperates at the Duchess' (Fleming) ranch. Believing that Ryder will bring law and order to Blue Springs, Palmer orders all the posse members murdered and after several killings Red infiltrates the gang by telling saloon owner Faro Carson (LeRoy Mason) he is really Reno, a wanted outlaw. Carson, who is in league with Palmer, hires Red and, along with gang member Adams (Kenne Duncan), they begin to terrorize the area although Ryder manages to warn the intended victims beforehand. Danny is blamed for the crimes and after Palmer prints an article accusing him of several murders, the young man comes to town and confronts the editor. Carson takes him prisoner. Red confides his activities to Palmer, who tells Carson. Ryder sets Danny free while Palmer tells Sheriff Walker (Tom London) that Boyd is out to murder him. Red, Gabby and Little Beaver ride to Blue Springs where Walker has arrested Boyd. Carson and his gang then steal the $40,000 the Duchess has left with the sheriff. As Danny tries to pursue the gang, Palmer incites the locals to capture him. When Danny is trapped in the hills, Red tries to help him but the young man does not believe Ryder. Palmer tells Kellogg to kill Danny but he only receives a flesh wound as Red, Gabby and Little Beaver surround the gang and capture them. Danny is exonerated, Palmer, Carson and Kellogg and the gang are sent to prison, and Blue Springs becomes the new county seat.

George "Gabby" Hayes left the Ryder series after *Marshal of Reno* and returned to the Roy Rogers series, appearing in fourteen features through 1946. Duncan Renaldo played the title role in the third Red Ryder feature, *The San Antonio Kid*, directed by Howard Bretherton and issued in the late summer of 1944. A part obviously written for Hayes was played by Earle Hodgins, with the character dubbed Happy Jack. The plot had petroleum scout Walter Garfield (LeRoy Mason) locating oil under property owned by rancher Ben Taylor (Jack Kirk). Figuring the oil must also be under other ranches in the area, Garfield sets out to force the locals off their land so he can sell it to his employer for a huge profit. He enlists the aid of saloon proprietor Ace Hanlon (Glenn Strange) and his men in terrorizing the ranchers. During a raid, Ben Taylor is killed. Taylor's daughter, Ann (Linda Stirling), comes to stay with the Duchess (Fleming) as Red (Elliott), Little Beaver (Blake) and ranch foreman Happy Jack (Hodgins), investigate the raids. When Red beats Hanlon in a fistfight, the saloon owner calls in Johnny Bennett (Duncan Renaldo), an outlaw known as the San Antonio Kid. While not an assassin, Bennett is in debt to Hanlon, who believes he can force Bennett to murder Red Ryder. Red,

Advertisement for *San Antonio Kid* (Republic, 1944).

Little Beaver and Happy Jack find oil in caves on the Taylor ranch and realize the motive for the lawlessness. Red then purchases the Taylor property from Ann so Hanlon cannot buy it as he has done with most of the other nearby ranches. When Garfield offers Ann twice what Red paid her, she thinks she was cheated until Ryder tells her and the Duchess about finding the oil. On his way to see Hanlon, Bennett is thrown by his horse and is nearly killed but is saved by Ryder. Going with Red to the Duchess' ranch, Bennett is attracted to Ann and is offered a job but before accepting it he rides to see Hanlon in order to pay off his gambling debts. When he finds out Hanlon wants him to murder Red, he refuses and tells Ryder. The two set up a plan to capture the crooks. While Bennett, Hanlon and Garfield play poker, Red rummages through Hanlon's office and gets proof of Garfield's oil discovery and his partnership with the saloon owner. The next day Bennett refuses to shoot Red and is wounded as he helps Ryder, Little Beaver and Happy Jack fight the outlaws. Trailing Garfield and Hanlon to the caves on the Taylor Ranch, Ryder shoots it out with the two crooks; Garfield is killed when a pool of oil ignites. Hanlon and his gang are put in jail and Bennett promises to go straight and help Ann and the Duchess with their ranches.

Lesley Selander directed the first of three Red Ryder adventures with *Cheyenne Wildcat*, which came out in the fall of 1944. The title apparently was taken from a plot ploy in which Little Beaver (Blake) uses a pet skunk to stop a bank run. The feature's rather complicated story told of Red (Elliott) and Little Beaver being summoned back to Blue Springs by the Duchess (Fleming), and along the way they see gunman Pete (Kenne Duncan) murder bank president Jason Hopkins (Tom Chatterton) at a remote relay station. Hopkins was there to meet Jim Douglas (Francis McDonald), a former partner he mistakenly had arrested and imprisoned for theft. Too late, Hopkins learned the real culprits were cashier Harrison Colby (Tom London) and another banker, Dandy Joe Meeker (Roy Barcroft). The two, who had been caught by Hopkins replacing gold certificates with bogus ones, escaped punishment by promising to reveal to Hopkins' foster daughter Betty Lou (Peggy Stewart) that Douglas is her real father. Pete was hired by Meeker to murder Hopkins and is captured by Red and Little Beaver but Douglas is arrested for the crime. The dying Hopkins asks Red to protect Betty Lou. Pete is murdered in his jail cell and the sheriff (Jack Kirk) frees Douglas. Colby hires Douglas as a bank guard and has him use the name Johnson. Betty Lou tries to keep the bank operating while Colby and Meeker undermine her efforts. Red and the Duchess join Betty Lou in investing their own funds in the bank. When outlaws steal a money shipment, Betty Lou is convinced that Johnson took part in the theft. Douglas leaves town as Red finds evidence that the man is Betty Lou's real father and that he was framed years before by Colby and Meeker. Ryder entices Douglas back to town with a news story that his daughter has been injured and he reunites Betty Lou with her real father. When Meeker tries to get the local citizens to lynch Douglas, Red reveals the evidence that he and Colby are crooks. The two men attempt to escape by taking the Duchess hostage; Meeker dies when he tries to stab Ryder. With Colby and the rest of the gang arrested, Betty Lou and her father announce they will keep the bank open.

Wallace Grissell returned to direct *Vigilantes of Dodge City*, a November 1944 release. Here Red (Elliott), Little Beaver (Blake) and their friend Denver Thompson (Tom London) come to the aid of the Duchess (Fleming), whose freight line is being robbed regularly. Unknown to her, banker Luther Jennings (LeRoy Mason) is in cahoots with insurance man Walter Bishop (Hal Taliaferro) in an attempt to get the freight line's insurance rates so high the Duchess will have to sell them the operation. The two men hire Ross Benteen (Bud Geary) and his gang to rob the franchise, which is kept going by money supplied by Red from his ranch. Jennings tells Benteen to raid Ryder's horse herd, which is supposed to be sold to the army. After the horses are rustled, Jennings informs Captain Glover (Stephen Barclay) that Ryder committed the robbery and plans to sell the herd to the highest bidder and that Ryder also committed the freight holdups. Glover places Red under arrest but when Benteen tries to murder the captain and place the blame on Ryder, he fails and Glover realizes Red is innocent. Glover convinces his commanding officer (Stanley Andrews) to let him and Red trap the outlaws. Following a colt he has nursed back to health, Little Beaver

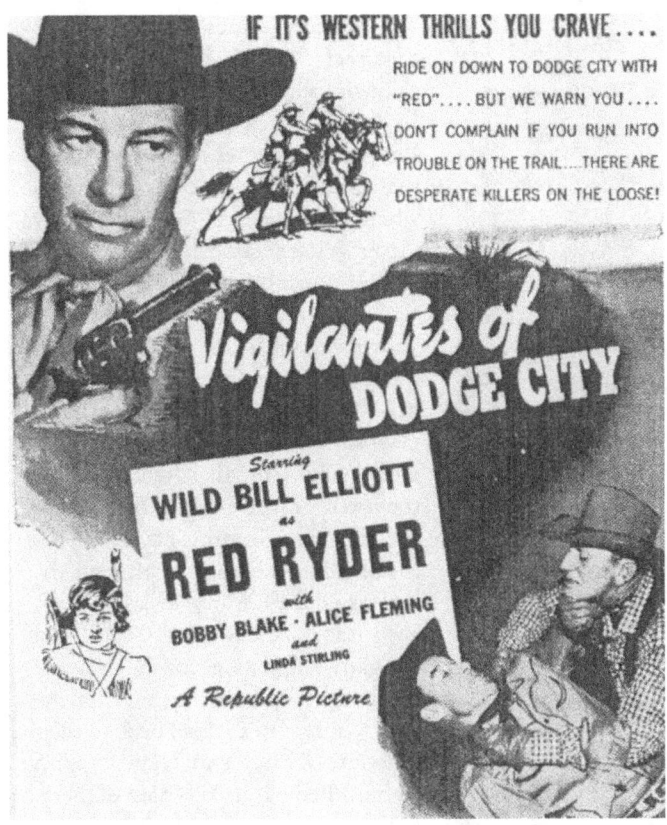

Advertisement for *Vigilantes of Dodge City* (Republic, 1944).

sweetheart of schoolmarm Ann Carter (Peggy Stewart). Tom has come under the influence of saloonkeeper Dan Sedley (William Haade), who stages a robbery to help his cohort, bank president Arthur Stanton (Selmer Jackson). Stanton has stolen money from his operation and to cover up the thefts he has Sedley's gang rob him, but they are thwarted by Red, who returns the money. When the judge announces he plans to cut his son out of his will, Stanton murders him and uses his securities to cover up the bank's money shortage. Tom is blamed for the murder and Red is forced to arrest him. Sensing that Tom is innocent, the sheriff places a bogus story in the local newspaper claiming to have evidence that the young man did not kill his father. Red hands Tom over to the Duchess for safekeeping and then tells Stanton where he has gone. Stanton orders Sedley to murder Tom but the saloon owner is shot by Red; before he dies, he confesses to murdering Judge Blackwell. When Stanton tries to ambush Tom, Red stops him, and the banker is arrested. Tom, who has learned his lesson, plans to marry Ann.

Issued in February 1945, *Great Stagecoach Robbery* had Red (Elliott) working with the Duchess (Fleming) in running her stagecoach line, which was robbed of $150,000 some years before by Con Hollister (Francis McDonald). Since a similar amount is about to be shipped, the Duchess is concerned but Red assures her that Con is still in jail, being unaware he has received an early parole. Red is disliked by Con's son Billy (John James) for helping send his father to prison, and Little Beaver (Blake) is at odds with Billy's little sister, Boots (Sylvia Arslan). Con's ex-partner, Joe Slade (Bud Geary), is in cahoots with criminal Jed Quinlan (Don Costello), who masquerades as a schoolmaster; Slade believes Hollister will be on the stagecoach and the money he is carrying is from the robbery. The two men get Billy to help them rob the coach but Red thwarts the trio and finds Con a reformed man who plans to return the stolen money to the bank. While

finds Red's missing horses and also overhears the crooks making plans to frame Ryder for another holdup. In Dodge City, Little Beaver tells Red and Captain Glover what he has learned, and in the gang's cave hideout Ryder forces henchman Brewster (Kenne Duncan) to confess to his involvement. When Red returns to Dodge City with Brewster, Jennings and Bishop try to make an escape and take Little Beaver with them. Red rescues the boy, and the two men are killed when their wagon tumbles over a cliff. Red's horses are recovered and he is given the government contract.

Sheriff of Las Vegas, released at the end of 1944, was directed by Lesley Selander, who would also helm its follow-up, *Great Stagecoach Robbery*. The title *Sheriff of Las Vegas* refers to the office held by Red (Elliott), who lives in the Nevada town with the Duchess (Fleming) and Little Beaver (Blake). Ryder tries to talk some sense into Tom Blackwell (Jay Kirby), the son of Judge Homer T. Blackwell (John Hamilton), and the

Reissue poster for *Sheriff of Las Vegas* (Republic, 1944).

Spencer Gordon Bennet returned to direct *Lone Texas Ranger*, which came to theaters in the spring of 1945. In this one Red (Elliott) is a Texas Ranger who comes to Silver City at the behest of the Duchess (Fleming) when her friend, mine owner Sally Carter (Helen Talbot), may be forced to shut down her operations due to a series of silver robberies. Unbeknownst to the locals, the men behind the lawlessness are popular Sheriff Iron Mike Haines (Tom Chatterton) and blacksmith Hands Weber (Roy Barcroft). The same day Red comes to town with Little Beaver (Blake), the sheriff's son, Tommy Haines (Jack McClendon), also arrives after finishing his education in the east. When gang leader Betcha (Bud Geary) and his gang rob a stagecoach, they are stopped by Ryder who trails henchman Whitey (Rex Lease) back to their hideout. Whitey and Haines try to ambush Red but he kills both of them. Before dying, Iron Mike asks Ryder not to tell his son the truth about him. Back in Silver City, Red announces the sheriff died trying to capture the outlaws and the citizens begin to raise money to build a memorial to Iron Mike Haines. Weber orders his henchman Baker (Dale Van Sickel) to sabotage Sally's mine so she will have to sell out. The explosion damages the property but miners agree to work for free until Sally can get out a new ore shipment. Betcha informs Weber that Red killed the sheriff and the blacksmith tells Tommy, who picks a fight with Ryder. Weber's men steal Sally's silver shipment and hide it in the blacksmith shop where it is later found by Red and Tommy. Realizing that Weber and his men stole the silver, Red tells Tommy the truth about his father. After the outlaws are arrested, Tommy refuses to participate in the memorial dedication to his father but eventually changes his mind.

For *Phantom of the Plains*, issued in the fall of 1945, Lesley Selander returned to direct and future series helmsman R.G. Springsteen served as executive producer. It told of the Duchess (Alice

Hollister and Boots try to fix up their ranch, the disappointed Billy joins Slade's gang. During a bank holdup, Red shoots Slade and wounds Quinlan, who escapes with the stolen money to Con's ranch. After Hollister finds the funds, Red suspects him of being involved in the robbery. Hollister locks Red in a closet and tries to prove his innocence. Little Beaver sets Red free and they go after Hollister as Boots finds the wounded Quinlan hiding in a barn and he shoots her. Quinlan later tells Con and Billy that Red killed Boots and they take Little Beaver hostage in order to provoke Red into fighting them. Red, however, proves to the Hollisters that Quinlan robbed the bank and killed Boots. Billy testifies against Quinlan, who receives the death sentence, and the young man is paroled to his father's custody. The brutal murder of the little girl was a surprisingly sadistic plot twist in this otherwise formula series outing.

Poster for *Great Stagecoach Robbery* (Republic, 1945).

cially after he sees him physically abusing a horse. While Red goes to town to wire the British consul for details about Champneys, Charlie offers Burdett and Hanlon half of his share of the Duchess' money if they will rid him of Ryder and Little Beaver. Telling the Duchess he has to go back to England and that they can be married on the way, Charlie has his two henchmen kidnap Red and Little Beaver after Celeste finds out they have contacted the British consul. Burdett and Hanlon want to keep Ryder and his pal alive until after the Duchess is out of the way so Charlie cannot double-cross them. Red and Little Beaver escape and go after the stagecoach with the Duchess, Charlie and Celeste. Just as Hanlon is about to shoot Charlie, Red stops him and Burdett and the two are arrested, along with Charlie. The Duchess then clobbers her ex-fiancé with the wedding cake.

Fleming) coming under the influence of cultured Englishman Talbot Wilberforce Champneys (Ian Keith), really con artist Fancy Charlie, who marries and murders wealthy women. Returning to Blue Springs following a trip, Red (Elliott) and Little Beaver (Blake) are shocked when they find out the Duchess is going to marry the Englishman. While at the Duchess' ranch with his cohort Celeste (Virginia Christine), who is posing as a designer, Charlie meets up with a former cellmate, Pete Burdett (Bud Geary), and his outlaw partner Ace Hanlon (William Haade). When Charlie refuses Burdett's demand to extort some of the Duchess' money, the outlaw fights with him but is stopped by the arrival of Red. Hanlon gets away and Charlie tells Red that Burdett owes him money from a gambling debt and insists he be set free. Ryder is suspicious of the Englishman, espe-

During its first nine entries, the Red Ryder films had various associate producers, including Edward J. White, Louis Gray, Stephen Auer and the previously mentioned R.G. Springsteen. Beginning with *Marshal of Laredo*, issued in the fall of 1945, Sidney Picker would take over as associate producer, a position he would hold for the remainder of the series. This feature would also introduce R.G. Springsteen as the series director and he would continue in that capacity for fourteen consecutive features, remaining with the series until its demise. Springsteen (1904–89), a native of Tacoma, Washington, came to films in 1930, working as an assistant director at Universal and Fox before joining Republic. *Marshal of Laredo* was his directorial debut and he went on to make over 70 feature films, most of them westerns, although he also helmed the highly regarded *Hellfire* (1949), which also starred Bill Elliott, *Geraldine* (1954) and *Come Next Spring* (1956), all for Republic. In the mid–1960s he directed a half dozen oaters for Paramount producer A.C. Lyles.

Marshal of Laredo came out in the fall of 1945 and told of Red (Elliott) being appointed the town's lawman and finding himself and Little Beaver (Blake) opposing crooked saloon owner

Denver Jack (Roy Barcroft) and his right hand man, the badly scarred Pretty Boy Murphy (Don Costello). When outlaw Ferguson (Bud Geary) robs a bank courier (Tom London), he is arrested by Red. Murphy obtains the stolen money and takes it to Jack. Pretty Boy beats the courier so he will not testify against Ferguson on the orders of Jack, who uses the services of lawyer Larry Randall (Robert Grady), much to the chagrin of Randall's fiancée Judy Bowers (Peggy Stewart). Because of Larry's involvement with Jack, Judy's father, banker Mel Bowers (George M. Carleton), refuses to let him see her but after the lawyer promises to lead a more honest life, Bowers says he can marry Judy in six months. The banker, however, is murdered by Pretty Boy, and Larry is arrested and convicted of the crime. The main witness against Larry was Dr. Allen (Wheaton Chambers); Red, who believes the lawyer is innocent, lets him break jail and trails him to the doctor's office. There Dr. Allen admits he lied and that he is being blackmailed by Denver Jack. As he is writing a confession, the doctor is killed by Pretty Boy; the saloon owner foments trouble with the locals, claiming Red is in cahoots with Larry. Along with Little Beaver, the two ride out of town. Red returns and finds evidence in Denver Jack's office that proves he has been blackmailing area residents as well as his own gang members. Ryder is caught by Jack and Pretty Boy, who also capture Larry and Little Beaver when they come to his aid. Randall goes back to jail as Pretty Boy guards Red and Little Beaver. Knowing that Pretty Boy is scared of fire, Red starts a blaze and forces the outlaw to confess to killing Mel Bowers and Dr. Allen. Just as the locals are about to lynch Larry, Red comes to his rescue and Denver Jack is arrested. The film gave Roy Barcroft a good role as the sadistic Denver Jack, who uses various methods, including photography, to obtain blackmail information in order to keep control of Laredo and carry out his criminal activities.

Colorado Pioneers, issued in November 1945, had Red (Elliott), and Little Beaver (Blake) going to Chicago to negotiate the sale of a herd of cattle to a meat packing company. In the Windy City they become involved in an attempted robbery involving two delinquents, Joe (Billy Cummings) and Skinny (Freddie Chapman), residents of a parish home. When the local priest (Tom Chatterton) tells the juvenile court the boys need a better environment, Red volunteers to take them on as summer help at the Duchess' (Fleming) ranch. Back home, Ryder finds out a wildfire has burned much of the ranch's grazing land with another rancher, Dave Wyatt (Frank Jaquet), offering to cover the Duchess' credit until she can get her cattle sold. When Little Beaver returns with Joe and Skinny, he also brings all of the parish residents with only Joe not liking the ranch. When Wyatt hires most of the Duchess' wranglers, Red becomes suspi-

Poster for *Colorado Pioneers* (Republic, 1945).

cious of him and, only finding aged Sand Snipe (Tom London) to help with the roundup, he puts the parish boys to work as cowboys. Wyatt and his foreman Bill Slade (Bud Geary) set off dynamite in an attempt to thwart the roundup, with one of the boys being injured. While the locals are displeased with Red for using teenagers as wranglers, he wins the town's annual buckboard race, defeating Slade. Joe, who worked with Bull Regan (Roy Barcroft) in Chicago, rejoins the crook, who has escaped jail, after wrongly concluding that Red cheated in winning the race. Ryder forces Slade to implicate Wyatt in the explosion, saying his boss wanted to buy the Duchess' ranch at a low price. The sheriff (Jack Rockwell) arrests Bull and Joe, since Bull stole Ryder's prize money. Realizing Red won the race honestly, Joe is set free since he did not know Bull had robbed Ryder. The boys go back to Chicago with Red promising them they can return the next summer.

It is interesting that in *Colorado Pioneers* the character of the Duchess was called Martha "The Duchess" Wentworth, a moniker that would be used in the next two series outing. Ironically, Martha Wentworth was the actress who played the part on radio and would take over the role of the Duchess in seven features with Allan Lane. The feature also reunited Bobby Blake with "Our Gang" alumnus Billie "Buckwheat" Thomas, who portrayed parish boy Smokey. While the film's plot of having juvenile delinquents reformed in the west was not a new one, the ploy of using them as cowboys when adult wranglers cannot be found proved to be a precursor to the 1972 John Wayne film *The Cowboys*.

Issued at the end of 1945, *Wagons Wheels Westward* was an entertaining effort in which Red (Elliott) leads a wagon train which includes the Duchess (Fleming), Little Beaver (Blake), old-time scout Pop Dale (Emmett Lynn), and a recently married couple, Bob (Jay Kirby) and Arlie Adams (Linda Stirling). When a rider, Lunsford (George J. Lewis), asks for sanctuary, Red agrees but Arlie is upset to see him since he is a newspaperman who once wrote a false story about her being involved with an outlaw. She won a libel suit against Lunsford's employer but her new husband is not aware of the scandal. Outlaw gang leader Dave McKean (Roy Barcroft) and his men rob a mail rider and find a letter from Ryder to Desert Springs realtor John Larkin (Bob McKenzie) asking him to find land for the travelers. McKean and his gang ride to the town but find it deserted and he decides to fleece the people on the wagon train by pretending to be Larkin. In town, McKean, pretending to be Larkin, greets Red and his party. When they are settling in at the hotel, Lunsford makes a pass at Arlie and gets into a fight with Bob. Ryder orders Lunsford to leave town and as he is going he recognizes gang member Butch (George Chesebro), who is masquerading as livery stable operator Sutton. Lunsford demands a cut of the gang's profits from the travelers but that night he is murdered and Bob is blamed; the crime was committed by another gang member, Tuttle (Dick Curtis). Although Bob is arrested by the fake sheriff (Bud Geary), Red proves his innocence but Bob finds out about McKean's criminal activities. Red also comes to realize that McKean is an imposter and, along with Little Beaver and Pop, he breaks Bob out of jail. Meanwhile Ryder has taken the rest of the travelers out of town but they are attacked by the outlaws. After a shootout, the gang members are captured; McKean tries to escape in a wagon but is chased by Red Ryder who beats him in a fistfight. Returning the outlaws to town, Red and his friends meet the real Larkin who says everyone left because of gold fever. The travelers then decide to stay in Desert Springs and Bob and Arlie move into their new house.

The first 1946 Red Ryder release, February's *California Gold Rush*, had the Duchess (Alice Fleming) sending for Red (Elliott) following the murder of the son of stagecoach line owner Colonel Parker (Russell Simpson) by outlaws. The letter sent by the Duchess is intercepted by Ernest Murphy (Joel Friedkin), a hotel clerk who is in league with whistling killer Chopin (Dick Curtis). Murphy is told to mail the letter by Chopin, who plans to have his henchman, the Idaho Kid (Wen Wright), ambush and replace Ryder. As they are riding toward town, Red and Little Beaver (Blake) are ambushed, and Red is forced to kill the Idaho Kid. Thinking his scheme has been successful, Chopin tells the Duchess that Red is dead and that he will kill Little Beaver if his plans to rustle cattle are halted. Red goes to see the Duchess and then takes on the guise of the Idaho Kid in order to infiltrate Chopin's gang. After thwarting a robbery, Red is recognized by gang member Felton (Kenne Duncan), the Idaho Kid's brother. As Ryder drives a shipment of gold, Chopin has the Duchess taken prisoner so she cannot tell the local sheriff (Tom London) her nephew's identity. Felton tells the sheriff that Red is really the Idaho Kid and when the gang attacks the wagon he is driving, they knock him out and steal the gold. The sheriff and his men find the unconscious Red and arrest him but Little Beaver comes to his rescue. The two trail Felton to the gang's hideout and free the Duchess. Red fights it out with the gang while Little Beaver summons the law. During the shootout, Ernest tries to kill Red but instead hits Chopin and is shot by Ryder. The sheriff and his men arrest the remainder of the gang.

Sheriff of Redwood Valley, issued in March 1946, was highlighted by the appearance of genre star Bob Steele as the Reno Kid. Although he had been starring in films for two decades, the still agile Steele looked young enough to play a character called Kid. The feature begins with the character breaking out of prison as the people in his home of Redwood Valley worry that he will try and steal a money shipment needed to pay for a railroad spur into the area. Businessman Bidwell (James Craven) and lawyer Harvey Martin (Arthur Loft) want the spur to go to rival Indian Gap, where they have illegally purchased land rights. Driving the wagon carrying the money, Bidwell gives it over to his henchmen Jackson (Kenne Duncan) and Strong (Bud Geary), who shoot the local sheriff (Tom London). Red (Elliott) and Little Beaver (Blake) have been guarding a decoy stagecoach, and the wounded sheriff appoints Red to take over his job. Ryder is shot trailing the two robbers but Little Beaver gets him to a remote shack where he is attended by Reno and his wife Molly (Peggy Stewart) and their small son Johnny (John Wayne Wright). Red recognizes Reno who tells him he was not guilty of the crimes for which he was incarcerated and that he had received poor legal advice from Martin. He also said he was forced to give the lawyer his ranch to pay his legal fees. When the Duchess (Fleming) comes to take care of him, she insists that Reno and his family join them at her ranch. Reno, however, rides away and is followed by Red and Little Beaver; after he forces Martin to sign his ranch back over to Molly, Ryder arrests him. Although Bidwell says Reno shot the sheriff and robbed him, Ryder does not believe him and the businessman decides to let Reno escape from jail so he can murder him. The Kid manages to get away unharmed while Red forces Martin to admit that he and Bidwell needed Reno's ranch for their land deal. When Ryder and Martin fight over a gun, a masked man arrives and Martin shoots him thinking it is the Kid, but it is really Bidwell. As Martin tries to run away he is captured by Reno, who gets back his ranch and is reunited with his family.

The background on how Red Ryder attained his horse Thunder is told in the next series outing, *Sun Valley Cyclone*, which came out in the spring of 1945. The plot also included the historical character of Theodore Roosevelt; he was played by the somewhat aged character actor Ed Cassidy. The story begins with Red (Elliott) and Little Beaver (Blake) on the trail of a wanted outlaw when a Mexican tries to shoot Red and is attacked by his horse Thunder. When the culprit demands the animal be killed, the marshal (Hal Price) agrees but Ryder then relates how he obtained the stallion. Some months before, he had broken the horse from a herd destined for Teddy Roosevelt's (Ed Cassidy) Rough Riders. Colonel Roosevelt asks Red to look into horse thefts in Sun Valley, the home of the Duchess (Fleming). Taking the horse, which he named Thunder, as his own, he returns home where his aunt is having a fence dispute with another rancher, Major Harding (Eddy Waller). The major's foreman, Blackie Blake (Roy Barcroft), is the leader of the gang rustling the horses. After he and Red have an altercation over an altered brand on one of the Duchess' horses, Ryder suggests his aunt and the major meet at her ranch. During the meeting, the outlaws steal Harding's horses and he blames the Duchess, who thinks he is behind the rustling. Thunder is also stolen. When Blake tries to ride the animal, it throws him and the foreman beats the horse, which runs away wearing a saddle belonging to Dow (Kenne Duncan), one of the gang. Thunder shows up with Dow's saddle, and Red realizes Blake is behind the rustling. When Dow tries to retrieve his saddle, the horse nearly kills him. After saving him, Red takes Dow to jail where he is released by other gang members.

Thunder goes back to the stolen herd and leads the horses through town as Ryder engages in a shootout with the outlaws. Only Blake manages to escape. After finishing his story Red unmasks Blackie as the man who tried to shoot him.

The sixteenth Red Ryder feature adventure, *Conquest of Cheyenne*, came out in the summer of 1946. The film begins with Red (Elliott) and Little Beaver (Bobby Blake) riding to the town of Muleshoe after being summed by the Duchess (Fleming). On the way they are fired upon by ranch foreman Daffy (Emmett Lynn), whose boss, Cheyenne Jackson (Peggy Stewart), is missing along with $2000. The townspeople fear that Cheyenne has met with foul play, especially after stranger Tom Dean (Jay Kirby), brought in by Deputy Sheriff Blake (Jack Kirk), is found with the young woman's horse. Cheyenne, however, shows up driving a horseless carriage but she soon takes a dislike to Tom, a geologist. Town banker Tuttle (Milton Kibbee) knows there is oil on Cheyenne's ranch and he wants it for himself and he orders his cohort Murdo (George Sherwood) to kill the young man. Tom escapes thanks to Ryder, and at the Jackson ranch he convinces Cheyenne and the Duchess to back his oil drilling project. Red goes to Dallas to close a cattle deal as Cheyenne finds out that Tom once served a prison term for fraud, but Tom tells her he was framed and she believes him. When Tuttle lies to Cheyenne and the Duchess that the girl's loans are overdue, several ranchers combine their resources to bring in an oil well. When Red returns and finds the cattle have not been rounded up, he becomes upset but Cheyenne says selling them will not make enough to cover her loans. Tuttle tells Murdo to destroy the oil rig, which he does with explosives, but he is seen by Ryder and chased into a cave where he is shot by Tuttle before he can talk. Tuttle brings in another geologist, McBride (Kenne Duncan), a crook who tells the investors about Tom's past. Sheriff Perkins (Tom London) arrests Dean and rides with him to Los Alvos and along the way they are attacked by Tuttle's henchman Long (Frank McCarroll) and two other men, who shoot the lawman. Tom, however, is rescued by Ryder who takes him back to work on the oil rig, which has been rebuilt. Tuttle and the gang ride to the drilling site and demand Tom's arrest for killing Perkins, but the wounded lawman arrives with Little Beaver, proving Dean's innocence. During a fight with Red on the rig's platform, McBride falls to his death and Tuttle shoots Long to keep him quiet. Red proves Tuttle is behind the lawlessness just as the oil well comes in, making Cheyenne and her investors rich.

Having become tired of the role of Red Ryder, Bill Elliott asked to be released from the series and Republic promoted him to "A" budget features. Billed as William Elliott, he starred in ten features for the studio between 1946 and 1950, with two of them, *The Last Bandit* and *Hellfire*, being filmed in color. Reverting to Bill Elliott, the actor headlined a quartet of westerns for Monogram in 1951–52 and when the studio became Allied Artists he starred in seven more oaters for them. After that he appeared in five detective films for Allied Artists between 1955 and 1957. During the 1950s he also starred in two unsold TV western series pilots, *Marshal of Trail City* and *Parson of the West*. Following the end of his film career, Elliott became a spokesman for Viceroy cigarettes before his death from lung cancer in Las Vegas in 1965. During the years he played Red Ryder, Elliott ranked in the top five western money-making stars in the annual *Motion Picture Herald* poll: In 1944 he was fifth, fourth in 1945 and second in 1946. In the similar *Boxoffice* poll he was fifth in 1945 and fourth the next year.

Replacing Elliott as Red Ryder was Allan Lane, who had just completed a half-dozen starring films in Republic's "Action Western" series. A native of Indiana, Lane (1904–73) was born Harry Albershart and played football at Notre Dame University before becoming a photographic illustrator and stage actor. He came to films with the coming of sound and by the late 1930s he was a leading man in "B" features at RKO Radio. After headlining a quartet of Republic cliffhangers, *King of the Royal Mounted* (1940), *King of the Mounties* (1942), *Daredevils of the West* (1943) and *The Tiger Woman* (1944), he was assigned his own series. His salary for the seven Red Ryder films was $350 per week.

Also new to the Red Ryder features was Martha Wentworth (1889–1974) as the Duchess, replacing Alice Fleming. As noted, her name had been used for that of the Duchess in three of the Elliott films and she also did the role on radio.

Billed on radio as the "actress of 100 voices," Wentworth appeared in over 40 feature films between 1935 and 1963 and she also worked in television.

Sidney Picker continued to produce the Allan Lane films with R.G. Springsteen staying on as director. The opening for the films changed, however: Red Ryder and Little Beaver were pictured on the cover of a Ryder book with them coming to life as Red shoots his guns. *Santa Fe Uprising*, released late in 1946, was the first feature to have this introduction in its tale of the Duchess (Martha Wentworth) becoming the heir to a Bitter Springs, New Mexico, toll road after her cousin Madison Pike (Edmund Cobb) is killed. Pike had been in league with newspaper editor Crawford (Barton MacLane) in charging area ranchers too much to use his road and at the same time using an outlaw gang lead by Bruce Jackson (Jack LaRue) and Luke Case (Dick Curtis) to harass the locals when they try to travel a free government turnpike. During a raid on rancher Lafe Dibble's (Tom London) herd, both Dibble and Pike are killed. Wanting the Duchess out of the way, Crawford orders Jackson and Case to wreck the stagecoach on which she is riding; Red Ryder (Lane) and Little Beaver (Blake) rescue her. After beating Case in a fight, Ryder is asked to become Bitter Springs' new marshal and he brings in ranch hand Hank (Emmett Lynn) as his deputy. When Jackson tries to ambush the lawmen by pretending to have his men drive a herd of cattle on the Duchess' road, Red diverts the herd and is seen by Sonny Dibble (Pat Michaels), the son of the murdered rancher, who realizes they were stolen from his family's ranch. In the melee that follows, Hank is shot by Jackson, and Sonny is blamed. In order to get the young man out of the way, Crawford and Jackson try to incite the locals to lynch him so he cannot reveal that they were the ones who stole the cattle. When this fails, Jackson abducts Little Beaver and offers to exchange him for Sonny. Red realizes the ransom note was written on paper from Crawford's office so he pretends to switch sides and join the newspaperman in his illegal activities. When the two get to the gang's hideout, Crawford shoots at Red, not knowing that Red has put blanks in his gun. Crawford then tries to murder Little Beaver but Red stops him, and he and his men arrest the gang members. Before returning home, the Duchess deeds her toll road to the town.

Released almost simultaneously with *Santa Fe Uprising* was *Stagecoach to Denver*; both were written by Earle Snell, who did thirteen of the Republic Red Ryder scripts. The plot had Red (Lane) driving the Duchess' (Wentworth) stagecoach with her and orphan Dickie Ray (Bobby Hyatt) as passengers. They stop in Elkhorn where Big Bill Lambert (Roy Barcroft) has just completed his own stage line to Denver, which does not compete with the Duchess since her line goes in the opposite direction. Although he pretends to be an upstanding citizen, Big Bill plans to use the stage line business to cover up his crooked land deals. Since Land Commissioner Felton (Ed Cassidy) has proof of Lambert's complicity, Big Bill orders his cohort Duke (Edmund Cobb) to wreck the stagecoach carrying Felton and Dickie to Denver, where the boy is to meet his aunt, May Barnes (Marin Sais), whom he has never seen. Duke tampers with the coach, causing it to crash, killing Felton and leaving Bobby paralyzed. Red, Little Beaver (Blake) and rancher Coonskin Boyd (Emmett Lynn) take the boy to Boyd's ranch where Dr. Kimball (Tom Chatterton) says he needs a delicate operation in order to walk again. Red rides to see telegrapher Joe (Budd Buster) to send a wire to Bobby's aunt. When Lambert's partner Silas Braydon (Wheaton Chambers) warns him, Big Bill orders Duke, Blackie Grubb (George Chesebro) and Ed (Lew Morphy) to kill him. Red manages to elude them, however, and the message is sent. Since Aunt May and the new land commissioner, Taylor (Frank O'Connor), are coming to Elkhorn on the same stagecoach, Lambert orders Duke to kidnap them and replace the duo with his cohorts Beautiful (Peggy Stewart) and Wally (Stanley Price), who will pretend to be Bobby's aunt and the new land commissioner. When this is successfully carried out, Beautiful goes to Coonskin's ranch where she sees Bobby and reluctantly gives her consent to the operation. The procedure is partially successful and Beautiful begins to become attached to the boy as the phony land commissioner's surveys result in an eviction notice for Coonskin. Red and Little Beaver conduct their own survey and realize that the ones done by the new commissioner are bogus. When Beautiful begins to defy Big Bill by demanding the boy be sent to a specialist in Denver, he plans to murder her but she is rescued by Red, who finds her purse in Lambert's office although he claims to hardly know her. Big Bill then has the crooked sheriff (Ted Adams) arrest Ryder for killing Blackie, who tried to ambush him. Beautiful flags down the stagecoach Duke is driving to Denver with the Duchess and Bobby, whom Lambert wants out of the way, as Coonskin helps Red in getting out of jail. When Beautiful realizes that Duke is supposed to kill the boy, she tries to stop him and helps Red in taking over the stagecoach. At the gang's hideout, Beautiful is killed by Lambert as she tries to protect the boy. Big Bill is shot by Red, as Coonskin, Little Beaver and the area ranchers arrive to arrest the outlaws. Bobby's aunt and Taylor are set free and later, following a successful operation, the boy receives a pony from Red.

Vigilantes of Boomtown, issued in February 1947, involved the 1897 heavyweight boxing championship between champion James J. Corbett and middleweight champion Bob Fitzsimmons. The script, however, so tangled the facts that the resulting feature, while entertaining, could hardly be called a true pictorial of the famous confrontation in which Fitzsimmons took the title. Taking place in Carson City, Nevada, the locale of the actual fight, it had Corbett (George Turner) incognito as rancher Jim McVey, with his daughter Molly (Peggy Stewart) not wanting him to return to the ring to battle Fitzsimmons (John Dehner). Red (Lane) becomes involved when he tries to stop a street fracas between the two boxers, not realizing it is a publicity gag. Outlaw McKean (Roy Barcroft) joins Fitzsimmons' entourage in hopes of evening a score with Ryder, who sent him to prison. He also joins forces with Billy Delaney (Roscoe Karns), Corbett's former manager. When Red spars with Corbett, McKean tries to shoot him. Red thinks Molly's ranch hands were behind the incident so he has the local judge (Harlan Briggs) set a high bail for them. When Little Beaver reports to Red that McKean and his gang are rustling cattle, Ryder recovers the herd and recognizes the outlaw. Molly's henchmen plan to kidnap her father to prevent the fight but instead end up taking Red; the next day, Molly sets him free. McKean plans to steal the gold bet on the boxing match, but Red and the sheriff (Ted Adams) replace the money with iron washers. Gang member Dink (George Chesebro) drives the wagon with the supposed gold but he has already told McKean the route of the actual shipment. The outlaws steal the money but are captured by Red Ryder and the law. The fight takes place with Corbett losing to Fitzsimmons, although Delaney has already scheduled another bout for the ex-champion. So convoluted was the plot, it had Corbett meeting with a group who want to get someone to challenge world champion John L. Sullivan, although James J. Corbett took the title from Sullivan in 1892, five years before the setting of the feature.

The next Ryder adventure, *Homesteaders of Paradise Valley*, which came out in the spring of 1947, harkened back to the type of rawboned pioneer epics Republic produced in earlier years in its tale of Red (Lane) leading a group of settlers in a wagon train. Among them are Little Beaver (Blake), the Duchess (Wentworth), and newspaperman Steve Hill (John James) and his sister Melinda (Ann Todd). Red decides to settle the group in Paradise Valley but is opposed by homesteader Bill Hume (Gene [Roth] Stutenroth), who with his brother Rufe (Mauritz Hugo) is in cahoots with A.C. Blaine (Milton Kibbee), a newspaper editor in Center City, who wants the water rights in the area so he can sell bonds to build a dam to rival the one planned for Paradise Valley. Due to the dry season, Red tells the homesteaders they must conserve water and he and Little Beaver find out the Humes are stealing water and are also trying to sabotage the dam project. Blaine convinces Ryder to write for his newspaper and urges him to support a bond issue although Blaine's henchman, banker Langley (Emmett Vogan), and his cohorts plan to take away the homesteaders' properties. Bill Hume accuses the Duchess, who operates a general store in Paradise Valley, of overcharging for supplies and Steve places the blame on Red for the passage of the bond issue. He tries to shoot Red but is stopped by Little Beaver. Steve leads a gang of angry settlers in blowing up the dam although the Duchess and Melinda try to stop him. Hume and his brother rob Blaine who refuses to tell Red who attacked him. Steve and the settlers converge on the Hume ranch just as Bill and Rufe are planning to escape. A gunfight ensues and Bill shoots

Rufe when he tries to surrender. Red diverts the settlers long enough for Bill to make a getaway and then follows him, defeating him in a fistfight and taking possession of Blaine's operating books, which the Hume brothers had also stolen. Blaine and his associates are indicted and the homesteaders get back their land.

The next month's *Oregon Trail Scouts* told another version of how Red (Lane) became Little Beaver's guardian. Here Red and his friend Bear Trap (Emmett Lynn) are fur trappers who make deal with Indian chief Running Fox (Frank Lackteen) for trapping rights in his territory along the Snake River. Dishonest trapper Bill Hunter (Roy Barcroft) is after the same rights and he attacks Red, who is saved by the Indians. Years before, Hunter was involved in a scheme to kidnap the chief's infant grandson and hold him for ransom but his cohort escaped with the baby. The man returns as a traveling druggist and Hunter kills him but escapes after fighting with Ryder. Red takes the dead man's wagon, in which the Duchess (Wentworth) and Little Beaver (Blake) have hidden, as Hunter plans another attack. Finding the two stowaways, Ryder takes Little Beaver back to town and they are attacked by Hunter's men, but they get away when Little Beaver wings Hunter with an arrow. Going back to camp, they find that the Duchess is missing. Little Beaver rides to Chief Running Fox and he and his braves surround the outlaw's camp. When Hunter tries to carry off Little Beaver, the Duchess knocks him out with a frying pan. Red and the Duchess now realize that Little Beaver is the chief's grandson but Running Fox wants him to stay with Red Ryder.

Rustlers of Devil's Canyon, issued in the summer of 1947, found Red (Lane) discharged after service in the Spanish-American War and returning to Sioux City, Wyoming, where he meets Dr. Cole (Arthur Space) at the Army's processing center. The physician tells him his old pal Blizzard (Emmett Lynn) is ailing and that rustlers are plaguing the area. When Blizzard is well, he and Red go in search of the rustlers and meet Little Beaver (Blake) who has seen a posse in pursuit of the outlaws. Red joins the sheriff (Tom London) in chasing the gang, lead by Matt (Pierce Lyden) and Frank (Bob Reeves). In town, Dr. Cole, the mastermind behind the lawlessness, urges the citizens to lead a major cattle drive to catch the culprits. Cole is also working with another physician, Dr. Glover (Forrest Taylor), the head of a veterans hospital, who recruits homesteaders to come to Sioux City, led by his assistant, land agent Clark (Roy Barcroft). When Red convenes a meeting of the homesteaders, which is attended by Bess Glazier (Peggy Stewart) and her brother Tad (Harry Carr), he remembers Clark, also in attendance, for having cheated earlier settlers. Red and Clark get into a fight that is halted when the rustlers break up the meeting, wounding both Tad and Clark. Cole attends to Tad's injury but also aids wounded rustlers. The next day

Poster for *Rustlers of Devil's Canyon* (Republic, 1947).

a warning note is thrown through the window of the Duchess' (Wentworth) ranch house. Red joins the settlers in the cattle drive but is forced to leave when he and Blizzard have to put out an arson fire in his aunt's barn. The sheriff suspects Bess and Tad of starting the fire. Disguised as settlers, the outlaws attack the trio and tie Tad to a horse and drag him. The sheriff and Tad blame Red, who escapes and hides in a cave. Little Beaver asks Dr. Cole to come to Red's aid but Bess stops the medical man from giving Ryder sleeping pills. The doctor locks her in a shed but she escapes as Cole and Matt try to subdue Red. Little Beaver, Blizzard and the sheriff show up and the crooks are arrested.

In the late summer of 1947 came *Marshal of Cripple Creek*. In Wyoming, Red (Lane) and Little Beaver (Blake) stop a stagecoach holdup and bring in the robber (Herman Hack). As a result, Red is made Cripple Creek's lawman, much to the chagrin of saloon owner Long John Lacey (Gene [Roth] Stutenroth) and his choice for the job, miner Baker (Tom London). Outlaw Tom Lambert (Trevor Bardette) joins Baker in a scheme to put gold ore in his mine and steal the shipment. Card dealer Link (Roy Barcroft) leads his men in staging the robbery but when Red follows with a posse, Lambert is injured and deserted by his cohorts. Lambert's wife Mae (Helen Wallace) and son Dick (William Self) are welcomed by Red and the Duchess (Wentworth), although Tom is sentenced to prison. Long John recruits Dick into his gang but Red tries to stop the young man from drinking and gets into a fight with Link, who is sent to prison when he tries to kill Ryder. In the penitentiary, Link informs Lambert that Ryder is picking on his son; he escapes and returns to Cripple Creek to confront the lawman. When Lambert tries to shot Red, Little Beaver knocks the gun out of his hand. During a gold shipment, Red hides in one of the wagons while Lambert joins his son as lookout for the gang. As Tom orders his son to quit the outfit, the outlaws take the wagon to Baker's mine where Red and Lambert fight. When Tom realizes the sheriff wants to help his son, he tries to escape with him but is shot by the mine owner. Baker then rides to Lacey to warn him that Ryder is out to arrest him. When Baker tries to kill Red, Little Beaver knocks him out with a bottle. Lacey and Baker are arrested and Red and Little Beaver return to their wandering ways.

Marshal of Cripple Creek proved to be the final Republic Red Ryder feature. The studio wanted to continue the successful series but due to a clerical error the option renewal date for the character passed and copyright owner Stephen Slesinger wanted a hefty increase in royalties. The studio refused.

Following the demise of the series, Lane starred in thirty-eight films in the studio's "Famous Westerns" series. In this well-made and highly regarded grouping, he portrayed an array of lawmen, not one continuing character. This series ran from 1947 to 1953 and after that he continued to appear in films and television. In the latter medium he provided the voice of the talking horse in the CBS-TV series *Mr. Ed* from 1961 to 1966. In 1955, Lane returned to the role of Red Ryder in the 30-minute television show *Gun Trouble Valley*, which was produced by Gene Autry's Flying A Productions. Directed by George Archainbaud, the unsold pilot co-starred Louis Lettieri as Little Beaver and Elizabeth Slifer as the Duchess.

Two years after the end of the Republic series, Equity Pictures produced a quartet of Red Ryder features filmed in color. Lensed at Iverson's Ranch in Chatsworth and the Monogram ranch at Newhall, these Eagle Lion releases starred Jim Bannon in the title role. A Missouri native, Bannon (1911–84) graduated from Rockhurst College and became a radio sportscaster before moving to Hollywood in 1938. There he became a radio announcer for many network programs; this led to acting parts, the most notable as Jack Packard on NBC's *I Love a Mystery* from 1939 to 1942 and on CBS during the 1943–44 season. After making *The Soul of a Monster* for Columbia in 1944, he played Jack Packard in a trio of "I Love a Mystery" features for the studio, *I Love a Mystery* (1945), *The Devil's Mask* and *The Unknown* (both 1946). He continued to appear in films like *Framed*, *The Thirteenth Hour* and *Johnny O'Clock* (all 1947) and he had the lead in the 1948 Republic serial *Dangers of the Canadian Mounted*, as well as supporting roles in Charles Starrett and Lash LaRue features. To win the role of Red Ryder, Bannon dyed his hair red.

Cast as the Duchess in the Equity Pictures

series was Marin Sais, who had appeared in a couple of the Republic Red Ryders. Sais (1890–1971) was a native of California (Marin County in that state was named for her family) who planned a career in opera before making films for Kalem in 1909. She became a star for the company and remained with Kalem for a decade, leaving to freelance and work with her husband, cowboy star Jack Hoxie. With the coming of sound she did supporting roles and remained a part of the movie industry into the early 1950s, appearing in over 225 movies.

Texas native Don Kay Reynolds (1937–) played Little Beaver in the Equity series. A rodeo trick rider, he came to Hollywood in 1944 and worked in westerns with Roy Rogers, Eddie Dean, Gene Autry and Charles Starrett before being cast as Little Beaver. After the series ended he made a few more westerns and worked in television before joining the rodeo circuit. After that he had a variety of jobs, including training animals for films; he trained the horse Shadowfax for *The Lord of the Rings: The Fellowship of the Rings* (2001) and *The Lord of the Rings: The Two Towers* (2002). In 2007 his memoir, *The Last Little Beaver*, was published. Reynolds was known as Little Brown Jug and this was how he was billed for the Ryder films.

Also a part of the series was Emmett Lynn, who was cast in the part of Red and Little Beaver's sidekick, Buckskin Blodgett. He had previously done supporting roles in five of the Republic Ryder films, two with Wild Bill Elliott and three with Allan Lane. Lynn (1897–1958) began working in films as a teenager, and also had a lengthy career on stage and radio. In 1940 Lynn made a quartet of westerns with Tim Holt at RKO and then supported Don "Red" Barry at Republic and Eddie Dean, with whom he had worked in radio in the 1930s, at PRC. Lynn also worked with genre stars Ken Maynard, Hoot Gibson, Charles Starrett and Buster Crabbe. Following the Red Ryder series he continued to appear in films and television until the mid–1950s.

Lewis D. Collins directed the quartet of Red Ryder features for Equity Pictures, beginning with *Ride, Ryder, Ride*, released in February 1949. Fred Harman worked as a technical advisor, mainly providing color sketches of the characters for authentic props and wardrobe. The story had Red (Bannon), Little Beaver (Little Brown Jug) and Buckskin (Lynn) stopping a stagecoach holdup on their way to Devil's Hole. The passengers include Libby Brooks (Peggy Stewart), a newspaper publisher, and her brother Gerry (Steve Pendleton), who believes the ringleader of the raiders is hotel owner Frenchy Beaumont (Edwin Max). When the Brookses write an article accusing Beaumont of fomenting the lawlessness, he orders his henchman Blackjack (Jack O'Shea) to start a fight with Gerry and then shoot him in self-defense. Red stops the fight but Beaumont challenges Gerry to a duel and kills him. In order to capture the hotel owner, Red tells Libby to write another article accusing him of being an outlaw. When Beaumont and Blackjack confront her about it, Buckskin gives him a fake copy and Blackjack strikes him. Iverson (Fred Coby), Beaumont's lawyer, advises him to sue for libel and when the case comes to trial Red acts as Libby's attorney. Since the article was never published, Red gets the charges dropped and Blackjack is sent to prison for assaulting Buckskin. Ryder then challenges Beaumont to fight a duel and receives only a slight wound. He is then able to prove Beaumont tampered with the dueling pistols; Red arrests him and he receives a manslaughter indictment. *Variety* asserted, "[T]he Ryder group stacks up as good Saturday matinee product"; regarding the star the trade paper opined, "Although physically a fine choice for the title role, Bannon isn't too convincing as an actor. However, his fistic prowess seems to more than compensate for his lack of histrionic finesse."

The next month's release of *Roll, Thunder, Roll*, found Red (Bannon) riding to town to tell the locals, including the Duchess (Sais), Little Beaver (Little Brown Jug) and Buckskin (Lynn), about finding a nearby ranch raided. Businesswoman Carol Loomis (Nancy Gates) tells him where to find her fiancé, Marshal Bill Faugh (Steve Pendleton), who is at the barbershop owned by her uncle, Happy Loomis (Lee Morgan). Having found a pair of conchas at the site of the raid as well as at other robbery locations, Ryder informs the lawman that they are associated with a California bandit called El Conejo (I. Stanford Jolley). The outlaw arrives in a nearby town with his cohort Felipe (Charles Stevens) and confronts bar owner Ace Hanlon (Glenn Strange) and gang member Wolf (Lane Bradford), accusing them of

Poster for *Roll Thunder Roll* (Eagle Lion, 1949).

In the third film with Bannon as Red, *The Fighting Redhead*, issued in the fall of 1949, he captures a rustler (Sandy Sanders) only to find out the man and his small daughter (Spooky Reynolds) are nearly starving; he offers the man a job on his ranch. Returning home, he finds the Duchess (Sais), Little Beaver (Little Brown Jug) and Buckskin (Lynn) repairing a fence and he suggests they all go on a fishing trip before the fall roundup. Red receives a message from rancher Dan O'Connor (Forrest Taylor) asking him to help prevent a range war which is about to be instigated by bar owner Faro Savage (John Hart) and his henchmen, Windy (Lane Bradford) and Goldy (Lee Roberts). The crooks rustle cattle belonging to rancher Evans (Billy Hammond) and shoot him; the murder is witnessed by O'Connor. Dan tells his daughter Sheila (Peggy Stewart) about the incident and then goes into town to meet Red, but Goldie shoots him. Realizing O'Connor had his gun, which he used to murder Evans, Savage rides to Dan's ranch where Red and Little Beaver have already arrived. Sheila tells Red of her dad's suspicions about Savage, whom Red knows from previous experience is dishonest. When Dan's horse shows up at the ranch, Red, Sheila, Little Beaver and Savage try to find him without success; the Duchess and Buckskin, who have followed Red and Little Beaver, find his corpse hidden in the brush. In the dead man's hand is a birthday card he gave his daughter. Goldy tries to quit the gang and Savage murders him, placing the blame on Sheila. The sheriff (Bob Duncan) tries to arrest the girl but she escapes. Red and Buckskin later find her at a remote shack; Ryder shows her the card and she tells him it refers to a tree stump where they find Savage's gun and a written statement by Dan. Red forces Windy to admit that Savage killed Dan for his ranch and that he also wants to get rid of Sheila. Cornering Savage in his office, Ryder tells the sheriff to arrest him and Windy verifies that his

framing him for robberies they committed. Ryder convinces the bandit to prove his innocence and puts him in jail but he is set free by Hanlon's gang. A posse is formed by Ryder and the marshal as Carol informs her uncle, who is secretly in cahoots with Hanlon, about a plan to take the bandit to a jail at the county seat. As a ruse, Buckskin masquerades as El Conejo while Red looks for evidence in Hanlon's office. He is spotted by Happy, whom Red confronts with the conchas, which he found in his barbershop. Happy tries to kill Ryder but is stopped by Buckskin. Red beats Hanlon in a fight; all the badmen go to jail.

boss committed several killings. The saloon owner tries to escape but after a fight he is subdued by Red and arrested. Sheila goes on the fishing trip with Red, Little Beaver, the Duchess and Buckskin.

Cowboy and the Prizefighter, released in December, 1949, proved to be the final Red Ryder feature film. It opened with Steve Stevenson (Don Haggerty) shooting a man who was about to kill Red (Bannon) after he had fired him. The grateful Red offers Steve a job on the ranch that he co-owns with the Duchess (Sais). Steve goes to work for Ryder and tells him that his gambler father, Miles Stevenson (Forrest Taylor), died mysteriously after becoming involved with boxing promoter Mark Palmer (John Hart). Ryder, Little Beaver (Little Brown Jug), Buckskin (Lynn) and Steve come upon a stagecoach robbery and save a gold payroll. Among the passengers are Palmer, his fighter Bull Mason (Lou Nova), and saloon singer Sue Evans (Karen Randle), who is going to work for bar owner Bart Osborne (Marshall Reed). Palmer and Osborne cook up a scheme to force Red into fighting Bull but Steve takes his place and is defeated after Mason uses a lead pipe in his glove. Before the fight, Buckskin overheard the two men and outlaw leader Duke Samson (Lane Bradford) make plans to steal the fight proceeds but they give him a beating that causes amnesia. When the outlaws pull off the robbery, Duke is killed and Palmer, Osborne and Mason divide the stolen money. Osborne spreads a rumor that Ryder is afraid of Mason and the two men square off but Red knocks the lead pipe out of Bull's glove and it hits Buckskin, relieving his amnesia. Due to Blodgett's testimony and Red's proof that illegal tactics were used in the fights, Palmer and Osborne are put in jail with Palmer later admitting he killed Steve's father. Steve has fallen in love with Sue, who was only working to pay off her brother's gambling debts, and he asks her to marry him.

After four efforts, Equity's Red Ryder series was halted due to the fact the features were not

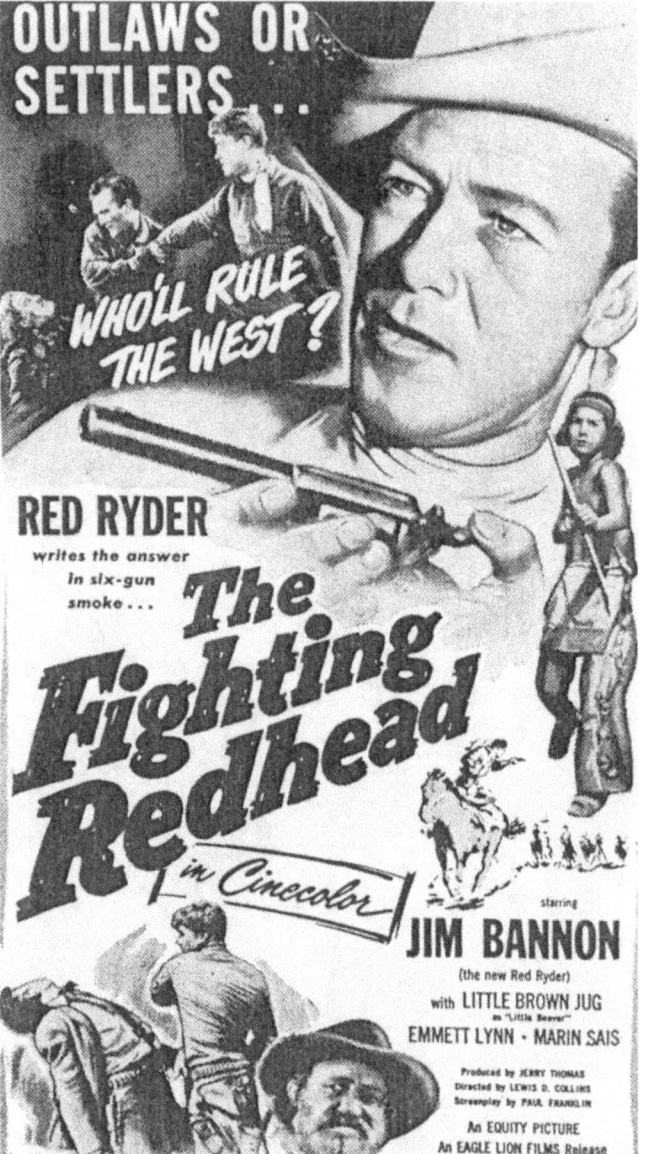

Poster for *The Fighting Redhead* (Eagle Lion, 1949).

profitable enough. Bannon, who had toured with the films in order to boost box office receipts, returned to the role of Red Ryder in the 1951 half-hour television series pilot *Whiplash*. Produced by Hal Roach, Jr., and directed by Thomas Carr, the unsold episode featured Olive Carey as the Duchess; the actor who played Little Beaver was billed under that name. The supporting cast included Monte Blue, Lyle Talbot and Dick Curtis. Following this unsuccessful effort to transfer the Fred Harman character to the small screen, Bannon appeared in films like *The Great Missouri Raid* and *Unknown World* (both 1951) and *Phantom from Space* (1953), as well as co-starring with Whip Wilson in five oaters at Monogram in 1951. During the 1954–55 television season he was a regular on the weekday NBC-TV soap opera *Hawkins Falls* and the next season he appeared in 26 episodes of the CBS-TV program *The Adventures of Champion*, made by Gene Autry's Flying A Productions. Bannon continued to appear in films and television until the mid–1960s and a decade later he made guest appearances at several western movie conventions. In the mid–1970s he self published his autobiography, *The Son That Rose in the West*. He died in 1984.

It is ironic that the character of Red Ryder, so successful as a newspaper comic strip and in comic books, radio, films and merchandising, did not become successful on television as did the Cisco Kid, the Lone Ranger, and Zorro (qq.v.). This is doubly dumbfounding considering the quality of the TV pilot film made by Allan Lane in 1955, which surprisingly never found a network or syndicated timeslot.

Filmography

Adventures of Red Ryder (Republic, 1940, 12 chapters) Associate Producer: Hiram S. Brown, Jr. Directors: William Witney & John English. Screenplay: Franklyn Adreon, Ronald Davidson, Norman S. Hall, Barney A. Sarecky & Sol Shor. Photography: William Nobles. Editor: William Thompson & Edward Todd. Music: Cy Feuer. Production Manager: Al Wilson. Unit Manager: Mack D'Agostino.

Cast: Don "Red" Barry (Red Ryder), Noah Beery (Ace Hanlon), Tommy Cook (Little Beaver), Maude Pierce Allen (The Duchess), Vivian [Austin] Coe (Beth Andrews), Harry Worth (Calvin Drake), Hal Taliaferro [Wally Wales] (Cherokee Sims), William Farnum (Colonel Tom Ryder), Bob Kortman (One-Eye Chapin), Carleton Young (Sheriff Dade), Ray Teal (Shark), Gene Alsace (Deputy Sheriff Lawson), Gayne Whitman (Harrison), Hooper Atchley (Commissioner Treadway), John Dilson (Railroad Official), Lloyd Ingraham (Sheriff Luke Andrews), Charles Hutchison (Brown), Gardner James (Barnett), Wheaton Chambers (Boswell), Lynton Brent (Len Clark), Billy Benedict (Dan Withers), Ernest Sarracino (Matt Grimes), Reed Howes (Slade), Ed Brady (Ed Madison), Edward Hearn (Colonel Lang), Joe de la Cruz (The Apache Kid), Jack O'Shea (Lem), Ed Cassidy (Ira Withers), Frankie Marvin, Chuck Baldra, Bob Card (Deputy Sheriffs), Roy Brent (Joe), Bob Jamison (Gus), Bob Burns (Deputy Sheriff Jones), Augie Gomez (Breed), Fred Burns (Jackson), Bud Geary (Pecos Bates), Budd Buster (Johnson), James Fawcett (Waiter), Frank O'Connor, James Carlisle (Railroad Board Members), Max Waizmann (Land Clerk), Matty Roubert (Pete), Charles Thomas (Lon Walker), Gus Shindle (Bat Mallory), Al Taylor (Slim), Kenneth Terrell (Bart Wade), Doc Adams (Hall), Jack Kirk (Stagecoach Guard Jack), Ted Mapes, Post Park, Charles Murphy, Eddie Juaregui (Stagecoach Drivers), Art Mix, Jack Rockwell, Roy Bucko, Silver Tip Baker, Victor Cox, James Sheridan [Sherry Tansey], Ray Jones, Jack Tornek (Saloon Customers), Duke Green (Janitor), Bruce Mitchell (Bartender), Bill Nestell (Waiter), Robert J. Wilke, Art Dillard, Bill Yrigoyen, Joe Yrigoyen, Bill Wilkus (Gang Members), Chick Hannon, Barry Hays (Poisoners), Walter Stiritz (Masked Man), Dan White, Rube Dalroy, Rose Plummer (Citizens).

Chapter titles: 1) Murder on the Santa Fe Trail; 2) Horsemen of Death; 3) Trail's End; 4) Water Rustlers; 5) Avalanche; 6) Hangman's Noose; 7) Framed; 8) Blazing Walls; 9) Records of Doom; 10) One Second to Live; 11) The Devil's Marksman; 12) Frontier Justice.

Tucson Raiders (Republic, 1944, 55 minutes) Associate Producer: Eddie [Edward J.] White. Director: Spencer [Gordon] Bennet. Screenplay: Anthony Coldeway. Story: Jack O'Donnell. Photography: Reggie Lanning. Editor: Harry Keller. Music: Mort Glickman, Paul Van Loan & Joseph Dubin. Art Director: Gano Chittenden. Sound: Thomas Carman. Sets: Otto Siegel. Assistant Director: Harry Knight.

Cast: Wild Bill Elliott (Red Ryder), George "Gabby" Hayes (Gabby), Bobby Blake (Little Beaver), Alice Fleming (The Duchess), Ruth Lee (Hannah Rogers), Peggy Stewart (Beth Rogers), LeRoy Mason (Jeff Stark), Stanley Andrews (Governor York), John Whitney (Tom Hamilton), Bud Geary (Deputy Sheriff One Eye), Karl Hackett (the Rev. George Allen), Tom Steele, Marshall Reed (Deputy Sheriffs), Tom Chatterton (Judge James Wayne), Ed [Edward] Cassidy (Sheriff Kirk), Edward Howard (Deputy Sheriff Logan), Charles Sullivan (Bartender), Frank McCarroll, Fred Graham, Bud Wolfe (Gang Members), Tommy Coats (Viewer), Kenne Duncan, Tom London, Jack Kirk (Voices of Gang Members).

Marshal of Reno (Republic, 1944, 58 minutes) Associate Producer: Louis Gray. Director: Wallace Grissell. Screenplay: Anthony Coldeway. Story: Anthony Coldeway & Taylor Caven. Photography: Reggie Lanning. Editor: Charles Craft. Music Director: Joseph Dubin. Art Director: Gano Chittenden. Sound: Thomas Carman. Sets: George Milo. Assistant Director: Joseph Dill.

Cast: Wild Bill Elliott (Red Ryder), George "Gabby" Hayes (Gabby), Bobby Blake (Little Beaver), Alice Fleming (The Duchess), Herbert Rawlinson (John Palmer), Jay Kirby (Danny Boyd), LeRoy Mason (Faro Carson), Blake Edwards (Lee Holden), Fred Graham

(Drake), Jack Kirk (Kellogg), Kenne Duncan (Adams), Bud Geary (Ward), Tom Steele (Crane), Tom London (Walker), Tom Chatterton (Judge Holmes), Edmund Cobb (Bob Wendall), Hal Price (Joe Richards), Al Taylor (Brownie), Marshall Reed (Wilson), Robert J. Wilke (Deputy Sheriff), Kenneth Terrell (Waiter), Charles Sullivan (Bartender), Charles King (Stagecoach Bandit), George Chesebro, Jack O'Shea, Chick Hannon, Pascale Perry, Jim Corey, Augie Gomez (Saloon Customers), Neal Hart, Horace B. Carpenter, Fred Burns (Citizens), Ted Wells (Rider), Carl Sepulveda (Stagecoach Driver), Roy Barcroft (Voice).

The San Antonio Kid (Republic, 1944, 59 minutes) Associate Producer: Stephen Auer. Director: Howard Bretherton. Screenplay: Norman S. Hall. Photography: William Bradford. Editor: Tony Martinelli. Music Director: Joseph Dubin. Art Director: Gano Chittenden. Assistant Director: Al [Allen K.] Wood.

Cast: Wild Bill Elliott (Red Ryder), Bobby Blake (Little Beaver), Alice Fleming (The Duchess), Linda Stirling (Ann Taylor), Earle Hodgins (Happy Jack), Glenn Strange (Ace Hanlon), LeRoy Mason (Walter Garfield), Duncan Renaldo (Johnny Bennett/The San Antonio Kid), Tom London (Long), Jack Kirk (Ben Taylor), Robert J. Wilke (Bailey), Jack O'Shea (Nick), Cliff Parkinson (Ed), Joe Garcia, Billy "Sailor" Vincent (Cowboys), Bud Geary (Mason), Herman Hack, Henry Wills, Bob Woodward (Gang Members), Tom Steele (Gunfighter), Tex Terry, Roy Bucko, Lew Morphy, Herman Nowlin (Saloon Customers).

Cheyenne Wildcat (Republic, 1944, 56 minutes) Associate Producer: Louis Gray. Director: Lesley Selander. Screenplay: Randall Faye. Photography: Ellis [Bud] Thackery. Editor: Charles Craft. Music Director: Joseph Dubin. Art Director: Fred Ritter. Sound: Thomas Carman. Sets: Otto Siegel. Assistant Director: Harry Knight.

Cast: Wild Bill Elliott (Red Ryder), Bobby Blake (Little Beaver), Alice Fleming (The Duchess), Peggy Stewart (Betty Lou Hopkins), Francis McDonald (Jim Douglas/Johnson), Roy Barcroft (Dandy Joe Meeker), Tom London (Harrison Colby), Tom Chatterton (Jason Hopkins), Kenne Duncan (Pete), Bud Geary (Chuck), Jack Kirk (Sheriff Brown), Sam Burton (Bank Teller), Frederick Howard (Bank Examiner), Jack O'Shea (Bank Customer), Dickie Dillon (Boy), Charles King, Lucille Ward, Horace B. Carpenter, Rudy Bowman (Citizens), Steve Clark (Station Agent Joe), Merlyn Nelson (Fred), Bob Burns (Clem), Forrest Taylor (Doctor), Franklyn Farnum (Evans), Robert J. Wilke (Deputy Sheriff Charlie), Bud Osborne (Dusty), Rex Lease, Frank Ellis (Deputy Sheriffs), Tom Steele, Jack Tornek, Tom Smith, Willie Keefer (Lynch Mob Members), Wade Crosby (Gang Member), Charles Morton (Bushwhacker).

Vigilantes of Dodge City (Republic, 1944, 54 minutes) Executive Producer: William J. O'Sullivan. Associate Producer: Stephen Auer. Director: Wallace Grissell. Screenplay: Anthony Coldeway & Norman S. Hall. Story: Norman S. Hall. Photography: William Bradford. Editor: Charles Craft. Music Director: Joseph Dubin. Art Director: Fred Ritter. Sound: Ed Borschell. Sets: Earl Wooden. Assistant Director: John Grubbs.

Cast: Wild Bill Elliott (Red Ryder), Bobby Blake (Little Beaver), Alice Fleming (The Duchess), Linda Stirling (Carol Franklin), LeRoy Mason (Luther Jennings), Hal Taliaferro [Wally Wales] (Walter Bishop), Tom London (Denver Thompson), Stephen Barclay (Captain James Glover), Bud Geary (Ross), Kenne Duncan (Dave Brewster), Robert J. Wilke (Bill), Stanley Andrews (General Wingate), Horace B. Carpenter (Jeff Moore), Post Park (Jim Evans), Roy Bucko (Guard), Dale Van Sickel (Gang Member).

Sheriff of Las Vegas (Republic, 1944, 55 minutes) Associate Producer: Stephen Auer. Director: Lesley Selander. Screenplay: Norman S. Hall. Photography: Ellis [Bud] Thackery. Editor: Charles Craft. Music Director: Richard Cherwin. Art Director: Fred Ritter. Sound: Ed Borschell. Sets: Earl Wooden. Assistant Director: Harry Knight.

Cast: Wild Bill Elliott (Red Ryder), Bobby Blake (Little Beaver), Alice Fleming (The Duchess), Peggy Stewart (Ann Carter), Selmer Jackson (Arthur Stanton), William Haade (Dan Sedley), Jay Kirby (Tom Blackwell), John Hamilton (Judge Homer T. Blackwell), Kenne Duncan (Whitey), Bud Geary (Nick), Jack Kirk (Buck), Dickie Dillon (Oliver Blake), Freddie Chapman (Ulysses Botts), Frank McCarroll (Sheriff Logan), Robert J. Wilke (Saloon Customer).

Great Stagecoach Robbery (Republic, 1945, 56 minutes) Associate Producer: Louis Gray. Director: Lesley Selander. Screenplay: Randall Faye. Photography: Bud Thackery. Editor: Charles Craft. Music Director: Richard Cherwin. Art Director: Fred Ritter. Sound: Ed Borschell. Sets: Charles Thompson. Assistant Director: Roy Wade.

Cast: Wild Bill Elliott (Red Ryder), Bobby Blake (Little Beaver), Alice Fleming (The Duchess), Don Costello (Jed Quinlan), Francis McDonald (Con Hollister), John James (Billy Hollister), Sylvia Arslan (Boots Hollister), Bud Geary (Joe Slade), Leon Tyler (Sneak), Freddie Chapman (Freddie), Dickie Dillon (Small Boy), Bobby Dillon (Boy on Plank), Raymond ZeBrack (Last Lost Boy), Patsy May (Girl), Chris Wren, Ginny Wren (Twins), Frederick Howard (Saunders), Grace Cunard (Mother), Hank Bell (Stagecoach Driver), Tom London, Horace B. Carpenter (Citizens), Fred Graham (Man Fighting in Bank), Henry Wills (Jake), Robert J. Wilke (Stagecoach Guard), Lucille Byron, Dorothy Stevens (Dancers).

Lone Texas Rangers (Republic, 1945, 56 minutes) Associate Producer: Louis Gray. Director: Spencer [Gordon] Bennet. Screenplay: Bob Williams. Photography: Bud Thackery. Editor: Charles Craft. Music Director: Richard Cherwin. Art Director: Russell Kimball.

Sound: Ed Borschell. Sets: George Milo. Assistant Director: Harry Knight.

Cast: Wild Bill Elliott (Red Ryder), Bobby Blake (Little Beaver), Alice Fleming (The Duchess), Roy Barcroft (Hands Weber), Tom Chatterton (Sheriff "Iron Mike" Haines), Jack McClendon (Tommy Haines), Helen Talbot (Sally Carter), Bud Geary (Betcha), Budd Buster (F.E. Murphy), Nelson McDowell (Henry Grimm), Larry Olsen (Payne), Rex Lease (Whitey), Jack Kirk (Bill Bradley), Frederick Howard (Bates), Earl Dobbins (Jenkins), Hal Price (Guard), Nolan Leary (Hills), Frank O'Connor (Horace Carter), Dale Van Sickel (Baker), Bill Stevens, Robert J. Wilke (Gang Members), Horace B. Carpenter (Mr. Hill), LeRoy Mason (Voice in the Crowd).

Phantom of the Plains (Republic, 1945, 58 minutes) Associate Producer: R.G. Springsteen. Director: Lesley Selander. Screenplay: Earle Snell & Charles Kenyon. Photography: William Bradford. Editor: Charles Craft. Music Director: Richard Cherwin. Art Director: Hilyard Brown. Sound: Ed Borschell. Sets: Charles Thompson. Makeup: Bob Mark.

Cast: Wild Bill Elliott (Red Ryder), Bobby Blake (Little Beaver), Alice Fleming (The Duchess), Ian Keith (Fancy Charlie/Talbot Wilberforce Champneys), William Haade (Ace Hanlon), Virginia Christine (Celeste), Bud Geary (Pete Burdett), Henry Hall (Jim), Fred Graham (Chuck), Jack Kirk (Sheriff), Jack Rockwell (Stagecoach Driver Buck), Earle Hodgins, Tom London (Ranchers), Neal Hart, Bob Burns, Jack Tornek, Rose Plummer (Citizens).

Working title: *Texas Manhunt*.

Marshal of Laredo (Republic, 1945, 56 minutes) Associate Producer: Sidney Picker. Director: R.G. Springsteen. Screenplay: Bob Williams. Photography: Bud Thackery. Editor: Charles Craft. Music Director: Richard Cherwin. Art Director: Hilyard Brown. Sound: Earl Crain. Sets: George Milo. Assistant Director: Ed Stein.

Cast: Wild Bill Elliott (Red Ryder), Bobby Blake (Little Beaver), Alice Fleming (The Duchess), Peggy Stewart (Judy Bowers), Robert Grady [Jack McClendon] (Larry Randall), Roy Barcroft (Denver Jack), Don Costello (Pretty Boy Murphy), Bud Geary (Ferguson), Sarah Padden (Mrs. Randall), Tom London (Barton), Tom Chatterton (the Rev. Parker), Wheaton Chambers (Dr. Allen), George Chesebro (Chief Deputy), George M. Carleton (Mel Bowers), Dorothy Granger (Suzanne), Dick Scott (Gambling Attendant), Mary Arden (Mrs. Paine), Jack Kirk (Stagecoach Driver), Lane Bradford (Stagecoach Guard), Jack O'Shea (Spud), Kenneth Terrell (Gang Member), Rose Marie Morei, Melva Anstead (Saloon Girls).

Colorado Pioneers (Republic, 1945, 57 minutes) Associate Producer: Sidney Picker. Director: R.G. Springsteen. Screenplay: Earle Snell. Story: Peter Whitehead. Photography: Bud Thackery. Editor: Charles Craft. Music Director: Richard Cherwin. Art Director: Frank Hotaling. Sound: Earl Crain. Sets: Otto Siegel. Special Effects: Howard & Theodore Lydecker. Assistant Director: Al [Allen K.] Wood.

Cast: Wild Bill Elliott (Red Ryder), Bobby Blake (Little Beaver), Alice Fleming (Martha "The Duchess" Wentworth), Roy Barcroft (Bull Reagan), Bud Geary (Bill Slade), Billy Cummings (Joe), Freddie Chapman (Skinny), Frank Jaquet (Dave Wyatt), Tom London (Sand Snipe), Monte Hale (Chuck), Buckwheat Thomas (Smokey), George Chesebro (Hank Disher), Emmett Vogan (Judge), Tom Chatterton (Father Marion), Ed Cassidy (Ramsey), Jack Rockwell (Sheriff), Fred Graham (Hoodlum), Howard M. Mitchell, Frank O'Connor, Cliff Parkinson (Chicago Policemen), Gary Armstrong, Bobby Anderson, Robert Goldschmidt, Romey Foley, Richard Lydon (Parish Boys), Jack Kirk (Wagon Owner), Wally West (Cowboys), Rose Plummer, Chick Hannon (Chicago Citizens), Jess Cavin, Horace B. Carpenter, George Morrell, Bud Wolfe (Citizens).

Wagon Wheels Westward (Republic, 1945, 55 minutes) Associate Producer: Sidney Picker. Director: R.G. Springsteen. Screenplay: Earle Snell. Story: Gerald Geraghty. Photography: William Bradford. Editor: Fred Allen. Music Director: Richard Cherwin. Art Director: Frank Hotaling. Sound: Earl Crain & Thomas Carman. Makeup: Bob Mark. Special Effects: Howard & Theodore Lydecker. Assistant Director: Al [Allen K.] Wood.

Cast: Wild Bill Elliott (Red Ryder), Bobby Blake (Little Beaver), Alice Fleming (Martha "The Duchess" Wentworth), Linda Stirling (Arlie Adams), Roy Barcroft (Dave McKean), Emmett Lynn (Pop Dale), Dick Curtis (Tuttle), Jay Kirby (Bob Adams), George J. Lewis (Lunsford), Bud Geary (Sheriff Brown), Tom London (Judge James Worth), Kenne Duncan (Joe), George Chesebro (Butch/Tom Sutton), Bob McKenzie (John Larkin), Jack Kirk (Outlaw), Jack Sparks (Jack), Cactus Mack (Stagecoach Driver), Frank Ellis, Tommy Coats, Pascale Perry (Gang Members), Frances Gladwin, Lucille Byron (Lobby Girls).

California Gold Rush (Republic, 1946, 56 minutes) Associate Producer: Sidney Picker. Director: R.G. Springsteen. Screenplay: Bob Williams. Photography: William Bradford. Editor: Charles Craft. Music Director: Richard Cherwin. Art Director: Frank Hotaling. Sound: Earl Crain. Makeup: Bob Mark. Assistant Director: Don Verk.

Cast: Wild Bill Elliott (Red Ryder), Bobby Blake (Little Beaver), Alice Fleming (Martha "The Duchess" Wentworth), Peggy Stewart (Hazel Parker), Russell Simpson (Colonel Parker), Dick Curtis (Chopin), Joel Friedkin (Ernest Murphy), Kenne Duncan (Felton), Tom London (Sheriff Peabody), Monte Hale (Pete), Wen Wright (The Idaho Kid), Dickie Dillon (Broken Arrow), Mary Arden, Jack Kirk, Nolan Leary (Stagecoach Passengers), Bud Osborne (Frank), Budd Buster (Bellhop), Freddie Chapman (Boy), Frank Ellis (Lobby Patron), Post Park (Stagecoach Driver), Pascale Perry,

Roy Bucko (Deputy Sheriffs), Henry Wills (Gang Member), Frances Gladwin, Dorothy Stevens, Marian Kerrigan, Beverly Reedy (Young Women), Neal Hart, Herman Hack, Jess Cavin, Kansas Moehring, James Mitchell (Citizens).

Sheriff of Redwood Valley (Republic, 1946, 57 minutes) Associate Producer: Sidney Picker. Director: R.G. Springsteen. Screenplay: Earle Snell. Photography: Reggie Lanning. Editor: Ralph Dixon. Music Director: Richard Cherwin. Art Director: Fred Ritter. Sound: Fred Stahl. Sets: John McCarthy, Jr., & Allen Alperin. Makeup: Bob Mark. Assistant Director: Don Verk.

Cast: Wild Bill Elliott (Red Ryder), Bobby Blake (Little Beaver), Bob Steele (The Reno Kid), Alice Fleming (The Duchess), Peggy Stewart (Molly), Arthur Loft (Harvey Martin), James Craven (Bidwell), Tom London (Sheriff), Kenne Duncan (Jackson), Bud Geary (Strong), John Wayne Wright (Johnny), Tom Chatterton (Doc Ellis), Budd Buster (Crump), Frank McCarroll (Pete), Frank Linn (Dog Man), Jack Kirk (Stagecoach Driver), James Linn (Jailer), Tex Cooper (Citizen).

Sun Valley Cyclone (Republic, 1946, 56 minutes) Associate Producer: Sidney Picker. Director: R.G. Springsteen. Screenplay: Earle Snell. Photography: Bud Thackery. Editors: Charles Craft & Harry Keller. Music Director: Richard Cherwin. Art Director: James Sullivan. Sound: Victor Appel. Sets: John McCarthy, Jr., & Marie Arthur. Assistant Director: Ed Stein.

Cast: Wild Bill Elliott (Red Ryder), Bobby Blake (Little Beaver), Alice Fleming (The Duchess), Roy Barcroft (Blackie Blake), Kenne Duncan (Dow), Eddy Waller (Major Harding), Tom London (Sheriff), Edmund Cobb (Luce), Edward [Ed] Cassidy (Colonel Theodore Roosevelt), Monte Hale (Jeff), George Chesebro (Shorty), Rex Lease (Sergeant), Frank O'Connor (Doctor), Jack Sparks (Junior Officer), Hal Price (Marshal Henry McGurin), Jack Rockwell (Deputy Marshal), Jack Kirk, Horace B. Carpenter, Bob Burns, Silver Tip Baker (Citizens), Tommy Coats, Tom Steele (Gang Members), LeRoy Mason (Voice).

Conquest of Cheyenne (Republic, 1946, 56 minutes) Associate Producer: Sidney Picker. Director: R.G. Springsteen. Screenplay: Earle Snell. Story: Joseph F. Poland & Bert Horswell. Photography: William Bradford. Editor: Charles Craft. Music Director: Richard Cherwin. Sound: Fred Stahl. Makeup: Bob Mark. Special Effects: Howard & Theodore Lydecker. Assistant Director: Eddie Stein.

Cast: Wild Bill Elliott (Red Ryder), Bobby Blake (Little Beaver), Alice Fleming (The Duchess), Peggy Stewart (Cheyenne Jackson), Jay Kirby (Tom Dean), Milton Kibbee (W.C. Tuttle), Tom London (Sheriff Dan Perkins), Emmett Lynn (Daffy), Kenne Duncan (McBride), George Sherwood (Murdo), Frank McCarroll (Long), Jack Kirk (Deputy Sheriff Blake), Tom Chatterton (Jones), Bob Burns (Rancher), Jack O'Shea, Bert Dillard (Citizens), LeRoy Mason (Voice Announcing Runaway).

Santa Fe Uprising (Republic, 1946, 56 minutes) Associate Producer: Sidney Picker. Director: R.G. Springsteen. Screenplay: Earle Snell. Photography: Bud Thackery. Editor: William P. Thompson. Music Director: Mort Glickman. Art Director: Fred Ritter. Sound: Victor Appel. Sets: John McCarthy, Jr., & Earl Wooden. Special Effects: Howard & Theodore Lydecker. Assistant Director: Don Verk.

Cast: Allan Lane (Red Ryder), Bobby Blake (Little Beaver), Martha Wentworth (The Duchess), Barton MacLane (Crawford), Jack LaRue (Bruce Jackson), Tom London (Lafe Dibble), Dick Curtis (Luke Case), Forrest Taylor (Moore), Emmett Lynn (Hank), Hank Patterson (Jake), Pat Michaels (Sonny Dibble), Edmund Cobb (Madison Pike), Kenne Duncan (Henchman), Edythe Elliott (Mrs. Dibble), George Chesebro (Stableman), Britt Wood (Bartender), Frank Ellis, Buck Moulton (Ranchers), Neal Hart (Plotter), Matty Roubert (Gang Member), Kansas Moehring (Deputy Sheriff), Fred Burns, Lee Reynolds (Cowboys), Art Dillard (Saloon Customer).

Stagecoach to Denver (Republic, 1946, 54 minutes) Associate Producer: Sidney Picker. Director: R.G. Springsteen. Screenplay: Earle Snell. Photography: Edgar Lyons. Editor: Les [Lester] Orleback. Music Director: Mort Glickman. Art Director: Pat Youngblood. Sound: Fred Stahl. Sets: John McCarthy, Jr., & Earl Wooden. Makeup: Bob Mark. Assistant Director: Don Verk.

Cast: Allan Lane (Red Ryder), Bobby Blake (Little Beaver), Martha Wentworth (The Duchess), Roy Barcroft (Big Bill Lambert), Peggy Stewart (Beautiful), Emmett Lynn (Coonskin Boyd), Ted Adams (Sheriff), Edmund Cobb (Duke), Tom Chatterton (Dr. Kimball), Bobby Hyatt (Dickie Ray), George Chesebro (Blackie Grubb), Edward [Ed] Cassidy (Commissioner Felton), Wheaton Chambers (Silas Braydon), Forrest Taylor (Matt Disher), Frank O'Connor (Commissioner Taylor), Stanley Price (Wally), Marin Sais (May Barnes), Budd Buster (Joe), Lew Morphy (Ed), Herman Hack, Chuck Baldra, Chick Hannon (Citizens), Cactus Mack (Rancher).

Vigilantes of Boomtown (Republic, 1947, 56 minutes) Associate Producer: Sidney Picker. Director: R.G. Springsteen. Screenplay: Earle Snell. Photography: Alfred Keeler. Editor: William P. Thompson. Music Director: Mort Glickman. Art Director: Fred Ritter. Sound: Fred Stahl. Sets: John McCarthy, Jr. Assistant Director: Eddie Stein.

Cast: Allan Lane (Red Ryder), Bobby Blake (Little Beaver), Martha Wentworth (The Duchess), Roscoe Karns (Bill Delaney), Roy Barcroft (McKean), Peggy Stewart (Molly McVey), George Turner (James J. Corbett/Jim McVey), Eddie Lou Simms (Sparring Partner), George Chesebro (Dick), Bobby Barber (Second), George Lloyd (Thug), Ted Adams (Sheriff), John

Dehner (Bob Fitzsimmons), Earle Hodgins (Governor), Harlan Briggs (Judge Seth), Budd Buster (Samuel Goff), Jack O'Shea (Referee), Pascale Perry, Herman Howlin (Gang Members).

Homesteaders of Paradise Valley (Republic, 1947, 53 minutes) Associate Producer: Sidney Picker. Director: R.G. Springsteen. Screenplay: Earle Snell. Photography: Alfred Keeler. Editor: Charles Craft. Music Director: Mort Glickman. Sound: Ed Borschell. Sets: John McCarthy, Jr., & Charles Thompson. Makeup: Bob Mark. Special Effects: Howard & Theodore Lydecker. Assistant Director: Nat Barrager.

Cast: Allan Lane (Red Ryder), Bobby Blake (Little Beaver), Martha Wentworth (The Duchess), Ann Todd (Melinda Hill), Gene [Roth] Stutenroth (Bill Hume), John James (Steve Hill), Mauritz Hugo (Rufe Hume), Emmett Vogan (Mr. Langley), Milton Kibbee (A.C. Blaine), Tom London (Rider), Edythe Elliott (Mrs. Hume), George Chesebro (E.J. White), Edward [Ed] Cassidy (Sheriff), Marshall Reed (Tim), Jack Kirk (Ed), Freddie Chapman (Bud Hume), Pat Hennigan (Jimmy Hume), Frank O'Connor (Doctor), Al Ferguson, Jack Sparks (Citizens), Bob Burns, Roy Bucko (Homesteaders), Herman Hack (Gang Member), Post Park (Tom).

Oregon Trail Scouts (Republic, 1947, 58 minutes) Associate Producer: Sidney Picker. Director: R.G. Springsteen. Screenplay: Earle Snell. Photography: Alfred Keller. Editor: Harold R. Minter. Music Director: Mort Glickman. Art Director: Pat Youngblood. Sound: William E. Clark. Sets: John McCarthy, Jr., & George Milo. Makeup: Bob Mark. Special Effects: Howard & Theodore Lydecker. Assistant Directors: Joe Kramer & Dick Moder.

Cast: Allan Lane (Red Ryder), Bobby Blake (Little Beaver), Martha Wentworth (The Duchess), Roy Barcroft (Bill Hunter), Emmett Lynn (Bear Trap), Edmund Cobb (Jack), Earle Hodgins (Judge), Edward [Ed] Cassidy (Mr. Bliss), Frank Lackteen (Chief Running Fox), Billy Cummings (Barking Squirrel), Jack Kirk (Stagecoach Driver), Jack O'Shea, Jack Sparks, Forrest Burns, Ted Elliott, Ernest "Tex" Young (Gang Members), Chief Yowlachie, John War Eagle (Indians).

Rustlers of Devil's Canyon (Republic, 1947, 58 minutes) Associate Producer: Sidney Picker. Director: R.G. Springsteen. Screenplay: Earle Snell. Photography: William Bradford. Editor: Harry Keller. Music Director: Mort Glickman. Art Director: Frank Arrigo. Sound: Victor Appel. Sets: John McCarthy, Jr., & Otto Siegel. Makeup: Bob Mark. Special Effects: Howard & Theodore Lydecker. Assistant Director: Eddie Stein.

Cast: Allan Lane (Red Ryder), Bobby Blake (Little Beaver), Martha Wentworth (The Duchess), Peggy Stewart (Bess Glazier), Arthur Space (Dr. Coe), Emmett Lynn (Blizzard), Roy Barcroft (Clark), Tom London (Sheriff), Harry Carr (Ted Glazier), Pierce Lyden (Matt), Forrest Taylor (Dr. Glover), Frank O'Connor (Stableman), Bob Reeves (Frank), Art Dillard, Pascale Perry (Homesteaders), Cactus Mack (Deputy Sheriff), Jack Montgomery (Rider), Tom Smith (Gang Member).

Marshal of Cripple Creek (Republic, 1947, 56 minutes) Associate Producer: Sidney Picker. Director: R.G. Springsteen. Screenplay: Earle Snell. Photography: William Bradford. Editor: Harold R. Minter. Music Director: Mort Glickman. Art Director: Frank Arrigo. Sound: Victor Appel. Sets: John McCarthy, Jr., & Helen Hansard. Makeup: Bob Mark. Special Effects: Howard & Theodore Lydecker. Assistant Director: Eddie Stein.

Cast: Allan Lane (Red Ryder), Bobby Blake (Little Beaver), Martha Wentworth (The Duchess), Trevor Bardette (Tom Lambert), Tom London (Baker), Roy Barcroft (Link), Gene [Roth] Stutenroth (Long John Lacey), William Self (Dick Lambert), Helen Wallace (Mae Lambert), Budd Buster (Joe), Frank O'Connor (Informer), Art Dillard, Silver Harr, George Russell, Jack Sparks, Leonard Wood (Gang Members), Herman Hack (Robber).

Ride, Ryder, Ride (Eagle Lion, 1949, 58 minutes) Producer: Jerry Thomas. Executive Producer: Jack Schwartz. Director: Lewis D. Collins. Screenplay: Paul Franklin. Photography: Gilbert Warrenton. Editor: Joseph Gluck. Music Director: Darrell Calker. Music Supervisor: David Chudnow. Art Director: Fred W. Kline. Sound: Victor Appel. Sets: Vin Taylor. Production Manager: Bartlett [Bart] Carre. Makeup: Herbert Offord. Special Effects: Ray Mercer. Costumes: Vern Murdock. Color Consultant: Henry J. Staudigl. Assistant Director: Ralph Slosser.

Cast: Jim Bannon (Red Ryder), Little Brown Jug [Don Kay Reynolds] (Little Beaver), Emmett Lynn (Buckskin Blodgett), Marin Sais (The Duchess), Edwin Max (Frenchy Beaumont), Peggy Stewart (Libby Brooks), Steve Pendleton (Gerry Brooks), Enva Doyle (Marge), Jack O'Shea (Blackjack), Fred Coby (Henry W. Iverson), William Fawcett (Judge Prescott), Steve Clark (Tom), Billy Hammond (Pinto), Stanley Blystone (Sheriff), Oscar Gahan, Chick Hannon (Saloon Customers), Ray Jones, Roy Bucko, Fess Reynolds (Citizens).

Roll, Thunder, Roll (Eagle Lion, 1949, 58 minutes) Producer: Jerry Thomas. Associate Producer: Lincoln A. Widder. Director: Lewis D. Collins. Screenplay: Paul Franklin. Photography: Gilbert Warrenton. Editor: Frank Baldridge. Music: Ralph Stanley [Raoul Kraushaar]. Music Supervisor: David Chudnow. Art Director: Vin Taylor. Sound: Earl Snyder. Makeup: Vern Murdock. Costumes: Don Wakeling. Technical Director: Fred W. Kline. Dialogue Director: Gloria Welsch. Color Consultant: Henry J. Staudigl. Assistant Director: Ralph Slosser.

Cast: Jim Bannon (Red Ryder), Little Brown Jug [Don Kay Reynolds] (Little Beaver), Emmett Lynn (Buckskin Blodgett), Marin Sais (The Duchess), I. Stanford Jolley (El Conejo), Nancy Gates (Carol Loomis), Glenn Strange (Ace Hanlon), Lee Morgan

(Happy Loomis), Lane Bradford (Wolf), Steve Pendleton (Marshal Bill Faugh), Charles Stevens (Felipe), William Fawcett (Josh Culvert), Dorothy Latta (Dorothy Culvert), Joe Green (Pat), Rocky Shanan (Fake Red Ryder), Carol Henry (Gang Member), George Chesebro (Ben Garson), Jack O'Shea (Bartender), Frank Ellis (Rider), Frank O'Connor (Gambler), Fess Reynolds (Citizen).

The Fighting Redhead (Eagle Lion, 1949, 55 minutes) Producer: Jerry Thomas. Associate Producer: Bart Carre. Director: Lewis D. Collins. Screenplay: Paul Franklin & Jerry Thomas. Photography: Gilbert Warrenton. Editor: Joseph Gluck. Music: Darrell Calker. Music Supervisor: David Chudnow. Sound: Earl Synder. Sound Supervisor: Glen Glenn. Sets: Vin Taylor. Makeup: Jack Casey. Special Effects: Ray Mercer. Production Assistant: Fred W. Kline. Costumes: Don Wakeling. Dialogue Director: Gloria Welsch. Assistant Director: Ralph Slosser.

Cast: Jim Bannon (Red Ryder), Little Brown Jug [Don Kay Reynolds] (Little Beaver), Emmett Lynn (Buckskin Blodgett), Marin Sais (The Duchess), Peggy Stewart (Sheila O'Connor), John Hart (Faro Savage), Lane Bradford (Windy), Forrest Taylor (Dan O'Connor), Lee Roberts (Goldy Grant), Bob Duncan (Sheriff), Sandy Sanders (Joe), Billy Hammond (Bill Evans), Spooky Reynolds (Spooky Reynolds), Ray Jones, Fess Reynolds (Citizens).

Cowboy and the Prizefighter (Eagle Lion, 1949, 59 minutes) Producer-Screenplay: Jerry Thomas. Associate Producer: Bartlett [Bart] Carre. Director: Lewis D. Collins. Photography: Gilbert Warrenton. Editor: Joseph Gluck. Music: Raoul Kraushaar. Music Supervisor: David Chudnow. Sound: Glen Glenn. Sets: Vin Taylor. Makeup: Jack Casey. Production Assistant: Fred W. Kline. Costumes: Bert Offord. Dialogue Director: Gloria Welsch. Assistant Director: Joseph Wonder.

Cast: Jim Bannon (Red Ryder), Little Brown Jug [Don Kay Reynolds] (Little Beaver), Emmett Lynn (Buckskin Blodgett), Marin Sais (The Duchess), Don Haggerty (Steve Stevenson), Karen Randle (Sue Evans), John Hart (Mark Palmer), Lou Nova (Bull Mason), Lane Bradford (Duke Sampson), Marshal Reed (Bart Osborne), Forrest Taylor (Miles Stevenson), Frank Ellis (Sheriff), Bud Osborne (Ernie), Steve Clark (Sam), Frank O'Connor (Jack), Herman Hack (Timekeeper), Ray Jones (Audience Member), Fess Reynolds (Citizen).

RENFREW OF THE ROYAL MOUNTED

Films about the Canadian Royal Mounted Police had been audience pleasers since the silent days but it was not until Nelson Eddy popularized the singing Mountie in *Naughty Marietta* (1935) and *Rose-Marie* (1936) that the concept of such a hero was transposed to the movie series format. Producer Phil Goldstone's Criterion Pictures Corporation obtained the rights to Laurie York Erskine's popular "Renfrew of the Royal Mounted" books and planned a series of low-budget efforts about a singing hero. Sans music the character was also popular on radio in the "Renfrew of the Mounted" program which starred House Jameson in the title role; it ran from 1936 to 1940, the first season on CBS and the last three on NBC's Blue Network.

For the movie outings, Criterion cast radio and band singer James Newill as Sergeant Renfrew. Born in Pennsylvania in 1911, Newill studied music at the University of California and in 1930 joined the Los Angeles Light Opera Company, whose roster also included George Houston, who later headlined PRC's "The Lone Rider" (q.v.) series. Billed as Jimmy Newell, he was a vocalist for the bands of Gus Arnheim, Eddy Duchin and Abe Lyman, and he performed the same chore for a time on George Burns and Gracie Allen's CBS radio program. He was first heard on film dubbing Ross Alexander in Warner Bros.' *Ready, Willing and Able* in 1937. The same year he made a good impression as a vocalist in two Grand National features, *Sing While You're Able* and *Something To Sing About*, thus leading to his being cast as Renfrew. Throughout the "Renfrew" series, David Sharpe was his stunt double.

Grand National released the first film in the series, *Renfrew of the Royal Mounted*, late in 1937. It was based on Erskine's 1922 novel of the same title with Al Herman taking both producer and director credit. Shot on location at Big Bear Lake in Northern California, the film greatly benefited from its scenic locales and well as Newill's ingratiating interpretation of the role of Sergeant Renfrew. In addition, his fine baritone singing voice lent itself well to the film's musical numbers which include the song "Mounted Men" by Betty Laidlaw and Robert Lively. It proved popular enough to become the series theme and was sung in all the remaining "Renfrew" films by its star.

Renfrew of the Royal Mounted's plot was about counterfeiters smuggling funny money across the Canadian border into the United States via frozen rainbow trout. When G-men ask the Mounties to help with the investigation, Renfrew (Newill) is assigned to the case. When another Mountie (Donald Reed) is murdered by Pierre (Chief Thundercloud), a henchman of the crooks, Renfrew vows to the murdered man's little boy (Dickie Jones) that he will catch the killer. Renfrew's friend George Poulis (William Royle), manager of the Totem Pole Lodge, is the brains behind the counterfeiters. Also working for the gang are Angel (Kenneth Harlan) and neurotic Dreamy (David Barclay [Dave O'Brien]). They enlist the unwilling aid of former engraver Bronson (Herbert Corthell) and promise to bring his daughter Virginia (Carol Hughes) to the lodge. Renfrew meets Virginia at a barbeque and follows her to the lodge, where she finds out her father is being forced to work for the gang. Dreamy, who likes Bronson, tries to help him and Virginia escape, but Poulis and Angel catch them. They kill Dreamy and imprison the Bronsons in a meat locker. Poulis then pretends to lead Renfrew to the counterfeiters' headquarters in an attempt to kill him, but Renfrew foils the plan and rescues Virginia and her father. The gang is rounded up and Bronson is promised he will not be prosecuted because he engraved an SOS on the bills he counterfeited.

In this initial outing, the Mountie hero was aided by his canine pal, Lightning. Also of interest is Dave O'Brien, billed as David Barclay, in the role of Dreamy Nolan. He played the character in the same wild-eyed manner he used the same year in the exploitation classic *Tell Your Children*, which is better known as *Reefer Madness*. O'Brien's real name was David Poole Fronabarger but he changed it legally to David Barclay in 1936. He would appear in six more "Renfrew" entries, five of them in the role of the hero's best pal, Constable Kelly.

On the Great White Trail, also called *Renfrew on the Great White Trail*, was issued late in the summer of 1938. It was the first of three series features to be based on Erskine's 1931 novel *Renfrew Rides North* and again Al Herman received both producer and director credit. The plot has Renfrew (Newill) assigned to escort Kay Larkin (Terry Walker) to a remote outpost to join her father, fur trader Andrew Larkin (Robert Frazer). Renfrew's commanding officer, Inspector Newcombe (Richard Tucker), has received word that a Mountie and Larkin's partner have both been found murdered and that Larkin is the main suspect. At first Kay does not like Renfrew. On their journey they are attacked by two thugs (Phil McCullough, Charles King) but they manage to escape and make it to their destination where Renfrew plans to arrest Larkin. With the aid of his dog Silver King, Renfrew sets up a ruse involving a local doctor (Richard Alexander), who has become a drunk, and is able to identify the real killer and his motive. During the proceedings, Newill sang the series theme "Mounted Men" along with "Je T'aime" and "Beautiful." *Variety* called it a "poor follow-up" to the initial "Renfrew" outing.

Criterion Pictures produced two more series films, *Fighting Mad* and *Crashing Thru*, for Grand National but the company folded in 1939 and a year after the release of *On the Great White Trail*, Criterion signed a deal with Monogram to release the two already made features plus four more. Thus the two finished films were issued by Monogram almost simultaneously in December, 1939, followed the next month by a fifth "Renfrew" affair, *Yukon Flight*.

Fighting Mad contained two new songs, "Trail's End" and "The Lady's in Distress," and it told of robbery witness Ann Fenwick (Sally Blane) being abducted by the crooks (Warner Richmond, Ted Adams) and being taken to Canada. When the trailer she is riding in breaks away and plunges into a lake, she is rescued by Renfrew (Newill) and Constable Kelly (Dave O'Brien). When Renfrew recognizes Ann from her picture on a wanted poster, she escapes and hides out in a cabin belonging to trading post operator Benny (Benny Rubin). Renfrew finds her but the crooks take him prisoner. Ann agrees to lead them to where she hid their stolen money in exchange for Renfrew's life. This was the first

"Renfrew" entry to feature O'Brien in the running role of Constable Kelly and was based on the 1927 novel *Renfrew Rides Again*.

Although *Fighting Mad* was officially released before *Crashing Thru*, it is probable the latter was the first to be produced. In it Renfrew's (Newill) pal is Corporal Kelly, played by Warren Hull. Dave O'Brien also appears, this time in the role of the heroine's brother. Milburn Stone is the lead villain, the same type of part he did in *Fighting Mad*. Here Renfrew and Kelly are taken prisoners aboard a steamer which is held up for its gold shipment belonging to mining company owner Herrington (Milburn Stone). Fellow passengers Ann Chambers (Jean Carmen) and her brother Fred (O'Brien) claim Herrington himself was behind the theft because he stole their father's gold mine. Renfrew and Kelly chase one of the robbers (Walter Byron) into the mountains but Kelly is shot and they have to return to town. There Renfrew arrests Ann for the robbery but she convinces him of her innocence and they set up a plot to trap Herrington and his gang. Again two new tunes, "Crimson Sunset" and "Easy on the Eyes," were featured and *Variety* proclaimed, "Good action film of the north in the Renfrew mountie series, with plenty of shooting, suspense, agreeable romantic flavor and a fist fight in a cabin among several men that has been very effectively staged."

With the first two Monogram releases, Philip N. Krasner took producer credit and he would continue to do so for the three "Renfrew" entries, which began with *Yukon Flight*, issued early in 1940. Ralph Staub directed the feature, as he would also do with *Danger Ahead* and *Sky Bandits*.

Left: Advertisement for *Renfrew of the Royal Mounted* (Grand National, 1937). **Above:** Advertisement for *Crashing Thru* (Monogram, 1939).

The second of three series features to be based on the 1931 novel *Renfrew Rides North*, *Yukon Flight* has Renfrew (Newill) investigating a plane crash which killed a pilot friend. He deduces that the owner (William Pawley) of the airline mail service is involved after he testifies the pilot was drunk. When Louise's (Louise Stanley) mine superintendent is murdered and an offer is made by the air service owner's friend (Karl Hackett) to buy her mine, Renfrew comes to believe that the two men are hijacking the gold shipments and flying them into the United States. After a shootout with the gang, he stows away on one of the air mail flights. Dave O'Brien resumed the role of Kelly and Warren Hull, who had the part in *Crashing Thru*, is cast as a pilot who helps Renfrew solve the case. Newill sings "My Weakness Is Eyes of Blue," "Mounted Men Are On Parade" and "The Old Grey Goose." *Variety* dubbed it, "Best of the Renfrew adventures screened to date...."

Danger Ahead, released in March, 1940, diminished the musical interludes with Newill singing on "Spare the Rod" in addition to the over-the-credits title song "Mounted Men." Based on the 1932 novel *Renfrew's Long Trail*, it had Renfrew (Newill) and Kelly (O'Brien) nearly getting killed when a truck they are driving is sabotaged (faulty brakes). The two are looking into the disappearance of an armored car gold shipment and due to the accident are able to find the missing vehicle submerged in a lake, but without the gold it was supposed to carry. The RCMP inspector's (Guy Usher) daughter Genevieve (Dorothea Kent) suspects Maxwell (Dick Rich), the owner of the armored car company, of being behind the thefts and Renfrew sets out to prove she is correct.

The 1931 novel *Renfrew Rides North* was for the third time the basis of another series entry, *Murder on the Yukon*, released in the spring of 1940. For this one, Johnny Lange, Lew Porter and Vick Knight wrote "Ah, Here's to Romance" and "Down the Yukon Trail" for Newill to sing; the di-

Poster for *Yukon Flight* (Monogram, 1939).

rection was handled by veteran Louis Gasnier, who had directed Dave O'Brien in *Tell Your Children* (*Reefer Madness*) in 1938. The leading lady was Polly Ann Young, whose sister, Sally Blane, had the same chore in the earlier *Fighting Mad*. Here Renfrew (Newill) and Kelly (O'Brien) are on vacation in the mountains where they find the body of murdered miner Jim Smithers (Budd Buster). After the dead man's brother is also found dead, Renfrew discovers fake money and deduces the two men were victims of counterfeiters. Kelly trails an Indian (Chief Thundercloud) to the crooks' headquarters but is captured. Renfrew spots the gang and retrieves the stolen money hidden in fur pelts. The gang captures Renfrew, but Kelly escapes with the aid of Jean (Polly Ann Young), the partner of the trading post owner

(William Royle), who is behind the crimes, and the two Mounties bring the gang to justice.

For the only time in the series, Criterion Pictures owner Phil Goldstone took producer credit for *Sky Bandits*, the final "Renfrew" entry. Taken from the 1928 novel *Renfrew Rides the Skies*, the film got little notice at the time of its release but today it may be the best known of the series films, due to its sci-fi subplot and the casting of horror film favorite Dwight Frye in a featured role. (Frye in fact appeared in both the first and last "Renfrew" films; *Renfrew of the Royal Mounted* gave him the small role of a hotel desk clerk.) Here he was Speavy, part of a gang of hijackers who force a professor (Joseph Stefani) to use his death ray to bring down planes carrying gold shipments. The story had Renfrew (Newill) and Kelly (O'Brien) looking into a series of mysterious crashes of planes carrying bullion from the Yukon Mining Company. Smuggler Morgan (Bill [William] Pawley) and his gang get coded messages via the radio from children's show host Uncle Dinwiddie (Dewey Robinson) and then force the professor to use his ray machine to bring down the planes so the gang can get the gold. Renfrew finds the operation but when he returns with reinforcements, the headquarters are vacant. With the professor's daughter (Louise Stanley) as a stowaway, Renfrew takes to the skies in order to unravel the mystery. Morgan orders the professor to shoot down their plane but the scientist instead turns his invention on the crooks.

Following the demise of the "Renfrew" series, Newill appeared as a singer in *The Great American Broadcast* in 1941 and had a dramatic role in *The Falcon's Brother* in 1942. That year he and Dave O'Brien re-teamed for PRC's "The Texas Rangers" (q.v.) series. In 1953 the two teamed again for the television series *Renfrew of the Royal Mounted*, which was syndicated in thirteen half-hour shows. Newill and O'Brien repeated their Renfrew and Kelly roles and the series utilized stock footage from the Criterion features. Louise Stanley, the leading lady in *Yukon Flight* and *Sky Bandits*, was featured as Renfrew's girlfriend, Carol Girard. Newill told John Brooker in *Film Collectors Registry* (March–April, 1972), "My ap-

Right: Advertisement for *Sky Bandits* (Monogram, 1940).

pearance had changed very little at that time and our new footage fitted OK with the old, but the producers spoiled the show's chances of big success by cutting every corner possible. I was part owner of the series, but I later sold my interest back to the producers, bought a ranch in the mountains and literally took to the woods."

Filmography

Renfrew of the Royal Mounted (Grand National, 1937; 57 minutes) Producer-Director: Al [Albert] Herman. Assistant Producer: Gordon S. Griffith. Screenplay: Charles Logue. Story: Laurie York Erskine. Photography: Francis Corby. Editor: Holbrook N. Todd. Production Manager: Harold Lewis. Music Supervisor: Arthur Kay. Sound: Glenn Rominger. Song: Robert Lively & Betty Laidlaw.

Cast: James Newill (Renfrew), Carol Hughes (Virginia Bronson), William Royle (George Poulis), Herbert Corthell (James Bronson), Kenneth Harlan (Roger "Angel" Carroll), Dickie Jones (Tommy MacDonald), [Chief] Thundercloud (Pierre), William Austin (Constable Holly), Donald Reed (Constable MacDonald), William Gould (Inspector Newcomb), David Barclay [Dave O'Brien] (Charles "Dreamy" Nolan), Robert [Bob] Terry (Duke), Forrest Taylor (Customs Agent), Dwight Frye (Desk Clerk), Earl Douglas (Mountie Constable), Marin Sais (Mrs. MacDonald), Arthur Millett (John), Otto Hoffman (Citizen), Buck Morgan (Henchman), Lightning the Dog (Himself).

On the Great White Trail (Grand National, 1938; 58 minutes) Producer-Director: Al [Albert] Herman. Screenplay: Joseph F. Poland & Charles Logue. Story: Laurie York Erskine. Photography: Ira Morgan. Editor: Duke Goldstone. Art Director: Fred Preble. Songs: Robert Lively, Betty Laidlaw & Bob Taylor. Sound: Corson Jowett.

Cast: James Newill (Renfrew), Terry Walker (Kay Larkin), Robert Frazer (Andrew Larkin), Richard Alexander (Dr. Howe), Richard Tucker (Inspector Newcombe), Robert [Bob] Terry (Sergeant Kelly), Eddie Gribbon (Constable Patsy), Walter McGrail (Garou), Philo McCullough (Williams), Charles King (LaGrange), Juan Duval (Pierre), Victor Potel (Parker), Roger Williams (Henchman), Herman Hack (Trapper), Carl Mathews (Indian Joe), Wally West, Gene Alsace, Bruce Warren, Jimmy Aubrey (Mounties), Silver King the Dog (Himself).

Also called *Renfrew on the Great White Trail.*

Fighting Mad (Monogram, 1939; 60 minutes) Producer: Philip N. Krasne. Director: Sam Newfield. Screenplay: George Rosener & John Rathmell, from the novel *Renfrew Rides Again* by Laurie York Erskine. Photography: Jack Greenhalgh. Editor: Martin G. Cohn. Songs: Robert Lively, Betty Laidlaw & Jack Brooks.

Cast: James Newill (Renfrew), Sally Blane (Ann Fenwick), Benny Rubin (Benny), Dave O'Brien (Constable Kelly), Milburn Stone (Cardigan), Walter Long (Frenchy), Warner Richmond (Trigger), Ted Adams (Leon), Chief Thundercloud (Wolf), Ole Olson (Joe), Horace Murphy (Smith).

Crashing Thru (Monogram, 1939; 65 minutes) Producer: Philip N. Krasne. Director: Elmer Clifton. Screenplay: Sherman L. Lowe, from the novel *Renfrew Rides the Range* by Laurie York Erskine. Photography: Edward Linden. Editor: S. Roy Luby. Songs: Robert Lively, Betty Laidlaw, Jack Brooks & Jules Loman. Sound: Hans Weeren. Assistant Director: Vincent Taylor.

Cast: James Newill (Renfrew), Warren Hull (Constable Kelly), Jean Carmen (Ann "Angel" Chambers), Milburn Stone (Delos Herrington), Walter Byron (McClusky), Stanley Blystone (Jim La Monte), Robert Frazer (Dr. Smith), Joseph Girard (Steamboat Captain), Dave O'Brien (Fred Chambers), Earl Douglas (Slant Eye), Ted Adams (Eskimo Pete), Roy Barcroft (Green), Iron Eyes Cody (Indian Joe), Horace Murphy (Boat Passenger), Wally West (Officer).

Yukon Flight (Monogram, 1940; 58 minutes) Producer: Philip N. Krasne. Director: Ralph Staub. Screenplay: Edward Halperin. Photography: Mack Stengler. Editor: Martin G. Cohn. Songs: Hy Heath, Johnny Lange, Lew Porter, Robert Lively & Betty Laidlaw. Assistant Director: Ben Chapman.

Cast: James Newill (Renfrew), Warren Hull (Bill Shipley), Louise Stanley (Louise Howard), William Pawley (Yuke Gradeau), Dave O'Brien (Constable Kelly), George Humbert (Nick), Karl Hackett (Mr. Raymond), Jack Clifford (Whispering Smith), Roy Barcroft (Lodin), Bob Terry (De Long), Earl Douglas (Smokie Joe), Ernie Adams (Henry), Jack Rutherford (James Benton), Eddie Fetherston (Rufe George).

Danger Ahead (Monogram, 1940; 60 minutes) Producer: Philip N. Krasne. Director: Ralph Staub. Screenplay: Edward Halperin, from the novel *Renfrew's Long Trail* by Laurie York Erskine. Photography: Mack Stengler. Editor: Martin G. Cohn. Song: Robert Lively, Betty Laidlaw, Johnny Lange & Lew Porter. Assistant Director: Ben Chapman.

Cast: James Newill (Renfrew), Dorothea Kent (Genevieve), Guy Usher (Inspector), Maude Allen (Mrs. Hill), Harry Depp (Jones), John Dilson (Thomas Hatch), Al Shaw (Yorgeson), Dave O'Brien (Sergeant Kelly), Dick Rush (Maxwell), Bob Terry (Gimpy), Lester Dorr (Lefty), Earl Douglas (Egg Face), David Sharpe (George Hill).

Murder on the Yukon (Monogram, 1940; 58 minutes) Producer: Philip N. Krasne. Director: Louis Gasnier. Screenplay: Milton Raison, from the story "Renfrew Rides North" by Laurie York Erskine. Photography: Elmer Dyer. Editor: Guy V. Thayer, Jr.

Music: Johnny Lange, Lew Porter & Vick Knight. Song: Robert Lively & Betty Laidlaw. Assistant Director: Ben Chapman.

Cast: James Newill (Renfrew), Polly Ann Young (Joan Manning), Dave O'Brien (Constable Kelly), Al St. John (Bill Smithers), William Royle (George Weathers), Chief Thundercloud (Monti), Karl Hackett (Hawks), Snub Pollard (Archie), Kenne Duncan (Tom), Earl Douglas (Steve), Budd Buster (Jim Smithers), Jack Clifford (Whispering Smith), Frank Campeau (Customer), Gertrude Chorre (Squaw).

Sky Bandits (Monogram, 1940; 62 minutes) Producer: Phil Goldstone. Director: Ralph Staub. Screenplay: Edward Halperin, from the novel *Renfrew Rides the Sky* by Laurie York Erskine. Photography: Mack Stengler. Editor: Martin G. Cohn. Assistant Director: Ben Chapman.

Cast: James Newill (Renfrew), Louise Stanley (Madeleine Lewis), Dave O'Brien (Constable Kelly), Bill [William] Pawley (Morgan), Ted Adams (Gary), Bob Terry (Hutchins), Dwight Frye (Speavy), Joseph Stefani [Joe De Stefani] (Professor Burton Lewis), Dewey Robinson (Dinwiddie), Jack Clifford (Whispering Smith), Jim [James] Farley (Inspector Warner), Karl Hackett (Hawthorne), Kenne Duncan (Brownie), Eddie Fetherston (Buzz Murphy), Don Brodie (Radio Operator), Harry Harvey (Greaseball), Snub Pollard, Marin Sais (Married Couple), Earl Douglas (Henchman).

THE ROUGH RIDERS

Following the success of the "Hopalong Cassidy" (q.v.) series at Paramount and "The Three Mesquiteers" (q.v.) at Republic, Monogram Pictures initiated its own triad hero concept with "The Rough Riders," starring Buck Jones, Tim McCoy and Raymond Hatton as the three leads. The trio headlined eight features during the 1941–42 theatrical season and Jones and Hatton played their parts in a final 1942 release, *Dawn on the Great Divide*, for a total of nine series outings. These features, as a whole, were very popular with fans and exhibitors. In a cinematograph on Tim McCoy published in *Views and Reviews* (Spring 1971), Jon Tuska stated, "They were the finest Westerns Monogram was associated with up to that time, and probably the best they ever would release."

The series was the brainchild of Monogram production supervisor Scott R. Dunlap, who with Buck Jones formed the production company that made the "Rough Riders" features. Dunlap and Jones had first worked together two decades before at Fox and by the time the series was produced Dunlap was also serving as the star's business manager. Adele Buffington, using the pseudonym Jess Bowers, did the scripts, Harry Neumann served as cinematographer and Edward Kay scored the features and composed "Rough Riders' Song," a rousing number sung by a male chorus over the opening credits of each film. The features were each shot in a week's time and were budgeted between $60,000 and $70,000. McCoy was paid $4,000 for each film while Jones got a percentage of the gross. Monogram even built a western town set for the productions at Prescott, Arizona.

McCoy had just finished a series for PRC when he signed to do "The Rough Riders," having previously headlined the "Lightning Bill Carson" (q.v.) films for Victory Pictures. Jones, on the other hand, had not starred in a cowboy series since the demise of his Columbia contract in 1938 although he had headlined the non-oater *Unmarried* for Paramount that year and co-starred as the villain in Republic's *Wagons Westward* (1939). In 1941 he appeared in two fifteen-chapter serials, starring in Columbia's *White Eagle* and co-starring in Universal's *Riders of Death Valley*. Hatton joined the series after having enacted the role of Rusty Joslin in nine episodes of "The Three Mesquiteers."

A native of Indiana, Jones (1891–1942) began appearing in films in 1918 after being in the military and working in Wild West shows. By the next year he was supporting Franklyn Farnum in a western series for Canyon Pictures; in 1920 he began starring in oaters for Fox, where he first worked with Scott R. Dunlap. In 1922 he acquired his famous horse Silver and as the decade progressed he rivaled the studio's chief star, Tom

Buck Jones, Tim McCoy and Raymond Hatton as "The Rough Riders."

Mix, in popularity. Jones did not renew his Fox contract in 1928 and instead produced *The Big Hop*, which was a financial failure, as was his "The Buck Jones Wild West Show and Roundup Days." With the coming of sound, Dunlap signed Jones to appear in features for Sol Lesser's Beverly Productions, which were released by Columbia. It was during this period that Jones made some of Hollywood's finest "B" westerns and in 1931 he signed exclusively with Columbia and stayed with the studio until 1934, even headlining some non-westerns. He then joined Universal, where he made 22 features and four serials, all westerns, before going back to Columbia for a half-dozen oaters in 1938. In 1936 the *Motion Picture Herald* poll of top moneymaking western stars listed him in the number one position. Dunlap (1892–1970), the son of actress Louise Dunlap, started as an actor in films in 1915 and four years later began directing, doing nearly 50 features, mostly westerns, as well as scriptwriting, until the coming of sound. After that he became a talent scout and Jones' financial manager, before going to work at Monogram as a producer.

The series kicked off with *Arizona Bound*, released in the summer of 1941. It opens with Buck Roberts (Jones), a retired U.S. marshal, enjoying the quiet life at his Arizona ranch when he receives a summons from Marshal Bat Madison (Bob Baker) to look into trouble in Mesa City. There he discovers Ruth Masters (Luana Walters) is about to lose her Wells Fargo contract because of constant attacks on her stagecoach by the outlaws who murdered her father. In the latest raid, her fiancé, Joe Brooke (Dennis Moore), is injured and his cargo of miners' gold stolen. Saloon operator Steve Taggert (Tristram Coffin) is behind the holdups in an effort to get control of Mesa City but he is unhappy to run into Buck, who once put him in prison. Also new in town is Parson Tim McCall (McCoy), who is dismayed to find Taggert's saloon open on the Sabbath. When Taggert's henchmen poke fun at the preacher, he forces them to back off at gunpoint and then beats the crook at his own game by winning a poker game with the saloon man's crooked deck and making him promise to build a new church in town. Hearing of Ruth's financial woes, Buck offers to drive her next gold shipment by taking a shortcut through Eagle Rock Pass but Taggert and his men hold up the stage, take the strongbox and make it look like Buck is a gang member. Buck is put in jail but escapes with the aid of cattle seller Sandy Hopkins (Hatton). Tim shows Ruth and Joe that Buck put rocks in the strongbox, with the gold remaining in the express office. Buck, Tim and Sandy, who are really undercover lawmen called the Rough Riders, formulate a plan to defeat the crooks. Buck runs a herd of horses through the town and then captures the gang, which is hold up in the saloon, as Tim captures two outlaws who have taken over the express office. Taggert tries to escape but is followed and shot by Buck. The Rough Riders then turn the gang over to Madison as Ruth and Joe plan to get married.

Arizona Bound was a nicely paced and entertaining effort that established some of the ground rules for the series. The three stars played lawmen who had once worked as a team in the past and who reunited for special assignments. At each film's end, the three would part, with Buck going back to his ranch in Texas, Tim to his spread in Wyoming and Sandy back home to marry a pretty widow. Buck's character also had the habit of chewing gum when angry. McCoy was featured in one of the film's best scenes in which his parson character forces a saloon full of crooks at gunpoint to sing "Bury Me Not on the Lone Prairie." Unfortunately there was a *faux pas* in the sequence as Tim fired a warning shot which broke some piano keys but when the scene concludes the piano is shown to be intact.

Next came *The Gunman from Bodie*, issued in the fall of 1941. Like the first outing it was directed by serial veteran Spencer Gordon Bennet. This one opened during a thunderstorm with Buck (Jones) taking refuge at a ranch house where he finds a murdered couple and their infant (Frederick Gee). He also locates a note written by the baby's mother before she died, implicating Bill Cook (John Merton) as one of the killers. After burying the couple the next day, Buck takes the baby to the neighboring ranch of Alice Borden (Christine McIntyre), who has returned home to the Circle B ranch following the killing of her father by marauders. She hires Joe Martin (Dave O'Brien), whose father was also murdered by the outlaws, as her new foreman. When Buck appears she takes custody of the baby, as he shows her the note naming Cook. Her father's lawyer, Wyatt (Robert Frazer), who owns the Larabee Land and Water Company, is disappointed when he learns that Alice will not sell her ranch to Jud Mason (Frank LaRue), who is cahoots with Wyatt in trying to acquire all the water rights in the area. As the ranch's new cook Sandy (Hatton) prepares a meal for Buck, Marshal McCall (McCoy) arrives at the ranch looking for outlaw Bodie Bronson, whom Alice and Joe recognize as Buck from his wanted poster. Although Joe tells the marshal about Cook, he does not reveal Bodie's presence at the ranch; Bronson then helps Cook break jail. In Larabee, Tim arrested Cook and placed him in the local jail although the sheriff (Max Waizman) works for Wyatt, who is the gang's leader. Bodie then ingratiates himself with Wyatt and takes over running the gang, much to the chagrin of former head Steve Dunn (Charles King). Disobeying Bodie's orders, Steve tries to rustle cattle from the Borden ranch and shoots Joe, whom Bodie takes back to the ranch house. Steve then tries to rob Wyatt's safe, thinking his boss has cheated him, and is shot by Tim. Sandy, who is really working with Buck and Tim as an undercover marshal, informs McCall about Joe being shot and they form a posse and go after Bodie, Wyatt and their men. Buck as Bodie, however, leads the outlaws into a blind canyon where they are captured by the lawmen.

Even better than its predecessor, *The Gunman from Bodie* gave Jones and McCoy good roles, although Hatton had little to do as the ranch cook. Buck was at his best in the tender scenes he shared with the orphaned infant and in the guise of outlaw Bodie Bronson, where he is particularly good in a showdown with gang member Charles King. King also was in one of McCoy's best scenes in the picture where the lawman is forced to kill the outlaw in the dark as he robs the utility company safe. An even better scene for McCoy occurred earlier in the film when he meets up with murderer Joe Cook in a saloon and meticulously details a hanging he witnessed as the killer slowly crumbles mentally.

Forbidden Trails, issued in December, 1941, "added considerable stunting and running inserts, elaborate truck shots, and excellent action photography to the series, and it would remain a staple of all the later entries" (Jon Tuska, *Views and Reviews*, Spring, 1971). The film opened in a penitentiary where prisoners Fulton (Charles King) and Joe Howard (Bud Osborne) vow to take revenge on the former U.S. marshal who sent them there, Buck (Jones), who has now retired to his Arizona ranch. Upon release, the two go to Yucca City where they meet their former partner, Jim Cramer (Dave O'Brien), a widower with two young children. Jim, who runs a freight company and plans to wed his employee Mary Doran (Christine McIntyre), wants no part of Fulton and Howard's plans since Buck took care of his children while he was in prison and got him an early parole. The crooks set a trap for Buck by dousing a remote cabin with kerosene, enticing him there and setting the building on fire. Buck manages to escape with the help of his horse Silver but is badly injured. His foreman, Steve Bunion (Hal Price), asks Buck's former lawmen partners, rancher Tim (McCoy) and Sandy (Hatton), who is about to be wed, to come to his aid. After meeting with Buck, Tim and Sandy go to Yucca City where Sandy pretends to be a teamster and Tim a gambler. Getting a job as a faro dealer at Ed Nelson's (Tristram Coffin) Red Moon Saloon, Tim spots Fulton and Howard, who work for Nelson. Sandy gets the two crooks to think he hates Buck, who arrives on the scene after Fulton accuses Tim of cheating. Sandy helps Fulton to escape from the saloon as Nelson tries to blackmail Jim into taking him as a partner or he will reveal Cramer's criminal past to Mary. When both men sign a contract, Buck arrests Nelson as Tim and Sandy round up Fulton and the remainder of Nelson's gang. The three partners again part ways, although Sandy is apprehensive about returning home to his jilted fiancée (Marin Sais). The feature was the final directorial effort of Robert North Bradbury, the father of Bob Steele. Incidentally, the first film on which Buck Jones and Scott R. Dunlap worked was also called *Forbidden Trails*. It was a 1920 Fox release that was Jones' second starring effort and it was written and directed by Dunlap.

The first 1942 series release, January's *Below the Border*, was directed by Howard Bretherton, who would helm the rest of the series, and told of U.S. Marshal Buck (Jones), masquerading as John Robbins, going to Border City to find out who murdered one of his colleagues, Marshal Ted Jordan. When the stagecoach he is riding is robbed, he tells Maria Garcia (Eva Puig) and her niece Rosita (Linda Brent) to give up their valuable jewels rather than be murdered. When they get to town, Rosita calls him a coward. Also arriving in the Mexican border community is Buck's partner Tim (McCoy), a supposed cattle buyer who contacts the third Rough Rider, Sandy (Hatton), who is working incognito for Border City Saloon proprietor Ed Scully (Roy Barcroft). After the three meet and form a plan of action, Robbins announces that the robbers will have to fence the stolen gems through him in order to get them sold. Tim goes to the Garcia ranch to sell cattle and meets foreman Joe Collins (Dennis Moore), who is in love with Rosita. Collins, who has been working with the gang which is led by Scully and Steve Slade (Charles King), tries to get back the jewels for Rosita but Slade, who is really wanted outlaw Blackie Johnson, gets the drop on him and forces him to stay with the gang. Meanwhile, Sandy tells the local sheriff (Jack Rockwell) that Robbins is a wanted outlaw as Buck ingratiates himself with Scully and takes over running the gang, much to Slade's chagrin.

Advertisement for *Forbidden Trails* (Monogram, 1941).

Poster for *Below the Border* (Monogram, 1942).

the outlaw. The Rough Riders then go after Scully and his gang with Tim and Sandy rounding up the outlaws as Buck chases Scully, who tries to escape with the jewels. Cornering the crook in the gang's cave, Buck arrests Scully and retrieves the gems that are returned to the Garcia family. Joe, who has only been wounded, promises to become honest as the Rough Riders return to their various homes. There is a mike boom shadow on the wall during a scene at the Garcia ranch. The feature reused the finale from *Arizona Bound* with the three Rough Riders going different trails back to their ranches.

Next came the spooky and atmospheric *Ghost Town Law*, which many consider the highlight of the series. Released in March 1942, it had the Rough Riders (Jones, McCoy, Hatton) investigating the killing of two of their comrades in the deserted town of Pickwick. Upon arrival, Tim finds out the town's founder, Nell Pickwick, has been murdered and that her relative, Ted Hall (Eddie Phillips), has disappeared. Nell owned the Lucky Hunch gold mine that she left to her niece Josie Hall (Virginia Carpenter); Tim helps her and miner Luke Martin (Milburn Morante) search for Ted. Sandy, pretending to be a prospector, comes to see Martin, and Buck also shows up at Josie's homestead, claiming to have lost his memory. He is permitted to stay by Josie and Tom Cook (Howard Masters), her foreman. During the night a phantom-like figure tries to steal Buck's money as well as gold belonging to Nell. Although Buck tells Josie to get away from Pickwick, she and Luke go to the mine looking for her brother. The Rough Riders learn that Judge Crail (Murdock MacQuarrie) is the next heir to the Pickwick properties. When he finds out they know he is in cahoots with outlaw Red Larkin (Ben Corbett) and his gang, the judge tries to shoot them. Although several of his cohorts die in a gunfight with the lawmen, Crail gets away and warns Larkin and his men, who have captured Josie and Luke. Cook manages to get the two free and the

Slade disobeys Buck's orders and rustles from the Garcia ranch and shoots Joe, who tells Tim it was Slade who murdered Gordon and that his gang has the jewels. While Rosita thinks Tim shot Joe, the sheriff arrests Buck for rustling the Garcia cattle. Tim overhears Slade tell Scully the jewels are at the gang's mine hideout and that Buck is an imposter. Meanwhile, the sheriff aids Buck in escaping jail. In a showdown with Slade, Buck kills

Rough Riders round up Crail, Larkin and the rest of their gang. They prove Larkin and his men murdered the two marshals and Ted Hall. With much of the film's action taking place in an eerie mansion, a maze of mine tunnels and a ghost town, *Variety* complained, "So much mystery surrounds the early part of the film, which is shot in shadow and inky blackness, that the story loses much of its effectiveness and becomes boresome. The speeding up of the action at the end of the film is insufficient to overcome its early faults and the improbable story." The trade paper also noted, "Much of the early mystery is never cleared up. Masked cowboys prowling in black shadows, and sudden attempts at killings are all tossed into the melting plot without much rhyme or reason."

Down Texas Way, which came to theaters in May 1942, found ex–Rough Rider Sandy (Hatton) settled down and running a hotel. He invites his former partners, ranchers Buck (Jones) and Tim (McCoy), to join him in celebrating his birthday but before they show up he is accused of murdering his friend, businessman John Dodge (Jack Daley). Outlaw Burt Logan (Harry Woods), who plans to take over the area with his gang, is the killer and Sandy tries to find him but is captured and held hostage in a cabin with Ann Dodge (Lois Austin), the estranged wife of the murdered man. In reality, the woman is Stella, who is working with Logan. Tim arrives in town and Mary Hopkins (Luana Walters), Sandy's niece, asks him to help her uncle, as she is engaged to Dave Dodge (Dave O'Brien), John's son. Pretending to be an ex-convict, Buck finds the cabin where Sandy is being held captive. Stella then helps Sandy get free and they head for town where Tim prevents his hanging and turns him over to the sheriff (Glenn Strange), who puts him in protective custody. Since Sandy owed John Dodge the final payment on his hotel, Dave comes to believe that Sandy murdered his father and he also learns that Ann Dodge is coming back to town to claim her husband's property. Buck uses a ruse to get Logan to reveal his plans and during a shootout with the gang, Logan manages to make a getaway. Dave trails Logan to an old mine where they engage in a fight with Logan being shot. The other outlaws go to the mine but are followed by Buck and Tim, who place them under arrest. Back in town, Stella is jailed and Sandy is given his freedom. The Rough Riders head back to their homes but promise to come back when Dave and Mary are wed.

In the late summer of 1942 the seventh series entry, *Riders of the West*, was issued. Taking place in Red Bluff, Wyoming, it had ranches being attacked by a gang, resulting in the owners not making their mortgage payments. One of the ranchers, Ma Turner (Sarah Padden), complains to cattleman John Holt (Robert Frazer) about the situation and he announces he is calling in a range investigator. Holt, however, plans to kidnap the lawman and replace him with an imposter since he is in cahoots with banker Miller (Walter McGrail) and the local sheriff (Lee Phelps) in trying to take over the fertile valley. Not trusting Holt, Ma sends for Buck (Jones) to look into the raids and he enlists the aid of Tim (McCoy) and Sandy (Hatton). Riding into Red Bluff, Buck and Tim see outlaws attacking a stagecoach carrying Jim Dodge (Ed Peil, Sr.), the investigator sent for by Holt. Dodge is saved by Tim while Buck rounds up the gang and unsuccessfully tries to get the truth out of them. Back in town, Holt finds out that Miller and Duke Mason (Harry Woods), the proprietor of the local saloon, plan to double-cross him and when he draws on them he is murdered by the sheriff. Holt's son Steve (Dennis Moore) then kills the lawman and is arrested by Buck after Miller claims John Holt was behind the lawlessness. Assuming the guise of the investigator, Tim comes to town and informs Mason he is a wanted outlaw and that he is taking over Holt's percentage of the gang's take. Red (Bud Osborne), one of Ma Turner's men who is actually working for Miller, learns the real investigator is hiding out on her ranch and he informs Miller and gang leader Hogan (Charles King). The two crooks decide to trap Tim by letting him join the outlaws; Tim tells Hogan he will break Steve out of jail. Carrying out the jailbreak, Tim gives him to Hogan who has ordered Buck's murder. Sandy finds out where Steve is being taken as Buck captures Red, who is shot by one of the gang before he can talk. Buck and Sandy head for the outlaw's lair where Tim and Steve, who was not aware of his father's activities, are being held prisoners. The two are set free by Buck and Sandy and the lawmen then trail Miller and Duke into Red Bluff where Tim nabs Mason and Buck forces

Miller to destroy the mortgages owed by the ranchers. With the outlaws arrested, Ma Turner is made acting sheriff and the Rough Riders go their separate ways.

The last Rough Riders outing with Jones, McCoy and Hatton was *West of the Law*, which came out in the autumn of 1942. Here the U.S. marshals (Jones, McCoy, Hatton) investigate a gang pulling off rustling and stagecoach holdups in the Gold Creek area. Opposing the lawlessness is newspaper editor Rufus Todd (Milt Moranti [Milburn Morante]) and his daughter Julie (Evelyn Cooke), their friend, businessman John Corbett (Jack Daley), and Julie's fiancé Ray Mason (Bud McTaggart). Rufus believes Red Diamond Saloon owners Jim Rand (Harry Woods) and Ludlow (Roy Barcroft) are behind the outlaw gang and denounces them in his newspaper, although the real culprit is Corbett. After his newspaper office is dynamited and his press destroyed, Todd sends for federal marshals. When Ray drives an ore shipment through Eagle's Pass, he is attacked and wounded by the gang but is saved by Buck. Rufus accuses Rand and Ludlow of the crimes but Tim, claiming to be a minister, arrives and stops the crooks from bothering him. Pretending to be an undertaker, Sandy rents office space from Rand. Buck and Sandy reveal their identities to Todd, as Sandy unveils a new printing press hidden in his coffins. After Buck tells Rufus to print a story saying the name of the real gang leader will be revealed in his next edition, Roberts takes the guise of outlaw Rocky Saunders and captures Tim, whom he claims is a lawman. Buck forces the saloon owners to make him a partner in their holdups and with Tim he goes with them to their hideout, a gold mine. When the newspaper comes out naming him the gang leader, Corbett confronts Rufus as Buck is taken prisoner by Rand and Ludlow who want him to take them to Ray's ore shipment wagon. Tim and Sandy, who have taken over the gang's hideout, free Buck, who then rides to Gold Creek and stops Corbett from killing Todd. In a shootout, Buck is forced to shoot Corbett. With the gang in jail, the Rough Riders return to their ranches.

While producer Scott R. Dunlap wanted to begin work on a second season of Rough Riders adventures, McCoy accepted the Republican nomination for the U.S. Senate from Wyoming, but he lost in the 1942 November general election. With World War II now underway the 51-year-old McCoy re-enlisted in the military and was commissioned as a lieutenant colonel. He served as a liaison officer between ground and tactical air forces in the European front and eventually became a full colonel. After the war he made personal appearances and starred in the educational television program *The Tim McCoy Show*, which was syndicated in the early 1950s and won an Emmy Award. He appeared in the 1951 film short *Injun Talk* as well as the features *Around the World in 80 Days* (1956) and *Run of the Arrow* (1957). He was also the headliner with a number of circuses and from 1962 to 1974 he was the featured attraction of Tommy Scott's Country Caravan and Wild West Show. His final feature, *Requiem for a Gunfighter*, was released in 1965, and he died January 29, 1978, the year after the publication of his autobiography, *Tim McCoy Remembers the West*.

Jones and Dunlap's production company made *Dawn on the Great Divide*, which is technically not a Rough Riders feature although Jones and Hatton played their Buck Roberts and Sandy Hopkins roles in it. McCoy was replaced by Rex Bell (1903–62), who had previously starred in cowboy series for Monogram, Resolute and Colony. Bell, who was married to Clara Bow, would later become lieutenant governor of Nevada. Made on a more elaborate budget than the Rough Riders entries and with a hefty supporting cast of familiar genre players, it had U.S. Marshal Jack Carson (Bell) learning that whites, pretending to be Indians, are attacking wagon trains in the vicinity of Lone Pine. He sends his scout, Alex Kirby (Steve Clark), to inform his comrades Buck (Jones) and Sandy (Hatton), who are in charge of a railroad wagon supply train on the way to Oregon. Among the passengers are railroad official Joe Wallace (Lee Shumway) and his nephew Terry Wallace (Robert Lowery), who is smitten with pretty Mary Harkins (Christine McIntyre), who is traveling with her mother, hard-bitten Sarah Harkins (Maude Eburne). Also on the wagon train are gambler Jack Rand (Tristram Coffin) and his wife Sadie (Mona Barrie), who are headed to Beaver Lake to start a gambling house, and Judge John Corkle (Robert Frazer) and his snobbish wife Elmira (Betty Blythe). Riding with the Rands is

Buck Jones, Mona Barrie and Roy Barcroft in *Dawn on the Great Divide* (Monogram, 1942).

pregnant Martha (Jan Wiley), who is snubbed by the Corkles. The judge and his wife are traveling to Beaver Lake with supplies for the judge's brother, Jim Corkle (Harry Woods), who runs the settlement and is behind the gang trying to stop the progress of the railroad. Just before reaching their destination, Martha dies giving birth to a son and the baby, nicknamed Tadpole, is cared for by the Rands, who learn the child's father is Tony Corkle (Dennis Moore), Jim's son. Alex arrives with the news from Carson when signal fires are spotted and Buck splits up the wagon train that is attacked by the marauders, led by Stevens (Reed Howes) and Chuck Loder (Roy Barcroft) dressed as Indians. Jack Rand and Alex Kirby are killed in the attacks and many of the settlers are slaughtered. Buck's supply wagons make it to Beaver Lake, where Jack joins them in the guise of a gambler and Sadie's friend. Sadie sets up her gambling operation and Jim is forced to go along with her after Jack shows him the marriage certificate between Martha and his son. Jack also makes Jim make him a partner, knowing the gambler plans to kill Buck and destroy the railroad supplies. Corkle orders Loder to attack the train and murder Buck but the renegades are surprised and captured as Jack arrests Jim and his son and the judge and his wife are taken into custody by Sandy. Gang member Ed (I. Stanford Jolley) manages to escape and warn Loder, who tries to get away but dies in a gunfight with Buck. While Buck and Sandy proceed with the wagon train to its destination in Oregon, Buck implies he will return to be with Sadie and the baby. With on-location shooting in forests of Northern California, the feature was "an all-around good job," according to *Variety*.

The feature was based on the James Oliver

Curwood story "Wheels of Fate" and in it Mona Barrie sang "Rock of Ages" at the funeral of the mother who died in childbirth. Fiddle player Spade Cooley played "Beautiful Dreamer" and accompanied Christine McIntyre and Robert Lowery when they sang a duet of the Stephen Foster classic.

Jones and Dunlap signed a contract with Monogram to continue the "Rough Riders" series with just two marshals, Buck and Sandy. Jones and Dunlap then went on a war bond selling and Navy recruiting tour that also promoted the upcoming new Rough Riders features. In Boston, the last city on the ten-city tour, on November 28, 1942, they were at the Coconut Grove night club where Buck was the guest of honor at a testimonial dinner. The papier mache decorations in the club caught fire and quickly turned into an inferno which killed or injured some 300 people. Jones reportedly made it to safety but returned to the club twice to save others and died two days later as a result of burns and smoke inhalation. Dunlap was also severely injured but survived. In the 1980s there was a movement to have a commemorative Buck Jones postage stamp but it was to no avail. The Postal Office apparently decided against honoring Jones, a true American hero.

With Jones' death, plans to continue the "Rough Riders" series were abandoned. Monogram produced "Trail Blazers" (q.v.) films starring Ken Maynard and Hoot Gibson in its stead and after he recovered, Scott R. Dunlap produced the "Nevada Jack McKenzie" (q.v.) movies with Johnny Mack Brown in the title role and Raymond Hatton continuing his Sandy Hopkins characterization. Some of the early entries in this new series were revamped by scripter Adele Buffington (as Jess Bowers) as they were originally intended to be used for the second season of "The Rough Riders."

Unlike most series westerns produced by Monogram and other smaller studios, "The Rough Riders" was the subject of an advertising campaign that featured the stars and their films in a variety of items like soft drinks, bicycles, toys, western paraphernalia and Dixie cup lids. In addition, Whitman Publishers released the Better Little Book *Buck Jones, Tim McCoy and Raymond Hatton's The Rough Riders* in 1943, the year after the series ended. The book's title page reads "Buck Jones and the Rough Riders in Forbidden Trails." No author credit is given.

Filmography

Arizona Bound (Monogram, 1941, 53 minutes) Producer: Scott R. Dunlap. Director: Spencer [Gordon] Bennet. Screenplay: Jess Bowers [Adele Buffington]. Story: Oliver Drake. Photography: Harry Neumann. Editor: Carl Pierson. Music: Edward Kay. Sound: Karl Zint. Production Manager: C.J. Bigelow. Technical Director: Vin Taylor. Assistant Director: William Drake.

Cast: Buck Jones (Buck Roberts), Tim McCoy (Tim McCall), Raymond Hatton (Sandy Hopkins), Luana Walters (Ruth Masters), Dennis Moore (Joe Brooke), Kathryn Sheldon (Miranda Masters), Tris [Tristram] Coffin (Steve Taggert), Horace Murphy (Bunion), Slim Whitaker (Red), Gene Alsace [Rocky Camron] (Mack), Ben Corbett (Luke), Jack Daley (Rogers), I. Stanford Jolley, Augie Gomez (Stage Line Workers), Bob Baker (Marshal Bat Madison), Budd Buster (Old Man), Murdock MacQuarrie (Zeke), Hal Price (Bill Hart), Buck Moulton (Slim), Victor Cox (Citizen), Matty Roubert (Saloon Customer).

Working title: *The Rough Riders*.

The Gunman from Bodie (Monogram, 1941, 63 minutes) Producer: Scott R. Dunlap. Director: Spencer [Gordon] Bennett. Screenplay: Jess Bowers [Adele Buffington]. Photography: Harry Neumann. Editor: Carl Pierson. Music: Edward Kay. Sound: Glen Glenn. Production Manager: C.J. Bigelow. Technical Director: Vin Taylor. Assistant Director: Chris Beute.

Cast: Buck Jones (Buck Roberts/Bodie Bronson), Tim McCoy (Tim McCall), Raymond Hatton (Sandy Hopkins), Christine McIntyre (Alice Borden), Dave O'Brien (Joe Martin), Robert Frazer (Mr. Wyatt), Charles King (Steve Dunn), Lynton Brent (Red), Max Waizman (Sheriff Cox), Gene Alsace [Rocky Camron] (Wrangler), John Merton (Bill Cook), Frank LaRue (Jud Mason), Ed Brady (Crane), Kernan Cripps (Al the Bartender), Wilbur Mack, Jerry Sheldon, Jack King, Earle Douglas, Billy Carr (Gang Members), Frederick Gee (Gibbs Infant).

Forbidden Trails (Monogram, 1941, 59 minutes) Producer: Scott R. Dunlap. Director: Robert North Bradbury. Screenplay: Jess Bowers [Adele Buffington]. Photography: Harry Neumann. Editor: Carl Pierson. Music: Edward Kay. Production Manager: Allen Wood. Technical Director: E.R. Hickson. Assistant Director: Mack V. Wright.

Cast: Buck Jones (Buck Roberts), Tim McCoy (Tim McCall), Raymond Hatton (Sandy Hopkins), Christine McIntyre (Mary Doran), Dave O'Brien (Jim Cramer), Tris [Tristram] Coffin (Ed Nelson), Charles King (Fulton), Bud Osborne (Joe Howard), Lynton

Brent (Bill Tooley), Jerry Sheldon (Sam), Hal Price (Steve Bunion), Frank Yaconelli (Tony), Marin Sais (Sue), Tom London (Marshal Tom), Ed Peil, Sr. (Faro Dealer), Eddie Phillips (Convict), Milburn Morante (Best Man), Bill Nestell (Gang Member), Lee Shumway, Kansas Moehring (Gamblers), Herman Hack, Silver Tip Baker (Citizens), Dan White, Lew Morphy, Tex Palmer, Jack Kirk, Jess Cavin, Jack Evans, Rube Dalroy (Saloon Customers).

Below the Border (Monogram, 1942, 53 minutes) Producer: Scott R. Dunlap. Director: Howard Bretherton. Screenplay: Jess Bowers [Adele Buffington]. Photography: Harry Neumann. Editor: Carl Pierson. Music: Edward Kay. Sound: Karl Zindt. Production Manager: Allen Wood. Technical Director: E.R. Hickson. Assistant Director: Mack V. Wright.

Cast: Buck Jones (Buck Roberts/John Robbins), Tim McCoy (Tim McCall), Raymond Hatton (Sandy Hopkins), Linda Brent (Rosita Garcia), Dennis Moore (Joe Collins), Charles King (Steve Slade/Blackie Johnson), Eva Puig (Aunt Maria Garcia), Roy Barcroft (Ed Scully), Bud Osborne (Bill), Merrill McCormick (Gus), Howard Masters (Captain Martini), Walter McGrail (Sam), Jack Rockwell (Sheriff J.B. Lawler), Reed Howes (Max), Tex Palmer (Stagecoach Driver), Kermit Maynard, Frank Ellis, Kansas Moehring (Gang Members), Bill Nestell (Blacksmith), Wally West, Jack Daley (Citizens), Denver Dixon, Foxy Callahan (Saloon Customers).

Ghost Town Law (Monogram, 1942, 62 minutes) Producer: Scott R. Dunlap. Director: Howard Bretherton. Screenplay: Jess Bowers [Adele Buffington]. Photography: Harry Neumann. Editor: Carl Pierson. Music: Edward Kay. Sound: Glen Glenn. Production Manager: Allen Wood. Technical Director: E.R. Hickson. Assistant Director: Mack V. Wright.

Cast: Buck Jones (Buck Roberts), Tim McCoy (Tim McCall), Raymond Hatton (Sandy Hopkins), Virginia Carpenter (Josie Hall), Murdock MacQuarrie (Judge Crail), Charles King (Gus), Tom London (Ace), Howard Masters (Tom Cook), Ben Corbett (Red Larkin), Milburn Morante (Luke Martin), Robert Walker (Marshal O'Neill), Jack Baxley (Marshal Bat Madison), Eddie Phillips (Ted Hall), Jack Ingram (Marshal), Frank Lackteen (Pawnee), Artie Ortego (Gang Member).

Working title: *Ghost Town*.

Down Texas Way (Monogram, 1942, 57 minutes) Producer: Scott R. Dunlap. Director: Howard Bretherton. Screenplay: Jess Bowers [Adele Buffington]. Photography: Harry Neumann. Editor: Carl Pierson. Music: Edward Kay. Sound: Glen Glenn. Production Manager: C.J. Bigelow. Technical Director: E.R. Hickson. Wardrobe: Louis Brown. Assistant Director: Mack V. Wright.

Cast: Buck Jones (Buck Roberts), Tim McCoy (Tim McCall), Raymond Hatton (Sandy Hopkins), Luana Walters (Mary Hopkins), Dave O'Brien (Dave Dodge), Lois Austin (Stella/Ann Dodge), Glenn Strange (Sheriff Trump), Harry Woods (Burt Logan), Tom London (Pete the Bartender), John Merton (Steve), Kansas Moehring (Luke), Jack Daley (John Dodge), Frank Ellis (Deputy Sheriff Red), Bill Nestell (Smitty), Jack Holmes (Mark), Blackie Whiteford (Lynch Mob Leader), Wally West, George Morrell, Foxy Callahan, Chick Hannon (Citizens), Ben Corbett, Artie Ortego, Charles Murphy, Jack Tornek (Gang Members), Milburn Morante (Hotel Worker).

Riders of the West (Monogram, 1942, 58 minutes) Producer: Scott R. Dunlap. Director: Howard Bretherton. Screenplay: Jess Bowers [Adele Buffington]. Photography: Harry Neumann. Editor: Carl Pierson. Music: Edward Kay. Sound: Glen Glenn. Production Manager: C.J. Bigelow. Technical Director: E.R. Hickson. Assistant Director: Mack V. Wright.

Cast: Buck Jones (Buck Roberts), Tim McCoy (Tim McCall), Raymond Hatton (Sandy Hopkins), Sarah Padden (Ma Turner), Harry Woods (Duke Mason), Christine McIntyre (Hope Turner), Charles King (Hogan), Milt [Milburn] Morante (Joe), Walter McGrail (Miller), Dennis Moore (Steve Holt), Robert Frazer (John Holt), Bud Osborne (Red), Tom London (Slim), Ed Peil, Sr. (Jim Dodge), Lee Phelps (Crooked Sheriff), Lynton Brent (Roy), Herman Hack (Herman), Jack Holmes (Lem Martin), George Morrell (Rancher), Kermit Maynard (Gang Member), Jack Kirk, Jimmy Aubrey, Denver Dixon, Roy Bucko (Citizens).

Working title: *Wyoming Roundup*.

West of the Law (Monogram, 1942, 60 minutes) Producer: Scott R. Dunlap. Director: Howard Bretherton. Screenplay: Jess Bowers [Adele Buffington]. Photography: Harry Neumann. Editor: Carl Pierson. Music: Edward Kay. Sound: Lyle Willey. Production Manager: C.J. Bigelow. Technical Director: E.R. Hickson. Assistant Director: William Strohbach.

Cast: Buck Jones (Buck Roberts/Rocky Saunders), Tim McCoy (Tim McCall), Raymond Hatton (Sandy Hopkins), Evelyn Cooke (Julie Todd), Harry Woods (Jim Rand), Jack Daley (John Corbett), Bud McTaggart (Ray Mason), Milt Moranti [Milburn Morante] (Rufus Todd), Roy Barcroft (Ludlow), Al Ferguson (Gang Member), George DeNormand (Pete), Tom London (Charlie), Eddie Parker (Joe), Bud Osborne (Ed), Artie Ortego (Bill), Warren Jackson, Tex Palmer, Foxy Callahan (Citizens), Horace B. Carpenter, Augie Gomez, Chick Hannon (Saloon Customers).

Dawn on the Great Divide (Monogram, 1942, 70 minutes) Producer: Scott R. Dunlap. Director: Howard Bretherton. Screenplay: Jess Bowers [Adele Buffington], from the story "Wheels of Fate" by James Oliver Curwood. Photography: Harry Neumann. Editor: Carl Pierson. Music: Edward Kay. Song: Stephen Foster. Sound: Glen Glenn. Art Director: E.R. Hickson. Production Manager: C.J. Bigelow. Technical Director: Vin Taylor. Assistant Director: Mack V. Wright.

Cast: Buck Jones (Buck Roberts), Mona Barrie

(Sadie Rand), Raymond Hatton (Sandy Hopkins), Robert Lowery (Terry Wallace), Rex Bell (Marshal Jack Carson), Maude Eburne (Sarah Harkins), Christine McIntyre (Mary Harkins), Betty Blythe (Elmira Corkle), Robert Frazer (Judge John Corkle), Harry Woods (Jim Corkle), Tristram Coffin (Jack Rand), Lee Shumway (Joe Wallace), Roy Barcroft (Chuck Loder), Steve Clark (Alex Kirby), Warren Jackson (Fred Cooke), Dennis Moore (Tony Corkle), Jan Wiley (Martha Turner Corkle), I. Stanford Jolley (Ed), Reed Howes (Stevens), Ben Corbett (Red), Spade Cooley (Fiddle Player), Bud Osborne (Stoney), Artie Ortego (Gus), George Morrell, Al Haskell (Settlers), Art Mix (Rider), Jack Daley (Gambler), Horace B. Carpenter, Ray Jones, Denver Dixon, George Sowards, Kansas Moehring, Rube Dalroy (Citizens), Herman Hack, Merrill McCormick (Saloon Customers), Chief Yowlachie, Iron Eyes Cody, Charles Soldani (Indians).

Working titles: *Beyond the Great Divide* and *Great Divide*.

ROUGH RIDIN' KIDS

By the early 1950s, television had made huge inroads into the production of "B" westerns. Republic Pictures made one last attempt at a continuing film series with "Rough Ridin' Kids," a juvenile version of Roy Rogers and Dale Evans. Michael Chapin and Eilene Janssen were cast as the teenage leads and James Bell portrayed Chapin's grandfather, Gramps White, a lawman. Although competently made and action-filled in the Republic tradition, the series lasted for only four installments. Don Miller in *Hollywood Corral* (1976) summed up the series' failure by noting, "[I]t was easy to see what the flaw was — when it came down to the necessary action, the film would have to fall back on grownups to carry it out.... Republic also erred in thinking that youngsters enjoy watching one of their own playing hero. They don't, preferring to imagine themselves as adults and transferring their allegiance to a 'Rocky' Lane or Rex Allen, instead of another juvenile."

Republic Pictures president Herbert J. Yates married Czech skating star Vera Ralston, who headlined many studio productions, often to an under-enthusiastic reception. Also on the studio payroll was her brother, Rudy Ralston, who served as associate producer of the "Rough Ridin' Kids" series. Philip Ford and Fred C. Brannon each directed two of the entries while William Lively wrote the scripts for three of the four features. Made with Valley Vista Productions, the series was filmed at the Iverson Ranch.

Michael Chapin (1936–) was a Hollywood native who made his film debut in 1944 and appeared in films like *Song of Arizona* (1944), *The Corn Is Green* (1945), *It's a Wonderful Life* (1946), *Call Northside 777* (1948) and *Summer Stock* (1949), before being hired to portray Red White in the "Rough Ridin' Kids" films. He was also did stage, radio and television work. After leaving acting in the mid–1950s he graduated from the Massachusetts Institute of Technology and was a paratrooper in the U.S. Army. He then worked in the education and computer professions. His brother, Billy Chapin, and sister, Lauren Chapin, also acted in films and television.

Eilene Janssen (1938–) was born in Los Angeles, California, and her father worked for Universal as a sound mixer. She made her film debut in *Sandy Gets Her Man* in 1940 and was in such features as *Since You Went Away* (1944), *Renegades* (1946), *Song of Love* (1947), *The Bride Goes Wild*, *On Our Merry Way* and *Borrowed Trouble* (all 1948). During World War II she was active in USO work and like Michael Chapin she also appeared on television in the 1950s. Her later screen credits included *The Search for Bridey Murphy* (1956), *Escape from Red Rock* (1958) and *Panic in the City* (1967). She married in 1965 and became the mother of five daughters.

James Bell (1891–1973), a Virginia native, appeared in scores of films between 1932 and 1964, including *I Walked with a Zombie*, *The Leopard Man* and *Gangway for Tomorrow* (all 1943), *The Spiral Staircase* (1945), *The Millerson Case* and *Brute Force* (both 1947). He was also very active in television from the early 1950s until his retirement in 1964.

The series kicked off with *Buckaroo Sheriff of Texas*, released in May 1951, and the adult heroics were left to Hugh O'Brian, who later gained genre fame in the title role of the TV series *The Life and Legend of Wyatt Earp* (ABC-TV, 1955–61). The story took place in Texas in the post–Civil War period with Sam White (Steve Pendleton) coming home to find his land has been taken over by a former friend, Jim Tulane (Tristram Coffin), who is in cahoots with outlaw gang leader Mark Brannigan (William Haade) in trying to control the area. Sheriff Tom "Gramps" White (Bell), Sam's father, asks the governor for help but is turned down as Sam plans to revive the locality by mining bauxite. In order to get back his ranch from Tulane, he sends for armaments and has his son Red (Chapin) take a message to his father in a birthday basket. The outlaws stop the stagecoach on which Red is riding and find the message but let the young man proceed to his grandfather. At the White ranch, the sheriff opens the gift in front of Red and his friend Judy Dawson (Janssen) and learns the route his son plans to take. Newspaperman Ted Gately (Hugh O'Brian), who is taken with Judy's sister Betty (Alice Kelley), gets harassed ranchers to remain on their land and plans to go with Gramps to meet Sam. Tulane's men capture Sam and torture him, causing amnesia. Gately and the sheriff rescue Sam as Tulane kidnaps Red and Judy, hoping the shock will return White's memory. The two youngsters get away from their captors but Sam is killed in a fight with Jim Tulane. Red uses the Morse Code taught him by this father to decipher a message he left in a wagon cover's seam and alerts his grandfather that the munitions are soon to arrive. The sheriff notifies the ranchers but Brannigan gets wind of the arrival and tells Tulane, who captures the wagons carrying the ammunition. He has his men take all of the wagons but one to Castle Rock for a showdown with the ranchers as he drives the other one, not knowing Gately is hidden in the back. When Ted is captured he is taken to the gang's mine hideout but Red rescues him and the two escape as a fire starts. Gramps and the ranchers chase the gang into the mine, where the outlaws are killed in an explosion. With law and order restored, Ted decides to stay and be near Betty. *Variety* commented, "If Michael "Red" Chapin and Eilene "Judy" Janssen are to find favor with juve ticket-buyers they will need more actionful sagebrushers than this one."

The Dakota Kid, the next "Rough Ridin' Kids" outing, came to theaters in the summer of 1951 and told of Ace Crandall (Robert Shayne) trying to take over the Paiute country in Arizona. He tries to force the locals to get rid of Sheriff "Gramps" White (Bell) and kidnaps the lawman's nephew, Cole White (Lee Bennett), putting escaped outlaw the Dakota Kid (Dann Morton) in his place. During a stagecoach holdup, Dakota saves the life of Red (Chapin), the sheriff's grandson. Since the lawman has never seen his nephew, he readily accepts Dakota as Cole. When the local schoolmarm, Mary Lewis (Margaret Field), wants to leave because her only pupils, Red and Judy (Janssen), are often absent from class, Dakota persuades her to stay. When Ace's men rob a payroll shipment, Dakota pretends to stop them and later he is shot by one of the gang members after he gives money to help Judy's father, Sam Dawson (House Peters, Jr.), save his ranch from Crandall. Dakota and Mary fall in love and as Cole he is nominated for the office of county sheriff. Ace orders Dakota to deliver a letter from the bank saying when money loaned to the sheriff will arrive. Red and Judy find out his real identity and they take the bank letter. The youngsters then ask Dakota to help the sheriff, whom Ace has accused of stealing the letter, and he delivers the information to Crandall but intends to aid the sheriff and his men in capturing the gang. During the holdup, Dakota is caught between the two sides and when he does not return, Red and Judy go hunting for him and find Cole White. Ace and his men are captured after a shootout with the sheriff and his posse and Dakota agrees to go back to prison although Gramps promises to ask the governor to parole him. Cole temporarily takes the county sheriff's job as Mary tells Dakota she will await his return. The Jule Styne-Eddie Cherkose song "What Cowboys Are Made Of" was performed in the feature.

After Philip Ford directed the first two series outings, Fred C. Brannon took over for the last two, beginning with *Arizona Manhunt*, issued in September 1951. The plot has Scar Willard (Stuart Randall) and his gang rob the Mesquite, Arizona, bank; during the escape they are spotted by

Red (Chapin) who tells his grandfather, Sheriff "Gramps" White (Bell). Scar hides the loot in a cave and is trailed to his cabin, where he lives with his niece Judy (Janssen), by the sheriff and his deputy, Jim Brown (John Baer); during a shootout Scar is killed. Judy rides away and is later found in the cave suffering from pneumonia. Banking commission secretary Clara Drummond (Lucille Barkley) arrives in town to investigate the holdup and meets secretly with Scar's brother Pete (Roy Barcroft), whom the sheriff has arrested. Pete tells her that Judy may know where Scar hid the money and later tries to get the remaining gang members to kidnap the girl. Dr. Sawyer (Harry Harvey) and the sheriff's niece, Jane Rowan (Hazel Shaw), nurse Judy back to health as the crooks' attempt to abduct her fails. Clara later helps Pete to escape from jail and the two take the girl away in a stagecoach. When Sheriff White and Red try to stop them, the outlaws take the lawman hostage and Judy makes a reference to the cave before leaving Red. The boy tells Jane to find Brown and then goes to the cave where he frees this grandfather and Judy. Clara and Pete locate the stolen money and shoot the sheriff but his deputy, who has been freed by Jane, arrives; Tom sends him after them. Jim manages to unhitch the horses from the stagecoach, throw off the money and jump away before the coach careens off a bridge and falls into a river, drowning Clara, Pete and the rest of the gang. Jim and Jane announce they plan to marry and adopt Judy and since Tom also wants to adopt her he suggests the three come to live with him and Red.

The final series entry, *Wild Horse Ambush*, came out in the spring of 1952. The story had Red (Chapin) and Judy (Janssen) becoming suspicious of cruel rancher Big John Harkins (Roy Barcroft), who captures wild horses he sells for fertilizer. Arrowfire, Red's horse, once belonged to the herd Harkins is capturing and the youngsters wonder why only the weak ones are sold while the others are broken. Harkins is using the animals to carry counterfeit pecos across the Mexican border and he has kidnapped engraver Enrico Espinosa (Julian Rivero) and his daughter Lita (Movita), forcing Espinosa to make the fake money for him. Bandit Jalisco (Richard Avonde) has been raiding the horse herds and Harkins and his cohort Mace Gary (Drake Smith) fail to capture him. When Jalisco tries to escape on Arrowfire, he is thrown. Red and Judy tie him up and take him to the boy's grandfather, Sheriff "Gramps" White (Bell), for his reward. Tom tells them Jalisco is really Captain Juan Reyes, a Mexican border patrol agent, who is working undercover to ferret out the money smugglers. The youngsters suggest that Reyes look into Harkins' activities and when they see horses from Big John's ranch heading south to the border, they tell Reyes who inspects the area and locates counterfeit currency. Judy goes to Harkins' ranch and finds more phony money and manages to escape with the help of Espinosa and Lita. Big John and Mace abduct Red and Judy and leave them to be trampled by the horse herd. Tom and Reyes form a posse and go to Harkins' ranch where the Espinosas direct them to the water hole where they youngsters are tied up. The lawmen shoot it out with the outlaws and capture all of the gang except Harkins and Mace as Arrowfire fights off a pinto leading the horse herd. Tom and Reyes shoot it out with Harkins and Mace with the crooks getting killed and the youngsters saved. The area is later made a wild horse reserve and Red reluctantly sets Arrowfire free.

After the release of the four "Rough Ridin' Kids" films, Republic sold the rights to the juvenile westerns to newspaper columnist Jimmie Fidler, who announced he planned to continue the features with Michael Chapin and Eilene Janssen. But there were no further outings in this mercifully short-lived series.

Filmography

Buckaroo Sheriff of Texas (Republic, 1951, 60 minutes) Associate Producer: Rudy Ralston. Director: Philip Ford. Screenplay: Arthur Orloff. Photography: John MacBurnie. Editor: Arthur Roberts. Music: Stanley Wilson. Art Director: Frank Arrigo. Sound: T.A. Carman. Sets: John McCarthy, Jr., & Charles Thompson. Makeup: Bob Mark.

Cast: Michael Chapin (Red White), Eilene Janssen (Judy Dawson), James Bell (Sheriff Tom "Gramps" White), Hugh O'Brian (Ted Gately), Steve Pendleton (Sam White), Tristram Coffin (Jim Tulane), William Haade (Mark Brannigan), Alice Kelley (Betty Dawson), Selmer Jackson (Governor), Edward [Ed] Cassidy, Bob Reeves (Ranchers), George Taylor (Governor's Secretary), Steve Dunhill (Stagecoach Guard),

Billy Dix (Wagon Driver), Eddie Dunn (Stagecoach Driver), Tommy Coats, Cactus Mack (Gang Members).

The Dakota Kid (Republic, 1951, 60 minutes) Associate Producer: Rudy Ralston. Director: Philip Ford. Screenplay: William Lively. Photography: John MacBurnie. Editor: Harry Keller. Music: Stanley Wilson. Song: Jule Styne & Eddie Cherkose. Art Director: Frank Hotaling. Sound: Earl Crain, Sr. Sets: John McCarthy, Jr., & Charles Thompson. Makeup: Bob Mark. Costumes: Adele Palmer. Special Effects: Howard & Theodore Lydecker.

Cast: Michael Chapin (Red White), Eilene Janssen (Judy Dawson), James Bell (Sheriff Tom "Gramps" White), Dann [Danny] Morton (Dakota Kid), Margaret Field (Mary Lewis), Robert Shayne (Ace Crandall), Roy Barcroft (Turk Smith), Mauritz Hugo (Squire Mason), House Peters, Jr. (Sam Dawson), Lee Bennett (Cole White), Michael Ragan [Holly Bane] (Messenger), Art Dillard (Ed).

Working title: *Tenderfoots on the Trail*.

Arizona Manhunt (Republic, 1951, 60 minutes) Associate Producer: Rudy Ralston. Director: Fred C. Brannon. Screenplay: William Lively. Photography: John MacBurnie. Editor: Irving M. Schoenberg. Music: Stanley Wilson. Art Director: Frank Hotaling. Sound: T.A. Carman. Sets: John McCarthy, Jr., & George Milo. Makeup: Bob Mark. Special Effects: Howard & Theodore Lydecker. Assistant Director: Herb Mendelson.

Cast: Michael Chapin (Red White), Eilene Janssen (Judy Dawson), James Bell (Sheriff Tom "Gramps" White), Lucille Barkley (Clara Drummond), Roy Barcroft (Pete Willard), John Baer (Deputy Sheriff Jim Brown), Hazel Shaw (Jane Rowan), Harry Harvey (Dr. Sawyer), Ted Cooper (Charlie), Stuart Randall (Scar Willard), Herman Hack, Foxy Callahan (Citizens).

Wild Horse Ambush (Republic, 1952, 54 minutes) Associate Producer: Rudy Ralston. Director: Fred C. Brannon. Screenplay: William Lively. Photography: John MacBurnie. Editor: Harold Minter. Music: Stanley Wilson, R. Dale Butts & Nathan Scott. Art Director: Frank Arrigo. Sound: Earl Crain, Sr. Sets: John McCarthy, Jr., & George J. Santoro. Makeup: Bob Mark. Special Effects: Howard & Theodore Lydecker. Assistant Director: Roy Wade.

Cast: Michael Chapin (Red White), Eilene Janssen (Judy Dawson), James Bell (Sheriff Tom "Gramps" White), Richard Avonde (Captain Juan Reyes/Jalisco), Roy Barcroft (Big John Harkins), Julian Rivero (Enrico Espinosa), Movita (Lita Espinosa), Drake Smith (Mace Gary), Scott Lee (Shorty), Alex Montoya (Pedro), John Daheim (Turk), Ted Cooper (Spy), Wayne Burson (Tom).

ROYAL CANADIAN MOUNTED POLICE

James Oliver Curwood (1878–1927), a Michigan native, began writing newspaper and magazine articles and short stories around 1900 and eight years later his first novel, *The Courage of Captain Plum*, was published. In the next two decades he wrote 32 more books, five of them published posthumously. His action stories of the Great Northwest made him one of the most read writers of his time and his works remain popular today. After becoming established as a best-selling author, Curwood made annual trips to Canada, Alaska and the Yukon for inspiration. In the 1910s he wrote scenarios for Hollywood films and to date nearly 200 films have been based on his works, making him one of the most filmed of fiction writers, along with Edgar Wallace and Peter B. Kyne.

Scores of feature films have been made about the Royal Canadian Mounted Police, but Curwood is the only writer to have three separate western film series based on his literary efforts. Kermit Maynard starred as a Mountie in nine features for Ambassador Pictures between 1934 and 1936; Russell Hayden did three such featurettes for Screen Guild in 1946–47; and Kirby Grant was the Mountie hero in ten films for Monogram-Allied Artists from 1949 to 1954, all the motion pictures being allegedly based on Curwood's works.

Maynard (1897–1971) was born in Indiana and was the younger brother of Ken Maynard. An All Western Conference halfback at Indiana University, after graduating in 1922 he worked for a packing company before joining his brother in Hollywood in the mid–1920s. He found work as an actor, double and stuntman and (billed as Tex

Maynard) he starred in a half-dozen westerns for Rayart Pictures in 1927. He continued to work in films and in the early 1930s he was twice named world champion in trick and fancy riding events. In 1934 Ambassador Pictures producer Maurice Conn signed him to star in a series of Northwest sagas based on Curwood works and Maynard brought along his horse Rocky. Each feature cost around $10,000 with location shooting mainly at Kernville and Big Bear Lake in Northern California.

The Ambassador series kicked off with *The Fighting Trooper*, based on Curwood's story "Footprints." Directed by Ray Taylor and released in November 1934, it not only featured Maynard's steed Rocky but also Rowdy, a German shepherd dog in the role of Dauntless. The story begins with rookie Mountie Burke (Maynard) losing an assignment to Sergeant Leyton (Walter Miller), who is ambushed and murdered. The chief inspector (Joseph Girard) tells Burke that Leyton took the duty to protect him and Burke requests the job of bringing in the suspect, trapper Andre La Farge (LeRoy Mason). Taking Constable Blackie (Charles Delaney) with him, Burke meets with Jim Hatfield (Robert Frazer), who offers a reward for LaFarge, who has robbed him several times. When an Indian (Artie Ortego) throws a knife at them, the Mounties trail him and learn from his smoke signals that Hatfield's trading post will be robbed. That night the lawmen see La Farge, his sister Diane (Barbara Worth) and their men enter the trading post where they rob Hatfield and his henchman Landeau (Charles King). Burke fires a gun, breaking up the robbery, and then helps the gang escape but he is shot by Hatfield's men and taken to La Farge's cabin hideout. Diane treats Burke's wounds and they fall in love. Blackie, who has trailed his partner, is captured by Rene (George Chesebro), one of La Farge's men. Burke pretends to shoot Blackie but La Farge sees through the ruse by feeling the "dead man's" pulse. When La Farge tries to help Burke bury Blackie, he is knocked out and put in a coffin with Burke making a getaway with it in a wagon which overturns when he is pursued by Rene and the rest of the La Farge gang. Burke takes the stunned La Farge to a nearby cabin that turns out to be owned by Hatfield, who shows up with Diane, whom he and his men have taken prisoner. After La Farge and Diane are locked in a room, Burke overhears Hatfield and Landeau arguing with Hatfield, admitting he ordered Landeau to kill La Farge's trader father and Sergeant Leyton. Burke helps the La Farges to escape and as the Mountie and La Farge overpower Hatfield and Landeau, Blackie rounds up the rest of the gang. With the Hatfield gang behind bars, La Farge and Diane return to running their trading post as Burke is made the commander of the local Mountie post so he can be near Diane.

Variety termed *The Fighting Trooper* an "effective drama with usual gun shooting and galloping steeds.... Outdoor stuff well photographed and performers meet expected standards." *Film Daily* opined, "Good western with enough action stuff to satisfy the outdoor drama clientele.... There is hardly a dull moment with a good number of fights well spaced.... Kermit Maynard does some clever trick riding." Kermit's riding skills were used to good advantage in the Ambassador films, as were Northern California locales that add scenic interest.

Kermit Maynard, the star of Ambassador Pictures' "Royal Canadian Mounted Police" series based on the works of James Oliver Curwood.

The second series outing, *Northern Frontier*, was issued in February 1935; it was a remake of the Curwood-scripted *Four Minutes Late: A Change of Heart*, a 1914 Selig release starring Tom Mix, Adda Gleason and Lafe McKee. With interiors lensed at Talisman Studios, *Northern Frontier* had Tyrone Power in one of his earliest screen roles as a Mountie. Directed by Sam Newfield, the plot told of RCMP Sergeant Mack McKenzie (Maynard) on the trail of counterfeiters, on the orders of post Inspector Stevens (J. Farrell MacDonald). With the help of saloon gal Mae (Gertrude Astor) he arrests trader Duke Milford (Russell Hopton) who works for the head of the gang, Bull Stone (LeRoy Mason). Parting from Beth Braden (Eleanor Hunt), the girl he loves, McKenzie takes on the guise of a furrier and infiltrates the gang, which uses Beth's father, Professor Braden (Lloyd Ingraham), to make the engravings for their phony money. Stone blackmails the professor, and his henchman Slink (Artie Ortego) carries messages for his boss to Beth from her father. Mack is able to arrest two of the gang members but Stone suspects Braden and his daughter are behind their disappearance and plans to murder them. He orders Slink to kill Beth while he plans to do away with the professor, but McKenzie finds out and rides to save his lover; along the way he meets Sam Keene (Ben Hendricks, Jr.), a wanted outlaw. Pete (Dick Curtis), another member of Stone's gang, abducts Beth and takes her to his boss who locks her up with the father. The gang then plans to kill McKenzie, who is aided by Keene, really a Secret Service agent. The two lawmen fight it out with the crooks and arrest them. After the professor and his daughter are set free, McKenzie and Beth are married by the inspector.

An interesting aspect of *Northern Frontier* is that its plot incorporated the popular theme of gangsters in the post–Prohibition era going into the counterfeiting racket with the Mounties teaming up with G-Men to fight them. *Variety* termed it "moderate entertainment" but complained, "Somewhat illogical that the Mountie could so easily become a member of a counterfeiting gang without being detected. His actions are too free and the suspicion of his gang associates too absent to make the story very convincing." The trade paper did concede that the feature contained "[c]onsiderable suspense ... and much fighting, narrow escapes and hard riding."

Wilderness Mail, released in March 1935, had the advantage of being filmed in scenic snow country. Directed by Forrest Sheldon, it was a remake of the 1914 Selig film of the same title written by Curwood and starring Bessie Eyton and Wheeler Oakman. Fred Kohler dominated the proceedings as the murderous villain Lobo McBain and his harrowing performance is in stark contrast to the feeble dramatics of leading lady Doris Brook, who played his stepdaughter. The story had Yukon trapper Rance Raine (Maynard) preparing for the return of his brother, RCMP Corporal Keith Raine (also Maynard), who comes upon a trapper Baptiste (Roger Williams) being ambushed by Lobo (Kohler) and his henchmen Mora (Syd Saylor) and Jacques (Dick Curtis). The three attackers leave the trapper for dead but he lives long enough to tell Keith that his partner Pierre (Merrill McCormick) is in danger. Lobo, Mora and Jacques go to the trappers' cabin where they shoot Pierre but are captured by Keith, whom they wound. As he marches them across the snow to a nearby village, Keith collapses and the sadist Lobo ties him to a tree, leaving the Mountie to the wolves. Rance, who has been mushing to meet his brother, finds Keith and takes him to a cabin where Lila Landau (Doris Brook) tries to help them and goes for a doctor. Lobo, who uses the name Landau, comes back to his cabin, where he lives with Lila, his stepdaughter, and finds the Raine brothers there but before Keith can identify him as his attacker, the Mountie dies. Seeking revenge for his brother's murder, Rance tells RCMP post Inspector Logan (Kernan Cripps) he will bring in the killer in his own way. When gang member Jules (Paul Hurst) gets drunk and brags about knowing Lobo, Rance trails him to his cabin and is about to beat a confession of him when Lobo shoots Jules through a window and runs away. Mora and Jacques, who fear the crazed Lobo, agree to desert him once a buyer comes for the furs they have stolen. Inspector Logan tells Rance the wilderness mail dogsled is bringing a picture of Lobo from the United States and Rance decides to intercept the sled. When he gives Lila a ride home, Rance mentions the photograph to her; they are overheard by Lobo and his men. They set out to get to the mail sled first, followed by Lila. The crooks steal the mail and Rance is winged by Lobo but is found by Lila, who takes him back to her cabin. There he recovers and finds snow shoes he gave to his brother. When Mora and Jacques return, he gets the drop on them and they confess that Landau is really Lobo. When an escort sled arrives in town with a gold shipment, Lobo robs the trading post and Rance helps him to escape. Taking him to the tree where Lobo tied his brother, Rance beats the madman in a fight and plans to leave him to the wolves but Logan and his men show up and arrest Lobo. Rance then returns to Lila.

The next two series outings, *The Red Blood of Courage* and *Code of the Mounted*, both came to theaters in June 1935, the former at the beginning of the month and the latter at its end. Like their two predecessors, the features were expanded versions of Selig Films written for the screen by Curwood. John English edited *Northern Frontier* and *Wilderness Mail* and he took over as director on *The Red Blood of Courage*, his directorial debut. It was a remake of the 1915 Selig movie starring Thomas Santschi, Bessie Eyton and Lafe McKee. During production, Maynard almost lost his life when a cabin caught fire prematurely. Maynard portrayed RCMP Constable Jim Sullivan who is looking for another Mountie who disappeared while on assignment. After being warned to stay out of the area by Bart Slager (Ben Hendricks, Jr.), Sullivan, who is working undercover as a lumberjack, goes to a nearby trading post where he asks about the Mountie and is overheard by Frenchy (George Regas), who works for Slager. Both crooks are in the employ of Pete Drago (Reginald Barlow), who is masquerading as Mark Henry in order to get control of the man's oil-rich property. He schemes to marry off Henry's niece and heir, Beth Henry (Ann Sheridan), to Slager so they can get rich. When Beth finds out about the scheme, she runs away and Sullivan stops Slager from capturing her. He ties Bart to a tree but he is freed by Frenchy and the two crooks take Sullivan and Beth back to the Henry cabin. Finding a wanted poster of Sullivan in his belongings, Drago decides to have Beth marry Jim so he can blackmail him into keeping silent. When Sullivan meets with Beth in her room, gang member Joe (Charles King) tells Drago and Bart, who go to the room with Bart killing Drago and placing the blame on Jim. After being freed by Beth's uncle, Mark Henry (also Barlow), whom Drago kept a prisoner, Sullivan cuts a telephone wire and calls Mountie headquarters for help. Going back to the cabin to save Beth, he is taken prisoner by Bart, who sets fire to the house. Bart and French abduct Beth but Sullivan escapes from the conflagration and rescues Beth as the Mounties bring in Bart and Frenchy. Jim Sullivan then tells his associates he plans to stay with Beth and continue his assignment. Leading lady Ann Sheridan appeared in the Ambassador production on loan-out from Paramount Pictures.

Code of the Mounted, which saw Sam Newfield return as director, was originally written by Curwood as the 1913 Selig two-reeler *Wheels of Fate* starring Thomas Carrigan. The story was later reworked for the final "Rough Riders" (q.v.) release *Dawn on the Great Divide* (1942). The plot had crook Raoul Martin (Roger Williams) being arrested for killing a trapper for his furs; he is set free by Snaky (Dick Curtis) who murders two Mounties in the process. Constable Jim Wilson (Maynard) re-captures Martin and he is sent to Fort Regina for trial but along the way he is freed by a gang led by Jean (Lillian Miles), who runs an outpost with Duval (Wheeler Oakman), who loves her. Inspector Mallory (Robert Warwick) assigns Wilson and Constable Rogers (Syd Saylor) to bring in the outlaws and at the trading post they see Duval kill an Indian trapper (Artie Ortego) because he refuses to sell his pelts for a low price. When Duval tries to silence Wilson, Jean comes to his rescue and he tells her he wants to control the local fur trade. Rogers informs everyone that Wilson is a well-known crook named Benet and leaves to bring back his lawmen cohorts. Jim makes a deal with Jean that leaves out Duval, who shows her a newspaper story saying Benet was hanged. Duval and his men set out to murder Jim as Rogers arrives with the Mounties who round up the gang. Raoul and Jean flee and Wilson chases them. When Raoul tries to murder Jim, Jean kills him and the Mountie lets her go free. *Film Daily* said this was a "pleasing action outdoor drama."

Sam Newfield also directed the mystery-laden *Trails of the Wild*, issued in August 1935. The scenario written by Curwood was first filmed by Selig in 1914 as *Caryl of the Mountains* and was remade by Reliable in 1936 under that title. The 1914 version was directed by Thomas Santschi who also starred with Kathlyn Williams, while the 1936 version headlined Rin-Tin-Tin, Jr., and Francis X. Bushman, Jr. Here Maynard was cast as RCMP Constable Jim McKenna who, along with fellow Mountie Windy Cameron (Fuzzy Knight), is after kidnappers who murdered one of their colleagues. He meets pretty Jane Madison (Billie Seward) whose father, Tom Madison (John Elliott), is missing. McKenna gets on the trail of a gang of crooks led by Larry Doyle (Monte Blue). Doyle wants to get possession of a lost gold mine located on the supposedly haunted Ghost Mountain, a once-active mining area that is now abandoned. The crooks try to do in McKenna and Windy but the Mounties find trap doors and secret passages leading them to the mine that is being worked by prospectors. They also locate Tom Madison, who had been kidnapped by Doyle and his gang. The two rescue Madison and round up the crooks with McKenna and Jane falling in love.

His Fighting Blood, directed by John English, came out in October 1935, and featured a group of singing Mounties (Glenn Strange, Jack Kirk, Oscar Gahan and Chuck Baldra). They performed "In the Valley Where the Yellow Moon Is Shining" and "The Mountie Song," on which they were joined by Maynard. It was based on the 1915 Selig production written by Curwood and starring Thomas Santschi, who also directed, and Bessie Eyton. Taking place in Ontario, it had businessman Tom Elliott (Maynard) finding out his young brother Phil Elliott (Paul Fix) has sold their Gold Rock Mining Company to Zale Ingram (Frank O'Connor). Young Elliott has become involved with an outlaw gang led by Marsden (Ted Adams) and he joins them in robbing jeweler Leslie (Theodore Lorch), who is a fence for Jim Bartlett. Mounties Black (Charles King) and Clark (Jack Cheatham) asks Tom's help in finding the gang and when he sees Phil leaving the scene of the crime, Tom tries to hide him. Since the two Mounties mistook Tom for Phil, they arrest him for the heist and he is sent to Kingston Penitentiary, although his loyal secretary Doris Carstairs (Polly Ann Young) believes he is innocent. When one of the gang is shot during another holdup, he exonerates Tom before dying and the warden (Edward Cecil) sets him free. Tom is able to realize his ambition of joining the RCMP; at the training camp, he is reunited with Doris whose brother Danny (John McCarthy) is also a member of the force. When a band of jewel thieves abduct Danny, Tom and his colleague Mac MacDonald (Ben Hendricks, Jr.) come to his aid and find Bartlett has been poisoned. Tom also learns that Phil was part of the gang which did in Barlett, and Marsden orders Phil to murder his brother. Unable to shoot Tom, Phil is captured by Mac and he tells the Mounties he did not kill Bartlett and agrees to lead them to Marsden, the real murderer. During a shootout, Phil takes a bullet in the back when he sees Marsden trying to kill Tom. The Mountie then shoots Marsden. *Film Daily* commented, "The scenery is nice and Kermit gives a fine exhibition of trick riding."

At this time, a major change took place in Maynard's series for Ambassador Pictures: He was not cast as a Mountie in his next release, *Timber War*, which came out in March 1936. Although based on the Curwood short story "Hell's Gulch," it had the star helping a young woman (Lucille Lund) save her sawmill business from saboteurs. Maynard then starred in the western *Song of the Trail*, which was directed by Russell Hopton, who had played the villain in *Northern Frontier*. It was released just three weeks after *Timber War*.

Maynard did star as Mounties in two more Ambassador releases, but these were evidently made before *Timber War* and *Song of the Trail* but issued after them. *Wildcat Trooper*, which came to theaters in July 1936, was directed by Elmer Clifton and was a remake of the 1914 Selig two-reeler *The Midnight Call* which was written by Curwood and starred Harold Lockwood. The new film's plot had Mounties Gale Farrell (Maynard) and Pat O'Hearn (Fuzzy Knight) getting involved in a feud between trappers Bob Reynolds (Eddie Phillips) and Jim Foster (Frank Hagney); the real culprit is saloon proprietor Henry McClain (John Merton) who wants the men's valuable furs. Gale captures a wanted outlaw called the Raven (Yakima Canutt) and uses his identity to work for McClain. After Reynolds is wounded, his sister Ruth (Lois Wilde) asks Farrell to help stop the lawlessness. When McClain plants stolen pelts with both men, Gale is able to prove to Reynolds and Foster that McClain is the one causing the trouble between them. Dr. Martin (Hobart Bosworth), who treated Bob's gunshot wound, is the real leader of the outlaws and he shoots both Reynolds and Foster. Bob is able to ride to Ruth for help and she gets him to Martin and tends to Jim; the doctor later tells her that her brother accused Foster of shooting him. Rogers (Ben Hendricks, Jr.), a fur buyer, informs McClain that Gale is an imposter and the Mountie escapes and finds Reynolds. Realizing the doctor was the shooter, he tells the medical man he will help him find the gang leader. Martin informs McClain where he can locate the Mountie. Gale and Pat lay a trap for McClain and Rogers and capture them after a gun battle, with Gale then arresting Dr. Martin. Gale is free to romance Ruth.

Phantom Patrol, the final Maynard Mountie movie, was directed by veteran serial star Charles Hutchison and released in the fall of 1936. It too was based on a 1914 Selig film, *Fatal Note: Jealous of His Own Love Letters*, written by Curwood and starring Adele Lane and Edwin Wallock. With a plot more akin to a gangster movie than a north woods adventure, the story had mobster Dapper Dan Geary (Harry Worth) escaping into the dense woods of Manitoba with his partner JoJo Regan (Paul Fix) and meeting lookalike author Stephen Norris (also Worth), at the latter's hotel retreat. Dan kidnaps the writer and takes over his identity but his cover is soon blown by the arrival of bandit Frenchie La Farge (Julian Rivero) and his gang. When Mountie Inspector McCloud's (George Cleveland) daughter Doris (Joan Barclay) takes her boyfriend, RCMP Sergeant Jim MacGregor (Maynard), to meet Norris, they actually see Dapper Dan who hires Doris as his secretary. When the inspector tells Geary about an upcoming payroll shipment, the gangster plans to rob the stagecoach carrying it but Frenchie and his gang get there first and steal the money, knocking out the Mountie escort, MacGregor. The lawman later trails a suspect that he sees climb into Norris' window and he tells Doris, who maintains that her boss is innocent. When she reads some of the writer's work to Jim, he recognizes it as having been written by Guy de Maupassant. At a party, Dapper Dan, JoJo and Frenchie team to steal a diamond necklace as MacGregor obtains Norris' fingerprints from a glass. When Doris finds the stolen necklace in her boss' room, she telephones the Mounties but the call is stopped by Dapper Dan. The real Norris manages to escape from LaFarge but is arrested by Jim who thinks he is Dapper Dan, whose fingerprints were matched with those on the glass. Geary abducts Doris and they go to the hideout that is surrounded by Mounties on La Farge's trail. Shooting JoJo, MacGregor uses tear gas to capture Frenchie and his men. He arrests Dapper Dan and frees Doris.

Although he no longer portrayed a Mountie, Maynard starred in seven more westerns for Ambassador Pictures before his contract expired in 1938. After that he returned to stunt work and minor roles in hundreds of features, and later television, until 1962, when he became a Screen Extras Guild official until his retirement in 1968.

In 1946–47, Russell Hayden starred in a quartet of Screen Guild Mountie movies advertised as being based on the works of Curwood. Hayden, who came to western film stardom as Lucky Jenkins in the "Hopalong Cassidy" (q.v.) series, headlined oaters at Columbia from 1941 to 1944 and he also did a couple for Universal in 1943–44. In one of the Columbia efforts, *Riders of the Northwest Mounted* (1943), he was a member of the RCMP and he did the same in three of the four features for Screen Guild. The four films ran around 40 minutes each and the first two, *'Neath Canadian Skies* and *North of the Border*, were produced by William B. David for Golden Gate Pictures with B. Reeves Eason directing. The second pair, *Where the North Begins* and *Trail of the Mounties*, were done by Bali Pictures with Carl K. Hittleman producing, and direction by Howard Bretherton. Regarding the four featurettes, James Robert Parish and I wrote in *The Great Western Pictures II* (1988), "These streamlined efforts were picturesque in their locales and speedy in plot due to their limited running time, but sometimes the action got in the way of proper plot development."

'Neath Canadian Skies, which came out in October 1946, packed a lot of story in its four reels as RCMP Sergeant Tim Ransom (Russell Hayden) is told by his commanding officer (Jack Mulhall) to look into the murders of a prospector and another Mountie. He arrives in the town of Blackwater in the guise of outlaw Joe Reed but is

recognized by salesman Wilbur Higgins (Cliff Nazarro), who promises he will not reveal his identity. Taking a room at a boarding house run by Linda Elliott (Inez Cooper), Ransom gets a job working in her gold mine that she has been told is worthless. In reality, her lawyer, Ned Thompson (Douglas Fowley), is in cahoots with saloon proprietor Bill Haley (I. Stanford Jolley) in trying to get the property because it contains a rich vein of gold. The two men had the prospector and the Mountie killed when they learned the truth about the mine's value. Thompson and Haley cause the mine to flood to keep Ramson from finding the ore vein but the water uncovers it and Ransom has Linda sign an affidavit retaining her claim to the property. Haley tells Ransom that the ore he found is fool's gold; when Ransom says he will see an assayer, he is told he will be turned over to the Mounties unless he helps Haley and Thompson rob the stagecoach and steal the affidavit. Ransom agrees to help but he gets word to his comrades and the Mounties thwart the holdup. When Haley finds out that Joe Reed is still in prison, he and his gang plan to go to the Elliott Mine and murder Ransom but Wilbur overhears them and tells Linda to ride to the mine to warn Ransom while he (Wilbur) goes for the Mounties. Ransom and Linda are trapped in the mine by the crooks but during a shootout Higgins arrives with the Mounties and the gang is surrounded and placed under arrest. Ransom then gets men to work the mine while he buys a wedding band from Wilbur so he and Linda can wed. Kermit Maynard, star of the earlier Ambassador series of Curwood films, was cast in 'Neath Canadian Skies as a gang member.

Hayden also starred in the second Golden Gate Production for Screen Guild, *North of the Border*, which was issued in November 1946, but he did not play a Mountie. Here he is cowboy Utah Hayes who comes to Canada to see his friend and partner Bill Lawton and ends up being accused of the man's murder that was actually committed by a gang of fur thieves and smugglers led by Nails Nelson (Douglas Fowley). Lyle Talbot portrayed a Mountie investigating the crime and Jack Mulhall was cast as his commanding officer.

For the final two Screen Guild Mountie releases, *Where the North Begins* and *Trail of the Mounties*, both issued in December 1947, Hayden portrayed RCMP Officer Lucky Sanderson. In the former, Sanderson is on the trail of outlaws who are trading whiskey to the Indians for their furs and is nearly ambushed by one of the gang, Henri (Keith Richards), who is warned off by his cohort Regan (Steve Barclay). Finding Mary Rockwell (Jennifer Holt) caught in a bear trap, Sanderson sets her free and takes her to her brother Rocky (Denver Pyle), who owns a hotel in the town of Caribou. Rocky is in cahoots with gang leader Mitch Arnold (Tristram Coffin) who blackmails him, having his sister to help get Sanderson out of the way. Rocky tells Mary to inform Sanderson about a whiskey shipment so he can be killed in an ambush but Regan, who is really a Mountie working undercover, tells his colleague. At the scene of the ambush, Sanderson fights with gang member Fergus (Frank Hagney), who is accidentally shot by Rocky. Arnold murders Regan for being a traitor. When Sanderson accuses Mary of being in league with the outlaws, she goes with him to where her brother is trading whiskey with the Indians; Rocky is arrested by Sanderson but later makes an escape. Sanderson chases Rocky and shoots him in the shoulder and after rescuing him from a creek takes him back to town. Because he is wearing Sanderson's red Mountie coat, Arnold thinks he is the lawman and shoots him. Before dying, Rocky reveals to his sister that Arnold killed Regan and plans to ambush Sanderson. Mary goes to tell Sanderson, who acts like he has been shot, and rounds up the gang while Arnold makes a getaway. When Sanderson shoots Arnold, he falls off his horse onto Regan's grave. With the lawlessness over, Sanderson asks Mary Rockwell to be his bride.

Trail of the Mounties cast Hayden in dual roles, that of Mountie Sanderson and his outlaw brother, Johnny. Here Sanderson is given the task of finding out who killed trapper Angus McVane (Jack Tornek), not knowing the outlaw gang that committed the crime is led by his twin brother, Johnny (also Hayden). When Johnny tries to steal some fur pelts, he is run off by trappers and takes a horse belonging to Kathie McVane (Jennifer Holt), the niece of the murdered trapper. Sanderson comes to the rescue of an old trapper, Gumdrop (Emmett Lynn), who has been attacked by two gang members who ride away and tell Johnny that his lookalike is in the area. Realizing the Mountie is his twin brother, Johnny puts on the uniform of the murdered lawman and, after diverting his brother to another location with a note about a dead man, he offers to deliver furs for some trappers to a nearby trading post. Finding no one at the site of the supposed murder, Sanderson returns and after talking to Kathie he concludes that his brother is involved with the outlaws. When the trappers thank Sanderson for protecting their furs, he sees gang member Nick (Terry Frost) and puts him under arrest. When the trappers learn their pelts never reached the trading post they want to hang Sanderson; Nick manages to get away. With Sanderson on his trail, Nick goes to the gang's hideout and the outlaws make plans to ambush the lawman over Johnny's protests. Sanderson takes a back trail to the hideout and surprises Johnny and makes him put on the coat of the murdered Mountie which he found in his saddlebags. Kathie and Gumdrop follow Sanderson to the hideout and when they call to him, Johnny is able to ride away but is gunned down by his own men who think he is a Mountie. Sanderson, Kathie and Gumdrop have a gun battle with the outlaws and round up the gang as the dying Johnny tells Sanderson he let himself be shot in order to save his life.

Hayden appeared in two 1948 westerns, *Albuquerque* and *Sons of Adventure*, along with two 1949 Lippert productions, *Deputy Marshal* and *Apache Chief*, before co-starring with James Ellison in the half-dozen 1950 Lippert "Irish Cowboys" (q.v.) series.

The third and final group of Curwood Mountie series westerns was done for Monogram–Allied Artists between 1949 and 1954. Lindsley Parsons was the producer on the majority of the features and William F. Broidy, Wesley Barry and Ace Herman co-produced various outings. The films are sometimes referred to as the "Chinook" series because all ten featured the beautiful white dog Chinook, who was trained by Sam Williamson. The human star of the productions was Kirby Grant, who portrayed RCMP Corporal Rod Webb in nine of the ten outings. A native of Montana, Kirby Grant (1911–85) was born Kirby Grant Hoon, Jr., and was a child prodigy violinist who later attended the University of Washington, Whitman College and the American Conservatory of Music. After leading a dance band and singing on radio and in nightclubs, he came to films in the mid–1930s and for a time was billed as Robert Stanton. Grant did supporting roles in several "B" series westerns and then headlined seven oaters for Universal in 1945–46 and two for Columbia in 1948 before beginning the Monogram series.

The initial Monogram Curwood series feature was *Trail of the Yukon*, issued in the summer of 1949; it was the first of two movies the studio based on Curwood's 1909 novel *The Gold Hunters*. Directed by William Beaudine under the name William X. Crowley and filmed at Big Bear Valley in the San Bernadino National Forest, it told of five men, Muskeg Joe (Anthony Warde), Buck (Maynard Holmes), Rand (Peter Mamakos), Matt Blaine (Guy Beach) and his son Jim (Bill Edwards), robbing the bank at Lebeck in northwest Canada of $150,000. Matt and his son joined the three outlaws in the holdup because Dawson (William Forrest), the bank president, had foreclosed on their mining claim. The Dawsons have a falling-out with the crooks over the money and try to escape from them in a canoe and are aided by Bob McDonald (Kirby Grant), a Mountie out of uniform, and his dog Chinook. During a shootout with the outlaws, Matt is killed, Jim is captured and McDonald is wounded with Chinook helping Jim to get free. At Lebeck, Jim gets help from Marie La Rue (Suzanne Dalbert), the daughter of saloon proprietor La Rue (Dan Seymour), and their Indian friend Poleon (Jay Silverheels). McDonald is taken to the Seymour home to mend as Marie and Jim begin a romance. When La Rue tells McDonald and Jim he is in debt to Dawson, Jim offers to return the money. McDonald identifies himself as a Mountie and says he believes the banker was involved in the robbery. After Dawson tries to convince the bank's stockholders to liquidate assets to cover the loss of the stolen money, he meets with Muskeg Joe who tells him that Jim escaped with a man and his dog. When the outlaws try to find the money at Jim's house, they alert Chinook who warns McDonald and Jim who roust the intruders. Chinook is sent to town to get La Rue and Poleon as McDonald enlists Jim's aid in trapping Dawson. The Mountie informs Dawson that he has arrested Blaine and that the stolen money has been turned over to the local RCMP constable (Bill Kennedy). Dawson tells Muskeg Joe and his men to kill Jim and get the money. When they try to get to Blaine they find the Mountie and Poleon, and during a fight the jail is set on fire. Muskeg Joe confesses to McDonald that it was Dawson who was behind the bank heist. Dawson shoots him and runs away but is killed by a knife thrown by Poleon. Jim then leaves with McDonald to stand trial but the Mountie tells Marie he will receive lenient treatment by the court. *Variety* called the film "laboriously-paced," adding, "Generous use of stock footage from previous Monogram film helps to pad out the minimum expenditure on this one but it still lacks production gloss and features amateurish direction." A few weeks later, however, the same trade paper again reviewed the movie and announced it "is budgeted higher than assembly-line westerns [and] should get a fair play in the action market." Kirby Grant sang "A Shantyman's Life."

For the remainder of the series, Grant would portray RCMP Corporal Rod Webb and the first film in which he did was *The Wolf Hunters*, based on Curwood's second novel. That 1908 book had been filmed previously in 1926 by Rayart with Robert McKim and Virginia Brown Faire as the stars and it was remade in 1934 by Monogram as *The Trail Beyond* starring John Wayne. In this one, Webb and his dog Chinook come to the aid of French-Canadian trapper Paul Latrec (Edward Norris) after he is shot by renegade Muskoka (Ted Hecht), who is chased off by the dog. Latrec came upon a couple who were murdered for their furs and he took their infant to his girlfriend, Renee (Jay Clayton), who is also romanced by trading post operator McTavish (Charles Lang), who ordered Muskoka to frame Latrec for the killings and then murder him. McTavish is criticized by trading post superintendent Cameron (Luther Crockett) for operating at a loss while Cameron's wife Marcia (Helen Parrish) fires servant Minnetaki (Elizabeth Root), who is taken in by Renee. Thinking Latrec is dead, Muskoka tells McTavish, who lets Cameron and Renee believe Paul murdered the married couple, stole their furs and escaped. Webb becomes suspicious of McTavish after he and Paul meet with Renee and she tells him of the traders' accusations. When Muskoka realizes Paul is still alive, he again tries to kill him but the trapper receives only a flesh wound. Renee thinks Chinook killed the infant after finding blood on the cabin floor. In reality, Muskoka tried to attack Minnetaki, who fled with the baby, when the dog came to her rescue and badly wounded her assailant. In the woods, Webb finds the dying Muskoka, who implicates McTavish in the robberies and killings. When Minnetaki returns with the baby, Renee stops Jim from hunting Chinook. Marcia informs McTavish that the Mountie is on his trail and he escapes into the woods but is followed by Webb and Chinook, who capture him after a fight.

Oscar (later Budd) Boetticher directed *The Wolf Hunters* with Frank McDonald taking over for the next five series outings, beginning with *Snow Dog*, issued in the summer of 1950. It was based on the Curwood short story "Tentacles of the North" and was filmed under that title in 1926 by Rayart with Gaston Glass and Alice Calhoun starring. The story had a wolf dog killing prospector Henri Blanchard, the uncle of fur trapper Louis Blanchard (Rick Vallin) and his sister Andree (Elena Verdugo). Webb (Grant) and Chinook come upon the wolf dog after he has killed the owner of a trading post and the two canines fight with Chinook tearing a collar off the killer dog's neck. The Mountie befriends the Blanchards who learn their uncle left them a map to a gold mine in the white woods, the domain of the killer wolf. Thieves steal the map and knock out Chinook, who the locals think is the wolf. When Rod tries to protect his dog, he is beaten but is treated by Dr. McKenzie (Milburn Stone). After hearing an Indian legend about the killer dog protecting the mine that is on sacred burial grounds, Webb goes to the area but the Mountie is shot by Antoine (Hal Gerard), a cohort of trapper Biroff (Richard Karlan). Louis finds Webb and takes him to the doctor who has his nurse, Red Feather (Jane Adrian), tend to him. After the Mountie, Andree and Louis reconstruct the map, Webb leaves for the trading post to get its duplicate but finds it has been stolen. Biroff murders Antoine to keep him quiet and blames the killing on Chinook but when Louis goes to find the real murderer he is captured by the crooks and tortured; Louis refuses to reveal the mine's location. Biroff and Red Feather abduct Andree as Chinook is trapped in a locked room. Webb returns and frees

Chinook and the two set out for the white woods in pursuit of Renee and the outlaws. When the Mountie locates them he is ambushed by Dr. McKenzie, the head of the gang. Chinook attacks the physician as Webb, Andree and Louis round up the rest of the gang. Andree and Louis then take control of the mine that Dr. McKenzie had coveted, using the killer dog he trained to keep away outsiders.

Coming out at the end of 1950, *Call of the Klondike* was allegedly based on an unnamed Curwood story and it had Webb assigned to go to Healy's Crossing with Nancy Craig (Anne Gwynne) in search of two missing men, one of them Nancy's prospector father. At a trading post owned by McKay (Russell Simpson), Nancy learns her father has not been seen in the area and she is taken in by miner Paul Mallory (Tom Neal) and his sister Emily (Lynne Roberts). McKay tells Webb that he is suspicious of miner Mencheck (Marc Krah) and when Nancy visits the man's cabin she finds her father's possessions. Escaping from Mencheck, Nancy returns to the village and gets help from McKay and some of the villagers. They go back to the Mencheck cabin where the prospector fires upon them before Webb arrives and stops the confrontation. Mencheck, an ex-convict, informs the Mountie that he and Nancy's father were partners in a mine but that Craig had disappeared and he had been forced to kill an assailant, the other missing man, in self-defense. Mallory and Fred Foley (Paul Bryar) have dug a tunnel under Mencheck's mine and are stealing his gold; when they learn that Webb is investigating the site, they rig it with dynamite and trap the Mountie and Chinook in an explosion. The dog slips through the rubble and goes for Mencheck who sets Webb free as Paul, Emily and Fred divide up the gold and prepare to escape. The trio takes Nancy hostage but Webb and Mencheck overpower the thieves and she is freed. Nancy decides to stay at Healy's Crossing and help Mencheck manage the mine as Webb, who is taking the prisoners back for trial, promises to return to her.

Released in the summer of 1951, *Yukon Manhunt* was a mystery melodrama that utilized the traditional plotlines of murder on a train and the gathering of all the suspects for interrogation. Again supposedly based on an unnamed Curwood story, it began on a train carrying a mine payroll in the Northwest Territory with Webb (Grant) and Chinook aboard to see that the money gets to its destination at Big Creek. Among the other passengers are Jane Kenmore (Gail Davis) and Mr. Kenmore, her uncle (Nelson Leigh), the owners of the mine sending the payroll; guard LeClerque (Paul McGuire); mining engineer Len (Rand Brooks) and his sister Polly (Margaret Field); Benson (John Doucette); payroll messenger Brown (Richard Barron); and miner Duval (Dennis Moore). During the night, Webb is knocked out, the other passengers suffer from chemical fumes inhalation, Brown is murdered and the payroll is stolen. When everyone comes to, Webb begins investigating and suspects LeClerque, but he has an alibi. At Bear Creek, Webb plans to question the passengers but Len is shot at. The Mountie and Chinook follow Duval, who gets away after wounding the dog. Later, Webb finds Len has been murdered and he fights with Duval, who is killed by Kenmore. The Mountie, Chinook and Jane go to Duval's cabin where the dog finds a notebook written in shorthand. Back at Bear Creek, Webb has all the passengers meet at Kenmore's office and announces that the notebook has been locked in the office safe until a transcriber arrives. That night, Webb sees Polly packing her clothes and she tells him her brother was an ex-convict who was starting a new life by putting new equipment in the Kenmore mine. Kenmore finds Benson trying to steal the notebook; he informs them that he is an insurance investigator working on the case. Benson is wounded by LeClerque, who thinks he has killed him and the Mountie. Webb and Benson then come to believe the Kenmores were working with LeClerque to get the insurance money from their theft of the payroll. Going back to Bear Creek, Polly informs Webb that she overheard Kenmore and his niece talk about the murders. The Mountie and Chinook take a land route to prevent the crooks from escaping by rail. As the Kenmores and LeClerque board a freight car, Chinook jumps LeClerque, who falls from the train and is killed during a fight with Webb. The Mountie then arrests Kenmore and his niece and begins a romance with Polly.

Coming to theaters at the end of 1951, *Northwest Territory* also claimed its origin was an unnamed Curwood story. This one had crooks

Kirby Grant, the star of Monogram-Allied Artists' "Royal Canadian Mounted Police" series.

LeBeau (John Crawford) and Dawson (Duke York) murdering prospector Pop Kellogg (Sam Flint) when he refuses to tell them the location of his gold mine. They set fire to his cabin but are spotted by Webb (Grant) and Chinook, who are bringing Dawson's grandson, Billy (Pat Mitchell), to live with him; Chinook rips material from the coat of one of the fleeing killers. Webb takes the boy to Fort McKenzie to stay with Ann Du Mere (Gloria Saunders), the clerk at Dan Morgan's

(Warren Douglas) trading post. When Webb and Ann search for a letter sent to Pop that might contain his mine claim location, they find that the missive has been stolen. The Mountie visits Pop's cabin, finds the map in a jar and is shot at by an unknown assailant. Webb goes undercover as a prospector and meets Morgan and mineralogist Kincaid (Tristram Coffin), who promises to give Billy his rightful share if he discovers Pop's claim. When Chinook spies Le Beau in town, he attacks him. Webb stops the man from killing his dog whom Morgan orders shot, but Webb promises to keep him under control. Webb tells Billy to trail Le Beau and he and Chinook follow him to Dawson's cabin where he overhears the two men talk about murdering Kellogg. Billy informs Ann and they head to Pop's cabin to warn the Mountie, but they are stopped by Dawson who fights with Chinook and falls off a cliff and is killed. Realizing that Pop's map shows a claim on Barrows Island, Webb goes there and finds crude oil, not gold. When the locals demand that Chinook be killed for Dawson's death, Billy informs Kincaid and Morgan that he overheard Dawson and LeBeau admit they killed his grandfather; Morgan agrees not to shoot Chinook. Billy takes the dog into the woods and ties him up so the locals cannot find him but they are trailed by Morgan and LeBeau; the two take Billy to Dawson's cabin. When Morgan's cohort Barton (Don C. Harvey) finds LeBeau at Pop's claim, he is shot by the outlaw but before dying he tells Webb the identity of his assailant. LeBeau then shoots Webb, who falls from a canoe but is unhurt, as Chinook breaks free, runs to Ann and leads her to Dawson's cabin. Webb takes Barton's body to Kincaid and they head to the cabin. When LeBeau captures Ann and attempts to kill Chinook, the Mountie stops him and LeBeau is killed in a fight with the dog. Kincaid gets the drop on Webb and admits to being behind the scheme to steal Kellogg's claim. Ann uses a log to knock him out. Webb arrests Morgan and Kincaid, and Ann becomes Billy's guardian.

Regarding the production, *Variety* complained, "For a product obviously aimed at the action market, pic is woefully lacking in the ingredient. Except for the denouement, pic consists mainly of a series of stalking chases through the northwest woods, with the villains stalking an old prospector, the hero following the villains, the villains following the hero, a boy and remarkable dog named Chinook stalking the villains, ad infinitum."

The seventh series entry, and the last to be directed by Frank McDonald, was *Yukon Gold*, released in August 1952. Some sources claim William Beaudine was an uncredited co-director. The feature was the second in the Monogram series to be based on Curwood's 1909 novel *The Gold Hunters*. Webb (Grant) and Chinook investigate the murder of a steamboat passenger with the Mountie questioning the dead man's sister, Marie Briand (Martha Hyer). Her brother was a prospector who lost all his money on a claim near Fort Le Beau. The two go there to investigate and find the area is controlled by businessman Clint McClay (Philip Van Zandt) and assayer Jud Powers (Mauritz Hugo). At her brother's cabin, Marie finds a love note from Nan Duvall (Frances Charles), who runs the Lucky Chance casino. When Webb shows Nan the note, she accuses him of murdering the prospector but he convinces her of his innocence and she agrees to help him find the killer. Ace Morgan (Harry Lauter), Nan's partner, is jealous of Webb and warns him to stay away from her as the Mountie tries to buy the dead man's claim from McClay. Since the only mine in the area producing gold is the North Star, Webb and Marie go there and get ore samples they find to be worthless. The Mountie then uses gold dust to make a fake ore brick which he uses in a poker game, provoking a fight with Ace who accuses him of cheating. Ordered out of the casino by Nan, Webb goes by canoe to the dead man's cabin, followed by Ace and later Marie and Clint. Later the Mountie finds Marie a prisoner of Powers. The two men fight and when a chair breaks, a false assayer's report, the evidence needed to convict the crooks, falls out. Powers plans to murder Webb and Marie but is attacked by Chinook; Ace arrives and aids the lawman. When Rod tells him he is a Mountie, Ace admits he was part of a plot to sell prospectors worthless claims based on faked assay reports, but he denies killing Marie's brother. McClay tries to get the drop on the two men but is stopped by Chinook and is shot by Webb. As Fort LeBeau closes down, Nan goes with Marie to Dawson City with Webb and Ace planning to follow them.

Rex Bailey, who had been assistant director on *Northwest Territory*, directed the next two series entries, *Fangs of the Arctic* and *Northern Patrol*, both 1953 releases. Again allegedly based on a Curwood short story, *Fangs of the Arctic* contained additional dialogue by Warren Douglas who played the villain. The story had Webb (Grant) and Mike Kelly (Robert Sherman) pretending to be trappers as they investigate a murder near Blackfoot Crossing. Mike once lived there and wants to see his childhood sweetheart, Sandra Borg (Lorna Hanson), the daughter of the murdered man. After chasing off some fur poachers, the two men see Sandra but her boyfriend, Matt Oliver (Warren Douglas), a mine superintendent, becomes jealous of Kelly. One of the poachers, Cheval (Richard Avonde), has words with Webb when Chinook growls at him. When the Mountie finds out that Howell (John Close), also one of the thieves, has purchased many large traps, he investigates the man's cabin and the two fight with Howell being killed when his gun accidentally fires. When Sandra sees Kelly trying to break into the trading post, he tells her he is a Mountie investigating her father's murder but he does not reveal Webb's identity. While he is looking around the trading post, Mike is killed by another of the poachers, Morgan (Leonard Penn). When Webb returns to the settlement, Chinook leads him to the post where he and its operator, MacGregor (Phil Tead), find Sandra unconscious and Kelly murdered. As he watches over Sandra's cabin, Webb is threatened by Cheval who wants the pelts he got from Howell's cabin. The Mountie then pretends to join the poachers and finds out that they substitute rabbit pelts for valuable furs after they have been inspected by MacGregor. Morgan learns MacGregor has sent for a Mountie to investigate Kelly's murder and when Sandra overhears the gang discuss the situation, she tells Oliver that Webb is one of the poachers with Morgan being their boss. When Rod, Morgan and Cheval attempt to switch rabbit pelts for beaver fur at the trading post, they are surprised by Oliver, who pulls a gun on the Mountie but is attacked by Chinook. MacGregor gets the drop on Morgan and Cheval as Webb stops Matt from being mauled by the dog. As the prisoners are taken away for trial, Webb accepts Sandra's apology and tells her that MacGregor knew his identity all along. In *Hollywood Corral* (1976), Don Miller noted that the film "showed signs of being shot on pocket money; dim lighting, rickety sets, weak cast support."

Northern Patrol was an improvement over *Fangs of the Arctic*; this time Warren Douglas supplied the screenplay although he did not appear in the film. It was based on Curwood's 1919 novel *Nomads of the North* that was filmed in 1920 by Associated First National Pictures with Betty Blythe, Lon Chaney and Lewis Stone. Released in the summer of 1953 under the Allied Artists banner, *Northern Patrol* had Webb (Grant) and Chinook investigating the mysterious hanging death of Tad Farrar. He gets assistance from the local constable, Gregg (Richard Walsh), and visits the dead man's fiancée Meg Stevens (Gloria Talbott), whose brother Frank (Bill Phipps) starts a fight with Webb. Frank tells Jason (Dale Van Sickel), a gambler, and the Quebec Kid (Marian Carr), a gunslinger, that the Mountie is looking into Farrar's death. Neither Jason or Quebec will help Webb but Oweena (Claudia Drake), an Indian maiden, meets with Rod and Meg and tells them she loved Tad and that he was killed because he would not reveal the location of the Valley of the Dead, an Indian burial ground rich in treasure. With Farrar dead, the killers kidnap Oweena's grandfather, Dancing Horse (Frank Lackteen), and torture him but he refuses to tell them the location of the burial grounds. When Webb comes upon the gang, Quebec fires a warning shot. When he attempts to arrest Jason, he is knocked out but revived by Chinook. The dog locates the trail of the outlaws, who are following the injured Dancing Horse, and Webb sends him to find Gregg. After Frank returns home, Meg wants to know the truth about Tad's death; the girl is killed when they struggle over a gun. When Quebec complains about being left out of the burial ground search, Frank beats her with a pistol and frames her for his sister's death. Frank then attempts to kill Webb but ends up wounding Gregg, who is wearing the Mountie's coat. After helping Gregg, Webb goes to the Stevens cabin and finds Quebec who admits being part of the robbery scheme but denies killing Farrar and Meg. When the Mountie leaves Oweena to guard Quebec, the gunslinger gets the drop on her and makes her go to the burial ground where

Webb has been captured by the gang. The crooks find out the relics have no value as Quebec and Oweena arrive and to avenge Farrar's death, Oweena pushes the Quebec Kid over a precipice. Webb defeats Jason in a fight as Chinook does the same with Frank. Before taking his prisoners to trial, Webb has Gregg help Oweena in looking after her grandfather.

William Beaudine, who had directed the initial series entry *Trail of the Yukon* in 1949 returned to helm the final outing, *Yukon Vengeance*, released early in 1954. Here Webb (Grant) and Chinook investigate a trio of mail carriers killed by a huge bear with their lumber company payrolls being stolen. At Quebec's Dear Creek, Webb and Chinook are attacked by a large bear prompted by trapper Schmidt (Henry Kulky) and his Indian cohort Gray Shadow (Fred Gabourie). As Schmidt steals a mailbag, the Mountie accidentally shoots Gray Shadow, and Chinook runs off the bear. Jim Barclay (Monte Hale), the boss of the local lumber camp, informs Webb that Gray Shadow was the son of Chief Lone Eagle (Billy Wilkerson). When they arrive at the trading post, Yellow Feather (Carol Thurston), the Indian's widow, accuses the Mountie of murdering her husband. Trading post manager MacLish (Parke MacGregor) does not believe Webb's story as Schmidt robs the mailbag. After he is shot at during the night, the Mountie finds bullets belonging to a gun owned by MacLish's employee, Madelon Duval (Mary Ellen Kay), and while searching her cabin he finds marked money taken during the holdups. When Schmidt wounds Rod, MacLish kills the bear and the Mountie is nursed back to health by Madelon, who finds out his true identity. She tells him the marked money was paid to her by McLish as wages and that the bear belonged to Schmidt. Going to Schmidt's cabin, Webb finds the stolen money and during a fight, Schmidt falls from the top of a water wheel. After McLish finds more of the stolen money in his safe and cash register, Madelon searches Barclay's office, finding still more of the stolen loot. She then accuses him of hiring Schmidt and his bear to do the killings and he takes her to the Indian reservation since he is a blood brother of the tribe. The Mountie and his dog follow them but Webb is captured. As Chinook sets Madelon free, Webb tells Lone Eagle that Barclay instigated the killings. The chief does not listen until the story is endorsed by Madelon and then he decides that Webb and Barclay must fight a trial by combat with tomahawks. When Barclay tries to run away, Yellow Feather kills him with a knife. Webb and Chinook bid farewell to Madelon and return to close the case.

Although the Kirby Grant Mountie series only averaged two films annually over five years, it outlasted most of the "B" western films series. Grant went on to greater fame starring in the TV series *Sky King* which ran on NBC-TV from 1951 to 1952 and on ABC-TV from 1952 to 1954. From 1959 to 1966 the episodes were rerun on CBS-TV on Saturday afternoons. Grant, who spent years making person appearances, sometimes with circuses, later worked in public relations and real estate. In the mid–1970s he ran the Sky King Youth Ranch in Florida before his death in a car crash in 1985.

Filmography

The Fighting Trooper (Ambassador, 1934, 61 minutes) Producer: Maurice Conn. Director: Ray Taylor. Screenplay: Forrest Sheldon, from the story "Footprints" by James Oliver Curwood. Photography: Edgar Lyons. Editor: Ted Bellinger. Sound: Corson Jowett. Production Manager: Martin G. Cohn. Sets: Ralph DeLacy.

Cast: Kermit Maynard (Trooper Burke), Barbara Worth (Diane La Farge), LeRoy Mason (Andre La Farge), Charles Delaney (Constable Blake), Robert Frazer (Jim Hatfield), George Regas (Henri), Walter Miller (Sergeant Leyton), Joseph W. Girard (Inspector O'Keefe), Charles King (Landeau), George Chesebro (Rene), Nelson McDowell (Nels), Lafe McKee (Trapper), Arthur [Artie] Ortego (Little Moose), Rowdy (Dauntless), Milburn Morante (Pete), Gordon De Main (Bartender), Merrill McCormick (Bearded Gang Member), George Morrell (Gang Member), George Hazel (Saloon Customer), Eva McKenzie (Citizen), Rose Plummer (Customer).

British title: *The Trooper*.

Northern Frontier (Ambassador, 1935, 57 minutes) Producer: Maurice Conn. Director: Sam Newfield. Screenplay: Barry Barringer, from the scenario "Four Minutes Late: A Change of Heart" by James Oliver Curwood. Photography: Edgar Lyons. Editor: Jack [John] English. Sound: Hans Weeren.

Cast: Kermit Maynard (Sergeant Mack McKenzie), Eleanor Hunt (Beth Braden), Russell Hopton (Duke Milford), J. Farrell MacDonald (Inspector Stevens),

Roy [LeRoy] Mason (Bull Stone), Ben Hendricks, Jr. (Sam Keene), Gertrude Astor (Mae), Lloyd Ingraham (Professor Braden), Walter Brennan (Cook), Lafe McKee, Henry Hall (Trappers), Nelson McDowell (Tobe), Kernan Cripps (Mike), Dick Curtis (Pete), Jack Chisholm (Durkin), Artie Ortego (Slick Garu), Charles King (Constable Wallace), Tyrone Power (Trooper).

Wilderness Mail (Ambassador, 1935, 55 minutes) Producer: Maurice Conn. Director: Forrest Sheldon. Screenplay: Bennett Cohen & Robert Dillon, from the story by James Oliver Curwood. Photography: Art [Arthur] Reed. Editor: Jack [John] English. Sound: Corson Jowett. Sets: Lewis J. Rachmil.

Cast: Kermit Maynard (Rance Raine/Corporal Keith Raine), Fred Kohler (Lobo McBain/Landau), Paul Hurst (Jules), Doris Brook (Lila Landau), Syd Saylor (Mora), Richard [Dick] Curtis (Jacques), Nelson McDowell (Mac), Kernan Cripps (Inspector Logan), Roger Williams (Baptiste), Merrill McCormick (Pierre), Julian Rivero, Ray Henderson (Gamblers), George Morrell (Customer).

The Red Blood of Courage (Ambassador, 1935, 55 minutes) Producer: Maurice Conn. Director: Jack [John] English. Screenplay: Barry Barringer, from the scenario by James Oliver Curwood. Photography: Arthur Reed. Editor: Richard G. Wray. Sound: Corson Jowett. Sets: Lewis J. Rachmil.

Cast: Kermit Maynard (Constable Jim Sullivan), Ann Sheridan (Beth Henry), Reginald Barlow (Pete Drago/Mark Henry), Ben Hendricks, Jr. (Bart Slager), George Regas (Frenchy), Nat Carr (Dr. Meyer), Charles King (Joe), Milburn Morante (Bushwhacker), Art Dillard (Gang Member), Carl Mathews (Indian).

Code of the Mounted (Ambassador, 1935, 60 minutes) Producer: Maurice Conn. Director: Sam Newfield. Screenplay: George Wallace Sayre, from the scenario "Wheels of Fate" by James Oliver Curwood. Photography: Edgar Lyons. Editor: John English. Art Director: Lewis J. Rachmil. Sound: Hans Weeren. Costumes: Jack Chisholm.

Cast: Kermit Maynard (Corporal Jim Wilson), Robert Warwick (Inspector Mallory), Jim Thorpe (Eagle Feather), Lillian Miles (Jean), Syd Saylor (Rogers), Wheeler Oakman (Duval), Eddie Phillips (Louie), Dick Curtis (Snakey), Stanley Blystone (Constable), Roger Williams (Raoul Martin), Jack Perrin (Mountie), Artie Ortego (Indian Trapper), George Morrell (Doctor), Pascale Perry (Mountie Escort), Frank McCarroll, Dick Botiller (Gang Members).

Trails of the Wild (Ambassador, 1935, 61 minutes) Producers: Maurice Conn & Sig [Sigmund] Neufeld. Director: Sam Newfield. Screenplay: Joseph O'Donnell, from the story "Caryl of the Mountains" by James Oliver Curwood. Photography: Jack Greenhalgh. Editor: Jack [John] English. Production Manager: Lewis J. Rachmil. Assistant Director: Samuel Diege.

Cast: Kermit Maynard (Mountie Jim McKenna), Billie Seward (Jane Madison), Monte Blue (Larry Doyle), Theodore Von Eltz (Inspector Kincaid), Fuzzy Knight (Windy Cameron), Matthew Betz (Hunt), Wheeler Oakman (Hardy), Robert Frazer (Bob Stacey), Charles Delaney (John D. Brent), Frank Rice (Missouri), John Elliott (Tom Madison), Roger Williams (Buck Hammond), Dick Curtis (Roper), William Desmond, Ted Mapes (Mounties), Eddie Phillips (Bushwhacker), Frank McCarroll (Jake), Dick Botiller, Clyde McClary, Artie Ortego (Gang Members), Ed Cassidy, Herman Hack (Saloon Customers).

His Fighting Blood (Ambassador, 1935, 56 minutes) Producers: Maurice Conn & Sig [Sigmund] Neufeld. Director: John English. Screenplay: Joseph O'Donnell, from the scenario by James Oliver Curwood. Photography: Jack Greenhalgh. Editor: Richard G. Wray. Art Director: Fred Preble. Sound: Hans Weeren. Sets: John McCarthy. Costumes: Harry Kusnick. Assistant Director: Samuel Diege.

Cast: Kermit Maynard (Tom Elliott), Polly Ann Young (Doris Carstairs), Paul Fix (Phil Elliott), Ben Hendricks, Jr. (Constable Mac MacDonald), Ted Adams (Marsden), Joseph W. Girard (Inspector), Frank LaRue (Al Gordon), Charles King (Constable Black), Frank O'Connor (Zale Ingram), John McCarthy (Constable Danny Carstairs), Ted [Theodore] Lorch (A. Leslie), Jack Cheatham (Constable Joe Clark), Glenn Strange (Davis), Oscar Gahan (Osborne), Chuck Baldra (Mountie), Al Baffert (Ed), Frank McCarroll (Sam), Milburn Morante, Tex Phelps, Barney Beasley (Saloon Customers).

Wildcat Trooper (Ambassador, 1936, 60 minutes) Producer: Maurice Conn. Director: Elmer Clifton. Screenplay: Joseph O'Donnell, from the scenario "The Midnight Call" by James Oliver Curwood. Photography: Arthur Reed. Editor: Richard G. Wray. Music Director: Lee Zahler. Songs: Didheart Conn. Sound: Hans Weeren. Production Manager: Martin G. Cohn. Sets: Frank Sylos.

Cast: Kermit Maynard (Sergeant Gale Farrell), Hobart Bosworth (Dr. Martin), Fuzzy Knight (Constable Pat O'Hearn), Lois Wilde (Ruth Reynolds), Jim Thorpe (Indian), Yakima Canutt (Raven), Eddie Phillips (Bob Reynolds), John Merton (Henry McClain), Frank Hagney (Jim Foster), Roger Williams (Slim Arnold), Richard [Dick] Curtis (Henri), Ted [Theodore] Lorch (C. Rogers), Hal Price, Ben Hendricks, Jr. (Buyers), Wally West, Ray Henderson, Art Dillard, Tex Phelps (Gang Members).

British title: *Wild Cat*.

Phantom Patrol (Ambassador, 1936, 60 minutes) Producer: Maurice Conn. Director: Charles Hutchison. Screenplay: Joseph O'Donnell, from the scenario "Fatal Note: Jealous of His Own Love Letters" by James Oliver Curwood. Photography: Arthur Reed. Editor: Richard G. Wray. Song: Didheart Conn. Art Director: Frank Sylos. Production Supervisor: Martin G. Cohn. Sound: Hans Weeren.

Cast: Kermit Maynard (Sergeant Jim McGregor),

Joan Barclay (Doris McCloud), Harry Worth (Dapper Dan Geary/Stephen Norris), Paul Fix (JoJo Regan), George Cleveland (Inspector McCloud), Julian Rivero (Frenchie La Farge), Eddie Phillips (Emile), Roger Williams (Gustav), Richard [Dick] Curtis (Josef), Lester Dorr (Officer).

'Neath Canadian Skies (Screen Guild, 1946, 41 minutes) Producer: William B. David. Associate Producer: Barney A. Sarecky. Director: B. Reeves Eason. Screenplay: Arthur V. Jones. Story: George H. Plympton. Photography: Marcel Le Picard. Editor: Roy Livingston. Art Director: Frank Dexter, Sr. Sound: Glen Glenn. Production Supervisor: William E. Strohbach. Makeup: Milburn Morante. Costumes: Albert Deano.

Cast: Russell Hayden (Sergeant Tim Ransom/Joe Reed), Inez Cooper (Linda Elliott), Douglas Fowley (Ned Thompson), Cliff Nazarro (Wilburn Higgins), I. Stanford Jolley (Bill Haley), Jack Mulhall (Captain Sharon), Kermit Maynard (Stony Carter), Richard Alexander (Pete Davis), Pat Hurst (Harding), Gil Patric (Kinney), Boyd Stockman (Real Joe Reed), Jimmie Martin (Lewis), Joe Bernard (T.M. Michaels), Bob Burns (Trapper).

North of the Border (Screen Guild, 1946, 42 minutes) Producer: William B. David. Associate Producer: Barney A. Sarecky. Director: B. Reeves Eason. Screenplay: Arthur V. Jones. Photography: Marcel Le Picard. Editor: Roy Livingston. Music Director: Carl Hoeffle. Art Director: Frank Dexter, Sr. Sound: Glen Glenn. Production Supervisor: William E. Strohbach. Special Effects: Ray Mercer. Makeup: Milburn Morante. Costumes: Albert Deano. Assistant Director: Kenneth Richert.

Cast: Russell Hayden (Bob "Utah" Hayes), Inez Cooper (Ruth Wilson), Douglas Fowley (Nails Nelson), Lyle Talbot (RCMP Sergeant Jack Craig), Jack Mulhall (Inspector Swanson), Anthony Warde (Jean Gaspee), I. Stanford Jolley (Ivy Jenkins), Guy Beach (George Laramie), Dick [Richard] Alexander (Tiny Muller).

Where the North Begins (Screen Guild, 1947, 40 minutes) Producer: Carl K. Hittleman. Executive Producer: Maury Nunes. Director: Howard Bretherton. Screenplay: Elizabeth [Betty] Burbridge. Story: Carl K. Hittleman, Harold [Kline] Klein & Jackie Schwabacher. Photography: Benjamin H. Kline. Editor: Paul Landres. Music Director: Carl Hoeffle. Sound: Ben Winkler. Special Effects: Ray Mercer. Makeup: Bob Cowan. Costumes: Albert Deano. Props: Everett Israelson. Assistant Director: Bob Farfan.

Cast: Russell Hayden (Sergeant Lucky Sanderson), Jennifer Holt (Mary Rockwell), Tristram Coffin (Mitch Arnold), Denver Pyle (Jim "Rocky" Rockwell), Steve Barclay (Constable Jeff Regan), Artie Ortego (Eagle Feather), Keith Richards (Henri), Anthony Warde (Joe), Frank Hagney (Andy Fergus), J.W. Cody (Two Arrows), Chris Willow Bird (Funeral Chanter), Billy Wilkerson (Indian Chief), Lew Morphy, Charly Cypert, Billy Cypert (Indians).

Working title: *Code of the North.*

Trail of the Mounties (Screen Guild, 1947, 45 minutes) Producer: Carl K. Hittleman. Executive Producer: Maury Nunes. Director: Howard Bretherton. Screenplay: Elizabeth [Betty] Burbridge. Story: Carl K. Hittleman & Harold [Kline] Klein. Photography: Benjamin H. Kline. Editor: Paul Landres. Song: Joseph E. Winner. Special Effects: Ray Mercer. Makeup: Bob Cowan. Costumes: Albert Deano. Assistant Director: Bob Farfan.

Cast: Russell Hayden (Sergeant David "Lucky" Sanderson/Johnny Sanderson), Jennifer Holt (Kathie McVain), Emmett Lynn (John "Gumdrop" Mason), Terry Frost (Nick), Harry Cording (Hawkins), Charles Bedell (Maurice), Zon Murray (Jacques), Pedro Regas (La Porte), Frank Lackteen (Pierre), Britt Wood (Musician), Felice Richmond (Mrs. McVane), Jack Tornek (Angus McVain), Herman Hack, George Morrell, Tom Smith (Trappers).

Working title: *Law of the Mounties.*

Trail of the Yukon (Monogram, 1949, 67 minutes) Producer: Lindsley Parsons. Associate Producer: William F. Broidy. Director: William X. Crowley [William Beaudine]. Screenplay: Oliver Drake, from the novel *The Gold Hunters* by James Oliver Curwood. Photography: William A. Sickner. Editor: Ace Herman. Music Director: Edward J. Kay. Art Director: Dave Milton. Sound: John Carter. Makeup: Ted Larsen. Assistant Director: Wesley Barry.

Cast: Kirby Grant (Mountie Bob MacDonald), Chinook (Himself), Suzanne Dalbert (Marie La Rue), Bill Edwards (Jim Blaine), Iris Adrian (Paula), Dan Seymour (La Rue), William Forrest (John Dawson), Anthony Warde (Muskeg Joe), Maynard Holmes (Buck), Peter Mamakos (Rand), Guy Beach (Matt Blaine), Stanley Andrews (Rogers), Dick Elliott (Sullivan), Jay Silverheels (Poleon), Bill Kennedy (Constable), Harrison Hearne (Frank), Al Bridge (Old Man), Burt Wenland (Red), Wally Walker (Miner), Roy Bucko (Saloon Customer).

The Wolf Hunters (Monogram, 1949, 70 minutes) Producer: Lindsley Parsons. Associate Producer: William F. Broidy. Director: Oscar [Budd] Boetticher. Screenplay: W. Scott Darling, from the novel by James Oliver Curwood. Photography: William A. Sickner. Editor: Ace Herman. Music Director: Edward J. Kay. Music: John T. Handley. Art Director: Dave Milton. Sound: Virgil Smith. Special Effects: Ray Mercer. Sets: Raymond Boltz, Jr. Set Continuity: Ilona Vas. Assistant Director: Wesley Barry.

Cast: Kirby Grant (Corporal Rod Webb), Chinook (Himself), Jan Clayton (Renee), Edward Norris (Paul Latrec), Helen Parrish (Marcia Cameron), Charles Lang (J.L. McTavish), Ted Hecht (Muskoka), Luther Crockett (Edward Cameron), Elizabeth Root (Minnetaki).

Snow Dog (Monogram, 1950, 63 minutes) Producer:

Lindsley Parsons. Associate Producer: William F. Broidy. Director: Frank McDonald. Screenplay: William Raynor, from the story "Tentacles of the North" by James Oliver Curwood. Photography: William A. Sickner. Editor: Ace Herman. Music Director: Edward J. Kay. Art Director: Dave Milton. Sound: John Carter. Production Manager-Assistant Director: Wesley Barry. Set Continuity: Bobbie Sierks.

Cast: Kirby Grant (Corporal Rod Webb), Chinook (Himself), Elena Verdugo (Andree Blanchard), Rick Vallin (Louis Blanchard), Milburn Stone (Dr. F.J. McKenzie), Richard Karlan (Biroff), Jane Adrian (Red Feather), Hal Gerard (Antoine), Richard Avonde (Philippe), Duke York (Duprez), Guy Zanette (Baptiste).

Call of the Klondike (Monogram, 1950, 66 minutes) Producer: Lindsley Parsons. Associate Producer: William F. Broidy. Director: Frank McDonald. Screenplay: Charles Lang. Photography: William A. Sickner. Editor: Ace Herman. Music Director: Edward J. Kay. Art Director: Dave Milton. Sound: Tom Lambert. Production Manager-Assistant Director: Wesley Barry. Script Supervisor: Eleanor Donahoe.

Cast: Kirby Grant (Corporal Rod Webb), Chinook (Himself), Anne Gwynne (Nancy Craig), Lynne Roberts (Emily Mallory), Tom Neal (Paul Mallory), Russell Simpson (Andrew "Andy" McKay), Marc Krah (Mencheck), Paul Bryar (Fred Foley), Pat Gleason (Billy), Duke York (Luke).

Yukon Manhunt (Monogram, 1951, 61 minutes) Producer: Lindsley Parsons. Associate Producer: William F. Broidy. Director: Frank McDonald. Screenplay: Bill [William] Raynor. Photography: William A. Sickner. Editor: Ace Herman. Music Director: Edward J. Kay. Art Director: Dave Milton. Sound: Tom Lambert. Set Continuity: Ilona Vas. Assistant Director: Wesley Barry.

Cast: Kirby Grant (Corporal Rod Webb), Chinook (Himself), Gail Davis (Jane Kenmore), Margaret Field (Polly), Rand Brooks (Len), Nelson Leigh (Mr. Kenmore), John Doucette (Benson), Paul McGuire (Jacques Le Clerque), Dick [Richard] Barron (Brown), Dennis Moore (Duval).

Northwest Territory (Monogram, 1951, 61 minutes) Producer: Lindsley Parsons. Associate Producer: William F. Broidy. Director: Frank McDonald. Screenplay: William Raynor. Photography: William A. Sickner. Editor: Ace Herman. Music Director: Edward J. Kay. Art Director: Dave Milton. Sound: Tom Lambert. Special Effects: Ray Mercer. Set Continuity: Bobbie Sierks. Assistant Director: Rex Bailey.

Cast: Kirby Grant (Corporal Rod Webb), Chinook (Himself), Gloria Saunders (Anne DuMere), Warren Douglas (Dan Morgan), Pat Mitchell (Billy Kellogg), Tristram Coffin (Kincaid), John Crawford (LeBeau), Duke York (Dawson), Don C. Harvey (Barton), Sam Flint (Pop Kellogg).

Yukon Gold (Monogram, 1952, 62 minutes) Producer: William F. Broidy. Associate Producer: Wesley Barry. Director: Frank McDonald. Screenplay: Bill [William] Raynor, from the novel *The Gold Hunters* by James Oliver Curwood. Photography: John J. Martin. Editor: Ace Herman. Music Director: Edward J. Kay. Art Director: Dave Milton. Sound: Frank Webster. Special Effects: Ray Mercer. Production Supervisor: A.R. Milton. Makeup: Charles Huber. Sets: Vin Taylor. Set Continuity: Eleanor Donahoe. Production Assistant: Jack Jungmeyer, Jr. Assistant Director: William Beaudine, Jr.

Cast: Kirby Grant (Corporal Rod Webb), Chinook (Himself), Martha Hyer (Marie Briand), Harry Lauter (Ace Morgan), Philip Van Zandt (Clint McClay), Frances Charles (Nan Duval), Mauritz Hugo (Jud Powers), James Parnell (Renault), Sam Flint (Mountie Captain), I. Stanford Jolley (Charlie), Hal Gerard, Roy Gordon, Ward Blackburn (Gang Members).

Fangs of the Arctic (Monogram, 1953, 62 minutes) Producer: Lindsley Parsons. Associate Producer: Ace Herman. Director: Rex Bailey. Screenplay: Bill [William] Raynor. Additional Dialogue: Warren Douglas. Photography: William A. Sickner. Editor: Leonard W. [Ace] Herman. Music Director: Edward J. Kay. Art Director: Dave Milton. Sound: Tom Lambert. Special Effects: Ray Mercer. Set Continuity: Lee Fredericks. Assistant Director: Joe Wonder.

Cast: Kirby Grant (Corporal Rod Webb), Chinook (Himself), Lorna Hanson (Sandra Borg), Warren Douglas (Matt Oliver), Leonard Penn (Morgan), Richard Avonde (Cheval), Robert Sherman (Constable Mike Kelly), John Close (Howell), Phil Tead (MacGregor), Roy Gordon (Briggs), Kit Carson (Andre Borg).

Northern Patrol (Allied Artists, 1953, 62 minutes) Producer: Lindsley Parsons. Associate Producer: Ace Herman. Director: Rex Bailey. Screenplay: Warren Douglas, from the novel *Nomads of the North* by James Oliver Curwood. Photography: William A. Sickner. Editor: Leonard W. [Ace] Herman. Music Director: Edward J. Kay. Art Director: Dave Milton. Sound: Tom Lambert. Special Effects: Ray Mercer. Sets: Ben Bone. Assistant Director: Art Lueker.

Cast: Kirby Grant (Corporal Rod Webb), Chinook (Himself), Marian Carr (Quebec Kid), Bill [William] Phipps (Frank Stevens), Claudia Drake (Oweena), Dale Van Sickel (Jason), Gloria Talbott (Meg Stevens), Richard Webb (Constable Ralph Gregg), Emmett Lynn (Old Man), Frank Lackteen (Dancing Horse), Frank Sully (Bartender).

Yukon Vengeance (Allied Artists, 1954, 68 minutes) Producer: William A. Broidy. Associate Producer: A. Robert Nunes. Director: William Beaudine. Screenplay: William Raynor. Photography: John J. Martin. Editor: Ace Herman. Music Director: Edward J. Kay. Art Director: George Troast. Sound: Ben Winkler. Special Effects: Ray Mercer. Sets: Harry Reif. Makeup: Charles Huber. Set Continuity: Eleanor Donahoe. Assistant Director: William Beaudine, Jr.

Cast: Kirby Grant (Corporal Rod Webb), Chinook (Himself), Monte Hale (Jim Barclay), Mary Ellen Kay (Madelon Duval), Henry Kulky (Schmidt), Carol Thurston (Yellow Flower), Parke MacGregor (Fergus McLish), Fred Gabourie (Gray Shadow), Billy Wilkerson (Chief Lone Eagle), Marshall Bradford (Commissioner).

THE SINGING COWGIRL

Grand National Pictures had been in business since 1936 and had, for a time, successfully competed with the major studios, especially after signing Warner Bros. refugee James Cagney to star in *Great Guy* in 1937. Cagney's second feature for the company, *Something to Sing About* (1938), however, failed to recoup its large budget and the studio found itself in financial trouble when the star returned to Warner Bros. Having already delved into the musical western filed with its "Renfrew of the Royal Mounted" (q.v.) series, the studio executives decided to try a new ploy by fashioning a group of films around a singing cowgirl. Grand National president George A. Hirliman formed Coronado Films to produce the features and radio singer Dorothy Page was signed to play the leading role. The concept did not catch on with the public and the series lasted for only three outings before Grand National folded.

Page (1904–61), a native of Pennsylvania, was born Dorothy Stofflett and majored in music at Cedar Crest College. After appearing on a *Saturday Evening Post* cover as one of the ten most beautiful women in the country, she married a doctor and had two daughters. She began singing on radio in Detroit in the early 1930s and later worked in Chicago and New York City where she appeared on several radio programs before coming to Hollywood in 1935. After appearing in *Manhattan Moon* and *King Solomon of Broadway* (both 1935) she became a regular on the NBC radio program *Plantation Party*, also known as *Paducah Plantation*, starring Irvin S. Cobb and Whitey Ford. In 1937 she returned to films with Republic's *Mama Runs Wild* and then signed to do the "Singing Cowgirl" series.

The initial series entry, *Ride 'Em Cowgirl*, was released early in 1939 and in it Page and leading man Milton Frome sang "A Campfire, a Prairie Moon and You" and "I Love the Wide Open Spaces." The feature's interiors were filmed at the Iverson Ranch and the exteriors were done in Kernville, California, with direction by Samuel Diege, who would helm all three series outings. Vince Barnett provided comedy relief while Arthur Hoerl wrote the scripts, Mack Stengler did the cinematography and Al Sherman, Walter Kent and Milton Drake composed the songs. *Ride 'Em Cowgirl* told of Bar X Ranch owner Rufe Rickson (Joseph Girard) being swindled out of his spread in a crooked poker game by gambler Sandy Doyle (Harrington Reynolds), who also runs a silver smuggling operation across the Mexican Border. When Rickson accuses Doyle of cheating him, a fight erupts and the old man is aided by electric linemen Oliver Shea (Milton Frome) and Dan Haggerty (Vince Barnett). To get even with Rufe, the gambler accuses him of stealing rodeo prize money, which Rickson's daughter Helen (Page) was keeping, in order to pay his gambling debt. Helen takes the blame for the theft but makes a getaway and is hidden by Oliver who enters her in a rodeo, which she wins. Riding into Mexico, Helen finds Doyle's henchmen Lingstrom (Pat Henning) and Philbin (Fred Cordova) smuggling silver and with Oliver's help she is able to prove the gambler is behind the thefts. Doyle captures Oliver and Dan as Helen enlists the aid of the sheriff (Frank Ellis) and together they arrest the gambler, with Oliver announcing he is a G-Man on the trail of the silver smugglers. *Variety* complained, "Story is so involved that it's almost impossible to tell what's going on." Regarding the female star, the reviewer wrote, "[S]he actually does nothing but toss a lariat once, ride and win a horserace, and throw a bit of lead at nothing in particular."

Dave O'Brien took over as leading man in

the second series film, *Water Rustlers*, which was issued shortly after *Ride 'Em Cowgirl*. It took nearly two weeks to film the series' initial feature but *Water Rustlers* was brought in on a five-day shooting schedule. The story had Tim Martin (Ethan Allen) and other ranchers up in arms when Robert Weylan (Stanley Price) dams up their water supply so he can increase productivity at his mine. With their cattle dying from lack of water, the ranchers decide to drive their herds through Weylan's spread. His foreman, Wiley (Warner Richmond), leads an ambush in which Martin is murdered. The dead man's daughter, Shirley (Page), hires Bob Lawson (O'Brien) as her new foreman and they try to take Weylan to court but his men use scare tactics to keep the ranchers from testifying against him. Finally, Shirley and Lawson unite the ranchers and they blow up the dam's retaining wall, supplying water for the area's cattle, and Weylan is brought to justice regarding his part in Tim Martin's shooting. Even less entertaining than its predecessor, the feature wasted Vince Barnett as a comic cook although it did give Page a chance to sing "I Feel at Home in the Saddle," "Let's Go On Like This Forever" and "When a Cowboy Sings a Dogie a Lullaby."

The Singing Cowgirl, the series' final outing, came out in June 1939. Here Page performed another trio of less than satisfying tunes, "I Gotta Sing," "Let's Round Up Our Dreams" and "Prairie Boy." This one had outlaw Gunhand Garrick (Warner Richmond) and his gang attacking the Circle H Ranch owned by Tom Harkins (Ed Peil, Sr.) with neighboring rancher Dorothy Hendrick (Page) telling him to consult lawyer John Tolen (Stanley Price). Harkins is unaware there is gold on his spread and Tolen, the actual leader of the outlaws, orders Garrick to murder the rancher and his wife, leaving young Bill Harkins (Dix Davis) an orphan. Cowpoke Dick Williams (Dave O'Brien) arrives on the scene but he is too late to save the couple; joined by Dorothy, they take the boy back to her ranch. When Dorothy discovers gold in a riverbed on the Harkins ranch, she begins to suspect the lawyer is behind the killings. Rex Harkins (Paul Barrett), Tom's younger brother, comes to look after Billy and meets Tolen's niece, Nora Bryde (Dorothy Short); the two fall in love. Garrick kidnaps Billy, Rex and Nora and when the boy does not return home, Dorothy goes to Tolen and demands his return. When the lawyer finds out that Garrick abducted his niece, he rides to the gang's hideout and the two men engage in a gunfight but are captured by Williams. With the outlaws behind bars, the two couples plan to marry.

Following the demise of the "Singing Cowgirl" series, Page left show business, married for a second time and went into the real estate business. After the death of her second husband, she married again and moved to a ranch near Fresno. She also owned land in Texas. She died in 1961 after a long battle with cancer. Although her starring series was brief, Page was certainly the highlight of the three films, especially when her fine contralto voice was displayed.

Filmography

Ride 'Em Cowgirl (Grand National, 1939, 53 minutes) Producer: Arthur Dreifuss. Executive Producer: George A. Hirilman. Associate Producer: Don Liberman. Director: Samuel Diege. Screenplay: Arthur Hoerl. Photography: Mack Stengler. Editor: Guy V. Thayer, Jr. Music Director: Ross DiMaggio. Songs: Al Sherman, Walter Kent & Milton Drake. Sound: William A. Wilmarth. Production Manager: Joseph Boyle. Special Effects: Howard A. Anderson. Assistant Director: Robert Richards.

Cast: Dorothy Page (Helen Rickson), Vince Barnett (Dan Haggerty), Milton Frome (Oliver Shea), Lynn Mayberry (Belle), Frank Ellis (Sheriff Larson), Harrington Reynolds (Sandy Doyle), Joseph Girard (Rufe Rickson), Fred Behrle (Deputy Sheriff Foster), Pat Henning (Lingstrom), Fred Cordova (Philbin), Eddie Gordon (Grigg), Lester Dorr (Announcer), Jack O'Shea, Blackjack Ward, Clyde McClary (Gang Members), Lionel Backus, Annabelle Driver (Citizens).

Working title: *Fury in the Saddle*.

Water Rustlers (Grand National, 1939, 54 minutes) Producer: Don Liberman. Executive Producer: George A. Hirilman. Director: Samuel Diege. Screenplay: Arthur Hoerl. Story: Don Laurie & Lawrence Meade. Photography: Mack Stengler. Editor: Guy V. Thayer, Jr. Music Director: Ross DiMaggio. Songs: Al Sherman, Walter Kent & Milton Drake. Sound: Hans Weeren. Production Manager: Joseph Boyle. Special Effects: Howard A. Anderson. Makeup: Louis Santee. Props: Lou Diege.

Cast: Dorothy Page (Shirley Martin), Dave O'Brien (Bob Lawson), Vince Barnett (Mike), Stanley Price (Robert Weylan), Ethan Allen (Tim Martin), Leonard Trainor (Andy Jurgens), Warner Richmond (Wiley), Edward R. [Eddie] Gordon (Sheehan), Edward [Ed]

Peil, Sr. (Lawyer), Lloyd Ingraham (Judge), Merrill McCormick (Sheriff).

The Singing Cowgirl (Grand National, 1939, 59 minutes) Producer: Don Liberman. Executive Producer: George A. Hirilman. Director: Samuel Diege. Story-Screenplay: Arthur Hoerl. Photography: Mack Stengler. Editor: Guy V. Thayer, Jr. Music Director: Ross DiMaggio. Songs: Al Sherman, Walter Kent & Milton Drake. Sound: Hans Weeren & Glen Glenn. Production Manager: Joseph Boyle. Special Effects: Howard A. Anderson. Props: Lou Diege.

Cast: Dorothy Page (Dorothy Hendricks), Dave O'Brien (Dick Williams), Vince Barnett (Kewpie), Dorothy Short (Nora Pryde), Dix Davis (Billy Harkins), Stanley Price (John Tolen), Warner Richmond (Gunhand Garrick), Edward [Ed] Peil, Sr. (Tom Harkins), Paul Barrett (Rex Harkins), Lloyd Ingraham (Dr. Slocum), Ethan Allen (Sheriff Teasley), Eddie Gordon (Trigger Williams), Merrill McCormick (Deputy Sheriff), Leonard Trainor (Sandy).

THE TEXAS RANGERS

Late in 1942, PRC launched its "Texas Rangers" series under the auspices of cousins Alfred Stern and Arthur Alexander. Twelve entries were issued through the summer of 1944 starring Dave O'Brien and Jim Newill, who had appeared earlier in the "Renfrew of the Royal Mounted" (q.v.) series. In 1944, Tex Ritter took over from Newill and eight more titles were released well into 1945.

Newill, billed as Jim Newill in the "Texas Rangers" features, and Dave O'Brien, billed as Dave "Tex" O'Brien in the series, were friends and in 1940 they purchased a ranch in Topanga Canyon, north of Hollywood. They sold the ranch in the mid–1940 to actor Jack Ingram. Continuing the tradition of the "Renfrew of the Royal Mounted" films, the "Texas Rangers" features contained musical interludes that took advantage of Newill's robust baritone voice. The two stars contributed a number of songs to the series, sometimes using the pseudonym Tex Coe.

To round out the triad hero concept, Guy Wilkerson (1901–79) was hired to portray the comedic character, Panhandle Perkins. A Texas native, he had formulated his comedy style after years of working in a variety of touring shows before coming to Hollywood in the mid–1930s. Thereafter he had supporting roles in films, including westerns like *Heart of the Rockies* and *Yodelin' Kid from Pine Ridge* (both 1937) and bucolic features such as *Mountain Justice* (1937) and *Kentucky Moonshine* (1938). Regarding the actor's screen persona, David Rothel wrote in *Those Great Cowboy Sidekicks* (1984), "Guy Wilkerson was a tall string bean of a galoot who generally drawled out his words at a molasses-in-winter tempo unless aroused to reluctant action because of some script consideration. The comedy that he provided was seldom of the slapstick variety and was often just a humorous touch to the proceedings. It was a rarity for comic sequences to be built into the scripts." Regarding the "Texas Rangers" films, Rothel said, "While the Texas Rangers series was a far cry from the highly respected and well-remembered Three Mesquiteers films made by Republic Pictures, it, nevertheless, was fairly popular in its time. The popularity it did have was primarily due to the on-screen rapport of its stars, and much of that can be placed at the large feet of Guy Wilkerson."

The series producers, Arthur Alexander (1909–89) and Alfred Stern (1911–79), were natives of Germany. With Arthur's brother, Max Alexander (1908–64), the cousins migrated to the United States in 1928 and went to work for another relative, Carl Laemmle, the head of Universal Pictures. The 1930 United States Census shows the three living together in Beverly Hills, with Max employed as a studio manager while Arthur and Alfred were listed as assistant directors. Max married Shirley Kassler, who left him to wed director Edgar G. Ulmer, causing Ulmer to be blacklisted by the major studios. The Alexanders co-founded two Poverty Row studios, Beacon and Colony, while Stern also worked as a production assistant, most notably on Universal's *The Invisible Ray* in 1936. During the course of the "Texas Rangers" series, Arthur Alexander and Alfred Stern would alternate as producer and associate producer and Alexander also did double duty as assistant director on several of the outings.

Alexander-Stern Productions also made a number of other features for PRC during the 1940s, including *The Ghost and the Guest* (1943), *Secrets of a Co-ed*, *Seven Doors to Death*, *Waterfront* (all 1944), *Arson Squad*, *The Lady Confesses* and *Navajo Kid* (all 1945).

Al Herman directed the initial "Texas Rangers" outing, *The Rangers Take Over*, which

Dave O'Brien as Ranger Tex Wyatt in "The Texas Rangers."

was released late in 1942. Herman had helmed the first entries in the "Renfrew" series and would do the same for the next two "Texas Rangers" features. The plot of the first feature has Tex Wyatt (O'Brien) and Panhandle Perkins (Wilkerson) joining the Texas Rangers, the outfit being under the command of Tex's estranged father, Captain Sam Wyatt (Forrest Taylor). The two are sent to investigate Pete Dawson (Bud Osborne), who is suspected of being involved in cattle rustling. When Tex gets into a fight with Dawson, his father expels him from the Rangers, telling a fellow officer, Sergeant Jim Steele (Newill), that the discipline will help his son. Gang leader Rance Blair (I. Stanford Jolley) hires Tex, hoping to use him to prevent being harassed by the Rangers. When the Rangers attack the outlaw gang, Captain Sam is wounded and taken prisoner by Blair. At a trading post run by Jean Lorin (Iris Meredith), Tex picks a fight with Jim under the guise of relaying information to him about Blair's next rustling scheme. Through Jean's efforts, the Rangers are warned of the outlaws' activities and Steele and Perkins find their hideout. Tex stops the gang from attacking his pals and the three subdue the outlaws, with Steele taking Blair prisoner. Tex sets his father free and as a result he is brought back into the Rangers unit.

Regarding the initial series entry, Don Miller wrote in *Hollywood Corral* (1976), "[F]rom the start it looked like a long, hard road. Newill and O'Brien had proved themselves before with weak material and production deficiencies; but Wilkerson, a cadaverous gent with a nasal twang, was no deft funster, far from it, and the dialogue written for him compounded the felony. Succeeding members of the series did nothing to cause any reassessment. Newill and O'Brien worked too much alike, and the attempted light banter between them sounded strained."

For *The Rangers Take Over*, Newill and O'Brien, writing under the name Tex Coe, contributed the title song, "High in the Saddle," and "Campfire on the Prairie." "Roll Along Cowboy" by Robert Hoag and Jack Williams was also included.

Bad Men of Thunder Gap (March, 1943) had Texas Ranger Tex Wyatt (O'Brien) observing crooks Ransom (Jack Ingram) and Holman (Charles King) robbing supplies from a mining company. They knock out Tex and escape and later, after Tex comes to, Ransom not only blames him for the robbery but also for the murder of the company guard. Back at headquarters, Tex, Jim (Newill) and Panhandle (Wilkerson) are assigned to work undercover as medicine show entertainers as they investigate supply wagon robberies in the vicinity of Thunder Gap. Trying to starve out area miners, store owner John Hobbs (Michael Vallon) and freight company owner Ransom are

Poster for *Bad Men of Thunder Gap* (PRC, 1943).

behind the scheme. Tex pretends to be looking for work and goes to Hobbs who sends him to Ransom, who does not recognize him. Meanwhile Jim is hired to give singing lessons to Hobbs' niece, Martha Stewart (Janet Shaw), and the two begin a romance. When she rides too near the gang's hideout, Holman shoots at her and she is rescued by Jim and Tex. The two Rangers then locate the stolen supplies but are taken prisoner by the outlaws. Panhandle tracks his friends to the hideout and hears Ransom's plans to murder them. He goes back to town and has Martha get together a posse while he and his medicine show co-workers ride back to the hideout. As Jim and Tex escape, Panhandle and the posse arrive and a shootout ensues, with the outlaws being captured.

Besides Newill's singing, musical interludes in the first two series features were provided by Cal Shrum and His Rhythm Rangers. For *Bad Men of Thunder Gap*, Shrum composed the song "Ride, Ride, Ride." The Newill-O'Brien moniker Tex Coe provided the film's trio of tunes "Medicine Man," "West Winds" and "The Moon is Yellow."

Released in May, 1943, the third series entry, *West of Texas*, had the Texas Rangers (Newill, O'Brien) going to New Mexico to set up a Rangers post in that territory. They have been informed that rancher Bent Yaeger (Henry Hall) has been trying to stop the building of a railroad through the area. Three men chase Yaeger's daughter, Ellen (Marilyn Hare), and the two Rangers save her. As a result they meet Bent, who tells them that two crooks, railroad man Bart Calloway (Robert Barron) and his lawyer Steve Conlon (Tom London), are trying to steal his land. When Conlon is murdered by Calloway's henchman Blackie (Jack Ingram), a note blames Yaeger, and Tex believes he is guilty, although Jim does not. When Panhandle (Wilkerson) arrives, he is arrested by Calloway whose lady friend, Marie Monette (Frances Gladwin), warns him that he is a suspect in Conlon's murder. Members of the new Rangers post, which has been set up by Jim and Tex, set Panhandle free and he tells the locals that Calloway is planning a stagecoach robbery. Hoping to entrap Bent, Tex orders him to rob the stagecoach carrying railroad money. Jim tries to stop Tex but is knocked out. Ellen revives Jim and the two signal Bent to return home. Bent tells Jim he plans to kill Tex but they are attacked by Calloway's gang. Panhandle arrives with the new Ranger recruits and the outlaws are arrested. Jim and Tex become pals again and the ranchers are promised their losses will be covered. For *West of Texas*, Newill and O'Brien composed three more tunes, "El Lobo," "Tired of Rambling" and "Whistle a Song." *West of Texas* was the first of four series features directed by Oliver Drake.

Border Buckaroos followed in June 1943. While on the way to Boulder City to investigate the murder of their friend, rancher Dan Clark, the Rangers (Newill, O'Brien, Wilkerson) capture gunman Trigger Farley (Reed Howes). Since his employer is a rancher, Cole Melford (Jack Ingram), who is a suspect in Clark's killing, Tex decides to impersonate Farley. On the way to town they find unconscious Tom Bancroft (Kenne Duncan), who later tells them he was attacked by unknown assailants and that he is supposed to inherit one-half of the Clark estate. For Tom's protection, Jim agrees to take his identity and the two Rangers leave Bancroft to guard Farley as they proceed to the Clark ranch for a midnight reading of the deceased's will. Along the way they prevent a stagecoach attack. Two of the passengers are Clark's daughter Betty (Christine McIntyre), the other inheritor, and her friend, Marge (Eleanor Counts). When Panhandle arrives in town, Melford fears he will discover that he murdered Dan Clark and he offers to buy the ranch from Betty but she refuses. Melford accepts Tex as Farley but henchman Hank Dugan (Ethan Laidlaw) is suspicious of the Ranger. At the Clark ranch, lawyer Higgins (Michael Vallon) begins reading the will, but Melford henchman Rance Daggett (Charles King) shoots out the light and steals the document. When Panhandle goes to take custody of Farley, he finds the gunman has tied up Tom and escaped. Tom and Panhandle rush to warn Tex but Farley beats them there and tells Bancroft that Tex is an imposter; the Ranger is taken prisoner. Panhandle and Tom free Tex and force Dugan to write a confession. Meanwhile, Daggett and Jim have a shootout at the ranch, with Melford and Farley helping their henchman to capture Jim and the two women. The crooks take their hostages to a deserted mine but Tex, Panhandle and Tom rescue them and round up Melford and his gang. When Betty and

Tom receive their inheritance, they find out it also includes the prosperous mine. For this entry, Newill and O'Brien wrote "Driftin,'" "Stay on the Right Trail" and "You're Here to Stay."

Released in August, 1943, *Fighting Valley* was not only written and directed by Oliver Drake, but he also composed the three songs used in the film: "Adios Vaquero," "I'm the Son of a Gun of a Son of a Gun" and "When Dreams Come True in Peaceful Valley." In addition to Newill's vocalizing, the film also offered an appearance by singer Tex Williams. The plot had the Texas Rangers (Newill, O'Brien, Wilkerson) thwart an ore shipment robbery by a gang led by Tucson Jones (Stanley Price) and Slim (Charles King). Reporting to smelting company manager Frank Burke (John Elliott), the trio is informed that a rash of such holdups is about to ruin the business Burke manages for Joan Manning (Patti McCarty). Tex believes that rival smelter Dan Wakely (John Merton) wants to force the Manning operation out of business and is behind the holdups. Joan arrives in town and announces that her fiancé, Paul Jackson (Robert Bice), is negotiating the sale of her business to Wakely but Burke objects, saying local miners cannot afford Wakely's high charges. A miners' meeting is called at the house of Ma Donovan (Mary MacLaren) but Joan still refuses not to sell to Wakely. Tex has the operation's creditors declare it insolvent and he takes over as its receiver, thus making it impossible for Joan to sell the business. Paul then tries to bribe Tex into giving up his receivership and when this fails he goes to Tucson and Slim and tells them the Rangers plan an ore shipment. The outlaws attack the ore wagon but are repelled by the Rangers. Tex learns that Tucson is the manager of one of Wakely's mines and he also tries to convince Joan that she is being double-crossed by her fiancé. When the gang steals ore belonging to a miner (Dan White), he goes to Ma's house with the local sheriff (Hal Price) and a judge (Budd Buster), who informs Tex he must claim the stolen ore or lose his receivership. Meanwhile, Paul accuses the Rangers of the ore theft but admits to Joan it was Wakely who gave him the money to bribe Tex. As a result, Joan breaks off her engagement to Paul. The Rangers and Jeff follow the stolen wagon's tracks to the mine run by Tucson and arrest the gang.

Oliver Drake wrote and directed his fourth and final "Texas Rangers" feature, *Trail of Terror*, released in September, 1943. Its three songs, "Along the Rio Grande," "Jog Along" and "Sleepy Hollow," were composed by Newill and O'Brien. Here O'Brien had a dual role, that of Ranger Tex Wyatt and his outlaw brother Curly, the lover of gang leader and saloon proprietor Belle Blaine (Patricia Knox). Curly and Nevada (Jack Ingram) follow Belle's orders and rob a relay station but realize the express box they took is empty. Tex, Jim (Newill) and Panhandle (Wilkerson) investigate the robbery with Tex being mistaken for his sibling. Masquerading as traveling dentists, the Ranger trio looks into a series of such robberies but after receiving a letter from his brother, Tex asks for a leave from his job. The brothers meet but Nevada and another gang member, Hank (I. Stanford Jolley), shoot Curly, who dies, but not before informing Tex that it was Hank who murdered an express agent. The outlaws mistake Tex for his murdered brother, who is discovered by Jim and Panhandle. In order to infiltrate the gang, Tex poses as Curly and tries to depose Nevada as the chief henchman. Belle realizes Tex is a fake and she and the gang force him to lead them to the hidden express box, which they find to be empty. Jim and Panhandle corner the gang and Belle is mortally wounded in a shootout. The gang is captured and Tex returns to the Rangers.

One of the major flaws of the "Texas Rangers" series was its technical inadequacies, which were quite apparent in *Trail of Terror*. In *Hollywood Corral* (1976), Don Miller said the sound recording "is not only faulty but deficient.... At one point, the sound equipment seems to have blown a gasket, and microphone thunks and thuds and crackles can be heard periodically throughout."

Beginning with the seventh series outing, *The Return of the Rangers*, issued in October, 1943, Elmer Clifton and Harry Fraser would alternate writing and directing for the rest of the series. Clifton (1890–1949) directed his first feature in 1917 and he helmed over eighty films, including four serials. During the silent days he worked for major studios but in the talkie era he often found himself toiling on Poverty Row, many times providing the script as well as directing. Fraser (1889–1974) also did screenplays, often under the names Harry Crist and Harry O. Jones, as well as directing. More so than Clifton, he majored in westerns for such companies as Monogram, Ajax, Resolute, Diversion and Commodore. His autobiography *I Went That-A-Way: The Memoirs of a Western Film Director* was published in 1990.

Clifton wrote and directed *The Return of the Rangers* which has the Texas Rangers (Newill, O'Brien, Wilkerson) investigating a rash of rustling. After Jim and Tex save pretty Ann Miller (Nell O'Day) from rustlers, she hires Jim to work on the Flying N which she has managed since the recent death of its owner. Frank Martin (Glenn Strange), the head of the local land company, tells Ann he plans to sell the ranch but she says he cannot until the arrival of lawyer Philip Dobbs (Harry Harvey), who represents the estate. Crooked lawyer Bolton (I. Stanford Jolley) and Dr. Vanner (Robert Barron) want the ranch for themselves and they plot to have Vanner impersonate Dobbs. They murder the lawyer; when Tex witnesses the killing, they accuse him of the crime. Panhandle then takes on the guise of circuit court judge Dean and releases Tex so he can prove his innocence. Panhandle also appoints Jim and Tex as managers of the land office, ousting Martin from the job. Martin offers Vanner a partnership in the sale of the ranch and land company. In the land office, the Rangers find proof that Martin is involved in the rustling. When Martin learns that Jim and Tex are Rangers, he orders a gunman (Charles King) to kill them but he fails. Captured, Bolton and gang member King (Richard Alexander) tell Jim and Tex that Vanner is impersonating the lawyer. The real Judge Dean (Henry Hall) arrives in town and finds out he is being impersonated; he rides with Martin and the sheriff (Emmett Lynn) to the ranch where the Rangers fill him in. Martin tries to escape but is captured by the Rangers. Besides the traditional "Home on the Range," the other songs used in the film were "Paradise Trail" by Oliver Drake and "Headin' Westward" by Newill and O'Brien.

Boss of Rawhide, released in November, 1943, was also written and directed by Elmer Clifton. Here the Texas Rangers (Newill, O'Brien, Wilkerson) are working undercover to stop landgrabbers led by Rawhide town boss Sam Barrett (Jack Ingram). After witnessing the robbery of a stagecoach and the murder of its driver who refused to pay a road toll, Tex pretends to be a drifter and is taken into town by ranch foreman Bill Holden (Karl Hackett). Barrett recognizes him as the son of Captain John Wyatt (Robert Hill), the head of the local unit of the Texas Rangers. Tex asks his father to run for the office of land commissioner to represent the area's smaller ranchers while Barrett puts up Holden for the same job in order to protect his own interests. When Holden orders his gang to attack a stagecoach carrying rancher Henry Colby (Ed Cassidy) and his daughter Mary (Nell O'Day), they are run off by Tex. At a town meeting, Holden and Barrett convince Colby that the small ranchers have destroyed his fences and are rustling his cattle. Barrett tries to shoot Captain Wyatt and then tells Colby the bullet was intended for him. When the Rangers realize the bullet fired at Captain Wyatt was the same caliber as the bullet that killed the stage driver, they suspect Barrett and they trail him. Mary sees Barrett attempt to shoot the lawmen and when he tries to capture her she is saved by the Rangers. Back in Rawhide, Barrett and his gang take Colby prisoner but they are captured by the lawmen with Colby throwing his support to Captain Wyatt. Three of Oliver Drake's songs, "I Got a Gal to Come Home To," "Stardust Trail" and "Ride On, Vaquero," the latter written with Herbert Myers, were used in the feature, which also included the Newill-O'Brien composition "High in the Saddle."

The part of Ranger Captain John Wyatt in *Boss of Rawhide* was portrayed by Robert Hill, a veteran director. Hill (1886–1966), who was often billed as Robert F. Hill or Bob Hill, was a director and scriptwriter who specialized in action features and serials. He began directing in 1919 and continued to do so until 1941, thereafter appearing in supporting roles. As a scripter, he often used the name Rock Hawkey.

The first of eight 1944 "Texas Rangers" films, *Outlaw Roundup*, was released in February of that year. Again written by Elmer Clifton, it was the first of the series to be directed by Harry Fraser. Featured in the cast as a musician was Aleth Hansen, who composed the three songs performed in the movie: "Forget Me Not," "Someone is Waiting" and "When the Western Sun is Sinking." Outlaws attack a stagecoach whose passengers include Texas Rangers Tex (O'Brien) and

Panhandle (Wilkerson), along with Ruth Randall (Helen Chapman), whose father, Jed Randall (Bud Osborne), is the sheriff of Cedar Bluff. The driver is shot, but Tex manages to take over the reins and elude the crooks. Gang leader Harkins (Charles King) rides into town to tell his boss, saloon proprietor Red Hayden (I. Stanford Jolley). Jim (Newill) is at the saloon; when Tex arrives to report the holdup attempt, Jim accuses him of being wanted outlaw Spade Norton. The Ranger leaves Tex with Hayden and goes for Sheriff Randall. While he is away, Hayden offers to let Tex go for one-half of the $200,000 he has buried in nearby Devil's Gulch; Tex agrees. When Jim comes back for him, he shoots the Ranger and makes a getaway. Panhandle and Randall take Steele to the sheriff's house; once there the Ranger reveals the shooting was a ruse to catch the outlaws. The real Spade Norton (Jack Ingram) comes to town and identifies himself to Hayden and his boss, barber Dude Merrill (Budd Buster). Panhandle hears Spade agree to lead Hayden to the buried loot and warns Jim and Tex, who arrest the barber. As Jim, Panhandle and Randall ride to Devil's Gulch, Harkins takes Tex to the gang's hideout, where the real Spade tells the outlaws that he is the Ranger who sent him to prison. As they go to dig up the money, Tex leaves a clue for his pals to follow and the gang is dispersed in a shootout. Hayden rides back to town with the money but Spade follows and kills him. The Rangers then capture Spade and the rest of the outlaw gang.

Elmer Clifton wrote and directed *Guns of the Law*, released in April, 1944. This time the Rangers (Newill, O'Brien, Wilkerson) come to the aid of ranchers who are being evicted by the Flint Land Company. Lillian Wilkins (Jennifer Holt), the daughter of ex–Confederate soldier Jed Wilkins (Budd Buster), sends for distant cousin Panhandle and he shows up just as the two are being evicted by Hyslop (Robert Kortman), Tyndall (Robert Barron) and Binns (Frank McCarroll). They beat the old man, giving him a head injury which makes him think he is again fighting in the Civil War. Lillian asks Perkins to convince her father to go to a nearby ranch where they can stay and Jed agrees. Jed has been forced out of his job as surveyor in favor of Sam Brisco (Jack Ingram), who is working for the Flint company and is changing boundary markers in favor of his employers. When Tyndall and Binns return to harass the Wilkinses, Jim arrives and stops them. Tex looks into the murders of three other ranchers and he talks with Brisco, who acts suspicious. The local ranchers ask lawyer Kendall Lowther (Charles King) to represent them, not knowing he is back of all the trouble. During a discussion, Tyndall arrives and, after making insulting remarks, is shot and killed by Jed. Hyslop charges Jed with murder but the Rangers hesitate in arresting him. Jed tells them about his survey maps which Tex locates in Lowther's office. The next day the Rangers check property boundaries and find the markers have been moved. When Brisco tries to kill the Rangers, they capture him and force him to admit that Lowther is behind the lawlessness. They take Brisco to McCloud's ranch where a shootout ensues with Lowther and his gang. McCloud is killed but a blow to Jed's head by Brisco brings back his memory. The Rangers capture Lowther and his gang, and Jed and Lillian return to their ranch. Walter Kittredge's classic "Tenting Tonight on the Old Camp Ground" was included in the film as were Aleth Hansen's "Old Arizona Moon" and the Newill-O'Brien song "Ranger A-Ridin."

Also released in April, 1944, was *The Pinto Bandit*, which was again written and directed by Elmer Clifton. Don Weston, who was cast as a relay rider, wrote its three songs: "It's Too Late to Say You're Sorry Now," "Listen to the Music of the Range" and "A Wanderer Wandering Home." A masked bandit riding a pinto horse has been robbing express riders in the vicinity of Yuba and Texas Rangers Jim (Newill), Tex (O'Brien) and Panhandle (Wilkerson) are sent to investigate. They rescue wounded express rider Walter Collins (James Martin) and take him to his sister Kitty (Mady Lawrence), who has the local mail franchise. Stage line owner Tom Torrant (Jack Ingram), Kitty's rival for the contract, wants to marry her but she refuses, thinking he may be the Pinto Bandit. After Walter is treated by Doc Carson (Edward Cassidy), the bullet which wounded him disappears; locals Spur Sneely (Charles King), Draw Dudley (Robert Kortman) and Heneberry (Budd Buster) accuse the Rangers of stealing it. Panhandle finds the missing bullet outside Kitty's house and it turns out to be an uncommon caliber. Doc informs Tom that Jim is trying to romance Kitty which causes a saloon brawl. Kitty tells Tom he needs to prove he is not the bandit and he agrees. The Rangers trail him as he rides out of town. Following the shooting of another express rider, they arrest Tom but he proves his innocence by showing his guns carry bullets not of the caliber used in the holdups. When it is announced that a new mail contract will given to the winner of a relay race, the Rangers agree to ride for Kitty. Tom sets up his own three-horse team as do Sneely, Dudley and Heneberry. Although outlaws try to stop Tex on the final leg of the race, Jim and Panhandle come to his rescue and Jim rides off with the mailbag only to be shot at by the Pinto Bandit. Tex and Panhandle capture the bandit who is Doc Carson. He admits being in cahoots with Sneely, Dudley and Heneberry, who are arrested by Jim and Panhandle. Tom wins the race and after doing so offers to make Kitty his partner.

The third "Texas Rangers" film in a row to be written and directed by Elmer Clifton, *Spook Town*, was issued in June, 1944. Its songs "El Lobo" and "Sleepy Hollow," composed by Newill and O'Brien, had been heard in previous series entries. Jim (Newill), Tex (O'Brien) and Panhandle (Wilkerson) are assigned to deliver a strongbox to Dry Valley, by Tex's father, Captain Wyatt (Edward Cassidy). While they spend the night in Mystic, a ghost town, they are attacked by Trigger Booth (Charles King) and his henchmen (John L. Cason, Richard Alexander, Bert Dillard). The Rangers thwart the holdup and the next day meet prospector Dry Wash Thompson (Harry Harvey) who goes with them to Dry Valley. There they lock the strongbox in Wells Fargo agent Sam Benson's (Dick Curtis) safe. Jim and Panhandle have dinner with Sam and his girlfriend Lucy Warren (Mady Lawrence), while Tex remains to guard the office. Booth, who has been hired by a masked man, ropes Tex and drags him into a nearby stream while his men steal the strongbox. As a result, Captain Wyatt drums his son, Jim and Panhandle out of the Rangers and the trio vow to recover the money. At the local café they meet Kurt Fabian (Robert Barron), whose money was in the strongbox. It was to be used to build a dam, with Fabian getting local ranchers to give him one-half of their income if the money was not repaid. They suspect Fabian of being involved in the holdup, especially when Trigger and his gang arrive at the café.

Poster for *Spook Town* (PRC, 1944).

Meanwhile Benson, who rode away following the robbery, is arrested by Captain Wyatt. Since Fabian owns the ghost town, they go back there looking for clues as Trigger accuses Fabian of being the masked man who hired him and demands to be made a partner. Fabian dies of heart failure after the gang threatens him. Released from jail, Sam goes to look for the stolen strongbox and he is followed by Trigger and his gang. Sam finds the strongbox in Mystic but the gang captures him, the event witnessed by Panhandle and Dry Wash. The latter goes for Jim and Tex and there is a shootout with the outlaws. Trigger goes back to town and fights Tex as Captain Wyatt arrives with a posse and the gang is captured. Jim, Tex and Panhandle are reinstated in the Rangers.

Brand of the Devil, released late in July, 1944, was directed by Harry Fraser and written by Elmer Clifton. Jim (Newill), Tex (O'Brien) and Panhandle (Wilkerson) are working undercover to expose the devil's brand rustling gang in the area of Willow Springs. Molly Dawson (Ellen Hall), a rancher, accuses Duke Cutter (Reed Howes) of stealing her white stallion, but Golden Ace Saloon keeper Jack Varno (I. Stanford Jolley) says she is mistaken. Panhandle masquerades as a branding iron salesman and joins Varno's gang, since the saloon owner is behind the rustling. Varno later takes back Molly's horse, claiming it has his brand while Panhandle slips a message to Jim that his boss is buying some new brands. Meanwhile, Henry Wilburn (Budd Buster), Molly's foreman, has put on her clothes and is seen branding cattle by rancher Palin (Karl Hackett), who believes the rustler is Molly. The Rangers arrest Wilburn while Palin forces the sheriff (Ed Cassidy) to arrest Molly. When Varno orders his men to murder Molly, they refuse and he decides to do the job. He shoots Molly through a jailhouse window, not realizing it is Wilburn. Varno sets a trap for the Rangers and tells his henchman Bucko Lynn (Charles King) to murder them. Bucko ambushes Jim and Tex, and Varno captures Panhandle, but after Varno leaves, Perkins and Tex manage to capture Bucko and set Jim free. The outlaw gang is stopped when the Rangers stampede cattle the gang has herded into Painted Canyon. Seeing he is defeated, Varno rides back to town to clean out his safe, planting dynamite in it so it will blow up when opened by the Rangers. During a fistfight, one of Varno's men falls, causing the safe to explode. The sheriff arrives and arrests the outlaws. Only the traditional western tune, "Goodbye Old Paint," was included in the feature.

Newill's final "Texas Rangers" film was *Gunsmoke Mesa* (September, 1941), again directed by Harry Fraser and written by Elmer Clifton. It had three songs by Aleth Hansen: "The Cradle That Used to Be Mine," "So the Spider Weaves His Web" and "Yippi Yi Oh." Jim (Newill), Tex (O'Brien) and Panhandle (Wilkerson) arrive at a cabin shortly after Sam Sneed (Kermit Maynard) and Frank Lear (Richard Alexander) murder a man and his wife. The arrival of the Rangers forces them to end their search for the couple's infant son. The lawmen find the baby along with

Poster for *Gunsmoke Mesa* (PRC, 1944).

the deed to the dead parents' mine. Panhandle takes the baby to a nearby cabin owned by a friend who is out prospecting. The murderers report to their employer, Henry Black (Jack Ingram), of their failure to find the baby; Black wants to become the guardian of the child so he can get control of the mine. When Sneed and Lear come across Jim and Tex bringing the dead bodies into town, they accuse them of murder; the crooks get the local judge (Michael Vallon) to issue warrants for their arrest. Meanwhile the Rangers borrow a cow to get milk for the baby; its angry owner, Joan Royal (Patti McCarty), forgives them when she sees the infant. In town, Jim tells Deputy Mace Page (Roy Brent) he wants to meet Black, since that name was on a note found in the murder cabin. Black and his men try to attack the Rangers, who get away. Joan tells Mace about the three strangers and the baby, and he innocently gives the information to Black. Hoping to record the baby's first words, Panhandle, who has been left in charge of the infant, puts a wax cylinder into a recording machine; when Black and his men show up, their conversation, which includes admitting the killings, is recorded. The gang abducts Panhandle and the baby and they leave the infant among some rocks, where it is found by Joan. Panhandle manages to escape from the gang and find his pals; the trio go back to the cabin where they hid the baby and find the cylinder proving Black's guilt. Joan takes the baby to the sheriff (Jack Rockwell) who turns it over to Black, since he is the legal guardian. The Rangers show up with the cylinder, which results in the arrest of Black and his gang. The judge then gives custody of the baby to Joan and Mace, who are planning to be married.

Newill left "The Texas Rangers" series to star in the musical adaptation of John Colton's play *Rain*, based on the short story by W. Somerset Maugham. He later worked in Europe with his wife and in the early '50s made a series of short musicals for television done by Snader Telescriptions. During that time, he and Dave O'Brien reunited for the 13-episode syndicated TV series *Renfrew of the Royal Mounted*, which used stock footage from their earlier "Renfrew" movies. After that, Newill concentrated on various business ventures. He died July 15, 1975, survived by his wife and three children.

Tex Ritter (1905–74) replaced Newill in the "Texas Rangers" series, causing some changes in character names and billing. In the Ritter films, O'Brien's character was now called Dave Wyatt and the nickname "Tex" was dropped from O'Brien's billing since the character played by Ritter was called Tex Haines. The series brought Ritter back into the poll of top money-making western stars for the 1944–45 theatrical season, a position he had previously held in 1937 and 1941. Ritter's increased salary probably came out of the series' overall budget because the eight films he did for Alexander-Stern Productions have even a shoddier look than earlier entries.

The "Texas Rangers" films were Ritter's final series westerns and in later years he expressed regret about making them, believing they were a comedown from his earlier oaters. Ritter, a native of Texas, had studied law before taking up singing as a career. He appeared on Broadway and in radio in the 1930s before being signed by Edward Finney's Boots & Saddles Productions in 1936 to star in a series for Grand National. He made a dozen entries in the "Range Rider" series for Finney, although he did not portray a continuing character. After Grand National folded in 1938, Ritter and Finney went to Monogram where Tex headlined twenty features between 1938 and 1940; in 1941 and 1942 he co-starred with Bill Elliott in the "Wild Bill Hickok" series (q.v.) for Columbia. After that he worked mostly with Johnny Mack Brown at Universal (from 1942 to 1944) before taking up the PRC series.

The initial Ritter series outing, *Gangsters of the Frontier*, came out in September, 1944, and again was written and directed by Elmer Clifton. Taking place in the town of Red Rock, it tells of escaped convicts Bart (I. Stanford Jolley) and Rad Kern (Marshall Reed) returning to attack Sheriff Tex Haines (Ritter), who originally sent them to jail, and mine owner Frank Merritt (Harry Harvey). When Texas Ranger Dave Wyatt (O'Brien) arrives and tries to stop the fight, he, Tex and Merritt are forced to take refuge in the telegraph office owned by Jane Deering (Patti McCarty). There they are aided by telegraph operator Panhandle (Wilkerson) and his homing pigeon Homer. The outlaws force the four men to hide in a barn where Wyatt tells the others he has been sent to capture the escaped convicts. Tex, Panhandle and Merritt agree to help him. Tex sneaks into Jane's house and plays his guitar and sings, diverting the outlaws while Dave and Panhandle ride away, but Merritt is captured by the badmen. When he tries to escape from the Kern brothers, Merritt is murdered and his widow (Betty Miles) vows revenge. She organizes the locals to fight the Kerns, and Tex swears them in as Rangers. The outlaws take control of Merritt's mine and decide to destroy the telegraph lines. The Kern gang captures Jane and shoots down Panhandle's pigeon who was being sent with a message for help. Panhandle is also taken prisoner by the gang but locates a downed telegraph wire and sends a message to Tex and Dave as to their whereabouts. Panhandle manages to escape his captors and joins Tex, Dave and the area Rangers; together they shoot the Kern brothers, bringing law and order back to Red Rock.

Not only did *Gangsters of the Frontier* have a mildewed look, it also had a rambling plotline which included the incredible scene of a pigeon pretending to be dead! With Ritter headlining the feature, it was only natural that music would be a dominant factor and the star's singing was certainly a plus for the proceedings. Tex's composition "Please Remember Me" was included as were two songs by Vern (Tim) Spencer, "He's Gone Up the Trail" and "Ride, Ranger, Ride." In England the film was called *Raiders of the Frontier*.

Dead or Alive (November, 1944), directed by Elmer Clifton and written by Harry Fraser, was somewhat better. Dave (O'Brien) and Panhandle (Wilkerson) are after an outlaw gang led by saloon owner Clint Yackey (Ray Bennett). Perkins pretends to be a marshal and Dave his prisoner and they plant the story that Dave has money hidden in a nearby town. A judge (Henry Hall) hires lawyer Tex Haines (Ritter), known as "The Idaho Kid," to bring law and order the area and Tex comes to town with his client, Arline Arthur (Marjorie Clements), who is claiming half-interest in Yackey's saloon. Because he has allegedly been losing Dave's money gambling in Yackey's saloon, Panhandle sets Dave free so he can join Clint's gang. Yackey tells the town's bank president (Ed Cassidy) that Arline also has a right to half the bank's assets, and to make sure she does not get them he has his men stage a holdup, with henchman Red (Charles King) killing the bank president. Tex chases Red and is able to retrieve the stolen money and then plans a ruse to get Yackey to rob the Wells Fargo office. During the robbery, Dave is arrested for being a member of the gang and he cannot prove his real identity since Panhandle has lost his Ranger credentials. Yackey captures Tex but ransoms him for Dave, but the local law enforcement committee refuses to set him free. Just as Dave is about to be hung, Panhandle finds the credentials and the two ride to the gang's hideout to rescue Tex. The lawyer manages to escape with the outlaws following him. Tex meets up with Dave and Panhandle and after fighting the gang at the saloon, the outlaws are brought to justice. Two Ritter songs, "I Don't Care Since You Told Me Goodbye" and "I'm Gonna Leave You Like I Found You," were included in the movie. In Great Britain it was retitled *Wanted By the Law*.

Due to its mystery angle, *The Whispering Skull*, issued early in 1945, is probably the best known of the Tex Ritter "Texas Rangers" features. Lawyer Tex Haines (Ritter) and Rangers Dave (O'Brien) and Panhandle (Wilkerson) are on the trail of a masked man, The Whispering Skull. Saloon keeper Duke Walters (I. Stanford Jolley) is warned by the Skull to get out of town, so he has his gang try to find the masked renegade. Instead they come upon Panhandle and accuse him of being the Skull; Tex and Dave save their partner from being lynched by the badmen. Dave goes undercover masquerading as outlaw Reno Carson and infiltrates Duke's gang. Walters plans to murder Sheriff Jackson (George Morrell) and blame the crime on the Skull. After hearing gunshots from the saloon owner's office, Tex and Dave find Jackson's body. Although Tex tells the sheriff's daughter Ellen (Denny Burke) that her father has been murdered, the lawmen realize the sheriff is still alive and they call in the town doctor (Ed Cassidy) to treat him but keep his condition a secret. Duke orders Ellers (Frank Ellis), a henchman, to put on the Skull's mask and rob the stagecoach but he is shot by Tex and Dave. The two then tell Ellen her father is alive and the sheriff identifies his attacker as Duke Walters. Dave finds the real Skull searching Duke's office and after a fight he learns the masked man is a prospector (Wen Wright) who is after minerals he thinks are valuable; he has been using the Skull

Poster for *The Whispering Skull* (PRC, 1944).

forces with Rangers Dave (O'Brien) and Panhandle (Wilkerson) in helping Sheriff Jim Whitlock (Henry Hall), Tex's one-time guardian, who is in the middle of a range war between cattlemen and sheep herders; one of the suspects is Pete Magoo (Charles King). While working as an traveling mender, Panhandle finds out Magoo is in cahoots with merchant Sam Taylor (Jack Ingram) and Bill Ganer (Wen Wright) in trying to control the area's range land. Taylor tells Ganer to kill cattleman Jed Moore (Frank Ellis) and as a result the dead man's partner, Dick Vernon (Ed Cassidy), blames Ruth Lane (Marilyn McConnell), who runs a sheep operation. The cattlemen attack Ruth's place and are arrested by the Rangers, who put Ruth and her men under protective custody. Taylor and his gang continue to cause trouble by rustling and cutting fences in hopes of further pitting the cattlemen and sheepherders against each other. Although the Rangers are unable to capture Ganer, they do force a confession out of Magoo, who says Taylor is behind the lawlessness. When the outlaws attack the jail, the Rangers unite the ranchers and the sheepherders and the gang is arrested after a gun battle.

Marked For Murder had Ritter performing four songs: "Long Time Gone," which he co-wrote; Smiley Burnette's "Great Grand Dad," Don Weston's "Tears of Regret" and the traditional "Froggie Went-a-Courtin.'" Tex recorded "Long

guise to frighten away ranchers. Duke has also been after the land for the minerals, which prove to be bogus. Because of his criminal activities, Duke and his gang are arrested. Two more songs co-written by Ritter were used in the movie, "In Case You Change Your Mind" and "It's Never Too Late." Both were recorded by Ritter for Capitol Records on September 27, 1944, although only "It's Never Too Late" was issued. He also waxed both numbers for Capitol Transcriptions.

Elmer Clifton wrote and directed *Marked For Murder*, which came out in February, 1945. Here lawyer and former Ranger Tex (Ritter) joins

Time Gone" for Capitol Records in 1945 and he did it and "Tears of Regret" for Capital Transcriptions. He recorded "Froggie Went-a-Courtin'" several times for Capital and he also filmed it in 1951 for Snader Telescriptions.

Harry Fraser wrote and directed *Enemy of the Law* which came to theaters in the spring of 1945. Tex (Ritter) joins his former Ranger partner Dave (O'Brien) in trying to find a strongbox hidden five years before by outlaw Wild Charlie Gray (Charles King). Panhandle (Wilkerson) is working undercover as Gray's prison cellmate, hoping to find the location of the hidden gold. Not trusting Panhandle, Gray draws a map to the gold on the bottom of Panhandle's boot while he is asleep. Upon their release from prison, Gray and Panhandle go to see the outlaw's former partner, saloon proprietor Steve Martin (Jack Ingram). Working at the saloon is Martin's niece Ruby Lawson (Kay Hughes); Dave, pretending to be a vagrant, asks Ruby for a job. When Steve becomes suspicious of Dave and pulls a gun on him, Tex, who once did legal work for Ruby, stops him. Meanwhile Gray goes to a local doctor (Karl Hackett) and has a scar removed and then he murders the medical man. Finding the map engraved on his boot, Panhandle presses it into a sock and throws it away. When a cowboy (Ben Corbett) picks up the sock, he is followed by Martin and Gray who recover it and then ride to the location of the hidden strongbox, the cellar of Steve's saloon. Martin tries to shoot Gray but Tex and Dave arrive and a fight takes place as Gray tries to get Panhandle to help him carry off the gold. Panhandle instead takes Gray to jail as Tex and Dave arrest Martin and his henchmen (Kermit Maynard, Frank Ellis). As a result of her uncle's arrest, Ruby becomes the proprietor of the saloon.

Like several other PRC titles, *Enemy of the Law* was issued on 16mm by Castle films in a cut version and given a new title, *Cowboy Reckoning*. Ritter sang "Teach Me to Forget" and "You Will Have to Pay," both of which he co-wrote. He waxed the former song for Capitol the year after the film was released; he had recorded "You Will Have To Pay" in 1944, before it went into production. He also did both numbers for Capitol Transcriptions.

Most of the films in the "Texas Rangers" series have only Dave and Panhandle as actual Rangers while Tex Haines is a lawyer and sometimes a former Ranger. Haines is neither in *Three in the Saddle*, which Harry Fraser directed and Elmer Clifton wrote. Released in the summer of 1945 it had Tex Haines (Ritter) working for ranch owner Peggy Barlow (Lorraine Miller) and being harassed by Bart Rawlins (Charles King) and his gang, who claim he is trespassing on land belonging to stage line owner John Rankin (Edward Howard). Rankin tells Peggy his state contract gives him right-of-way through her property and he offers to buy her ranch but she refuses to sell. Tex (O'Brien) and Panhandle (Wilkerson), who came to Tex's rescue, are working undercover to stop Rankin from robbing the ranchers of their lands. The next day Peggy is given an eviction notice by a local deputy sheriff (Frank Ellis) and when her foreman, Dan Brown (Bob Duncan), protests, he is shot by Rankin's henchman, Dugan (Art Fowler), who in turn is killed by Tex. Trading post owner Jim Manning (Ed Cassidy) is Rankin's secret partner and he convinces the sheriff (Bud Osborne) to arrest Tex; the cowboy flees. Later, at a remote hideout, Dave tells Tex and Panhandle he plans to ambush Rankin who is on his way back from the state capitol. Disguising himself, Dave robs Rankin and finds papers which show he plans to sell the ranchers' land to a syndicate. Dave suspects Manning is involved in the scheme but has a falling-out with Tex when he tries to take him to jail. Panhandle pretends to be a land syndicate representative and demands that Rankin and Manning sign a contract. Bart arrives and identifies Panhandle, and Rankin orders him to kill the Ranger. The two crooks plan to evict Peggy and sell her ranch to the syndicate but Tex, Dave and Panhandle ride to the woman's ranch and stop the eviction. Rankin and Manning try to escape but Dave and Panhandle arrest them. The two Rangers then go on to their next assignment, leaving behind Tex and Peggy. This outing had Ritter singing "I Done the Best I Could," which he co-wrote, and Ernest Tubb's "Try Me One More Time." He recorded "I Done the Best I Could" at his first Capitol Records session in 1942 and he waxed the Tubb song three years later for Capitol (he also did it for Capitol Transcriptions).

Frontier Fugitives, called *Fugitives of the Frontier* in England, was released in the fall of 1945. It was again directed by Harry Fraser and scripted by Elmer Clifton. It is the only film in the series in which the character of Tex Haines is an actual Ranger. Texas Rangers Tex (Ritter), Dave (O'Brien) and Panhandle (Wilkerson) investigate a series of Indian attacks which turn out to be perpetrated by white men. Two supposed Indians murder trapper Williams (George Morrell) and one of them is shot by Dave while the other is followed by Tex who sees him rummaging through the dead man's papers. Before he can arrest the outlaw, he is shot by cohorts Sneed (I. Stanford Jolley) and Donner (Frank Ellis), who escape. Indian agent Fain (Jack Ingram), who is really a crook in cahoots with the outlaws, arrests Tex for the killing. Dave goes to see Williams' daughter Ellen (Lorraine Miller), who has found Sneed and Donner searching her property. While she and Dave argue, the outlaws escape. Fain arrives and arrests Dave, then takes both Tex and Dave to jail. Ellen gets a judge to set the Rangers free and she tells them she suspects her father left a map to his hidden fur cache, which is being sought by the crooks. Panhandle and Sneed dress themselves as Indians and try to find the map but fail. Tex realizes that Fain is an imposter who tries to escape when told that the body of the real Indian agent has been located. The Rangers come to realize the clue to the furs is at Jim Gar's (Jack Hendricks) trading post; Gar is also associated with Sneed and Donner. The crooks kidnap Ellen and are chased by the Rangers but the outlaws return with her to the trading post where a fight ensues with Ellen being freed. Panhandle finds the map but it is stolen by Sneed, who with his gang heads to a nearby ghost town. The Rangers follow and arrest the crooks after a gunfight. The furs are located, making Ellen a rich woman. Two Al Dexter songs, "Too Late to Worry, Too Blue to Cry" and "I'll Want to See You, Dear," were sung in the feature by Ritter. He recorded the first song for Capitol Transcriptions. The feature included an amusing scene in which both hero Panhandle and henchman Sneed masquerade as Indians with the crook smoking a peace pipe laced with happy weed.

The final "Texas Rangers" outing, *Flaming Bullets*, written and directed by Harry Fraser, came out in October, 1945. Like the previous entry, it contained quite a bit of comedy, especially in the casting of Charles King in the role of buffoon Porky Smith and the use of laughing gas at the finale. Tex (O'Brien) arrives in Alkalai Springs with lawyer Tex (Ritter), whose friend has been falsely arrested, sprung from jail and then murdered for the reward money. Panhandle (Wilkerson) comes to town disguised as a traveling dentist and he enlists the aid of Porgy Smith (Charles King) in bringing him clients. Dave takes on the guise of his lookalike, outlaw Steve Carlson (also O'Brien), whose fiancée, Belle (Patricia Knox), operates the town saloon. Dave is accepted as Carlson by both Belle and the leader of the murder gang, Sid Tolliver (I. Stanford Jolley), but he is arrested by the marshal (Bud Osborne) and put in jail. Tex is knocked out in a riding accident; when the Tolliver gang go through his coat, they find a Ranger badge which belongs to Dave, and assume that Tex is a Ranger out to bring in Carlson, who they think is in jail. Back in town, Tex gets into a fight with Tolliver in the saloon and is arrested but he and Dave persuade the lawman they are after the outlaw gang. When the real Carlson comes to town, the marshal arrests him but the gang breaks Dave out of jail, still thinking he is their henchman. At the outlaw hideout, Dave tries to arrest the gang but is knocked out by henchman Luke (Kermit Maynard) and left for dead. Tex trails the outlaws and, finding Dave supposedly murdered, he tells Tolliver and Luke they can collect the reward money for Carlson. Dave reveals his identity to Belle but is exposed by henchman Jim (John L. Cason). When Tex arrives at the saloon, a fistfight breaks out. During the melee, one of the bottles of laughing gas used by Panhandle in his dentistry is broken and everyone is overcome with laughter. Tex, Dave and Panhandle manage to subdue the crooks and later Tex agrees to Belle's request to help Carlson.

During the course of *Flaming Bullets*, Ritter sang "Be Honest with Me" and "I Hang My Head and Cry," both of which were popularized at the time by Gene Autry on Columbia Records. Autry co-wrote "Be Honest with Me" with Fred Rose, while Rose and Ray Whitley composed "I Hang My Head and Cry." Tex waxed the latter song for one of his Capitol Transcriptions in the late 1940s.

While the finish of the "Texas Rangers" series spelled the end of Ritter's days as a "B" western star, he would continue to entertain for the rest of his life. He had many hit records for Capitol, with whom he had a lifetime contract, and he appeared in other movies as well as singing the background song in the classic *High Noon* (1952). He headlined the radio and TV series *Town Hall Party* in the 1950s; partnered with Johnny Bond to form Vidor Publications, a music publishing firm; and in 1964 he was elected to the Country Music Hall of Fame. Moving to Nashville, Tennessee, in 1965, he starred on radio for station WSM as well as joining the Grand Ole Opry. In 1970 he unsuccessfully ran for the Republican nomination for the U.S. Senate from Tennessee. He died January 2, 1973, as he was preparing to go on still another singing tour. His son John Ritter (1948–2003) was a noted actor in films and television. His wife, Dorothy Fay [Southworth] (1915–2003), who married Tex in 1939, appeared in 15 feature films, most of them "B" westerns. They were together in three films: *Sundown on the Prairie* and *Rollin' Westward* (both 1939) and *Rainbow Over the Range* (1940).

While working in the "Texas Rangers" series, Dave O'Brien also starred in two 1945 features for the studio, *The Man Who Walked Alone* and *Phantom of 42nd Street*. He also began working at MGM in 1942 in the "Pete Smith Specialties" short subject series, and for the next 13 years he did scores of these films, both as a writer and actor. After that he worked as a comedy writer for TV's *The Red Skelton Show*, winning an Emmy Award. His hobby was boat racing, and after winning a race he died on November 8, 1969, at Catalina Island's Avalon Harbor.

Guy Wilkerson continued to work in films after the "Texas Rangers" features, eventually appearing in over 160 movies, mostly in supporting and bit roles. He even played a character called Panhandle in the 1946 Universal western, *The Scarlet Horseman*. Also active in television, his last film was *The Todd Killings* (1971). He died in Hollywood on July 15, 1971.

Filmography

The Rangers Take Over (PRC, 1942, 60 minutes) Producers: Alfred Stern & Arthur Alexander. Director: Al Herman. Screenplay: Elmer Clifton. Photography: Robert Cline. Editor: Charles Henkel, Jr. Sound: Corson Jowett. Music Director: Lee Zahler. Songs: Robert Hoag, Jack Williams & Tex Coe [Jim Newill & Dave O'Brien].
Cast: Dave "Tex" O'Brien (Tex Wyatt), Jim Newill (Jim Steele), Guy Wilkerson (Panhandle Perkins), Iris Meredith (Jean Lorin), Forrest Taylor (Captain John Wyatt), I. Stanford Jolley (Rance Blair), Charles King (Kip Lane), Carl Mathews (Weir Slocum), Harry Harvey (Bill Summers), Lynton Brent (Brock Nelson), Bud Osborne (Pete Dawson), Slim Whitaker (Sheriff Jake), Hank Bell (Bartender), Jess Cavin, Rube Dalroy, Art Dillard, George Morrell, Jack Tornek (Saloon Customers), Cal Shrum's Rhythm Rangers [Cal Shrum, Rusty Cline, Don Weston & Art Wenzell] (Musicians).

Bad Men of Thunder Gap (PRC, 1943, 59 minutes) Producers: Alfred Stern & Arthur Alexander. Director: Al Herman. Screenplay: Elmer Clifton. Photography: Robert Cline. Editor: Charles Henkel, Jr. Sound: Hans Weeren. Music Director: Lee Zahler. Songs: Cal Shrum & Tex Coe [Jim Newill & Dave O'Brien]. Assistant Director: Lou Perlof.
Cast: Dave "Tex" O'Brien (Tex Wyatt), Jim Newill (Jim Steele), Guy Wilkerson (Panhandle Perkins), Janet Shaw [Ellen Clancy] (Martha Stewart), Jack Ingram (Ed Ransom), Charles King (Pete Holman), Michael Vallon (John Hobbs), Lucille Vance (Mathilda Matthews), Tom London (Hank Turner), I. Stanford Jolley (Bill Horne), Bud Osborne (Clem), Jimmy Aubrey (Frank Rand), Kermit Maynard, Hank Bell, Artie Ortego, Carl Mathews (Henchmen), Cal Shrum's Rhythm Rangers [Cal Shrum, Robert Hoag, Rusty Cline, Don Weston & Art Wenzell] (Musicians).
Reissued in 1947 in a 39-minute version called *Thundergap Outlaws*.

West of Texas (PRC, 1943, 56 minutes) Producers: Alfred Stern & Arthur Alexander. Director-Screenplay: Oliver Drake. Photography: Ira Morgan. Editor: Charles Henkel, Jr. Sound: Corson Jowett. Music Director: Lee Zahler. Songs: Tex Coe [Jim Newill & Dave O'Brien]. Assistant Director: Arthur Alexander.
Cast: Dave "Tex" O'Brien (Tex Wyatt), Jim Newill (Jim Steele), Guy Wilkerson (Panhandle Perkins), Frances Gladwin (Marie Monette), Marilyn Hare (Ellen Yeager), Henry Hall (Bent Yeager), Robert Barron (Bart Calloway), Tom London (Steve Conlan), Jack Rockwell (Gabe Jones), Jack Ingram (Clem), Roy Butler (Sheriff Tom McCallister), Charles King (Blackie), Chuck Morrison, Victor Cox, Wally West, Carl Mathews (Henchmen), Chick Hannon, Hank Bell, Curley Dresden, Jack Tornek, Matty Roubert (Rangers), Herman Hack (Rider), George Morrell, Rube Dalroy, Jack Evans (Saloon Customers).
Reissued in 1947 in a 40-minute version called *Shootin' Irons*.

Border Buckaroos (PRC, 1943, 60 minutes) Producers: Alfred Stern & Arthur Alexander. Director-Screenplay: Oliver Drake. Photography: Ira Morgan. Editor: Charles Henkel, Jr. Music Director: Lee Zahler. Songs: Jim Newill & Dave O'Brien.
Cast: Dave "Tex" O'Brien (Tex Wyatt), Jim Newill (Jim Steele), Guy Wilkerson (Panhandle Perkins), Christine McIntyre (Betty Clark), Eleanor Counts (Marge Leonard), Jack Ingram (Cole Melford), Ethan Laidlaw (Hank Dugan), Charles King (Rance Daggert), Michael Vallon (Seth Higgins), Kenne Duncan (Tom Bancroft), Reed Howes (Trigger Farley), Slim Whitaker (Sheriff McAllister), Kermit Maynard, Roy Brent (Henchmen), Bud Osborne (Stage Driver).

Fighting Valley (PRC, 1943, 60 minutes) Producers: Alfred Stern & Arthur Alexander. Director-Screenplay-Songs: Oliver Drake. Photography: Ira Morgan. Editor: Charles Henkel, Jr. Music Director: Lee Zahler.

Art Director: Fred Preble. Sets: Harry Reif. Sound: Corson Jowett. Special Effects: Ray Mercer. Properties: George Bahr.

Cast: Dave "Tex" O'Brien (Tex Wyatt), Jim Newill (Jim Steele), Guy Wilkerson (Panhandle Perkins), Patti McCarty (Joan Manning), John Merton (Dan Wakely), Robert Bice (Paul Jackson), Stanley Price (Tucson Jones), Mary McLaren (Ma Donovan), John Elliott (Frank Burke), Charles King (Slim), Budd Buster (Judge Hawkins), Hal Price (Sheriff Losen), Dan White (Jeff Kelly), Jess Cavin, Curley Dresden, Jimmy Aubrey (Henchmen), Tex Williams (Singer), Don Weston (Musician).

Trail of Terror (PRC, 1943, 60 minutes) Producers: Alfred Stern & Arthur Alexander. Director-Screenplay: Oliver Drake. Photography: Ira Morgan. Art Director: Fred Preble. Sound: Corson Jowett. Sets: Harry Reif. Properties: Sam Gordon. Music Director: Lee Zahler. Songs: Jim Newill & Dave O'Brien.

Cast: Dave "Tex" O'Brien (Jim Wyatt/Curly Wyatt), Jim Newill (Jim Steele), Guy Wilkerson (Panhandle Perkins), Patricia Knox (Belle Blaine), Jack Ingram (Nevada Simmons), I. Stanford Jolley (Hank), Budd Buster (Monte), Kenne Duncan (Tom), Frank Ellis (Poe), Robert Hill (Captain Curtis), Dan White (Al), Jimmy Aubrey (Patient), Slim Whitaker (Messenger), Wally West (Cowboy), Rose Plummer, Artie Ortego, Tom Smith (Citizens).

The Return of the Rangers (PRC, 1943, 60 minutes) Producer-Assistant Director: Arthur Alexander. Associate Producer: Alfred Stern. Director-Screenplay: Elmer Clifton. Photography: Robert Cline. Editor: Charles Henkel, Jr. Music: Lee Zahler. Songs: Jim Newill & Dave O'Brien. Sound: Corson Jowett. Sets: Harry Reif.

Cast: Dave "Tex" O'Brien (Tex Wyatt), Jim Newill (Jim Steele), Guy Wilkerson (Panhandle Perkins), Nell O'Day (Ann Miller), Glenn Strange (Frank Martin), Emmett Lynn (Sheriff Summers), I. Stanford Jolley (Don Bolton), Robert Barron (Dr. Robert "Doc" Vanner), Henry Hall (Judge Dean), Art Fowler (Deputy Sheriff), Dick [Richard] Alexander (Sam King), Charles King (Bill Thorn), Harry Harvey (Phillip Dobbs), Wally West (Stagecoach Driver), Hank Bell (Wagon Driver), Tex Cooper (Man on Wagon), Curley Dresden (Al), Herman Hack (Man in Court), Horace B. Carpenter, Rose Plummer (Citizens), Art Wenzel (Musician).

Boss of Rawhide (PRC, 1943, 57 minutes) Producer: Alfred Stern. Associate Producer: Arthur Alexander. Director-Screenplay: Elmer Clifton. Photography: Robert Cline. Editor: Charles Henkel, Jr. Music: Lee Zahler. Songs: Jim Newill, Dave O'Brien, Oliver Drake & Herbert Myers. Sound: Lyle Willey. Sets: Harry Reif. Assistant Director: Clark L. Paylow.

Cast: Dave "Tex" O'Brien (Tex Wyatt), Jim Newill (Jim Steele), Guy Wilkerson (Panhandle Perkins), Nell O'Day (Mary Colby), Edward [Ed] Cassidy (Henry Colby), Jack Ingram (Sam Barrett), Billy Bletcher (Jed Bones), Charles King [Jr.] (Frank Hade), George Chesebro (Joe Gordon), Robert Hill (Captain John Wyatt), Dan White (Minstrel Man), Lucille Vance (Mrs. Perriwinkle), Karl Hackett (Bill Holden), Frank Ellis (Jim Davis), Bud Osborne (Frank), Slim Whitaker (Jeffries), Jimmy Aubrey (Pawn Shop Owner), Robert Kortman, Curley Dresden (Henchmen), Wally West (Stagecoach Driver), Budd Buster, Herman Hack, Fred Burns, Tex Cooper, Rose Plummer (Citizens).

Top, above and following page: Advertisements for re-edited versions of the "Texas Rangers" films.

Outlaw Roundup (PRC, 1944, 55 minutes) Producer: Alfred Stern. Associate Producer: Arthur Alexander. Director: Harry Fraser. Screenplay: Elmer Clifton. Photography: Ira Morgan. Editor: Charles Henkel, Jr. Sound: Lyle Willey. Sets: Harry Reif. Music Director: Lee Zahler. Songs: Aleth Hansen. Assistant Director: Clark L. Paylow.

Cast: Dave "Tex" O'Brien (Tex Wyatt), Jim Newill (Jim Steele), Guy Wilkerson (Panhandle Perkins), Helen Chapman (Helen Randall), Jack Ingram (Spade Norton), I. Stanford Jolley (Red Hayden), Charles King (Frank Harkins), Reed Howes (Rod Laidlow), Bud Osborne (Sheriff Jed Randall), Frank Ellis (Sam Panzer), Budd Buster (Duke Merrill), Dan White (Louie the Bartender), Cal Shrum, Aleth Hansen (Musicians), Frank McCarroll (Lookout), Jimmy Aubrey, Jess Cavin, Jack Tornek (Saloon Customers).

Guns of the Law (PRC, 1944, 56 minutes) Producer-Assistant Director: Arthur Alexander. Associate Producer: Alfred Stern. Director-Screenplay: Elmer Clifton. Photography: Edward Kull. Editor: Charles Henkel, Jr. Sound: Arthur B. Smith. Sets: Harry Reif. Music Director: Lee Zahler. Songs: Jim Newill, Dave O'Brien & Aleth Hansen.

Cast: Dave "Tex" O'Brien (Tex Wyatt), Jim Newill (Jim Steele), Guy Wilkerson (Panhandle Perkins), Jennifer Holt (Lillian Wilkins), Budd Buster (Jed Wilkins), Charles King [Jr.] (Kendall Lowther), Jack Ingram (Sam Brisco), Robert Kortman (Joe Hyslop), Robert Barron (Dan Tyndall), Frank McCarroll (Tom Binns), Slim Whitaker (Sheriff), Bud Osborne (Henry McCloud), Dan White (Henchman).

The Pinto Bandit (PRC, 1944, 56 minutes) Producer: Alfred Stern. Associate Producer-Assistant Director: Arthur Alexander. Director-Screenplay: Elmer Clifton. Photography: Edward Kull. Editor: Charles Henkel, Jr. Sound: Arthur B. Smith. Sets: Harry Reif. Music Director: Lee Zahler. Songs: Don Weston.

Cast: Dave "Tex" O'Brien (Tex Wyatt), Jim Newill (Jim Steele), Guy Wilkerson (Panhandle Perkins), Mady Lawrence (Kitty Collins), James Martin (Walter Collins), Jack Ingram (Jack Torrant), Edward [Ed] Cassidy (Doc Carson), Budd Buster (P.T. Heneberry), Karl Hackett (Sheriff Bisbee), Charles King [Jr.] (Spur Sneely), Robert Kortman (Draw Dudley), Jimmy Aubrey (Tommy the Bartender), Kermit Maynard, Don Weston (Riders), Herman Hack, Carl Mathews, Ray Henderson (Saloon Customers).

Spook Town (PRC, 1944, 59 minutes) Producer: Arthur Alexander. Associate Producer: Alfred Stern. Director-Screenplay: Elmer Clifton. Photography: Robert Cline. Editor: Charles Henkel, Jr. Sound: Arthur B. Smith. Sets: Harry Reif. Music Director: Lee Zahler. Songs: Jim Newill & Dave O'Brien. Animal Trainer: Lionel Comport.

Cast: Dave "Tex" O'Brien (Tex Wyatt), Jim Newill (Jim Steele), Guy Wilkerson (Panhandle Perkins), Mady Lawrence (Lucy Warren), Dick Curtis (Sam Benson), Harry Harvey (Dry Wash Thompson), Edward [Ed] Cassidy (Captain Wyatt), Charles King (Trigger Booth), Robert Barron (Kurt Fabian), Dick [Richard] Alexander, Bert Dillard (Henchmen), John L. Cason (Breed), Kermit Maynard, Chick Hannon (Texas Rangers), John Elliott (Homesteader), Jack Tornek (Citizen).

Brand of the Devil (PRC, 1944, 62 minutes) Producer: Arthur Alexander. Associate Producer: Alfred Stern. Director: Harry Fraser. Screenplay: Elmer Clifton. Photography: Edward Kull. Editor: Charles Henkel, Jr. Sound: Arthur B. Smith. Sets: Harry Reif. Music Director: Lee Zahler. Special Effects: Ray Mercer. Assistant Director: Lou Perlof.

Cast: Dave "Tex" O'Brien (Tex Wyatt), Jim Newill (Jim Steele), Guy Wilkerson (Panhandle Perkins), Ellen Hall (Molly Dawson), I. Stanford Jolley (Jack Varno), Charles King (Bucko Lynn), Reed Howes (Duke Cutter), Budd Buster (Henry Wilburn), Karl Hackett (Jeff Palin), Kermit Maynard (Gripper Joe), Ed Cassidy (Sheriff Parker), Wally West (Deputy Sheriff), John L. Cason (Ed), Hank Bell (Hank the Bartender), Rose Plummer (Housekeeper), Jess Cavin, Jack Evans, Jack Tornek (Saloon Customers).

Gunsmoke Mesa (PRC, 1944, 59 minutes) Producer: Arthur Alexander. Associate Producer: Alfred Stern. Director: Harry Fraser. Screenplay: Elmer Clifton. Photography: Ira Morgan. Editor: Charles Henkel, Jr. Sound: Lyle Willey. Sets: Harry Reif. Music Director: Lee Zahler. Songs: Aleth Hansen.

Cast: Dave "Tex" O'Brien (Tex Wyatt), Jim Newill (Jim Steele), Guy Wilkerson (Panhandle Perkins), Patti McCarty (Joan Royal), Jack Ingram (Henry Black), Kermit Maynard (Sam Sneed), Robert Barron (Moore), Dick [Richard] Alexander (Frank Lear), Michael Vallon (Judge Ezra Plymouth), Roy Brent (Deputy Sheriff Mace Page), Jack Rockwell (Sheriff Horner), Budd Buster (Grandpa), Don Weston (Tom Andrews), Rose Plummer (Mrs. Summers).

Gangsters of the Frontier (PRC, 1944, 56 minutes) Producer: Arthur Alexander. Associate Producer: Alfred Stern. Director-Screenplay: Elmer Clifton. Photography: Robert Cline. Editor: Charles Henkel, Jr. Sound: Arthur B. Smith. Sets: Harry Reif. Music Director: Lee Zahler. Songs: Tex Ritter, Bob McJimsey [Robert MacGimsey] & Vern [Tim] Spencer. Special Effects: Ray Mercer. Assistant Director: Harold E. Knox.

Cast: Tex Ritter (Tex Haines), Dave O'Brien (Dave Wyatt), Guy Wilkerson (Panhandle Perkins), Patti McCarty (Jane Deering), Harry Harvey (Mayor Frank Merritt), Betty Miles (Mrs. Merritt), I. Stanford Jolley (Bart Kern), Charles King (Haner), Charles Stevens (Shade), Marshall Reed (Rad Kern), Henry Hall (Rogers), Wally West (Driver), Robert Barron, Herman Hack, Victor Cox, Ray Henderson, Lew Morphy (Henchmen), Dan White, George Morrell, Jack Evans (Citizens).

British title: *Raiders of the Frontier*.

Dead or Alive (PRC, 1944, 56 minutes) Producer: Arthur Alexander. Associate Producer: Alfred Stern. Director: Elmer Clifton. Screenplay: Harry Fraser. Photography: Robert Cline. Editor: Hugh Winn. Sound: Arthur B. Smith. Sets: Harry Reif. Music Director: Lee Zahler. Songs: Tex Ritter, Lt. Frank Harford & Bonnie Dodd. Special Effects: Ray Mercer. Assistant Director: Harold E. Knox.

Cast: Tex Ritter (Tex Haines), Dave O'Brien (Dave Wyatt), Guy Wilkerson (Panhandle Perkins), Marjorie Clements (Arlene Arthur), Rebel Randall (Belle Loper), Ray Bennett (Clint Yackey), Charles King (Red Avery), Bud Osborne (Committee Man), Henry Hall (Judge Henry Wright), Ted Mapes (Luke Brown), Reed Howes, Frank Ellis (Henchmen), Ed Cassidy (John Ealey), Jimmy Aubrey (Bank Teller), Wen Wright (Guard), Ray Henderson (Juror).

British title: *Wanted by the Law*.

The Whispering Skull (PRC, 1945, 56 minutes) Producer: Arthur Alexander. Associate Producer: Alfred Stern. Director: Elmer Clifton. Screenplay: Harry Fraser. Photography: Edward Kull. Editor: Hugh Winn. Sound: Arthur B. Smith. Sets: Harry Reif. Music Director: Lee Zahler. Songs: Tex Ritter, Lt. Frank Harford & Bonnie Dodd. Special Effects: Ray Mercer. Assistant Director: Sidney Smith.

Cast: Tex Ritter (Tex Haines), Dave O'Brien (Dave Wyatt), Guy Wilkerson (Panhandle Perkins), Denny Burke (Ellen Jackson), I. Stanford Jolley (Duke Walters), Henry Hall (Judge), George Morrell (Sheriff Marvin Jackson), Ed Cassidy (Doc Henderson), Wen Wright (Arkansas Mike Coram), Frank Ellis (Ellers), Jimmy Aubrey (Bartender), Ray Henderson (Henchman).

Marked for Murder (PRC, 1945, 58 minutes) Producer: Arthur Alexander. Associate Producer: Alfred Stern. Director-Screenplay: Elmer Clifton. Photography: Edward Kull. Editor: Holbrook N. Todd. Sound: Arthur B. Smith. Sets: Harry Reif. Music Director: Lee Zahler. Songs: Tex Ritter, Lt. Frank Harford, Smiley Burnette & Don Weston. Special Effects: Ray Mercer. Assistant Director: Sidney Smith.

Cast: Tex Ritter (Tex Haines), Dave O'Brien (Dave Wyatt), Guy Wilkerson (Panhandle Perkins), Marilyn McConnell (Ruth Lane), Ed Cassidy (Dick Vernon), Henry Hall (Sheriff Jim Whitlock), Charles King (Pete Magoo), Jack [Ingram] Ingraham (Sam Taylor), Wen Wright (Bill Ganer), Robert Kortman, Kermit Maynard, Wally West (Henchmen), The Milo Twins (Entertainers), Frank Ellis (Jed Moore), Ray Henderson (Nord Collins), Art Felix (Brandy Smith), Jack Evans (Jack), Jimmy Aubrey (Bartender), Herman Hack (Sheepman), Chick Hannon, Roy Bucko (Cattlemen), George Soward (Cowboy).

Enemy of the Law (PRC, 1945, 59 minutes) Producer: Arthur Alexander. Associate Producer: Alfred Stern. Director-Screenplay: Harry Fraser. Photography: Jack Greenhalgh. Editor: Holbrook N. Todd. Sound: Glen Glenn. Sets: Harry Reif. Music Director: Lee Zahler. Songs: Tex Ritter, Lt. Frank Harford, Bonnie Dodds & Sarah Jane Cooper. Special Effects: Ray Mercer. Assistant Director: Sidney Smith.

Cast: Tex Ritter (Tex Haines), Dave O'Brien (Dave Wyatt), Guy Wilkerson (Panhandle Perkins), Kay Hughes (Ruby Lawson), Jack Ingram (Steve Martin), Charles King [Jr.] (Wild Charlie Gray), Frank Ellis (Red), Kermit Maynard (Mike), Henry Hall (Sheriff), Ed Cassidy (Ranger Captain), Karl Hackett (Dr. Carey), Ben Corbett (Cowboy), Jack Evans (Saloon Customer).

16mm. title: *Cowboy Reckoning* (Castle Films).

Three in the Saddle (PRC, 1945, 61 minutes) Producer: Arthur Alexander. Associate Producer: Alfred Stern. Director: Harry Fraser. Screenplay: Elmer Clifton. Photography: Robert Cline. Editor: Holbrook N. Todd. Sound: Glen Glenn. Sets: Harry Reif. Music Director: Lee Zahler. Songs: Tex Ritter, Lt. Frank Harford & Ernest Tubb. Special Effects: Ray Mercer. Assistant Director: Sidney Smith.

Cast: Tex Ritter (Tex Haines), Dave O'Brien (Dave Wyatt), Guy Wilkerson (Panhandle Perkins), Lorraine Miller (Peggy Barlow), Charles King (Bart Rawlins), Edward Howard (John Rankin), Edward [Ed] Cassidy (Jim Manning), Bud Osborne (Sheriff), Bob Duncan (Dan Brown), Art Fowler (Bill Dugan), Jimmy Aubrey (Jimmy the Bartender), Frank Ellis (Deputy Sheriff), Herman Hack, Ray Henderson (Henchmen), Jack Tornek (Rancher), Post Park (Stagecoach Driver).

Frontier Fugitives (PRC, 1945, 57 minutes) Producer: Arthur Alexander. Associate Producer: Alfred Stern. Director: Harry Fraser. Screenplay: Elmer Clifton. Photography: Robert Cline. Editor: Holbrook N. Todd. Sound: Glen Glenn. Sets: Sidney Moore. Music Director: Lee Zahler. Songs: Al Dexter. Special Effects: Ray Mercer. Assistant Director: Sidney Smith.

Cast: Tex Ritter (Tex Haines), Dave O'Brien (Dave Wyatt), Guy Wilkerson (Panhandle Perkins), Lorraine Miller (Ellen Williams), I. Stanford Jolley (Frank Sneed), Jack Ingram (Allen Fain), Frank Ellis (Mert Donner), Jack Hendricks [Ray Henderson] (Jim Gar), Karl Hackett (Agent), Budd Buster (Sheriff Wilson), Charles King (Henchman), Carl Mathews (Fred), George Morrell (Williams).

British title: *Fugitives of the Frontier*.

Flaming Bullets (PRC, 1945, 57 minutes) Producer: Arthur Alexander. Associate Producer: Alfred Stern. Director-Screenplay: Harry Fraser. Photography: Robert Cline. Editor: Holbrook N. Todd. Sound: Lyle Willey. Sets: Sidney Moore. Music Director: Lee Zahler. Songs: Gene Autry, Fred Rose & Ray Whitley. Special Effects: Ray Mercer. Assistant Director: Sidney Smith.

Cast: Tex Ritter (Tex Haines), Dave O'Brien (Dave Wyatt/Steve Carson), Guy Wilkerson (Panhandle Perkins), Patricia Knox (Belle), Charles King [Jr.] (Porky Smith), I. Stanford Jolley (Sid Tolliver), Bob Duncan (Eddie the Bartender), Bud Osborne (Marshal), Robert Hill (Ranger Captain), Richard Alexander (Dick), Kermit Maynard (Luke), John L. Cason (Jim), Dan White (Henchman).

THE THREE MESQUITEERS

William Colt MacDonald (1891–1968) was one of the most popular and prolific writers of western fiction in the 20th century. A native of Detroit, Michigan, he started working as a writer for trade publications. In the mid–1920s he began writing western stories for pulp magazines and in 1929 his first novel, *Gun Country*, was published. After that, for more than thirty years, he turned out numerous western novels, although he is best remembered today for his Three Mesquiteers characters, which were popularized on film by Republic Pictures. The Mesquiteers solidified the popularity of the triad hero concept in films, which had its roots in the "Hopalong Cassidy" (q.v.) series, and spawned such imitators as "The Range Busters," "The Texas Rangers," "The Trail Blazers," "The Rough Riders" and "Frontier Marshals" (qq.v.). MacDonald also scripted several Tim McCoy oaters for Columbia including *Texas Cyclone* and *Two-Fisted Law* (both 1932).

Republic Pictures was organized in 1935 by combining Monogram, Mascot, Liberty, Supreme and a few other smaller studios with Herbert J. Yates' Consolidated Film Industries, a film laboratory service. The new company was housed at the Mascot-leased Mack Sennett Studios and it utilized the 39 city exchanges set up by Monogram. With the merger, Republic acquired producer Paul Malvern's "Lone Star" Western series with John Wayne, along with Bob Steele and Johnny Mack Brown cowboy pictures from A.W. Hackel's Supreme Pictures. With these established stars, along with a schedule of features and serials, Republic gambled on two new series, one headlining singing cowboy Gene Autry, the other "The Three Mesquiteers." These ventures paid off handsomely, quickly establishing Republic as the top independent studio in Hollywood.

The reason for Republic's almost immediate success was noted by Sam Sherman in "Republic Studios: Hollywood Thrill Factory" in *Screen Thrills Illustrated* (January, 1963):

> Technically, Republic in their "independent" way was second to none. Consolidated Film Industries ranked among moviedom's best labs and together with RCA "High Fidelity" sound recording, gave the Republic films a polish others lacked. The camera work was also fantastic! Speedy camera trucks, good composition, quick moving panning and numerous studio dolly shots gave all Republic productions a feeling of movement that the "static" films of the major studios lacked. In the music department, compositional geniuses wrote film scores that rivaled serious classical works. While most of the other companies let dramatic and action run without music, Republic scored to the hilt.... In combination with well paced direction, ace camera work, and skilled editing, Republic's music brought out the best in their films.

When Republic Pictures was founded, Nat Levine, the former chief of Mascot, was placed in charge of production. In that capacity he produced the first five "Three Mesquiteers" features with Sol C. Siegel as associate producer. After that Siegel took over production until 1938. Siegel (1903–82) was a New York City businessman who helped organize Republic and stayed on there as a producer until going to Paramount in 1940. Several years later he moved to 20th Century–Fox and in 1956 he became the vice-president in charge of production at MGM. An independent producer in the 1960s, he retired in 1968.

There was a trio of features made based on William Colt MacDonald's characters prior to the Republic series. *The Law of the 45s*, based on the 1934 novel of the same title, was issued on a states rights basis by Normandy Pictures Corporation late in 1935. Made by producer Arthur Alexander's Beacon Productions, it contained only two Mesquiteers, Tucson Smith and Stony Martin, not Brooke. It told of Tucson ([Guinn] Big Boy Williams) and Stony (Al St. John) coming to the aid of an old rancher (Lafe McKee) and his daughter (Molly O'Day) who are being harassed by a mysterious outlaw gang. Alexander also produced Normandy's *Too Much Beef* (1936), which starred Rex Bell as Tucson Smith. The other two Mesquiteers did not appear in the feature which was allegedly based on a story by MacDonald. The plot had Cattlemen's Association agent Johnny Argyle (Bell) working undercover as Tucson Smith while trying to determine who is trying to frame rancher Rocky Brown (Forrest Taylor) for rustling (he has refused to sell his ranch to make way for a railroad).

The first full-fledged Three Mesquiteers feature was *Powdersmoke Range*, based on MacDonald's 1934 novel. Released by RKO Radio Pictures in the fall of 1935, it was a well-made and fairly faithful adaptation of the book. It began with Tucson Smith (Harry Carey), Stony Brooke (Hoot Gibson) and Lullaby Joslin (Guinn Williams) witnessing the robbery of a stagecoach by Fin Sharkey (Ethan Laidlaw), who also murders the driver. The Mesquiteers catch Sharkey rifling through a mail bag and in it Tucson finds a letter addressed to him which gives him a thirty-day option on the Tresbarro ranch. The Mesquiteers take Sharkey to a way station where the owner (Bob McKenzie) warns them to be wary of Steve Ogden (Sam Hardy) and the local deputy sheriff, Brose Glasgow (Adrian Morris). Another employee, Bud Taggart (Wally Wales), tells them Ogden and Glasgow are crooks but is told to be quiet by Sharkey. In town the Mesquiteers force a reluctant Glasgow to put Sharkey in jail and they go looking for their pal, ex-outlaw Jeff "Guadalupe Kid" Ferguson (Bob Steele). At Happy Hopkins' (William Desmond) saloon they meet Sourdough Jones (Frank Rice), the cook at the Tresbarro ranch, who tells them that Jeff was arrested for the murder of the ranch owner three days before. Tucson goes to Ogden's saloon and demands he release Jeff, who is not in jail. When Jeff is brought in by Glasgow, he and Tucson are attacked by Ogden's men but are saved by Stony, Lullaby and three cowboys (Buffalo Bill, Jr., Art Mix, Buzz Barton) whom Tucson hired to help work the ranch.

Advertisement for *The Law of the 45s* (Normandy Pictures, 1935).

Jeff tells the trio he had outbid Ogden for the Tresbarro ranch and then put the option in Tucson's name. At the ranch, the Mesquiteers meet Carolyn Sibley (Boots Mallory), the ward of the late owner and Jeff's sweetheart. To put an end to the Mesquiteers, Ogden hires notorious gunman Sundown Saunders (Tom Tyler) to force a showdown with Tucson. Saunders agrees to do the job but makes it known he dislikes Ogden. Tucson finds out the deed records to the ranch are missing and plans to go to the county courthouse when he is challenged to a gunfight by Saunders. Jeff tries to talk Saunders out of the meeting with Tucson but the gunman refuses. Getting a new set of guns with lightweight bullets, Tucson meets Saunders that evening and uses the distance between them to outshoot and wound the outlaw, who is removed to the Tresbarro ranch to recover. When Ogden's men, led by Jake Elliott (Eddie Dunn), bring a cattle herd onto the Tresbarro range, the Mesquiteers and their men rout them in a gun battle but during the shooting Saunders is fatally wounded, taking a bullet intended for Tucson. Tucson, who has been appointed a deputy by the county marshal, heads back to town and is forced to shoot Glasgow who, thinking he is dying, confesses and blames Ogden for all their crimes. Ogden, meanwhile, hires two gunmen (Buddy Roosevelt, Ray Mayer) to shoot Tucson but he kills them instead; he also eliminates Ogden, but not before being wounded. Carolyn nurses Tucson back to health and decides to stay on at the ranch and marry Jeff.

Today *Powdersmoke Range* is best remembered for its cast of veteran western stars. While he was probably two decades too old for the part of Tucson Smith, Harry Carey is excellent in the role, as are Hoot Gibson and Guinn Williams as Stony and Lullaby. Bob Steele and Tom Tyler, both popular "B" western stars, are outstanding in their roles, a foreboding of the fine character work both would do in later films. Other genre stars in the cast were Wally Wales, Buffalo Bill, Jr., Art Mix and Buzz Barton on the side of the Mesquiteers, Buddy Roosevelt as a hired gunman and William Farnum in the small role of the town banker.

The 53 Republic Three Mesquiteers features, however, are considered the epitome of the MacDonald characters. The formula for the success of the series was noted in *Wildest Westerns* (May, 1961):

> Each story was unique and all of them filmed as top productions. The motion picture industry set up and took notice of this high quality series. All of the films were expertly photographed against the backdrop of some of the most scenic Western locations ever used in the movies. Top directors with interesting stories and extremely capable actors turned out these films which have never been equaled.

Robert Livingston (1904–88) was signed to play Stony Brooke in the Mesquiteers series. A native of Illinois, his real name was Robert Randall and he went from newspaper work to stage acting and by the mid–1920s he was in Hollywood doing extra and bit parts (he doubled for Colin Clive in the final scene in 1931's *Frankenstein*). Republic cast him as the masked hero, "The Eagle," in the 1936 serial *The Vigilantes Are Coming* and this led to his work with the Mesquiteers. His younger brother Jack Randall (1906–45) starred in 22 westerns for Monogram from 1937 to 1940.

Cast as Tucson Smith in the Republic series was Ray Corrigan (1902–76), a physical culture instructor who was born Raymond Bernard. In the early 1930s he was signed by MGM where he doubled for Johnny Weissmuller in *Tarzan, the Ape Man* (1932) and *Tarzan and His Mate* (1934). He also appeared in Fox's *Dante's Inferno* and Universal's *Night Life of the Gods* (both 1935) as well as in the latter studio's serial *Flash Gordon* (1936). Stardom came for the actor when he portrayed the character Crash Corrigan in Republic's cliffhanger *Undersea Kingdom* (1936) and after that he was often billed as Ray "Crash" Corrigan.

Republic cast Syd Saylor in the role of Lullaby Joslin, but he proved unsatisfactory in the part and appeared only in the initial entry, *The Three Mesquiteers*, in 1936. Born Leo Sailor in Chicago, Saylor (1895–1962), sometimes billed as Sid Saylor, came to talkies from the stage and for over 30 years he appeared in scores of features as well as headlining a series of short comedies for Universal. He was also active in television and was one of the first actors to portray Bozo the Clown on the small screen.

The production of the series got off to a bad start when Robert Livingston received a gunshot wound to the leg and *The Three Mesquiteers* had to be halted for several weeks for him to recover. Released theatrically late in the summer of 1936, it was directed by Ray Taylor and supervised by Mack V. Wright. Taking place in 1919, it told of a group of war veterans coming to New Mexico to homestead government land. The settlers have a 90-day land preference, much to the chagrin of rich rancher Brack Canfield (J.P. McGowan), who wants to discourage them from settling on open range. The homesteaders are led by Bob Brian (Gene Marvey) and his sister Marian (Kay Hughes) and they are aided by cowpokes Stony (Livingston) and Tucson (Corrigan) and their pal Lullaby (Saylor). Canfield has his men dynamite the trail used by the settlers but the Mesquiteers lead them to safety. Once they are settled, Canfield continues to harass the homesteaders, resulting in Bob being tortured to death. This leads to a showdown between Canfield and the settlers with the Mesquiteers using hand grenades to smoke the gang out of its hideout, with Canfield being killed. The Mesquiteers then ride away to new adventures. During the course of the feature, George M. Cohan's song "Over There" is performed, as is "Wagon Team," written by Gene Autry and Smiley Burnette.

Unfortunately there was little on-screen charisma between the three leads in *The Three Mesquiteers* and for the second feature, *Ghost Town Gold*, Saylor was replaced by Max Terhune. As a result, the triad concept caught on immediately with the natural interplay between Livingston, Corrigan and Terhune as the Mesquiteers. Terhune (1891–1973) was a native of Franklin, Indiana, who began doing rustic comedy in touring shows and later in vaudeville. By 1932 he was a regular on radio's "National Barn Dance" in Chicago. Also featured on the program was Gene Autry; when he came to Hollywood, he brought Terhune to Republic to appear in his feature *Ride, Ranger, Ride* in 1936. This led to Terhune's being cast in the role of Lullaby in the Mesquiteers series. In addition to being adept in comedy, card tricks and animal imitations, Terhune was an accomplished ventriloquist and the inclusion of his doll Elmer Sneezewood added much to the overall popularity of the Mesquiteer series. Terhune's successful ventriloquism on film paved the way for Edgar Bergen's screen stardom.

Max Terhune as Lullaby Joslin and Elmer.

Ghost Town Gold, released in October, 1936, not only introduced Terhune to the Mesquiteers, it was the first of four series films directed by Joseph Kane. Filmed on location in Chatsworth, California, it showed how Lullaby acquired his ventriloquist doll Elmer in a card game. It also contained an extremely well-staged climactic shootout in a tale of cattlemen versus sheepherders, with the sympathy definitely being with the former in Oliver Drake and John Rathmell's script. With the obvious on-screen camaraderie of its trio of stars, along with its high-grade production values, the film propelled the Mesquiteers series towards future success.

The film begins with the Three Mesquiteers (Livingston, Corrigan, Terhune) getting their annual pay in a large check from their rancher employer (Bob Burns). Although they have misgivings, Stony and Tucson allow Lullaby to take the check for deposit to the bank at Prospect while they ride through the ghost town of Nemesis, where they meet its owner, prospector Jake Rawlins (Milburn Morante). While there, they see a poster advertising a prize fight that day in Prospect so they head for that town before Lullaby can bet away their earnings. The boxing match, between champion Thunderbolt O'Brien (Robert C. Thomas) and Wild Man Kamatski (Frank Hagney), is being promoted by saloon owner Barrington (LeRoy Mason). Thornton (Burr Caruth), the bank president and town mayor, is unhappy about the rowdy element being brought into the town by the match and he has the sheriff (Ed Peil, Sr.) order the fight stopped. To get even, Barrington orders his henchmen Buck (Yakima Canutt) and Stubby (Harry Tenbrook) to rob the bank; after doing so they hide the stolen money in Nemesis. The next day, Thornton and his daughter Sabina (Kay Hughes) discover the robbery; when the Mesquiteers arrive to deposit their check, they are told the bank has no funds. The Mesquiteers agree to help the Thorntons, and Stony cons Tucson into fighting Kamatski, since O'Brien has pulled out of the match. The Mesquiteers will then use the money they get from betting on Tucson to win to keep the bank open. At the fight, Lullaby sees Jake Rawlins try to bet with money from a sack belonging to the bank. During the match, Barrington orders the lights shot out and he and his henchmen steal the fight proceeds and head to Nemesis to get the bank money. Jake beats them to the ghost town, which he has booby-trapped, and he is followed by Stony and Tucson, with Lullaby and Sabina trailing them. The eerie noises and traps set up by Jake scare off the crooks and Sabina convinces Jake to hand over the bank money to the Mesquiteers. Meanwhile in town, the citizens of Prospect are up in arms and blame Thornton for the robberies. They engage him in a shootout but the Mesquiteers show up with the money, forcing a confession out of Barrington, who is chased out of the area.

Mack V. Wright had supervised *The Three Mesquiteers*; the third series entry, *Roarin' Lead*, issued late in 1936, was the first of a quartet of Mesquiteers features he would direct. Sam Newfield got co-director credit. Based on MacDonald's 1935 novel of the same name, it had the Mesquiteers (Livingston, Corrigan, Terhune) as the trustees of an estate which is in charge of the local cattlemen's protective group as well as financing an orphanage run by Doris Moore (Christine Maple). The general manager of the cattlemen's group, Hackett (Hooper Atchley), has been stealing cattle and paying the ranchers back with association funds, thus nearly bankrupting the operation and endangering the orphanage's existence. Following a raid on a rancher (Bob Burns), the Mesquiteers begin to suspect Hackett and they remove him from office. They also stop the adoptions at the orphanage to save the youngsters from being used for child labor. When the outlaws attack another ranch, the Mesquiteers try to stop them and they are seen by an orphan, Bobby (Tommy Bupp), who is rescued by Lullaby. The boy tells the Mesquiteers that Hackett's henchman Captain Gardner (George Chesebro) is the leader of the gang. At a fundraiser for the orphanage, Stony uses his mental act to extract a confession from one of the gang, whom Hackett kills. The outlaws go to Hackett's ranch but there the Mesquiteers subdue them and retrieve the stolen association funds. The orphanage is saved and Bobby joins the Mesquiteers.

Early in January, 1937, Republic issued *The Riders of the Whistling Skull* which was also directed by Mack V. Wright. It was based on two MacDonald works, the 1934 novel of the same title and another book published the same year, *The Singing Scorpion*. Because of its deft combination of the western, mystery and horror genres, it is one of the best-regarded entries in the series. It begins with the Three Mesquiteers (Livingston, Corrigan, Terhune) finding Professor Faxon (C. Montague Shaw) wandering in the desert. They take him to a trading post run by Rutledge (Roger Williams) and there they find out that Faxon was part of an expedition (looking for a lost Indian city) led by Professor Marsh (John Van Pelt). Also at the trading post looking for March are his daughter, Betty (Mary Russell), and her companion Henrietta McCoy (Fern Emmett), along with professors Fronc (George Godfrey), Cleary (Earle Ross), Brewster (John Ward) and Coggins (Frank Ellis). The delirious Faxon tells them about a whistling skull rock formation and a city of gold, and says that Professor March is being held prisoner by an ancient Indian cult. Faxon is later stabbed to death. The Mesquiteers agree to go along with the group which will be led by Rutledge and his Indian guide Otah (Yakima Canutt). A notebook containing a map to the Whistling Skull is divided among the members but Cleary is also killed and his part of the map stolen. Later Fronc is tortured and branded by the cult and his part of the map is also missing. Although some of the group want to return to the trading post, Betty insists they go on and soon their horses are scattered. The group locates the Whistling Skull and soon find themselves trapped in a cavern. Rutledge, who is really the leader of the Sons of Anatazia cult, and Otah lead an attack on the expedition members, who find Professor March. The professor informs them that he has been held prisoner so that he could not reveal the location of the ancient treasures. The Mesquiteers go for help but Stony is captured. Tucson returns with the local sheriff (Ed Peil, Sr.) and a posse, and Stony is set free. An avalanche buries the cult members, and the treasure of Luckachakai is brought back to civilization.

Particularly memorable is the scene where the expedition members are trapped in the Whistling Skull's cave after the cult members have taken away their escape ladders. There they find the haggard professor a prisoner among crumbling skeletons and mummies. One of the mummies comes to life and attacks the group but is killed by Tucson. Later Tucson races for help being pursued by Otah and other cult members in a nerve-wracking sequence in which the pursuers and the pursued vie with each other and the elements to see who will survive. In *Forgotten Horrors: The Definitive Edition* (1999), George E. Turner and Michael Price wrote, "In addition to the pleasing lead performances, *Riders* offers a harrowing and imaginative story, high production values, beautifully shot locations near St. George, Utah, plenty of stirring action music and a large helping of Yakima Canutt's great stunt work. Perfectly crafted glass shots position the Whistling Skull atop existing pinnacles. The mysterious members of the lost tribe are introduced through ominous drumming and glimpses of distorted shadows moving among the rocks."

Oliver Drake co-wrote the story and screenplay for *The Riders of the Whistling Skull* and in 1949 he reworked the plot into a Charlie Chan mystery, *The Feathered Serpent*, released by Monogram. Robert Livingston, who was hero Stony Brooke in *Riders*, was cast as a villain in the remake. The Monogram Chan did not give credit to MacDonald.

The fifth Republic Mesquiteers feature, *Hit the Saddle*, issued in March, 1937, was also directed by Mack V. Wright and written by Oliver Drake. The Mesquiteers (Livingston, Corrigan, Terhune) aid Sheriff Miller (Ed Cassidy) in capturing Buck (Yakima Canutt), Harvey (Harry Tenbrook) and their gang for rustling wild horses from a government preserve. The rustlers work for real estate agent Rance McGowan (J.P. McGowan) who tells Miller that his men were only looking for strays. The sheriff releases McGowan's men who are then ordered by their boss to steal 1,000 more horses needed for a promised sale. Friction develops between the Mesquiteers over Stony's girlfriend, saloon dancer Rita (Rita [Hayworth] Cansino), who Tucson and Lullaby believe is a gold digger. On McGowan's orders, Harvey paints a killer stallion, Volcano, to look like the leader of a wild horse herd and then tries to get the animal to trample Sheriff Miller to death. Tucson is then appointed the new sheriff and he orders the real wild stallion killed although Stony believes the animal is innocent. The incident with the wild stallion and his planned marriage to Rita causes a rift between Stony and Tucson. Lullaby tells Rita that Tucson has power of attorney over Stony's money and offers her $1,500 and a ticket to New York City, an offer she promptly accepts. Stony blames Tucson for Rita's departure; the two argue and he steals the wild stallion and rides out of town. McGowan's gang captures Stony, and Harvey orders Volcano to trample him, but the wild stallion comes to his defense. Tucson and Lullaby rescue Stony from the gang and, during a shootout with McGowan and his men, Lullaby feigns an injury, causing his two pals to reconcile. The Mesquiteers capture the gang but McGowan tries to escape riding Volcano, who throws and tramples him. *Variety* reported, the "picture offers some nice outdoor scenics and the Mesquiteers themselves are a likable trio."

Hit the Saddle was the last film Rita Hayworth made under her real name, Rita Cansino. By this time she was somewhat of a western heroine veteran, having already appeared with Tom Keene in Crescent Pictures' *Rebellion* (1936) and *Old Louisiana* (1937) and with Tex Ritter in Grand National's *Trouble in Texas* (1937). After becoming Rita Hayworth, she co-starred with George O'Brien in *The Renegade Ranger* (1939).

Joseph Kane returned to direct the next Mesquiteers adventure, *Gunsmoke Ranch*, which came to theaters in the spring of 1937. It was the fifth series feature to be scripted by Oliver Drake. This time Stony (Livingston), Tucson (Corrigan) and Lullaby (Terhune) try to aid flood-stricken families by selling their spread to land developer Phineas Flagg (Kenneth Harlan). Flagg is secretly behind a scheme to sell land to settlers and then have it condemned and resold to the government for a huge profit. When the trio finds out what Flagg is up to, they try to warn the families but they are ignored. The settlers, who are given free bus transportation to Gunsmoke Valley by Flagg, are led by Judge Warren (Burr Caruth) and Williams (Bob Walker) with Stony romancing the judge's daughter, Marion (Julia Thayer). The people build a new town called Three Score and Ten and improve the land only to have it condemned for the construction of a dam. To stop Flagg, the Mesquiteers buy Warren's land and as a result the judge and Williams are abducted and the deed to the Warren ranch is the ransom for their return. The deed is returned and Warren is found near death; before dying, he tells the Mesquiteers that Williams is in league with Flagg. When Stony, Tucson and Lullaby pretend to take Warren's body to a hospital, they are attacked by Flagg's gang but the settlers unite and come to their rescue. Flagg and his henchman Duke Madden (Jack Padjan) are killed and Williams and another cohort, Reggie Allen (Allen Connor), are arrested. During the course of the film, Robert Livingston reluctantly crooned the song "When the Campfire Is Low on the Prairie" while the settlers on the way to Gunsmoke Valley sang "When You and I Were Young, Maggie." Lullaby and Elmer have several comedic exchanges during the proceedings and there is an amusing sequence in which Lullaby gets into a fight with a mannequin. There is also some rather forced comedy provided by the hayseed team of Oscar and Elmer.

Also released in the spring of 1937 and directed by Joseph Kane was *Come On, Cowboys!*, written by Betty Burbridge. Here the Mesquiteers are performers in a circus with Stony (Livingston) doing a sharpshooting act, Tucson (Corrigan) a strongman, and Lullaby (Terhune) a ventriloquist and card trickster. When circus co-owner Jeff Harris (Ed Cassidy) refuses to sell out to his partner Thomas Rigby (Edward Peil, Sr.), he is framed for counterfeiting by Rigby and sent to prison for a decade. Harris appoints the Mesquiteers guardians of his little daughter Nancy (Anne Bennett) but they are forced to prove their competence and the child stays with her governess, Ellen Reed (Maxine Doyle). The Mesquiteers find counterfeit money on some of Rigby's men but after a fight with them, a judge (Horace Murphy) decides to send Nancy to an orphanage unless one of the trio marries. Ellen reluctantly agrees to wed Stony while Lullaby plays cards with Jake (Yakima Canutt), one of Rigby's gang, and ends up winning counterfeit money. As a result he is captured by the gang but he leaves a trail of cards. Stony, who was about to wed Ellen, and Tucson come to his rescue. The trio captures Rigby and his gang and prove Harris' innocence.

Range Defenders, issued in the summer of 1937, was the last series feature to be directed by Mack V. Wright. Like most of the entries, it was a well-made and fast-paced feature, and contained a particularly amusing scene in which Elmer Sneezewood trades barbs with a crooked and none-too-bright sheriff (Earle Hodgins). The film featured an exciting finale in which the Mesquiteers use dynamite to end a shootout between cattlemen and the crooks trying to take over their range. Included in the cast was future genre director Thomas Carr in the role of Stony Brooke's younger brother George. The son of actress Mary Carr, Thomas began directing at Republic in the mid–1940s and thereafter he helmed over thirty westerns for that studio and Monogram, Lippert (where he directed the "Irish Cowboys" [q.v.] series in 1950), and Allied Artists. Between 1947 and 1951 he co-directed seven serials, one for Republic and the rest at Columbia.

The feature begins with Tucson (Corrigan) and Lullaby (Terhune) having problems with a young hothead who challenges Tucson to a shootout. The showdown is stopped, however, when Stony (Livingston) realizes the troublemaker is his younger brother George (Carr). The young man tells the Mesquiteers he has fled the Brooke ranch in Green Valley because he was falsely accused of murdering rich sheepman John Ashton. The four men head to Silver City; before getting there, Stony tells George to hide out in a cave in the nearby hills while he and his pals check out the situation. They see a poster advertising the auction of the Brooke ranch with the proceeds going to Sylvia Ashton (Eleanor Stewart), the murdered man's daughter. At the auction, Stony shows that the deed to the ranch is in his name, which upsets the plans of John Harvey (Harry Woods), the manager of the Ashton Estates, who wants to marry Sylvia. Harvey orders his cohort, dishonest Sheriff Gray (Earle Hodgins), to locate George while the Mesquiteers learn from ranch hand Pete (Horace B. Carpenter) that Harvey and his gang are after the Brooke ranch's water rights. Tucson is persuaded to run against Gray in the election for sheriff in order to insure that George gets a fair trial. Stony and Sylvia meet and are attracted to each other but the young woman snubs him when she finds out he is George's brother. George is captured and brought back to town but Sylvia prevents him from being lynched by demanding that he be given a fair trial. Stony realizes that his brother will not get justice and tries to break him out of jail but he fails and ends up behind bars himself. Tucson and Lullaby ride all night to corral ranchers whom they bring to town to vote in the election. Realizing that Gray will lose, Harvey has his men barricade the main street to keep out the cattlemen. During a shootout, Tucson is able to get Stony and George out of jail. Harvey decides to flee as Sylvia overhears him admit that he murdered her father. She joins forces with the Mesquiteers, with Harvey and his gang being captured. Sylvia tells the Mesquiteers she plans to start raising cattle.

Director Joseph Kane and scripter Oliver Drake returned to the series for its autumn 1937 release *Heart of the Rockies*, which had a more rustic setting than previous entries. Here Stony (Livingston), Tucson (Corrigan) and Lullaby (Terhune) find Enoch Dawson (Maston Williams) trapping on their land and they accuse him of

Ray Corrigan, Max Terhune and Bob Livingston as "The Three Mesquiteers."

killing their cattle. He claims the culprits are bears dwelling in the nearby national park but when the four men go there to hunt the animals they are forbidden to do so by Ranger Brady (Hal Taliaferro). The men go to see Enoch's father, Big Ed Dawson (J.P. McGowan), whom they hire to get rid of the predators. The Mesquiteers learn that Big Ed plans to marry his young stepdaughter Lorna (Lynne Roberts) to an older man, Charley Coe (Yakima Canutt), and that he is forcing the girl and her mother (Georgia Simmons) into the arrangement. The Mesquiteers inform Dawson that Lorna is not of legal age to marry and return to their ranch. Big Ed and his clan continue their clandestine raids on the Mesquiteers' ranch. One day Davey Dawson (Sammy McKim), Lorna's younger brother, is about to be attacked by a mountain lion and he is saved by the Mesquiteers. When the trio finds out that Big Ed plans to carry out the wedding plans, they warn Coe to stay away from Lorna. The Mesquiteers, who now suspect Big Ed of being behind their cattle thefts, set a trap by asking him to watch their herd while they go away on business. Big Ed, Enoch and Coe rustle the cattle and are ambushed by the Mesquiteers, but the Dawsons flee and are followed by Tucson and Lullaby while Stony rides after Coe. Ranger Brady captures Stony and Coe, but Charley murders the lawman and wounds Stony. Lorna hides Stony from rangers looking for him and then she goes for Tucson and Lullaby, who explain the situation to Ranger Clayton (Ranny Weeks) and his men. The Dawson clan is rounded up and Coe is arrested for murder.

While doing a high riding dive off a bridge during the early filming of the next series outing, *Trigger Trio*, Robert Livingston was injured when he fell on some rocks and he was replaced by Ralph Byrd, who was cast in the role of Tucson Smith's brother, Larry. Oliver Drake's quickly rewritten script had Stony away in Mexico, with Larry Smith (Byrd) visiting with Tucson (Corrigan) and Lullaby (Terhune) at their 3M ranch. Tucson is the deputy to state cattle inspector John Evans (Robert Warwick) who has found evidence of hoof and mouth disease. He orders Tucson to enforce a quarantine which angers Tom Brent (Cornelius Keefe) and his foreman Luke (Hal Taliaferro), who are trying to transport their racing horse. Luke tries to buy Larry's horse but he is rebuffed. When Larry sees him abusing his dog Buck, he agrees to race the foreman, the winner getting the animal of his choice. Thanks to some tampering with a marker by Lullaby, Larry wins the race and takes Buck. Brent, the owner of the infected cattle, murders Evans when he refuses to take a bribe. Brent then changes the brands on his dead cattle to that of the Evans ranch, forcing Tucson to order the destruction of the rest of the herd. This causes a falling-out between him and Anne Evans (Sandra Corday), the murdered inspector's daughter, and his brother Larry, who then agrees to work for Brent. Lullaby finds out about Brent and Luke putting the sick cattle on the Evans ranch and he warns Larry, who has joined Brent's cattle drive. Larry sends Lullaby to find Tucson. During a fight with Luke, both men fall into a ravine and are trapped by a rockslide. Larry sends Buck for help while Luke confesses that it was Brent who murdered Evans. Tucson rescues Larry, who then shoots Brent when he tries to escape.

Although it appeared that Byrd would continue in the role of Larry Smith, Livingston made a quicker than expected recovery from his injuries and was back in the saddle for the next Mesquiteers adventure, *Wild Horse Rodeo*, which was released late in 1937. It was the first of twenty series entries to be directed by George Sherman, who made his directorial debut with the feature. A native of New York, Sherman (1908–91) began in films as an assistant director and moved to directing in 1938. He remained with Republic until 1944; beginning in 1940, he also got associate producer credit on most of his movies. In the mid–1940s he moved to Columbia and from 1948 to 1955 he worked at Universal; thereafter he directed for various companies, his last feature being the 1971 John Wayne starrer *Big Jake*.

Wild Horse Rodeo had the Three Mesquiteers (Livingston, Corrigan, Terhune) on the verge of losing their 3M ranch. Stony decides to capture wild stallion Cyclone and star him in Colonel Nye's (Walter Miller) rodeo in order to make enough money to save the ranch. Tucson is in love with artist Alice Harkley (June Martel), whose magazine paintings of Cyclone has made the horse famous, and he opposes Stony's plan. Stony and Alice have opposite views about taming the horse but they find they are attracted to each other. Cyclone is captured and Tucson tries to ride him at the rodeo but is thrown. Stony manages to stay on the horse and win the prize money. When Stony refuses to stay with the rodeo, Nye tries to steal Cyclone but is thwarted by Lullaby, as the horse makes it back to the range. When Stony learns that Tucson wants to marry Alice, he tries to break off his romance with her, causing friction between the trio. Stony leaves and Lullaby tells Tucson about his pal's feelings toward Alice; the two go after Stony. Nye hires an airplane to find Cyclone while some of his men attack the Mesquiteers who want to save the animal. When the plane crashes, Nye and his gang are captured. Alice decides to go to New York City to exhibit her artwork and Cyclone remains free.

In the film's supporting cast was Dick Weston, who would soon gain fame at Republic as Roy Rogers. Here he sings the song "Riding High" while star Robert Livingston crooned "My Madonna of the Trail." The final series release for 1937, the film helped to make the series one of the most popular of "B" western theatrical offerings and the "Three Mesquiteers" series ranked eighth in that year's *Motion Picture Herald Poll* of top money-making westerns. The Mesquiteers would remain in the top ten of that poll for the rest of its run through 1943. The series would rank fifth in 1938, sixth in 1939, eighth in 1940 and 1941, tenth in 1942 and seventh in 1943.

George Sherman next directed *The Purple Vigilantes*, released in January, 1938, from a script by Oliver Drake and Betty Burbridge. This time the Mesquiteers (Livingston, Corrigan, Terhune) agree to help businessman David Ross (Earl Dwire) and his vigilante committee clean up the town of Trail's End. During a raid on the saloon, some of the vigilantes rob the customers and then start raiding the area, blaming Ross and his committee for their crimes. The sheriff (Ed Cassidy) knows Ross is innocent but suggests he leave town for a while. When he refuses, Stony files a phony murder charge against him so he will be safe in the county jail. The lawman, however, is killed and his deputy, Tracy (Frank O'Connor), has Ross put on trial; he is found guilty before the Mesquiteers can testify in his defense. The trio captures a vigilante who turns out to be railroad detective William Jones (Francis Sayles), whose daughter Jean (Joan Barclay) is being romanced by Stony. Jones tells the trio he is investigating Ross' partner McAllister (Earle Hodgins), the beneficiary of the convicted man's estate. To see if McAllister is guilty or not, the Mesquiteers arrest him wearing vigilante garb and later the gang break Stony out of jail, thinking he is McAllister. They take him to a cave where their masked leader orders Jones killed after they find out he is an imposter. Stony manages to escape with Jones' journal which proves useless although the Mesquiteers pretend it contains valuable information in order to trap the vigilantes. Local attorney Drake (Robert Fiske) tells McAllister to leave town and then orders the vigilantes to capture Stony. This fails, however, when Tucson, Lullaby and Tracy round up the gang and arrest their ringleader, Drake, who was out to kill both Ross and McAlister in order to get their property and insurance proceeds. Ross is then set free. *Variety* reported, "Those 'Three Mesquiteers' are still crusading for law and order in this latest of Republic western dualers, but are now doing it with greater and more believable conviction ... probably the best effort they have made in the series."

William Berke took over as the series' associate producer with *Call the Mesquiteers*, issued in March, 1938. Born in Wisconsin, Berke (1903–58) studied to be a civil engineer but came to Hollywood in the silent days doing photography and writing. As Lester Williams he produced and directed two 1935 Fred Kohler, Jr., Westerns for Commodore and the next year he performed the same chores in two Jack Perrin starrers for Atlantic. He and the star partnered in Perrin-Berke Productions for which he also produced two other Atlantic Westerns starring Perrin. After joining Republic he was production supervisor on the Mesquiteers' feature *Ghost Town Gold* and when he left Republic he returned to directing in 1942 at Columbia. By the mid–1940s he was working at various studios, turning out features in a variety of genres; his final film was *The Lost Missile* in 1958.

Call the Mesquiteers was the first of eight series films to be directed by John English, a native of Canada; it was the first of many features and serials he would helm for the company. English (1903–69) first directed Kermit Maynard in two of his "Northwest Mountie" (q.v.) series for Ambassador in 1935 and two years later he directed

Maynard in one of that company's westerns, *Whistling Bullets*, along with the Tex Ritter feature *Arizona Days* for Grand National the same year. English would direct over two dozen features for Republic before going with Gene Autry to Columbia in 1947 where he helmed 18 of the singing cowboy's features through 1951. English, however, is best remembered for the 19 serials he did for Republic from 1937 to 1944, all but two of which were co-directed by William Witney.

Silk smuggling was the basis of the plot of *Call the Mesquiteers* which had Stony (Livingston), Tucson (Corrigan) and Lullaby (Terhune) being mistaken for train robbers after recovering their truck which was taken from them by smugglers who had just robbed the Desert Express of a silk shipment. On the run from the police, who mistakenly believe the Mesquiteers are the robbers, the trio meet medicine show operator Dr. Aurelius Irving (Earle Hodgins) and his youngsters, Madge (Lynne Roberts) and Tim (Sammy McKim), who are stranded without gasoline. Due to Lullaby's ventriloquist abilities, the trio convince the Irvings they are show people and ask for work. They travel to the ghost town of Canyon Springs where the only resident is a friendly hermit, Hardy (Eddy Waller). When the law shows up after a call from Hardy, the Mesquiteers elude them but Dr. Irving believes them to be the silk thieves. Tim and his dog Flash explore an old mine shaft and learn that Hardy is the leader of the silk smugglers and that the town is the hideout for him and his gang. The boy is discovered and taken prisoner as the gang plans to escape with the stolen furs; Flash follows as do the Mesquiteers. The trio takes Phillips (Maston Williams), Hardy's assistant, into custody and rescues Tim, who tells them that Hardy is the leader of the gang. Stony and Tucson shoot out the tires on the truck carrying Hardy, and Lullaby shows up with the other truck, locking up the gang members.

Sherman returned to direct April's *Outlaws of Sonora*, the first of 13 straight series film he would helm. Here Robert Livingston not only portrayed Stony Brooke but also his lookalike, outlaw Dude Brannen. Stony becomes Brannen's prisoner while transporting bank funds and the outlaw takes his identity and tries to get money from Pierce (Edwin Mordant), the Red Rock bank president. Realizing that Dude is not Stony, Pierce refuses and Dude murders him, then rides out of town, with Stony being blamed for the killing. A reward is put on Stony's head while the gang continues its series of robberies in Mesquite County. An injured Stony manages to escape from the gang's hideout and make it to the 3M ranch where he is hidden by Tucson (Corrigan) and Lullaby (Terhune). The Mesquiteers get Dr. Martin (Jack Mulhall) to attend to Stony's wounds. Dude, who originally had planned to turn in Stony for the reward, decides instead to have surgery to change his face and he orders Martin to perform the operation. The Mesquiteers arrive in town with everyone thinking Stony is Dude. When the outlaw comes to the doctor's office for the operation, he is captured by Stony, as the sheriff, Tucson and Lullaby round up Dude's gang. The Mesquiteers then collect the reward money for Brannen.

Riders of the Black Hills, which came to theaters early in the summer of 1938, had the Three Mesquiteers (Livingston, Corrigan, Terhune) capturing a wild stallion, Mesquite, which looks like a recently stolen thoroughbred race horse, Black Knight. Sheriff Brown (Roscoe Ates) arrests the trio for having the horse which he believes is the animal which really has been stolen by bookie Rod Stevens (Tom London). Peg Garth (Maude Eburne), who co-owns Black Knight with her niece Joyce (Ann Evers), realizes that Mesquite is not her horse and the Mesquiteers are set free. Since Black Knight's winnings from a big race will go to a children's hospital, Stony suggests putting Mesquite in the race in his place. Joyce opposes the action but her fiancé, Don Weston (Frank Melton), tells her to agree but not inform her aunt. When Mesquite wins the race, Weston, who is in league with Stevens in kidnapping Black Knight, secretly demands a ransom from Peg or the truth of the horse substitution will be made known. Joyce delivers the ransom money but the Mesquiteers chase the kidnappers and capture Weston, Stevens and their gang. As a result, Black Knight is returned and the two women are allowed to keep the prize money.

Livingston took a hiatus from the Mesquiteers series after starring in *Heroes of the Hills*, released in August, 1938. Here Stony (Livingston), Tucson (Corrigan) and Lullaby (Terhune) volunteer their 3M ranch as the site of a prisoner parole program. Robert Beaton (Roy Barcroft), who has a state contract to build a new prison, opposes the plan and he enlists the aid of actress Madeline Roberts (Priscilla Lawson), Connors (Carleton Young) and Crane (John Beach) in helping him stop the operation. First they try scaring off the parolees by shooting at them, but prisoner Red (LeRoy Mason) easily brings them back to the ranch. Madeline flirts with Stony and drugs him as Tucson and Lullaby are lured away from the ranch and their horses are stolen. Meanwhile, Benton's gang commits robberies dressed as the prisoners but their plans to raid the 3M ranch is overheard by another parole, the Kid (James Eagles), whom Connors shoots. Dying, the Kid tells Red of the plot and he reports it to Stony. Stony tries to stop Madeline from leaving town but she accuses him of kidnapping her; the sheriff (Forrest Taylor) arrests him but he manages to escape. When the locals demand the parolees be sent back to prison, the Mesquiteers and Red capture the sheriff and make him send for Beaton. Red accuses Beaton of being behind the Kid's murder and the lawlessness, to which he confesses. Connors and Crane rescue Beaton but are chased by the Mesquiteers with Connors falling to his death from a mountainside. Beaton and his gang are captured and the parole plan is allowed to continue.

John Wayne replaced Livingston as Stony Brooke in the Mesquiteers series while Livingston remained at Republic to star in a series of non-westerns: *Arson Racket Squad*, *Ladies in Distress*, *The Night Hawk*, *Orphans of the Street* and *Federal Manhunt*, all 1938 releases. He also had the title role in the studio's 1939 cliffhanger *The Lone Ranger Rides Again*.

Wayne (1909–79) had been a staple of the Western cinema since starring in *The Big Trail* in 1930. After that he supported Buck Jones and Tim McCoy at Columbia before headlining a series of oaters for Warner Bros. in 1932–33. In 1933 he signed with producer Paul Malvern to star in 16 "Lone Star" Westerns released by Monogram. When Monogram became part of Republic, Wayne stayed with the Malvern unit to make another eight slickly produced cowboy films before heading to Universal with the same production outfit to headline a half-dozen action features. After starring in Paramount's 1937 western *Born to the West*, he returned to Republic for the Mesquiteers series. While he got bigger billing than his two co-stars in the Mesquiteers movies, the return to Republic could be called a comedown for the actor had it not been for the fact that in the midst of the productions he got the nod from director John Ford to star in his classic *Stagecoach* (1939). George Sherman directed all eight of Wayne's series outings.

Pals of the Saddle, released in August, 1938, was the first of eight Mesquiteer films starring Wayne. It was also one of the first "B" westerns in the pre–World War II era to deal with foreign spies working their nefarious activities on the open range. Stony (Wayne), Tucson (Corrigan) and Lullaby (Terhune) attempt to come to the aid of dude ranch guest Ann Cameron (Doreen McKay), whose horse bolts during a ride with fellow guest Paul Hartman (George Douglas). Ann is not grateful and rides away with Hartman, leaving her purse behind. The trio heads to the dude ranch, which is run by Judge Hastings (Josef Forte), to return the purse and Stony ends up being accused by Ann of killing Hartman, who was actually shot by another guest, Frank Paige (Frank Milan), who escapes after being wounded by Hartman. Lullaby takes the guise of the local lawman and pretends to arrest Stony but when the real sheriff (Jack Kirk) arrives, Stony makes a quick departure. Later he finds Ann at a remote cabin tending Paige, who dies. She tells Stony she is a Secret Service agent and that Paige was her partner. The two were on the trail of foreign agents smuggling monium, a chemical found in the desert and used to make poison gas, in violation of the Neutrality Act. Stony agrees to aid Ann by posing as a hillbilly trying to get the reward money on his head and then pretending to be Hartman in order to make contact with Gordon (Ted Adams), a smuggler working with the spies who are headquartered at Acme Salt Refinery. Tucson and Lullaby trail Stony, thinking he is the man who killed their pal, and are relieved to find him still alive. When they are captured by the gang, Stony sets his pals free but his cover is spoiled when he is recognized by Hastings and he is locked in one of the gang's wagons carrying monium. Before the spies can cross the Mexican border they are spotted by Tucson, Lullaby and Ann. Tucson and Lullaby free Stony and try to hold off the wagons from crossing the border while Ann goes for the cavalry. The Mesquiteers manage to destroy two of the gang's five wagons, the cavalry arrives and the spies are arrested. One amusing sequence had Stony and Ann masquerading as hillbillies Ezeckial Saunders and his wife Mirandi. The finale with the gun battle between the Mesquiteers and the spies trying to get the monium carrying wagons across the border was well-staged and quite exciting.

Next came *Overland Stage Raiders*, issued the next month. Today it is best remembered as the final feature of actress Louise Brooks (1906–85) who attained cult status by starring in features like *Beggars of Life* (1928), *Diary of a Lost Girl*, *Pandora's Box* (both 1929), and *Prix de Beaute* (1930). She was paid $300 for her work in the Republic feature. Its rather complicated plot had aviator Stony (Wayne) parachuting from his plane and stopping a bus robbery, with help from fellow Mesquiteers Tucson (Corrigan) and Lullaby (Terhune). The trio use their reward money to invest in an air express so that mining owner Harmon (Roy James) can make gold shipments without worrying about being robbed. Stony urges Harmon to use pilot Ned Hoyt (Anthony Marsh), who works with his sister Beth (Brooks). Needing a co-pilot, Ned hires Bob Whitney (Ralph Bowman [John Archer]) over radio operator Joe Waddell (Archie Hall), who also wants the job. Unhappy about the loss of the gold shipment franchise, bus company owner Mullins (Gordon Hart) hires Waddell to work undercover at the airfield and then has his gang hold up a cattle train. Later the gang members pull a robbery on the plane, kill Whitney, and force the passengers to parachute out. Ned, whose real name is Knight and who is an ex-convict, empties the plane's fuel so the hijackers will be forced to land. Thinking the robbery is an inside job, the Mesquiteers question Joe and force him to confess and then go to find the hijacked plane. They leave Waddell tied

John Wayne, George Plues, George Sherwood and Ray Corrigan in *Overland Stage Raiders* (Republic, 1938).

up but Beth finds him and he tells her he has been robbed; she sets him free. He then radios Mullins about the Mesquiteers who find the plane and fight with the hijackers, with Ned being wounded. Mullins arrives with his gang but the crooks are defeated by the Mesquiteers using smoke bombs just as Beth shows up with a posse. Ned, who was blamed for the sky robbery, is exonerated and plans to join another air service.

One of the best of the series, *Santa Fe Stampede*, was released in November, 1938. The Mesquiteers (Wayne, Corrigan, Terhune) have grubstaked Dave Carson's (William Farnum) mining operation. He makes a big gold strike and asks the trio to help him register his claim since he fears Santa Fe Junction's corrupt mayor, Byron (LeRoy Mason), will try to take the mine for himself. Upon arriving at Carson's ranch, the Mesquiteers stop two of Byron's men, Moffitt (Richard Alexander) and Ben (Charles King), from stealing Carson's horses. Ben escapes with ore samples from the mine and takes them to Byron while the Mesquiteers escort the captured Moffit to drunken Judge Hixon (Ferris Taylor), who is in cahoots with Byron. After a shady trial, the judge sets Moffitt free. The local citizens want to form a vigilante group to clean up the town but Stony convinces them to sign a petition of appeal asking the state government for help. When the petition is signed by most of the locals, Stony rides with Dave and his youngest daughter, Julie Jane (Genee Hall), who are going to register the mine claim. After Stony separates from them in order to ride to Placerburg with the petition, Moffitt and another Byron henchman, Tex (Jerry Frank), attack the Carson wagon which crashes, killing Dave and Julie Jane. Byron and his crooked lawyer advisor Harris (Walter Wills) claim that Stony murdered Carson and his daughter so he could have the mine for himself, and the local sheriff (Dick Rush), another Byron cohort, wires Placerburg sheriff Jim Wood (Tom London) to arrest Stony. Not believing Stony guilty of murder, Wood escorts him back to Santa Fe Junction where Stony tells Carson's two survivors, adult Nancy (June Martel) and her little brother Billy (Martin Spellman), that he is innocent. Byron then incites the locals against Stony while Moffitt and Tex abduct Tucson and Lullaby and tie them up in a remote shack. Billy sets them free as Nancy tries to get Stony out of jail. She becomes entrapped with him as Byron has the citizens set fire to the building. Judge Hixon, distressed by the Carson murders, wires the governor for help, as Tucson and Lullaby arrive in town to see the jail torn apart by a dynamite explosion. Stony and Nancy, however, escape and he gets the drop on Byron and his gang. When Byron finds out that Hixon double-crossed him, he shoots the judge but is captured by Stony when he tries to get away.

A fast-paced and entertaining feature, *Santa Fe Stampede*, is also a very violent western. Particularly sadistic is the sometimes cut sequence where Dave Carson and his little girl are ambushed and die when their wagon overturns on them. Equally disturbing are the scenes in which Stony and Nancy are left to roast in the jail set afire by the enraged citizens. *Variety* noted, "All the ingredients of a good western are here. Given an almost airtight script, terrific suspense, some rootin'-tootin' hard-fisted sorrel-saddlers on the side of the law and order, and a ruthless thorough-going villain, western producers can't go wrong.... Action scenes are handled in straightforward dramatic style with few attempts at humor to lighten things up.... Mob scenes at the jail and a near lynching is the punch sequence of the yarn, and will have fans sitting on the edge of their seats."

The final 1938 series feature, *Red River Range*, came out at the end of the year. Here the Mesquiteers (Wayne, Corrigan, Terhune) are working undercover for the Cattlemen's Association in trying to stop a rash of cattle thefts. Near the town of Red River they rescue an old friend, Tex Reilly (Kirby Grant), who has been wounded after trying to infiltrate the rustling gang. Tex agrees to go with Tucson and Lullaby to a ranch owned by Pop Mason (Burr Caruth), whose daughter Jane (Lorna Gray) loves Tex. Stony checks in at a local dude ranch under an assumed name but he is soon recognized as Killer Madigan because of wanted posters put out by the association. Tucson uncovers evidence that faked cattle rustling used to entertain ranch guests is the real thing and he manages to convey the information to Stony, who then tries to join the outlaws after finding out that their leader, Payne (William Royle), is the dude ranch manager. Thinking Stony is Madigan, Payne offers him $500 to eliminate the Mesquiteers. The trio then concocts a ruse in which the Mesquiteers are murdered and a big funeral is planned for them. Stony as Madigan tells Payne this will be a good time to hijack the rest of the cattle (all the locals will be at the funeral). A member of the Cattlemen's Association, Randall (Stanley Blystone), reveals the plans to local banker Hartley (Perry Ivins), not realizing he is in cahoots with Payne. Tucson, however, finds out about Hartley and the plans are altered with the gang being arrested.

Upon the completion of filming *Red River Range*, Wayne took leave from the series to do *Stagecoach*, which was released theatrically early in 1939. He then returned to Republic to finish out his contract to film four more Mesquiteer features. Since *Stagecoach* was a tremendous hit at the box office, Republic held back the release of Wayne's final four entries in order to reap bigger payoffs from his association with the series. Thus the next Mesquiteers feature, *The Night Riders*, was not released until the spring of 1939, some four months after *Red River Range* went into theaters.

The Night Riders, made as *Lone Star Bullets*, took place in the early 1880s with the Mesquiteers (Wayne, Corrigan, Terhune), passengers on a riverboat, witnessing a fight between Talbot (George Douglas) and another gambler (Glenn Strange) who accuses Talbot of cheating. Talbot is cut on the wrist and thrown overboard. He seeks sanctuary with forger Hazleton (Walter Wills) and his companion, Soledad (Doreen McKay). Hazleton has expertly counterfeited a 1744 Spanish land grant which gives the owner over thirteen million acres in the Southwest and he persuades Talbot to assume the guise of the supposed rightful owner of the grant, Don Luis de Serrano. The courts uphold Serrano's claim and with Hazleton, now called Roberto, as his advisor, he sets himself up as a dictator with Soledad impersonating his wife, Senora de Serrano. Don Luis sends his thugs, led by Jackson (Tom Tyler), to collect taxes and evict those who fail to pay. Among those losing their ranches are the Mesquiteers, who become caped riders called Los Capaqueros. They rob the tax collectors and give the money to ranchers about to be evicted. During a raid they accidentally meet President James A. Garfield (Francis Sayles) who is on a tour of the West; he tells them to bring him proof of Don Luis' duplicity and he will give them federal support. Serrano offers a reward for Los Capaqueros and the Mesquiteers go undercover by joining the tax collecting gang after they save Soledad from an angry mob. Don Luis makes them officers in his army and it is then that Stony recognizes him as Talbot. Hazleton, however, is suspicious of the Mesquiteers and when their capes are found in their room, the trio is captured and sentenced to death by firing squad. Susan Randall (Ruth Rogers), one of the ranchers harassed by the tax collectors, gets evidence of Serrano's background and prison record and sends it to President Garfield. Garfield, however, is assassinated before he can help the Mesquiteers, who are led before a firing squad and shot. This causes the locals to attack Serrano's hacienda with the local sheriff (Kermit Maynard) setting the

Poster for *The Night Riders* (Republic, 1939).

Mesquiteers free, since he had the firing squad use blanks to fake the executions. The trio then rides to Serrano's hacienda and force him and Hazelton to sign confessions, thus returning all the lands to their rightful owners.

The film proved to be fast-paced and actionful but unfortunately the Mesquiteers' garb as Los Capaqueros made them look like Klansmen. Also, the subplot of Soledad becoming Serrano's wife had interesting connotations, since she appeared to be physically involved with both Hazelton and Talbot. It is a wonder that such an obviously erotic situation got past the Hays Office at that time.

Three Texas Steers, issued in May, 1939, was Max Terhune's final series feature and the last time the Lullaby Joslin character would appear in the Mesquiteers features for several entries. Terhune had signed with Phoenix Productions to co-star with Ray Corrigan, whose Republic contract also was about to expire, in the "Range Busters" (q.v.) series, released by Monogram. The feature had the Mesquiteers (Wayne, Corrigan, Terhune) coming to the aid of Nancy Evans (Carole Landis) and her beleaguered circus which has been harassed by a series of raids and "accidents." Nancy plans to settle her troupe on a ranch she owns in Mesquite County and mistakenly thinks the Mesquiteers' 3M ranch belongs to her. The Evans ranch is actually rundown but the Mesquiteers decide to fix it up for Nancy and then they are forced to tell her the truth when a gang tries to burn down a barn. The trio loans her money with the mortgage on her ranch as collateral but Lullaby sells it to businessman Abbott (John Merton) for a profit and is then robbed. When Nancy finds out the government wants to buy her land for a large amount of money, she thinks the Mesquiteers have swindled her. The trio learns that Nancy's circus manager, George Ward (Ralph Graves), and his cohort Steve (Ted Adams) knew about the government offer and were trying to sabotage the circus in order to force Nancy into selling them her ranch. They also find out that the duo are in cahoots with Abbott. When Nancy refuses to believe them about Ward, the Mesquiteers abduct her horse Rajah and train him for a big race since they plan to use the winnings to save Nancy's circus and ranch. When Ward attempts to stop Rajah from winning the race, Nancy realizes he is guilty and he is arrested along with Steve and Abbott. The horse wins the race and Nancy sells her ranch to the government, which wants it for a dam site. She then makes plans to take the now solvent circus back on the road.

In his last series outing, Terhune gets more onscreen time with Elmer; additional comedy is provided by Roscoe Ates' addled sheriff. Like the previous entry, *Three Texas Steers* was fast-paced with a number of fight sequences as well as such suspense grippers as a runaway circus wagon and the climactic horse race. *Variety* noted that the feature "leans heavily on novel story angles which set the picture off the beaten track" and added, "[John] Wayne as usual hits the top with first-rate riding and carries his teammates along at a fast clip throughout." Stock footage from Republic's *Circus Girl* (1937), starring Robert Livingston, was used to illustrate the fire which decimated most of the Evans circus early in the proceedings.

With *Wyoming Outlaw*, issued in June, 1939, Raymond Hatton joined the series as Rusty Joslin, presumably a relative of Lullaby. Dominating the feature, however, was Donald Barry, who was so impressive in this outing that Republic soon elevated him to stardom in the 1940 serial *Adventures of Red Ryder* and thereafter he was billed most of the time as Don "Red" Barry. Barry's role as good-badman Will Parker was a precursor to the one portrayed by Humphrey Bogart two years later in *High Sierra*. The two films even have a similar scene in which the outlaw is in the hills stalked by a posse with radio broadcasters bringing the event to a nationwide listening audience. The feature also deals with farmers being victimized by the Dust Bowl, a theme best exemplified on the screen the next year in *The Grapes of Wrath*. Early in the film the song "Dust" by Gene Autry and Johnny Marvin is heard as the Mesquiteers take refuge from a dust storm.

Raymond Hatton (1887–1971), a native of Iowa, was a versatile character actor who started out in vaudeville and stock companies before coming to the movies in 1912. In a career that spanned over a half-century, he appeared in scores of films; during the late 1920s he and Wallace Beery co-starred in a series of popular comedies for Paramount and he also appeared in many Cecil B. DeMille productions. With the coming of sound he most often appeared in character roles in dramatic films and as a sidekick in westerns. In the latter capacity he not only worked in the "Three Mesquiteers" series but he also co-starred with Roy Rogers and Johnny Mack Brown, with whom he made 45 features for Monogram between 1943 and 1948, including the "Nevada Jack McKenzie" (q.v.) series, and he was co-star of the "Rough Riders" and "Irish Cowboys" (qq.v.) series. He was also quite active in television, again mostly in Western series.

Wyoming Outlaw had the Mesquiteers (Wayne, Corrigan, Hatton) taking refuge in an old house during a dust storm and afterward finding one of their cows has been slaughtered. Riding to the town of Mesquite, Stony stops Joe Balsinger's (LeRoy Mason) henchman Sims (Yakima Canutt) from making improper advances to pretty Irene Parker (Adele Pearce [Pamela Blake]). Balsinger is the head of a public works program which fleeces farmers hit hard by the dust storms. Stony takes Irene home and he finds Tucson and Lullaby there since the thief turned out to be Irene's brother Will (Donald Barry), who was trying to get food for his starving family. Irene and Will's father, Luke (Charles Middleton), was fired by Balsinger as foreman of the local road gang because he refused to collect bribe money for him. The Mesquiteers confront Balsinger at his office, which is destroyed in a fight, and Stony goes to testify against him before state officials. Will is hired by the Mesquiteers but is forced to give up the job because of his past record for poaching and he is then arrested for capturing a deer in violation of federal game laws. Although a hearing is scheduled in Mesquite, Balsinger also has the Mesquiteers arrested for destroying his office and his gang intimidates the locals so that they will not appear at the probe. Enraged, Will breaks out of jail and takes sanctuary in the hills after killing two deputies; a U.S. marshal (Elmo Lincoln) orders the cavalry to bring him to justice. The Mesquiteers try to reason with Will but he eludes them and goes to say goodbye to his folks before returning to town. There Will takes Balsinger prisoner and they both are killed in a crossfire. The relief racket is ended and the dust victims are promised new farms.

Wayne and Corrigan's final Mesquiteers feature was *New Frontier*, which came to theaters in August, 1939. When NTA sold the Republic film package to television in the 1950s, its title was changed to *Frontier Horizon* to avoid confusion with another John Wayne film done for the studio in 1935, *The New Frontier*. The film begins in the Civil War Reconstruction period when people pushed off their land went West to homestead. Major Steven Braddock (Eddy Waller) leads a band of citizens to an area they dub New Hope Valley and a half-century later a jubilee is planned to celebrate the occasion. On the way to the event, a buckboard with Gilbert (LeRoy Mason) and local representative Bill Proctor (Harrison Greene) goes out of control due to a stampede and is stopped by the Three Mesquiteers (Wayne, Corrigan, Hatton). At the jubilee, Gilbert and Proctor announce that the nearby city of Metropole needs more water and that the valley has been condemned so a dam can be built on the site. The

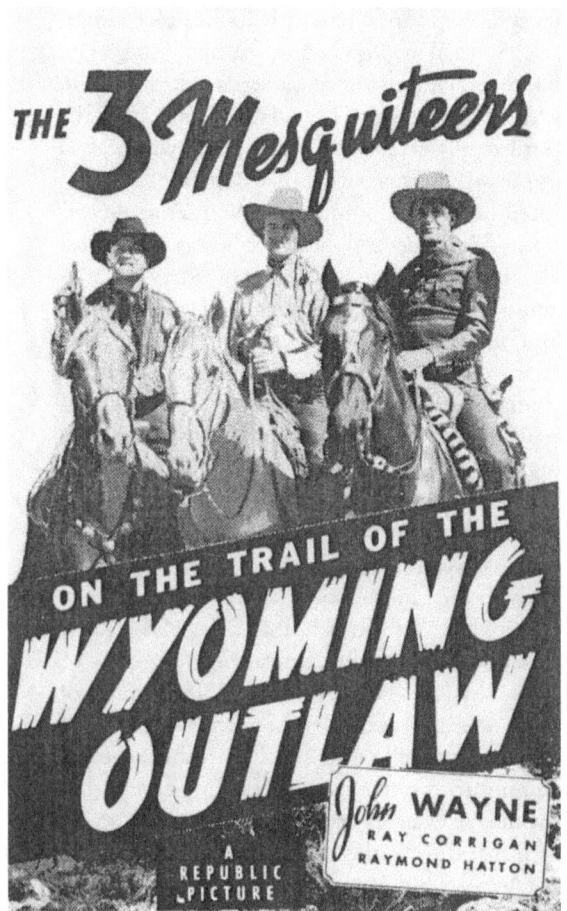

Poster for *Wyoming Outlaw* (Republic, 1939).

citizens protest having to take monetary compensation for their land but a judge (Reginald Barlow) rules in favor of the Abbott Construction Company, which is headed by Gilbert. The citizens have a showdown with construction foreman Harmon (Jack Ingram) and his men who try to wipe them out with a burning wagon. The Mesquiteers, upon the urging of Braddock's pretty granddaughter Celia (Phyllis Isley [Jennifer Jones]), join with the settlers and they all end up in jail. Realtor Dodge (Wilbur Mack), who is in cahoots with Gilbert and Proctor, convinces the Mesquiteers to lead the citizens in buying land in nearby Devil's Acres, promising them that the arid land will be made fertile from water piped in from the dam. With the completion of the dam, the Mesquiteers learn the pipeline has never been installed and ride to warn the locals who are about to relocate to Devil's Acres. They are captured by Gilbert's men and imprisoned in a cellar but manage to escape and warn the citizens before they can be caught in the floodwaters Gilbert has unleashed by opening up the dam's reservoir. The ranchers attack the dam site and during a fight with Stony, Gilbert is drowned. Stony manages to stop the floodwaters. When Devil's Acres has been made fertile, the people resettle there as Proctor and Dodge are sentenced to ten years in prison.

With the departure of Wayne and Corrigan, the role of Stony Brooke was reclaimed by Robert Livingston while the third member of the trio was now played by Duncan Renaldo. His character was first called Renaldo and then after a couple of entries it came Rico Rinaldo. Renaldo (1904–80) was a European native who came to films in the late 1920s after a spell as a portrait painter. With the coming of sound he scored a big hit in *Trader Horn* in 1930 but marital problems a few years later caused a run-in with the Immigration Department and he served a brief term in federal prison. Returning to Hollywood, the only work he could get was as a stagehand until Herbert J. Yates put him back in front of the camera at Republic. After that he worked in a number of features and serials, appearing in seven Mesquiteers offerings in the 1939–40 season. His greatest fame came when he portrayed "The Cisco Kid" (q.v.) in both film and television.

George Sherman continued directing the Mesquiteers series with *The Kansas Terrors*, released in October, 1939. Here Stony (Livingston) and Rusty (Hatton) deliver a shipment of horses to a Caribbean island but are accosted by rebel leader Renaldo (Renaldo), who warns them if they sell the horse as planned to the local commandante (George Douglas) they will be helping him oppress the local citizens. The duo does not believe what they have been told but they reconsider after being attacked and robbed by soldiers. Renaldo then joins them in trying to find the thieves. At a cantina, a fight breaks out in which the rebel leader is injured and Rusty takes care of him while Stony goes to the commandante to report the robbery. While there he overhears a plan to assassinate the island's governor general (Howard Hickman); he puts on a mask and goes to warn the official but the commandante carries out the killing. The governor's daughter, Maria (Jacqueline Wells [Julie Bishop]), blames the masked man. Trying to prove Stony's innocence, Rusty sets up a meeting between her and Renaldo but the young woman informs the commandante, and the rebel leader is arrested and sentenced to die before a firing squad. Realizing the truth, Maria joins forces with the rebels, and Stony and Rusty recruit men to attack the commandante's stronghold. The revolutionaries are successful and the commandante and his men are arrested for tax fraud. With a new government in place, Renaldo returns to the United States with Stony and Rusty. *Variety* opined, "It is purely and simply designed for the hinterland hamlets where a cow caddy is big stuff and it stacks up favorably with other quickie product of its ilk."

The Kansas Terrors was the 25th Mesquiteers film and with it came a new associate producer, Harry Grey. A native of New York City, Grey (1905–63) joined Republic in 1936 as a music supervisor; he performed that function for the first five Mesquiteer films. The next year he became an associate producer and he produced nine Mesquiteer features during the 1939–40 season. He remained an associate producer until the mid–1940s and from 1947 to '49 he produced the "Musical Parade" series of shorts for which he received two Academy Award nominations. He was also a composer, probably best remembered for the song "Dream Valley."

Oliver Drake wrote *Cowboys from Texas*, the

Bob Livingston, Raymond Hatton and Duncan Renaldo as "The Three Mesquiteers."

final series feature for 1939; it was released late in the year. Like earlier Mesquiteer films, it had its basis in a historical subject, this time the 1902 Reclamation Act, which was designed to irrigate arid lands in the West. The Mesquiteers (Livingston, Hatton, Renaldo) welcome homesteaders to the Wood River area, especially pretty June Jones (Carole Landis), who arrives with her father, Kansas Jones (Charles Middleton), and younger brother, Tim (Harry McKim). Saloon owner Belle Starkey (Betty Compson) and her cohort Duke Plummer (Ethan Laidlaw) lead area ranchers in opposing the influx of settlers since Belle and Duke plan to get their lands and re-sell the real estate. Clay Allison (Ivan Miller), the new irrigation supervisor, pretends to offer jobs to the locals but really is in cahoots with Belle and Duke. The trio foment a range war between the ranchers and the settlers, and during one of their gang's raids, Tim is badly injured. To find out who is behind all the trouble, Stony takes to gambling in Belle's saloon which apparently causes a rift between him and his partners. He also dons a mask and takes relief fund money that the gang has stolen and gives it to the locals, revealing that Allison is behind the robbery. When Allison tears off Stony's mask, the people refuse to believe his story because he and the Mesquiteers are cattlemen. Rusty and Renaldo arrive with engineers who were kidnapped so they could not help with the irrigation project and a fight ensues with the crooks being arrested. Newspaper editor Jefferson Morgan (Walter Wills), June's employer, becomes the new irrigation supervisor as the Mesquiteers ride off to a new adventure.

The first of eight series outings in 1940, *Heroes of the Saddle*, was released in January. William Witney returned for the directorial chores in the story of the Mesquiteers (Livingston, Hatton, Renaldo) agreeing to look after little Peggy Bell

(Patsy Lee Parsons) after her father is killed performing at a rodeo. Not having funds to adopt the girl, the Mesquiteers are forced to put her in an orphanage run by Melloney (Byron Foulger), who is stealing public funds along with welfare director J.D. Crone (William Royle). When Peggy needs a brace for her injured foot, public money is not available and Stony ends up getting the needed funds by winning a boxing match with Killer McCully (Jack Roper). The Mesquiteers come to believe that the orphanage officials are mistreating the children and a masked Stony, along with Rusty and Rico, is assisted by nurse Ruth Miller (Loretta Weaver) in taking the orphans to their 3M ranch. At a state commission hearing, Peggy and the other children testify that they were forced to do manual labor; when Melloney and his men try to stop the proceedings, they are subdued by the Mesquiteers. Ruth becomes the new head of the orphanage and Melloney and his cohorts go to prison. An interesting plot ploy had the heroes being aided in the finale fight by several orphans whom Rico had taught to use a bolo.

Heroes of the Saddle was edited by Lester Orlebeck, who had edited ten previous Mesquiteers features. He took the director's chair for the next entry, *Pioneers of the West*, and he would helm seven more films in the series. Sometimes billed as Les Orlebeck, he was born in Wisconsin in 1907 and entered films in 1925 as a technician for Bennett Laboratories. He joined Mascot Pictures as an editor in 1930 and stayed with Republic after its 1935 formation. During World War II he also directed government training films. After his final Mesquiteers feature, *Shadows on the Sage* (1942), he returned to editing and later worked in that capacity in television on such series as *Gunsmoke*, *Wanted: Dead or Alive* and *The Rifleman*. He died in 1970.

Noah Beery appeared in *Pioneers of the West*, released in March, 1940, as a crooked judge out to fleece settlers of their newly settled lands. In 1876 a wagon train led by Dr. Bailey (George Cleveland) and his daughter Anna (Beatrice Roberts) is saved from an Indian attack by the Mesquiteers (Livingston, Hatton, Renaldo). Since the trail guide (Hal Taliaferro) was killed during the attack, the trio agrees to lead the settlers to their new homes, which they have bought at a bargain price from Judge Platt (Noah Beery), who is in league with Steve Carson (Lane Chandler), Anna's fiancé. Disappointed at the poor quality of the land they bought, the pioneers nevertheless clear the area, build homes, plant crops and begin to make a living. To help them, the Mesquiteers round up yearlings and build a cattle herd. Platt and his cohort, Sheriff Gorham (Joe McGuinn), find out that the railroad wants the settlers' land so they get the tax rate made so high the people will have to sell their homes. The Mesquiteers lead a cattle drive for the settlers but after selling the herd they are robbed by Platt's gang. After fighting with the sheriff and his men, they are brought into Platt's court on fraud charges but the settlers refuse to prosecute so the judge sentences them to 30 days hard labor on a road project. When Anna finds a letter proving Steve is in cahoots with Platt in cheating the settlers out of their land, she gets it to the Mesquiteers who make an escape. A masked Stony takes the tax proceeds from Platt and returns it to the settlers who pay off their debts. Platt then orders his men to force the settlers to move, but while trying to harass Dr. Bailey, henchman Nolan (Yakima Canutt) is accidentally killed by Stony. The sheriff arrests him and he is taken to jail while Rico rounds up the settlers for a showdown with Platt and the sheriff. The crooks move into the courthouse, planning to ambush the settlers when they arrive in town, but during the shootout Rusty arrives with a cattle herd and the gang is captured. Platt, Gorham and their gang is arrested, settler Mack (Earl Askam) is made sheriff and Dr. Bailey is the town's new judge. The Mesquiteers then ride off to a new adventure in Arizona. *Variety* termed it "one of Republic's better westerns."

George Sherman was back to direct *Covered Wagon Days*, an April, 1940, release. Earle Snell's script had the area along the Mexican border being closed by military officials due to silver smuggling. When the Mesquiteers (Livingston, Hatton, Renaldo) attempt to go into Mexico to attend the wedding of Rico's brother Carlos (Paul Marion), they are forced to elude a border guard (Richard Alexander). At the Rinaldo hacienda, Rico introduces his friends to Carlos and his fiancée, Maria (Kay Griffith), as well as his mother (Ruth Robinson) and his uncle, Don Diego (Guy D'Ennery), the owner of the long-abandoned

Raymond Hatton, Bob Livingston and Duncan Renaldo as "The Three Mesquiteers."

Juanita silver mine. Unbeknownst to them, mining supply business operator Ransome (George Douglas) is the head of the smuggling operation. He uses an underground tunnel between his Santa Rosa mine and the Juanita property to ship the silver. He invites Carlos and Don Diego to his store with an offer to buy the Juanita; when Don Diego refuses, he has a henchman (John Merton) knock out Carlos and murder Don Diego, blaming the crime on Carlos. Ransome then instigates a lynch mob against Carlos but the Mesquiteers save him and hide him in the hills. He then sends Maria with a message for Carlos and has his gang follow her but the Mesquiteers hold them off as Maria and Carlos flee; Carlos is wounded during the escape. Maria takes him to a local fort for treatment and he is arrested. While Carlos is standing trial, Stony looks for the secret passage to the Juanita mine under Ransome's store but is captured by the gang. He soon escapes with Rico's help. Carlos is found guilty by the court and sentenced to die by firing squad. Donning a mask, Stony returns to Ransome's store and finds the secret tunnel and he is joined by Rusty and Rico. Ransome and his men are subdued when a dynamite keg explodes. Ransome tries to escape but Stony captures him and forces the crook to confess to ordering the murder of Don Diego. Carlos is set free and the smuggling ring is smashed.

Rocky Mountain Rangers, also directed by Sherman, was issued in May, 1940. This fairly slow-paced feature had the Mesquiteers (Livingston, Hatton, Renaldo) leading a contingent from their Ranger post to join Texas counterparts in opposing lawlessness. Raids on towns in the area near the Panhandle are being led by King Barton (LeRoy Mason) and his gang. The Mesquiteers find a wagon full of dead men with only one survivor, injured teenager Danny Burke (Sammy McKim). They take him to the Ranger

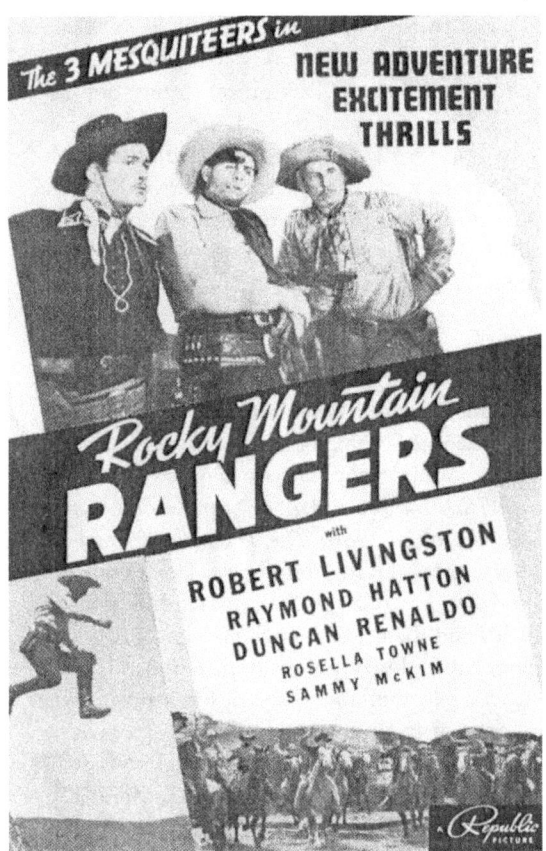

Poster for *Rocky Mountain Rangers* (Republic, 1940).

headquarters where he tells them about Barton and his gang murdering his family and anyone else who opposes them. The trio agrees to bring in Barton and offer to make Danny a Ranger since he tells them he is 18. When he is better, Danny goes to San Carlos to get the Rangers' mail and while he is there, Barton and his gang pull a raid with Danny being fatally wounded. Barton's brother Jim (Dennis Moore) is captured. In order to infiltrate Barton's gang, Stony takes the guise of outlaw The Laredo Kid and he and Rico break Jim out of jail and head for the Panhandle. Because they freed Jim, Barton accepts Laredo and Rico into his gang. At the local gun shop, Stony reveals his identity to gunsmith Joseph Manners (John St. Polis), who is trying to arm the locals against Barton, and his daughter Doris (Rosella Towne). When Barton's gang plans to rob a stagecoach, Stony wears a mask and commits the robbery himself but later gives back the money. Rusty arrives in Panhandle posing as a snake oil salesman but the real Laredo Kid (Livingston) also shows up and the Mesquiteers are captured. Laredo tells Barton he wants his help in robbing a stagecoach of $500,000 in gold, government money sent to set up martial law in the Panhandle. Barton shoots Laredo and orders Jim to kill the Mesquiteers while he and the gang pull off the robbery. Dying, Laredo kills Jim, thus saving Stony, Rusty and Rico. While Rusty goes for the Rangers, Stony and Rico try to thwart the gang by blocking them at Red Rock Pass after they have robbed the stagecoach. The two hold off the gang as Rusty arrives with reinforcements. The outlaws are captured and Barton falls to his death off a cliff during a fight with Stony. Martial law is declared in the Panhandle and it becomes part of Oklahoma.

Director Nate Watt's only Mesquiteers effort, *Oklahoma Renegades*, was issued late in August of 1940. It was also the last series film to feature Livingston, Hatton and Renaldo as the Mesquiteers. Taking place in the early 1900s, it had Spanish-American War veterans coming West to homestead land in Oklahoma, much to the chagrin of cattle ranchers led by Mace Liscomb (William Ruhl) and his brother Orv (Harold Daniels). The Mesquiteers (Livingston, Hatton, Renaldo), who have encouraged the veterans to make the move West, find that others, including rancher Marian Carter (Florine McKinney), also oppose the homesteaders settling near the community of Cottonwood. There the group is attacked but saved by the Mesquiteers, but later their supplies are destroyed in a dynamite explosion. Two former showmen, Jim Keith (Lee "Lasses" White) and Hank Blake (Al Herman), give a performance to raise funds for the settlers but Liscomb's gang rob the proceeds. While being chased by the Mesquiteers, Orv is killed. Mace then takes revenge by murdering Jim Keith, thus bringing Marian to the side of the veterans. Stony and Rico hunt Mace but his men pin them down in an old building as Rusty and Marian unite the veterans in fighting the gang. Following a shootout, Mace and his men are captured with Marian planning to marry blind veteran Carl (James Seay).

When the next series affair, *Under Texas Skies*, came to theaters in the fall of 1940, it was with a change in the lineup of stars playing the Mesquiteers. While Livingston remained as Stony

Brooke, Bob Steele took over the role of Tucson Smith and Rufe Davis took over as Lullaby. The addition of Steele and Davis brought new life to the series as Livingston, Steele and Davis had better camaraderie than Livingston, Hatton and Renaldo.

Steele had been starring in PRC's "Billy the Kid" (q.v.) series when he signed to play Tucson, and his genre popularity certainly added to the outings. Davis was a newcomer to Westerns, although he had been in films since 1937. Born Rufus Davidson in 1908 in Oklahoma, he was reminiscent of Max Terhune in that he was an accomplished animal imitator. His comedy was more in the Smiley Burnette vein although age-wise he better fit the Lullaby character as written by William Colt MacDonald. Still, his Lullaby was more of a buffoon than the mild, more relaxed character played by Terhune. Davis came to films after working in vaudeville; after leaving the Mesquiteers series in 1942, he returned to the stage and also worked in radio and television. In the latter medium he is best remembered for the role of train engineer Floyd Smoot in the CBS-TV series *Petticoat Junction* from 1964 to 1968. Davis died in 1974 not long after his 66th birthday.

In some ways, *Under Texas Skies* was a rebirth of the series, not only in its new combination of leading players but also plotwise. It began with Tucson (Steele) accused of murdering Sheriff Brooke (Wade Boteler), Stony's father, and sentenced to be hanged. Returning after being away for several years, Stony (Livingston) finds Tucson, who has been wounded while escaping from jail with the aid of his friend Jim Marsden (Rex Lease). Stony takes Tucson to his ranch where his sister Helen (Lois Ranson) bandages his wounds. Tucson flees when Sheriff Blackton (Henry Brandon) arrives with a posse looking for him. Blackton, who had been deputy to Stony's father, tells him that Tucson murdered his dad and Stony joins the posse looking for him. Stony trails Helen to Tucson's hideout but does not believe him that Blackton is the real killer. Tucson escapes again and Helen tells Stony a court hearing will set her brother free. Judge Craig (Burr Caruth), who is set to hold the hearing, is mysteriously slain and Stony begins to believe in Tucson's innocence. He continues as a deputy to Blackton but works undercover and asks barber shop owner Lullaby (Davis) to aid him in the investigation. When Lullaby hears that Tucson is going to Marsden's ranch, he informs Blackton but Stony prevents his pal from being ambushed. Stony and Tucson set a trap for Blackton by telling him the ranchers want him to guard their cattle drive. Blackton plans to inform his gang of the drive so they can rustle the cattle but his emissary is abducted by Stony. When the outlaws attack the cattle drive, the sheriff is caught in the crossfire. As a result, Blackton confesses to the killing of Sheriff Brooke and then is fatally wounded. Tucson is set free and the Mesquiteers are reunited.

George Sherman directed *Under Texas Skies* as he would do the last two 1940 series entries, *The Trail Blazers* and *Lone Star Raiders*. Issued in November, 1940, *The Trail Blazers* had the Mesquiteers (Livingston, Steele, Davis) meeting Jim Chapman (Carroll Nye), his wife Alice (Mary Field) and their little boy, Stony's godson, who is named after him. Jim has been assigned to construct a telegraph line from the local fort in order to prevent lawlessness. After the trio leaves the Chapman convoy, it is attacked by outlaws with the telegraph equipment destroyed. Major Kelton (Tom Chatteron), commander of the fort, does not believe the telegraph will help the cavalry and opposes its construction, as does local newspaperman Jeff Bradley (Weldon Heyburn), who is secretly the leader of the outlaws. While the town committee refuses funds for the telegraph line, the Mesquiteers convince Jim to continue construction although raids are made on his camp. When the trio tries to question Bradley, they are arrested by soldiers and detained at the fort until they manage to escape. Bradley sends his gang, led by henchman Mason (John Merton), to murder all the construction workers, with only Jim's son surviving. Kelton's daughter, Marcia (Pauline Moore), tells the Mesquiteers of the tragedy and promises to take care of little Stony. She also convinces her father to provide money for the telegraph line. A new engineer, Reynolds (Rex Lease), arrives to complete the project. When the line is completed, Bradley has a fake message sent saying a nearby fort is being attacked, and Kelton and his troops ride to help while Bradley, Mason and the gang plan to destroy the construction camp. Stony and Tucson, who had been jailed by Kelton, escape, join Lullaby and head for the camp. They fight with the gang and Stony repairs the line and sends a message to Kelton, who returns with his men and captures the gang.

Like the previous year's *Wyoming Outlaw*, *Lone Star Raiders*, which came out at the end of 1940, had its plot origins in Dust Bowl conditions. The Three Mesquiteers (Livingston, Steele, Davis) work for the Circle H Ranch, which is about to go under due to drought and dust conditions. The only hope is for the ranch to win a government contract to sell horses to the cavalry, but Henry Martin (George Douglas) wants the contract for himself and hires punchers Dixon (John Merton) and Fisher (Rex Lease) to sabotage the Circle H operation. The new owner of the ranch, Lydia "Granny" Phelps (Sarah Padden), who has inherited the property, arrives from a welfare home and the Mesquiteers and foreman Cameron (John Elliott) and his daughter Linda (June Johnson) do not have the heart to tell her of the ranch's plight. One day Granny tries to set free a recently captured black stallion but the entire herd of mustangs escapes. The Mesquiteers follow the stallion who leads them to a huge mustang herd which is brought back to the ranch. After Dixon and Fisher try to scatter the herd, Stony fires them. Martin orders the duo to poison the Circle H watering troughs. Cameron catches them and Dixon kills him, blaming the death on the wild stallion, which Stony has broken in order to win the race that will determine the cavalry contract. Because of Cameron's death, Granny decides to sell the ranch to Martin but the Mesquiteers stop the sale and destroy Martin's office in a fistfight. Martin has the sheriff (Hal Price) arrest the Mesquiteers for assault and battery and they are put in jail. Granny, however, pulls a gun on the lawman and sets them free; they take part in the race which Stony wins riding the stallion. The sheriff tries to take the Mesquiteers back to jail just as the stallion corners Dixon, who admits murdering Cameron and then implicates Martin in the lawlessness. Martin tries to run but is captured by Stony. The Circle H is awarded the cavalry contract. During the course of the feature, Davis sang "Little White Mule," which included a number of animal imitations.

Lone Star Raiders was the first feature on which Louis Gray served as associate producer. He would continue in that position until the series' demise in 1943. He stayed with Republic as an associate producer and during the 1948–49 theatrical season he produced Jimmy Wakely Westerns for Monogram. In the early 1950s he produced 85 episodes of *The Gene Autry Show* for CBS-TV and he also produced several other TV series for Autry's production company.

Lester Orlebeck directed the next three Mesquiteer features, beginning with *Prairie Pioneers*, released in February, 1941. This one took place in California in the aftermath of the Mexican War. The Mesquiteers (Livingston, Steele, Davis) bring in settlers to homestead areas which were once part of Spanish land grants. At Rancho Ortega, owner Don Miguel (Guy D'Ennery) is told by his friend, Don Carlos Montoya (Davison Clark), that the settlers will take over his property. In reality, Montoya is an agent for strip miner Fields (Kenneth MacDonald) who wants the land to expand his operations. Don Miguel's son, Roberto (Robert Kellard), tries to stop Fields' henchmen Wade (Jack Ingram) and Morrison (Yakima Canutt) from trespassing on his father's land and a fight ensues, which is stopped by the Mesquiteers. Stony blames Ortega for causing the problem but it turns out Roberto is a boyhood friend of Tucson. To quell any further problems, Don Miguel invites everyone to a fiesta at his hacienda the next day but Fields takes a note from Tucson to Roberto and lures him away from the rancho and he is ambushed. Meanwhile, Wade, Morrison and their men attack the settlers' camp and massacre those present, blaming the killings on Roberto, who is also accused of murdering settler Nelson (Lee Shumway), the killing actually being done by Wade. Tucson helps Roberto escape from a lynch mob, but Stony believes he is guilty. When the mob attacks Don Miguel, Stony saves the old man and convinces his daughter Dolores (Esther Estrella) to reveal Roberto's hiding place so he can bring him to his father. Montoya finds out and sends for the cavalry with Roberto being arrested and Tucson and Dolores blaming Stony for his capture. Roberto is tried and convicted of murder and sentenced to die before a firing squad, but Stony becomes suspicious of Fields' offer to buy the Ortega property without any knowledge of ranching. Tucson trails Montoya to Fields' El Dorado Hydraulic Mining Company headquarters and confronts the two men. Later Stony and Tucson patch up their differences when they realize Fields and Montoya are in league to take over the Ortega rancho. While the area governor denies Roberto's request for a reprieve, Stony and Tucson ride to Fields' headquarters and find the evidence needed to clear him. They are ambushed by the gang and trapped in one of the buildings but Lullaby comes to their rescue by subduing the outlaws with a hydraulic mining hose. The trio forces a confession out of Wade and they take him to the fort just in time to save Roberto from execution. Tucson and Lullaby capture Fields and Montoya, who have been exposed by Nelson. One amusing sequence had Lullaby doing a Mexican hat dance.

Pals of the Pecos, released in the spring of 1941, took place just before the Civil War with the Mesquiteers (Livingston, Steele, Davis) working with Daniel Burke (Pat O'Malley) in setting up the Sierra Express Company, a stagecoach business, in Sacramento. Burke's son, Larry (Dennis Moore), owes gambling debts to saloon keeper Keno Hawkins (Roy Barcroft), who is in league with Stevens (Robert Frazer), a steamship operator who wants to put Burke out of business. Also working with Stevens is attorney Buckley (John Holland). When Burke assigns his son to carry payroll money to the stagecoach road construction site, Keno makes Larry use the money to pay off his debts and claim he was robbed. The Mesquiteers trail Keno and his gang, who (along with Larry) rob a relay station and shoot a guard. Gang member Nevada (Bud Osborne) is captured by the Mesquiteers and he tells them Larry was involved in the holdup. At the relay station they have a shootout with the remaining gang members; Keno kills Larry and escapes. The Mesquiteers think they are to blame and they inform his family that Larry died trying to thwart

Rufe Davis, Bob Steele and Bob Livingston in *Pals of the Pecos* (Republic, 1941).

the robbery. Larry's sister June (June Johnson) tells the sheriff (Tom London) the Mesquiteers killed her brother and they are arrested after Keno notifies the lawman that the trio tried to pass the stolen money at his saloon. While Burke agrees to sell his stagecoach franchise, his youngest son, Tim (Robert Winkler), believes the Mesquiteers are innocent and helps them escape. The trio retrieves the stolen money from Keno and use it to pay off the road construction workers. The next day, they drive the Burke stagecoach in order to win a mail contract. They force Buckley and the sheriff to go along with them and, fearing he will be killed, the lawyer tells them Keno shot Larry and that he also plans to dynamite Apache Pass along the travel route. Although Keno succeeds in blowing up the pass, the Mesquiteers manage to detour and get the stagecoach to town and win the contract. Uniting with the sheriff, the trio brings in Keno and the rest of the gang with Stevens and Buckley also being arrested. During the proceedings, Davis performed the comedy number "Don Juan Pestachio."

A cowboys-and-Indians excursion for the series took place in *Saddlemates*, issued in May, 1941. Stony (Livingston), Tucson (Steele) and Lullaby (Davis) are scouts for the Texas Rangers stationed along the Mexican border. When the Ranger company is replaced by the cavalry, the Mesquiteers decide to leave but become enamored with Susan Langley (Gale Storm), the daughter of Colonel Langley (Forbes Murray), who wants to negotiate with Wanechee (Peter George Lynn), the leader of marauding Indians. Unbeknownst to the cavalry, Wanechee is masquerading as the post's interpreter, LeRoque. Wanechee incites his people to rid the area of settlers but is opposed by Thunder Bird (Marty Faust), who wants to negotiate with the cavalry. The renegade then leads his braves in attacking a wagon train and stealing rifles. When the Mesquiteers are assigned to go with LeRoque on a peace mission, one of the soldiers is killed and the trio is blamed. Susan convinces her father to set them free but after he is in a saloon fight, Stony loses his job as a scout. Tucson and Lullaby also quit the cavalry but are captured by Wanechee, not recognizing him as LeRoque. The Indian leader later kills two of his men previously captured by Stony, Tucson and Lullaby, and the Mesquiteers are accused of murder and arrested. Thunder Bird is told by LeRoque to attack a wagon train carrying rifles along with Langley's wife (Marin Sais) and son. LeRoque then captures Langley and his men, who were on their way to a meeting with the chiefs. At the post, Susan tries to get Lieutenant Manning (Cornelius Keefe) to release the Mesquiteers and he refuses, but they manage to escape. Stony and Lullaby ride to find Langley and his men, whom they set free, and Tucson goes to assist the wagon train. LeRoque and his braves attack the wagons and are nearly victorious until Stony arrives with Langley and the cavalry. With LeRoque unmasked as Wanechee and placed under arrest, Langley begins negotiations with Thunder Bird. *Variety* called it "standard stuff for action runs, average cowboy and Indian fare with a little too much talkin' and too little shootin.'" Davis performed the song "Just Imagine That" and comedy subplots had Lullaby trying to avoid an old maid (Ellen Lowe) as well as a scalp-seeking Indian (Glenn Strange).

John English was back directing the series with *Gangs of Sonora*, which came out in the summer of 1941. In Wyoming Territory in 1890, the Mesquiteers (Livingston, Steele, Davis) are hired by newspaper editor Ward Beecham (William Farnum) to guard his new printing press after his earlier equipment was destroyed in a raid. The deed was ordered by commissioner Sam Tredwell (Robert Frazer), who is afraid of losing his power if Beecham's petition for statehood is passed. Working with Tredwell is young lawyer David Conners (Ward "Bud" McTaggart); his mother, famed newspaperwoman Kansas Kate Conners (Helen McKellar), has come to town with her daughter June (June Johnson) to visit David. Kate tells David he is betraying his late father's work by being associated with Tredwell, and she and June take over Beecham's petitions after he is slain by one of Tredwell's henchmen. Although the outlaws try to stop it, the Mesquiteers get the petitions aboard a train to Washington, D.C. Meanwhile David is blamed for killing printer Jed Pickins (Budd Buster), with whom he argued, but the deed was really done by Tredwell henchman Drennon (Bud Geary). David is arrested while Tredwell hides the knowledge that an election has been ordered for the next day since Pickins was killed because he also knew about the election.

The Mesquiteers steal the printing press and put out an extra claiming David's innocence. After questioning the telegrapher (Max Waizmann), they find out about the election and the motive for Pickins' murder. The trio spreads the word about the election which is held at the newspaper office but Treadwell wants to nullify the results by declaring martial law. He organizes a mob to hang David but Stony arrives and forces Drennon to admit killing Jed and implicate Tredwell in the crimes. As a result of the vote, Wyoming is made a state.

Livingston's Republic contract ended with *Gangs of Sonora* and he went to PRC to take over the lead in the "Lone Rider" (q.v.) series. Hired to replace him as Stony Brooke was veteran genre star Tom Tyler. Born Vincent Markowski in New York state, Tyler (1903–54) first gained fame as a weight lifter before coming to movies. In 1925 he began starring in a series of oaters for Films Bookings Office and he would continue to do so for the rest of the decade, making his talkie debut in 1930 in the Mascot serial *Phantom of the West*. After that he headlined series for Syndicate, Monogram, Monarch, Reliable and Victory along with having good character roles in *Powdersmoke Range* (1935), the first Mesquiteers feature, and *The Last Outlaw* (1936). He was a villain in the 1939 Mesquiteers outing *The Night Riders* and the same year he was impressive as gunman Luke Plummer in *Stagecoach*. In 1940 he was Kharis in *The Mummy's Hand* at Universal and the next year he had the title role in the Republic cliffhanger *Adventures of Captain Marvel*, which led to his being given the part of Stony Brooke in the Mesquiteers series.

Lester Orlebeck was back to direct the next three series features, beginning with *Outlaws of the Cherokee Trail*, released in the fall of 1941. Like the earlier *Rocky Mountain Rangers* it dealt with lawlessness in territory out of the jurisdiction of the Texas Rangers. Tucson (Steele), Stony (Tyler) and Lullaby (Davis) join the Rangers in order to thwart the activities of gang leader Val Lamar (Roy Barcroft), who uses the Cherokee Strip as his headquarters. The trio captures Lamar's younger brother, Pete (John James), who is found guilty of murder and hanged. Lamar vows revenge and has two of the jurors who convicted his brother murdered. The Mesquiteers convince Ranger Captain Sheldon (Tom Chatterton) they need to raid the no man's land and capture Lamar and his gang. The outlaws, however, murder James Warren, the governor's nephew, and replace him with one of their own, Harvard (Philip Trent). Lamar fakes a letter from the governor telling Sheldon to stay out of the Cherokee Strip but the Mesquiteers decide to take action themselves after the murder of a judge (Joel Friedkin). Disguised as Indians, the trio goes to Lamar's saloon where they overhear him make plans to abduct Sheldon's daughter Doris (Lois Collier). Receiving a letter, supposedly written by her father but actually penned by Harvard, Doris leaves convent school and takes a stagecoach to the military post. When the Mesquiteers do not find Doris at school, they follow the stagecoach, which is attacked by the outlaws. Lullaby and Doris are taken hostage by the gang but Stony and Tucson escape and take a message to Sheldon that he is to come alone to the Cherokee Strip. Seeing a picture of the real James Warren, Tucson realizes Harvard is a fake and he forces the outlaw to go with him and Stony to Lamar's saloon where Sheldon is about to be hung. Aided by the Texas Rangers,

Tom Tyler as Stony Brooke of "The Three Mesquiteers."

the Mesquiteers capture Lamar and his gang and the Sheldons are set free.

Duncan Renaldo returned to the series in *Gauchos of El Dorado*, which came to theaters in October of 1941, but not as one of the Mesquiteers. Instead he was cast as Jose Ojara, also known as The Gaucho, an outlaw who turns on Bart Branden's (Norman Willis) after finding that his boss holds the mortgage to his family's ranch. Jose takes the money from the gang and rides away, meeting up with old friends Tucson (Steele), Stony (Tyler) and Lullaby (Davis). When the outlaw gang nears, looking for Jose, he rides away but returns to save the Mesquiteers from being ambushed. Jose, however, is fatally wounded and before dying he gives the trio a medal for his mother along with the money to pay off her mortgage. At the Ojara ranch, the Mesquiteers meet Jose's mother, Isabel (Rosina Galli), who believes Tucson is her long-lost son, and they do not have the heart to disappoint her by telling her the truth. When the trio tries to pay off the mortgage, they find out the money is stolen currency and are arrested. They are released, however, when they say they did not know the money was stolen and vow to get the funds to pay off the mortgage. The money had been taken from Samuel Tyndal's (William Ruhl) bank and he is in league with Branden and his pal Monk Stevens (Ray Bennett), all of whom want the Ojara ranch for its rich bauxite deposits. Branden, however, is captured by the Mesquiteers who plan to use his reward money to pay off the mortgage, but the trio is soon arrested for allegedly murdering Jose. Meanwhile, Jose's sister-in-law, Ellen (Lois Collier), has brought his small son to the rancho and he is captured for ransom by the gang. The Mesquiteers break out of jail and foil the kidnap plot, capturing crooks and paying off the Ojara mortgage.

West of Cimarron, released late in 1941, takes place in the Reconstruction Era in Texas following the Civil War. The Mesquiteers (Steele, Tyler, Davis) come to the aid of a trooper being chased by bushwhackers. One of the attackers, Ken Morgan (James Bush), is an old friend of Tucson's but he is not happy about the Mesquiteers interfering since the trooper was one of three soldiers trying to force his father (Budd Buster) to pay high taxes. The civilian attaché, Charles Bentley (Hugh Prosser), and Captain Hawkes (Roy Barcroft) have been forcing the locals to play exorbitant taxes but this is not known by the post commander, Colonel Conway (Guy Usher), whose daughter Doris (Lois Collier) is attracted to Ken. When Ken and his brother Jimmy (Mickey Rentschler) are about to be shot by troopers, the Mesquiteers come to their rescue, but Jimmy is killed. Stony has Tucson and Lullaby join the troopers so they can work undercover; when they tell Conway that Jimmy was murdered, he arrests Hawkes. Bentley orders a trooper (Bud Geary) to kill Conway, and Ken is blamed. Taking over command of the post, Bentley has Ken arrested along with Tucson and Stony. Lullaby then asks Doris to ride for help from the local inspector general, Colonel Briggs (Stanley Blystone), while he sneaks guns to his pals. Ken's father gets the bushwhackers together and they join Briggs' men who aid the Mesquiteers in defeating the crooks in a shootout.

Code of the Outlaw, issued early in 1942, was the first of four series features in a row to be directed by John English. A mysterious gang is carrying out a series of holdups and Sheriff Ed Stoddard (John Ince) sends for the Three Mesquiteers (Steele, Tyler, Davis) to help him stop the lawlessness. Following a stagecoach payroll robbery, the trio comes to the aid of a young boy, Tim Hardin (Bennie Bartlett), not knowing he was helping his father, Bart Hardin (Weydon Heyburn), and his gang carry out the holdup. The boy escapes and joins his father in hiding the stolen money. The Mesquiteers trail a gang member to their hideout and during a shootout Bart Hardin is killed by one of his own men, but Tim thinks the Mesquiteers shot him. Upon the instigation of newspaper reporter Sue Dayton (Melinda Leighton), Tim is sent to a boy's work farm but the Mesquiteers are able to get him released in their custody. He grows to like Tucson, Stony and Lullaby and decides to help them recover the stolen money but later runs away after hearing the trio argue with Sue and Boyle (Phil Dunham), the work farm boss, over his custody. He is captured by gang member Taggart (Donald Curtis), who shoots Lullaby, but Tim is able to leave a note in Lullaby's pocket giving the location where the money is hidden. Lullaby is not badly hurt and he joins Tucson and Stony in going to a Wells Fargo office where the money was hidden only to find it taken by Taggart. The outlaw takes over a stagecoach as the Mesquiteers trail him. Tim escapes by jumping onto Lullaby's horse. Taggart is captured and the stolen money is retrieved by the Mesquiteers with Tim agreeing to go to military school.

Next came *Raiders of the Range* in March, 1942. Here the Mesquiteers (Steele, Tyler, Davis) come to the aid of Dr. Higgins (Tom Chatterton), the owner of the Valley Oil Company. Raiders have been attacking the project and rancher John Travers (Charles F. Miller) is considering withdrawing funding even though the railroad has promised to build in the area once the well produces. Higgins fires foreman Plummer (Fred Kohler, Jr.) for allowing drinking on the job, unaware that the man is in cahoots with Daggett (Frank Jaquet), who has a second lease on the oil site. Another worker, Ned Foster (Dennis Moore), is made foreman but that night he gets into a rigged poker game with Daggett and is forced to sign several IOUs. When Higgins comes looking for Foster in Daggett's saloon, a fight breaks out between him and Plummer but is broken up by the Mesquiteers. During the melee, the doctor's medical bag falls open and Foster accidentally mixes up pills which have been spilled. When the fight is over, Higgins treats Plummer for a head wound but accidentally gives him the wrong medicine, resulting in his death. Although Higgins is cleared of purposely killing Plummer, suspicion about him remains. Daggett takes advantage of this and blackmails Foster into helping him to sabotage the drilling site. After new equipment has been installed at the well, a gas pocket is found, necessitating a new blowout valve. The Mesquiteers go to a nearby town to get a new valve, which is stolen by Daggett's gang, but the trio manages to retrieve it. With the aid of workers Todd (Jack Ingram) and Jensen (Al Taylor), Foster tries to slow up the project but Travers sees them putting rocks into the well shaft. Foster goes to Travers' home and there switches the pills Higgins has given him, resulting in the rancher's death. This time Higgins is arrested for murder but the Mesquiteers help him to escape and all four men are hunted by the sheriff (Hal Price) and his deputies. Lullaby, masquerading as a scrubwoman, rummages through Daggett's office and finds the IOUs from Foster. Travers' daughter, Jean (Lois Collier), sees the Mesquiteers and Higgins riding to the well site and goes for the sheriff. Daggett tries to poison Foster to get him out of the way, but Higgins substitutes knockout drops. The Mesquiteers fight it out with Daggett and his gang until the sheriff arrives. Foster accuses Daggett of trying to kill him and admits his part in Travers' death, thus exposing Daggett's schemes. Tucson and Lullaby bring in the oil well with dynamite.

Released in April, 1942, *Westward Ho* found the Mesquiteers (Steele, Tyler, Davis) in the town of Spring Valley. The area has been plagued by an outlaw gang and the local bankers' organization puts up a $5,000 reward for their capture. Mrs. Healey (Evelyn Brent), president of the bankers' group, is really the head of the gang, along with her henchman Rick West (Donald Curtis). To get the heat off of the gang and collect the reward money, Mrs. Healey has West set up Wayne Henderson (Tom Seidel), who has just returned home from school. After meeting his sister Anne (Lois Collier) and brother Jimmy (John James), Wayne is asked to make a bank deposit for a drunk, not knowing he is carrying a robbery note. As a result he is killed, allegedly trying to rob the bank. Lullaby becomes the gang's next target but another person gets shot; Lullaby is arrested by the sheriff (Emmett Lynn). Jimmy, who saw the gang members approach Lullaby, rides out of town and is accused of being part of the robbery scheme. To get Lullaby out of the way, Mrs. Healey and West try to get him lynched but Tucson and Stony come to his rescue and they also stop the sheriff from arresting Jimmy. The four men hide out in an old mine and Lullaby goes into town in the guise of a fortune teller; he finds out the gang plans to rob a stagecoach. The Mesquiteers beat the gang to the money and Tucson and Stony, after turning the proceeds over to the sheriff, infiltrate the gang. The lawman takes the money to Mrs. Healey and informs her of the Mesquiteers' activities. She then makes plans with West to get the trio out of the way by trapping them in her bank. Realizing the woman is a crook, the Mesquiteers have a gun battle with the gang. Mrs. Healey shoots West when he tries to stop her from making a getaway. Dying, West tells the truth about Mrs. Healey and she and the rest of the gang are arrested. *Variety* called it "an above-average Western with much action and a novel

Tom Tyler, Rufe Davis and Bob Steele as "The Three Mesquiteers."

story.... Film is tight and never lets up a minute from an opening blast of gunfire. Direction is rapid-paced and acting is all good."

The Mesquiteers' next outing, *The Phantom Plainsmen*, released in June, 1942, returned the trio to contemporary times. Here Tucson (Steele), Stony (Tyler) and Lullaby (Davis) work for Cap Marvin (Charles F. Miller), a horseman who refuses to sell his stock for military purposes. Unbeknownst to Cap, Kurt Redman (Alex Callam), broker for the local cattlemen, is selling his herds to Germany. Tad Marvin (Richard Crane), Cap's son, wins a scholarship to study veterinary medicine in Germany and he goes abroad, leaving behind his fiancée Judy Barrett (Lois Collier), Redman's secretary. When Muller (Monte Montague) mistreats one of the horses, he and Tucson fight, and Cap fires Muller, who is secretly working with Redman. While taking a bill of sale to the exchange office, Lullaby overhears Redman and Muller discuss shipping Cap's horses to the Germans and he informs Tucson and Stony. The trio tells Cap, who refuses to let Redman handle any more of his sales. As a result, Redman reports to his superior in New York City, Colonel Eric Hartwig (Robert O. Davis), who has the Gestapo take Tad into custody. When he is informed of these events by Redman, Cap agrees to work with the Germans in order to protect his son. The Mesquiteers then quit their jobs and begin sabotaging shipping operations, with Muller rehired as Cap's foreman. When Cap goes to the trio's cave hideout, Redman has the sheriff (Ed Cassidy) follow him, and the Mesquiteers are arrested. During a fight, Cap is accidentally wounded and the Mesquiteers are put in jail. The trio escape and with Judy's help search Redman's office, breaking the code he uses to send message to Hartwig. As the sheriff and his men chase the Mesquiteers, Judy sends a coded message to Hartwig ordering

Tad's release. Redman is taken prisoner by the Mesquiteers and kept at Cap's ranch. Muller informs Hartwig, who flies West and takes control of the situation by informing Cap that his son is still a prisoner. He then forces the Mesquiteers to help round up a horse herd for shipment and orders Muller to kill Stony and Lullaby; Tucson comes to their rescue. Judy arrives at Cap's ranch with the news that Tad has been set free and is on his way home. Tucson subdues Redman as Stony chases Hartwig, who tries to escape in a car with Cap. Stony overtakes the German, defeats him and rescues Cap. Returning home, Tad informs his father that Germany is ready to fight and Cap decides to sell his horses to the government.

Released more than six months after the United States entered World War II, *The Phantom Plainsmen* still proved to be a good propaganda piece. It marked Davis' final appearance as Lullaby Joslin; with the next entry, *Shadows on the Sage*, he was replaced by Jimmie Dodd. A native of Ohio, Dodd (1910–64) was a character actor who also appeared with John Wayne in Republic's *Flying Tigers* (1942), the same year he joined the Mesquiteers. He began working in radio in 1933 and came to Hollywood four years later. Today he is best remembered as the host of the daily television series *The Mickey Mouse Club* (ABC-TV, 1955–59); he wrote "The Mickey Mouse March." Like Davis, Dodd composed and performed comedy songs in the Mesquiteers films.

Shadows on the Sage, issued in August, 1942, was the last film in the group to be directed by Lester Orlebeck. It also gave star Bob Steele a chance to play dual roles. The story takes place in a lawless area of Colorado where Steve Jackson's (Griff Barnett) mining company has been the site of a number of holdups. After four sheriffs are murdered, the job goes to the aging Lippy (Harry Holman), who is idolized by Jackson's son

Lobby card for *Shadows on the Sage* (Republic, 1942) picturing Tom Tyler, Jimmie Dodd and Bob Steele.

Johnny (Freddie Mercer). During a gold shipment, Steve and Lippy are attacked by bandits but are rescued by Tucson (Steele), an old friend of Lippy's, Stony (Tyler) and Lullaby (Dodd). Lippy is injured during the holdup so Stony and Lullaby escort the stagecoach to town while Tucson trails the bandits. He finds their hideout but is captured by John Carson (Bryant Washburn), the town banker behind the robberies, and his gang. Since Tucson is a dead ringer for gang leader Curly (also Steele), Carson orders his henchman to infiltrate the Mesquiteers. Curly goes to meet Stony and Lullaby at the Carson ranch and that night Johnny catches him fighting with his father, who found him trying to rob his safe. Steve is shot and killed by Curly, who escapes, and Johnny thinks Tucson murdered his father. Lippy resigns as sheriff and tracks Tucson while Stony and Lullaby barely escape being lynched by the angry locals. Lippy finds Carson at the gang's hideout but is captured; he and Tucson are ordered killed but they are saved by the arrival of Stony and Lullaby. Since Jackson's daughter Doris (Cheryl Walker) is about to sell the family ranch to Carson, Stony tells Lippy to take the captured Curly and the retrieved stolen gold to her and stop the sale. Doris and Johnny refuse to believe Carson is not Tucson but the outlaw escapes and is killed while being chased by the Mesquiteers. The trio rounds up the rest of the gang and Carson is arrested.

Like earlier series features *Pals of the Saddle* and *The Phantom Plainsmen*, the next entry, *Valley of Hunted Men*, issued in November, 1942, dealt with foreign spies on the range. It also marked director John English's return to the series. A solid addition to the Mesquiteers features, it begins in 1941 before the U.S. entry into World War II. A trio of German fliers, Captain Curt Baum (Roland Varno), Franz Toller (Richard French) and Willie Schmidt (Louis Adlon), escape from a Canadian military internment camp by digging under a high voltage fence. They flee across the border into Wyoming where they shoot a young man (Billy Benedict) and steal clothes and weapons. Citizens are up in arms and rancher Clem Parker (Hal Price) claims that Germans are hiding them. Among those he suspects are refugees Dr. Heinrich Steiner (Edward Van Sloan) and his daughter Laura (Anna Marie Stewart). Steiner has been brought to Wyoming by the Three Mesquiteers (Steele, Tyler, Dodd) in order to perfect a chemical that can help extract rubber from the culebra plant. After Lullaby admires a pistol in Jed Carson's (Budd Buster) general store, the three Germans rob and kill Carson, which results in a manhunt. Toller and Schmidt are killed by a posse but Baum manages to hitch a ride with Paul Schiller (George Neise), who has come to visit his uncle, Dr. Steiner, whom he has not seen since he was a child. Baum murders Schiller and takes his identity, planning to steal the doctor's formula. Since Steiner was proven not to have hidden the Germans, the locals, including Parker, agree to participate in an experiment to see if his formula works. Meanwhile, Baum is kidnapped by local Nazi leader Von Breckner (Arno Frey), who thinks he is Schiller. When they learn his true identity, Von Breckner and his cohorts agree to aid Baum in stealing the formula. The Nazis learn that Steiner has sent for his sister, Elizabeth Schiller (Edythe Elliott), Paul's mother, and they waylay the woman and warn her to play along with them or her son will be killed. Baum puts acid in Steiner's formula spray, resulting in the culebra plants burning up in the fields and the ranchers turning against the doctor. The Mesquiteers are surprised at Mrs. Schiller's strange behavior, since she has accepted Baum as her son thinking her real son is held hostage, and they get her to tell them the truth. As the ranchers, who have just heard about the Pearl Harbor attack, plan to hang Steiner, he and Lullaby prevent the Nazis from stealing his formula with Lullaby finding the gun which killed Carson. Baum, pretending to be Schiller, claims it belongs to him and the Mesquiteers become suspicious. When Mrs. Schiller tells them her story, the ranchers turn on the Nazis. Baum tries to escape in an airplane but is shot down by Stony. The dying Baum admits he killed Schiller, and Von Breckner is arrested. The ranchers are notified the government will compensate them for their lost crops and they agree to again try Steiner's formula.

Director English's final Mesquiteers feature, *Thundering Trails*, came out early in 1943. This one had the Mesquiteers (Steele, Tyler, Dodd) as Texas Rangers in a small unit commanded by Stony's father, Captain Sam Brooke (Charles F. Miller). A local judge, Morgan (Sam Flint), refuses more funds for the Rangers, forcing Sam to ride solo guard on a stagecoach carrying a gold shipment for Ben Walker (Forrest Taylor). Also on board is Sam's other son, New Mexico policeman Johnny Brooke (John James), who is escorting Walker's daughter Edith (Nell O'Day). At the border, Johnny decides to remain with the stagecoach; a little later it is ambushed and Sam is badly wounded although Johnny is able to shoot the gun out of the hand of his assailant. The Mesquiteers arrive on the scene and the dying Sam asks Stony to maintain their Ranger unit. While Stony wants Johnny to join the Rangers, he decides to hunt for his father's killer, a man with an injured gun hand. The Mesquiteers go to the state capitol to get more funds but their plea is rejected. Judge Morgan appoints Johnny the head of the local police, but unbeknownst to him it is really an extortion gang headed by Morgan and his cohort Jeff Cantrell (Reed Howes). When Ben Walker complains to the Mesquiteers that the local police are trying to get him to pay protection money, the trio tries to explain to Johnny that the group is dishonest but he refuses to believe it. Edith asks Johnny to guard another of her father's gold shipments but Morgan and Cantrell overhear and have their gang rob the stage; they are thwarted by the Mesquiteers. Johnny arrives after the robbery attempt and, seeing the Mesquiteers taking the gold off the stage, he mistakenly believes they committed the robbery. He arrests the Mesquiteers while Cantrell hires gunman Mollison (Karl Hackett) to murder Walker. The Mesquiteers break jail and trail Mollison, who turns out to have a scarred gun hand. When Johnny arrives with Cantrell and his men, he does not believe the Mesquiteers until he is shown Mollison's scarred hand. While the gang is tying up Johnny, Tucson and Stony, Lullaby makes a break, resulting in a fight, with the outlaws being defeated. Stony is commissioned captain of the local Texas Ranger unit and he arrests Judge Morgan.

Veteran director Elmer Clifton helmed the next series outing, *The Blocked Trail*, issued in March of 1943. Martin (Walter Soderling), a recluse with a trained dwarf horse called Brilliant, is ambushed and murdered on the eve of his niece Ann's (Helen Deverell) return home from school. Ann, her boyfriend, stagecoach driver Freddie (George J. Lewis), and her lawyer Frank Nolan

Tom Tyler, Jimmie Dodd and Bob Steele as "The Three Mesquiteers."

(Charles F. Miller) hunt for the animal because they believe it may hold the clue to her late uncle's gold mine. The Three Mesquiteers (Steele, Tyler, Dodd) find the horse, but only after Lullaby has been bilked out of money by a fake Indian (Earle Hodgins). Because the murder weapon is found in the horse's saddlebag, the sheriff (Hal Price) arrests the Mesquiteers. During the night, crooks Lon Henderson (Bud Geary), Scott Rankin (Pierce Lyden) and Reese (Kermit Maynard) murder the deputy sheriff (Budd Buster) and steal the horse. Witnessing the crime, the Mesquiteers escape from jail; Stony manages to recover Brilliant and capture Henderson, who is then murdered by Reese. The sheriff re-arrests the trio but they again manage to break jail. They go to Martin's cabin looking for clues and find Freddie already searching the premises. Ann shows up, gets the drop on the Mesquiteers and goes for the sheriff, leaving Freddie to guard the trio. They overpower Freddie and find a paper with a code. Later, in Nolan's office, they recover a partially burned book written in Braille. As a result they figure that Martin was going blind and that he used Brilliant as a guide to his gold mine. When they learn that Ann and Nolan are going to Whisper Canyon with Brilliant, the Mesquiteers and Freddie follow them but at the mine they are captured by Rankin and Reese. Nolan, who killed Martin to get possession of the mine, orders his men to tie up the Mesquiteers and Freddie and then blow up a mineshaft with dynamite. He plans to follow Ann, whom he has sent back to town for the sheriff, and kill her. Nolan double-crosses his men and locks them in the mine but the Mesquiteers get Brilliant to kick down the door and they manage to escape before the explosion. Nolan causes Ann to be thrown from her horse but she is not hurt; he is captured by Stony, who turns him over to the sheriff. Ann gets possession of the mine and Nolan is later sentenced to life in prison for murdering her uncle.

The final two Mesquiteers productions, *Santa Fe Scouts* and *Riders of the Rio Grande*, were directed by Howard Bretherton, a prolific helmsman in the Western genre who steered some of the earliest, and best, "Hopalong Cassidy" (q.v.) features. *Santa Fe Scouts*, issued in April, 1943, had Tucson (Steele), Stony (Tyler) and Lullaby (Dodd) getting fed up with the antics of carefree cowboy Tim Clay (John James), whose mother Nervy Clay (Elizabeth Valentine) gives him her other ranch in Santa Fe. Mrs. Clay asks the trio to drive a head of cattle to her son's new spread; when they get there, they find three men, Billy Dawson (Tom London), Wid Lighton (Budd Buster) and Tom Howard (Jack Ingram), charging ranchers a fee for watering their herds. They fight with the men and are joined by Tim, who is engaged to Claire Robbins (Lois Collier). The three crooks report to their boss, Judge Neil Morgan (Tom Chatterton), who wants possession of the Clay ranch. He tells them to stay put so they can claim squatter's rights and get legal control of the property. When Tim refuses to let them stay, they stage a false shooting in which it appears that Claire killed Wid. In order to prevent Claire from being arrested, Tim agrees to let Dawson remain at the water hole. When the Mesquiteers find Dawson still charging for water, they take his money and return it to area ranchers only to be arrested for theft. They escape from the sheriff (Ed Cassidy) but are captured by Wid and Tom and taken to the gang's hideout, but again they manage to escape. Overhearing the judge tell Wid that Dawson needs only one more day to claim squatter's rights on the Clay ranch, Tucson and Stony go to find Nervy and Claire while Lullaby follows Wid. The crooks try to block the road and, during a shootout with them, Tim tells his mother about Wid supposedly being killed. Wid, on the run from Lullaby, is seen by Tim, who captures him as the Mesquiteers round up the gang. Tim and Claire are then married.

The final Three Mesquiteers movie, *Riders of the Rio Grande*, came out in May, 1943. Taking place in the town of Owensville, it had the mayor and bank president, Pop Owens (Edward Van Sloan), upset at the behavior of his son Tom (Rick Vallin), who is in debt to gunfighter gambler Sam Skelly (Harry Worth). To get the money he needs to pay off Skelly, Tom robs his father's bank but is caught by Skelly's henchman Berger (Jack Ingram), who wounds him. Realizing that Tom has been involved in the robbery, Pop decides to replace the money with proceeds from a trust fund he set up for Tom and his sister Janet (Lorraine Miller). Making the bank his beneficiary, Pop asks Skelly to have him killed so the money from the trust fund can be collected. A delighted Skelly goes along with the plan and hires the Cherokee Boys (Charles King, Roy Barcroft, Jack O'Shea) to carry out the assassination. The three gunmen, however, get into a saloon brawl with the Three Mesquiteers (Steele, Tyler, Dodd), who take away their weapons and end up being mistaken for the killers. Thinking the Mesquiteers are the Cherokee Boys, Pop takes them to his bank and orders them to shoot him. They decide to pretend they killed Pop in order to conceal the fact he is still alive from the gunmen. When Tom orders Skelly to return the stolen money, he agrees, but instead tells the Cherokee Boys to murder Tom; he is saved by the Mesquiteers. The trio, however, is arrested by the sheriff (Bud Osborne) for supposedly killing Pop, who confides the scheme to Tom, who admits his part in robbing the bank. Pop and Tom go for the sheriff but are abducted by the gang as the Mesquiteers break jail and locate the outlaws' hideout. A gunfight ensues between the Mesquiteers and Skelly and his men, with the outlaws being captured as Janet arrives with the sheriff. The Mesquiteers are exonerated and ride away to participate in a rodeo. Dodd sang "I've

Got Those Wailin' in the Jailhouse Blues," a song he composed.

With the demise of the Mesquiteers, Steele was signed by Monogram to join Ken Maynard and Hoot Gibson in the "Trail Blazers" (q.v.) series. For Tyler, however, the end of the Mesquiteers spelled the finish to his career as the star of Western film series. While he did have the lead in the 1945 Columbia feature *Sing Me a Song of Texas*, he mainly appeared in supporting roles in Westerns, including "A" features like *San Antonio* (1945), *Red River* (1948) and *She Wore a Yellow Ribbon* (1949). In 1950 he portrayed himself in the Roy Rogers feature *Trail of Robin Hood* and he also worked in a number of Western television series before ill health forced him to retire in the early 1950s. He died in 1954.

Today it is somewhat difficult to understand why the "Three Mesquiteers" series came to a halt in 1943. It ended on a high note with *Riders of the Rio Grande* and was still among the top ten money-making "B" Westerns. Perhaps Republic just decided the series had run its course and wanted to concentrate on its other series with solo stars like Roy Rogers, Don "Red" Barry and Wild Bill Elliott, along with its ill-fated "John Paul Revere" (q.v.) films starring Eddie Dew. Whatever the reason, the Mesquiteers films must rank as one of the finest and most popular of all Western film series.

Filmography

Powdersmoke Range (RKO Radio, 1935, 71 minutes) Associate Producer: Cliff Reid. Director: Wallace Fox. Screenplay: Adele S. Buffington, from the novel by William Colt MacDonald. Photography: Harold Wenstrom. Editor: James Morley. Music: Alberto Columbo. Art Directors: Van Nest Polglase & Feild Gray. Sound: Hal Bumbaugh. Assistant Director: Sid Fogel.

Cast: Harry Carey (Tucson Smith), Hoot Gibson (Stony Brooke), Guinn Williams (Lullaby Joslin), Bob Steele (Jeff "Guadalupe Kid" Ferguson), Tom Tyler (Sundown Saunders), Boots Mallory (Carolyn Sibley), Sam Hardy (Steve Ogden), Adrian Morris (Deputy Brose Glascow), Buzz Barton (Bat Wing), Wally Wales (Aloysius "Bud" Taggart), Art Mix (Rube Phelps), Buffalo Bill, Jr. [Jay Wilsey] (Tex Malcolm), Buddy Roosevelt (Auringer), Ray Mayer (Chap Bell), Franklyn Farnum (Jim Reece), William Desmond (Happy Hopkins), William Farnum (Sam Orchan), Ethan Laidlaw (Fin Sharkey), Eddie Dunn (Jake Elliott), Irving Bacon (Gunsmith), Barney Furey (Gus Trout), Henry Roquemore (Clem Jones), Frank Rice (Sourdough Jenkins), Bob McKenzie (Winters), Frank Ellis (Blacksmith), Phil Dunham (Barber), Jim Mason (Jordan), Nelson McDowell (Man at Bar), Tex Palmer, George Sowards, Lem Sowards (Saloon Customers), Silver Tip Baker, Charles Murphy, Silver Harr (Citizens).

The Law of the 45s (Normandy Pictures, 1935, 56 minutes) Producer: Arthur Alexander. Associate Producer-Production Manager: Max Alexander. Director: John P. McCarthy. Screenplay: Robert Emmett Tansey, from the novel by William Colt MacDonald. Photography: Robert Cline. Editor: Holbrook N. Todd. Music Director: Myron Marsh. Song: Jack Kirk.

Cast: [Guinn] Big Boy Williams (Tucson Smith), Molly O'Day (Joan Hayden), Al St. John (Stony Martin), Ted Adams (Gordon Rentel), Lafe McKee (Charlie Hayden), Fred Burns (Sheriff), Curley Baldwin (Deputy Sheriff), Martin Garralaga (Joe Sanchez), Broderick O'Farrell (Sir Henry Sheffield), Sherry Tansey [James Sheridan] (Toral), Glenn Strange (Monte), The Singing Wranglers [Jack Kirk, Jack Jones] (Musicians), Merrill McCormick (Gunman), Ace Cain (Saunders), William McCall (Doctor), George Morrell (Wounded Man), Bill Patton (Angry Rancher), Francis Walker (Wrangler), Herman Hack, Tex Palmer, Jack Evans, Art Felix, Buck Morgan, Ralph Bucko (Gang Members), Budd Buster (Station Agent), Chuck Baldra (Guitarist).

British title: *The Mysterious Mr. Sheffield*.

Too Much Beef (Normandy Pictures, 1936, 69 minutes) Producers: Arthur Alexander & Max Alexander. Director: Robert Hill. Screenplay: Rock Hawkey [Robert Hill]. Story: William Colt MacDonald. Photography: Harry Forbes. Editor: Charles Harris. Music: Lee Zahler. Sound: Joe Lapis. Production Manager: William L. Nolte. Assistant Director: William O'Connor.

Cast: Rex Bell (Johnny Argyle/Tucson Smith), Coney [Connie] Bergen (Ruth Brown), Forrest Taylor (Rocky Brown/Hugh Stanford), Lloyd Ingraham (Dynamite Murray), Peggy O'Connell (Sheila Murray), Vincent Dennis (Senator Rogge), George Ball (Tracy Paine), Jimmy Aubrey (Shorty Rawlins), Jack Cowell (George Thompson), Fred Burns (Judge), Steve Clark (Prosecutor), Horace Murphy (Sheriff), George Morrell (Bartender), John Elliott (Cattlemen's Association Head), Budd Buster (Railroad Worker), Frank Ellis (Arrested Gang Member), Denny Meadows [Dennis Moore] (Cowboy), William McCall (Court Worker), Ace Cain (Defense Lawyer), Jack Kirk (Player), Jack King (Gang Member).

The Three Mesquiteers (Republic, 1936, 58 minutes) Producer: Nat Levine. Associate Producer: Sol C. Siegel. Director: Ray Taylor. Screenplay: Jack Natteford. Story: Charles Condon. Photography: William Nobles. Editor: William Thompson. Supervising Editor: Murray Seldeen. Production Supervisor: Mack V.

Wright. Music Supervisor: Harry Grey. Sound: Terry Kellum. Production Manager: Al Wilson.

Cast: Robert Livingston (Stony Brooke), Ray Corrigan (Tucson Smith), Syd Saylor (Lullaby Joslin), Kay Hughes (Marian Brian), J.P. McGowan (Brack Canfield), Al Bridge (Olin), Frank Yaconelli (Pete), John Merton (Bull), Gene Marvey (Bob Brian), Milburn Stone (John), Duke York (Chuck), Nena Quartaro (Rosita), Allen Connor (Milt), George Plues (Ed), Stanley Blystone, Wally West, Tracy Layne, Ray Henderson, Ralph Bucko, Roy Bucko (Henchmen), Oscar Gahan, Cactus Mack, Rudy Sooter (Musicians), John Ince (Bartender), Jack Evans (Saloon Customer), Rose Plummer (Citizen).

Ghost Town Gold (Republic, 1936, 57 minutes) Producer: Nat Levine. Associate Producer: Sol C. Siegel. Director: Joseph Kane. Screenplay: Oliver Drake & John Rathmell. Story: Bernard McConville. Photography: Jack Marta & William Nobles. Editor: Lester Orlebeck. Supervising Editor: Murray Seldeen. Music Supervisor: Harry Grey. Sound: Harry Jones. Production Supervisor: William Berke. Assistant Directors: Harry Knight & Louis Germonprez.

Cast: Robert Livingston (Stony Brooke), Ray Corrigan (Tucson Smith), Max Terhune (Lullaby Joslin), Kay Hughes (Sabina Thornton), LeRoy Mason (Barrington), Burr Caruth (Mayor Thornton), Robert Kortman (Monk), Milburn Morante (Jake Rawlins), Frank Hagney (Wild Man Kamatski), Don Roberts (Manager), F. Herrick (Catlett), Robert C. Thomas (Thunderbolt O'Brien), Yakima Canutt (Buck), Hank Worden (Mr. Crabtree), Harry Tenbrook (Stubby), Bob Burns (J.B. Brand), I. Stanford Jolley (Bystander), Harry Harvey (Card Sharp), Earle Hodgins (Referee), Horace Murphy (Judge), Budd Buster (Street Fighter), Wally West (Timekeeper), Charles Sullivan (Kamatski's Handler), Billy Franey (Fight Watcher), Ed Peil, Sr. (Sheriff), Horace B. Carpenter, Jess Cavin, Bill Hickey, Art Dillard, Rube Dalroy (Citizens).

Roarin' Lead (Republic, 1936, 57 minutes) Producers: Nat Levine. Associate Producer: Sol C. Siegel. Directors: Mack V. Wright & Sam Newfield. Screenplay: Oliver Drake & Jack Natteford, from the novel by William Colt MacDonald. Photography: William Nobles. Editor: William Thompson. Supervising Editor: Murray Seldeen. Music Supervisor: Harry Grey. Songs: Ned Washington & Sam H. Stept. Sound: Harry Jones.

Cast: Robert Livingston (Stony Brooke), Ray Corrigan (Tucson Smith), Max Terhune (Lullaby Joslin), Christine Maple (Doris Moore), Hooper Atchley (Hackett), Yakima Canutt (Canary), George Chesebro (Captain Gardner), Tommy Bupp (Bobby), Mary Russell (Blondie), Jane Keckley (Mrs. Perkins), Tamara Lynn Kauffman (Baby Mary), Beverly Luff (Prima Donna), Theodore Frye, Katherine Frye (Apache Dancers), Frank Austin (Mr. Perkins), The Meglin Kiddies (Dancers), Burr Caruth (Mr. Morris), Maston Williams (Rankin), Bob Burns (Wilson), Murdock MacQuarrie (Sims), Forbes Murray (Official), Bobby Burns (Audience Member), Jack Kirk (Citizen), Harry Tenbrook, Pascale Perry, George Plues (Gang Members).

The Riders of the Whistling Skull (Republic, 1936, 56 minutes) Producer: Nat Levine. Associate Producer: Sol C. Siegel. Director: Mack V. Wright. Screenplay: Oliver Drake & John Rathmell. Story: Oliver Drake & Bernard McConville, from the novel by William Colt MacDonald. Photography: Jack Marta. Editor: Tony Martinelli. Supervising Editor: Murray Seldeen. Music Supervisor: Harry Grey. Sound: Harry Jones & John Stransky. Assistant Director: Louis Germonprez.

Cast: Robert Livingston (Stony Brooke), Ray Corrigan (Tucson Smith), Max Terhune (Lullaby Joslin), Mary Russell (Betty Marsh), Roger Williams (Rutledge), Fern Emmett (Henrietta McCoy), C. Montague Shaw (Professor Faxon), Yakima Canutt (Otah), John Ward (Brewster), George Godfrey (Professor Fronc), Earle Ross (Professor Cleary), Frank Ellis (Coggins), Chief Thundercloud (High Priest), John Van Pelt (Professor Marsh), Ed Peil, Sr. (Sheriff), Jack Kirk (Deputy Sheriff), Tracy Layne (Rancher), Ken Cooper (Rider), Iron Eyes Cody, Wally West, Tom Steele (Cult Members).

Hit the Saddle (Republic, 1937, 57 minutes) Producer: Nat Levine. Associate Producer: Sol C. Siegel. Director: Mack V. Wright. Screenplay: Oliver Drake. Story: Oliver Drake & Maurice Geraghty. Photography: Jack Marta. Editor: Tony Martinelli. Supervising Editor: Murray Seldeen. Music Supervisor: Harry Grey. Sound: Terry Kellum.

Cast: Robert Livingston (Stony Brooke), Ray Corrigan (Tucson Smith), Max Terhune (Lullaby Joslin), Rita [Hayworth] Cansino (Rita), J.P. McGowan (Rance McGowan), Edward [Ed] Cassidy (Sheriff Miller), Sammy McKim (Tim Miller), Yakima Canutt (Buck), Harry Tenbrook (Joe Harvey), Robert Smith (Hank), Ed Boland (Pete), George Plues, Tex Palmer (Gang Members), Jack Kirk, Bob Burns, Russ Powell (Ranchers), Allan Cavan (Judge), Budd Buster (Drunk), Oscar Gahan, Rudy Sooter, Robert Hoag, Harley Luse (Musicians), Sheila Terry (Woman in Cantina), Kernan Cripps (Bartender), Herman Hack, George Morrell, Jack Tornek, Tex Phelps (Saloon Customers), Wally West (Patron).

Gunsmoke Ranch (Republic, 1937, 54 minutes) Associate Producer: Sol C. Siegel. Director: Joseph Kane. Screenplay: Oliver Drake. Story: Oliver Drake & Jack Natteford. Photography: Gus Peterson. Editor: Russell Schoengarth. Supervising Editor: Murray Seldeen. Music Supervisor: Raoul Kraushaar. Sound: Terry Kellum. Assistant Director: William O'Connor.

Cast: Robert Livingston (Stony Brooke), Ray Corrigan (Tucson Smith), Max Terhune (Lullaby Joslin), Kenneth Harlan (Phineas T. Flagg), Julia Thayer [Jean Carmen] (Marion Warren), Sammy McKim (Jimmy Warren), Oscar & Elmer [Ed Platt, Lou Fulton] (Themselves), Burr Caruth (Judge Jonathan Warren),

Allen Connor (Reggie Allen), Yakima Canutt (Spader), Horace Carpenter (Joe Larkin), Jane Keckley (Mathilda Larkin), Bob [Robert] Walker (Seth Williams), Jack Ingram (Jed), Jack Kirk (Sheriff), Loren Riebe (Hank), Vinegar Roan (Zeke), Jack Padjan (Charles "Duke" Madden), Wes Warner, Jack O'Shea, Ed Peil, Sr., Bud McClure, William McCall, Eva McKenzie, Bob Card, Silver Tip Baker, Bobby Burns (Settlers), John Merton (Clem Jurgens), June Johnson, Peggy McKim (Settler Girls), Richard Beach (Surveyor), Fred Burns (Livery Stable Man), Lee Ford (Perkins), Bob McKenzie (Shop Keeper), Fred "Snowflake" Toones (Snowflake), Al Taylor (Gang Member).

Come On, Cowboys! (Republic, 1937, 58 minutes) Associate Producer: Sol C. Siegel. Director: Joseph Kane. Screenplay: Betty Burbridge. Photography: Ernest Miller. Editor: Lester Orlebeck. Supervising Editor: Murray Seldeen. Music Director: Alberto Columbo. Song: Smiley Burnette & Oliver Drake. Production Manager: Al Wilson.

Cast: Robert Livingston (Stony Brooke), Ray Corrigan (Tucson Smith), Max Terhune (Lullaby Joslin), Maxine Doyle (Ellen Reed), Willie Fung (Fong), Edward [Ed] Peil, Sr. (Thomas Rigby), Horace Murphy (Judge Blake), Anne Bennett (Nancy Harris), Ed Cassidy (Jefferson "Jeff" Harris), Roger Williams (Harry), Fern Emmett (Spinster), Yakima Canutt (Jake), George Burton (Sheriff), Merrill McCormick (Dan), Loren Riebe (Red), Victor Allen (Jim), Al Taylor (Tim), George Plues (Mike), Carleton Young (Lawyer), Jack O'Shea (Deputy Sheriff), Ernie Adams, Henry Hall, Tom Smith, Rose Plummer (Citizens), George Morrell (Shop Keeper), James A. Marcus (Judge), Milburn Morante (Zeke), Oscar Gahan (Fiddler), Jack Kirk, Jim Corey (Ambushers).

Range Defenders (Republic, 1937, 56 minutes) Associate Producer: Sol C. Siegel. Director: Mack V. Wright. Screenplay: Joseph F. Poland. Photography: Jack Marta. Editor: Lester Orlebeck. Supervising Editor: Murray Seldeen. Music Supervisor: Raoul Kraushaar. Song: Fleming Allen. Sound: Terry Kellum. Assistant Director: William O'Connor.

Cast: Robert Livingston (Stony Brooke), Ray Corrigan (Tucson Smith), Max Terhune (Lullaby Joslin), Eleanor Stewart (Sylvia Ashton), Harry Woods (John Harvey), Earle Hodgins (Sheriff Dan Gray), Thomas Carr (George Brooke), Yakima Canutt, Frank Ellis, Al Taylor (Gang Members), John Merton (Craig), Harrison Greene (Auctioneer), Horace B. Carpenter (Pete), Fred "Snowflake" Toones (Cook), Lafe McKee (Grandpa), Jack Kirk (Bill), Hank Bell (Man with Rifle), Lew Meehan, George Morrell, Ernie Adams, Charles Brinley (Citizens), Jack Lowe (Parrot Shooter), Jack Rockwell (Bidder), Jack O'Shea (Deputy Sheriff), Curley Dresden (Trunk Hauler).

Heart of the Rockies (Republic, 1937, 57 minutes) Associate Producer: Sol C. Siegel. Director: Joseph Kane. Screenplay: Oliver Drake & Jack Natteford. Story: Bernard McConville. Photography: Jack Marta. Editor: Lester Orlebeck. Music Director: Raoul Kraushaar. Assistant Director: William O'Connor.

Cast: Robert Livingston (Stony Brooke), Ray Corrigan (Tucson Smith), Max Terhune (Lullaby Joslin), Lynn[e] Roberts (Lorna Dawson), Sammy McKim (Davey Dawson), J.P. McGowan (Big Ed Dawson), Yakima Canutt (Charley Coe), Hal Taliaferro [Wally Wales] (Captain Brady), Maston Williams (Enoch Dawson), Ranny Weeks (Ranger Captain), Georgia Simmons (Ma Dawson), Herman's Mountaineers (Musicians), Guy Wilkerson, Frankie Marvin, Slim Whitaker, Nelson McDowell, Blackie Whiteford (Dawson Clansmen), George C. Pearce (Old Man).

Trigger Trio (Republic, 1937, 55 minutes) Associate Producer: Sol C. Siegel. Director: William Witney. Screenplay: Oliver Drake & Joseph F. Poland. Story: Joseph F. Poland & Houston Branch. Photography: Ernest Miller. Editor: Tony Martinelli. Music Supervisor: Raoul Kraushaar. Production Supervisor: John T. Coyle. Assistant Director: Peter Jones.

Cast: Ray Corrigan (Tucson Smith), Max Terhune (Lullaby Joslin), Ralph Byrd (Larry Smith), Sandra Corday (Anne Evans), Robert Warwick (John Evans), Cornelius Keefe (Tom Brent), Sammy McKim (Mickey Evans), Hal Taliaferro [Wally Wales] (Luke), Willie Fung (Cook), Buck the Dog (Himself), Harry Semels (Nick Popupopolis), Jack Ingram (Cowboy), Henry Hall (Rancher), Bob Burns, Fred Burns (Cattlemen), Jerry Frank (Trooper), Ted Billings (Spectator).

Wild Horse Rodeo (Republic, 1937, 55 minutes) Associate Producer: Sol C. Siegel. Director: George Sherman. Screenplay: Betty Burbridge & Oliver Drake. Story: Oliver Drake & Gilbert Wright. Photography: William Nobles. Editor: Lester Orlebeck. Music Supervisor: Alberto Columbo. Production Supervisor: John T. Coyle.

Cast: Robert Livingston (Stony Brooke), Ray Corrigan (Tucson Smith), Max Terhune (Lullaby Joslin), June Martel (Alice Harkley), Walter Miller (Colonel Nye), Edmund Cobb (Hank Bain), William Gould (Mr. Harkley), Jack Ingram (Jim), Dick Weston [Roy Rogers] (Singer), Henry Isabell (Slim), Art Dillard (Bud), Ralph Robinson (Announcer), Fred "Snowflake" Toones (Snowflake), Jack Kirk (Joe), Bob Burns, Bob Card (Rodeo Judges), Jerry Frank (Pilot), Charles Murphy (Timer), June Gittelson (Dancing Partner), Harry Willingham (Guest), Duke Green (Masters), Frank Ellis (Cowboy).

The Purple Vigilantes (Republic, 1938, 58 minutes) Associate Producer: Sol C. Siegel. Director: George Sherman. Screenplay: Oliver Drake & Betty Burbridge. Photography: Ernest Miller. Editor: Lester Orlebeck. Music Director: Alberto Columbo. Production Manager: Al Wilson. Unit Manager: Arthur Siteman. Assistant Director: Harry Knight.

Cast: Robert Livingston (Stony Brooke), Ray Corrigan (Tucson Smith), Max Terhune (Lullaby Joslin),

Joan Barclay (Jean McAllister), Earl Dwire (David Ross), Earle Hodgins (J.T. "Mack" McAllister), Francis Sayles (William Jones), George Chesebro (Eggers), Robert Fiske (George Drake), Jack Perrin (Duncan), Ernie Adams (Blake), William Gould (Jenkins), Harry Strang (Murphy), Ed Cassidy (Sheriff Jim Dyer), Frank O'Connor (Deputy Sheriff Tracy), Jason Robards (Prosecuting Attorney), Niles Welch (State Attorney), Allan Cavan (Judge Hiram Wells), Jack Kirk (Tom Purdy), George [Montgomery] Letz (Gambler), Lee Shumway (Roulette Attendant), Ed Peil, Sr. (Deputy Sheriff), Frank Ellis (Bartender), Billy Bletcher (Voice of Number One), Curley Dresden (Mob Leader), Murdock MacQuarrie (Juror), Bob Burns (Vigilante Recruit), Frankie Marvin (Cowboy), Merrill McCormick (Informer), Dot Farley (Suffragette), Bill Patton, Jim Corey, Wally West, Fred Burns, Brandon Beach, Herman Hack, Tom Smith (Citizens).

Call the Mesquiteers (Republic, 1938, 55 minutes) Associate Producer: William Berke. Director: John English. Screenplay: Luci Ward. Story: Bernard McConville. Photography: William Nobles. Editor: Lester Orlebeck. Music Director: Alberto Columbo. Production Manager: Al Wilson. Unit Manager: Arthur Siteman. Assistant Director: Harry Knight.

Cast: Robert Livingston (Stony Brooke), Ray Corrigan (Tucson Smith), Max Terhune (Lullaby Joslin), Lynn[e] Roberts (Madge Irving), Earle Hodgins (Dr. Aurelius Irving), Sammy McKim (Tim Irving), Eddy Waller (Hardy), Maston Williams (Phillips), Eddie Hart (Lefty), Pat Gleason (Joe), Roger Williams (Frank), Warren Jackson (Mac), Hal Price (Sheriff Benton), Flash the Dog (Himself), Ralph Peters, Jim Corey (Deputy Sheriffs), Ethan Laidlaw (Brakeman Henley), Curley Dresden (Al), Jack Ingram, Bob Burns, Al Taylor, Bob Card (Posse Members), Frank Ellis (Policeman), Tom Steele (Bert), Francis Walker, Loren Riebe (Gang Members).

Working titles: *Calling the Mesquiteers* and *Desert Trail Riders*.

Outlaws of Sonora (Republic, 1938, 55 minutes) Associate Producer: William Berke. Director: George Sherman. Screenplay: Betty Burbridge & Edmond Kelso. Story: Betty Burbridge. Photography: William Nobles. Editor: Tony Martinelli. Music Director: Alberto Columbo. Song: Eduardo Durant, Harold Peterson & Carlos Ruffino. Production Manager: Al Wilson. Unit Manager: Arthur Siteman. Assistant Director: Harry Knight.

Cast: Robert Livingston (Stony Brooke/Dude Brannen), Ray Corrigan (Tucson Smith), Max Terhune (Lullaby Joslin), Jack Mulhall (Dr. George Martin), Otis Harlan (Newt), Jean Joyce (Miss Burke), Sterlita Peluffo (Rosita), Tom London (Sheriff Trask), Gloria Rich (Jane), Edwin Mordant (Pierce), Ralph Peters (Gabby), George Chesebro (Slim), Frank La Rue (Coroner), Jack Ingram (Nick), Merrill McCormick (Pete), George Cleveland (Agent), Tommy Coats, Art Dillard (Deputy Sheriffs), Curley Dresden (Joe), Earl Dwire (Jake), Jack Kirk (Jim), Horace B. Carpenter (Merchant), George [Montgomery] Letz (Bank Teller), Bob Burns, Fred Burns, Bob Card, Herman Willingham (Ranchers), Bob Reeves, Jack O'Shea, Blackjack Ward (Saloon Customers).

Riders of the Black Hills (Republic, 1938, 55 minutes) Associate Producer: William Berke. Director: George Sherman. Screenplay: Betty Burbridge. Story: Betty Burbridge & Bernard McConville. Photography: William Nobles. Editor: Lester Orlebeck. Music Director: Alberto Columbo. Unit Manager: Al Wilson.

Cast: Robert Livingston (Stony Burke), Ray Corrigan (Tucson Smith), Max Terhune (Lullaby Joslin), Ann Evers (Joyce Garth), Roscoe Ates (Sheriff Brown), Maude Eburne (Peg Garth), Frank Melton (Don Weston), Johnny Lang Fitzgerald (Buck), Jack Ingram (Lefty), Edward Earle (Steward), Monte Montague (Deputy Sheriff Sam), Ben Hall (Ethelbert), Frank O'Connor (Doctor), Tom London (Rod Stevens), Fred "Snowflake" Toones (Snowflake), John Wade (Ed Harvry), John Merton (Theater Patron), Dick Elliott, Gloria Rich, Lester Sharpe, Jette White (Movie Actors), George Magrill (Pilot), David Sharpe (Co-Pilot), Jack O'Shea, Milburn Morante (Race Spectators), Bud Osborne, Art Dillard (Gang Members), Slim Whitaker (Posse Member).

Heroes of the Hills (Republic, 1938, 56 minutes) Associate Producer: William Berke. Director: George Sherman. Screenplay: Betty Burbridge & Jack Natteford. Story: Jack Natteford & Stanley Roberts. Photography: Reggie Lanning. Editor: Tony Martinelli. Music: Cy Feuer. Song: Eddie Cherokee & Alberto Columbo. Production Manager: Al Wilson. Unit Manager: Arthur Siteman. Assistant Director: Harry Knight.

Cast: Robert Livingston (Stony Brooke), Ray Corrigan (Tucson Smith), Max Terhune (Lullaby Joslin), Priscilla Lawson (Madeline), LeRoy Mason (Red), James Eagles (The Kid), Roy Barcroft (Robert Beaton), Barry Hays (Regan), Carleton Young (Jim Connors), Forrest Taylor (Sheriff), John Wade (Board Chairman), Maston Williams (Nick), John Beach (Crane), Jerry Frank (Slim), Roger Williams (Warden), Kit Guard (Mac), Gloria Rich (Singer), I. Stanford Jolley (Dance Patron), Bob Card (Deputy Sheriff), Jack Kirk (Merchant), Buck Morgan (Convict), Lew Meehan, Tommy Coats, Art Dillard, Curley Dresden, Chuck Baldra (Gang Members).

Pals of the Saddle (Republic, 1938, 55 minutes) Associate Producer: William Berke. Director: George Sherman. Screenplay: Stanley Roberts & Betty Burbridge. Photography: Reggie Lanning. Editor: Tony Martinelli. Music Director: Cy Feuer. Production Manager: Al Wilson. Unit Manager: Arthur Siteman. Assistant Director: Harry Knight.

Cast: John Wayne (Stony Brooke), Ray Corrigan (Tucson Smith), Max Terhune (Lullaby Joslin), Doreen McKay (Ann Cameron), Josef [Joe] Forte (Judge Hastings), George Douglas (Paul Hartman), Frank Milan (Frank Paige), Ted Adams (Henry C. Gordon), Harry Depp (Desk Clerk), Dave Weber (Russian Musician), Don Orlando (Italian Musician), Charles Knight (English Musician), Jack Kirk (Sheriff Johnson), Philip Kieffer (Army Officer), Bob Burns (Coroner), Yakima Canutt, Olin Francis, John Beach, Art Dillard, George Plues, Herman Nowlin (Gang Members), George [Montgomery] Letz (Rider), Monte Montague, Curley Dresden, Tex Palmer (Refinery Gang Members), Otto Hoffman, Kenner G. Kemp (Citizens).

Overland Stage Raiders (Republic, 1938, 55 minutes) Associate Producer: William Berke. Director: George Sherman. Screenplay: Luci Ward. Story: Bernard McConville & Edmond Kelso. Photography: William Nobles. Editor: Tony Martinelli. Production Manager: Al Wilson. Unit Manager: Arthur Siteman. Assistant Director: Harry Knight.

Cast: John Wayne (Stony Brooke), Ray Corrigan (Tucson Smith), Max Terhune (Lullaby Joslin), Louise Brooks (Beth Hoyt/Beth Vincent), Anthony Marsh (Ned Hoyt/ Ned Vincent), Ralph Bowman [John Archer] (Bob Whitney), Gordon Hart (W.T. Mullins), Roy James (Frank Harmon), Olin Francis (Jake), Fern Emmett (Ma Hawkins), Henry Otho (Sheriff Mason), George Sherwood (Clanton), Archie Hall (Joe Waddell), Frank LaRue (Hank Milton), Dirk Thane (Dutch), Yakima Canutt (Bus Driver), Edwin Gaffney (Gat), Slim Whitaker (Pete Hawkins), Burr Caruth (Evans), Jack Kirk, Tommy Coats, John Beach, Chuck Baldra, Duke R. Lee, George Plues (Gang Members), Bud Osborne, Fred Burns, Curley Dresden, Charles Brinley, George Morrell, Bud McClure, Bill Wolfe (Ranchers), Milton Kibbee (Airplane Passenger).

Santa Fe Stampede (Republic, 1938, 56 minutes) Associate Producer: William Berke. Director: John English. Screenplay: Luci Ward & Betty Burbridge. Story: Luci Ward. Photography: Reggie Lanning. Editor: Tony Martinelli. Music: William Lava. Production Manager: Al Wilson.

Cast: John Wayne (Stony Brooke), Ray Corrigan (Tucson Smith), Max Terhune (Lullaby Joslin), June Martel (Nancy Carson), William Farnum (Dave Carson), LeRoy Mason (Mayor Gilbert Byron), Martin Spellman (Billy Carson), Genee Hall (Julie Jane Carson), Walter Wills (Harris), Ferris Taylor (Judge Henry J. Hixon), Tom London (Marshal Jim Wood), John F. Cassidy (Jed Newton), Dick Rush (Sheriff Tom), Yakima Canutt (Ben Carey), Griff Barnett (Henry Jones), Richard Alexander (Joe Moffitt), Charles King (Ben), Bud Osborne (Mac), Jerry Frank (Tex), Nelson McDowell (John Franklin), George Morrell (Timothy), Ralph Peters (Store Owner), Curley Dresden (Witness), Marin Sais (Angry Woman), Charles Murphy (Rancher), Robert Milasch (Miner), Chick Hannon (Spectator), George Chesebro, Blackjack Ward, Cliff Parkinson (Gang Members), Horace B. Carpenter, John Elliott, Jim Corey, Russ Powell, Frank O'Connor, George Sowards, Tex Driscoll, Murdock MacQuarrie, Duke R. Lee, Tex Phelps, Fred Parker, Bud McClure (Citizens).

Red River Range (Republic, 1938, 56 minutes) Associate Producer: William Berke. Director: George Sherman. Screenplay: Stanley Roberts, Betty Burbridge & Luci Ward. Story: Luci Ward. Photography: Jack Marta. Editor: Tony Martinelli. Music: William Lava. Production Manager: Al Wilson.

Cast: John Wayne (Stony Brooke), Ray Corrigan (Tucson Smith), Max Terhune (Lullaby Joslin), Polly Moran (Mrs. Maxwell), Lorna Gray [Adrian Booth] (Jane Mason), Kirby Grant (Tex Reilly), Sammy McKim (Tommy Jones), William Royle (Payne), Perry Ivins (Hartley), Stanley Blystone (Randall), Lenore Bushman (Evelyn Maxwell), Burr Caruth (Pop Mason), Roger Williams (Sheriff Woods), Earl Askam (Morton), Olin Francis (Kenton), Fred "Snowflake" Toones (Bellhop), Bob McKenzie (Justice of the Peace), Ed Cassidy (Marshal), Curley Dresden, John Beach (Rustlers), Theodore Lorch (Rancher), Al Taylor (Slick), Joe Whitehead (Gang Member), Jack Montgomery (Cattleman), Chuck Baldra (Dude Ranch Cowboy).

The Night Riders (Republic, 1939, 58 minutes) Associate Producer: William Berke. Director: George Sherman. Screenplay: Betty Burbridge & Stanley Roberts. Photography: Jack Marta. Editor: Lester Orlebeck. Music: William Lava. Production Manager: Al Wilson. Assistant Director: Philip Ford.

Cast: John Wayne (Stony Brooke), Ray Corrigan (Tucson Smith), Max Terhune (Lullaby Joslin), Doreen McKay (Soledad/Senora de Serrano), Ruth Rogers (Susan Randall), George Douglas (Talbot Pierce/Don Luis de Serrano), Tom Tyler (Jackson), Kermit Maynard (Sheriff Pratt), Sammy McKim (Tim Randall), Walter Wills (Hazelton/Roberto), Ethan Laidlaw (Andrews), Edward [Ed] Peil, Sr. (Harper), Tom London (Wilson), Jack Ingram (Wilkins), William Nestell (Allen), Georgia Summers (Aunt Martha Randall), Glenn Strange (Riverboat Gambler), Horace Murphy (Captain Asa Beckett), Hugh Prosser (Government Man), Francis A. Sayles (James A. Garfield), John Ince (Captain Timmons), Yakima Canutt, Curley Dresden, Art Dillard, George [Montgomery] Letz (Mob Members), Hal Price, Lee Shumway, Hank Worden, Bob Card (Ranchers), Eva McKenzie, Jane Keckley (Ranchers' Wives), David McKim (Messenger), Francis Walker, Olin Francis (Enlistees), Allan Cavan (Judge), Frank O'Connor (Telegrapher), Bud Osborne (Gunman), Jack Kirk (Tavern Owner), David Sharpe, Al Taylor, Cactus Mack (Gang Members).

Working title: *Lone Star Bullets*.

Three Texas Steers (Republic, 1939, 56 minutes) Associate Producer: William Berke. Director: George Sherman. Screenplay: Betty Burbridge & Stanley Roberts. Photography: Ernest Miller. Editor: Tony Martinelli. Music: William Lava. Music Director: Cy Feuer. Production Manager: Al Wilson.

Cast: John Wayne (Stony Brooke), Ray Corrigan (Tucson Smith), Max Terhune (Lullaby Joslin), Carole Landis (Nancy Evans), Ralph Graves (George Ward), Roscoe Ates (Sheriff Brown), Collette Lyons (Lillian), Billy Curtis (Hercules), Ted Adams (Steve), Stanley Blystone (Rankin), David Sharpe (Tony), Ethan Laidlaw (Morgan), Lew Kelly (Postman), Ray Corrigan, billed as Naba (Willie the Gorilla), John Merton (Mike Abbott), Dave Willock (Desk Clerk), Jack Kirk, Bob Burns (Citizens), Ted Mapes, John Beach (Gang Members).

Wyoming Outlaw (Republic, 1939, 58 minutes) Associate Producer: William Berke. Director: George Sherman. Screenplay: Betty Burbridge & Stanley Roberts. Story: Stanley Roberts. Photography: Reggie Lanning. Editor: Tony Martinelli. Music: William Lava. Production Manager: Al Wilson. Assistant Director: Harry Knight.

Cast: John Wayne (Stony Brooke), Ray Corrigan (Tucson Smith), Raymond Hatton (Rusty Joslin), Donald [Don "Red"] Barry (Will Parker), Adele Pearce [Pamela Blake] (Irene Parker), LeRoy Mason (Joe Balsinger), Charles Middleton (Luke Parker), Katherine Kentworthy (Mrs. Parker), Elmo Lincoln (U.S. Marshal Gregg), Jack Ingram (Sheriff Nolan), David Sharpe (Newt), Jack Kenny (Amos Doyle), Yakima Canutt (Ed Simms), Dave O'Brien (Park Game Warden), Allan Cavan (Senator Roberts), John Hiestand (Radio Broadcaster), Frankie Marvin (Shorty), Tommy Coats (Curly), Malcolm "Bud" McTaggart (Park Ranger), Ralph Peters (Newspaper Reader), Jack Rockwell, Bob Burns (Ranchers), Budd Buster (Bank Teller), Curley Dresden, John Beach, George De Normand (Gang Members), Jack Kirk, Al Taylor (Posse Members), Ed Payson (Citizen).

Working title: *Oklahoma Outlaws*.

New Frontier (Republic, 1939, 57 minutes) Associate Producer: William Berke. Director: George Sherman. Screenplay: Betty Burbridge & Luci Ward. Photography: Reggie Lanning. Editor: Tony Martinelli. Music: William Lava. Production Manager: Al Wilson. Assistant Director: William O'Connor.

Cast: John Wayne (Stony Brooke), Ray Corrigan (Tucson Smith), Raymond Hatton (Rusty Joslin), Phyllis Isley [Jennifer Jones] (Celia Braddock), Eddy Waller (Major Steven Braddock), Sammy McKim (Stevie Braddock), LeRoy Mason (M.C. Gilbert), Harrison Greene (William "Bill" Proctor), Wilbur Mack (Mr. Dodge), Reginald Barlow (Judge Morse), Burr Caruth (Dr. William Hall), Dave O'Brien (Jason Braddock), Hal Price (Sheriff), Jack Ingram (Harmon), Bud Osborne (Dickson), Charles [Slim] Whitaker (Jed Turner), George Chesebro (Deputy Sheriff), Frankie Marvin, Oscar Gahan (Musicians), Jody Gilbert (Large Woman), Herman Hack (Jim), Charles Murphy (Zeke), Curley Dresden (Guard), Fred Burns (Fiddler), Cactus Mack (False Indian), William Nestell, Victor Cox (Men at Dance), Bob Reeves, John Elliott, Frank Ellis, Walt LaRue, Bud McClure, Bill Wolfe (Citizens), Jim Corey (Bushwhacker), Bob Burns, Chuck Baldra (Jailed Ranchers), George Plues (Gang Member).

Television title: *Frontier Horizon*.

The Kansas Terrors (Republic, 1939, 57 minutes) Associate Producer: Harry Grey. Director: George Sherman. Screenplay: Betty Burbridge & Jack Natteford. Story: Luci Ward. Photography: Ernest Miller. Editor: Tony Martinelli. Music: William Lava. Production Manager: Al Wilson.

Cast: Robert Livingston (Stony Brooke), Raymond Hatton (Rusty Joslin), Duncan Renaldo (Renaldo), Jacqueline Wells [Julie Bishop] (Maria), Howard Hickman (Governor General), George Douglas (Commandante), Frank Lackteen (Captain Gonzales), Myra Marsh (Duenna), Yakima Canutt (Sergeant), Ruth Robinson (Juanita), Richard Alexander (Miguel), Ann Baldwin (Senorita), Merrill McCormick (Juan), Artie Ortego (Sentry), Henry Wills, Al Haskell (Bandits), Rosa Turich (Peon's Wife), Curley Dresden (Paymaster), Dick Botiller, Jose Dominguez (Guards), Billy Bletcher (Masked Rider's Voice).

Working title: *Heroes of the Saddle*.

Cowboys from Texas (Republic, 1939, 57 minutes) Associate Producer: Harry Grey. Director: George Sherman. Screenplay: Oliver Drake. Photography: Ernest Miller. Editor: Tony Martinelli. Music: William Lava. Production Manager: Al Wilson.

Cast: Robert Livingston (Stony Brooke), Raymond Hatton (Rusty Joslin), Duncan Renaldo (Renaldo), Carole Landis (June Jones), Charles Middleton (Kansas Jones), Ivan Miller (Clay Allison), Betty Compson (Belle Starkey), Ethan Laidlaw (Duke Plummer), Yakima Canutt (Tex Dawson), Walter Wills (Jefferson Morgan), Edward [Ed] Cassidy (Jed Tyler), Charles King (Beau), Bud Osborne (Gang Leader), David Sharpe (Courier), Horace Murphy (Constable Dan), Forbes Murray (Governor), Jack O'Shea (Gambler), Harry McKim (Tim Jones), Jack Kirk (Guard), Murdock MacQuarrie (Congressman), Harry Strang (Settlers' Leader), William Nestell (Bartender), Al Haskell (Saloon Customer), Lew Meehan (Homesteader).

Heroes of the Saddle (Republic, 1940, 56 minutes) Associate Producer: Harry Grey. Director: William Witney. Screenplay: Jack Natteford. Photography: William Nobles. Editor: Lester Orlebeck. Supervising Editor: Murray Seldeen. Music: Cy Feuer. Production Manager: Al Wilson.

Cast: Robert Livingston (Stony Brooke), Raymond Hatton (Rusty Joslin), Duncan Renaldo (Rico Rinaldo), Patsy Lee Parsons (Peggy Bell), Loretta Weaver (Ruth Miller), Byron Foulger (Melloney), William Royle (J.D. Crone), Vince Barnett (Zach), Jack Roper (Killer McCully), Reed Howes (Wilson), Ethel May Halls (Miss Dobbs), Al Taylor (Hendricks), Patsy Carmichael (Annie), Kermit Maynard (Montana Bill Bell), Tex Terry (Rancher), Harry Strang, Tommy Coats (Gang Members), Douglas Deems, Darwood Kaye (Orphans), Harrison Greene, Tom Hanlon (Radio

Announcers), Art Dillard, Bob Card (Men at Rodeo), Chief Big John Tree (Rodeo Indian), Bob Burns (Café Patron).

Covered Wagon Days (Republic, 1940, 56 minutes) Associate Producer: Harry Grey. Director: George Sherman. Screenplay: Earle Snell. Photography: William Nobles. Editor: Bernard Loftus. Music: Cy Feuer. Production Manager: Al Wilson.

Cast: Robert Livingston (Stony Brooke), Raymond Hatton (Rusty Joslin), Duncan Renaldo (Rico Rinaldo), Kay Griffith (Maria), George Douglas (Ransome), Ruth Robinson (Señora Rinaldo), Paul Marion (Carlos Rinaldo), John Merton (Assassin), Tom Chatterton (Major J.A. Norton), Guy D'Ennery (Don Diego), Tom London (Martin), Reed Howes (Store Henchman), David Newell (Lieutenant Weaver), Edward Hearn (Captain Hudson), Richard Alexander (Border Guard Sergeant), Elias Gamboa (Amigo), Jack Kirk, Bob Card (Deputy Sheriffs), Arthur Loft (Official), Rosa Turich (Cook), Al Taylor (Store Clerk), Jack Montgomery (Smuggler), Art Mix, Barry Hays, Herman Hack, Ken Terrell, Tex Palmer, Pascale Perry, Herman Nowlin, Roy Bucko (Gang Members), Frank McCarroll, Chick Hannon (Lynch Mob Members), Lee Shumway (Sheriff), Henry Wills, Bud McClure (Citizens).

Pioneers of the West (Republic, 1940, 56 minutes) Associate Producer: Harry Grey. Director: Lester Orlebeck. Screenplay: Jack Natteford, Karen De Wolf & Gerald Geraghty. Photography: Jack Marta. Editor: Tony Martinelli. Music: Cy Feuer. Production Manager: Al Wilson.

Cast: Robert Livingston (Stony Brooke), Raymond Hatton (Rusty Joslin), Duncan Renaldo (Rico Rinaldo), Noah Beery (Judge Platt), Beatrice Roberts (Ann Bailey), George Cleveland (Dr. "Doc" Bailey), Lane Chandler (Steve Carson), Hal Taliaferro [Wally Wales] (Jed Clark), Yakima Canutt (Nolan), John Dilson (Morgan), Joe McGuinn (Sheriff Gorham), Earl Askam (Mack), Ray Jones, Art Dillard (Deputy Sheriffs), Chief Big John Tree (Indian Chief), George Chesebro, Frankie Marvin, Herman Hack, Duke Taylor (Gang Members), Bob Burns (Tom), Jack Kirk, Tex Terry, Chuck Baldra, Jane Keckley, Hansel Warner, Cecil Weston (Settlers), Artie Ortego, Iron Eyes Cody (Indians).

Working title: *Oklahoma Outlaws*.

Rocky Mountain Rangers (Republic, 1940, 58 minutes) Producer: Harry Grey. Director: George Sherman. Screenplay: Barry Shipman & Earle Snell. Photography: Jack Marta. Editor: Lester Orlebeck. Music: Cy Feuer. Production Manager: Al Wilson. Assistant Director: Harry Knight.

Cast: Robert Livingston (Stony Brooke/The Laredo Kid), Raymond Hatton (Rusty Joslin), Duncan Renaldo (Rico Rinaldo), Rosella Towne (Doris Manners), Sammy McKim (Danny Burke), LeRoy Mason (King Barton), Pat O'Malley (Captain Taylor), Dennis Moore (Jim Barton), John St. Polis (Joseph Manners), Robert Blair (Sergeant Bush), Burr Caruth (John), Jack Kirk (Harris), Bud Osborne (Slade), Mary MacLaren (Mrs. Logan), Kernan Cripps (Doctor), Brandon Beach (State Official), Ted Mapes (Stagecoach Driver), Carey Loftin (Ranger Guard), Fred Burns (Shotgun Rider), Frank Ellis, Silver Tip Baker (Texas Rangers), Frankie Marvin, Chuck Baldra, Tommy Coats, Curley Dresden, Buck Morgan, Pascale Perry, Lew Morphy, Vinegar Roan, Tex Harper, Augie Gomez (Gang Members), Pat McKee (Panhandle Bartender), William Nestell (Fat Bartender), Hank Bell, Budd Buster, Betty Roadman (Citizens).

Oklahoma Renegades (Republic, 1940, 57 minutes) Associate Producer: Harry Grey. Director: Nate Watt. Screenplay: Doris Schroeder & Earle Snell. Story: Charles R. Condon. Photography: Reggie Lanning. Editor: Tony Martinelli. Production Manager: Al Wilson.

Cast: Robert Livingston (Stony Brooke), Raymond Hatton (Rusty Joslin), Duncan Renaldo (Rico Rinaldo), Lee "Lasses" White (Jim Keith), Florine McKinney (Marian Carter), William Ruhl (Mace Liscomb), Al Herman (Hank Blake), James Seay (Carl), Eddie Dean, Jack Lescoulie, Art Dillard (Veterans), Harold Daniels (Orv Liscomb), Frosty Royce (Mort), Yakima Canutt (Rancher), Harry Strang (Bartender), Ken Terrell (Cowboy), Frankie Marvin, Hank Bell, Jack Lawrence, Tom Smith (Citizens), Al Taylor, Ted Mapes, Pascale Perry (Gang Members).

Under Texas Skies (Republic, 1940, 57 minutes) Associate Producer: Harry Grey. Director: George Sherman. Screenplay: Betty Burbridge & Anthony Coldeway. Story: Anthony Coldeway. Photography: William Nobles. Editor: Tony Martinelli. Music: Cy Feuer. Production Manager: Al Wilson. Assistant Director: Louis Germonprez.

Cast: Robert Livingston (Stony Brooke), Bob Steele (Tucson Smith), Rufe Davis (Lullaby Joslin), Lois Ranson (Helen Smith), Henry Brandon (Tom Blackton), Wade Boteler (Sheriff Brooke), Rex Lease (Jim Marsden), Jack Ingram (Finley), Walter Tetley (Theodore), Yakima Canutt (Talbot), Earle Hodgins (Barber Smithers), Curley Dresden (Jackson), Burr Caruth (Judge Craig), Forrest Taylor (Harley Richards), Bob Burns (Andy Foster), Donald Kerr (Express Agent), Fred Burns (Stagecoach Driver), Charles King, Jack Kirk, Frank Ellis, Jim Corey (Ranchers), John Beach, Matty Roubert, Ken Terrell, Chuck Baldra, Chick Hannon, Augie Gomez, Herman Nowlin, Vester Pegg (Gang Members), Franklyn Farnum, Bob Card, Herman Hack, Al Haskell, Pascale Perry, Silver Tip Baker, Lew Morphy (Citizens).

The Trail Blazers (Republic, 1940, 58 minutes) Associate Producer: Harry Grey. Director: George Sherman. Screenplay: Barry Shipman. Story: Earle Snell. Photography: William Nobles. Editor: Tony Martinelli. Music: Cy Feuer. Production Manager: Al Wilson.

Cast: Robert Livingston (Stony Brooke), Bob Steele (Tucson Smith), Rufe Davis (Lullaby Joslin), Pauline Moore (Marcia Kelton), Weldon Heyburn (Jeff Bradley), Tom Chatterton (Major R.C. Kelton), Si Jenks (T.L. Johnson), Mary Field (Mary Chapman), John Merton (Mason), Rex Lease (Reynolds), Robert Blair (Foster), Forrest Taylor (Graves), Barry Hays (Talbot), Harrison Greene (Rogers), Pascale Perry (Milligan), Horace B. Carpenter (Walters), Brandon Beach (Official), Jack Kirk (George), Bud Osborne (Sentry), Post Park (Stagecoach Driver), Harry Strang (Sergeant), Cactus Mack (Soldier), Herman Hack, Merrill McCormick, Tom Smith (Laborers), Matty Roubert, Al Taylor, Curley Dresden, Chuck Baldra, Roy Bucko (Gang Members), Ray Teal (Code Man), William Nestell (Line Worker).

Lone Star Raiders (Republic, 1940, 57 minutes) Associate Producer: Louis Gray. Director: George Sherman. Screenplay: Barry Shipman & Joseph Moncure March. Story: Charles Francis Royal. Photography: William Nobles. Editor: Tony Martinelli. Music: Cy Feuer. Production Manager: Al Wilson.

Cast: Robert Livingston (Stony Brooke), Bob Steele (Tucson Smith), Rufe Davis (Lullaby Joslin), June Johnson (Linda Cameron), George Douglas (Henry Martin), Sarah Padden (Lydia "Granny" Phelps), John Elliott (Dad Cameron), John Merton (Dixon), Rex Lease (Fisher), Bud Osborne (Blake), Jack Kirk (Bixby), Tom London (Jones), Hal Price (Sheriff), Tommy Coats (Sam), John Beach (Official), Bob Card, Matty Roubert, Chick Hannon (Deputy Sheriffs), Harrison Greene (Racing Official), Al Haskell (Rider), Reed Howes, Herman Hack, Bert Dillard, Cactus Mack (Gang Members), Art Dillard, Bud McClure, George Sowards, Fox Callahan, Augie Gomez, Herman Nowlin, Duke Taylor, Roy Bucko, Bill Wolfe (Cowboys).

Prairie Pioneers (Republic, 1941, 58 minutes) Associate Producer: Louis Gray. Director: Lester Orlebeck. Screenplay: Barry Shipman. Original Idea: Karl Brown. Photography: Ernest Miller. Editor: Ray Snyder. Music: Cy Feuer. Production Manager: Al Wilson.

Cast: Robert Livingston (Stony Brooke), Bob Steele (Tucson Smith), Rufe Davis (Lullaby Joslin), Esther Estrella (Dolores Ortega), Robert Kellard (Robert Ortega), Guy D'Ennery (Don Miguel Ortega), Davison Clark (Don Carlos Montoya), Jack Ingram (Wade), Ken [Kenneth] MacDonald (Fields), Lee Shumway (W.M. Nelson), Mary MacLaren (Martha Nelson), Yakima Canutt (Morrison), Jack Kirk (Al), Carleton Young (Army Officer), Leander De Cordova (Padre), Wheaton Chambers (Lawyer), Cactus Mack (Johnson), Frank Ellis (Haines), Rosa Turich (Cook), Pascale Perry (Driller), Bob Burns, Dan White, Al Taylor, Tom Smith (Settlers), Silver Tip Baker (Wagon Driver), Frank McCarroll (Man in Wagon), Roy Bucko (Vaquero), Chuck Baldra, Jim Corey, George Plues (Gang Members), Ray Henderson (Soldier).

Pals of the Pecos (Republic, 1941, 56 minutes) Associate Producer: Louis Gray. Director: Lester Orlebeck. Screenplay: Oliver Drake & Herbert Dalmas. Story: Oliver Drake. Photography: Reggie Lanning. Editor: Ray Snyder. Music: Cy Feuer. Production Manager: Al Wilson.

Cast: Robert Livingston (Stony Brooke), Bob Steele (Tucson Smith), Rufe Davis (Lullaby Joslin), June Johnson (June Burke), Robert Winkler (Tim Burke), Pat O'Malley (Dan Burke), Dennis Moore (Larry Burke), Robert Frazer (Stevens), Roy Barcroft (Keno Hawkins), John Holland (Buckley), Tom London (Sheriff), Eddie Dean (Gang Member), Bud Osborne (Nevada), George Chesebro (Slim), Frank Ellis (Deputy Sheriff), Jack Kirk (Laborer), Chuck Morrison (Monk), William Nestell (Davis), Forrest Taylor (Postmaster), Neal Hart (Saloon Customer), Tom Smith (Citizen).

Saddlemates (Republic, 1941, 56 minutes) Associate Producer: Louis Gray. Director: Lester Orlebeck. Screenplay: Albert DeMond & Herbert Dalmas. Story: Bernard McConville & Karen De Wolfe. Photography: William Nobles. Editor: Tony Martinelli. Music: Cy Feuer. Production Manager: Al Wilson.

Cast: Robert Livingston (Stony Brooke), Bob Steele (Tucson Smith), Rufe Davis (Lullaby Joslin), Gale Storm (Susan Langley), Forbes Murray (Colonel Langley), Cornelius Keefe (Lt. Bob Manning), Peter George Lynn (Chief Wanechee/LeRoque), Marin Sais (Mrs. Langley), Marty Faust (Chief Thunder Bird), Glenn Strange (Little Bear), Ellen Lowe (Aunt Amanda), Iron Eyes Cody (Black Eagle), Rex Lease (Settler), Ed Cassidy (Captain Miller), Slim Whitaker (Huggins), Chief Yowlachie (Indian Council), Bill Keefer (Sergeant), Yakima Canutt (Wagon Driver), Jack Kirk (Hank), Spade Cooley (Fiddler), Art Dillard (Trooper), Kansas Moehring (Soldier), Henry Wills (Captured Indian), Bob Woodward (Driver), Bill Hazlett (Chief), Chick Hannon (Gambler), Tex Cooper (Man at Fort), Roy Bucko, William Nestell, Herman Hack, Jess Cavin, Victor Cox (Saloon Customers), Bert Dillard, Lew Meehan (Brawlers).

Gangs of Sonora (Republic, 1941, 56 minutes) Associate Producer: Louis Gray. Director: John English. Screenplay: Albert DeMond & Doris Schroeder. Photography: Bud Thackery. Editor: Ray Snyder. Music: Cy Feuer. Production Manager: Al Wilson.

Cast: Robert Livingston (Stony Brooke), Bob Steele (Tucson Smith), Rufe Davis (Lullaby Joslin), June Johnson (June Conners), [Malcolm] Ward "Bud" McTaggart (David Conners), Helen MacKellar (Kansas Kate Conners), Robert Frazer (Commissioner Sam Tredwell), William Farnum (Ward Beecham), Budd Buster (Jed Pickins), Hal Price (Sheriff J.D. Lawson), Wally West (Deputy Sheriff), Burr Caruth (Town Leader), Bud Geary (Drennon), Max Waizmann (Butler the Telegrapher), Jack O'Shea (Voter), Al Taylor (Jordan), Buddy Roosevelt, Bud Osborne (Gang Members), Griff Barnett (Stagecoach Rider), Curley Dresden

(Wagon Driver), Jack Kirk, Herman Hack, Jack Lawrence (Citizens).

Outlaws of Cherokee Trail (Republic, 1941, 56 minutes) Associate Producer: Louis Gray. Director: Les [Lester] Orlebeck. Screenplay: Albert De Mond. Photography: Ernest Miller. Editor: Ray Snyder. Supervising Editor: Murray Seldeen. Music: Cy Feuer. Production Manager: Al Wilson.

Cast: Bob Steele (Tucson Smith), Tom Tyler (Stony Brooke), Rufe Davis (Lullaby Joslin), Lois Collier (Doris Sheldon), Tom Chatterton (Captain Sheldon), Joel Friedkin (Judge), Roy Barcroft (Val Lamar), Phillip Trent (James Warren/Harvard), Rex Lease (Marshal), Peggy Lynn (Belle), John James (Pete Lamar), Eddie Dean (Guard), Bud Osborne (Hank), Henry Wills (Lefty), Billy Curtis (Papoose), Karl Hackett (Lawyer), Bob Burns (Jones), Griff Barnett (Foreman), Sarah Padden (Nun), Lloyd Ingraham (Victim), Lee Shumway (Decker), Iron Eyes Cody, Chief Yowlachie (Gamblers), Wally West, Bud Geary (Convicted Outlaws), Chuck Morrison, Cactus Mack (Gang Members), Ernest Sarracino (Indian), Ethyl May Halls (Citizen).

Gauchos of El Dorado (Republic, 1941, 56 minutes) Associate Producer: Louis Gray. Director: Lester Orlebeck. Screenplay: Albert DeMond. Story: Oliver Drake & Earle Snell. Photography: Reggie Lanning. Editor: Charles Craft. Supervising Editor: Murray Seldeen. Music: Cy Feuer. Song: Jule Styne & Sol Meyer. Production Manager: Al Wilson.

Cast: Bob Steele (Tucson Smith), Tom Tyler (Stony Brooke), Rufe Davis (Lullaby Joslin), Lois Collier (Ellen Ojara), Duncan Renaldo (Jose "The Gaucho" Ojara), Rosina Galli (Isabel Ojara), Norman Willis (Bart Braden), William Ruhl (Sam Tyndal), Tony Roux (Miguel), Ray Bennett (Monk Stevens), Yakima Canutt (Snakes), John Merton (Curly Kid), Virginia Farmer (Aunt Agatha), Jack Holmes (Casey), Si Jenks (County Clerk), Edmund Cobb (Sheriff), Eddie Dean, Terry Frost, Al Taylor, Bud Geary (Gang Members), Matty Roubert, Ted Mapes (Deputy Sheriffs), Bob Woodward (Killer), Roy Bucko (Gambler), Ray Jones (Saloon Customer), Lynton Brent, Bob Burns, Horace B. Carpenter (Citizens).

West of Cimarron (Republic, 1941, 56 minutes) Associate Producer: Louis Gray. Director: Les [Lester] Orlebeck. Screenplay: Albert DeMond & Don Ryan. Photography: Ernest Miller. Editor: Howard O'Neill. Music: Cy Feuer. Assistant Director: George Webster.

Cast: Bob Steele (Tucson Smith), Tom Tyler (Stony Brooke), Rufe Davis (Lullaby Joslin), Lois Collier (Doris Conway), James Bush (Dr. Ken Morgan), Guy Usher (Colonel Conway), Hugh Prosser (Charles Bentley), Cordell Hickman (Rastus Brown), Roy Barcroft (Captain Hawkes), Budd Buster (Col. Grant Morgan), Mickey Rentschler (Jimmy Conway), Cactus Mack (Guard), Stanley Blystone (Col. Briggs), John James (Dick Morgan), Eddie Dean, Eddie Dew (Riders), Nick Stewart (Jason Brown), Bud Geary (Trooper Tompkins), James Gillette (Jimmy Morgan), Tommy Coats (Gate Trooper), Sonny Bupp (Boy).

Code of the Outlaw (Republic, 1942, 57 minutes) Associate Producer: Louis Gray. Director: John English. Screenplay: Barry Shipman. Photography: Reggie Lanning. Editor: Charles Craft. Music: Cy Feuer. Song: Hy Heath. Assistant Director: George Webster.

Cast: Bob Steele (Tucson Smith), Tom Tyler (Stony Brooke), Rufe Davis (Lullaby Joslin), Weldon Heyburn (Bart "Pop" Hardin), Bennie Bartlett (Tim Hardin), Melinda Leighton (Sue Dayton), Don [Donald] Curtis (Taggart), John Ince (Sheriff Ed Stoddard), Kenne Duncan (Plug), Phil Dunham (Boyle), Max Waizmann (Dr. Horace M. Beagle), Chuck Morrison (Martin), Carleton Young (Garson), Richard Alexander (Morgan), Robert Frazer (Billings), Pascale Perry (Burke), Al Taylor (Joe), Hank Worden (Lars), Bud Osborne (Rider), Chuck Baldra (Bill), Sonny Bupp, Harry McKim (Work Farm Boys), Ed Peil, Sr. (Sam), Forrest Taylor (Wells Fargo Clerk), Wally West, Jack Kirk, Jack Ingram (Payroll Guards), Bob Burns, Cactus Mack (Citizens), Adele Smith (Blonde Woman), George Billings (Spike), Merlyn Nelson (Stagecoach Driver).

Working title: *Riders of the Sunset Trail*.

Raiders of the Range (Republic, 1942, 55 minutes) Associate Producer: Louis Gray. Director: John English. Screenplay: Barry Shipman & Albert DeMond. Photography: Ernest Miller. Editor: John Lockert. Music: Cy Feuer. Song: Raoul Kraushaar & Sol Meyer.

Cast: Bob Steele (Tucson Smith), Tom Tyler (Stony Brooke), Rufe Davis (Lullaby Joslin), Lois Collier (Jean Travers), Frank Jaquet (Samuel Daggett), Tom Chatterton (Dr. "Doc" Higgins), Charles F. Miller (John "Pop" Travers), Dennis Moore (Ned Foster), Fred Kohler, Jr. (Plummer), Max Waizmann (Coroner), Hal Price (Sheriff), Jack Ingram (Todd), Al Taylor (Jensen), Joel Friedkin (Ambrose), Cactus Mack (Deputy Sheriff), Richard Alexander (Big Brawler), David Sharpe (Brawler), Monte Montague, Frank McCarroll, Bud Geary, Chuck Morrison, Bob Woodward, John Tyrrell, Pascale Perry (Gang Members), William Nestell (Oil Well Worker).

Westward Ho (Republic, 1942, 56 minutes) Associate Producer: Louis Gray. Director: John English. Screenplay: Doris Schroeder. Photography: Reggie Lanning. Editor: William Thompson. Music: Cy Feuer. Art Director: Russell Kimball.

Cast: Bob Steele (Tucson Smith), Tom Tyler (Stony Brooke), Rufe Davis (Lullaby Joslin), Evelyn Brent (Mrs. Healey), Donald Curtis (Rick West), Lois Collier (Anne Henderson), Emmett Lynn (Sheriff), John James (Jimmy Henderson), Tom Seidel (Wayne Henderson), Jack Kirk (Deputy), Kenne Duncan (Dallas), Budd Buster, Bud Osborne, Monte Montague, Jack Montgomery, Al Taylor (Gang Members), Milton Kibbee, Jayne Hazard (Photographers), Edmund Cobb,

Horace B. Carpenter (Citizens), John L. Cason (Cowboy), Roy Bucko (Deputy Sheriff Ed), Jack O'Shea (Lynch Mob Member).

The Phantom Plainsmen (Republic, 1942, 56 minutes) Associate Producer: Louis Gray. Director: John English. Screenplay: Robert Yost & Barry Shipman. Story: Robert Yost. Photography: Bud Thackery. Editor: William Thompson. Art Director: Russell Kimball.

Cast: Bob Steele (Tucson Smith), Tom Tyler (Stony Brooke), Rufe Davis (Lullaby Joslin), Robert O. Davis [Rudolph Anders] (Col. Eric Hartwig), Lois Collier (Judy Barrett), Charles F. Miller (Captain "Cap" Marvin), Alex Callam (Kurt Redman), Monte Montague (Muller), Henry Rowland (Lindrick), Richard Crane (Tad Marvin), Jack Kirk (Joe), Vince Barnett (Deputy Sheriff Short), Ed Cassidy (Sheriff), Lloyd Ingraham (Doctor), Al Taylor, Bud Geary (Gang Members), Herman Hack (Citizen).

Shadows on the Sage (Republic, 1942, 57 minutes) Associate Producer: Louis Gray. Director: Les [Lester] Orlebeck. Screenplay: J. Benton Cheney. Photography: Edgar Lyons. Editor: William Thompson. Music: Jimmie Dodd & Mort Glickman. Art Director: Russell Kimball.

Cast: Bob Steele (Tucson Smith), Tom Tyler (Stony Brooke), Jimmie Dodd (Lullaby Joslin), Cheryl Walker (Doris Jackson), Harry Holman (Lippy), Bryant Washburn (John Carson), Griff Barnett (Steve Jackson), Freddie Mercer (Johnny Jackson), Tom London (Franklin), Yakima Canutt (Red Harvey), Rex Lease (Reluctant Deputy Sheriff), Johnnie Morris (Little Man), William Nestell (Cherokee Bill), Fred Burns (Sheriff Blink), Burr Caruth (Doc Selby), Eddie Dew (Deputy Sheriff Thompson), Frank Brownlee (Johnson), John L. Cason (Cowboy), Jack Rockwell, Horace B. Carpenter, Tommy Coats (Citizens), Betty Farrington (Young Mother), Cactus Mack, Pascale Perry (Gang Members).

Valley of Hunted Men (Republic, 1942, 60 minutes) Associate Producer: Louis Gray. Director: John English. Screenplay: Albert DeMond & Morton Grant. Photography: Bud Thackery. Editor: William Thompson. Music: Mort Glickman. Art Director: Russell Kimball. Sets: Otto Siegel.

Cast: Bob Steele (Tucson Smith), Tom Tyler (Stony Brooke), Jimmie Dodd (Lullaby Joslin), Edward Van Sloan (Dr. Heinrich Steiner), Roland Varno (Captain Carl Baum), Anne Marie Stewart (Laura Steiner), Edythe Elliott (Elizabeth Schiller), Arno Frey (Von Breckner), Richard French (Franz Toller), Bob Stevenson (Kruger), George Neise (Paul Schiller), Hal Price (Clem Parker), Budd Buster (Jed Carson), Kenne Duncan (Curley), Jack Kirk (Hank Carlson), Mickey Rentschler (Danny), Hank Worden (Hank), Oscar "Dutch" Hendrian (Wessel), Charles Flynn (S.W. Tomsen), Louis Adlon (Willie Schmidt), Billy Benedict (Ranch Boy), Arvon Dale (Reporter), John Frazer (Radio Announcer), Kermit Maynard (Roberts), Jack O'Shea (Radio Operator), Tex Terry, Bob Card, Charles Graham, Henry Morris, James Mitchell (Posse Members), Rose Plummer (Citizen).

Thundering Trails (Republic, 1943, 56 minutes) Associate Producer: Louis Gray. Director: John English. Screenplay: Norman S. Hall & Robert Yost. Photography: Reggie Lanning. Editor: William Thompson. Music: Mort Glickman. Art Director: Russell Kimball. Sets: Otto Siegel.

Cast: Bob Steele (Tucson Smith), Tom Tyler (Stony Brooke), Jimmie Dodd (Lullaby Joslin), Nell O'Day (Edith Walker), Sam Flint (Judge Morgan), Karl Hackett (Mollison), Charles F. Miller (Captain Sam Brooke), John James (Johnny Brooke), Forrest Taylor (Ben Walker), Edward [Ed] Cassidy (Jim Patterson), Forbes Murray (Arthur Howland), Reed Howes (Jeff Cantrell), Bud Geary (Blake), George Chesebro (Charlie), Vince Barnett (Jailer), Lane Bradford (Jim), Budd Buster (Jupiter Jones), John Carpenter, George DeNormand (Gang Members), Art Mix, Jack O'Shea, Tex Cooper (Citizens), Eddie Parker, Al Taylor (Troopers).

The Blocked Trail (Republic, 1943, 55 minutes) Associate Producer: Louis Gray. Director: Elmer Clifton. Screenplay: John K. Butler & Jacquin Frank. Photography: Bud Thackery. Editor: Edward Schroeder. Music: Mort Glickman. Art Director: Russell Kimball. Sets: Otto Siegel. Assistant Director: Harry Knight.

Cast: Bob Steele (Tucson Smith), Tom Tyler (Stony Brooke), Jimmie Dodd (Lullaby Joslin), Helen Deverell (Ann Martin), George J. Lewis (Freddie), Walter Soderling (Martin), Charles F. Miller (Frank Nolan), Kermit Maynard (Reese), Pierce Lyden (Scott Rankin), Carl Mathews (Lon), Hal Price (Sheriff Pillsbury), Budd Buster (Deputy Sheriff "Bets" McGee), Brilliant (Horse), Earle Hodgins (Chief Plenty Harvest), Ellen Lowe (Chief Plenty Harvest's Wife), Bud Geary (Henderson), Bud Osborne (Deputy Sheriff on Stagecoach), Matty Roubert, Al Taylor (Deputy Sheriffs), Art Dillard (Posse Deputy Sheriff), Nolan Leary (Drunk), Cliff Parkinson, Roy Bucko (Gang Members), Jess Cavin, Rose Plummer, Bill Wolfe (Citizens), Kelly Flint (Stagecoach Passenger).

Santa Fe Scouts (Republic, 1943, 55 minutes) Associate Producer: Louis Gray. Director: Howard Bretherton. Screenplay: Betty Burbridge & Morton Grant. Photography: Reggie Lanning. Editor: Charles Craft. Music: Mort Glickman. Art Director: Russell Kimball. Sets: Charles Thompson. Sound: Fred Stahl. Assistant Director: Kenneth Holmes.

Cast: Bob Steele (Tucson Smith), Tom Tyler (Stony Brooke), Jimmie Dodd (Lullaby Joslin), Lois Collier (Claire Robbins), John James (Tim Clay), Elizabeth Valentine (Minerva "Nervy" Clay), Tom Chatterton (Judge Neil Morgan), Tom London (Billy Dawson), Budd Buster (Wid Lighton), Jack Ingram (Tom Howard), Kermit Maynard (Ben Henderson), Rex Lease (Gang Member), Reed Howes, Kenne Duncan, Al Taylor (Hoodlums), Ed Cassidy (Sheriff), Curley

Dresden (Red), Edmund Cobb (Citizen), Bud Geary (Brawler).

Riders of the Rio Grande (Republic, 1943, 55 minutes) Associate Producer: Louis Gray. Director: Howard Bretherton. Screenplay: Albert DeMond. Photography: Ernest Miller. Editor: Charles Craft. Music: Mort Glickman. Song: Jimmie Dodd. Art Director: Russell Kimball. Sets: Charles Thompson. Sound: Tom Carman.

Cast: Bob Steele (Tucson Smith), Tom Tyler (Stony Brooke), Jimmie Dodd (Lullaby Joslin), Lorraine Miller (Janet Owens), Edward Van Sloan (Timothy "Pop" Owens), Rick Vallin (Tom Owens), Harry Worth (Sam Skelly), Roy Barcroft (Cherokee Boy Sarsaparilla), Charles King (Cherokee Boy Thunder), Jack Ingram (Berger), Jack O'Shea (Cherokee Boy Butch), Bud Osborne (Sheriff), Yakima Canutt (Deputy Sheriff), Chester Conklin, Curley Dresden (Saloon Customers), Budd Buster (Jed), Robert Kortman (Zeke), Charles Sullivan (Bartender).

THE TRAIL BLAZERS

Following the tragic death of Buck Jones in Boston's Coconut Grove fire on November 28, 1942, Monogram Pictures abandoned its popular "The Rough Riders" (q.v.) series. Wanting to continue the successful pattern of teaming established cowboy stars in a series, the studio assigned one of its production supervisors, Robert Emmett Tansey, to produce a new one called "The Trail Blazers." Tansey signed Ken Maynard and Hoot Gibson to star in these productions; the budgets were considerable less than had been designated for "The Rough Riders." The "Trail Blazers" movies did not measure up critically or with fans as did its predecessor.

A native of Brooklyn, New York, Tansey (1897–1951) was an actor, producer, director, writer and production manager who began his career in front of the camera in 1911. With the coming of sound he switched to the production side of filmmaking, writing over 80 features, directing around 50 movies and producing another 40 films, plus being production manager on three dozen outings and assistant director on sixteen films. He worked under a number of names, including his full name, shortened versions like Robert Emmett and Robert Tansey, plus Al Lane, John Foster and Craig Hutchison. His mother, Emma Tansey, also acted in films, as did his brother, Sherry Tansey, who was also known as James Sheridan. Tansey's reputation as a filmmaker is mediocre at best, with his productions often relying on excess stock footage and general incongruity. In the "Trail Blazers" production *Westward Bound*, Tansey's general lack of concern for a quality product was evident in the scene where Hoot Gibson uses dynamite to hold off an outlaw gang. Regarding the sequence, Don Miller noted in *Hollywood Corral* (1976), the dynamite sticks were seen landing on the ground "then the charges go off several feet away from the dummy sticks, in plain view." Frances Kavanaugh would supply either the story or screenplay, or both, for all eight "Trail Blazers" features and Betty Miles would be the leading lady in half of them.

Hoot Gibson (1892–1962) had not been on the screen since co-starring in the 1937 Republic serial *The Painted Stallion*. In the interim he had made personal appearances as well as touring with circuses and he operated Hoot Gibson's Trading Post in Hollywood, but he hankered to be back on the big screen, where he had been since 1910, having previously been a performer in Wild West shows. Ken Maynard (1895–1973) also made his reputation as a horseman before coming to films in 1923 and, like Hoot, he too has been off the screen for a time, his Colony series having ended in 1940. He also had kept busy on the sawdust trail and with his own outfit, Ken Maynard's Diamond K Ranch Wild West Show. Unlike his friend Hoot, Maynard had no yen to return to the screen and only did the "Trail Blazers" series as a favor to his pal since Tansy would not finance the features with Gibson as a solo star. With each of the films budgeted at around $15,000, the series was a comedown for both men, considering their earlier palmy days at Universal, since they each averaged about $800 per film from Tansey. The stars also aged, with Gibson looking older than his 50 years while Maynard had gained weight. Both still showed their stuff in the required action sequences, although the rigorous stunt work was done by Cliff Lyons.

The "Trail Blazers" features were filmed at Corriganville with five- to six-day shooting schedules. For the first two, Tansey hired director Alan James (Alvin J. Neitz), who had previously worked with both Maynard and Gibson. He had directed Ken at both World Wide and Universal and he had helmed Hoot in two of his 1936 Grand National features. The initial series release, *Wild Horse Stampede*, which came out in April, 1943, was a mixed bag in that it was fairly action-filled and had a good story line but was plagued with excessive stock footage, including a lengthy sequence depicting a raid on a horse herd. Taking place near the western town of Cold Springs, it told of raiders attacking the supply trains of the Southwestern Railroad as its workers struggle to complete 40 miles of track in a limited time. The foreman of the project, Bill Borman (Kenneth Harlan), and railroad commissioner Brent (I. Stanford Jolley) seek help from Marshal Cliff Tyler (Forrest Taylor), whose son Bob (Bob Baker) is the U.S. marshal in Cold Springs. The elder Taylor enlists the aid of ex-lawmen Ken Maynard and Hoot Gibson, planning to put patrolmen in the area to stop the sabotage as Deputy Sheriff Hanley (Kenne Duncan) makes a deal to buy a herd of horses for the riders from Betty Wallace (Betty Miles). Betty's ranch foreman, Tip (Glenn Strange), is in cahoots with stagecoach line operator Carson (Ian Keith) who is working with corrupt Judge Black (John Bridges) and lawyer Puckett (Bob McKenzie) in stopping the railroad's progress. Tip and his men rustle the herd, murder the railroad men and steal the money for the sale of the horses, unaware that the bills are marked. Ken and Hoot arrive in town and are made deputies by the incompetent Bob, whom Ken has to rescue from a saloon fight with Carson's henchman Westy (Tom London). Carson orders the new deputies killed but Ken escapes an ambush and Hoot becomes suspicious of Tip. After winning money from Carson in a poker game, Ken realizes it is from the robbery and he and Hoot trick Tip and the gang into leading them to the hidden herd. There they use a ruse to make the outlaws think they are surrounded as the two corral the horses and head them toward town. With the aid of her little brother Don (Don Stewart), Betty rounds up a crew to help him with the drive as Hoot goes back to town and gets proof of Carson's guilt from the cowardly Puckett. As the herd arrives in town, a gunfight takes place between the lawmen and Carson and his gang. Most of the outlaws are shot as Ken beats Carson in a fistfight and Marshal Bob does the same to Tip after learning the art of self-defense from peddler Rawhide (Si Jenks). The money is retrieved from Carson's safe and used to purchase the Wallace horses as Ken and Hoot ride off to new adventures.

Apparently producer Tansey had planned to continue the triad hero concept from "The Rough Riders" with "The Trail Blazers" because he cast another cowboy star, Bob Baker, in the role of the U.S. marshal. Baker (1910–75), who was christened Stanley Leland Weed, had starred in a series of westerns for Universal before teaming with Johnny Mack Brown at that studio. A cowboy crooner, he later had supporting roles in a couple of the "Rough Riders" segments for Tansey, who was probably hoping to return him to screen stardom in *Wild Horse Stampede*. Unfortunately, Maynard allegedly took a dislike to Baker and the triad hero concept was dropped for the next couple of films until Bob Steele joined the series in *Death Valley Rangers*.

The camaraderie between Maynard and Gibson was a plus in *Wild Horse Stampede*, which was followed in the summer of 1943 by *The Law Rides Again*. Here Ken and Hoot are United States marshals investigating a series of Indian raids near Prescott, Arizona, in violation of a government treaty. Hoot talks Ken into releasing convict Duke Dillon (Jack LaRue) so he can help them find the culprit who is inciting the Indians. They ride to escort a stagecoach carrying Dillon and a lawman (Roy Brent), but the coach, which is being driven by Betty Conway (Betty Miles), is attacked by Indians. Dillon kills the marshal and escapes as Ken and Hoot run off the attackers and escort Betty and the coach into town. The sheriff (Kenne Duncan) accuses Ken and Hoot of killing the marshal and locks them in jail but they manage to escape and find Dillon. He agrees to help them and, back in town, the outlaw confronts Indian agent John Hampton (Kenneth Harlan), who stole his business when he was sent to prison. Hampton, who is in league with tribe member Barking Fox (Chief Many Treaties), has been selling cattle intended for the Indian reservation. When Ken comes looking for him, Dillon escapes from Hampton's office through a secret panel as Hoot meets with the tribe's leader (Chief Thunder Cloud) and finds out they are being cheated by Hampton. Ken gets evidence of the thefts from the agent's receipts and, when Hampton tries to make a getaway, he is murdered by Dillon. The outlaw is chased by the lawmen, who are followed by Dillon's henchman Spike (John Merton) and Hampton's band. When Dillon and Spike try to murder Ken, Hoot shoots Spike, who falls from a cliff. The cavalry, sent by Betty, arrives and joins forces with the Indians, who rout the gang. In the gun battle, Dillon is killed.

After having acted as assistant director using the name Robert Emmett on the first two entries, producer Tansey, billed as Robert Tansey, took over the directorial reins for the rest of the series with *Blazing Guns*, issued in the fall of 1943. Here Maynard and Gibson are United States marshals assigned by Governor Brighton (Lloyd Ingraham) to break up an outlaw gang that has murdered two of their comrades near the town of Willow Springs. Rancher Jim Wade (Roy Brent) finds out his brother Duke Wade (LeRoy Mason) and his gang have stampeded his cattle because he will not pay to have them graze on his sibling's land. When Jim kills one of Duke's men, his brother orders his men to get him; Jim takes refuge at a ranch owned by Mary Baxter (Kay Forrester). Ken and Hoot arrive on the scene, run off the outlaws and tell Jim to stay hidden while they look into the matter. When the band tries to ambush the lawmen, they are rounded up and put in jail but a crooked judge (John Bridges) sets them free. Hoot asks the governor to release a quartet of gunmen, Eagle Eye (Emmett Lynn), Cactus Joe (Eddie Gribbon), Weasel (George Kamel) and Lefty (Frank Ellis), to aid him and Ken in battling the outlaws. Ken and Duke fight it out in the town saloon and, after beating the crook, the lawman orders the Wade gang to leave town. Weasel, however, double-crosses Ken and Hoot and joins up with Duke, whose men follow the marshals to Mary's ranch. During a shootout, Hoot and Jim make a getaway as Ken remains to fight the gang. The gunmen kill Weasel when they find out he betrayed them and then follow Hoot and Jim back town where they shoot it out with Duke and his men. During the melee, Eagle Eye is killed but the gang is defeated. Emmett Lynn played the character of Eagle Eye in both *The Law Rides Again* and *Blazing Guns*, but in the former he was a scout and not a gunslinger.

The series got a real boost with its next entry, *Death Valley Rangers*, released late in 1943, with Bob Steele riding in as a third star. Steele had finished his work in Republic's "The Three Mesquiteers" (q.v.) films and would remain with "The Trail Blazers" for the rest of its run. The story had Death Valley stage line owner Edwards (Bryant Washburn) enlisting the aid of Ranger Captain Ainsley (Forrest Taylor) when his gold shipments are hijacked. He also sends for government lawmen Ken, Hoot and Bob, with Bob falling for Ainsley's daughter Lorna (Linda Brent). When his horse becomes lame, Bob hitches a ride on one of Edwards' coaches and is attacked by outlaws. Ken

Advertisement for *Blazing Guns* (Monogram, 1943) showing Hoot Gibson and Ken Maynard.

and Hoot help Bob in running off the marauders who are able to find the strongbox containing gold after Bob tosses it off the coach. For the next run, Hoot substitutes an empty strongbox but the driver (Steve Clark) warns the gang not to rob the stage and then refuses to talk. Morgana Mine owner Jim Kirk (Weldon Heyburn) is behind the robberies and he is working with escaped convict Doc Farn (Karl Hackett), whom Ken later recognizes. In order to infiltrate the outlaws, Bob claims to be a former member of Farn's gang and Kirk hires him to murder Ken and Hoot. At the mine, Hoot locates a chemistry laboratory and Ken finds the stolen gold in a safe but he is captured by Farn, who has concocted a formula that turns reheated gold back into ore. When Kirk finds out that Bob double-crossed him by only pretending to kill his pals, he and his men get on his trail, but Steele unites with Maynard and Gibson and the three rout the outlaws as Kirk tries to escape on the stagecoach carrying the gold. Hoot takes over as the driver and the mine owner is captured. Steele's presence added a romantic twist to the series since Ken and Hoot were a bit too old to romance the young leading ladies. He also brought his physical prowess to the proceedings, excelling in the fight sequences.

The series' first 1944 release was *Westward Bound*, a fairly pleasing affair in which U.S. marshals Maynard, Gibson and Steele come to the aid of Wyoming Territory ranchers Jasper Tuttle (Hal Price) and Enid Barrett (Betty Miles), who are being forced off their lands by marauders. The outlaws work for Territorial Commission Secretary Albert Lane (Weldon Heyburn), who is in cahoots with Big Horn banker-politician Roger Caldwell (Harry Woods) and tax collector Henry Wagner (Karl Hackett), who want the area for themselves since property values are due to rise (Montana is about to become a state). When Lane orders one of his men, Judd (Frank Ellis), to cut off the ranchers' water supply, Enid confronts the crook and his cohorts. During the struggle, she is rescued by the newly arrived lawmen. Caldwell hires Ken as the new town marshal, thinking he will carry out his orders. When Judd and his pal Wade (Dan White) threaten Enid, they are placed under arrest. Caldwell tries to dismiss Ken, who refuses to give up the marshal's job. The banker orders his men to murder Ken, Hoot and Bob, but the three escape. Judd and Wade break jail; Wade is recaptured while Judd makes a getaway as Wade confesses that Lane is behind the lawlessness. Since statehood is to be decided the next day, Lane orders his men to kill the lawmen but the trio fights the gang with Hoot using dynamite to subdue the crooks.

Arizona Whirlwind (February, 1943) began with undercover lawmen Maynard, Gibson and Steele rescuing stagecoach passengers Ruth Hampton (Myrna Dell) and Jim Lockwood (Dan White) after they are attacked by Indians. They take the coach into Sonora where Lockwood joins Ted Hodges (Charles Murray, Jr.) in planning the completion of a telegraph line. The attack was actually carried out by white men masquerading as Indians under the guidance of Ace (George Chesebro), henchman of banker Steve Lynch (Karl Hackett). Lynch is after uncut diamonds which are secreted in a bucket of grease and sends another of his cohorts, Duke Rollins (Charles King), to find the contraband. The marshals also realize that something valuable is on the stagecoach and they try to search it but are stopped by Lynch as Duke removes the diamonds. The lawmen then team with Lockwood and Hodges in completing the telegraph line as diamond cutter Warren (Ernie Adams) comes to town to process the gems so they can be sold. When Bob romances Ruth at her mother's eatery, young Donny Davis (Don Stewart), his pal, reveals he is a lawman, alerting criminal Polini (Ian Keith), who has come to Sonora to buy the polished stones. Polini orders Duke and his men to trail Bob, who leads them to an abandoned mine where Ken, Hoot and Lockwood have their headquarters. Ruth and Donny, on Bob's orders, spy on the crooks and they see Lynch put the diamonds in his safe. Attempting to retrieve the gems, Donny is locked in the vault. As the outlaws surround the mine, Ruth has Hodges contact Lockwood by telegraph, telling the lawmen of Donny's predicament. Bob sneaks out of the mine and gets the attention of the gang as Ken, Hoot and Lockwood ride for town. Upon their arrival, Lynch turns coward and Polini kills him as the lawmen fight it out with the gang. As Ken tries to open the safe, Polini starts to shoot him but is killed by Hoot. Ken rescues the boy and the diamonds are recovered.

One particularly amusing scene in *Arizona Whirlwind* had Duke and his gang ordering Ken to stop stringing telegraph wire with Hoot using electrified wire to shock the gunmen. The film also presented an impressive array of bad men, with the gang members being enacted by Charles King, George Chesebro, Al Ferguson, Frank Ellis and Bud Osborne. The outing proved to be Ken Maynard's last in the series as he quit following a salary dispute with Tansey. Apparently there was no animosity between the two since Tansey would direct Maynard in his final starring western, *Harmony Trail*, a Walt Mattox production released later in 1944. Maynard continued to make personal appearances, often with circuses, into the 1960s and in 1955 he starred in the syndicated radio series "Tales from the Diamond K." His final films were *Bigfoot* (1970), in which he played himself, and the unissued *Marshal of Windy Hollow* (1971).

Maynard was replaced in "The Trail Blazers" by Chief Thunder Cloud (1899–1955), whose character used that name in the series' two final entries, *Outlaw Trail* and *Sonora Stagecoach*. Born Victor Daniels in Oklahoma, a member of the Cherokee tribe, he attended the University of Arizona at Tucson and worked at various occupations before becoming a movie stuntman in 1929. He went on to portray Native Americans in 75 feature films, mostly notably as Tonto in the Republic serials *The Lone Ranger* (1938) and *The Lone Ranger Rides Again* (1939) and the title role in the 1939 Paramount feature *Geronimo*. His final film was *The Searchers* in 1956. Also added to the cast of the last two series features was Rock Camron. Camron (1902–67), who also used the screen name Gene Alsace, usually played villains in westerns but he did star as Buck Coburn in Willis Kent's 1935 production *Gunsmoke on the Guadalupe* and he also appeared in other Robert Emmett Tansey films, including *Harmony Trail* (1944) with Ken Maynard and *Wildfire* (1945) with Bob Steele.

Released in the spring of 1944, *Outlaw Trail* was from a story by Alvin Neitz, who as Alan James had directed the first two "Trail Blazers" episodes. U.S. marshals Hoot, Bob and Thunder Cloud come to the aid of Alice Thornton (Jennifer Holt), who has inherited the Flying T Ranch from her father, who was killed by outlaws. The murdered man was a friend of the marshals who are also investigating the disappearance of Carl Beldon (George Eldredge) who had come to Johnstown with cash to buy cattle for his packing company employer. In town, Bob gets into a fight with Blackie (Bud Osborne) and Spike (Jim Thorpe) who work for banker Travers (Cy Kendall), who controls the area and issues his own currency. Hoot, who has met with Sheriff Rocky Camron (Camron), and Thunder Cloud help Bob fight the gunmen and then ride to the Flying T, which is deserted. Blackie finds out about Alice's impending arrival and tries to kidnap her but the marshals come to her defense. Camron's deputy Bud (Charles Murray, Jr.) frees Blackie, who informs his boss about Alice's arrival. The lawmen

Poster for *Outlaw Trail* (**Monogram, 1944**).

take Alice to her ranch where they find a paper containing Beldon's name. When the sheriff arrives, Hoot suggests he investigate Travers, but the lawman is reluctant since the banker has been kind to him. When the marshals find out that Travers is making ranchers join his cattle drive, Bob enlists the aid of Jud Hanson (Warner Richmond), who has refused to take orders from the banker's henchmen and join the drive. Bob convinces Hanson to rally the other ranchers in stopping Travers as the banker orders Camron to arrest Steele. The sheriff refuses Travers' request and informs him that Bob is a U.S. marshal. The lawmen later find the banker murdered and his money stolen. Hoot and Bob suspect that Travers was murdered by his henchman, Chuck Walters (Charles King), who has hidden the money in an abandoned mine where it is discovered by Thunder Cloud. Hoot, Bob, Thunder Cloud and Camron go back to town to have it out with Walters and his gang and there Rocky forces his deputy to admit that Walters killed both Travers and Beldon. Bob beats Walters in a fistfight while Hoot and Thunder Cloud shoot it out with Blackie and the rest of the gang. The lawmen round up the outlaws, give the stolen money to the ranchers for the sale of their cattle, and Rocky agrees to help Alice run her ranch.

Sonora Stagecoach, released in the early summer of 1944, ended the series on a satisfactory note. U.S. marshals Hoot, Bob and Thunder Cloud, taking prisoner Rocky Camron (Camron) to Sonora, are attacked by Blackie Reed (Charles King) and his gang. The four men manage to escape from the outlaws and at a relay station run by Pop Carson (John Bridges), they meet Rocky's girlfriend Betty Miles (Betty Miles), who says he is being framed on a robbery charge. Rocky relates how money was stolen from the Sonora Express Office, run by Paul Kenton (Glenn Strange), with some of the money being found in his mattress. He escaped after being accused of the robbery by Blackie; Betty tells the lawmen she believes that Blackie and his cohort Steve (Bud Osborne) framed Rocky on orders from Kenton and his brother Joe (Karl Hackett), a banker. In order to get a confession from Steve, Hoot has the man, who is also a driver for the stage line, take Rocky and Betty to town; along the way Rocky escapes and joins Hoot, Bob and Thunder Cloud. Two gang members, Weasel (Charles Murray, Jr.) and Red (Al Ferguson) wound Steve and are arrested by the lawmen. The two outlaws admit that Kenton and Blackie were behind the robbery. Back in town, Weasel, who makes a getaway, is killed by Blackie for promising to turn state's evidence against the gang. With the aid of Judge Crandall (Forrest Taylor), the lawmen, Rocky and Betty shoot it out with the crooks and arrest them. Rocky is then set free and remains in Sonora with Betty.

Although the series was at an end, Steele and Gibson co-starred in three more 1944 Monogram releases, *Marked Trails*, *the Utah Kid* and *Trigger Law*. Hoot went on to portray a sheriff in the spy drama *Flight to Nowhere* (1946) and he closed out his screen career with a co-starring role in *The Marshal's Daughter* (1952), a supporting part in *The Horse Soldiers* (1959) and a guest bit in *Ocean's Eleven* (1960). Steele did two Cinecolor features directed by Tansey, *Wildfire* and *Northwest Trail* (both 1945), before ending his "B" Western starring career in a quartet of PRC productions released in 1945–46. Thereafter he became a character actor, continuing to appear in features until his retirement in 1973.

Betty Miles and Bob Steele in *Sonora Stagecoach* (Monogram, 1944).

Poster for *Sonora Stagecoach* (Monogram, 1944).

In 1950, the original three "Trail Blazers," Maynard, Gibson and Steele, became the subjects of a series of comic books, although none had tie-ins with the Tansey productions. Fawcett Comics published *Ken Maynard Westerns* for eight issues between 1950 and 1952 and during the same time period the company also did ten issues of *Bob Steele Westerns*. Fox Features released three issues of *Hoot Gibson* comics in 1950 and later did the one-shot *Hoot Gibson's Western Roundup*.

While the "Trail Blazers" series came out at a time when the triad hero concept was beginning to wane at the Saturday matinees, it was a welcome one if only for the fact that it brought Ken Maynard and Hoot Gibson back to the screen for a final bow and briefly teamed them with Bob Steele. Made on the cheap but containing fairly interesting plots, the films were not the best of their ilk, but certainly they were not the worst. Popular enough in their day, the features hold up surprisingly well and have remained favorites with "B" Western collectors.

Filmography

Wild Horse Stampede (Monogram, 1943, 59 minutes) Producer: Robert [Emmett] Tansey. Director: Alan James. Screenplay: Elizabeth Beecher. Story: Frances Kavanaugh. Photography: Marcel Le Picard. Editor: Fred Bain. Music Director: Frank Sanucci. Sound: Glen Glenn. Production Manager: Fred Hoose. Assistant Directors: Robert Emmett [Tansey] & William L. Nolte.

Cast: Ken Maynard (himself), Hoot Gibson (himself), Betty Miles (Betty Wallace), Bob Baker (U.S. Marshal Bob Tyler), Ian Keith (Carson), Si Jenks (Rawhide), Bob McKenzie (Puckett), John Bridges (Judge Black), Ken [Kenneth] Harlan (Bill Borman), Forrest Taylor (Marshal Cliff Tyler), Ken [Kenne] Duncan (Deputy Sheriff Hanley), Glenn Strange (Tip), Tom London (Westy), Reed Howes (Tex), Don Stewart (Don Wallace), Tex Palmer, Chick Hannon, George Sowards, Augie Gomez (Gang Members).

The Law Rides Again (Monogram, 1943, 58 minutes) Producer: Robert [Emmett] Tansey. Director: Alan James. Screenplay: Frances Kavanaugh & Gina Kaus. Story-Assistant Director: Robert Emmett [Tansey]. Photography: Marcel Le Picard. Editor: Carl Pierson. Music Director: Frank Sanucci. Sound: Lyle Willey. Production Manager: Fred Hoose.

Cast: Ken Maynard (himself), Hoot Gibson (himself), Jack LaRue (Duke Dillon), Betty Miles (Betty Conway), Emmett Lynn (Eagle Eye), Ken [Kenneth] Harlan (John Hampton), Chief Thunder Cloud (Thunder Cloud), Chief Many Treaties (Barking Fox), Bryant Washburn (Commissioner Lee), Fred Hoose (Stagecoach Driver Hank), Ken [Kenne] Duncan (Sheriff Jeff), Roy Brent (Murdered Marshal), John Bridges (Jess), John Merton (Spike), Hank Bell (Tex), Charles Murray, Jr. (Gang Member), Steve Clark (Pete Conway), Budd Buster (Commissioner's Aide), Wally West (Deputy Sheriff), Chick Hannon, Foxy Callahan (Cowboys).

Blazing Guns (Monogram, 1943, 54 minutes) Producer-Director: Robert [Emmett] Tansey. Screenplay: Frances Kavanaugh & Gina Kaus. Story: Robert Emmett [Tansey]. Photography: Marcel Le Picard. Editor: Carl Pierson. Music Director: Frank Sanucci. Sound: Glen Glenn. Production Manager: Fred Hoose. Assistant Director: Art Hammond.

Cast: Ken Maynard (himself), Hoot Gibson (himself), LeRoy Mason (Duke Wade), Emmett Lynn (Eagle Eye), Weldon Heyburn (Vic), Roy Brent (Jim Wade), Eddie Gribbon (Cactus Joe), Lloyd Ingraham (Governor Brighton), George Kamel (Weasel), Kay Forrester (Mary Baxter), Robbie Kavanaugh (Virginia), Frank Ellis (Lefty), Charles King (Blackie), Ken [Kenne] Duncan (Red Higgins), Dan White (Trigger), Charles Murray, Jr. (Mack), Robert Allen [Lee Roberts] (Hodge), John Bridges (Judge Foster), Wally West (Messenger), Victor Cox (Gang Member).

Death Valley Rangers (Monogram, 1943, 59 minutes) Producer-Director: Robert [Emmett] Tansey. Screenplay: Elizabeth Beecher. Story: Frances Kavanaugh & Robert Emmett [Tansey]. Photography: Edward Kull. Editor: Carl Pierson. Music Director: Frank Sanucci. Sound: Glen Glenn. Production Manager: Fred Hoose. Assistant Director: George Tobin.

Cast: Ken Maynard (himself), Hoot Gibson (himself), Bob Steele (himself), Weldon Heyburn (Jim Kirk), Linda Brent (Lorna Ainsley), Bryant Washburn (Edwards), Glenn Strange (Marshal), Forrest Taylor (Captain Ainsley), Karl Hackett (Doc Farn), Lee Roberts (Ranger Michaels), Charles King (Blackie), George Chesebro (Red), John Bridges (Cal Wilkins), Al Ferguson (Ross), Steve Clark (Stagecoach Driver Hank), Wally West (Stagecoach Guard Wally), Frank Ellis (Gang Member).

Westward Bound (Monogram, 1944, 54 minutes) Producer-Director: Robert [Emmett] Tansey. Screenplay: Elizabeth Beecher & Frances Kavanaugh. Story: Frances Kavanaugh & Robert Emmett [Tansey]. Photography: Marcel Le Picard. Editor: John C. Fuller. Music Director: Frank Sanucci. Sound: Corson Jowett. Production Manager: Fred Hoose. Assistant Director: Art Hammond.

Cast: Ken Maynard (himself), Hoot Gibson (himself), Bob Steele (himself), Betty Miles (Enid Barrett), Harry Woods (Roger Caldwell), Weldon Heyburn (Albert Lane), Karl Hackett (Henry Wagner), Hal Price (Jasper Tuttle), John Bridges (Ira Phillips), Roy Brent (Will), Frank Ellis (Judd), Curley Dresden (Monte), Al Ferguson (Curley), Charles Murray, Jr. (Jess), Dan White (Webb), Horace B. Carpenter (Dr. Bernard Adrian), Chick Hannon (Rancher), Denver Dixon, Foxy Callahan (Citizens).

Arizona Whirlwind (Monogram, 1944, 59 minutes) Producer-Director: Robert [Emmett] Tansey. Screenplay: Frances Kavanaugh. Story: Robert Emmett [Tansey]. Photography: Edward Kull. Editor: John C. Fuller. Music Director: Frank Sanucci. Sound: Glen Glenn. Production Manager: Fred Hoose. Assistant Director: Art Hammond.

Cast: Ken Maynard (himself), Hoot Gibson (himself), Bob Steele (himself), Ian Keith (Polini), Myrna Dell (Ruth Hampton), Don Stewart (Donny Davis), Charles King (Duke Rollins), Karl Hackett (Steve Lynch), John Bridges (Tomkins), George Chesebro (Ace), Dan White (Jim Lockwood), Charles Murray, Jr. (Ted Hodges), Frank Ellis (Lefty), Ernie Adams (Warren), Al Ferguson (Bates), Bud Osborne (Mack), George Eldredge (Davis), Chris Willow Bird, Charles Soldani (Indians).

Outlaw Trail (Monogram, 1944, 54 minutes) Producer-Director: Robert [Emmett] Tansey. Screenplay: Frances Kavanaugh. Story: Alvin Neitz [Alan James]. Photography: Edward Kull. Editor: John C. Fuller. Music Director: Frank Sanucci. Sound: Glen Glenn. Production Manager: Fred Hoose. Assistant Director: Art Hammond.

Cast: Hoot Gibson (himself), Bob Steele (himself), Chief Thunder Cloud (Thunder Cloud), Jennifer Holt (Alice Thornton), Cy Kendall (Honest John Travers), Rocky Camron [Gene Alsace] (Sheriff Rocky Camron), George Eldredge (Carl Beldon), Warner Richmond (Jud Hanson), Charles King (Chuck Walters), Bud Osborne (Blackie), Jim Thorpe (Spike), John Bridges (Ed Knowles), Hal Price (Marshal H.A. Fraser), Charles Murray, Jr. (Deputy Sheriff Bud), Al Ferguson (Skeeter), Lee Roberts (Marshal), Frank Ellis (Fred), Fred Hoose (Joe), Evelyn Selbie (Nomi), Rose Plummer (Mrs. Martin), Bert Dillard (Stagecoach Driver), Tex Palmer, Artie Ortego (Gang Members), Herman Hack (Citizen), Denver Dixon, Lynton Brent, Roy Bucko (Saloon Customers).

Sonora Stagecoach (Monogram, 1944, 61 minutes) Producer-Director: Robert [Emmett] Tansey. Screenplay: Frances Kavanaugh. Photography: Edward Kull. Editor: John C. Fuller. Music Director: Frank Sanucci. Sound: Glen Glenn. Production Manager: Fred Hoose. Assistant Director: Art Hammond.

Cast: Hoot Gibson (himself), Bob Steele (himself), Chief Thunder Cloud (Thunder Cloud), Rocky Camron [Gene Alsace] (Rocky Camron), Betty Miles (Betty Miles), Glenn Strange (Paul Kenton), George Eldredge (Larry Payne), Karl Hackett (Joe Kenton), Henry Hall (Sheriff Hampton), Charles King (Blackie Reed), Bud Osborne (Steve Martin), Charles Murray, Jr. (Weasel), John Bridges (Pop Carson), Forrest Taylor (Judge Crandall), Al Ferguson (Red), Hal Price (Sheriff Paulson), Horace B. Carpenter (Doc Brady), John L. Cason (Gunman), Frank Ellis (Tex), Fred Hoose (Citizen), Augie Gomez (Gang Member), Rodd Redwing (Indian).

Working titles: *The Roaring West* and *Sonora Kid*.

WILD BILL ELLIOTT

In 1943, after attaining cowboy film stardom at Columbia, Bill Elliott signed a contract with Republic Pictures that stated he was to appear only in feature films, with a specific clause that he would not have to make serials. The studio then starred him in eight westerns in which he played a character called Wild Bill Elliott *and* was billed under that name. He was paid $2,750 for each film. Further, the first entry, *Calling Wild Bill Elliott*, incorporated the star's name and character in its title. All eight oaters co-starred George "Gabby" Hayes as the hero's sidekick and in each of them Anne Jeffreys was the leading lady. Summing up the series, Don Miller wrote in *Hollywood Corral* (1976), "Elliott appeared comfortable among his new surroundings.... The series soon became a worthy companion to Republic's other range sagas." Most of the features contained a song, all in public domain, with the majority composed by Stephen Foster.

Hayes (1885–1969) was a New York native who went on stage as a teenager and worked in vaudeville as a song and dance man as well as acting in plays. He settled in Hollywood in the late 1920s and began working in films where he easily made the transition to sound. He worked extensively in the early 1930s with producers Trem Carr and Paul Malvern, often in "B" westerns, eventually developing the old codger character that would make him famous. The Windy Halliday role in Paramount's "Hopalong Cassidy" (q.v.) series made him very popular with movie audiences and after a salary dispute with producer Harry Sherman he left the Cassidy films and signed with Republic. Sherman refused to let Hayes use the Windy Halliday character so he developed the guise of Gabby Whitaker, and "Gabby" became part of his on-screen name. At Republic, Hayes made 25 features with Roy Rogers between 1939 and 1942 before being signed to appear in the "Wild Bill Elliott" series, where his character was called Gabby, Gabby Hayes and Gabby Whittaker.

Anne Jeffreys was born Anne Carmichael in 1923 in North Carolina. She began singing on local radio at age ten and after finishing high school traveled to New York where she worked as a model and studied opera. She came to Hollywood in the early 1940s and made her film debut in the PRC oater *Billy the Kid Trapped* (1941). After two more films she signed with Republic and was assigned to the "Wild Bill Elliott" series.

Action ace Spencer Gordon Bennet directed the first "Wild Bill Elliott" feature, *Calling Wild Bill Elliott*, which was released in the spring of 1943. Rancher John Culver (Fred Kohler, Jr.) is ordered off his land by Captain Carson (Roy Barcroft) and Dean (Bud Geary), henchmen of territorial governor Steven Nichols (Herbert Heyes), after he is unable to pay excessive taxes. Since federal judge Anson Richards (Forbes Murray) is due in the area, Cactus Jim Culver (Barr Caruth) and young son Demi-John Culver (Buzzy Henry), along with family friend Gabby Hayes (Hayes), decide to bring the matter to his attention. Braggart Gabby has told young Demi-John about fictitious adventures he had in the past with Wild Bill Elliott (Elliott), and when they meet the famous westerner in Eagle Junction, Bill pretends Gabby is an old friend. Carson, who has been sent by his boss, shoots Cactus Jim and later the governor has Bill arrested for the crime. When John finds out about his father's killing, he too blames Bill and joins Carson, who has incited a lynch mob; Bill manages to escape. Gabby and the boy tell Culver the truth and, with Bill, they also try to convince the judge and his daughter Edith (Anne Jeffreys) of his innocence. When Carson ambushes and kills the judge, Edith thinks it was Bill who committed the murder. As Bill makes a getaway, Culver tries to tell Edith he is innocent but John is arrested as the fugitive's accomplice. The governor decrees that John Culver is to be hanged as John's wife Mary (Eve March), Gabby and Demi-John convince Edith that Bill did not kill her father. When Edith faces Nichols, he takes her and Mary hostages as Gabby goes to a nearby army post for help and Bill unites the ranchers. During a shootout with Nichols and his militia, Bill helps John escape and Culver frees his wife and Edith. Gabby arrives with soldiers and shoots Carson while Bill captures Nichols. Although Edith offers to back Bill as the new territorial governor, he declines; he and Gabby, now sidekicks for real, head for a new adventure.

John English directed the second series outing, *The Man from Thunder River*, which came out in the early summer of 1942. Bill (Elliott) and Gabby (Hayes) leave their Thunder River ranch to buy cattle from rancher Jack Ferguson (John James) and his Aunt Bess (Georgie Cooper). While Bill claims it is a business trip, Gabby believes he also wants to see Jack's sister, Nancy (Anne Jeffreys). Jack tells the two cowboys he wants to reopen the family mine but Aunt Bess is

Anne Jeffreys, Wild Bill Elliott and George "Gabby" Hayes.

opposed to the idea since nearby rancher Henry Stevens (Ian Keith) told her the enterprise would be too expensive. Jack gets financial backing from banker Bates (Ed Cassidy) but he is murdered and Ferguson is arrested for the crime. The real killer is Jason (Bud Geary) who works for Stevens and carried out the killing on his orders. Stevens has been working the Ferguson mine with plans to pass off the ore as being from his own claim that he plans to sell to a mining syndicate. When a lynch mob tries to hang Jack, Bill and Gabby save him and hide him out while they investigate the killing. When Stevens finds out Bill is bringing Jack home the following day, he tells the sheriff (Jack Rockwell) who arrests them. While Gabby helps his friends break jail, Culver is wounded and captured while Bill makes a getaway; he and Gabby locate the secret tunnel Stevens' men use to work the Ferguson mine. An explosive is set off in the mineshaft but the two men manage to escape, and Bill turns Stevens over to the sheriff.

When Stevens is convicted of the banker's murder, Jack is set free. Bill and Gabby tell him they will return after their cattle drive to help him work his mine.

The next two "Wild Bill Elliott" adventures, *Border City Gun Fighters* and *Wagon Tracks West*, were issued in the summer of 1943 and directed by Howard Bretherton. The former had Bill (Elliott), an undercover Secret Service agent, and Gabby (Hayes) being arrested by Deputy Sheriff Jack Gatling (Roy Barcroft) for the murder of Roland Clark (Wheaton Chambers), a New Mexico state official. The two are taken into custody by federal marshal Dave Strickland (Harry Woods), who knows that Bill is a government agent and reveals to them that Clark was investigating the Lone Star Lottery, an operation jilting New Mexico residents. Bill and Gabby go to Washington D.C. to meet with the head (Edward Earle) of the Secret Service and then return on a train where they meet Anita Shelby (Anne Jeffreys), the niece of

Cameo Shelby (Ian Keith), the crook behind the lottery and Gatling's boss. When Anita tells her uncle about meeting Bill and Gabby, he questions Gatling as to why they did not go to trial and orders him to trail them. Bill finds out that Cameo plans to send a shipment of fake lottery tickets via tannery owner Frank Holden (Karl Hackett); when Gabby attempts to find the contraband, he is knocked out and taken to Las Palmas. Bill trails the gang, rescues Gabby and takes the tickets. Cameo then puts another shipment of tickets in Anita's saddlebag but Bill finds them as Gatling informs his boss that Bill is a government agent. When Gabby and Strickland find out that Cameo has ordered Gatling to kill Bill when he tries to resist being arrested, they warn Bill, and in a gunfight with the crooks Strickland is wounded as Bill kills Gatling. Cameo tries to run away but is followed by Bill; Shelby dies falling from a cliff. Bill, Gabby and Anita travel back to the nation's capitol where Bill receives a medal for cleaning up the lottery racket.

Bordertown Gun Fighters was issued as part of a double-bill with the re-release of the 1937 Gene Autry starrer *Boots and Saddles* in which Elliott, then billed as Gordon Elliott, was the bad guy. An interesting aspect of the third "Wild Bill Elliott" feature is that it cast usual genre villain Harry Woods in the part of a federal marshal who helps the hero round up the crooks. Appearing briefly as a messenger is future Oscar winner Ben Johnson, who was Elliott's stunt double during the production.

Six weeks after *Bordertown Gun Fighters* came to movie screens, *Wagon Tracks West* was issued in mid–August 1943. The film cast genre star Tom Tyler in the role of a cruel, corrupt Indian medicine man while Anne Jeffreys played Moon Hush, a beautiful tribal maiden who helps bring the shaman to justice. Set in 1891, it has John Fleetwing (Rick Vallin), a Pawnee Indian, graduating from medical college and returning to his home to practice medicine. When Bill (Elliott) and Gabby (Hayes) attempt to escape pursuing Indians, they are forced to jump into a lake with Gabby becoming ill from swallowing contaminated water. In town, the newly arrived Dr. Fleetwing tries to help Gabby but is harassed by Laird (Roy Barcroft), a thug who is thwarted by Bill. After tending Gabby, the doctor learns that members of his tribe have died from drinking the lake's water and he and Bill determine the cause is an irrigation system used by area ranchers. Bill goes with the doctor to the Indian camp where Fleetwing finds Chief Brown Bear (Charles Miller), his father, has the fever but before he can help him, the chief is murdered by medicine man Clawtooth (Tom Tyler). Clawtooth, who wants to be chief, is in the pay of Indian commissioner Robert Warren (Robert Frazer) and his henchman Laird who want the tribe's rich land. Bill informs the ranchers that their irrigation system is causing a backwash that is poisoning the lake's waters and the doctor tells them they too will get the fever when the seasonal rains begin. Warren, who has been causing trouble between the ranchers and the Indians, orders Laird to kill cattleman Lem Martin (Tom London) and place the blame on the doctor. When Fleetwing is arrested for the crime, Bill and Gabby help him to escape but he is later found by the sheriff (Jack Rockwell) and taken to jail. Bill and Gabby have a showdown with Clawtooth and Laird with the medicine man being killed and Laird accidentally drinking some polluted water. Knowing the doctor can save him, Laird implicates Warren in Martin's murder and Bill and Gabby get him back to town in time to save Fleetwing from being lynched. When the ranchers are shown evidence of Warren's guilt, the Indian commissioner is arrested. The cattlemen agree to stop the lake's pollution and they also plan to set up Dr. Fleetwing's medical office.

John English directed the next two films, *Death Valley Manhunt* and *Overland Stage Robbery*. The former, released in the fall of 1943, had Elliott as a U.S. marshal planning to retire but declining Gabby's (Hayes) offer of sharing oil property in Death Valley. While Bill prefers being a rancher, Gabby and his dog Teabone ride to the drilling area where he is warned by Tex Benson (Davison Clark) to avoid Ross Petroleum Company field manager Richard Quinn (Weldon Heyburn), whom Benson claims is involved in a stock swindle. When Quinn's henchmen steal equipment from Benson's property, he does the same from the Ross operation and Quinn forces Judge Hobart (Herbert Heyes) to order his arrest. When the local marshal (Jack Kirk) attempts to carry out the arrest order, Benson accidentally shoots him. Quinn then has the judge order Benson arrested for murder but Gabby helps him to escape jail. In Chicago, the head (Edward Keane) of the Ross oil operation hires Bill to look into the matter; he travels to Death Valley where he gets Quinn to drop the charges against Benson and back the local drillers. If the oilmen cannot bring in their wells in 30 days, the land they are working will go back to the Ross Petroleum Company. Bill meets and falls in love with the judge's niece, Nicky (Anne Jeffreys), although the locals begin to believe he is in cahoots with Quinn, who does not deliver needed equipment. Gabby and Teabone go to get the equipment but Sid Roberts (Bud Geary) and deputy marshals Blaine (Eddie Phillips) and Lawson (Al Taylor), who work for Quinn, attack his wagon with the dog being killed and Gabby left for dead. Gabby survives and tells Bill that Blaine was one of the men who attacked him. Bill accuses Blaine of murder and he blames Quinn and Hobart. When Bill faces the judge with the confession, he agrees to turn state's evidence against Quinn. After killing Blaine, Quinn and Roberts head to the drilling site that belongs to Gabby and Benson but Bill arrives and beats Roberts in a fight. He then follows a fleeing Quinn up the oil rigging, where they fight. Quinn falls off and lands on a detonator with the explosion causing a gusher. Bill, Gabby and Nicky travel to Chicago where the oil company gives Bill a ranch in payment for his services and Gabby gets a replacement for Teabone.

In *Overland Mail Robbery* (November 1943), stage line foreman Gabby (Hayes) tries to help Judith Goodrich (Anne Jeffreys) keep her business in operation following the murders of her father and his partner during a robbery. One of the company drivers, Slade (Bud Geary), is working with David Patterson (Roy Barcroft) in trying to force the company out of business so it can be purchased by David's mother, Mrs. Patterson (Alice Fleming). Her other son, John Patterson (Weldon Heyburn), is a banker who is also working with his mother and brother in trying to take over the stage line operation. Texas Ranger Jim Hartley (Peter Michael) and his Boston businessman brother Tom (Kirk Alyn), the sons of Judith's father's partner, are expected to arrive and help her save the business but when Jim shows up he is murdered by David Patterson. Before dying, Jim tells Gabby to send his badge to Ranger headquarters as Mrs. Patterson orders her sons to rob Tom Hartley. When the stagecoach driver (Hank Bell) is shot during the holdup, Tom faints but is saved by Bill (Elliott), a Texas Ranger working incognito. Bill talks Tom into letting him take over his identity and for him to pretend to be an old childhood friend of Anne's, Tim Jordan. When Slade tries to get Judith's drivers to quit, Bill bests him in a fight and convinces them to stay on the job. Bill and Gabby teach Tom the ways of the west, including self-defense, and when David and Slade try to shoot Bill, they realize he is not the man who fainted when they robbed the stagecoach. Mrs. Patterson enlists the aid of her niece Lola (Nancy Gay), who gets Tom to admit his real identity, and after he puts $30,000 in the stage line safe she asks him to let her put her purse in the safe, not knowing it contains a bomb. John Patterson holds Tom hostage, and Bill and company employee Hank (Kenne Duncan) are knocked out when the safe explodes. David takes the money and murders Hank with Bill being accused of the crime by the sheriff (Tom London). Gabby, who finds Bill's Ranger badge, helps him get away. Thinking Bill has turned on her, Judith agrees to sell her business to Mrs. Patterson, who tells David and John to force Tom to also sign the bill of sale. After getting the truth about the Pattersons from Lola, Bill and Gabby ride to their hideout and save Tom, and he joins them in a shootout with the gang. John Patterson tries to escape but falls off a cliff and Mrs. Patterson, her other son David and their gang are arrested. Judith and Tom plan to marry but Tom faints when his fiancée kisses him.

It is noteworthy that Alice Fleming is cast in the villainous role of Mrs. Patterson since she played Red Ryder's kindly aunt, the Duchess, when Bill Elliott starred in the title role of that series following the end of the Elliott films.

Spencer Gordon Bennet returned to direct the seventh "Wild Bill Elliott" outing, *Mojave Firebrand*, the title referring to the hero's reputation as a peace officer. Issued in March 1944, the feature took place in Arizona in the mid–1870s with the town of Epitaph, which Gabby (Hayes) founded after discovering a rich silver strike, being taken over by crooks Tracy Dalton (LeRoy Mason), Sheriff Barker (Forrest Taylor) and Mayor

Frisbie (Hal Price). Much to Gabby's chagrin, his ward Johnny Taylor (Harry McKim) looks up to Dalton, and when some of the gambler's men, including Red Collins (Bud Geary), try to beat up the religiously devout Gabby, Bill (Elliott) comes to his rescue. After Gabby tells Elliott about the situation in town, Bill asks schoolteacher Abigail Holmes (Anne Jeffreys) to tutor Johnny. Lawman Bill then informs Dalton that he knows he is really outlaw Turkey Dameron and that his man Red tried to kill him but the gambler gives Collins an alibi. In order to clean up the town, Bill tells Gabby and Abigail to have the citizens say they were forced to vote for Frisbie and then request a new election. When Dalton assigns Sheriff Barker to make the mine owners pay protection money, miner Frank Brady (Fred Graham) refuses and Red murders him. At the crime scene, Bill and Gabby find a collection book belonging to Barker that details the miner's protection payments. After Dalton accepts marked money, which he destroys after being seen by Bill, the gambler tries to kill Gabby but the bullet is deflected by his Bible. When enough petitions are collected for a new election, Mayor Frisbie tries to leave the gang and Dalton shoots him. The crime is witnessed by Johnny. Bill and Gabby find the dying mayor who tells them Dalton plans to rob the bank which contains the mine owners' payrolls. The miners aid Bill and Gabby in thwarting the holdup with Dalton, Barker and their gang being arrested. Marshal Tom Scott (Larry Steers), who assigned Bill to clean up Epitaph, takes custody of the prisoners and makes Johnny a deputy sheriff.

Howard Bretherton returned to direct the final "Wild Bill Elliott" outing, *Hidden Valley Outlaws*, which came out in the spring of 1944. Taking place in the post–Civil War southwest, it had a homesteaders group called the "Head Righters" being taken over by crooked lawyer Gilbert Leland (Roy Barcroft), who wants to get all the land around the area of San Pablo. With his cohorts Bannion (Kenne Duncan), Canary (LeRoy Mason), Gridley (Charles Morton) and Coulter (Frank McCarroll) he tries to move in on ranchers, including Clark (Charles Miller). When the rancher orders the gang members off his land, Canary murders him. Since the only witnesses are Clark's grown children, Judy (Anne Jeffreys) and Danny (John James), the court sets the killer free. Danny then shoots Gridley and Coulter as Leland sends for lawmen Bill (Elliott) and Gabby (Hayes) to capture the young man. After Bill and Gabby trail Judy to Danny's hideout, they are followed by Canary who kills Danny. The two lawmen are then arrested by Sheriff McBride (Tom London) for murdering Danny. Ned Murphy (Budd Buster), the foreman of the Clark ranch, wants to lynch them, but when the vigilantes raid the jail, the lawmen escape by wearing masks and infiltrating the group. Judy asks Bill to get rid of the crooked homesteaders and he appeals to the governor (Forbes Murray) who demands an end to vigilantism. Hoping to destroy the vigilantes, Leland has actor Eddie Purchell (Earle Hodgins) file a land claim and then pretend to be murdered. When the sheriff investigates the supposed crime, he locates Bill and Gabby and arrests them for killing both Danny and Purchell. The two make a getaway, find the actor and force him to confess while Judy sells her ranch to the lawyer. As Leland travels by train to the state capitol to register his land claims, he is followed by Canary, who realizes he has been double-crossed. Bill and Gabby follow the two crooks and during a fight Canary falls from the train and dies. Elliott then places Leland under arrest and the ranchers' lands are returned to them.

After the series' end, Republic cast Elliott (still using the screen name Wild Bill Elliott) in the lead role in its new "Red Ryder" (q.v.) series. Gabby Hayes appeared in the first two efforts, *Tucson Raiders* and *Marshal of Reno* (both 1944), before returning the studio's Roy Rogers films, co-starring in 14 of them between 1944 and 1946. In 1944, Hayes was a regular on the ABC radio series "The Andrews Sisters Eight-to-the-Bar Ranch," playing the singing trio's foreman. During the 1946–47 season he was co-starred with Rogers, Dale Evans and the Sons of the Pioneers on NBC's "Saturday Night Roundup" and from 1948 to 1950 he was a regular on "The Roy Rogers Show" on the Mutual network. Over the years, Hayes had appeared in several "A" productions for Republic, including *Dark Command* (1940), *In Old Oklahoma* (1943) and *Tall in the Saddle* (1944). In 1946 he did not renew his studio contract but instead began to freelance, appearing in features such as *Badman's Territory* (1946),

Wyoming (1947), *Albuquerque* (1948), *El Paso* (1949) and *The Cariboo Trail* (1950). From 1950 to 1952 he starred on NBC-TV's *The Gabby Hayes Show*, a weekly series, as well a weekday show on which he featured cowboy movies. Quaker Oats, which sponsored his weekly TV program, did the same with radio's *The Gabby Hayes Show*, which was broadcast by Mutual during the 1951–52 season. Hayes served as guest host on the NBC-TV program *Howdy Doody* in1954 and '55. The actor also had his own comic book series, *Gabby Hayes Western*, which Fawcett published from 1948 to 1953 for a total of 50 issues. Toby Press did one issue of "Gabby Hayes Adventure Comics" in 1953 and the next year Charlton Comics revived *Gabby Hayes Western* for another nine issues until 1957. Hayes retired in the mid–1950s and died in 1969.

After appearing in RKO Radio's *Step Lively* in 1944, Anne Jeffreys left Republic and signed with RKO where she made *Nevada* (1944), *Zombies on Broadway, Those Endearing Young Charms, Sing Your Way Home* (all 1945), *Genius at Work, Step By Step, Dick Tracy vs. Cueball* (all 1946), *Trail Street, Riffraff* (both 1947) and *Return of the Badmen* (1948), which reunited her with Gabby Hayes. After that, she returned to the stage to star in *The Merry Widow, Kiss Me Kate, Street Scene* and *Three Wishes for Jamie*. Perhaps her greatest fame came as Marian Kirby in the NBC-TV series *Topper* (78 episodes in 1955–56), with her husband Robert Sterling, and Leo G. Carroll in the title role. She and Sterling also headlined the 1958 ABC-TV comedy *Love That Jill*. During the 1960s Jeffreys appeared on stage and returned to films in *Boys' Night Out* (1962) and *Panic in the City* (1968), as well as making a recording of "Kismet" for RCA. After that she kept active in the TV soap operas *Bright Promise, The Guiding Light, Finder of Lost Loves* and *General Hospital*. Starting in the 1980s, she became a popular guest at film festivals.

Following the "Red Ryder" series, Elliott went on to star in nine "A" productions for Republic billed as William Elliott (1946 to 1950). After that he signed with Monogram and reverted to his Wild Bill Elliott billing for 11 oaters between 1951 and 1954, the first four coming out under the Monogram banner and then seven Allied Artists releases. In 1951 he also headlined the 15-minute syndicated radio series *Wild Bill Elliott*. From 1950 to 1955 Dell published 18 issues of its *Wild Bill Elliott* comic book. The character was also featured in Dell's *Western Roundup* comic book series from 1952 to 1957.

Filmography

Calling Wild Bill Elliott (Republic, 1943, 55 minutes) Associate Producer: Harry Grey. Director: Spencer [Gordon] Bennet. Screenplay: Anthony Coldeway. Story: Luci Ward. Photography: Ernest Miller. Editor: Edward Schroeder. Music: Mort Glickman. Song: Thomas Haynes Bayly. Art Director: Russell Kimball. Sets: Charles Thompson. Assistant Director: Harry Knight.

Cast: Wild Bill Elliott (Wild Bill Elliott), George "Gabby" Hayes (Gabby Hayes), Anne Jeffreys (Edith Richards), Herbert Heyes (Governor Steven Nichols), Buzzy Henry (Demi-John Culver), Fred Kohler, Jr. (John Culver), Roy Barcroft (Captain Carson), Eve March (Mary Culver), Burr Caruth (Cactus Jim Culver), Bud Geary (Dean), Lynton Brent (Weldon), Al Taylor (Carson), Yakima Canutt, Budd Buster, George Hazel (Militiamen), Hank Bell (Stagecoach Driver), Charles King (Ace), Frank Hagney (Gambler), Forbes Murray (Judge Anson Richards), Bill Nestell (Saloon Customer), Fred Burns (Churchman), Horace B. Carpenter, Rose Plummer (Ranchers), Foxy Callahan, Lew Morphy (Gamblers), Frank McCarroll, Jack Evans, Roy Bucko (Citizens).

The Man from Thunder River (Republic, 1943, 57 minutes) Associate Producer: Harry Grey. Director: John English. Screenplay: J. Benton Cheney. Photography: Bud Thackery. Editor: Harry Keller. Music: Mort Glickman. Art Director: Russell Kimball. Sound: Earl Crain, Sr. Assistant Director: Abe Abrams.

Cast: Wild Bill Elliott (Wild Bill Elliott), George "Gabby" Hayes (Gabby Whittaker), Anne Jeffreys (Nancy Ferguson), Ian Keith (Henry Stevens), John James (Jack Ferguson), Georgie Cooper (Aunt Bess Ferguson), Jack Ingram (Les Foster), Eddie Lee (Wong), Charles King (Peters), Jack Rockwell (Sheriff Thompson), Ed Cassidy (Daniel Bates), Bud Geary (Jason), Roy Brent, Al Taylor (Deputy Sheriffs), Robert Barron (Clerk), Edmund Cobb (Jim), Alan Bridge (Prospector), Jack O'Shea, Curley Dresden, Frank McCarroll (Gang Members).

Working title: *Overland Mail Robbery*.

Bordertown Gun Fighters (Republic, 1943, 56 minutes) Associate Producer: Eddy [Edward J.] White. Director: Howard Bretherton. Screenplay: Norman S. Hall. Photography: Jack Marta. Editor: Richard Van Enger. Music: Mort Glickman. Song: Stephen Foster. Art Director: Russell Kimball. Sound: Dick Tyler. Assistant Director: George Blair.

Cast: Wild Bill Elliott (Wild Bill Elliott), George "Gabby" Hayes (Gabby Hayes), Anne Jeffreys (Anita Shelby), Ian Keith (Cameo Shelby), Harry Woods (Dave Strickland), Edward Earle (Daniel Forrester), Karl Hackett (Frank Holden), Roy Barcroft (Jack Gatling), Bud Geary (Buck Newcombe), Carl Sepulveda (Red Dailey), Charles King (Sheriff Barnes), Charles Sullivan (Grady), Wheaton Chambers (Roland Clark), Jack Kenney (Conductor), Nino Bellini (Croupier), Kenneth Terrell (Stevens), Ben Johnson (Messenger), Budd Buster, Pascale Perry (Saloon Customers), Frank McCarroll (Gang Member), Post Park (Stagecoach Driver), Jack Rockwell, Herman Willingham (Gamblers), Marshall Reed, Neal Hart, Al Haskell, Foxy Callahan, Frosty Royce, Rose Plummer, James Mitchell, Jim Massey, Ralph Bucko (Citizens).

Wagon Tracks West (Republic, 1943, 55 minutes) Associate Producer: Louis Gray. Director: Howard Bretherton. Screenplay: William Lively. Photography: Reggie Lanning. Editor: Charles Craft. Music: Mort Glickman. Art Director: Russell Kimball. Sound: Tom Carman. Assistant Director: Kenneth Holmes.

Cast: Wild Bill Elliott (Wild Bill Elliott), George "Gabby" Hayes (Gabby Whittaker), Tom Tyler (Clawtooth), Anne Jeffreys (Moon Hush), Rick Vallin (Dr. John Fleetwing), Robert Frazer (Robert Warren), Roy Barcroft (Laird), Charles Miller (Chief Brown Bear), Tom London (Lem Martin), Cliff Lyons (Matt), Jack Rockwell (Sheriff Summers), Bill Nestell (Burns), Kenne Duncan (Gregg), J.W. Cody (Blue Feather), Jack Ingram (Joe), Hal Price (Cattleman), Minerva Urecal (Mrs. Perkins), Bryant Washburn (Medical School Superintendent), Roy Butler, Marshall Reed, Frank Ellis, Jack O'Shea, Frank McCarroll, Jack Montgomery, Ben Corbett, Hank Bell (Citizens), Curley Dresden (Blacksmith), Bob Burns, Pascale Perry (Ranchers), Bill Hazlett (Indian), Dick Rush (Hangman), Tom Steele (Rider).

Death Valley Manhunt (Republic, 1943, 55 minutes) Associate Producer: Eddy [Edward J.] White. Director: John English. Screenplay: Norman S. Hall & Anthony Coldeway. Story: Fred Myton & Eddy [Edward J.] White. Photography: Ernest Miller. Editor: Harry Keller. Music: Mort Glickman. Song: James Bland. Art Director: Russell Kimball. Sound: Howard Wilson.

Cast: Wild Bill Elliott (Wild Bill Elliott), George "Gabby" Hayes (Gabby), Anne Jeffreys (Nicky Hobart), Weldon Heyburn (Richard Quinn), Herbert Heyes (Judge Jim Hobart), Davison Clark (Tex Benson), Pierce Lyden (Clayton), Charlie Murray, Jr. (Danny), Jack Kirk (Marshal Hugh Ward), Eddie Phillips (Deputy Marshal Blaine), Bud Geary (Sid Roberts), Al Taylor (Deputy Marshal Lawson), Jesse Graves (Henry), Charles Sullivan (Bartender Ed), Walter McGrail (Richards), Edward Keane (Kingdon Ross), Neal Hart (Neal), Franklyn Farnum (Frank), Frank Ellis (Masked Outlaw), Art Dillard (Deputy Sheriff), Marshall Reed, Kansas Moehring, Silver Harr (Oil Drillers), Curley Dresden (Saloon Customer).

Overland Mail Robbery (Republic, 1943, 56 minutes) Associate Producer: Louis Gray. Director: John English. Screenplay: Bob Williams & Robert Yost. Story: Robert Yost. Photography: John MacBurnie. Editor: Charles Craft. Music: Mort Glickman. Art Director: Fred Ritter. Sound: Earl Crain, Sr. Assistant Director: Joe Dill.

Cast: Wild Bill Elliott (Wild Bill Elliott), George "Gabby" Hayes (Gabby Hayes), Anne Jeffreys (Judith Goodrich), Alice Fleming (Mrs. Patterson), Weldon Heyburn (John Patterson), Kirk Alyn (Tom Hartley/Tim Jordan), Roy Barcroft (David Patterson), Nancy Gay (Lola Patterson), Peter Michael (Jim Hartley), Bud Geary (Slade), Tom London (Sheriff), Jack Kirk (Guard), Kenne Duncan (Hank), Maxine Doyle (Mrs. Bradley), Hank Bell (Murdered Stagecoach Driver), Jack Rockwell, Jack O'Shea, Frank McCarroll (Stage Line Drivers), Diane Henry (Maxine), LeRoy Mason, Frank Ellis (Citizens), Al Taylor, Tom Steele, Cactus Mack, Ray Jones (Gang Members).

Mojave Firebrand (Republic, 1944, 55 minutes) Associate Producer: Eddy [Edward J.] White. Director: Spencer [Gordon] Bennet. Screenplay: Norman S. Hall. Editor: Harry Keller. Music: Mort Glickman. Song: Stephen Foster. Art Director: Fred Ritter. Sound: Fred Stahl. Assistant Director: Joe Dill.

Cast: Wild Bill Elliott (Wild Bill Elliott), George "Gabby" Hayes (Gabby Hayes), Anne Jeffreys (Abigail Holmes), LeRoy Mason (Tracy Dalton/Turkey Dameron), Jack Ingram (Matt Ganton), Harry McKim (Johnny Taylor), Karl Hackett (Luke Reed), Forrest Taylor (Sheriff Barker), Hal Price (Mayor Frisbie), Marshall Reed (Nate Bigelow), Kenne Duncan (Tony Webb), Bud Geary (Red Collins), Jack Kirk (Jeff Butler), Fred Graham (Frank Brady), Tom London (Joshua Henderson), Larry Steers (Marshal Tom Scott), Bud Osborne (Clem Sawyer), Bob Burns (Miner), Horace B. Carpenter (Banker), Jess Cavin, Jack Tornek, Art Dillard (Citizens), Frank Ellis, Silver Harr (Gang Members), Bill Nestell, Tom Smith, Victor Cox (Saloon Customers).

Hidden Valley Outlaws (Republic, 1944, 56 minutes) Associate Producer: Louis Gray. Director: Howard Bretherton. Screenplay: John K. Butler & Bob Williams. Story: John K. Butler. Photography: Reggie Lanning. Editor: Tony Martinelli. Music: Mort Glickman. Song: Stephen Foster. Art Director: Fred Ritter. Sound: Dick [Richard] Tyler. Assistant Director: Harry Knight.

Cast: Wild Bill Elliott (Wild Bill Elliott), George "Gabby" Hayes (Gabby Hayes), Anne Jeffreys (Judy Clark), Roy Barcroft (Gilbert Leland), Kenne Duncan (Ben Bannion), Charles Miller (Daniel Montoya Clark), John James (Danny Clark), Fred Toones (Snowflake), Budd Buster (Ned Murphy), Tom London (Sheriff MacBride), LeRoy Mason (Canary), Earle Hodgins

(Eddie Purchell), Yakima Canutt (Tracy), Jack Kirk (Deputy Sheriff Rawlins), Charles Morton (Gridley), Frank McCarroll (Coulter), Bud Geary (Jackson), Ed Cassidy (Marshal Bud Masterson), Forbes Murray (Governor Walker), Bob [Robert J.] Wilke (Rancher), Frank O'Connor, Tom Smith, Harry Leroy (Train Passengers), Tom Steele (Torrence), Kansas Moehring (Vigilante).

WILD BILL HICKOK

While most western film heroes were fictional, Wild Bill Hickok was a real person whose exploits in the Old West placed him in the category of folk hero. As a result, many of Hickok's deeds, both real and fictional, were embellished for the silver screen. Beginning in the silent days, Hickok was portrayed in a number of feature films and during the sound era he was the subject of a Columbia series starring Bill Elliott. During the 1950s, the *Wild Bill Hickok* television program was so popular that dozens of its episodes were fashioned into 16 features that were released theatrically.

Wild Bill Hickok (1837–76) was born James Butler Hickok in Homer, Illinois. During the Civil War he was a soldier in the Union army, also serving as a spy. When the war ended he became a civilian scout for the military but in 1868 he had to give up the job when he was severely wounded by a Cheyenne warrior's lance. Hickok then parlayed his frontier reputation into a job as sheriff of the cow town of Abilene, Kansas. He fought the lawless in Abilene although he was in reality a trigger-happy gunman and a chronic gambler. After his sheriff's contract in Abilene ended, he wound up in the Black Hills of South Dakota where he supposedly romanced Calamity Jane. He became a western legend in 1876 after being shot in the back by Jack McCall while playing cards.

William S. Hart renewed the lawman's legacy when he portrayed him in the 1923 production *Wild Bill Hickok*; the next year, Jack Padjan played Hickok in the classic *The Iron Horse*, and J. Farrell MacDonald enacted the role in *The Last Frontier* in 1926. In the sound era, Gary Cooper was Hickok in Cecil B. DeMille's *The Plainsman* in 1936. Others playing the part included George Houston in Grand National's *Frontier Scout* (1938), Roy Rogers in *Young Bill Hickok* (1940), Richard Dix in *Badlands of Dakota* (1941), Bruce Cabot in *Wild Bill Hickok Rides Again* (1942), Howard Keel in the musical *Calamity Jane* (1953), Tom Brown in *I Killed Wild Bill Hickok* (1956), Robert Dix in *Deadwood '76* (1965), Don Murray in the 1966 remake of *The Plainsman*, Charles Bronson in *The White Buffalo* (1977) and Jeff Bridges in *Wild Bill* (1995).

Following the success of Gary Cooper's portrayal of Wild Bill Hickok in 1936's *The Plainsman*, Columbia Pictures decided to make a cliffhanger about the lawman's exploits called *The Great Adventures of Wild Bill Hickok*. The studio's fourth chapterplay, it starred little-known Gordon Elliott in the title role and its success launched him on the road to western film stardom. Opinions regarding the serial vary today. Buck Rainey in *Serials and Series: A World Filmography, 1912–1956* said it "is considered by most serial buffs as probably the best of Columbia's chapterplays. Both the budget and production values were above par at Columbia." Don Miller in *Hollywood Corral* (1976) noted that the serial was "riddled with flaws" but added, "[I]t made the right noises." In *The Western* (1983), Phil Hardy opined, "[T]he script is childish, but [Mack V.] Wright and [Sam] Nelson's energetic direction papers over the story's flaws efficiently enough. Even more significantly, Columbia's promotion department got behind the serial. The result was Columbia's first really successful serial outing and the real beginning of Elliott's career in the saddle."

Gordon Elliott (1904–65), née Gordon Nance, was a Missouri native who grew up near the Kansas City stockyards where his father was employed. At an early age he learned to ride, rope and work with cattle and this led to his traveling the rodeo circuit as a young man. Wanting to act, he came to Hollywood in the mid-1920s and began working in films, mainly doing bit roles. He had no trouble making the transition to sound and during the 1930s he was a contract player at Warner Bros. where he appeared in numerous films, eventually playing villains in the Dick Foran series westerns *Moonlight on the Prairie* (1935), *Trailin' West* and *Guns of the Pecos* (both 1936), and continuing as the bad guy in Gene Autry's *Boots and Saddles* (1937) at Republic and *Roll Along, Cowboy* (1937), a 20th Century–Fox oater starring crooner Smith Ballew. Shaving his moustache, Elliott won the title role in *The Great Adventures of Wild Bill Hickok* and thereafter he was a screen hero. In the serial, Elliott used a gimmick that would remain with him for the rest of his cowboy film career: Not only did the wear two guns, he wore them backwards in his holsters.

Jack Fier, who also made many of Charles Starrett's westerns at Columbia, was the producer of *The Great Adventures of Wild Bill Hickok*. The plot had land baron Morrell (Robert Fiske) out to keep cattle from coming into his territory via the Chisholm Trail; he also wants to stop the railroad from reaching Abilene. To carry out his plans he forms the Phantom Raiders, a group of marauders harassing the railroad, cattlemen and settlers. To restore peace to the area, Hickok (Elliott) is made the U.S. marshal and to aid his cause he brings together a group of young boys called the Flaming Arrows, led by Little Brave Heart (Frankie Darro), Buddy (Dickie Jones) and Boots (Sammy McKim). Morrell and his raiders want to stop a major cattle drive and a wagon train, which is led by Kit Lawson (Kermit Maynard), an army scout. After 14 action-filled chapters, Hickok, Lawson and the Flaming Arrows, with the aid of a cavalry detachment, bring Morrell and his Phantom Raiders to justice. This leads to the success of both the cattle drive and the completion of the railroad.

Thanks to the popularity of the cliffhanger, Elliott was signed by Columbia Pictures and his first name was changed from Gordon to Bill. He began his "B" western feature starring career working for producer Larry Darmour, who had previously made oaters for the studio with Ken Maynard, Bob Allen and Jack Luden. Elliott headlined four films for Darmour, *In Early Arizona* and *Frontiers of '49* (both 1938) and *Lone Star Pioneers* and *The Law Comes to Texas* (both 1939), the quartet being based on historical subjects. Following this, Elliott starred in the serial *Overland with Kit Carson* (1939) along with four "Wild Bill Saunders" (q.v.) efforts for producer Leon Barsha. In 1940 the character he played in that series reverted back to the Wild Bill Hickok moniker. Dub Taylor, who had played comedy sidekick Cannonball in the Saunders outings, continued the role in the Hickok features.

The first "Wild Bill Hickok" series film was *Prairie Schooners*, issued in the fall of 1940. Sam Nelson, who had helmed Elliott's Hickok serial, directed this tale of Hickok (Elliott) coming to the aid of rancher Virginia Benton (Evelyn Young) and her foreman Cannonball (Dub Taylor), who are trying to stop homesteaders from hanging money lender Dalton Stull (Kenneth Harlan). Due to drought conditions in Kansas, Stull has been forced to call in the settlers' loans so Hickok tells the people to pay Stull their debts and homestead in Colorado. Virginia urges the settlers to agree and she helps them form a wagon train that Stull and his fur business partner Wolf Tanner (Ray Teal) plan to sabotage. The two give the Pawnee tribe guns so they can attack the wagon train and Virginia is taken prisoner by Dalton. At the Indians' camp, Hickok tries to get Chief Sanche (Jim Thorpe) to stop harassing the settlers but he refuses until Cannonball tells him that Tanner sold guns to an enemy tribe, the Sioux, which used them to attack the Pawnees. Hickok is then able to bring Stull and Tanner to justice and Chief Sanche vows not to molest the wagon train as it crosses his tribe's territory. *Variety* thought it a "rambling, implausible yarn" but noted of star Elliott, "Besides looking like a cowboy, he also is a first-rate thespian," adding, "Dub Taylor, his aide, is effective for comic relief."

Lambert Hillyer directed the next effort, *Beyond the Sacramento*, and he would helm seven more features in the series. Released in November 1940, it told of Cannonball (Dub Taylor) sending for his friend Hickok (Elliott) to come to the town of Lodestone after he recognizes saloon owner Cord Crowley (Bradley Page) and newspaperman Jeff Adams (Frank LaRue) as crooks now using aliases. Hickok tries to get banker Jason Perry

(John Dilson) and his daughter Lynn (Evelyn Keyes) to help him get rid of the two swindlers but Perry refuses to help, claiming the men are honest. Cord tries to force Hickok out of town; Hickok and Cannonball clandestinely put a story in Adams' newspaper about his corrupt past as Shark Lambert. When the story is published, Adams kills himself and Crowley robs the bank and shoots Lynn. The banker, who was really working with Crowley and Adams, sets out to avenge his daughter's injury but the bar owner murders him. Hickok and Crowley then shoot it out in the saloon with Cord being killed. The song "The West Gets Under My Skin" was performed in the feature by Taylor.

The last 1940 series release, *The Wildcat of Tucson*, came out in late December. Here Hickok (Elliott) comes to the aid of his brother Dave (Stanley Brown), a rancher who is jailed for shooting Gus Logan (Sammy Stein) in self-defense, after the gunman tried to throw Seth Harper (Edmund Cobb) off his land. Logan worked for Rance McKee (Kenneth MacDonald) who files homestead claim against area ranchers with the help of Judge Barlow (Ben Taggart). Dave's pal Cannonball (Taylor) breaks him out of jail and sends for Bill Hickok, who goes to his brother's hideout with Vivian Barlow (Evelyn Young), the judge's daughter and Dave's girlfriend. Dave becomes jealous over Vivian and orders his brother to go away. When Rance's gang attacks Harper's ranch, Seth goes after the judge but Hickok stops him from shooting Barlow. Hickok then has the judge make a written confession as to his dishonest dealings with McKee. When Rance finds out, he tells Logan to kill the judge. The next day, Logan instead shoots Dave, who has stopped to apologize to Hickok, and is in turn killed by Cannonball. Hickok is blamed for Logan's death by the U.S. marshal (George Lloyd) as Seth Harper tries to get the locals to oust the judge. Hickok informs them that McKee is behind their troubles, and Harper and the ranchers overpower Rance's gang as Hickok bests McKee in a gunfight. Hickok then rides away, not informing the recovering Dave and Vivian of her father's duplicity.

Director D. Ross Lederman took over for the next outing, *Across the Sierras*, issued in February 1941. It told of ex-convict Mitch Carew (Dick Curtis) coming to Arroyo and killing storekeeper Dan Woodworth (John Dilson), one of the two men responsible for putting him behind bars. He also vows to kill the other man, Hickok (Elliott), who has come to the area with plans to homestead. Hickok stops a mob from hanging his friend Larry Armstrong (Richard Fiske) for cattle rustling and also halts Carew's henchman Stringer (LeRoy Mason) from forcing Mrs. Woodworth (Ruth Robinson), the murdered merchant's widow, to sell his boss her store. Hickok falls in love with her niece Ann (Luana Walters), who is skeptical of his believing in the code of western justice. Hickok tries to dissuade Larry from joining Carew's gang but he does so and takes part in a stagecoach holdup. When Hickok goes to confront Larry at the gang's camp, Stringer shoots at him and Hickok accidentally kills his friend. Grief-stricken, Hickok offers to set aside his guns if Ann will marry him but when he finds out Carew and his men are gunning for him he tells her he must face them. Mitch mistakenly wings Hickok's friend Cannonball (Taylor) and is killed in a shootout with Hickok, who says goodbye to Ann and leaves Arroyo. Two songs, "I Gotta Make Music" and "Honeymoon Ranch," were performed in the feature by Taylor.

Lambert Hillyer came back to direct the next four series entries, beginning with *North from the Lone Star*, which came to theaters at the end of March 1941. Again Hickok (Elliott) is summoned to a frontier town, this time Deadwood, by Cannonball (Taylor), who wants him to help his friend Clint Wilson (Richard Fiske) and his sister Madge (Dorothy Fay). The siblings decide to auction their horse stable and leave Deadwood, which has been taken over by crooked businessman Flash Kirby (Arthur Loft) and his gang. Arriving in town, Bill outbids Kirby's man Rawhide Fenton (Jack Roper) for the stable and the two get into a fight that Hickok wins. When Hickok tries to buy land from Kirby, he is refused, but Flash offers him the job of town marshal, hoping to keep him under his control. At first Hickok declines but after he sees Rawhide trying to force Joan to sell her business, he agrees to serve as the town's lawman. When Clint shoots Spike (Chuck Morrison), one of Kirby's men, Hickok puts him in jail and Joan tries to get the locals to help her set her brother free. Hickok stops the crowd and then has Cannonball escort Clint out of town while he closes down Kirby's crooked gambling tables at his saloon and arrests Rawhide, who tries to stop him. When Flash finds out that his gambling operations have been closed and Rawhide is behind bars, he orders Hickok to leave town but Cannonball arrives with the news that Clint Wilson has gotten away from him. Lucy Belle (Claire Rochelle), a dance hall girl in love with Hickok, warns him that Kirby, her boss, plans to ambush him at Wilson's stables. Hickok knocks out Clint, who believes that the sheriff is in cahoots with the crooks, and leaves him with Lucy Belle as he and Cannonball go to a showdown with Kirby and his men. Coming to, Clint is apprised of Hickok's honesty by Lucy Belle, and he runs to join Hickok and Cannonball but is wounded by Kirby, whom he kills. The gang surrenders and Hickok makes Cannonball the new sheriff before leaving Deadwood. Two songs by Taylor, "Of Course, It's Your Horse" and "Saturday Night in San Antone," slowed up the film's action.

Hands Across the Border, which came to theaters in June 1941, found Hickok (Elliott) involved in a dispute between crook Juno Jessup (Kenneth MacDonald) and cowpoke Johnny Peale (Stanley Brown) over Marsha Crawley (Mary Daily), the niece of brothers Rufe (Frank LaRue), Dade (Donald Curtis) and Hi (Tom Moray) Crawley. Juno wants to marry the girl in order to keep her quiet since she saw him murder Cannonball's (Taylor) father, and he offers the siblings $2,000 if they will agree to the nuptials. Coming to the town of Independence by stagecoach are Cannonball and his pal Hickok; during the trip, Hickok recognizes one of the passengers, outlaw Cash Jennings (Hugh Prosser), and hands him over to the law. In town, Hickok and Cannonball stop Rufe from abusing Marsha with his riding crop when he sees her ride into town with Johnny. Rufe then claims that Peale kidnapped his niece and has the marshal (Slim Whitaker) arrest him as Marsha is taken back to the Crawley cabin. Hickok pretends to be a lawyer in order to defend Johnny, who will not talk to him; when he and Cannonball try to see Marsha, they are run off by the Crowley brothers. The next day Hickok argues Johnny's case before an armed judge (Eddy Waller) and after Rufe testifies that Peale kidnapped his niece, Bill has the girl examined and gives the court proof it was Rufe's riding crop that caused her scars. The judge drops the charges against Johnny and orders Rufe to prison for ten years for lying under oath. When Hickok asks the judge to put Jessup on trial for murdering Cannonball's father, Juno tries to run away but is shot by Hickok. As Marsha and Johnny plan to wed, Hickok and Cannonball head out to recapture Cash Jennings, who escaped from jail. Two silly songs were performed by Taylor during the proceedings, "Ro-Ro-Rollin'" and "While the Stage Went Bumpin' Along."

The series got a boost with its next entry, *King of Dodge City*, when Tex Ritter joined Elliott as co-star. Ritter had already starred in over 30 westerns for Grand National and Monogram and his popularity added to the series' appeal. Another plus was Tex's singing, which added authenticity to the western songs he performed. As a result of his joining the Hickok series, Ritter returned to the *Motion Picture Herald*'s annual list of the top ten money-making stars, joining Elliott on the honor roll.

Released in August 1941, *King of Dodge City* had Abilene crook Morgan King (Guy Usher) trying to take over Kansas after its admission to the Union. Stephen Kimball (Harrison Greene) puts together a citizen's group to oppose King and he makes Hickok (Elliott) a special agent in charge of compiling information on the crook's illegal actions. Riding into town looking for the man who stole his horse, cowboy Tex Rawlings (Ritter) is appointed the new sheriff by Judge Lynch (Rick Anderson) after he stops a gunfight in which his predecessor (Ed Coxen) was killed. Hickok arrives in Abilene to meet with blacksmith Cannonball (Taylor), who is allied with Kimball, and stops Reynolds (Pierce Lyden) and Carney (Francis Walker), two of King's henchmen, from ambushing Tex. King wants to make Reynolds the new lawman but Tex refuses to give up the job as Hickok entrusts Cannonball with his credentials. When bank customer Thomas Samuels (Steve Clark) is murdered, Hickok tells Tex that King is to blame but the sheriff does not believe him. Hickok and Cannonball secretly examine the records in King's bank and see he is embezzling customers' deposits. Hickok then has Cannonball spread the rumor that the bank is insolvent and has bank teller Carruthers (Kenneth Harlan) put in jail for his own protection. When Tex finds out about the rumor, he arrests Hickok and put him in a cell next to Carruthers, who is murdered, with Hickok being blamed. Cannonball tells Judge Lynch about Bill's credentials, which he thought were stolen by Reynolds and Carney, but he cannot prove his claims due to Kimball's sudden demise from natural causes. Breaking Hickok out of jail, Cannonball finds the authorization letter from Kimball and shows it to the judge and Tex. Tex then joins forces with Hickok and the two stop the outlaws in a showdown, with Hickok killing Morgan King. Hickok and Tex agree to combat lawlessness in other towns. Ritter sang the Johnny Marvin tunes, "Empty Chair," "The Horse Thief Song" and "The Trail That Leads Home."

Next came *Roaring Frontiers*, released in the fall of 1941. In it Frank Mitchell replaced Dub Taylor as Cannonball; he would stay in the part for the remainder of the series. The storyline had the mayor of Gold Field murdered and his son, Tex Rawlings (Ritter), vowing revenge. The chief suspect is the town's new mayor, gang leader Hawk Hammond (Bradley Page), and when he and Tex fight in Hammond's Golden Nugget Saloon, the sheriff (George Eldredge) is shot and Tex is arrested for murder. He escapes into the hills and Hickok (Elliott) takes over as the town's lawman, stopping Knuckles (Joe McGuinn), one of Hawk's men, from shooting a prospector, Cannonball (Mitchell). When Hickok convinces Tex to return to Gold Field and face trial, Hammond tries to rig the court and jury, and his gang shoots Tex while he is in jail; the injured man escapes with Hickok's help. They board a stagecoach and at a rest stop one of the passengers, ticket agent Reba Bailey (Ruth Ford), tends to Tex's wound. Tex then accuses another passenger, Flint Adams (Tristram Coffin), of murdering the sheriff and he makes a getaway; Hickok and Tex follow him back to town. There they shoot it out with the outlaws with Tex killing Hammond and Adams. As Hickok leaves town, Tex is sworn in as the new mayor. In this one, Ritter performed another trio of tunes composed by crooner Johnny Marvin, "Jail House Hanging Song," "Oh, You've Got to Come and Get Me" and "A Part of the West."

Wallace Fox took over as the director of the next two entries, *The Lone Star Vigilantes* and *Bullets for Bandits*. The former, issued early in 1942, began with Hickok (Elliott), Tex (Ritter) and Cannonball (Mitchell), members of the Confederate Army, returning home to Texas at the end of the Civil War and being ambushed by their former commanding officer, Colonel Sam Monroe (Budd Buster), who mistook them for Yankees. Realizing his mistake, Monroe invites the trio to his ranch where lives with his daughter Shary (Virginia Carpenter). When they find out Monroe's horses have been rustled, the three ex–Confederates go with him to Mexico to recover them and there they engage in a gun battle with the rustlers, Cobb (Edmund Cobb) and Benson (Ethan Laidlaw). During the fracas, the colonel is wounded; they take him to Dr. Banning (Forrest Taylor), who was run out of Texas with his daughter Marcia (Luana Walters) by Monroe. The doctor and Marcia go back with the four men to the town of Winchester, which they find under the control of Major Harlan Clark (Gavin Gordon) and his State Police, whose ranks include Cobb and Benson. Clark levies heavy taxes on the area ranchers and when they cannot pay he confiscates their cattle. Marcia, who wants revenge for the treatment previously given her father, joins forces with Clark in return for gold. The disgruntled locals aid Tex in forming a vigilante group while Hickok rides to a nearby army post with information revealing Clark to be an imposter and a wanted outlaw. Going back to get proof about Clark, Hickok finds Tex is jail and the colonel murdered. Hickok suspects Marcia of helping the police break up the vigilante meeting and tells her he plans another one to recruit men to break Tex and his cohorts out of jail. Marcia takes the news to Clark who sends his gang to the meeting while Hickok frees Tex and the other captives. Hickok then makes Peabody (Lowell Drew), a carpetbagger in league with Clark, confess that the major is a criminal and they take the evidence to the army post. After telling Clark about the jailbreak, Marcia is killed when she gets caught between his men and the ranchers. Hickok and Tex return to town with the cavalry and Clark and his outlaws are arrested. Hickok, Tex and Cannonball then decide to become Texas Rangers. Two Johnny Marvin songs, "Headin' Home to Texas" and "The Moon is Shining on the Old Corral," were sung in the film by Ritter.

Bullets for Bandits, which came out in February 1942, was filmed at Corriganville with actor Lane Bradford, the son of genre villain John Merton, as Elliott's stunt double. The feature offered Ritter a chance to perform another trio of Johnny Marvin tunes, "Reelin,' Rockin,' Rollin Down the Trail," "Somewhere on the Lone Prairie" and "With My Boots on When I Die." The plot had Cannonball (Mitchell) asking Sheriff Tex Martin (Ritter) to help him find Prince Katey (Elliott), who has been missing for many years. Prince is the son of Cannonball's boss, elderly ranch owner Queen Katey (Edythe Elliott), whose range is sought by crook Clem Jeeter (Ralph Theodore), the man who, years before, branded Prince. When Hickok (Elliott) sees a man with a brand on his arm cheat at cards, he steps in and the two have a gunfight with the gambler being killed. Cannonball mistakes Hickok for Prince and the two ride out of town while the sheriff deduces the gambler was shot twice, once in the front by Hickok and again in the back. Hickok goes with Cannonball to Queen's ranch, where the old woman accepts him as her son, while Beetle (Joe McGuinn), who fired the shot that killed the gambler, tells Jeeter that Prince is out of the way. Jeeter then gets a court order to become the old woman's guardian, but Hickok defies him and the two fight. While looking for Hickok, Sheriff Martin rides by a burned house belonging to Bert Brown (Forrest Taylor) and his daughter Dakota (Dorothy Short) and they tell him Queen's men destroyed their homestead. Jeeter tells the sheriff that Hickok is a fake, something Queen also comes to realize, but having learned to trust Hickok she informs him that Jeeter ordered the destruction of the Browns' property in order to blame her so the locals would become her enemies. Tex meets with Hickok who agrees to turn himself in. Beetle tries to shoot the lawman, who thinks his assailant was Hickok. When he finds out that Hickok is innocent, Martin joins forces with him to find the murderer. At Queen's ranch, Jeeter and his men try to murder Hickok but the old lady starts shooting at the outlaws as Cannonball goes for the law. The posse arrives at the ranch with Cannonball, surrounding Jeeter and his gang, who are forced to surrender. Hickok then rides off knowing Dakota will care for Queen as Tex takes the crooks to jail.

Lambert Hillyer returned to direct the final two "Wild Bill Hickok" series films, *The Devil's Trail*, issued in May 1942, and *Prairie Gunsmoke*, which came out in July. The former had its basis in the "Bloody Kansas" confrontation over slavery and free soil in its tale of a group called the Broken U, formed by crook Buck McQuade (Noah Beery, Sr.) to keep settlers out of the territory so it will become a slave state. Marshal Tex Martin (Ritter) runs into the group when he is shot at while camping for the night. In the town of

Poster for *Bullets for Bandits* (Columbia, 1942).

Tiburon, wanted outlaw Hickok (Elliott) learns of the gang from blacksmith Dawson (Paul Newlan), who is a member. In the local saloon, Ella (Ruth Ford), who works for McQuade, claims Hickok is not loyal to the slavery cause and he learns that several free state proponents, including Cannonball (Mitchell), Dr. Willoughby (Joel Friedkin) and his daughter Myra (Eileen O'Hearn), are kept under house arrest by Buck's gang. When McQuade's henchman Randall (Joe McGuinn) tries to beat up Cannonball, Hickok stops him and is stabbed. Ella takes him to Dr. Willoughby for treatment and Myra scolds him for being loyal to the slave-holding interests. Denying the charges, Hickok offers to free the locals who oppose McQuade in order to prove his innocence. Wanting to get rid of Hickok, Buck sends him to guard a pass and later turns him over to Tex, who has a warrant for his arrest. When Tex refuses to believe Hickok's story about the Broken U, Cannonball jumps him and the two leave the star packer tied up. After escaping, the sheriff warns McQuade about Hickok but Buck decides to get the lawman out of the way and the doctor tells his daughter to warn Tex. Ella tries to set a trap for Tex by telling him to meet Hickok at a remote cabin, but Myra warns him and he escapes. Myra then rides with Tex to the cave where Hickok and Cannonball have taken refuge. When Buck's gunman Howland (Edmund Cobb), who followed them, tries to kill the sheriff, he is shot by Hickok. Hickok, Tex, Cannonball and Myra ride back to Tiburon to free the girl's father and there a shootout takes place with Buck and his men, with Ella being killed. Since they are running low on bullets, Hickok and Tex start a fire and cease firing. When McQuade and his men go after them, they are shot. In this one, Ritter did two more Johnny Marvin compositions, "Hi Diddle Dum Diddle Um Diddle Ay" and "When the Sun Goes Down."

The final series entry, *Prairie Gunsmoke*, had Dan Whipple (Rick Anderson) murdered by Jim Kelton (Tristram Coffin) and Spike Allen (Joe McGuinn), who steal the money he had to pay off his mortgage to Kelton and a pair of custom-made gun handles. In reaction to Whipple's slaying, his neighbor Henry Wade (Hal Price) and daughter Lucy Wade (Virginia Carroll) hold a ranchers' meeting attended by Tex Terrell (Ritter) and his pal Cannonball (Mitchell). When Hickok (Elliott) shows up, the ranchers think he is Kelton's hired gun. Jim offers to pay Hickok to get Tex to sell his land. Hickok investigates and finds out both Whipple and Terrell's properties are near an old mine where he finds a rich vein of ore. Hickok returns to town and forces Kelton into making him a partner as Tex stops the outlaw gang from burning down Wade's barn. Cannonball tells Tex some men are killing his cattle and when he rides away, Allen knocks out Cannonball and abducts Wade. When Lucy goes for help, she is captured by the gang and taken to the Whipple ranch. Tex goes to have a showdown with Kelton as Hickok rifles the bad man's office and finds the gun handles stolen from Dan Whipple. Hearing Spike tell Jim about Lucy being at the Whipple place, Hickok then shows Tex the gun handles and tells him that Whipple was his uncle. Hickok sets Wade free as Tex rides to the Whipple ranch where he and Lucy are surrounded by Kelton and his men. Just as Jim is about to dynamite the ranch house, Hickok stops him and, after defeating him in a fight, makes Kelton confess to his uncle's killing. Two more Johnny Marvin songs were sung in the feature by Ritter, "Someone" and "Where the Buffalo Roam."

Following the demise of the "Wild Bill Hickok" series, Elliott and Ritter made two more features for Columbia, *North of the Rockies* and *Vengeance of the West*, both 1942 releases directed by Lambert Hillyer. After that, Ritter went to Universal where he made 11 features, seven with Johnny Mack Brown, before replacing Jim Newill in PRC's "Texas Rangers" (q.v.) series. After starring in the 1942 serial *The Valley of Vanishing Men*, Elliott left Columbia and signed with Republic where he headlined in eight features in the studio's "Wild Bill Elliott" (q.v.) series, playing a character of the same name.

Nine years after the end of the Columbia series, the legendary lawman came to television in *The Adventures of Wild Bill Hickok*, starring Guy Madison in the title role and Andy Devine as his hefty sidekick Jingles P. Jones. Made by William F. Broidy Productions, the series was syndicated from 1951 to 1956; it was also telecast on CBS-TV from 1955 to 1958 and on ABC-TV during the 1957–58 season. A total of 113 half-hour episodes were filmed, 61 in black and white and 52 in color. After 100 episodes were made, production on the series was halted in 1957 due to Broidy's fatal illness. The next year, Screen Gems filmed another 13 episodes. The series was done at various locales, including Corriganville, the Iverson Ranch and Melody Ranch. From 1951 to 1953, David Sharpe served as Guy Madison's stunt double. He was followed by several other stuntman, including Richard Farnsworth, who worked on the series during the 1955–56 season. The horse ridden by Hickok in the series was called Buckshot while Jingles' mount was named Joker.

The Adventures of Wild Bill Hickok was such a success that a merchandising campaign was launched; among the items offered were toys, cereal box-top premiums, puzzles, lunch boxes, clothes, belts, records and the Wild Bill Hickok and Jingles Official Diamond Cowboy Outfit, which included a holster with two toy guns. There were also children's books like Elf's *Wild Bill Hickok and Deputy Marshal Joey* (1954) and *Wild Bill Hickok and the Indians* (1956), both written by Ethel B. Stone, and the Wonder publication *Wild Bill Hickok* (1956) by Felix Sutton. In addition, the show's popularity spawned a radio series called "Wild Bill Hickok" which was broadcast on the Mutual network from the spring of 1951 through December 1954. Madison and Devine repeated their TV roles in over 270 episodes of the series that was initially broadcast on Sunday and from 1952 to 1954 on Wednesday and Friday, with repeats on Monday.

Madison (1922–96) had been a matinee idol in the late 1940s and playing Wild Bill Hickok rejuvenated his career. Born Robert Moseley, Madison was a California native who first gained attention in a small but flashy role in *Since You Went Away* (1944). After military service he starred in features like *Till the End of Time* (1946), *Honeymoon* (1947) and *Massacre River* (1949). During the production of the Hickok series he also starred in such films as *The Charge at Feather River* (1953), *The Command* (1954), *The Last Frontier* (1955), *Hilda Crane* (1956) and *Bullwhip* (1958). In the early 1960s he relocated in Europe where he headlined a variety of feature films for a decade, including several westerns. Devine (1905–77) was born Jeremiah Schwartz in Arizona and after playing football in college came to Hollywood in the mid–1920s. With the coming of sound films he became an in-demand character actor. Besides playing Jingles on the Hickok series, he also starred in *Andy's Gang* (NBC-TV, 1955–60).

Due to the popularity of *The Adventures of Wild Bill Hickok*, 16 theatrical feature films were made up of episodes culled from the series (the advertising did not refer to their small screen origins). Each telefeature contained two series segments and were released in batches of four from 1952 through 1955. In November 1952, Monogram issued *Behind Southern Lines, Ghost of Crossbones Canyon, Trail of the Arrow* and *Yellow Haired Kid*. Within the year the Monogram logo was phased out and was replaced by Allied Artists, and they released *Border City Rustlers, Secret of Outlaw Flats, Six Gun Decision* and *Two Gun Marshal* in November 1953. Thirteen months later the studio had *Marshals in Disguise, Outlaw's Son, Trouble on the Trail* and *Two Gun Teacher* in theaters. The final batch, *Match-Making Marshal, Phantom Trails, Timber Country Trouble* and *The Titled Tenderfoot*, were released in April 1955.

Guy Madison as "Wild Bill Hickok."

Filmography

The Great Adventures of Wild Bill Hickok (Columbia, 1938, 15 Chapters) Producer: Jack Fier. Associate Producer: Harry S. Webb. Directors: Sam Nelson & Mack V. Wright. Screenplay: G.A. Durlam, Dallas Fitzgerald, Tom Gibson, Charles Arthur Powell & George Rosener. Story: John Peere Miles. Photography: Benjamin H. Kline & George Meehan. Editor: Richard Fantl. Sound: George Cooper & Lambert Day. Assistant Directors: Milton Carter & Thomas Flood.

Cast: Gordon [Bill] Elliott (Wild Bill Hickok), Monte Blue (Mr. Cameron), Carole Wayne (Ruth Cameron), Frankie Darro (Jerry/Little Brave Heart), Dickie Jones (Buddy), Sammy McKim (Boots), Kermit Maynard (Kit Lawson), Roscoe Ates (Snake Eyes Smith), Reed Hadley (Jim Blakely), Monte Collins (Danny), Chief Thunder Cloud (Chief Gray Eagle), [Ray] Mala (Little Elk), Robert Fiske (Morrell), Walter Wills (Joshua Bruce), J.P. McGowan (Scudder), Eddy Waller (Stone), Jack Perrin (Breen), Edmund Cobb (Sam), Art Mix (Dolan), George Chesebro (Deputy Sheriff Metaxa), Ernie Adams (Professor), Earle Hodgins (Editor Kimball), Edward Hearn (Tom Stedman), William Gould (J.W. Johnson), Ed Brady (Station Agent Wilson), Al Bridge (Blackie), Frank Lackteen (The Vulture), Jesse Graves (Jasper), Charles Brinley (Reardon), Allan Cavan (Colonel Roberts), Buck Connors (Parson), Earl Dwire (Jenkins), Kenne Duncan (Blacksmith), Hal Taliaferro [Wally Wales] (Talkative Citizen), Jack Evans (Riddle), Ethan Laidlaw (Stagecoach Guard Williams), Tom London (Kilgore), Blackie Whiteford (Moran), Ted Mapes (Brown), Artie Ortego (Silver Cloud), Slim Whitaker (Cactus), Lee Phelps (Blacksmith Gally), Frank Ellis (Carter), Robert Walker (Morton), David McKim (Billy), George Morrell (Harrington), Hank Bell (Clerk), Walter Miller, Lew Meehan, Bill Patton, Gene Alsace, Ray Jones, Art Dillard, Ray Henderson, Curley Dresden, Herman Hack, Chick Hannon, Carl Mathews, Bud McClure, Julian Rivero, Jack Montgomery, Blackjack Ward (Gang Members), Francis Walker, Dick Botiller, Al Haskell, Augie Gomez, Jim Corey, Bob Burns, Joe McGuinn, Tex Palmer (Phantom Raiders), Silver Tip Baker (Abilene Citizen), Budd Buster, Al Thompson, Art Fowler (Citizens), Bruce Lane (Lieutenant), Jack Rockwell (Sheriff), Richard Cramer (Apache Killer), Tom Steele (Trail Driver), Horace B. Carpenter (Texan), Steve Clark (Outrider), A.R. Haysel (Bartender), Iron Eyes Cody (Warrior), Chuck Hamilton (Saloon Customer).

Chapter titles: 1) Law of the Gun; 2) Stampede!; 3) Blazing Terror; 4) Mystery Canyon; 5) Flaming Brands; 6) The Apache Killer; 7) Prowling Wolves; 8) The Pit; 9) Ambushed!; 10) Savage Vengeance; 11) Burning Waters; 12) Desperation; 13) Phantom Bullets; 14) The Lure; 15) Trail's End.

Prairie Schooners (Columbia, 1940, 58 minutes) Producer: Leon Barsha. Executive Producer: Irving Briskin. Director: Sam Nelson. Screenplay: Fred Myton & Robert Lee Johnson, from the story "Into the Crimson West" by George Cory Franklin. Photography: George Meehan. Editor: Al Clark. Assistant Director: Thomas Flood.

Cast: Bill Elliott (Wild Bill Hickok), Evelyn Young (Virginia Benton), Dub Taylor (Cannonball), Kenneth Harlan (Dalton Stull), Ray Teal (Wolf Tanner), Bob Burns (Jim Gibbs), Netta Packer (Cora Gibbs), Richard Fiske (Adams), Edmund Cobb (Blacksmith Rusty), Jim Thorpe (Chief Sanche), Sammy Stein (Dude Getter), Ned Glass (Skinny Hutch), Lucien Maxell (Indian Boy), Lee Shumway (Gambler), Merrill McCormick (Mack), George Morrell, Bud McClure (Settlers), Art Dillard, Blackjack Ward (Gang Members), Jim Corey (Farmer).

Beyond the Sacramento (Columbia, 1940, 58 minutes) Producer: Leon Barsha. Executive Producer: Irving Briskin. Director: Lambert Hillyer. Screenplay: Luci Ward. Photography: George Meehan. Editor: James Sweeney. Music Director: Morris Stoloff. Sound: Ed Bernds. Assistant Director: Thomas Flood.

Cast: Bill Elliott (Wild Bill Hickok), Evelyn Keyes (Lynn Perry), Dub Taylor (Cannonball), John Dilson (Jason Perry), Bradley Page (Cord Crowley/Mark Bradley), Frank LaRue (Jeff Adams/Shark Lambert), Norman Willis (Nelson), Steve Clark (Curley Wollson), Jack Clifford (Sheriff), Don Beddoe (Warden McKay), Harry Balley (Merchant), Art Mix, Blackjack Ward (Gang Members), Bud Osborne (Joe), George McKay (Bartender George), Jack Low (Prison Guard), Olin Francis (Tom Jimson), Clem Horton (Barlow), Ned Glass (Bank Teller), Chick Hannon (Gambler), Eddie Laughton, George Morrell, Tex Phelps, Jack Tornek (Citizens), Tex Cooper (Stagecoach Driver Tex), Tom Moray (Saloon Customer).

Working title: *Ghost Guns*; British title: *Power of Justice*.

The Wildcat of Tucson (Columbia, 1940, 59 minutes) Producer: Leon Barsha. Executive Producer: Irving Briskin. Director: Lambert Hillyer. Screenplay: Fred Myton. Photography: George Meehan. Editor: Charles Nelson. Sound: George Cooper. Assistant Director: Milton Carter.

Cast: Bill Elliott (Wild Bill Hickok), Evelyn Young (Vivian Barlow), Stanley Brown (Dave Hickok), Dub Taylor (Cannonball), Kenneth MacDonald (Rance McKee), Ben Taggart (Judge John Barlow), Edmund Cobb (Seth Harper), George Lloyd (U.S. Marshal Jim), Sammy Stein (Gus Logan), Francis Walker (Butch), Robert Winkler (Bobby), Forrest Taylor (Editor Charlie), Murdock MacQuarrie (Doctor), George Chesebro (Bart), Jim Corey (Jim), Archie Ricks (Archie), Steve Clark, Bob Burns (Ranchers), John Daheim, Art Dillard, Ray Jones, Newt Kirby, Bert Young (Gang Members), Dorothy Andre (Citizen).

Working title: *Cimarron Trail*; British title: *Promise Fulfilled*.

Across the Sierras (Columbia, 1941, 57 minutes) Producer: Leon Barsha. Executive Producer: Irving Briskin. Director: D. Ross Lederman. Screenplay: Paul Franklin. Photography: George Meehan. Editor: James Sweeney. Songs: Milton Drake. Sound: Frank Goodwin. Assistant Director: Milton Carter.

Cast: Bill Elliott (Wild Bill Hickok), Luana Walters (Ann Woodworth), Richard Fiske (Larry Armstrong), Dub Taylor (Cannonball), Dick Curtis (Milt Carew), Milt Kibbee (Sheriff), LeRoy Mason (Stringer), Ruth Robinson (Lu Woodworth), John Dilson (Dan Woodworth), Ralph Peters (Hobie), Eddie Laughton (Ed), Carl Knowles (Woody), Tom London (Hopkins), Jim Pierce (Wilson), Eddie [Edmund] Cobb (Mac Fawcett), Art Mix (Stagecoach Driver Ed), Ed Coxen (Doctor), Lew Meehan (Bartender), Blackjack Ward (Blackjack), Curley Dresden, Rube Dalroy, Tex Cooper, Jack Tornek (Citizens).

British title: *Welcome Stranger*.

North From the Lone Star (Columbia, 1941, 58 minutes) Producer: Leon Barsha. Executive Producer: Irving Briskin. Director: Lambert Hillyer. Screenplay: Charles Francis Royal. Photography: Benjamin Kline. Editor: Mel Thorsen. Songs: Milton Drake. Art Director: Perry Smith. Assistant Director: Bud Brill.

Cast: Bill Elliott (Wild Bill Hickok), Richard Fiske (Clint Wilson), Dorothy Fay (Madge Wilson), Dub Taylor (Cannonball), Arthur Loft (Edward "Flash" Kirby), Jack Roper (Rawhide Fenton), Chuck Morrison (Spike), Claire Rochelle (Lucy Belle), Al Rhein (Slats), Edmund Cobb (Dusty Daggett), Hank Bell (Bartender), Art Mix, Dick Botiller, Steve Clark (Gang Members), Francis Walker (Brawler), Lane Bradford, Oscar Gahan, Ray Jones, Jack Evans, Barney Beasley, Joe Garcia, Clem Horton (Saloon Customers), George Morrell, Tex Cooper (Citizens).

Hands Across the Rockies (Columbia, 1941, 56 minutes) Producer: Leon Barsha. Executive Producer: Irving Briskin. Director: Lambert Hillyer. Screenplay: Paul Franklin, from the story "A Gunsmoke Case for Major Cain" by Norbert Davis. Photography: Benjamin Kline. Editor: Mel Thorsen. Sound: Ed Bernds. Assistant Director: Milton Carter.

Cast: Bill Elliott (Wild Bill Hickok), Mary Daily (Marsha Crawley), Dub Taylor (Cannonball Taylor), Kenneth MacDonald (Juno Jessup), Frank LaRue (Rufe Crawley), Donald Curtis (Dade Crawley), Tom Moray (Hi Crawley), Stanley Brown (Johnny Peale), Slim Whitaker (Sheriff Bemis), Harrison Greene (Abel Finney), Art Mix (Red), Eddy Waller (Judge Plunkett), Hugh Prosser (Cash Jennings), Edmund Cobb (Ranger), John Tyrrell (Stagecoach Passenger), George Morrell (Jury Foreman), Eddie Laughton (Court Clerk), Ethan Laidlaw (Bartender), George Chesebro, Buck Moulton, Tex Cooper (Jurors), Kathryn Bates (Carrie), Curley Dresden (Gang Member).

King of Dodge City (Columbia, 1941, 62 minutes) Producer: Leon Barsha. Executive Producer: Irving Briskin. Director: Lambert Hillyer. Screenplay: Gerald Geraghty. Photography: Benjamin Kline. Editor: Jerome Thoms. Songs: Johnny Marvin. Art Director: Arthur Royce. Sound: Tom Lambert. Assistant Director: Milton Carter.

Cast: Bill Elliott (Wild Bill Hickok), Tex Ritter (Tex Rawlings), Judith Linden (Janice Blair), Dub Taylor (Cannonball Taylor), Guy Usher (Morgan King), Rick Anderson (Judge Lynch), Kenneth Harlan (Jeff Carruthers), Pierce Lyden (Reynolds), Francis Walker (Carney), Harrison Greene (Stephen Kimball), Jack Rockwell (Martin), Russ Powell (Merchant), Frosty Royce, Tex Cooper (Citizens), George Chesebro, Tristram Coffin, Edmund Cobb (Gamblers), Jack Ingram (Bill Lang), Steve Clark (Thomas Samuels), Ed Coxen (Sheriff Daniels), Lee Prather (Wilson), Ned Glass (Bank Teller), Jay Lawrence (Mitchell).

Roaring Frontiers (Columbia, 1941, 61 minutes) Producer: Leon Barsha. Executive Producer: Irving Briskin. Director: Lambert Hillyer. Screenplay: Robert Lee Johnson. Photography: Benjamin Kline. Editor: Mel Thorsen. Songs: Johnny Marvin. Sound: Frank Goodwin. Assistant Director: Milton Carter.

Cast: Bill Elliott (Wild Bill Hickok), Tex Ritter (Tex Rawlings), Ruth Ford (Reba Bailey), Frank Mitchell (Cannonball), Bradley Page (Hawk Hammond), Tristram Coffin (Flint Adams), Hal Taliaferro [Wally Wales] (Link Twiddle), Francis Walker (Boot Hill), Joe McGuinn (Knuckles), George Chesebro (Red Thompson), Charles Stevens (Moccasin), Rick Anderson (Pewitt), Hank Bell, Fred Burns (Stagecoach Drivers), Steve Clark (Stagecoach Guard), George Eldredge (Sheriff), Lew Meehan, Jim Corey, Dick Botiller, George Hazel, Tom Moray, Clem Horton, Earl Gunn (Gang Members), Ernie Adams (Jailer), Sammy Stein (Bad Guy), Jess Cavin (Saloon Customer), Tex Cooper (Citizen).

The Lone Star Vigilantes (Columbia, 1942, 57 minutes) Producer: Leon Barsha. Executive Producer: Irving Briskin. Director: Wallace Fox. Screenplay: Luci Ward. Photography: Benjamin Kline. Editor: Mel Thorsen. Songs: Johnny Marvin. Art Director: Perry Smith. Sound: Jack Haines. Assistant Director: Milton Carter.

Cast: Bill Elliott (Wild Bill Hickok), Tex Ritter (Tex Martin), Frank Mitchell (Cannonball Boggs), Virginia Carpenter (Shary Monroe), Luana Walters (Marcia Banning), Budd Buster (Colonel Sam Monroe), Forrest Taylor (Dr. Mark Banning), Gavin Gordon (Major Harlan Clark), Lowell Drew (Peabody), Edmund Cobb (Sergeant Charlie Cobb), Ethan Laidlaw (Benson), Rick Anderson (Lige Miller), Eddie Laughton (Matson), John Tyrrell (Nolan), Buel Bryant (Skinner), Francis Walker (Kellogg), Steve Clark (Jones), Charles Hamilton (Hawkins), Dick Botiller (Pedro), Paul McVey (Colonel Knapp).

Working title: *Law of the Winchester*; British title: *The Devil's Price*.

Bullets for Bandits (Columbia, 1942, 55 minutes) Producer: Leon Barsha. Executive Producer: Irving Briskin. Director: Wallace Fox. Screenplay: Robert Lee Johnson. Photography: George Meehan. Editor: Mel Thorsen. Songs: Johnny Marvin. Art Director: Perry Smith. Sound: Frank Goodwin. Assistant Director: Milton Carter.

Cast: Bill Elliott (Wild Bill Hickok), Tex Ritter (Tex Martin), Frank Mitchell (Cannonball), Dorothy Short (Dakota Brown), Ralph Theodore (Clem Jeeter), Edythe Elliott (Queen Katey), Forrest Taylor (Bert Brown), Joe McGuinn (Beetle), Tom Moray (Whip), Art Mix (Spur), Hal Taliaferro [Wally Wales] (Gaming Attendant), Eddie Laughton (Bartender), John Tyrrell, Bud Osborne (Cowboys), Harry Harvey (Gambler).

Working title: *Honor of the West*.

The Devil's Trail (Columbia, 1942, 60 minutes) Producer: Leon Barsha. Executive Producer: Irving Briskin. Director: Lambert Hillyer. Screenplay: Robert Lee Johnson, from the story "The Town in Hell's Backyard" by Philip Ketchum. Photography: George Meehan. Editor: Charles Nelson. Music Director: Morris Stoloff. Songs: Johnny Marvin. Art Directors: Lionel Banks & Perry Smith. Sound: George Cooper. Assistant Director: George Rhein.

Cast: Bill Elliott (Wild Bill Hickok), Tex Ritter (Tex Martin), Eileen O'Hearn (Myra Willoughby), Frank Mitchell (Cannonball), Noah Beery [Sr.] (Buck McQuade), Ruth Ford (Ella), Joel Friedkin (Dr. Willoughby), Joe McGuinn (Jim Randall), Edmund Cobb (Sid Howland), Tristram Coffin (Ed Scott), Paul Newlan (Blacksmith Ed Dawson), Sarah Padden (Belle), Bud Osborne (Harris), Stanley Brown (Guard), Art Mix, Steve Clark, Buck Moulton, Art Dillard (Gang Members).

Prairie Gunsmoke (Columbia, 1942, 56 minutes) Producer: Leon Barsha. Executive Producer: Irving Briskin. Director: Lambert Hillyer. Screenplay: Fred Myton. Story: Jack Ganzhorn. Photography: Benjamin Kline. Editor: Arthur Seid. Music Director: Morris Stoloff. Songs: Johnny Marvin. Art Directors: Lionel Banks & Perry Smith. Sound: Frank Goodwin. Assistant Director: Milton Carter.

Cast: Bill Elliott (Wild Bill Hickok), Tex Ritter (Tex Terrell), Frank Mitchell (Cannonball), Virginia Carroll (Lucy Wade), Tristram Coffin (Jim Kelton), Hal Price (Henry Wade), Joe McGuinn (Spike Allen), Frosty Royce (Sam), Rick Anderson (Dan Whipple), Steve Clark (Buck Garrett), Paul Conrad (Red), Art Mix, Francis Walker, Herman Hack (Gang Members), Horace B. Carpenter, Milburn Morante, George Morrell, Fred Parker (Ranchers), Jack Evans, Ray Jones, Tex Cooper (Citizens).

Behind Southern Lines (Monogram, 1952, 51 minutes) Producer: Wesley Barry. Executive Producer: William F. Broidy. Director: Thomas Carr. Photography: John Martin. Supervising Editor: Ace Herman. Music: Lee Zahler.

Cast: Guy Madison (Wild Bill Hickok), Andy Devine (Jingles P. Jones).

Episodes:

"BEHIND SOUTHERN LINES"
Screenplay: Melvin Levy.
Guest Cast: Rand Brooks, Gloria Saunders, Murray Alper, Jonathan Hale, William Ruhl, Parke MacGregor, Bill McKenzie.

"THE SILVER MINE PROTECTION STORY"
Screenplay: Maurice Tombragel.
Guest Cast: Milburn Stone, Robert Shayne, Duke York, Lee Phelps, Bill Meader, Orley Lindgren.

The Ghost of Crossbones Canyon (Monogram, 1952, 56 minutes) Producer: Wesley Barry. Executive Producer: William F. Broidy. Director: Frank McDonald. Photography: John Martin. Supervising Editor: Ace Herman. Music: Lee Zahler. Assistant Director: William Beaudine, Jr.

Cast: Guy Madison (Wild Bill Hickok), Andy Devine (Jingles P. Jones).

Episodes:

"THE TAX COLLECTING STORY"
Screenplay: Maurice Tombragel & Dwight V. Babcock.
Guest Cast: Gordon Jones (Curley Wolf), Mike Ragan [Holly Bane] (Gus), Ray Bennett (Sheriff), Marjorie Bennett (Widow), Sam Flint (Judge), Joe Greene (Rancher), James Guilfoyle (Old Rancher), Billy Bletcher (Waiter).

"GHOST TOWN STORY"
Screenplay: Maurice Tombragel.
Guest Cast: Russell Simpson (Sam Overman), John Doucette (Stopes), Bart Davidson (Manager).

Trail of the Arrow (Monogram, 1952, 54 minutes) Producer: Wesley Barry. Executive Producer: William F. Broidy. Director: Thomas Carr. Screenplay: Maurice Tombragel. Photography: John Martin. Supervising Editor: Ace Herman. Music: Lee Zahler.

Cast: Guy Madison (Wild Bill Hickok), Andy Devine (Jingles P. Jones).

Episodes:

"INDIAN BUREAU STORY"
Guest Cast: Monte Blue, Raymond Hatton, Wendy Waldron, Terry Frost, Steve Pendleton, Neyle Morrow, Jack Reynolds.

"INDIAN PONY EXPRESS"
Guest Cast: Wendy Waldron (Jeannie), Francis Ford (Zeke), Rory Mallinson (Owens), Dick Rich (Dillon), David Sharpe (Lenny), Tom Steele (Falk), Ferris Taylor (Gorman), Rodd Redwing (Red Horse), Tito Renaldo (Little Deer), Anthony Sydes (Ned).

Yellow Haired Kid (Monogram, 1952, 56 minutes) Producer: Wesley Barry. Executive Producer: William F. Broidy. Director: Frank McDonald. Photography:

John Martin. Supervising Editor: Ace Herman. Music: Lee Zahler.

Cast: Guy Madison (Wild Bill Hickok), Andy Devine (Jingles P. Jones).

Episodes:

"YELLOW HAIRED KID"
Screenplay: Dwight V. Babcock.
Guest Cast: David Bruce (Charles), Marcia Mae Jones (Amy), Bill [William] Phipps (Yellow Haired Kid), Wade Crosby (Lard), Tom Hubbard (Collins), John Carpenter (Guard), Alice Ralph (Citizen).

"JOHNNY DEUCE"
Screenplay: Maurice Tombragel.
Guest Cast: Alan Hale, Jr. (Johnny Deuce), Renie Riano (Bedelia), Tom Tyler (Sheriff), Riley Hill (Cowboy), Tommy Ivo (Timmy), Emory Parnell (Mayor).

Border City Rustlers (Allied Artists, 1953, 54 minutes) Producer: Wesley Barry. Executive Producer: William F. Broidy. Director: Frank McDonald. Screenplay: William Raynor. Photography: John Martin. Editor: Richard C. Currier. Supervising Editor: Ace Herman. Music: Lee Zahler. Art Director: Dave Milton. Sound: Tom Lambert. Sets: Vin Taylor. Special Effects: Ray Mercer. Makeup: Charles Hurber. Assistant Director: William Beaudine, Jr.

Cast: Guy Madison (Wild Bill Hickok), Andy Devine (Jingles P. Jones).

Episodes:

"BORDER CITY"
Guest Cast: Gloria Talbott (Consuelo), George J. Lewis (Ramon), Steve Pendleton (Larson), Murray Alper (Kirby), Jerome Sheldon (Marshal), George Eldredge, Don Turner.

"HEPSIBAH"
Guest Cast: Isabel Randolph (Hepsibah), Douglas Evans (Grogan), Robert Bice (Branton), George Eldredge (Judge), Larry Johns (Collins), Billy Griffith (Jenkins).

Secret of Outlaw Flats (Allied Artists, 1953, 54 minutes) Producer: Wesley Barry. Executive Producer: William F. Broidy. Director: Frank McDonald. Screenplay: William Raynor. Photography: William A. Sickner. Editor: Richard C. Currier. Supervising Editor: Ace Herman. Music: Lee Zahler. Art Director: Dave Milton. Sound: Tom Lambert. Sets: Vin Taylor. Special Effects: Ray Mercer. Makeup: Charles Hurber. Assistant Director: William Beaudine, Jr.

Cast: Guy Madison (Wild Bill Hickok), Andy Devine (Jingles P. Jones).

Episodes:

"OUTLAW FLATS"
Guest Cast: Tris [Tristram] Coffin (Mr. Otis), Kristine Miller (Cindy Howard), Bobby Jordan (Sandy Smith), John Crawford (King Bradshaw), Richard Avonde (Dick Howard), Ed Clark (Jeb Randall), Bill Hale (Ted), William Haade (Tony).

"SILVER STAGE HOLDUP"
Guest Cast: Jane Adams (Peggy), Reed Howes (Mr. Slate), Wade Crosby (Canfield), William Haade (Guard), Riley Hill (Outlaw), Lennie Geer.

Six Gun Decision (Allied Artists, 1953, 54 minutes) Producer: Wesley Barry. Executive Producer: William F. Broidy. Director: Frank McDonald. Photography: William A. Sickner. Editor: Richard C. Currier. Supervising Editor: Ace Herman. Music: Lee Zahler. Art Director: Dave Milton. Sound: Tom Lambert. Sets: Vin Taylor. Special Effects: Ray Mercer. Assistant Director: William Beaudine, Jr.

Cast: Guy Madison (Wild Bill Hickok), Andy Devine (Jingles P. Jones).

Episodes:

"BORDER CITY ELECTION"
Screenplay: Maurice Tombragel.
Guest Cast: Lyle Talbot (Blackburn), Gloria Saunders (Jane), Dave Sharpe (Johnny Powers), Robert Bice (Art), Fred Hoose (Matt Thompson), Zon Murray (Carson), Jim Connell (Frank).

"PONY EXPRESS VS. TELEGRAPH"
Screenplay: William Raynor.
Guest Cast: Peggy Stewart (Jane), Fred Kohler, Jr. (Jordan), Tom Steele (Barton), Michael Vallon (Charlie Rogers), Don Hayden (Bob Ridgeway), Hank Patterson (Pop Clancy), Tom Steele (Barton), Parke MacGregor (Bennett).

Two Gun Marshal (Allied Artists, 1953, 54 minutes) Producer: Wesley Barry. Executive Producer: William F. Broidy. Director: Frank McDonald. Photography: John Martin. Editor: Richard C. Currier. Music: Lee Zahler. Sound: Tom Lambert. Sets: Vin Taylor. Special Effects: Ray Mercer. Makeup: Charles Hurber. Assistant Director: William Beaudine, Jr.

Cast: Guy Madison (Wild Bill Hickok), Andy Devine (Jingles P. Jones).

Episodes:

"PAPA ANTONELLI"
Screenplay: William Raynor.
Guest Cast: Michael Vallon (Papa Antonelli), Pamela Duncan (Connie), Francis McDonald (Blake Cody), Minerva Urecal (Mama Antonelli), Ray Hyke (Landers), Wes Hudman (Burke).

"THE SLOCUM FAMILY"
Screenplay: Maurice Tombragel.
Guest Cast: Raymond Hatton (Pa Slocum), Frankie Darro (Clint Slocum), Carole Mathews (Miss Jennings), Sara Haden (Ma Slocum), Richard Tyler (Gus Slocum), Danny Mummert (Al Slocum), Gregory Marshall (Gabe Slocum), Noralee Norman (Tessie Slocum).

Marshals in Disguise (Allied Artists, 1954, 54 minutes) Producer: Wesley Barry. Executive Producer: William F. Broidy. Director: Frank McDonald. Photography: John Martin. Editor: Richard C. Currier. Supervising Editor: Ace Herman. Music: Lee Zahler.

Cast: Guy Madison (Wild Bill Hickok), Andy Devine (Jingles P. Jones).
Episodes:

"Lost Indian Mine"
Screenplay: William Raynor.
Guest Cast: Bud Osborne (Floyd), John Eldredge (Jim Hawks), Guy Beach (Old Dan), John Reynolds (Randall), Anthony Sydes (Bobby), David Sharpe, James Bush, Don Turner.

"Civilian Clothes"
Screenplay: Maurice Tombragel.
Guest Cast: Tris [Tristram] Coffin, Norma Eberhardt, Rick Vallin, John Merton, Leonard Penn, Fred Kelsey, Bill Hale, Pat Mitchell.

Outlaw's Son (Allied Artists, 1954, 54 minutes) Producer: Wesley Barry. Executive Producer: William F. Broidy. Director: Frank McDonald. Screenplay: Maurice Tombragel. Photography: John Martin. Music: Lee Zahler.
Cast: Guy Madison (Wild Bill Hickok), Andy Devine (Jingles P. Jones).
Episodes:

"The Outlaw's Son"
Guest Cast: Ralph Reed (Drew), Anne Kimball (Sally), Steve Darrell (Big Jack), Dan White (Pinto).

"Wild White Horse"
Guest Cast: Sally Fraser (Nancy Latham), Bobby Hyatt (Tommy Latham), Pierce Lyden (Powers), Frank Fenton (Jed Latham), Fred Kelsey (Old Timer), Guy Wilkerson (Hunter), Wes Hudman (Stuart).

Trouble on the Trail (Allied Artists, 1954, 54 minutes) Producer: Wesley Barry. Executive Producer: William F. Broidy. Director: Frank McDonald. Photography: John Martin. Editor: Richard C. Currier. Supervising Editor: Ace Herman. Music: Lee Zahler.
Cast: Guy Madison (Wild Bill Hickok), Andy Devine (Jingles P. Jones).
Episodes:

"Blacksmith Story"
Screenplay: William Raynor.
Guest Cast: Robert Livingston (Nate Finch), Carole Mathews (Anne Hardy), Richard Alexander (Luke Barstow), Sam Flint (Doc Higgins), William [Merrill] McCormick (Sam Peters).

"The Professor's Daughter"
Screenplay: Maurice Tombragel.
Guest Cast: Martha Hyer (Elsa Gray), James Bush (Drago), Bobby [Robert] Blake (Rain Cloud), Byron Foulger (Professor Gray), Bud Osborne (Stagecoach Driver), Henry Rowland (Spike).

The Two Gun Teacher (Allied Artists, 1954, 52 minutes) Producer: Wesley Brady. Executive Producer: William F. Broidy. Director: Frank McDonald. Screenplay: William Raynor. Supervising Editor: Ace Herman. Music: Lee Zahler.
Cast: Guy Madison (Wild Bill Hickok), Andy Devine (Jingles P. Jones).
Episodes:

"Mexican Gun Running Story"
Guest Cast: Rand Brooks (Ed Chandler), Theodora Lynch (June Chandler), Sujata (Marguerita), Tom Tyler (Sheriff), Monte Montague (Williams), Murray Alper (Ace Parker), Paul Fierro (Ramon), Bud Osborne (Denton).

"Schoolteacher Story"
Guest Cast: Don C. Harvey (Sykes), Anne Carroll (Betty), Rory Mallinson (Sam Roca), Emory Parnell (Professor Kleinberg), Steve Pendleton (Bailey), Nadine Ashdown (Pam), Isa Ashdown (Marsha), Jim Flowers (Jim).

The Matchmaking Marshal (Allied Artists, 1955, 54 minutes) Producer: Wesley Ruggles. Executive Producer: William F. Broidy. Supervising Editor: Ace Herman. Music: Lee Zahler.
Cast: Guy Madison (Wild Bill Hickok), Andy Devine (Jingles P. Jones).
Episodes:

"Marriage Feud of Ponca City"
Director-Editor: S. Roy Luby. Screenplay: Maurice Tombragel. Sets: Mowbray Berkeley.
Guest Cast: Anne Carroll (Ada Manson), Louise Lorimer (Martha Ward), Paul McGuire (Mort Ramsey), Robert Jordan (Steve Manson), Nelson Leigh (Clyde Manson), Forrest Taylor (Ira Beecher), Ed Cassidy.

"Wrestling Story"
Director: Frank McDonald. Screenplay: William Raynor.
Guest Cast: Lyle Talbot (Bank Teller), Douglas Fowley (Three Finger Jack Ruskin), Rand Brooks (Bob Purdy), Karl "Killer" Davis (Abdul), Henry Kulky (Opponent), House Peters [Jr.] (Jason), Frank Scannell (Otis).

Phantom Trails (Allied Artists, 1955, 54 minutes) Producer: Wesley Barry. Executive Producer: William F. Broidy. Photography: John S. Martin. Editor: Carl Pierson. Music: Lee Zahler. Art Director: Dave Milton. Sound: Frank Webster. Sets: Vin Taylor & Mowbray Berkeley. Special Effects: Ray Mercer. Makeup: Charles Huber. Production Supervisor: A.R. Milton. Assistant Director: William Beaudine, Jr.
Cast: Guy Madison (Wild Bill Hickok), Andy Devine (Jingles P. Jones).
Episodes:

"A Close Shave for the Marshal"
Director: Frank McDonald. Screenplay: Maurice Tombragel.
Guest Cast: Steve Brodie (Matt), Harry Harvey (Sheriff), Byron Foulger (Hooper), Robert Filmer (Wade), Burt Wenland (Thug).

"Ghost Rider"
Director: Wesley Barry. Screenplay: William Raynor.

Guest Cast: Steve Pendleton (Curt Lesley), Hank Patterson (Jess Morgan), Ethan Laidlaw (Ben Lesley), Paul Bryar (Ed Grannis), William Vedder (Pops Garroway).

Timber Country Trouble (Allied Artists, 1955, 54 minutes) Producer-Director: Wesley Barry. Executive Producer: William F. Broidy. Photography: John J. Martin. Editor: Carl Pierson. Music: Lee Zahler. Art Director: Dave Milton. Sound: Frank Webster. Sets: Vin Taylor. Special Effects: Ray Mercer. Makeup: Charles Hurber. Production Supervisor: A.R. Milton. Assistant Director: Eugene Anderson, Jr.

Cast: Guy Madison (Wild Bill Hickok), Andy Devine (Jingles P. Jones).

Episodes:

"The Boy and the Bandit"

Screenplay: William Raynor.

Guest Cast: Edmund Cobb (Sheriff Lober), Buddy Roosevelt (Blacksmith Judd), Bruce Edwards (Whitey Peters), John Merton (Ed Hartman), Henry Blair (Jimmy Peters), Michael Vallon.

"Lumber Camp Story"

Screenplay: William Raynor & Sam Roeca.

Guest Cast: Harry Lauter (Webb), Kenne Duncan (Ben), Frances Charles (Cissy), George Barrows (LaFarge), Fred Krone.

The Titled Tenderfoot (Allied Artists, 1955, 54 minutes) Producer: Wesley Barry. Executive Producer: William F. Broidy. Director: Frank McDonald. Photography: John J. Martin. Editor: Carl Pierson. Supervising Editor: Ace Herman. Music: Lee Zahler. Art Director: Dave Milton. Sound: Frank Webster. Sets: Vin Taylor. Special Effects: Ray Mercer. Makeup: Charles Hurber. Production Supervisor: A.R. Milton. Assistant Director: William Beaudine, Jr., & Eugene Anderson, Jr.

Cast: Guy Madison (Wild Bill Hickok), Andy Devine (Jingles P. Jones).

Episodes:

"A Joke for Sir Anthony"

Screenplay: Maurice Tombragel.

Guest Cast: Dick Cavendish (Sir Anthony Aldershot), I. Stanford Jolley (Logan), Dick Elliott (Mayor), Parke MacGregor (Doc Miller), Gerald O. Smith (Equerry), Russ Whiteman (Apperson), Marshall Reed, Guy Teague.

"The Trapper Story"

Screenplay: William Raynor.

Guest Cast: Clayton Moore (Larson), Jeanne Cagney (Doris), Marshall Reed (DuBois), James Bell (Corbett), Jack Reynolds (Douglas), Hal Gerard (Doc Barton).

Wild Bill Saunders

Following his success in the leading role in the 1938 Columbia serial *The Great Adventures of Wild Bill Hickok*, Bill Elliott signed with producer Larry Darmour to star in a series of "B" westerns for release by the studio. Darmour had previously done cowboy pictures with Ken Maynard, Bob Allen and Jack Luden for Columbia; the quartet Elliott did for him were melodramas loosely based on historical events. The second set of four, however, had Elliott playing a continuing character, Will Bill Saunders, with Leon Barsha taking over as producer and Dub Taylor providing comedy relief in the role of Cannonball. Between them, Elliott headlined a second Columbia cliffhanger, *Overland with Kit Carson* (1939).

Released late in 1939, *The Taming of the West* was the initial "Wild Bill Saunders" release and it presented the character as a frontier crusader trying to bring law and order to the wild west. When the marshal (Hank Bell) of Prairie Port, an area plagued by lawlessness, is murdered in a barroom fight, newcomer Saunders (Elliott) rides after the killer, Turkey (Lane Chandler). The two battle and Turkey falls over a cliff. Saunders is given the job of the town's lawman. Outlaws Rawhide (Dick Curtis) and Handy (James Craig) rob and murder Mary Jenkins (Irene Herndon) and Saunders puts them in jail. Their boss, banker Carp Blaisdale (Kenneth MacDonald), promises them they will be set free. Carp has his men intimidate all the witnesses but Mrs. Gardner (Stella Le Saint), whose husband was beaten by the gang, testifies against the two accused men. Judge Bailey (Ethan Allen) recesses the court in order to get Gardner's testimony but Handy, along with another gang member, Slim (Stanley Brown), silences him. Restaurant proprietor Pepper Jenkins (Iris Meredith) see the two outlaws kill Gardner and they try to get rid of her but are stopped by Saunders. When Pepper sees gang member Shifty

(Bob Woodward) going into Carp's bank, she tells the sheriff who sets out to catch Blaisdale. He has jailer Cannonball (Taylor) tell Rawhide and Shifty that Handy and Slim have been transferred to the county seat when, in reality, they have been locked in Pepper's cellar. The two outlaws then go to Carp and all three of the badmen are arrested by Saunders. *Variety* felt it was "an above average horse opera" and in regards to the star added, "Bill Elliott, on top, is a type likely to become quite popular. He's more along the line of William S. Hart and somewhat of a slugger, with punches not always pulled."

Norman Deming directed *The Taming of the West*; Sam Nelson took over to helm *Pioneers of the Frontier*, issued early in 1940. This one had Saunders (Elliott) riding to the ranch of his uncle, Mort Saunders (Lafe McKee), only to find the old man dead and his foreman, Matt Brawley (Dick Curtis), running the spread. Brawley, who ordered Mort's killing, also murders settler Jim Darcy (Carl Stockdale); the other homesteaders, led by Cannonball Sims (Taylor), want to get rid of the tyrant. Saunders, who has agreed to help the settlers, is put in jail on a murder charge after a gunfight with some of Brawley's gang. Cannonball gets help from Joan Darcy (Linda Winters [Dorothy Comingore]), Jim's daughter, and with the homesteaders they plan to free Bill. Brawley has his men take Saunders to his ranch but along the way Cannonball manages to help him get away. When the settlers go to Brawley's ranch, Saunders realizes they will be massacred so he pretends to come to terms with Matt. Cannonball helps Saunders escape from the Brawley spread, and the two go to Joan with a plan to bring in the outlaw and his gang. They try to corner the crooks in a box canyon but Brawley finds out and attacks the settlers. Cannonball rides to town to get Bill. There the two men fight with other gang members as the homesteaders defeat their attackers and ride to town, catching Brawley and the remainder of his men in a crossfire. The outlaws are captured as Saunders kills Brawley, bringing an end to the lawlessness. After seeing the settlers obtaining their land claims, Saunders and Cannonball ride off to another adventure.

Joseph H. Lewis took over as director for the series' final two releases, *The Man from Tumbleweeds* and *The Return of Wild Bill*. In the former, issued in May 1940, Saunders (Elliott) comes to Gun Sight at the behest of Cannonball (Taylor), whose freight company owner boss (Edward LeSaint) was murdered during a holdup by outlaw Powder Kilgore (Raphael [Ray] Bennett) and his gang. Saunders gets permission from the state's governor (Don Beddoe) to form a band of deputies made up of prisoner recruits. Arriving in town, Saunders stops Kilgore's henchman Lightning Barlow (Francis Walker) from trying to extort protection money from Spunky Cameron (Iris Meredith), the daughter of the

Poster for *The Man from Tumbleweeds* (Columbia, 1940).

murdered freight company owner. When Powder's gang tries to hold up Spunky's gold shipment, they are confronted by Saunders and his men, who are hiding in the wagon. Lightning, however, is allowed to escape by Deputy Shifty Sheldon (Ernie Adams), who is in cahoots with Kilgore. Suspicious of Shifty, Saunders tells him to join the outlaw gang. Sheldon and Kilgore plan to kill the sheriff but he is warned by another deputy, Webster (Al Hill). Saunders and Webster shoot Lightning, arrest Shifty and ride to the ranch of another gang member, Dixon (Robert Fiske). Looking for stray cattle, Spunky and Cannonball locate the gang's hideout at the Dixon spread; when Cannonball rides for help, Spunky is captured. The lawmen ride to her rescue as Kilgore plans to ambush them at the hideout, but Spunky escapes and brings back the other deputies. During a gunfight, the gang is rounded up and Saunders arrests Kilgore.

In the next month's *The Return of Wild Bill*, Saunders (Elliott) returns to his father's (Edward LeSaint) ranch only to find him mortally wounded by outlaws Matt Kilgore (George Lloyd) and his brother Jake (Francis Walker). Their gang has been attacking and robbing all the area ranchers and Saunders vows revenge. He shoots Jake and stops Matt and his gang from hanging another rancher, Ole Mitch (Frank LaRue). Saunders meets Sammy Lou Griffin (Iris Meredith), the daughter of another murdered rancher (John Ince), and the two are attracted to each other and unite in their quest to avenge their fathers' killings. Matt assumes the guise of the local lawman with plans to murder Saunders but Kate Kilgore (Luana Walters), who detests her brothers' murderous ways, finds out and with Ole Mitch and several ranchers, she rides to help Saunders. In a shootout with the gang, Kate is killed but Saunders avenges her death and arrests the remainder of the gang.

The Return of Wild Bill had the interesting subplot of the hero having two girlfriends, the traditional heroine whose father was murdered by the bad men, and the villains' sister. Iris Meredith, who was the leading lady in three of the series' four entries, gave her usual competent performance in the first part, but it was Luana Walters who was most memorable in the film, playing a young woman who also fancied Saunders but ended up losing her life for betraying her lawless kin.

Although the "Wild Bill Saunders" series came to a halt after only four outings, Elliott essentially continued to play the character for producer Leon Barsha in the "Wild Bill Hickok" (q.v.) features with Dub Taylor continuing in the role of Cannonball. Since Elliott had portrayed Hickok in Columbia's 1938 serial, the producer no doubt felt the historical significance of the famed lawman's name would add to the box office receipts. Despite the name change, there appeared to be little difference in the "Wild Bill Saunders" and "Wild Bill Hickok" outings. Both were so popular with moviegoers that in 1940 Bill Elliott made it to the *Motion Picture Herald*'s poll of the top ten moneymaking western stars and he would stay there through 1954.

Filmography

The Taming of the West (Columbia, 1939, 55 minutes) Producer: Leon Barsha. Executive Producer: Irving Briskin. Director: Norman Deming. Screenplay: Charles Francis Royal & Robert Lee Johnson. Story: Robert Lee Johnson. Photography: George Meehan. Editor: Otto Meyer. Sound: George Cooper. Assistant Director: Walter McGaugh.

Cast: Bill Elliott (Wild Bill Saunders), Iris Meredith (Pepper Jenkins), Dick Curtis (Rawhide), Dub Taylor (Cannonball), James Craig (Handy), Stanley Brown (Slim), Ethan Allen (Judge Bailey), Kenneth MacDonald (Carp Blaisdale), Victor Wong (Cholly Wong), Charles King (Jackson), Lane Chandler (Turkey), Art Mix (Blackie Gilbert), Richard Fiske (Blake), John Tyrrell (Coleman), Bob Woodward (Shifty), Hank Bell (Marshal Bates), Stella Le Saint (Mrs. Gardner), Irene Herndon (Mary Jenkins), Francis Walker (Gang Member), Fred Burns (Rancher), Horace B. Carpenter, Fred Parker, George Morrell, Ray Jones, Al Haskell (Citizens), Jack Evans (Parolee), Jack Kirk (Gun Checker).

Working title: *Sundown in Helldorado*.

Pioneers of the Frontier (Columbia, 1940, 58 minutes) Producer: Leon Barsha. Executive Producer: Irving Briskin. Director: Sam Nelson. Screenplay: Fred Myton. Photography: George Meehan. Editor: James Sweeney. Music Director: Morris Stoloff. Sound: George Cooper. Assistant Director: Milton Carter.

Cast: Bill Elliott (Wild Bill Saunders), Linda Winters [Dorothy Comingore] (Joan Darcey), Dick Curtis (Matt Brawley), Dub Taylor (Cannonball Sims), Stanley Brown (Dave), Richard Fiske (Bart), Carl Stockdale (Jim Darcey), Lafe McKee (Mort Saunders), Ralph McCullough (Lem Watkins), Al Bridge (Marshal Larsen), Blackjack Ward (Shorty), George Chesebro (Appleby), Eddie [Edmund] Cobb (Ed Carter), Ralph Peters (Jack Harvey), Ed Coxen (Hardrock), Hank Bell (Harper), Jay Wilsey [Buffalo Bill Jr.] (Durango), Buddy Cox (Tommy), Francis Walker (Joe), Jack Kirk (Rancher), Lynton Brent (Carter), Art Dillard (Deputy Sheriff), George Morrell, Jim Corey, Ray Jones, Bob Card (Citizens).

Working title: *Gun Lord of the Frontier.*

The Man from Tumbleweeds (Columbia, 1940, 59 minutes) Producer: Leon Barsha. Executive Producer: Irving Briskin. Director: Joseph H. Lewis. Screenplay: Charles Francis Royal. Photography: George Meehan. Editor: Charles Nelson. Sound: George Cooper. Assistant Director: Milton Carter.

Cast: Bill Elliott (Wild Bill Saunders), Iris Meredith (Spunky Cameron), Dub Taylor (Cannonball), Raphael [Ray] Bennett (Powder Kilgore), Francis Walker (Lightning Barlow), Ernie Adams (Shifty Sheldon), Al Hill (Honest John Webster), Stanley Brown (Slash), Richard Fiske (Kid Dixon), Edward LeSaint (Jeff Cameron), Don Beddoe (Governor Dawson), Eddie Laughton (Jackson), John Tyrrell (Ranch Gang Member), Edward [Ed] Cecil (Butler), Jack Lowe, Jay Lawrence, Buel Bryant, Olin Francis (Deputy Sheriffs), Bruce Bennett (Prison Warden), George Chesebro (Bank Robber), Steve Clark (Marshal), Hank Bell (Stagecoach Driver), Frank McCarroll (Stagecoach Guard), Art Dillard, Jack Evans, Blackie Whiteford, Herman Howlin, Ray Jones, George Fiske, Jack King, George Hazel, Billy Wilson (Gang Members), Tex Cooper, Jack Tornek (Citizens).

The Return of Wild Bill (Columbia, 1940, 60 minutes) Producer: Leon Barsha. Executive Producer: Irving Briskin. Director: Joseph H. Lewis. Screenplay: Fred Myton & Robert Lee Johnson, from the story "Block K Rides Again" by Walt Coburn. Photography: George Meehan. Editors: Charles Nelson & Richard Fantl. Assistant Directors: Milton Carter & Bob [Robert] Farfan.

Cast: Bill Elliott (Wild Bill Saunders), Iris Meredith (Sammy Lou Griffin), George Lloyd (Matt Kilgore), Luana Walters (Kate Kilgore), Edward LeSaint (Lige Saunders), Frank LaRue (Ole Mitch), Francis Walker (Jake Kilgore), Chuck Morrison (Bart), Dub Taylor (Cannonball), Buel Bryant (Deputy Sheriff Mike), William Kellogg (Deputy Sheriff Hep), John Ince (Sam Griffin), Jack Rockwell (Sheriff), John Merton (Dusty Donahue), Donald Haines (Bobby), Jim Corey (Mike), Bill Nestell (Blacksmith), Tex Cooper (Citizen).

Working title: *Block K Rides Again.*

WINNETOU

Karl May (1842–1912) is one of Germany's all-time best-selling authors, with sales of over 200 million copies worldwide. Although many of his works were set in the Middle East and the Orient, he is best remembered for his novels about the American West, these having been greatly influenced by the writings of James Fenimore Cooper. Between 1962 and 1968, eleven films were produced from May's books, focusing on the Apache chief Winnetou and his blood brothers Old Firehand, Old Shatterhand and Old Surehand. These features are credited with spawning the popularity of the Spaghetti Westerns as well as reviving the western film series concept. Among May's followers were Adolf Hitler, Albert Einstein and Hermann Hesse.

Pierre Brice portrayed Winnetou in all eleven outings about this "noble savage" while Lex Barker played his white blood brother Old Shatterhand in seven features, Stewart Granger was Old Surehand in three and Rod Cameron made a solo effort as Old Firehand. The term "Old" was used by May to refer to the heroic backgrounds of these legendary frontiersmen. Most of the features were made in Yugoslavia in order for the terrain to match that of the American West.

Brice (1929–), a native of France whose real name is Baron Pierre Louis de Bris, was best known as the hero of the horror classic *Mill of the Stone Women* (1960) before taking the Winnetou role in 1962. He also portrayed Zorro in *Zorro Contro Maciste* (q.v.) in 1963. Although he appeared in a number of feature films throughout his career, Brice always returned to the Winnetou role, not only on film but also in live appearances and on television.

New York native Lex Barker (1919–73) played Old Shatterhand to Brice's Winnetou in the first series outing, *Der Schatz im Silbersee* (The Treasure of Silver Lake), which was released in

1962. Up to that time, Barker was best known for having portrayed Tarzan in five features from 1949 to 1953; in 1957 he also had the lead in James Fenimore Cooper's *The Deerslayer*. By the late 1950s he had relocated to Europe where his popularity soared after he began appearing in the May movies, which besides the "Winnetou" series included *Der Schut* (The Shoot) (1964), *Der Schatz der Aztcken* (The Treasure of the Aztecs), *Die Pyramide des Sonnengottes* (The Pyramid of the Sun Gods) and *Durchs wilde Kurdistan* (Wild Kurdistan) (1965).*

The 1960s May features were produced by the Berlin company Rialto Film-Preben Philipsen, which was formed in 1960 by producer Horst Wendlandt (1923–2002) and Preben Philipsen. Wendlandt, who had been in films since 1939 and had formerly worked for Central Europa Film and CCC–Filmkunst, launched a series of features in 1959 based on the works of Edgar Wallace and these films became the most successful produced in West Germany. Wendlandt then tapped into the works of May, producing another highly successful series, making him one of Europe's best known film producers. Rialto also did a series of "Dr. Mabuse" features in the early 1960s, two of which starred Lex Barker.

Der Schatz im Silbersee (The Treasure of Silver Lake), issued in Europe in 1962 and based on May's 1890 novel, told of a legendary Indian treasure being buried near Silver Lake. A map leading to the treasure has been torn into two pieces, with one half being stolen during a stagecoach robbery in Arkansas by outlaw leader Colonel Brinkley (Herbert Lom) and his gang of marauders. The other half of the map belongs to settler Fred Engel (Gotz George), whose father was murdered for possessing its companion. Fred enlists the aid of his friends, frontiersman Old Shatterhand (Barker) and his blood brother, Apache chief Winnetou (Brice), in capturing the killers. The trio go to see Engel's partner Patterson (Jan Sid), since he has possession of the second part of the map. Before they arrive, Brinkley and his men raid Patterson's farm and kidnap his daughter Ellen (Karin Dor), Fred's fiancée. As a result, Brinkley forces Fred to lead them to Silver Lake. Old Shatterhand and Winnetou are ambushed by a hostile Indian tribe but Winnetou convinces them to join the two in pursuing Brinkley and his gang. At Silver Lake, Brinkley plans to hang Fred and torture Ellen but Old Shatterhand sets them free. Winnetou and the Indians round up the outlaws as Brinkley falls through a secret trap and is entombed with the gold.

Leading lady Karin Dor's husband, Harald Reinl, directed *Der Schatz im Silbersee* in a fast-paced and highly entertaining style. The film proved to be a sensation and not only resulted in ten follow-ups but also sparked a European craze about the American West. It revived Barker's career, making him a matinee idol in Europe, and it made Brice a star. Its Yugoslavian locales were very impressive as was the camerawork of Ernst W. Kalinke. Composer Martin Bottcher's theme for the film, "Old Shatterhand-Melodie," sold over 100,000 records as an instrumental and Brice, among others, recorded a vocal version. Among the many awards won by the feature was the Bambi, for being West Germany's big box-office winner in 1963. In the United States the feature was issued by Columbia as *The Treasure of Silver Lake* in 1965 but it was shorn of nearly thirty minutes of its running time.

Harald Reinl next helmed *Winnetou I*, which was released in West Germany in 1963, and it proved to be a prequel to *Der Schatz im Silbersee* in that it showed how Old Shatterhand and Winnetou met and became blood brothers. Here the Apache Indians have their lands violated by the Great Western Railroad; the plot was actually hatched by outlaw Santer (Mario Adorf), who is allied with the Kiowa tribe in trying to steal Apache gold. Winnetou (Brice), the son the Apache chief (Milivoje Popovic-Mavid), leads his tribe's warriors in trying to stop the incursion but Santer captures and tortures him. He is saved by Old Shatterhand (Barker), the railroad's special investigator, but Winnetou escapes without knowing who rescued him. When Old Shatter-

---

The Old Shatterhand character first appeared in the 1939 German feature Wasser für Canitoga *(Water for Canitoga) and was played by Hans Mierendorff. The character of Winnetou does not appear in the production, which starred Hans Albers as the head of a fledgling mining town that badly needs water and attempts to get it by constructing a pipeline. In* The Western *(1983), Phil Hardy called it "an unsatisfactory film, the real significance of which lies in its celebration of the indomitable Aryan spirit."*

hand tries to stop Santer, Winnetou and his braves raid the headquarters of the railroad and the investigator is badly hurt. He is saved by Nschotschi (Marie Versini), Winnetou's sister. After he recovers he agrees to go through several trials in order to prove his loyalty to the Apaches. Surviving the trials by tomahawk and canoe, Nschotschi proves he saved her sibling's life and Old Shatterhand and Winnetou become blood brothers. The two then shoot it out with Santer and his gang, resulting in the deaths of Nscho-tschi and her father, but Santer is killed and his gang routed.

Based on May's 1893 novel *Winnetou, der rote Gentleman* (*Winnetou, the Red Gentleman*), the feature was released in the United States in 1965 by Columbia as *Apache Gold*, running ten minutes less than its original 101 minutes. It was also called *Winnetou the Warrior.*

The third Winnetou feature, *Old Shatterhand*, came out in 1964 and was directed by Hugo Fregonese, a native of Argentina, who had previously helmed Westerns like *Saddle Tramp* (1950), *Apache Drums* (1951) and *Untamed Frontier* (1952) and would go on to make *Savage Pampas* (1965). Lensed in 70mm Superpanorama, this visually impressive feature was about a band of renegades, made up of whites and their Comanche allies, attacking small ranches and placing blame on the Apaches in order to get their lands. When General Taylor (George Fawcett) leaves for Washington, D.C., the local army post is left in the command of Captain Bradley (Guy Madison), who is really the leader of the marauders. Young Tom (Burschi Putzgruber) sees his father (Dusko Rajojcic) murdered and their ranch raided by the outlaws while Tujunga (Alain Tissier), Winnetou's (Brice) adopted son, is blamed for the crimes and nearly hanged; he is saved by Old Shatterhand (Lex Barker). Tom goes to stay with Paloma (Daliah Lavi), an Indian princess whose father was white, and Old Shatterhand escorts them to a wagon train being protected by Bradley and his men. Along the way they meet Sam Hawkens (Ralf Wolter) and his men, who are scouts for the travelers. When the wagon train is attacked, two Indians identified as Apaches are killed and Old Shatterhand goes to see Winnetou. At the council, Tujunga wants to kill all whites but Old Shatterhand says that it was Comanches who attacked the wagon train. The frontiersman reports this information to the recently returned General Taylor who wants to meet with Winnetou, but Bradley opposes the idea. Winnetou engages in hand-to-hand combat with the Comanche chief and kills him as Old Shatterhand tells the general he has a witness to the raids, one who will prove the Apaches' innocence. Since Tom is that witness, Bradley has his cohort Barker (Mirko Ellis) murder the boy, with Hawkens being blamed for the crime. The scout proves his innocence and then saves Old Shatterhand, who has been ambushed by Bradley's man Dixon (Rik Battaglia), who confesses he sold horses to the Comanches. Winnetou orders Tujunga to take Paloma back to her sanctuary while Bradley and Corporal Bush (Gustavo Rojo) set fire to a farm, blaming the Apaches, and murdering Barker. Winnetou is given safe conduct to the fort and then is taken prisoner by Bradley, who claims that the new commander, Colonel Hunter (Jim Burke), died of snake bite. When Bradley learns of Barker's confession from Old Shatterhand, he lets the blood brothers go but his men capture Tujunga at Paloma's sanctuary and she rides to tell Old Shatterhand. The frontiersman attempts to rescue Tujunga but fails and is captured. Winnetou and his Apache warriors attack the fort and during the fierce fight Tujunga sets off a munitions explosion. Hawkens and his men escort the returning General Taylor back to the fort, ending the fighting. Taylor arrests Bradley and then signs a peace treaty with the Apaches.

Goldstone Film Enterprises issued *Old Shatterhand* in the U.S. as *Shatterhand* with over thirty minutes excised from the running time. In England it was called *Apache's Last Battle*. While the film's plot was a bit complicated, it did contain some very fine action sequences, especially the well-staged and exciting climactic battle scenes. Leading lady Daliah Lavi (or a double) had a brief nude bathing scene. Many viewers and critics consider *Old Shatterhand* the best film in the Winnetou series.

Like *Winnetou I*, *Winnetou II* was based on May's 1893 novel *Winnetou, der rote Gentleman*. Issued in West Germany in the fall of 1965, it saw release a year later in the United States by Columbia as *Last of the Renegades* but this time the feature's running time was not trimmed. Harald Reinl, who directed several of the Edgar Wallace

Pierre Brice as Winnetou in *Old Shatterhand* (Constantin, 1964).

thrillers for Rialto, was back helming this Winnetou series entry as was his wife, Karin Dor, who starred in a half dozen of the Wallace films. Klaus Kinski, who enacted villainous roles in several Wallace thrillers, had a similar part in *Winnetou II*, as did Eddi Arent, here seen as the silly kind of character he portrayed in the *Krimis*. He played Lord Castlepool, a part he did first in *Der Schatz im Silbersee*. A further Wallace series connection comes from the fact that Siegfried Schurenberg, who portrayed the bumbling Scotland Yard chief Sir John in the thrillers, dubbed the voice of Colonel Merrill for the West German release of the feature.

Winnetou II told of the chief (Rikard Brzeska) of the Assiniboin tribe waging a war against white settlers trying to take over his tribe's lands. Winnetou (Brice), the chief of the Apaches, rescues Ribanna (Karin Dor), the Assiniboin chief's daughter, from his enemies and promises to keep the peace between the warring factions. He then helps to set free a trio of soldiers, including Lieutenant Merril (Mario Girotti [Terence Hill]), the son of the local fort commander, Colonel Merril (Renato Baldini). Oil man Bud Forrester (Anthony Steel) is behind all the troubles and he sends his men and several renegade Indians, led by henchman Lucas (Klaus Kinski), to massacre a Ponca village. Lieutenant Merril is almost captured during the raid but is saved by the arrival of scout Old Shatterhand (Barker) who is accompanying British adventurer Lord Castlepool (Eddi Arent) on a tour of the West. Old Shatterhand then tells Forrester's oil workers that their boss is behind the lawlessness and his wells are set on fire. To get revenge, Forrester kidnaps Lord Castlepool while Colonel Merril tells Winnetou he will help him find those responsible for the Ponca massacre.

To further strengthen the peace, Lieutenant Merril agrees to marry Ribanna. After Old Shatterhand and Winnetou set Lord Castlepool free, they uncover evidence that Forrester's gang attacked a wagon train and blamed the Apaches for the crime. The outlaws trap Lieutenant Merril, Ribanna and a number of Assiniboin women and children in a cave, but Winnetou leads his warriors in rescuing them.

The end of 1964 saw the West German release of *Unter Geiern* (Among Vultures), the first of three features starring Stewart Granger in the role of Old Surehand, a character very similar to Old Shatterhand. Brice continued in the part of Winnetou and in all three features with Granger his voice was dubbed by Thomas Eckelmann in the West German versions. Heinz Engelmann dubbed Granger's voice while this time Siegfried Schurenberg dubbed the voice of the leader of the Vultures gang. Based on the 1914 novel by May, the film was released in the United States in 1966 by Columbia as *Frontier Hellcat* with publicity emphasis on co-star Elke Sommer, who (after the film was made) had come to American prominence in *The Victors* and *The Prize* (both 1963), *A Shot in the Dark* (1964) and *The Art of Love* (1965).

Granger (1913–93) was a native of Great Britain whose real name was James Stewart. Entering features as a bit player in 1933, he changed his name in order to avoid confusion with the American actor James Stewart. By the late 1930s he was a star in England and during the 1940s he became one of the country's most popular players. Coming to Hollywood in 1950, he headlined rugged action features like *King Solomon's Mines* (1950), *The Wild North*, *Scaramouche* and *The Prisoner of Zenda* (all 1952), *All the Brothers Were Valiant* (1953), *The Last Hunt* (1956) and *North to Alaska* (1960). He worked mainly in Europe in the 1960s and in 1966 he co-starred with Barker and Brice in the spy melodrama *Killer's Carnival*.

Set in Arizona, *Unter Geiern* (Among Vultures) begins with Apache chief Winnetou (Brice) helping hunter Bauman (Walter Barnes) and his son Martin (Gotz George) kills a large bear which has been menacing the vicinity. While they are away, the Bauman ranch is ransacked by a gang called the Vultures, white men masquerading as Indians. They set the place on fire and kill Bauman's wife and small daughter. When the Baumans return home and find the carnage, the blame is placed on Shoshone Indians, and Winnetou vows to find the killers. Meanwhile Old Surehand (Granger) joins Old Wabble (Milan Srdoc) and his men who are accompanying beautiful Annie Dillman (Elke Sommer), who is carrying a money belt containing diamonds to her father in Arizona. When they see an Indian, Wokadeh (Gojko Mitic), being attacked by riders, Old Shatterhand comes to his rescue and is soon joined by Winnetou. At the ranch, Bauman refuses to believe Winnetou's story about fake Indians killing his family, especially when a preacher (Miha Baloh) arrives and claims he saw the massacre and says that Indians were to blame. Old Shatterhand proves the man is a fake and he runs away; his real name is Weller and he is one of the Vulture gang. When the gang murders the Shoshone chief, the new leader, Wokadeh, places the blame on Bauman and vows to kill him; Winnetou tells him he will bring the real killer to justice. Gang members kidnap Annie and take her to their hideout but she is followed by Martin, who has fallen in love with her. He infiltrates the gang and ingratiates himself with the leader (Renato Baldini), pretending to be a horse trader and gunman, but he is soon recognized by one of the outlaws and captured. Winnetou, who has trailed Martin to the hideout, sets off an explosion which allows Martin and Annie to escape. The Shoshones capture Bauman, and Old Surehand tries to rescue him but fails. He then must shoot down three arrows fired at him and when he is successful in this test, Wokadeh agrees to help him fight the Vulture gang. Martin and Annie join a wagon train only to find it under the control of Weller and other gang members. They try to hang Martin but Annie comes to his rescue as Old Surehand arrives. When Wokadeh and his braves see that the Vulture gang has desecrated the tribe's burial grounds, he sets Bauman free along with the captive Old Wabble and his men. Old Surehand forces a confession out of Weller as the Vulture gang attacks the wagon train. Winnetou, Wokadeh and his braves, along with Bauman, Old Wabble and his gang, come to the train's rescue and Old Surehand kills the gang leader. Weller takes Bauman prisoner but is killed as Martin and Annie are reunited.

Granger, who introduced a modicum of underplayed humor as Old Surehand, returned in the role in *Der Ölprinz* (The Oil Prince), which was first shown in West Germany in August, 1965. It was based on May's 1893 novel of the same title and was shown in a dubbed version on the U.S. by Columbia as *Rampage at Apache Wells*. The plot had outlaws called the Finger Gang attack a wagon train and kill its leader, Billy Forner (Zvonimir Crnko). When frontiersman Old Surehand (Granger) and Apache chief Winnetou (Brice) find out about the murder, Old Surehand takes over as the train's wagon master. The settlers on the wagon train are headed for new homes near Lake Shelly, and Winnetou convinces the Navajo tribe in the area to let them alone as they travel to their destination. The Oil Prince (Harald Leipnitz), the leader of the outlaws, wants the settlers' property and, to incite the Navajos, he frames the chief's son for robbery and then murders him, placing the blame on the settlers. The Indians retaliate and attack the wagon train but Old Surehand proves to them that it was the Oil Prince who was behind the crimes. With the aid of Winnetou, Old Surehand brings the Oil Prince and his gang to justice and the wagon train proceeds to its destination.

Barker was back as Old Shatterhand in *Winnetou III*, which like *Winnetou I* and *Winnetou II*

Pierre Brice and Lex Barker in *Winnetou III* (Constantin, 1965).

Lex Barker and Pierre Brice in *Winnetou III* (Constantin, 1965).

was based on the 1893 May novel *Winnetou, der rote Gentleman*. Released originally in West Germany in the fall of 1965, it was screened in America by Columbia in a dubbed version called *The Desperado Trail*. Here Winnetou (Brice) and Old Shatterhand (Barker) try to aid the territorial governor (Carl Lange) in arranging a peace treaty with rival tribe chief White Buffalo (Dusan Antonijevic). White Buffalo and his tribe have come under the influence of Rollins (Rik Battaglia), a crook who operates a land trust. Dealing in corrupt land speculation, Rollins tries to stir up trouble between the Indiana tribes by bribing White Buffalo and his people with fire water and guns. Learning of the governor's plan, Rollins has his men ambush Old Shatterhand and Winnetou but they fail. Rollins frames Winnetou for the murder of White Buffalo's son. Scout Sam Hawkens (Ralf Wolter) rescues Winnetou, who then leads his Apache warriors against a combined force of Rollins' outlaws and White Buffalo and his braves. Nearly defeated, Winnetou and his men are saved by the arrival of the cavalry but the Apache chief dies, taking a bullet intended for Old Shatterhand.

Although the title character dies at the end of *Winnetou III*, the Apache chief was back in *Old Surehand*, which came out in West Germany at the end of 1965. It saw release in the United States in 1968 as *Flaming Frontier*, a dubbed version released by Warner Bros.-7 Arts. It was the third and last film in which Granger enacted the part of the frontiersman and it was based on the 1894 May novel *Old Surehand*. This time out, Old Surehand (Granger), who has been on a three-year search for this brother's killer, comes to the aid of victims of a mail train robbery. The act was committed by a gang led by an outlaw called the General (Larry Pennell), whose men then slaughter buffalos on Comanche land and murder the chief's son. When the Comanches threaten war on the settlers, Old Surehand seeks the aid of Winnetou (Brice) in preventing an uprising. The General murders a prospector and steals the map to his gold mine as the man's daughter, Judith (Leticia Roman), and her fiancé, Toby (Mario Girotti [Terence Hill]), also seek the treasure. The two becomes prisoners of the Comanches, but Old Surehand obtains their freedom in exchange for a promise to find the killer of the chief's son. Scout Old Wabble (Paddy Fox) tells Old Surehand that it was the General who murdered his brother, and when the outlaw tries to set a trap for the frontiersman, Old Surehand escapes and brings back the cavalry which captures the outlaw gang. The General escapes to an abandoned mine where he is found by Old Surehand and Old Wabble. Old Surehand shoots it out with the General, kills him and retrieves the map to the gold mine which he gives to Judith and Toby.

The next series feature, *Winnetou und das Halbblut Apanatschi* (Winnetou and the Half Blood Apanatschi), was shown first in West Germany in the late summer of 1966 but it did not get U.S. release until 1973 as *Half Breed*. Probably the most obscure of the Winnetou films, it told of Apanatschi (Ursula Glas), the daughter of a white settler and an Indian woman, who is given a gold mine as a twenty-first birthday present by her father (Walter Barnes), with the blessing of Winnetou (Brice). Crooks want the mine for themselves and try to stir up trouble between settlers and the Indians in order to get the property. Although under the protection of railroad agent Old Shatterhand (Barker), Apanatschi is kidnapped by the crooks but she is rescued by Winnetou and his warriors. Old Shatterhand has a showdown with the bandits and kills them, restoring peace to the land.

The tenth Winnetou feature, *Winnetou und sein Freund Old Firehand* (Winnetou and His Friend Old Firehand), was a departure from previous entries in that it took place on the plains of the American Southwest (although still filmed in Yugoslavia) and not in the Rocky Mountains as had been the case with most of the series' other films. Here the white hero was called Old Firehand and the role was ably enacted by western veteran Rod Cameron. A native of Canada, Cameron (1910–83), whose real name was Nathan Cox, came to Hollywood in the late 1930s as a bit player after working in the construction industry. He soon became popular as a western star in a series for Universal in 1944–45 and then graduated to bigger productions like *Salome, Where She Danced* and *Frontier Gal* (both 1945), *The Runaround* (1946), *Pirates of Monterey* (1947), *River Lady* (1948), *Brimstone* (1949), *Oh! Susanna* (1951), *Ride the Man Down* (1952), *San Antone* (1953), *Southwest Passage* (1954) and *Spoilers of the Forest* (1957). He continued making genre appearances well into the 1970s but found his greatest fame on television, headlining and co-producing three highly successful syndicated series: *City Detective*, *State Trooper* and *Coronado 9*.

Released in the United States in 1967 by Columbia as *Thunder at the Border*, *Winnetou und sein Freund Old Firehand* was first shown in West Germany late in 1966. Winnetou (Brice) and his sister Nscho-tschi (Marie Versini) team with frontiersman Old Firehand (Cameron) in defending a Mexican village, Miramonte, against a band of bloodthirsty marauders led by Silers (Harald Leipnitz). After fighting off the onslaughts of the outlaws, Old Firehand and Winnetou are able to rout the bandits and restore peace to the area. Phil Hardy in *The Western* (1983) refers to Brice and Cameron "as a sort of Magnificent Two" and noted that the film "omits the obligatory [Karl] May ending, with Winnetou and his braves riding to the rescue, in favor of dynamite and individual heroics." Marie Versini repeated the role of the Apache chief's sister which she first played in *Winnetou I*.

Barker and Brice teamed on film as Old Shatterhand and Winnetou for the last time in *Winnetou und Shatterhand im Tal der Toten* (Winnetou and Shatterhand in the Valley of Death), released in West Germany late in 1968. It was shown stateside as *In the Valley of Death*. The plot had a fort commander, Major Kingsley (Jan Sid), saving a fortune in gold after the fall of his garrison. He takes the treasure to a remote area and hides it but dies after being found by Winnetou (Brice). The major's daughter, Mabel (Karin Dor), arrives at the fort looking for her father and hears rumors that he took the government gold for his own use. Scout Old Shatterhand (Barker) agrees to lead Mabel in search of her father's gold and they are joined by amateur botanist Lord Castlepool (Eddi Arent) and Winnetou. Along

Poster for *Winnetou und sein Freund Old Firehand* (Winnetou and His Friend Old Firehand) (Constantin, 1968).

the way the party is harassed by outlaws and Winnetou is forced into hand-to-hand combat with his old enemy, Sioux chief Red Buffalo (Wojo Govedarizu). Finally reaching the Valley of Death, Old Shatterhand and Winnetou are able to help Mabel find the gold and clear her father's name. Eddi Arent portrayed Lord Castlepool for the third and last time in this film, which was directed by Harald Reinl. *Winnetou und Shatterhand im Tal der Totem* was his fifth and last series entry and the third series film for his wife Karin Dor.

There was to be one more teaming of Barker and Brice as Old Shatterhand and Winnetou as they did the parts on the West German television program "Die Rudi Carrell Show," telecast June 5, 1971.

The soundtracks to *Winnetou I*, *Winnetou II* and *Winnetou III* were issued in Europe on the PEG label, and Europa Records issued a series of LPs dramatizing the Winnetou series with Michael Poelachau as Old Shatterhand and Konrad Haloes as Winnetou. In 1996 the German label Bear Family Records released a CD called "Winnetou du Warst Mein Freund," a compilation of two dozen songs about the Apache chief, including nine vocals by Brice and two by Barker. Four years later, Sony BMG released the two-CD set "Winnetou und Old Shatterhand."

Following the last Winnetou feature in 1968, Brice continued to portray the role of the Apache chief in various West German open air stage productions until 1991. During that time he also starred in the TV series *Ein Schloss am Wörthersee* (A Castle on the Wo-

Siegfried Rauch and Pierre Brice in *Winnetou le Mescalero* (Winnetou the Mescalero) (Antenne-2, 1980), also called *Winnetou in Mexico*.

erthersee), *Die Hütte am See* (The Hut on the Lake) and *Die Mädchen aus dem Weltrau* (Star Maidens). In 1979 he had the title role in the French television series *Winnetou le Mescalero* (Winnetou the Mescalero), which was also called *Mein Freund Winnetou* (My Friend Winnetou). This outing (not based on a Karl May work) told of Winnetou (Brice) coming to the aid of a young Arapaho kidnapped by outlaw Sammy Cook (Jose Antonio Marros) and his gang. When the Apache chief is injured in a shootout with the gang, he is left for dead but found by a traveling photographer (Jean-Claude Deret), who is blamed by the Paiutes. Old Shatterhand (Siegfried Rauch) convinces the Indians the photographer is innocent and then tends to his friend's wounds. Once he recovers, Winnetou, Old Shatterhand and the Paiutes hunt down the outlaws. The teleseries was filmed in Mexico.

The Treasure of Silver Lake was remade as an animated feature in East Germany in 1989 as *Die Spur führt zum Silbersee* (The Trail Leads to the Silver Sea) with Henry Hübschen providing the voice of Winnetou and Gert Grasse enacting the part of Old Shatterhand.

In 1998, Brice again starred as Winnetou in the two-part German television series *Winnetous Rückkehr* (The Return of Winnetou). The story began with the Apache chief living as a recluse in the mountains and having nothing to do with people. When outlaws harass settlers and local Indian tribes, he agrees to help them fight back. Again the plot was not based on a May work and purists were not happy with the program since the Winnetou character had been killed off in *Winnetou III*.

Another animated Winnetou venture, this time a TV series called *Winnetoons*, was telecast in Europe in 2002. Its thirty-minute episodes had Sascha Draeger as the voice of Winnetou and Michael Lott as Old Shatterhand.

As noted, Brice portrayed Winnetou in theatrical productions for many years and one of the places he worked was at the open air theater in Bad Segeberg, Germany. Located in Schleswig-Holstein, the theater is solely dedicated to staging Karl May works. He played Winnetou there from 1988 to 1991 and continued to work at the theater until 1999 as a director. When Brice left the part of Winnetou at Bad Segeberg, he was succeeded by Gojko Mitic, who did the role in fifteen plays and over one thousand performances before a combined audience of 3.6 million spectators. He continued to play Winnetou through the 2006 season. Mitic had appeared in five of the Rialto features, cast in Native American roles.

Beginning in 2002, a Bad Segeberg production was filmed annually and shown on German television as feature films; Mitic was Winnetou in all the productions. These were *Im Tal des Todes* (In the Valley of Death) (2002) with Reiner Schone as Old Firehand; *Old Surehand* (2003) with Wayne Carpendale in the title role and Joshy Peters as Old Shatterhand; *Unter Geiern — Der Sohn des Bärenjägers* (Among Vultures — The Son of the Barenjagers) (2004) with Joshy Peters repeating as Old Shatterhand; *Winnetou und das Geheimnis der Felsenburg* (Winnetou and the Secret of the Rock Castle) (2005) with Joachim Kretzer as Old Shatterhand; and *Winnetou III* (2006) with Joachim Kretzer again appearing as Old Shatterhand.

A German television special about the character of Winnetou was telecast on November 11, 2004. Produced and directed by Axel Klawuhn, "Auf den Spuren Winnetous" (In the Footsteps of Winnetou) featured Brice along with fellow series actors Gotz George and Ralf Wolter, who portrayed scout Sam Hawkens in five of the Rialto features and in the 1980 telefilm, and composer Martin Bottcher. Archive footage featured Lex Barker, Marie Versini, Herbert Lom, director Alfred Vohrer and producer Horst Wendlandt.

Released in 2005, the German short feature *Winnetou und der Schatz der Marikopas* (Winnetou and the Treasure of the Marikopas), featuring both professional and amateur actors, was a homage to the Karl May series of the 1960s. It had outlaws after the gold of the Marikopas tribe with the chief's daughter (Barbara Weinreich) being kidnapped by the gang leader (Dietmar Roske) and his men, with the blame being placed on Winnetou (Mike Dietrich) and Old Surehand (Eugen Brahler). The Indians vows to kill all whites but Old Shatterhand (Thomas Vogt) intervenes and joins Winnetou and Old Surehand in destroying the criminals and bringing peace back to the Rocky Mountains. As he had done with the 1960s Winnetou films, Martin Bottcher composed the film's score.

Filmography

Der Schatz im Silbersee (The Treasure of Silver Lake) (Constantin-Filmverleih, 1962, 111 minutes) Producers: Horst Wendlandt & Leif Feilberg. Executive Producers: Erwin Gitt, Zvonko Kovacic & Stipe Gurdulic. Director: Harald Reinl. Screenplay: Harald G. Petersson, from the novel by Karl May. Photography: Ernst W. Kalinke. Editor: Hermann Haller. Music: Martin Bottcher. Special Effects: Erwin Lange. Production Manager: Erwin Drager. Sound: Erik Molnar. Production Design: Dusan Jericevic. Costume Design: Irms Pauli. Makeup: Willi Nixdorf & Charlotte Schmidt-Kersten. Assistant Directors: Charles Wakefield & Slavko Andres.

Cast: Lex Barker (Old Shatterhand), Pierre Brice (Winnetou), Herbert Lom (Colonel Brinkley), Gotz George (Fred Engel), Karin Dor (Ellen Patterson), Ralf Wolter (Sam Hawkens), Eddi Arent (Lord Castlepool), Marianne Hoppe (Mrs. Butler), Mirko Boman (Uncle), Jan Sid [Sima Janicijevic] (Patterson), Jozo Kovacevic (Wolf), Slobodan Dimitrijevic (Donner), Branko Spoljar (Dr. Jefferson Hartley), Milivoj Stojanovic (Knox), Velemir Hill (Woodward), Ilija Ivezic (Hilton), Sime Jagarinac (Chief Osagen), Antun Nails (Bruns), Vladimir Medar (Saloon Owner).

Released in the United States in 1965 by Columbia as *Treasure of Silver Lake* (82 minutes).

Winnetou I (Constantin, 1963, 101 minutes) Producer: Horst Wendlandt. Director: Harald Reinl. Screenplay: Harald G. Petersson, from the novel *Winnetou, der rote Gentleman* by Karl May. Photography: Ernst W. Kalinke. Editor: Hermann Haller. Music: Martin Bottcher. Production Design: Vladimir Tadej. Production Manager: Erwin Gitt. Makeup: Gerda Wegener & Walter Wegener. Assistant Directors: Charles Wakefield & Slavko Andres.

Cast: Lex Barker (Old Shatterhand), Pierre Brice (Winnetou), Marie Versini (Nscho-tschi), Mario Adorf (Frederick Santer), Walter Barnes (Bill Jones), Chris Howland (Lord Tuff-Tuff), Ralf Wolter (Sam Hawkens), Milivoje Popovic-Mavid (Intschu-tschuna), Dunja Rajter (Belle), Niksa Stefanini (Bullock), Branko Spoljar (Bancroft), Husein Cokic (Will Parker), Demeter Bitenc (Dick Stone), Tomoslav Erak (Tangua), Krvoje Svob (Klekih-petra), Dusko Dobudj (Black Adler), Vlado Krstulovic (Harvey), Ilija Ivezic (Joaquin), Teddy Stotsek (Randolph), Antun Nalis (Bartender Hicks), Vladimir Bosnak (Lemmy), Ana Kranjcec (Vollmond), Sime Jagarinac (Apache), Ivo Kristof (Trail Guide), Gojko Mitic (Indian).

Released in the United States in 1965 by Columbia as *Apache Gold* (91 minutes).

Old Shatterhand (Constantin, 1964, 122 minutes) Executive Producer: Artur Brauner. Director: Hugo Fregonese. Screenplay: Ladislas Fodor & Robert A. Stemmle, from the novel by Karl May. Photography: Siegfried Hold. Editor: Alfred Srp. Music: Riz Ortolani. Art Director: Veljko Despotovic. Sound: Vladimir Dodig. Production Design: Otto Pischinger. Costumes: Mira Glisic & Trude Ulrich. Visual Effects: Zoran Djordjevic & Erwin Lange. Makeup: Raimund Strangl, Alfred Rasche & Susi Krause. Assistant Directors: Herta Friedel & Stevo Petrovic.

Cast: Lex Barker (Old Shatterhand), Pierre Brice (Winnetou), Guy Madison (Captain Bradley), Daliah Lavi (Paloma/The White Dove/Amy Wilkins), Rik Battaglia (Dixon), Gustavo Rojo (Corporal Bush), Ralf Wolter (Sam Hawkens), Kitty Mattern (Rosemary), Bill Ramsey (Timpe), Alain Tissier (Tujunga), Charles Fawcett (General Taylor), Nikola Popovic (Sheriff Brandon), Mirko Ellis (Joe Barker), Burschi Putzgruber (Tom), Jim Burke (Colonel Hunter), Dusko Radojcic (Murdered Farmer), Zivojin Denic (Schmeid), Nikola Illic (Lieutenant Boyd), Stevo Petrovic (Bandit), Uwe Rehse (Bartender), Vladimir Sovanovic (Medicine Man), Georg Attifeliner (Barbier), Mirko Boman (Dick Stone), Gojko Mitic (Apache), Vojkan Pavlovic (Will Parker), Andrea Scotti (Sergeant Flanner), Milivoje Popovic-Mavid (Lata Nalgut), Ulla Moritz (Trail Girl), Dusan Tadic (Porucnik Bakster).

Released in the United States in 1967 by Goldstone Film Enterprises as *Shatterhand* (89 minutes). British title: *Apache's Last Battle*.

Winnetou II (Constantin, 1964, 94 minutes) Producers: Horst Wendlandt, Erwin Gitt & Stipe Gurdulic. Executive Producer: Wolfgang Kuhnienz. Director: Harald Reinl. Screenplay: Harald G. Petersson, from the novel *Winnetou, der rote Gentleman* by Karl May. Photography: Ernst W. Kalinke. Editor: Hermann Haller. Music: Martin Bottcher. Art Director: Zeljko Sitaric. Production Manager: Eberhard Junkdesdorf. Production Design: Vladimir Tadej. Assistant Directors: Charles Wakefield & Slavko Andres.

Cast: Lex Barker (Old Shatterhand), Pierre Brice (Winnetou), Anthony Steel (Bud Forrester), Karin Dor (Ribanna), Klaus Kinski (David "Luke" Lucas), Renato Baldini (Colonel J.F. Merril), Mario Girotti [Terence Hill] (Lieutenant Robert Merril), Eddi Arent (Lord Castlepool), Marie Noelle (Susan Merril), Ilija Ivezic (Red), Velemir Chytil (Carter), Stole Arandjelovic (Caesar), George Heston [Djorje Nenadovic] (Captain Bruce), Mirko Boman (Uncle), Rikard Brzeska (Tah-Sha-Tunga), Gojko Mitic (White Bird), Sime Jagarinac (Ponca), Jozo Kovacevic (Ponca Chief), Antun Nalis (Sergeant Wagner), Ivo Kristof (Bandit), Curt Ackerman (Narrator).

Released in the United States in 1966 by Columbia as *Last of the Renegades*.

Unter Geiern (Among Vultures) (Constantin, 1964, 103 minutes) Producer: Horst Wendlandt. Executive Producers: Erwin Gitt & Stipe Gurdulic. Director: Alfred Vohrer. Screenplay: Eberhard Keindorff & Johanna Sibelius, from the novel by Karl May. Photography: Karl Lob. Editor: Hermann Haller. Music: Martin Bottcher. Production Managers: Herbert Kerz & Eberhard Junkdersdorf. Sound: Matija Barbalic. Special Effects: Erwin Lange. Makeup: Irmgard Forster & Erich L. Schmekel. Production Design: Vladimir Tadej. Second Unit Director: Stipe Delic. Assistant Director: Eva Ebner.

Cast: Stewart Granger (Old Surehand), Pierre Brice (Winnetou), Gotz George (Martin Bauman), Elke Sommer (Annie Dillman), Renalto Baldini (Leader of the Vultures), Walter Barnes (Bauman), Mario Girotti [Terence Hill] (Junior Baker), Gojko Mitic (Wokadeh), Miha Baloh (Weller/the Rev. Stephen Fox), Sieghardt Rupp (Preston), Paddy Fox [Milan Srdoc] (Old Wabble), Louis Velle (Gordon), Voja Miric (Stewart), Stole Arandjelovic (Milton), George Heston [Djordje Nenadovic] (Miller), Dunja Rajter (Betsy), Dusan Bulajic (Bloomfield), Ilija Ivezic (Jackie), Davor Antolic (Rod), Mirko Kraljev (Billy), Boris Dvornik (Fred), Milan Micic (Jimmy), Joza Seb (Bob), Sime Jagarinac (Schoschone), Gordana Cosic (Wokadeh's Sister), Vladimir Bacic (Jeremy), Mirko Boman (Davy), Margot Leonard (Annie), Vladimir Medar (Senior Baker), Marinko Cosic (Trail Boy).

Released in the United States in 1966 by Columbia as *Frontier Hellcat* (98 minutes).

Der Ölprinz (The Oil Prince) (Constantin, 1965, 91 minutes) Producer: Horst Wendlandt. Director: Harald Philipp. Screenplay: Harald Philipp & Fred Denger, from the novel by Karl May. Photography: Heinz Holscher. Editor: Hermann Haller. Music: Martin Bottcher. Art Directors: Zeljko Sitaric & Tihomir Peletic. Production Design: Dusan Jericevic. Costume Design: Irms Pauli. Sound: Matija Barbalic. Special Effects: Erwin Lange & Nikola Vujasinovic. Makeup: Claire Fussbach & Erich L. Schmekel. Stunt Director: Allen Pinson.

Cast: Stewart Granger (Old Surehand), Pierre Brice (Winnetou), Walter Barnes (Bill Campbell), Harald Leipnitz (The Oil Prince), Macha Meril (Lizzy), Antje Weissgerber (Mrs. Ebersbach), Mario Girotti [Terence Hill] (Richard Forsythe), Heinz Erhardt (Kantor Aurelius Hampel), Paddy Fox [Milan Srdoc] (Old Wabble), Milivoje Popovic-Mavid (Mokaschi), Gerd Frickhoffer (Kovacz), Slobodan Dimitrijevic (Knife), Dusan Janicijevic (Butler), Davor Antolic (Paddy), Veljiko Maricic (Bergmann), Ilija Ivezic (Webster), Zvonimir Crnko (Billy Forner), Marinko Cosic (Tobby), Petar Dobric (Nitsas-Ini), Sloban Vedernjak (John Campbell), Petar Petrovic (Jimmy Campbell), Branko Supek (Jack Campbell), Vladimir Leib (Duncan), Antun Nalis (Jenkins), Sime Jagarinac (Mokaschi's Son), Tihomir Polanec, Jovan-Burdus Janicijevic, Stole Arandjelovic (Bandits).

Released in the United States by Columbia as *Rampage at Apache Wells*.

Winnetou III (Constantin, 1965, 93 minutes) Producers: Horst Wendlandt, Erwin Gitt & Stipe Gurdulic. Director: Harald Reinl. Screenplay: Harald G. Petersson & J. Joachim Bartsch, from the novel *Winnetou, der rote Gentleman* by Karl May. Photography: Ernst W. Kalinke. Editor: Jutta Hering. Music: Martin Bottcher. Art Director: Vladimir Tadej. Production Manager: Wolfgang Kuhnlenz. Costumes: Irms Pauli. Assistant Director: Charles Wakefield.

Cast: Lex Barker (Old Shatterhand), Pierre Brice (Winnetou), Rik Battaglia (Rollins), Ralf Wolter (Sam Hawkens), Carl Lange (Governor), Mihail Baloh (Gomez), Dusan Antonijevic (White Buffalo), Aleksandar Gavric (Kid), Ilija Ivezic (Clark), Veljko Maricic (Vermeulen), Slobodan Dimitrijevic (Quick Panther), Sophie Hardy (Ann), Gojko Mitic (Jicarilla), Milan Micic (Lieutenant O'Hara), Dusan Vujisic (Scotter), Sime Jagarinac (Red Arrow), Dragomir Felba (Brown), Ivo Kristof, Miroslav Buhin (Bandits), Joachim Nottke (Narrator).

Released in the United States by Columbia as *The Desperado Trail*.

Old Surehand (Constantin, 1965, 93 minutes) Producers: Horst Wendlandt & Wolfgang Kuhnienz. Director: Alfred Vohrer. Screenplay: Eberhard Keindorff & Fred Denger, from the novel by Karl May. Photography: Karl Lob & Kreso Grcevic. Editor: Hermann Haller. Music: Martin Bottcher. Production Manager: Erwin Gitt. Sound: Max Galinsky & Matija Barbalic. Special Effects: Erwin Lange. Makeup: Kate Koopmann & Erich L. Schmekel. Assistant Director: Eva Ebner.

Cast: Stewart Granger (Old Surehand), Pierre Brice (Winnetou), Larry Pennell (General Jack O'Neal), Leticia Roman (Judith), Mario Girotti [Terence Hill] (Toby), Paddy Fox [Milan Srdoc] (Old Wabble), Wolfgang Lukschy (Dick Edwards), Erik Schumann (Captain Miller), Bata Zivojinovic (Jim Potter), Dusan Antonijevic (Maki-moteh), Vladimir Medar (Ben O'Brian), Hermina Pipinic (Molly), Jelena Zigon (Delia), Voja Miric (Joe), Dusan Janicijevic (Clinch), Nikola Gec (Cat), Veljko Maricic (Mac Hara), Miroslav Buhin (Bob Hara), Sime Jagarinac (Tou-Wan), Martin Sagner (Bonoja), Predrag Ceramilac (Old Surehand's Scout), Marijan Habazin (Buster), Lujo Knezevic (Bini), Mate Ivankovic (Wynand), Ivan Novak (Brewster), Marin Ercegovic (Medicine Man), Leo Butorac (Waiter), Stjepan Jurcevic (Stall Owner), Djani Segina (Blackie), Josip Zappalorto (Unhappy Man), Ivo Kristof (Outlaw).

Released in the United States in 1968 by Warner Bros.-7 Arts as *Flaming Frontier*.

Winnetou und das Halbblut Apanatschi (Winnetou and the Half-Blood Apanatschi) (Constantin, 1966, 90 minutes) Producer: Horst Wendlandt. Executive Producers: Erwin Gitt & Stipe Gurdulic. Assistant Producer: Charles Wakefield. Director: Harald Philipp. Screenplay: Fred Denger, from the novel by Karl May. Photography: Heinz Holscher. Editor: Jutta Herring. Music: Martin Bottcher. Sound: Matija Barbalic. Production Managers: Dusko Ercegovic, Bosko Mitrovic, Wolfgang Kuhnlenz & Herbert Kerz. Production Design: Vladimir Tadej. Costume Design: Irms

Pauli. Assistant Directors: Stipe Delic, Slavko Andres & Gundula V. Seelen.

Cast: Lex Barker (Old Shatterhand), Pierre Brice (Winnetou), Gotz George (Jeff Brown), Ursula [Uschi] Glas (Apanatschi), Ralf Wolter (Sam Hawkens), Walter Barnes (Mac Haller), Ilija Dzuvalekovski (Curly Bill), Mihail Balon (Judge), Marinko Cosic (Happy), Petar Dobric (Sloan), Vladimir Leib (Pinky), Nada Kasapic (Bessie), Abdurrahaman Shala (Hank), Marija Crnobori (Mine-Yota), Sime Jagarinac (Blackie), Zvonko Dobrin (Bryan), Ivo Kristof (Buster), Branko Spoljar (Doc), Rikard Brzeska (Smith), Mile Gatara (Bartender), Adam Vedernjak (Outlaw).

Released in the United States in 1973 by Hampton Films as *Half Breed*.

Winnetou und Sein Freund Old Firehand (Winnetou and His Friend Old Firehand) (Columbia, 1966, 98 minutes) Producer: Horst Wendlandt. Executive Producers: Erwin Gitt & Stipe Gurdulic. Director: Alfred Vohrer. Screenplay: Harald G. Petersson, David DeReszke & C.B. Taylor, from the novel by Karl May. Photography: Karl Lob. Editor: Jutta Herring. Music: Peter Thomas. Sound: Matija Barbalic. Special Effects: Erwin Lange. Production Managers: Herbert Kerz & Wolfgang Hantke. Production Design: Vladimir Tadej. Costume Design: Irms Pauli. Makeup: Erich L. Schmekel. Assistant Directors: Slavko Andres, Eva Ebner & Vili Caklec.

Cast: Rod Cameron (Old Firehand), Pierre Brice (Winnetou), Marie Versini (Nscho-tschi), Todd Armstrong (Tom), Harald Leipnitz (Silers), Viktor de Kowa (Robert Ravenhurst), Nadia Gray (Michele Mercier), Rik Battaglia (Captain Mendoza), Jorg Marquardt (Jace Mercier), Vladimir Medar (Caleb), Miha Baloh (Captain Luis Sanchez Quilvera), Aleksandar Gavric (Derks), Emil Kutijaro (Puglia), Illja Ivezic (Moses), Dusan Antonijevic (Leon Mercier), Walter Wilz (Billy Bob Silers), Milan Bosiljcic (Vince), Aleksanadar Stojkovic (German Joe), Marija Crnobori (Joanna), Tana Mascarelli (Indian Woman), Aleksandar Belaric (Hernando), Adela Podjed (Julia), Boris Dvornik (Padre), Dado Habazin (Callaghan), Nikola Gec (Wirz), Emil Mikuljan (Merz), Stejepan Spoljaric (Wallace), Ivo Kristof (Kaylurr), Vladimir Simac (Ben), Franc Ursic (Lem), Jovan Vukovic, Zvonko Dobrin (Officers), Sime Jagarinac (Outlaw).

Released in the United States in 1967 by Columbia as *Thunder at the Border*.

Winnetou und Shatterhand im Tal der Toten (Winnetou and Shatterhand in the Valley of Death) (Constantin, 1968, 89 minutes) Producers: Artur Brauner, Zvonko Kovacic & Sulejman Kapic. Executive Producers: Rolf Meier & Gotz Dieter Wulf. Director: Harald Reinl. Screenplay: Harald Reinl & Alex Berg [Herbert Reinecker]. Photography: Ernst W. Kalinke. Editor: Hermann Haller. Music: Martin Bottcher. Sound: Matija Barbalic. Production Managers: Marko Vrdoljak, Franz Achter, Georg M. Reuther, Joseph Thuis & Dusko Ercegovic. Production Design: Vladimir Tadej. Costume Design: Irma Pauli. Makeup: Erich L. Schmekel. Assistant Directors: Charles Wakefield & Stipe Delic.

Cast: Lex Barker (Old Shatterhand), Pierre Brice (Winnetou), Karin Dor (Mabel Kingsley), Ralf Wolter (Sam Hawkens), Eddi Arent (Lord Castlepool), Rik Battaglia (Murdock), Wojo Govedarizu (Red Buffalo), Clarke Reynolds (Captain Cummings), Vladimir Medar (Sheriff), Branco Spoliak (Cranfield), Kurt Waitzmann (Colonel Bergson), Heinz Welzel (Richter), Vladimir Leib (Man in Stagecoach), Llija Ivezic (Davis), Jan Sid [Sima Janicijevic] (Major Kingsley), Ivo Kristof (Craigh), Nikola Gec (Boone), Vladimir Bacic (Brown), Sime Jagarinac (White Feather), Miroslav Buhin, Valent Borovic (Soldiers), Mirko Kraljev (Settler Adams), Dusko Ercegovic (Bartender), Rajko Zakarija (Piano Player), Drago Sosa (Outlaw), Vladimir Simac, Stjepan Spoljaric (Stagecoach Drivers), Slavica Orlovic (Slender Deer), Vida Jerman (Saloon Girl).

Released in the United States as *In the Valley of Death*.

Winnetou le Mescalero (Winnetou the Mescalero) (Antenne-2, 1980, 364 minutes) Producer: Otto Fisher. Director: Marcel Camus. Screenplay: Jean-Claude Deret & Jean Gerard. Photography: Pierre Petit & Leon Sanchez. Music: Peter Thomas.

Cast: Pierre Brice (Winnetou), Siegfried Rauch (Old Shatterhand), Eric Do Hieu (Tashunko), Ralf Wolter (Sam Hawkens), Arthur Brauss (Lieutenant Robert Merril), Jean-Claude Deret (Napoleon Charbonneau), Leopoldo Frances (Ambrose), Jose Antonio Marros (Sammy Cook), Noe Murayma (Chief Paiute), Ana Laura (Winona), Carlos East (Skerbeck), Roger Cudney (Vincent), Monica Miguel (Nalin Vincent), Jesus Alvaro (Peter Vincent), Miguel Angel Fuentes (Yaqui), Vincente Lara (Old Bear), Ignacio Martinez (Chihuahua), Ramon Menendez (Captain Stone), Gerard Buhr (Major Turner), Rene Barrera (Lobo Dent), Armando Soya (Little Lobo), Jacques Francois (Stevens), Chad Hastings (Fowler), Elpidia Carrillo (Wetatoni), Jorge Reynoso (Hehaka Pa), Rosenda Monteros (Hehaka Win), Aurora Clavel (Mother), Salvador Godinez (Old Cheyenne), Rodrigo Puebla (Sergeant Hount), Reto Babst (Robinson), Antonio Zubiaga (Bessette), Carlos Camara (Mortimer), Luis Guevara (Fatty Morrison), Gerardo Moscoso (Sergeant Miller), Jesus Gomez (McKenna), George Segal (Gottlieb), Richard Duffour (Barbier), Mario Luraschi (Magic Man), Jose Vicente Huerta (Vittorio).

Alternate titles: *Mein Freund Winnetou* (My Friend Winnetou) and *De Sable et de Sang* (Of Blood and Sand).

Die Spur Führt zum Silbersee (The Trail Leads to the Silver Sea) (Deutsche Film, 1989, 81 minutes) Producer–Production Manager: Helga Kurth. Director: Gunter Ratz. Screenplay: Gunter Ratz, from the novel *Der Schatz im Silbersee* by Karl May. Photography: Rudof Uebe. Music: Addy Kurth. Animators-Puppeteers: Sybille Hartel & Barbel Hasselbarth.

Cast: Gert Grasse (Voice of Old Shatterhand), Henry Hubschen (Voice of Winnetou), Dieter Wien (Voice of Colonel Brinkley), Victor Deiss (Voice of Hobble-Frank), Hans-Jurgen Hanisch (Voice of Tante Droll), Klaus Manchen (Voice of Big Bear), Reinhard Michalke (Voice of the Sheriff).

Winnetous Rückkehr (The Return of Winnetou) (Regina Ziegler Film-production, 1998, 171 minutes) Producer: Mariette Rissenbeek. Director: Marijan D. Vajda. Screenplay: Pierre Brice, Jean-Claude Deret & Werner Waldhoff. Photography: Martin Stingl & Eberhard Geick. Editor: Renate Engelmann. Music: Martin Bottcher. Production Design: Beatrice Behrens & Ulrich Bergfelder. Set Decorators: Maarten van der Meijden, Gabriella Ausonio, Nelja Stump & Guido Konin. Costume Design: Claudia Bobsin. Assistant Directors: Stephan Wagner & Andreas Drost.

Cast: Pierre Brice (Winnetou), Candice Daly (Mary), Pierre Semmler (John Mayotte), Tobias Hoesl (Spencer), Christoph Moosbrugger (Hermann), Manuel Trausch (Timmy Mayotte), Juraj Kukura (Robert DeWill), Diego Wallraff (Steven Shagan), Calvin Burke (Balthasar), Buffalo Child (Tanka), Lowell Raven (Little Biber), Jimmy Herman (Tah-Sha-Tunga), Jonathan Joss (Wash-Ti), Patrice Martinez (Kish-Kao-Ko), Katy Martohy (Heather), Erwin Leder (Fred), Paco Fuentes (Chif Crows), Bernhard Bettermann (Gunman), Cornelia Corba (Erika Hanson), Ady Berber (Older Assiniboin), Nikolaus Grobe (Sven), Detief Bothe, Martin Dutrop, Sylvie Nogler (Quakers), Carlos Lucas.

Im Tal des Todes (In the Valley of Death) (NDR Television, 2002, 90 minutes) Director: Norbert Schultze, Jr. From the novel by Karl May.

Cast: Gojiko Mitic (Winnetou), Reiner Schone (Old Firehand), Allegra Curtis (Senorita Miranda), Yokes Baumert (Sam Hawkens), Jorg Bundschuh (Hobble-Frank), Anderson Farah (Juanito Alvarez), Michael Grimm (Lata Naigut), Vanida Karun (Paloma), Nicolas King (Iron Arrow), Thorsten Laussch (Dr. Hartley), Joshy Peters (Roulin), Clemens von Ramin (Martin).

Old Surehand (NDR Television, 2003, 90 minutes) Director: Norbert Schultze, Jr. From the novel by Karl May.

Cast: Gojiko Mitic (Winnetou), Wayne Carpendale (Old Surehand), Joshy Peters (Old Shatterhand), Jurgen Mai (General Douglas), Dunja Rajter (Mother Thick), Frank Weiczorek (Old Wabble).

Unter Geiern — Der Sohn des Bärenjägers (Among Vultures — The Son of the Barenjagers) (NDR Television, 2004, 90 minutes) Director: Norbert Schultze, Jr. From the novel by Karl May.

Cast: Gojiko Mitic (Winnetou), Joshy Peters (Old Shatterhand), Patrick Bach (Martin Baumann), Anderson Farah (Wokadeh), Tanja Szewczenko (Mary Lou Carson), Vanida Karun (Pashewa), Ben D. Bremer (Tokvi-Tey), Dirc Simpson (Heavy Moccasin), Frank Wieczorek (Long Davy), Jochen Baumert (Chubby Jeremy).

Winnetou und das Geheimnis der Felsenberg (Winnetou and the Secret of the Rock Castle) (NDR Television, 2005, 90 minutes) Producer: Stefan Tietgen. Director: Norbert Schultze, Jr. From the novel by Karl May.

Cast: Gojko Mitic (Winnetou), Joachim Kretzer (Old Shatterhand), Saskia Valencia (Judith Steinberger), Joshy Peters (Vete-Ya), Helmut Krauss (Don Geronimo), Gotz Otto (Harry Melton), Frank Schroder (Jurisconsulto), Thomas Schunke (Yuma-Setar), Oliver Utecht (Don Timoteo Purchillo/Hermann), Jochen Baumert (Juggle-Fred), Marvin Bottcher (Benito), Friedhelm Wolff (Ramon Ramirez), Clara Velez (Felisa), Anderson Farah (The Player).

Winnetou und der Schatz der Marikopas (Winnetou and the Treasure of the Marikopas) (WVG Median GmbH, 2005, 45 minutes) Director: Eugen Brahler. Screenplay: Gene Carpenter. Music: Martin Bottcher.

Cast: Mike Dietrich (Winnetou), Thomas Vogt (Old Shatterhand), Eugen Brahler (Old Surehand), Meike Anders (Ribanna), Frank Zimmerman (Grinley), Dietmar Roske (Frank Mason), Stefan Luckert (Barenjager), Barbara Weinrich (Para-Angare), Jutta Kochling (Mah-Tschom-Pah), Fritz Heier (Carter), Uwe Mertel (Pedro).

Winnetou III (NDR Television, 2006, 90 minutes) Producer: Stefan Tietgen. Director: Norbert Schultze, Jr. From the novel *Winnetou, der rote Gentleman* by Karl May.

Cast: Gojko Mitic (Winnetou), Joachim Kretzer (Old Shatterhand), Winfried Glatzeder (Santer), Alexandra Kamp-Groeneveld (Dr. Kate Brody), Joshy Peters (Ko-Itse), Jorg Zick (Stephen Moody), Anderson Farah (Ma-Ram), Jochen Baumert (Sam Hawkens), Thomas Bestvater (Fred Morgan), Gesa Dreckmann (Hi-La-Dih), Ben D. Bremer (To-Kei-Chun/Mark Jorrocks), Volker Brandt (Father Hillmann).

ZORRO

For some nine decades, the character of Zorro, the masked avenger protecting the helpless against injustice, has been a popular cinematic figure. Two people, Johnston McCulley and Douglas Fairbanks, deserve the credit for popularizing this dashing freedom fighter. McCulley first conceived the character in print in 1919 and Fairbanks brought him to the screen in 1920, thus launching a movie hero whose past and present exploits continue to delight audiences in theaters and on television. Few characters have had the lengthy popularity of Zorro, ranging from Fairbanks' *The Mark of Zorro* in 1920 to *The Legend of Zorro* in 2005.

Johnston McCulley (1883–1958), a native of Illinois, was a prolific writer whose output included books, magazine stories, pulp fiction and screenplays. Although he wrote over fifty novels and used several pseudonyms, he is best remembered for creating Zorro, the "Fox," who first appeared in the five-part *All-Story Weekly* story "The Curse of Capistrano" in 1919. Following the immense popularity of the movie *The Mark of Zorro* in 1920, he revived the character in 1922 in the six-installment *Argosy* magazine story "The Further Adventures of Zorro." He returned to the character in 1931 in the *Argosy* four-part serial "Zorro Rides Again" and thereafter he wrote over sixty more Zorro stories, most of which were published in *West* magazine from 1944 to 1951. His final effort about the masked hero, "The Mask of Zorro," was published in *Short Stories for Men* in 1959.

There are many who feel the character of Zorro might well have drifted into obscurity had not Douglas Fairbanks purchased the rights to "The Curse of Capistrano" and filmed it as *The Mark of Zorro*, the year after its publication. Fairbanks (1883–1939) was born Douglas Ulman and made his Broadway debut in 1902, working his way to stardom by 1910. Five years later he came to Hollywood, contracted by Triangle; in 1916 he formed Douglas Fairbanks Film Corporation and four years later he helped found United Artists. The actor established his film popularity in light-hearted comedies but *The Mark of Zorro* changed his image to that of a swashbuckler and he would remain in that mold for the rest of his career. Not only did he play the title role in *The Mark of Zorro* but he also helped adapt the McCulley story to the screen, using the name Elton Thomas.

Joe Franklin noted in *Classics of the Silent Screen* (1959), "*The Mark of Zorro* remains one of the best of Doug's cloak-and-sword adventures because it is essentially a product of the *old* Doug. It has the zip and pace of his early films, is fairly short ... and doesn't allow spectacle and décor to swamp the action.... As the famous Mexican Robin Hood, Doug had a chance to masquerade as a fop, with many delightful comedy touches of his own ... and to spring into frequent action as Zorro, crusader for the rights of the oppressed Mexicans. There are a couple of fine duel sequences, and a wonderful chase towards the end, in which Doug eludes his pursuers with some fantastic acrobatics." In *Zorro Unmasked: The Official History* (1998), Sandra Curtis wrote, "Fairbanks gave a life to Zorro that in turn imbued his own life with a dream. McCulley's fox was in large part the beneficiary of Fairbanks's genius as a performer and visionary. Many men have played Zorro, but no actor has imbued the California defender of justice with such panache or given Diego such a contrasting, humorous persona. These were Fairbanks's unique gifts and his contributions to McCulley's creation."

The Mark of Zorro, released late in 1920, takes place a century before in Southern California where the governor, Alvarado (George Periolat), has levied heavy taxes on the people. His actions are being opposed by a masked avenger called Zorro. One of the landowners who is against the governor is Don Alberto Vega (Sydney De Gray) whose foppish son, Don Diego Vega (Fairbanks), has returned home from Spain, but is a bitter disappointment to this father. Unbeknownst to all, Don Diego is really Zorro. A ten thousand peso reward is posted for the capture of Zorro, and Sergeant Gonzales (Noah Beery) promises to collect it, but at a road house the masked man duels with the officer, humiliates him and escapes. Don Alberto wants a marriage for his son with the beautiful Lolita (Marguerite de la Motte), whose parents, Don Carlos Pulido (Charles Hill Mailes) and Dona Catalina Pulido (Claire McDowell), are land poor from heavy taxation. While Lolita is unimpressed with Don Diego, as Zorro he romances her and wins her heart. Seeing Zorro on their grounds, the Pulidos send for Captain Juan Ramon (Robert McKim) and his men in order to win favor with the governor. Zorro, however, escapes but returns when the captain makes unwanted advances to Lolita. The Pulido family moves to Don Diego's town house but Juan Ramon soon intrudes and tries to force himself on Lolita. Again Zorro intervenes, defeats the captain in a duel and forces him to apologize to the young woman. When Don Carlos tries to get Don Diego to defend Lolita's honor in a duel with the captain, the young man feigns boredom. The governor arrives with a cortege intent on ruling the area and when a priest (Walt Whitman) is falsely accused of swindling for bribes he orders the holy man beaten. Don Carlos stops the punishment while Zorro writes letters to local caballeros asking them to band together and fight the government oppression. When Juan Ramon tells the governor that Don Carlos and his family have been aiding Zorro, they are put in prison. Zorro then rallies the caballeros in fighting the governor and sets the Pulidos free. Taking their men to Don Diego's home, Juan Ramon and the governor realize the supposedly cowardly Vega is really Zorro. Don Diego defeats Juan Ramon in a sword fight as the caballeros back him, taking away the governor's power. Gonzales and his men also join forces with Don Diego, who wins Lolita's love.

After making the swashbucklers *The Three Musketeers* (1921), *Robin Hood* (1922) and *The Thief of Baghdad* (1924), Fairbanks returned to the Zorro character in 1925's *Don Q, Son of Zorro*, which he also produced. Directed by Donald Crisp, who also portrayed the villainous Don Sebastian, the feature gave Fairbanks dual roles, that of Don Diego Vega and his son, Don Cesar de Vega. Based on Hesketh and Kate Prichard's 1925 novel *Don Q's Love Story*, the film, which was released in the fall of that year, told of devil-may-care Don Cesar de Vega (Fairbanks) being sent to Spain by his father, Don Diego Vega (also Fairbanks), to learn the art of being a soldier and a gentleman. Arriving in Spain, Don Cesar immediately falls in love with beautiful Dolores de Muro (Mary Astor) and he is soon popular at the Spanish court of the queen (Stella De Lanti). He also

Advertisement for *The Mark of Zorro* (United Artists, 1920).

becomes friendly with the Archduke (Warner Oland), a visitor from Austria. The Archduke is murdered by one of the queen's guards, and the conniving Don Fabrique (Jean Hersholt) blackmails the culprits behind the assassination while laying the blame for the killing on Don Cesar. In order to clear his name and find those behind the assassination, Don Cesar pretends to kill himself as Don Diego arrives hoping to help his son. When Don Diego realizes his son is still alive, the two men unite to unmask the murderous rogues with Don Cesar winning Dolores' heart.

In *The New York Times*, Mordaunt Hall noted, "It is a swift picture with plenty of pleasing surprises and action. Mr. Fairbanks appears to have trained down to a very slender figure for the part. He springs into the saddle with amazing ease, and never makes a false move. It is an ideal part for Mr. Fairbanks, who as usual has put in no end of work in mastering the great whip as well as in showing that he is just as agile as he was years ago when he first startled audiences by his remarkable leaps." While Don Diego used a sword in *The Mark of Zorro*, Don Cesar brandishes a whip in this sequel although there is a scene in which father and son, via well-done camera tricks, stand side by side and duel with court soldiers. Just as lighthearted and actionful as its predecessor, *Don Q, Son of Zorro* proved to be another potent box office success for Fairbanks.

When the film was first previewed in New York City in June, 1925, it had a prologue in which stock whip expert Fred Lindsay gave several demonstrations. These included lassoing a woman around the neck and waist and taking a cigarette out of a man's hand.

An obscure feature, *A la Manière de Zorro* (The Way of Zorro), was made in Belgium in 1926, starring William Elie in the title role.

In 1933, Fairbanks announced he and his son, Douglas Fairbanks, Jr., along with Alexander Korda, would form a production company in Great Britain to produce a film to be called either *Zorro and Son* or *Zorro Rides Again* to star the two Fairbankses. The production company nor the project ever materialized.

Zorro did not come to sound films until 1936 when Republic Pictures produced *The Bold Caballero*, which was released in February of that year. Filmed in Magna Color, it was called *The Bold Cavalier* in the United Kingdom. Although McCulley supplied the story idea, it was director Wells Root who adapted it to film from his screen story "The Return of Zorro." Robert Livingston portrayed Don Diego Vega, alias Zorro, in the feature and it was his first starring effort for Republic. The year 1936 proved to a banner one for the actor as he followed up the Zorro part with the role of another masked avenger, "The Eagle," in the studio's twelve-chapter cliffhanger *The Vigilantes Are Coming* and then he starred as Stony Brooke in the first trio of "Three Mesquiteers" (q.v.) adventures. In both the serial and the Zorro feature, Livingston wore a full-face mask when portraying the hero.

Taking place in Santa Cruz in Old California, *The Bold Caballero* had Don Diego Vega (Livingston) moonlighting as Zorro, aiding the poor Indian peons who have been taxed unmercifully by the corrupt Commandante Sebastian Golle (Sig Rumann), a cruel expatriate Austrian. Having been captured, Zorro is about to be hung when word arrives that a new governor, Palma (Robert Warwick), is nearby. In the confusion, Zorro makes his escape. Upon Palma's arrival, Vega shows up asking to be a part of the governor's entourage. Palma takes an immediate dislike to the young man and decides to offer him up as bait for Zorro, despite the objections of his daughter Isabella (Heather Angel). Golle, realizing his theft of the king of Spain's tax money will get him hung, murders Palma and places the blame on Zorro. Isabella takes over as governor and vows to hang Zorro. Vega ingratiates himself with Golle by showing him how to court Isabella, whom he wants to marry so he can continue to rule Santa Cruz. When the new governor finds Golle's men making slaves of those who cannot pay their taxes, she offers a reward in gold for the capture of Zorro, who steals the money, thus setting the peons free. The masked man saves a priest (Ian Wolfe) Golle had planned to kill and then humiliates the commandante by tying him up and dressing him in Zorro's garb. To get even, Golle stages a bullfight on Isabella's birthday and uses a child matador as a trick to bring Zorro out into the open. When Isabella begs Vega to save the child, he does so and then proclaims his love for her. Golle attacks Vega, who beats him in a sword fight and leaves the mark of Zorro, a "Z," on him.

Realizing Don Diego is Zorro, Isabella, who has fallen in love with him, sets out to avenge her father's killing and helps Golle and his men capture the masked man. When she refuses to marry Golle, Isabella and her lady in waiting (Emily Fitzroy) are thrown in a dungeon with Zorro. Vega convinces her it was Golle who killed her father, and the commandante whips her lady in waiting and leaves the sign of the Z on her. As a ruse, Isabella consents to marry Golle as Vega changes clothes with the lady in waiting, who is taken to the gallows to be hung as Zorro. The peons, lead by the priest, attack Golle and his men and Don Diego kills the commandante in a duel. Santa Cruz is freed of tyranny as the priest blesses the upcoming nuptials of Isabella and Don Diego Vega.

Not only was *The Bold Caballero* the first Zorro film in color, it was also the first to have the masked avenger sing. Robert Livingston serenades Isabella with "The Stars in Your Eyes" and, in a very humorous sequence, he stays off to the side singing "La Paloma" while the bumbling Golle tries to romance the young woman. This was followed by the commandante proposing marriage to the foppish Vega with Isabella wishing them happiness.

Although MagnaColor failed to catch on, *The Bold Caballero* proved successful enough for Republic to launch a series of cliffhangers based on the exploits of the Masked Fox, beginning with *Zorro Rides Again*, which came to theaters in November, 1937. The first of seventeen serials co-directed by the team of William Witney and John English, it was similar to *The Bold Caballero* in that Zorro wore a full-face mask and he also sang. John Carroll starred as James Vega, the great-grandson of Zorro, who is represented by a huge wall picture which bears a striking resemblance to Douglas Fairbanks. For the first time, a Zorro adventure was set in the present.

The twelve chapter serial told of the machinations of ruthless magnate J.A. Marsden (Noah Beery), who is trying to take control of the California-Yucatan Railroad, co-owned by Don Manuel Vega (Nigel de Brulier), the grandson of Zorro. In the pay of Marsden is the notorious outlaw El Lobo (Richard Alexander), who with his gang, raids railroad property, trying to put the franchise out of business. In desperation, Don Manuel sends for his nephew, businessman James Vega (Carroll). James displays none of the manly qualities associated with the Vega family. Unbeknownst to everyone except old family retainer Renaldo (Duncan Renaldo), James takes on the guise of Zorro and prevents El Lobo and his men from burning down the Vega hacienda. He also stops an attack by the marauders on the railroad construction site but in the shootout Don Manuel is mortally wounded. Before his uncle dies, Zorro reveals his true identity to him and vows to grant his final request by defeating Marsden and his minions. When the outlaws try to rob the payroll train, Zorro shoots down the plane on which El Lobo had planned to bomb the conveyance, thus saving Vega's business partners, Phillip Andrews (Reed Howes) and his sister Joyce (Helen Christian). Zorro, aided by Phillip, Joyce and Renaldo, continue to thwart Marsden and El Lobo's plans to kill them and wreck the railroad. Eventually Vega goes to the big city to search Marsden's office and he is nearly killed in a fall from a skyscraper but is saved by using his whip to swing to safety. Finally, Zorro is captured by El Lobo and his gang and is unmasked. Renaldo confides to Joyce his master's true identity and they lead a posse to his rescue with Zorro's horse, El Rey, trampling El Lobo to death.

Noah Beery, who played the bombastic Sergeant Gonzales in 1920's *The Mark of Zorro*, here is cast as the villainous Marsden, who communicates with El Lobo from his skyscraper office via the wireless. Beery's scenes were shot in one day and his character, although the main bad guy, apparently gets away in the end. The script of the film was attributed to five writers (Barry Shipman, John Rathmell, Franklyn Adreon, Ronald Davidson, Morgan B. Cox), and some sources say that uncredited Sherman L. Lowe also contributed. *Zorro Rides Again* was issued in a feature version in 1938 and 1959, making it the only Republic cliffhanger to two theatrical releases as a feature film. It was also released to television in a half-dozen 26-minute installments. Its working title was *The Mysterious Don Miguel*.

Two years after the release of *Zorro Rides Again*, Republic issued one of its all-time best chapterplays, *Zorro's Fighting Legion*, starring Reed Hadley as Zorro. Hadley was so good in the part that he ranks with Fairbanks and Guy Williams,

Poster for *Zorro's Fighting Legion* (Republic, 1939).

fight off foreign enemies. Local Governor Felipe (Leander De Cordova) and his henchmen, mine supervisor Manuel Gonzalez (Edmund Cobb), Commandante Manuel (John Merton) and Chief Justice Pablo (C. Montague Shaw), have joined forces in order to keep the gold for themselves. Further complicating matters are the local Yaqui Indians, who worship the recently revived three-century-old god, Don Del Oro, who tells them the mine's gold is theirs as he uses them in his plans to take control of the country. (One of the four conspirators dresses in a metal suit and pretends to be the Yaqui god.) Rancho owner Don Francisco (Guy D'Ennery) has formed a band of men called the Fighting Legion to combat the lawlessness and he hopes his visiting nephew, Don Diego Vega (Reed Hadley), will help him, but the young man shows no interest in the cause. When Don Francisco is killed by the marauders, Don Diego secretly becomes Zorro and leads the fight to wipe out the crooks, joined by his friend Ramon (William Corson) and servant Juan (Budd Buster). Successfully getting the gold shipment who later did the role on television for Walt Disney Productions, as one of the best Zorros. With Zorro wearing a shorter mask than in the two previous Republic productions, the story was set in the early 1800s with Mexico winning its independence from Spain in 1810 only to have a madman in the guise of Yaqui Indian god Don Del Oro trying to become emperor of the nation. Set in 1824, the serial had Mexican President Benito Juarez (Carleton Young) trying to keep gold shipments coming through from the San Mendolita Mines in order to pay off his country's debts and through to Juarez, Zorro and his men are constantly at odds with Don Del Oro and his legions, with the masked man rescuing Ramon and his sister Volita (Sheila Darcy), who thinks Don Diego is a fop, when they are captured by the Yaquis. Zorro saves Yaqui chief Kala (Paul Marion) from being murdered and proves to him that Don Del Oro is not a god but a man masquerading as the deity. Zorro and Kala stop the Indians from attacking the mine and Zorro unmasks Don Del Oro with the Yaquis taking a terrible revenge on the imposter. Don Diego returns home to Cal-

Reed Hadley in *Zorro's Fighting Legion* (Republic, 1939).

ifornia after the Indians and the Mexican government sign a peace treaty.

Again directed by the ace serial team of William Witney and John English, *Zorro's Fighting Legion* was action-packed from start to finish through a dozen explosive chapters. Running true to form with the cliffhanger format, Zorro escaped such climaxes as a landslide, an exploding building, a falling elevator, a cut suspension bridge, an exploding wagon, moving walls, a runaway stagecoach, a water-filled mine shaft, an arrow attack, a runaway wagon and capture by the Indians. Interestingly, the serial had Zorro using the sword as a weapon, something not done in other Republic serials based on the character. The cliffhanger was reissued theatrically in 1958 and, like *Zorro Rides Again*, to which it was a pre-

quel, it was shown on TV in six 26-minute chapters. Although only one of the four conspirators was revealed in Chapter Twelve as Don Del Oro, the producers tried to avoid his identification by using another actor's voice for the character. Republic files show Billy Bletcher was hired to supply the voice of Don Del Oro but some sources claim it was Gayne Whitman. The serial also used the triad hero concept for the first time in a Zorro outing, emulating Republic's popular feature series "The Three Mesquiteers" (q.v.).

20th Century–Fox acquired the rights to the Johnston McCulley story "The Curse of Capistrano" and remade *The Mark of Zorro*, releasing it to theaters in November, 1940. Tyrone Power assumed the role of Don Diego Vega in this well-mounted, rather leisurely production, which was directed by Rouben Mamoulian. The feature proved to be very popular, especially in Latin America where it was dubbed into six different Spanish dialects, but it lacked the panache of the Fairbanks version done two decades before. The highlight of the production is a well-staged and highly exciting duel sequence, between Power and villain Basil Rathbone. Fred Cavens, the fencing expert who tutored both Fairbanks and Robert Livingston, did the same with Power. Rathbone, an able fencer in his own right, added much to the excitement of the sequence.

The feature begins with Don Diego Vega (Power) proving to be a top swordsman at his military training school in Spain. He is suddenly summoned home to California by his father, Don Alejandro Vega (Montagu Love), who has been replaced as alcalde of Los Angeles by Don Luis Quintero (J. Edward Bromberg). Upon arrival, Don Diego finds that the peasants blame his father for the cruel treatment meted out to them by Quintero's troops under the command of the cruel Captain Esteban Pasquale (Rathbone). While Don Diego pretends to be a snobbish aristocrat, he becomes the masked Zorro, who posts a notice that Quintero is a thief who will face his revenge. Zorro holds up Quintero and takes gold from him which was intended for the king of Spain. He hides the money in the local church and soon reveals his identity to the priest, Fray Felipe (Eugene Pallette). While in the guise of Zorro, Don Diego sees and romances Quintero's lovely niece Lolita (Linda Darnell) while as a fop he flirts with Quintero's wife Inez (Gale Sondergaard), the mistress of Esteban. While Esteban is paid to protect Quintero, the corrupt but bumbling governor is afraid of Zorro, especially after the masked man orders him to return to Spain so Don Alejandro can resume the office of alcalde. The scheming Quintero proposes a marriage between Don Diego and Lolita, while Inez wants to go back to Spain with Don Diego. Lolita, however, finds Don Diego revolting until she comes to realize he is really Zorro. When Esteban finds the money Zorro left in the church, he arrests Fray Felipe. Lolita tells Don Diego, who challenges the captain to a duel. Don Diego kills Esteban but when Quintero finds a secret stairway in his study, which Zorro has used to previously escape capture, he orders Vega arrested and sentences him and the priest to face a firing squad. Don Diego is able to escape and he rallies the local caballeros and peasants to rise up and fight Quintero and his soldiers. The troops are defeated, Don Diego forces Quintero to resign and his father returns to the position of alcalde while Vega is free to marry Lolita.

While *The Mark of Zorro* made Power one of the top five box office attractions of 1940, the actor paled in comparison to Fairbanks as Zorro. As Hector Arce noted in *The Secret Life of Tyrone Power* (1979), Power "could never match Fairbanks's acrobatic skill and physical comedy." Arce added, however, "[Director] Mamoulian tapped Ty's comedic talents more fully than any of his previous roles had done. He was required to play an everyday fop who is transformed into a Spanish nobleman at night.... With his characteristic adaptability, Ty wore both guises so naturally and with such subtle changes in gestures and body carriage that his masquerade allayed suspicion far longer than it should have." The author also noted that Power's "fencing scenes were natural and convincing, looking more like someone trying to kill an opponent with a sword than someone flailing a prop for a Hollywood camera."

In 1941 the first of several Mexican Zorro films appeared; hardly any of them ever credited Johnston McCulley as the character's creator. *El Zorro del Jalisco* (The Fox of Jalisco) starred Pedro Armendariz as Leonardo Torres, an attorney who returns to his hometown only to find himself denied entrance to his family's hacienda. Isabel (Consuelo de Alba) sees her father murdered by outlaws who are terrorizing the area. Leonardo learns that their leader is Ernesto (Emilio Fernandez), Isabel's cousin, and while pretending to be a mild-mannered bookworm, he becomes the masked Zorro, defending the locals against the crooked government officials. This modern-day adventure has an amusing sequence early with Leonardo and Isabel sharing a train car; he reads a scholarly book while she prefers pulp magazines featuring Doc Savage and Fu Manchu.

Republic returned with another Zorro serial in 1944, *Zorro's Black Whip*, although Don Diego Viega was nowhere to be seen in its action-filled twelve chapters. Directed by genre veterans Spencer Gordon Bennet and Wallace Grissell, it

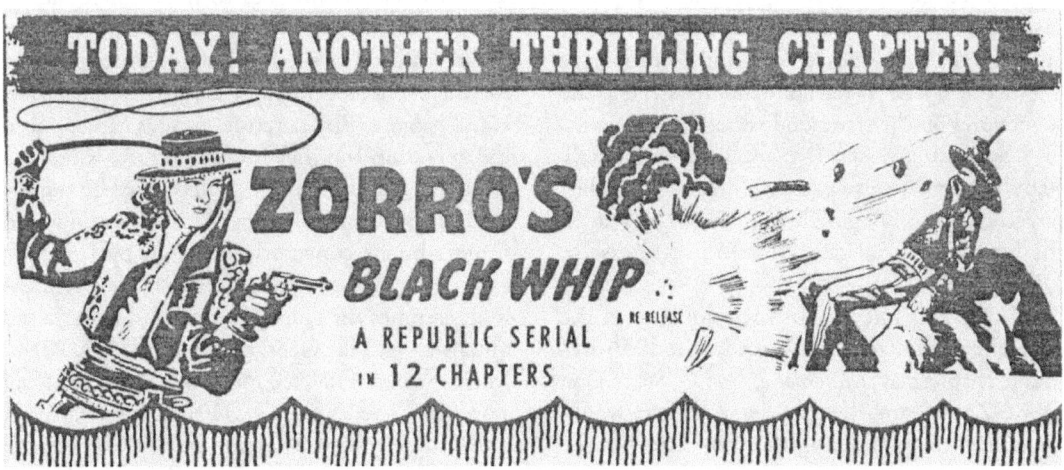

Advertisement for *Zorro's Black Whip* (Republic, 1944).

starred Linda Stirling as a female Zorro, known as The Black Whip. Here the whip-wielding heroine wore a mask which covered the lower half of her face but not the eyes or nose. In 1889 Idaho, the area around Crescent City is plagued by a reign of terror by those opposing statehood. The secret leader of the gang is stagecoach line owner Tom Hammond (Francis McDonald), who orders his gang to rob the local bank. Since the funds stolen included federal money, Commissioner James Bradley (Tom London) is sent to investigate. While being escorted to town by Barbara Meredith (Stirling), Bradley is ambushed and mortally wounded by members of the Hammond gang, Baxter (Hal Taliaferro) and Harris (John Merton). Arriving on the scene is railroad surveying engineer Vic Gordon (George J. Lewis), who is really an undercover agent. Before dying, Bradley orders Gordon to carry out his work and makes Barbara Vic's deputy. Barbara's brother, newspaper editor Randolph Meredith (Jay Kirby), has endorsed statehood, and to stop the lawlessness he dons a black outfit and mask and has become known as the Black Whip. While trailing one of the gang members, he is ambushed; he returns to his hideout, located behind a waterfall in a cave next to the Meredith ranch house, and Barbara finds him there dead. She vows revenge on his killers and takes his place as the Black Whip. Hammond orders Baxter and Harris to destroy the newspaper office and they harass typesetter Jackson (Lucien Littlefield) but end up in a fight with Gordon. Later the gang captures the undercover agent along with Barbara's new printing press, and the Black Whip comes to the rescue. Eventually, the Black Whip and Gordon have a showdown with Hammond and his gang as the town votes on the statehood issue.

Surprisingly, *Zorro's Black Whip* is the only Republic serial to give author Johnston McCulley screen credit although Zorro does not appear in the film. The serial saw theatrical re-release in 1957.

An even more tenuous relationship to the McCulley character took place in the 1946 Republic chapterplay, *Daughter of Don Q*. Since Don Q was Zorro's son, the title character here would have been his granddaughter, but that was the only link the movie had to Zorro. Instead it was a modern-day thriller about a crook (Roy Barcroft) who wants to murder all the people who could lay claim to an old Spanish land grant. The mastermind wants the grant for himself so he can control the city which is located on the tract of land in the grant and he is opposed by an heir (Adrian Booth), the title character, and her reporter boyfriend (Kirk Alyn). Spencer Gordon Bennet co-directed with Fred C. Brannon, who followed it the next year with *Son of Zorro*.

The title *Son of Zorro* is a misnomer since the character played by George Turner was explained to be distantly related to Zorro by his mother's line. The plot had lawyer Jeff Stewart (George Turner) coming home from the Civil War to Box County only to find the area has been taken over by three crooks, Boyd (Roy Barcroft), Sheriff Moody (Edward Cassidy) and Judge Hyde (Ernie Adams), all of whom work for a mysterious leader called "The Chief" (Tom London). Donning the black outfit and full-face mask of Zorro, Jeff teams with his ranch foreman Pancho (Stanley Price) and local postmistress Kate Wells (Peggy Stewart) to stop the crooks from harassing the locals with high taxes, road tolls and attacks on those who oppose their regime. Made as *Zorro Strikes Again*, the serial was later cut down to six 26-minute episodes when shown on television.

Republic's final Zorro chapterplay was *Ghost of Zorro*, released in 1949. Here Clayton Moore played engineer Ken Mason, the grandson of the masked avenger. Directed solo by Fred C. Brannon, the story involved the construction of telegraph lines between the towns of St. Joseph and Twin Bluffs. Mason goes to work for Jonathan White (Steve Clark) and his daughter Rita (Pamela Blake) as the head of construction crew for the Pioneer Telegraph Company but crook Hank Kilgore (Roy Barcroft) and his gang oppose the operation and they murder White. Kilgore is afraid his lawless activities will be hurt by the arrival of the telegraph. Rita plans to continue the project but is constantly harassed by Kilgore's gang until Mason, who pretends to be a tenderfoot, assumes the guise of Zorro and thwarts the outlaw gang. Like George Turner in *Son of Zorro*, Moore wore a full-face mask when riding as the avenger. *Ghost of Zorro* was issued theatrically in a 69-minute feature version in 1959. The same year the serial saw release, leading man Moore began his tenure as another famous masked man, the Lone Ranger, on ABC-TV. Ironically, it is claimed the Fran Striker–created character of the Lone Ranger was based on Zorro. Fourth-billed in *Ghost of Zorro* was George J. Lewis as Moccasin, an Indian ally of Mason.

Regarding Republic's last two official Zorro serials, *Son of Zorro* and *Ghost of Zorro*, Jim Harmon and Donald F. Glut wrote in *The Great Movie Serials: Their Sound and Fury* (1972), "Both of these new Zorros were nothing more than black-masked cowboys, using six-guns instead of swords. Those unmasked alter egos were about all the actors did play in the photoplays. When Zorro put on a mask, it was incomparable stunt expert, Tom Steele, beneath the silk."

As early as *Son of Zorro*, Republic had used stock footage from earlier serials, including *Zorro's Black Whip*, as chapter endings. The ploy of using stock shots with new footage filmed to match was apparent in two further studio cliffhanger efforts, *Don Daredevil Rides Again* (1951) and *Man with the Steel Whip* (1954). Both used footage from the studio's earlier Zorro chapterplays. The former starred Ken Curtis in the title role, with most of the older shots coming from *Zorro's Black Whip*. The plot revamped the Spanish land grant angle from *Daughter of Don Q* only with the setting in the Old West with "meek" rancher Lee Hadley (Curtis) becoming the masked Don Daredevil to save his cousin's (Aline Towne) ranch from crook

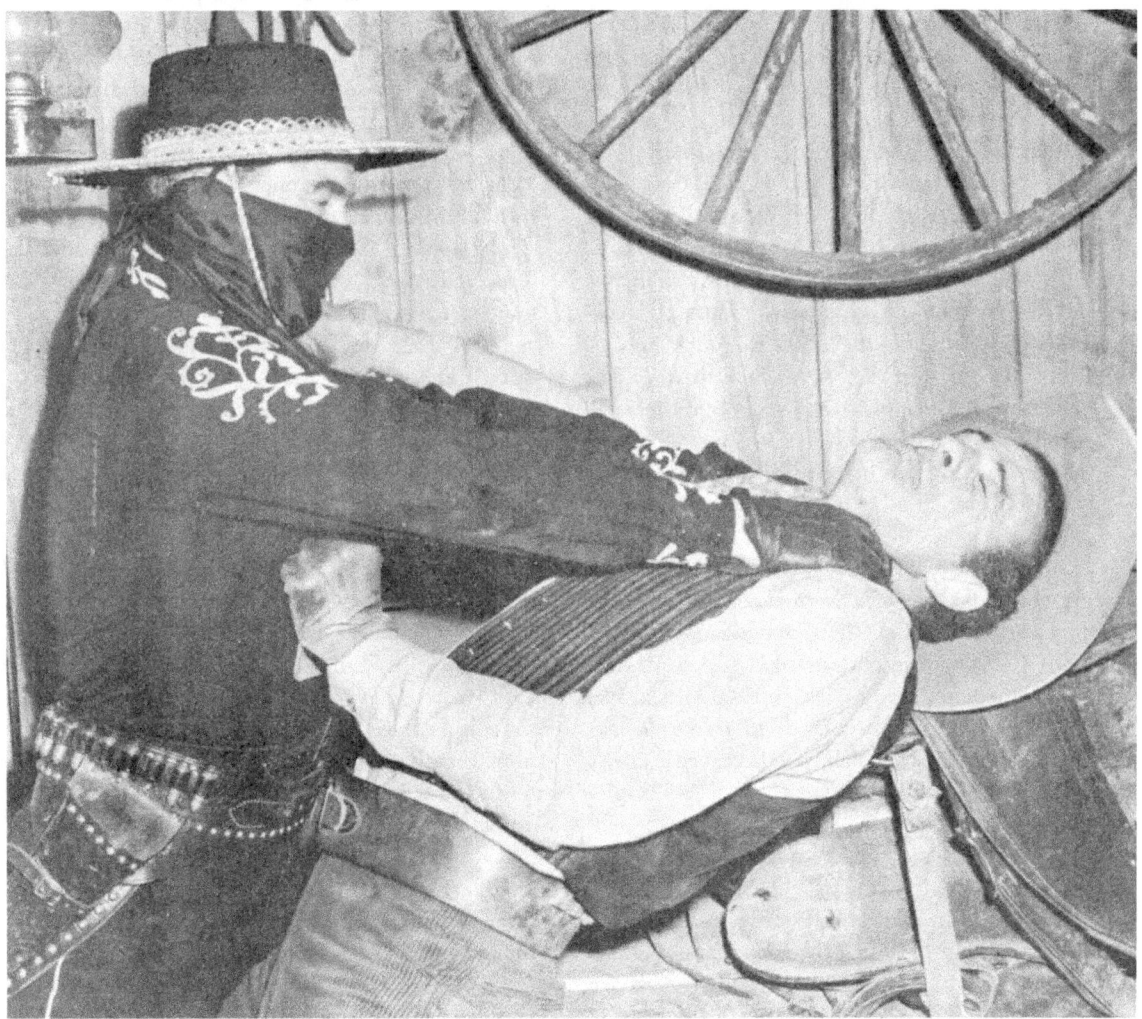

Richard Simmons (left) as El Latigo, throttles Price (Guy Teague), in *The Man with the Steel Whip* (Republic, 1954), issued in France as *Le Triomphe de Zorro* (The Triumph of Zorro).

Stratton (Roy Barcroft). *Man with the Steel Whip* headlined Richard Simmons, later famous as Sergeant Preston of the Yukon on the TV series of the same name, as El Latigo, the Whip. The character was created by rancher Jeff Randall (Richard Simmons) and schoolteacher Nancy Cooper (Barbara Bestar) to make the local Indians believe the spirit of their protector had returned to thwart the activities of crooks out to obtain reservation lands containing gold. The masked character of El Latigo was revived in the 1970s for the Mexican features *El Latigo* (The Whip), *El Latigo contra Santana* (The Whip versus Satan) (both 1976), and *El Latigo Contra los Momias* (The Whip versus the Mummies) (1980).

Sandwiched between the last two official Republic serials was the Mexican satire *El Nieto del Zorro* (The Grandson of Zorro), released in 1948. This comedy has two touring actors, Restores (Adalberto Martinez) and Otilio (Leopoldo "Chato" Ortin), having a run-in with Zorro, who is fleeing from pursuers. After he forces the two to change clothes with him, Restores is mistaken for the masked avenger and ends up helping a beautiful woman (Alicia Revel) whose inheritance is coveted by a crook (Humberto Osuna). In another Mexican take-off, 1950's *La Marca del Zorilla* (The Mark of the Skunk), German Valdes, better known as Tin Tan, played a bumbler who given a formula by which he turns himself into a swordsman and this helps him to defeat the bad guys and win the heart of the heroine (Silvia Pinal).

The Zorro character was also kidded in two Argentine features, *El Zorro Pierde el Pelo* (The Fox Loses His Hair) (1950) and *Los Sobrinos del Zorro* (The Nephews of Zorro) (1952), both starring comedian Pepe Iglesias. In 1946 Iglesias had starred in the mystery-comedy *El Tercer Huésped* (The Third Guest), which was also called *El Zorro en Peligro*. In *Si Usted No Puede, Yo Si* (1952) Iglesias billed himself as "El Zorro."

In 1951 Columbia Pictures purchased the screen rights to McCulley's "The Curse of Capistrano" from the Fairbanks estate with the intention of making a feature called *The Crimson Mask*. When the feature was finally released the next year as *California Conquest*, it dealt with the Spanish and Americans fighting an attempt by Russia to take over the area and had nothing to do with Zorro. Directed by Lew Landers, the film starred Cornel Wilde and Teresa Wright with George Eldredge as John C. Frémont. The same year, the first of several Italian Zorro features was released. *Il Sogno de Zorro* (The Dream of Zorro) starred Walter Chiari in the title role. The film featured Sophia Loren in a supporting role billed as Sofia Scicolone. This farce had Zorro's grandson taking a fall from a horse as a child and striking his head, making him timid. As an adult, Raimundo (Walter Chiari) takes another fall, this time transforming into a swordsman who takes up the cause of fighting tyranny.

Another Zorro feature was made in Mexico in 1953; *La Montaña Sin Ley* (The Mountain Without Law) starred Jose Suarez as the masked avenger, out to expose the head of a gang of pirates by revealing his own identity. In France it was called *Zorro se Demasque* (Zorro Unmasked). Two years later the Spain-Mexico co-production *El Coyote* (The Coyote) appeared, starring Abel Salazar as the mild-mannered Cesar who returns to California in the mid–1800s and takes the guise of the masked Coyote in fighting corrupt local leaders. In 1956 a sequel, *La Justicia del Coyote* (The Justice of the Coyote), followed with Salazar again as Cesar, this time becoming El Coyote to oppose U.S. military men trying to evict Spanish ranchers. Both features were filmed in Spain by director Joaquin Luis Romero Merchant; Jess Franco provided the stories as well as working as assistant director.

In 1957 the character of El Zorro Escarlata (The Scarlet Fox) appeared in Mexican cinemas, resulting in a trio of horror-westerns, *El Zorro Escarlata* (The Scarlet Fox) (1957), *El Regresso del Monstruo* (The Return of the Monster) (1958) and *El Zorro Vengador* (The Avenging Fox) (1962), all starring Luis Aguilar. Each of the features were filmed in three episodes with *El Zorro Escarlata* telling of a witch who revives her hanged son Tomas (Jaime Fernandez), who takes revenge on those who sent him to the gallows. Meek Luis (Aguilar) becomes the dashing Zorro Escarlata to save Gloria (Irma Dorantes) from the clutches of the monster. The feature was reissued in 1959 as *La Venganza del Ahorcado* (The Vengeance of the Hanged). *El Regreso del Monstruo* had the Luis (Aguilar) donning the black mask and costume of Zorro Escarlata to fight a mad doctor (Arturo

Martinez) who is set on mating a young woman (Teresa Velaszquez) with a monster he has brought back to life. The final Zorro Escarlata effort, *El Zorro Vengador* found the masked Luis (Aguilar) coming to the aid of his fiancée (Marla Eugenia San Martin) whose gold mine is coveted by a mysterious group called the Brotherhood of the Scorpion.

A huge Zorro revival took place in the mid-1950s when Walt Disney Studios acquired the rights to the character and cast Guy Williams in the title role for the ABC-TV series *The Adventures of Zorro*. Running for 78 half-hour episodes from 1957 to 1959, the series was very popular and resulted in a plethora of merchandise based on the character, including toys, watches and clothing. Co-starred in the series were Henry Calvin as the bumbling Sergeant Garcia, Britt Lomond as the evil Monastario, Gene Sheldon as Don Diego's servant Bernardo and Don Diamond as Corporal Reyes. There were also connections to the Republic serials in that George J. Lewis, who was the hero in *Zorro's Black Whip* and a sidekick in *Ghost of Zorro*, played Don Diego Vega's father, Don Alejandro, and the music for the series was done by veteran Republic composer William Lava, who scored *Zorro's Fighting Legion*. The theme song for the program was written by series director Norman Foster and George Bruns and it resulted in a hit record for the Chordettes on the Cadence label in 1958. Following the unexpected cancellation of *The Adventures of Zorro* in 1959, Guy Williams returned as the character in four one-hour programs on ABC's *Walt Disney Presents* during the 1960–61 TV season; the first two were directed by William Witney who co-directed the first two Republic serials, *Zorro Rides Again* and *Zorro's Fighting Legion*. The half-hour series went into syndication in 1965 and returned to TV on the Disney Channel in 1983. The black-and-white program was colorized in 1992.

Guy Williams (1924–89) was a native New Yorker whose real name was Armando Catalano. He learned fencing at an early age, which gave him a big advantage when he tested for the role of Zorro. He changed his name to Guy Williams and signed a contract with MGM in 1948, playing bit parts before returning to New York City and working in live television. He signed with Universal-International in 1952 and went back and forth between the stage and films before being signed to the Zorro role in 1957. After the series ended he headlined the features *Damon and Pythias* (1962) and *Captain Sinbad* (1963) and in 1964 he portrayed Will Cartwright in five episodes of the NBC-TV series *Bonanza*. Next to Zorro, he is best known for playing Professor John Robinson in eighty-four episodes of CBS-TV's *Lost in Space* (1965–68). In the 1970s *The Adventures of Zorro* became very popular in Argentina where Williams made many personal appearances as well as developing a stage show around the character.

The popularity of the TV series resulted in the theatrical feature *The Sign of Zorro*, released by Buena Vista in 1959. Cobbled together from episodes of the television show, the film told of Don Diego Vega (Williams) returning to his California home in 1820 only to find the area under the domination of the corrupt Commandant Monastario (Britt Lomond). Pretending to be a coward, Don Diego enlists the aid of his mute servant Bernardo (Gene Sheldon) in taking on the guise of the masked Zorro, who opposes the despot. When his father, Don Alejandro (George J. Lewis), is arrested for leading a revolt against Monastario, Zorro orders the judge at his father's trial to proclaim him innocent. Monastario then comes to believe that Don Diego is Zorro and tries to force him into the open by hiring another to impersonate him. When this fails, the commandant challenges Diego to a duel but Bernardo impersonates Zorro, causing the Viceroy (John Dehner) to order Monastario's arrest, replacing him with the rotund Sergeant Garcia (Henry Calvin). Regarding this telefeature, Leonard Maltin complained in *The Disney Films* (1973), "While the *Zorro* TV series seemed enjoyable, this feature-film patchwork is rather clumsy and not terribly exciting.... Because it is strung together from several TV episodes, there are several climaxes and resolutions, making for a very uneven flow of continuity. What is more, the plot material becomes repetitious and, inevitably, dull." Nonetheless, *The Sign of Zorro* was still being shown in theaters well into the 1970s.

A second feature culled from *The Adventures of Zorro* was *Zorro the Avenger*, issued in 1959 but only to theaters abroad where the series had not yet been televised. Taken from six TV episodes

Advertisement for *The Sign of Zorro* (Buena Vista, 1958).

directed by Charles Barton, the plot had Zorro (Williams) doing battle with a villain called The Eagle (Charles Korvin) who is trying to take over Southern California. The year 1959 also saw the reissue of the Republic serials *Zorro Rides Again* and *Ghost of Zorro*.

In 1961, an obscure Mexican Zorro title, *Zorro nella Valle dei Fantasmi*, also called *El Valle de los Desaparecidos*, appeared with Jeff Stone in the title role and direction by Rafael Baldeon, who previously helmed *El Zorro Escarlata*. Though little-seen today, this feature apparently began an avalanche of Zorro movies made abroad, due to the popularity of the Walt Disney television series. The plot had Zorro (Stone) after a criminal gang which has taken over a gold mine and imprisoned its owner. It was reissued in 1964 as *Vendetta de Zorro* (Vendetta of Zorro).

Most of the new Zorro movies were made in Europe and one of the first was *L'Ombra di Zorro* (The Shadow of Zorro), directed by Joaquin Luis Romero Merchant and released in 1961. Jess Franco contributed to the script under his real name, Jesus Franco Manera, and is thus credited on a version of the film called *La Venganza del Zorro* (The Vengeance of Zorro). Corrupt officials plunder churches and murder locals, and try to capture the masked avenger (Frank Latimore) by committing violent acts and blaming them on him. Allied Artists dubbed it and released it in the U.S. as *Shadow of Zorro*. In 1975, director Marius Lesoeur, billed as James Gartner, added erotic footage to the feature, turning Zorro into a woman played by Monica Swinn, and Eurocine issued it as *La Marque de Zorro* (The Mark of Zorro). Some sources claim the new footage was directed by Jess Franco.

The 1962 Italian production *Zorro alla Corte di Spagna* (Zorro in the Court of Spain) told of Zorro (George Ardisson) coming to the aid of the queen of Spain after her brother-in-law (Alberto Lupo) kidnaps her daughter and holds her for ransom, trying to force the queen to bend to his will. Zorro falls in the love with the heiress (Nadia Marlowe) and fights to save her fortunes. It was shown on U.S. television as *The Masked Conqueror*.

Five Zorro movies were released theatrically in 1963, five of them made in Europe. The Italian production *L'Invincible Cavaliere Mascherato* (The Invincible Masked Cavalier) starred Pierre Brice, best known for playing the title role in the "Winnetou" (q.v.) series, as Don Diego, the timid stepson of tyrant Don Luis (Daniele Vargas), who rules 17th century Higuera with an iron hand. His evil ways, however, are opposed by the masked Zorro, really Don Diego, who has been betrothed to Carmencita (Helene Chanel), whose late father was deposed by Don Luis as governor. The feature was released in the United States in 1967 by Embassy Pictures.

Errol Flynn's son, Sean, took on the guise of the masked avenger in *Il Segno di Zorro* (The Sign of Zorro), an Italian-Spanish co-production, issued in the spring of 1963. In the U.S. it saw release as both *The Sign of Zorro* and *Duel at the Rio Grande*. Pretty much a rehash of the much-filmed storyline, it had young Don Ramon (Flynn) returning to early California and finding his father has been killed and the area ruled by a despot (Enrique Diosdado). As Zorro, Don Diego defeats the tyrant, avenges his father's murder, and brings back law and order to his homeland. In the swashbuckling tradition of Errol Flynn, the film contained a great deal of swordplay.

Many of the foreign-made Zorro features kept the Fox in Europe and not California, as exemplified by another 1963 release, *Zorro e i Tre Moschiettieri* (Zorro and the Three Musketeers), produced in Italy and starring Gordon Scott, best known for his roles as Tarzan and for European sword-and-sandal epics. Here he plays Zorro, who teams with the Three Musketeers (Livio Lornzon, Roberto Risso, Giacomo Rossi-Stuart) and D'Artagnan (Nazzareno Zamperla) to rescue a princess (Maria Grazia Spina) from the clutches of the Spanish emissary (Jose Greci) who has kidnapped her. American International Pictures released it directly to U.S. TV as *Mask of the Musketeers*. Pierre Brice portrayed Zorro in a second 1963 Italian feature, *Zorro Contra Maciste* (Zorro vs. Hercules), which American International distributed to U.S. cinemas as *Samson and the Slave Queen*. He was cast as poet Ramon, really Zorro, the lover of Princess Isabella (Maria Grazia Spina), who is a rival of the wicked Princess Malva (Moira Orfei) for the throne of Navarre. Zorro, who comes to the aid of Isabella, must do battle with strongman Samson (Alan Steel), who is hired by Malva to find a royal treasure chest which contains the will naming the new queen. Finally, Zorro and Samson team to stop Malva and place Isabella on the throne. When the film was released in the U.S., it contained a new music score by Les Baxter.

Another 1963 Italian production was *Le Tre Spade di Zorro* (The Three Swords of Zorro), which takes place in 1830 when a group of tyrants try to take over the recently independent Mexico and a landowner teaches his son (Guy Stockwell) and daughter (Gloria Milland) to defy them. The son takes the guise of Zorro but soon finds his family threatened by the despots. On U.S. television it was shown as *Sword of Zorro*.

A variation of the serial *Zorro's Black Whip* came out in Mexico in 1963: *Las Hermanas X* (The Sisters X), in which Kitty de Hoyos portrayed Christine, a traveling entertainer who secretly becomes the whip-wielding avenger who seeks the killer of her parents a dozen years before. She is aided by her sister Teresa, played by Dacia Gonzalez. The next year the two sisters (de Hoyos, Gonzalez) continued their adventures in *Las Vengadoras Enmascaradas* (The Masked Women Avengers) in a story about a silver shipment robbery which results in the killing of Teresa's fiancé. Federico Curiel directed both features as he would do with two 1964 Mexican Zorro films, *Las Hijas del Zorro* (The Daughters of Zorro) and *Las Invencibles* (The Invisible Women), both again starring de Hoyos and Gonzalez.

Las Hijas del Zorro was made in three episodes and took place in 19th century California with Zorro (Rafael Bertran) being jailed as his wife dies giving birth to twin girls, Lupe (de Hoyos) and Rosa (Gonzalez). Eighteen years later, the girls take their father's place and oppose the evil Captain Gonzalo (Eduardo Fajardo), who was responsible for capturing their father. The two female masked avengers try to set Zorro free as Gonzalo has him murdered but Lupe avenges his death by killing the governor in a duel. The sequel, *Las Invencibles* (The Invincible Women), was also filmed in three segments and had many of the same cast members, but here Bertran, who played Zorro in the first film, was cast in a villainous role. The plot had Lupe (de Hoyos) and Rosa (Gonzalez) joining forces with Juan (Dagoberto Rodriguez), the protector of the local country people, in fighting the mysterious "El Maestro," who had ordered underling Rodrigo (Bertran) to kidnap Rosa and force her to impersonate his niece (Celia Viveros) in order to control her estate. Some sources list a third feature, *Le Sorelle Zorro*, directed by Federico Curiel and starring de Hoyos, but this 1966 release is probably a reissue of one of the two above features.

In 1965, the Italian-Spanish co-production, *El Zorro Cabalga Otra Vez* (The Fox Rides Another Time), starred Tony Russell in the title role. Directed by Richard Blasco, who had previously done *Le Tre Spade di Zorro* (The Three Swords of Zorro) two years before, it had Patricio (Russell) pretending to be a butler, Antonio, for the governor in California, but really working as an undercover agent and donning the mask of Zorro to capture Don Esteban (Maria Jose Alfonso), a bandit fomenting revolution.

The 1966 Italian release *Zorro il Ribelle* (Zorro the Rebel) told of the corrupt governor of Lucca, Don Alvarez (Arturo Dominici), wanting his son Louis (Charles Borromei) to marry the lovely Isabel (Dina De Santis), whose father places her in a convent for protection. A family friend, Don Ramiro (Howard Ross), advises the girl to accept the marriage proposal but that night the masked Zorro convinces her to marry Don Ramiro. Before the marriage can be consummated, the governor orders Don Ramiro killed but it is the assassin who ends up dead, dressed in Don Ramiro's clothes. Isabel is now forced to marry Louis but at the ceremony Zorro appears and defeats Louis in a duel while his rebels overpower the governor's soldiers. Zorro then reveals himself to be Don Ramiro, and he and Isabel plan to marry.

Three more Zorro features came out in 1968, one from the Philippines and two more from Italy. The Filipino action-comedy *The Magnificent Zorro* starred Chiquito in the title role. Less obscure is the first of two Zorro features starring the Italian comedy team of Franco Franchi and Ciccio Ingrassia, *I Nipoti di Zorro* (The Nephews of Zorro). This silly affair has Franco La Vacca (Franchi) and Ciccio La Vacca (Ingrassia) sailing to California in order to search for gold. They arrive in Las Palmas which is under the control of the despot Judge Ramirez (Mario Maranzana) and his cohort Captain Martinez (Ivo Staccioli), an imposter who has taken the place of a man (Enzo Andronico) who sailed with the LaVaccas. The two try to get a loan from their uncle, Don Diego Vega (Franco Fantasia), who once defended the helpless as Zorro. Now his son, Raphael (Dean Reed), is the masked avenger and he asks his father to give them the loan in order to get the pests out of the area. Don Diego refuses, and the two crazies complicate Zorro's life and even make a play for Raphael's fiancée, Carmencita (Agata Flory), by telling her they are Zorro. Martinez arrests Franco and Ciccio, not for masquerading as Zorro, but because they know the identity of the real captain. Zorro shows mercy and, against his better judgment, rescues the two zanies. The final 1968 Zorro feature was *La Volpe* (The Fox), in which George Ardisson returned to the role. In Spain it was called *La Spada del Zorro* (The Sword of Zorro) and on U.S. TV it was shown as *Zorro the Fox*. Here Zorro (Ardisson) protects villagers in a small Mexican town from a governor who keeps them under the yoke of oppression. Zorro undermines the corrupt official's actions and leads the peons in revolt against him.

A half-dozen Zorro features came in 1969, three from Italy and three from Turkey. *El Zorro Justiciero* (The Severe Zorro) was an Italian-Spanish co-production, directed by Rafael Romero Merchant, who had co-scripted *L'Ombra di Zorro* (The Shadow of Zorro), which was helmed by his brother Joaquin Romero Merchant. Martin Moore starred in the title role, the son of a hacienda owner who has been kidnapped by a crook (Frank Brana) who takes control of the property. As Zorro, the young man steals the money made from the auctioning of his father's rancho and uses it to pay off the property. The crook tries to force Dominguez (Antonio Gradoli), Zorro's friend, to reveal the masked man's true identity. Romana Film, which produced most of the 1960s Italian Zorro features, then released *Zorro alla Corte d'Inghilterra* (Zorro at the Court of England), starring Spyros Focas as Zorro. This time the action takes place in Central America, where Pedro Suarez (Focas), who pretends to be a frivolous nobleman, is really the masked Zorro, who protects the people from the abuses of the local governor (Daniele Vargas). Queen Victoria (Barbara Carroll) gets word of the corruption in the British colony and sends Lord Percy Moore (Franco Ressel) as her emissary but he soon joins forces with the governor and offers a former pupil, the beautiful Rosanna (Dada Gallotti), to the official in return for his sending a good report to the queen. Zorro saves the girl from Moore and she falls in love with the masked man whose aid is enlisted by Luisa (Angela De Leo), the governor's mistress, in stopping the wedding. When the two finally reveal the alliance between the governor and Moore, the villains try to escape and take Rosanna with them, but Zorro comes to her rescue, killing the governor and arresting Moore. As a result, Queen Victoria gives Pedro a title and her blessings for his marriage to Rosanna.

Nadir Moretti starred as Zorro in the third 1969 release, also produced by Romana Film, called *Zorro Marchese di Navarra* (Zorro, Marquis of Navarra). Here nobleman Oste (Moretti) works for Spanish King Ferdinand VII (Renato Montalbano) in trying to defeat the French troops invading the country. When Colonel Brizard (Daniele Vargas), the leader of the invaders, wants to massacre a group of patriots, the plan is learned by Carmen (Melisa Longo), the niece of the alcalde of Pamplas, who helps Zorro prevent the killings. As a result, the French army is routed and Brizard flees, taking Carmen as his prisoner. Zorro defeats the colonel and rescues Carmen, and the king makes him the marquis of Navarra. The feature was released to U.S. TV as *Zorro, Marquis of Navarre*, eleven minutes shy of its original running time.

Three Zorro features made in Turkey were also released in 1969: *Zorro disi Fantoma'ya Karsi*, *Zorro'nun Intikami* and *Zorro Kamcili Suvari*, the latter two directed by Yilmaz Atadeniz and starring Tamer Yigit as Zorro.

In 1971 Charles Quiney starred in two Zorro adventures co-produced by Spanish and Italian companies, *Zorro il Cavaliere della Vendetta* (Zorro, the Cavalier of Revenge) and *El Zorro de Monterrey* (The Fox of Monterrey). Both were co-scripted by Jose Luis Merino who co-directed the first with Luigi Capuano and helmed the second solo. *Zorro il Cavaliere della Vendetta* was called *El Zorro, Caballero de la Justicia* (The Fox, Gentleman of Justice) in Spain and *Zorro, Rider of Vengeance* in the United States. *El Zorro de Monterrey* was dubbed *Zorro the Dominator* in the U.S. *Zorro il Cavaliere della Vendetta* told of adventurer Zack (Arturo Dominici) cheating Alfaro (Ignazio Balsamo) and his daughter Gladys (Malisa Longo) out of a map which leads to the place where Indians hid a diamond they believe to be a talisman. Working with Alfaro and Gladys, David Sandoval (Quiney) becomes Zorro to delay Zack and his gang from finding the gem. In order to stop the masked man, Zack hires Pinkerton agent Berta Cooper (Maria Mahor) to uncover Zorro's true identity. Zorro talks Alfaro and Gladys into giving up the search for the diamond and at the same time rallies the local Comanches in defeating Zack and his men. *El Zorro de Monterrey* had Antonio Sandoval (Quiney) returning home to his California village after completing studies in Spain, and finding it under the rule of the ruthless alcalde, Jose Arellano (Vidal Molina). While pretending to be a gentleman of leisure, David becomes Zorro and works to defend the locals with the aid of traveler Borracha (Pasquale Basile). The alcalde, who thinks David and Zorro are the same person, sets a trap but Zorro is rescued by Borracha and the beautiful Berta (Lea Nanni). Zorro then leads the people in a revolt which overthrows Arellano.

The early 1970s also saw the release of a couple of "adult" Zorro features. These films basically retold the usual story but were heavily spiced with sex sequences. In *The Erotic Adventures of Zorro* (1972), Don Diego Vega (Douglas Frey) pretends to be a gay cavalier who rides a white mule and carries a parasol. At night he turns into the lusty Zorro, who beds all the town's beautiful women while fighting the area's evil governor (Jude Farese). Michael J. Weldon in *The Psychotronic Video Guide* (1996) noted, "It's the usual Zorro story with lots of dumb gags and jokes plus sex and full nudity.... It was shot on the old Selznick lot used for *Duel in the Sun* and has high production values." *Les Aventures Galantes de Zorro* (The Gallant Adventures of Zorro), also a 1972 release, was a French-Belgian co-production which re-edited an older Spanish western and added sex scenes. Also called *Red Hot Zorro* and *Affairs of Zorro*, it had the masked avenger (Jean-Michel Dhermay) winning all the women he meets in 19th century California, including the evil governor's (Ghislaine Kay) mistress (Alice Arno).

The 1974 Italian-Spanish production *Il Figlio di Zorro* (The Son of Zorro) starred Robert Widmark in the title role as a nobleman who teams with an army colonel (Fernando Sancho) to defeat tyranny in Old California. It was reissued as *Man with the Golden Winchester*. The same year, Frank Langella appeared as Don Diego Vega in the ABC-TV telefeature *The Mark of Zorro*, a new version of Johnston McCulley's story "The Curse of Capistrano." The telefilm even used Alfred Newman's music score from the 1940 version with Tyrone Power. Unfortunately the retelling was a lame one, with Langella making a vapid hero. Yvonne De Carlo, as Don Diego's mother, and Louise Sorel, as his sweetheart, were pretty much wasted, although Ricardo Montalban as Captain Esteban, Gilbert Roland as Don Alejandro Vega and Robert Middleton as the governor were outstanding. Regarding Roland as Don Diego's father, James Robert Parish and I noted in *The Great Western Pictures* (1976), "Roland engaged in a sword duel with the villain and, despite his advanced middle age, was as dashing and athletic as he had been as a star in the silent cinema."

The grating Italian "comedians" Franco Franchi and Ciccio Ingrassia made a second Zorro feature, released in 1975, called *Il Sogno di Zorro* (The Grandsons of Zorro), which found sparse release in the U.S. as *Dream of Zorro* and *Grandsons of Zorro*. The plot had Paco (Franchi) daydreaming about being Zorro while the lecherous General Ruarte (Gianni Musi) makes advances to his fiancée Zaira (Paola Tedesco). A servant (Ingrassia) gives Paco a sleeping potion which causes him to turn into the master swordsman and defeat the general and his men.

French star Alain Delon took on the swashbuckling role in the 1975 French-Italian co-production *Zorro*, directed by Duccio Tessari. Although it unfortunately included a talking dog named Assassin in its plot, it was an otherwise good rendering of the saga with the newly appointed governor of California murdered and his assistant, Don Diego (Delon), taking over his identity. The crime was ordered by Colonel Huerta (Stanley Baker), the despotic ruler who finds himself facing the wrath of Zorro, really Don Diego in disguise, who leads the peons in overthrowing the general and his troops. Allied Artists issued the film in a dubbed version in the U.S.

In 1975 a second TV series, *Zorro*, was shown in India on Mondo TV. Fifty-two episodes featured Navin Nichol as the legendary hero.

The year 1976 saw the release of Zorro features from Mexico and Europe. The first, *La Gran Aventura del Zorro* (The Great Adventure of Zorro), had the evil Emilio (Pedro Armendariz, Jr.) buying a ranch and then killing the former owner and stealing back his money, then blaming the crime on Zorro, who is really nobleman Don Diego (Rodolfo de Anda). Zorro sets a trap to capture the villain, one involving his wounded father and his brother's fiancée. The action took place in California in the 1820s. The Italian-Spanish satire *Ah Si? E Io Lo Dico a Zzzzorro!* (Who's Afraid of Zorro!) starred George Hilton, who headlined over twenty Spaghetti Westerns in the 1960s and 1970s, as a bumbler named Philip MacKintosh, who masquerades as Zorro although all of his heroics are orchestrated by a monk, Padre Donato (Lionel Stander). The usual plot had Zorro spearheading a revolution by the people in frontier California, overthrowing a tyrannical ruler (Antonio Pica). In Spain it was called *Nuevas Aventuras de Zorro* (New Adventures of Zorro) and in the United States a dubbed version was issued as *Mark of Zorro*.

In 1976 the first of three Mexican features was released. This time the hero was called El Latigo (The Whip) and in all three films the role was enacted by Juan Miranda. The first outing, *El Latigo* (The Whip), released in 1976, had the avenger at odds with El Dios Tigre (The Tiger God) over a hidden treasure, while the sequel, *El Latigo Contra Santana* (The Whip vs. Satan), issued the same year, had the hero saving a young woman (Yolanda Ochos), accused of being a witch, from a cult of Satan worshippers. In 1979 a third feature, *El Latigo Contra los Momias* (The Whip vs. the Mummies), told of the Zorro-like El Latigo fighting a quartet of mummies who try to become immortal by killing off all the members of a family. Another Mexican feature, *El Zorro Blanco* (The White Fox), a 1978 release, was a modern-day thriller in which the hero, again played by Miranda, saves his fiancée (Hilda Aguirre) from the clutches of her evil stepfather (Carlos Agosti) who wants her murdered so he can take her inheritance. Two more Zorro-like features were made in Spain, starring Fernando Allende as El Lobo Negro (The Black Wolf), another masked hero fighting injustice. Released in 1980, both *El Lobo Negro* (The Black Wolf) and *La Venganza del Lobo Negro* (The Vengeance of the Black Wolf) had the masked swordsman battling government oppression in California in the mid–1800s. Like the El Latigo features, they were Zorro ripoffs; both were produced by Lotus Films and released internationally by Televicine.

A spoof of the 1940 film *The Mark of Zorro* came to theaters in 1981 as *Zorro, the Gay Blade* and it was dedicated to the director of the earlier feature, Rouben Mamoulian. George Hamilton not only starred as Don Diego Vega, alias Zorro, and his gay brother Ramon, aka Bunny Wigglesworth, he enacted the part of Margarita Wigglesworth and also served as the film's co-producer. While the film satirized the McCulley character, it also remained true to the original's overall story line, with Zorro fighting oppression in frontier California. The feature proved to be Hamilton's second stab at poking fun at a classic, as in 1979 he had great success starring as Dracula in *Love at First Bite*.

Zorro, the Gay Blade had lustful Don Diego Vega (Hamilton) ordered home from Spain by his father. Upon his arrival, he finds the father dead and the area under the rule of the despotic alcalde, Esteban (Ron Leibman), and his wife Florinda (Brenda Vaccaro). A letter from his late father tells Don Diego that, in the guise of Zorro, he is to protect the locals from the wrath of the alcalde. Diego wears the costume to Florinda's ball where he befriends reformer Charlotte (Lauren Hutton) and humiliates Esteban in a sword fight. Diego, who injured his foot in a fall while escaping from Esteban's palace, is unable to carry out his duties as Zorro and he also must fight off unwanted attention from Florinda, which makes Esteban suspicious. Appearing on the scene is Diego's long-lost brother, Ramon, now known as Bunny, who takes over the Zorro role but insists on using a whip instead of a sword, and dresses in bright colors. Charlotte falls in love with Bunny, who does not respond (Diego truly loves the young woman). At another ball given by Florinda, Esteban sets a trap for Zorro but Bunny arrives disguised as Margarita Wigglesworth and charms the alcalde. He also steals Florida's diamond necklace, gives it to Diego and announces he is going back to England. Esteban arrests Charlotte because he thinks she is in league with Zorro, who will try to rescue her. As Charlotte is about to be executed, Zorro, disguised as a monk, is captured and he offers his life for the woman he loves. At that moment, Bunny returns and he and Diego fight Esteban and his men. With aid from the peasants they overthrow the corrupt alcalde. Charlotte realizes that she is in love with Diego and they ride off together.

In *Zorro Unmasked: The Official History* (1998), Sandra Curtis wrote, "*Zorro, the Gay Blade* was an amusing, playful romp that showed a strong parallel between the Scarlet Pimpernel and Zorro." The feature, however, was nowhere as success as *Love at First Bite*.

In 1981 the Fox also returned to television in the animated cartoon series *The New Adventures of Zorro*, produced by Filmation Associates. Henry Darrow provided the voice of Don Diego/Zorro. Darrow then appeared as Don Diego de Vega in the half-hour CBS-TV series, *Zorro and Son*, with Paul Regina as Don Carlos de Vega. The series was produced by Walt Disney Pictures and ran for only five episodes with Bill Dana appearing in the role of Zorro's helper, Bernardo. Darrow's third Zorro series, this time portraying Don Alejandro de la Vega, was the 87-episode *Zorro*, which was on the Family Channel from 1990 to 1993, starring Duncan Regehr in the title role. (During the series' first season, Efrem Zimbalist, Jr., had the Don Alejandro role but when he left he was replaced by Darrow.) In 1997, another animated series, *Zorro*, was telecast for 26 episodes on Warner Bros. TV stations, with Michael Gough providing the voice of Don Diego and Zorro. Also called *The New Adventures of Zorro*, its plots often included the supernatural and futuristic weapons. There was also a 1992 Italian animated series from Mondo TV called *The Legend of Zorro* in which the masked hero was a teenager. In 1996, the Japanese anime TV series *Kaiketsu Zorro* retold the legend.

The McCulley character returned to the screen in 1998 in the big-budget *The Mask of Zorro*. It begins with Don Diego de la Vega, alias Zorro (Anthony Hopkins), being captured and imprisoned by his archenemy, Don Rafael Montero (Stuart Wilson), the cruel Spanish governor ruling California. In a duel between the two men, Don Diego's beloved wife Esperanza (Julieta Rosen) is killed. After the grieving Diego is arrested, his infant daughter, Elena, is stolen by Montero. Two decades later Montero returns to California from Spain, just as Don Diego escapes from prison and befriends Alejandro Murrieta (Antonio Banderas), whose brother has just been murdered by the evil Captain Love (Matt Letscher). Years before, as youths, Alejandro and his brother had helped Zorro escape an execution plot. Recognizing the young man by a medallion he had given him at the time, Don Diego begins training Alejandro to take over as Zorro, the defender of the people. Diego had planned to kill Montero but he soon realizes the now-grown Elena (Catherine Zeta-Jones) thinks he is her father. At a banquet, Alejandro vies with Captain Love for the attentions of Elena and also wins the confidence of Montero, who tells him he plans to purchase California from Mexico with gold from a mine worked by prisoners. To thwart the plan and save the people, Don Diego has Alejandro steal the map to the gold mine from Montero and then announces he plans to kill his nemesis. When he confronts Montero, Don Diego is nearly killed by Captain Love but saved by Elena. When Montero and Love try to destroy the mine, to keep Mexican president Santa Anna from finding out they planned to buy California with his own gold, Zorro arrives to stop them. Elena releases Don Diego from a wine cellar where Montero ordered him held, and the two go to the mine, where Diego saves Zorro from being shot by Montero. When Montero threatens to kill Elena, the young woman realizes Don Diego is her real father. Elena again stops Montero from shooting Diego as Alejandro pursues Captain Love. The two engage in a sword fight which results in Love being killed. Elena releases the prisoners as Diego does battle with Montero, who dies when he becomes entangled in the harness of a wagon which rolls off a cliff. Diego, who has been mortally wounded by Montero, blesses Elena and Alejandro and urges the young man to carry on the fight for justice as Zorro. The feature proved to be a huge box office success with a worldwide take of over $230 million.

In 2000 the Mexican feature *La Mascara de Zorro* (The Mask of Zorro) starred Mario Colli as Don Diego Vega and Bruno Bichir as Alejandro Murrieta, with both characters donning the mask of Zorro. Two years later the Fox was back on U.S. television in the Nickelodeon Network's *The Amazing Zorro*, an animated retelling set in old California. In 2007 Christian Meier portrayed the hero in the Columbian TV series *Zorro: La Espada y la Rose* (Zorro: The Sword and the Rose). This soap opera was produced by Sony Pictures and Telemundo and was filmed at the colonial village of Villa de Leyva in Columbia. A further Zorro TV series, the animated *Zorro: Generation Z* was set for showing in 2008 in the United States.

Antonio Banderas returned to the role of Alejandro, alias Zorro, in 2005 in *The Legend of Zorro*. Set in California in 1850, the film had Alejandro (Banderas) stopping gunslinger McGivens (Nick Chinlund) from stealing votes which might decide whether or not California joins the union. He takes the ballots to Governor Riley (Pedro Armendariz) and later learns from his wife Elena (Catherine Zeta-Jones) that statehood has been approved. When Elena finds out her husband is still masquerading as Zorro, she throws him out of the house and the next day sends their son Joaquin (Adrian Alonso) away to school. After three months, Frey Felipe (Julio Oscar Mechoso) urges Alejandro to attend a party at the mansion of French Count Armand (Rufus Sewell) and he finds Elena has been seeing him. After McGivens steals the deed to a peasant family's home, Alejandro, as Zorro, learns the gunman is allied with

Armand who is the head of a secret society which wants to take over the United States. When Pinkerton agents abduct Alejandro, he is saved by Joaquin as Elena learns about Armand's duplicity. Armand and his cohorts have smuggled nitroglycerin into the country in bars of soap and intend to use it to bring down the government. Zorro plans to blow up the train carrying the nitro but stops when he finds out Armand has taken Elena prisoner. McGivens captures Joaquin. Frey Felipe, who has been shot by McGivens, is able to stop the gunman from killing Alejandro, and it is McGivens who is killed by the nitro. The next day Zorro boards the train carrying Armand, Elena, Joaquin and the nitro and engages the count is a swordfight; Joaquin escapes on Zorro's horse, Tornado. As the governor is about to sign the bill making California a state, Joaquin is able to change a track switch, causing the train to go around the governor's party. Zorro defeats Armand and saves Elena. Armand is killed when the train crashes and the nitro explodes. Alejandro and Elena are reconciled and she agrees to let him continue as Zorro.

The Legend of Zorro made around $120 million worldwide, almost one-half the box office take of *The Mask of Zorro*. Daniel Eagan wrote in *Film Journal* that the sequel "sacrifices the earlier film's tongue-in-cheek wit for broader, more family-oriented humor. Gone, too, is any semblance of a serious story.... Apart from the leads, the film feels utterly heartless, from the absurdly scattershot script to the peculiarly bright production design to the perfunctory supporting cast.... Filmmaking this slack may be one reason why box-office receipts have been dropping."

Perhaps the most outlandish aspect of *The Legend of Zorro* is its historical inaccuracies. Although the film takes place in 1850, the group trying to take over the country is the Confederacy, which was not formed until 1861. Abraham Lincoln is depicted in the feature as an election inspector although he never traveled that far west; Confederate general Pierre G.T. Beauregard is shown being killed at the finale (he actually died in 1893). There are also continuity problems. In *The Mask of Zorro*, the hero was called Alejandro Murrieta, a supposed brother to actual outlaw Joaquin Murrieta, but in the sequel he is Alejandro de la Vega, although in the first film he was no relation to Don Diego de la Vega, who was portrayed by Anthony Hopkins.

In addition to the numerous theatrical films and television series, there were several stage productions about Zorro in the 1990s, including *Zorro, the Musical*, which was done in London in 1995 and the next year in Mexico City. Over the years there have been at least three "Zorro" radio series, the first broadcast in the United States in 1944. In 1957, "Preview Theater of the Air" presented a Zorro story and this was followed by several episodes of the series "The Adventures of Zorro." The character returned to the airwaves in July, 1997, in the British BBC Radio 4 five-part series "The Mark of Zorro" which featured Mark Arden in the title role with Louise Lombard as Lolita and Glyn Houston as Friar Felipe.

Over the years the Zorro character has been used for all types of merchandising and there have been at least fifteen books published by various authors since 1942. Zorro has also been very popular in the comic book field, beginning in 1949 when Dell published the first Zorro comics. In 1958 the series began featuring likenesses from the *Adventures of Zorro* TV series with Guy Williams on the covers and this continued until Dell discontinued the Zorro comics in 1961. Between 1966 and 1968 Gold Key issued Zorro comics in connection with the syndication of the Walt Disney TV series and two of these issues were reprinted by Top Comics in 1967. In 1962–63 Zorro headlined five issues in "Walt Disney's Comics of Stories" and the character was featured in four issues of "Walt Disney Comic Digest" between 1969 and 1975. In addition Zorro was the star of "Walt Disney Showcase" #49, a Dell reprint. In 1986, the Eclipse Graphic Album series issued "Zorro in Old California" followed by "Zorro: The Complete Classic Adventures" in two volumes. In 1990, Marvel Comics did a dozen issues of Zorro comics, a tie-in with the television series starring Duncan Regehr. Zorro was back for thirteen issues in 1993 from Topps Comics and in the late 1990s the character was featured in a daily comic strip syndicated in a number of newspapers. Beginning in 2005, Papercutz began issuing a series of Zorro comic books and Dynamite Entertainment announced it would do the same in 2007.

Filmography

The Mark of Zorro (United Artists, 1920, 90 minutes) Producer: Douglas Fairbanks. Director: Fred Niblo. Screenplay: Eugene Miller & Elton Thomas [Douglas Fairbanks], from the story "The Curse of Capistrano" by Johnston McCulley. Photography: William McGann & Harry Thorpe. Art Director: Edward Langley. Assistant Director: Theodore Reed.

Cast: Douglas Fairbanks (Don Diego Vega/Zorro), Marguerite de la Motte (Lolita Pulido), Robert McKim (Captain Juan Ramon), Noah Beery (Sergeant Pedro Gonzales), Charles Hill Mailes (Don Carlos Pulido), Claire McDowell (Dona Catalina Pulido), George Periolat (Governor Alvarado), Walt Whitman (Frey Felipe), Sidney De Grey (Don Alejandro), Tote du Crow (Bernardo), Snitz Edwards (Innkeeper), Gilbert Clayton (Soldier with Carved Face), Charles Stevens (Beaten Peon), Noah Beery, Jr., Milton Berle (Boys).

Don Q, Son of Zorro (United Artists, 1925, 111 minutes) Producer: Douglas Fairbanks. Director: Donald Crisp. Screenplay: Jack Cunningham, from the novel *Don Q's Love Story* by Hesketh & Kate Prichard. Photography: Henry Sharp. Editor: William Nolan. Costume Design: Paul Burns. Technical Effects: Ned Mann. Assistant Director: Frank Richardson.

Cast: Douglas Fairbanks (Don Cesar de Vega/Don Diego Vega/Zorro), Mary Astor (Dolores de Muro), Jack McDonald (General de Muro), Donald Crisp (Don Sebastian), Shella De Lanti (Queen), Warner Oland (Archduke Paul), Jean Hersholt (Don Fabrique Borusta), Albert MacQuarrie (Colonel Matsado), Lottie Pickford Forrest (Lola), Charles Stevens (Robledo), Tote du Crow (Bernardo), Martha Franklin (Duenna), Juliette Belanger (Dancer), Roy Coulston (Admirer), Enrique Acosta (Ramon).

À la Manière de Zorro (The Way of Zorro) (Associated Actors, 1926) Producer-Director-Screenplay: Paul Flon. Photography: Deviller & Freddy Smekens.

Cast: William Elie (Zorro), Suzanne Christy, Jacques Manuel, Georges Gersan.

The Bold Caballero (Republic, 1936, 67 minutes) Producer: Nat Levine. Associate Producer: Albert E. Levoy. Director-Screenplay: Wells Root. Photography: Jack Marta & Alvin Wyckoff. Editor: Lester Orlebeck. Supervising Editor: Murray Seldeen. Music: Carl [Karl] Hajos. Music Supervisor: Harry Grey. Sound: Harry Jones. Costume Design: Eloise.

Cast: Robert Livingston (Don Diego Vega/Zorro), Heather Angel (Isabella Palma), Sig Rumann (Commandante Sebastian Golle), Ian Wolfe (Priest), Robert Warwick (Governor General Palma), Emily Fitzroy (Lady in Waiting), Charles Stevens (Captain Vargas), Walter Long (Chato), Ferdinand Munier (Innkeeper), Chris King [Chris-Pin] Martin (Pedro), Carlos De Valdez (Alcalde), Soledad Jiminez, Louise Carter (Indian Women), Yakima Canutt (Angry Peon), John Merton (Rider Sergeant), Chief Thundercloud (Zorro's Ally), Chief Big Tree (Indian at Inn), Joe Dominguez (Guard), I. Stanford Jolley, Jack Kirk, Al Haskell, Slim Whitaker, Pascale Perry, George Plues, Henry Morris, Vinegar Roan (Soldiers), Jack Roberts (Second Sergeant), Artie Ortego, Iron Eyes Cody, Chris Willow Bird, Gurdial Singh (Indians), William Emile (Dueler), Juan Medina, Andres Blando (Bullfighters).

British title: *The Bold Cavalier*.

Zorro Rides Again (Republic, 1937, 12 chapters) Supervisor: Robert Beche. Associate Producer: Sol C. Siegel. Directors: William Witney & John English. Screenplay: Barry Shipman, John Rathmell, Franklin Adreon, Ronald Davidson & Morgan Cox. Photography: William Nobles. Editors: Helene Turner & Edward Todd. Music Director: Alberto Columbo. Songs: Walter Hirsh, Alberto Columbo, Eddie Cherokee & Lou Handman.

Cast: John Carroll (James Vega/Zorro), Helen Christian (Joyce Andrews), Reed Howes (Philip Andrews), Duncan Renaldo (Renaldo), Noah Beery (J.A. Marsden), Richard Alexander (Brad "El Lobo" Dace), Nigel de Brulier (Don Manuel Vega), Robert Kortman (Trellinger), Jack Ingram (Carter), Roger Williams (Manning), Edmund Cobb (Larkin), Mona Rico (Carmelita), Tom London (O'Shea), Harry Strang (O'Brien), Jerry Frank (Pilot Duncan), Lane Chandler (Chief Engineer Malloy), Jason Robards (Citizen), Dirk Thane (John), Frank Leyva (Gonzalez), Hector Sarno (Senor Lerda), Ray Teal (Pete), Rosa Turich (Tia), Brooks Benedict (Starcroft), Vinegar Roan, Art Felix, Ray Henderson, Forrest Burns, Al Taylor, Duke Taylor, Henry Isabell, Loren Riebe (Raiders), Frank Cannon (Cannon Firer), Al Haskell, Merrill McCormick, Jack Kirk, Bob Jamison (Gang Members), Paul Lopez (Rurales Captain), Murdock MacQuarrie (Night Watchman Jones), Frankie Marvin (Wounded Citizen), Josef Swickard (Watchman), Frank McCarroll (Railroad Worker), Tony Martelli (Rurale), George Mari (Boy).

Chapter titles: 1) Death from the Sky; 2) The Fatal Minute; 3) Juggernaut; 4) Unmasked; 5) Sky Pirates; 6) The Fatal Shot; 7) Burning Embers; 8) Plunge of Peril; 9) Tunnel of Terror; 10) Trapped; 11) Right of Way; 12) Retribution.

Released in feature versions in 1938 and 1959 (69 minutes).

Zorro's Fighting Legion (Republic, 1939, 12 chapters) Associate Producer: Hiram S. Brown, Jr. Directors: William Witney & John English. Screenplay: Ronald Davidson, Franklin Adreon, Morgan Cox, Sol Shor & Barney A. Sarecky. Photography: Reggie Lanning. Editor: Edward Todd, Bernard Loftus & William Thompson. Music: William Lava. Production Manager: Al Wilson. Unit Manager: Mack D'Agostino.

Cast: Reed Hadley (Don Diego Vega/Zorro), Sheila Darcy (Volita), William Corson (Ramon), Leander De Cordova (Governor Felipe), Edmund Cobb (Manuel Gonzalez), John Merton (Commandante

Miguel), C. Montague Shaw (Chief Justice Pablo), Budd Buster (Juan), Carleton Young (Benito Juarez), Guy D'Ennery (Don Francisco), Paul [Marion] Marian (Kala), Joe Molina (Tarmac), Jim [James] Pierce (Moreno), Helen Mitchel (Dona Maria), Curley Dresden (Tomas), Charles King (Valdez), Al Taylor (Rico), Joe De La Cruz (Rope Cutter), Jason Robards (Cantina Owner), Theodore Lorch (Councilman), Jack O'Shea, Blackjack Ward, Millard McGowan (Cave Outlaws), Augie Gomez (Indian), Cactus Mack (Cisco), Bud Geary (Dungeon Outlaw), George Plues (Garcia), Jack Carrington (Lieutenant Antonio Gomez), Victor Cox (Pistolero), John Wallace (Jailer), Bert Dillard (Jaimo), Jimmy Fawcett (Jose), Martin Faust (Mabesa), Kenneth Terrell (Dungeon Guard), Wylie Grant (Martinez), Carl Sepulveda (Orlando), Eddie Cherkose (Pedro), Charles Murphy (Carriage Driver), Max Marx (Presidio Guard), Buel Bryant (Renaldo), Norman Lane (Ricardo), Ralph Faulkner (Rodriguez), Alan Gregg (Salvador), Ernest Sarracino (Sebastian), Clayton Moore (Fernando), Bert Dillard (Jaimo), Bob Mabesa (Hernandez), Yakima Canutt, Reed Howes, Barry Hays, Joe McGuinn (Troopers), Bill Yrigoyen (Coachman), Jerry Frank (Throne Guard), Henry Wills (Legionnaire), Ted Mapes (Armory Outlaw), Gordon Clark (Miguel Torres), Frank Ellis, Joe Yrigoyen (Men).

Chapter titles: 1) Golden God; 2) The Flaming Z; 3) Descending Doom; 4) The Bridge of Peril; 5) The Decoy; 6) Zorro to the Rescue; 7) The Fugitive; 8) Flowing Death; 9) The Golden Arrow; 10) Mystery Wagon; 11) Face to Face; 12) Unmasked.

Reissued in 1958.

The Mark of Zorro (20th Century–Fox, 1940, 94 minutes) Director: Rouben Mamoulian. Screenplay: John Taintor Foote, Bess Meredyth & Garrett Fort, from the story "The Curse of Capistrano" by Johnston McCulley. Photography: Arthur Miller. Editor: Robert Bischoff. Music: Alfred Newman. Art Directors: Richard Day & Joseph C. Wright. Sound: Roger Heman & W.D. Flick. Sets: Thomas Little. Costume Design: Travis Banton.

Cast: Tyrone Power (Don Diego Vega/Zorro), Linda Darnell (Lolita Quintero), Basil Rathbone (Captain Esteban Pasquale), Gale Sondergaard (Senora Inez Quintero), Eugene Pallette (Fray Felipe), J. Edward Bromberg (Don Luis Quintero), Montagu Love (Don Alejandro Vega), Janet Beecher (Senora Isabella Vega), George Regas (Sergeant Gonzales), Chris-Pin Martin (Turnkey), Robert Lowery (Rodrigo), Belle Mitchell (Maria de Lopez), John Bleifer (Pedro), Frank Puglia (Proprietor), Eugene Borden (Officer of the Day), Pedro de Cordoba (Don Miguel), Guy D'Ennery (Don Jose), Paul Sutton (Morales), Charles Stevens (Jose), William Edmunds (Peddler), Hector Sarno (Moreno), Stanley Andrews (Commanding Officer), Robert Cauterio (Manuel), Rafael Corio (Don Diego Vega's Servant), Frank Yaconelli (Don Alejandro Vega's Servant), Fortunio Bonanova (Sentry), Gino Corrado, George Sorel, Lucio Villegas, Harry Worth (Caballeros), Ralph Byrd, Francisco Maran (Officers), Fred Malatesta, Jean Del Val (Sentries), Franco Corsaro (Orderly), Victor Kilian (Boatman), Art Dupuis (Soldier).

El Zorro de Jalisco (The Fox of Jalisco) (FICSA/Pegaso Film, 1941, 68 minutes) Director-Screenplay: Jose Benavides, Jr. Photography: Raul Martinez Solares. Editor: Emilio Gomez Muriel. Music: Rafael Jiminez & Tomas Pouce Reyes. Music Director: Rafael de Paz. Production Design: Jorge Fernandez.

Cast: Pedro Armendariz (Leonardo Torres/Zorro), Consuelo de Alba (Isabel), Emilio Fernandez (Ernesto), Lucha Reyes, Agustin Isunza, Tito Junco, Alfonso Bedoya, Manuel Pozos, Miguel Indan, Manuel Donde, Julio Ahuet.

Zorro's Black Whip (Republic, 1944, 12 chapters) Associate Producer: Ronald Davidson. Directors: Spencer [Gordon] Bennet & Wallace Grissell. Screenplay: Basil Dickey, Jesse Duffy, Grant Nelson & Joseph Poland. Photography: Bud Thackery. Editors: Harold Minter & Cliff Bell. Music Director: Richard Cherwin. Art Director: Fred Ritter. Sets: Charles Thompson. Unit Manager: George Webster. Sound: Ed Borschell. Special Effects: Theodore Lydecker. Second Unit Director: Yakima Canutt.

Cast: George J. Lewis (Vic Gordon), Linda Stirling (Barbara Meredith/The Black Whip), Lucien Littlefield (Tenpoint Jackson), Francis McDonald (Dan Hammond), Hal Taliaferro [Wally Wales] (Baxter), John Merton (Ed Harris), John Hamilton (Banker Walsh), Tom Chatterton (Councilman), Tom London (Commissioner James Bradley), Jack Kirk (Marshal Weatherby), Jay Kirby (Randolph Meredith), Si Jenks (Zeke Hayden), Stanley Price (Hedges), Tom Steele (Ed), Duke Green (Evans), Dale Van Sickel (Carl/Danley), Cliff Lyons, Post Park, Duke Taylor, Kenneth Terrell (Gang Members), Roy Brent (Wagner), Bill Yrigoyen (Stagecoach Driver/Pete), Forrest Taylor (Becker), Fred Graham (Black), Marshall Reed, Horace B. Carpenter, Herman Hack, Carl Sepulveda (Citizens), Augie Gomez (Mob Member), Carey Loftin (Dirk), Cliff Parkinson (Ed), Nolan Leary (Payne), Robert Wilke (Bill Slocum), Vinegar Roan (Ambusher), Jack O'Shea (Defender).

Chapter titles: 1) The Masked Avenger; 2) Tomb of Terror; 3) Mob Murder; 4) Detour to Death; 5) Take Off That Mask!; 6) Fatal Gold; 7) Wolf Pack; 8) The Invisible Victim; 9) Avalanche; 10) Fangs of Doom; 11) Flaming Juggernaut; 12) Trail of Tyranny.

Reissued in 1957.

Son of Zorro (Republic, 1947, 13 chapters) Associate Producer: Ronald Davidson. Directors: Spencer [Gordon] Bennet & Fred C. Brannon. Screenplay: Franklin Adreon, Basil Dickey, Jesse Duffy & Sol Shor. Photography: Bud Thackery. Editors: Cliff Bell & Sam Starr. Music Director: Mort Glickman. Art Director: Fred Ritter. Sets: John McCarthy, Jr. & Perry Murdock. Unit Manager: Roy Wade. Sound: William E. Clark.

Special Effects: Howard & Theodore Lydecker. Makeup: Bob Mark.

Cast: George Turner (Jeffrey "Jeff" Stewart/Zorro), Peggy Stewart (Kate Wells), Roy Barcroft (Boyd), Edward [Ed] Cassidy (Sheriff Moody), Ernie Adams (Judge Hyde), Stanley Price (Pancho), Edmund Cobb (Stockton), Kenneth Terrell (George Thomas), Wheaton Chambers (Caleb Baldwin), Fred Graham (Quirt), Eddie Parker (Melton), Si Jenks (Fred), Jack O'Shea (Hood), Jack Kirk (Charlie Graham), Tom Steele (Spike/Leach), Dale Van Sickel (Forney), Tom London (Mark Daniels), Mike J. Frankovich (Auctioneer), Pierce Lyden (Lem Carter), Rocky Shahan (Clark), Charles King, Ted Adams, John Daheim, Pascale Perry (Gang Members), Gil Perkins, Ted Mapes (Ranch house Thugs), Tex Terry (Cattleman), Art Dillard, Joe Philips, George Bell (Deputies), Duke Taylor (John Dixon), Post Park (Wagon Driver), Al Ferguson, Cactus Mack (Deputy Inspectors), Bud Wolfe (Haskell), Newton House (Haines), Frank O'Connor (Turnkey), Tommy Ryan (Messenger), Carl Sepulveda (Milt), George Chesebro (Tom), Howard Mitchell (Louie Wells), Frank Ellis, Tommy Coats, Silver Harr, Ralph Bucko, Roy Bucko, Doc Adams, Joe Balch (Citizens).

Chapter titles: 1) Outlaw County; 2) The Deadly Milestone; 3) Fugitive from Injustice; 4) Buried Alive; 5) Water Trap; 6) Volley of Death; 7) The Fatal Records; 8) Third Degree; 9) Shoot to Kill; 10) Den of the Beast; 11) The Devil's Trap; 12) Blazing Wells; 13) Check Mate.

Reissued in 1956.

Ghost of Zorro (Republic, 1949, 12 chapters) Associate Producer: Franklin Adreon. Director: Fred C. Brannon. Screenplay: William Lively, Royal K. Cole & Sol Shor. Photography: John MacBurnie. Editors: Harold Minter & Cliff Bell. Music: Stanley Wilson. Art Director: Fred Ritter. Sets: John McCarthy, Jr., & James Redd. Unit Manager: Roy Wade. Sound: Dick Tyler. Special Effects: Howard & Theodore Lydecker. Makeup: Bob Mark.

Cast: Clayton Moore (Ken Mason/Zorro), Pamela Blake (Rita White), Roy Barcroft (Hank Kilgore), George J. Lewis (Moccasin), Eugene [Gene] Roth (George Crane), John Crawford (Agent Mulvaney), I. Stanford Jolley (Paul Hobson), Steve Clark (Jonathan White), Steve Darrell (Marshal Ben Simpson), Dale Van Sickel (Mike Hodge), Tom Steele (Bruce), Alex Montoya (Yellow Hawk), Marshall Reed (Fowler), Frank O'Connor (Doctor), Jack O'Shea (Freight Agent), Holly Bane (Larkin), Bob Reeves (Gang Member in Cave), John Daheim (Black), Eddie Parker (Jim Cleaver), Post Park (Stagecoach Driver/Zeke), Stanley Blystone (Dan Foster), Joe Yrigoyen (Indian with Dynamite), George Chesebro (Mob Leader), Charles King (Wagon Driver), Roger Creed (Mike), Kenneth Terrell (Morley), Robert Wilke, Frank Ellis (Citizens), Wally West, Roy Bucko (Laborers), Art Dillard (Rider), Bob Robinson (Winch Operator).

Chapter titles: 1) Bandit Territory; 2) Forged Orders; 3) Robber's Agent; 4) Victims of Vengeance; 5) Gun Trap; 6) Deadline at Midnight; 7) Tower of Disaster; 8) Mob Justice; 9) Money Lure; 10) Message of Death; 11) Runaway Stagecoach; 12) Trail of Blood.

El Nieto del Zorro (The Grandsons of the Fox) (Producciones Cuauhtemoc, 1948, 96 minutes) Producers: Henry A. Lube & Modesto Pasco. Director-Screenplay: Jaime Salvador. Photography: Augustin Jiminez. Editor: Rafael Portillo. Music: Manuel Esperon. Production Design: Carlos Toussaint.

Cast: Adalberto "Restores" Martinez (Restores/Zorro), Leopoldo "Chato" Ortin (Otilio), Alicia Ravel (Aurora), Delia Magana, Lala Gil, Eduardo Casado, Miguel Manzano.

El Zorro Pierde el Pelo (The Fox Loses His Hair) (Argentina Sono Film S.A.C.I., 1950, 77 minutes) Assistant Producer: Carmelo Vecchione. Director: Mario C. Lugones. Screenplay: Carlos A. Petit. Photography: Alberto Etchebehere. Editors: Enrique Vico Caarre & Jose Serra. Music: Anatole Pietri. Sound: Mario Fezia & Jose Maria Paleo. Production Design: Jorge Beghe. Makeup: Vincenta Miguel.

Cast: Pepe Iglesias (Pedro Medina/Zorro), Fidel Pinto (Enrique), Maria Esther Gamas (Vicky), Homero Carpena (Cayetano Orloff), Nathan Pinzon (Assassin), Pedro Pompillo (Mr. Medina), Angel Prio (Man in House), German Vega (Internode), Nelly Panizza (Maquilladora), Celia Geraldy (Nurse), Alberto Quiles, Nicolas Taricano (Doormen), Aida Villadeamigo (Medina's Secretary), Tessia Raines (Fabiola), Olga Gatti (Teresa Pinto), Eduardo de Labar (Tantaro), Fernando Fields, Ernesto Meliante, Aurelio Molina, Sara Santana, Virginia de la Cruz, Fernando Campos, Adolfo Linvel, Jaime Saslavsky.

Il Sogno di Zorro (The Dream of Zorro) (Titanus, 1952, 93 minutes) Director: Mario Soldati. Screenplay: Mario Amendola, Marcello Marchesi, Sandro Continenza, Ruggerio Maccari & Vittorio Metz. Story: Mario Amendola & Marcello Marchesi. Photography: Carlo & Mario Montuori. Editor: Enrique Cinquini. Music: Mario Nascimbene. Production Design: Guido Fiorini. Costumes: Vittorio Nino Novarese.

Cast: Walter Chiari (Don Raimundo Esteban/Zorro), Delia Scala (Gloria/Estrella/Dolores), Vittorio Gassman (Don Antonio/Juan), Carlo Minchi (Don Esteban Contrero), Nietta Zocchi (Dona Hermosa Alcazan), Luigi Pavese (Don Garcia Fernandez), Gualtiero Tumiati (Don Cesar Alcazan), Sofia Scicolone [Sophia Loren] (Conchita), Anna Arena (Innkeeper), Claudio Ermelli (Music Maestro), Umberto Aquilino (Jose), Sandro Bianchi (Pablo/Ramon), Juan de Landa (Cesar/Pedro), Gisella Monaldi (Luisa/Consuelo), Michele Philippe (Maria/Marta), Pietro Capanna (Manuel), Giorgio Costantini (Captain), Augusto Di Giovanni (Don Formoso), Giovanni Dolfini Don Alonzo), Giacomo Furia (Panchito), Michele Malaspina (Perez), Guido Morisi (Ignazio), Luigi Pavese (Don Garcia Fernandez), Riccardo Rioli (Notaio).

Los Sobrinos del Zorro (The Nephews of the Fox) (Argentina Sono Film S.A.C.I., 1952, 77 minutes) Director: Leo Fleider. Screenplay: Carlos A. Petit. Photography: Fulvio Testi. Editor: Jose Serra. Music: Silvio Vernazza. Production Design: Jorge Beghe.

Cast: Pepe Iglesias (Zorro), Mirtha Torres, Pedro Pompillo, Chola Oses, Jose Comellas, Hugo Lanzilotta.

La Montaña Sin Ley (The Mountain Without Law) (Ignacio Ferres Iquano, S.A., 1953, 95 minutes) Director: Miguel Lluch. Photography: Pablo Ripoll. Editor: Ramon Quadreny.

Cast: Jose Suarez (Zorro), Isabel de Castro (Maria), Francisco Martinez Soria, Luis Induni, Jorge Morales, Carlos Otero, Maria Zaldivar.

French title: *Zorro se Demasque* (Zorro Unmasked).

El Zorro Escarlata (The Scarlet Fox) (Clasa-Mohme, 1957) Director: Rafael Baledon.

Cast: Luis Aguilar (Luis/Zorro Escarlata), Irma Dorantes (Gloria Carrion), Jaime Fernandez (Tomas), Fernando Fernandez (Captain Antonio Orellana), Pascual Garcia Pena (Pascual), Jose Eduardo Perez (Riccardo Carrion), Fanny Schiller (Witch), Emma Roldan.

The Sign of Zorro (Buena Vista, 1958, 91 minutes) Producer: Bill Anderson. Associate Producer: Walt Disney. Directors: Norman Foster & Lewis R. Foster. Screenplay: Norman Foster, John Meredyth Lucas, Ian Hay & Bob Wheling, from the story "The Curse of Capistrano" by Johnston McCulley. Editors: Hugh Chaloupka, Roy V. Livingston, Cotton Warburton & Stanley E. Johnson. Music: William Lava. Art Director: Marvin Aubrey Davis. Sound: Robert O. Cook. Sets: Hal Gausman & Emil Kuri. Costume Design: Chuck Keehne. Visual Effects: Peter Ellenshaw. Fencing Instructor: Fred Cavens.

Cast: Guy Williams (Don Diego de la Vega/Zorro), Henry Calvin (Sergeant Garcia), Gene Sheldon (Bernardo), Romney Brent (Padre Felipe), Britt Lomond (Captain Monastario), George J. Lewis (Don Alejandro de la Vega), Tony [Russell] Russo (Carlos Martinez), Jan Arvan (Don Nacho Torres), Than Wyenn (Licenciado Pino), John Dehner (Viceroy), Lisa Gaye (Constancia), Nestor Paiva (Innkeeper), Madeleine Holmes (Luisa Torres), Elvera Corona (Pilar Fuentes), Eugenia Paul (Elena Torres).

Zorro the Avenger (Buena Vista, 1959, 90 minutes) Producer: Bill Anderson. Director: Charles Barton. Screenplay: Lowell S. Hawley & Bob Wehling. Music: William Lava. Sound: Robert O. Cook. Costume Design: Chuck Keehne. Fencing Instructor: Fred Cavens.

Cast: Guy Williams (Don Diego de la Vega/Zorro), Charles Korvin (Jose Sebastian Varga/The Eagle), Henry Calvin (Sergeant Garcia), Gene Sheldon (Bernardo), George J. Lewis (Don Alejandro de la Vega), Jay Novello (Juan Greco), Ralph Clanton (George Brighton), Henry Rowland (Count Kolinko), Michael Pate (Salvador Quintna), Jonathan Hole (Alfredo).

El Regreso del Monstruo (The Return of the Monster) (Clasa-Mohme, 1959, 63 minutes) Producer: Luis Manrique. Director: Joselito Rodriguez. Screenplay: Fernando Oses, Luis Manrique & Antonio Orellana. Photography: Carlos Najera. Sound: Consuelo Rodriguez. Music Editor: Enrique Rodriguez. Production Manager: Fernando Oses.

Cast: Luis Aguilar (Luis/Zorro Escarlata), Teresa Valazquez (Teresita), Pascual Garcia Peria (Pascual), Jaime Fernandez (Esteban), Yolanda del Valle (Estate Owner), Arturo Martinez (Dr. Kraken), Roger Lopez (Dr. Morantes), Fanny Schiller, Sergio Murrieta.

Zorro nella Valle dei Fantasmi (Zorro in the Valley of Ghosts) (Mexico, 1961, 85 minutes) Director: Rafael Baledon.

Cast: Jeff Stone (Zorro), Maria Rivas, Pedro de Aguillon, William Carey, Charles Stanford, John Tompkins, Elizabeth Dixon, Ted Briggs, Robin Call, Frank Curtis, Pedro Diaguillon, Anthony Sanders, Robert Seward.

Also called *El Valle de los Desaparecidos* (The Valley of the Desperadoes).

El Zorro Vengador (The Avenging Fox) (Alameda Film, 1962, 87 minutes) Producers: Cesar Santos Galindo, Luis Manrique & Alfredo Ripstein, Jr. Director: Zacarias Gomez Urquiza. Photography: Agustin Martinez Solares. Editor: Alfredo Rosas Priego. Music: Sergio Guerrero.

Cast: Luis Aguilar (Luis/Zorro Escarlata), Maria Eugenia San Martin (Carolina), Arturo Martinez (Garcia), Jaime Fernandez, Fernando Soto, Victorio Blanco, Emilio Garibay, Jesus Gomez, Pascual Garcia Pena, Carlos Leon.

L'Ombra di Zorro (The Shadow of Zorro) (Centauro Film, 1962, 87 minutes) Producer: Alberto Grimaldi. Executive Producer: Attilo Tosato. Director: Joaquin Luis Romero Merchant. Screenplay: Joaquin Romero Hernandez, Jose Mallorqui Figueroa, Rafael Romero Marchent & Jesus Franco Manera [Jess Franco]. Story: Joaquin Romero Hernandez & Jose Mallorqui Figueroa. Photography: Rafael Pacheco & Enrico Franco. Music: Manuel Parada. Production Managers: Attilio Tosato & Norberto Solino. Unit Manager: Carlo Caiano. Production Design: Luciano Vicenti. Sets: Cubero-Galicia. Costume Design: Paquita Pons. Makeup: Cesare Pacelli & Antonio Florido. Assistant Director: Rafael Romero Marchent.

Cast: Frank Latimore (Don Jose de la Torre/Zorro), Maria Luz Galicia (Maria), Paul Piaget (Dan), Robert Hundar [Claudio Undari] (Billy), Ralph [Raf] Baldassarre (Chinto), Howard Vernon (General), Gianni Santuccio (Minister), Marco Feliciani (McDonald), Maria Silva (Irene), Marco Tulli (Tom Gray), Xan das Bolas (John), Pierro Lulli, Diana Lorys, Miguel Merino, Jose Marco Davo, Jesus Tordesillas, Jose Marco.

Spanish title: *La Venganza del Zorro* (The Vengeance of Zorro); U.S. title: *Zorro the Avenger*.

Zorro alla Corte di Spagna (Zorro in the Court of Spain) (Starlight, 1962, 94 minutes) Producer: Ferdinand Felicioni. Director: Luigi Capuano. Screenplay: Nino Scolaro & Arpad DeRiso. Photography: Oberdan Troiani. Editor: Antonietta Zita. Music: Carlo Savina. Production Design: Alfredo Montori. Costume Design: Camillo Del Signore. Assistant Director: Gianfranco Baldanello.

Cast: George Ardisson (Riccardo Di Villa Verde/Zorro), Alberto Lupo (Miguel), Nadia Marlowa (Bianca Rodriguez), Tullio Altamura (Count of Toledo), Carlo Tamberlani (Marquis Pedro Di Villa Verde), Gianni Rizzo (Don Carlos), Adreina Paul (Queen Maria Cristina), Maria Letizia Gazzoni (Princess Isabella), Franco Fantasia (Manuel Garcia), Maria Grazia Spina (Consuelo), Nerio Bernardi (Colonel Vargas), Carla Calo (Francisca Di Villa Verde), Livio Lorenzon (Captain Morales), Gloria Parri (Rosita), Nazzareno Zamperia (Paquito), Pasquale De Filipp (Valet), Antonio Gradoli (Innkeeper), Ugo Sasso (Dignitary), Amedeo Trilli (Friar).

Released in the U.S. by American International Pictures as *The Masked Conqueror.* U.S. TV title: *Zorro in the Court of Spain.* Also known as *Zorro the Intrepid.*

L'Invincible Cavaliere Mascherato (The Invincible Masked Cavalier) (Romana Film, 1963, 96 minutes) Producer: Fortunato Misiano. Executive Producer: Nino Misiano. Director: Umberto Lenzi. Screenplay: Gino De Santis, Guido Malatesta & Umberto Lenzi. Photography: Adalberto Albertini. Editor: Jolanda Benvenuti. Music: Francesco De Masi. Sets: Peppino Piccolo.

Cast: Pierre Brice (Don Diego/Zorro), Daniele Vargas (Don Luis), Helene Chanel (Carmencita), Gisella Arden (Maria), Aldo Bufi Landi (Francisco), Carlo Latimer (Tabuca), Massimo Serato (Don Rodrigo), Nerio Bernardi (Don Gomez), Romano Ghini (Maurilio), Tulio Alamura (Dr. Bernarinis), Attilo Torelli (Innkeeper), Amedeo Trilli (Merchant), Salvatore Campochiaro (Alvarez), Guido Celano (Dr. Aquilero), Gino Marturano (Ortega), Elenora Morana (Rosaria), Giovanni Pazzafini (Alonzo), Gino Soldi (Miguel).

Released in the United States in 1967 by Embassy Pictures as *Terror of the Black Mask.*

Il Segno di Zorro (The Sign of Zorro) (Exisa S.A., 1963, 90 minutes) Producer: Benito Perojo. Director: Mario Caiano. Screenplay: Guido Malatesta, Andre Tabet, Arturo Rigel, Luis Marquina & Casey Robinson. Story: Guido Malatesta & Casey Robinson. Photography: Adalberto Albertini & Antonio Masasoli. Editors: Alberto Galliti & Antonio Ramirez de Loaysa. Music: Gregorio Garcia Segura. Sound: Mario Morigi & Enzo Silvestri. Production Manager: Luigi Nannerini. Production Design: Enrique Alacron & Alberto Boccianti. Sets: Bruno Cesari. Costume Design: Virgilio Ciarlo. Assistant Director: Alfonso Brescia.

Cast: Sean Flynn (Don Ramon Martinez y Rayol/Zorro), Danielle De Metz (Manuela), Folco Lulli (Jose), Gaby Andre (Senora Gutierrez), Enrique Diosdado (Governor), Armando Calvo (General Gutierrez), Mino Doro (Don Luis), Mario Petri (Captain Martin), Helga Line, Carlo Tamberlani, Walter Barnes, Piero Lulli, Alfredo Rizzo, Ugo Sasso, Gigi Bonos, Manrico Melchiorre, Elena Barrios.

U.S. TV titles: *Sign of Zorro* and *Duel at the Rio Grande.*

Zorro e i Tre Moschiettieri (Zorro and the Three Musketeers) (Starlight, 1963, 101 minutes) Producers: Ferdinand Felicioni & Marino Vacca. Director: Luigi Capuano. Screenplay: Roberto Giaviti & Italo De Tuddo. Photography: Carlo Bellero. Music: Carlo Savina.

Cast: Gordon Scott (Zorro), Maria Grazia Spina (Manuela), Jose Greci (Emissary), Giacomo Rossi-Stuart (Athos), Livio Lorenzon (Porthos), Roberto Risso (Aramis), Nazzareno Zamperla (D'Artagnan), Franco Fantasia (Count of Seville), Mario Pisu (Count of Tequel), Gianni Rizzo (King Philip), Nerio Bernardi (Cardinal Richelieu), Amina Pirani Maggi.

U.S. TV title: *Mask of the Musketeers.*

Le Tre Spade di Zorro (The Three Swords of Zorro) (Hispamer/Roder/Cepicsa Italica Films, 1963, 89 minutes) Director: Richard Blasco. Screenplay: Jacques Dumas, Mario Amendola, Luis Lucas Ojeda, Daniel Ribera, Ricardo Blasco & Jose Gallardo. Story: Mario Amendola. Photography: Antonio Borghesi. Music: Jose Pagan, Antonio Ramirez Angel & Aldo Piga.

Cast: Guy Stockwell (Zorro), Gloria Milland (Virginia), Mikaela Wood (Maria), Antonio Prieto (Governor), John McDouglas [Giuseppe Addobbati] (Father Geronimo), Franco Fantasia (Juan Ortiz), Rafael Vaquero, Felix Fernandez, Robert Dean, Antonio Gradoli.

U.S. TV title: *Sword of Zorro.*

Zorro Contro Maciste (Zorro vs. Maciste) (Romana Film, 1963, 86 minutes) Producer: Fortunato Misiano. Director: Umberto Lenzi. Screenplay: Umberto Lenzi & Guido Malatesta. Photography: Augusto Tiezzi. Editor: Iolanda Benvenuti. Music: Angelo Francesco Lavagnino. Sets: Salvatore Giancotti. Costume Design: Walter Patriarca. Production Manager: Nino Misiano.

Cast: Pierre Brice (Ramon/Zorro), Alan Steel [Sergio Ciani] (Maciste/Samson), Moira Orfei (Malva), Maria Grazia Spina (Isabella de Alazon), Andrea Aureli (Rabek), Massimo Serato (Garcia de Higuera), Antonio Corevi (Don Manuel), Loris Gizzi (Don Alvarez), Rosy di Leo (Carmencita), Attilio Dottesio (General Saveria), Nello Pazzafini (Rabek's Lieutenant), Andrea Scotti (Pedro), Amedeo Trilli (Innkeeper), Nazzareno Zamperla (Sadoch), Gianni Gaghino (Paco), Ignazio Balsamo (Joaquim), Gianni Baghino (Paco), Aldo Bufi Landi (Deikor).

Released in the U.S. by American International Pictures as *Samson and the Slave Queen.*

Las Hijas del Zorro (The Daughters of Zorro) (Peliculas Rodriguez, S.A., 1964, 87 minutes) Director: Federico Curiel. Screenplay: Federico Curiel & Alfredo Ruanova. Photography: Alfredo Uribe. Editor:

J. Juan Mungula. Music: Enrico Cabiati. Sound: Consuelo J. de Rendon. Production Manager: Luis Quintanilla Rico. Production Design: Arcadi Artis Gener. Makeup: Antonio Ramirez. Special Effects: Ricardo Sainz. Assistant Director: Tito Novaro.

Cast: Kitty de Hoyos (Lupe), Dacia Gonzalez (Rosa), Rafael Bertrand (Rodrigo/Zorro), Eduardo Fajardo (Captain Gonzalo), Santanon (Dwarf), Eric de Castillo, Alvaro Ortiz, Pancho Cordova, Luz Marquez, Rogelio Guerra, Tito Novaro.

Las Invencibles (The Invincible Women) (Peliculas Rodriguez, S.A., 1964, 86 minutes) Director: Federico Curiel. Screenplay: Federico Curiel & Alfredo Ruanova. Photography: Alfredo Uribe. Editor: J. Jose Mungula. Music: Enrico Cabiati. Sound: Consuelo J. de Rendon. Production Manager: Luis Quintanilla Rico. Production Design: Arcadi Artis Gener. Makeup: Antonio Ramirez. Special Effects: Ricardo Sainz. Assistant Director: Tito Novaro.

Cast: Kitty de Hoyos (Lupe), Dacia Gonzalez (Rosa), Dagoberto Rodriguez (Juan), Eduardo Fajardo (Captain Gonzalo), Eric del Castillo (Aldo), Pancho Cordova (Victor), Rafael Bertrand (Rodrigo), Celia Viveros (Ana), Rogelio Guerra, Gmo. Alvarez Vianchi, Fernando Curiel, Federico Curiel, Jorge Arvizu, Jose de Estancia, Roberto Porter, Noe Murayama, Fanny Schiller.

El Zorro Cabalga Otra Vez (Zorro Rides Another Time) (Duca/Hispamer/Promidex Film, 1965, 106 minutes) Producers: Tullio Bruschi & Sergio Newman. Director: Richard Blasco. Screenplay: Richard Blasco, Mario Amendola, Jose Gallardo, Luis Lucas Ojeda & Daniel Ribera. Story: Jose Gallardo, Luis Lucas Ojeda & Daniel Ribera. Photography: Julio Ortas. Music: Ramirez Pagan Angel.

Cast: Tony Russel (Patricio/Alfonso/Zorro), Rosita Yarza (Serafina), Jesus Puente (General Esteban Garcia), Maria Jose Alfonso (Manuela), Jose Maria Seoane (Don Antonio), Agustin Gonzalez (Captain), Mireya Merauigilia (Alicia), Jose Rubio (Marcel), Felix Garcia Sancho (Juan), Roberto Paoleti, Naria Seoane, Angel Soler.

U.S. TV titles: *Behind the Mask of Zorro* and *Oath of Zorro*.

Zorro il Ribelle (Zorro the Rebel) (Romana Film, 1966, 95 minutes) Director: Piero Pierotti. Screenplay: Piero Pierotti & Gianfranco Clerici. Photography: Augusto Tiezzi. Music: Angelo Francesco Lavagnino.

Cast: Howard Ross [Renato Rossini] (Don Ramiro/Zorro), Dina De Santis (Isabel), Charles Borromel (Louis), Arturo Dominici (Don Alvarez), Gabriella Andreini (Nina), Ted Carter (Cobra), Rosy De Leo, Nello Pazzafini.

The Magnificent Zorro (Sotang Bastos Productions, 1968) Director: Artemio Marquez.

Cast: Chiquito (Zorro), Sofia Moran, Bella Flores.

La Volpe (The Fox) (Magic Films, 1968, 89 minutes) Director: Guido Zurli. Screenplay: Guido Zurli, Guido Leoni, Ambrogio Molteni & Angelo Sangermano. Photography: Franco Delli Colli. Editor: Romeo Ciatti. Music: Gino Peguri.

Cast: George Ardisson (Riccardo de Villaria/Zorro), Consalvo Dell'Arti, Jack Stuart [Giacomo Rossi-Stuart], Pedro Sanchez [Ignazio Spalla], Evaristo Maran, Femi Benussi, Spartaco Battisti, Artemio Antonini.

U.S. TV title: *Zorro the Fox*. Spanish title: *La Spada del Zorro* (The Sword of Zorro).

El Zorro Justiciero (The Severe Zorro) (Copercines/Italian International Film, 1969, 78 minutes) Director: Rafael Romero Marchent. Screenplay: Rafael Romero Marchent, Fulvio Lucisano & Fernando Mateo. Photography: Marcello Masciocchi. Music: Lallo Gori.

Cast: Martin Moore (Zorro), Simoneta Blondell (Isabel), Fabio Testi (Don Diego), Antonio Gradoli (Buck), Frank [Francisco] Brana (Patterson), Luis Induni (Sheriff), Ana Maria Saijar (Senorita Simpson), Eduardo Baldi (Judge), Emilio Rodriguez (Brad), Piero Lulli, Carlos Romero Marchent, Richard Garrone.

I Nipoti di Zorro (The Nephews of Zorro) (Flora Film/Variety Film, 1969, 96 minutes) Producers: Gino Mordini, Leo Cevenini & Vittorio Martino. Director: Frank Reed [Marcello Cioriolini]. Screenplay: Marcello Cioriolini, Roberto Gianviti, Vittorio Metz & Dino Verde. Photography: Tino Santoni. Editor: Giuliana Atttenni. Sound: Pietro Vesperini. Special Effects: Gino Vagniluca. Makeup: Sergio Angeloni. Production Manager: Sergio Borelli. Production Design: Enzo Bulgarelli. Assistant Director: Teodoro Ricci.

Cast: Franco Franchi (Franco La Vacca), Ciccio Ingrassia (Ciccio La Vacca), Dean Reed (Raphael/Zorro), Agata Flory (Carmencita), Ivano Staccioli (Fake Captain Martinez), Pedro Sanchez [Ignazio Spalla] (Sergeant Alvarez), Mario Maranzana (Giudice Ramirez), Umberto D'Orsi (Commandante della Nave), Franco Fantasia (Don Diego de la Vega), Enzo Andronico (Captain Martinez), Antonietta Fiorito (Manuela), Evi Farinelli (Rosita).

Zorro alla Corte d'Inghilterra (Zorro at the Court of England) (Romana Film, 1969, 92 minutes) Producer: Fortunato Misiano. Director: Franco Montemurro. Screenplay: Arpad De Riso & Franco Montemurro. Photography: Augusto Tiezzi. Music: Angelo Francesco Lavagnino.

Cast: Spyros Focas (Pedro Suarez/Zorro), Anna Maria Guglielmotti (Isabel), Daniele Vargas (The Governor), Franco Ressel (Lord Percy Moore), Dada Gallotti (Rosanna Gonzales), Massimo Carocci (Cortez), Barbara Carroll (Queen Victoria), Franco Fantasia (Captain Wells), Carole Wells (Patrizia Scott), Angela De Leo (Luisa), Mirella Pamphili (Cortez's Daughter), Liana Del Balzo (Party Guest), Spartaco Conversi.

U.S. TV title: *Zorro at the Court of England.*

Zorro, Marchese di Navarra (Zorro, Marquis of Navarre) (Romana Film, 1969, 102 minutes) Producer: Fortunato Misiano. Director: Jean Monty [Franco

Montemurro]. Screenplay: Piero Pierotti & Francesco [Franco] Montemurro. Photography: Augusto Tiezzi. Editor: Iolanda Benvenuti. Music: Angelo Francesco Lavagnino.

Cast: Nadir Moretti (Oste/Zorro), Maria Luisa Longo (Carmen de Mendoza), Daniele Vargas (Colonel Brizard), Loris Gizzi (Don Ignazio), Renato Montalbano (King Ferdinand VII), Dada Gallotti (Linda), Ugo Adinolfi (Lieutenant Bombardi), Mimmo Poli (Friar Pistola), Fortunato Arena (El Moko), Gisella Arden, Ignazio Balsamo, Rosy De Leo.

U.S. TV title: *Zorro, Marquis of Navarre* (91 minutes).

Zorro Disi Fantoma'ya Karsi (Kimiz Film, 1969) Producer-Screenplay: Feridun Kete. Directors: Feridun Kete & Alpay Ziyal. Photography: Erhan Canan.

Cast: Nehahat Cehre (Zorro), Hasan Demirtas, Turgut Ozatay, Tansu Savin, Reha Yurdakul, Behcet Nacar, Zuhal Yildiz, Yasar Sener, Faruk Panter.

Zorro'nun Intikami (Atadeniz Film, 1969) Producer-Director: Yilmaz Atadeniz. Screenplay: Melih Gulgen. Photography: Kaya Ererez.

Cast: Tamer Yigit (Zorro), Nebahat Cehre, Mujgan Agrali, Reha Yurdakul, Atilla Ergun, Mine Soley, Ahmet Turgutlu, Danyal Topatan, Gani Dede, Mehmet Buyukgungor, Kudret Karadag, Huseyin Sayan, Yilmaz Bora, Ihsan Gedik, Gunay Guner, Cemal Konca.

Zorro Kamcili Suvari (Atadeniz Film, 1969, 68 minutes) Producer-Director: Yilmaz Atadeniz. Screenplay: Melih Gulgen. Photography: Kaya Ererez.

Cast: Tamer Yigit (Zorro), Nebahat Cehre, Reha Yurdakul, Mujgan Agrali, Dalyan Toptanan, Atilla Ergun, Gani Dede, Cemal Konca, Mehmet Buyukgungor, Kudret Karadag, Yilmaz Bora, Ihsan Gedik, Gunay Guner, Huseyin Sayan.

Zorro il Cavaliere della Vendetta (Zorro, the Cavalier of Vengeance) (D.C. Films/Hispamer Films, 1971, 92 minutes) Directors: Luigi Capuano & Jose Luis Merino. Screenplay-Story: Jose Luis Merino & Maria del Carmen Martinez Roman. Photography: Emanuele Di Cola. Music: Francesco De Masi.

Cast: Charles [Carlos] Quiney (David Sandoval/Zorro), Malisa Longo (Gladys), Maria Mahor (Berta Cooper), Arturo Dominici (Zack), Ignazio Balsamo (Alfero), Anna Farra, Fernando Hilbeck, Jose Cardenas, Enrique Avila, Pasquale Basile.

U.S. TV title: *Zorro, Rider of Vengeance*. Spanish title: *El Zorro, Caballero de la Justicia* (Zorro, Gentleman of Justice). Also called *Zorro and the Comanches*.

El Zorro de Monterrey (Zorro of Monterrey) (Rosa Films, S.A., 1971, 89 minutes) Producer: Maria Angel Coma Borras. Director: Jose Luis Merino. Screenplay: Jose Luis Merino, Jose Luis Damiani, Enzo Gicca, Maria del Carmen Martinez Roman & Mario Merino. Story: Jose Luis Damiani, Enzo Gicca & Maria del Carmen Martinez Roman. Photography: Emanuele Di Cola & Antonio Modica. Editor: Giuseppe Giacobino. Music: Alessandro Alessandroni. Production Design: Tedy Villalba. General Manager: Angel Rosson.

Cast: Charles [Carlos] Quiney (Antonio Sandoval/Zorro), Lea Nani (Berta), Vidal Molina (Alcalde Jose Arellano), Pasquale Basile (Borracha), Antonio Jiminez Escribano, Alex Marco, Juan Cortes, Pasquale Simeoli, Santiago Rivero, Jose Jaspe, Luis Marin, A.G. Scribano.

U.S. TV title: *Zorro the Dominator*.

The Erotic Adventures of Zorro (Entertainment Ventures, 1972, 102 minutes) Producers: David F. Friedman & William Allen Castlemen. Director: Colonel Robert Freedman. Screenplay: David F. Friedman. Photography: Ferd Sebastian. Music: Sam Kopetzky.

Cast: Douglas Frey (Don Diego de Vega/Zorro), Roby Whiting (Maria), Penny Boran (Helena), Jude Farese (Luis Bonasario), Robert W. Creese (Sergeant Felipio Latio), Michelle Simon (Margarita), Bruce Gibson (Alejandro), Sebastian Gregory (Fred Felipe), Mike Perratta (Don Manuel), Ernie Dominy (Rodriguez), Allen Bloomfield (Academy Commander), Becky Pearlman (Graciola), Kathy Hilton (Esmeralda), Gerald Broulard (Pablo), Cory Brandon (Manuel), David Villa (Scarred Soldier), Fermin Castillo del Muro (Chico), Jesus Valdez (Ortiz), David F. Friedman (Snake Soldier).

British title: *The Sexcapades of Zorro*; French title: *Les Chevauchées Amoureuses de Zorro*.

Les Avenures Galantes de Zorro (The Gallant Adventures of Zorro) (Brux International/Eurocine, 1972, 85 minutes) Producers: Marius Lesoeur & Pierre Querut. Director: William Russell [Gilbert Roussel]. Screenplay: Henri Bral de Boitselier & Pierre Querut. Photography: Johan Vincent. Editor: Beatrice De la Porthe du Theil & Denise De Spigeler. Music: Gilbert Gardet. Sound: Edouard Servapi. Production Supervisor: Pierre Querut. Makeup: Francoise Roussel.

Cast: Jean-Michel Dhermay (Zorro), Evelyne Scott (Angelica), Alice Arno (Marie-France Broquet), [Roger] Darton (Captain Pedro), Ghislaine Kay (Governor), Mikaela Wood, Fatou, Evelyne Gatou, Rose Kiekens, Christine Chantrel.

Also called *Affairs of Zorro* and *Red Hot Zorro*.

Il Figlio di Zorro (The Son of Zorro) (Films Triunfosa, 1974, 86 minutes) Producers: Marcello Simoni & Lorenzo Piani. Director: Frank G. Carroll [Gianfranco Baldanello]. Screenplay: Mario DeRiso, Joaquin Luis Romero Marchent, Guido Zurli & Gianfranco Baldanello. Photography: Franco Delli Colli. Editor: Gianmaria Messeri. Music: Marcello Gigante. Production Design: Mario Speriduti. Sets: Mario Speriduti. Costume Design: Maria Luisa Panaro. Production Manager: Tony Biddau. Makeup: Duilio Giustini. Assistant Director: Ennio Marzocchini.

Cast: Robert Widmark [Alberto Dell'Acqua] (Don Ricardo Villaverde/Zorro), Fernando Sancho (Colonel

Michel Leblanche), Elisa Ramirez (Conchita Herrara), William Berger (Mathias Boyd), George Wang (Pedro Garcia), Marina Malfatti (Mathilda), Marco Zuanelli (Sergeant Marat), Franco Fantasia, Giorgio Dolfin, Marcello Monti, Mario Dardanelli, Marcello Simoni, Lorenzo Piani, Pietro Riccione, Andrea Fantasia, Carlos Bravo.

U.S. titles: *Man with the Golden Winchester* and *Son of Zorro.*

The Mark of Zorro (ABC-TV/20th Century–Fox, 1974, 78 minutes) Producers: Robert C. Thompson & Rodrick Paul. Director: Don McDougall. Screenplay: Brian Taggert, from the story "The Curse of Capistrano" by Johnston McCulley. Photography: Jack Woolf. Editor: Bill Martin. Music Supervisor: Lionel Newman. Art Director: Walter McKeegan. Sets: Frank Lombardo. Sound: John Speak. Production Supervisor: Mark Evans. Assistant Director: Joseph M. Ellis.

Cast: Frank Langella (Don Diego/Zorro), Ricardo Montalban (Captain Esteban), Gilbert Roland (Don Alejandro Vega), Yvonne De Carlo (Isabella Vega), Louise Sorel (Inez Quintero), Robert Middleton (Don Luis Quintero), Anne Archer (Teresa), Tom Lacy (Fray Felipe), Jorge Cervera, Jr. (Sergeant Gonzales), Jay Hammer (Antonio), John Rose (Rodrigo), Robert Carricart (Dockworker), Alfonso Tafoya (Don Miguel), Inez Perez (Duenna Maria), Frank Soto (Proprietor).

Il Sogno di Zorro (The Grandsons of Zorro) (Dania Film/Medusa, 1975) Director: Mariano Laurenti. Screenplay: Mario Mariani, Mariano Laurenti & Luci Tortelli. Photography: Mario Vulpiani. Editor: Alessandro Peticca. Music: Ubaldo Continiello.

Cast: Franco Franchi (Paco/Zorro), Ciccio Ingrassia (Ciccio), Mario Colli (Don Diego), Gianni Musi (General Ruarte), Pedro Sanchez [Ignazio Spalla] (Sergeant Garcia), Paola Tedesco (Zaira), Maurizio Arena (Friar Miguel), Vito Pecory, Ugo Bonardi, Rod Licari, Mario Carotenuto, Grazia Di Marza, Renato Malavasi, Vittorio Daverio.

U.S. titles: *Dream of Zorro* and *Grandsons of Zorro.*

Zorro (Titanus, 1975, 124 minutes) Producer: Mondial Tefi. Executive Producer: Luciano Martino. Director: Duccio Tessari. Screenplay: Duccio Tessari & Giorgio Arlorio. Photography: Guilio Albonico. Editor: Mario Morra. Music: Guido & Marizio De Angelis. Production Managers: Maurizio Pastrovich & Averoi Stefani. Production Supervisors: Vittorio Goliano & Benamino Sterpetti. Sets: Riccardo Domenici. Production Design: Enzo Bulgarelli. Costume Design: Luciano Sagoni. Makeup: Alfredo Marazzi & Michael Duruelle.

Cast: Alain Delon (Don Diego/Miguel de la Serna/Zorro), Stanley Baker (Colonel Huerta), Adriana Asti (Aunt Carmen), Giacomo Rossi Stuart (Fritz von Merkel), Ottavia Piccolo (Contessina Ortensia Pulido), Moustache (Sergeant Garcia), Enzo Ceruscio (Joaquin), Giampiero Albertini (Brother Francisco), Marino Mase (Real Miguel de la Serna), Rajka Jurcec (Senorita de la Serna), Yvan Chiffre (Thug).

Released in the United States by Allied Artists.

La Marque de Zorro (The Mark of Zorro) (Eurocine, 1975, 82 minutes) Director: James Gartner [Marius Lesoeur]. Photography: Alain Hardy.

Cast: Monica Swinn (Guy Gilbert/Zorro), Howard Vernon (General), Roger Darton, Clint Douglas, Rene Gaillard, Jean-Pierre Bouyxou, Madame Caillard, Mary Stanford.

La Gran Aventura del Zorro (Zorro's Great Adventure) Cine Vision/Estudios America S.A./Radiant Films, 1976, 90 minutes) Director: Raúl de Anda. Screenplay: Raúl de Anda, Raúl de Anda, Jr. & Rodolfo de Anda. Photography: Raul Dominguez. Editor: Francisco Chiu.

Cast: Rodolfo de Anda (Don Diego/Zorro), Pedro Armendariz, Jr. (Emilio), Ricardo Carrion (Pedro), Helena Rojo, Jorge Russek, Carlos Lopez Montezuma, Jorge Arvizu, Carlos Leon, Jorge Mateos, Jose L. Murillo.

Ah si? E Io Lo Dico a Zzzzorro! (Who's Afraid of Zorro) (Starlight, 1976, 97 minutes) Producer: Jose Maria Cunilles. Director: Franco Lo Cascio. Screenplay: Francisco Lara & Augusto Finocchi. Story: Augusto Finocchi. Photography: Franco Villa & Juan Geipi Puig. Editor: Renzo Lucidi. Music: Gianfranco Plenizio.

Cast: George Hilton (Philip MacKintosh/Don Alba de Mendoza), Lionel Stander (Padre Donato), Charo Lopez (Rosita Florenda), Rod Licari (Count Manuel de Pas), Antonio Pica (Major de Colignac), Flora Carosello, Tito Garcia, Gino Pagnani.

U.S. title: *Mark of Zorro*; Spanish title: *Nuevas Aventuras de Zorro* (New Adventures of Zorro).

El Zorro Blanco (The White Fox) (Producciones Filmicas Agrasanchez S.A./Solis Hermanos S.A., 1978, 90 minutes) Producer: David Agrasanchez & Ernesto Solis. Director: Jose Luis Urquieta. Screenplay: Adolfo Martinez Solares. Photography: Armando Castillon. Editor: Jose Liho. Music: Ernsto Cortazar. Songs: Jesus Gomez & Tony de la Rosa. Sound: Salvador Topete. Production Manager: Ernesto Fuents.

Cast: Juan Miranda (Gaston/Zorro), Hilda Aguirre (Vicky), Carlos Agosti (Roberto), Fredy Fernandez "Pichi" (Adrian), Ernesto Solis, Rene Agrasanchez, Rebeca Sixton, Antonio Moreno, Josefina Sosa, Luis A. Elizondo.

Zorro, the Gay Blade (20th Century–Fox, 1981, 93 minutes) Producers: C.O. Erickson & George Hamilton. Executive Producer: Melvin Simon. Associate Producer: Don Moriarty & Greg Alt. Director: Peter Medak. Screenplay: Hal Dresner. Story: Hal Dresner, Greg Alt, Don Moriarty & Bob Randall. Photography: John A. Alonzo. Editor: Hilary Jane Kranze. Art Director: Adrian Gorton. Sets: Jim Payne. Production Design: Herman A. Blumenthal. Costume Design: Gloria Gresham. Special Effects: Allan Hall. Makeup: Bob Mills.

Cast: George Hamilton (Don Diego Vega/Bunny Wigglesworth/Ramon Vega/Margarita Wigglesworth), Lauren Hutton (Charlotte Taylor Wilson), Brenda Vaccaro (Florinda), Ron Leibman (Captain Esteban), Donovan Scott (Paco), James Booth (Velasquez), Helen Burns (Consuelo), Clive Revill (Garcia), Carolyn Seymour (Dolores), Eduardo Noriega (San Jose Don Francisco), Jorge Russek (San Diego Don Francisco), Eduardo Alcaraz (San Bernadino Don Jose), Carlos Bravo (Don Luis Obisbo), Robert Dumont (Ferraro), Jorge Bolio (Pablito), Dick Balduzzi (Old Man), Ana Elisa Perez Bolanos (Granddaughter), Francisco Mauri (Guard), Julian Colman (Martinez), Paco Morayta (Ramirez), Pilar Pellicer (Senora Don Francisco), Owen Lee (Firing Squad Sergeant), Gustavo Ganem (Bartender), Armando Duarte (Soldier), Norm Blankenship (Whipping Master), Frank Welker (Narrator).

The Mask of Zorro (Columbia/Tri-Star, 1998, 136 minutes) Producers: David Foster, Doug Claybourne & John Gertz. Executive Producers: Walter F. Parkes, Laurie MacDonald & Steven Spielberg. Associate Producer: Tava R. Maloy. Director: Martin Campbell. Screenplay: John Eskow, Ted Elliott & Terry Rossio. Story: Ted Elliott, Terry Rossio & Randall Jahnson. Photography: Phil Meheux. Editor: Thom Noble. Music: James Horner. Art Director: Michael Atwell. Production Design: Cecilia Montiel. Sets: Denise Camargo. Costume Design: Graciela Mazon.

Cast: Anthony Hopkins (Don Diego de la Vega/Zorro), Antonio Banderas (Alejandor Murrieta/Zorro), Catherine Zeta-Jones (Elena), Matt Letscher (Captain Harrison Love), William Marquez (Fray Felipe), Pedro Armendariz [Jr.] (Don Pedro), L.Q. Jones (Three Fingered Jack), Jose Perez (Corporal Armando Garcia), Tony Amendola (Don Luiz), Julieta Rosen (Esperanza de la Vega), Victor Rivers (Joaquin Murrieta), Maury Chaykin (Prison Warden), Moises Suarez (Don Hector), Humberto Elizondo (Don Julio), Erika Carlson (Don Pedro's Wife), Vanessa Bauche (Indian Girl), Eduardo Lopez, Manolo Pastor, Rudy Miller, Fernando Becerril, Alberto Carrera, Gonzalo Lora (The Six Dons), Paul Ganus (Prison Guard), Enrike Palma (Bartender), Diego Sieres (Young Joaquin Murrieta), Jose Maria de Tavira (Young Alejandro Murrieta), Paco Morayta (Undertaker), Pedro Altamirano (Squad Leader), Luisa Huertas (Nanny), Tony Genaro (Proprietor).

La Máscara de Zorro (The Mask of Zorro) (Mexico, 2000)

Cast: Mario Colli (Don Diego de la Vega/Zorro), Bruno Bichir (Alejandro Murrieta/Zorro), Jamie Taylor (Elena), Paco Morayta (Don Rafael Montero), Catherine Salviat (Nanny).

The Amazing Zorro (Nickelodeon Network, 2002, 72 minutes) Executive Producers: Andy Heyward and Michael Maliani. Director: Scott Henning. Screenplay: Bob Forward, from the story "The Curse of Capistrano" by Johnston McCulley. Voice Coordinator: Paul Quinn. Music: John Campbell and Andrea Franklin. Production Supervisor: Shannon Nettleton.

Cast: Cusse Mankuma (Voice of Don Diego/Zorro), Nancy Cortes (Voice of Luisa), Mark Acheson, Carmen Aquirre, Kathleen Barr, Eli Gabay, Santo Lombardo, John Novak, Sylvia Maldonado, Dale Wilson.

The Legend of Zorro (Columbia, 2005, 129 minutes) Producers: Walter F. Parkes, Laurie MacDonald, Lloyd Phillips, John Gertz, Amy Reid Lescoe & Marc Haines. Executive Producers: Gary Barber, Roger Birnbaum & Steven Spielberg. Director: Martin Campbell. Screenplay: Roberto Orci & Alex Kurtzman. Story: Roberto Orci, Alex Kurtzman, Ted Elliott & Terry Rossio. Photography: Phil Meheux. Editor: Stuart Baird. Music: James Horner. Art Director: Philip Ivey & Tomas Owen. Production Design: Cecilia Montiel. Sets: Jon Danniells. Costume Design: Graciela Mazon. Makeup: Ken Diaz. Production Supervisor: Gregor Wilson. Assistant Director: Choke Correa Cristopher.

Cast: Antonio Banderas (Alejandro de la Vega/Zorro), Catherine Zeta-Jones (Elena), Rufus Sewell (Count Armand), Nick Chinlund (Jacob McGivens), Pedro Armendariz [Jr.] (Governor Riley), Julio Oscar Mechoso (Frey Felipe), Mary Crosby (Mrs. Riley), Leo Burmester (Colonel Pierre Beauregard), Adrian Alonso (Joaquin), Alberto Reyes (Brother Ignacio), Gustavo Sanchez Para (Cortez), Giovanna Zacarias (Blanca), Carlos Cobos (Tabulador), Michael Emerson (Harrigan), Mauricio Bonet (Don Verdugo), Fernando Becerril (Don Diaz), Xavier Marc (Don Robau), Tony Amendola (Father Quintero), Brandon Wood (Ricardo), Alejandro Galan (Constable), Pedro Altamirano (Saloon Keeper), Philip Meheux (Lord Dillingham), Pedro Mira (Abraham Lincoln), Raul Mendez (Ferroq), Mar Carrera (Marie), Silverio Palacios (Jailer), Matthew Stirling (Stoker), Shuler Hensley (Pike), Pepe Olivares (Phineas Gendler), Alexa Benedetti (Lupe).

Bibliography

Books

Alvarez, Max Joseph. *Index to Motion Pictures Reviewed by Variety, 1907–1980.* Metuchen, NJ: Scarecrow Press, 1982.

Barbour, Alan G. *Cliffhanger: A Pictorial History of the Motion Picture Serial.* New York: A & W Publishers, 1977.

_____. *The Serials of Columbia.* Kew Gardens, NY: Screen Facts Press, 1967.

_____. *The Serials of Republic.* Kew Gardens, NY: Screen Facts Press, 1965.

Black, Bill. *Roy Rogers and the Silver Screen Cowboys.* Longwood, FL: AC Comics/Paragon Publications, 1997.

Brooks, Tim, and Earle Marsh. *The Complete Dictionary to Prime Time Network TV Shows 1946 to the Present.* New York: Ballantine Books, 1988.

Copeland, Bobby. *B-Western Boot Hill.* Madison, NC: Empire Publishing, 1999.

Curtis, Sandra [S.R.]. *Zorro Unmasked: The Official History.* New York: Hyperion, 1998.

Eyles, Allen. *The Western.* South Brunswick, NJ: A.S. Barnes, 1975.

Hardy, Phil. *The Western.* New York: William Morrow, 1983.

Harmon, Jim, and Donald F. Glut. *The Great Movie Serials: Their Sound and Fury.* Garden City, NY: Doubleday, 1972.

Heide, Robert, and John Gilman. *Box Office Buckaroos: The Cowboy Hero from the Wild West to the Silver Screen.* New York: Abbeville Press, 1982.

Hickerson, Jay. *The New, Revised, Ultimate History of Network Radio Programming and Guide to All Circulating Shows.* Hamden, CT: Jay Hickerson, 1996.

Katz, Ephraim. *The Film Encyclopedia.* New York: Harper Perennial, 1994.

Maltin, Leonard. *The Disney Films.* New York: Crown, 1973.

_____. *Our Gang: The Life and Times of the Little Rascals.* New York: Crown, 1977.

Martin, Len D. *The Republic Pictures Checklist: Features, Serials, Cartoons, Short Subjects and Training Films by Republic Pictures Corporation, 1935–1959.* Jefferson, NC: McFarland, 1998.

McClure, Arthur F., and Ken D. Jones. *Heroes, Heavies and Sagebrush: A Pictorial History of the "B" Western Players.* South Brunswick, NJ: A.S. Barnes, 1972.

Miller, Don. *B Movies.* New York: Curtis Books, 1973.

_____. *Hollywood Corral.* New York: Popular Library, 1976.

Nareau, Bob. *Kid Kowboys: Juveniles in Western Films.* Madison, NC: Empire Publishing, 2003.

Parish, James Robert, and Michael R. Pitts. *The Great Western Pictures II.* Metuchen, NJ: Scarecrow Press, 1988.

Petzel, Michael. *Das Grosse Album der Karl-May-Filme* (two volumes). Berlin: Schwarzkopf & Schwarzkopf Verlag, 2003–04.

Pitts, Michael R. *Poverty Row Studios, 1929–1940.* Jefferson, NC: McFarland, 1997.

_____. *Radio Soundtracks: A Reference Guide.* 2d ed. Metuchen, NJ: Scarecrow Press, 1986.

_____. *Western Movies: A TV and Video Guide to 4200 Genre Films.* Jefferson, NC: McFarland, 1986.

Quinlan, David. *Quinlan's Film Directors: The Ultimate Guide to Directors of the Big Screen.* London: B.T. Batsford, 1999.

Rainey, Buck. *Heroes of the Range: Yesteryear Saturday Matinee Movie Cowboys.* Waynesville, NC: The World of Yesterday, 1987.

_____. *Saddle Aces of the Cinema.* San Diego, CA: A.S. Barnes, 1980.

_____. *Serials and Series: A World Filmography 1912–1956.* Jefferson, NC: McFarland, 1999.

_____. *Sweethearts of the Sage: Biographies and Filmographies of 258 Actresses Appearing in Western Movies.* Jefferson, NC: McFarland, 1992.

_____. *Those Fabulous Serial Heroines: Their Lives and Films.* Metuchen, NJ: Scarecrow Press, 1990.

Rothel, David. *Those Great Cowboy Heroes.* Metuchen, NJ: Scarecrow Press, 1984.

Rutherford, John A., and Richard B. Smith III. *More Cowboy Shooting Stars.* Madison, NC: Empire Publishing, 1992.

Weiss, Ed, and John Goodgold. *To Be Continued.* New York: Crown, 1972.

Weisser, Thomas. *Spaghetti Westerns—The Good, the Bad and the Violent: 558 Eurowesterns and Their Personnel, 1961–1977.* Jefferson, NC: McFarland, 1992.

Weldon, Michael J. *The Psychotronic Film Guide.* New York: St. Martin's Griffin, 1996.

Wilt, David E. *The Mexican Filmography, 1916 Through 2001.* Jefferson, NC: McFarland, 2004.

Periodicals

Filmfax (Evanston, IL)
Filmograph (Alexandria, VA)
The Films of Yesteryear (Waynesville, NC)
Screen Facts (Kew Gardens, NY)
Screen Thrills Illustrated (Philadelphia, PA)
Under Western Skies (Waynesville, NC)
Variety (New York, NY)
Western Clippings (Albuquerque, NM)
Western Revue (Maitland, FL)
Wildest Westerns (Philadelphia, PA)
Wrangler's Roost (Bristol, England)

Websites

American Film Institute (www.afi.com)
B.Westerns (www.b.westerns.com)
Internet Movie Database (www.imdb.com)

Index

À la Manière de Zorro (The Way of Zorro) 431, 448
Abrahams, Derwin 56, 69, 80, 82, 83, 142, 145
AC Comics 91
Ace of the Saddle 37–38, 42
Aces Wild 34, 39–40, 43
Across the Badlands 93–94, 110
Across the Border 217
Across the Sierras 401, 408
"Action Westerns" 1, 271
Adair, Phyllis 24, 77, 248
Adams, Betty *see* Adams, Julie
Adams, Ernie 128, 181, 222, 225, 257, 387, 414, 436
Adams, Jane 56
Adams, Julie 175–178
Adams, Ted 23, 24, 27, 29, 66, 117, 124, 125, 147, 184, 185–188, 210, 273, 285, 307, 351, 355
Adelson, Lenny 199
Adlon, Louis 371
Adorf, Mario 416
Adreon, Franklyn 191, 193, 437
Adrian, Jane 311
The Adventures of Champion 279
Adventures of Red Ryder 260–261, 279, 355
The Adventures of Wild Bill Hickok 405–406
The Adventures of Zorro 439
Affairs of Zorro 444, 454, 477
Agosti, Carlos 445
Aguilar, Luis 438, 439
Aguirre, Hilda 445
Ah Si! E Io Lo Dico a Zzzzorro! (Who's Afraid of Zzzzorro!) 444, 455
Albers, Hans 416
Alcaide, Chris 101
Alexander, Arthur 322–323, 341
Alexander, Ben 261
Alexander, Betty 157
Alexander, Max 322
Alexander, Richard (Dick) 97, 159, 161, 222, 285, 327, 329, 330, 352, 359, 432
Alexander, Ross 284
Alexander-Stern Productions 323, 331
Allen, Alfred 37
Allen, Bob (Robert) 142, 254–258, 400, 412
Allen, Drew 51
Allen, Ethan 321, 412
Allen, Gracie 184
Allen, Judith 129
Allen, Maude Pierce 260
Allen, Rex 300
Allende, Fernando 445
Along the Sundown Trail 117, 118
Alonso, Adrian 446
Alonso, Maria Jose 442
Alsace, Gene *see* Camron, Rocky
Alyn, Kirk 154, 395, 436
Amann, Betty 133
The Amazing Zorro 446, 448
Amendola, Tony 58
Ames, Ramsay 51, 52
Anderson, G.M. "Broncho Billy" 1
Anderson, George 138
Anderson, Rick 137, 242, 405
Andrews, Dana 46
Andrews, Stanley 93, 141, 159, 160, 191, 262, 264
Andy's Gang 406
Angel, Heather 431
Ankrum, Morris 137, 139, 141, 142, 143 *see* Morris, Stephen
Ansara, Michael 197
Antonijevio, Dusan 421
Apache Gold 417, 425
Apache's Last Battle 417, 425
Apfel, Oscar 127
Arbuckle, Roscoe "Fatty" 22
Arcand, Nathaniel 202
Arce, Hector 435
Archainbaud, George 147, 152, 153, 154, 275
Archer, John 352
Arden, Mark 447
Ardisson, George 441, 442
Arent, Eddi 418, 422, 423
Arizmendi, Yareli 59
Arizona Bound 226, 291–292, 298
The Arizona Kid 45
Arizona Manhunt 301–302, 303
Arizona Stagecoach 244–245, 253
Arizona Whirlwind 387–388, 391
Armendariz, Pedro 435
Armendariz, Pedro, Jr. 444, 446
Armetta, Henry 44
Armida 50, 55
Arms, Russell 87
Arnell, Red, & the Western Aces 86
Arnheim, Gus 284
Arno, Alice 444
Arnold, Bert 100
Arslan, Sylvia 265
Askam, Earl 125, 359
Astor, Gertrude 305
Astor, Mary 430
Atadenz, Ylimaz 443
Atchley, Hooper 47, 344
Ates, Roscoe 350, 355
Atkinson, Tex 78
Atterbury, Malcolm 197
Aubrey, Jimmy 9, 14, 212, 256
Auer, Stephen 267
Auf den Spuren Winnetous (In the Footsteps of Winnetou) 424
Austin, Frank 145
Austin, Little Jean 249
Austin, Jim 249
Austin, Lois 295
Austin, Vivian 260
Austin Family 249
Autry, Gene 1, 75, 84, 86, 101, 117, 124, 147, 178, 233, 255, 276, 279, 335, 340, 343, 350, 355, 363, 394, 400
Les Aventures Galantes de Zorro (The Gallant Adventures of Zorro) 444, 454
Avonde, Richard 302, 315

Bacon, Irving 124
Bad Men of Thunder Gap 324–325, 336
Badlands of Dakota 399
Baehr, Theodore *see* Allen, Bob (Robert)
Baer, John 202
Bailey, Bernard 58
Bailey, Buck 56
Bailey, Dick 158
Bailey, Rex 315
Bailey, Richard 78, 92
Bailey, William Norton 94
Baker, Bob 179, 291, 385
Baker, Stanley 444
Bakewell, William 54
Baldeon, Rafael 440
Baldini, Renato 418, 419
Baldra, Chuck 307
Baldwin, Alan 146
Baldwin, Walter 55
Ballew, Smith 400
Baloh, Mike 419
Balsamo, Ignazio 443
Banderas, Antonio 446
Bandits of El Dorado 90, 109
Bane, Holly 158
Banning, Leslie 91
Bannon, Jim 86, 87, 96, 275–279
Bar 20 150–152, 172
Bar-20 123, 133
Bar 20 Justice 128, 132, 163
Bar 20 Rides Again 121, 122, 163–164
Bar-20 Rides Again 121
Barclay, David *see* O'Brien, Dave
Barclay, Joan 24, 26, 27, 185, 186, 308, 349
Barclay, Stephen (Steve) 79, 156, 182, 264, 309
Barcroft, Roy 134, 135, 138, 143, 148, 152, 212, 220, 221, 234, 264, 266, 268, 269, 270, 272–275, 293, 296, 297, 302, 351, 364, 366, 367, 373, 392–396, 436, 438

459

Bardette, Trevor 47, 89, 91, 96, 126, 133, 191, 275
Bare Fists 37, 42
Bari, Lynn 45
Barkeley, Lucille 302
Barker, Lex 415–424
Barlow, Reginald 306, 357
Barnes, Walter 370
Barnett, Griff 370
Barnett, Vince 320, 321
Barrat, Robert 45, 46
Barrett, Curt, & the Trailsmen 78
Barrett, Paul 321
Barrie, Mona 296, 297
Barron, Kirk 225
Barron, Richard 311
Barron, Robert 71, 325, 327–329
Barry, Don "Red" (Donald) 152, 276, 355, 356, 374
Barry, Patricia 86
Barry, Wesley 310
Barsha, Leon 400, 412, 414
Bartlett, Bennie 367
Barton, Buzz 341, 342
Barton, Charles 440
Basile, Pasquale 443
Batchelor, George R. 22
Battaglia, Rik 417, 421
Baucin, Escolastico 245
Baxter, George 95
Baxter, Les 199
Baxter, Warner 43–46
Beach, Guy 310
Beach, John 55, 127, 131, 132, 351
Beach, Rex 126
Beaudine, William 310, 314, 316
Beauty and the Bandit 52, 62
Bechdolt, Frederick R. 36
Beck, Jackson 56
Beck, John 124
Beddoe, Don 413
Beebe, Ford 56
Beecher, Janet 47
Beemer, Brace 190
Beery, Noah (Sr.) 260, 359, 404, 429, 432
Beery, Wallace 355
Behind Southern Lines 406, 409
Bell, Hank 240, 395, 412
Bell, James 300–302
Bell, Rex 296, 341
Belmont, Virginia 159
Below the Border 294, 299
Beneath Western Skies 182, 183, 216
Benedict, Billy 371
Bennet, Spencer Gordon 254, 261, 266, 392, 395, 435, 436
Bennett, Anne 346
Bennett, Bruce *see* Brix, Herman
Bennett, Edna 248

Bennett, Lee 301
Bennett, Ray (Raphael) 9, 12, 47, 64, 71, 214, 222, 225, 226, 228, 332, 367, 413
Berke, William 65, 247, 349
Bernerd, Jeffrey 53
Bernie, Ben 233
Berrell, George 35
Bertram, Rafael 442
Bestar, Barbara 438
Bettger, Lyle 196
Beyond the Last Frontier 180–181, 182–183
Beyond the Sacramento 400–401, 407
Bice, Robert 326
Bichir, Bruno 446
Big Boy Rides Again 238
Bigelow, Charles J. 224
Billingsley, Barbara 55
Billy Carson 1, 3–21, 34, 216
Billy the Kid 1, 3, 21–34, 113, 208, 362
Billy the Kid (1930) 21
Billy the Kid (1940) 21, 22
Billy the Kid in Blazing Frontier 30, 34
Billy the Kid in Cattle Stampede 29, 34
Billy the Kid in Fugitive of the Plains 29, 33
Billy the Kid in Law and Order 27, 32–33
Billy the Kid in Santa Fe 24–25, 31
Billy the Kid in Texas 23, 31
Billy the Kid Outlawed 23, 30–31
Billy the Kid Rides Again 29
Billy the Kid Wanted 25–26, 31–32
Billy the Kid's Fighting Pals 24, 31
Billy the Kid's Gun Justice 23–24, 25, 31
Billy the Kid's Law and Order 27, 32–22
Billy the Kid's Range War 24, 25, 31
Billy the Kid's Round-Up 26, 27, 32
Billy the Kid's Smoking Guns 27, 32
Bishop, Julie *see* Wells, Jacqueline
Black Buttes 128
Black Market Rustlers 248, 249, 254
The Black Raven 213, 244
Blackmer, Sidney 124, 136
Blair, Henry 261
Blair, Robert 241
Blake, Bobby (Robert) 261–275
Blake, Pamela 356, 436

Blanc, Mel 58
Bland, James A. 84
Blane, Sally 285, 287
Blasco, Richard 442
Blazing Across the Pecos 86, 108
Blazing Frontier 3, 30, 34
Blazing Guns 386, 390–391
Blazing the Western Trail 74, 103
The Blazing Trail 89, 109
Bletcher, Billy 191, 434
Bliss, Sally 72
The Blocked Trail 372–373, 383
Blue, Monte 96, 278, 307
Blystone, Stanley 354, 367
Blythe, Betty 151, 296, 315
Boetticher, Oscar (Budd) 355
Bogart, Humphrey 355
The Bold Caballero 194, 431–432, 448
Bonanza Town 96, 97, 111–112
Bond, Johnny 145, 248, 249
Bond, Raymond 94
Bonney, William "Billy the Kid" 21
Boot Hill Bandits 245, 253
Booth, Adrian 436; *see also* Gray, Lorna
Boots and Saddles 394
Border Bandits 227, 231–232
Border Buckaroos 325–326, 336
Border Caballero 185
Border City Gunfighters 393–394, 397–398
Border City Rustlers 406, 410
Border Patrol 148–149, 171
Border Roundup 212, 218
Border Terror 43, 59
Border Vigilantes 142, 169
Borderland 126, 133, 164–165
Borromei, Charles 442
Borrowed Trouble 160–161, 174
Boss of Rawhide 327, 337
Bosworth, Hobart 308
Boteler, Wade 362
Both Barrels Blazing 71–72, 84, 96, 103
Botiller, Dick 71
Bottcher, Martin 416
Bow, Clara 296
Bowers, Jess *see* Buffington, Adele
Bowlly, Al 124
Bowman, Ralph *see* Archer, John
Boyd, Bill (Cowboy Rambler) 113–117
Boyd, William (Bill) 1, 101, 113, 118–163

Boyd, William (Stage) 113, 119
Bradbury, James, Jr. 45
Bradbury, Robert North 293
Bradford, Lane 199, 251, 276, 277, 403
Bradley, Grace 163
Brady, Edward (Ed) 238
Brahler, Eugen 424
Brana, Frank 443
Brand of the Devil 330, 338
Branded a Coward 178
Brandes, Alaine *see* Randall, Rebel
Brandon, Henry 362
Brannon, Fred C. 300, 301, 436
Breese, Frank 261
Brent, Evelyn 53, 124, 143, 368
Brent, Linda 293, 386
Brent, Roy 10, 216, 331, 385, 386
Bretherton, Howard 121, 137, 141, 145, 180, 308, 373, 393, 396
Brian, Edwin 28, 237
Brice, Pierre 415–424, 441
Bridge, Alan (Al) 72, 74, 84, 123, 130, 236
Bridges, Jeff 399
Bridges, John 385, 386, 389
Briggs, Harlan 273
Bring Me His Ears 126
Britt, Elton 89
Britton, Barbara 146
Brix, Herman 191, 193
Broidy, William F. 310, 405, 406
Bromberg, J. Edward 434
Bronson, Charles 399
Brook, Doris 305
Brooke, Hillary 209
Brooks, Jean 243, 244
Brooks, Louise 352
Brooks, Rand 155–161, 312
Brooks, Ted 35, 39
Brown, Anita 202
Brown, Johnny Mack 1, 21, 178, 179, 220–228, 250, 298, 331, 340, 356, 385, 405
Brown, Lew 43
Brown, Milt 35
Brown, Stanley 66, 401, 402, 412
Brown, Tom 399
Brown Jug *see* Little Brown Jug
Brunas, George 439
Bryan, Arthur Q. 261
Bryant, Joyce 187, 188
Bryar, Paul 312
Brzeska, Rikard 418
Buchanan, Edgar 162, 163
Buck Peters, Ranchman 132
Buckaroo from Powder River 83, 107

Index

Buckaroo Sheriff of Texas 301, 302–303
Bucking Broadway 35–36, 41
Buckley, Kay 94
Buckskin Rangers 250
Buffalo Bill, Jr. 256, 257, 341, 342
Buffington, Adele 219, 290, 298
Bulldog Courage 185
Bullet 91
Bullets and Saddles 249–250, 254
Bullets for Bandits 403, 404, 409
Bupp, Sonny 135
Bupp, Tommy 344
Burbridge, Betty 346, 349
Burgess, Dorothy 44
Burke, Caroline 28
Burke, Danny 332
Burke, James 46
Burke, Jim 417
Burlando, Joseph 51
Burnette, Smiley 1, 75–102, 180–182, 333, 343
Burns, Bob 343, 344
Burns, George 284
Burns, Tex *see* L'Amour, Louis
Burt, Frederick 45
Burton, Frederick 135
Bush, James 367
Bushman, Francis X., Jr. 307
Buster, Budd 6, 9, 10, 14, 15, 24, 27, 182, 187, 209, 210, 213, 215, 240, 243, 245, 247–249, 272, 287, 326, 328, 330, 365, 367, 371–373, 396, 403, 433
Buster, John L. 15
By Whose Hand? 103
Byrd, Ralph 348
Byron, Walter 286

The Caballero's Way 43, 59
Cabanne, Christy 53
Cabot, Bruce 399
Cactus Mack 255
Cagney, James 320
Calamity Jane 399
Calhoun, Alice 311
California Conquest 438
California Gold Rush 269–270, 281–282
Call of the Klondike 312, 319
Call of the Prairie 122–123, 164
Call the Mesquiteers 349–350, 377
Callam, Alex 369
Callejo, Cecilia 49
Calling Wild Bill Elliott 392, 397
Calvert, John 71, 74

Calvin, Henry 439
Cameron, Rod 178, 181, 182, 388, 415, 422
Campbell, Paul 83, 84, 86, 88, 95, 98
Campeau, Frank 44, 119
Camron, Rocky 388, 389
Cansino, Rita *see* Hayworth, Rita
Canutt, Yakima 89, 247, 307, 344–346, 348, 356, 359, 363
Captain Gallant of the Foreign Legion 16, 179
Capuano, Luigi 443
Card, Virginia 210
Cardigan, Thomas 306
Carey, Hal 185
Carey, Harry 2, 34–41, 341–342
Carey, Olive 34, 35, 278
Carleton, Claire 56
Carleton, George M. 268
Carlin, Jean 14
Carmen, Jean 286; *see also* Thayer, Julia
Carpendale, Wayne 424
Carpenter, Horace B. 224, 347
Carpenter, Virginia 294, 403
Carr, Harry 274
Carr, Marian 315
Carr, Mary 346
Carr, Stephen 176, 177
Carr, Thomas 175, 278, 346
Carr, Trem 120, 392
Carrell, Rudi 423
Carrillo, Leo 54–58
Carroll, Barbara 443
Carroll, John 432
Carroll, Leo G. 397
Carroll, Virginia 115, 405
Carson, Sunset 75
Carter, Cathy 54
Carter, Harry 36
Carter, Julie 138–139
Caruth, Burr 344, 346, 353, 362, 392
Carver, Lynne 224
Caryl of the Mountains (1914) 306–307
Caryl of the Mountains (1936) 307
Case, Kathleen 110
The Case of the Missing Medico 61
Cason, John L. (Bob) 8–12, 15, 84, 87, 93, 175–178, 225, 328, 335
Cass, Maurice 134
Cass County Boys 84, 87
Cassidy, Edward (Ed) 4, 7, 11, 30, 40, 76, 215, 216, 249, 260, 262, 270, 272, 327–330, 332, 334, 345, 346, 349, 369, 373, 393, 436

Cassidy of Bar 20 130–131, 166
Castle, Anita 85
Castle, Mary 95
Cattle Stampede 29–30, 33–34
Cavendish, Robert S. 94
Cavens, Fred 434
Cecil, Edward 307
The Challenge 110
Challenge of the Range 78, 87, 108–109
Chambers, Wheaton 268, 272, 393
Champions of Justice 200, 204
Chandler, Lane 7, 77–79, 92, 132, 193, 196, 213, 214, 257, 359, 412
Chanel, Helene 441
Chaney, Lon (Sr.) 315
Chapin, Billy 300–302
Chapin, Lauren 300
Chapin, Michael 300
Chapman, Freddie 268
Chapman, Helen 328
Charles, Frances 314
Chase, Alden (Stephen) 55, 131, 185, 186, 209
Chatterton, Tom 75, 262, 264, 266, 268, 272, 362, 366, 368, 373
The Cheat 106
Cheatham, Jack 307
The Cheat's Last Throw 105
Cheney, J. Benton 85
Cherkose, Eddie 51, 301
Chesebro, George 5, 14, 15, 24, 30, 75, 81–85, 87–90, 93, 100, 126, 175–178, 196, 212, 235, 237, 239, 242, 246, 248, 249, 269, 272, 273, 304, 344, 384
Les Chevauchées Amoureuses de Zorro 454
Cheyenne Harry 2, 34–43
Cheyenne Wildcat 264, 280
Cheyenne's Pal 35, 41
Chiari, Walter 438
Chief Big Tree 127
Chief Many Treaties 386
Chief Thundercloud 86, 191, 193, 194, 285, 287, 386, 388–389
Chinlund, Nick 446
Chinook 310–316
Chiquito 442
The Chordettes 439
Christian, Helen 432
Christine, Virginia 267
Christy, Jan 148
Circus Girl 355
Cisco and the Angel 62
The Cisco Kid 2, 43–63, 357
The Cisco Kid and the Lady 46, 60
The Cisco Kid in Old New Mexico 61

The Cisco Kid in South of the Border 61
The Cisco Kid Returns 48–49, 61
The Cisco Kid Rides Again 48
Claire, Roy *see* Luby, S. Roy
Clark, Cliff 160, 161
Clark, Colbert 68
Clark, Davidson (Davison) 78, 139, 363, 394
Clark, Harvey 130
Clark, Steve 4, 12, 72, 83, 221, 223, 224, 226, 227, 239, 241, 243–245, 247–249, 296, 387, 402, 436
Clarke, Richard 181
The Claw Strikes 105
Clayton, Jane (Jan) 133–135, 137, 311
Clemente, Steve 127
Clements, Curley, & His Rodeo Rangers 85
Clements, Marjorie 332
Clements, Steve 35
Clements, Zeke 78
Cletro, Eddie, & His Roundup Boys 91
Cleveland, George 143, 191, 308, 359
Clifton, Dorinda 158
Clifton, Elmer 307, 326–328, 330–334, 372
Clinton, Larry 193
Clinton, Walter 49
Clive, Colin 342
Close, John 315
Clyde, Andy 139–162
Cobb, Edmond 55, 64, 67, 69, 74, 76, 184, 191, 220–223, 225, 240, 272, 401, 403, 405, 433
Cobb, Irvin S. 320
Cobb, Lee J. 127, 147
Coburn, Buck *see* Camron, Rocky
Coby, Fred 276
Code of the Cactus 185–186, 189
Code of the Mounted 306, 317
Code of the Outlaw 367–368, 382
Code of the Plains 20, 30, 34
Cody, J.W. 256
Coe, Tex 322, 324, 325
Coe, Vivian *see* Austin, Vivian
Coffin, Tristram (Tris) 51, 88, 98, 101, 194, 234, 240, 291, 293, 296, 309, 314, 403
Cohan, George M. 343
Colli, Mario 446
Collier, Lois 366–369, 373
Collins, Lewis D. 276
Colmans, Edward 198

Colorado Pioneers 268–269, 281
Colorado Rangers 177, 179–180
Colt, Lee *see* Cobb, Lee J.
Colt Comrades 150, 172
Colton, John 331
Come On, Cowboys! 346, 376
Comingore, Dorothy 413
Compson, Betty 358
Condemned in Error 108
Conn, Maurice 304
Connor, Allen 346
Conquest of Cheyenne 271, 282
Conquistador 47
Conrad, Mikel 85
Conrad, Paul 71
Conrad, William 200
Consolidated Film Industries 340
Conway, Lita 234, 239
Coogan, Jackie 178
Cook, John 36
Cook, Tommy 260, 261
Cooke, Evelyn 296
Cooley, Spade 71, 73–75
Cooper, Gary 399
Cooper, Georgie 392
Cooper, James Fenimore 415, 416
Cooper, Inez 52, 309
Coppin, Douglas D. 84
Corbett, Ben 183–188, 223, 294, 334
Corbett, James J. 273
Corby, Ellen 145
Corday, Sandra 348
Cording, Harry 157, 158
Cordova, Fred 320
Corey, Jeff 158
Corey, Jim 67
Correll, Mady 153
Corrigan, Ray 232–245, 342–357
Corriganville 99, 250, 385, 404, 406
Corson, William 433
Corson of the JC 133
Cortez, Ricardo 47
Corthell, Herbert 285
Coslow, Sam 124
Costello, Don 48, 153, 154, 265, 268
Cotton, Carolina 73, 75, 100
Cottonwood Gulch 127
Count the Clues 200, 204
Counts, Eleanor 325
Covered Wagon Days 359–360, 380
Cowboy and the Prizefighter 278, 284
Cowboy Commandos 248–249, 254
Cowboy Reckoning 334
Cowboys from Texas 357–358, 379

A Cowboy's Holiday 117
Cox, Buddy 257
Cox, Morgan B. 432
Coxen, Ed 402
El Coyote (The Coyote) 438
Crabbe, Buster 3–21, 25–30, 276
Crabbe, Cullen "Cuffy" 16
Craig, James 132, 412
Cramer, Richard 152, 235, 257
Crane, Richard 369
Crashing Thru 285, 286, 289
Craven, James 161, 237, 270
Crawford, Joan 183
Crawford, John 313
The Crimson Mask 438
Cripps, Kernan 221, 305
Crisp, Donald 430
Crist, Harry *see* Fraser, Harry
Crno, Zvonimir 420
Crockett, Luther 97, 311
Crooked Creek 176, 178, 179
Cross, Alexander 129
Cummings, Billy 268
Cummings, Irving 43, 45
Curiel, Federico 441, 442
Currie, Louise 23, 155
The Curse of Capistrano 429, 434, 438
Curtis, Dick 139, 144, 269, 272, 278, 305, 306, 329, 401, 412, 413
Curtis, Donald 66, 367, 368, 402
Curtis, Jack 246
Curtis, Joann 226
Curtis, Ken 437
Curtis, Sandra 429, 445
Curwood, James Oliver 1, 297–298, 303–308, 310–312, 314, 315
Cyclone Fury 78, 97–98, 112

D'Acosta, Don Barry *see* Barry, Don "Red" (Donald)
Daily, Mary 402
The Dakota Kid 301, 303
Dalbert, Suzanne 310
Daley, Jack 220, 221, 295, 296
Dalya, Jacqueline 46, 47
Danger Ahead 286, 287, 289
Dangerous Venture 157–158, 173–174
Daniels, Harold 125, 361
Daniels, Victor *see* Chief Thundercloud
Darcy, Sheila 237, 433
Darien, Frank 130
The Daring Adventurer 61
The Daring Caballero 55–56, 63
The Daring Rogue 63

Darmour, Larry 254, 258, 400, 412
Darnell, Linda 434
Darrell, Steve 14, 15, 83, 85, 87–89, 95, 98
Darro, Frankie 400
Darrow, Henry 445
Daughter of Don Q 436, 437
David, William B. 308
Davidson, Ronald 191, 193, 432
Davis, Art 113–117, 185
Davis, Dix 321
Davis, Gail 89, 91, 312
Davis, Robert O. 369
Davis, Rufe 362–370
Davis, Wee Willie 156
Dawn on the Great Divide 290, 296–298, 299–300, 306
Dawson, Joe 221
Dax, Donna 10
DC Comics 162
The Dead Don't Dream 159–160, 174
Dead or Alive 332, 339
De Alba, Consuelo 435
Dean, Eddie 87, 136, 138, 236, 250, 276
De Anda, Rodolfo 444
Dearing, Edgar 94, 96, 98
Death Rides the Plains 214, 215, 219
Death Valley Manhunt 394–395, 398
Death Valley Rangers 386–387, 391
De Brulier, Nigel 46, 432
De Carlo, Yvonne 444
De Cordoba, Pedro 47, 53, 55, 136
De Cordova, Leander 433
Deeds, Jack 190
De Gray, Sydney 429
Dehner, John 90, 92, 96, 100, 273, 439
De Hoyos, Kitty 441, 442
De Kova, Frank 197
De La Motte, Marguerite 430
Delaney, Charles 304
De Lanti, Stella 430
De Lay, Melville 22, 113, 214
De Leo, Angelo 443
Dell, Myrna 216, 387
Dell Comics 58, 191, 220, 228, 259
Delon, Alain 444
Del Rosario, Rosa 227
De Mario, Donna *see* Martell, Donna
Demetrio, Anna 133, 137
De Mille, Cecil B. 118, 126, 163, 175, 355, 399
Deming, Norman 413
D'Ennery, Guy 359, 363, 433

Dennis, Mark 83
De Normand, George 56
Dent, Vernon 69
The Deputy Sheriff 131
Deret, Jean-Claude 424
De Santis, Dina 442
Desert Bandit 152
The Desert Horseman 78, 105
Desmond, William 341
The Desperado Trail 421, 426
Desperate Men 108
Deste, Luli 145
De Sylva, Buddy 43
De Val, Jean 145
De Valdez, Carlos 140
Deverell, Helen 372
The Devil Bat 7–8
Devil Riders 3, 4–5, 16
The Devil's Playground 155–156, 173
The Devil's Trail 404–405, 409
Devine, Andy 405–406
Dew, Eddie 75, 179, 180–182, 221, 374
Dexter, Al 335
Dhermay, Jean-Michel 444
Diablo 57
Diamond, Don 439
Dickinson, Dick 125, 132
Diehl, Jim 83
Dietrich, Mike 424
Dillard, Art 215
Dillard, Bert 329
Dillon, John Webb 45
Dilson, John 401
Diosado, Enrique 441
Dix, Richard 399
Dix, Robert 399
Django 2
Doc Monroe *see* Dr. Monroe
Dr. Monroe 64–68, 69
The Doctor's Alibi *see The Medico of Painted Springs*
Dodd, Jimmie 370–374
Dominici, Arturo 443, 443
Don Amigo 63
Don Daredevil Rides Again 437
Don Q, Son of Zorro 430–431, 448
Doomed Caravan 141, 169
Dor, Karin 416, 418, 422, 423
Dorantes, Irma 438
Doret, Nica 214
Double Alibi 27, 33
Doucette, John 90, 312
Douglas, George 351, 354, 357, 360, 363
Douglas, Warren 314, 315
Down Texas Way 295, 299
Doyle, Maxine 181, 346
Draeger, Sascha 424
Drago, Harry Sinclair *see* Lomax, Bliss

Drake, Claudia 148, 152, 315
Drake, Milton 320
Drake, Oliver 325–327, 343, 345–349, 357
Dream of Zorro 444, 455
Dresden, Curley 24
Drew, Lowell 403
Duchin, Eddy 284
Duel at the Rio Grande 441, 452
Dumbrille, Douglass 152–154
Duna, Steffi 136
Duncan, Bob 334
Duncan, Julie 115, 117, 213, 215, 238, 244, 247, 249
Duncan, Kenne 23, 181, 182, 214, 234, 235, 263–265, 270, 271, 325, 385, 395, 396
Duncan, Slim 89, 92, 95, 97
Duncan, Tommy 25, 90
Duncan, William 128, 132, 133, 136
Dunham, Phil 39, 40, 467
Dunlap, Scott R. 50, 53, 219, 290, 291, 293, 296, 298
Dunn, Eddie 342
Dunn, Ralph 194
Dunn, William R. 43
The Durango Kid 1, 56, 67, 68–113, 102, 182
Duval, Joe 162
Dwire, Earl 40, 349

Eagles, James 351
The Eagle's Brood 120–121, 162
Earle, Edward 308
Eburne, Maude 296, 350
Eby, Lois 191
Echaverria, Gerald 53
Eddy, Nelson 212, 284
Edwards, Bill 310
Edwards, Blake 262
Edwards, Cliff (Ukulele Ike) 66, 67, 69
Edwards, Thornton 139, 209
Einstein, Albert 415
El Dorado Pass 87, 108
Eldredge, George 72, 87, 161, 388, 403, 438
Elliott, Bill (William/Wild Bill) 1, 179, 261–271, 276, 331, 334, 391–397, 399–405, 412–414
Elliott, Dick 94
Elliott, Edythe 64, 371, 404
Elliott, Gordon *see* Elliott, Bill (William/Wild Bill)
Elliott, John 7, 8, 26, 34, 115, 125, 130, 131, 188, 210, 212–214, 237, 238, 242, 246, 256, 307, 326, 363

Elliott, Robert 155
Elliott, Wild Bill *see* Elliott, Bill (William/Wild Bill)
Ellis, Frank 5, 8, 10, 15, 24, 30, 115, 186, 211, 214, 215, 234, 237, 244, 245, 248, 249, 320, 332–334, 344, 386–388
Ellis, Mirko 417
Ellison, James (Jimmy) 119–121, 123–126, 175–178, 228, 310
Emmett, Fern 344
Emmett, Robert *see* Tansey, Robert Emmett
Emory, Richard 89
Enemy of the Law 333–334, 339
English, John (Jack) 181, 193, 260, 306, 349, 365, 371, 394, 432, 434
Enstedt, Howard 37
The Erotic Adventures of Zorro 443–444, 454
Erskine, Laurie York 284, 285
Estrella, Esther 116, 140, 146, 363
Ethier, Alphonse 134
Evans, Charles 93
Evans, Dale 300, 396
Evans, Douglas 157
Evans, Muriel 123, 127
Evers, Ann 350
Everybody's Dancin' 178
Eyton, Bessie 305–307

Fairbanks, Douglas 190, 429–431, 432, 435
Fairbanks, Douglas, Jr. 431
Faire, Virginia Brown 318
Faith Baldwin Broadcast Theatre 95
Fajardo, Eduardo 442
Falcon 3, 4
False Colors 152, 172
False Hero 104
False Paradise 161, 174–175
Famous Westerns 1
Fangs of the Arctic 315, 319
Farese, Jude 444
Farnsworth, Richard 201, 406
Farnum, Dustin 151
Farnum, Dustine 151
Farnum, Franklyn 290
Farnum, William 120, 191, 260, 342, 353, 365
Farr, Lynn 85
Fast on the Draw 178, 180
Fatal Note: Jealous of His Own Love Letters 308
Faust, Marty 365
Fawcett, George 417
Fawcett Comics 162, 390, 397
Fay, Dorothy 336, 401
The Feathered Serpent 345

Felker, Rex 234
Fenton, Frank 93, 95
Fenton, Mark 37
Ferguson, Al 23, 127, 147, 388, 389
Fernandez, Emilio 435
Fernandez, Jaime 438
Fidler, Jimmie 302
Field, Charlotte 132
Field, Elvin 69, 79
Field, Margaret 301, 312
Field, Mary 362
Field, Virginia 46
Fields, Stanley 46
Fier, Jack 69, 400
A Fight for Love 37, 42
Fighting Bill Carson 11, 12, 19
The Fighting Frontiersman 79–80, 81, 106
Fighting Mad 285–286, 289
The Fighting Redhead 277–278, 284
The Fighting Renegade 187–188, 189–190
The Fighting Trooper 304, 316
Fighting Valley 326, 336–337
Il Figlio di Zorro (The Son of Zorro) 444, 454–455
Filmer, Robert 79, 85, 88
Findlay, Ruth 41
Finlayson, Jimmy 139
Finley, Evelyn 6, 7, 12, 225, 246, 248, 249
Finney, Edward 331
Fisher, Valerie 100
Fiske, Richard 401
Fiske, Robert 131, 134, 222, 349, 400, 414
Fitzroy, Emily 133, 432
Fitzsimmons, Bob 273
Fix, Paul 121, 307, 308
Flaming Bullets 335, 340
Flaming Frontier 421, 426
Flash 350
Flavin, James 185
Fleischer, Max 232
Fleming, Alice 261–271, 395
Flicker, Ted 201
Flint, Sam 55, 83, 85, 96, 99 152, 220, 221, 371
Flores, Iris 52
Flory, Agata 442
Flynn, Errol 441
Flynn, Sean 441
Focas, Spyros 443
Foo, Lee Tung 146, 161
Fool's Gold 156, 173
Foran, Dick 400
Forbidden Trails 293, 298–299
Ford, Glenn 80
Ford, John (Jack) 3, 37, 38, 39, 351
Ford, Philip 300, 301

Ford, Ruth 403
Ford, Whitey 320
The Forged Will 109
Forrest, William 310
Forrester, Kay 386
The Fort 110
Fort Savage Raiders 96, 111
Forte, Josef (Joe) 351
Forty Thieves 154–155, 173
Foster, John *see* Tansey, Robert Emmett
Foster, Morris 35
Foster, Norman 439
Foster, Stephen 79, 80
Foulger, Byron 57, 148, 359
Four Minutes Late: A Change of Heart 305
Fowler, Art 223, 224, 240, 249, 334
Fowler, Wally 250
Fowley, Douglas (Doug) 63, 91, 146, 147, 150, 309
Fox, Paddy 422
Fox, Wallace 220, 403
Fox Features 390
Franchi, Franco 442, 444
Franco, Jess 438, 440, 441
Frank, Jerry 352
Franklin, Joe 429
Fraser, Harry 326–327, 330, 332–334
Frazer, Robert 155, 221–223, 285, 292, 295, 296, 304, 364, 365, 394
Frederic, Norman 199
Fredericks, Dean *see* Frederic, Norman
Free, Bill 84
Fregonese, Hugo 417
Fremont, John C. 438
French, Richard 371
French, Ted 223
Frey, Arno 114, 371
Frey, Douglas 443
Frome, Milton 370
Frontier Feud 227, 231
Frontier Fighters 20, 29, 33
Frontier Fugitives 334–335, 340
Frontier Fury 210, 217
Frontier Gun Law 75, 77, 104
Frontier Hellcat 419, 426
Frontier Horizon 356, 379
Frontier Marshals 26, 113–118, 209, 340
Frontier Outlaws 5–6, 16–17
Frontier Outpost 95, 111
Frontier Phantom 16
Frontier Scout 208, 399
Frontiers of '49 400
The Frontiersman 128, 133–134, 167
Frost, Terry 7, 310
Frye, Dwight 288
Fugitive of the Plains 20, 29, 33

Index

Fugitive Valley 238, 249, 252
Fung, Willie 132, 239
Fuzzy Settles Down 7, 17

The Gabby Hayes Show 397
Gable, Clark 119
Gabourie, Fred 316
Gabriel, Bob 159
Gabriel, Lynn 124
Gadoli, Antonio 443
Gahan, Oscar 307
Gale, Clita 37
Galindo, Nacho 51
Gallagher, Glen 156
The Gallant Defender 68
Galli, Rosina 367
Galloping Thunder 78, 87, 90, 97, 104, 105
Galloti, Dada 443
Gangs of Sonora 365–366, 381–382
Gangsters' Den 11, 18–19
Gangsters of the Frontier 331–332, 339
Garcia, Al 133
Garcia, Joe 249
Garralaga, Martin 48, 49, 51–53, 141
Gartner, James *see* Lesoeur, Marius
Gasnier, Louis 287
Gates, Nancy 276
Gatzert, Nat 254
Gauchos of El Dorado 367, 382
Gay, Nancy 182, 395
The Gay Amigo 55, 63
The Gay Caballero 47, 60
The Gay Cavalier 51, 61–62
Gaze, Gwenn 129, 132, 234, 237, 241, 246
Geary, Bud 79, 182, 260, 264, 265, 267–270, 365, 367, 372, 392, 393, 395, 396
Gee, Frederick 292
Gentlemen with Guns 14, 19
George, Gotz 416, 419, 424
George, Jean 240
George, John 155
The Georgia Crackers 88
Geraghty, Gerald 193
Gerard, Hal 311
Gerard, Helen 51
Gerould, Katherine Fullerton 47
Gest, Ina 221
Gettinger, Bill 35, 36
Ghost Guns 224, 225, 230–231
Ghost of Crossbones Canyon 406, 409
Ghost of Hidden Valley 14–15, 19–20
Ghost of Zorro 436–437, 439, 440, 450
The Ghost Rider 220, 228–229

Ghost Town 34, 40–41, 43, 217
Ghost Town Law 294–295, 299
Gibson, Helen 176
Gibson, Hoot 34, 35, 276, 298, 341–342, 374, 384–390
Gifford, Frances 142
Gilmore, Art 261
Girard, Joseph 37, 304, 320
The Girl from San Lorenzo 56–57, 67
Girotti, Mario *see* Hill, Terence
Gladstone, Marilyn 12
Gladwin, Frances 5, 11, 30, 215, 325
Glas, Ursula (Uschi) 422
Glason, Ada 305
Glass, Gaston 311
Gleason, James 118
Glut, Donald F. 190, 437
Godfrey, George 344
The Gold Hunters 310, 314
Golden, Olive 34, 35; *see also* Carey, Olive
Golden Lady 106
Goldin, Pat 53
Goldstone, Phil 284, 288
Gombell, Mina 141
Gomez, Augie 247
Gonzales, Aaron 133
Gonzalez, Dacia 441, 442
Goodwin, Cousin Harold 239
Goodwin, Harold 46
Gordon, Gavin 403
Gordon, Richard 49
Gough, Michael 446
Gould, William 52, 92, 194, 256
Govedarizu, Wojo 423
Gradville, Marcelle 53
Graham, Fred 396
La Gran Aventura del Zorro (The Great Adventure of Zorro) 444, 455
Grandsons of Zorro 444, 455, 456
Granger, Stewart 45, 419–420, 421–422
Grant, Kirby 179, 221, 223, 310–316, 353
Granville, Bonita 196, 210
The Grapes of Wrath 355
Graser, Earl 190
Grasse, Gert 424
Graves, Ralph 355
Gray, Beatrice 226
Gray, Lorna 353; *see also* Booth, Adrian
Gray, Louis 269, 363
Grayson, Donald 69
The Great Adventures of Wild Bill Hickok 399, 400, 407, 412
Great Stagecoach Robbery 265–266, 280

Great Western Productions 219
The Greatest Story Ever Told 163
Greci, Jose 441
Greene, Harrison 356, 402
Greene, Joseph J. 153
Greenhalgh, Jack 22, 113
Grey, Harry 357
Grey, Zane 25, 181
Gribbon, Eddie 386
Griffin, Frank 96
Griffith, D.W. 34, 118, 149
Griffith, Kay 359
Grissell, Wallace 262, 264, 435
The Guadalajara Trio 50
The Guardsmen Quartet 143
Gubitoski, Mickey *see* Blake, Bobby (Robert)
Guilbert, Nina 145
A Gun Fightin' Gentleman 38, 42
Gun Smoke 225–226, 231
Gun Trouble Valley 275
The Gunman from Bodie 292–293, 298
Gunning for Vengeance 77–78, 93, 104
Guns of Fury 63
Guns of the Law 328, 338–339
Gunsmoke Mesa 330–331, 338–339
Gunsmoke on the Guadalupe 388
Gunsmoke Ranch 346, 375–376
Guthrie, Jack 75
Gwynne, Anne 312

Haade, William 92, 142, 265, 267, 301
Hack, Herman 184, 275
Hackel, A.W 340
Hackett, Karl 5, 9–12, 14–16, 24, 25, 29, 30, 72, 114, 116, 129, 147, 184, 185, 209, 212–214, 235, 262, 287, 327, 330, 334, 372, 387, 389, 394
Hadley, Reed 261, 432–434
Haggerty, Don 160, 161, 278
Hagney, Frank 34, 114, 116, 210, 211, 307, 309, 344
Hale, Bill 250
Hale, Monte 316
Half Breed 422, 427
Hall, Archie (Arch, Sr.) 10, 12, 210, 212, 352
Hall, Edward 10
Hall, Ellen 153, 221, 222, 330
Hall, Genee 352
Hall, Henry 88, 142, 144, 325, 327, 332, 353

Hall, Lois 80, 92, 95
Hall, Mordaunt 431
Hall, Norman S. 86
Halligan, Tom 125
Haloes, Kenneth 423
Halop, Billy (William) 88
Halton, Charles 55
Hamilton, Chuck 64
Hamilton, George 445
Hamilton, John 265
Hammond, Billy 277
Hanby, Benjamin Russell 79
Hands Across the Border 402, 408
Hannon, Chick 215
Hansen, Aleth 327, 328, 330
Hanson, Lorna 315
Harding, Tex 71–75, 88, 89
Hardy, Phil 201, 399, 416, 422
Hardy, Sam 341
Hare, Marilyn 325
Harlan, Kenneth 125, 132, 134, 136, 137, 285, 346, 385, 386, 400, 402
Harlan, Russell 132, 143
Harman, Fred 259, 278
Harmon, Jim 190, 437
Harmonica Bill 94, 98
Harmony Trail 388
Harr, Silver 249
Harrigan, William 152
Harris, Joseph (Joe) 36, 37, 39
Harris, Roy 244
Harrison, James 159
Hart, Gordon 146, 352
Hart, John 194, 200, 201, 277, 278
Hart, William S. 64, 399, 413
Hartigan, Pat 44
Harvey, Don C. 56, 91, 95, 314
Harvey, Harry 302, 327, 329, 331
Harvey, Paul 48
Hatton, Raymond 175–178, 188, 194, 219–228, 290–298, 355–361
The Haunted Mine 227–228, 232
Haunted Ranch 247–248, 254
The Hawk of Powder River 99, 112
Hawkey, Rock *see* Hill, Robert
Hawkins, Georgia 141
Hayden, Russell 69, 126–143, 175–178, 179, 303, 308–310
Hayes, Bernadene 127, 137
Hayes, George "Gabby" 119–129, 132, 134, 135, 261–268, 392–397

Hayes, Margaret 141
Hayworth, Rita 345–346
Heading West 78–79, 105
Healey, Myron 97, 101, 163
Hearn, Edward 255
Heart of Arizona 131–132, 166
Heart of the Rockies 347–348, 376
Heart of the West 124, 125, 164
Hecht, Ted 52
Hell Bent 36, 42
Hellfire 271
Hell's Heroes 39
Henaberry, Joseph E. 149
Henderson, Ray 43
Hendricks, Ben, Jr. 305–308
Hendricks, Jack 335
Henning, Pat 320
Henry, Bill (William) 199
Henry, Buzz (Buzzy) 82, 255, 256, 392
Henry, Gloria 94
Hensley, Harold 78, 90
Herman, Ace 310
Herman, Al 284, 285, 323, 361
Las Hermanas X (The Sisters X) 441
Herndon, Irene 412
Heroes of the Hills 350–351, 377
Heroes of the Saddle 358–359, 379–380
Herrick, Virginia 251
Hersholt, Jean 431
Hesse, Herman 415
Heyburn, Weldon 75, 141, 145, 243, 362, 367, 387, 394, 395
Heyes, Herbert 392, 394
Hi Yo, Silver 194, 203
Hickman, Howard 375
Hickok, James Butler "Wild Bill" 399
Hidden Gold 138, 168
Hidden Valley Outlaws 396, 398–399
High Noon 335
High Sierra 355
High Stakes 105
Las Hijas del Zorro (The Daughters of Zorro) 441, 442, 452–453
Hill, Al 123, 130, 414
Hill, Riley 78, 225–228
Hill, Robert (Bob) 215, 327
Hill, Terence 418, 422
Hill, Tex 200
Hills of Old Wyoming 126–127, 165
Hillyer, Lambert 49, 64, 69, 220, 400, 401, 404, 405
Hilton, George 444
Hirliman, George A. 320

His Brother's Ghost 9–10, 18
His Fighting Blood 307, 317
Hit the Saddle 345–346, 375
Hitler, Adolf 415
Hittleman, Carl K. 308
Hively, George 36, 37
Hoag, Robert 78, 324
Hodgins, Earle 132, 136, 137, 147–150, 152, 153, 156, 158–160, 235, 263, 346, 347, 349, 350, 372, 396
Hoerl, Arthur 320
Hoffman, Gertrude W. 131
Hohl, Arthur 48
Holden, William 86
Holiday, Nan 224
Holland, John 364
Holman, Harry 370
Holmes, Jack 115, 116, 237, 239, 242
Holmes, Jack M. 212
Holmes, Maynard 310
Holt, Jacqueline *see* Holt, Jennifer
Holt, Jennifer 144, 181, 225, 226, 309, 388
Holt, Tim 89, 99, 101
Homesteaders of Paradise Valley 273–274, 283
Hop-Along Cassidy 119–120, 121, 163
Hopalong Cassidy 1, 56, 68, 71, 85, 90, 118–175, 181, 199, 290, 308, 340, 373, 392
Hopalong Cassidy and the Eagle's Brood 120
Hopalong Cassidy Enters 119, 163
Hopalong Cassidy Returns 124–125, 164
Hopalong Cassidy's Protégé 122
Hopalong in Hoppy Land 163
Hopalong Rides Again 128–129, 130, 165
Hope, Bob 250
Hopetown 250
Hopkins, Anthony 446, 447
Hoppy Serves a Writ 147–148, 154, 171
Hoppy's Holiday 158–159, 174
Hopton, Russell 135, 305, 307
Horse, Michael 301
Horsemen of the Sierras 90–91, 93, 109
Horvath, Charles 96, 97
Hostile Country 176, 179
Houck, Doris 78, 79
Houston, George 22, 208–213, 399
Houston, Glyn 447
Houston, Norman 132

Howard, Edward 262, 334
Howes, Reed 185, 186, 188, 204, 214, 238, 325, 330, 372, 432
Hoxie, Jack 276
Hubschen, Henry 424
Hudman, Wes 56
Hudson, Larry 99
Hughes, Billy 67
Hughes, Carol 285
Hughes, Charles "Tony" 133
Hughes, Kay 12, 334, 343, 344
Hughes, Mary Beth 47, 48
Hugo, Mauritz 74, 101, 273, 314
Hull, Henry 45
Hull, Warren 286, 287
Hunnicutt, Arthur 69
Hunt, Eleanor 305
Hunter, Bill 153
Hunter, Jerry 91
Hunter, Virginia 83–85
Hurst, Patrick 86
Hurst, Paul 305
Hutchison, Charles 308
Hutchison, Craig *see* Tansey, Robert Emmett
Hutton, Lauren 445
Hyatt, Bobby 272
Hyer, Martha 92, 314

I Killed Wild Bill Hickok 399
I Was That Masked Man 210
Iglesias, Pepe 438
Im Tal der Todes (In the Valley of Death) 424, 428
In Early Arizona 400
In Old Arizona 1, 43–45, 59
In Old Colorado 141–142, 169
In Old Mexico 133, 166
In Old New Mexico 49, 50, 61
In the Valley of Death 422, 427
Ingraham, Llloyd 222, 224, 260, 305, 386
Ingram, Jack 5, 6, 15, 29, 86, 93, 115, 117, 215, 222, 223, 225–227, 244, 257, 322, 324–328, 331, 333–335, 357, 363, 368, 373
Ingrassia, Ciccio 442, 444
Las Invencibles (The Invisible Women) 441, 442, 453
L'Invincible Cavaliere Mascherato (The Invincible Masked Cavalier) 441, 452
The Irish Cowboys 126, 175–180, 213, 228, 310, 346, 356

The Iron Horse 399
Irwin, Boyd 54
Isley, Phyllis *see* Jones, Jennifer
Iverson Ranch 406
Ivins, Perry 254
Ivo, Tommy 87, 89–91, 96, 100

Jaccard, Jacques 34
Jackson, Selmer 265
Jackson, Thomas 86
Jail Break 104
James, Alan 385, 388
James, John 55, 152, 265, 273, 366, 368, 372, 373, 392, 396
James, Roy 352
Jameson, House 284
Janes, Elizabeth 35
Janney, William 124
Janssen, Eilene 300–302
Jaquet, Frank 56, 182, 268, 368
Jara, Maurice 199
Jeffreys, Anne 27, 175, 392–397
Jenks, Frank 98
The Jesters 71
Jewell, James 190
Jiminez, Soledad 44, 45, 50
The Jimmy Wakely Trio 144, 145; *see also* Wakely, Jimmy
John Paul Revere 180–183, 216, 374
Johnny Nelson 132
Johnson, Ben 394
Johnson, June 363, 365
Johnson, Linda 227
Jolley, I. Stanford (Stan) 11, 12, 30, 73, 82, 116, 208, 212–214, 234, 243, 276, 297, 309, 324, 326–328, 330–332, 334, 335, 385
Jones, Buck 64, 128, 188, 219, 255, 290–298, 351, 384
Jones, Dickie 133, 194, 285, 400
Jones, Harry O. *see* Fraser, Harry
Jones, Jennifer 357
Jordan, Ted 97
Jory, Victor 142–144, 148–151
Judge Roy Bean 178
Junction City 100–102, 113
La Justicia del Coyote (The Justice of the Coyote) 438
Justice of the West 200, 204

Kadell, Carlton 261
Kaiketsu Zorro 446
Kalinke, Ernst W. 416
Kane, Joseph 343, 346, 347

The Kansas Terrors 357, 379
Karlan, Richard 311
Karns, Roscoe 273
Kassler, Shirley 322
Katzman, Sam 184, 188
Kay, Bernice *see* Williams, Cara
Kay, Edward J. 290
Kay, Ghislaine 444
Kay, Mary Ellen 93, 316
Keach, James 201
Keane, Edward 144, 395
Keane, Robert Emmett 156
Keays, Vernon 74
Keckley, Jane 184
Keefe, Cornelius 348, 365
Keel, Howard 399
Keene, Tom 52, 142, 251, 345
Keith, Ian 267, 385, 387, 393, 394
Kellard, Robert 363
Kelley, Alice 301
Kellogg, John 160
Kennedy, Bill 311
Kennedy, Douglas 199
Kent, Dorothea 287
Kent, Walter 320
Kent, Willis 53, 232
Kenyon, Gwen 49
Kerby, Marian 237
Keyes, Evelyn 401
Keyes, Stephen 224
Kibbee, Milton (Milt) 24, 27, 29, 34, 115, 271, 273
The Kid from Amarillo 98, 112
The Kid from Broken Bow 101–102, 113
The Kid Rides Again 26
The Kid's Last Ride 236–237, 251
Kimberley, Billy 94
King, Brad 143–146, 152, 155
King, Charles 4, 5, 7, 10–12, 14, 15, 23, 24, 26–30, 72, 115–117, 208, 209, 211, 212, 216, 220, 221, 224, 225, 244–248, 285, 292, 293, 295, 304, 306, 307, 324–330, 332–335, 352, 373, 387–389
King, Claude 123
King, John 232–247, 250
King, Pee Wee, & His Golden West Cowboys 96, 100
King, William (Billy) 128, 129, 131, 132
King of Dodge City 402–403, 408
King of the Bandits 53–54, 62
King of the Range 174
The King's Men 135, 138, 139
Kingsford, Guy 245

Kinski, Klaus 418
Kirby, Jay 146–150, 152, 155, 262, 263, 265, 269, 271, 436
Kirk, Jack 78, 181, 262, 264, 271, 307, 351, 394
Kirke, Donald 137, 158
Kittredge, Walter 328
Knight, Fuzzy 16, 175–179, 307
Knight, Vick 287
A Knight of the Range 34–35, 41
Knox, Patricia 14, 15, 212, 326, 335
Kohler, Fred 124, 305
Kohler, Fred, Jr. 55, 349, 368, 392
Korda, Alexander 431
Kortman, Robert (Bob) 11, 77, 129, 144, 238, 249, 255, 260, 328
Korvin, Charles 440
Krah, Marc 311
Kramer, Wright 137
Krasne, Philip N. 48, 54, 286
Kretzer, Joachim 424
Kuhn, Mickey 76
Kulky, Henry 316
Kyne, Peter B. 38, 39

Lackteen, Frank 139, 274, 315
Laemmle, Carl 322
Lagunes, Teresa 59
Laidlaw, Betty 285
Laidlaw, Nathan 84, 93, 325, 341, 358, 403
Laird, Effie 182
L'Amour, Louis 162
Land of Hunted Men 248, 254
Land of the Outlaws 224, 230
Landers, Lew 438
Landis, Carole 355, 358
Landrush 79, 93, 97, 105
Lane, Adele 308
Lane, Al *see* Tansey, Robert Emmett
Lane, Allan 1, 269, 271–275, 279, 300
Lane, Lola 147
Lane, Nora 45, 126, 128, 146, 185
Lane, Vicky 49
Lang, Carl 311
Lang, Harry 58
Lang, Howard 121, 123
Lang, Melvin 69
Lange, Carl 421
Lange, Johnny 22, 115–117, 185, 208, 235, 236, 249, 287
Langella, Frank 444
Laramie 89, 109
Laramie Mountains 99–100, 112

The Laramie Trail 182
Larson, Bobby 69, 149
La Rue, Frank 4, 23, 51, 67, 74, 75, 81, 185, 224–227, 235, 292, 400, 402, 414
La Rue, Jack 53, 272, 385
La Rue, Lash 16, 238
La Sadio, Sojo 136
The Last Bandit 271
Last Days of Boot Hill 84, 107
The Last Frontier 399
Last of the Renegades 417, 425
The Last Time I Saw Archie 210
El Latigo (The Whip) 438, 444–445
El Latigo Contra los Momias (The Whip vs. the Mummies) 438, 445
El Latigo Contra Santana (The Whip vs. Satan) 438, 445
Latimore, Frank 440
Laurence, Mady 9, 328, 329
Lauter, Harry 98, 314
Lava, William 439
Lavi, Daliah 417
Law, Mildred 74
Law and Order 27, 32–33
The Law Comes to Texas 400
Law Men 223, 230
Law of the Canyon 82, 106
The Law of the 45s 341, 374
Law of the Pampas 128, 136–137, 167–168
Law of the Ranger 256–257, 258–259
Law of the Saddle 22, 214, 216, 219
Law of the Valley 224–225, 230
The Law Rides Again 385–386, 390
The Lawless 200, 204–205
Lawless Empire 74–75, 103–104
Lawrence, Mady *see* Laurence, Mady
Lawson, Priscilla 351
Leary, Nolan 74, 77, 79, 82
Lease, Rex 23–25, 240, 247, 248, 266, 362, 363
The Leather Burners 149–150, 171
Lederman, D. Ross 401
Lee, Duke R. 35–37
Lee, Jennie 37
Lee, Ruth 262
Leeds, Herbert I. 45–47
The Legend of the Lone Ranger 194, 196, 200–201, 203, 207–208

The Legend of Zorro 429, 446–447, 448
Leiber, Fritz 49, 157
Leibman, Ron 445
Leicester, William F. 161
Leigh, Nelson 153, 312
Leighton, Linda 314
Leighton, Melinda 367
Leipnitz, Harald 420, 422
Le Moyne, Charles 39
Leonard, David 55
Le Saint, Edward J. 39
Le Saint, Stella 412
Leslie, Maxine 28, 29, 211
Lesoeur, Marius 440
Lesser, Sol 291
Lester, Bill 56
Lester, Vickie 211
Letscher, Matt 446
Lettieri, Louis 97, 275
Letz, George 191 *see* Montgomery, George
Levine, Nat 341
Lewis, Eugene B. 36, 37
Lewis, George J. 49, 51, 90, 145, 175, 177, 178, 194, 269, 322, 436, 437, 439
Lewis, Joseph H. 413
Lewis, Sheldon 8
Lewis, Texas Jim, & His Lone Star Cowboys 82, 83
Lightnin' Bill Carson 184, 185, 188–189
Lightning Bill Carson 1, 183–190, 290
Lightning Carson Rides Again 184–185, 186, 189
Lightning Guns 94, 111
Lightning Raiders 14, 19
Lincoln, Elmo 356
Litel, John 55
Little, Mickey 55
Little Brown Jug 86, 93, 276, 278
Littlefield, Lucien 436
Littlefield, Ralph 196
Lively, Robert 285
Lively, William 300
Livingston, Robert (Bob) 181–182, 193, 194, 213–216, 342–351, 355, 355–366, 431–432, 434
Lloyd, Christopher 201
Lloyd, George 401, 404
El Lobo Negro (The Black Wolf) 445
Lockwood, Harold 307
Loco 57
Loftus, Arthur 270, 401
Logan, Sydney 11
Lollier, George 140
Lom, Herbert 416, 424
Lomax, Bliss 146, 149, 150
Lombard, Louise 447
Lomond, Britt 439
London, Tom 30, 145, 193, 209, 234, 238, 241, 250,

256, 263, 264, 268–272, 274, 275, 325, 350, 353, 365, 373, 385, 394, 396, 436
The Lone Hand Texan 81–82, 106
The Lone Ranger 114, 190–206, 208
The Lone Ranger and the Lost City of Gold 199–200, 203–204
The Lone Ranger Rides Again 193–194, 196, 203
The Lone Rider 3, 22, 113, 208–219, 366
The Lone Rider Ambushed 210–211, 219
The Lone Rider and the Bandit 211–212, 217–218
The Lone Rider Crosses the Rio 209, 210, 217
The Lone Rider Fights Back 211, 217
The Lone Rider Galloping to Glory 209
The Lone Rider in Border Roundup 212, 218
The Lone Rider in Cheyenne 212, 218
The Lone Rider in Frontier Fury 209–210, 217
The Lone Rider in Ghost Town 209, 217
The Lone Rider in Law of the Saddle 214, 219
The Lone Rider in Texas Justice 212, 218
The Lone Rider Rides On 209, 216–217
Lone Star Pioneers 400
Lone Star Raiders 362, 363, 381
Lone Star Vigilantes 403, 408
Lone Texas Ranger 266, 280–281
Long, Walter 132, 138
The Long, Long Trail 253
Longo, Melissa (Malisa) 443
Lopez, Perry 196
Lorch, Theodore (Ted) 39, 307
Loren, Sophia 438
Loring, Teala 52
Lornzon, Livio 441
Lost Canyon 147, 171
The Lost Trail 226–227, 231
Lott, Michael 424
Love, Montagu 434
Love at First Bite 445
Lovecraft, H.P. 8
Lowe, Edmund 44, 45
Lowe, Ellen 365
Lowe, Sherman L. 432
Lowery, Robert 48, 296, 298

Luby, S. Roy 232, 247, 248
Lucas, Nick 43
Lucas, Wilfred 39
Lucky Cisco Kid 46–47, 60
Luden, Jack 258, 400, 412
Lugosi, Bela 7
Lumberjack 153–154, 172–173
Lund, Lucille 307
Lupo, Alberto 441
Lyden, Pierce 84, 149, 152–154, 274, 372, 402
Lyman, Abe 284
Lynn, Emmett 5, 10, 11, 72, 79, 84, 85, 269, 271, 272, 274, 276–278, 309, 327, 368, 386
Lynn, Peter George 365
Lyons, Cliff 89, 385
Lytton, J. Courtland 84

MacDonald, Edmund 47
MacDonald, J. Farrell 37, 138, 144, 153, 161, 176, 194, 305, 396
MacDonald, Kenneth 55, 69, 182, 221, 224, 226, 363, 401, 402, 412
MacDonald, William Colt 340–342, 344, 345, 362
MacGregor, Casey 84
MacGregor, Parke 316
Mack, Wilbur 357
MacLane, Barton 272
MacLaren, Mary 221, 257, 326
MacQuarrie, Murdock 294
MacRae, Henry 36
Madison, Guy 405–406, 417
Magna Color 431, 432
The Magnificent Zorro 442, 453
Mahan, Leo J. 126
Mahoney, Jock (Jack) 81, 89–91, 93, 94, 98–101
Mahor, Maria 443
Mailes, Charles Hill 36, 430
Malcolm, Robert 89
Mallinson, Rory 87, 99
Mallory, Boots 342
Malone, Dorothy 35, 36
Maltin, Leonard 439
Malvern, Paul 120, 340, 351, 392
Mamakos, Peter 310
Mamoulian, Rouben 434, 435, 445
The Man from Bar 20: A Story of Cow-Country 129
The Man from Thunder River 392–393, 397
The Man from Tumbleweeds 413–414, 415
Man with the Golden Winchester 454

Man with the Steel Whip 437–438
Manera, Jesus Franco *see* Franco, Jess
Manners, Marjorie 29, 116, 213, 345
Manning, Mildred 39
Mapes, Ted 76, 79, 81, 223, 227, 240, 242, 251
Maple, Christine 344
Maranzana, Mario 442
The Marauders 158, 174
La Marca del Zorilla (The Mark of the Skunk) 438
March, Eve 392
Marcus, James 44
Mari, George 120
Marin, Cheech 58
The Marines Are Coming 177
Marion, Paul 94, 359, 433
Mark of Zorro 429–430, 431, 434–435, 441, 444, 445, 447–449, 455
Marked for Murder 333, 339
A Marked Man 35, 41
Marked Men 38–39, 42–43
Marked Trails 389
Marlowe, Nora 441
La Marque de Zorro (The Mark of Zorro) 455
Marquis, Margaret 131
Marros, Jose Antonio 424
Marsh, Anthony 352
Marshal of Cripple Creek 275, 283
Marshal of Heldorado 176, 179
Marshal of Laredo 267–268, 281
Marshal of Reno 262–263, 279–280
Marshal of Trail City 271
Marshall, George 80
Marshals in Disguise 406, 410–411
Martel, June 348, 353
Martell, Donna 53
Martin, Charles 124
Martin, Chris-Pin 45–48, 53, 146
Martin, James 328
Martin, Jill 188; *see also* Wood, Harley
Martin, Johnny 115
Martinez, Adalberto 438
Martinez, Arturo 438–439
Martinez, Nana *see* Woodbury, Joan
Marvey, Gene 343
Marvin, Johnny 355, 403–405
La Máscara de Zorro (The Mask of Zorro) 446, 456
Mask of the Musketeers 441
The Mask of Zorro 446, 447, 456

The Masked Conqueror 443
Mason, LeRoy 181, 182, 235, 262–264, 304, 305, 344, 351, 352, 356, 360, 386, 395, 396, 401
Masquerade 200, 205
Masters, Frankie 237
Masters, Howard 24, 26, 117, 209, 294
Match Making Marshal 406, 411
Mather, Jack 58
Mathews, Carl 234, 241–244, 249
Mathews, Carole 73, 74
Mattox, Martha 36
Mattox, Walt 388
Max, Edwin 276
Maxey, Virginia 87
Maxwell, Edwin 48
May, Karl 415–417, 419, 420–422, 424
May, Princess Neola 37
Mayer, Ray 342
Maynard, Ken 8, 142, 250, 254, 256, 276, 298, 303, 374, 384–388, 390, 400, 412
Maynard, Kermit 5, 8, 11–13, 90, 138, 145, 220, 244, 246, 251, 303–309, 330, 334, 335, 349–350, 354, 372, 400
Maynard, Tex *see* Maynard, Kermit
McCall, Jack 399
McCarroll, Frank 8, 79, 84, 86, 217, 328, 396
McCarthy, John 307
McCarthy, John P. 48
McCarty, Patti 4, 7, 15, 67, 326, 331
McClendon, Jack 266
McConnell, Marilyn 333
McConnell, Molly 37
McCormick, Merrill 243, 305
McCoy, Tim 1, 69, 128, 183–188, 255, 290–296, 340, 351
McCullough, Philo 285
McCulley, Johnston 49, 141, 190, 221, 222, 429, 431, 434–436, 438, 444
McDonald, Francis 50, 136, 151, 153, 155, 157, 159, 161, 264, 265, 436
McDonald, Frank 251, 311, 314
McDowell, Claire 430
McGlynn, Frank, Jr. 119
McGlynn, Frank, Sr. 191
McGovern, Johnny 261
McGowan, J.P. 343, 345, 348
McGrail, Walter 23, 27, 295
McGuinn, Joe 23, 66, 359, 403–405

McGuire, Paul 94, 97, 312
McIntyre, Christine 221, 222, 227, 242, 292, 293, 296, 298, 325
McKay, Doreen 351, 354
McKay, Wanda 27, 115, 145, 212
McKee, Lafe 256, 257, 305, 306, 341, 413
McKellar, Helen 365
McKenzie, Robert (Bob) 153, 269, 341, 385
McKim, Harry 358, 396
McKim, Robert 39, 318, 430
McKim, Sammy 193, 348, 350, 360, 400
McKinney, Florine 361
McKinney, Mira 91
McMahon, Leo J. 131
McTaggart, Malcolm "Bud" (Ward) 27, 188, 296, 365
Meadows, Denny *see* Moore, Dennis
Mechoso, Julio Oscar 446
The Medico of Painted Springs 64–65, 67
The Medico on the Trail 67
The Medico Rides 65
Meier, Christian 446
Mein Freund Winnetou (My Friend Winnetou) 424, 247
Melody Ranch 406
Melton, Frank 350
Menacing Shadows 104
Menken, Shepard 200
Mercer, Freddie 371
Merchant, Joaquin Luis Romero 438, 440, 442
Merchant, Rafael Romero 442
Meredith, Charles 196
Meredith, Iris 29, 255, 324, 412–414
Meredith, John 14
Meredith, Robert 8
Merino, Jose Luis 443
Merton, John 4, 7, 23, 27, 28, 51, 78, 87, 121, 135, 153, 184, 191, 224–227, 243, 248, 249, 256, 257, 292, 307, 326, 355, 360, 362, 363, 386, 403, 433, 436
Mesquite Jenkins, Tumbleweed 124, 135
Messinger, Gertrude 39
Michaels, Pat 272
Middleton, Charles 119, 144, 356, 358
Middleton, Robert 444
The Midnight Call 307
Mierendorff, Hans 416
Mike and Ike 11
Milan, Frank 351
Miles, Betty 214, 332, 385, 387, 389

Miles, Lillian 306
Miljan, John 199
Milland, Gloria 441
Miller, Charles 181, 182, 394, 396
Miller, Charles F. 368, 369, 371, 372
Miller, Don 3, 69, 74, 80, 114, 115, 121, 208, 214, 282, 300, 315, 325, 326, 384, 392
Miller, Eve 84
Miller, Ivan 358
Miller, John "Skins" 139
Miller, Lorraine 12, 334, 335, 373
Miller, Walter 256, 304, 348
Millett, Arthur 257
Miranda, Juan 444
Mr. Ed 275
Mitchell, Frank 403–405
Mitchell, Pat 313
Mitchell, Peter 395
Mitchell, Yvette 43
Mitchum, Robert (Bob) 143, 150–152, 180, 181, 210
Mitic, Gojko 419, 424
Mix, Art 215, 221, 255, 341, 342
Mix, Tom 64, 290–291, 305
Moehring, Kansas 226
Mojave Firebrand 395–396, 398
Molieri, Lillian 50
Molina, Vidal 443
Montague, Monte 369
Montalban, Ricardo 444
Montalbano, Renato 443
Montana, Montie 232
La Montaña Sin Ley (The Mountain Without Law) 438, 451
Montell, Lisa 199
Montenegro, Conchita 45
Montgomery, George 46; *see also* Letz, George
Moody, Ralph 199
Moonlight Raid 109
Moore, Clayton 90, 97, 99, 194–201, 436–437
Moore, Dennis 24, 26, 142, 175, 177, 211–213, 215, 224, 227, 248–250, 291, 293, 295, 297, 312, 361, 364, 368
Moore, Martin 442
Moore, Pauline 362
Moorhead, Natalie 131
Moran, Betty 136
Morango, Louis 190
Morant, Edwin 350
Morante, Milburn 226, 234, 243, 294, 296, 343
Moranti, Milt *see* Morante, Milburn
Moray, Tom 402

More Than Magic 200, 205
Moreno, Antonio 146
Moretti, Nadir 443
Morey, Elaine 9
Morgan, Boyd "Red" 91, 97
Morgan, Lee 94, 96, 276
Morin, Alberto (Albert) 145, 161
Morison, Patricia 47, 48
Morphy, Lew 272
Morrell, George 256, 257, 332, 334
Morris, Adrian 341
Morris, Philip 86
Morris, Stephen 124–127; *see also* Ankrum, Morris
Morrison, Chuck 39, 40, 401
Morrow, Neyle 157
Morton, Charles 153, 396
Morton, Dann 301
Movita 302
Mowery, Helen 79, 94
Mulford, Clarence E. 118–135, 146, 151
Mulhall, Jack 239, 308, 309, 350
Mummert, Danny 66
Murder Over the Yukon 287–288, 289–290
Murietta, Joaquin 211, 447
Murietta and the Lone Rider 211
Murphy, Horace 235, 256, 261, 346
Murray, Chad Michael 202
Murray, Charles, Jr. 387–389
Murray, Don 399
Murray, Forbes 67, 148, 149, 152, 159, 191, 365, 392, 396
Murray, Zon 14, 79, 82, 85, 98, 99, 161
Musi, Gianni 444
Mustard & Gravy 82, 90
"My Tonia" 43, 45
Myers, Charlotte 134
Myers, Herbert 327
The Mysterious Rider 28–29, 33
Mystery Man 142, 154, 173

Nace, Anthony 134
Nance, Gordon *see* Elliott, Bill (William/Wild Bill)
Nanni, Lea 443
Naranjo, Ivan 200
Nash, Noreen 199
The Navajo Trail 225, 231
Nazarro, Cliff 142, 309
Nazarro, Ray 74, 76, 80, 83, 93, 95, 96, 98–100
Neal, Tom 64, 312
'Neath Canadian Skies 308–309, 318
Neise, George 371
Neitz, Alvin J. *see* James, Alan

Nelson, James T. "Bud" 71
Nelson, Sam 399, 400, 413
Neufeld, Ruth 22
Neufeld, Sigmund 3, 16, 22, 113, 184, 188, 214, 305
Neumann, Harry 290
Nevada Jack McKenzie 1, 50–51, 219–232, 298, 356
Neville, Marjean 77
The New Adventures of Hopalong Cassidy 163, 175
The New Adventures of Zorro 445, 446
The New Frontier 356–357, 379
Newell, Jimmy *see* Newill, James (Jim)
Newfield, Joe 26, 27
Newfield, Sam 3, 7, 16, 22, 24, 29, 113, 114, 184, 185, 188, 214, 306, 375
Newill, James (Jim) 284–289, 322–331, 405
Newlan, Paul 405
Newman, Alfred 444
Newman, Bob 80
Newman, Hank, & the Georgia Crackers 80, 81
Newton, Mary 81, 84, 88, 100, 158
Nichol, Navin 444
El Nieto del Zorro (The Grandsons of Zorro) 438, 450
De Nieuwe Avonturen von Hopalong Cassidy (The New Adventures of Hopalong Cassidy) 163, 175
Nigh, William 51, 53
The Night Riders 354–355, 366, 378
Night Stage to Galveston 86
Nilsson, Anna Q. 144
I nipoti di Zorro (The Nephews of Zorro) 442, 453
No Man's Range 176
Noble, Ray 124
Nolan, Bob 69
Nolan, Dani Sue 98
Nolte, William L. 238, 250–251
Nomads of the North 315
Norris, Edward 311
North from the Lone Star 401, 408
North of the Border 308, 309, 318
North of the Rio Grande 127, 165
North of the Rockies 405
Northern Frontier 305, 306, 307, 316–317
Northern Patrol 315–316, 319

Northwest Mounties see Royal Canadian Mounted Police
Northwest Territory 313–314, 315, 319
Northwest Trail 389
Not Above Suspicion 200, 205–206
Les Nouvelles Aventures d'Hopalong Cassidy (The New Adventures of Hopalong Cassidy) 163, 175
Nova, Lou 278
Novak, Jane 40
Nuevas Aventuras de Zorro (New Adventures of Zorro) 444, 455
Nye, Carroll 362

O. Henry (William Sydney Porter) 43, 48, 51, 58
Oakman, Wheeler 64, 305, 306
Oath of Vengeance 9, 17–18
O'Brian, Hugh 301
O'Brien, Dave (Tex) 24, 26–28, 186, 187, 285–288, 292, 293, 295, 320, 321, 322–336
O'Brien, George 346
O'Brien, Pat J. 132, 141
Ochos, Yolanda 445
O'Connor, Frank 99, 222, 307, 349
O'Connor, Kathleen 38
O'Connor, Una 157
O'Day, Molly 341
O'Day, Nell 253, 327, 372
O'Dell, Doye, & His Radio Rangers 86, 238
Ogg, Sammy 261
O'Hearn, Eileen 65, 66, 105
Oklahoma Renegades 361, 380
Oland, Warner 431
Old Shatterhand 417, 418, 425
Old Surehand 421–422, 426
Der Ölprinz (The Oil Prince) 420, 426
O'Mahoney, Jock see Mahoney, Jock (Jack)
O'Malley, Pat 86, 88, 101, 364
L'Ombra di Zorro (The Shadow of Zorro) 440–441, 442, 451
On Boot Hill 107
On the Great White Way 285, 289
On the Trailing of the Tumbling T 135
One Mask Too Many 200, 206
O'Neal, Anne 160
Orefi, Moira 441

Oregon Trail Scouts 274, 283
Orlean, Will 160
Orlebeck, Lester (Les) 359, 363, 366, 370
Ormond, Ron 16, 175
Ormont, Dave 255
Ortego, Artie 29, 304–306
Ortin, Leopold "Chato" 438
Osborne, Bud 4, 15, 16, 49, 78, 79, 95, 175, 227, 234, 241, 247, 248, 257, 293, 295, 324, 328, 334, 335, 364, 373, 388, 389
O'Shea, Jack 276, 373
Osuna, Humberto 438
Outcasts of Black Mesa 91–92, 110
Outlaw Roundup 327–328, 338
Outlaw Trail 388–389, 390
Outlaws of Boulder Pass 121–213, 218
Outlaws of Sonora 350, 377
Outlaws of Stampede Pass 221, 229
Outlaws of the Cherokee Trail 366–367, 382
Outlaws of the Desert 145, 170
Outlaws of the Plains 15, 21
Outlaws of the Rockies 73–74, 103
Outlaws' Paradise 186–187, 189
Outlaw's Son 406, 411
Overland Riders 15, 21
Overland Stage Raiders 352–253, 378
Overland Stage Robbery 394, 395, 398
Overland Stagecoach 213, 215, 218
Overland Trail 250
Overland with Kit Carson 400
Owen, Michael 11
Owen, Seena 37

Padden, Sarah 27, 141, 223, 225, 295, 363
Padjan, Jack 346, 399
Page, Bradley 400, 403
Page, Dorothy 320–321
The Painted Stallion 384
Paiva, Nestor 53
Palange, Inez 46, 47
Pallette, Eugene 434
Palmer, Joseph L. 225
Palmer, Tex 247
Pals of the Pecos 364–365, 381
Pals of the Saddle 351–352, 371, 377–378
Panhandle Trail 29, 33
Parish, James Robert 308, 444

Parker, Carol 9
Parker, Eddie 83, 86
Parker, Edwin 227
Parkinson, Cliff 149
Parks, Nanette 75
Parrish, Helen 87, 311
Parrish, John 156, 159, 160
Parrish, Pat 72
Parson of the West 271
Parsons, Lindsley 310
Parsons, Patsy Lee 359
Partners of the Plains 129–130, 166
Partners of the Trail 222–223, 229–230
Patterson, Hank 196
Patterson, Shirley 222
Pawley, William (Bill) 287, 288
Payne, Bruce 58
Payne, Edna 43
Payne, Leon 115
Pearce, Adele see Blake, Pamela
Pearce, Peggy 37
Pecos River 98, 112
Pegg, Vester 35, 36, 43
Peil, Ed, Sr. (Edward) 24, 29, 209, 238, 241, 295, 321, 345, 346
Pendleton, Steve 89, 276, 301
Penn, Leonard 56, 158, 159, 315
Pennell, Larry 421
Penny, Hank 89, 95
Penny, Hank, & His Plantation Boys 78
Periolat, George 429
Perlman, Ron 58
Perrin, Jack 257, 349
Perry, John Bennett 201
"Pete Smith Specialties" 336
Peters, House, Jr. 301
Peters, Joshy 424
Peters, Ralph 188
Pettie, Graham 39
Phantom of the Plains 266–267, 281
Phantom Patrol 308, 317–318
The Phantom Plainsmen 369–370, 371, 383
The Phantom Riders 36, 41–42
Phantom Trails 406, 411–412
Phantom Valley 85, 107–108
Phelps, Lee 56, 295
Philipsen, Preben 416
Phillips, Eddie 27, 244, 294, 307, 395
Phillips, Jean 145
Phipps, Bill 315
Phoenix Productions 232, 355
The Phynx 200
Pica, Antonio 444

Pickard, John 197
Picker, Sidney 267, 272
Pickrell, June Terry 153
The Pinto Bandit 328–329, 338
Pioneers of the Frontier 413, 414–415
Pioneers of the West 359, 380
Pirates on Horseback 142–143, 169
The Plainsman 126, 175, 399
Plowright, Hilda 129
Plues, George 352
Plummer, Rose 49
Poelachau, Michael 423
Popovic-Mavid, Milivoje 416
Porter, Lew 22, 115–117, 185, 208, 235, 236, 287
Porter, William Sydney (O. Henry) 43
Powder River 104
Powdersmoke Range 39, 341–342, 366, 374
Powell, Lee 113–117, 191–193, 209
Power, Tyrone 305, 434–435, 444
Power of Possession 104
Prairie Badmen 15, 20
Prairie Gunsmoke 404, 405, 409
Prairie Pals 116–117, 118
Prairie Pioneers 363–364, 381
Prairie Raiders 82–83, 97, 106–107
Prairie Roundup 95–96, 111
Prairie Rustlers 12–14, 19
Prairie Schooners 400, 407
Prairie Stranger 65, 67, 68
Preble, Fred 22
Preston, Lew, & His Ranch Hands 67
Price, Hal 7, 9, 27–29, 71, 146, 211, 222, 225, 249, 270, 293, 326, 363, 371, 405
Price, Michael H. 213, 345
Price, Stanley 175–178, 214, 222, 223, 244, 321, 326, 372, 387, 396, 436
The Price of Crime 106
Prickett, Maudie 81
Pride of the Plains 182, 183
Pride of the West 132–133, 166,
Prosser, Hugh 83, 84, 87, 93, 147, 152, 223, 224, 367, 402
Pryor, Roger 49
Puig, Eva 146, 293
The Purple Vigilantes 349, 376–377
Putzgruber, Burschi 417
Pyle, Denver 309

Quick on the Trigger 87, 108
Quiney, Charles 443
Quinn, Jack 157
Quinn, Tom 224, 225, 227

Rachmil, Lewis J. 155
Raider 70
Raiders of Red Gap 216, 218
Raiders of Red Rock 20, 29, 33
Raiders of Sunset Pass 181, 183
Raiders of the Border 222, 229
Raiders of the Frontier 332
Raiders of the Range 368, 382
Raiders of the West 115–117
Raiders of Tomahawk Creek 94, 110–111
Rainey, Buck 68, 399
Rainger, Buck 126, 145
Rajojcic, Dusko 417
Ralston, Rudy 300
Ralston, Vera 300
Rambeau, Marjorie 137
Rampage at Apache Wells 420, 426
Ramsey, Quen 237
Randall, Jack 52, 142, 342
Randall, Karen 278
Randall, Lorraine 127
Randall, Rebel 209
Randall, Robert *see* Livingston, Robert (Bob)
Randall, Stuart 301
Randolph, Jane 156
The Range Busters 1, 50, 213, 226, 232–254, 340
Range Defenders 346–347, 376
Range Law 223–224, 230
Range Rider 1
Range War 136, 137
Ranger Bob Allen 254–259
Ranger Courage 256, 258
The Rangers Step In 257–258, 259
The Rangers Take Over 323–324, 336
Ranson, Lois 30, 362
Rathbone, Basil 434–435
Rathmell, John 343, 432
Rattenberry, Harry 35
Rauch, Siegfried 423, 424
Rawlinson, Herbert 147, 150, 152, 153, 155, 160, 161, 262
Raymond, Paula 88
Reckless Ranger 257, 259
Red Blood of Courage 306, 317
Red Hot Zorro 444, 454
Red River Range 353–354, 378
Red Ryder 87, 199, 259–284, 396, 397

The Red Skelton Show 336
Reed, Dean 442
Reed, Donald 285
Reed, Marshall 99, 100, 221–228, 331
Reeves, Bob 274
Reeves, George 148–152
Regas, George 306
Regas, Pedro 50
Regehr, Duncan 445, 447
Regina, Paul 445
El Regreso del Monstruo (The Return of the Monster) 438–439, 451
Reinl, Harald 416, 417, 423
Remember Me 110
Renaldo, Duncan 48–50, 54–58, 145, 148, 194, 263, 357–361, 367, 432
Renaldo, Tito 50
The Renegade 21, 30, 34
The Renegade Trail 135–136, 167
Renegades of the Sage 91, 110
Renfrew of the Royal Mounted 284–290, 320, 322, 329
Renfrew on the Great White Trail 285, 289
Renfrew Rides Again 286
Renfrew Rides North 285, 287
Renfrew Rides the Skies 288
Renfrew's Long Trail 287
Rentschler, Mickey 367
Ressel, Franco 443
Return of the Cisco Kid 45, 59–60
The Return of the Durango Kid 69–70, 72, 103
Return of the Lone Ranger 200
The Return of the Rangers 326–327, 337
The Return of Wild Bill 414, 415
Revel, Alicia 438
Revier, Dorothy 21
Reynolds, Don Kay *see* Little Brown Jug
Reynolds, Harrington 320
Rice, Frank 342
Rich, Dick 47, 287
Richards, Addison 120
Richards, Grant 124
Richards, Keith 146, 309
Richmond, Warner 285, 321, 389
Ride 'Em Cowgirl 320, 321
Ride on Vaquero 47, 48, 61
Ride, Ryder, Ride 276, 283, 343
Rider of the Law 176
Rider of the Plains 217
Riders of the Black Hills 350, 377
Riders of the Deadline 152–153, 172

Riders of the Lone Star 83, 107
Riders of the Northwest Mounted 308
Riders of the Rio Grande 373–374, 384
Riders of the Timberline 142, 143–144, 153, 170
Riders of the West 295–296, 299
The Riders of the Whistling Skull 344–345, 375
Riders of Vengeance 37, 42
Ridges, Stanley 135
Riding the California Trail 52–53, 62
Riley, Elaine 155, 160, 161, 163
Rin-Tin-Tin, Jr. 307
Rio Grande Ranger 255–256, 258
Riordan, Marjorie 51
Ritter, John 336
Ritter, Tex 1, 142, 147, 179, 250, 331–336, 345, 350, 402–405
River of Poison 109
Rivero, Julian 24, 53, 209, 213, 302, 308
Roach, Hal, Jr. 278
Roadman, Betty 71
Roarin' Lead 344, 375
Roaring Frontiers 403, 408
Roaring Rangers 75, 76, 77, 104
Robards, Jason (Jr.) 210
Robards, Jason (Sr.) 90
Roberson, Chuck 91, 96
Roberts, Adelle 76, 78
Roberts, Beatrice 359
Roberts, Lee 90, 197, 277
Roberts, Lynne (Lynn) 47, 48, 191, 311, 348, 350
Robertson, Willard 45, 47, 136
Robin, Leo 126, 145
Robin Hood of Monterey 53, 62
Robinson, Dewey 288
Robinson, Rad 138, 139
Robinson, Ruth 359, 401
Roche, Aurora 49
Rochelle, Claire 212, 402
Rock River Renegades 242–243, 253–253
Rockwell, Jack 30, 66, 73, 76, 78, 116, 135, 137, 144–146, 154, 155, 184, 224, 227, 257, 258, 269, 293, 331, 393, 394
Rocky 304
Rocky Mountain Rangers 360–361, 366, 380
Rogers, Jean 46
Rogers, Jimmy 152–154, 155
Rogers, Roy 1, 75, 101, 120, 147, 233, 263, 276, 300, 349, 356, 374, 396, 399
Rogers, Ruth 135, 138, 354

Rogers, Smokey 75
Rogers, Will 152
Roland, Gilbert 51–54, 444
Roll, Thunder, Roll 276–277, 283–284
Rolling Down the Great Divide 115, 117–118
Roman, Leticia 422
Romance of the Rio Grande 47–48, 60–61
Romary, Fred 123, 125, 132
Romero, Cesar 45–48
Roosevelt, Buddy 342
Root, Elizabeth 311
Root, Wells 431
Roped 37, 42
Roper, Jack 359, 401
Rose, Fred 117, 335
Rosen, Julieta 446
Rosen, Phil 49
Roske, Dietmar 424
Rosoff, Charles 51
Ross, Earle 344
Ross, Howard 442
Roth, Gene 55, 273, 275
Rothel, David 3, 136, 228, 322
The Rough Riders 1, 188, 219, 290–300, 306, 340, 356, 384, 385
Rough Ridin' Kids 1, 300–303
The Round-Up 126
Rouverol, Jean 121
Roux, Tony 146
A Roving Rogue 103
Rowdy 304
Royal Canadian Mounted Police 1, 303–320
Royle, William 285, 288, 353, 359
Rub, Christian 149
Rubel, James L. 64, 65, 67
Rubin, Benny 285
Ruhl, William 361, 367
Rumann, Sig 431
Rush, Dick 353
Russell, Mary 344
Russell, Tony 442
Rustlers' Hideout 7, 8, 17
Rustlers of Devil's Canyon 274–275, 283
Rustlers of the Bad Lands 72–73, 103
Rustlers' Valley 127–128, 147, 165
Rutherford, Jack 235
Rutherford, John 124, 127, 128
Ryan, Sheila 47
Rye, Michael 200

Sabata 2
Saddle Mountain Roundup 238–239, 245, 252
Saddlemates 365, 381
Sagebrush Heroes 69, 102–103

St. Brendan Boys Choir 134
St. John, Al 1, 3–16, 21–30, 121, 208–216, 341
St. Polis, John 123, 361
Sais, Marin 5, 9, 12, 24, 272, 276–278, 293, 365
Salazar, Abel 438
Sale, Virginia 74
Samson and the Slave Queen 441, 452
The San Antonio Kid 263–264, 280
Sancho, Fernando 454
Sande, Walter 196
Sanders, Sandy 99, 277
San Martinez, Marla Eugenia 439
Santa Fe Marshal 137, 168
Santa Fe Scouts 373, 383–384
Santa Fe Stampede 353, 378
Santa Fe Uprising 272, 282
Santschi, Thomas (Tom) 44, 306, 307
Saracino, Ernest 261
Sartana 2
Satan's Cradle 56, 63
Saunders, Gloria 313
Saunders, Nancy 82–84, 97
Savage, Ann 63
Sawyer, Joseph (Joe) 47, 55
Sayles, Francis 349, 354
Saylor, Syd 305, 306, 342, 343
Schade, Betty 37
Der Schatz im Silbersee (The Treasure of Silver Lake) 415–416, 418, 425
Schone, Reiner 424
Schroeder, Edward 121
Schurenberg, Siegfried 418, 419
Sciolone, Sofia *see* Loren, Sophia
Scott, Fred 22, 117
Scott, Gordon 441
Scott, Randolph 120
Scott, Robert 82
Scott, Robert E. 97
Scott, Sherman *see* Newfield, Sam
Scott, Tommy 296
The Search 200, 206
Sears, Fred F. 81, 82, 85, 86, 89, 90, 93, 95–101
Seay, James 142, 361
The Secret Man 35, 41
Secret of Outlaw Flats 406, 410
Secret of the Wastelands 145–146, 170–171
Il Segno di Zorro (The Sign of Zorro) 441, 452
Seidel, Tom 152, 220, 368
Selander, Lesley 128, 129, 137–139, 141, 148, 150, 154, 199, 264, 267
Self, William 275
Selman, David 129
Sennett, Mack 139
Sepulveda, Carl 211, 249
Sergeant Preston of the Yukon 182
Seward, Billie 307
Sewell, Rufus 446
The Sexcapades of Zorro 454
Seymour, Dan 310
Shadow of Zorro 440
Shadows of Death 10, 18
Shadows on the Sage 359, 370–371, 383
Shannon, Frank 121
Sharpe, David 40, 66, 245–247, 250, 261, 284, 406
Shatterhand 417, 425
Shaw, C. Montague 47, 344, 433
Shaw, Hazel 302
Shaw, Janet 325
Shayne, Robert 301
Sheffield, Johnny 47
Sheldon, Forrest 305
Sheldon, Gene 439
Sheldon, Julie 187
Sheldon, Kathryn 134
Shepard, Elaine 255, 256
Sheridan, Ann 306
Sheridan, Gail 125, 127
Sheridan, James *see* Tansey, Sherry
Sheriff of Las Vegas 265, 266, 280
Sheriff of Redwood Valley 270, 282
Sheriff of Sage Valley 28, 33
Sherman, Al 320
Sherman, George 348–351, 357, 359, 362
Sherman, Harry "Pop" 118, 126, 130, 136, 146, 148, 150, 152, 155, 392
Sherman, Lois 150
Sherman, Robert 315
Sherman, Sam 340
Sherry, J. Barney 38
Sherwood, Choti 26
Sherwood, Gale (Dale) 212
Sherwood, George 271, 352
Shields, Everett 155
Shipman, Barry 76, 84, 89, 90, 191, 193, 432
Shipman, Gwynne 125
Shirley, Arthur 37
Shor, Sol 193
Short, Dorothy 131, 185, 211, 235, 321, 404
The Showdown 137–138, 168
Shrum, Cal 149
Shrum, Cal, & His Rhythm Rangers 66–67, 227, 325
Shrum, Walt, & the Colorado Hillbillies 78, 227
Shumway, Lee 40, 296, 363
Sid, Jan 416, 422
Sidney, Delores 98
Siegel, Sol C. 341
Sigmund Neufeld Productions 22, 208, 209, 213, 216
The Sign of Zorro 439–440, 441, 451
Silent Conflict 159, 174
Silver King 191
Silverheels, Jay 89, 194, 196–201, 310
Simmons, Georgia 348
Simmons, Richard 437, 438
The Simp-Phonies 64
Simpson, Russell 148, 149, 153, 269, 312
The Singing Cowgirl 1, 320–322
The Singing Scorpion 344
Sinister Journey 160, 174
Six Gun Decision 406, 410
Six Gun Gospel 221, 229
Six Gun Law 84, 107
Six Gun Trail 185, 189
Sky Bandits 286, 288, 289
Sky King 319
Slesinger, Stephen 259
Slifer, Elizabeth 275
The Slippery Pearls 45
Small, Louise 255, 257
Smith, Drake 302
Smith, Sharon 49
Smits, Jimmy 58
Smoky Canyon 98–99, 112
Snake River Renegades 96–97, 111
Snell, Earle 359
Snow Dog 311–312, 318–319
Los Sobrinos del Zorro (The Nephews of Zorro) 438, 451
Soderling, Walter 372
El Sogno de Zorro (The Dream of Zorro) 438, 450–451, 444, 455
Sommer, Elke 419
Son of Zorro 436, 437, 449–450, 455
Sondergaard, Gale 434
Song of the Border 61
Song of the Trail 307
Songs and Bullets 117
Sonny, the Marvel Horse 39, 40
Sonora Stagecoach 389, 391
The Sons of the Pioneers 69, 396
Sooter, Rudy 244
Sorel, Louise 444
Le Sorelle de Zorro 442
Sorin, Louis 58
Sotello, Dimes 226
The Soul Herder 35, 41
South of Death Valley 89–90, 109
South of Monterey 51–52, 62
South of the Chisholm Trail 80–81, 106
South of the Rio Grande 49–50, 61
Space, Arthur 234
La Spada del Zorro (The Sword of Zorro) 442, 453
Spellman, Martin 353
Spence, Sebastian 202
Spencer, Shelley 149
Spencer, Tim (Vern) 69, 332
Spilsbury, Klinton 201
Spina, Mario Grazia 441
Spook Town 329, 338
The Sportsmen Quartette 147
Spriggins, Deuce 73
Springsteen, R.G. 267
Die Spur Führt zum Silbersee (The Trail Leads to Silver Lake) 424, 427–428
Srdoc, Milan 419
Staccioli, Ivo 442
Stagecoach 89, 138–139, 168, 351, 354
Stagecoach Outlaws 11, 19
Stagecoach to Denver 272–273, 282
Stagecoach War 138–139, 168
Stander, Lionel 444
Stanley, Forrest 145
Stanley, Louise 287, 288
Stanton, Robert *see* Grant, Kirby
Stapp, Marjorie 89
Starrett, Charles 64–67, 68–102, 129, 182, 276
State Police 108
Staub, Ralph 286
Steel, Alan 441
Steel, Anthony 418
Steele, Bob 22–25, 142, 176, 208, 270, 340, 341–342, 362–374, 385, 386–390
Steers, Larry 396
Stefani, Joseph 288
Stein, Sammy 401
Steiner, Howard 237
Stengler, Mack 156, 320
Stephens, Harvey 139
Sterling, Robert 47, 397
Stern, Alfred 322–323
Stern, Jack 125
Sternbach, Bert 22, 113
Stevens, Angela 101
Stevens, Charles 45, 99, 227, 276
Stevens, Jean 71, 75
Stevens, Onslow 123
Stevens, Robert 81
Stevens, Rev. W. D. 75
Stewart, Anna Marie 371
Stewart, Don 385, 387

Stewart, Eleanor 142–144, 154, 255, 257, 347
Stewart, James 419
Stewart, Peggy 88, 262, 254, 265, 268, 270–274, 276, 277, 436
Stewart, Peter *see* Newfield, Sam
Stewart, Redd 100
Stewart, Roy 39, 44
Stick to Your Guns 144–145, 170
Stirling, Linda 263, 269, 436
Stockdale, Carl 413
Stolen Time 103
Stone, Jeff 446
Stone, Lewis 315
Stone, Milburn 286, 311
Stone, Paula 119
Storm, Gale 365
Storm Over Wyoming 99
Stout, Archie 121
Straight Shooter 187, 189
Straight Shooting 35, 41
Strang, Harry 160, 256
Strange, Glenn 7, 26, 27, 29, 30, 52, 87, 115, 134, 136, 139, 143, 152, 154, 194, 196, 211, 213, 236–238, 243, 244, 247, 249, 263, 276, 295, 307, 354, 365, 385, 389
Strange Gamble 161, 175
The Stranger from Pecos 220–221, 229
The Stranger from Ponca City 83, 107
Stranger from Santa Fe 226, 231
Strauch, Joe, Jr. 182
Streets of Ghost Town 79, 93, 110
Striker, Fran 190, 191
Stuart, Glenn 82
Stutenroth, Gene *see* Roth, Gene
Styne, Julie 301
Suarez, Jose 438
Sullivan, John L. 273
Sully, Frank 80, 95
Sun Valley Cyclone 270–271, 282
Sunset Trail 134–135, 167
The Sunshine Boys 85, 87, 88, 95, 100
Suspected 110
Sutton, Paul 48, 132, 133, 255
Swinn, Monica 441
Sword of Zorro 441, 452

Taggart, Ben 401
Talbot, Helen 266
Talbot, Lyle 87, 278, 309
Talbott, Gloria 315
Tale of Gold 200, 206
Tales from the Diamond K 388

Tales of the Texas Rangers 98, 100
Taliaferro, Hal 79, 85, 142, 144, 148, 154, 191, 255–257, 261, 264, 348, 359, 436; *see also* Wales, Wally
Talisman Studios 305
Talmadge, Richard 247
The Taming of the West 412–413, 414
Tansey, Emma 384
Tansey, Robert Emmett 245, 247, 384–386, 388, 389, 390
Tansey, Sherry 384
The Tarzan/Lone Ranger Adventure Hour 200
Tate, Lincoln 201
Tate, Patricia 157
Taylor, Al 368, 395
Taylor, Dub 71–75, 83, 400–403, 412–414
Taylor, Ferris 352
Taylor, Forrest 23, 69, 75, 84, 95, 99, 154, 185–188, 235, 237, 241, 243, 245, 248, 250, 274, 277, 278, 324, 341, 351, 372, 385, 386, 389, 395, 403, 404
Taylor, Ray 304, 343
Taylor, Robert 21, 22
Tead, Phil 315
Teague, Guy 437
Teal, Ray 260, 400
Tedesco, Pedro 444
Temple, Brooke 261
Tenbrook, Harry 36, 344, 345
Tentacles of the North 311
El Tercer Huésped 438
Terhune, Max 228, 232–250, 343–355, 362
Terror of the Black Mask 452
Terror Trail 79, 105
Terrors on Horseback 15, 20–21
Terry, Bob 184, 186
Tessari, Duccio 444
Tex 129
Texas 80
Texas Dynamo 92–93, 110
Texas Justice 218
The Texas Kid 221–222, 229
Texas Manhunt 114–115, 117
Texas Marshal 185
Texas Masquerade 153, 172
Texas Panhandle 75, 104
The Texas Rangers 1, 288, 322–340, 405
Texas Renegades 188
Texas to Bataan 245, 248, 253
Texas Trail 129, 165–166
Texas Trouble Shooters 244, 253
Texas Wildcats 186, 189

Thane, Dirk 257
Thayer, Julia 346; *see also* Carmen, Jean
Theodore, Ralph 404
Thieves' Gold 36, 42
Thomas, Billie "Buckwheat" 269
Thomas, Robert C. 344
Thomerson, Tim 58
Thompson, Nick 212
Thompson, Peter 96
Thompson, Shorty 87
Thomson, Kenneth 119
Thorpe, Jim 388, 400
The Three Godfathers 38, 39, 232
Three in the Saddle 334, 339
Three Men from Texas 139–141, 168–169
The Three Mesquiteers 1, 25, 142, 194, 213, 260, 290, 340–384
Three Mountain Men 36–37, 42
Three on the Trail 123–124, 164
Three Texas Steers 355, 378–379
Thunder at the Border 422, 423, 427
Thunder Over the Prairie 65–66, 67
Thunder River Feud 241–242, 252
Thundering Gun Slingers 5–6, 17
Thundering Trails 371–372, 383
Thurston, Carol 316
Tibbetts, Martha 255, 256
Tim McCoy Remembers the West 292
The Tim McCoy Show 296
Timber Country Trouble 406, 412
Timber War 307
Tin Tan (German Valdes) 438
Tissier, Alain 417
The Titled Tenderfoot 406, 412
Tobey, Kenneth (Ken) 157
Tobias, Harry 125
Todd, Ann 273
Todd, Dick 193
Todd, Holbrook N. 22, 113
Todd, John 190
Toler, Sidney 136, 155
Tombes, Andrew 159
Tombragel, Maurice 175
Tombstone Canyon 8
Tonto Basin Outlaws 239–240, 248, 252
Too Much Beef 341, 274
Toones, Fred "Snowflake" 39, 247, 248
Topper 120
Tortosa, Jose Luis 141

Towne, Aline 437
Towne, Rosella 361
Townsend, Mrs. Anna 35, 37
Trace, Al, & His Silly Symphonists 71, 73, 75
Trackers 200, 206–207
Trader Horn 39, 357
The Trail Beyond 318
The Trail Blazers 1, 298, 340, 362–363, 374, 380–381, 384–391
Trail Dust 125, 164
Trail of Terror 326, 337
Trail of the Arrow 406, 409
Trail of the Lonesome Pine 179
Trail of the Mounties 308, 309–310, 318
Trail of the Rustlers 91, 110
Trail of the Silver Spurs 234–236, 251
Trail of the Yukon 310–311, 316, 318
Trail Riders 245–246, 248, 253
Trail to Laredo 86–87, 108
Trailing Double Trouble 234, 251
Trails of the Wild 306–307, 317
Travis, Merle, & His Bronco Busters 76, 78, 97
Le Tre Spade di Zorro (The Swords of Zorro) 441, 442, 452
Treadwell, Laura 54
The Treasure of Silver Lake 417, 424, 425
Trendle, George W. 190
Trent, Philip 366
Trevor, Claire 80
Trigger Fingers 188, 190
Trigger Law 389
Trigger Man 24, 31
Trigger Trio 348, 376
Trinity 2
Le Triomphe de Zorro (The Triumph of Zorro) 436
Trouble on the Trail 406, 411
The Truth 200, 207
Tubb, Ernest 69
Tucker, Mary 159
Tucker, Richard 285
Tucson Raiders 261–262, 279, 396
Tumble Down Ranch in Arizona 237, 251
Tumbleweed Trail 26, 115–116, 118
Turner, George 273, 436
Turner, George E. 213, 345
Tuska, Jon 34, 290, 293
Twilight on the Trail 145, 170
Twitchell, Archie 67
Two-Fisted Agent 112

Two-Fisted Stranger 78, 105
Two-Gun Justice 246–247, 253
Two Gun Marshal 406, 410
Two Gun Teacher 406, 411
Tyler, T. Texas 90
Tyler, Tom 144, 175–178, 341–342, 354, 366–374, 394

Ulmer, Edgar G. 322
Under Arrest 108
Under Texas Skies 361–362, 380
Undercover Man 146–147, 171
Underground Rustlers 240–241, 252
Unexpected Guest 156–157, 173
Ung, Tommy (Tom) 145
University of Arizona Glee Club 237
The Unknown Ranger 255, 258
Unter Geiern (Among Vultures) 419, 425–426
Unter Geiern — Der Sohn des Barenjagers (Among Vultures — The Son of the Barenjagers) 424, 428
Usher, Guy 146, 287, 367, 402
The Utah Kid 389

Vaccaro, Brenda 45
Valdes, German (Tin Tan) 438
Valdez, Luis 58, 59
Valentine, Elizabeth 373
Valez, Kippee 56
The Valiant Hombre 54, 55, 62
El Valle de los Desaparecidos 440
Vallee, Rudy 136
Valley of Hunted Men 371, 383
The Valley of Vanishing Men 405
Valley of Vengeance 6–7, 17
Valley Vista Productions 300
Vallin, Rick 311, 373, 394
Vallon, Michael 324, 325, 331
Van Peet, John 344
Van Sickel, Dale 266, 315
Van Sloan, Edward 371, 373
Van Zandt, Philip 73, 142, 314
Vargas, Daniele 441, 443
Varno, Roland 371
Vejar, Harry 87
Venable, Evelyn 47, 133
Vendetta de Zorro (Vendetta of Zorro) 440

Las Vengadoras Enmascaradas (The Masked Women Avenger) 441
La Venganza de Lobo Negro (The Vengeance of the Black Wolf) 445
Venganza del Ahoreado (Vengeance of the Hanged) 438
La Venganza del Zorro (The Vengeance of Zorro) 440
Vengeance in the Saddle 254
Vengeance of the West 405
Vengeance Vow 200, 207
Venturini, Edward D. 133
Verdugo, Elena 87, 311
Verria, Roquell 209
Versini, Marie 416, 422, 424
Vickers, Sunny 96
Victoria, Lorena 58
Vidor Publications 335
The Vigilantes Are Coming 431
Vigilantes of Boomtown 273, 282–283
Vigilantes of Dodge City 264–265, 280
Villegas, Lucio 227
The Virginian 128
Viva Cisco Kid 46, 60
Viveros, Celia 442
Vogan, Emmett 273
Vogt, Thomas 424
Vohrer, Alfred 424
La Volpe (The Fox) 442, 453
Vosper, John 146

Wagon Tracks West 393, 394, 398
Wagon Wheels Westward 269, 281
Waizmann, Max 292, 366
Wakely, Jimmy 69, 88, 213, 363 *see also* The Jimmy Wakely Trio
Wales, Ethel 138
Wales, Wally 341, 342; *see also* Taliaferro, Hal
Walker, Bob 346
Walker, Cheryl 371
Walker, Cindy 83
Walker, Francis 40, 41, 255, 402, 413, 414
Walker, Terry 23, 64, 285
Wallace, Edgar 90, 416, 417–418
Wallace, Helen 275
Wallace, Morgan 139, 142
Waller, Eddy 141, 270, 250, 356, 402
Wallingham, Lopez 67
Wallock, Edwin 308
Walsh, Raoul 43
Walsh, Richard 315
Walt Disney Presents 439
Walters, Luana 69, 235–237, 291, 295, 401, 403, 414
Wanger, Walter 258
Wanted By the Law 332
War Eagle, John 99
Warburton, John 129
Ward, Anna Bell 232
Ward, John 344
Warde, Anthony 49, 54, 152, 310
Ware, Helen 36
Warwick, Robert 119, 306, 348, 431
Washburn, Beverly 196
Washburn, Bryant 371, 386
Wasser für Canitoga (Water for Canitoga) 416
Water Rustlers 321–322
Waters, Ozie, & His Colorado Rangers 69, 79, 82, 85, 92, 93, 154
Watson, Minor 46, 138
Watt, Nate 125, 136, 361
Watters, Bice 237
Watts, Charles 199
Wayne, Billy 55
Wayne, Frank 185
Wayne, John 89, 121, 269, 318, 340, 351–357, 370
Weaver, Loretta 359
Weaver, Marjorie 46
Weeks, George 323
Weeks, Ranny 348
Weeren, Hans 22, 113
Weinreich, Barbara 424
Weisser, Thomas 2
Weissmuller, Johnny 342
Weldon, Michael J. 444
Wells, Jacqueline 357
Wells, L.M. 35, 36
Wells, Ted 143
Wendlandt, Horst 416, 424
Wentworth, Martha 261, 269, 271–275
Werner, Hansel 29
West, Wally 3, 11, 12, 187
West of Brazos 177–178, 180
West of Cimarron 367, 382
West of Dodge City 82, 97, 106
West of Pinto Basin 234, 245, 251
West of Sonora 85, 108
West of Texas 325–326, 336
West of the Law 296, 299
West of the Rio Grande 224, 230
Western Cyclone 20, 29, 33
The Westerners 39, 42
Weston, Dick *see* Rogers, Roy
Weston, Don 328, 333
Westover, Winifred 39
Westward Bound 384, 387, 391
Westward Ho 368–369, 382–382
Wheels of Fate 298, 306

Where the North Begins 308, 309, 318
Whiplash 278
Whirlwind Riders 86, 97, 108
The Whispering Skull 332–333, 339
Whitaker, Slim 15, 16, 26, 115, 185, 186, 212, 215, 216, 245, 402
White, Dan 326, 387
White, Edward J. 267
White, Gloria Ann 46
White, Lee "Lasses" 49, 55, 361
White, Patricia *see* Barry, Patricia
The White Buffalo 399
Whitehead, Joe 144
Whitley, Ray 335
Whitman, Gayne 434
Whitney, Claire 227
Whitney, John 153, 262
Who Killed Waring? 103
Wide Open Town 143, 169–170
Widmark, Robert 454
Wild Bill 399
Wild Bill Elliott 391–399, 405
Wild Bill Hickok 175, 331, 399–412, 414
Wild Bill Hickok Rides Again 399
Wild Bill Saunders 400, 412–415
Wild Horse Ambush 302, 303
Wild Horse Phantom 7–9, 17
Wild Horse Rodeo 348–349, 376
Wild Horse Rustlers 213–214, 218–219
Wild Horse Stampede 385, 390
Wild Women 36, 42
The Wildcat of Tucson 401, 407
Wildcat Trooper 307–308, 317
Wilde, Cornel 438
Wilde, Lois 128, 307
Wilderness Mail 305–306, 317
Wildfire 388, 389
Wiley, Jan 49, 223, 240–242, 297
Wilke, Robert J. (Bob) 84, 85, 89, 94, 97, 99, 197
Wilkerson, Billy 316
Wilkerson, Guy 1, 196, 322–336
Wilkins, Paul 148
William Boyd Productions 162
Williams, Cara 143
Williams, Curly, & His Georgia Peach Pickers 83

Williams, Guinn (Big Boy) 238, 341
Williams, Guy 324, 432, 439–440, 447
Williams, Kathlyn 307
Williams, Lester *see* Berke, William
Williams, Maston 191, 347–350
Williams, Robert B. 157, 161
Williams, Roger 39, 40, 257, 305, 306, 344
Williams, Tex 4, 5, 78, 326
Williamson, Sam 310
Willis, Norman 49, 79, 145, 367
Wills, Bob, & His Texas Playboys 71, 74
Wills, Chill, & His Avalon Boys 121, 123
Wills, Walter 352, 354, 358
Wilson, Charles 86
Wilson, Stuart 446
Wilson, Whip 179
Winkler, Bobby (Robert) 209, 365
Winner, Joseph E. 80
Winnetou 2, 415–428, 441
Winnetou I 416–417, 420, 423, 425
Winnetou II 417–419, 420, 423, 425
Winnetou III 420–421, 423, 424, 426
Winnetou der Rote Gentleman 417, 421
Winnetou in Mexico 423
Winnetou le Mescalero 423, 424, 427
Winnetou Ruckkehr (The Return of Winnetou) 424, 428
Winnetou und das Geheimnis der Felenburg (Winnetou and the Secret of the Red Castle) 424, 428
Winnetou und das Habblut Apanatschi (Winnetou and the Half Breed Apanatschi) 422, 426–427

Winnetou und der Schatz der Marikopas (Winnetou and the Treasure of Marikopas) 424, 428
Winnetou und Sein Freund Old Firehand (Winnetou and His Friend Old Firehand) 422, 423, 427
Winnetou und Shatterhand im Tal de Toten (Winnetou and Shatterhand in the Valley of Death) 422–423, 427
Winters, Linda *see* Comingore, Dorothy
Wiseman, Scotty 90
Withers, Isabel 223
Witney, William 193, 3\260, 350, 432, 434
The Wolf Hunters 311, 318
Wolfe, Ian 158, 431
Wolter, Rolf 417, 421, 424
Wolves of the Range 214–216, 219
Wood, Britt 71, 136–138, 142
Wood, Edward D., Jr. 52
Wood, Harley *see* Martin, Jill
Woodbury, Joan 48, 120
Woods, Craig 222
Woods, Harry 51, 180, 220, 221, 255, 295–297, 347, 387, 393
Woodward, Bob 224, 413
Woodward, Frances 152
Worden, Hank 249
Worth, Barbara 304
Worth, Constance 69
Worth, Harry 121, 128, 184, 260, 308, 373
Wranglers' Roost 238, 245, 252
Wrather, Jack 210
Wrather Corporation 196, 200
Wright, John Wayne 270
Wright, Mack V. 343–346, 399
Wright, Teresa 438
Wright, Wen 139, 226, 269, 332, 333
Wyatt, Al 97
Wyatt, Charlotte 126
Wynters, Charlotte 135

Wyoming Outlaw 260, 355, 356, 363, 379

Yaconelli, Frank 52
Yates, George Worthington 191
Yates, Herbert J. 300, 340, 357
The Yellow Haired Kid 406, 409–410
The Yellow Streak 103
Yigit, Tamer 443
York, Duke 313
Yong, Soo 146
Young, Carleton 22–24, 131, 188, 242, 260, 351, 433
Young, Clara Kimball 127, 133
Young, Evelyn 400, 401
Young, Ned (Nedrick) 155, 157
Young, Polly Ann 287, 307
Young, Victor 124
Yukon Flight 285, 286–287, 289
Yukon Gold 314, 319
Yukon Manhunt 312, 319
Yukon Vengeance 316, 319–320

Zahler, Lee 255
Zamperla, Nazzareno 441
Zeta-Jones, Catherine 446
Zimbalist, Efrem, Jr. 445
Zorro 2, 49, 141, 194, 221, 238, 429–456
Zorro alla Corte d'Inghilterra (Zorro in the Court of England) 443, 453
Zorro alla Corte di Spagna (Zorro in the Court of Spain) 441, 452
Zorro and Son 445
Zorro and the Comanches 454
El Zorro Blanco (The White Fox) 445, 455
El Zorro, Caballero de la Justicia (The Fox, the Gentleman of Justice) 443, 454
Zorro, il Cavaliere della Vendetta (Zorro, the Cavalier of Revenge) 443, 454

Zorro Contra Maciste (Zorro vs. Maciste) 425, 441, 452
El Zorro de Monterey (The Fox of Monterey) 443, 454
El Zorro del Jalisco (The Fox of Jalisco) 435, 449
Zorro Disi Fantoma'ya Karsi 443, 454
El Zorro en Peligro 438
El Zorro Escarlata (The Scarlet Fox) 438, 440, 451
Zorro: La Espada y la Rose (Zorro: The Sword and the Rose) 446
Zorro: Generation Z 446
Zorro i Tre Moschiettieri (Zorro and the Three Musketeers) 441, 452
Zorro il Ribelle (Zorro the Rebel) 442, 453
El Zorro Justiciera (The Severe Zorro) 442, 453
Zorro, Marchese di Navara (Zorro, Marquis of Navarre) 443, 453–454
Zorro 'mun Intikami 443, 454
Zorro nella Valle dei fantasmi 440, 451
El Zorro Pierde el Pelo (The Fox Loses His Hair) 438, 450
Zorro Rides Again 432, 434, 439, 440, 448
Zorro Se Demasque (Zorro Unmasked) 438
Zorro the Avenger 439–440, 451
Zorro the Fox 442
Zorro, the Gay Blade 445, 456–457
Zorro, the Musical 447
El Zorro Vengador (The Avenging Fox) 438, 451
Zorro's Black Whip 435–436, 437, 439, 441, 449
Zorro's Fighting Legion 432–434, 439, 448–449

www.ingramcontent.com/pod-product-compliance
Lightning Source LLC
Chambersburg PA
CBHW080752300426
44114CB00020B/2714